To Danielle & Raphi:

With Best Wishes from the Author,

Kurt F. Stone

THE
CONGRESSIONAL
MINYAN:
THE JEWS OF CAPITOL HILL

by

Kurt F. Stone

THE
CONGRESSIONAL
MINYAN:
THE JEWS OF CAPITOL HILL

by

Kurt F. Stone

KTAV PUBLISHING HOUSE, INC.

in association with

AMERICAN JEWISH HISTORICAL SOCIETY

Stone, Kurt F.
    The Congressional minyan : the Jews of Capitol Hill,
by Kurt F. Stone.
        p.   cm.
    Includes bibliographical references and index.
    ISBN 0-88125-659-5
    1. Jewish legislators--United States Biography Dictionaries.
2. Jews--United States Biography Dictionaries. 3. Legislators-
-United States Biography Dictionaries. 4. United States. Congress
Biography Dictionaries. I. Title.
E184.37.A17 1999
328.73'092'3924--dc21
[B]   99-22735
                                                               CIP

Manufactured in the United States of America
Distributed by Ktav Publishing House, Inc.
900 Jefferson Street, Hoboken, NJ 07030

Table of Contents

Acknowledgments

A work of this magnitude could not have come to fruition without the help of many people. The author hereby wishes to express his gratitude to:

The Hon. Harry Johnston, former United States Congressman from Florida, for acting as the "godfather" of this work.

Cheri Harris, my "on-line queen," for teaching me everything worth knowing about the Internet.

Art Galietti, for time and again saving my cyber sanity and being a wonderful sounding-board for ideas, both ethereal and graphic.

The late Dr. Jacob Rader Marcus, my mentor, for his wisdom and advice ("Stick to the main river; there are far too many tributaries out there.").

The late Professor Page Smith, who made American history come alive.

Professor Jonathan Sarna, friend, former congregant, and *mentsch* for his encouragement during the early stages of this work.

Dr. Steven Wexner, surgeon extraordinaire, for giving me a livable life.

Greg Lewen, who makes politics an honorable profession.

Daniel D. Cantor, the lover of ideas, for his wit, friendship and extreme generosity.

My elder daughter, Ilana Chaya and son-in-law Jason. Ilana, your love, class and literacy never cease to amaze me.

My younger daughter Nurit, who has been most understanding of all the thousands of hours that "Abba" wasn't available.

Alice and Henry Stone, my parents, who first sparked my interest in politics by naming me after a President (the "F." is for Franklin).

James Ragsdale, Office of the Congressional Historian, for his encouragement.

Alan Weiss, my best friend, who has taught me the meaning of *mentschlichkeit*.

Alan Sheinfeld, for always being there when I need him.

The following who made themselves available for interviews, either in person, over the Internet, or through correspondence:

Bella Abzug, Gary Ackerman, Anthony Beilenson, Shelly Berkley, Howard Berman, Benjamin Cardin, Meyer Cardin, Aaron Chudoff, William S. Cohen, Sam Coppersmith, Peter Deutsch, Isidore Dollinger, Joshua Eilberg, Judith (Spector) Ellenbogen, Eliot L. Engel, Sylvia ("Seroy") Engel, Ben Erdreich, Eli N. Evans, Mickey Edwards, Russell Feingold, Rabbi Dena Feingold, Bob Filner, Jon Fox, Barney Frank, Martin Frost, Sam Gejdenson, Benjamin Gilman, Milton Glickman, Barry Goldwater, Bill Gradison, Bill Green, Dan Hamburg, Jacob "Chic" Hecht, Bob Heller, Lester Holtzman, Leo Isacson, Joan (Javits) Zeeman, Charles Joelson, Herb Klein, Herbert Kohl, Ken Kramer, Tom Lantos, Frank Lauteberg, Carl Levin, Mel Levine, Elliott Levitas, Ellen Lieberman, Joseph Lieberman, Nita Lowey, Marjorie Margolies-Mezvinsky, Mildred Margolies, Edward Mezvinsky, Abner Mikva, John Miller, Bertram Podell, Howard Rayfiel, Fred Richmond, Lola (Rosenthal) Ostreicher, Steve Rothman, Bernard Sanders, Jan Schakowsky, Lynn Schenk, James Scheuer, Rabbi Emanuel Schenk, Steven Schiff, Charles Schumer, Selma Schumer, Iris Weinshall (Schumer), Robert Shamansky, Brad Sherman, Norman Sisisky, Larry Smith, Sam Steiger, Richard Stone, Herbert Tenzer, Gilbert Toll, Henry Waxman, Anthony Weiner, Ted Weiss, Paul Wellstone, Robert Wexler, Lester Wolfe, Howard Wolpe, Edith Wyden, Peter Wyden, Dick Zimmer.

Sam Elowitch, and Robert Milch, who vetted the manuscript with skill, precision and a critical eye.

My agent, Marianne Strong, for her gracious hospitality, encouragement and strength.

Bernard Scharfstein of KTAV, for his patience, insights and friendship.

Lastly, to Anna Zamosc-Stone, my wife, soul mate, companion, sounding board and editor, the patron who made this book possible. To her is this work dedicated with love and deep affection.

A Note to the Reader...

For the convenience of readers, names of members of the minyan mentioned in articles about other members of the minyan are printed in italic.

It is the intention of the author to publish updated editions of *The Congressional Minyan: The Jews of Capitol Hill* in the future. The reasons behind this are obvious; minyanaires die, are defeated for reelection, or retire from office, and newly elected members move on to other posts.

Additionally, new information about those in the current volume may become available. This is where the reader comes in. Anyone having any information, reminiscences, memorabilia, or documents concerning individuals who are (or should be) in *The Congressional Minyan* are cordially invited to contact the author. My postal address is:

Kurt F. Stone
P.O. Box 771326
Coral Springs, FL 33071

Or, you can reach me via cyberspace at:

CongMinyan@aol.com

Thank you.

minyan (min-yan) *noun. plural:* **min-ya-nim**. In Jewish religious service, the quorum of persons necessary for the conducting of public worship, no less than ten adults; among the Orthodox, only men are required.

Foreword

On any given day on Capitol Hill, members of Congress meet in dozens of groups and caucuses that target a vast array of causes. These groups range from the notable to the obscure. You probably have heard of the Congressional Black Caucus and the Women's Caucus. Other groups may have escaped your notice, like the Congressional Caucus on Sri Lanka, the Bipartisan Bike Caucus, the Auto Parts Task Force, and the Congressional Wine Caucus. There are literally dozens of official members' caucuses, defending the rights and extolling the virtues of everything from minor league baseball to Interstate 69. Nowhere to be found among these many diverse groups is an official caucus of Jewish members.

However, the Jewish members of Congress often meet as friends and colleagues in a relaxed and unofficial setting. We come together not to debate the merits of the latest tax-cut proposal or to argue the specific details of a new health care plan; we come together as Jewish Americans, reflecting upon our shared religion, culture, and history. Our discussions and interactions differ widely from meeting to meeting. On some occasions, we read and study the Torah. On others, we get together simply to talk and eat deli sandwiches brought down from New York by Congressman Gary Ackerman. Occasionally, the group gathers under more solemn circumstances, to form a minyan to pray for a bereaved family, or to attend a screening of *The Last Days*, a film recounting Representative Tom Lantos's personal tale of strength and courage during the Holocaust.

The Jewish members of the House of Representatives all have very distinct identities and backgrounds. Some of us represent large Jewish constituencies, others do not. Our Congressional districts are spread throughout the entire nation, from California to Florida through New York.

We represent older Americans, burgeoning high-tech communities, as well as rural America. Perhaps because of our shared history as a group, we tend to rally for human rights or to fight genocide in Africa or Europe. However each Jewish member is completely independent, each motivated by a unique agenda and the specific concerns of his or her district, region, and state.

A wise friend of mine recently made a statement that resonated strongly with me. He said, "We should never think of people as Conservative Jews, Orthodox Jews, or Reform Jews. We are all, quite simply, Jewish Jews." This statement relates intimately to the group of distinct individuals who make up the Jewish members of Congress. Our goals and priorities may collide or they may coalesce perfectly. On politics we may vehemently disagree or we may, and often do, join together to champion vitally important issues. But ultimately, we share a common bond that is fundamental and basic to our identity: We are Jewish Jews.

I give Rabbi Kurt Stone tremendous credit for undertaking a project that is difficult, probably unprecedented, and may prove, above all else, that we, the Jewish members of Congress, like all good members, are committed to serving the people who elected us and this nation that honors the dignity of every individual.

Robert Wexler
Member of Congress
Washington, D.C.
March 2000

In the Beginning . . .
(1654–ca. 1840)

In early October 1998, the House Judiciary Committee met behind closed doors to consider the fate of President Bill Clinton. At stake was whether the President, who, after months of strenuous public denial had finally confirmed that he had had an "inappropriate relationship" with White House intern Monica Lewinsky, should be impeached. Chaired by Republican Henry Hyde of Illinois, the committee was described by the *Washington Post* as "a sharpened and amplified image of the nation's cultural and ideological extremes," a panel "laced with zealous, tart-tongued veterans of ideological battles that most divide the nation."[1]

Political observers noted that the makeup of this committee was the bi-polar opposite of the one that had met nearly a quarter-century earlier to draw up articles of impeachment against President Richard Nixon. In 1974, The House Judiciary Committee was made up of moderate Republicans and conservative Democrats. As such, it "blurred the ideological and cultural edges of the parties."[2] In comparison to the relatively civil deliberations of the Watergate-era panel, the committee sitting in judgment of President Clinton engaged in what one observer termed "a partisan food fight." Over the course of two decades, Judiciary had become politically polarized, due mainly to the rise of such issues as busing, abortion, prayer, and the status of gays in the military.

Among the committee's twenty GOP members were many outspoken ideological conservatives, including:

- Representative Bob Barr of Georgia, who advocated impeachment hearings even before the Lewinsky scandal became front-page news,
- James E. Rogan of California, who, as a state legislator, had pushed a bill that would allow police to spank graffiti vandals, and
- Chairman Hyde, who had championed the 1996 Defense of Marriage Act, which stipulated that states were not required to recognize gay marriages.

Included among the committee's fifteen Democrats were six of the House's twenty-four Jewish members. Speaking on behalf of his Jewish colleagues, Representative Robert Wexler of Florida noted with great dismay that the release of more than 2,800 pages of grand jury testimony and sexually explicit material (detailing the Clinton-Lewinsky "relationship") took place on Rosh Hashanah, the Jewish New Year. Representative Barney Frank, another of the committee's Jewish members, called the timing of the release "inconsiderate." Responding to the pique expressed by the committee's Jewish members, Republicans averred that the timing and nature of the disclosures was "a sign that Republican conservatives listen to different voices than . . .liberal Democrats."[3] That six Jewish Representatives should find themselves center stage in one of the hottest issues of a generation is not surprising. From antebellum times to the present, Jewish members of the House and Senate have played pivotal roles in most, if not all, of the great political issues in American history.

The Republican-controlled One Hundred and Fifth Congress contained twenty-four Jewish Representatives and ten Jewish Senators. Hailing from California and New York, Vermont, Wisconsin, and Texas, and more than a dozen other states, the members of this "Congressional Minyan" contained a fascinating amalgam of individuals. Their stories, along with those of their colleagues over the years, form the heart and substance of *The Congressional Minyan: The Jews of Capitol Hill*.

A question arises at the outset: who is a Jew? According to Jewish law (*halacha*), a Jew is anyone born of a Jewish mother or converted according to clearly delineated rites and rituals. In recent years, liberal Jews have sought to extend this definition by including anyone born of a Jewish father as well. As a partial result, the debate over "who is a Jew" has reached a vituperative crescendo, with segments of the ultra-Orthodox going so far as to essentially declare that Reform and Conservative Jews are members of an entirely different faith.

With few exceptions, members of the *Congressional Minyan* are Jewish according to *halacha*—born of a Jewish mother. In those very limited cases where the individual was not born of a Jewish mother (Senators Goldwater, Cohen of Georgia, and Cohen of Maine, and Representative Pulitzer of New York), or was raised in a different faith (Fiorello LaGuardia), the classical definition has been "waived." Senator Goldwater (who was buried in a "mixed" Jewish-Episcopalian funeral) is included because of his family's deep and well-documented Jewish roots. Senator Cohen of Maine's inclusion comes from the fact of his upbringing: he was raised and educated as a Jew up until the time of his bar mitzvah. Senator Cohen of Georgia was descended from an old Jewish family; Representative Pulitzer, athough the son of a non-Jewish mother, was the target of vicious anti-Semitic barbs throughout his life. And despite the fact that LaGuardia, the "little flower," seemed to be the quintessential Italian, he was, in fact, the son of a Jewish mother. In all events, the author has chosen to follow the lead established by his mentor, the late Professor Jacob Rader Marcus. When Dr. Marcus (1896–1996) declared someone "Jewish enough" to be included in his *American Jewish Biography*, his students listened. The author gladly obeys his mentor's dictate.

In the nearly 160 years since the first Jew went to Congress, 179 Jewish men and women have served in either the House or the Senate. Some were so unrecognizable as Jews as to be all but invisible. Others were the products of families steeped in the religious practices, customs, and traditions of their ancestors. The Congressional Minyan has included members born in the West Indies, Germany, Russia-Poland, and Palestine, New York, Kansas, and Alabama. Among them have been Harvard-trained doctors and self-taught lawyers, journalists and high school teachers, children of poverty and scions of unimaginable wealth. They have been Democrats and Republicans, Whigs and Socialists, radicals and reactionaries. In short, the *dramatis personae* comprising the Congressional Minyan are a microcosm of America.

The Jewish contribution to America is a story as vast and sweeping as any Hollywood epic. Ever since that early autumn day in 1654 when the *Ste. Catherine*, the Jewish *Mayflower*, sailed into New Amsterdam harbor with twenty-three Jewish refugees aboard, Jews have played a pivotal role in the shaping of America. The American landscape is heavily overrepresented with the names and accomplishments of Jews who helped make this country the wealthiest, most industrious, and most creative in the history of humankind. From the smelting of ore to the creation of blue jeans; from the invention of the atomic bomb to the creation of the motion picture industry; from the financing of wars to the underwriting of the nation's largest manufacturing enterprises; from Wall Street, the stage, the classroom, and the laboratory to the pressroom, boxing arena, corporate boardroom, and halls of government, Jewish men and women have made incalculable contributions to our nation's health and well-being. When their zest for learning and indomitable spirit were given the chance to flourish in the *goldene medina*, pushcart peddlers became philanthropists, hat makers became Hollywood moguls, children of immigrants became confidants to Presidents, cap makers became Congressmen. In retrospect, it seems to have happened overnight. In reality, it took time, talent, and tenacity.

From 1654 until the American Revolution, the great majority of Jews in this country were Sephardim, descendants of the Spanish and Portuguese Jewries that came to an end with the great expulsions of the fifteenth century. In 1776 there were perhaps 2,500 Jews among the no more than 5 million people comprising the populace of the thirteen colonies.[4] This group was more or less equally divided between the cities of New York, Newport, Philadelphia, Savannah, and Charleston. Because they rejected the divinity of Christ, Jews were not allowed to reside in Massachusetts, Connecticut, or New Hampshire. In the colonies where they were welcome, the Sephardim quickly established themselves as merchants, traders, and, occasionally, communal leaders. In his massive *History of the Jews in America*, Howard M. Sachar notes that "In 1718, Jews served as constables in three of New York's seven wards. . . . In 1765 two Jews were elected port officials of Savannah."[5]

Jews fought on both sides in the Revolutionary War, with the great majority being patriots. Beginning a tradition that would continue for more than two centuries, Jewish merchants and contractors supplied the Continental Army with everything from uniforms and tents to saddles and musket balls, while privateers owned and outfitted by Jewish shipowners plied the seven seas searching for

British prizes. These entrepreneurs—men named Lopez, Sheftal, Scixas, Moses, and Franks—did not become rich as a result of their wartime commerce. As Sachar remarks, "nearly every Jewish . . . financier of note came out of the Revolution with his fortune either gone or painfully diminished."[6] More than 100 Jews fought in the Revolution, with several rising to ranks of prominence and prestige. Lieutenant Colonel David Franks was an aide to Benedict Arnold. General George Washington and his men had their medical needs attended to at Valley Forge by the Jewish physician Moses Russell.

It was a non-Sephardi, the Polish-born Philadelphian Haym Salomon, whose financial acumen kept the fledgling nation from going under. Salomon (1740–1785) brokered Continental bills of exchange for hard currency, charging an inconsequential quarter of a percent for his services. He also made personal interest-free loans to many of the Founding Fathers. Despite the personal and official gratitude of the Continental Congress, its members, and the people of the United States, Salomon owed his creditors in excess of $600,000 at the time of his death. To this day, there are those who believe that the geometric figure floating above the eagle's head in the Great Seal of the United States is a Star of David, placed there in memory of the Jewish broker who kept the nation's finances afloat.[7]

During the Federal period, the Jewish community grew at a slow but steady pace. Since they were relatively unencumbered by the kinds of religious and political barriers erected against them in almost every other part of the world, Jews found that they could enter into avenues of commerce and community heretofore strictly off-limits. In New York City, both Tammany Hall and the Stockbrokers' Guild (the forerunner of the New York Stock Exchange) were founded, at least in part, by Jews. In Philadelphia, Moses Levy was elected to the state legislature and eventually served as presiding judge of the city's district court. Reuben Etting was appointed federal marshal for Maryland, and Mordecai M. Noah (see below) was appointed American consul to Tunis.

From earliest times, Jewish traders and trappers left the security of big cities and ventured out into the untamed American frontier. These wandering merchants and frontiersmen reached the territories of Michigan, Wisconsin and Illinois by the end of the eighteenth century, often helping to establish new towns and settlements along the way. The Jewish lumberman Jacob Franks arrived in the Wisconsin territory by 1792, and was one of the founders of Green Bay. John Hays is thought to have been the first permanent settler in Illinois. Jewish traders freely entered into transactions with Indians, occasionally being adopted into tribes with elaborate ceremonies. Being few in number, Jews found themselves more the objects of curiosity than targets of obloquy. To many of the people they encountered, these bearded itinerant peddlers and traders were the living, breathing remnants of the Old Testament.

The newly enacted Constitution guaranteed the civil and political rights of Jews and other non-Christians. No religious tests or oaths would be tolerated. To Jews, coming from countries where social, political, and religious inequality were both *de facto* and *de jure*, America truly was a land of promise. There were, however, still flaws to be worked out in the constitutions of the various states.

Drawing upon their heterogeneous religious roots, many states legislated through Christian eyes and Christian *weltanschauung*. In consequence, Jews and other non-Christians often found themselves relegated to second-class status before the bar of justice and in matters of local import. The challenge to full equality often stemmed from the long-standing tradition of taking a religious oath upon the Christian Bible; the declarant being made to swear steadfastness in Jesus. Despite the fact that Jewish religious practice was beginning to take on a less rigorous, decidedly American cast and coloration, there were limits to what individual Israelites would tolerate. Swearing fealty to Jesus on a Christian Bible went beyond those limits. When Jacob Henry was elected to the North Carolina House of Commons in 1809, that body sought to remove him from his seat because he denied "the divine authority of the New Testament," and refused to take the prescribed religious oath. After much rancorous debate, he was allowed to remain a member of the Commons, but was debarred from holding any civil office. As historian Stanley Feldstein observed in *The Land That I Show You*, "In effect, Jews could enact laws but could not execute them."[8] Maryland, which likewise had strictures against those refusing to take a Christian oath (Maryland was a predominantly Catholic state), debated a so-called "Jew Bill" for almost thirty years. In 1825, the Maryland legislature decided that non-Catholics could hold office so long as they declared their belief in "a future state of rewards and punishments." Gradually, religious tests were eliminated in all of the original thirteen colonies. Massachusetts finally came around in 1833; North Carolina did not drop the matter from its constitution until three years after the Civil War.

Jews faced other problems as well. Many refused to testify in court or transact business on Saturday, the Jewish Sabbath. It was not only theology that caused problems for Jews; there was also the matter of religious custom and practice. In one of many such situations, Jonas Phillips refused to be called as a witness in a trial that was held on a Saturday. He was held in contempt and subsequently fined ten pounds by a Pennsylvania court. At a subsequent hearing on the contempt citation, his religious scruples were found to be inconsequential. The fine stood; the law was the law.

Jewish merchants likewise found themselves running afoul of local blue laws by keeping their places of business open on Sunday. Why, they argued, should they be penalized when Sunday was not their holy day of rest? In order to serve both God and man, they argued, they would have to keep their shops closed two days instead of one, thus giving their competitors an unfair advantage. Many Jews sought relief before the bar of justice, though most state and local courts were unwilling to see the Jewish point of view and regularly fined Jewish merchants for violating the Lord's Day.

Despite these disabilities, America offered Jews more freedom and greater opportunity for advancement than ever before. The freedom Jews discovered in the new land permitted them to practice (or not practice) the religion of their ancestors without the fear of persecution. So alluring was the new land that more than one Hebrew tried to establish a Jewish homeland on American soil.

Moses Levy, the father of David Levy Yulee, was a prosperous merchant and landowner. Between 1818 and 1829, he purchased nearly 90,000 acres in Alachua and Marion Counties,

Florida, some 10 miles south of present-day Gainesville. Levy's partners in these transactions, Abraham M. Cohen and Antonio Meir (Meyer), were both Jewish. On this land Levy established a plantation called "Pilgrimage." A utopian dreamer, Moses Levy sought to transform Pilgrimage into a haven for Jews yearning to escape the shackles of European oppression. In furtherance of this dream, he wrote New York's Shearith Israel congregation in 1820, proposing the development of a Jewish agricultural colony. In his letter, he declared his intention to pledge a sizable portion of his land for the colony. Levy's proposal fell on deaf ears. Undeterred, he left for Europe in late 1820, to recruit settlers for his Florida colony. He returned from Europe the next year with fewer than fifty people, all of whom were brought over at his expense. Attempting to breathe life into his dream, Levy built twenty-five houses, 45 miles of road, and three plantations on 300 acres of cultivated land. He had a cargo of sugar roots and seeds brought over from Cuba, envisioning that one day these plantations would produce sugarcane and tropical fruits. The plan came to naught. Moses Levy returned to Europe in the hope of finding more settlers for his Jewish utopia. One more journey, one more failure.

Moses Levy was certainly not the only Jew who dreamed of establishing a Jewish homeland on American soil. Many other Jews in the nineteenth century tried and failed. The most famous plan was the brainchild of the era's best-known Jew, Mordecai Manuel Noah. The mercurial Noah (1785–1851) was a fascinating amalgam of politician and playwright, popular journalist and professional Jew. Before breaking ranks to become a Whig, Noah served as both grand sachem of Tammany Hall and sheriff of New York City. As mentioned above, he was also the first American Jew to hold a major diplomatic post—American consul in Tunis. In 1825, he boldly unveiled his plan to establish a Jewish state under the aegis of the American Constitution. Toward that end, he purchased a considerable tract of land on Grand Island, near Buffalo, New York. Taking a page from the Bible, Noah named his Jewish republic "Ararat," after the mountain upon which his eponymous ancestor had landed when the waters of the great Flood receded. On September 15 of that year, Noah staged a gala Ararat inaugural at

Buffalo's St. Paul's Episcopal Church(!). Resplendently garbed like a Shakespearean monarch, Noah, in the company of a group of dignitaries (none of them Jewish) that included an Indian chief, dedicated Ararat's cornerstone, which contained the words:

> I Mordecai Manual Noah, Citizen of the United States of America, late Consul of said States for the City and Kingdom of Tunis, High Sheriff of New York, Counselor at Law, and by the grace of God Governor and Judge of Israel, do hereby proclaim the establishment of the Jewish State of Ararat.

Unlike Moses Levy, who evinced a singular degree of sincerity and lack of ego in his project, the pompous Noah gave himself the title of Emperor. In what amounted to his coronation address at St. Paul's, he decreed that all Jews everywhere would be assessed a head tax of three shekels. The Jewish world briefly considered Noah's plan; it was found to be both untenable and repugnant, its creator a buffoon. Like Moses Levy's Pilgrimage, Noah's Ararat was a complete failure. Today, all that remains of Ararat is its cornerstone, housed in the town hall on Grand Island.[9] Moses Levy gave up his Zionist dream and settled down to run his own 50,000-acre plantation in Volusia County.

A totally different response to the freedom America offered was the act of reinvention. Case in point: August Belmont.

Born Auguste Schoenberg, Belmont (1816–1890) was reputed to be the scion of a distinguished Dutch Sephardi family of poets and diplomats. He spent his youth in Alzey (Hesse), and while still in his teens, went to work for the House of Rothschild. He rose rapidly through the financial ranks of that distinguished Jewish banking concern, and in 1837, barely twenty years of age, was sent to New York to oversee its financial interests in the United States. Short and dapper, with a decidedly Continental flair heretofore unseen in the New World, the young Belmont (as Schoenberg now called himself) took New York by storm. By the early 1840s, he had not only established his own highly successful banking concern, August Belmont & Co., but had become the arbiter of social style and custom. Belmont went on to represent the United States as chargé d'affaires (1853–55) and minis-

ter (1855–58) at The Hague.[10] During the Civil War, he used his international banking connections to successfully enlist the support of European bankers for the Union cause. By the time he became chairman of the Democratic National Committee in 1860 (a post he held until 1872), few people remembered that the wealthy, influential banker, married to the daughter of Commodore Matthew C. Perry, was, in fact, a Jew from Central Europe. One wonders if even Belmont himself remembered his roots.[11]

August Belmont was neither the first nor the last Jew to reinvent himself in America. He was the harbinger of a new wave of Jewish immigration that would soon eclipse the might and prestige of the Sephardim, America's first Jewish families. By the early nineteenth century, a majority of the Jews residing in America were from Germany and German-speaking areas of Central Europe like Bohemia and Posen. Restless, ambitious, and willing to take risks, these newcomers were, in the main, markedly less pious, less attached to Jewish ritual and practice, than the families that had reared them. Although Jewish life in America continued to be centered around the synagogue, new alliances were forged in commerce and politics.

From the time of the American Revolution through the Age of Jackson, most of the German Jews, or Ashkenazim, found a political home in the party of Jefferson. Then as now, most called themselves Democrats. It was as Democrats that Ashkenazim were elected to state legislatures, boards of aldermen, and city councils. Predictably, most resided in places of relatively dense Jewish settlement. Ironically, though, it was two Sephardi Whigs, David Levy Yulee and Judah P. Benjamin, from the distinctly non-Jewish states of Florida and Louisiana, who first entered the Halls of Congress.

1. *Washington Post*, Sept. 27, 1998, A-1.
2. Ibid.
3. Ibid.
4. Jacob R. Marcus, *To Count a People: American Jewish Population Data, 1585–1984* (Lanham, Md.: University Press of America, 1990).
5. Howard M. Sachar, *A History of the Jews of America* (New York: Alfred A. Knopf, 1992), pp. 18–20.
6. Ibid., p. 25.
7. *Dictionary of American Biography*, vol. 16 (1935)

pp. 313–314. Jacob R. Marcus, *Early American Jewry*, vol. 2 (1953) pp. 132–164. See also Howard Fast's marvelous children's book, *Haym Salomon, Son of Liberty* (New York: Julian Messner, 1941).

8. Stanley Feldstein, *The Land That I Show You: Three Centuries of Jewish Life in America* (New York: Anchor Press/Doubleday, 1976), p. 34.

9. Ibid., pp. 59–61. Sachar, pp. 45–48. The great English-Jewish writer Israel Zangwill wrote a satirical short story on the Ararat project entitled "Noah's Ark," published in *They That Walk in Darkness* (Philadelphia: Jewish Publication Society, 1899), pp. 79–127.

10. Belmont was not the first American Jew to serve in a diplomatic post. President James Madison appointed Mordecai M. Noah counsel to Tunis in 1815. He was quickly relieved of his position when it was discovered that he had used embassy funds to ransom several French-speaking hostages from Moroccan pirates. Noah explained that they claimed to be American citizens. In his letter of dismissal, President Madison also cited the fact that "At the time of your appointment . . . it was not known that the Religion you profess would form any obstacle to the exercise of your Consular function." Madison's unfortunate choice of words caused many Jews to label him an anti-Semite.

11. Irving Katz, *August Belmont: A Political Biography* (New York, 1968). See also *Encyclopaedia Judaica*, vol. 4, col. 442.

ABZUG, BELLA SAVITZKY (1920–1998): *Democrat from New York; served three terms in the House (Ninety-second through Ninety-fourth Congress; January 3, 1971–January 3, 1977).*

It seems only fitting that Bella Abzug's name should appear first on the Congressional Minyan's roster. During her years in the political limelight, Bella was one of the most easily recognized members of Congress and perhaps the best-known woman in America. She was known as much for her flamboyance, trademark wide-brimmed hats, and dynamic speaking style as for her idealistic forthrightness. In her heyday, she was variously called Battling Bella, Hurricane Bella, Mother Courage, and "a Jewish mother with more complaints than Portnoy." In her last term in office (1977), she was chosen by her congressional peers in a *U.S. News and World Report* survey as the "third most influential" member of the House.

Bella Abzug, the second daughter of Emanuel and Esther Savitzky, was born in New York City on July 24, 1920 (the same year women won the right to vote). Her father, an immigrant from Russia who owned and operated the "Live and Let Live Meat Market" on Ninth Avenue in Manhattan, was known as the "humanist butcher". At age thirteen, when her father died, Bella insisted on saying Kaddish for him in synagogue every morning for a year, a privilege traditionally reserved for males. She graduated from Walton High School in the Bronx, where she was class president, and then entered Hunter College, from which she graduated with an A.B. in 1942. While an undergraduate, she was elected president of the student council and was an active Zionist. Denied admission to Harvard Law School (women were not accepted in those days), she attended Columbia University Law School on a scholarship. Her legal education was interrupted by World War II, when she went to work in a shipyard. After the war she completed her education, receiving her LL.B. in 1947. One of but a handful of women students at Columbia Law, she served as an editor of the *Columbia Law Review*. She also did graduate work at the Jewish Theological Seminary. She was admitted to the New York bar in 1947 and practiced in New York City, where she specialized in labor law, representing fur and restaurant workers, auto workers, and striking longshoremen.

During her legal career, Abzug worked *pro bono* for such organizations as the ACLU and the Civil Rights Congress. She gained worldwide attention in the late 1940s when she served as chief counsel in the two-year death sentence appeal of Willie McGee, a young Mississippi black convicted of raping a white woman. Despite her best efforts, McGee was executed in 1951. In the 1950s, Abzug represented numerous individuals accused of leftist activities by the late Senator Joseph McCarthy. She was a founder and member of the National and State New Democratic Coalition in 1968, and an initiator and national legislative representative of the Women's Strike for Peace movement from 1961 to 1971. She was an active participant in the 1967 Dump Johnson Movement, which had been spearheaded by *Allard Lowenstein*, a member of the Congressional Minyan. Abzug then became a founder of the Coalition for a Democratic Alternative, which supported the presidential candidacy of Senator Eugene McCarthy. Abzug served as a delegate to the Democratic National Convention in 1972 and 1980, and was elected as a Democrat from the ethnically diverse Nineteenth Congressional District to the Ninety-second Congress. Running on the slogan "This woman's place is in the House—the House of Representatives," Abzug defeated Democrat *Leonard Farbstein*, a fourteen-year incumbent known as a "solid but somewhat somnolent liberal." She went on to serve in the lower house a total of three terms, from January 3, 1971 to January 3, 1977.

On her first day in Congress, Bella Abzug introduced a resolution calling for the withdrawal of all troops from Vietnam by July 4, 1971. Despite an all-out campaign to win a seat on the House Armed Services Committee, she was assigned to the committees on Government

Operations and Public Works. While in the House, Abzug became one of the earliest supporters of an Equal Rights Amendment and co-sponsored legislation for the federal financing of twenty-four-hour-a-day childcare centers. As chair of the House Subcommittee on Government Information and Individual Rights, she helped write and pass the landmark Freedom of Information and Privacy Acts, and the milestone Government in the Sunshine Law. The latter opened up government inquiries into covert and illegal activities of the CIA, FBI, Internal Revenue Service, and other agencies. Abzug was also the first member of Congress to call for President Richard Nixon's impeachment in the Watergate scandal.

Forever tilting at windmills, Bella Abzug launched a drive to obtain statehood for New York City, and had the audacity to question the competence of Washington icon J. Edgar Hoover. According to a 1977 Gallup Poll, she was one of the twenty most influential women in the world. Although not a candidate for reelection to the House of Representatives in 1976, Abzug unsuccessfully sought the Democratic nomination to the United States Senate. Defeat followed defeat: She ran unsuccessfully in the New York mayoral primary and was an unsuccessful candidate for the Ninety-fifth Congress in a special election held February 14, 1978. She failed in a later bid for election to the One Hundredth Congress, and was denied her party's nomination to replace Representative *Ted Weiss* when he died. *Jerrold Nadler* eventually took the seat.

When not running for office, Bella Abzug continued working on behalf of a multiplicity of issues. In 1977, President Jimmy Carter appointed her to head the National Commission on the Observance of International Women's Year. She went on to preside over the first (and only) federally funded National Women's Conference in Houston in 1977. She served as co-chair of the Women's Environment and Development Organization, and presided over the World Women's Congress for a Healthy Planet in 1991. This Congress drew more than fifteen hundred women from eighty-three countries and produced and approved "Women's Action Agenda 21," a blueprint for incorporating the women's

dimension into local, national, and international environmental-policy decision-making.

Bella Abzug was married for forty-one years to Martin Abzug, a stockbroker and novelist. The two met on a bus in Miami, Florida, on the way to a Yehudi Menuhin concert. Martin Abzug had little interest in politics. Once, while his wife was out of the room, he quietly told an interviewer, "The political bug is a curious bug." His two published works were *Spearhead* (1946), a novel about the Battle of the Bulge, and *Seventh Avenue Story*. At the time of his death, two months before Bella Abzug's unsuccessful 1986 race for Congress, he had just completed a novel about a man's lifetime search for his Nazi persecutor. The Abzugs had two daughters, Isobel (Liz) and Eve, both of whom are active in New York political circles. In her last years, Bella Abzug spent a great deal of time working on environmental and women's issues, lecturing and speaking on behalf of United Jewish Appeal.

During the last decade of her life, Bella suffered from a host of physical ailments, including breast cancer, but continued to practice law. Of her time in Congress, she once stated: "Outside of Martin and the kids, I don't feel very related to most people at this point. I feel detached in social situations. I'm always thinking about other things, about Congress, about the issues, about the political coalition I'm trying to organize. It never leaves me." Abzug died in New York City on March 31, 1998 from complications following heart surgery. Hearing of her death, New York Representative Charles Rangel said, "She was one of the most exciting, enlightened legislators that ever served in Congress."

Bella Abzug's funeral was held at the Riverside Memorial Chapel on Manhattan's Upper West Side. The eulogists included Jane Fonda, Shirley MacLaine, and Geraldine Ferraro. Speaking of her political mentor, Ferraro said: "Let's be honest about it: she did not knock politely on the door. She took the hinges off of it." Actor Joseph Bologna predicted that Abzug's first action upon arriving in the next world would be "to immediately begin petitioning God for better conditions for the people in hell."

References

Bella Abzug, *Bella! Ms. Abzug Goes to Washington*, edited by Mel Ziegler (New York: Saturday Review Press, 1972).

Current Biography, 1971, pp. 1–3.

Doris Faber, *Bella Abzug* (New York: Lothrop, 1976).

New York Times, April 1, 1998, p. A1.

Women in Congress, 1917–1990 (Washington, D.C.: Office of the Historian, U.S. House of Representatives, 1991).

ACKERMAN, GARY (1942–): *Democrat from New York; served nine terms in the House (Ninety-eighth to One Hundred and Sixth Congress; March 1, 1983–present).*

Over the past generation, Congress has subdivided itself into numerous caucuses—bipartisan collectives that reflect commonalties of geography, ethnicity, or regional self-interest. The early 1970s saw New York Democrat *Elizabeth Holtzman* and Massachusetts Republican Margaret Heckler forming the Woman's Caucus; the racial tensions of the 1960s gave rise to the Black Caucus. Additionally, there are groups that center around coal mining, timber, the Rust Belt, and the arts. Somewhat surprisingly, there is no official Jewish Caucus. Given the plethora of political cliques on Capitol Hill, the question "why no Jewish caucus?" is obvious.

When asked this question, members of the Congressional Minyan come up with a variety of responses ranging from "we don't really need one" and "we weren't elected as Jews, but as representatives of our states and districts," to "why antagonize the anti-Israel crowd?" Most seem to agree that organizing a formal Jewish caucus would not add any more cohesion or collective strength to their numbers. Many add that despite the lack of a *de facto* caucus, the Jews on Capitol Hill often act, speak, and vote as if one existed.

This is not to say that the Hill is totally devoid of a Jewish group. Once or twice a month, a dozen or more Jewish representatives gather in a second-floor suite in the Rayburn House Office Building to study Torah, *siddur* (prayer book), and a little Talmud with a rabbi brought down from New York. The informal group, which actually calls itself the Congressional Minyan, was the brainchild of two New York Democrats: Gary Ackerman and *Chuck Schumer*. Ackerman's involvement in the Minyan comes despite the fact that, in his own words, he "didn't have a very extensive religious background." As a matter of fact, Ackerman, who is one of the few Congressional Minyanaires who keeps a mezuzah on his office door, did not learn how to *daven* (pray in the tra-

ditional Jewish manner) until he was an adult.

Gary Ackerman, the son of Max and Eva (Barnett) Ackerman, was born in Brooklyn on November 19, 1942. Max's parents had come from Poland around the turn of the century; the Barnetts (originally Bandrema) had also emigrated from the Jewish Pale. Gary and his younger brother Alan (who today resides in Phoenix) were raised in Queens in a nonkosher home where Yiddish was spoken "only when our parents didn't want us to understand what they were talking about." Gary Ackerman was educated in the New York public schools and started his Jewish education at the Orthodox Young Israel. When the venue proved to be too far from the Ackerman home, Gary moved on to a Conservative Hebrew school. He graduated from Brooklyn Technical High School and then went on to Queens College, where he met his future wife, Rita Tewel. As a college student, Ackerman was involved in various campus organizations. Graduated from Queens in 1965, he spent the next four-plus years teaching social studies at a local junior high school.

In 1970, Rita gave birth to the first of the Ackermans' three daughters. Gary petitioned the Board of Education for an unpaid leave of absence in order to spend time with his newborn daughter. His request was denied; under then-existing policy, maternity leave was solely for women. In what was to be a forerunner of the Clinton-era Family Leave Act, teacher Ackerman successfully sued the Board of Education in a landmark case which established the right of either parent to claim unpaid maternal leave. (More than a quarter-century later, Representative Ackerman, serving on a House-Senate Conference Committee, signed the report of the Family and Medical Leave Act which became the law of the land.)

At the end of his unpaid leave, Ackerman left his teaching position in order to start a weekly community newspaper, the *Flushing Tribune*. Renaming his paper the *Queens Tribune*, Ackerman brought out editions covering local news events throughout the borough. During his years as a publisher (1970–78), Ackerman "had run-ins with the Queens Democratic machine." In 1977, he campaigned unsuccessfully as an independent against a New York City Council incumbent. Ackerman wound up running the *Queens Tribune* for eight years before selling it to publisher Jerry Finkelstein, the father of Andrew Stein, the president of the New York City Council. The Ackerman-Finkelstein connection continued for many years. Shortly before the 1992 New York Democratic primary, *Newsday* reported that Ackerman had "negotiated a $45,000 yearly consulting contract for his wife with Finkelstein . . . an attempt to evade outside income restrictions." Ackerman successfully sidestepped the charge and went on to win his primary with 60 percent of the vote.

Gary Ackerman was elected to the New York State Senate in 1978. Shortly after his reelection in November 1982, Seventh District (Queens) Representative *Benjamin S. Rosenthal* died after a long bout with cancer. Ackerman quickly jumped into the campaign to replace the widely popular Rosenthal, who, despite his terminal illness, had won his last election with 77 percent of the vote. In a four-candidate field, Ackerman's chief rival was pollster Douglas Schoen, "a wealthy independent candidate." Ackerman won the special election without need of a runoff, pulling in precisely 50 percent of the vote. Sworn in on March 1, 1983, Ackerman was seated on the Foreign Affairs and the Post Office and Civil Service Committees.

During his early years in Congress, Gary Ackerman was "identified mainly with his idiosyncrasies: his glib wit, considerable girth, goatee, boutonniere and unusual residence." With regard to the last "idiosyncrasy," Ackerman lived (and still does) on a houseboat moored in the Potomac. He purchased his first houseboat soon after arriving in Washington, but twenty-four hours later it sank. Told of the mishap, Ackerman retorted, "I guess I didn't ask the right questions when I bought it." All that was left was a life preserver. Ackerman then spent $25,000 on a second houseboat, despite the fact that he had never even "taken a nap in a canoe." He called the new craft, a 42-footer, the *Unsinkable II*, which, Ackerman quipped to a *New York Times* reporter "makes for a lot of questions about what happened to number one." Ackerman told the reporter that "the advantage

of owning a houseboat in Washington is that I'm always reminded that I want to go home. And it symbolizes I'm not putting roots down here." Gary Ackerman and Alabama Republican Sonny Callahan are the only two members of Congress who live on houseboats. They call themselves the "sea caucus."

During 1987, Ackerman lost two of his idiosyncrasies by shedding more than 100 pounds and shaving off his goatee. He persists in wearing a carnation in his lapel every day, and his wit is as glib as ever. In January 1991, after U.S. forces began the bombing campaign against Iraq, Ackerman read a poem on the House floor:

Slam, bam, thanks Saddam
You should have took the letter.
Now take the loss, reverse the course
Because it ain't going to get no better.

Once, during a discussion on a constitutional ban on flag desecration, Ackerman sought to "convey its impracticality" by displaying "swimming trunks, pantyhose and other paraphernalia emblazoned with a flag motif." In January 1995, Congress voted for a new Speaker. Called in alphabetic order, Gary Ackerman followed Neil Abercrombie of Hawaii. Being Democrats, both men voted for Missouri Representative Dick Gephardt. As soon as Ackerman cast his vote he shouted out, "Move to close the roll!" The House rocked with laughter.

From his position on the House Post Office and Civil Service Committee, Ackerman was "one of the few congressmen willing to stand up during the almost hysterical drive against drugs . . . to argue that drug tests are unreliable." Furthermore, Ackerman authored legislation to prevent indiscriminate drug testing of federal employees. He was also one of the leading opponents of the move, popular during the early Reagan years, to privatize and contract out government jobs. As a member of the House Foreign Affairs (now the International Relations) Committee, Ackerman traveled the world on its Subcommittees on Europe/Middle East and Human Rights/International Operations. In his travels, Ackerman drew attention to the rescue of Soviet and Ethiopian Jews and "relieving government-caused famines in Ethiopia and Sudan." Ackerman says he "makes it [his] business to go to shul in every country" he visits. One of his most emotional moments, he recalled in a 1994 interview, was "davening with the Ethiopian Jews in Gandar." Additionally, Ackerman was "one of the few Americans ever to meet with North Korean dictator Kim Il Sung."

In 1990, Ackerman added the Select Committee on Hunger to his work assignment. At one point, he posed as a homeless person on the streets of New York in order to gain information for pending legislation. In 1992, Ackerman became chair of a subcommittee on worker compensation. From this position, he steered through a pay-raise plan that "help[ed] close the gap between public- and private-sector salaries." In 1993, he acceded to the chair of the Asian and Pacific Affairs Subcommittee. Asked by a *New York Times* reporter why he had sought this particular chairmanship, Ackerman, true to form, quipped: "I love Asian food. That's probably the overriding reason for becoming chairman. Lots of good restaurants." As often will occur, Ackerman's subcommittee chairmanship had a price: accepting a slot on the Committee on Standards and Official Conduct (Ethics)—a post few members seek and even fewer accept.

Public pronouncements and demeanor to the contrary, Gary Ackerman has always been popular with the people of his district. Each year he brings his "Taste of New York" gathering-cum-fundraiser to Capitol Hill, which features "pastrami sandwiches and stuffed cabbage with waiters imported from New York." As a result, Ackerman is generally well-heeled when election time comes around. From 1984, when he was reelected by a better than three-to-one margin, to 1988 and 1990, when he ran unopposed, Gary Ackerman's moderately liberal voting record struck an obviously responsive chord with voters in the Seventh (soon to be Fifth) District. The year 1992, however, was "near-fatal." Ackerman "suffered a double blow" from the House Bank investigation. Not only did he have 111 overdrafts; he was accused by Democrat Representatives Edward Feighan of Ohio and Charles Hayes of Illinois (both of whom were retiring) of "leaking a preliminary list of the worst bank offenders," presumably because the list included his political rivals. The two requested a probe into whether Ackerman had leaked the House Bank list. Although

Ackerman "absolutely and unequivocally" denied being the source of the leak, the accusation forced him to resign his position ("a thankless task") on the Ethics Committee. Published reports later indicated that the letter was actually the work of retiring New York Democrats Robert Mrazek and *James H. Scheuer.*

Added to the House Bank imbroglio, Ackerman was faced with running in a new district: "An urban liberal, Ackerman was placed in a district that removed much of his base in . . . Queens and gave him new voters in suburban (and more conservative) Long Island." Ackerman had his work cut out for him; only 9 percent of the new district had been part of his old constituency. For the first time since the special election in 1983, he had to fend off a primary challenger in the person of Rita-Louise Morris, "a grandmotherly college librarian who had never run for office." Morris had three things in her favor: she had $500,000 in life savings that she was willing to dump into her campaign; her son Hank Morris was a highly regarded campaign consultant; she was running in "the year of the woman." Ackerman wound up defeating Morris 60 percent to 40 percent. In the November general election, he won by the narrowest margin of his career, besting Republican/Conservative Allan E. Binder by only 7 points. In both 1994 and 1996, Ackerman faced Republican Grant Lally. In their first face-off, Ackerman won by the not-overwhelming margin of 55 percent to 43 percent. Ackerman finally secured his position with the voters of the Fifth District in 1996, when he beat Lally by a more impressive 64 percent to 35 percent.

In 1996, Ackerman steered to passage the so-called Baby AIDS Bill, requiring HIV testing of newborns and disclosure of the results to the mother. The legislation also barred insurers from terminating coverage because of AIDS test results. Manhattan liberals, despite the fact that many HIV positive newborns could be saved if identified in time, opposed the measure. Ackerman's marshaling of the measure earned him plaudits from the *Almanac of American Politics* (1998), which noted that "it took courage for Ackerman to brave the wrath of New York's left wing."

Gary Ackerman has another problem lurking in his political future: further redistricting. A federal court has ordered a redrawing of the

"Bullwinkle Hispanic"-majority Twelfth District that will surely force changes in Ackerman's district. Despite his overwhelming victory (65 percent to 33 percent) in 1998, redistricting after the 2000 census will undoubtedly present him with a new roster of voters to impress. But Gary Ackerman has overcome challenges in the past—even having his home sink into the Potomac.

References

Interview with Gary Ackerman, Washington, D.C., July 21, 1994.

Almanac of American Politics (1984–98).

Politics in America (1988–96).

New York Times, March 26, 1993, LI, 3:1.

ANSORGE, MARTIN CHARLES (1882–1967):
Republican from New York; served one term in the House (Sixty-seventh Congress; March 4, 1921–March 3, 1923).

A one-term conservative Republican from Manhattan's Twenty-first District, Martin Ansorge had his moment in the sun—five years after he lost his congressional seat. In 1927, he was, ironically, retained by auto magnate Henry Ford to negotiate out-of-court settlements in legal suits that charged Ford with slander, libel, and disseminating anti-Semitic propaganda.

Martin Ansorge was born into a German Jewish family in Corning, New York, on New Year's Day, 1882. His father, a clothing manufacturer in Corning, moved the family to New York City in 1885. He would eventually become the owner of Ansorge Brothers and Company in Scranton, Pennsylvania, and see his son Herbert become president of the Wholesale Clothing Manufacturers Association.

One of seven children born to Mark Perry and Jennie (Bach) Ansorge, Martin grew up in a prosperous household: "We always lived in a private house, and we had two servants—what we called the cook and the upstairs girl—and they were always German." For all intents and purposes, German was the family's *lingua franca*. Martin attended public schools, and graduated from Columbia University (1903) and Columbia University Law School (1906). While at Columbia, Ansorge lettered in both track and football, and made a nice living selling advertising space in the *Columbia Spectator* on the side: "I purchased a white page, minimum . . . at a ten-cent rate per inch. I had my `representatives' selling space to stores at fifty cents an inch—the regular `retail' rate. . . . I always made $75 or so a week while I was at Columbia, without working!"

After practicing law with the firm of Hays, Hershfield and Wolf for six years ("I managed to get in through my father's friendship with Hays"), Ansorge ran as a Republican for Congress in 1912 against Bull Moose candidate, Jerome Reilly, and incumbent, Democrat Henry George, Jr. Representative George was reelected, with Ansorge coming in third. In 1914, Ansorge ran once again, this time as the nominee of both the Republicans and the Progressives. Another campaign, another defeat; this time to Murray Hulbert. Ansorge lost by less than fifteen hun-

dred votes. Without either asking or seeking, Ansorge was "handed" the Republican nomination for Congress in 1916. Once again, Hulbert defeated Ansorge—this time by a wide margin.

Taking time out to serve the last few months of World War I in the Transportation Corps, Ansorge ran for Congress a fourth time in 1920. Along with a host of other Republican candidates, he was swept into Congress on the coattails of Harding and Coolidge. Martin Ansorge truly believed that Warren Gamaliel Harding was one of the outstanding American Presidents. At the time of Harding's death in August 1923, Ansorge was quoted by the *New York Times* as saying: "Next to Lincoln, Harding was the most human man who ever occupied the executive chair. By training and natural ability, he was one of the best qualified. . . . Posterity will remember him as one of our best Presidents." When Martin Ansorge was interviewed for the Columbia University Oral History Project some twenty-five years later, he held the same opinion: "I still believe what I then said—that he [Harding] was one of our best Presidents."

Ansorge's one legislative accomplishment in the Sixty-seventh Congress was sponsoring and floor-managing passage of the resolution establishing the New York Port Authority. Ansorge also introduced two anti-lynching bills. Both passed the House by overwhelming majorities but went down to defeat in the Senate. He also introduced several bills to repeal the Volstead (Prohibition) Act. They were never even reported out of the Judiciary Committee, which happened to be chaired by none other than Representative Volstead himself.

Ansorge was defeated for reelection in the Democratic landslide of 1922. While Democratic gubernatorial candidate Al Smith was carrying Ansorge's district by some twenty-two thousand votes, Ansorge managed to lose to Royal Weller by precisely ten votes. This marked the apogee of Ansorge's political career. From there he lost elections in 1924, 1927, and 1928 for positions as judge on the Court of General Sessions and the New York Supreme Court, respectively.

As mentioned above, Martin Ansorge was retained by Henry Ford to negotiate out-of-court settlements stemming from the Aaron Sapiro case. This famous million-dollar libel case involved publications against Sapiro in Ford's notorious anti-Semitic paper, the *Dearborn Independent*. The first trial, held in Detroit, resulted in a mistrial. At that point, it was suggested to Ford that he negotiate an out-of-court settlement. Martin Ansorge was brought to Ford's attention by one Joe Palma, formerly chief of the United States Secret Service in Detroit and subsequently New York. Ansorge successfully negotiated a settlement for an undisclosed amount, plus a public retraction from Ford.

Ansorge was also hired to represent Ford in another libel case against Herman Bernstein. In this case, Ansorge went up against Bernstein's attorney of record, the brilliant Samuel Untermeyer, who refused to deal with him, claiming that Ansorge was not Ford's attorney of record. This case was also settled out of court, though Martin Ansorge apparently played no part in its conclusion.

Following this episode, which received wide play in the newspapers, Martin Ansorge returned to the practice of law. He went on to serve as a director of United Airlines from 1934 to 1961. He died at age eighty-five on February 4, 1967, and was buried in Temple Israel Cemetery, Hastings-on-Hudson, New York. He, like four of his brothers, had never married.

References

American Jewish Year Book, vol. 24, p. 115.

New York Times, February 6, 1967, 29:3.

"The Reminiscences of Martin C. Ansorge," Special Collections Department, Columbia University, January 1950.

Universal Jewish Encyclopedia.

Who's Who in American Jewry, 1926, 1928, 1938.

Who Was Who in America, vol. 4.

For a fine summary of the Henry Ford libel case, see Abraham M. Sachar, *A History of the Jews in America* (New York: Alfred M. Knopf, 1992), pp. 308–319.

BACHARACH, ISAAC (1870–1956): *Republican from New Jersey; served eleven terms in the House (Sixty-fourth through Seventy-fourth Congress; March 4, 1915–January 3, 1937).*

Certain cities and states are known for their political "dynasties"—families that year in, year out, and from one generation to the next, provide a specific locale with its civic, political, and communal leaders. Some are well-known, like the Adamses and Kennedys of Massachusetts, and the Tafts of Ohio. Other political dynasties are known only to political cognoscenti and the locals: Detroit has been represented in Congress for more than sixty years by the Dingels, *père et fils*. Five generations of Fishes, all named Hamilton, have represented New York's political interests for the past 150 years; New Jersey has had a Frelinghuysen in the House or Senate ever since pre-Revolutionary times. Then there is Atlantic City, New Jersey, one of the few cities able to boast of a dynasty that was Jewish: the Bacharachs.

Originally from Philadelphia, the Bacharachs were among the first Jewish families to settle in Atlantic City. Prior to 1880, the only Jews to be found on Absecon Island (less than 5 miles from downtown Atlantic City) were vacationing Philadelphians. The Bacharachs, brothers Benjamin, Isaac, and Harry, were brought to the seaside resort community a year later, in 1881. Their father quickly made his mark in the community by becoming a founder of Atlantic City's first synagogue, the Reform Beth Israel. The Bacharachs would lead and succor that temple for the next seventy-five years, with Benjamin (1865–1936), the oldest of the three boys, serving as its president for more than twenty years.

The Bacharachs started out with a single clothing store, originally owned by their father. Over the years, they expanded their interests into banking, real estate, and lumber. The brothers put together a syndicate that developed Brigantine, a resort community on the northern tip of Absecon Island, and built the seaside resort's first hotel.

As their wealth increased, they became more active in civic affairs. In 1900, Harry (1873–1947), the youngest of the brothers, became president of the Atlantic City Council. The following year President William McKinley appointed him postmaster; he continued to serve in that posi-

tion for the next decade. In 1911, Harry was elected mayor of Atlantic City, an office to which he was reelected three times. He returned to the mayoralty in 1930, and served until 1935, at which time he was appointed to the New Jersey State Public Utilities Commission.

In addition to his long tenure as president of Beth Israel, Benjamin served as president of the Atlantic City Chamber of Commerce and, along with his brothers, founded and helped underwrite the Jewish Community Center of Atlantic City.

Without question, the most prominent of the three was the middle brother, Isaac (1870–1956). Although limited to a high-school education, Isaac Bacharach excelled in both business and politics. Before he turned thirty, he had become president of the Second National Bank of Atlantic City and a director of the city's Safe Deposit Company.

In 1907, Isaac joined brother Harry on the Atlantic City Council. Five years later, he was elected as a Republican to the New Jersey State Assembly. In November 1914, Isaac Bacharach was elected to Congress as representative from the Second District. A man of immense popularity, he was easily reelected ten times. During the Republican Bacharach's first two terms in Congress (1915–1919), he languished as a relatively unknown member of the minority party. Things began looking up from the moment the Republicans captured both Houses of Congress in the Harding landslide of 1920. Speaker James Beauchamp "Champ" Clark of Missouri was replaced by the Republican Frederick H. Gillett of Massachusetts. Speaker Gillett liked Bacharach's political instincts and appointed the third-term representative to a seat on the powerful Ways and Means Committee. He was reappointed to Ways and Means throughout the rest of his congressional career. Bacharach was also named to a three-man Building Commission, appointed to oversee the construction of what was then the New House Office Building. The other two members were former Speaker Nicholas Longworth of Ohio and future Speaker (and future Vice President) John Nance Garner of Texas. The "new" building, which cost more than $10 million to construct, is today known as the Longworth House Office Building—LHOB for short.

A down-the-line fiscal conservative, Bacharach could generally be counted upon to support high tariffs and low taxes. In 1931, he secured passage of a bill that would lend World War I veterans up to 50 percent of the face value of their adjusted service insurance policies. This was one of the first attempts to provide an early bonus payment for the doughboys. With unemployment rising at an alarming rate, the veterans were calling for immediate payment of the war bonuses promised for 1945. When the bonuses failed to materialize by the summer of 1932, between ten and twenty thousand men, women, and children converged on Washington, D.C., setting up "flats" beside the Anacostia River. Unemployed, hungry, and filled with rage, the impoverished ex-soldiers sang:

> Mellon pulled the whistle
> Hoover rang the bell,
> Wall Street gave the signal
> And the country went to hell.

The Bonus Army's rally ended in tragedy. Federal troops, under the command of Army Chief of Staff Douglas MacArthur (and his subordinates, Major Dwight D. Eisenhower and Captain George S. Patton), dispersed the ragtag army at the point of bayoneted rifles. The soldiers, with the assistance of the D.C. police, set the veterans' shacks ablaze and dispersed them with tear gas. Two infants died, and the sight of U.S. soldiers attacking American war veterans was truly ghastly. Political shock waves resounded throughout the land. The first to fall was President Herbert Hoover, who, as Commander in Chief, was held ultimately responsible for the debacle.

Isaac Bacharach managed to hold on to his House seat during the first Roosevelt Administration (1932–1936). He was soundly defeated in the Democratic landslide of 1936, when the Republican presidential candidate, Kansas Governor Alf Landon, was able to carry only two states, Kansas and Vermont. Isaac Bacharach returned to Atlantic City and his many business interests.

In 1924, the three Bacharach brothers (along with their two sisters) built and dedicated a Home for Afflicted Children in Longport, New Jersey. They named it in memory of their mother, Betty, who had recently died.

Isaac was married for many years to Florence Scull. They remained childless. The Bacharachs lavished attention on their many nieces and nephews, one of whom, Dr. David B(acharach) Allman, would one day serve as the second Jewish president of the American Medical Association. Dr. Allman, who grew up in the mansion built by his grandfather and uncles, was installed in a service held at Congregation Beth Israel, the synagogue his family had built, succored, and led for more than seventy-five years.

Of average height, with broad shoulders, steel gray hair, and a full mustache, Isaac Bacharach was a handsome, photogenic man. He outlived his brothers by more than ten years, finally succumbing on September 5, 1956 at age eighty-six. He is buried in Mount Sinai Cemetery in Philadelphia.

References

American Jewish Year Book, vol. 24, p. 116.
Encyclopaedia Judaica (1972).
New York Times, September 6, 1956, 25:5.
Universal Jewish Encyclopedia.
Who Was Who in America, vol. 3.
Who Was Who in American Jewry, 1926, 1928, 1938.

BEILENSON, ANTHONY CHARLES (1932–):
Democrat from California; served ten terms in the House (Ninety-fourth through One Hundred and Fourth Congress; January 3, 1977–January 3, 1997).

When Representative Tony Beilenson retired from the House of Representatives in January 1997, Capitol Hill said goodbye to a man that Roll Call named one of the "20 Smartest Members of the United States Congress." *U.S. News & World Report* called him one of the House's "Straight Arrows," a group of twelve Representatives "whose integrity is beyond reproach." Throughout his twenty-year congressional career, Beilenson was known not only for his honesty, integrity, and political savvy, but also for the fact that, unlike the vast majority of his colleagues, he refused to accept either political action committee (PAC) money or honoraria.

Peter and Edna Beilenson, the future Congressman's parents, were both first cousins of Moshe Beilenson (1889–1936), a noted Hebrew writer, journalist, and "one of the chief spokesmen of the labor movement in Eretz Israel." Originally from Veprika, Russia, Moshe Beilenson earned a medical degree before emigrating to Palestine. Under the tutelage of Zalman Shazar and Beryl Katznelson, he became a committed Zionist. From Russia, he moved to Italy. There he published a series of Hebrew translations of books of Jewish interest, including Martin Buber's *Reden über das Judentum* and R. Travers Herford's *The Pharisees*. Moving to Petach Tikvah, Palestine, in the mid-1920s, he joined the editorial board of the newly founded newspaper *Davar*. As a journalist in pre-1948 Palestine, he specialized in articles about the Jewish labor movement. When he died in 1936, one of the main hospitals in the Tel Aviv area was named after him.

Like their multi-talented cousin, Peter and Edna Beilenson were also involved in the publishing industry. Their firm, the Peter Pauper Press, was one of the handful of fine small presses in the United States from the 1930s through the 1950s. The Beilensons lived in Mount Vernon, New York, where, according to Tony

Beilenson, they "hung around with an interesting crowd." Their son, Anthony Charles Beilenson, was born in New Rochelle, New York, on October 26, 1932. The Beilensons were a totally assimilated family. Although most of their friends, drawn largely from the world of publishing and the arts, were Jewish, Judaism played almost no role in their lives. Young Tony Beilenson, whose parents neither belonged to nor attended synagogue, received virtually no Jewish education. The only Jewish aspect of their lives was the family Passover seder, which abruptly ended with the death of Edna Beilenson's father in the mid-1940s.

Beilenson attended the Wilson Elementary School in Mount Vernon, New York. In 1948, the Beilensons sent their son to Phillips Academy in Andover, Massachusetts, for his last two years of high school. The alma mater of, among others, George Herbert Walker Bush (class of '42) and Humphrey DeForest Bogart (expelled, 1916), Phillips was the quintessential WASP prep school in America. The Beilensons' decision to send their son to Andover was likely based on a family connection; Tony's cousin Lawrence Beilenson of Arkansas, a graduate of Harvard and Harvard Law School, had been a student there. "I don't really remember what my parents did with me originally or why they did it [sending him to Phillips]. I was a compliant child; if they wanted to send me away that was all right with me." Following his graduation from Phillips in 1950, Beilenson likewise headed off for Harvard, where, for four years, he roomed with the son of Max Macoby, rabbi of the Free Synagogue of Westchester. Remembering his roommate's father, Beilenson commented: "If he hadn't been a rabbi, you wouldn't have known he was Jewish."

Following his graduation from Harvard in 1954 (A.B. in American government), Tony Beilenson entered Harvard Law School ("the worst three years of my life . . . I don't think I ever picked up anything in law school, frankly"). Upon receiving his LL.B. in 1957, he headed for California, where he spent the next two years working for his cousin Lawrence in a Beverly Hills law firm. In 1960, Beilenson got his first taste of government work when he was appointed counsel to the California Assembly's Committee on Finance and Insurance. The next two years he served as staff attorney for the California Compensation and Insurance Fund. During his early days in California, Beilenson met Delores Martin, a public elementary-school teacher. Martin, who was born in Brooklyn, had moved to Los Angeles at age fourteen. Raised in the predominantly Jewish sections of Boyle Heights and Fairfax, she graduated from the University of California at Berkeley. Tony and Delores were married in 1959. They have three children: Peter Lowell, born in 1960; Dayna Anne, born in 1961; and Adam Laurence, born in 1963.

Tony Beilenson was elected to the California State Assembly from a Beverly Hills district in 1963. After one term in the Assembly, he ran successfully for the California State Senate, where he would continue to serve until his election to Congress in 1976. Shortly after his election to the State Senate, Beilenson ran for the U.S. Senate seat occupied by moderate Republican Thomas Kuchel. In the Republican primary, Kuchel was defeated by ultraconservative Dr. Max Rafferty, the California State superintendent of public instruction. Beilenson lost the Democratic primary to former state controller Alan Cranston, who then went on to defeat Rafferty and become a power in the United States Senate. Following his defeat, Beilenson settled down to a highly successful career in the State Senate.

During his decade in the Senate (1967–1976), Beilenson authored more than 200 pieces of legislation and served as chairman of the Committees on Health and Welfare (1968–1974) and Finance Committee (1975–1976). Among his more notable legislative efforts were the first reform of California's abortion laws since the late nineteenth century, the Auto Repair Fraud Act of 1971, the Funeral Reform Act of 1971 ("the most comprehensive family planning program in the nation"), and California's first state law to tax church-owned businesses. Highly esteemed by both his fellow legislators and members of the Sacramento press, Beilenson was named "Best All-Around Senator" by the Capitol press corps and "Most Effective Senator" in a poll of

his Senate colleagues. In a 1974 poll of legislative aides, he was the only state legislator (out of 120) to rate in the top three of each of the named categories: "Most Intelligent," "Most Honest," and "Most Effective."

In 1976, Beilenson gave up his State Senate seat in order to run for the Congress from California's Twenty-third District, the most heavily Jewish congressional district outside New York City. Situated on Los Angeles' West Side, it included the pricey enclaves of Bel Air, Beverly Hills, Brentwood, Century City, Malibu, Topanga Canyon, Westwood (home of UCLA), Pacific Palisades, and West Hollywood. It also extended over into the San Fernando Valley communities of Canoga Park, Reseda, Tarzana, Woodland Hills, Encino, Sherman Oaks, and West Hills—site of a devastating earthquake in January 1994. Until 1976, the Twenty-third Congressional District had never elected a Jewish representative. It had, however, been represented by a string of famous people, the three most notable being former actress Helen Gahagan Douglas, the wife of actor Melvin Douglas; James Roosevelt, the son of FDR; and Samuel Yorty, a three-term mayor of Los Angeles. Left-leaning Douglas, who served in Congress from 1945 to 1951, was the hapless opponent of Richard Nixon in the 1950 California Senate race, when he smeared her as the "Pink Lady."

In 1976, Thomas Rees, who had represented the Twenty-third District since 1965, announced his retirement from Congress. Rees, like Beilenson, a former state senator, holds the unique distinction of having represented more constituents than any state legislator in American history. In the days before the "one man, one vote" law went into effect, Rees was state senator for all of Los Angeles County— more than 7 million people. Beilenson entered a three-candidate race for the Democratic nomination, and won with 58 percent of the vote. He won the November general election going away, and was regularly reelected to nine more terms.

Following a one-term stint on House Foreign Affairs and Judiciary, Beilenson, with the help of Speaker Thomas P. "Tip" O'Neill and Congressman Richard P. Bolling, was appointed to the strategic and powerful House Rules Committee. Leaders of the California congressional delegation had wanted the seat to go to

Representative Jerry Patterson; O'Neill "didn't want to let others decide these things." Rules is the committee, in the words of the *Almanac of American Politics*, "best suited to a legislator willing to remain anonymous; it allows a skilled operator to exert important influence on many different kinds of legislation, but often silently and seldom with any fanfare." This suited Tony Beilenson's personality just fine, for he was a low key politician. On House Rules, Beilenson became known as "the most independent of the committee's Democrats." His reputation as an independent thinker led the authors of the *Almanac of American Politics* to conclude: "He is one who seems to vote almost entirely on the merits of legislation, without much regard to who is backing or opposing it." Beilenson also became the House's "closest student of the budget process." In the mid-1980s, he was already urging the House to "prepare a plan to erase the budget deficit by 1989." He also quickly became the House's leading advocate of full public financing of congressional elections.

In his third term (1981–1983), Tony Beilenson was appointed to the House Permanent Select Committee on Intelligence, and became chair of its Oversight and Evaluation Subcommittee. By the beginning of the One Hundred and First Congress (January 1991), he had become chairman of the full committee. From that position, Beilenson "tried to promote bipartisan cooperation and amity with the Bush Administration." His efforts often met with frustration, as when he sought to create "covert action language" for federal intelligence-gathering agencies. In this case, Beilenson was "whipsawed between demands by liberal Barbara Boxer and opposition from President Bush, who unexpectedly vetoed Beilenson's compromise measure."

The House Permanent Select Committee on Intelligence has a five-term limit on service. Beilenson asked Speaker Thomas Foley for a waiver at the end of the One Hundredth Congress, so that he could remain committee chair; Foley refused, as did Beilenson's own Rules Committee. Transferring off Intelligence, Beilenson picked up a spot on the equally strategic House Budget Committee, where he chaired the Task Force on the Budget Process, Reconciliation, and Enforcement.

On the Budget Committee, Beilenson "urged changes which make good policy but bad politi-cal sense." Chief among these were his call for a 50-cent gas tax increase over five years ("we can pay now . . . or pay OPEC later") and a proposal to make cuts in Social Security (as well as other programs) in order to cut the deficit. Beilenson was an early opponent of the ill-fated Catastrophic Health Care bill. In opposing the measure, he argued that it did not provide coverage for long-term nursing home care, was redundant in its provision for drug expenses, and "given its expense, it should have covered the young and old."

One of Tony Beilenson's most exotic causes was his African Elephant Conservation Act of 1988, which restricted U.S. imports of elephant ivory. As the first action taken by an ivory-importing nation to stem the decline of the species, Beilenson's legislation was the catalyst for a major international campaign to save the elephant. It resulted in the October 1989 decision at the Convention on International Trade in Endangered Species to ban worldwide trade in elephant ivory. In 1990 and 1991, he managed to secure $8.3 million for projects aimed at preventing the elephant's extinction.

Following the 1990 census, Beilenson's district became more Republican—so much so that he gave thought to running in the West Side Twenty-ninth District. Rather than face fellow Democrat Henry Waxman in the primary, Beilenson decided to "take his chances" in the newly reshaped (and renamed) Twenty-fourth District. The new district included most of the southern and western San Fernando Valley, "from the hillside mansions of Encino to the gang territory around the old Van Nuys General Motors plant." Despite the fact that he took no PAC contributions, Beilenson was able to raise nearly $680,000 for his campaign against Ventura County Assemblyman Tom McClintock, who had come in first in nine-candidate Republican primary. McClintock, a conservative, sought to "privatize street lights and prisons" and was a "fierce critic" of tax increases, abortion, and gun control. Beilenson, enjoying the advantages of incumbency, won with 56 percent of the vote.

In Beilenson's last race (1994), he faced Richard Sybert, a former aide to Republican Governor Pete Wilson. Although Sybert actually "outspent and outhustled" him, Beilenson managed to eke out a 4,500-vote victory. Beilenson's razor-thin victory was most likely the product of "residual goodwill toward [him for] his help in delivering federal disaster aid following the 1994 earthquake, plus Jewish and showbiz voters' antipathy to the cultural conservatism of national Republicans." Following his victory, Beilenson announced that this election would be his last; after nearly thirty years in office, he would retire from public life.

On the weekend of January 25–27, 1991, the Ramah Academy, a Jewish camp north of Los Angeles, held an unprecedented conclave with the area's four Jewish members of Congress: Tony Beilenson, *Henry Waxman, Mel Levine*, and *Howard Berman*. The weekend came on the heels of the House's historic vote on military engagement in the Persian Gulf. Beilenson voted against going to war. During the session on that vote and developments in the Gulf, Beilenson outlined the thinking that went into his no vote: "I don't like Americans systematically inflicting great violence and punishment on another people without absolutely compelling reasons for doing so," Beilenson explained to the several hundred people who attended the weekend session. "I don't like the fact that we are killing thousands of human beings who have not harmed any of us, who have no capability of doing so, and whose threat to our own national interests was contained months ago without the need of hostilities." In Beilenson's opinion, the Gulf War sent the wrong message to the world at large: "By unilaterally ratcheting up the level of rhetoric and U.S. response, we sent absolutely the wrong signal to the rest of the world: that we would be happy to do the job for them, that we would take care of the problem for them." Upon reflection, Beilenson believed that President George Bush's policy of diplomatic containment would have been the best way to go: "Sanctions were working," he said, "and would succeed in weakening Saddam considerably if we were patient. We had succeeded in cutting off Iraq's

oil exports, almost its entire source of income; that had reduced Iraq's GNP by 50 percent, and would reduce it by 70 percent in the near future. Sanctions would have weakened Iraq's military capability as shortages of spare parts and needed materiel develop[ed]." Although Beilenson saw the necessity of protecting Israel at all costs, he concluded: "I regret that the first major world problem since the end of the Cold War is being resolved in this manner: by military force, rather than by diplomacy and economic and political pressure. I regret that we didn't have the sense, the imagination, the wit, to deal with the problem in a way that could have produced the desired results without going to war."

During his many years on the Rules Committee, Tony Beilenson was the point man on Israel-related issues. On his many trips abroad (which, unlike most of his colleagues, he generally paid for out of his own pocket), he regularly had the State Department set up meetings with local Jewish groups and then have prominent Jews invited to American embassy dinners. On one trip to Eastern Europe, he escorted members of the Intelligence Committee to Auschwitz and Birkenau. One of the people on the trip, Jean Hyde (the late wife of Illinois Republican Henry Hyde), went back to Illinois and talked to her Catholic women's group about the camps. "She had them in tears," Beilenson remembers. While on a 1993 visit to troops in Saudi Arabia, Beilenson took his group back through Israel. For most, it was the first time they had ever visited the Jewish state.

References

Interview with Anthony Beilenson, Washington, D.C., February 1992.

Almanac of American Politics (1980–1996 editions).

Politics in America (1980–1996 editions).

Ramah Institute Weekend, January 25–27, 1991 (transcript).

BENJAMIN, JUDAH PHILLIP (1811–1884): *Whig (turned Democrat) from Louisiana; served eight years in the Senate (Thirty-fourth through Thirty-sixth Congress; March 4, 1853–February 4, 1861).*

One of the most fascinating and talented men ever to grace the American political stage, Judah P. Benjamin was both a successful attorney and a plantation owner; a man who would serve as United States Senator and as Attorney General, Secretary of War, and Secretary of State of the Confederate States of America. Benjamin played a pivotal role in the C.S.A.'s brief life, for which he was variously labeled "the brains of the Confederacy," "Judas Iscariot Benjamin," and, most snidely, "Mr. [Jefferson] Davis' pet Jew." Stephen Vincent Benét referred to him as "the dark prince . . . with the perpetual smile."

Judah Benjamin (1811–1884), like *David Levy-Yulee*, the first member of the Congressional Minyan, was born in the Caribbean to a Sephardic family of English origin. Like Levy-Yulee, he spent most of his childhood in Charleston. The chances of their having been acquainted in youth seems rather remote; Levy-Yulee, the son of a wealthy landowner, was sent to Charleston specifically to receive an education. From all indications, his contacts with the approximately 650-strong Jewish community were, at best, infrequent. Benjamin, on the other hand, was the son of a largely unsuccessful fruit merchant. Where Levy-Yulee spent his Charleston years being schooled, Benjamin whiled away countless hours playing on the docks of that bustling seaport.

The future United States Senator was the eldest of seven Benjamin children. His mother, Rebecca Mendes Benjamin, was descended from a distinguished Jewish family known for its scholars, physicians, and international traders. His father, Phillip, whom one writer described as a "small, intelligent, olive-skinned Sephardic" was well-known in the Jewish community of Charleston. He was not a pious Jew in the traditional sense; the Benjamins, much to the consternation and displeasure of their more Orthodox Jewish neighbors, kept their shop open on the Sabbath. Phillip Benjamin was "committed to changing Judaism to conform to the realities of the modern world." He was one of the forty-seven members of Congregation Beth Elohim to petition the synagogue's board of trustees for changes in the liturgy, including the use of English for some of the prayers and the weekly sermon. When the board tabled the request, the dissenters, Phillip Benjamin among them, broke away and formed America's first liberal congregation, the Reformed Society of Israelites. Phillip was selected to serve on the all-important committee on correspondence, more in tribute to his leadership skills and abilities than his financial standing. Eventually, however, he was banished from the Reformed Society of Israelites, most likely for his continued desecration of the Sabbath.

Judah Benjamin was an intellectually gifted child; one account depicts him reciting Shakespeare while playing marbles. The future Senator and statesman was "discovered" by a Jewish merchant of Charleston, Moses Lopez, who advised the boy's parents about their son's extraordinary gifts. They both agreed that young Judah deserved a more thorough education than could be obtained in Charleston. And so, at fourteen, armed with a Hebrew copy of the Book of Psalms, Judah Benjamin set out for Yale. He was by far the youngest member of the class of 1829. It had been seventeen years since the last Jew had attended that school. Indeed, in the first half of the nineteenth century, Jews made up less than one-tenth of one percent of Yale's student body. While a student in New Haven, Benjamin was consistently ranked number one in his class. Known in later life as an orator of spellbinding proportions, young Benjamin joined "Brothers in Unity," one of Yale's two great debating societies. While a member of this group, he debated such issues as "Ought Missouri to have been admitted to the Union with the privilege of holding slaves?" and "Ought the United States take immediate measures for the manumission of the slaves of our Country?"

At the end of his second year at Yale, the enormously popular Benjamin was expelled. The reasons for his expulsion have never been adequately explained, although in his biography, *Judah P. Benjamin: Southern Confederate*, Eli Evans quotes a letter the sixteen-year-old Benjamin wrote to Yale president Jeremiah Day. In it, he expressed his gratitude for "their kind indulgence to my father in regard to pecuniary affairs," and expressed the fervent hope that he might soon be reinstated. Day did not respond; Benjamin never returned to Yale.

Judah Benjamin's return to Charleston was short-lived. Acting in accordance with the age-old Hebrew adage *m'shaneh makom, m'shaneh mazal* ("A change of place changes luck"), Benjamin opted to relocate to New Orleans, the young nation's fourth-largest city. It turned out to be a very wise choice. In the mid-1820s, New Orleans had a Jewish population of no more than 700 families. Of these, only four kept kosher and but two observed the Sabbath. Nonetheless, New Orleans was a place well-suited for Judah Benjamin's skills and temperament. Native ability, drive, and determination meant as much as social standing, religion, or family connections in antebellum New Orleans.

Young Benjamin worked at a series of odd jobs while reading law and preparing for his future. One of his part-time jobs found him tutoring sixteen-year-old Natalie St. Martin in exchange for French lessons, an essential skill in Creole-dominated New Orleans. Before the year was out, the beautiful, sloe-eyed Natalie was affianced to the young, up-and-coming Jewish attorney-to-be. She called him "Philipe."

Natalie's father, the prosperous Auguste St. Martin, demanded that his future son-in-law convert to Catholicism. Benjamin refused. After much give-and-take, they reached a compromise: Benjamin could remain a Jew but would have to permit Natalie to raise any children they might have as Catholics. Judah and Natalie were married in 1833.

"Philipe" and Natalie lived with her parents for the first three years of their marriage, during which time Judah worked on a massive legal text. Aiding him in his research was a future Chief Justice of the Louisiana Supreme Court, Thomas Slidell. Tom's brother, John Slidell (1793–1871), sensing a spark of greatness in the young Jewish lawyer, quickly became Judah's mentor. He would eventually become Benjamin's Senate colleague. During the Civil War, he would serve the Confederacy as ambassador to both England and France. A native New Yorker, John Slidell was a graduate of Columbia College and a member of that state's bar. He was also related by marriage to Jewish financier August Belmont. As a result of his close association with two Jews, John Slidell would often be accused of being a Jew himself. Slidell laughed off the charge as ridiculous and continued to be Judah Benjamin's political champion. The Slidell brothers were political focal points in antebellum New Orleans—slick, corrupt, and absolutely fearless. The name "Slidell" in Louisiana was uttered with the same political reverence (or contempt) as "Tammany" in New York.

Judah Benjamin's legal casebook proved to be an immediate success. It permitted the twenty-three-year-old attorney to enter doors that otherwise would have been firmly locked and barred. Almost overnight, he acquired a measure of *gravitas* that men twice his age would never attain. He began taking on extremely complex, and lucrative, cases. Within a few short years he was in the enviable position of being able to select only cases and clients that appealed to him. He took on issues running the gamut from railroads to land disputes, and from international law to the intricacies of Louisiana's unique Napoleonic Code. By his fortieth birthday (1851), Benjamin was making as much as $50,000 a year, easily more than a million tax-free dollars by today's inflated standards.

Judah Benjamin's rapid ascent in the legal world brought him wealth, social position, and respect. It also ruined his marriage. Like many ambitious young men, Judah spent less and less time at home. Natalie, forever restless, coquettish, and self-absorbed, responded to the isolation and neglect by promenading through New Orleans society on the arms of dashing young men. Quite understandably, her suspected trysts and affairs became the subject of gossip in polite society. As liberated as antebellum New Orleans seemed on the surface, it was still a provincial Catholic town. When Judah Benjamin heard the gossip about his wife, he quickly recognized that he was partly to blame; he had become too absorbed in his work. He also knew that Natalie's peccadilloes, whether real or imagined, could easily damage his career. In response to this dicey situation, Benjamin decided to take a break from the law and change his lifestyle.

In 1842, Benjamin purchased a magnificent plantation named Bellechasse. Upon completion, it would house some 140 slaves and one of the grandest, most architecturally significant mansions in all the South. Benjamin believed that Bellechasse would make a new woman out of Natalie by giving her life added focus. He envisioned her taking on the role of planter's wife. Benjamin also knew that it would make good civic sense to become a member of the planter class; no Southerner with political ambitions could "arrive" without first becoming a successful landowner. Judah moved his mother and sisters to Bellechasse. His sister Rebecca met and married a Jewish lawyer, Abraham Levy. Benjamin now lived in a house of women. Natalie found life on the plantation even more stultifying than in New Orleans. At least there she had been with her family and friends.

In 1843, after ten years of marriage, Natalie gave birth to Judah Benjamin's only child, a girl named Ninette. From all accounts, Judah was ecstatic. Within two short years, however, Natalie's ennui had gotten the best of her; she took baby Ninette and moved to Paris, where, with the exception of one brief interlude, they would remain for the rest of their lives, generously supported by America's most famous Jew. Over the next forty years, Judah Benjamin would spend but one month in twelve with his wife and daughter. All that remains of Natalie's correspondence to "Philipe" is one revealing line: "Oh talk to me not of economy, it is so fatiguing."

Judah Benjamin discovered that he loved the challenge of plantation life. Like Thomas Jefferson before him, he turned out to be an agronomist of noteworthy proportions. He all but single-handedly introduced sugarcane to the South, and successfully ushered in new, more efficient techniques of drainage, fertilization, and extraction of sugar from molasses. Benjamin was known as a kind and enlightened slaveowner. He looked upon the "peculiar institution" as a regional economic necessity rather than a divinely ordained fact.

Like David Levy-Yulee, Judah P. Benjamin first entered politics under the Whig banner. He was elected to the Louisiana legislature in 1842, where he opposed both the reopening of the slave trade and the admission of more slave states. Despite this, his political star rose rapidly. In 1844, he was a delegate to the state's Constitutional Convention. In 1846, with the outbreak of the Mexican-American War, the federal government sent him to California, where he was appointed land commissioner. In that capacity he untangled the complex mess of disputed land claims arising out of the war. From all indications, he performed his duties with both skill and aplomb. In 1848, in his capacity as a Whig elector, he traveled to Washington, D.C. to attend the inauguration of President Zachary Taylor.

Taylor wanted the thirty-seven-year-old lawyer for his cabinet but apparently demurred upon receiving reports of Mrs. Benjamin's "scandalous" behavior. What troubled the proper Virginian most was the fear that she would never be accepted by polite Washington society. President Taylor need not have concerned himself; Natalie and little Ninette had already been living in Paris for nearly three years prior to his election. Had Judah P. Benjamin been appointed to Taylor's cabinet, there is no telling what road his career might have taken. Taylor died less than a year and a half into his term, and was succeeded by Millard Fillmore.

Bellechasse continued turning a profit until 1852, when a series of financial reverses forced Benjamin to sell. His days as a planter and slaveowner were over. With the proceeds of the sale he purchased a fine home in Washington, where he would live throughout his career as United States Senator. Today, after nearly 150 years, the scarred structural remains of Bellechasse stand mutely amid the weeds and brambles, a pale ghost of its former glory.

On December 5, 1853, Judah P. Benjamin and John Slidell were duly sworn in as United States Senators from the sovereign state of Louisiana. Both would serve until February 4, 1861, when they became the final members of the Southern delegation to resign their seats. During his seven years in the Senate, Benjamin earned a reputation for being one of that body's truly great minds and easily its most powerful orator. Short and stocky with dark curly hair and an olive complexion, Benjamin sported a closely cropped beard and what appeared to be a perpetual smile. Although well-respected by his Senate colleagues, Benjamin, like David Levy-Yulee, was nonetheless the target of anti-Jewish barbs. Unlike Senator Levy-Yulee however, the Senator from Louisiana refused to hide behind a mask of denial. Quite the contrary; the Benjamin riposte was a thing of Senate legend. Once, during a heated colloquy on the possible extension of slavery into Kansas, an exasperated Ben Wade (Senator from Ohio) attacked Benjamin's religion. Benjamin is reported to have looked directly at Wade and replied: "It is true that I am a

Jew, and when my ancestors were receiving their Ten Commandments from the immediate hand of Deity, the ancestors of my opponent were herding swine in the forests of Great Britain!"

In 1858, Natalie returned from Paris and moved back in with her "Philipe." Almost immediately, the old rumors began to resurface; Natalie's dissatisfaction was apparent. Fresh from the liberated atmosphere of Paris, she found Washington both provincial and terribly stultifying. By early 1859, she was back in Paris for good.

One issue of specifically Jewish concern cropped up during Benjamin's first Senate term: a proposed Swiss-American commercial treaty that included a provision effectively restricting the right of Jews to reside in Switzerland. According to the terms of the treaty, each of Switzerland's cantons would have the right to adopt its own Jewish policy. This may at first have seemed harmless enough, but in 1857, when an American Jewish businessman was "invited" to leave one of the cantons, the issue took on a life of its own. Voices across America were raised in protest. Moreover, despite the hue and cry emanating from the Jewish community, most people in Washington saw it as a singularly American issue. Secretary of State Lewis Cass lodged an eloquent, impassioned protest with the Swiss government on behalf of the American people:

In their migrations [the Jews] have at length reached a continent by whose rivers they may sit down without weeping in the language of their psalmist, even when remembering Zion, and where the law secures equal rights to all, be they Jew or Gentile. . . . Beside their legal right to equal protection there is no portion of our population whose peaceable and law-abiding conduct better proves than theirs does, that they are well entitled to all the privileges secured to every American by our system of government.

The Jewish community, seeking to find its voice, also protested the treaty, but with neither the volume nor the efficacy of its non-Jewish allies. *Phillip Phillips*, a former one-term Representative from Alabama, and Jonas Levy (see article on *Jefferson Monroe Levy*) became the major Jewish lobbyists/organizers against the treaty. A lengthy debate ensued in both the House and the Senate. Judah Benjamin, despite his position as America's most recognizable, if not influential, Jew, played less than a minor role in the ongoing drama. Throughout the weeks of debate, the *Congressional Globe* (fore-runner of the modern *Congressional Record*) carried but one reference to the Senate's lone Jew:

Mr. Benjamin presented . . . a petition of citizens of the United States, professing the Jewish religion, praying that measures may be taken to secure to American citizens of every religious creed, residing or traveling abroad, their civil and religious rights; which was referred to the Committee on Foreign Relations.

Judah Benjamin's lack of involvement in "L'Affaire Suisse" strikes one as both curious and unconscionable. Who better to take the lead and manage floor debate over the treaty than the chamber's one Jew? Was his silence a mark of disinterest or merely smart politics? It is possible that Benjamin, seeing the matter already in capable hands, decided to stand back. Then again, Benjamin had neither the desire nor the temperament to become the political spokesman for the American Jewish community. Whatever the case, it is obvious that Judah P. Benjamin was not going to become "The Jewish Senator." Nonetheless, the Senate did not ratify the Swiss-American treaty until its restrictive language had been reworded. The Swiss Constitution was amended in 1866, ever after ensuring equality for citizens, residents, and travelers of all religious persuasions.

Until 1913, the U.S. Constitution empowered the various state legislatures, and not the people of the states, to elect members of the United States Senate. It was only with the ratification of the Seventeenth Amendment that Senators were popularly elected. In essence, under the pre-1913 protocol, he who was able to muster the greatest number of political IOU's from members of the state legislature stood the best chance of becoming a United States Senator. Such was the case with Judah P. Benjamin. The Louisiana legislature reelected him for another six-year term in 1859, although until it was final, his victory was by no means a sure thing. During the campaign in the legislature, word went out that Benjamin, chairman of the Senate Committee on Private Land Claims, had helped his friend Senator Slidell make a huge profit from a questionable land deal. The charges were never proven. More to the point, powerful political forces in the upstate region were tired of having two Senators from New Orleans. Benjamin's reelection did not come until the forty-second ballot, and only then by the slimmest of margins. There is no indication that Benjamin's Jewishness became an issue in an otherwise brutal campaign of vilification preceding his election.

In October 1859, John Brown and his band captured the arsenal at Harper's Ferry, Virginia. Judah Benjamin's second term began in December; he was still that body's only self-professed Jew. (Senator Levy-Yulee of Florida, refusing to admit his Jewish antecedents, claimed to be of Moroccan parentage.) In the early days of 1860, the Senate was ablaze with the fiery, combative rhetoric of Secessionists like Yulee and the more reasoned states' rights arguments of Judah Phillip Benjamin. The Republicans were selecting a former one-term Congressman from Illinois to lead their party in the upcoming presidential election. Two of the three men placing Lincoln's name before the Republican convention were Jewish: Morris Pinner of Missouri and Louis N. Dembitz of Kentucky.

Judah Benjamin, who, until virtually the eleventh hour, had sought to bring about a rapprochement between North and South, would go on to play a central role in the Civil War. He was also the last Southern Senator to resign his seat. His farewell address is considered one of the great speeches in American history. Delivered before a hushed Senate chamber on New Year's Eve, 1860, it was that rare combination of finely crafted words being delivered by a masterful orator:

> And now, Senators, within a few weeks we part, to meet as Senators in one common council chamber of the nation no more forever. We desire, we beseech you, let this parting be in peace . . . indulge in no veiled delusion that duty or conscience, interest or honor imposes upon you the necessity of invading our States or shedding the blood of our peo-

ple. We have not possible justification for it . . . what may be the fate of this horrible contest no man can tell . . . but this much, I will say: the fortunes of war may be adverse to our arms, you may carry despolation into our peaceful land, and with torch and fire you may set our cities in flame . . . you may, under the protection of your advancing armies, give shelter to the furious fanatics who desire, and profess to desire, nothing more than to add all the horrors of a servile insurrection to the calamities of civil war; you may do all this—and more too, if more there be—but you never can subjugate us; you never can convert the free sons of the soil into vassals, paying tribute to your power; and you never, never can degrade them to the level of an inferior and servile race. Never! Never!

Were one not aware that Judah Benjamin was speaking about the South, one might well imagine that he was referring to his fellow Jews, never subjugated or degraded "to the level of an inferior and servile race." The Northern press's response to Benjamin's speech was singularly hostile; it upbraided Southern Jews for supporting the Secessionist cause.

Judah Benjamin spent the war years serving the Confederate States of America in a variety of high-level posts. As Secretary of War, he was regularly pilloried by the Southern press for "his" army's military setbacks and defeats, and denounced for not supplying the troops with all the materiel and ordnance they required. It was even suggested that "the Jew Benjamin" was making a personal profit. More than one Southern editorialist discovered how easy it was to transmute "Judah" into "Judas".

Benjamin's tenure as Secretary of War was brief; he was soon made Secretary of State. As his cause's chief internationalist, Benjamin busied himself getting the British and French to supply Confederate forces with the goods they needed. He even proposed the arming of slaves to fight for the South. This proposal was roundly defeated. Toward the end of the war, he ventured through Northern lines in order to begin setting the stage for eventual surrender.

A tireless, ebullient statesman, he made a perfect counterbalance to the sickly, depressive Jefferson Davis. According to Davis's wife, Varina, the Confederate President leaned heavily upon his Secretary of State and deeply respected his judgment. Surprisingly, Benjamin merited but a single reference in Davis's voluminous memoirs. At war's end, members of the Davis cabinet went their separate ways, seeking to keep a few steps ahead of their Northern pursuers. Judah Benjamin's tale of escape and relocation to England has, over the past century, taken on an almost mythical quality. An obituarist, writing in the *Times* of London, provided a synopsis of the perilous journey:

> After many hairbreadth escapes he got in an open boat, old and leaky, from Florida to the Bahamas, where he landed. He was shipwrecked on his way to Nassau, in a vessel laden with sponges. A British man-of-war rescued the unfortunate passengers and carried them to St. Thomas. The steamer in which he started from this island caught fire and had to be put back. At length Mr. Benjamin reached England.

Benjamin arrived in London in 1865, armed with native intelligence, irrepressible spirit and wit, and one hundred bales of cotton. These he quickly sold for $20,000, which permitted him to send money to his sisters back home and to continue supporting his wife and daughter in Paris. Desiring admittance to the English Bar, he first had to pay his dues by studying British common law. On January 13, 1866, Benjamin was admitted as a student to the ironically named Lincoln's Inn, where aspiring British barristers studied law, took their meals, and lived together communally. The former United States Senator and C.S.A. Secretary of State was now thrown into a community where he was, on average, twenty-five to thirty years older than his fellows, who, for the most part, were the products of English public schools (Harrow, Eton, Rugby) and either Oxford or Cambridge.

One is reminded of the great Rabbi Akiva, sitting at a tiny desk beside his three-year-old son, surrounded by little boys beginning their first day of school. Jewish tradition recounts that by the end of his first year of study, Akiva was teaching the class. In like manner, Benjamin completed the three-year course of legal study in less than six months, and was called to the bar on June 6, 1866. While one cannot doubt that Benjamin's intellectual prowess and innate drive

made his rapid progress possible, he also made use of personal connections. The *Times* of London reported that "due to the intercession of Lords Justice Turner and Gifford, and of Lord Hatherley and Sir Fitzroy Kelley, he was allowed to forego the normal three years of 'unprofitable dining' and to enter the bar after a very short stint."

Shortly after he began studying at Lincoln's Inn, Benjamin suffered severe financial reverses. In order to pay for his education and maintain a semblance of civilized living, he was driven to newspaper work. He became a writer for the *London Daily Telegraph*, specializing in stories on international affairs. Despite the success he would eventually realize as a British barrister, Benjamin continued on as a working journalist until the end of his life.

Benjamin's first legal assignment was in the northern circuit, which included Liverpool. He was no doubt chosen for this post because of his connections in the American South. Liverpool was the market where most of the South's prewar cotton crop had been sold. Understandably, his first clients were solicitors representing Liverpudlian cotton merchants.

It will be recalled that Benjamin's early career skyrocketed after he published a compendious work on the law. History repeated itself on the other side of the Atlantic. As he was building up a clientele, Benjamin was also doing research on another legal tome. In August 1868, he published a book that would propel him into the first rank of British barristers: *Treatises on the Law of Sale of Personal Property, with Reference to the American Decisions to the French Code and Civil Law*. Known by the shorthand title *Benjamin on Sales*, it went through three printings during his lifetime and is still considered a classic.

In 1869 Benjamin became a "Palatine Silk"—Queen's Counsel for the County Palatine of Lancaster. Within three years, he had his pick of cases, and actually was in a position to decline any matter that was not to be heard before either the House of Lords or the Judicial Committee of the Privy Council. In the decade between 1872 and 1882, he appeared as counsel in more than 135 cases before these two tribunals of last resort.

In 1880, Judah Benjamin was thrown from a moving streetcar in Paris and suffered numerous injuries. Despite his advanced age (sixty-nine) and the slow pace of recovery, he refused to remain idle. He soon returned to the practice of law. In December, 1882, he suffered a heart attack, brought on by diabetes. In early 1883, he announced that, due to poor health, he would retire from the bar and move permanently to Paris. News reports of this announcement included the fact that he was returning more than $100,000 in retainers to the clients he would no longer be able to serve. His retirement was noted in all the major newspapers. The English bar threw him an unprecedented "collective farewell" banquet.

Benjamin moved across the English Channel to Paris, where he took up residence with Natalie in a glorious three-story mansion he had built at 41 Avenue d'Iléna, one of the six avenues radiating out from the Place de l'Etoile, near the site of the Arc de Triomphe. He died at home on May 6, 1884. History records that Natalie brought in a Catholic priest to administer the last rites; there is no indication, however, that he consented to a conversion. Funeral services were held at St. Pierre de Chaillot, the same church where Ninette had married a French army captain, Henri de Bousignac, in 1874. Judah P. Benjamin, the first professing Jew to serve in the United States Congress, was buried in Père Lachaise cemetery under a marker with the simple inscription "Philipe Benjamin."

For more than half a century, passersby would have absolutely no idea that the individual buried in this lovely Parisian cemetery was in fact a Jew who had been one of the more accomplished men of the nineteenth century. In 1938, the Paris chapter of the Daughters of the American Confederacy rectified the situation by providing a new headstone for the almost anonymous grave. It read:

Judah Phillip Benjamin
Born St. Thomas West Indies August 6, 1811
Died in Paris May 6, 1884
United States Senator From Louisiana
Attorney General, Secretary of War
And Secretary of State of the Confederate States
Of America, Queen's Counsel, London

References

American Jewish Year Book, vol. 2 (1900–1901), p. 517.

Dictionary of American Biography.

Eli N. Evans, *Judah P. Benjamin: The Jewish Confederate* (New York: Free Press, 1988).

Jewish Encyclopedia.

New York Times, May 8, 1884, 1:6.

Dan A. Oren, *Joining the Club: A History of Jews and Yale* (New Haven: Yale University Press, 1985).

Publications of the American Jewish Historical Society, vol. 12, pp. 63–85; vol. 38, pp. 153–171.

Universal Jewish Encyclopedia.

BERGER, VICTOR LUITPOLD (1860–1929):
Socialist from Wisconsin; served five terms in the House (Sixty-second, Sixty-sixth, Sixty-eighth through Seventieth Congress; March 4, 1911–March 3, 1913, March 4, 1923–March 3, 1929).

The first of three Socialists elected to Congress, Victor Berger seemingly spent more time in federal court than on the House floor. Sentenced by Judge Kenesaw Mountain Landis in 1919 to twenty years in the federal penitentiary for subversive activities, Berger waged a long and costly legal battle not only for exoneration, but for the right to be officially seated in Congress.

Victor Berger was born in Nieder-Rehbach, Austria, on February 18, 1860, the eldest of Ignatz and Julia Berger's four children. When he was seven, the family moved to Leutschau, a small town in the mountains of Hungary, where his parents operated the village inn. Unlike many Jews of that era, the Bergers were staunchly royalist in their sympathies. For a while, the family prospered, and Victor attended private schools. When the family's finances took a sudden downturn, he found himself attending the local public school. After graduating secondary school, Victor Berger attended both the University of Vienna and the University of Budapest, where he studied philosophy, political science, and history. In 1878, he left for America and settled in Bridgeport, Connecticut. After trying his hand at various pursuits (metal polisher, boiler mender, and leather-goods salesman), he moved on to Milwaukee, where he became a teacher of German in the public schools. There, on December 4, 1897, he married one of his former students, Meta Schlichting, the daughter of one of the local school commissioners. They had two daughters. The elder, Doris, who married a physician named Colin G. Welles, became an attorney. Jane, the younger, married a man named Edelman, and became the first woman ambulance surgeon in Washington, D.C. Meta served many years on the Milwaukee school board, and at one time was trumpeted for the Vice Presidency on the Socialist Party ticket.

In the late nineteenth century, Milwaukee had the highest percentage of foreign-born residents of the twenty-eight largest cities in America. By 1900, more than 150,000 of the city's 285,000 inhabitants were German by birth or parentage. As such, Milwaukee became a cradle for socialism. At the time of his arrival in Milwaukee, Victor Berger was an ardent supporter of Henry George's single-tax theory. According to George, excessive riches came unearned to individuals and companies that owned land, natural resources (like water, coal, oil, etc.), and franchises (such as railroads and streetcar companies), which, being common wealth to start with, became more and more valuable as the growing population increased the need for and value of these natural monopolies. George's solution to this growing problem was for government to recover the increased value "by taxing nothing but the values of the land, natural resources and monopolies."

As a member of a German debating club, Berger was selected to argue the case for the single-tax doctrine against socialism. The ensuing debate changed his life, for as he read and studied the question and then successfully debated against the shoe worker defending socialism, he felt in his heart that he had not won. From that point on, Berger gradually was transformed into a committed socialist.

Berger's leftist politics got him in trouble with the school board, and he was suspended for ten days for his radical ideas. Only through the assistance of the South Side *Turnverein,* a political club to which he belonged, did the suspension not turn into a permanent dismissal. In 1892, Berger left teaching and founded a German-language paper, the *Milwaukee Daily Vorwaerts.* In 1898, he became the editor of the *Social Democratic Herald,* continuing to run the paper when, in 1911, it became a daily and was renamed the *Milwaukee Leader.* Berger was the paper's editor until his death. Through his pen, he brought the concepts, ideals, and arguments of socialism to the people of Milwaukee.

Unlike many of his leftist colleagues in that era, Victor Berger was anything but an inspired orator. He was forever hampered by a voice that did not carry. In an era antedating amplification, this proved to be a serious problem. In appearance, he was short and stocky. His mustache and steel-rimmed glasses made him look like a European academic. Indeed, he was, to a great extent, an intellectual aristocrat. His sense of dignity—call it elitism—made it impossible for him to become a backslapping sort of politician.

Nonetheless, he did possess a self-deprecating sense of humor and was known to poke fun at himself, his accent, and his peculiar constituency.

It took a while for Victor Berger to find a comfortable niche on the socialist spectrum. Dissatisfied with the dogmatic Marxism of Socialist Labor Party founder Daniel De Leon, Berger was likewise uncomfortable with the conservatism of the Progressives, who supported William Jennings Bryan for President in 1896. Berger believed in gradual reform and cooperation. At one point, he thought he had found a home in a group called Social Democracy in America. This organization, an amalgam of what remained of Eugene V. Debs's American Railway Union (after the Pullman Strike) and J. A. Wayland's Brotherhood of the Cooperative Commonwealth, suffered a political split in 1899, with Berger and Debs leaving to form the Social Democratic Party. Despite the close political association between Berger and Debs, the two were never personally close or cordial. Indeed, there was an antagonism between the two that stemmed as much from their disparate personalities as from their doctrinal and policy disputes.

In addition to "educating" the public through his daily articles and editorials, Berger was an active trade unionist, heading up the Milwaukee local of the International Typographical Workers' Union. Berger gave the people of Milwaukee a daily lesson in the need for reform, preaching socialism and attacking both socialists and non-socialists alike when they failed to agree with him. When Milwaukee elected a Socialist mayor in 1910, the Republican Sentinel gave Berger full credit: "Social Democracy in Milwaukee is what it is, either for good or ill, chiefly because of Mr. Berger." In April 1910, Berger was appointed alderman-at-large; in November, he was elected to the Sixty-second Congress, defeating Henry F. Cochens, a devoted follower of the Progressive Robert M. La Follette. On March 4, 1911, Berger was sworn in as the first Socialist elected to the United States Congress.

As a member of Congress, Victor Berger confined himself to two major areas of activity: measures to improve working conditions and direct attacks on the capitalist system. Upon entering Congress, his first official act was to vote "present" rather than for or against either candidate for Speaker of the House. His first resolution called for the removal of all American troops from the Mexican border. His second resolution called for the abolition of both the United States Senate and the veto powers of the President. Through this resolution, he sought to minimize the role of elected officials who faced the voters on what he termed "an infrequent basis" (Senators at six-year intervals, Presidents at four, as compared to the two-year terms of Representatives). He also entered bills calling for old-age pensions, home rule for the District of Columbia, and limitations on working hours. Interestingly, his Socialist colleagues saw his being elected to Congress as a form of co-optation, and missed few chances to rail against him. Berger was defeated for reelection in 1912, and was unable to reclaim his seat again in 1914.

Victor Berger opposed American involvement in World War I "on principle," and wrote innumerable articles and editorials in the *Leader* to this effect. He viewed the war as an imperialist struggle between rival capitalist nations, and believed that American involvement would ultimately sacrifice the rights of labor and hinder the advance of socialism. When his paper was barred from the mails under the terms of the Espionage Act, Victor Berger found himself in deep trouble. He was indicted no fewer than five times and eventually sentenced to twenty years in the federal penitentiary at Leavenworth by Judge Landis.

At the time of his indictment, Victor Berger had won election to the Sixty-sixth Congress. But his colleagues, in a resolution passed 309 to 1, declared him "not entitled to take the oath of office as a Representative or to hold a seat therein as such." The seat was subsequently declared vacant. When the Governor of Wisconsin called for a special election to fill the vacated seat, Berger again won. Again, he was denied the right to be seated. When the Supreme Court, in 1921, overturned his conviction, Berger was finally permitted back into the House of Representatives. He served three consecutive terms until he was defeated for reelection by William Stafford in 1928. Berger supported Alfred E. Smith for President that year, largely because Smith stood firmly for repeal of Prohibition.

On July 16, 1929, Berger was struck by a streetcar in Milwaukee and suffered grave internal injuries. He lingered for three weeks, finally succumbing on August 7. Ironically, Berger's only Socialist colleague in the House, *Meyer London*, had died precisely thirty-eight months to the day earlier under similar circumstances.

References

American Jewish Year Book, vol. 32, p. 153.

Dictionary of American Biography.

Edward J. Muzik, "Victor Berger's Early Career," *Historical Messenger* (Milwaukee), 17 (March 1961).

Encyclopaedia Judaica (1972), vol. 4, col. 613.

New York Times, August 8, 1929, 25:1.

Sally M. Miller, *Victor Berger and the Promise of Constructive Socialism* (Westport, Conn.: Greenwood Press, 1973).

Who Was Who in America, vol. 1.

Who Was Who in American Jewry, 1928.

BERKLEY, ROCHELLE (1951–): *Democrat from Nevada; served in the One Hundred and Sixth Congress (January 4, 1999–present).*

Few, if any, members of the Congressional Minyan can be said to have grown up with their district. Rochelle Berkley, who was elected to the One Hundred and Sixth Congress in November 1998, can easily make that claim. When Rochelle and her family first arrived in Las Vegas in the early 1960s, the gambling mecca (and indeed the entire state of Nevada) was undergoing explosive population growth. In 1960, Nevada was home to no more than 275,000 people. By the time of Berkley's election to Congress nearly forty years later, more than 850,000 people lived in the metropolitan Las Vegas area alone. Although the third least densely populated state in the union (approximately four people per eleven square miles), Nevada has for many years been this nation's fastest-growing state. Now home to more than 1.7 million, nearly half of its residents are represented by Berkley, a product of Las Vegas' Sands by way of the Catskills' Concord.

Rochelle "Shelley" Levine, the first of William and Estella (Colonomos) Levine's two daughters, was born in New York City on January 20, 1951. Her father's side of the family, Russian immigrants, had arrived at Ellis Island in the early years of the twentieth century. Her paternal grandmother, Ana Berkowitz Levine, left Russia with one child shortly after her husband froze to death while hiding from the tsar's troops. Shortly after her arrival in New York, she married a widower with children named George Levine. Six months after their son William was born, George died. Ana, who was left to raise all the children ("hers, his, and theirs") on her own, never remarried.

Shelley's mother's side of the family were Sephardic Jews from Salonika, Greece. Shelley's great-grandmother, a woman named Torres, came to America with eight children at the turn of the century. Like Grandmother Levine, Shelley's maternal grandmother, Rachel Colonomos, reared her children by herself after the death of her husband.

At the time of Shelley's birth, the family lived at 42 Rivington Street. Within a short period, the family picked up and moved to the Catskills community of South Fallsburg. William Levine worked at the Concord Hotel, rising from waiter to coffee shop manager. In the early 1960s, the family (which now included Shelley's sister Wendy) packed up and drove out west, intent on settling in California. Stopping in Las Vegas "in the middle of the night," William Levine decided to remain for a short stay. He found employment at the Sands Hotel as a waiter, and the family rented an apartment on a monthly basis. Before too long, they moved to a better neighborhood. The family's short stay turned into a permanent move; William remained at the Sands for thirty-six years, the last ten as the hotel's maître d'.

During the years Shelley was growing up in Las Vegas, the city's Jewish population was somewhere around 2,500 people. The Levines belonged to the Conservative Temple Beth Shalom, where Estella was active in the sisterhood and president of Hadassah. Reflecting on her teenage years, Shelley says, "it [the temple] was the center of my entire social life." While attending public school, Shelley served as president of the Las Vegas B'nai B'rith Girls. "I never dated a non-Jew," Berkley said in a 1998 interview, "which is really something, considering the size of the Jewish community in Las Vegas during the 1960s and early '70s."

Shelley Levine attended the University of Nevada at Las Vegas, becoming student body president in her senior year. "I can never remember a time when I was not involved in politics," she said, hearkening back to her years at UNLV. "I always planned on having a life in public service. I knew when I was president of UNLV that I would be running for public office some day. I guess you could call it a debt owed to America. I mean, my family came here as immigrants with nothing, and was able to make something of themselves. I thought I could have a value by working harder than anyone else . . . my method of leaving a thumbprint."

After graduating from UNLV with honors in 1972, Shelley Levine was admitted to the University of San Diego School of Law, from which she received her LL.B. in 1976. In 1973, she interned for Senator Howard Cannon. While attending college and law school, Berkley spent summers working at the Sands Hotel as a waitress and occasional keno runner. "It was a great job," she said. "I could earn enough in tips in one summer to pay for an entire year's tuition." While in San Diego, Shelley Levine met Fred Berkley, a fellow law student from Queens, New York. The two married shortly after receiving their law degrees, and moved back to Las Vegas; Fred's family would eventually move from Queens to Las Vegas to be with their son and daughter in-law. The Berkleys, who were divorced in 1995, had two boys: Max, born in 1982, and Sam, born in 1985. Despite their divorce, the Berkleys have maintained close and cordial relations; Fred Berkley attended the press conference where his ex-wife officially announced her candidacy for Congress.

As a young attorney, Shelley Berkley worked as deputy director of the Nevada State Commerce Department and then as counsel for Southwest Gas Corporation. In 1982, Berkley was elected to a two-year term in the Nevada state legislature. During her single term, Democrat Berkley sponsored consumer protection laws, lemon laws, and anti-drunk driving measures. She was also instrumental in creating the Senior Law Project, which provided "affordable legal help for seniors." Midway through her legislative term, Berkley announced her candidacy for the state senate. Running a race she was "supposed to win," Berkley lost. She and her staff had been so certain of victory that they had scheduled a mass press gathering for the day after the election. When Berkley lost, the press naturally assumed that she would cancel her "victory conference." Much to their surprise, she honored her press commitments, thereby gaining a large measure of respect from members of the fourth estate.

Shortly after losing her bid for the state senate, Shelley Berkley went back to work for the Sands—this time as vice president for government and legal affairs. In this position, she worked directly under Sands chairman Sheldon Adelson. The son of a Boston cab driver, Adelson was the founder and driving force behind Comdex, the firm that virtually invented the computer trade show. According to an article in Adelson's hometown paper, the *Boston Globe*, these trade shows became "a vital link between the manufacturer and the retailer, every bit as important to a budding computer firm as advertising and sales staff." Adelson's plan was nothing short of brilliant; in addition to taking

over (sometimes even buying) space for his conventions, Comdex brokered travel arrangements and hotel accommodations. Comdex's flagship convention site was Las Vegas. Before too long, Adelson was investing in hotels and casinos along the strip, winding up as the undisputed boss of the Sands. Without question, Comdex was a gigantic moneymaker; he eventually sold the firm for an estimated $900 million. In 1998, Forbes Magazine estimated Sheldon Adelson's personal fortune to be in excess of $550 million.

As Adelson's in-house counsel for nearly a decade, Shelley Berkley flourished. Spreading her wings beyond the Sands, she became deeply involved in local and state affairs. Over the next decade, she served variously as chair of the Nevada Hotel and Motel Association, president of the Las Vegas Public Broadcasting affiliate, and director emeritus of the National Conference of Christians and Jews. In 1990, Nevada Governor Bob Miller appointed Shelley Berkley to a vacant seat on the university's board of regents. Berkley was successfully reelected to the position in 1994 and 1996.

In 1994, Republican John Ensign, a Las Vegas veterinarian and former general manager of the Gold Strike Hotel (which his family owns), upset First District Representative James Bilbray. Ensign attacked Bilbray, a moderate Democrat, for supporting President Clinton's budget and tax package in 1993, and his health care and crime bills in 1994. In turn, Bilbray trumpeted his opposition to NAFTA and the Brady bill. Ensign managed to raise more than $900,000 to Bilbray's $690,000. Shortly before the election, the *Las Vegas Review-Journal* reported that a key Bilbray political advisor stood to gain more than $7 million on a land investment if the congressman's bill to expand the Red Rock Canyon National Conservation Area passed. Despite the damaging disclosure, Bilbray came within 1,436 votes of victory.

Although a political novice, Ensign won a seat on the House Ways and Means Committee and was instrumental in forming a Gaming Caucus. Ensign supported the Republicans' Contract With America, led a fight to weaken the national commission on gaming, and successfully urged House Speaker Newt Gingrich to separate the welfare and Medicaid issues and pass a separate welfare bill. A formidable fundraiser, Ensign put together a war chest of nearly $2 million for his reelection in 1996. Running against state senator Bob Coffin, Ensign managed to eke out a 50 percent to 44 percent victory and immediately started making plans to challenge Nevada's senior senator, Harry Reid, in 1998.

Shelley Berkley bided her time, waiting for Ensign to make his formal entry into the 1998 Senate race. Within days of Ensign's announcement, Berkley held a rally on the steps of the university's Ham Hall. In announcing her candidacy for the First District seat, Berkley "edged away from the Democratic Party's liberal wing," proclaiming that she backed "smaller government, less burdensome regulation and fair, sensible taxation." She also called for more teacher accountability and higher standards for teachers and students. She promised to push for "performance audits setting educational goals and measuring achievements at the federal level." From day one, Berkley was perceived as being the Democratic front-runner.

Berkley's Republican opponent, Clark County District Judge Don Chairez, reacted to her announcement saying, "She's in the wrong party because their party doesn't believe in that. She sounds more Republican than me right now." Ironically, Chairez, who had been appointed to the bench by a Democratic governor in 1994, had not become a Republican until just days before filing for the First District race.

The race between Berkley and Chairez turned out to be as acrimonious and heated as any in the nation. It all hinged on Sheldon Adelson, Berkley's old boss. Adelson had originally urged her to run as a Republican, promising that in return he would "bankroll her campaign." Berkley refused, explaining to Adelson that the campaign finance law made it virtually impossible for him to contribute more than $5,000 to her campaign.

Shortly before the primary election (in which Berkley had only nominal opposition), the *Las Vegas Review-Journal* reported the existence of a tape recording of Berkley telling Adelson that "judges will do favors for campaign contributors," and that "Clark County commissioners' votes can be bought with jobs." Berkley quickly apologized for her "ill-chosen words," explaining that she had been giving her employer her

"best advice" about how to get Adelson's $1.2 billion Venetian Casino project the necessary votes of approval from the commission. Leading Republicans immediately jumped on the issue. Representative John Linder, chair of the Republican National Congressional Campaign Committee, said, "I think the people of Las Vegas ought to accept her apology and urge her to find another line of work." Berkley claimed that "something very insidious is going on here . . . I seem to be a victim of a `Linda Tripp' with an unlimited bankroll right here in Las Vegas," referring to the woman who had taped former White House intern Monica Lewinsky's conversations about President Clinton. When asked if she was specifically accusing Adelson (who had fired her in 1997) of taping her conversation, she said, "I believe it is self-evident what's going on here and who is behind it. You draw your own conclusions." Berkley all but dared her opponents to use the issue against her, insisting "whoever goes negative ends up the loser."

The contest between Berkley and Chairez was long on finger pointing and vituperation and short on substantive issues. Berkley scored Chairez for leaving the bench during the middle of what she called "one of the court's highest profile murder cases in years"—the trial of Jeremy Strohmeyer, accused of strangling and sexually assaulting seven-year-old Sherrice Iverson. Chairez's departure, said Berkley, showed "a lack of commitment." Republicans ran six television commercials focusing solely on Berkley's alleged ethical problems. The National Rifle Association, a term-limits group, and anti-abortion activists produced issue-oriented ads on behalf of Chairez as well.

Toward the end of the campaign, Berkley and Chairez staged a televised debate. Chairez, who insisted that he "disliked the negative tenor of the campaign," held up several newspaper headlines trumpeting his court rulings. Turning to Berkley, he said, "I don't think we need to remind people of when you made the front page of the newspaper." Chairez also managed to bring Berkley's two sons into a question about education. Chairez told viewers that his two daughters attended public schools, "with the unspoken implication that Berkley's sons did not." Berkley recoiled, calling Chairez's tactic "offensive to the point of abusive." "This is a campaign of ideas between two adults," she said. "To start dragging children through the mud is most unfortunate." Shoring up support from core Democratic groups—unions, Hispanics, blacks, and women—Berkley wound up defeating Chairez 49 percent to 46 percent.

During the campaign Shelley Berkley was diagnosed with osteoporosis, a potentially debilitating disease that attacks the bones. Being without health insurance after her ouster from the Sands Corporation, Berkley said she had "learned a great deal about the plight of more than 37 million Americans who also have no medical coverage." Learning that most insurance carriers refused to cover the costs of a simple bone scan (essential in the diagnosis and treatment of osteoporosis), Berkley said, "I believe it is time for Congress to guarantee that medical decisions will be made only by doctors and patients. We must ensure that our doctors' offices and clinics do not become assembly lines, as they have already in some cases." As a result, she came out strongly in favor of the Democrats' "Patient Bill of Rights" legislation, which would extend broad coverage options for people covered by HMOs and managed-care groups. As of early 1999, Berkley's medical condition had improved dramatically.

Berkley's campaign brought several leading Democrats out to Las Vegas, including House Minority Leader Richard Gephardt. He promised Berkley that, should their party reclaim leadership in the One Hundred and Sixth Congress (it did not), she would be appointed to Ways and Means. As a member of the One Hundred and Sixth's minority, Berkley was appointed to the Infrastructure and Transportation and the Veteran's Affairs Committees.

Just two weeks after her election to the House, Shelley Berkley's younger son, Sam, became bar mitzvah at Temple Beth Shalom. Recently, she was remarried to Las Vegas nephrologist Larry Lehrner.

References

Interview with Shelley Berkley, December 1998.

Boston Globe, May 19, 1985, A89.

Las Vegas Review-Journal, April 2, 1998, 1B; June 12, 1998, 1B; August 2, 1998, 2B; August 24, 1998, 1D; October 15, 1998, 4B; November 4, 1998, 1B.

BERMAN, HOWARD LAWRENCE (1941–):

Democrat from California; has served nine terms in the House (Ninety-eighth through One Hundred and Sixth Congress; January 3, 1983–present).

When Howard Berman entered UCLA in September of 1959, the race for the Democratic presidential nomination was in its earliest stages. At the head of the pack were Senators John F. Kennedy of Massachusetts, Lyndon B. Johnson of Texas, and Stuart Symington of Missouri. Trailing somewhat behind the front-runners was former Illinois Governor Adlai E. Stevenson, the man who had lost the presidency to Dwight Eisenhower in both 1952 and 1956. While the smart money was on Kennedy, youthful idealists threw their support behind Stevenson. At UCLA, the Draft Stevenson movement was headed by a twenty-year-old under-graduate named *Henry Waxman*. Waxman befriended Berman, who like himself was a native Angelino. The two were drawn together by political values and a point of personal commonality: "not having a lot of dates." Together with Howard's brother Michael, they forged an "alliance" that over the next thirty-five-plus years changed the face of California politics: the Waxman-Berman "mach-ine." Waxman and Berman are quick to argue whenever their "alliance" is called a "machine." Berman defines it as "a coalition of friends who share political goals."

Joseph Berman, the future Congressman's father, was a clothing salesman. While still a youngster in Poland, Joe peddled fabrics door-to-door. At age twelve, he arrived in New Jersey, speaking not a word of English. Within six years, Joe Berman had mastered the language and was a student at New York University. In 1934, he married Eleanor Shapiro, a fellow student. The two moved to Los Angeles, where their first son, Howard Lawrence, was born on April 15, 1941. Six years later, a second son, Michael, was born. Despite the differences in age and outward style (Howard playing Dr. Jekyll to Michael's Mr. Hyde), the brothers have had an indelible impact on each other.

Howard grew up in the "middle-class heavily Jewish" Beverlywood section of West Los Angeles. The "single most important Jewish experience" in his life came in the summer of 1956, when he went to camp Machene Yehuda in the Santa Susanna Mountains, just northeast of the San Fernando Valley. At the time, the camp's head counselor was a young rabbi named Chaim Potok, who would one day gain international fame as the author of such novels as *My Name Is Asher Lev*, *The Chosen*, and *The Promise*. Berman started learning conversational Hebrew at Machene Yehuda. The next summer, he went back—as a dishwasher, because "I didn't speak enough Hebrew to be a waiter." "To this day," Berman once quipped, "I know all the Israeli songs written before 1956."

Joseph Berman, who at one time had studied to be a rabbi, remained an Orthodox Jew throughout his life. Coming from Poland, "the notion of anti-Semitism loomed large in his perspective." In the Berman household, "Israel was very important, not simply as the fulfillment of biblical prophecy, but because what happened in Germany could happen any-where."

Following his graduation from Hamilton High School, Howard Berman went off to UCLA, where he majored in political science and became active in the California Federation of Young Democrats. Graduated in 1962, he immediately entered law school at UCLA, receiving his LL.B. three years later. By this time (1965), Henry Waxman, also a UCLA Law School graduate, was president of the California Federation of Young Democrats (CFYD). With Waxman at its head, the CFYD gravitated toward the party's insurgent faction led by future United States Senator Allan Cranston, and against the party's more established wing controlled by California Assembly Speaker Jesse ("Big Daddy") Unruh. After leading the California delegation at the contentious 1968 Democratic National Convention in Chicago, Unruh ran for California Governor, losing by more than a half-million votes to Ronald Reagan.)

Howard Berman spent his first year out of law school working as a Visa volunteer. In 1967, he took over the presidency of the Young Democrats. Entering private practice, he specialized in labor law. Meanwhile, brother Michael was masterminding Henry Waxman's election to the California State Assembly in 1969. Two years later, when Waxman became chair of the Assembly panel that oversaw reapportionment, he invited Michael to join the committee's staff. The two tried to create an Assembly district for Howard right in his own backyard of Beverlywood, but Governor Ronald Reagan vetoed the plan. Undaunted, Howard moved into a district that ran along the Santa Monica Mountains from Hollywood through the San Fernando Valley. This was in March 1972, just three months before the Democratic primary. Ironically, in view of the outcome, the move hardly seemed to make political sense. Even if Howard won in the crowded Democratic primary, he had to face a twenty-six-year incumbent, Charles Conrad, in the general election. As a Republican, Conrad was likely to benefit from Richard Nixon's coattails in what everyone predicted was going to be a landslide victory.

Against all odds, Howard Berman came in first in the eleven-candidate primary. Concerned that Hubert Humphrey's impending loss would drag him down to defeat, brother Michael managed to get him an endorsement from a local GOP group. He used it in a mailer he then sent to more than five thousand registered Republicans. Under the banner headline "Republicans for Nixon-Berman," the slick brochure proclaimed: "Mr. Berman and President Nixon have many traits in common. Both are hardworking, practical men who avoid radical extremes." Berman went on to easily defeat Conrad. At age thirty-two, Howard Berman was now a member of the California Assembly. Speaking of that mailer more than twenty years later, Howard Berman said: "It certainly was expedient. I never said I was pure, and I never said I was proud of everything that I did."

Berman arrived in Sacramento just as the Assembly was about to elect a new Speaker. The freshman legislator threw his support behind Bay Area Assemblyman Leo McCarthy. When McCarthy won, he rewarded the freshman legislator by naming him Majority Leader—the youngest in California history. As Majority Leader, Berman worked closely with both Speaker McCarthy and Governor Edmund G. "Jerry" Brown to enact the nation's first agricultural labor law. He also "steered measures to Brown's desk creating the Santa Monica Mountains Conservancy and imposing stiff penalties on California banks that joined the Arab boycott against Israel."

One day in 1979, Howard Berman marched into Speaker McCarthy's office and demanded that he step down. McCarthy refused, and the fight was on. Brother Michael moved up to Sacramento to aid in the political tussle, assisted by Congressman Waxman, who returned frequently from Washington to lend a hand. Berman's case against his former ally McCarthy was simple: he contended that McCarthy was "more interested in raising money for a 1982 governor's race than for Democratic Assembly members in 1980." Berman's argument carried the day. The Assembly's Democratic caucus voted 26 to 24 against McCarthy, who then backed out of the race. When the issue came to the Assembly floor, however, San Francisco Assemblyman (and future mayor) Willie Brown "picked off several Berman backers and also got Republican support to win" the speakership for himself. It looked like the bottom had fallen out of Howard Berman's political career.

After his defeat for speaker, Berman allied himself with Representative Phillip Burton (the husband of *Sala Burton*) in the 1982 reapportionment plan. Burton, working alongside brother Michael, got Howard a congressional seat that "stretched from south of Mulholland Drive over the Hollywood Hills to Studio City and Sherman Oaks and into the northeast San Fernando Valley." "The Valley," as it is known both locally and across the nation, has an aura all its own. At one time, it was "classic suburban territory, filled with "Leave It to Beaver" families; working fathers, homemaker mothers, two or three or four kids walking every day to the local public school." By the time Howard Berman ran for Congress, the Valley had drastically changed.

The Twenty-sixth District was ideally suited to the reform-minded Berman. It included "the Democratic middle class neighborhoods of Van Nuys and Panorama City, the more Democratic parts of Granada Hills, the black neighborhood of Pacoima and the mostly Mexican-American neighborhoods on either side of the Golden State Freeway." Howard Berman easily won his first congressional race with 60 percent of the vote— a figure that he has either equaled or bettered ever since. By leaving the California State Assembly for the United States Congress, Howard Berman was "giving up more real power than most congressmen ever achieve."

Upon entering the House, Berman quickly broke out of the freshman pack by executing "something of a political coup"—beating Texas Representative John Bryant for a seat on the Democratic Steering and Policy Committee. This is the body that makes Democratic committee assignments. Berman was given seats on both Foreign Affairs and Judiciary. Throughout his congressional career, Howard Berman has allied himself with "others traditionally shut out of the ruling elite—Blacks and Latinos," becoming in the process a "champion of historically under-represented groups [from] farm workers to immigrants."

From his position on Judiciary, Berman has been able to see to the needs of "showbiz types" in matters of copyright and licensing laws. Another of his pet concerns is laws affecting immigration. In 1986, Berman, along with New York Representative *Charles Schumer*, worked up a compromise on the so-called guest worker amendment. Berman had opposed the amend-ment in its original form, as introduced in both 1982 and 1984 by his California colleague Leon Panetta (one day to be Bill Clinton's White House chief of staff). The Berman-Schumer com-promise permitted a large number of "guest workers" into the United States and "opened the way for them to become U.S. citizens." When it looked as if the issue had reached a political impasse, Berman volunteered to become its floor manager—a position which few members relish. Two years later, he sponsored a provision allow-ing twenty thousand visas for immigrants with-out close relatives in the United States. They were to be randomly selected by computer. Among the masses of potential immigrants mak-ing application, these came to be known as "Berman Visas." In 1990, Berman worked to pro-vide more family reunification slots so as to expedite the immigration of Soviet Jews. His bill also provided amnesty provisions which allowed more family members to remain in the country. In 1994, Howard Berman authored an amendment to the crime bill that required the federal government to "either repay state and local governments for the cost of imprisoning criminals who are illegal immigrants or transfer-ring them to local custody."

From his position on the Foreign Relations Committee, Berman, along with old friend *Mel Levine* (whom he had met when the latter was a volunteer lawyer for the Anti-Defamation League and Berman was working on legislation to keep businesses from complying with the Arab boycott), became an ardent, outspoken supporter of Israel, and an equally vocal critic of Iraqi dictator Saddam Hussein. As early as 1988, he was leading the fight for a House bill barring U.S. oil purchases from Iraq and opposing American trade credits and loans by internation-al banking organizations to that nation, "unless its leaders [swear] off using chemical weapons." The bill was killed when Senator Jesse Helms lodged an objection from his seat on the Senate Foreign Relations Committee.

Nearly a year before the Persian Gulf War, Berman began calling for sanctions against Saddam Hussein as a man he termed "danger-ous and unpredictable." Berman took the Iraqi dictator to task for his use of chemical weapons, development of a nuclear capability, and egre-gious human rights violations. As late as August 1990, Berman's bill to put sanctions in place was "stoutly opposed" by the Bush Administration, a position that Bush later said he "absolutely regret[ted]." Along with Representative Henry Hyde, an Illinois Republican, Berman co-authored a law "allowing imposition of arms embargoes on nations that support terrorism." On the eve of the Persian Gulf vote, Berman told the House: "If we do not deal with Saddam Hussein now, the United States and the world will be facing a more heavily armed, a more powerful, more dangerous Saddam Hussein five or ten years from now. . . . There is a man who is hell-bent on establishing hegemony over the entire Middle East." In his peroration, Berman said: "I can't get out of my mind the notion that this man [Hussein] is a very dangerous, poten-tially very powerful tyrant, and even though there is inadequate burden-sharing, and even though it sickens me that some of our allies are not participating the way they should . . . we have to deal with him now. If we don't, we'll pay a much greater price in the future."

Needless to say, Berman voted in favor of the Gulf resolution.

Of Howard Berman, the editors of the *Almanac of American Politics* write: "There are few House members who have made such an imprint on legislation in so many areas . . . and he has done it without any important chairmanship or powerful mentor." Another source refers to him as "one of the most talented and creative legislators in the House—and one of the most clear-sighted and aggressive operators in American politics."

In Los Angeles, Berman is well-known as one half of the powerful "Waxman-Berman Machine," which the *Los Angeles Times* describes as a "loose-knit confederation." Unlike Tammany Hall or the old Tweed Ring, Waxman and Berman dole out no patronage jobs and do not fix parking tickets. Rather, they raise enormous sums of money, mainly from Jewish liberals. Most of the donors come from the entertainment industry. As far back as their days in the California State Legislature, both Waxman and Berman were making contributions to the campaigns of other, like-minded liberals. Although the donations were not technically illegal, many thought them to be blatantly self-serving. In a sense, they were right. As the late Jesse Unruh was fond of saying: "Money is the mother's milk of politics." For all their contributions, Waxman and Berman have been able to influence votes and get favorable hearings from colleagues. Case in point: In 1989, Berman decided that he wanted a seat on the House Budget Committee. After extensive lobbying and the liberal sprinkling of campaign donations, he received 23 out of a possible 31 votes from the Democratic Steering Committee.

Anchored by brother Michael's B.A.D. Campaigns organizations, Waxman and Berman have literally changed the face of California politics. They are not always successful, however. In 1992, they threw their support behind Mel Levine in the race for United States Senate. Despite employing the "machine's" classic strategy—lying low and raising money for a last-minute barrage of commercials—Levine stumbled badly, coming in third in a three-candidate race. The Democratic primary went to Representative *Barbara Boxer*, who defeated Levine by a two-to-one margin. Waxman-Berman have also backed losers in races for Los

Angeles mayor and California governor. The "machine" is not without its detractors. An *L. A. Times* writer characterized Waxman-Berman as having "a kind of swagger that has bred resentment among Democrats as well as Republicans. The Bermans have tenaciously clung to power, pushed partisan advantage to the hilt, turned their backs on personal and ideological allies—even taken them on."

Howard and brother Michael are, as noted above, a study in opposites. One close friend summed up their differences with a metaphor: "Howard's game is poker, where his ability to read his opponents and mask his own hand parallels his legislative skills. Michael is such an adept blackjack card counter that . . . he has been asked to leave Las Vegas casinos." Howard is variously described as a *mensch*, "liked even by political adversaries," and "charmingly unassuming." He has also been labeled "the cold-blooded boss of a ruthless political machine." Howard is a stylish dresser; Michael "must spend $200 to get his clothes pre-wrinkled."

At the beginning of the One Hundred and Second Congress, Howard Berman became chair of the House Foreign Affairs Subcommittee on International Operations, which oversees State Department and other U.S. diplomatic functions. He came under fire when, during consideration of a bill to reauthorize the State Department for fiscal 1994 and '95, his subcommittee approved his proposal "to lift a number of restrictions on cultural and educational exchanges with Cuba and other nations that are subject to U.S. economic embargoes." Attacking Berman's "Free Trade in Ideas Act," Republicans charged that "such exchanges could provide Castro's regime with desperately needed hard currency." In response, Berman argued that his proposal would actually weaken Castro's rule "by exposing the Cuban people to democratic ideas." The "Free Trade in Ideas Act" was passed by Berman's subcommittee. Before it could come to the House floor for a vote, Berman, reacting to pressure from the Clinton Administration, agreed to withdraw the motion. In 1994, the House passed a modified version of the act, but only after Berman's personal intercession with officials of the Cuban American National Foundation (the preeminent Cuban-American exile organization). The compromise entailed the addition of "nonbinding language," sought by the anti-Castro lawmakers and groups, that "urged the president to seek a U.N. trade embargo against Cuba."

Berman has never encountered a difficult reelection. Voters in the Twenty-sixth District have regularly returned him to office by margins of better than 60 percent. One key in his string of successful races, of course, has been his ability to raise enormous amounts of campaign cash.

Howard Berman is married to the former Janis Schwartz. Their marriage ceremony was performed by Rabbi David Lieber, who was president of the University of Judaism, the West Coast branch of the Jewish Theological Seminary. The Bermans have two daughters, Brinley and Lindsey. During the months when they reside in Washington, Mrs. Berman is involved in a bi-weekly Jewish study group that brings a rabbi in from New York once a fortnight. The Bermans' California home is in Sherman Oaks. Joseph Berman died during surgery after a heart attack on Thanksgiving Day, 1989. Joining Howard Berman in the minyan during *shiva* at his parents' home were colleagues Henry Waxman and Mel Levine, a trio of old friends who have made a consummate mark on American politics in the twentieth century.

References

Almanac of American Politics (1982–98 editions).

Brandeis-Bardin Weekend Seminar, January 25–27, 1991, Los Angeles (transcript).

Los Angeles Times, October 29, 1990, A16:1. June 5, 1992, B1:2.

New Republic, July 17, 1986, pp. 17–19.

New York Times Magazine, March 29, 1992; pp. 18–21, 34–38.

Politics in America (1984–96 editions).

BLOOM, SOL (1870–1949): *Democrat from New York; served thirteen terms in the House (Sixty-ninth through Eighty-first Congress; January 30, 1923–March 7, 1949).*

By any stretch of the imagination, Sol Bloom must be considered one of the most colorful and unlikely members of the Congressional Minyan. An entrepreneur and impresario of great note, he had at least three highly successful careers before entering Congress at age fifty-three, where he remained for more than a quarter of a century, eventually chairing the House Committee on Foreign Relations.

Born in Pekin, Tazewell County, Illinois, on March 9, 1870, Sol Bloom was the sixth and youngest child of Gershom and Sarah Bloom, Orthodox Jews who had immigrated to America from Poland in about 1860. Gershom, also known as Garrison, was an itinerant peddler. Although intelligent and industrious, he could never earn enough to feed his large family. In 1875, his small clothing store having gone bankrupt, Gershom packed the family onto a train and headed west to San Francisco. More than seventy years later, Sol Bloom would recall that train trip: how the family lived on eggs and fruit purchased from the Indians at railroad stops because they could not obtain kosher food.

Sol Bloom's formal education lasted precisely one day; his family could not afford to purchase the requisite texts for their son (a common practice in those days), and were too proud to ask for assistance. Therefore, at age seven, Sol found himself working in a brush factory. By age ten, he was keeping the factory's books. At night, he sold programs at local theaters, acted in occasional bit parts, and became involved in a series of schemes he would later term "legitimate chiseling." As a youngster he became friends with the equally young David Belasco, who would go on to become one of America's premier theater producers. They remained lifelong friends.

At age fifteen, Bloom was hired by San Francisco newspaper publisher H. H. de Young to be assistant treasurer of the Alcazar Theater. Over the next four years, he sold advertising, got into merchandising and production, and by age nineteen, had amassed more than $80,000 in savings. At this point, he "retired" and took the grand tour of Europe. While there, he became fascinated by a troupe of Algerian sword swal-

lowers, glass and scorpion eaters, and signed them to a personal contract. Upon his return to the United States, he was hired by his old mentor, de Young, to run the Midway Plaisance at the World's Columbian Exposition in Chicago. For this he was paid the princely sum of $50,000. During the Exposition, Bloom introduced America to the Ferris Wheel and the exotic dancer "Little Egypt," for whom he wrote the famous "Hootchy Kootchy" tune. The song took the country by storm and made young Sol Bloom an even wealthier man.

When the Exposition closed, Bloom remained in Chicago and opened up the country's first mail-order music store. He renamed himself "Sol Bloom, the Music Man." Between 1896 and 1903, he built a chain of eighty music stores from coast to coast; by 1903 he was a millionaire.

In Chicago, Bloom was introduced to Evelyn Hechheimer, an aspiring songwriter from San Francisco. The two soon fell in love and were married. Sol's only concern was how she would be received by his family: the Blooms were Orthodox Jews; Evelyn and her family belonged to San Francisco's Temple Emanuel, a classical Reform synagogue. Despite their religious differences, they were married on June 22, 1897. At the reception following, they were serenaded by two of Sol Bloom's better-known songwriter clients: Paul Dresser, who sang "On the Banks of the Wabash," and Charles K. Harris, who crooned "After the Ball Is Over"—both published by Sol Bloom. The Blooms had one child, a daughter named Vera.

A genius at self-promotion, Sol Bloom managed to take out the first copyright of the twentieth century, a song called "I Wish I Was in Dixie Tonight." He managed this minor coup by sending agents to stand in line at the copyright office starting on December 29, 1899, and to remain there until the office opened for business on January 2, 1900.

Moving on to New York in 1903, Bloom became national distributor for Victor Talking Machines. Always restless, he also became a theater builder and a backer of stage productions. Over the course of fewer than ten years, he either built or renovated more than a dozen theaters along Broadway's Great White Way. Among the theaters he built were the Apollo and the Harris. Bloom's partners in these ventures were Asa Candler, the founder of Coca-Cola, Edgar Selwyn, a movie pioneer, and Ed Bowes, one day to become famous as radio's Major Bowes. As a theater angel, Bloom backed the early works of playwright Elmer Rice (Reizenstein) and the then-unknown John Galsworthy.

Moving into real estate, Bloom became a speculator and builder of apartment houses. When he learned that the Pennsylvania Railroad was going to bore a Hudson River tunnel in order to carry passengers into the heart of New York City, he took an option on all the land between 31st and 33rd Streets west of Seventh Avenue. He then made yet another fortune selling the land that was to become Penn Station. Bloom always considered this to be his shrewdest real estate investment.

Sol Bloom got out of the music business in 1910, and by 1920, at age fifty, was ready to "retire" once again. The retirement proved to be shortlived. In the off-year elections of 1922, Democrat *Samuel Marx* was elected to Congress from New York's Nineteenth District but died before taking office. A special election ensued, in which Tammany Hall convinced Sol Bloom to throw his hat into the ring. Bloom had no illusions about why the boys from Tammany had selected him: "I knew a lot of people, and I had no serious enemies. . . . I had been chosen to run because I was an amiable and solvent Jew." The Nineteenth District, one of America's wealthiest, soon became Bloom's. He would serve in Congress until his death in 1949.

Bloom's first decade and a half in Congress was largely undistinguished, and his colleagues looked upon him as a bit of a buffoon. He spoke out against radio advertising, fought Sunday blue laws, advocated putting baseball under federal control, and railed against the tax on boxing match admissions. In the late 1920s, he became interested in the so-called Eastman Plan for reforming the calendar, a brief craze that soon went out of fashion.

In 1926, Henry Ford published a series of anti-Semitic articles in his newspaper, the *Dearborn Independent*, under the collective title "The International Jew." They purported to show that Jews were "in direct control of all financial centers of government." Incensed by Ford's malicious and scurrilous charges, Representative Bloom introduced a resolution in the House calling for the appointment of a committee to inquire into their truth or falsity. Threatened with a subpoena and plagued by numerous court battles, Ford issued a public apology and finally shut down his anti-Semitic paper. Bloom believed that he had been largely responsible for putting Ford's tirade to an end.

Sol Bloom's first taste of national exposure came when he was appointed director of the George Washington Bicentennial Commission in 1932. Given a budget of $350,000 and a staff of 125, he produced and directed a yearlong gala that put the name, face, and ideals of America's first President on every school bulletin board—as well as newspapers, movie theaters, and radio. Much to everyone's surprise, he turned a million-dollar profit. So closely tied was Sol Bloom with the Father of Our Country that for years to come, the New York Democrat received mail from schoolchildren addressed simply to "George Washington." Bloom also headed the Constitution Sesquicentennial Commission. As commissioner, Bloom "produced" and distributed a free copy of his book, *The Story of the Constitution*, to every schoolchild in America.

Through attrition and seniority, Sol Bloom became chairman of the House Foreign Relations Committee in 1939. This caused a shudder in Washington because most cognoscenti believed that Bloom was incapable of anything but theatrics. In his first year as committee head, Bloom led the unsuccessful fight for President Roosevelt's revision of the Neutrality Act, but gained the respect of his colleagues in the process. After the beginning of World War II, Bloom successfully pushed through both Lend-Lease and the Selective Service Act. His role in reintroducing a military draft earned him the undying enmity of American isolationists, who picketed his home as Bloom was sitting *shiva* for his wife. He was vilified as a "Jewish warmonger" in the press, and received enough threats on his life that J. Edgar Hoover assigned him a personal retinue of bodyguards.

Bloom was the only Jew selected for the eight-man American delegation that went to San Francisco in April 1945 to write the United Nations Charter. At the sessions of the nascent world body, Bloom, viewed by more than one prominent historian as a "perennial court Jew," argued vociferously on behalf of refugees. It was too little, too late. In 1943, Bloom had been the sole Jew on the American delegation to the Bermuda Conference, convened to discuss the single issue of wartime immigration. No aid was forthcoming for the Jews of Europe; Bloom's presence on the delegation was mere window dressing. Additionally, during the innumerable congressional battles over increased immigration quotas, Sol Bloom, House Foreign Relations Committee chairman, did virtually nothing to help the Jews of Europe to escape Hitler's ovens. It was Bloom, acting at the behest of the State Department, who buried a 1943 House resolution to create a U.S. government agency to rescue Jews from Hitler. But the agency—the War Refugee Board—was established anyway, when Jewish protests forced FDR's hand despite the non-action of Bloom's committee. One wonders how in the world Congress could again and again have barred increases in the number of European refugees allowed into America, especially since the three committees most directly responsible for this type of legislation (Foreign Relations, Immigration, and Judiciary) were chaired by Jews: Bloom, *Dickstein*, and *Celler*.

Throughout his long congressional career, Bloom was both an ardent liberal and a vociferous supporter of Roosevelt's New Deal. Despite his vast wealth and opulent lifestyle, Bloom could always be counted on to vote for the interests of the downtrodden and the have-nots—with the bothersome exception of the Jews of Europe.

Short and thin, with slick black hair, Bloom was known for his impeccably tailored clothing, his omnipresent walking stick, and the gold pince-nez attached with a flowing black ribbon. One of the most notable characters on Capitol Hill, Bloom used to walk up the steps of the Capitol each morning "strewing pennies, nickels and dimes along his path like Hansel and Gretel had done with crumbs in the fairy tale." After repeatedly observing this, House Doorkeeper "Fishbait" Miller asked him what he was doing. "He said, 'Shhhh. Let the little children find them when they come to see the Capitol. In this Depression, someone has to show them that good things can happen.'" Till the end of his days, Bloom called himself an Orthodox Jew, observed the Sabbath as a day of total rest, and was easily able to converse in Yiddish. He served as honorary president of the Hebrew Convalescent Home in the Bronx, and was a life member of the West Side Institutional Synagogue. From all indications, he kept a kosher home till the last day of his life. Sol and Evelyn's daughter, Vera Tova, became an author, a prominent Washington hostess, and a songwriter of some note.

Sol Bloom succumbed to a heart attack in Washington on March 7, 1949, just two days shy of his seventy-ninth birthday. His seat in Congress was taken by Franklin Delano Roosevelt, Jr. He is buried in Mount Eden Cemetery, Pleasantville, New York.

References

American Jewish Year Book, vol. 51, p. 519.

Sol Bloom, *The Autobiography of Sol Bloom* (New York: G. P. Putnam's Sons, 1948).

Vera Bloom, *There's No Place Like Washington* (New York: G. P. Putnam's Sons, 1944).

Current Biography, 1943.

Encyclopaedia Judaica (1972), vol. 4, col. 1132.

New York Times, March 8, 1949, 1:6.

Universal Jewish Encyclopedia.

Who Was Who in America, vol. 2.

Who's Who in American Jewry, 1926, 1928, 1938.

BOSCHWITZ, RUDOLPH ELI (1930–):
Republican from Minnesota; served two terms in the Senate (January 3, 1978–January 3, 1991).

The 1990 Minnesota election for United States Senate featured a unique first in American history: the first race in which a Jewish challenger ran against a Jewish incumbent. That year the challenger, Carlton College professor *Paul David Wellstone*, defeated the two-term Republican incumbent, Senator Rudy Boschwitz. What makes the scenario even more remarkable is that the election, held in a state with a Jewish population of less than 1 percent, hinged in large part on the question of who was the "better" Jew. Six years later, Wellstone and Boschwitz met on the field of battle a second time. Once again, Wellstone—by now a seasoned member of the "World's Most Exclusive Club"—defeated Boschwitz. In the mind of Rudy Boschwitz, the better Jew had lost yet again.

Rudy Boschwitz's personal story is extremely compelling. It is also proof positive that the American Dream is still alive. Rudolph Eli, the son of Ely and Lucy (Dawidawicz) Boschwitz, was born in Berlin on November 7, 1930, where Ely was a stockbroker. On January 30, 1933, Adolf Hitler was appointed Chancellor of Germany. Less than a month later, the Reichstag building burned to the ground, precipitating the total Nazi takeover of the German government. Ely Boschwitz had seen enough; he fled with his family to Czechoslovakia. Over the next two years, the Boschwitzes kept moving farther west: from Czechoslovakia to Switzerland, and on to the Netherlands, England, and finally, in 1935, the United States of America.

The family settled in New Rochelle, New York, where young Rudy received his early education. At age sixteen, he entered Johns Hopkins University. At the end of his sophomore year (1948), he transferred to New York University, where he earned a B.S. in business in 1950 at age twenty, and a Bachelor of Laws in 1953. Shortly after passing the New York bar exam in 1954, Boschwitz served a two-year hitch in the United States Army Signal Corps. Returning to New York in 1955, he practiced law for two years before moving out to Wisconsin, where he joined his brother's growing plywood business. Seven years later, he moved on to Minnesota, where he founded "a retail store for do-it-your-self building items, stocking paneling, lumber, and assorted building items." He called it "Plywood Minnesota." It was the first store of its kind and made Rudy Boschwitz a multimillionaire. By the time he was forty-five, Boschwitz had sixty-seven "Plywood Minnesota" franchises throughout the upper Midwest.

Plywood Minnesota brought Boschwitz more than wealth; it also brought him great name recognition in his adopted state. Beginning in the 1960s, a "folksy, flannel-shirted Boschwitz" began appearing in a series of television ads pitching do-it-yourself home furnishings. In his downhome ads, Boschwitz would use such "deliberately ridiculous," attention-grabbing slogans as "Keep Bullfighting Out of Minnesota" and "Unite the Twin Cities—Fill in the Mississippi." There was a definite method to the young businessman's madness, for not only were Boschwitz's attention-grabbing commercials making his business a household name; they were also setting the stage for a political career. As Boschwitz's name recognition and visibility soared, he became increasingly active in statewide Republican politics. By 1968, he was a delegate to the Minnesota Republican Convention. Three years later, he was elected a Republican national committeeman. In 1972 and again in 1976, he represented the Gopher State at the Republican National Convention. Minnesota politicians began wondering how long it would take for the plywood king to run for office. More importantly, which office? It is likely that not even Rudy Boschwitz knew the answer to that question—until December 30, 1976.

Boschwitz's road to Washington began nearly two years before the 1978 election, when Minnesota Senator Walter Mondale resigned his seat in order to be sworn in as Jimmy Carter's Vice President. Governor Wendell Anderson desperately wanted Mondale's seat. According to Minnesota law, the governor has the power to fill vacant congressional seats. Anderson understood that to name himself would be tantamount to political suicide. Instead, he hit upon a slightly different ploy. Anderson resigned, but not before arranging that his successor, Lieutenant Governor Rudy Perpich, would name him as Mondale's replacement. Undoubtedly, Anderson felt he could perform well enough in the job to overcome "the jinx that follows most 'self-appointed' senators." He was wrong; the voters of Minnesota were furious with this naked deception. Had Anderson only studied a little political history, he would have realized what a difficult task he had set out for himself: only one senator-governor has been elected in his own right in the past sixty years.

When it became clear that Senator Anderson was going to be in electoral trouble, Rudy Boschwitz entered the race on the Independent-Republican ticket. With his vast name recognition and ability to raise almost unlimited amounts of cash, Boschwitz made a formidable opponent. A born campaigner, Boschwitz made the rounds of Minnesota county fairs, wearing his trademark flannel shirts. As the race progressed, it became apparent that Boschwitz's campaign was sticking more closely to personalities than issues. While endorsing the "standard G.O.P. campaign themes," he said little that was controversial. In November, Boschwitz defeated the hapless Anderson 57 percent to 40 percent.

Rudy Boschwitz entered the United States Senate in January 1979 having had virtually no governmental experience. As a result, he "found it hard to focus his efforts on a limited enough range of topics to have a consistent impact on any of them." He was appointed to the Senate Committees on Agriculture (a key post for Minnesota), Small Business, Foreign Relations, and Budget. One of the first areas to which he lent his time and talents was the issue of refugees—not surprising, considering his personal history. As a member of the Senate Foreign Relations Committee, Boschwitz traveled to Thailand to learn about Cambodian and Hmong refugees, and "helping those in the United States stay there." This issue also resonated well with the voters at home; Minnesota, a state long known for its tolerance and strong economy, had attracted a sizeable refugee population.

As a member of the Agriculture Committee, Boschwitz became a champion of the dairy industry—so much so that, in a game of free association, the word "Boschwitz" could easily elicit the response "milk" among most people on Capitol Hill. During his first term, Boschwitz authored—and President Reagan signed—a bill to help limit milk production. Boschwitz's legislation sought to maintain milk prices by paying dairy farmers to cut their output.

Simultaneously, Boschwitz contended that "the real problem with milk is underconsumption, not overproduction." In keeping with his understanding of the problem, Boschwitz became well-known both on Capitol Hill and back in Minnesota for the banana-, root beer–, cherry-, and amaretto-flavored milk drinks he would hand out. Each year, he sponsored "Rudy's Super-Duper Milk House" at the Minnesota State Fair.

On Foreign Affairs, Boschwitz was a strong, though not thoroughly uncritical, supporter of Israel. When Israel bombed the Osirak nuclear reactor near Baghdad in June 1981, Boschwitz remarked that "they [the Israelis] probably did us a favor." The Minnesota Senator waged a furious fight against the Reagan administration's sale of AWACS radar planes and missiles to Saudi Arabia, and played a pivotal role in forcing the administration to withdraw its proposal to sell arms to Jordan. Boschwitz developed a good working relationship with the committee's other pro-Israel supporters, most notably California's Senator Alan Cranston. In 1984, however, Boschwitz disagreed with Cranston over the Californian's amendment to "guarantee that annual U.S. payments to Israel at least equal that country's repayment of past loans." Among other arguments, Boschwitz warned that what Cranston had intended to be a minimum payment might at some future date be interpreted as a maximum.

In the 1984 election, Boschwitz faced liberal Minnesota Secretary of State Joan Anderson Growe. The "feisty and shrill" Growe was not a widely popular choice even within her own party. In order to get the Democratic-Farmer-Labor nomination, she had to outlast a field that included former Senator Anderson and Representative James L. Oberstar. At the state convention, Growe did not receive the DFL endorsement until the nineteenth ballot. In the general election race, Growe "peppered Boschwitz with a wide array of issues, ranging from his strong support of Reagan defense policies to his personal finances." Candidate Growe repeatedly scored Boschwitz for refusing to release his income-tax returns, and charged him with benefiting from some of the Reagan tax cuts that he had supported. Boschwitz managed to largely deflect the issue by using his accountant to selectively disclose "highlights" of his tax returns. Outspending Growe by a more than three-to-one margin, Boschwitz went on to a solid 56 percent to 43 percent victory.

During his second six-year term, Rudy Boschwitz began to attain positions of importance. When the Republicans captured the Senate in 1984, Boschwitz was named to chair two subcommittees: Near Eastern Affairs and Foreign Agriculture Policy. At the beginning of the session, Boschwitz ran for GOP Conference secretary. He lost to Mississippi Senator Thad Cochran. Although he was well-liked, many of his colleagues found him a bit too eccentric for their taste: in addition to his passion for flavored milk drinks, Boschwitz was also well-known for appending smiley faces to his signature on letters. In 1988, Senate Republicans selected Boschwitz as chair of their Senate Campaign Committee. The indefatigable Boschwitz crisscrossed the country, raising enormous sums of cash and inducing highly qualified candidates to run. Convinced that the Republicans were about to field an excellent slate of Senate candidates, Boschwitz publicly predicted that the GOP would recapture control of the upper chamber. He was wrong. Despite George Bush's overwhelming victory over Massachusetts Governor Michael Dukakis, the Republicans suffered a net loss of one seat. Notwithstanding this poor showing, few Republicans held Boschwitz responsible. He had done his job; it was the voters who had not done theirs.

As a ten-year veteran of the Budget Committee, Boschwitz often fought the supply-side economics of the Reagan-Bush administrations. Time and time again, Boschwitz urged "giving priority to the deficit over tax revision." One of his pet economic schemes was a "fair play" budget—one that would limit the annual growth in federal spending to 5 percent. It failed to pass. Boschwitz also pushed for the earned income tax credit as "an alternative to the minimum wage increase." The proposal garnered little support, as most attention went to raising the minimum wage and instituting a subminimum training wage of some kind. In the main, though, Boschwitz remained a solid freemarket Republican.

Friendly, garrulous, and impulsive, Rudy Boschwitz once remarked: "I do my own thing. I'm impatient and I don't want to sit still."

To Minnesota Democrats, Boschwitz's defeat became a paramount cause. They believed that, in order to topple the two-term incumbent in 1990, they would have to have a political heavyweight as a challenger. Their first choice, former Senator and Vice President Walter Mondale, turned them down. So did their second choice, department store heir Mark Dayton. Eventually, the nomination went to Carlton College political science professor Paul Wellstone. The campaign was a study in opposites: Wellstone, the "hyperactive little man with a high-pitched voice who wants to kiss every baby he sees and shake every hand he can reach," and Boschwitz, "tall, thin, grayhaired and more reserved."

Although the battle lines between liberal and conservative were clearly drawn, the election hinged on an ancillary issue: which man was more Jewish. The week before the election, the Boschwitz campaign sent out a letter signed by his Jewish supporters to a mailing list of Jewish voters. The letter suggested that "in this first Senate race between two Jewish candidates," Boschwitz was the better Jew because "Wellstone took no part in Jewish affairs and had not raised his children as Jews." Boschwitz, on the other hand, does take his Jewishness seriously. Although a Reform Jew, he has donated vast sums to the ultra-Orthodox Lubavitch House in St. Paul, and has served as state chair of the Minneapolis Jewish Fund. Within the Senate he was well-known for "playing matchmaker with single Jews on his and other Capitol Hill staffs." Nonetheless, the letter struck a negative chord with the voters of Minnesota. To many Christians, it sounded "uncomfortably close to an appeal to religious prejudice." Wellstone went on to defeat Boschwitz by slightly more than 47,000 votes.

In 1996, the two squared off against each other a second time. After six years in the Senate, the "La Guardia-like" Wellstone had toned down his act. Now wearing tailor-made suits and sporting neatly trimmed hair, he was able to campaign on political, not emotional, issues. Boschwitz ran negative ads, but none that attacked Wellstone's Judaism—or lack thereof. Once again, Wellstone emerged victorious. The final tally showed Wellstone capturing 50 percent of the vote (1,093,734) to Boschwitz's 41 percent (897,305). It is likely that without a relatively strong showing by a third-party candidate,

Boschwitz might have defeated Wellstone; Dean Berkley, running as the candidate of H. Ross Perot's Reform Party garnered 7 percent (151,738).

During 1997–1999, Boschwitz served as chairman of the Committee For a Secure Peace, a group that took out newspaper ads and distributed articles supporting Israeli government policies and critical of Palestinian violations of the Oslo accords.

Rudy Boschwitz is married to the former Ellen Lowenstein. Residing in the Twin Cities suburb of Plymouth, they have four children.

References
Almanac of American Politics (1980–90 editions).
New York Times, October 24, 1996, A14:2.
Politics in America (1980–90 editions).
Murray Polner, *American Jewish Biographies* (New York: Facts on File, 1983), pp. 45–46.

BOXER, BARBARA LEVY (1940–): *Democrat from California; served five terms in the House (Ninety-eighth through One Hundred and Third Congress; January 3, 1983–December 31, 1992), and two terms in the Senate (January 3, 1993–).*

Barbara Boxer and *Dianne Feinstein* share the unique distinction of being the first Jewish women elected to the United States Senate. Neither can really claim to be the first Jewish woman in the history of that body; both were elected on the same day and from the same state. Beyond this similarity, they have little in common; they have substantially different political philosophies and styles, and, in truth, share little affection for one another. Unlike Feinstein, or any other member of the Congressional Minyan for that matter, Boxer can claim a distinction all her own: she is the only Jewish member of Congress ever to be related through marriage to the First Family. On Saturday, May 29, 1994, Senator Boxer's daughter, Nicole, married First Lady Hillary Rodham Clinton's younger brother, Tony Rodham, in a White House ceremony.

A decade before her election to the House of Representatives (and a full twenty years before she was elevated to the Senate), Barbara Boxer wrote a novel (still unpublished) that painted an eerily accurate portrait of her future:

The television announcer's voice came in clearly over the noise and excitement of the crowd: "The California U.S. Senate race is still too close to call." . . . In the middle of the crowd at campaign headquarters stood Carol Wynn. At five feet, three, with shining black hair and blue eyes—"like Elizabeth Taylor's," her mother would say—Carol could have been the attractive woman selling soap, cereal, or sewing machines. . . . But Carol Wynn wanted to be a U.S. senator from the most populous state in the union. . . . Carol looked at the nervous, anxious faces of the people hovering around the TV. Exhausted . . . she . . . climbed to the podium to address her campaign workers. Immediately there was silence.

"My beautiful people," she began . . . "for six months we have followed a path together. I was placed on that path by you, and you have guided me along it. It has been difficult and sometimes hazardous, but because of you, I found my way. And whatever happens tonight, I'll continue to find my way."

"Bobby" Levy was born in Brooklyn on November 11, 1940. Her parents, Ira R. and Sophie (Silvershein) Levy, were close enough to their European roots to have lost family members in the Holocaust. In later life, Boxer would claim that hearing those horrifying references to her murdered relatives taught her "the importance of standing up for what you believe." Her father had gone to night school in order to become a lawyer and accountant. As a candidate for the United States Senate forty years later, she often cited his life "as an example of the American dream that now eludes too many." A self-described "child of the fifties," Bobby Levy's basic goal in life was "to get a good education, fall in love, and get married." Imbued with a streak of independence, she circumvented her high school's ban on female participation in sports by coaching an all-boys baseball team. Following high school, Barbara Levy went to Brooklyn College, where she was one of the few women to major in economics. One day, while on a basketball court, she met Stewart Boxer, "a big, good-looking guy with a frank, amused countenance." They married in 1962, while still students. During her senior year, she was sexually harassed by an economics professor, who tried to kiss her. She told no one but her husband about the unsettling incident for more than thirty years. It was only after Anita Hill's public revelations before the Senate Judiciary Committee that Boxer decided to go public with her story. It added an even greater degree of credibility to the lead she has taken on women's issues throughout her political career.

The newlyweds moved into a small apartment at 770 Ocean Parkway in Brooklyn. The only downside to their new home was that the carpet in the building's lobby was worn and musty. The landlord assured them that it would be replaced within a day or two. When months passed and nothing had been done, Barbara Boxer organized the building's tenants into an effective protest group. The carpet was replaced. In a sense, that was the beginning of Barbara Boxer's political career. Following her graduation from Brooklyn College, she worked for three years as a secretary at a Wall Street brokerage firm, thus enabling her husband to attend Fordham Law School. While working, she studied on her own for her stockbroker's license. She passed the exam, got her NASD license, but was not promoted, because she was a woman.

In 1965, Barbara Boxer moved to the San Francisco area. Her husband remained in New York, finishing his bar exam. On the day after she arrived in California, Barbara gave birth to their son, named Doug, who was born two months prematurely, and was given only a fifty-fifty chance of survival. He lived, and two years later the Boxers had a daughter, Nicole.

Three years later, in 1968, the Boxers moved to Greenbrae in trendy, affluent, Marin County, just across the Golden Gate Bridge from San Francisco. That year, the war in Vietnam, coupled with the assassinations of Martin Luther King and Robert F. Kennedy, put Barbara Boxer into a distressing funk. She felt she had two choices: "I could either psychologically withdraw into a 1950s'-type bomb shelter, and put my family into it . . . or reach out and try to change things."

She chose the second course. Like the young woman who organized the apartment house tenants, Boxer invited women from her neighborhood to gather in her backyard and asked them a simple question: "Are you feeling what I'm feeling?" The answer was yes, but what were they going to do? What could they do to overcome their collective feeling of powerlessness? As Boxer recalls: "I wanted to do something and didn't know what. I don't know how it all happened, but what we decided was [that] the politics of the world was too large for us. So what we would do was try to do something in the community that would help some people."

What they did was to organize a project called the Education Corps of Marin, a program aimed at high school dropouts. Their project, which involved trying to reduce the dropout rate and providing job training for those who had already left school, was an unqualified success. By year's end, the Marin school system took it over. From there, Boxer launched a women's political group and a day-care center. In 1970, she helped publicize a peace initiative that would "send a message to President Richard Nixon to end the war in Vietnam." It passed, even though Marin County was mostly Republican.

Energized by her positive political experiences, Barbara Boxer ran for the Marin County Board of Supervisors in 1972. From the very first day she began campaigning, people tried to discourage her. "How can you run for office when you have young children at home?" they asked. One of her opponents, unhinged by the very idea of a woman competing in a "man's arena," had the nerve to tell her that "only the oppressor can free the oppressed." If she truly wanted to do something for women, she was told, she should stay home, raise her children, and take care of her husband. Despite an exhausting door-to-door campaign, she lost. To this day, Boxer believes that her defeat was due to gender—and perhaps her height as well; she stands in at a mere four feet, eleven inches.

Barbara Boxer spent the next two years covering the Board of Supervisors as a reporter for a local paper, the *Pacific Sun*, getting an insider's view of their work. In 1974, she joined the San Francisco office of Congressman John Burton, the brother of Democratic powerhouse Phil Burton. (John Burton was well-known in the Bay Area for his years in the California State Assembly. Once, during a debate on a measure making it a crime to desecrate the American flag, Burton entered the Assembly chamber wearing a necktie made out of the Stars and Stripes.)

After working for Burton for two years, and armed with greater name recognition and political acumen, Boxer ran for the Board of Supervisors once again. This time she won, and served for the six years from 1977 until her election to Congress in 1983. In 1980, she was elected the first female president of the Marin County Board of Supervisors in its 131-year history. Concurrently, she served on the Bay Area's Air Quality Management Board, the board of directors of the Golden Gate Bridge Highway and Transportation District, and the Marin National Women's Political Caucus.

In 1983, just a few days before the filing deadline, Representative John Burton announced that he would not run for reelection for his safe Sixth District seat. Suffering from a myriad of health problems and not too keen on remaining in Washington after five terms, Burton just wanted to return to San Francisco. (Today, Burton is happy, healthy, and, as of February 1998, President pro tem of the California State Senate, the second most powerful position in state government.) The Sixth Congressional District, comprising Marin County, the waterfront edge of San Francisco (with most of its black neighborhoods), and the working-class suburbs of Daly City and Vallejo, was, in essence, a gift from Phil Burton to his brother John. Phil, who drew up California's new districts after the 1980 census, wanted to make sure his younger brother had a safe Democratic seat in the new decade.

Facing four other Democrats in the primary, Boxer avoided a runoff by winning 50 percent of the vote. In the general election she faced Republican Dennis McQuaid, who had been defeated by John Burton in 1980. In 1982, McQuaid, stressing his strong support of the nuclear freeze and environmental measures (Marin Republicans tend to be moderate to liberal), carried Marin County. Boxer, benefiting from a huge margin in San Francisco, managed to win 54 percent to 45 percent.

Barbara Boxer was one of eighteen women serving in the House during the Ninety-eighth Congress. Assigned to Government Operations, Merchant Marine, and the Select Committee on Children, Youth and Families, she immediately made it known that henceforth, women would no longer be second-class citizens in the House. First, annoyed at Speaker Thomas P. "Tip" O'Neill's frequent references to "the men in Congress" and "you guys," she sent him a letter firmly requesting that, in the future, he employ the term "men and women of the House." O'Neill, impressed with Boxer's forthrightness, changed his terminology. Next, fed up with the House women's gym, a small room with a Ping Pong table and a couple of old-style hooded hairdryers, Boxer formed a women's Gym Committee. The group presented the male members of the House with a song that humorously emphasized the women's predicament in not having access to the men's state-of-the-art gymnasium.

In 1983, Barbara Boxer came to national prominence when she single-handedly took on Pentagon procurement policies. For weeks, she focused the attention of the House and the country on the spectacle of a Pentagon that was purchasing $7,622 coffeepots, $640 toilet seats, and $400 hammers. "Even though I was just a freshman member of Congress," she wrote in *Strangers in the Senate*, "I knew no one else was doing anything about publicizing this scandal. I also knew that if you want to be effective on an issue, you have to take it to the people. So I did." Her outrage led to legislation. Along with Iowa Representative Berkeley Bedell, Boxer coauthored a bill to open up competition in the spare parts industry. Over the next ten years, her legislation saved the taxpayers an estimated $1 billion. For her efforts, Boxer was named cochair of the Military Reform Caucus.

During her decade in the House of Representatives, Barbara Boxer had her share of legislative successes and failures. As one of the House's acknowledged leaders on women's issues, she became a perennial sponsor of the doomed Equal Rights Amendment. She also wrote the House version of the Violence Against Women Act, which funded shelters and rape-prevention education centers. In her speech introducing the bill, Boxer said: "People need to learn that if a woman smiles at them, it doesn't mean that she invites sex." She was speaking from personal knowledge. The bill never passed. In 1989, along with Illinois Republican Henry Hyde, she cosponsored a bill that would "punish brokers who set up surrogate motherhood arrangements." According to their legislation, "no penalties would be assessed the women or the adoptive parents," only those who acted as brokers. Speaking on the House floor, Boxer said: "In the case of surrogacy, there is a desperate childless couple and a surrogate mother desperate for money. Into this circumstance a commercial brokerage business has emerged which would lead to the creation of a new class of women in our society—paid breeders—and eventually a new class of children who will be forced to accept the reality that their natural mothers sold them."

Later that year, in the fall of 1989, Boxer went head-to-head with both pro-life forces and the Democratic leadership of the House. During a rancorous, emotional debate over the abortion issue, Boxer called for an immediate vote on what had come to be known as the "Boxer Amendment," a measure allowing the federal government to pay for the abortions of poor women whose pregnancies were the result of rape or incest. The House Democratic leadership asked her to postpone the vote, feeling that her action was precipitate. To the disbelief of her "seniors," the Boxer Amendment passed by ten votes, "giving pro-choicers their first legislative win in a decade." Although President Bush vetoed the amendment, he found himself "in a most unwelcome spotlight, courtesy of Barbara Boxer." Reveling in her heady move, Boxer exclaimed: "we caught the anti-choice people flat-footed."

An ardent environmentalist, Barbara Boxer sponsored a measure establishing criteria for dolphin-safe tuna fishing and banning drift nets. This had the result of pressuring canners to voluntarily label their products, while providing for penalties if they misled consumers. As a budget watchdog, Boxer criticized NASA about the projected cost of the space station. NASA claimed it would cost $30 billion; research provided by her subcommittee estimated the cost to be at least six times that amount. When a space station proponent invoked JFK's vision of space exploration, Boxer fired back: "When John Kennedy made his speech, we didn't have a $3.5 trillion debt or 100,000 kids who'll go to sleep tonight without a roof over their head."

Boxer denounced the Gulf War Resolution with "more ardor than probably any other member" of Congress, and proposed that exemptions from combat be granted to single parents who were serving in the military and to one parent of military couples. When Defense Secretary Richard Cheney opposed her proposal, she publicly chided him by bringing up the fact that during Vietnam, he had received an exemption on the basis of being an expectant father. Nonetheless, it went down to defeat. Always quick with a rhetorical barb, Boxer, responding to Republicans who said it would embarrass the United States to shrink from fighting Saddam Hussein, said: "It's not about egg on our face, it's about blood on our kids." During her race for the Senate in 1992, she told audiences: "I'm really proud of my vote on the war. The more time passes, the more people tell me, 'My God, you were right.'"

In 1991, Barbara Boxer announced that she would run for the Senate seat being vacated by Alan Cranston. At the time of her announcement, she was well-known in the Bay Area but a virtual unknown to the voters of Southern California. To make her uphill journey even more difficult, her primary opponents were Los Angeles-area Congressman *Mel Levine* and former Assembly Speaker Leo McCarthy. But luck, talent, and the issues were on her side. Boxer was able to raise substantial money from the liberal, mostly Jewish Democrats of the West Side, and counted among her ardent supporters Barbara Streisand, Lloyd Bridges, Ted Danson, Rita Moreno, Richard Dreyfuss, and former Music Corporation of America head Sid Sheinberg. In addition to these financial heavyweights, Boxer came up with the novel idea of selling souvenir yellow-and-black boxer shorts to raise needed dollars.

Her campaign was given an unexpected boost during the Clarence Thomas confirmation hearings. When the members of the Senate Judiciary Committee were reluctant to have Anita Hill testify, Boxer took matters into her own hands, leading a "bipartisan squadron of female House members" over to the Senate side to protest. The photo of a grim, determined-looking Boxer striding at the head of a group of distinguished female members of Congress made newspapers across the country. The Anita Hill issue did her campaign wonders: "Hill led women to political empowerment, as women finally made the ultimate connection between their lack of power and the lack of women in high political office."

Boxer campaigned relentlessly, hammering away at the issues that had brought her to prominence: cutting the defense budget, protecting the rights of women and children, and safeguarding the environment. At the same time she was running for her Senate seat, Dianne Feinstein was running for California's other Senate position. Although the two appeared together toward the end of the primary, there was a bit of bad blood between them: Boxer had supported Feinstein's male opponent in the 1990 gubernatorial primary. Boxer came in first in the Democratic primary with 44 percent to McCarthy's 31 percent and Levine's 22 percent; it was the lowest voter turnout in more than fifty years.

In the general election, Boxer squared off against conservative Los Angeles–area television commentator and former Nixon speech writer Bruce Hirschensohn. The political gap between Boxer and Hirschensohn was of "Grand Canyon proportions." While Boxer called for defense cuts of up to $150 billion over five years and reinvesting the so-called "peace dividend" in education and environmental protection, Hirschensohn advocated eliminating the Federal Reserve Bank and the Environmental Protection Agency, as well as the Departments of Energy and Education. Hirschensohn, described by columnist George F. Will as "part basset hound, part pixie," scored points by publicizing Boxer's 143 overdrafts on the House bank, her having missed 40 percent of the recorded votes in the One Hundred and Second Congress, and her having charged the government $1,565 for limousine service to the airport. His campaign was dealt a fatal blow, however, when, in the early days of October, it was revealed that he was a devotee of nude dance clubs. On election day, Boxer, buoyed by a huge margin in the Bay Area, won by a margin of 48 percent to 43 percent.

Even before Boxer won the election, Senate Judiciary Committee chair Joseph Biden, a Delaware Democrat, hand delivered a dozen red roses, with a note saying: "Welcome to the Senate Judiciary Committee." Boxer declined the offer, instead joining the committees on Banking, Environment, and Budget. As a Senator, Boxer began moving to the political center. While in the House, she had been an ardent supporter of single-payer national health insurance. In the Senate, she declined to support Senator Paul Wellstone's single-payer legislation. This raised the hackles of her liberal supporters, who, in late 1993, called for a "Boxer rebellion." The rebels accused Boxer of selling out on a host of liberal issues.

For her part, Boxer flatly rejected the notion. She pointed to her fight to allow openly gay people serve in the military, as well as her support for continued government funding of the National Endowment for the Arts. Likewise, she hyped her vote to confirm Roberta Achtenberg, the first openly gay official, to a top federal post. In 1994, Boxer hoped to get a seat on the Finance Committee by playing an active role in the contest to select the new Senate Democratic leader.

She failed after siding with Connecticut Senator, Chris Dodd, who lost to Tom Daschle. From almost the moment of her election, Boxer knew she would face the fight of her life in 1998. She got that fight, somewhat surprisingly, in the person of California State Treasurer Matt Fong.

The nation's highest-ranking Asian-American Republican holding elected office, Matt Fong was the adopted son of California's long-time Democratic state Treasurer, March Fong Eu. A political centrist who supported abortion rights in the first trimester, Fong was challenged in the Republican primary by political newcomer Darrell Issa, a multimillionaire auto alarm magnate from San Diego. During the Republican primary, Senator Boxer watched quietly as Issa spent a record $10 million painting a picture of himself as a man whose "Horatio Alger-like business success" could more than offset his lack of elective experience. Fong challenged his opponent's rosy hagiography, suggesting that there was indeed a worm in the apple of Issa's success. A week before the primary election, allegations surfaced that Issa's rise to wealth had been accompanied by "questionable events," including a fire at one of his businesses that first was "suspected to be arson." Despite being outspent by a better than five-to-one margin, Fong defeated Issa by nearly 135,000 votes.

Boxer, who had been biding her time and saving money, went into the general election with an enormous financial edge. From almost the moment he won the Republican primary, Fong charged Boxer with being a dangerous, out of touch, "tax-and-spend" liberal. For her part, the better-financed Boxer ran television ads defining Fong as a political extremist. Running neck-and-neck with Boxer, Fong actually pulled out to a slight lead in the campaign's closing days. Then disaster struck. Shortly before election day, it was revealed that Fong, who had sought and received the endorsement of the "Log Cabin" group–made up of gay Republicans–had sent a substantial contribution to an Orange County-based "family values" group that did extensive lobbying against issues important to the gay community. Boxer also charged Fong with having accepted a $50,000 contribution from an Indonesian businessman in 1995—a clear violation of state and federal law. Boxer wound up overwhelming Fong 53 percent to 43 percent.

In their post-election analysis, pollsters and strategists opined that more than the "Log Cabin/Family Values/Indonesian Businessman" flap, Fong was done in by the September 21st release of President Clinton's videotaped testimony before a grand jury investigating the Monica Lewinsky scandal. "Until then" (i.e., September 21st), Boxer's campaign manager said, "we had a flood of Monica, and all of a sudden the rain stopped and we got questions from reporters about issues. We knew if we could keep the campaign on issues, we'd be all right."

Throughout her career in Washington, Barbara Boxer has been one of Capitol Hill's most ardent liberals. Without question, she voted for more dollars in federal spending than any other member in the early 1990s. She is not terribly comfortable with the "L word," preferring the "passionate progressive" label pinned on her by columnists Evans and Novak. At the same time, she has developed a reputation for being one of Washington's most pugnacious budget watchdogs. Possessed of a verbal style "as snappy and direct as a jolt of horseradish," Boxer has always had a "laser-like instinct" for finding platforms that allow her to play her "cherished watchdog role to best advantage."

Boxer has never truly become part of the Washington social scene. During her ten years in the House, she commuted back and forth to Northern California, where Stewart is a labor lawyer in Oakland. Their son Doug is an attorney in the Bay Area. Nicole Boxer Rodham, a graduate of NYU's Tisch School of the Arts, is an executive with a film company in Los Angeles. As mentioned above, Nicole married Hillary Rodham Clinton's brother in a White House ceremony on May 29, 1994. It was the first White House wedding in the twenty-three years since Tricia Nixon's 1971 marriage to Edward F. Cox. Judge Peter Capua, a family friend from Miami, officiated "under a white canopy with remarks from a Methodist minister and a Jewish layperson." Bobby Levy had come a long, long way from Brooklyn.

References

Barbara Boxer and Nicole Boxer, Strangers in the Senate: *Politics and the New Revolution of Women in America* (Washington, D.C.: National Press Books, 1994).

Almanac of American Politics (1984–98 editions).

Chicago Tribune, November 3, 1991, 6, 1:2.

Current Biography, 1994, pp. 63–6.

Harper's Magazine, November 1995, pp. 16–17.

Lears, November 1991, p. 90.

Los Angeles Times, August 8, 1993, 3:1.

Politics in America (1984–98 editions).

BURTON, SALA, (1925–1987): *Democrat from California; served three terms in the House (Ninety-eighth through One Hundredth Congress; June 21, 1983–February 1, 1987).*

As a little girl growing up in pre-war Poland, Sala Galante got a terrifying lesson in politics: "I saw and felt what happened in Western Europe when the Nazis were moving. You learn that politics is everyone's business." From almost the moment she arrived in San Francisco as a teenager to the last day of her life, Sala Burton lived by that creed. With her "grandmotherly air" and distinctive accent, Mrs. Burton seemed anything but the astute political animal she was. Sala Burton married into politics: she was the widow of Representative Phillip Burton (1926–1983), who the *Almanac of American Politics* (1986) termed "one of the two or three most important congressmen in the past 20 years." Like her late husband, Sala Burton was a thoroughgoing liberal, giving her support to a whole host of programs that would benefit the poor, the forgotten and the dispossessed. And like her husband, she died before her time.

Of Sala Burton's life in Poland precious little is known. She was born in Bialystok on April 1, 1925. Her family left Poland while she was still a child, and made their way to San Francisco, where Sala attended public school and San Francisco State University. In 1948, at age twenty-three, she became associate director of the California Public Affairs Institute—a position she held until 1950. That year, while attending a convention of the California Young Democrats, she met Phil Burton, a twenty-four-year-old law student at San Francisco's Golden Gate School of Law. The two were married shortly after Phil received his law degree in 1952. The honeymoon would have to wait because Phil went off with the Air Force to Korea. Returning at war's end, Phil went into private practice while Sala raised their daughter Joy.

Along with Phil, Sala helped found the California Democratic Council—the state party's most liberal wing—and served as its vice president from 1951 to 1954. Two years later, Phil Burton was elected to the California State Assembly. While her husband was carving out his political career, Sala continued concentrating on party affairs. In 1956, Sala Burton attended her first Democratic National Convention. She would return as a delegate to the 1976, 1980, and 1984 conventions. In 1957, Sala was elected president of the San Francisco Democratic Women's Forum, and served in that post until 1959, when her husband was appointed to represent the United States at the North Atlantic Organization conference in France.

In 1964, Congressman John F. Shelly resigned his Fifth District seat, having been elected Mayor of San Francisco. California's Fifth Congressional District takes in almost three-fourths of San Francisco, from the rich enclaves of Nob Hill, Russian Hill, and Pacific Heights, to the low income Mission District. In the special election to fill Shelly's seat Phillip Burton won, beginning a congressional career that would last nearly twenty years. Mrs. Burton, as had by then become custom, acted as her husband's campaign manager. During his two decades in the House, Phil Burton was one of the true leaders of that body. An anti-war labor liberal, Burton ran for House majority leader in 1976, losing by a single vote to Thomas P. "Tip" O'Neil of Massachusetts. Despite the loss, Burton "still did more to change the way business is done in the House, and channeled more money and benefits to poor people than any other congressman." During his years in congress, Phil Burton "vastly expanded the number and size of the national park system, helped to establish the Supplemental Security Income (SSI) program, made strikers eligible for food stamps, established the Black Lung Compensation program for coal miners, increased the minimum wage ... engineered the abolition of the House Un-American Activities Committee and established the rule that all House committee chairmen must be elected by the Democratic Caucus, by secret ballot, every two years." This last accomplishment represented an historic change in the way the House did business; it effectively brought the seniority system to a screeching halt. Lastly, Phil Burton was responsible for drawing California's redistricting plans after both the 1970 and 1980 censuses, thus insuring the continued growth of liberal Democratic representation from the Golden State.

While Phillip Burton served in Congress, getting reelected every two years with little effort, his wife remained politically active. In Washington, she served as legislative chair of the Women's National Democratic Club, and helped organize the Bipartisan Wives Task Force, a research group of members' wives interested in issues relating to "families, children and the elderly." Perhaps her most important role though, was acting as her husband's chief political operative, "often salving bruised egos after he had run over them."

Phillip Burton died suddenly and unexpectedly in San Francisco on April 10, 1983. He was not quite fifty-seven years old. Four days after her husband's funeral, Sala Burton announced that she would try to succeed him in Congress. Although there were many prominent San Francisco-area politicians waiting in the wings, by the end of the filing period, Mrs. Burton was the only well-known candidate on the ballot. Still, there were ten minor contenders vying in the special election. Under California law, special elections are open to candidates from all parties; the winner has to take more than fifty percent in order to avoid a runoff. Rebuilding the campaign organization that had helped her husband win so many elections, Burton and her volunteers "set up phone-canvassing and door-to-door leafleting operations," spreading the word that Sala Burton, holding the same views as her late husband and just as familiar with the Washington scene, would be "effective from the start." Sala Burton wound up winning the special election with 57 percent of the vote.

Sworn in on June 21, 1983, Representative Burton was given her husband's old seats on the Education and Labor and Interior Committees. One of her first acts was to add her name as co-sponsor of the Equal Rights Amendment. On Education and Labor she "repeatedly defended social welfare programs, working to stave off cuts in child nutrition spending and bilingual education." She was also one of just three members of the full committee to vote against "equal access" legislation, which permitted religious groups to meet on public school property.

After successfully running for reelection to a full two-year term just a few months later (winning with 72 percent of the vote), Mrs. Burton sought a seat on the House Appropriations Committee: "Taking a leaf from Phillip Burton's book, she launched a concerted lobbying effort aimed at members of the Steering and Policy Committee, which made the assignments." The pressure and phone calls were intense. One member of the Policy Committee, considering a statewide campaign in 1986, was promised access to "tens of thousands of dollars in California contributions" if he supported Burton. Despite the active efforts of Representatives Jim Wright and *Henry Waxman*, the Appropriations seat went to a candidate backed by House Ways and Means Chair Dan Rostenkowski. Instead of Appropriations, Burton "got what Speaker O'Neill wanted her to have in the first place: a seat on Rules."

In 1986, Sala Burton was diagnosed with cancer. Despite her weakened condition, she decided to run for reelection. Her condition was not kept secret from her constituents, who reelected her to a third term just a few days after she had undergone surgery. Shortly after being sworn in as a member of the One Hundredth Congress, she announced her retirement, and endorsed her successor, Nancy Pelosi, who has held the seat ever since. Sala Burton died on February 1, 1987. Sixty-three members of Congress attended funeral services at San Francisco's Temple Emanuel. Sala Burton was buried next to her husband in the National Cemetery of the Presidio of San Francisco. She was survived by her daughter Joy Temes.

References

Almanac of American Politics (1978–88 editions).
New York Times, Feb. 2, 1987; II, 7:4.
Politics in America (1980–88 editions).

CANTOR, JACOB AARON (1854–1921): *Democrat from New York; served one term in the House (Sixty-third Congress; November 4, 1913–March 3, 1915).*

Once one of the most prominent and durable Jewish politicians in late-nineteenth- and early-twentieth-century New York, Jacob Aaron Cantor is today no more than a footnote in modern texts. Once an ardent and loyal water-carrier for the boys from Tammany Hall, Cantor eventually had a change of heart and allied himself with the reform-minded Seth Low. In 1901, he became the first of seven Jews to be elected Manhattan borough president.

Jacob Aaron Cantor was born on the Lower East Side of New York on December 6, 1854. At the time, New York City was home to about 30,000 Jews (out of a total city-wide population of approximately 630,000) and about twenty synagogues. Jacob's mother, Hannah (Hanau) Cantor, was the daughter of the rabbi of London's Duke Place Synagogue. His father, Henry Cantor, was likewise, an English Jew. According to available biographic evidence, young Jacob Cantor attended public school until only his fourteenth birthday. He left school in order to become a clerk in a law office and a cub reporter on the *New York World.* Cantor spent five years as a reporter for the *World,* getting to know the ins-and-outs of New York City politics and meeting the powerful and influential bosses who would one day give his career a boost. Leaving his position with the *World,* Cantor entered the law department of the City College of New York, from which he received his LL.B. in 1875.

Cantor practiced law in New York City for the next ten years. In 1885, the thirty-year-old was elected as a Democrat to the New York State Assembly. Two years later he moved up to the State Senate, in which he would serve until 1898. In most of those years, the Democrats were the minority party in New York State. In 1893, when the Democrats regained control of the legislature, Cantor was elected Senate president and acting Lieutenant Governor—the first Jew to occupy either of those posts. As a member of the State Senate, Cantor was intensely interested in prison conditions as they affected Jewish inmates. As a director of the Society for the Aid of Jewish Prisoners and the Jewish Protectory,

he advocated legislation according equal rights to inmates, and saw to it that rabbis officiating as chaplains in prisons and reformatories were given compensation.

As noted above, Cantor spent many years as a dedicated lieutenant in the Tammany Hall faction of the Democratic Party. Because he had a basic instinct for reform, the Tammany *modus operandi* began wearing thin. In 1901, Cantor joined forces with the Citizens' League—a reform-minded organization dedicated to the dismantling of Tammany Hall. His eventual election as Manhattan borough president owed as much to his opposition to "King Richard" Croker's high-handed policies as to his support for reform mayoral candidate Seth Low. Declining renomination, Cantor served but a single term as borough president. His disaffection proved to be short-lived: within a few years, he was back in the good graces of Tammany Hall.

In 1910, Mayor Gaynor appointed Cantor chairman of the New York Committee on Congestion of Population, a position he held for the next three years. On September 1, 1913, Representative Francis B. Harrison resigned from Congress in order to become Governor General of the Philippines. Cantor ran for his seat. An easy victor, Jacob Cantor was sworn in as a member of the Sixty-third Congress on November 4, 1913. Two years later, Cantor was narrowly defeated for reelection by *Isaac Siegel.* Cantor contested Siegel's victory, claiming voter fraud, but was rebuffed. He returned to private practice after serving his single term in the House.

In 1918, Mayor Hylan appointed Cantor president of the Tax Commission Board of New York, a position he held until his death on July 2, 1921. Cantor, who had married Lydia Greenbaum in September, 1897, had no children. Funeral services were conducted by Reform Rabbi M. H. Harris. He is buried in Mount Hope Cemetery, Westchester, New York.

References

American Jewish Year Book, vol. 6 (1904–1905), pp. 72–73; vol. 24, p. 101.
Encyclopaedia Judaica (1972), vol. 5, col. 134.
Jewish Encyclopedia.
Universal Jewish Encyclopedia.

CARDIN, BENJAMIN LOUIS (1942–):
Democrat from Maryland; served seven terms in the House (One Hundredth through One Hundred and Sixth Congress, January 3, 1987–present).

In nine cases out of ten, election to Congress must be considered a step up in the world—especially for a state legislator. One's circle of influence becomes magnified; the stage upon which one acts is far more grand. In nine cases out of ten, that is. In the tenth case, election to Congress can mean trading in stature, tenure, and power for a position at the very bottom of the "greasy pole." Benjamin Louis Cardin, Democrat from Maryland, is undoubtedly that tenth man. For when Ben Cardin was elected to the One Hundredth Congress in November 1986, he had been at the very pinnacle of legislative power in his state for almost twenty years.

As Speaker of the Maryland House of Delegates for nearly a decade, he had been a first among equals. As a freshman member of the One Hundredth Congress, he was a relatively unknown junior among 435 ambitious politicos. But Cardin, a man of uncommon political instincts, soon broke out of the pack, making a name for himself in his new surroundings.

Ben Cardin comes by his knack for politics and public service as a matter of inheritance. His father, Meyer Cardin, who turned ninety in July, 1997, served as a Baltimore city judge for more than forty years. The Kardinskys originally came from Lithuania in 1902. Ben's paternal grandfather settled in Baltimore, where he ran grocery stores. Ben's maternal grandparents, the Greens, also came from Lithuania and also ran a grocery store. Meyer's brother Jack, the first attorney in the family, received his law degree in 1918. That year he legally changed the family name to Cardin.

Meyer and Dora Cardin have two sons, who both grew up to be attorneys: Howard, born in 1941, and Benjamin Louis, born on October 5, 1943. Ben Cardin grew up in Baltimore's Lake Ashburton area, where his parents maintained an observant, kosher household. The Cardins belonged to the Orthodox Beth Tefilah, where Meyer served as both president and chairman of the board. Ben became bar mitzvah at Beth Tefilah in 1956, the year after his father became chief judge of the Police Court in Baltimore.

Following his graduation from public high school, Ben Cardin entered the University of Pittsburgh, where he majored in political science. He received his B.A., *cum laude*, in 1964, and immediately entered the University of Maryland School of Law. In 1966, a full year before receiving his law degree, the twenty-three-year-old Cardin was elected to represent a suburban Baltimore district in the Maryland House of Delegates. Cardin's election was not as surprising as one might think; the seat had previously been held by his uncle. Nonetheless, he was easily the youngest member of that legislative body. The next year, Cardin received his LL.B., graduating first in his class. Along with his duties in the state legislature, he went into private practice.

In the Maryland legislature, which is known for having a fast track and a dizzying pace, Cardin soon attracted the attention of his colleagues, demonstrating "great finesse and skill as well as complete honesty." In 1974, he became an original sponsor of Maryland's public financing law. After less than a decade in the House of Delegates, he became Ways and Means Committee chair. In that position, he "established himself as an expert on issues of state finance." In 1979, at age thirty-five, he became the youngest Speaker in the history of the Maryland House.

As Speaker, Ben Cardin established a Spending Affordability Committee to rein in the growth of state spending. An article in the *Baltimore Sun* described Cardin's political *modus operandi* as Speaker: "Cardin widened the circle of House leadership, including as many of the body's 141 members as possible into the inner circle and then, gently, making every vote a test of loyalty. He preached the value of a 'group result.'" Although Cardin was generally well-liked by his colleagues in Annapolis, some legislators complained that he "planted pliable allies in chairmanships and rushed favored bills through without debate." In 1984, Cardin led a fight to reform Maryland's "then-generous and largely underfunded pension system" for teachers and state employees. Despite pressure from unions that threatened to retaliate by opposing those who voted for reform, Cardin persuaded his colleagues to enact the measure.

Well-known statewide for his strong legislative record and expertise on fiscal matters, Cardin began setting his sights on the 1986 governor's race. Harry Hughes, the outgoing governor, had served two four-year terms, and was leaving office with two significant accomplishments to his credit: cleaning up Chesapeake Bay and eliminating scandal from "the quaint 18th-century capital of Annapolis." Cardin's plans abruptly changed when longtime (1971–1986) Baltimore mayor William Donald Schaeffer–a "near mythic figure on the Maryland political stage"—decided to enter the Democratic primary to succeed Hughes. During his tenure as mayor, Schaeffer (1921–) restored the city's Inner Harbor, built Harborplace (with its world-famous aquarium), "strengthened the city's diversified local economy," and "bridged the gap between black and white." His popularity and notoriety—one time he jumped into the tank at the aquarium fully clothed—were so great that when introduced at an Orioles' World Series game, he received a greater ovation than the team's best players. Cardin was smart enough to realize that to remain in the primary race against Schaeffer would be "foolhardy, not brave." "I don't run to lose," he was quoted as saying. "I run to win. I don't run to make a statement. I'm very calculating."

Once out of the governor's race, Cardin set his sights on a seat in the United States House of Representatives. In 1986, Third District Representative Barbara Mikulski vacated her House seat in order to run for the Senate seat being vacated by moderate Republican Charles McC. Mathias, Jr. Mikulsi had initially won her House seat following Paul Sarbanes' elevation to the Senate in 1976. Cardin quickly jumped into the race, where victory in the Democratic primary is the only challenge. Maryland's Third

Congressional District is centered in Baltimore, and takes in the Jewish suburbs of Pikesville and Owings Mills, the mostly Polish Highlandtown area, and the "planned community" of Columbia. Raising nearly a half-million dollars, Cardin swamped his closest opponent, Edward Ellison, garnering 82 percent of the vote. Predictably, Speaker Cardin rolled to victory in the general election as well, capturing nearly 80 percent of the final vote.

Ben Cardin entered the One Hundredth Congress with a reputation as "a legislative deal-maker and budgetary expert." Cardin lobbied hard—"a bit too hard, perhaps"—for a seat on either Budget or Ways and Means. He wound up receiving assignments on Judiciary and Public Works. During his first term in the House, Ben Cardin did a lot of "listening to the proceedings and talking with members one-on-one." What few speeches he did give in these early days, were generally about the plight of individual Soviet Jewish refuseniks. Cardin compiled a solidly liberal voting record during his first term (A.D.A. of 90), and was reelected with 73 percent of the vote. In its editorial of endorsement, the *Baltimore sun* said Cardin was "probably the finest legislator to come out of the Annapolis State House since World War II."

Working quietly behind the scenes with the party leadership, Cardin was rewarded with a seat on Ways and Means at the beginning of the One Hundred and Second Congress. He was concomitantly appointed to the Committee on Official Conduct—Ethics. One of Ben Cardin's greatest assets, according to his colleagues, is his ability to work with both Democrats and Republicans. As an example, in 1990, he joined Florida Republican E. Clay Shaw, Jr. to press for repeal of a tax enacted on luxury items, including boats. Although the tax was ostensibly aimed at the wealthy, it also contributed to a serious decline in the boat-building industry—a major employer in Maryland. After the Republicans took over the House following the 1994 elections, Cardin quickly contacted newly elected Speaker Newt Gingrich, offering to be of assistance. Gingrich did not reply. Instead, Cardin's Democratic colleagues chose him to oversee the logistics of moving the party from majority to minority status. As noted in the *Almanac of American Politics* (1996): "As the

Democrats' transition team leader, Cardin tried to make sure that the now-reigning Republicans treated the new minority fairly." To that end, he denounced the GOP's intention to fire some Hill administrative workers, most of whom had worked for the Democrats, and provide them with no severance pay for accrued vacation time. The Republicans eventually backed down when Cardin "forcefully reminded them that such actions would never be tolerated in the private sector."

With the advent of the Republican majority, Ben Cardin actually found himself coming into even greater prominence. As the second-ranking Democrat on the Ways and Means Subcommittee on Health, Cardin is the one Republicans look to for support when they are seeking to give legislation "the patina of bipartisanship." When the Health Subcommittee was creating a new Medicare bill, Cardin was actually able to get a measure enacted—a rare accomplishment in the highly partisan One-Hundred and Fifth Congress. Cardin proposed a package of preventive medical benefits, including mammograms and Pap smears, as well as screening for colon cancer, prostate cancer, and diabetes. Cardin had a strong enough relationship with Subcommittee Chair Bill Thomas, a California Republican, that Thomas "adopted Cardin's benefits package as his own on the first day of Congress . . . and made sure money was available for it in the balanced-budget deal with the White House."

An assistant party whip and member of the Democratic Caucus Steering and Policy Committee (the panel which makes committee assignments), Cardin finally moved into the national spotlight in 1997 from his position on House Ethics. Cardin played a pivotal role in the two-year investigation of Speaker Newt Gingrich's part in a fundraising scheme. The investigation resulted in the Speaker being fined $300,000. According to a *Baltimore Sun* article: "Cardin...was the one GOP committee members found they could work with most comfortably on what for them was a particularly wrenching task." Cardin gets ribbed from time to time by his Democrat colleagues about his "close association" with Republicans. Cardin took quite a bit of good-natured heat when he became the only Democrat to have an amendment passed in the

GOP tax bill—a $150 tax break for tutoring expenses.

Beginning in early 1997, Maryland political insiders began spreading the word that Ben Cardin might run for Governor in 1998–"the public office he's always wanted most." Speculation was rife that Cardin might challenge incumbent Governor Paris N. Glendening in the Democratic primary. Glendening, weakened by reports of campaign finance irregularities, was seen as being particularly vulnerable. When questioned, Cardin said he was not sure what his future would bring. At one point he was quoted as saying, "I've completed my health care agenda. Got done what I wanted to do on Ethics. I have nothing else to do but go fishing." By June 1997, Cardin had formed an exploratory committee. Within six months, however, he changed his mind and announced that he would run for reelection to the House. Running against Republican Colin Harby, Cardin won election to a seventh term by a 78 percent to 22 percent margin.

Ben Cardin is married to the former Myrna Edelman. They have two children, Michael, an attorney, and Deborah, who has a degree in Art History and works in museums. Unlike most members of Congress, Ben Cardin is not part of the "Washington scene." He returns to his suburban Baltimore home every night. The Cardins belong to Beth Tefilah, an Orthodox congregation in Baltimore. Ben Cardin has participated in Jewish communal affairs virtually all his life. He has been actively involved in the Jewish National Fund, Bonds for Israel, the Jewish Relations Council of Greater Baltimore, and B'nai B'rith. A man of moderate height, a bit portly, and balding, Ben Cardin is a fine poker player and a motorist who "tends toward the A. J. Foyt school of driving." According to a close friend, "with him driving . . . you quickly develop a closer relationship with your god."

Ben Cardin is, by all accounts, something of a practical joker as well: Some years back, he purchased one of the first cars with remote-control door locks and lights. One day, he stopped in the parking lot and said to an aide, "You won't believe what this car will do." If the aide would say, "Ben," the congressman said, the car's lights would go on.

"Ben," said the aide.

"Louder," advised the Congressman.

"BEN!" shouted the aide. On came the lights as the Congressman hit the "magic button" hidden in his hand. Only later, when a friend of the aide purchased a similarly equipped automobile, did she get her boss's joke.

References

Interview with Hon. Meyer Cardin, July 1997.
Interview with Benjamin Cardin, July 1997.
Almanac of American Politics (1990–98 editions).
Baltimore Sun, December 18, 1996; June 22, 1997.
Politics in America (1990–98 editions).

CELLER, EMANUEL (1888–1981): *Democrat from New York; served twenty-five terms in the House (Sixty-eighth through Ninety-second Congress; March 4, 1923–January 3, 1973); chairman, House Judiciary Committee, Eighty-first, Eighty-second, and Eighty-fourth through Ninety-second Congress.*

In late 1924, as the thirty-six-year-old Emanuel Celler was finishing his first term in Congress, he was uncertain whether or not he wanted to stand for reelection. Simply stated, he didn't like Washington all that much. Moreover, he was a bit chary about what Washington was doing to him as a person: "I was not a happy man. I didn't like the Washington climate; I didn't like Washington ideas. I was intolerant, impatient and lost. I seemed to be climbing a greased pole." After much soul searching, he decided to run one more time. That "one more time," turned out to be the beginning of the second longest Congressional tenure in all American history—forty-nine years and nearly ten months. Only Mississippi's Jamie Whitten—fifty years and two months—served in Congress longer.

Celler not only grew to love Congress; he even developed a humorous attitude toward that which he had originally found repugnant. Toward the end of his illustrious career, speaking before the freshman class of a new Congress, he advised: "To be a successful Congressman, one must have the friendliness of a child, the enthusiasm of a teenager, the assurance of a college boy, the diplomacy of a wayward husband, the curiosity of a cat and the good humor of an idiot." He concluded his little chat by telling them to "Learn the rules and listen. Remember that God gave you two ears and one mouth. The fish that opens its mouth is the one that gets caught."

The Cellers lived in a frame house on Sumner Avenue and Floyd Street in Brooklyn. In the basement there was a 25,000 gallon tank, filled with the whiskey that Manny's father, Henry H. Celler, rectified and then sold under the name "Echo Spring." At the time of his son Manny's birth on May 6, 1888, "Echo Spring" was already a flourishing family enterprise. Manny, along with his sisters Jessie (Anixter) and Lillien (Masch) and his brother Mortimer, worked for their father, pasting labels on an endless supply of bottles.

Manny Celler was a good student, graduating from Brooklyn Boy's High School in June 1906, and looking forward to entering Columbia College in the fall. Just about the time he was ready to matriculate, his father's business failed; Manny became dependent on an uncle for financial support. Shortly after he entered Columbia, Manny's father, Henry, died; his mother, Josephine (Müller), passed away less than five months later. Suddenly, the college freshman was faced with a whole new set of challenges. As he wrote in his autobiography, *You Never Leave Brooklyn*: "I became head of the household. Following his failure, my father had given up his business and become a wine salesman. I took up his route. I went to school in the mornings and sold wines all afternoon until seven o'clock in the evening." Even with his increased responsibilities, Manny Celler managed to graduate on time, receiving a B.A. in 1910. He then breezed through Columbia University Law School in two years, receiving his LL.B. in 1912.

Following his admission to the New York bar in 1912, Emanuel Celler began practicing with the firm Meyer Krashauer. His first clients were, not surprisingly, his wine customers. His first case involved a Polish immigrant who had been arrested for voting without first having become a naturalized citizen. This would set the stage for one of Celler's lifelong interests: the plight of the immigrant.

In June 1914, Manny Celler married Stella B. Barr, and became a partner in the new firm of Kaufman, Weitzner and Celler. The Cellers, who were married for fifty-two years until Stella's death in 1966, had two daughters, Judith and Jane (Mrs. Sidney) Wertheimer. Jane, afflicted with cerebral palsy, predeceased her parents. In a March 1969 interview with T. H. Baker of the Lyndon Baines Johnson Library, Celler offered the following encomium to his late wife: "Whatever modicum of success I have, some of which I certainly can lay at her door. She assuaged my sorrow when sorrows came. She tempered my anger when anger came forward, and set me right on many, many an occasion. That kind of an overseer, or helpmate . . . is of overwhelming, staggering advantage to a man in public life."

During the First World War, Emanuel Celler got his first taste of government work when he was appointed an appeal agent under the Draft Act of 1917. In this capacity, he sat as a member of his local draft board, hearing entreaties from young men seeking to change or challenge their draft status.

Following the war, Celler's practice flourished and his interests expanded. In addition to acting as counsel for various butchers' organizations (Brooklyn Retail Butchers' Corporation, the Retail Butchers' Holding Company, and the Butchers' Mutual Casualty Company), he became involved in banking. Celler organized both the Brooklyn National Bank and the Madison State Bank of New York City—of which he was vice president—served as counsel for the Reliance Investment Company, and was trustee and joint counsel of the Queensboro Savings Bank. In 1928, Celler, by then a three-term member of Congress, was forced to sell the Brooklyn National Bank to one of the nation's larger and more powerful banks. Although his stockholders were protected, Celler himself took a financial hit: "it resulted in the loss to me of a most substantial sum of money. For many years thereafter it took a major portion of my earnings to repay it."

In 1922, during the midst of the Harding Administration, Emanuel Celler's friend, New York City Tax Commissioner James J. Sexton, urged him to run for Congress from New York's Tenth District. Although previous attempts to wrest the district from Republican hands had failed, Celler agreed to become the Democratic candidate. Running on the slogan "It's time for a change," and stressing "the evils of prohibition and the virtues of the League of Nations," Celler defeated the Republican incumbent by slightly more than 3,000 votes. Celler was sworn in as a member of the Sixth-eighth Congress on March 4, 1923, and continued to represent the district (variously numbered the Tenth, Eleventh, Fifteenth, and again the Tenth) for the next half century.

Celler languished as a member of the minority party through the Harding, Coolidge, and Hoover administrations, and was assigned to the relatively minor committees on Accounts Claims and Civil Service. His first major debate concerned the Johnson Immigration Act of 1924. In 1921, Congress had passed the so-called Quota Law, which limited immigration in any one year to 3 percent of the number of each nationality according to the census of 1910, with an absolute maximum of 356,000. Of this act, historian Page Smith wrote: "Its unabashed purpose was to limit the number of Southern and Eastern European immigrants." The Johnson Act

of 1924 sought to cut the quota in half, further restricting immigration to 2 percent of the "nationals" in the 1890 census. Again quoting Page Smith, the Johnson Immigration Act "demonstrated the growing hostility both to immigration per se and to such nationals as Italians, Poles, Serbs, and other Slavs." Representative Celler argued forcefully against its passage, but to no avail. This was merely the first act in a drama that would not reach its conclusion until the mid-1960s. Celler continued railing against any form of the "Quota Law" or "national origins theory of immigration," under seven different presidential administrations for the next four decades.

It was not until 1965, during the Johnson administration, that Celler finally got Congress to "get that idea [national origins] ripped out of the immigration fabric" by passing the Celler-Hart Immigration Act. Although the final bill did not call for any significant increase in the then-current annual immigration level of 300,000, it did eliminate altogether—and forthwith—the old national quotas framework. Signed into law by President Lyndon B. Johnson at a dramatic ceremony held at Ellis Island in New York harbor, it marked the end of a long and—often lonely—crusade for the gentleman from Brooklyn.

Always a staunch liberal, Celler came into his own with the advent of the New Deal, and supported the vast majority of the F. D. R.-sponsored legislation. By the mid-1930s, Celler was garnering a reputation for being one of Congress' leading defenders of civil rights and constitutional liberties. Celler's entry in *Current Biography* noted: "As early as 1935 [he] had scented danger in a proposed measure to make mere advocacy of the overthrow of the government a crime." To Celler's way of thinking the bill invited potential punishment for "merely harboring radical opinions." Celler fought a losing battle to keep the Special Committee on Un-American Activities (formerly known as the Dies Committee) from becoming a standing committee under the chairmanship of Mississippi's notoriously anti-Semitic John Rankin. Throughout his long and illustrious Congressional career, Celler consistently voted against every extension of the House Committee on Un-American Activities (HUAC). In the late 1940s, as chairman of the House Judiciary

Committee, he tried to get his colleagues to jettison HUAC in favor of a civil rights committee that would investigate not only Communists, but the Ku Klux Klan and Fascists as well. This was not to be; the McCarthy era, with its mass hysteria and "Communists under every bed" pathology was just beginning. Joining with other House liberals, Celler voted against both the Mundt-Nixon Communist Registration Bill (1948) and the Internal Security Act of 1950. As Judiciary Committee chair, he invariably voted to recommit (i.e., kill or delay) any proposal calling for loyalty checks on federal employees. Horrified by the excesses of McCarthyism, Celler tried to get the Republican-controlled House to enact legislation that would deny Senators and Representatives immunity from civil liability for any defamatory articles or undelivered statements they might include in the *Confressional Record*. Celler's proposal fell on deaf ears.

While Celler was unable to convince Congress to open America's doors to the oppressed Jews in Europe, it was not for lack of trying. In addition, his frequent speeches about the Nazi genocide helped rouse public consciousness of the Holocaust—a significant accomplishment. But Celler was up against a State Department predisposed to keeping the status quo on matters of immigration—especially in the persons of Secretary of State Cordell Hall and his adjutant, Assistant Secretary Breckinridge Long. Descended from the Breckinridges of Kentucky and the Longs of Virginia, and married to the wealthy Francis Preston Blair (a granddaughter of the 1868 Democratic Vice Presidential nominee), Long oversaw no fewer than twenty-three of the Department of State's forty-two divisions. These included the Visa Division. Faced with repeated requests to speed up the visa process for those in imminent danger, Long ground the bureaucratic wheels to a virtual halt. This brought out Celler's ire. On the House floor, he sarcastically stated that "Frankly, Breckinridge Long, in my humble opinion, is the least sympathetic to refugees in all the State Department. I attribute to him the tragic bottleneck in the granting of visas. . . . It takes months and months to grant the visa and then it usually applies to a corpse." Celler tried in vain to exercise influence with his good

friend, President Franklin Roosevelt, but to no avail. Tragically, the fact remains that throughout the Nazi era, neither Celler nor Dickstein nor Bloom could get a single act of refugee legislation through Congress.

Emanuel Celler served a record eleven terms as Judiciary Committee chair. During his tenure, he steered four constitutional amendments through the House of Representatives:

1. Amendment 23, which granted citizens of the District of Columbia the right to vote in Presidential elections.

2. Amendment 24, which barred the poll tax as a prerequisite in federal elections.

3. Amendment 25, which detailed the procedures to be followed in the event of the death or disability of the President.

4. Amendment 26, which lowered the voting age to eighteen.

In 1957, Celler shepherded through the first civil rights legislation Congress had enacted in eighty-two years. This landmark act created a six-member Civil Rights Commission that was empowered to "subpoena and to investigate denial of voting rights." Three years later, Celler authored the Civil Rights Act of 1960, which made the obstruction of court orders for school desegregation a federal crime. As Judiciary Committee chair, Celler played a major role in the passage of the historic 1964 Civil Rights Act, which once-and-for-all ended segregated public facilities. Toward the end of his Congressional service, Celler's Judiciary Committee held hearings on the proposed "Equal Rights Amendment" (ERA), which the chairman adamantly opposed.

Emanuel Celler became a Zionist in 1917, when he read Theodor Herzl's *The Jewish State*. During his decades in Congress, Celler spoke forcefully against any and all attempts to weaken the emerging Jewish homeland. Near the end of World War II, Celler strenuously objected to Franklin Roosevelt's reluctance to urge Great Britain to consent to the creation of a Jewish homeland in Palestine. When after the war, President Truman urged massive postwar aid to England, Celler led the opposition, arguing that such aid should be linked to a British withdrawal from Palestine. Celler also led a valiant albeit unsucessful fight at the Democratic Party's 1948 convention to insert a plank opposing the

Truman administration's arms embargo on the newborn State of Israel.

Traditionally reelected by overwhelming margins, Celler looked a bit vulnerable in 1968. That year, he drew competition in the Democratic primary from Edna Kelley and twenty-seven-year-old attorney Bob Heller, the son of Celler's former House colleague *Louis B. Heller*. With virtually no political experience (save for being the son of a prominent public official), Heller unaccountably received the *New York Times'* endorsement. Although Celler wound up winning the primary, the myth of his invincibility had finally been pierced. Celler finally met his match four years later in the person of fellow Brooklynite *Elizabeth Holtzman*. Holtzman, a thirty-one-year-old Democratic State committeewoman and former assistant to New York City mayor John V. Lindsay, decided to challenge the eighty-four-year-old Celler in the 1972 Democratic primary. A complacent campaigner (he hadn't had a serious primary challenge since his first campaign in 1922), Celler refused to take Holtzman seriously. Running a low-key, direct-mail campaign, Celler privately referred to Holtzman as a "political nonentity." Publicly, he described her as "irritating as a hangnail," and confidently asserted "which nail I am going to cut off." Running a vigorous campaign with the aid of a small army of volunteers, Holtzman defeated the senior member of Congress by the slimmest of margins—15,557 to 14,995. An historic career had come to an end.

Following his defeat, Celler resumed practicing law with the firm he had created thirty-six years earlier—Weisman, Celler, Allan, Spett and Sheinberg. From 1973 to 1975, he served as a member of the Commission on the Revision of the Federal Appellate Court System. Celler also busied himself with the Jewish community, in which he had always played an active role. As a member of Congress, Celler had taken the initiative for funding a Semitics division at the Library of Congress. Celler served as an honorary director of the Jewish Family Welfare Society and the American Red Mogen David Fund, and was a member of the American Jewish Congress, American Jewish Committee, and B'nai B'rith. Celler was also a devotee of the arts, most notably opera, for which he had a passion.

Emanuel Celler died on January 15, 1981, just a few months short of his ninety-third birthday. He is buried in Mount Nebo Cemetery in Cypress Hills, New York.

References

American Jewish Year Book, vol. 83, p. 533.

Biographic Encyclopedia of American Jewry, 1926, 1928, 1938.

Emanuel Celler, *You Never Leave Brooklyn* (New York: Day, 1953).

Dictionary of American Biography.

Encyclopaedia Judaica (1973–82).

Oral History Interview with Lyndon B. Johnson Library, March 19, 1969.

Oral History Interview with John F. Kennedy Library, April 11, 1972.

New York Times, January 26, 1981, 1:1.

Universal Jewish Encyclopedia.

Who Was Who in America, vol. 7.

Who Was Who in American Jewry, 1926, 1928, 1938.

CHUDOFF, EARL (1907–1993): *Democrat from Pennsylvania; served five terms in the House (Eighty-first through Eighty-fifth Congress; January 3, 1949–January 5, 1958).*

Although Earl Chudoff spent over thirty five years in the public eye—as state legislator, member of Congress, and judge—little is known of his private life. Among the Chudoffs of the second and third generations, there exists only a vague knowledge that they had a relative who was "a somebody" from Philadelphia.

What is known is that Earl, the son of Morris and Jenny Chudoff, was born in Philadelphia on November 15, 1907. The family lived in the Jewish enclave known as "Strawberry Mansion," where Morris first sold ladies' dresses, then gravitated to the dental supply business. They had one other child: a daughter named Meryl. Earl Chudoff was educated in the Philadelphia public school system and received an undergraduate degree in economics from Wharton in 1929. Three years later, he received his law degree from the University of Pittsburgh. Passing the bar a year later, he went into private practice in Philadelphia. From 1936 to 1939, he served as a building and loan examiner for the Pennsylvania State Department of Banking. With the coming of war he entered the United States Coast Guard Reserve, where he served as a chief boatswain's mate from December 1942 until September 1945. Prior to the war he had married and had two children: Steven, who became a schoolteacher, and Diane.

A year before he entered the Coast Guard Reserve, Earl Chudoff was elected to the Pennsylvania State House of Representatives. He served in that body from 1941 to 1948, at which time he ran for Congress from Philadelphia's Fourth District. Chudoff's opponent, incumbent Franklin J. Maloney, had won the seat just two years earlier—the first Republican to represent the Fourth District in nearly a generation. Chudoff won election to the Eighty-first Congress in November 1948, and wound up spending nine years in the House. In Congress, he served on the House District Committee and the House Operations Committee. At one point, he chaired the Public Works subcommittee on resources.

On January 5, 1958—midway through his fifth term—Chudoff resigned his seat in order to take a position as judge on the Philadelphia Court of Common Pleas. Elected to a ten-year term in 1958, he served on that body until his retirement in 1978. While on the bench, he was known for "often holding defendants, lawyers and witnesses in contempt of court for failing to act respectfully in his courtroom." Upon retirement, he moved to Miami Beach, Florida, where he died on May 17, 1993.

According to Aaron Chudoff, the judge's elderly first cousin, the Chudoff family practiced "a middle-of-the-road-Conservative brand of Judaism." As young men, the two spent many hours playing tennis. The place of Earl Chudoff's interment is publicly unknown, as are the current whereabouts of his children.

References

Interview with Aaron Chudoff, Miami, Florida, March 1998.

Biographical Directory of the United States Congress: 1774–1989, p. 775.

Washington Post, May 19, 1993, C6.

CITRON, WILLIAM MICHAEL (1896–1976):
Democrat from Connecticut; served two terms in the House (Seventy-fourth through Seventy-fifth Congress; January 3, 1935–January 3, 1939).

William Michael Citron, the son of Benjamin and Dora (Newmark) Citron, was born in New Haven, Connecticut, on August 29, 1896. Turn-of-the-century New Haven contained more than half of Connecticut's total Jewish population—estimated at 8,000. In 1899, the family moved to Middletown, which had only a handful of Jewish families. There, William Citron attended the city's public schools. Remaining at home, he attended Wesleyan University, from which he received his B.A. in June 1918. On September 16 of that year, he was commissioned a second lieutenant and began training as a field artillery officer. Three months later, the Armistice concluded, he was discharged. Following his brief military career, he attended law school at Harvard University, from which he received an LL.B. in 1921. Successfully passing the Connecticut bar, Citron went into private practice in Middletown.

William Citron was elected to a two-year term in the Connecticut House of Representatives in 1927. Somewhat unusually, Citron served as minority leader during his first term. In 1928, Citron was appointed city corporation counsel of Middletown. From all indications, he also maintained his private practice. That year, he decided that, rather than run for reelection to the state house, he would try for the United States Congress. The year 1928 was not a good one for young, relatively unknown Democrats running in historically Republican districts. Besides having to battle the traditional advantage given to incumbents, Democrats were also saddled with having New York Governor Al Smith at the top of the ticket. In 1928, the "Happy Warrior's" Catholicism was a decided albatross for his fellow Democrats. Running against the odds, Citron was handily defeated by Republican James P. Glynn, a two-term incumbent. Two years later, Citron regained his seat in the Connecticut state house. Following the 1930 census, Connecticut's Congressional delegation was expanded from five to six seats. The new sixth slot was declared

an "at-large" position. William Citron ran for this at-large seat in the more Democrat-friendly year of 1932. Again, he lost—this time to Charles M. Bakewell of New Haven. Bakewell (1867–1957) taught philosophy at Yale from 1905 to 1930; a preeminent philosopher, he was elected president of the American Philosophical Association in 1910. Two years later, Citron, who was now in his sixth year as city corporation counsel, waged his third race for Congress. This time he won the at-large position, defeating Representative Bakewell.

Citron served two quiet terms in the House, losing his seat to Republican Boleslaus J. Monkiewicz in 1938. Following his Congressional service, Citron spent two years (1940–1942) as chairman of the Housing Authority of Middletown. In July 1942, the nearly forty-six-year-old William Citron returned to military service. This time he entered as a captain in the military police. A year later, he was promoted to major. In October 1943, he retired from the Army for reasons of "physical incapacity." Citron then returned to his law practice and various civic responsibilities, serving as a member of the Connecticut Veterans Reemployment and Advisory Commission and as commander of the Connecticut Disabled American Veterans. In 1952, another great year for Republicans, Citron waged his final campaign for Congress, losing to Antoni M. Sadlak. Connecticut would continue to have an at-large seat until 1964. In the twelve years from 1952 to 1964, voters in the state elected two men of obvious ethnicity to their single at-large position: the aforementioned Antoni M. Sadlak, and Frank Kowalski.

The 1952 race was Bill Citron's last stab at elective office. Retiring in the late 1960s, he died in Titusville, Florida, on June 17, 1976, just two months before his eightieth birthday. William Citron is buried in Middletown at the Adath Israel Cemetery.

References
New York Times, June 9, 1976.
Universal Jewish Encyclopedia.
Who Was Who in America, vol. 7.
Who Was Who in World Jewry, 1938.

COHEN, JOHN SANFORD (1870–1935):

Democrat from Georgia; served part of an unexpired term in the Senate (April 25, 1932–January 11, 1933).

Senator John S. Cohen of Georgia was the product of uniquely mixed parentage. His father, Phillip Lawrence Cohen (1845–1882), was descended from Portuguese Jews who had settled in Savannah in the early eighteenth century. His mother, Ellen Gobert (Wright) Cohen, was the daughter of Major General Ambrose Ransom Wright, "a distinguished commander in the Confederate army and a lieutenant-governor of Georgia," and Mary Hubbell Savage, "a descendant of Thomas Savage (1594–1627), who came from England and settled in Virginia in 1607." John Sanford, the Cohens' second child, was born on February 26, 1870 in Augusta, Georgia, where his father was a private banker and broker. As a teenager, the senior Cohen had served in the Confederate army, surrendering with Lee at Appomattox.

John Sanford Cohen received a private education at the Richmond Academy in Augusta, Maupin's School for Boys in Ellicot City, Maryland, and the Shenandoah Valley Academy in Virginia. In 1885, the fifteen-year-old John Sanford Cohen entered the United States Naval Academy. John's brother, Ambrose Ransom Wright Cohen, who was two years John's senior, had died at Annapolis the year before. John Cohen resigned from the Naval Academy after only one year and returned to Augusta, where he served an apprenticeship on the *Augusta Chronicle*. One of the South's oldest and most respected newspapers, the *Chronicle* had long been owned by Cohen's maternal grandparents; his grandfather and his uncle (Henry Gregg Wright) had been editors. After fulfilling his apprenticeship, the eighteen-year-old Cohen spent 1888 in Mexico as secretary to Captain William G. Raoul, the builder of the Mexican National Railroad. In 1889, he moved to New York, becoming a reporter on *Joseph Pulitzer's New York World*. The following year, Cohen returned to Georgia, where he found employment with the *Atlanta Journal*, a connection he would maintain for the next forty-five years.

During the second Cleveland administration (1893–97), Cohen became Washington correspondent for the *Journal* and private secretary to Interior Secretary Hoke Smith. With the outbreak of the Spanish-American War in 1898, Cohen sailed to Cuba with the American fleet as a correspondent for the *Journal*. When the call went out for volunteers, he returned to Georgia and was commissioned a first lieutenant in the Third Georgia United States Volunteer Infantry. Promoted to major, he went with the army of occupation to Cuba. After the war, Cohen became the *Journal's* managing editor, eventually becoming its president. Under his guidance, the paper became the first in the South (and the second in the nation) to establish a radio station—WSB, the "Voice of the South"—which went on the air from the roof of the Journal Building on March 15, 1922. A visionary, Cohen started using wire-photos as early as 1935.

"The Major," as he was known, was elected Democratic National Committeeman for Georgia in 1924. He was reelected to that post in 1928 and 1932. On April 18, 1932, Georgia's senior Senator, William J. Harris, died unexpectedly. Cohen, who was appointed to replace him until a special election could be held, was officially sworn in a week later. Cohen's tenure in the Senate actually amounted to a little over two months; the Senate's second session did not commence until December 5, 1932. Well before then, Cohen was appointed vice chairman of the Democratic National Committee, and decided to put his energies into campaigning for Franklin D. Roosevelt. He therefore declined nomination for the remaining four years of his Senate term; the seat was won by the thirty-five-year-old Richard Brevard Russell, Jr. (1897–1971), who went on to have one of the most distinguished careers in the history of the United States Senate. One of the Senate's three office buildings is named in his honor.

Despite the fact that John Cohen's father was the scion of a distinguished Jewish family, the "Major" was a practicing Episcopalian. He married the former Julia Lowry Clarke in 1887, and had two children, John, Jr., and Mary. A "patron of art, music and education," John S. Cohen was instrumental in reestablishing the Lee School of Journalism at Washington and Lee University in Virginia. He died on May 13, 1935, and was buried in West View Cemetery, in Atlanta, Georgia.

References

Atlanta Journal, May 14, 1935.

Biographical Directory of the United States Congress, 1774–1989, p. 805.

Dictionary of American Biography.

Josephine Mellichamp, "John Cohen," in *Senators from Georgia* (Huntsville, Ala.: Strode Publishers, 1976), pp. 240–244.

COHEN, WILLIAM S. (1940–): *Republican from Maine; served three terms in the House (Ninety-third through Ninety-fifth Congress; January 3, 1973–January 3, 1979); three terms in the Senate (January 3, 1979-December 1, 1996). Secretary of Defense (December 15, 1996-present).*

Growing up in Bangor, Maine, the son of a Russian-Jewish immigrant father and an Irish Protestant mother, Bill Cohen had the worst of two worlds: reviled as a "Jew boy" by bigots, and not fully accepted by the close-knit Jewish community as a "member of the tribe." An excellent Hebrew school student for seven years, he nonetheless could not become bar mitzvah unless his mother converted and he went through a symbolic *bris*. Cohen knew nothing of this until just before his thirteenth birthday. He was floored. "Why didn't he [the rabbi] tell me this right at the beginning—seven years ago?" Cohen complained to his father. Neither event—his mother's conversion or his symbolic *bris*—ever occurred; Bill Cohen never became bar mitzvah. The trauma of his religiously bifurcated childhood led the adult Bill Cohen to affiliate with the Unitarian Universalist Church.

William S. Cohen was born in Bangor on August 28, 1940 to Reuben and Clara (Hartley) Cohen. His father ran a small bakery, arriving each night at his shop at 9:30 P.M. and working eighteen-hour days. One of three children, the young Bill Cohen was torn between playing basketball at the local YMCA and attending Shabbat services at the local shul. Cohen worked out a deal with his father; he would play basketball at the Y one weekend a month and attend synagogue the other three. As Cohen remembers, "It became two and two, then it became three and one, and then, finally, I stopped going to services altogether and just played basketball." This caused hard feelings among the children in his Hebrew school class, who were rewarded for their collective attendance at Shabbat worship services. Cohen recalls that his many absences "led to fisticuffs and a lot of brawling."

Cohen was considered an outcast by the Jewish community until he began making a name for himself as a stellar basketball player at Bangor High.

There he co-captained the varsity team and earned All-State honors. When the local newspaper ran a banner headline "Coyne Scores 33," the Jewish community got up in arms; how dare the paper deliberately misspell the name of "one of ours"? Cohen was confused. In his mind he was "taking all the grief and [receiving] none of the comfort [of the Jewish community]."

In 1958, Cohen entered Bowdoin College, where he excelled both in his major, Latin, and on the basketball court, where he was named to both the All-State and the New England Hall of Fame teams. While a freshman at Bowdoin, he met Diane Dunne of Fairfield, Maine. The two were married in January, 1962, and had two sons, Kevin and Christopher. The Cohens were divorced after twenty-five years of marriage. On February 14, 1996, Bill Cohen married the non-Jewish Janet Langhart, a fifty-three-year-old journalist who had a thirty-year career as anchor, correspondent, and talk show host on ABC, NBC, CBS, and the Black Entertainment Television.

Following his graduation in 1962, he entered Boston University Law School to study for his LL.B., which he received, *cum laude*, in 1965. While a student at BU, he was a member of the law review and served on its editorial board. His first year out of law school, he was employed as assistant editor-in-chief of the *Journal of the American Trial Lawyers Association.*

Returning to Bangor, Cohen began the practice of law. Because attorneys could not advertise their services in those days, Cohen became involved in a host of community activities: parks and recreation committee, zoning board of appeals, and city council. At the same time, he was an instructor at both Husson College in Bangor and the University of Maine at Orono, and assistant county attorney for Penobscot County. In 1971, he was elected mayor of Bangor.

In 1972, when incumbent Representative William Dodd Hathaway announced his intention to run for Margaret Chase Smith's Senate seat, Cohen decided to run for the House. During the ensuing campaign, he walked more than 600 miles across the district, in order to "find out what is on people's minds." He was elected to the Ninety-second Congress with better than 53 percent of the vote. Cohen came to national attention during his first term when, as a member of the House Judiciary Committee, he "resisted political pressure by voting to recommend the impeachment of President Richard Nixon for complicity in the Watergate cover-up." Crossing party lines, Cohen cast what turned out to be the deciding vote on a Democrat motion that informed President Nixon of his failure to comply with the committee's subpoena of White House documents and tapes. Cohen was also one of the few Republicans on the committee to vote in favor of the first two articles of impeachment. The people of Maine, decidedly Republican in their politics, saw Cohen's votes as a matter of conscience. He was reelected in 1976 and again in 1978, this time with 77 percent of the popular vote.

During his three terms in the House, Cohen had the reputation of being a moderate-to-liberal Republican. He supported the proposed Equal Rights Amendment and the minimum wage, and opposed Nixon's proposed cuts in social welfare programs. As the years progressed, he became more conservative, especially on fiscal and defense issues.

In 1978, Cohen was elected to the United States Senate, defeating incumbent Senator Hathaway, with 56 percent of the vote. Cohen was appointed to a seat on the Senate Armed Services Committee, where he became a leader, along with Senators Gary Hart and Sam Nunn, and Representative *Mel Levine*, of the so-called "Military Reform Caucus." This ad-hoc group advocated strengthening America's defense posture through increased but more efficient military spending.

In October 1980, Cohen ran afoul of the Jewish community when, at the last moment, he somewhat reluctantly voted in favor President Reagan's proposed sale of five Airborne Warning And Control System (AWACS) surveillance planes to Saudi Arabia. Heretofore a committed Zionist ("I am a very strong Zionist . . . at least half of my mind is still there."), his last-minute vote in favor of the AWACS was seen as a betrayal of the Jewish community, which in

this instance chose to see him as being "one of the family." Cohen commented that "the reaction of the Jewish community [to his vote] was just vicious." Having been forthrightly against the sale, how could he change his mind at the last minute, the Jewish community wanted to know. Apparently, Cohen changed his vote after consultation with the Israeli ambassador, who told him, "off the record," that the Israelis were, in fact, more concerned about other defense issues. They had somehow become publicly committed to opposing the sale. But truth be told, they weren't that concerned about it. Cohen was angered that the Israelis had turned to him in this instance—one whose relationship with the Jewish community was "unique," to say the least. Since those days, Cohen has apparently mended fences with his Jewish supporters; he was easily reelected twice, the last time (1990) with 61 percent of the vote.

In addition to being a senior member of the United States Senate, William Cohen was also an accomplished writer, having published two spy novels, poetry (*Of Sons and Seasons*), and several nonfiction works, including *Roll Call: One Year in the United States Senate*, and a 1988 account of the Iran-Contra investigation, coauthored by then Senate Majority Leader George Mitchell. Early in 1996, Cohen announced that he would not run for reelection to a fourth term. On December 5, 1996, President Bill Clinton announced that Cohen was his choice for Secretary of Defense in his second term. Cohen was easily confirmed by his former colleagues in the United States Senate.

References

Private correspondence with author.
Almanac of American Politics (1980–96 editions).
William S. Cohen, *Roll Call: One Year in the United States Senate* (Boston: Houghton Mifflin, 1988).
Current Biography, 1982, pp. 71–74.
New York Times, October 24, 1996; March 21, 1999, A14:1.
Politics in America (1980–96 editions).
Murray Polner, *American Jewish Biographies* (New York: Facts on File, 1983), pp. 45–46.
Howard Simons, *Jewish Times: Voices of the American Jewish Experience* (New York: Simon & Schuster, 1981), pp. 387–392.

COHEN, WILLIAM WOLFE (1874–1940):
Democrat from New York; served one term in the House (Seventieth Congress; March 4, 1927–March 3, 1929).

A one-term member of Congress from New York's Seventeenth District, William Wolfe Cohen was born in New York City on September 6, 1874. His father, Benjamin, was a prosperous shoe manufacturer. His mother, Fredericka (Kronacher) Cohen, like her husband, was a German Jew. Following a public-school education, William entered his father's business, being made a partner on his twenty-first birthday. Shortly after his twenty-eighth birthday, Cohen married Sophie Dazian, the daughter of David Wolf Dazian, a silk manufacturer. The next year, tiring of his father's business, William went into business for himself, forming the stock broker-age firm of William W. Cohen & Co., in which he was active until his death some thirty-seven years later.

Cohen prospered as a stock broker, even purchasing a seat on the New York Stock Exchange. Greatly respected by his fellow brokers, Cohen became a director of the New York Cotton Exchange and the Chicago Board of Trade, and a member of the Commodity and New York Curb exchanges. Always interested in diversification, Cohen bought in to the Copper Canyon Mining Company and presided over a consortium called the Brooklyn National Corporation. Shortly after the beginning of the Harding Administration, Cohen decided to sell his seat on the N.Y.S.E., netting a nearly $100,000 profit. He was set for life.

Always active in Democratic political circles, Cohen served as Chairman of the Tammany Hall Finance Committee for more than a decade. In 1926, when Seventeenth District Representative Ogden L. Mills (1884–1937) decided to leave Congress and challenge New York Governor Al Smith—who won an unprecedented fourth term—Cohen ran for the open seat. (Despite his defeat, the patrician Mills went on to serve as President Herbert Hoover's last Secretary of the Treasury). Cohen won the election, and found himself representing a district with a distinguished history: its Congressmen had included Henry B. George, Jr., the son of the famous economist and social reformer; the aforementioned Mills (of the Newport Mills);

and Herbert C. Pell, Jr., the great-great-grand-nephew of two signers of the Declaration of Independence, FDR's wartime Minister to Hungary and father of longtime Rhode Island Senator Claiborne de Borda Pell.

During his one term in Congress (1927–1929), Cohen was the junior-most member of the minority party. His chances for making a distinctive mark on the lower house were nil. He did manage to introduce a pension bill for members of the U.S. Coast Guard that was eventually passed in the next Congress. Aside from that, Cohen's two years in Congress went by without much fanfare. At the end of his term he decided to return to New York. His seat was taken over by Republican Ruth Sears Baker Pratt (see article on *Theodore Peyser*).

Aside from his many business ventures, William Cohen was a lifelong supporter of the New York City Fire Department, which named him an honorary deputy fire chief. He was also a member of all the principal firemen's organizations. Active in Jewish communal organizations, Cohen served as president of the Jewish Council of Greater New York and the New York branch of the American Jewish Congress. He was also a member of Temple Emanu-el and president of the American Committee for the Settlement of Jews in Birobidjan (a remote Soviet region near Siberia). Cohen continued working as a broker until his death on October 12, 1940. Unfortunately, his death received little notice; he had the bad fortune of passing away on the same day that movie great Tom Mix was killed in an automobile accident. The Cohens, who were married for thirty-eight years, had no children. In addition to his wife, William Cohen was survived by his brother Clarence, who had changed the spelling of the family surname to "Cone." He was interred in Mount Nebo Cemetery, in Brooklyn, New York.

References
American Jewish Year Book, vol. 43, p. 356.
Biographical Directory of the United States Congress 1774–1989, p. 805.
National Cyclopedia of American Biography, vol. 30, pp. 183–184.
New York Times, Oct. 13, 1940, 49:3.
Universal Jewish Encyclopedia.
Who Was Who in American Jewry, 1926, 1928, 1938.

COPPERSMITH, SAM (1955–): *Democrat from Arizona; served one term in the House (One Hundred and Third Congress; January 3, 1993–January 3, 1995).*

In the twenty-three biennial Congressional elections between 1952 and 1998, the voters in Arizona's First District sent only one Democrat to Washington—Sam Coppersmith. In the twenty-two other elections the victor was named Rhodes. From 1953 to 1983, the seat was held by John Jacob Rhodes (1916–), who served as House Minority Leader in the Ninety-third through Ninety-sixth Congress. Upon his retirement in 1983, his seat was taken over by his son, John Jacob Rhodes III (1943–). Sam Coopersmith's 1992 victory over John Rhodes III was noteworthy not only for breaking the Republican hold on that First District seat, but in toppling the Rhodes' political hegemony.

Sam Coppersmith's paternal grandfather, Samuel Kuperschmidt, emigrated to the United States from Odessa, Russia. According to Representative Coppersmith, the family name was changed at Ellis Island. Kuperschmidt/Coppersmith moved to Johnstown, Pennsylvania, where he met and married Bella Glosser, an immigrant from the village of Antapol in what is now Belarus. The Coppersmiths worked in a dry goods store that later became a department store called "Glosser Brothers." Bella Glosser Coppersmith, "a quiet but well-respected lay leader in the Johnstown Jewish community," was president of the family department store until her retirement. Representative Coppersmith's maternal grandfather, David Evans, emigrated to Boston from Leeds, England, where he met and married the Russian-born Lena Saievetz.

The Coppersmith's son, W. Louis, married the Evans' daughter, Bernice Barbara, and settled in Johnstown. The Coppersmiths had three children: Susan, Beth, and Sam, who was born in Johnstown on May 22, 1955. Sam was educated in the local public schools, and attended religious school from kindergarten through confir-

mation, at the end of tenth grade. Coppersmith became bar mitzvah at Johnstown's Conservative synagogue. According to Representative Coppersmith, his family was moderately observant.

The Coppersmiths were and are a family of overachievers: One of Sam Coppersmith's sisters, Dr. Susan N. Coppersmith, is currently a professor of physics on the faculty of the University of Chicago; his other sister, Beth, is a professional chef in Philadelphia. Their father, W. Louis Coppersmith, served twelve years (1969–1981) in the Pennsylvania State Senate, where he chaired the Public Health and Welfare Committee, and was known as the "Conscience of the Senate." As a teenager, Sam Coppersmith got an early exposure to politics, "spend[ing] much of his spare time working on his father's state Senate campaigns."

Sam Coppersmith attended Harvard University, where he graduated *magna cum laude* in 1976. Following his four years at Harvard, Coppersmith spent two years (1977–79) working in the Foreign Service, assigned to the United States Embassy in Port of Spain, Trinidad. Detached from the Foreign Service, Coppersmith attended law school at Yale, from which he received a J.D. in 1982. Following law school, Coppersmith moved to Phoenix, Arizona, where he clerked for Judge William C. Canby, Jr., of the U.S. Court of Appeals.

As an attorney in private practice, Sam Coppersmith became involved in Democrat Terry Goddard's successful 1983 Phoenix mayoral campaign. Following Goddard's victory, Coppersmith became one of his top aides. Coppersmith also joined the local Planned Parenthood Association, eventually becoming president of the Central/Northern Arizona region. Looking ahead, Coppersmith gave some thought to eventually running for Phoenix City Council—perhaps in 1994.

All that changed in 1992, when a federal court in Arizona finished drawing the lines for the state's new congressional districts. The court's redistricting plan made the heretofore-Republican stronghold more politically moderate. This occurred when the court effectively "shift[ed] some of the Phoenix area's most conservative Republicans into the newly created Sixth District." Despite the fact that 53 percent of the newly drawn district was still nominally Republican, two factors were working in Coppersmith's (or any moderate Democrat's) favor:

• The more moderate Republicans of West Mesa, Tempe and Phoenix, "under certain circumstances [would] consider voting for a Democrat," and

• incumbent Jay Rhodes had managed to "rankle many conservatives" by his support of both the 1989 congressional pay raise and the 1990 budget summit agreement—the one that broke George Bush's "Read my lips: No new taxes!" promise.

Prodded by the local Democratic elite, Sam Coppersmith entered the Democratic primary one week before the filing deadline. Running as a "new-generation Democrat" (pro-choice and business-oriented), Coppersmith coasted to an easy (nearly three-to-one) victory over primary opponent, David J. Sanson, III. Rhodes, on the other hand, turned in a surprisingly poor performance in the Republican primary, winning only 33 percent of the vote in a five-candidate race.

In the general election, Coppersmith called for "deficit reduction and public investment, congressional reform and preserving the environment." He came out against "single-payer national health insurance," favoring a plan that would "give states more leeway in adopting their own plans." He also contrasted his pro-choice stand on abortion with Rhodes's pro-life position. On election day, First District voters split their tickets, giving George Bush a 40 percent to 33 percent (with 26 percent for Ross Perot) victory over Bill Clinton, and Sam Coppersmith a 51 percent to 45 percent victory over Jay Rhodes.

As a member of the One Hundred and Third Congress, Sam Coppersmith was one of fifteen freshmen Democrats assigned to the committees on Public Works and Science, Space and Technology. During his one term in the House, Coppersmith kept a unique campaign promise: he turned down the congressional pay raise, by "writing a check each month to the U.S.

Treasury." He also gained some attention with his leadership of an effort to eliminate the "Advanced Liquid Metal Reactor Program," an effort that "united budget-cutters, environmentalists, and foreign policy experts concerned about plutonium policy."

In 1994, Coppersmith, entered the Democratic primary for the seat being vacated by three-term Senator Dennis DeConcini. Coppersmith's major opponents were Arizona Secretary of State Dick Mahoney and State Senate Minority Leader Cindy Resnick. The race turned out to be "excruciatingly close": Coppersmith wound up winning the primary by 59 votes out of more than 255,000 cast. Meanwhile, Republican Congressman Jon Kyl, unopposed in his primary, was blanketing the state with television ads showing him "travelling through the desert countryside in a Chevy Suburban, dressed in jeans and working on ranches, while talking about how he and his wife first fell in love with the state." Outspending Coppersmith by a better than two-to-one margin, he also out-polled the Democrat 54 percent to 40 percent. After two years on the Hill, Sam Coppersmith returned to Arizona. Coppersmith's First District seat reverted to the G.O.P., with the election of conservative Republican Matt Salmon.

Since his defeat, Sam Coppersmith has practiced business and real estate law with the firm of Coppersmith and Gordon in Phoenix. He is also an officer of the Arizona Internet Access Association. From 1995 to 1997, he served as Chair of the Arizona Democratic Party. During that tenure, the Clinton/Gore ticket carried Arizona—the first time for a Democrat since Harry S. Truman in 1948. In 1996, Coppersmith headed the Arizona delegation to the Democratic National Convention.

Sam Coppersmith married Beth Schermer on August 28, 1983. Schermer, an attorney specializing in health care law, grew up in St. Louis, the daughter of J. Leonard and Thelma (Bushman) Schermer. As an attorney, Beth Schermer "represents both local and national health care organizations, and heads the health care section at her firm, Lewis and Roca, in Phoenix." The Coppersmiths have three children: Sarah Bernice (born 1986), Benjamin Evans (born 1988), and Jacob Louis (born 1991). The Coppersmiths belong to Temple Solel (Reform), which they joined "because our children went to preschool there, and they wound up having their friends there." "As one of our major goals in joining a congregation was to raise our children Jewish," Coppersmith notes, "it made sense to join where their friends (and soon ours) belonged." Sam and Beth Coppersmith are active members of their synagogue, and participate in "various Jewish community activities." Referring to his "synagogue skills," Coppersmith notes: "I can read and speak Hebrew as in reading prayers. . . . I do not read or speak Yiddish, and understand only enough, as the old joke says, to get around Harvard Yard."

References

Private correspondence with author.
Almanac of American Politics (1994–96 editions).
Politics in America (1994 edition).

DAVIDSON, IRWIN DELMORE (1906–1981):
Democrat from New York; served most of one term in the House (Eighty-fourth Congress; January 3, 1955–December 31, 1956).

In the 1985 bestseller *Inside, Outside*, author Herman Wouk tells the story of I. David Goodkind, "counselor-at-law and lifelong Democrat." Goodkind, a Nixon-era White House speechwriter, starts out his professional life as scriptwriter for a famous radio personality in the 1930s. In an eerie sense, Wouk's I. [for Yehudah] David Goodkind could be based, at least in part, on the life of "counselor-at-law and lifelong Democrat" I. [for Irwin] Delmore Davidson, who likewise wrote scripts for a famous radio personality—Fred Allen.

Irwin Delmore Davidson was born in New York City, on January 2, 1906, the son of Lafayette and Tillie (Bechstein) Davidson. He attended the public schools of New York, and the Washington Square campus of New York University. Following his graduation in 1927, the dean of NYU nominated him to go to a special school sponsored by Metro-Goldwyn-Mayer, in order to study dramatics. Tempted by the chance to become a professional actor, Davidson thought long and hard, but eventually decided to enroll in the NYU School of Law. Unable to totally turn his back on acting and performing, Davidson earned his way through law school as an entertainer on the borscht circuit. According to a *New York Times* article from May 1960, Davidson was "an extraordinary actor and raconteur; [he] wrote, acted, produced and directed." In one biographic sketch, Davidson listed "magic" as his chief hobby.

Davidson graduated from law school in less than two years, and by 1929, was in private practice. Because it was terribly difficult for a twenty-three-year-old attorney to make a living in the earliest days of the Depression, Davidson supplemented his meager earnings by writing scripts for radio legend Fred Allen. Like Wouk's Goodkind, Irwin Davidson became an after-dinner speaker in great demand, who, also like his fictional counterpart, would regale audiences with finely crafted tales of his days in radio.

Davidson first entered the world of politics in 1935, when he was appointed counsel for the Legislative Drafting Commission. The following year he became special counsel to the New York Mortgage Commission. In 1936, he was elected to the New York State Assembly, where he served six two-year terms. As a liberal member of that body, he introduced the state's first slum-clearance legislation, as well as bills dealing with rent control, workmen's compensation, and civil rights.

Irwin Davidson resigned from the State Assembly in 1948 in order to run for Justice of the Court of Special Sessions. Successfully elected, Davidson served on the court for the next 6 years, earning a reputation for compassion and generosity. Davidson might have been the first judge to maintain a private fund for helping needy defendants buy clothing for trial. In one trial, he deferred sentencing a convicted auto thief until the young man's malformed hand—it had been purposely burned by his mother—could be operated on by an orthopedic surgeon. Davidson was quoted as saying "I will personally look for a doctor to perform the operation. The boy is entitled to one break."

In 1954, Irwin Davidson resigned his position on the Court of Special Sessions in order to run for the United States Congress. Running as a Democrat-Liberal, Davidson was elected to the Eighty-fourth Congress, and served from January 3, 1955 until his resignation less than two years later, on December 31, 1956. Davidson's heart really wasn't in Congress; he longed for a return to the bench. He was elected to a fourteen-year term on the New York Court of General Sessions in 1956, and left that post seven years later when he was elected to the New York Supreme Court, where he served until 1974.

While on the Supreme Court, Davidson participated in the famous trial of seven teenaged gang members charged with the killing of one Michael Farmer, a fifteen-year-old polio victim. Davidson sentenced all seven teenagers to prison terms of between five years and life. In 1959, Davidson published a book about the trial entitled *The Jury Is Still Out*.

Irwin Davidson married Beatrice Feltenstein on June 4, 1936. They had two sons, James Sylvan and Mark Lewis. Later in life, Davidson married a second time to Marion Doniger, who brought into their union her two children, Dr. Joy Osofsky, late of Topeka, Kansas, and William R. Doniger, of Greenwich, Connecticut.

A Reform Jew, Davidson served on the board of Temple Rodeph Shalom on West 83rd Street in Manhattan. Irwin Davidson died on August 1, 1981. In accordance with his final will and testament, his remains were cremated and scattered over Long Island Sound by seaplane.

References

New York Times, March 8, 1960; August 2, 1981, 28:1.

Who Was Who In American Jewry, 1938.

DEUTSCH, PETER (1957–): *Democrat from Florida; has served four terms in the House (One Hundred and Third through One Hundred and Sixth Congress; January 3, 1992–present).*

The word "ambition" derives from the Latin *ambire*—literally "to go about." In Roman times, candidates who went about the city soliciting votes for office were said to be *ambitio*. Webster's unabridged defines ambition as "an eager and sometimes inordinate desire for something, as . . . power, or [the] desire to distinguish oneself in some way." Webster's might well have added an addendum reading: "See Peter Deutsch." For in the now nearly two-decade political career of the young Representative from Florida's Twentieth Congressional District, one finds a drive, a single-mindedness that the early Romans might well have understood.

The future Congressman's paternal grandparents, Isidore and Celia Deutsch, were, respectively, from Minsk and Bryansk, in Russia. His maternal grandparents, Isidore and Minnie Brandeis, hailed from Russia as well. Both couples came to the United States in the final years of the nineteenth century, where the men settled on the Lower East Side as tailors. Their children, Arthur Leo Deutsch and Beulah Rachel Brandeis, married and eventually moved to Riverdale, the Bronx, where Arthur prospered as the head of his own maintenance construction business. Their first son, Michael, was born in 1955. Their second son, Peter, was born in New York, on April 1, 1957.

Young Peter Deutsch was educated in the public schools of New York. The Deutsch family belonged to the Reform Riverdale Temple on Independence Avenue in the Bronx, and a Conservative synagogue at their summer home on the New Jersey shore. Peter was bar mitzvah at the Riverdale Temple in 1970.

Following his high school graduation in 1975, Peter Deutsch entered Swarthmore College, in Swarthmore, Pennsylvania. During his four years there, Deutsch majored in psychology, was named a Swarthmore National Scholar, and

captained the school's sailing team. He graduated in June 1979 as a member of Phi Beta Kappa. From Swarthmore, Deutsch headed off to the Yale Law School, where he won honors in "Regulatory Reform and Business Units," and graduated with a J.D. in June 1982. Here is where the ambition comes in . . .

Upon graduating from law school, most young attorneys spend the next several months cramming for a bar examination. Upon his graduation, Peter Deutsch moved from New Haven, Connecticut, to Broward County, Florida, where he found employment with the South Broward Jewish Federation. It happened that State Representative Fred Lippman, one of the first Jews elected to the Florida State Legislature, had his offices right next door to those of the Jewish Federation. Peter quickly became a fixture in Lippman's office, learning the political ropes, and getting himself introduced to all the appropriate people. Within a few short months, Peter Deutsch announced his candidacy for state representative from Florida's Ninetieth District.

Deutsch brought a "new kind of campaign" to Broward County, according to political consultant Barbara Miller. "Peter was the first to launch a one-on-one campaign, where he literally walked from house to house, apartment to apartment, condo to condo, meeting the people of the district." Moreover, within a few days after the young candidate's visit, he would send each person he had visited a postcard, stating how nice it had been to meet them, and add some personal touch that easily pointed out that the postcard was not mass-produced. A few days later, each individual received a potholder. Aided by family money and his mother, who also went door-to-door, Deutsch won the four-way Democratic primary without a runoff. Within five months of his graduation from Yale Law School, Peter Deutsch found himself an elected member of the Florida State Legislature.

Shortly before the beginning of the legislature's annual two-month session, Deutsch took the Florida Bar examination. It is difficult to appreciate just how much drive and discipline it takes to undergo a grueling examination at precisely the time one is making final preparations for the beginning of a legislative career. Somehow Deutsch accomplished both; he passed the bar, and at the close of the legislative session in Spring 1983, entered private practice. Representing a district with a high concentration of elderly Jewish voters, Deutsch "introduced bills prohibiting nursing home evictions, allowing the investment of state pension funds in Israeli bonds and extending grandparents' visitation rights." As one of the legislature's youngest members, Deutsch quickly earned a reputation for being what a *Miami Herald* reporter termed "bright but abrasive . . . an expert at using procedural rules to advance or torpedo legislation." Arrogance and abrasiveness aside, Deutsch struck a thoroughly responsive chord with his constituents, and was reelected in 1984 with the largest vote in Florida. He was unopposed in his next three elections.

Throughout his career in the Florida Legislature, Deutsch wrote a weekly question-and-answer column for the local Jewish press dealing with health-care issues. Through literally hundreds of columns, Deutsch managed to maintain a high level of visibility with his constituents, even as he was progressing in the legislature: from 1988 to 1990, he chaired the legislature's Insurance Committee; from November 1990 until his election to the Congress in November 1992, he chaired the all-important Congressional Reapportionment Committee.

Never one to shy away from a political challenge, Deutsch decided in early 1992 to run for Congress from South Florida's newly created Twentieth District. Three-quarters of this district included "most of South Broward County . . . most of Hollywood, some of Fort Lauderdale . . . and most of the newer towns" in the area. The other quarter was "divided between the southern and western parts of Dade County, including some of the neighborhoods hit hardest by Hurricane Andrew, and Monroe County, which includes the Florida Keys, from the fishing center of Key Largo to the heavily gay and charmingly restored old city of Key West."

This district, as drawn by a federal court, contained the homes of two congressional incumbents: Dante Fascell and *Larry Smith*. Where another man or woman might have thought long and hard about engaging in such a "David versus Goliath" struggle, Deutsch plunged in headlong, seemingly unfazed. Deutsch immediately made a bit of history by becoming the first congressional candidate in state history to get on the ballot by petition. His self-confidence—some called it *chutzpa*—was rewarded by an immediate stroke of luck: Smith, who had 161 overdrafts on the House bank and "faced questions about possible diversion of his campaign funds," announced his retirement. That left just Deutsch and Fascell—a daunting, uphill struggle to say the least.

Fascell, a thirty-eight-year House veteran was both a South Florida institution and Chairman of the House Committee on Foreign Affairs. When asked what he thought his chances of besting Fascell in the Democratic primary, Deutsch responded "he's going to have to beat me." At age seventy-five, and faced with running in a district that he had never represented, Fascell also chose to retire—but not before taking a parting shot at Peter Deutsch. Fascell, along with retiring representatives Larry Smith and *William Lehman*, issued a formal letter endorsing Deutsch's newly announced primary opponent, Broward County Commissioner Nicki Englander Grossman—the scion of a prominent political family and wife of a well-known local judge. In their letter, the three lame duck representatives said that Grossman alone possessed the "knowledge and temperament" to represent the Twentieth District. Deutsch's reputation for arrogance seemed to be catching up with him.

As the primary campaign progressed, virtually the entire Democratic political establishment of the Twentieth District endorsed Nicki Grossman. Because the two had few differences on matters of political substance—"both supporting abortion rights, Israel and universal health care"—the campaign became personal and deeply contentious. Grossman attacked Deutsch for accepting funds from out-of-state lobbyists and for being "one of the least effective legislators in Tallahassee." For his part, Deutsch, who had the clear edge in campaign money (he began the campaign by lending it $350,000), fought back with an "eleventh-hour blitz of mail and television ads." One flier depicted a "bountiful table spread, with the caption 'Nicki Grossman put this meal on our tab.'" Many thought this was going too far—Grossman being rather "Rubenesque" in stature. In another broadside, Deutsch charged Grossman with entertaining at the local taxpayers' expense. Outspending Grossman by a nearly ten-to-one margin, Deutsch easily won the primary with 63 percent of the vote. In the November general election, Deutsch bested Republican business consultant Beverly Kennedy by a 55 to 39 percent margin. Kennedy, the wife of the only Republican member on the Broward County Commission, would, in 1996, lose a congressional race to *Robert Wexler*. During that campaign, Kennedy, known as a devout born-again Christian, announced that she had been born and raised an Orthodox Jew.

Peter Deutsch entered the House carrying the third highest campaign debt ($343,000) of any freshman. He made immediate headlines in the local South Florida press when he hired nineteen-year-old Henry Ellenbogen as his chief of staff. Ellenbogen, who had managed Deutsch's campaign, is the grandson of the late Pennsylvania Congressman *Henry Ellenbogen*. During the years that Ellenbogen worked for Deutsch, he managed to earn three degrees (A.B., LL.B., and M.B.A.) from Harvard.

In his first term, Deutsch sought a seat on the powerful Energy and Commerce Committee. To his disappointment, he was assigned to Banking, Foreign Affairs, and Merchant Marine. Upon his reelection to the One Hundred and Fourth Congress in 1994, he traded in these three seats for the coveted post on Commerce, receiving assignments on subcommittees that deal with Commerce, Trade and Hazardous Materials, Energy and Power, and Health and Environment. Deutsch's "elevation" to the Commerce Committee position was not quite the plum it might have been in previous sessions of Congress; in the One Hundred and Fourth Congress, Democrats became the minority party. Instead of working with a Democrat chair—Michigan's John Dingell—Deutsch now had to butt heads with Republican chair Thomas Bliley of Virginia.

Always in a hurry, Deutsch (whom the *Almanac of American Politics* termed "a veritable and seemingly unstoppable engine of political ambition") entered a bill on his very first day in Congress. While most freshmen legislators were either being sworn in or finding their way

through the underground labyrinth that is the Capitol, Deutsch was holding a press conference. At the conference, he announced the introduction of a bill to increase flood insurance benefits—something desperately needed in south Florida, which had recently been ravaged by Hurricane Andrew. Following shortly on the heels of this measure came a bill to prohibit members of Hamas, an Islamist terrorist organization, from entering the United States.

Now at the end of his fourth term in Congress, Deutsch has put together a moderate-to-liberal voting record. Deutsch was one of many cosponsors of the Balanced Budget Amendment and of the bill that would regulate "cop-killer" ammunition. Not surprisingly, he has been "pro-Israel, pro-choice and pro-universal health care." On other issues, Deutsch "favors an increase in federal funding for AIDS research, amending the 1964 Civil Rights Act to include sexual orientation as a discriminatory classification, and lifting the ban on gays in the military." In the One Hundred and Fourth Congress, the liberal Americans for Democratic Action gave Deutsch a rating of 60 (out of 100), while the Christian Coalition rated him at 15—agreeing with him on the single vote for the Balanced Budget Amendment.

Always a seeker after philosophical truth, Peter Deutsch went to Israel for the first time in 1985. He came back a changed man. Although raised a Reform Jew, Deutsch began searching for a more satisfying, "authentic" form of Jewish expression. Following his return from the Jewish State, Deutsch began spending time discussing broad philosophical and theological issues with various south Florida rabbis, looking for a path that would add meaning to his life. His "quest" led to the Young Israel movement. Today, Peter Deutsch is an "evolving" Orthodox Jew. He keeps kosher, observes the Sabbath, and has made arrangements, when necessary, to vote by nonelectronic means when Congress holds Saturday or holiday sessions.

Following his return from Israel, Deutsch formed a Friday-night Jewish single's group with friends Bernie Friedman and Steve Geller. (Geller is currently a member of the Florida State Legislature; Friedman is director of government affairs for the Florida Association of Jewish Federations). One of the main reasons why the three friends started the group was that they were all single and interested in meeting eligible Jewish women. Within a short period of time, the group became a smashing success with more and more people attending their Friday evening conclaves. It was at one of these Friday evening sessions that Deutsch met his wife, Laurie Coffino. Today, the Deutsches have two children, Jonathan (born in 1990) and Danielle (born in 1992). The Deutsches chose to move to a neighborhood where they could walk to synagogue. The Deutsch children attend the Orthodox Hillel Hebrew Day School in North Miami.

For several years, Florida political insiders speculated that Deutsch would run for Senator Bob Graham's seat, if Graham decided to run for Florida Governor. Toward that end, Deutsch amassed a sizable war chest, and traveled the state from one end to another. Shortly after Deutsch's reelection in November 1996, Graham announced that he would run for a third Senate term in 1998.

In early March 1999, Florida's Senator Connie Mack caught everyone off-guard by announcing that he would not seek a third term. Within hours of Mack's statement, Peter Deutsch began publicly ruminating about a run for the open seat. His comments set the stage for a possible round of political "musical chairs" in south Florida. Whether or not Deutsch runs for the United States Senate (or, indeed, Broward County mayor, as some have predicted) in 2000 is besides the point. With his drive, talent, intelligence, and ambition, one can easily see him on the political scene for many years to come.

References

Interview with Peter Deutsch, November 1996.
Almanac of American Politics (1994–96 editions).
Broward Jewish Journal, January 7–13, 1993, pp. 4-5.
Interview with Barbara Miller, November 19, 1996.
Politics in America (1994 edition).

DICKSTEIN, SAMUEL (1885–1954): *Democrat from New York; served eleven terms in the House (Sixty-eighth through Seventy-eighth Congress; March 4, 1923 December 30, 1945); Chairman, House Committee on Immigration and Naturalization, Seventy-second through Seventy-eighth Congress.*

American history is filled with myth and irony—especially when it comes to "parentage." Consider the following: George Washington, the Father of Our Country, himself never sired any offspring. Colonel Abner Doubleday (1819–1893), credited with being the Father of Baseball, had virtually nothing to do with the birth or development of America's Pastime. The House Un-American Activities Committee (HUAC), which specialized in investigating domestic Communist activities, was actually the brainchild of a liberal New York Jew, whose chief aim was the ferreting out of seditionists on the Right.

The Father of HUAC, Samuel Dickstein, was born in Vilna, Lithuania, on February 5, 1885. One of five children born to Rabbi Israel and Slata B. (Gordon), Dickstein was brought to the New York's Lower East Side in 1887, where his father had accepted a position as cantor of the Orthodox Norfolk Street ("Bialystoker") Synagogue—Beis Hamedrash Hagadol. Young Sam attended both *cheder* and the public schools of New York City. After attending the City College of the City of New York, Dickstein graduated from the NYU School of Law in 1906. He was admitted to the New York bar in 1908, and immediately went into private practice. Dickstein became a specialist in tenant's rights law. It is claimed that during his legal career, he offered *pro bono* representation to nearly 30,000 East Side tenants.

In 1911, Dickstein got his start in Democratic Party politics with an appointment as Special Deputy Attorney General for the State of New York. In 1917, he was elected to the city's Board of Aldermen, and two years later, became a member of the New York State Legislature. During his three years in the state legislature (1919–1922), Dickstein sponsored New York's first kosher food laws, which were eventually adopted by more than twenty states.

In 1922, Samuel Dickstein was elected to the House of Representatives from a district that ran along the East River from Chatham Square to East Houston Street. A Democratic Party loyalist, Dickstein was easily reelected each year between 1922 and 1944. During his twenty-two years in the House, no cause took more of his time, energy or passion than the creation of a committee to investigate subversive activities. When Dickstein spoke of "subversion" or "conspiracies," he was invariably referring to the seditious activities of pro-Nazis. This is not to say that he was totally blind or unmindful of problems on the Left: In 1930, Dickstein was cosponsor of a resolution (submitted by the patrician Hamilton Fish of upstate New York) condemning religious persecution in Russia. Two years later, he joined forces with the demagogic Martin Dies of Texas in an attempt to outlaw Communist Party membership in America. After the failed supposed attempt to assassinate President-elect Franklin Delano Roosevelt in 1933, Dickstein called for a Congressional investigation of anarchists. Despite this seemingly even-handed approach to investigation, Dickstein had a dark secret: He was, for many years, a "devoted and reliable" Soviet agent whom his handlers nicknamed "Crook."

In the 1930s, when Nazi storm troopers were goose-stepping their way through most of Europe, America was being victimized by its own version of Brown Shirts and jack-booted thugs. Men like Fritz Kuhn, leader of the German-American Bund and William Dudley Pelley of the Silver Shirts held mass public rallies, organized youth camps, and disseminated vitriolic broadsides against Jews, Jewish bankers, and Jewish conspirators. Sensitive to the looming tragedy in Europe (and with an undeniable flare for self-promotion), Dickstein went on the attack. Appointed chairman of the House Immigration Committee in 1931, Dickstein conducted an "unofficial" inquiry into Nazi propaganda in America. These hearings received vast publicity, as Dickstein paraded a series of secret letters, smuggled documents, and a secret witness called "Mr. X" before his committee. Dickstein claimed that the revelations he would bring forth would "shock the country." Since the hearings were both unofficial and unsanctioned, little came of them.

In January 1934, the New York Representative tried to launch an official investigation of pro-Nazi activities in the United States. Dickstein's proposal was unique; heretofore, when faced with a perceived wrong, Congress resorted to its legislative—rather than it's investigative—authority. In calling for a special committee of the Congress to examine and investigate pro-Nazi, anti-Semitic activities in the United States, Dickstein was breaking new ground. The Dickstein Resolution was supported by his New York colleague, Hamilton Fish. During floor debate on his proposed resolution, a representative from Nebraska suggested that "the whole thing was a scheme by Jews to offend German-Americans like those in [my] state who admire the Führer." Others chimed in that the real danger facing America from within stemmed from Communists and their fellow travelers—a buzz word for Jews and other "foreigners." Despite the rancor and acrimony aroused during debate, Congress passed the Dickstein resolution by a vote of 168 to 31. Although the panel would be known as the "Dickstein Committee," Speaker Henry T. Rainey chose the mild-mannered John McCormack of Massachusetts to be its first chair. Dickstein, viewed as a bit of a loose cannon, was appointed committee vice-chair. Although Dickstein would later claim that he had been passed over "in deference to his own feeling that a non-Jew should conduct this particular inquiry," he was being a bit disingenuous. Dickstein was too much a firebrand to accept playing second-fiddle to McCormack. He was attempting, in modern political parlance, to put a proper "spin" on events in order to save face.

The "McCormack-Dickstein" (or "Dickstein-McCormack") hearings were held during the summer and fall of 1934. When the cool, detached McCormack wielded the gavel, hearings had a proper air of decorum and respect. When Dickstein assumed the chair (often sitting as a committee of one), things got wild and woolly. On more than one occasion, Dickstein got into shouting matches with the subpoenaed witnesses. At the final hearing, held at the American Bar Association building in New York, several hundred German-Americans packed the hearing room, cut radio wires, and shouted "Down with Dickstein." The meeting ended in a flurry of Nazi salutes and boisterous shouts of "Heil Hitler!" Dickstein made the front page of the *New York Times*.

Little emerged from the raucous committee sessions. McCormack, ever the moderate, was of the opinion that pro-Nazi sympathizers were few in number and constituted more sound than fury. Dickstein, on the other hand, spoke incessantly of Nazi plots, of "Nazi rats, spies and agents." In light of the bombast that would spring from McCarthy's mouth less than a decade-and-a-half later, Dickstein's words have a haunting similarity: "I will name you one hundred spies." This is not to say that the hearings were totally without merit. Two laws did emerge out of the McCormack-Dickstein hearings: the compulsory registration of foreign agents disseminating propaganda in the United States, and an extension of subpoena power to Congressional investigating committees holding hearings outside of the District of Columbia.

In 1937, Sam Dickstein submitted the bill that would lead to the creation of the infamous House Un-American Activities Committee. By terms of this bill, Congress would establish a committee that would investigate all organizations "found operating in the United States for the purpose of diffusing propaganda of religious, racial or subversive political prejudices which tends to incite the use of force and violence or which tends to incite libelous attacks upon the President of the United States or other offices of the Federal Government, whether such propaganda appears to be of foreign or domestic origin." In short, Dickstein was calling for a probe of any and all "un-American" activities.

Debate on the resolution revolved around the question of what was meant by "un-American" activities. Witch hunters on the right warned Dickstein that his bill could only lead to a renewed outbreak of anti-Semitism. Colleagues on the left decried potential harm to First Amendment guarantees. The real issue was Sam Dickstein. The little New Yorker had simply offended too many of his colleagues with his brash, self-aggrandizing style. The resolution went down to defeat 184 to 38.

Several weeks later, Dickstein teamed up with Texas Representative Martin Dies to resubmit the issue for Congressional consideration. This time it was called the "Dies Resolution," an obvious snub to the gentleman from New York. Unlike Dickstein, Martin Dies, a firebrand from Lufton, Texas, was "one of the boys." A backslapper of the old school, Dies wanted nothing so much as to ferret out subversives on the left. While Dickstein was going around proclaiming that "you can find almost 200,000 men of the [German-American] Bund ready to put on uniforms and to use a gun," Dies spoke of "danger on the left."

Many members of Congress were unwilling to vote in favor of the Dies resolution, fearful lest "an alien" like Dickstein be named committee chair. When assurances were given that Dies, not Dickstein, would be named chairman, the resolution passed 191 to 41. Flush with victory, Dickstein rose to request permission to address his colleagues on the House floor. He asked for a scant three minutes. In a rare breach of Congressional etiquette, he was unceremoniously turned down. A week-and-a-half later, Chairman Dies named the members of his new committee: Sam Dickstein, the Father of HUAC, was not among them.

Within a year, Dickstein would denounce "The Committee" (as it came to be known) for its political excesses. As the years went by, Sam Dickstein would see his beloved child become an out-of-control monster, chaired by a succession of reactionaries and virulent anti-Semites like Martin Dies, John Rankin of Mississippi, and J. Parnell Thomas of New Jersey. As one conservative stated: "I love [this] committee because of the enemies it has made." Certainly one of it's most outspoken enemies would be the defeated Sam Dickstein.

As chairman of the House Committee on Immigration and Naturalization, Samuel Dickstein was at the center of another political maelstrom: saving the potential victims of Nazi atrocities. From the distance of more than a half century, one is shocked by the apparent lack of action or concern taken by the American government on behalf of the millions who would be gassed, starved, and cremated. Historical apologists claim that the President, the press, and the American people were largely unaware of the true nature of Nazi intentions. They are wrong.

In Spring 1939, Chairman Dickstein scheduled hearings on the Child Refugee Bill, known also as the Wagner-Rogers Bill. This bill, named after its two main sponsors, New York Senator Robert F. Wagner and Massachusetts Representative Edith Nourse Rogers, proposed that a maximum of ten thousand children under the age of fourteen be admitted to America in both 1939 and 1940. By terms of the bill, their entry would be considered separate and distinct from—and in addition to—the regular German immigration quota.

During the hearings, Chairman Dickstein entertained testimony from a wide variety of witnesses. Their input ran the gamut from the emotionally/intellectually/politically supportive to the downright bizarre. Secretary of State Cordell Hull sent a letter stating that granting the twenty thousand additional German visas in addition "to an estimated 30,000 immigration visas now being issued annually in that country will inevitably necessitate increased clerical personnel, unfamiliar with the law and regulations as well as additional office accommodations." As might be expected, additional opposition came from such groups as the American Legion, United Daughters of the Confederacy, Society of Mayflower Descendants, and Daughters of the American Revolution. Most did not believe that the Jews of Germany were in any real danger. Some worried that the addition of the 20,000 children would lead to increased anti-Semitism and labor unrest.

In one fascinating exchange, Chairman Dickstein questioned the American journalist Quentin Reynolds, who had made two extended stays in Nazi-ruled Germany:

> *Dickstein*: Do you contemplate . . . that there will be another pogrom?
> *Reynolds*: I not only contemplate it, but I am confident the complete pogrom is not very far away.
> *Dickstein*: In other words, there will be a new slaughter?
> *Reynolds*: Yes, there is no doubt about that.
> *Dickstein*: Annihilation?
> *Reynolds*: Yes, a complete pogrom.

Despite the reasoned attempts of Dickstein, Wagner, and Rogers, the bill could not even find sufficient support within the Committee on Immigration and Naturalization itself. When it was finally reported out of committee in July 1939, the bill had essentially been gutted by an amendment: the children's visas over the next two years would be issued *against*—not in *excess of*—the German quota. Senator Wagner couldn't live with the change and withdrew his bill. The issue died and 20,000 Jewish (and non-Jewish) children perished.

The failure of the Wagner-Rogers bill cannot be laid solely at the feet of Chairman Dickstein. Despite his best efforts, the tide of isolationism and nativist sentiment was simply too strong. The defeat of Wagner-Rogers (and other legislation of similar intent) is a permanent blot on the escutcheon of American moral rectitude and compassion.

In a 1998 book entitled *The Haunted Wood: Soviet Espionage in America—The Stalin Era*, authors Allen Weinstein and Alexander Vassilev revealed that for the three years between 1937 and 1940, Representative Dickstein was a paid agent of the NKVD—the forerunner of the KGB. Moreover, as Dickstein himself told his Soviet contact, he had previously been a paid agent of both the British and the Poles. Dickstein, who repeatedly haggled over the monthly fee he expected for his services, was nicknamed "Crook" by his Communist handler, a man known to him as "Igor."

Writing about Dickstein, "Igor" noted: "Crook is completely justifying his code name. This is an unscrupulous type, greedy for money, consented [*sic*] to work because of money, a very cunning swindler." When Dickstein failed to be appointed to the newly created HUAC, his value to the Soviets diminished. During his three-year relationship with the Soviets, Dickstein passed along committee transcripts and names of possible double agents—information the Russians found to be of negligible importance. Nonetheless, Dickstein was paid somewhat over $12,000—$135,000 in 1999 dollars. Despite this, when Dickstein's will was probated in 1954, he was found to have had a net worth of only $2,500.

Sam Dickstein would remain in Congress until December 30, 1945. Three days later, he took his seat on the New York State Supreme Court, to which he had been elected in a landslide. He remained on the bench until his death, on April 22, 1954. He was survived by his wife Essie (Tevers), whom he had married in June 1932, and daughter Marlene Eloise. Dickstein was buried in Union Field Cemetery, New York. More than five hundred people attended the funeral.

References

American Jewish Year Book, vol. 24, p. 132; vol. 56, p. 569.

Biographic Encyclopedia of American Jewry.

Encyclopaedia Judaica.

Walter Goodman, *The Committee* (New York: Farrar, Straus and Giroux, 1968), chap. 1.

Arthur D. Morse, *While Six Million Died: A Chronicle of American Apathy* (New York: Random House, 1968).

New York Times, April 23, 1954, 27:1.

Howard M. Sachar, *A History of the Jews in America* (New York: Alfred A. Knopf, 1992), chaps. 14–15.

Universal Jewish Encyclopedia.

Allen Weinstein and Alexander Vassilev, *The Haunted Wood: Soviet Espionage in America—The Stalin Era* (New York: Random House, 1998), pp. 140–150.

Who Was Who in America, vol. 3.

Who Was Who in American Jewry, 1926, 1928, 1938.

DOLLINGER, ISIDORE (1903–): *Democrat from New York; served six terms in the House (Eighty-first through Eighty-sixth Congress; January 3, 1949–December 31, 1959).*

As the old bromide goes: "When a dog bites a man, that is not news, because it happens so often. But if a man bites a dog, that is news." The 1947 election for Congress from New York's Twenty-fourth District was definitely the political equivalent of a man biting a dog. For in that election, in contravention of the age-old tradition of partisan politics, the Democratic nominee, Isidore Dollinger, ran with the blessing of not only his own party, but of the Republican and Liberal parties as well. Dollinger's triple endorsement had as much to do with the incumbent's perceived political radicalism as with the challenger's acknowledged political strengths. What brought the three philosophically disparate parties together was their mutual antipathy for the politics of incumbent *Leo Isacson*—one of two American Labor party members in Congress. Elected on February 17, 1947 to fill the unexpired term of Representative *Abraham Multer,* Isacson's defeat had so obsessed the Democrats, Republicans, and Liberals that for once, they managed to put their political differences aside. What makes this coalition all the more remarkable is the fact that at no time was its reality denied or papered over; it was an overt alliance all the way. Indeed, a case of "man bites dog."

The beneficiary of this unusual act of political accommodation, Isidore Dollinger, was born in Manhattan on November 13, 1903. Dollinger's father, Emanuel (1874–1925), an immigrant from Horodenka (Gorodënka), Galicia, was originally an insurance broker and notary with offices on Rivington Street. When "Izzie" and his brother Abraham (born 1908) were youngsters, their father began a steamship business. The concern's primary focus was sending money and tickets to Jews in Galicia—particularly Horodenka—so that they could come to America. Izzie Dollinger's mother, Jenny Weidler, had come to America from Stanislau, also in Galicia. Emanuel Dollinger came from a religious family. "Once he arrived in New York, he was forced to work seven days a week, so his religious practice sort of went by the wayside," Dollinger remembered in 1998. The Dollingers

did belong to an Orthodox synagogue on Clinton Street, where the senior Dollinger was active "from time to time." Both his sons were bar mitzvah at that synagogue. A four-pack-a-day smoker, Emanuel Dollinger dropped dead of a heart attack at age fifty-nine.

Izzie Dollinger was educated in the Bronx public schools and received a B.S. from New York University in 1925—the year his father died. Three years later, he earned his LL.B. from New York Law School. In 1929, the year the stock market crashed, Dollinger began practicing law out of an office at 170 Broadway. As a young attorney, Dollinger married the former Rose Zahn. Ironically, Rose's mother, like Isidore Dollinger's father, came from Horodenka, although the two did not meet until they both lived in New York.

Isidore Dollinger served in the New York State Assembly from the Fourth District from 1937 to 1945, and in the State Senate from the twenty-sixth District from 1945 to 1948. During his twelve-year legislative career in Albany, Dollinger was always a member of the minority, where he "generally followed New Deal lines." The 1947 race against Leo Isacson was "a bitter contest in which both he and Mr. Isacson sought to establish themselves with the voters as the better friend of Zionism and of the underprivileged." Voters in the Twenty-fourth Congressional District, composed largely of "low-income and poor families, many of the Jewish faith," found little that separated the two candidates. According to the *New York Times* post-election analysis, "virtually the only difference on issues was on foreign policy. Mr. Dollinger supporting and Mr. Isacson opposing, Marshall Plan aid and the Truman Doctrine."

Dollinger's Republican and Liberal Party endorsements were largely orchestrated by Walter Kirschenbaum, a local political power, and David Dubinsky, president of the International Ladies Garment Workers Union. Dubinsky (1892–1982), a native of Brest-Litovsk, immigrated to New York in 1911, after having been arrested and sent off to Siberian exile. A tough-minded organizer with a genius for politics, Dubinsky started as a knee-pants cutter, eventually making his way to the top of his union. Concerned with what Isacson's upset victory meant for Democrat Harry Truman's chances in the upcoming 1948 presidential election, Dubinsky and Kirschenbaum went to work putting together the unique tripartite coalition for Dollinger. Dollinger also employed the services of journalist Victor Lasky as his campaign press officer. Lasky would go on to become an arch-conservative and one of Richard Nixon's early biographers. On Election Day, Isidore Dollinger out-polled Leo Isacson by more than 6,000 votes.

Representative Dollinger was originally assigned to the House Banking Committee. During his second term, he rotated on to Interstate and Foreign Commerce, chaired by Democrat Harley Staggers of West Virginia. During his ten years in Congress, Dollinger voted a fairly straight Democratic line, spending the lion's share of his time seeing to his constituents' needs. As a member of Congress, Dollinger was paid $12,500—plus $75 per month for his district office in the Bronx. Rose Dollinger convinced her husband that he could make more money by returning to New York. As luck would have it, Daniel V. Sullivan, the Democratic Bronx District Attorney, decided not to run for reelection in 1959. Heeding his wife's wishes, Dollinger entered the race for Bronx

D.A. Dollinger defeated Republican Michael Sibilio and Liberal Hyman Bravin by a better than two-to-one margin in November 1959. Dollinger was reelected in both 1963 and 1967. In retrospect, Dollinger says, he would have preferred to remain in Congress. At the time of his departure from the House (December 31, 1959), Dollinger was the second-ranking Democrat on the Interstate and Foreign Commerce Committee. Had he remained on Capitol Hill, he likely would have become committee chair.

In 1968, Isidore Dollinger was elected to the first of two ten-year terms on the New York State Supreme Court. He retired from the court on December 31, 1975, having reached the mandatory age of retirement. As of 1999, Isidore Dollinger is a spry, ninety-six-year old with a powerful memory. His wife Rose died in 1994. Son Edmund, an attorney in Tenafly, New Jersey, is married to the former Ruth Sherry.

References
Interview with Hon. Isidore Dollinger, March 1998.

New York Times, November 3, 1948; November 4, 1959.

EDELSTEIN, MORRIS MICHAEL (1888–1941):
Democrat from New York; served one term in the House (Seventy-seventh Congress; February 6, 1940–June 4, 1941).

On June 4, 1941, New York Representative M. Michael Edelstein engaged in a heated colloquy with the House's most notorious anti-Semite, Representative John Rankin of Mississippi. Responding to Rankin's charge that the pro-interventionist faction in America (i.e., those who favored entering the war in Europe) was being orchestrated, financed, and led by "a little group of our international Jewish brethren," Edelstein went on the attack. He accused Rankin of demagoguery and hate-mongering. His voice rising with emotion, Edelstein cried out: "Mr. Speaker, Hitler started out by speaking about 'Jewish brethren' and 'international bankers.' The last speaker speaking about international bankers coupled them with our Jewish brethren. The fact of the matter is that the number of Jewish bankers in the United States is infinitesimal. . . . I deplore the idea that any time anything happens . . . men in this House and outside this House attempt to use the Jews as their scapegoat." Edelstein began to sway; his face was quickly losing color. Nonetheless, he continued on to his peroration: "I say it is unfair and I say it is un-American. . . . All men are created equal, regardless of race, creed, or color; and whatever a man be, Jew or Gentile, he may think what he deems fit." Edelstein staggered from the House floor, collapsed in the Capitol lobby, and, within seconds, had succumbed to a massive heart attack—murdered, some say, by Rankin, the "Great American Earache."

Born in Messeritz, Poland, on February 5, 1888, Michael Edelstein immigrated to New York with his parents, brother, and four sisters in 1891. His father, a toolmaker, died just after Michael's bar mitzvah. Although his family's financial straits kept him from completing a high school education, he studied nights at Cooper Union, while working days in a bowling alley, as a Western Union messenger, and as a runner for a brokerage firm. He eventually qualified for admission to the Brooklyn Law School of St. Lawrence University, from which he graduated in 1909. With the establishment of Prohibition, his legal practice began to flourish. His clients during the 1920s included many exclusive night-

clubs, and such personalities as Texas Guinan and Belle Livingston. Often, Edelstein was the first one called when their establishments were raided.

Edelstein spent more than thirty years as a Tammany Hall stalwart. Starting as a poll watcher in the Eighth Assembly District, he soon became an assistant district captain, district captain, and member of the law committee. In 1939, he succeeded Charles A. Schneider as the Tammany leader of the Eighth Assembly District. So, it was not surprising that when, on December 17, 1939, incumbent Congressman *William Sirovich* died, the boys of Tammany offered Edelstein the Democratic nomination to replace their fallen colleague. In the special election held in early February 1940, Edelstein, with the endorsements of Mayor *Fiorello La Guardia*, Senator Robert Wagner, and Tammany boss James A. Farley, defeated both Louis Lefkowitz, the Republican candidate, and Earl Browder, the Communist candidate. Edelstein took his seat in the Seventy-sixth Congress on February 6, 1940. He was easily reelected in November 1940 in the "regular" election.

At the time of Edelstein's arrival on Capitol Hill, Congressional anti-Semitism was on the rise. The halls of Congress resounded with the hate-inspired warnings of such populist demagogues as the aforementioned Rankin of Mississippi, as well as Senators Gerald Prentice Nye of North Dakota and Burton K. Wheeler of Montana, and Representatives Paul Shafer of Michigan, Jacob Thorkelson, of Montana and William Lambertson of Kansas. These super-patriots and populist arch-conservatives loathed the "riffraff" of Central and Eastern Europe and firmly believed that they "add to the trouble we already have, pad our relief rolls, and stir dissension and discontent here as they have done abroad." With war raging in Europe and America debating whether or not to enter the fight, populists had a field day, condemning Jews as being part and parcel of a monolithic, international conspiracy. Representative Edelstein, who represented one of the most polyglot Congressional districts in America, was deeply affronted by these baseless attacks. His Lower East Side district was composed largely of Eastern European Jewish immigrants; it also contained sizable numbers of Hungarians, Poles,

Irish, and Italians. To attack immigrants as the source of American problems, was to attack "his" people.

In April 1941, Rankin's invective hit a new low, when he accused the great American journalist Walter Lippmann of being an "international Jew." Rankin was apoplectic over what he saw as Lippmann's treachery in encouraging President Roosevelt to declare war on Germany. Lippmann was vilified as "the mouthpiece of international Jewish financiers who controlled the world's gold." Rankin claimed that "they have controlled the world through the gold standard ever since Rothchilds [sic] got financial control of England during the Napoleonic war." Rankin concluded his comments in words echoing the late William Jennings Bryan: "They are now crucifying civilization on a cross of gold."

The Mississippi representative characterized his constituents as being "old-line Americans, Anglo-Saxon, people whose folks have been here for 200 years." As their representative, he was unalterably opposed to any legislation that would permit more of the European "riffraff" into America. Again, Edelstein saw in Rankin's invective a calumny against *his* constituents.

Edelstein's emotional plea on behalf of his constituents was perfectly in keeping with his Congressional *raison d'être*. Throughout his brief tenure in the House, he spent the lion's share of his time and energies attending to refugee problems and defending his "brethren." On one occasion he said: "It is with regret" that the populists and nativists refuse to see that "the great majority of aliens in this country are law-abiding, substantial people, most of whom have become citizens. To accuse them of faults or weaknesses which they do not have, as a group, is not consistent with the facts and ignores the rights which those aliens and their children have under our form of government." Edelstein's East Side constituents would long remember him as a man who gave his life attempting to defend their rights, their humanity, and their dignity.

Michael Edelstein's tragic death brought forth a virtual torrent of commentary in the nation's press. Edelstein's New York colleague, Representative *Samuel Dickstein* likened his fallen colleague to an ancient prophet of Israel, railing against "those forces of evil which ever threaten to engulf American democracy."

Representative *Adolph Sabath*, the dean of the Congressional Minyan, characterized Edelstein's final words as "one of the most dramatic as well as most significant utterances ever made by a Jew in Congress." One commentator noted that Edelstein had died "while the House Chamber still resounded with the noblest American principles expressed by him in his final words."

Newspapers across the country pilloried Rankin, one editorial writer going so far as to compare the Mississippian to Joseph Goebbels, Hitler's propaganda minister. Rankin's hometown newspaper, the *Tupelo Journal*, roundly thrashed him in an editorial headlined "We Are Ashamed of This."

When told of Edelstein's death, Rankin tried to seem as if he were genuinely shaken. He sat quietly, face in hands, during the eulogies held on the House floor. "Later . . . he told reporters that his remarks about 'Jewish brethren' did not have Edelstein in mind, that he deeply regretted his death, and that the New Yorker had been 'a good man, a good citizen, and a worthy representative of his district.'" Shaken though he may have been, Edelstein's untimely death did little to harness Rankin's bitter anti-Semitism. From his position as Chairman of the House Un-American Activities Committee, Rankin would continue blasting away at the "Jewish-Communist Conspiracy" and "flannel-mouthed agitators." With America's entry in World War II, however, Rankin would find himself more and more isolated, as his brand of anti-Semitism began to fade from the mouths, if not the hearts and minds, of American nativists and hate-mongers. Never again, would such calumnies against the Jewish people be heard on the floor of Congress.

Michael Edelstein's funeral on June 6, 1941 was held at the Gramercy Park Memorial Chapel on New York's the Lower East Side. The *New York Times* estimated that more than 15,000 people were in attendance. Edelstein, who never married, still lived with his eighty-five-year-old mother at the time of his death. He was survived by his brother Joseph, and sisters Ella (Montag), Mildred (Winter), Beatrice (Greenberg), and Pauline (Strull). M. Michael Edelstein was buried at Mount Zion Cemetery, in Maspeth, Long Island.

References

American Jewish History, vol. 74, no. 1, September 1984, pp. 45-65.

Memorial Services Held in the House of Representatives of the United States, Together with Remarks Presented in Eulogy of Morris Michael Edelstein, Late a Representative of New York (Washington, D.C.: U.S. Government Printing Office, 1943).

New York Times, June 5 and 7, 1941.

EDWARDS, MARVIN HENRY (1937–): *Republican from Oklahoma; served eight terms in the House (Ninety-fifth through One Hundred and Second Congress, January 3, 1977 –January 3, 1993).*

During the last decades of the twentieth century, the emergence of the so-called religious right as a force in American politics caused many to begin equating political conservatism with issues rather than with ideology. Whereas in former times one might regularly expect the term "political conservatism" to educe responses such as states' rights, diffusion of power, or free-market economy, the more modern mutation came to be associated with prayer in the public schools, pro-life, line-item veto, and term limits. The new-fashioned conservatives (sometimes called "neocons") began to press positions that saw the federal government not as an adversary, but as a means to enforce the standards of a "proper society." While "family-values" issues (i.e., prayer, abortion, the nuclear family) had always occupied some conservatives, they now began taking center stage.

The roots of "classical" (i.e., ideologically based) American conservatism go back to the days of Alexander Hamilton and the issues raised in the *Federalist Papers*. As with all political movements or ideologies, conservatism has waxed and waned, found voice, and suffered from "political laryngitis." In the twentieth century, political conservatism reached an apogee in the presidencies of Harding, Coolidge, and Hoover, and then bottomed out with the advent of Roosevelt's New Deal. The liberal notion that a strong centralized government can best do that which people cannot do for themselves, continued, in the main, to exert a hold on the American electorate for nearly a generation after Roosevelt's death. The seeds of conservatism's rebirth would not be planted until the mid-1960s—ironically, at the very nadir of its electoral popularity.

In the 1964 presidential election, Lyndon Johnson defeated Arizona Senator *Barry Goldwater* by the greatest popular-vote margin in U.S. history. Carrying just five southern states and his own Arizona, Goldwater—"Mr. Conservative"—captured a mere 39 percent of the vote. Goldwater's defeat was so overwhelming that even Vermont—a state that had not gone Democrat since the creation of the G.O.P.—sup-

ported Johnson by a better than two-to-one margin. Moreover, Democrats increased their Senate membership from 66 to a veto-proof 68 and their House roster from 259 to 295. According to one political historian, "pundits had all but completed their obituaries for conservatism as a meaningful force" in the United States. However, to paraphrase Mark Twain, reports of its demise were greatly exaggerated.

Just five days after the Goldwater debacle, a handful of conservatism's brightest stars assembled to "pick up the pieces and assess the movement's future." Those who attended the election post-mortem were determined "not merely to paper over the damage, but to craft and forge a new vehicle through which the ideas and ideals articulated [by Goldwater] could be advanced in the political arena." Out of their deliberations was born a new force on the political right: the American Conservative Union (ACU). Founded by such figures as writers John Dos Passos (1896–1970), William F. Buckley, Jr., and L. Brent Bozell, Republican Representatives John Ashbrook (1928–1982), Donald C. Bruce (1921–1969), and future Maryland Congressman Robert E. Bauman (1937–), the ACU staked itself to a three-fold mission:

- consolidate the overall strength of the American conservative movement through unified leadership and action.
- mold public opinion.
- stimulate and direct responsible political action.

In its first dozen years, the ACU's activities included rating state legislatures and individual members of Congress, tax-limitation campaigns, and the creation of state and regional CPACs—"conservative political action conferences." Unlike the neocons and evangelicals who would take up the mantle of leadership in the 1980s and 1990s, these conservatives were more motivated by the ideology of diffusion and decentralization than the allure of partisan politics. During its first fifteen years, leadership of the ACU was generally vested in Republican members of Congress: John Ashbrook of Missouri, Phillip Crane of Illinois, and Robert E. Bauman of Maryland.

In November 1980, following a well-publicized personal scandal that contributed to his defeat for reelection to Congress, Bauman resigned his post as head of the ACU. He was replaced by Mickey Edwards, a forty-three-year-old Representative from Oklahoma City, Oklahoma. Edwards would be the last member of Congress to chair the group; following his resignation in 1984 (and indeed, his resignation from the ACU itself), the Union's membership passed a by-law guaranteeing that future chairmen would be "public citizens rather than government employees."

Nothing in Mickey Edwards's background suggested that one day he would grow up to become one of the nation's most thoughtful, articulate, passionate conservatives. The son of Isidore and Rosalie (Widetsky) Yarnowsky, Marvin Henry Yanowsky (Mickey Edwards) was born in Cleveland on July 12, 1937. Isidore, the orphaned son of Polish immigrants, was raised at the Jewish Orphanage Home in Cleveland; Rosalie, whose family changed their name to Miller, was the daughter of Lithuanians. Mickey's father worked for the Shoe Corporation of America (SCA). As Isidore progressed up the ranks of the company, SCA moved him first to Toledo and then Chicago, where he managed the shoe department at the Boston Store. Shortly after World War II, Isidore was given the choice of moving his family to Washington, D.C. or Oklahoma City. Isidore chose the latter. Remembering that move more than fifty years later, Mickey Edwards would comment wryly: "There is no telling how much different my life would have been had we moved to [Washington] D.C. instead of Oklahoma. I might have even turned out to be a liberal."

The Yarnowskys moved into a small house on the city's south (read: poor) side; most of the city's approximately 1,600 Jews (and its handful of synagogues) were on the north side. Because the Yarnowskys did not own a car (Isidore generally took a bus or taxi to work), it was next to impossible for young Mickey to attend either school or services at the north-side Temple B'nai Israel. Consequently, Mickey Edwards never became bar mitzvah. Despite the fact that the Yarnowskys "did not participate in Jewish rituals," the family was "very conscious of [their] Jewishness." "I would say that we [Mickey and his sister Sheila] were raised in an ethnic way," Edwards explained in 1999.

As a young college graduate living in Muskogee, Oklahoma (where he had gone to take a job as a reporter for the *Muskogee Daily Phoenix*), Edwards "participated as a reader at the High Holiday services." After moving back to Oklahoma City in the late 1950s—where he went to work as a reporter for the *Daily Oklahoman*—Edwards joined B'nai Israel and taught "youth classes in the Sunday school."

Nowhere in Edwards's *curriculum vitae* is there even a hint that he is Jewish or born of Jewish parents. Both the *Almanac of American Politics* and *Politics in America* listed him as an Episcopalian up until 1986. Beginning with their 1988 editions, both publications identified him as a Presbyterian. In a 1999 interview, Edwards explained that during the time he belonged to B'nai Israel in Oklahoma City, he found that services (replete with a Christian choir he nicknamed the "Hessians") "were not related to the modern world or issues of the day." He found himself becoming "filled with theological difficulties." Increasingly he sensed "a dichotomy between the religion and the ethnicity." In the end, he feels, he "drifted away from the religion, but not the ethnicity." When contacted in late 1999 and questioned about his Jewish roots and antecedents, Edwards commented, "Although I drifted away from my religion, I am really quite Jewish."

Mickey Edwards received preuniversity education in the Oklahoma City public schools. In high school, he worked on the school paper, often covering the sports beat. Not imbued with great athletic skill, he became (and still is) a diehard Cleveland Indians fan. Indeed, Edwards began a 1995 assessment of "the media's ability to report on politics in a fair manner" by writing at length about then-Clevelands Indian star outfielder Albert Belle. In writing of Belle—a player who throughout his career has had "little use for the press"—Edwards displayed a true fan's knowledge of statistics. He noted that in the recently completed season (1995), Belle "hit 50 home runs and 50 doubles—something no other player had ever done . . . nobody—not Babe Ruth, not Ted Williams—had ever had such a season before."

Edwards attended the University of Oklahoma in Norman, where he served as managing editor of the college newspaper, belonged to the student senate, and was an officer of Sigma

Alpha Mu, a Jewish fraternity. As mentioned above, Edwards moved to Muskogee following his college graduation (1958) in order to take a job with the *Muskogee Daily Phoenix*. While living in Muskogee, he joined the local Masonic lodge. Before moving back to Oklahoma City, he had completed Masonry's first two degrees. Once back in Oklahoma City, he sought out a lodge where he could continue working toward his next degree. He was told that he could complete his degree with the local lodge, but would not be permitted to join because they did not admit Jews. "To the best of my recollection," Edwards noted, "this was my only brush with anti-Semitism."

From 1958 to 1963, Edwards worked as a reporter/editor for the *Daily Phoenix* and the *Oklahoma City Times*. In 1964, he left the *City Times* to go into advertising. For the next four years, (1964–1968), he worked as advertising director for the Beale Agency. While working for Beale, Edwards attended the law school of Oklahoma City University, from which he received his J.D. in 1969. From 1968 to 1973, he worked as managing editor of *Private Practice Magazine*, "a socio-political magazine for doctors." While working as the magazine's managing editor and commencing the practice of law, Edwards also found time to write a book about the health-care industry entitled *Hazardous to Your Health: A New Look at the "Health Care Crisis" in America* (1972). Eleven years later, while a member of Congress, Edwards authored a second book, *Behind Enemy Lines*.

According to Edwards, his fascination with politics and history went back to his early years in Chicago: "The libraries in Chicago used to award kids with ribbons for reading lots of books. I really wanted to earn those ribbons, so I began reading. I became fascinated with books about Revolutionary War heroes, which got me to thinking about how things worked." In 1960, Edwards sided with Richard Nixon over John F. Kennedy because he favored Nixon's stand on foreign policy issues. Shortly after the election, he went to a meeting of the local Republican Party where they were selecting precinct leaders. After speaking out on the issue of redistricting, Edwards came to the attention of a local Republican leader. Taking Edwards under his wing, he told the young reporter that he had a

future in politics. Edwards began making his way up the political ladder and before too long was viewed as a "comer." In 1972, his days at *Private Practice Magazine*, coming to an end, Edwards moved to Washington, D.C., where he became special legislative counsel for the Republican Steering Committee. From this position, Edwards began meeting national Republicans who would, within less than five years, help him win a seat in Congress.

In 1974, Mickey Edwards ran unopposed for the Republican nomination for Congress from Oklahoma's Fifth District. Containing the northern reaches of Oklahoma City (which has working oil wells on grounds of the state capitol) and several oil-rich outlying towns, the Fifth District—and indeed the entire city—had originally been a Democrat stronghold. Between 1920 and 1948, Oklahoma County had supported a Republican presidential nominee only once—Herbert Hoover in 1928. Following the end of World War II however, the district became increasingly Republican. Between 1952 and 1998, only one Democrat—Lyndon Johnson—carried the district. Despite its shift in political allegiance, two Democrats represented the Fifth District in the thirty-seven years between 1939 and 1976: Almer Stillwell "Mike" Monroney (1902–1980), who served six terms in the House (1939–1951) and three terms in the Senate (1951–1969), and John Jarman (1915–1982), a graduate of Harvard Law School. Edwards's decision to challenge the conservative Jarman in 1974—a year made difficult for Republicans because of Watergate—was viewed as quixotic at best, suicidal at worst. Widely supported by the local newspapers (most of which were run by the elderly E. K. Gaylord), "distinguished looking with an Ivy League education," Jarman was a high-ranking member of the House Commerce Committee who, despite chairing a subcommittee on health, made a move to the subcommittee on Aeronautics and Transportation. As the full committee's third-ranking Democrat (behind Chairman Harley Staggers of West Virginia and Tobert MacDonald of Massachusetts), Jarman was "in a good position to protect some of Oklahoma City's interests." (The district boasted an Air Force base and the FAA Aeronautical Center).

By the 1970s, Jarman's political string was about to run out. Publisher Gaylord's death at

101 took away the incumbent's best source of media support and protection. Although consistently conservative and only in his late fifties, Jarman was beginning to be viewed as out of step with his constituents. He began attracting challengers in Democrat primaries—something from which a twenty-plus-year incumbent is normally immune. In 1972, Jarman won reelection with a rather anemic 60 percent of the vote. This, coupled with his having won the primary with only 65 percent, caused political eyebrows to rise throughout the district. In 1974, the year Mickey Edwards won his primary without opposition, Jarman was down to 61 percent in his Democrat race. Edwards did surprisingly well against Jarman, losing by a mere 3,402 votes (52%–48%). Jarman's thirteenth (and final) term was beset with difficulties. Freshmen Democrats (the historic "Watergate class") staged a coup in the Commerce Committee, passing over a senior subcommittee chair in favor of a junior member. Jarman concluded that "young, liberal Democrats would not allow [him] to accede to the full committee chairmanship, and indeed might oust him from the post he held." Sensing that his seniority within the Democratic Party was quickly losing value (and looking over his shoulder at Mickey Edwards, who was gearing up for another race), Jarman announced that he would not seek reelection in 1976. On January 25, 1975—shortly after announcing his retirement—Jarman switched party affiliation. Despite having served in Congress longer than any other Republican in the House at the time, he was only given the number-three position on the Science and Technology Committee—a sure sign that the Republicans "didn't have to pay a particularly high price to get him."

Edwards did not get a free ride in the 1976 Republican primary. To the contrary, he faced off against former state Attorney General G. T. Blankenship. Campaigning almost nonstop for two years, Edwards managed to eke out a 1,087-vote margin in what one writer termed an "acrimonious struggle." Victory in hand, Edwards faced the even more daunting task of running against thirty-one-year-old Tom Dunlap, a hospital administrator and son of the highly popularly state chancellor of higher education. Dunlap, a political moderate, had broad support among the district's lower-income voters. Edwards, by this

point well known for his articulate conservatism, ran as a supporter of Ronald Reagan. Former Texas Governor and Secretary of the Treasury John Connally and other national Republican heavyweights came to Oklahoma City to campaign for Edwards. Edwards, the conservative "star-in-the-making," won with a bare 51 percent of the vote. According to the *Almanac of American Politics*, the election was "decided more by the mistakes of the candidates than anything else." At thirty-nine, Cleveland-born Marvin Henry Yanowsky had become Mickey Edwards, United States Representative from the Fifth District in Oklahoma.

Edwards quickly gained a reputation among his House colleagues as being one of that body's "most steadfast ideological conservatives." In the words of the *Almanac of American Politics* (1982), he was "a 'New Rightist' before the emergence of the New Right." Described as "a man who loves a good fight," Edwards was assigned to two committees "most uncongenial to his own thinking," Education and Labor and Interior. During his first term, he organized a "truth squad" of Republican colleagues to go around the country speaking against U.S. transfer of the Panama Canal—a hot issue in the late 1970s. Overwhelmingly reelected in 1978, Edwards gave serious considering to running for the seat being vacated by two-term Republican Senator Henry Bellmon. Sensing that his future lay in the House, Edwards left the senate race even before it began. Bellmon's seat was taken by thirty-one-year-old Don Nickles, a member of the Oklahoma State Senate from Ponca City. Reelected to a third term with 68 percent of the vote, Edwards was rewarded with a seat on the House Appropriations Committee, and concomitantly elected president of the American Conservative Union—a position, as mentioned above, that he would hold for four years.

With the advent of the Reagan administration, Edwards's brand of conservatism came into style. This is not to say that he supported every administration proposal or program. From his seat on Appropriations, he became a leading critic of the World Bank. He called the International Development Agency (IDA)—the World Bank arm that lends money to the poorest nations—"a concept of aiding the poorest of the poor through a giant, worldwide welfare program." During

Reagan's first year in office (1981), Edwards opposed the administration's request for IDA funding in the amount of $850 million. The Oklahoman—who had managed Reagan's campaign in the Sooner State—offered a counterproposal of $520 million. After much back-and-forth maneuvering, a House/Senate conference committee agreed on $700 million—over Edwards's strenuous objection. Edwards was one of the few Republicans to vote against Reagan's 1982 tax hike—on the grounds that raising taxes went counter to a consistent conservative agency. Edwards was also the leading (at times, the only) conservative critic of the line-item veto, which he termed "a scheme for concentrating power in the hands of a single chief executive." In a February 1980 op-ed piece in the *Washington Post*, Edwards wrote that he found it "incongruous" that President Reagan, "the nation's leading principled spokesman against big government," should ask for such power. "The problem with propositions such as the line-item veto," he noted, "is the certainty of change. Powers delegated to the presidency to be dispensed according to the wisdom and conscience of a Ronald Reagan will remain in place for the time, certain to come, when a Democrat again ascends to that increasingly lofty presidential throne." "Opposition to the concentration of power in Washington," he chided, "is the root of American political conservatism." Pointing to a potential risk (that would become a full-blown reality within a few years), Edwards prophetically concluded: "Unfortunately, the philosophical roots of what we are about are sometimes forgotten in the pragmatic rush to achieve immediate ends. Conservatives, who ought to be champions of the congressional veto—increasing the power of the elected representatives of the people to block regulations imposed by the federal bureaucracy—find themselves opposing congressional interference with bureaucrats appointed by 'our guys.' They do so oblivious to the enduring nature of laws and precedents (meaning that what we do to them they will later be able to do to us). This acquiescence to the imperial presidency for the immediate short-term gain threatens the foundation of our form of government—a system carefully designed to balance powers and limit central authority. To set constitutional protections aside for short-

term expediency is to win temporary advantage at a very high long-cost." Edwards would continue fighting against the line-item veto proposal even after his congressional career ended. As he has noted in various articles and speeches, "It's a constitutional issue, not a policy one."

Edwards also parted company with the Reagan administration over the issue of South African apartheid. In 1984, he joined thirty-four other conservatives in sending a letter to South Africa denouncing its politically repressive regime. "Freedom cannot be demanded for our enemies," he noted, "if we ignore its suppression by those we count as friends." Speaking on the House floor, Edwards thundered, "Mr. Speaker, no nation which represses its citizens and denies basic human freedoms is a friend of mine or of the principles on which this country was founded."

After the 1980 census, the Oklahoma state legislature rewarded Edwards by reshaping his district—making it even more solidly Republican. As a perhaps unwitting result, the legislature also created new centers of Democrat strength. This caused the state's Republican Party to take the unusual step of sponsoring a state referendum to overturn it. They were narrowly defeated (51%–49%). The editorial writers of the *Wall Street Journal* wrote that as a result of the redistricting (which Edwards claimed to have no hand in), he had become a "GOP member in perpetuity . . . and a profile in the problem of congressional power." The *Journal* belittled Edwards for his penchant for writing articles that "managed to cite Locke, Blackstone, Jefferson, Hamilton, Montesquieu, Toqueville and Burke," and noted "Mr. Edwards knows that the Oklahoma gerrymander has made his House seat as safe as any in the Soviet Politburo (whoops, now make that safer)." The editorialist even challenged the purity of Edwards's motives in opposing the line-item veto, noting that as a member of a subcommittee (Foreign Operations) that doled out "pork barrel goodies" Appropriations was the committee "most threatened by any line-item veto."

As congressional Republican ranks swelled in the 1980s and early 1990s with the addition of dozens of New Rightists, Edwards began taking a more statesmanlike posture. He also began feeling disaffected from these new conservatives.

Gone were the days of political "bomb throwing." By the late 1980s, Edwards was garnering a reputation for having "evolved into an increasingly pragmatic conservative," one who "issu[ed] appeals for moderation and unity in pursuit of tangible legislative success." On more than one occasion, Edwards referred to the "neocons" as "New Age monarchists," and chided many of his old-time colleagues for "engaging in useless guerilla warfare in the name of ideological purity." "While the noise and fury of a strategy of confrontation may be cathartic for frustrated Republicans," he noted in 1985, "it serves only a limited usefulness politically." In 1984, he cut all ties with the American Conservative Union, believing that the organization had "gotten away from its original causes—limits on taxation and regulation and a strong national defense."

In the spring of 1987, Buffalo-area Representative Jack Kemp resigned his position as chair of the House Republican Conference Committee in order to devote more time to his nascent presidential campaign. His departure brought about an upward shift in Republican ranks, with Dick Cheney of Wyoming (who had been chair of the Policy Committee) moving up to take Kemp's spot, Jerry Lewis of California vacating his leadership of the Republican Research Committee to take over Cheney's spot, and Mickey Edwards moving into Lewis's post. Defeating Representatives Steve Bartlett of Texas and Steve Gunderson of Wisconsin, Mickey Edwards became the number-four man in the Republican hierarchy.

Mickey Edwards was regularly reelected by overwhelming margins. For sixteen years, his seat was indeed "as safe as any in the Soviet Politburo." That all began to change after the 1990 election. Several factors led to his downfall. First, Oklahoma was not the same place, economically speaking, that it had been when Edwards was first elected in 1976. During the worst years of the nation's recession (1978–1980) Oklahoma had the nation's lowest unemployment rate–a scant 4 percent. Starting in the mid-1980s, the Sooner State began experiencing an economic downturn; by 1986, its unemployment rate had more than doubled. Working oil rigs—a prime indicator of the state's economic health—had gone from 882 in 1982 to 128 by 1986.

Edwards also fell afoul of Fifth District voters when he was listed among the twenty-two worst abusers of the House Bank. In April 1992, the *Washington Post* reported that he had written 386 overdrafts for more than $54,000. Edwards quickly admitted that the charges were true, but blamed the overdrafts on the fact that he "didn't have a lot to live on. . . . We had loans out the kazoo." This did not sit well with his constituents, most of whom could not fathom how a man making $129,500 a year could have trouble making ends meet. Mike Hunter, an Oklahoma City attorney and former state representative, spoke for many when he said, "How can you balance the federal budget . . . if you don't have the patience to balance your own checkbook?" Speaking on his behalf, Edwards's exwife, Lisa Reagan, said: "A lot of congressmen had businesses or family wealth before they ran. Mickey had nothing but brains." Edwards found himself being "pummeled" at town meetings and on radio talk shows. Then there was the issue of his personal life.

In 1992, Mickey Edwards was going through his fourth divorce. For a man long associated with family-values issues this proved to be an insurmountable obstacle to overcome. When questioned as to whether his personal problems would adversely affect him in the coming election, Edwards told the *Washington Post*: "People know me—they know my family. I have not had a great deal of success at married life. Some people may hold that against me. Some people may feel sorry for me." Responding to Edwards, Oklahoma State Democrat Party chair Peter White was quoted as saying, "I don't think people thought he meant multifamily when he talked about family values."

Mickey Edwards wound up coming in third (26 percent) in a five-way race for the Republican nomination. The eventual victor, state Representative Ernest Istook, Jr., ran as a hardline Christian conservative. Since entering the House in 1993, Istook (who like Edwards received a seat on the Appropriations Committee) has proposed measures on prayer, abortion, condom distribution, and birth-control counseling.

Shortly after leaving the House, Mickey Edwards was appointed to a lectureship at the John F. Kennedy School of Government at

Harvard University. Extremely popular with his students (in 1997, students at the school voted him outstanding teacher), he was named the John Quincy Adams Lecturer in Legislative Politics in February 1999. At the Kennedy School, Edwards teaches courses on "Congress, political leadership, issue advocacy, election strategies, conservative political theory and the constitutional separation of powers."

Over the past seven years, Edwards has taught, written a syndicated newspaper column, and appeared as a regular political commentator on National Public Radio's *All Things Considered*. As one of America's most thoughtful (and quotable) conservatives, he is often called upon to explain the conservative philosophy to the public. In a September 1997 article for the *Chronicle of Higher Education*, Edwards wrote: "Conservatives are less inclined to strive for equal, or more nearly equal, outcomes, whether through quota systems (in admissions and hiring) or through progressive taxation. Their goal is not 'equality' but 'equity.' If all players are given equal opportunity to compete, conservatives generally oppose policies designed to shape the final outcome. [Conservatives] oppose the very concept of redistributing wealth, whatever the cause to be served. They prefer individual action and the action of the private sector—induced by incentives. To many liberals, this is proof of conservatives' indifference to the well-being of those who are not well off. But even that definition is hard to sustain. . . . The emphasis is on reduced public mandates and public subsidies, not necessarily a reduced commitment to solving public problems."

Edwards is not averse to scoring other conservatives who he believes have traduced its philosophy. In September 1999, when word spread that conservative columnist Pat Buchanan might leave the Republican fold for Ross Perot's Reform Party, Edwards urged him to follow his heart. Writing in the *Boston Globe*, Edwards likened Buchanan's policies to those of the political left. In speaking of Buchanan's signature positions—high-tariff protections and America-First isolationism ("rooted in the worst nostrums of the radical left"), Edwards noted: "In opposing NAFTA Buchanan seems to have concluded that the global economy is a pie of pre-ordained size. One more slice for Canada means one less slice for us. Like the Victor Reuthers of labor's old leftist fringe, Pat Buchanan apparently believes that if one man eats, another must starve." Referring to Buchanan's hostility to deploying American troops "in aid of oppressed peoples overseas," Edwards flatly stated: "Buchanan is decidedly neutral in the struggle between freedom and oppression. Amazingly, he attempts now to convince us that this disinterest in the cause of human liberty is somehow a conservative point of view. Nonsense. It is George McGovern all over again. We heard it about Vietnam. We heard it about Nicaragua."

One of three founding trustees of the Heritage Foundation, a conservative Washington-based think tank, he has also worked for the liberal-leaning Brookings Institution as cochair of their Task Force on Resources for International Affairs. One of Edward's more high-visibility projects is Citizens for the Constitution, a national organization he cochairs with former Representative and White House counsel *Abner Mikva*. This group is concerned with "limiting the use of constitutional amendments as a substitute for the normal legislative process." In May 1999, Mikva and Edwards released *Developing Guidelines for Constitutional Change* (New York: Century Foundation Press), a work that urged "restraint in the constitutional amendment process." They advised that legislators contemplating new amendments consider:

- Whether the goals of a proposed amendment can be realized in other ways and are likely to be recognized as of abiding importance to succeeding generations.
- Whether a proposed amendment damages the cohesiveness of existing constitutional provisions or makes the system less politically responsive.
- Whether a proposed amendment has been fully considered and fairly debated, has a nonextendable deadline, and is fully enforceable.

In May 1999, Mickey Edwards remarried. His new wife, Elizabeth, who has a Ph.D. in sociology, is director of the Center for Women in Politics and Public Policy at the University of Massachusetts. Edwards is quick to note that his new wife is "a thorough-going liberal."

Mickey Edwards has three children: Patrick (named for Patrick Henry), a student in Virginia; Barry, who holds a Ph.D. in English literature (with a specialty in the poetry of William Butler Yeats), is a law student in Minnesota; and Ellen, the mother of Edwards's two grandchildren, who lives in Oklahoma City.

When asked what gave him the greatest pride from his sixteen years in Congress, Edwards says: "Two things actually. First, that I was voted 'one of the ten smartest' members of Congress by *Roll Call*. Second, is a little private bill I had passed. It permitted a young girl to be airlifted from the Philippines back to Oklahoma, where she had life-saving surgery. Its little things like that which make you feel that maybe, just maybe, you have made a difference."

Although he has not practiced Judaism in nearly thirty-five years, Mickey Edwards is proud to proclaim: "I am quite Jewish. My parents are buried in a Jewish cemetery in Oklahoma City and my current wife (who is a non-Jew) is as proud as I am of my Jewish faith." When asked if he sees any dichotomy between his arch-conservatism and being Jewish, Edwards responds: "Knowing what I know the history of Jews and Judaism, I cannot conceive of how any Jew can be a liberal. Think about it." That is Mickey Edwards: a man who challenges thinking by being consistently thoughtful.

References

Interview with Mickey Edwards, December 1999.

Almanac of American Politics (1976–1994).

Boston Globe, September 20, 1999, p. A13; August 27, 1992, p. A21; April 2, 1992, p. A3

Chronicle of Higher Education, September 9, 1997, pp. B4 ff.

Congressional Quarterly, March 3, 1990, p. 714; June 6, 1987, pp. 1185–86.

Jeff Hollingworth, "The History of the American Conservative Union," Internet.

Nieman Reports, Summer 1996, pp. 12 ff.

Politics in America (1980–1994).

Street Journal, November 21, 1989, p. 18.

Washington Post, August 27, 1992, p. A9; April 2, 1992, p. A1; October 2, 1985, p. D3; February 8, 1984, p. A19;

Washingtonian, February 1999, pp. 59 ff.

EILBERG, JOSHUA (1921–): *Democrat from Pennsylvania; served six terms in the House (Ninetieth through Ninety-fifth Congress; January 3, 1967–January 3, 1979).*

In the midst of Joshua Eilberg's 1978 campaign for reelection to Congress, the House Ethics Committee charged the six-term Pennsylvania Democrat with "accepting more than $100,000 from his law firm and two affiliated firms which were helping a Philadelphia hospital get a federal grant." Sensing victory in November, the Republicans ran a strong, attractive candidate, Charles Daugherty, who represented a substantial portion of Eilberg's district in the Pennsylvania State Senate. Shortly before the election, Eilberg was indicted. As a result, Daugherty won with 56 percent of the vote. Eilberg's political career came to a crashing end. After the election, Eilberg pleaded guilty and was given five years probation.

Today, more than twenty years after losing his House seat, Joshua Eilberg is remembered largely for his legal and ethical problems. What is forgotten is that for nearly a half-dozen years, beleaguered Soviet Jews had perhaps no better or more effective friend—and former Nazis no worse enemy—on Capitol Hill than the gentleman from Pennsylvania's Fourth District. From his position as Chairman of the House Judiciary Subcommittee on Immigration and Nationality, Eilberg (along with his Senate counterpart, Edward M. Kennedy) was often the last word on "parole authority"—that political maneuver which permits immigration in excess of legally established limits. "It got to the point that when Justice would call and say: 'We are seeking parole authority for an additional 10,000 Vietnamese,' they would quickly add 'we will of course add an additional 10,000 Soviet Jews at the same time,'" Eilberg recalled in a July 1997 interview. "It was as if I was the final word," he said.

The Eilbergs were originally from Lithuania. Leaving the Pale of Settlement in the 1880s, some emigrated to America, others to Palestine. Like those immigrants who came into America through New York, Baltimore, or Charleston, those who arrived through Philadelphia settled close to their point of disembarkation. In late nineteenth- and early twentieth-century Philadelphia, that area was on the city's South Side, close to the South Street pier. Joshua

Eilberg's father, David Benjamin Eilberg, was born and grew up on Philadelphia's South side, along with eight siblings. The Congressman's mother's family, the Jaspans, originally came to America from Russia in the 1860s. For reasons unknown, they went back to Russia, and did not return to America for nearly thirty years. Miriam Jaspan Eilberg, the Congressman's mother, was born in Philadelphia; she was one of eight children. David and Miriam Eilberg's only child, Joshua, was born in Philadelphia on February 12, 1921.

In the 1920s, David Eilberg worked as a life insurance agent for the Metropolitan Insurance Company of America. With the coming of the Depression, David, along with millions of other Americans, lost his job. He eventually managed to find work as a janitor in the Philadelphia school system. During those years, the Eilberg family lived on Philadelphia's North Side in an area called North Liberties—a mile above Market Street. Joshua Eilberg was educated in the Philadelphia public schools. He attended an Orthodox *cheder*, and was privately tutored for his bar mitzvah. The Eilberg family was "Orthodox by training, but without much learning."

When it came time for Joshua Eilberg to enter college in the late 1930s, he chose the University of Pennsylvania. Because of their straitened financial situation, the Eilbergs could not afford to send their son to college. Fortunately, one of Eilberg's uncles, H. Jerome Jaspan, was a Pennsylvania state senator. Through his uncle's good offices, Eilberg was able to secure a four-year scholarship to Penn. He received a B.A. from the University's famed Wharton School in 1941.

Following his graduation, Joshua Eilberg entered the United States Naval Reserves. Serving for more than three years, he was sent to Okinawa shortly after the American invasion. Eilberg, who rose to the rank of lieutenant, senior grade, received an honorable discharge in 1945, and entered the University of Pennsylvania School of Law. Following his first year at Penn, he transferred to Temple University. While completing his legal education at Temple, he met Gladys Greenberg, a social worker. The two married shortly thereafter, in 1948, and moved to Philadelphia's Northeast Side—the area where many newlyweds were establishing homes. Eilberg quickly set up a legal practice and began "greeting people as they moved into the neighborhood." The young attorney also became active in local reform Democratic politics, working his way up through the ranks of what was "essentially an Irish-Catholic area." In 1952, Joshua Eilberg went to work as an assistant D.A. for Richardson Dilworth, an emerging power in local Democratic circles. Eilberg's growing reputation in the Northeast neighborhoods led to his 1954 election to the Pennsylvania Legislature. He was easily reelected five times. During his last term in the state legislature (1965–66), he served as majority leader.

In 1966, four-term Congressman *Herman Toll* (1907–1967) announced that declining health would force him to retire his Fourth District seat. Joshua Eilberg quickly announced his candidacy. Facing Republican Robert Cohen, Eilberg waged a vigorous campaign. He won by the rather slender margin of 7,000 votes. Eilberg's new district—the Fourth—was, in 1966, the "most middle-class, prosperous, and indeed . . . . still growing part of Philadelphia." More than half of Philadelphia's Jews lived within the Fourth District's lines. Ironically, the Fourth District has always been the least Democratic of Philadelphia's four districts (it was the only one to support Richard Nixon against George McGovern in 1972).

Appointed to the House Judiciary Committee, Joshua Eilberg compiled a moderate-to-liberal voting record and attracted little attention either in his district or on Capitol Hill. He was reelected five times by margins ranging from 56 to 72 percent. In 1972, Eilberg became chairman of the Judiciary Committee's Subcommittee on Immigration, Citizenship and International Law. During his tenure as subcommittee chair, Eilberg held hearings that uncovered the government's penchant for admitting former Nazis to America. "After World War II," Eilberg recalled, "the government would admit virtually anyone, so long as they proclaimed themselves to be anti-Communist. That meant that a heck of a lot of former Nazis got entry permits. The extent to which the government concealed their actions was truly astounding." As a result of the work done by Eilberg's subcommittee, the Office of Special Investigations was established. OSI was mandated to seek out for-

mer Nazis and, once they were identified, to effect their deportation.

As mentioned above, Joshua Eilberg also used his position as subcommittee chair to come to the assistance of literally tens of thousands of Soviet Jews. In an attempt to learn more about their plight, Eilberg led a Congressional delegation to Russia. Included in his group were Representatives Christopher Dodd, *Elizabeth Holtzman*, and *Edward Mezvinsky*. While in Russia, the group met openly with such "enemies of the state" as Anatoly (Natan) Sharansky and Andrei Sakharov. "It amazed me that despite all their troubles, they were willing to meet with us in public. It was as if they were challenging the authorities to take action against them. Little did we know that shortly after our return to America, Sharansky would be in prison," Eilberg said in a July 1997 interview.

From Russia, the group went on to the Hebrew Immigrant Aid Society (H.I.A.S.) way station in Vienna. Here, Jews in transit from Soviet Russia received temporary shelter prior to their departure for Israel or America. The group arrived in Vienna on a Friday. As Eilberg recalls: "I spoke with a group of newly arrived émigrés through a translator. I said, 'since this is your first Sabbath in the free world, perhaps you would like to go to a synagogue here in Vienna.' They were outraged at the suggestion, and quickly told me that because of all the pressures put on them in Russia because of their being Jewish, they really had no interest in having anything to do with the religion! It was a real eye-opening experience," the chairman recollected.

Shortly after winning the 1974 Democratic primary, Eilberg was thrust into the national spotlight; the House Judiciary Committee began considering the impeachment of President Richard M. Nixon. As noted in the 1974 edition of the *Almanac of American Politics*: "Eilberg did nothing that was especially surprising. He wound up, as all the Committee's Democrats did, voting against Nixon; he made speeches decrying the President's conduct and that of his men. He did not shine or generate a national fan club, as some Judiciary members did; but by his general competence he strengthened the impression that so many people gained, that the House is composed of intelligent, decent men and women." Eilberg made far fewer public statements than other members of the committee.

When he did, his sentiments tended to be terse and to the point: "I feel that he [Nixon] doesn't have the character to be President." Eilberg's participation in the House Watergate hearings struck a responsive chord with his constituents. His margin of victory, which had never been more than 60 percent, suddenly jumped to 72 percent in 1974.

Within a year, Joshua Eilberg's political career began moving in a downward spiral. In 1975, he became embroiled in the "Osser Affair": Maurice Osser, a former Philadelphia City Commissioner, had been convicted of receiving kickbacks. Representative Eilberg wrote the United State Parole Board on Osser's behalf, requesting a pardon for his political friend—a potential impropriety. When confronted with the charge, Eilberg issued a denial: "As a member of the Judiciary Committee of the House of Representatives, this would have been an improper act, because the committee has jurisdiction over the Federal prison system." Shortly after issuing his denial, the *Philadelphia Inquirer* obtained a letter in which Mr. Eilberg said that Mr. Osser's "reputation in the community has been, and as far as I know, continues to be high." When confronted with the letter, Eilberg said his original denial was the result of an "office mix-up."

Later that year, Eilberg's name turned up in a federal trial in Massachusetts dealing with kickbacks. Thomas Graham, a Philadelphia businessman, testified that in 1966, he had paid then-Majority Leader Eilberg $5,000 in return for Eilberg's help in obtaining a $1.8 million state architecture contract. The next year, Eilberg was charged with attempting to thwart an investigation of allegations that Philadelphia hospital administrators had paid his law firm $500,000 to help the hospital obtain $65 million in funds for a building extension. Eilberg compounded the problem by calling then-President Jimmy Carter and "urg[ing] him to 'expedite' the removal of (United States Attorney) David W. Marston . . . a Republican holdover whose office was investigating the charges." Finally, in September 1978, as mentioned above, the House Ethics Committee leveled charges against the Pennsylvania Democrat. This turned out to be the final straw; in November 1978, Joshua Eilberg was defeated 56 percent to 44 percent by Republican Charles F. Daugherty.

Since leaving Congress in January 1979, Joshua Eilberg has served his five-year probationary period, resumed the practice of law, and gone into retirement. The Eilbergs have two children: son William, a Harvard-trained patent lawyer, and daughter Amy. William Eilberg received his undergraduate education at Swarthmore, and earned another degree in Hebrew Literature at Graetz College in Philadelphia. Amy Eilberg occupies a unique position in Jewish history: She is the first woman to be ordained a Conservative Rabbi by the Jewish Theological Seminary of America (JTS).

During his days in Congress, Joshua Eilberg and his family belonged to Congregation Beth Emeth, "a relatively poor-man's synagogue in the heart of my district." During her teenage years, Amy became increasingly interested in Jewish religious practice. After a summer tour with a Jewish group, she came home and requested that their home be made kosher; Mrs. Eilberg *kashered* the kitchen. Upon graduating from Brandeis University, Amy Eilberg entered JTS as a graduate student. When the conservative Rabbinical Assembly of America decided that women should be admitted to JTS as rabbinical students, Amy entered the program. Upon hearing of Amy's decision, the family rabbi back at Philadelphia's Beth Emeth began "ostracizing us," Joshua Eilberg recalls. As a result of the rabbi's rejection of their daughter's career path, the Eilbergs left Beth Emeth and joined another synagogue. Today, Rabbi Amy Eilberg teaches "Jewish Healing" in Palo Alto, California. She is the mother of a girl, Penina, who in 1999 was studying for bat mitzvah.

Joshua and Gladys Eilberg live just outside of Philadelphia in Beaver Hill, where the Congressman is on his condominium's board of directors. Ironically, the attorney for the 1,000-plus unit condo community is Gilbert Toll, the son of the man Joshua Eilberg replaced in Congress more than thirty years ago.

References
Interview with Joshua Eilberg, July 1997.
Almanac of American Politics (1972–80 editions).
New York Times, January 31, 1978.

EINSTEIN, EDWIN (1842–1905): *Republican from New York; served one term in the House (Forty-sixth Congress; March 4, 1879–March 3, 1881).*

In the decades following the Civil War, America went through one of its semiperiodic bouts of Christian-nativist fervor. Ethnic Americans, especially those who were not members of the "true faith," were finding more and more doors being shut—literally. This was true even for acculturated Jews who had been in America for one, two, three generations or more. As nativist sentiment grew, Jews found themselves being excluded from the better hotels, resorts, and clubs. As maddening and inexplicable as such insults were, however, they did not pose a serious threat to the legal or political security of the Jewish community. That was to come from a different source. For running parallel to these exclusionary practices, was a "movement favoring a constitutional amendment that would recognize the authority of God, Jesus, and scriptural law." The movement, spearheaded by United States Supreme Court Justice William Strong, included both members of the clergy and "an impressive number of governors, state judicial officials, and academicians." For those following Mr. Justice Strong's lead, 1892 was a watershed year. In that year, another Supreme Court Justice—David Brewer—asserted in an *obiter dictum* reading (passing remark), that the United States was, without question, a Christian nation. This caused nativists throughout the land to stand up and cheer.

Ironically, 1892 was also the year that a Jew, Edwin Einstein, chose to run for mayor of New York City. A Republican, Einstein decided that, after being out of elective politics for more than a decade, the time was right to take on Tammany Hall in order to clean up the mess they had made of the city. Needless to say, Einstein was defeated by a combination of anti-Jewish sentiment and Tammany ruthlessness. But as will often occur in politics, one man's defeat can lead to another man's triumph. Just two years later, a new reform candidate, William L. Strong (no relation to Justice Strong), managed to take the mayoralty away from Tammany. Although Einstein had not conquered the enemy, he had delivered a mortal blow.

The details of Edwin Einstein's life are rather sketchy. He was born in Cincinnati, Ohio, on November 18, 1842, and moved with his parents to New York City in 1846. While working as a store clerk, he took classes at both the City College of New York and Cooper Union. Apparently, he became a successful businessman with diverse interests, for by the end of his life, he was president of both the New River Mineral Company and the Raritan Woolen Mills, and served as a director of the Alabama Mineral Land Company and Trustee of the Texas Pacific Land Trust.

In 1878, Einstein defeated first-term incumbent Democrat Anthony Eickhoff, thereby becoming the first Republican to represent the Seventh Congressional District. Like Eickhoff and the preceding ten representatives from the Seventh Congressional District, Einstein served but a single term, declining to run for reelection in 1880. Returning to his mercantile interests, Einstein next surfaced in 1892, in the aforementioned race for mayor of New York City. Mayor Strong apparently believed that he owed Einstein's failed run in 1892 for his own success, for shortly after taking over as mayor, Strong named Edwin Einstein dock commissioner of New York City—a plum assignment. It should be noted that Strong appointed the up-and-coming Theodore Roosevelt police commissioner.

From this point on, the record once again becomes rather hazy. Edwin Einstein died of a sudden heart attack at age sixty-two on January 24, 1905, and was buried in Shearith Israel Cemetery in Brooklyn. His one certain involvement in the Jewish community came just before his term in Congress, when he served on the board of directors of New York's Mount Sinai Hospital.

References
Biographical Directory of the United States Congress, 1789–1989, p. 956.
New York Times, January 25, 1905, 9:4.

ELLENBOGEN, HENRY (1900–1985): *Democrat from Pennsylvania; served three terms in the House (Seventy-third through Seventy-fifth Congress; March 4, 1933–January 3, 1938).*

For those who were not alive sixty-five or more years ago, it is difficult to imagine just how much deprivation and poverty the Depression caused. The nation's unemployment rate reached a staggering 25 percent. Long Island potatoes rotted in the fields because, at the price of twenty-four cents a bushel, it did not pay to pick them. In England, Arkansas, a band of 500 farmers armed with shotguns and rifles pleaded with a Red Cross administrator for food. When told that he had no more requisition blanks, they invaded the town's only grocery store and intimidated the grocer into giving them more than $900 worth of groceries. More than 5,650 college professors were unemployed. Medical school graduates had to forsake their chosen profession because doctors simply could not make a living. Millions of Americans took to the road or traveled the rails, drifting from place to place, looking for odd jobs or handouts. From September 1931 to April 1932, the Southern Pacific Railroad reported that its brakemen and yard police had rousted 416,915 transients from their trains.

There was no security to be found anywhere. Oscar Ameringer, a keen observer of the times wrote about the "brokers, bank clerks, counter-jumpers, A.B.s, M.D.s, Ph.D.s, D.D.s, shoveling snow in the lowly company of bricklayers, cellists, hod carriers, oboists, garment workers, concert masters, stevedores, dramatists, and dock wallopers." The Depression was, in Ameringer's words, "a nightmare of woe and despair."

One enduring image of the Depression is the forlorn apple peddler, standing out on a street corner, often clad in suit and tie, selling fruit for a nickel, a penny—whatever he could get. This "phenomenon" came about when an officer of the International Apple Shipper's Association, faced with a glut of apples, got the idea of providing the unemployed with apples on credit. Within two months, there were more than 6,000 apple sellers in New York City alone.

During the early days of the Depression, Henry Ellenbogen, then a Pittsburgh attorney, arbitrator, and author, was greatly moved by the plight of the impoverished, the unemployed, and the dispossessed. In 1932, he was asked by a dynamic, politically active priest, Father James R. Cox, to join a group of prominent, influential Pittsburghers whose common goal would be to seek solutions to the severe problems at hand. Father Cox was the founder of the "Jobless Party," and its announced candidate for President of the United States. Leading the Pittsburgh contingent during the Bonus Army march on Washington in the summer of 1932, Cox managed to obtain an audience for his group with President Herbert Hoover. Father Cox, Ellenbogen, and the rest urged the president to appropriate funds for public works and unemployment relief. Hoover turned a deaf ear on their proposal. A kind man at heart, Hoover was, nonetheless, both philosophically and politically against any form of public assistance. Hoover explained to the group that, "a voluntary deed by a man impressed with the sense of responsibility and the brotherhood of man is infinitely more precious to our National ideals and National spirit than a thousandfold poured from the Treasury of the Government under compulsion of law."

Stunned by what he saw as Hoover's blindness—or insensitivity—Ellenbogen then and there decided that he must do something to aid the "forgotten man." Shortly after his return to Pittsburgh, the thirty-two-year-old attorney announced his candidacy for the United States Congress. Only one obstacle was standing in his way: in 1932, Henry Ellenbogen had yet to receive his final American citizenship papers.

A native of Vienna, Henry Ellenbogen was the fourth of five children born to Samson and Rose (Francoz) Ellenbogen. Henry was born on April 3, 1900. Samson died in 1911. Coming from a solidly middle-class family, Henry was able to attend the University of Vienna Law School; he received his law degree shortly after his nineteenth birthday. Just before graduating, his mother and youngest brother, Theodore, emigrated to the United States, settling in Pittsburgh, where they had relatives. At age nineteen, feeling that there was no future in Europe for a young Jewish lawyer, Henry uprooted himself and joined his mother and Theodore in Pennsylvania. Henry's elder siblings—Doris, Adolph, and Joseph would all eventually make their way to America. Joseph was the last to come. Imprisoned by the Nazis in 1938, Henry, by then a judge, contacted the American Ambassador to Austria, former Pennsylvania Governor George Earle, who managed to secure Joseph Ellenbogen's release. He arrived in America in 1939.

Once in Pittsburgh, Henry Ellenbogen found work as a bookkeeper at Kaufman's Department Store, going to Duquesne University Law School at night. Within four years of his arrival in America, he earned both an A.B. and J.D. Ellenbogen passed the Pennsylvania bar in 1924, receiving the highest score of anyone taking the exam. According to his daughter, Judith, his score was not equaled for another thirty-five years. Despite his high test score, the Allegheny County Bar Association, responding to a periodic wave of anti-immigrant sentiment, challenged his right to be admitted to practice, on the grounds that Ellenbogen was not a United States citizen. Ellenbogen took the bar association to court, arguing that nowhere did the Constitution of the United States or the laws of Pennsylvania state that an attorney must be a citizen. Ellenbogen won his case. Entering private practice, Ellenbogen defended labor unions and workers, acting as cocounsel with the great Clarence Darrow in one strike case. In 1927, Ellenbogen was appointed an arbitrator and public panel chair by the National War Labor Board. He spent the next several years arbitrating labor disputes. He also began writing and publishing articles on economic, social, and legal issues.

In the late 1920s, Henry Ellenbogen was introduced to Rachel Savage, the daughter of Nathan Savage, a Polish immigrant and one of Pittsburgh's most learned Jewish educators. They met on the steps of the YMHA, and married in 1928. Nathan Savage served for many years as the principal of one of that city's premier Hebrew schools.

In his first race for Congress, Ellenbogen took on two-term incumbent Republican Harry A. Estep. Benefiting from the Roosevelt landslide, Ellenbogen was easily elected to the Seventy-third Congress. Estep contested the election, arguing that since his American citizenship papers had not been finalized, Ellenbogen could not legally be seated in Congress. Estep's challenge failed. In an unusual move, House Speaker Henry T. Rainey permitted Ellenbogen to be sworn in as a duly elected member of Congress, but without the right to vote (or receive his salary or any mileage compensation) until he received his final citizenship papers. This occurred some three months later, in June 1933.

As a member of Congress, Henry Ellenbogen pursued a progressive, pro-New Deal course. He was among the first to sponsor social security legislation for the nation's elderly and champion unemployment insurance. Ellenbogen worked along with New York Senator Robert F. Wagner toward the creation of a United States Housing Authority that would work for lost-cost housing and slum clearance. According to Ellenbogen's daughter, Judith Specter, the idea for the Housing Authority was originally her father's. President Roosevelt, realizing that the young man from Pittsburgh carried little political weight in Congress, urged the powerful and well-known Senator Wagner to come on board. Originally known as the "Wagner-Ellenbogen" bill, the latter name soon began to fade from memory. Sadly, few histories of the era include the name of Henry Ellenbogen on this critical piece of New Deal legislation.

Henry Ellenbogen was given a relatively minor committee assignment—District of Columbia. In the 1930s, that appointment carried no political rewards—District residents could not vote. Nonetheless, Ellenbogen successfully sponsored legislation that provided pensions for the District's blind and financial assistance for its unemployed. Ellenbogen must have struck a responsive chord with his constituents, for he was reelected in 1934 with 98.7 percent of the vote.

During his second term in the House, Henry Ellenbogen was one of two legislators to sponsor legislation that resulted in the availability of thirty-year mortgages. Commenting on this nearly a half-century later, Ellenbogen's grandson and namesake said: "He really believed that owning a house was one of the most important things that anyone could do." Again, history played a cruel trick on Henry Ellenbogen. Had he been a more prominent member of Congress, it is likely that today he would be known as the "Father of the thirty-year mortgage."

During his legal career, Henry Ellenbogen appeared as counsel for the defense in many disputes involving immigration and naturalization.

As such, many of his clients were European leftists—Socialists and Communists. In one case, Ellenbogen defended one John Tapolcsanyi, a Pittsburgh-area barber, who had become a naturalized citizen. Upon discovering that Tapolcsanyi had been, in his own words, "a pure red Communist," the Justice Department sought to have his citizenship revoked. The Communist Party of America came to Tapolcsanyi's aide, providing him with legal counsel and publicizing his plight in their national press organ. Although Ellenbogen and his cocounsel, a Mr. Wallerstein, eventually lost the case, it was used against Ellenbogen in his 1936 campaign for reelection. In a September 26, 1936 radio address, former Assistant United States District Attorney Raymond D. Evans, speaking on behalf of Ellenbogen's opponent, Edward O. Tabor, charged the Congressman with being a Communist Party stooge: "I am convinced that there is no person in the United States holding high office today who knows more about COMMUNISM than HENRY ELLENBOGEN." Evans continued, saying: "I regret that a man with his background and political tendencies should represent the people of this district in the United States Congress." In his peroration, Evans asked, "Can a man who uses his professional talents to retain the citizenship of an admitted Communist himself be attached to the principles of the Constitution and the laws of the United States? Are you going to vote for an attorney who uses his professional talents to fight for the citizenship of a man who states under oath that he would have our Government taken away from us and placed in the hands of a class; a man who is a Communist; a man who believes there is only one country—Soviet Russia?" Despite Evans' rhetorical broadside, reissued as a printed document to the voters of the district, Ellenbogen was easily reelected to a third term.

During his years in Congress, Henry, Rachel, and daughter Naomi (soon to be joined by their second daughter, Judith) lived in Washington, D.C. Henry commuted back to Pittsburgh every weekend. By the time Naomi was of school age, Rachel began urging her husband to find a way for the family to return to Pittsburgh. After a bit of investigation, Henry decided to run for the bench. Not only would that allow him to return home, but the position for which he was running carried a ten-year term—decidedly more appealing than having to run every two years. In November 1937, he was elected to a ten-year term on the Allegheny County Court of Common Pleas. He resigned his seat in Congress, effective January 3, 1937. Judge Ellenbogen was reelected to the Court of Common Pleas in 1947 and again in 1957. During his final four years on the bench (1963–1966) he served as Chief Judge. Retiring from the bench at the end of his third term, Henry and Rachel Ellenbogen moved to Miami, Florida, where they spent the remaining years of their lives.

An ardent Zionist, Judge Ellenbogen was an officer of the Zionist Organization of America and an active member of the American Jewish Congress. He served for more than twenty years as the president of the Jewish National Fund in Pittsburgh, and was honored by having a forest dedicated in his name. Henry Ellenbogen was also the long-time president of the American Friends of the Hebrew University. In his honor, that institution named a forestry institute after him. He died in Miami on July 4, 1985, and was buried in West View Cemetery of Rodef Sholom Congregation, Squirrel Hill, Pennsylvania. He was survived by two daughters, Naomi Chase and Judith Specter, and five grandchildren. Judge Ellenbogen's grandson—also named Henry—became something of a celebrity when, in 1993, at age nineteen, he was appointed Administrative Assistant to United States Representative Peter Deutsch of Florida's Twentieth Congressional District. At the time of his appointment, it was written that "he may be the youngest person ever to hold that title on Capitol Hill."

References

Interview with Judith (Specter) Ellenbogen, March 1996.

American Jewish Year Book, vol. 44, p. 112.

Ft. Lauderdale New Sun Sentinel, January 5, 1993, 8B.

Page Smith, *Redeeming the Time: A People's History of the 1920s and the New Deal* (New York: Penguin, 1991).

Universal Jewish Encyclopedia.

Who Was Who in American Jewry, 1938.

ELLISON, DANIEL (1886–1960): *Republican from Maryland; served one term in the House (Seventy-eighth Congress; January 3, 1943–January 3, 1945).*

Daniel Ellison was born in Russia on February 14, 1886. His family emigrated to Baltimore before his first birthday. Educated in the Baltimore public schools, Ellison went on to earn both a B.A. from Johns Hopkins University in 1907 and a law degree from the University of Maryland. Admitted to the Maryland bar in 1909, Ellison went into private practice. Starting in 1923, Ellison was elected to five four-year terms on the Baltimore City Council. He resigned his seat in 1942 in order to run for Congress from Maryland's Fourth District. Ellison defeated one-term Democrat John Ambrose Meyer, becoming the first Republican to represent that district in forty years.

As a freshman Republican in a Democrat-controlled House, Ellison had virtually no visibility. Coming from an overwhelmingly Democratic district, Ellison's chances for reelection in 1944 were slim at best. True to the district's history, Ellison only served one term; he was defeated for reelection by Democrat George Hyde Fallon, who went on to hold the seat until 1970. After twelve terms, Fallon lost the Democratic primary to an up-and-coming thirty-seven-year-old Rhodes Scholar—Paul Sarbanes. After serving three terms in the House (1970–76), Sarbanes was elected to the Senate. As of 1997, Sarbanes was still Senator from Maryland.

Following his defeat, Daniel Ellison returned to the practice of law. In 1946, he was elected to a four-year term in the Maryland Senate. Never married, Daniel Ellison died in Baltimore on August 20, 1960. He is buried in the Hebrew Friendship Cemetery in Baltimore.

References

American Jewish Year Book, vol. 50, p. 645.
Biographical Directory of the United States Congress: 1774 1989, p. 962.
Who Was Who in American Jewry, 1938.

EMERICH, MARTIN (1846–1922): *Democrat from Illinois; served one term in the House (Fifty-eighth Congress; March 4, 1903–March 3, 1905).*

As a general rule, today's voting public tends to cast ballots for candidates they know or feel "kinship" toward. In terms of campaigning for office, it is most advantageous to be able to say: "I was born in this district, educated in its schools, and have been one of you virtually from day one." There are, of course, exceptions to the rule. South Floridians, many of whom are displaced New Yorkers, have no problem voting for a non-native; Californians often elect men and women born elsewhere.

Martin Emerich, who served a Chicago constituency for a single term at the turn of the century, was unique in two respects: first, he did not move to Illinois until he was past age forty; second, he was one of the few members of the Congressional Minyan elected to office in two different states. A native Marylander, Emerich was born in Baltimore on April 27, 1846, the son of German immigrants. He had at least one sister. Little is known of his early years, save that he attended public school. Entering the importing business, Emerich became involved in local communal affairs. Shortly after his twenty-forth birthday, he was appointed ward commissioner of the poor, a patronage position. The following year, Emerich married Lena Strauss. They had three children: Melvin L., Frank, and Corinne. Melvin, also known as M. L., became the Chicago resident partner of the New York investment banking firm of Hallgarten and Company. Daughter Corinne married one Alexander Marcuse.

Emerich served a single term (1881–1883) in the Maryland House of Delegates, and spent seven years (1880–1887) as aide-de-camp to Governors William T. Hamilton and Elihu E. Jackson. Leaving Jackson's employ, Emerich inexplicably moved to Chicago in 1887, where he spent the next ten years engaged in "mercantile pursuits." A civic-minded individual, Emerich quickly became involved in communal affairs. Within five years of his arrival in Chicago, he was elected to the Cook County Board of Commissioners. After a single two-year term (1892–1894), Emerich decided not to run for reelection. Leaving the Board, he was named tax assessor for South Chicago. In 1896, the fifty-year-old Martin Emerich became a brick manufacturer—a much-needed commodity in the rapidly growing "Windy City."

In 1903, Martin Emerich was elected to the Fifty-eighth Congress from Chicago's First District. As in the case of his election to the Maryland House of Delegates and the Cook County Board of Commissioners, Emerich decided that one term was enough; he decided not to be a candidate for reelection. Returning to Chicago, Emerich sold his brick-manufacturing concern, and retired at age sixty. His was an active presence in the Chicago Jewish community: he served several terms as grand president of the District Grand Lodges of the Independent Order of B'nai B'rith, as that organization used to be known. He also served as a director of both the Chicago Home for Jewish Orphans and the Orthodox Jewish Home for the Aged.

Martin Emerich died at the New York City home of his sister, Mrs. Isaac Kapp, September 27, 1922. His body was returned to Chicago, where he was interred in Rosehill Cemetery.

References

Biographical Directory of the United States Congress: 1774–1989, p. 966.
New York Times, September 28, 1922, 21:4.

ENGEL, ELIOT L. (1947–): *Democrat from New York; has served six terms in the House (One Hundred and First through One Hundred and Sixth Congress; January 3, 1989–present).*

By all accounts, Eliot L. Engel has lived the American Dream: the product of public housing and public schooling, by age forty-one, he was a member of the United States Congress. To this day, he continues to live in the same district in which he was born and bred.

The Engels and the Bleends (the Congressman's maternal grandparents) were all from Eastern Europe. The Engels came to New York from the Ukraine in 1913. Their son, Eliot's father Pinchas ("Pinya," or "Phillip" as he was known in English), was born the following year. Eliot's mother, Sylvia ("Seroy") Bleend, was likewise the product of an immigrant home; her mother emigrated from Belarus in 1908, her father from Odessa in 1913. When Seroy was four, her father, Joe Bleend, died, leaving her mother, a dressmaker, with the task of raising three children alone. When Seroy married Phillip, a welder, Mrs. Bleend came to live with the newlyweds.

The Engel's first child, Eliot L., was born in New York City on February 18, 1947; his sister, Dori (Kaplan) was born eight years later. From birth to age twelve, Eliot and his family lived on the third floor of a Bronx tenement. At age twelve, the family moved to "Eastchester Homes," a middle-income housing project. While receiving a public school education, Eliot attended an afternoon Hebrew school at a local Orthodox synagogue in the West Bronx. Eliot grew up in a home that was "traditional but not religious." So long as grandmother Bleend lived with them, the Engels kept a kosher home. In 1960, Eliot became bar mitzvah at a Reform synagogue.

Seroy Engel was, and remains, a bit of a "live wire." As a young woman, she was a speed skater, and at one time aspired to skate with the Roller Derby. While Phillip earned his living as a welder, Seroy sewed dresses, worked with retarded young adults, and acted in off-Broadway shows. For several seasons, she toured with a production of The World of Sholom Aleichem. As a teenager, young Eliot spent summers touring with the company as an actor. Following his graduation from high school in 1965, Engel, who lived at home until age twenty-four, attended Hunter-Lehman College in New York City, from which he earned a bachelor's degree in history in 1969. In 1973, he received a master's degree in guidance and counseling from Lehman College of the City University of New York. Two years before his college graduation, Engel made his first trip to Israel, where his mother has relatives: her sister's son is a rabbi there.

Although he came from a fairly nonpolitical family, Eliot Engel was intrigued with Democratic politics from an early age. Like many youngsters of his generation, he was greatly influenced by President John F. Kennedy: "By his own account," the *New York Times* reported, "Mr. Engel's affection for Democratic politics goes back to his early teens, when he fell under the spell of John F. Kennedy, taking a subway from the Bronx to 59th Street to pick up lapel buttons at the Kennedy-for-President headquarters. He sold them as fund-raising items, and said wryly that he turned in all the money."

Eliot Engel spent the years 1969–1977 working as a teacher and guidance counselor in the New York City public schools. In 1977, following the conviction of the local incumbent assemblyman, Engel decided to run for his open seat. Running as an insurgent Democrat-Liberal, Engel easily captured the seat; he was reelected five times. Described as a "low-key figure" during his days in the New York Assembly, Engel worked his way up to chair a committee on drug and alcohol abuse and a subcommittee that handled moderate-income housing matters. As the writers of *Politics in America* noted, these positions "served him well in his initial House race."

While serving in the New York State Legislature, Engel married Patricia Ennis. The two had originally met in politics and had been friends for many years. Before their marriage, Ennis, a Catholic, was converted to Judaism by a Conservative rabbi. According to Eliot Engel, his wife had given serious thought to converting long before they decided to marry: "it's almost as if she were Jewish in a previous life," he quips. The Engels have two children: Julia Ann, born in 1981, and Jonathan Bradley, born in 1986.

From 1968 to 1988, Eliot Engel's congressman was Nineteenth District Representative Mario Biaggi. Biaggi (1917–), at one time the most decorated member of the New York City police department, was best known for his sponsorship of the law banning "cop-killer" bullets. Widely popular (for years Biaggi had run unopposed as the candidate of *both* the Democrats and Republicans), Biaggi had been a serious candidate for mayor in 1977. His chances of election to that post were severely hampered when it was discovered that "contrary to his own statement, [he had] taken the Fifth Amendment before a grand jury."In September 1987, Biaggi was convicted of accepting illegal gratuities: "he accepted expenses for a quick Florida vacation for himself, and someone who seems to have been a girlfriend, from Brooklyn Democratic boss Meade Esposito, and did some favors for Esposito in return," according to the *Almanac of American Politics*. To make matters far worse, Biaggi was convicted nearly a year later of having accepted a bribe from Wedtech, a now-defunct Bronx defense contractor. Prior to going on trial in the Wedtech case, Eliot Engel decided to gamble and take on Biaggi in the Democratic primary. With his conviction in August 1988, Biaggi was forced to resign his seat. Nonetheless, his name remained on the ballot. Rather than attacking Biaggi for being a convicted felon, Engel treated the ten-term Congressman with kid gloves, "praising him for his good works in the past, but making it clear his time was over." Engel hit upon the strategy of evoking Biaggi's legal woes by stating that a Congressman, no matter how good a legislator he might be, could not offer his constituents effective representation from a courtroom or jail cell. Engel's strategy worked: on election day, he won the Democratic primary with 48 percent to Biaggi's 26 percent and Assemblyman Vincent Marchiselli's 26 percent. Engel faced Biaggi again in the November general election—Biaggi had won the Republican primary. Engel once again trounced Biaggi, this time with 56 percent of the vote. By the time Eliot Engel was sworn in as a member of the One Hundred and First Congress, Mario Biaggi was in jail.

Engel sought, and received, a seat on the House Foreign Affairs Committee (now renamed International Relations). From that post he has spent the lion's share of his time working on international affairs. Coming from an ethnically diverse district, he has followed what the *Almanac of American Politics* termed the "three I's strategy in New York politics": Israel, Ireland, and Italy. By means of this "strategy," Engel

• introduced a bill to ban weapons sales to the Royal Ulster Constabulary in Northern Ireland,

• passed the first resolution honoring "cultural" contributions by Italian-Americans, and,

• introduced a successful joint resolution stating that Jerusalem "is and should remain" the capital of Israel.

As an internationalist, Engel was one of the earliest advocates for "greater U.S. intervention" in the civil war in the former Yugoslavia. As early as February 1993, he joined a bipartisan group of legislators who urged the Clinton administration to take sides against the Bosnian Serbs. In September 1993, he went on a fact-finding trip to Croatia and came back with dire predictions of what might happen in that region if the United States did not take a stance against the Bosnians. In May 1994, Engel warned his fellow House members that "by standing aside in the Bosnian war," the United States and Europe were "showing the Serbs that aggression does pay and that brutality does pay and genocide does pay, and here it is 50 years after the Nazi era, and we are seeing the same kinds of atrocities committed on civilian populations, and the world wrings its hands. Nobody can agree and so nobody does anything." Engel has also been a constant critic of both the Bush and the Clinton administration's policy of repatriation of Haitian emigrants. As a member of the Foreign Affairs Africa Subcommittee, Engel attended the inauguration of Nelson Mandela as president of South Africa—an event which he termed the "greatest honor." Engel was one of the only Democrats in the New York Congressional delegation to vote in favor of sending U.S. troops into the Gulf in 1991.

Engel, who has been regularly reelected with anywhere between 61 percent and 80 percent of the vote from his Bronx district (which after the 1990 census was renamed the Nineteenth), easily has one of the most liberal voting records in the House. He regularly receives a perfect 100 score from the Americans for Democratic Action and a 0 rating from the Christian Coalition.

In 1994, Engel had his first (and so far only) serious reelection challenge from renowned salsa singer Willie Colon. Colon, who was supported by the Reverend Al Sharpton, attempted to portray himself as a "son of the streets," and Engel as a fat cat insider. Voters in the district, knowing of Engel's upbringing in a public housing project, reelected him with 61 percent of the vote—his lowest total to date.

In 1984, Engel attended the Democratic National Convention as a delegate for Walter Mondale. As with all delegates, he was asked to fill out a questionnaire. Asked about his ethnicity, he wrote down the word "Jewish." "Sorry," the questioner explained, "that's not a proper answer. Where does your family come from?" When Engel said that originally they had come from the Russian Ukraine, the party functionary replied, "Oh, so your ethnic background would be Ukrainian. That makes you a Ukrainian-American." "Try as I might," Engel recalled "I couldn't convince her that I was an American Jew."

Engel is a popular speaker for Jewish organizations, especially on the subject of Israel. He regularly ends his speeches by saying: "America is our home, but Israel is our Homeland." He firmly believes in the importance of identifying as a Jew publicly and regularly advises: "Don't be timid, don't be afraid. Its up to us to combat anti-Semitism. Don't worry about charges of 'dual loyalty.' Stand up and be proud." Engel is co-chair of the Peace Accord Monitoring Group in the House of Representatives, which monitors and challenges Palestinian violations of the Oslo accords.

Eliot Engel cruised to a 88 percent to 12 percent victory in 1998. Now serving his sixth term in the House, he can probably look forward to remaining in Congress virtually as long as he pleases.

References

Interview with Eliot L. Engel, February 1992, Washington, D.C.

Interview with Mrs. Phillip Engel, October 1996, Tamarac, Fla.

Almanac of American Politics (1990–96 editions).

New York Times, September 17, 1988.

Politics in America (1990-1996 editions).

ERDREICH, BEN LEADER (1938–): *Democrat from Alabama; served four terms in the House (Ninety-eighth through One Hundred and First Congress; January 3, 1983–January 3, 1991).*

To many, Alabama, the Heart of Dixie, conjures up a melange of disturbing political images: George Wallace standing at a schoolhouse door loudly proclaiming, "Segregation now, segregation forever;" Rosa Parks, "tired and footsore," bravely refusing to move to the back of a public bus; Bull Connor unleashing police dogs and fire hoses on young civil rights protesters; Martin Luther King, Jr., marching in Selma, much to the chagrin of Sheriff Jim Clark. This Alabama is deeply ingrained on the canvas of American political history. Yet there is another Alabama—that of the "Big Mules": men like Senators Hugo Black, John Sparkman, and Lister Hill; Congressmen Carl Elliott, Albert Rains, Kenneth Roberts, and Robert Jones. For nearly half of the twentieth century, these men were at the forefront of what was arguably "the nation's most legislatively productive House delegation." It is this Alabama, the Alabama of Black, Sparkman, et al., that produced the state's sole member of the Congressional Minyan: Ben Leader Erdreich of Birmingham.

The question must be asked: What brought the Leader and Erdreich families to Alabama in the first place? Why not New York, Boston, Philadelphia, or Chicago? Why Birmingham, Alabama? Birmingham was founded a mere half-dozen years after the end of the Civil War. Situated in a valley, the city sits at the base of a mountain made entirely of iron ore. Birmingham once housed the South's biggest steel mills. These mills required tens of thousands of workers. Many were imported from places like Czechoslovakia, Hungary, and Poland, and settled in dozens upon dozens of little towns. The explosive growth of Alabama mining brought a need not only for miners and steelworkers; it also created opportunities for literally thousands of peddlers, shopkeepers, and merchants. Among these were a handful of Eastern European Jews.

Ben Erdreich's maternal grandparents, Ben Leader and Mary Levine, were born within a few dozen miles of each other in Polish Lithuania. Ben Leader's precise birthplace is not known; Mary was born in Kabrinn. Ben Leader's father immigrated to Brookwood, Alabama, around 1880; Mary's settled in West Blockton at about the same time. Both men went to work for distant relatives who were merchants in their respective towns. When Leader and Levine had saved enough money, they sent for their families. Ben Leader came to Brookwood (Jefferson County) at age four; Mary Levine arrived in West Blockton (Tuscaloosa County) at age two. In the 1870s and 1880s, Brookwood, which had a population of several thousand, attracted a fairly sizable number of Russians and Lithuanians; its onion-domed Russian Orthodox church is still standing in 1998. Today, Brookwood was about 6 miles from downtown Birmingham; West Blockton is within sight of a gigantic Daimler-Chrysler plant.

Ben Leader grew up in Brookwood, where his father ran a store. Around 1903 or 1904, Ben Leader met Mary Levine. He was instantly smitten. The Levines had moved away from West Blockton, first to Warrior, and finally to Birmingham. At the time of their meeting, the twenty-year-old Ben was working as a bookkeeper in his father's shop. Mary declared that he was wasting his talents and encouraged him to go to law school. Taking his girlfriend's advice, Ben Leader made application to the University of Alabama School of Law. Despite never having attended college, Ben Leader was admitted, and became an attorney in 1909. That same year, he and Mary married. Ben Leader hung out his shingle in Birmingham, where he would practice law for more than a half-century. Deeply involved in Alabama politics, Ben Leader became both friend and trusted advisor to more than two generations of Alabama senators, congressmen, and local elected officials. Ben and Mary had a daughter, Corinne ("Corinne from Kobrinn," they used to chant, even though she was born in

West Blockton). The Leaders were stalwart members of Birmingham's Reform Temple Emanu-El.

The roots of the Erdreich/Marx side of the family are not so well known. From all appearances, the first Erdreichs (German for "rich realm") came to Selma, Alabama, prior to the Civil War. Ben Erdreich believes they came from "the eastern part of Germany, somewhere around Dresden." Likewise, the Marxes, the Congressman's paternal grandmother's family, came to Selma in the 1840s or early 1850s, most likely from eastern Germany. Maurice Kohn ("M. K.") Erdreich and Blanche Marx Erdreich were both born and raised in Selma. They had two sons: M. K. (named after his father—an uncommon practice among Ashkenazi Jews), and Stanley, whom they raised in Birmingham, where the senior M. K. ran a store. Stanley Erdreich and Corinne Leader married in Birmingham and had two sons. Their first, Stanley, arrived in 1935. Three years later, on December 9, 1938, their second son was born. They named him Ben Leader.

At the time of Ben's birth, Stanley Erdreich did the advertising for several local department stores. In 1939, he bought Porter's Clothing Store in downtown Birmingham. When brother M. K. returned from World War II (Stanley having been exempted due to diabetes), he went into partnership with Stanley. Together, they ran the store until Stanley's death in 1963.

Ben Erdreich attended public school in Birmingham and was confirmed by Rabbi Milton Grafman at Temple Emanu-El. "In those days," Erdreich recounted, "few if any of the boys I knew ever became bar mitzvah. The Reform Jews just weren't doing that sort of thing." Following his graduation from Shades Valley High School in 1956, Ben Erdreich headed off to Yale. After earning his B.A. in 1960, he headed back home, where he attended the University of Alabama School of Law. While a student at Tuscaloosa, he served as editor-in-chief of the *Alabama Law Review*. He graduated with honors in 1963. From 1963 to 1965, Erdreich was in the United States Army with the rank of first lieutenant; he was sent to New York City, where he acted mostly as a courier. When Erdreich mustered out of the army in 1965, he thought long and hard about whether to remain in New York or return home to Birmingham.

After a bit of deliberation, Erdreich decided to remain in Manhattan. He had good reason; his high school girlfriend, Ellen Cooper, was living in New York.

Jerome Cooper, Ellen's father, hailed from Brookwood, Alabama. A graduate of Harvard and Harvard Law School, he had been Supreme Court Justice Hugo Black's first law clerk. Following her graduation from Wellesley, Ellen headed for Manhattan, where she pursued a master's degree in art history at the New York Institute of Fine Arts. Ben Erdreich and Ellen Cooper were married on May 30, 1965. They have two children: Jeremy Cooper Erdreich, born in 1969, and Anna Bertha, born in 1972. Jeremy, who, like his father, graduated from Yale, earned an advanced degree in architecture from the Harvard University School of Design. He currently works as an architect in Birmingham. Anna, who like her mother graduated from Wellesley, worked in the White House for First Lady Hillary Clinton, and served three years on the staff of Secretary of Education Richard Riley. Like her brother, she too went back home to live and work in Birmingham.

Ben Erdreich practiced law with a large firm in New York City for a few years before joining his father-in-law's firm, Cooper, Mitch and Crawford in Birmingham. In 1970, he was elected to the Alabama House of Representatives. While in the state legislature, Erdreich sponsored Alabama's Clean Air Act and drew up a bill that "helped to foster special education programs throughout the state." After just two years in the state legislature, he ran an unsuccessful race for the Sixth District congressional seat against incumbent Republican John Buchanan, a Baptist minister. Buchanan (1928–) had originally won his seat in the Goldwater debacle of 1964. Now running for a fifth term, he had a moderate voting record and was able to win over Democratic voters. He dispatched the thirty-four-year-old Erdreich with ease.

Two years later, growing tired of a "part-time political career"—the legislature held regular sessions only once every two years—Erdreich accepted appointment as Jefferson County Commissioner of Public Welfare. He was then elected to the first of two four-year terms on the Jefferson County Commission. As a commissioner, Erdreich was "widely credited with gearing up the county's services to senior citizens including a 'Meals on Wheels' program and 'Eldergarden,' a downtown Birmingham gathering place for the elderly." Erdreich had a "low-key style" that garnered him only "modest name recognition."

In 1978, Representative John Buchanan barely survived a primary challenge by Birmingham insurance underwriter Albert Lee Smith, Jr. Buchanan's political moderation made him a target of increasingly conservative Republicans. Running again in 1980, Smith beat Buchanan in the primary and then went on to a narrow victory in the November general election. Following his eight terms in Congress, Buchanan went on to become president of People for the American Way, a national grass-roots lobbying organization.

After sixteen years of moderate Republicanism, voters in Alabama's Sixth District (Birmingham and most of its Jefferson County suburbs) now had a rock-ribbed conservative representing their interests in the House.

Albert Smith's two years on Capitol Hill coincided with an economic downturn in Birmingham. Because of the narrowness of his 1980 victory, and the shape of the economy (Birmingham had an unemployment rate in excess of 15 percent), Smith looked to be vulnerable in 1982. Surprisingly, no Democrat stepped forward to challenge him. Erdreich, coming to the end of his second four-year term on the County Commission, was giving serious thought to leaving politics and "going back to law and making a living." Local Democratic officials went to work on Erdreich, eventually persuading him that he stood a good chance of defeating Smith.

Erdreich ran unopposed in the Democratic primary and then set his sights on Smith. The Republican ran a well-financed ($528,000) campaign. Erdreich, by comparison, had so little money that he could only afford one poll. Instead, he relied heavily on volunteer phone banks. Well-known for supporting senior and health-care issues (which earned him the sobriquet "the Claude Pepper of Alabama"), Erdreich ran a heavily grass-roots campaign "tapping a pool of volunteers to help go door-to-door in neighborhoods throughout the city." His efforts on behalf of the elderly gave him a built-in pool of supporters.

During the campaign, Erdreich discovered that Smith's telephone squad was going out of its way to inform prospective voters, "You know, Erdreich is a Jew." One Erdreich supporter, incensed at the Smith campaign's tactic, quickly organized a group to respond in kind. She happily reported back to Erdreich that now, whenever one of Smith's people called one of her friends and made the comment,"You know, he's a Jew," they would respond: "Well, I'm going to support him then, because the Jews are the Chosen People!"

Despite being outspent by a nearly three-to-one margin, Erdreich defeated Smith 53 percent to 46 percent, an amazing figure when one considers that just two years earlier, Reagan won the district with 51 percent of the vote. Erdreich's victory was aided by redistricting, which added some industrial and heavily black suburbs on Birmingham's West Side, and by an unusually high turnout among blacks. In winning, Ben Erdreich became the first Democrat to represent the Sixth District in twenty years.

Ben Erdreich was assigned to Banking, Finance and Urban Affairs, Government Operations, and the Select Committee on Aging. He saw himself as a champion of his district's languishing steel interests. Shortly after joining the Ninety-eighth Congress, Erdreich introduced the Unfair Foreign Competition Act, which would have "enabled U.S. steel companies to seek damages in federal court from foreign concerns they suspected of having illegally sold products in American markets." He also pushed for a federal Department of Trade and Industry, which would likewise aid American steel interests.

Known to his House colleagues as a "good-natured man with a cautious, deliberative style," Erdreich spent his first term "performing a difficult balancing act . . . carefully cultivat[ing] conservative interests at home while keeping up his credentials as a national Democrat." He compiled a moderate-to-liberal record (by far the most liberal in his delegation), while voting with the Republicans on defense and foreign policy issues "just enough to maintain the comfort level of the Sixth District's conservative majority." Throughout his decade in the House, Ben Erdreich consistently walked a political tightrope, receiving 50 ratings from both the liberal Americans for Democratic Action and the Americans for Conservative Action—an all but unheard of accomplishment.

In 1984, GOP leaders back home persuaded longtime Democratic State legislator J. T. "Jabo" Waggoner to switch parties and run against Erdreich. Wagoner raised $355,000 (to Erdreich's $567,000), and "relied on robot-like Reagan loyalty to cover ineffective local efforts." With Reagan crushing Walter Mondale 59 percent to 41 percent in the Sixth, Erdreich won his reelection in a cakewalk with 60 percent of the vote. Erdreich's next two reelection campaigns featured only token Republican opponents.

At the start of the One Hundred and First Congress, Ben Erdreich was named acting chair of the newly formed Policy, Research and Insurance Subcommittee, which was created during a reorganization of the parent Banking Committee. Erdreich's new panel had the broad mandate to "review problem issues in banking, finance, housing and insurance." His elevation to the post came as something of a surprise; he had leapfrogged over three Democrats with greater seniority. New York's Robert Garcia, the most senior of the three, was barred from serving as chair because of his indictment in the Wedtech bribery case; Bruce Morrison of Connecticut opted to chair another panel's subcommittee; Marcy Kaptur of Ohio won a seat on the Budget Committee.

In 1990, Ben Erdreich won reelection with 93 percent of the vote; the Republicans didn't even field a candidate. Two years later, he lost his seat to Alabama Republican Party Chairman Spencer Bachus, 52 percent to 45 percent. What truly defeated Ben Erdreich was redistricting. For years, the Sixth District had consisted of all or most of Birmingham and surrounding Jefferson County. In this guise, the district included "heavily Democratic black precincts" and "heavily Republican wealthy and not-so-wealthy white areas." The prevalent interpretation of the 1982 Voting Rights Act required the creation of a new black-majority district. Prior to redistricting, 37 percent of the voters in the Sixth District were black; its median house value was $40,000.

After redistricting, the percentage of black voters was cut to less than 9 percent, while the median house value shot up to nearly $73,000. Where the old district would have given only 57 percent to George Bush (which Ben Erdreich could have lived with politically), the new district gave Bush a whopping 76 percent. Within two years, Ben Erdreich's district had become one of the most Republican in the country.

Speaking of Ben Erdreich's ill-fated 1992 election, the *Almanac of American Politics* noted: "What is amazing is not that he lost, but that he fought gamely and almost won." Without redistricting, Erdreich would have easily won. In point of fact, Erdreich was leading Bachus in most of the polls until the very end of the campaign. He attacked his Republican opponent for "breaking a pledge not to negatively campaign," and for "missing 3,000 votes during his tenure in the legislature." Toward the end of the campaign, the *Birmingham News* endorsed Bachus, thus sounding Erdreich's death knell.

During the decade her husband served in Congress, Ellen Cooper Erdreich, who had been a professor back home in Alabama, earned a Ph.D. in art history from Johns Hopkins University. Today (2000), she is a part-time professor of Renaissance Art at American University in Washington, D.C. On July 2, 1993, President Bill Clinton appointed Ben Erdreich to a nonrenewable seven-year term as chairman of the United States Merit Service Protection Board, an independent agency in the executive branch of the federal government that adjudicates all federal civil service suits.

Ben Erdreich's term expired on March 1, 2000, at which time he decided to move back to Birmingham. "There's just something wonderful about living there. After all, its home."

References
Interview with Ben Erdreich, February 1998.
Almanac of American Politics (1980–94 editions).
"Introduction to the MSPB" (a publication of the United States Merit Service Protection Board, transmitted via the Internet).
Politics in America (1980–92 editions).

FARBSTEIN, LEONARD (1902–): *Democrat from New York; served seven terms in the House (Eighty-fifth through Ninety-first Congress; January 3, 1957–January 3, 1971).*

Leonard Farbstein won his first election—a race for the New York State Assembly—in 1932, the year Franklin D. Roosevelt initially captured the White House. Farbstein suffered his one and only defeat at the hands of *Bella Abzug* thirty-eight years later, during the Nixon administration. In between, he won eighteen straight elections, including seven congressional races, often by margins of nearly three-to-one. Farbstein's extraordinary success at the polls was due as much to the makeup of his district as to his own political skills. His congressional district (at first the Nineteenth, later the Twentieth)was so overwhelmingly Democratic that his first opponent, Maurice G. Henry, Jr., took to "handing his campaign cards to people upside down. The underside contain[ed] all the 'Facts About Henry' except one—his political affiliation."

Leonard Farbstein, the son of Louis and Yetta (Schlanger) Farbstein, was born in New York City on October 12, 1902. Louis, like many other Jewish immigrants from Russia-Poland, was a tailor. At the time of his son's birth, he was engaged in an "oil cloth and carpet business." Reflecting on his early days on Norfolk Street Farbstein recalled: "It was a very rough childhood. . . . I sold newspapers and handkerchiefs after school and worked at the Audubon Society during high school." During the First World War, the teenaged Farbstein served in the United States Coast Guard Reserve. Farbstein graduated from New York's High School of Commerce at war's end, and began taking night classes at both City College and the Hebrew Union Teacher's College.

Despite his lack of an undergraduate degree, Farbstein was admitted to the New York University School of Law, from which he received an LL.B. in 1924. Admitted to the bar, he eventually went into partnership with Jacob Markowitz, a future justice of the New York State Supreme Court. Farbstein married Blossom Langer, and had one son, named Louis, after his father. The Farbsteins lived in an "older union-built cooperative—Amalgamated's Hillman Houses at 500 Grand Street," just a few blocks from where he was born and raised.

Shortly after graduating from law school, Farbstein, though admittedly apolitical, joined friends in campaigning for, and electing, Louis J. Lefkowitz to the New York State Assembly. Lefkowitz would go on to serve many terms as New York State Attorney General. After Lefkowitz won a second term in the Assembly, Farbstein decided, "Maybe I should try to see what I could do for myself." He became assistant to the district captain in his own Fourth Assembly District. Within five years, he had become the machine's candidate for the Assembly seat. As noted above, Farbstein was elected to the New York State Assembly in 1932. During his twenty-four years in that body, he sponsored legislation establishing the State Judicial Conference, the Youth Court, and a system of youth rehabilitation centers. Farbstein was also active in the local community, serving as vice chairman of the philanthropic East River Day Camp.

In 1956, Nineteenth District Representative *Arthur Klein* vacated his seat in order to wage a successful run for the New York State Supreme Court. (Klein's Nineteenth District predecessor, *Samuel Dickstein*, likewise ran for the State Supreme Court.) At the time that Leonard Farbstein announced his candidacy for Klein's seat, the Nineteenth Congressional District included "Manhattan from West 21st and East 20th Streets down to the islands off the Battery." The district's heaviest voter concentration was centered on the Lower East Side with its large and politically active Jewish population. Running against Maurice G. Henry, Jr. (he of the upside-down cards), Farbstein captured the seat by a better than two-to-one margin.

Leonard Farbstein went on to enjoy a fourteen-year career in the House of Representatives. A moderate-to-liberal Democrat, he voted against the Landrum-Griffin labor reform law, for federal aid for education, home-building, and public-housing projects, and for increasing the minimum wage. As noted above, Farbstein was generally reelected by overwhelming margins. Nonetheless, he was regularly targeted by reform-minded Democrats as an "organization cipher" who had significant ties with the "old-line Democratic leaders" on the Lower East Side. As Farbstein's 1964 opponent, Liberal Party candidate Edward Morrison said: "There's nothing special about him, no fire in him. He's just another Congressman."

Despite the fact that the Reform Democrats had few objections to Farbstein's voting record, they nonetheless ran candidates against him in his last four campaigns. In 1966, Farbstein was challenged by New York City Councilman *Ted Weiss*, a darling of the Reform Democrats. At first, it appeared that Farbstein had lost by 61 votes. When the ballots were recounted, he emerged victorious by a 151-vote margin. Upon hearing the news that defeat had been snatched from the jaws of victory, Weiss appeared before the press charging "wholesale fraud . . . perpetrated by Tammany Hall." Weiss retained the firm of Paul, Weiss [no relation], Rifkind, Wharton and Garrison to petition the State Supreme Court for an order "requiring the Board of Elections to show cause why it should certify Mr. Farbstein as the nominee." The court eventually ordered a new primary, which Farbstein won by an even more convincing margin. The next year, 1968, Weiss again challenged Farbstein for the Democratic nomination. Once again he lost.

All the while, Leonard Farbstein was gaining seniority in the House. By 1966, he was a ranking member of the House Foreign Affairs Committee and chairman of its subcommittee on Foreign Economic Policy. As a senior member of the committee, Farbstein supported President Lyndon Johnson's handling of the Vietnam War.

A short (5 feet, 7 inches), solid (160 pounds) man, Farbstein was an avid golfer and tennis player. As a member of Congress, he noted, his only form of exercise was "an almost daily quarter-mile swim in the pool of the Rayburn Office Building."

Leonard Farbstein suffered his one and only election loss in June 1970, when he was defeated by Bella Abzug in the Democratic primary. Farbstein returned to New York City, where he has lived in retirement ever since. In October 1999, Farbstein celebrated his ninety-seventh birthday.

References

New York Times, November 2, 1956, 21:1; November 3, 1960, 35:3; February 19, 1966, 56:2; July 2, 1966, 9:2.

FEINGOLD, RUSSELL D. (1953–): *Democrat from Wisconsin; elected to two six-year terms in the Senate (January 3, 1992–present).*

Among many people, religion and politics are the two things never to be discussed at dinner. By ignoring this ancient dictum, Leon and Sylvia Feingold wound up raising both a United States Senator and an ordained rabbi.

The southern tier of Wisconsin, just a stone's throw from Illinois, used to be prime dairy country. Originally settled by Yankee and German farmers in the 1840s, the area, which extends from Lake Michigan inland to the Rock River Valley, eventually became a prime center for factories. Today, Racine houses a Johnson Wax operations center; Janesville, Senator Russ Feingold's birthplace, is the manufacturing home of the Parker Pen Corporation.

Max and Dina (Katz) Feingold, the Senator's paternal grandparents, settled in Janesville in 1917. Max, a grocer, had emigrated from Russia in the late 1890s. Before reaching Janesville, the Feingold's spent a short time in Rochester, New York, where their son Leon was born. Leon (1912–1980) grew up to be an attorney, and "among the most prominent progressive Democrats in southern Wisconsin—pals with the likes of [Senator Gaylord] Nelson and Tom Fairchild." In the 1930s, Leon ran for district attorney of Rock County. Losing heavily, he "turned his energies to helping other progressive politicians."

Isaac and Rachel (Rosenfield) Binstock, Senator Feingold's maternal grandparents, emigrated to America from Austria-Hungary in 1896. Settling originally in Memphis, Tennessee, they eventually moved to Denver. While attending the University of Wisconsin in Madison, their daughter Sylvia met and married Leon Feingold. Sylvia and Leon had four children: Nancy, David, Russell, and Dena. Before her retirement, Sylvia worked as an abstractor.

Russell Dana Feingold was born in Janesville on March 2, 1953. One of the formative events in his life occurred in 1960, at age seven. As a second-grader, his class held a mock presidential election. Russ came home from school in tears; he

was the only student who had supported John F. Kennedy. Greatly agitated, he told his parents that if JFK didn't win the real election, he "didn't think he would ever be able to return to school." As history records, Kennedy did win the presidency, thereby turning a youngster's thoughts to politics.

Janesville has a tiny Jewish population and no synagogue. As a result, the Feingold children were *schlepped* (Yiddish for "dragged") to Madison each week—a 90-mile round trip—in order to attend religious school at a Reform temple. Russ attended Hebrew school from kindergarten through confirmation. In 1971, the eighteen-year-old Feingold, a senior at Janesville's Crag High School, won the state high school debate championship and headed off to the University of Wisconsin in nearby Madison. Four years later, he earned a B.A. with honors in history and political science. From 1975 to 1977, Feingold was a Rhodes Scholar at Oxford University, where he earned first-class honors in Final Honours from the School of Jurisprudence. Returning to the United States, he enrolled in Harvard Law School, from which he received his J.D. in 1979.

Returning to Janesville, Russ Feingold practiced law as a litigator with Wisconsin's largest and most prestigious law firm, Foley & Lardner. He married in the late 1970s. From this first marriage (he was later divorced), he had two daughters: Jessica, born on March 29, 1980, and Ellen, born on March 8, 1983. Feingold married a second time to Mary Erpenbach, who had two children—Sam and Ted Speerschneider—from her first marriage. Moving to nearby Middleton, the Feingolds and the Speerschneiders lived within a few blocks of each other.

In 1982, Russ Feingold decided to make a run for the Wisconsin State Senate against incumbent Republican Cy Bidwell. Running a cash-starved, grass-roots campaign, Feingold at first appeared to have suffered a razor-thin defeat. A recount gave Feingold the victory by a mere 31 votes out of more than 47,000 cast. A few weeks after his upset victory, Russ's father Leon succumbed to cancer. He was sixty-eight. Despite his evident appetite for politics, Leon, according to some accounts, was "uncomfortable with the notion that his son would get in the electoral arena himself." His reasoning was straightforward enough; Leon feared that as an elected official, Russ would not have enough time to be a successful husband and father.

As a member of the Wisconsin Senate, Russ Feingold, former litigator, now earned slightly more than $30,000—a decided drop in income. The family lived (and continues to live) in a modest ranch-style home in Middleton. Positioning himself as an earnest liberal on social and cultural issues, and a moderate on economics, Feingold chaired one of the State Senate's most powerful committees—the panel on Aging, Banking, Communications and Taxation. Nonetheless, by all indications Feingold was never what one would call a Senate insider. During his ten years in the Wisconsin State Senate (he was reelected in 1986 with 63 percent of the vote), Feingold waged an unsuccessful (some called it quixotic) campaign to prevent out-of-state banks from coming into Wisconsin. On the positive side, he led a successful fight to impose a moratorium on the use of synthetic hormones in cows to increase milk production—an obvious hot-button issue in the Dairy State.

On the same night that Russ Feingold was reelected to the State Senate (1986), voters across the state were giving Republican Robert W. Kasten, Jr., a narrow victory in his bid for a second six-year term in the United States Senate. Gathering with his family and campaign staff, Feingold watched the returns on television. When news of Kasten's narrow (50 percent to 48 percent) victory came on, Feingold reportedly pointed at the screen and said: "I want him." Thus was born a nearly half-decade long campaign for the United States Senate.

Robert W. Kasten, Jr. (1942–), was a Milwaukee native. Rich, a "product of a country club atmosphere," Kasten had originally been elected to the House of Representatives in 1974 at age thirty-two, and reelected two years later. Following a loss in the 1978 gubernatorial primary at the hands of Lee Sherman Dreyfus, Kasten came back in 1980 to eke out a 50 percent to 48 percent victory over three-term Democratic Senator (and former governor) Gaylord Nelson, long a liberal icon. According to the *Almanac of American Politics* (1986 edition), Kasten was helped by the fact that Nelson, despite possessing a world of respect on Capitol Hill, had "little of the personal ambition and motivation that keeps so many candidates working overtime." As United States Senator, Kasten compiled a mostly conservative record. He was the leading opponent of withholding from savings and brokerage accounts, and served as cosponsor of the Republican alternative to the Bradley-Gephardt tax reform plan. Kasten also served as the prime sponsor of tort reform—the effort to set federal standards limiting product liability. A fiscal conservative, he favored deep cuts in both the capital gains and Social Security payroll taxes. During his first term, Kasten got involved in a civil suit "involving partnerships he had with a bankrupt real estate speculator who went to jail." Shortly before his 1986 reelection campaign, he was arrested for drunk driving.

In 1986, Kasten ran against Democrat Ed Garvey in "one of the year's least edifying brawls." Garvey, onetime attorney for National Football League players (who had involved them in a long and fairly unsuccessful strike), attacked Kasten for being "remote from the public and for drinking on the job." Garvey went so far as to hire a private detective who posed as a reporter to investigate Kasten's financial affairs. Kasten responded with ads attacking Garvey's handling of the football players' fund. When the smoke had cleared, Kasten won by a none-too-impressive margin of 51 percent to 47 percent. Russ Feingold, sensing that Kasten's lack of popularity might make him vulnerable, decided, in November 1986, to make a six-year run for the United States Senate.

For the next five years, Russ Feingold "quietly began organizing a grass-roots movement." Feingold tirelessly crisscrossed the state, visiting each of Wisconsin's seventy-two counties—an annual practice he religiously maintains as a United States Senator. As the 1992 Democratic primary neared, two high-profile candidates threw their hats into the ring: Fifth District Representative Jim Moody, and millionaire businessman Joseph Checota. Within a month of the primary election, Feingold was still running a distant third. But Feingold had both a plan and a strategy: "The plan was to take advantage of the fact that I didn't have money, to make every weakness a strength, to be the one guy in the race who didn't look big and powerful and have the money."

Taking a page from the successful 1990 campaign of Minnesota Senator *Paul Wellstone*, Feingold began running a series of commercials that the *National Journal* likened to "whimsical, low-budget cinema verité." In one two-minute commercial, Feingold visited Checota's mansion, knocked on the door, and then held up a travel brochure on Jamaica, where Jim Moody, Feingold's other Democrat rival, had a vacation home. The commercial ended with a tour of the Feingolds' modest home in Middleton. As he opened the door to one closet, he turned around, looked into the camera, and quipped: "Look, no skeletons!" In another tongue-in-cheek commercial, Elvis Presley endorsed his candidacy. This one caused the *Chicago Tribune* to label Feingold "the Jerry Seinfeld of the 1992 campaign season." Other commercials featured Feingold talking to a man standing on a 12-foot ladder in a hardware store, and another with a man hanging upside-down in a Velcro suit. All the while, Moody and Checota were "cutting each other into shreds with a series of nasty, 'intemperate' ads."

Beneath the levity, Feingold was actually running a deeply serious campaign in which he took a classically liberal approach to many issues—favoring abortion rights, a national health care system, and large defense cuts, and opposing the death penalty, congressional term limits, the balanced budget amendment, the line-item veto, school vouchers, and NAFTA. The political centerpiece of his campaign was "a work of fiscal conservatism": a detailed 82-point plan to reduce the federal deficit by $1 trillion in five years by slashing spending and upping taxes on corporations and the wealthy. The *National Journal* termed it "the sort of proposal that gives pork barrelers a migraine."

Despite being outspent by a better than ten-to-one margin, Feingold pulled off the upset of the year, winning the primary with an unbelievable 70 percent of the vote. Feingold's entry into the general election was likened to a "heat-seeking missile." In the general election campaign, Feingold was able to raise slightly more than $2 million. Senator Kasten, who began the general election campaign behind Feingold by more than 20 points, had, for all intents and purposes, an unlimited supply of cash. Kasten attempted to

paint Feingold as a sixties-type liberal who favored bigger government, higher taxes, and was soft on crime. Eschewing negative tactics, Feingold responded with humor, creativity, and facts, facts, facts. People driving past the Feingold home in Middleton couldn't help but notice that their garage door contained a message painted in bold black letters: Feingold's "contract with the people of Wisconsin." In his "contract," Feingold promised that he would:

- continue to live in Wisconsin;
- continue to send his children to the public schools of Middleton;
- rely on Wisconsin residents for most of his campaign contributions;
- accept no pay raise during his six years in office.

Responding to Kasten's charge that he was soft on crime, Feingold said: "Senator, it's ten days to Halloween. It's a little too early to be scaring people."

Kasten's negative campaign almost worked; from being down more than 20 points in the polls, he pulled to within single digits with just days remaining. It proved to be too little, too late. On election day, Robert Kasten became one of just three incumbent senators to lose his seat in 1992 (the others were Democrats Sanford of North Carolina and Fowler of Georgia). Russell Feingold had turned in "one of the great political stories of a year."

Entering the Senate in January 1993, Russell Feingold sought positions on Appropriations and Human Resources—the committees that primarily control the federal budget and health care—as well as Agriculture. He wound up on the latter, as well as Budget, Foreign Relations, Judiciary, and the Special Committee on Aging. Feingold delivered his maiden speech in the Senate on February 17, 1993. In the speech (heard when only Senator Edward Kennedy was on the floor) the junior Senator from Wisconsin endorsed a bill providing more money for research at the National Institutes of Health for AIDS and women's health issues.

In his first two years in the Senate, Russell Feingold voted less frequently with the Clinton administration than any other Democrat. Mindful of his promise to do everything in his power to reduce the deficit, he "attacked spending wherever he could find it." The objects of his attacks ranged from the Pentagon's medical coverage to helium subsidies and the Superconducting Super Collider. The one issue that kept Feingold's name before the public was campaign finance reform. Along with Arizona Republican John McCain, Feingold fashioned a bill that attempted to place stringent limits on both campaign spending and soft-money contributions. Hotly debated, filibustered, and amended, the bill, as of the first session of the One Hundred and Sixth Congress, was still pending. As Congress became increasingly involved in the Clinton-Lewinsky imbroglio, issues such as McCain-Feingold were put on the political backburner. Despite the inability to get their measure passed, McCain and Feingold said they would not give up.

Arguing that consistency is a crucial aspect of integrity, neither Senator Feingold nor his staff will accept gifts from lobbyists. Any and all gifts that reach his office are handed over to charity. On those occasions when he is invited to a free political dinner for which reimbursement is not feasible, Feingold writes a personal check to the United States Treasury. True to his campaign promise, he did not move Mary and the children to Washington. They still live in Middleton, where Russ manages to return every weekend. True to his campaign promise, Senator Feingold has managed to visit each of Wisconsin's seventy-two counties at least once a year. True to his campaign promise, he has not accepted a raise.

Feingold's 1998 reelection campaign turned out to be a cliffhanger. Running against the representative from his own home First District, conservative Republican Mark W. Neumann, Feingold started the election season with a 15–20 point lead. Running as if the proposed McCain-Feingold bill had already become law, the Senator set himself a "one-dollar-per-voter" spending limit, raising more than three-quarters of his money in-state. His campaign quickly took on the feel of a crusade. Political insiders considered Feingold's stand on campaign finance to be political suicide.

Neuman, bankrolled by conservative interests across the country, managed to raise nearly three times as much money as Feingold. Throughout the fall, Feingold saw his once comfortable lead shrink until, less than a week before election day,

the two were in a virtual dead heat. When questioned as to the wisdom of his campaign fundraising strategy, Feingold told a reporter: "I am happy to risk my seat in the name of trying to change what I believe to be a completely corrupt system."

Sensing that Feingold's chief issue—campaign finance reform—would fail to energize Wisconsin voters, Neumann decided that he was in a perfect position to define the issues to his advantage. Running on a smorgasbord of classic conservative positions and issues—lower taxes, banning partial birth abortion, and Social Security—Neumann began making giant strides in statewide polls. Neumann made such judicious use of his television spots that, shortly before election day, the race was virtually neck-and-neck. When representatives of the national Democratic Party came to Feingold with an offer to pump nearly $500,000 of "soft money" into his campaign, the senator's response was both terse and unequivocal: "Get out of my state." On election day, Russell Feingold managed to eke out a 3-point (51 percent to 48 percent) victory. He will next face reelection in 2004.

Mary Feingold, a former executive assistant to the Wisconsin Broadcasters Association, recently earned a degree in English at the University of Wisconsin, Madison. The Senator's sister, Nancy, is a practicing psychotherapist; brother David is an attorney in Janesville. Dena, the baby of the family, is the first female rabbi to serve a pulpit in the Dairy State. She is currently the spiritual leader of Temple Beth Hillel in Kenosha. Tall and boyish with a sprinkling of gray in his closely cropped black hair, Russell Feingold is "an enthusiastic and untalented golfer."

References

Interview with Rabbi Dena Feingold, February 1998.

Additional biographical information provided by Senator Feingold.

Almanac of American Politics (1982–98 editions).

Janesville Gazette, May 8, 1993, A-1.

Milwaukee Journal, March 3, 1993.

National Journal, January 30, 1993, p. 242.

New Republic, November 23, 1998, pp. 14–15.

Politics in America (1986–98 editions).

Washington Post, November 11, 1992, D-1. 1993.

FEINSTEIN, DIANNE (1933–): *Democrat from California; elected to the remaining two years of an unexpired Senate term, and then a full six-year term (November 4, 1992–present).*

The child of a Jewish father and a Catholic mother, Dianne Emiel Goldman was raised in two religious traditions. As a teenager, she attended the exclusive Convent of the Sacred Heart, where she was the only Jewish student, and went to synagogue on Friday nights. It was the Goldmans' desire that Dianne and her younger sisters, once grown, would make their own choice as to religious affiliation. Speaking about her dual upbringing from the distance of more than twenty-five years, Dianne Feinstein said: "I was brought up supposedly with some Catholic religion and some Jewish, and I was to choose . . . but I don't think that works very well. You are what you are." When she was twenty, Dianne Goldman decided what she was; she officially converted to Judaism.

Born in San Francisco on June 22, 1933, the future Dianne (the unusual spelling is said to be in tribute to her late maternal aunt, Anne) Feinstein was the eldest child of Dr. Leon and Betty (Rosenburg) Goldman. Her father, a prominent surgeon and professor at the University of California at San Francisco, was the son of Orthodox Jews who had immigrated to California from Poland at the end of the nineteenth century. Her mother, who claimed to have been born Pasha Pariskovia in St. Petersburg, Russia, modeled clothes at one of San Francisco's trendiest and most exclusive shops.

Mrs. Goldman suffered from an undiagnosed brain disorder; "she was prone to great bouts of hostility and irrationality that sometimes manifested themselves in really undeserved punishments for us." As a result of their mother's unpredictability, Dianne and her younger sisters, Yvonne and Lynn, "lived in a great deal of fear." Late in her life, with the invention and perfection of the CAT scan, the source of Mrs. Goldman's troubles was finally diagnosed as chronic brain syndrome. Speaking about her

childhood in a 1990 interview, Dianne Feinstein remembered: "It was not always easy with my mother, but she was still a good mother. She took good care of me and my sisters. I think I can say I was happy growing up."

It is apparent that the two stabilizing influences in her young life were her father, a kindly man, and her father's brother Morris, a clothing manufacturer with a passion for politics. Uncle Morris would take his teenage niece to Monday-afternoon sessions of the San Francisco Board of Supervisors, which he derisively referred to as the Board of "Stupidvisors". It was Uncle Morris who planted the seeds of his niece's political ambitions. "Dianne, you get an education and you can do this job," he would tell her.

In 1951, following her graduation from the Convent of the Sacred Heart, Dianne entered Stanford University. After a brief fling at premed—and a D in genetics—she changed majors to political science and history. While at Stanford, she modeled clothes on her uncle's television show, played golf, taught horseback riding, and joined the Young Democrats. As a senior, she ran successfully for student body vice president. While campaigning at a fraternity house, she was severely heckled, picked up, and carried into a shower stall, where she was drenched. Rather than lash out, Feinstein took things in stride; she turned up the heat in her campaigning, and, once in office, used her new-found influence to deny the culprit fraternity a much-sought-after permit for an overnight party.

Upon graduating in 1955, Dianne became an intern at the San Francisco–based CORO Foundation, an organization dedicated to providing promising young adults with concrete experience in the realm of politics and public service. While on assignment to the San Francisco district attorney's office, Dianne met and began working for a thirty-three-year-old prosecutor named Jack Berman. They were married on December 2, 1956. Just a few days shy of eight months later, July 31, 1957, Dianne gave birth to her only child, a daughter named

Katherine Anne. The Bermans were divorced in 1959, leaving Dianne alone with a two-year-old child to raise.

For the next several years, Dianne Goldman Berman took care of her daughter, explored various career paths, and worked as a volunteer in the 1960 presidential campaign of John F. Kennedy. She also studied the Stanislavsky method of acting. After a few less-than-stellar acting appearances and a trip to New York, she put her acting ambitions out to pasture. In 1961, she approached California Governor Edmund G. ("Pat") Brown about the possibility of working for the state. Soon thereafter, Brown appointed the twenty-eight-year-old to the California Women's Board of Terms and Parole, the body that set prison terms and parole conditions for female inmates in the California penal system. Feinstein (known at the time as Berman, of course) served on the board for the next five years, formulating her positions on such issues as abortion and capital punishment.

While serving on the Board of Terms, Feinstein became vehemently opposed to the death penalty: "though you may owe it to your fellow-man to put a criminal out of commission, there is no moral or religious ground that gives you the right to terminate the life of another human being." Years later, she would change her point of view and come to support capital punishment as a means of deterring certain types of heinous crimes: "In those days I saw the criminal justice arena very differently than I do now [1990]. The nature of the problem has changed. . . . I began to see that there are people who have no regard for other people's lives— and over time came to forge the view that by your acts you can abrogate your own right to life." This change of heart, derided by her political opponents as waffling or mere opportunism, would be used against her in future campaigns.

On November 11, 1962, twenty-nine-year-old Dianne Berman married a forty-eight-year-old neurosurgeon named Bertram Feinstein. In 1968, San Francisco Mayor Joseph Alioto appointed her to a blue-ribbon committee on crime. With her increased visibility, she decided to chance a run for the eleven-member San Francisco Board of Supervisors. Bucking the odds—no woman had been elected to the board in nearly half a century—Feinstein, spending an estimated

$100,000, overwhelmed the eighteen other candidates, capturing more votes than any of them. In one fell swoop, she became both a member and president of the Board of Supervisors.

Dianne Feinstein went on to serve nearly nine years on the Board of Supervisors. Additionally, she was its president three times: 1970 to 1972, 1973 to 1976, and in 1978. Not having to work for a living, she became the board's first full-time supervisor. During her tenure, she gained a reputation for being its most knowledgeable authority on criminal justice issues. She pushed for an increase in the number of police officers patrolling the city's streets and sought much-needed revamping of the entire criminal justice system.

San Francisco, often referred to as "Baghdad by the Bay," has long been known as a wide-open city—one eminently tolerant of the aberrant, the wild, and the woolly. Over the years it has been the home of such "dens of iniquity" as the Barbary Coast, Haight-Ashbury, the Castro District, and North Beach.

In 1970, Supervisor Feinstein made the politically unpopular move of tightening zoning restrictions "in order to limit or abolish adult nightclubs and movie theatres." Going against the prevailing political wisdom, which would have had her simply look the other way and maintain the status quo, she instead did what she thought was right. After visiting a local pornographic movie house with members of her staff, the supervisor reported: "We have become a kind of smut capital of the United States. . . . As a woman I feel very strongly about it, because part of what is happening, what is shown on the screens, works to the basic denigration and humiliation of the female." At the same time, Dianne Feinstein was developing quite a following in San Francisco's politcially active gay community. "She conferred legitimacy on many gay activist groups by attending rallies during her campaign, authored and obtained passage of a measure to ban job and hiring discrimination against gays, and favored a state law that would legalize all private sexual conduct between or among consenting adults."

Soon, Dianne Feinstein was the most visible member of the Board of Supervisors. In 1971 and 1975, she ran unsuccessfully for mayor, placing third in both races. The 1975 mayoral race went to State Senator George Moscone. By that time, San Francisco was going through a particularly difficult time of political upheaval. These were the days of the Reverend Jim Jones's People's Temple, the attempted assassination of President Gerald Ford, the Symbionese Liberation Army (which kidnapped heiress Patty Hearst), and the New World Liberation Front. Feinstein herself was the target of two separate bomb attacks, in 1976 and 1977. After the second failed attempt—this at her vacation home in Monterey—she took to carrying a .38-caliber pistol for protection. Feinstein's personal life was particularly difficult as well. In 1975, her father died from cancer. In April 1978, her husband succumbed to the same disease.

The violence of the era began cresting on November 18, 1978, when nine hundred members of Jones's People's Temple committed mass suicide in the wilds of Guyana. Nine days later, November 27, both Mayor Moscone and Supervisor Harvey Milk (the city's first openly gay supervisor) were gunned down in their City Hall offices by a deranged former supervisor named Dan White. Just hours before the double assassination, Feinstein had told a reporter that she would be retiring at the end of her term. By the end of the day, she was the city's acting mayor. She garnered high marks for the manner in which she led San Francisco during its days of shock, anguish, and disbelief. An editorial in the San Francisco Chronicle stated, simply: "She was poised. She was eloquent. She was restrained. And she was reassuring and strong."

Dianne Feinstein served as mayor of San Francisco from 1978 to 1988. Early in her first term, she married Richard C. Blum, a wealthy investment banker. Blum's wealth (reported at somewhere between $40 million and $50 million) would become a source of difficulty a decade later. During her mayoralty, Dianne Feinstein (she maintained the name under which she had entered elective politics) was twice reelected and survived a vicious recall drive. The latter occurred in early 1983, after she had angered the far right by supporting tighter restrictions on handguns, and the far left by vetoing a domestic-partners law "which would have granted some benefits such as insurance, to unmarried couples (straight and gay) who registered at city hall."

Feinstein easily survived the recall drive, receiving more than 80 percent of the vote. This victory all but guaranteed her winning her next election as mayor. During her second term, Feinstein, although popular, angered gays and women by closing gay bathhouses and refusing to close off a street for an abortion rights rally. When questioned about some of her supposedly anti-feminist positions, she stated flatly: "I've lived a feminist life. I had to quit a job because there was no maternity leave. I raised a child as a single mother. I put together legislation. I haven't been a marcher, but I've lived it."

By 1984, Feinstein's popularity and respect among her colleagues had risen to the point that Walter Mondale seriously considered asking her to run for Vice President with him on the Democratic ticket. Feinstein was eventually passed over for another woman, New York Congresswoman Geraldine A. Ferarro. It appears that what ultimately kept Her Honor, the Mayor off the ticket was concern about her husband's finances. Ironically, Ferarro came under repeated attack during the 1984 campaign about *her* husband's financial dealings.

Dianne Feinstein left the office of mayor after 1988, San Francisco City law permitting only two consecutive terms. In 1990, she became the first woman to run for governor of California. She drew as her opponent Republican United States Senator Pete Wilson. Running on a "pro-environment, abortion rights platform that also [included] a plank in favor of the death penalty," Mayor Feinstein was hard-pressed to say precisely where and how she and the Senator differed. He attacked her for leaving San Francisco with a $172 million deficit. Feinstein countered that the shortfall was nothing out of the ordinary—a fact that Wilson, himself a former mayor of San Diego, certainly knew. The Republicans also questioned the finances of Feinstein's husband, Richard Blum, who was underwriting a goodly proportion of his wife's campaign. Feinstein angrily replied: "This is all his business. I have nothing to do with it. It's his—and it was before we were married. . . . Clearly there's a strategy here that's really basically pretty sexist. It's sort of implicit that somehow the woman can't be doing all this by herself."

With few issues dividing or distinguishing them, the campaign devolved into a series of personal charges and countercharges. In the end, Feinstein held Wilson to less than an absolute majority—49 to 46 percent.

In American political history, 1992 will go down as the Year of the Woman. On November 10 of that year, Dianne Feinstein and *Barbara Boxer* were both elected to the United States Senate, thereby becoming the first Jewish women to serve in that body. Feinstein handily defeated (54 to 38 percent) Senator John Seymour, a wealthy political consultant and former state senator from Orange County, whom Wilson appointed to fulfill the final two years of his own six-year term. In winning the election, Feinstein garnered more votes than any senatorial candidate in U.S. history—5,853,621. By previous arrangement, Feinstein was sworn in ahead of Boxer, thereby becoming California's senior Senator.

Feinstein got a seat on the Appropriations Committee, where she could watch out for California's multifaceted economic interests, and the Judiciary, where, after the Clarence Thomas/Anita Hill debacle, it seemed prudent for committee chair Joseph Biden of Delaware to appoint a woman. Although Feinstein did not support the North America Free Trade Agreement (NAFTA) and quietly opposed President Clinton's health-care plan (which she had originally supported), she carved out a generally liberal position on most issues. In her first term, she managed to append an assault weapons ban onto the Clinton crime bill. When Idaho Republican Larry Craig, who was against the ban, challenged Senator Feinstein's knowledge of firearms, she froze him in his tracks by responding: "I know something about what firearms can do; I came to be Mayor of San Francisco as a product of assassination." The assault weapons ban was enacted into law.

In 1994, Senator Feinstein easily won the Democratic primary for the Senate, leading the field with 74 percent of the vote. In the general election, she squared off against multimillionaire Representative Michael Huffington of Santa Barbara. The Republican Huffington, who had spent more than $5 million of his own money to capture his House seat in 1992, spent nearly $30 million of his own funds in 1994, making their Senate race the most expensive in U.S. history. Huffington, who had grown up in modest circumstances in Houston, Texas, went on to attend Stanford and Harvard Business School, and made a fortune in his father's oil and gas business. Huffington and his former wife, Arianna Stassinopolous, a biographer of Pablo Picasso and Maria Callas, moved to Santa Barbara just one year before his race for the U.S. House.

Michael Huffington began the Senate race with an advertising barrage extolling former Secretary of Education William Bennett's *Book of Virtues*. In his commercials, he sought to take the moral high ground, arguing that California suffered from a moral malaise. Feinstein came under attack for casting the deciding vote for the 1993 tax increase, and for being a "career politician." The press had a field day with the Huffingtons, deriding Arianna for being the "Edmund Hillary of social climbing," and publishing stories about her involvement in the Movement for Spiritual Awareness.

Amidst the charges and countercharges, Huffington made a fatal mistake: he endorsed Proposition 187—a measure that would have banned all state spending on illegal immigrants. Feinstein opposed it. Less than a month before the election, it was revealed that the Huffingtons had employed an illegal alien as a nanny—a charge hurled against many people seeking office that year. Even though Huffington offered proof that Feinstein had likewise employed an illegal alien, the charge failed to stick.

On election day, Feinstein eked out a 47 to 45 percent victory. Demanding a recount, Huffington refused to concede defeat until February 1995. Undecided as to whether he would run against Feinstein in 2000 or Barbara Boxer in 1998, Huffington began running negative ads almost as soon as he conceded defeat. In 1998, Huffington effectively ended his political career when he publicly announced that he, the outspoken defender of family values, was gay and divorced his wife.

In early 1998, *Roll Call* magazine estimated Feinstein and Blum's net worth to be $50 million—the fifth-highest in Congress. In 1996, Feinstein was appointed to the Committee on Foreign Relations, where she is the ranking minority member on the Near Eastern and South Asian Affairs subcommittee.

Throughout 1996 and 1997, speculation was rife that Senator Feinstein would run a second time for governor. Public opinion polls were consistently showing her outdistancing any potential Democratic nominee and well ahead of the Republican heir apparent, California Attorney General Dan Lungren. President Clinton took the highly unusual step of calling the Senator and urging her to run—"even at the expense of irritating other Democratic candidates." As pressure continued to mount, Feinstein kept her own counsel. Finally, on January 20, 1998, she announced that she would not run for the office that many assumed she had always wanted. "These are big races, and you really have to want to do them," Mrs. Feinstein said in a telephone conference call with reporters from San Francisco. Her call from President Clinton urging her to run, she averred, had made her realize "the depth of my ambivalence about it." Once she made her decision, she said, it felt like "a huge weight off my shoulders."

The Senator and her husband live in a Tudor house directly across the street from where Dianne Goldman grew up. Feinstein's daughter, Katherine, a former assistant district attorney in San Francisco, is married to Rick Marino. On September 18, 1992, Dianne Feinstein became a grandmother when Katherine gave birth to Eileen Feinstein Marino. The Senator also has three stepchildren: Heidi, Annette, and Eileen. Among her numerous honors and awards are citations from the American Friends of Hebrew University and the Paulist Fathers—somewhat fitting for one raised as both a Jew and a Catholic.

References

Almanac of American Politics (1994–96 editions).

Current Biography, August 1995, pp. 22–27.

New Republic, August 13, 1990, pp. 23 f.

New York Times, January 21, 1998, A10:1.

Jerry Roberts, *Dianne Feinstein: Never Let Them See You Cry* (New York: Harper Collins, 1994).

FIEDLER, ROBERTA FRANCES (1937–):
Republican from California; served three terms in the House (Ninety-seventh through Ninety-ninth Congress; January 3, 1981–January 3, 1987).

Variously described as an outspoken populist and a one-issue candidate, Roberta Frances "Bobbi" Fiedler built a successful political career on an issue that was, strictly speaking, not a congressional issue at all: school busing. A conservative Republican who represented the San Fernando Valley region of Los Angeles, Fiedler was best known as that city's leading opponent of mandatory busing of schoolchildren.

Roberta Frances Horowitz was born in Santa Monica, California, on April 22, 1937. Her father, Jack Horowitz, to whom she was very close, was an energetic man of many interests. During his life, he helped construct the Empire State Building, did movie stunt work, ran a laundry, and started his own construction business. Most important in Bobbi's eyes, her father was also a middleweight boxer. Fighting under the name of Jack "the Milling" Miller (his stepfather's surname), Horowitz became middleweight champ of the Pacific Coast and Mexico. Bobbi loved going to the fights with her father, where "a spectator often gets sprayed with blood and sweat." Unlike her older sister Esther, Bobbi was a tomboy. Despite having to wear leg braces and high-top shoes for a number of years in order to correct severely pigeon-toed feet, Bobbi turned out to be a pretty good athlete. As a child, she played on boys' baseball teams. Years later, she determined that she must have broken her nose—"it takes a little turn in the middle." At thirteen, she lied about her age and joined a women's semi-pro softball team. She played until they found out that the nearly 5-foot, 7-inch girl was five years too young to be a member of their league. By the time she was eighteen, Bobbi had reached her full height of nearly 5 feet, 10 inches.

Since the Horowitzes were the only Jewish family in the area where she grew up, Bobbi was subjected to "name-calling and rock-throwing" during her formative years. She is fairly philosophical about the bigotry: "Although it hurts at the time, it also helps you to build some strength and resiliency about the realities of life . . . that helps you to identify what really is important in your life, what the values are that you have. And you learn to step away from that kind of super-

ficial thing." She turned to her father for direction, and he taught her his philosophy of life: you are as good as, but no better than, anyone else.

Bobbi Horowitz started working by the time she reached eighth grade. Her first job, at age thirteen, was wrapping gifts at the Brentwood Market and Toy Shop. She continued working odd-jobs through high school and while attending both Santa Monica City College and Santa Monica Technical School, where she majored in advertising art and minored in philosophy. Originally intending to go into advertising, she soon found out "that would mean drawing cans of beans and electric cameras." Unhappy with advertising, she did some interior decorating, worked for an accounting firm, and, at age twenty-two, married a young pharmacist. Interestingly, nowhere in the many interviews she has granted has she mentioned her former husband's first name—only that his surname was Fiedler. Within a year of their marriage, Bobbi Fiedler gave birth to her daughter Lisa. Two years later came son Ron. She stayed at home raising the children while her husband ran his pharmacy. This arrangement lasted until Ron was six years old. Then Bobbi joined her husband, becoming the pharmacy manager.

In 1976, a local court issued a district-wide busing order, which produced "some of the most absurd—and for parents, maddening—results imaginable." Fiedler, now living in Northridge in the San Fernando Valley, learned that her children might be subjected to the court order, which would mean being bused to a school nearly fifty miles away. Irate, she soon became active in her local PTA, attending meetings and becoming politicized. After a few months of getting the lay of the land, Fiedler helped found an anti-busing group known as BUSTOP. As one of the group's leading spokespersons, Fiedler's visibility began growing in the Valley; soon she became a candidate for the board of education.

A series of crucial developments ensued for the forty-year-old Fiedler. She sold the pharmacy, divorced her husband after eighteen years of marriage, and ran for the Los Angeles Board of Education. Of her divorce, Fiedler said: "It had nothing to do with becoming active in politics. . . . Often there are problems when there are two careers, but this just happened to be a situation where that was not the case, where we were just moving in different directions."

Running as a Republican (she was a Democrat until 1970) against pro-busing board member Robert Doctor, Bobbi Fiedler turned her campaign into a one-woman crusade. On election day, she easily defeated Doctor. In her nearly three years on the board of education, Bobbi Fiedler helped pass Proposition I, which led directly to the end of mandatory busing in Los Angeles. Turning her sights beyond the City of Angels, Fiedler traveled to Washington in 1979, to help Representative Ron Mottl, an Ohio Democrat, lobby Congress for a federal anti-busing amendment. As mentioned above, busing is not really a congressional issue. While Congress might vote for a statute or constitutional amendment forbidding busing in various circumstances, it is, politically speaking, a rather clumsy way to address an inherently local situation. Nonetheless, Mottl was spearheading the effort to pass just such a constitutional amendment.

While making the rounds lobbying members of Congress, Bobbi Fiedler came to the office of her own representative, James C. Corman, chairman of the House Democratic Campaign Committee. A ten-term incumbent and high-ranking member of the powerful Ways and Means Committee, Corman perturbed Fiedler by his "lack of responsiveness to her views." Once she returned to the Valley, Fiedler looked into Corman's record on other issues, and concluded that "his views did not jibe with those of his constituency." Buoyed by the young Valley families that had supported her candidacy for the board of education, Fiedler decided to challenge Corman for the Twenty-first District seat.

In 1979, the Twenty-first Congressional District was a decidedly family-oriented district, taking in the northeastern corner of the San Fernando Valley. Excluding the high-income enclaves of Sherman Oaks and Encino, it contained North Hollywood with its large Jewish population, the middle-class suburbs of Van Nuys and Northridge, and Pacoima, which housed the Valley's small black ghetto. Fiedler easily won the Republican primary over Patrick O'Brien and then set her sights on Corman. Riding the crest of voter anger over the busing issue, Fiedler attacked Corman for being out of touch with his constituents, especially on the issue of "massive forced busing." Corman, in turn, portrayed Fiedler as a one-issue candidate who did not have the skills, ability, or knowledge to be an effective member of Congress.

Fiedler kept pounding away on the busing issue. "As for the voters, what issue could be more important? The assumptions on which they built their lives, selected their neighborhoods, and planned their families were all under challenge." She responded to the one-issue charge by swearing allegiance to the Republican platform of candidate Ronald Reagan. On election day, while Reagan was beating Carter 51 percent to 38 percent in the Twenty-first Congressional District, Fiedler found herself elected by the slimmest of margins—752 votes out of more than 150,000 cast. Political analysts believe that Corman would have won the election if Jimmy Carter had not conceded defeat while the polls in California were still open. (Once people in California heard that Carter had conceded, hundreds—perhaps thousands—left the voting lines, neglecting the other issues and candidates on the ballot.)

In her first term, Fiedler lobbied for, and received, a seat on the House Budget Committee—the first-ever Republican freshman appointed to the panel. Within a matter of months, she became well known to her House colleagues through two false starts: the "incident," and "deep meow." The "incident" involved a breach of House protocol. During floor debate on the defense budget, North Carolina Democrat Bill Hefner offered an amendment that would raise defense spending in the Democratic budget alternative. Fiedler publicly called Hefner down for not having supported the amendment in committee. Moreover, Fiedler charged, Hefner had conveniently absented himself from the committee room at the time of the original vote. By pointing out that Hefner had left the room when the vote came up, Fiedler was implying that his amendment was a partisan last-ditch effort to entice conservatives away from the Reagan-backed proposal. In effect, she was calling his motives and integrity into question. House Majority Leader Jim Wright, a Texas Democrat, interrupted debate to tell Fiedler that House tradition discourages members from "impugning the honor or the integrity or the intentions" of other distinguished members. Fiedler was unrepentant.

"Deep meow" was a contretemps between Fielder and Colorado Representative Pat Schroeder. The Democrat Schroeder, a member of the House Armed Services Committee, introduced an amendment that would require the President to cut $8 billion worth of fraud and waste from the defense budget. Fiedler voiced her opposition, calling Schroeder's amendment "a meat-ax approach to the defense budget." "The Gentlelady's amendment," Fielder said, "cuts blindly." According to one reporter covering the colloquy, "this applied the old meat-ax to any bond of sisterhood that might have been struck between Fiedler and Schroeder."

Schroeder, who had already served three terms in the House, believed that the eighteen women members of Congress had to "hang together or we all hang separately." She had already become perturbed some months earlier when Fiedler would not contribute $2,500 of her government House allowance to join the Congressional Women's Caucus. Said Schroeder: "She let the other side [Republicans] use her to counter [my amendment] and make us look like two fighting cats. Women never did that [to each other] before. We've tried to avoid that media image of two women scratching at each other. You don't go around reinforcing stereotypes. It was really nasty. You could almost hear the hissing in the microphone."

Despite her false start, Fiedler was ultimately named Outstanding Freshman in the Republican class of 1980. With reapportionment after the 1980 census, her district was merged with that of Barry Goldwater, Jr. Luckily for Fiedler, Goldwater decided to give up his House seat in order to run for the United States Senate. With Goldwater out of the way, Fiedler beat her Democratic opponent, George Margolis, by a better than three-to-one margin.

In her second term, Fiedler supported most of the Reagan administration's budget and tax proposals, and received a perfect 100 rating from the American Conservative Union. Despite her strong support for the president's programs, the *Almanac of American Politics* described her as being "the California Republican most likely to vote against the Reagan administration, although she certainly does not belong in the ranks of Northeastern liberals." The one area where Fiedler did exercise a modicum of independence was on "womens" issues. In 1983, she was one of six GOP women in Congress to write the President, urging prompt consideration of the Equal Rights Amendment and passage of a Women's Economic Equity Act.

In 1984, Bobbi Fiedler was chosen to second Ronald Reagan's nomination at the Republican National Convention in Dallas. That November, she was once again reelected by a better than three-to-one margin. Bobbi Fiedler's political star was on the rise. In 1985, she decided that the time was right to run for the United States Senate seat held by liberal Democrat Alan Cranston. Fiedler faced a tough Republican primary battle against no fewer than three strong candidates. Her campaign collapsed before it really began, when in January 1986, she and her campaign manager (and future husband), Paul Clarke, were charged with bribery under an obsolete state law never previously invoked. Clarke and Fiedler were indicted after State Senator Ed Davis charged that they had tried to bribe him by offering to help retire his campaign debt if he withdrew. The amount of the bribe, according to Davis, was $100,000. Although the indictment was dropped in February, Fiedler's chances of winning the primary were irreparably damaged. Palo Alto Congressman Ed Zschau won the Republican primary in a walk (Fiedler received only 8 percent), and then lost to Cranston by less than 120,000 votes out of more than 7.2 million cast. It turned out to be the most expensive Senate election in American history up to that time: the two candidates spent nearly $23 million between them.

Shortly after their indictment was quashed, Bobbi Fiedler and Paul Clarke married. With her congressional career over, Fiedler returned to Northridge, where she became a business consultant. In January 1987, she became a twice-weekly political commentator on the local ABC affiliate. In this role, she engaged liberal commentator Bill Press in "spirited verbal sparring on topics ranging from the death penalty to surrogate motherhood." While working for KABC, she began thinking about running for mayor of Los Angeles. These plans came to an end when she was abruptly fired by the television station in July 1987. Although the station said her removal was due to financial concerns, it was able to hire a new sportscaster for a reported $750,000 annually, and made its anchor, Paul Moyer, the city's first $1-million-a-year newscaster.

In the mid-1990s, Fiedler took the lead in a campaign aimed at splitting the sprawling, population-rich San Fernando Valley from Los Angeles. Claiming that "for every $1 we send to Los Angeles we get back less than 40 cents," Fiedler argued that "the only way we are going to get our fair share of the tax pie is [to break away]." In 1997, Fiedler estimated that if Valley voters managed to pass the secession bill, a new city could be created in "from five to eight years." "This is ultimately going to land in the Supreme Court," she told the *Los Angeles Times:* "there will be that many legal challenges that will merit taking it there."

In December 1993, Governor Pete Wilson appointed Fiedler to the State Lottery Commission for a five-year term.

In August 1993, Paul Clarke died of lung cancer. Nearly five years later, in May 1998, Bobbi Fiedler wed political activist Harry Coleman in a ceremony that was billed "the social/political event of the season." Coleman, also active in the Valley-secession movement, said he hoped to spend "many happy years together promoting the biggest, nastiest divorce since Donald and Ivana Trump [i.e., that of the Valley from Los Angeles]."

References

Almanac of American Politics (1980–88 editions).

Los Angeles Times, November 29, 1981, III, 11:6; January 30, 1986, II, 3:3; August 26, 1987, II, 1:1; December 28, 1993, II 2:1.

Politics in America (1980–88 editions).

FILNER, BOB (1942–): *Democrat from California; has served four terms in the House (One Hundred and Third through One Hundred and Sixth Congress; January 3, 1993–present).*

To the American mind, sunny Southern California is the nation's most laid-back, most anything-goes part of the country. It is the home of surfers and swingers, of Hollywood actors and environmental activists. As with all stereotypes, this one carries a grain of truth. But there is another Southern California—populated by white supremacists and anti-Semites, John Birchers and neo-Nazis. Just ask Fiftieth District Representative Bob Filner of San Diego.

In his first race for the House in 1992, Filner's Republican opponent, Tony Valencia, took great pains to remind voters that Filner was a Jew. When one debate turned to a discussion of imprisoned junk bond dealer Michael Milken (of Los Angeles' San Fernando Valley, about 110 miles to the north), Valencia said: "Let me state that Michael Milken is of the Jewish religion, as is Bob Filner." On another occasion, Valencia said that Jews "tend to turn on each other" because Milken was "turned in by a fellow of the same religion in New York," and that "the process is cyclical . . . like Judas and Jesus Christ." A lesser man might have gone off like a Roman candle. Not Filner. As a young man, he had faced even greater prejudice and bigotry—in the jails of Mississippi.

The Filner family came to the United States from Lithuania in 1906. The Congressman's maternal grandparents, the Frishmans, came from Russia around the same time. Both families settled in Pittsburgh. Bob Filner was born in Pittsburgh on September 4, 1942. Both Bob and his brother, Bernard, were educated in the Pittsburgh public school system and received formal Jewish training through age thirteen. The Frishman side of the family was devoutly Orthodox.

Following his high school graduation, Bob Filner went off to Cornell University, where he received a B.A. in chemistry. During the summer of 1961, he traveled south as a Freedom Rider in Mississippi. Joining a group staging a sit-in at a lunch counter, the nineteen-year-old Filner was arrested and spent nearly two months in a Mississippi jail. This experience helped shape Filner's continuing commitment to social change in the name of human progress.

In 1969, Filner received an M.A. from the University of Delaware. The next year, he moved to San Diego, where he became an assistant professor of history at San Diego State University. Three years later, in 1973, he received his Ph.D. in the history of science from Cornell. In addition to his teaching duties, Bob Filner quickly became active in the San Diego Jewish community, serving on the boards of both the Jewish Community Relations Council and the Anti-Defamation League. Additionally, while working on his Ph.D., he served a short stint as an aide to Senator Hubert H. Humphrey, Democrat of Minnesota. By the time of his election to Congress in November 1992, Filner was the director of the University's Lipinsky Institute for Judaic Studies.

In 1979, Bob Filner won a seat on the San Diego School Board. As a school board member, he worked for "mandatory homework, tougher graduation requirements, stricter discipline and attendance regulations." In 1983, he gave up his school board seat in order to wage an unsuccessful campaign for the San Diego City Council. Four years later, after Councilman Uvaldo Martinez pleaded guilty to "misusing credit cards," Filner ran again and won—despite the fact that the district was heavily Latino. In 1991, Filner's Latino constituents reelected him with a rousing 70 percent of the vote. While on the city council, he focused attention on joint local-federal concerns and formed a "graffiti patrol with a graffiti hotline" to address the problem of "street artists" fouling up local neighborhoods. Among his more successful ventures were the creation of a local defense conversion plan (San Diego is a Navy town) and the building of more parks.

Following the 1990 census, San Diego got several new congressional districts. Filner decided to run in the newly created Fiftieth District, which had a near minority-majority constituency of blacks and Hispanics. Filner faced two well-known Democrats in the June 1992 primary: former four-term Representative Jim Bates and longtime (since 1966) State Assemblyman and Senator Waddie Deddeh. Luckily for Filner, both candidates carried negative baggage into the primary. Bates had lost his seat in 1990 to Republican Randy ("Duke") Cunningham, after having been disciplined by the House on charges of sexual harassment. He also had eighty-nine overdrafts on the House bank.

Deddeh, seventy-one years old, had recently undergone open heart surgery, was pro-life, and "apparently failed to make timely payment of income taxes."

Filner campaigned tirelessly, and earned the strong backing of blacks, Latinos, and labor unionists. On election day, he took the primary with 26 percent to Senator Deddeh's 23 percent and Bates's 20 percent. The lone Latino candidate, Juan Carlos Vargas, ran last with 19 percent. As mentioned above, Tony Valencia, Filner's Republican opponent in the general election took great pains to remind Latino voters of the professor's religion. His attempts at outright bigotry failed; Filner won with 57 percent of the vote.

As a new member of the House, Filner immediately went to work to make his voice heard among his freshman colleagues. They elected him freshman class treasurer, but failed to heed his plea that they vote as a bloc on reform proposals. Filner was assigned to Public Works and Transportation and Veterans' Affairs—two important posts for a city in which more than 20 percent of the economy is directly tied to the defense industry. (Next to the United States Navy, San Diego's biggest employers are General Dynamics, Hughes Aircraft, and Teledyne.)

During his first term in the House, Filner devoted an inordinate amount of time and energy to the issue of defense conversion. He advocated "requiring the federal government to return dollar for dollar whatever is lost to local economies due to defense cuts." This aid, he argued, should be in the form of "job training, health care, crime prevention and construction of public infrastructure." Filner opposed the North American Free Trade Agreement (NAFTA), calling it "a trickle-down treaty designed to benefit big corporations and exploit our continent's resources—both human and environmental," and was one of the founders of the congressional anti-NAFTA caucus. After the treaty passed, Filner "tried to get trade facilities working on the border [and] worked to fund construction of an international treatment plant for raw sewage coming into San Diego from Mexico." At the same time, he attempted to get his city exempted from Clean Water Act standards. Filner was easily reelected in 1994 with 57 percent of the vote.

Filner, whose political pedigree is "practical politics defined by a true commitment to progressive ideals," regularly received 100 percent ratings from the AFL-CIO and the liberal Americans for Democratic Action. Pat Robertson's Christian Coalition regularly gave him a zero rating.

During his second term in the House, Filner ran afoul of the politically powerful insurance industry. In sponsoring a bill to end the "$1 billion to $1.5 billion tax advantage for the immensely profitable mutual life insurance companies," Filner courted political suicide. Enter Juan Carlos Vargas, the man who had come in last in the 1992 primary. Although Filner's bill got nowhere in the House, the insurance industry got behind Vargas's candidacy in 1996, pumping untold tens of thousands of dollars into his campaign coffers. Their message was clear: don't mess with the life insurance lobby. To make matters worse, leading California Republicans endorsed Vargas rather than their own candidate—Baptist minister Jim Baize.

Filner sent an SOS to the White House political officer, Deputy Chief of Staff Harold Ickes, Jr. Despite the fact that Filner had supported the Clinton administration 91 percent of the time, Ickes claimed that his hands were tied. "Rules are rules," Ickes told Filner. "That means no interference in contested primaries." In place of President Bill Clinton and Vice President Albert Gore, the White House did manage to send then-Housing Secretary Henry Cisneros out to San Diego on Filner's behalf. With only weeks to go, Vargas looked to be in the lead. But he had not considered Bob Filner's formidable political skills. On election day, Filner bested Vargas 18,809 to 15,673.

During the general election against Jim Baize, anti-Semitic fliers referring to Filner as the "Anti-Christ Jew for Congress" began showing up all over the Fiftieth District. The pamphlets, containing "swastikas, racial epithets and a local San Diego phone number," were found inside school newspapers, and both on and near the campus of San Diego State University. A reporter from *Roll Call* dialed the number on the pamphlet and reached the answering machine of a group calling itself the White Preservation Congress. The voice on the machine proclaimed the organization to be "devoted to the genetic survival of the white race as the one and only way we can re-establish a progressive civilization, nation and religion." When informed of the pamphlets, Republican Baize merely commented: "I'm sorry to hear this." Despite the opposition's crude tactics, Filner beat Baize nearly two-to-one, and was returned to Washington for a third term. Filner ran unopposed for a fourth term in 1998.

Bob Filner is married to the former Jane Merrill. Raised as a Catholic, she became a convert to Judaism. The Filners have two children: daughter Erin, born in 1970, and son Adam, born in 1973. Erin is currently working as a middle-school teacher in Westchester, New York; Adam is a college student in Northern California.

References

Correspondence with Bob Filner.
Almanac of American Politics (1994–98 editions).
Politics in America (1994–98 editions).
Roll Call, November 4, 1996, p. 13.
Washington Post, March 21, 1996, A-17:1.

FINE, SIDNEY ASHER (1903–1982): *Democrat from New York; served three terms in the House (Eighty-second through Eighty-fourth Congress; January 3, 1951–January 2, 1956).*

In the summer of 1950, shortly after being renominated to the congressional seat he had held since 1940, Congressman Walter A. Lynch decided instead to run for governor of New York. By vacating his Twenty-third District seat (for what turned out to be an unsuccessful gubernatorial bid), Lynch opened the way for State Senator Sidney Fine to move from Albany to Washington. Lynch went on to be elected to the New York State Supreme Court in 1954. Two years later, Fine became Lynch's colleague on the court.

Sidney Asher Fine was born in New York City on September 14, 1903. Little is known of his family or early life. He graduated from City College of New York in 1923 and received his law degree from Columbia University in 1926. While building up his legal practice, Fine became a Democratic stalwart. He was elected to the New York State Assembly in 1945, and moved up to the State Senate in 1947. During his years in the state legislature, Fine specialized in civil service and labor affairs. Upon Walter Lynch's retirement from Congress, Fine, a candidate running on both the Democratic and Liberal Party tickets, easily won election to the Eighty-second Congress from the Bronx. During his brief congressional career (1951–56), Fine was a member of the House Judiciary Committee and the Committees on Interior and Insular Affairs, and Government Operations.

While serving his third term in the House, Fine decided to run for the New York State Supreme Court. Following his election to that body in November 1955, he resigned his congressional seat on January 3, 1956, at the beginning of the second session of the Eighty-fourth Congress. His seat was taken by Tammany Democrat James C. Healy, who would be defeated eight years later by *James H. Scheuer*. Fine went on to spend two decades (1956–75) as an associate justice of the Appellate Division. His brightest hour came in 1973, when he was given the lion's share of the credit for mediating a quick settlement of a strike by New York City firefighters. Fine retired from the high court in 1975, and spent the next several years as special counsel to the Manhattan firm of Fine, Tofei, Saxl, Berelson & Berandes; the Fine in the firm's name being his son, Burton Fine.

Sidney Fine was married twice. His first wife, Libby, who predeceased him, was the mother of Fine's two sons—the aforementioned Burton, and Ralph, who became a judge in Milwaukee. Following his first wife's death, Fine married Annette, who survived him. Sidney Fine died at New York's Mount Sinai Hospital on April 13, 1982, and was buried at Old Montefiore Cemetery in Queens, New York.

References
Biographical Directory of the United States Congress, 1774–1989, p. 996.
New York Times, April 14, 1982, 31:1.

FINGERHUT, ERIC D. (1959–): *Democrat from Ohio; served one term in the House (One Hundred and Third Congress; January 3, 1993–January 3, 1995).*

Even before he was elected to the House of Representatives, Eric Fingerhut announced that when (not if) he took his seat in the One Hundred and Third Congress, he would seek to lead the freshman class of 1992. True to his word, the sixty-three Democratic freshmen chose him to be their unofficial chief. Moreover, once Congress went into session, Fingerhut was named co-chair of the Democratic freshmen's Task Force on Reform. That mixture of *chutzpa* and absolute self-assurance certainly helped get him elected; it also, to a great extent, brought about his defeat after only one term. "[Eric] likes to think he's the moral conscience and the only one who knows what's right," a former colleague lamented.

Eric Fingerhut was born in the University Heights section of Cleveland on May 6, 1959. Politics was something in his blood; his aunt was a union organizer who once ran for Ohio secretary of state on the Socialist ticket. His parents were "more conventional Democrats." He received his Jewish education at Congregation Beth Am, where, as an adult, he became a Sunday School teacher. Following his graduation from Cleveland Heights High School (where he was inducted into the Hall of Fame), Fingerhut went on to Northwestern University, where he got his bachelor's degree with highest honors, and Stanford University, where he was a member of the law review. Receiving his law degree in 1984, Fingerhut returned to Cleveland, where he became a staff attorney for the Older Persons Law Office of the Cleveland Legal Aid Society. Moving into private practice, he joined the Cleveland firm of Hahn, Loeser & Parks.

From 1986 through 1989, Fingerhut was chairman of Common Cause Ohio, chaired Cleveland Works, a "welfare recipients' job training program," and headed a local group trying to close a toxic waste facility. In 1989, he managed Michael White's successful campaign for mayor of Cleveland. Following his election, White named Fingerhut director of his transition team and Special Assistant to the Mayor. In November 1990, Eric Fingerhut was elected to the Ohio Senate, where he served until his election to Congress. While in the Senate, he worked on recycling, clean air, campaign finance reform, and gun control. On this latter issue, Fingerhut authored a gun safety bill that "required all first-time gun buyers to take a one-time gun safety course."

During the early days of the One Hundred and Second Congress, Cleveland-area representatives Dennis Eckart and Ed Feighan announced that they would not be running for reelection. The forty-one-year-old Eckart's announcement came as a bit of a shock; he was widely popular, had a seat on the Energy and Commerce Committee, and could easily have been reelected. Feighan's retirement came as no surprise; with 397 overdrafts, he had been named as one of the twenty-two abusers of the House bank. Fingerhut, fresh from his successful election to the Ohio State Senate, joined eight rival Democrats in seeking the nomination for Feighan's Nineteenth District seat.

The Nineteenth Congressional District of Ohio takes in a "very irregularly-shaped hunk" of northeastern Ohio and the old Western Reserve—the part of Ohio that once belonged to Connecticut. It includes all of Lake and Ashtabula Counties, as well as "a motley collection of the Cuyahoga County suburbs of Cleveland," including the predominantly Jewish Pepper Pike and Beachwood.

Though Fingerhut's official residence was outside the district, he won the Democratic nomination with 24 percent of the vote. His closest rivals in the nine-candidate race were Cuyahoga auditor Tim McCormack and former Cleveland mayor Dennis ("The Menace") Kucinich. The winner in the five-way Republican primary, Lake County commissioner Robert Gardner, gave Fingerhut a run for his money. Fingerhut ran on the issues of job creation and health-care reform, "and added a strong emphasis on campaign finance reform." Fingerhut backed NAFTA with some changes, and said that Israel must become economically self-sufficient. Gardner ran into trouble with the Jewish voters in the district by calling for a U.S. policy in the Middle East that was "balanced" rather than clearly "pro-Israel." Fingerhut's campaign was greatly aided when both Dennis Eckart and House Majority Leader Richard Gephardt, a Missouri Democrat, came to the district to speak on his behalf. Though vastly outspent and "less articulate and polished than Fingerhut," Gardner managed to run a surprisingly successful campaign, losing by less than 12,000 votes out of nearly 165,000 votes cast.

Fingerhut came into the House like a ball of fire. His "aggressive efforts on behalf of the freshmen" hurt him in the eyes of the Democratic leadership, who admonished him to be realistic. Fingerhut was passed over for his first-choice committee assignment, Public Works and Transportation, but landed his two other choices—Science, Space, and Technology and Foreign Affairs. The former assignment was critical to his district: the NASA/Lewis Research Center, employing thousands of locals, was located near Cleveland–Hopkins International Airport.

Overflowing with ideas, Fingerhut produced a 16-page outline for economic revitalization for his district, boldly entitled "A New Deal for the 19th," and came out with "a stringent welfare bill" that "didn't go anywhere." Fingerhut learned the painful lesson that, in Congress, "the best way to get along is to go along." He was persuaded to vote for President Clinton's budget and tax plans, and to water down his draconian ban on lobbyists' gifts to members and their staffs. He also got himself into trouble with the people back home. After inviting H. Ross Perot to come speak at a town forum, Fingerhut raised the ire of a local labor union executive who said: "I think Eric has a short memory of how he got elected."

Worse, he embarrassed himself when, "after he had long denounced franked mail, he decided to send out his own in the election year." When queried by the local press as to why he had gone back on his former position, he weakly responded: "The level of misunderstanding of what we did and didn't do is astounding. The positive aspects got overwhelmed by the painful parts." During his reelection campaign, Fingerhut was taken to task by the *News Herald* of local Lake County, which wryly commented: "Fingerhut . . . talks a great game about being in favor of change and heading in new directions, but his votes reveal the fundamental hypocrisy of his words."

Fingerhut also enraged many of his senior colleagues with his good-government efforts. He became known on Capitol Hill as "the [jerk] who said we couldn't park at the National Airport." He also introduced a pay freeze for Congress, legislation forbidding lobbyists from presenting gifts to members, and a bill making the body "subject to the same civil rights and workers' rights laws as private-sector employees."

In his ill-fated reelection campaign, Fingerhut faced Lake County Prosecutor Steve LaTourette, who had gained renown for winning thirteen convictions in a cult murder case. Fingerhut attacked the Republican LaTourette for opposing gun control with the accusation that "Washington will never change [him]." For his part, LaTourette charged Fingerhut with being "soft on crime, and hypocritically using the frank." In November 1994, Eric Fingerhut's brief congressional career came to an end; LaTourette defeated him 48 percent to 43 percent.

Following his defeat, Fingerhut rejoined Hahn, Loeser & Parks, and spent the next four years working as an analyst for the Federation for Community Planning, "a research and advocacy organization that deals with health and human service issues." In November 1998, Eric Fingerhut was reelected to his old seat in the Ohio State Senate. When asked if history would repeat itself and he would once again use his state senate seat as a launching pad for an eventual return to Congress, Fingerhut said "absolutely not." Speaking of his return to Columbus, Fingerhut said: "I see a real continuity here. State and local governments are taking on increased importance as government-funded programs are being spun off to states, cities and counties."

References

Almanac of American Politics (1994–96 editions).
New Republic, October 11, 1994, p. 22.
Politics in America (1994–96 editions).

FISCHER, ISRAEL FREDERICK (1858–1940):
Republican from New York; served two terms in the House (Fifty-fifth and Fifty-sixth Congress; March 4, 1895–March 3, 1899).

Historians generally point to Louis D. Brandeis, Benjamin N. Cardozo, and Felix Frankfurter as the three titans of American-Jewish jurisprudence. Brandeis (1856–1941), the first Jew named to the Supreme Court, received his nomination from President Woodrow Wilson in 1916, and served until 1939. Cardozo (1870–1938) and Frankfurter (1882–1965), both FDR appointees, served on the nation's highest court from 1932 to 1938 and from 1939 to 1962, respectively. A full sixteen years before Brandeis's appointment, a Jew was already presiding in the federal judiciary: Israel Frederick Fischer. Moreover, the unknown Fischer served longer than any of the aforementioned judicial icons—a full thirty-three years.

The son of Isaac and Hannah Sarner Fischer, Israel F. Fischer was born on Lewis Street in New York City on August 17, 1858. Educated at Cooper Union, Fischer read law for three years in the offices of Henry S. Bennett and was admitted to the New York bar in 1879. Shortly after his thirtieth birthday, he moved to the Prospect Park section of Brooklyn, where, in September 1895, he married Clara Groedel. They had one daughter, Ruth (Thurston) Fischer. From 1880 to 1886, he practiced law with the firm of Davidson and Fischer. In 1886, he formed a new firm, Cook, Salmon, and Fischer, with which he remained until 1895.

In 1889, Fischer succeeded another Jew, Ernst Nathan, as chairman of the Republican executive committee of Kings County. Simultaneously, he served as a member of the party's state executive committee. As the Republican leader of his county, he was easily elected to Congress from the Fourth District in 1894 and again in 1896. No significant records exist of Fisher's congressional activities.

Israel Fischer was defeated for reelection in 1898. The next year, President William McKinley nominated him to be a member of the United States Board of General Appraisers, a nine-member tribunal that acted on appeals and interpretations of the tariff laws by local boards of appraisers throughout the United States and its territories. Fischer's nomination ran into immediate problems because of his religion. Representatives of at least three large national firms tried to persuade McKinley to remove Fischer's name from consideration, arguing that "a Jew could not be trusted in such a delicate position." To his credit, McKinley turned a deaf ear to this allegation and Fischer's nomination was approved. After he had served on the board for three years, McKinley's successor, Theodore Roosevelt, appointed Fischer as one of the American representatives to the International Customs Congress.

In 1926, Congress reorganized the Board of General Appraisers by establishing the United States Customs Court. President Calvin Coolidge appointed Fischer its first chief judge, a position he retained until his retirement in 1931. From 1931 until his death, he served as senior judge, assigning other members of the court to the country's various judicial districts. In his latter years, Judge Fischer would occasionally travel to a district court in order to hear a case.

A Reform Jew, Israel Fischer was for many years a leader of the Union Temple on Brooklyn's Eastern Parkway. Fischer died in New York City on March 16, 1940, and was buried in Maimonides Cemetery in Brooklyn.

References
American Jewish Year Book, vol. 24, p. 139; vol. 42, p. 478.
Biographical Directory of American Jews.
New York Times, March 17, 1940, 48:7.
Universal Jewish Encyclopedia.
Who's Who in America, vol. 4.
Who Was Who in American Jewry, 1926, 1928, 1938.

FOX, JON D. (1947–): *Republican from Pennsylvania; served two terms in House (One Hundred and Fourth and One Hundred and Fifth Congress; January 3, 1995–January 4, 1999).*

The midterm election of 1994 was one of the most dramatic in American history. Running on a conservative platform it called the "Contract With America," the Republican Party wrested control of both houses of Congress from the hands of the Democrats for the first time in forty years. Of the eighty-four newly elected Republicans (eleven in the Senate, seventy-three in the House), only one was Jewish: Representative Jon D. Fox of Pennsylvania's Thirteenth District. Defeated in his first run for the House (1992) by *Majorie Margolies Mezvinsky* (by a mere 1,373 votes), Fox campaigned hard throughout the next two years in order to win a rematch against the woman known locally as "MMM." His margin of victory in 1994 was a slightly more comfortable 8,181 votes (he received 49 percent) out of nearly 195,000 cast.

Jon Fox was born in Philadelphia on April 22, 1947, one of William L. and Elaine (Brickman) Fox's three children. Jon's paternal grandfather, Benjamin Fox, had emigrated from Russia in the late nineteenth century, while his maternal great-grandfather Brickman had come from Germany at about the same time. Jon Fox, along with his brother Lawrence and sister Caren (Fires), was educated in the public schools of suburban Philadelphia.

Among the students at Jon's high school, Cheltenham, was one Benjamin Netanyahu, destined to become Prime Minister of Israel. Although the two didn't really know each other (Netanyahu was two years ahead of Fox), the future Congressman watched the young Israeli play soccer. "Bibi studied assiduously; Jon like[ed] to enjoy himself, like the rest of us," a friend commented when asked if the two had known each other. Shortly after Netanyahu's election as Israel's Prime Minister in 1996, Fox was chosen to chair the congressional host committee for the Israeli leader's first official visit to

Capitol Hill. At a luncheon in Philadelphia, Fox told about having watched Bibi play high school soccer; Fox noted that even in high school, Netanyahu was "a very focused young man, very competitive. . . . we knew he was a man of destiny."

Fox received his formal religious education at the Conservative Adath Jeshurun of Greater Philadelphia, the synagogue to which his family has belonged for four generations. He was bar mitzvah at Adath Jeshurun in 1960 and confirmed in 1963. While in high school, he was an officer of the local United Synagogue Youth. Jon Fox graduated from Pennsylvania State University in 1969, where he was class president. He received his J.D. from Widener University in Chester, Pennsylvania, in 1975, and was admitted to the Pennsylvania bar shortly thereafter. Between 1969 and 1975, Fox served in the United States Air Force Reserve and did a stint as an intern in Washington, D.C. After serving four years (1976–80) as a Montgomery County assistant district attorney, Fox was elected to the Abington Township Board of Commissioners. From that position, he went on to serve four terms in the Pennsylvania House of Representatives, where he was a member of the Education and Appropriations Committees, and was appointed Republican chairman of the Special Education Subcommittee. Leaving the Pennsylvania House in 1991, Fox was elected to the Montgomery County Board of Commissioners, where he established a reputation as a fiscal conservative and social moderate. Fox paid particular attention to the needs of his constituents, becoming, in the words of the *Philadelphia Inquirer*, a "zen master of constituency service."

During his first run for the U.S. House of Representatives (1992), Fox was held to 52 percent in the Republican primary. Running against Democrat Margolies-Mezvinsky, Fox was attacked as "a political animal [who] runs and runs and runs from political feeding to political feeding." While Fox boasted of all the things he had done for the voters of the Thirteenth

District, MMM attacked him for lacking a political center: "Pro-choice, that's me; multiple choice, that's Jon Fox." Following his defeat, Fox returned to the county board, where he supported a 3 percent tax cut. This would prove to be a critical issue in the 1994 election.

The Thirteenth Congressional District is a collection of "mostly middle- and upper-middle income bedroom communities northwest of Philadelphia," where "Republican voters outnumber Democrats more than 2 to 1 and tend to be more moderate than conservative." In his next race against MMM, Fox stressed his fiscal conservatism against his opponent's "tax and spend" philosophy. MMM was especially vulnerable because she had supported the 1993 Clinton budget and tax package; she had originally declared herself against the proposal, but wound up casting the deciding vote in its favor. In the Thirteenth District, which had a 1994 median household income of $44,764, and more high-income taxpayers than 95 percent of the nation's political districts, MMM's vote was tantamount to political suicide. Backed by much of the local political establishment, and benefiting from a large Jewish vote, Fox was elected in an expensive political nail-biter.

Fox was appointed to the House Committees on Banking and Financial Services, Government Reform and Oversight, and Veterans' Affairs. In his short time on Capitol Hill, Jon Fox began to establish himself in the area of criminal justice, calling for an expansion in the number of crimes punishable by the death penalty and fighting to prosecute as adults juveniles who commit violent crimes. In the One Hundred and Fourth Congress, he, like most Republican freshmen, voted with the Republican majority on all "Contract With America" issues. During the first session, he voted with the Republican majority 91 percent of the time—the lowest percentage among all Republican freshmen. Fox also took a special interest in the issue of American citizens killed by Palestinian Arab terrorist attacks in Israel. He initiated a House Resolution urging Yasir Arafat to surrender suspects in such attacks to the United States for prosecution, and met personally with the parents of the victims.

Because of his razor-thin margin of victory in the 1994 race, Fox was considered a highly vulnerable incumbent for the 1996 election. Going into the election, the Democratic strategy was to tie Fox to House Speaker Newt Gingrich, who was viewed as too conservative by a clear majority of the district's voters. Fox's eventual Democratic opponent, Joseph Hoeffel, was well known to voters in the Thirteenth District. A county commissioner, Hoeffel had run strong races in both 1984 and 1986 against Republican incumbent Lawrence Coughlin. True to form, Hoeffel attacked Fox for voting 91 percent of the time with Speaker Gingrich. (As noted above, Fox voted against Gingrich more than any other Republican freshman.) Fox countered by saying: "This is not Newt Gingrich country. This is a moderate, progressive community in both political parties. And this is the home of the proverbial soccer moms."

Both candidates campaigned indefatigably—Fox with his wife and mother and "Adlai Stevenson–style holes in his shoes." On election day, the Thirteenth District proved to be the closest race in the nation: the initial tally showed Fox winning by a mere ten votes. Nine days after the election, he was declared the victor by a margin of 84 votes. Following his victory, Fox began speaking in less partisan terms: "Neither party holds the patent on good ideas and both Republicans and Democrats want to act in the best interests of the people they are sworn to serve."

Facing Hoeffel once again in 1998, Fox ran a surprisingly sluggish campaign, and lost his seat by a 52 to 46 percent margin. He was one of only five incumbent Republicans to be defeated in that election.

Married to Judithanne (Judi) Fox, Congressman Fox lives in Abington, where he and his wife are still active members of Adath Jeshurun.

References

Private correspondence with Jon Fox, March 1995.
Almanac of American Politics (1994–96 editions).

FRANK, BARNEY (1940–): *Democrat from Massachusetts; has served ten terms in the House (Ninety-seventh through One Hundred and Sixth Congress;, January 3, 1981–present).*

A self-described pragmatic zealot who once ran on the slogan "Neatness isn't Everything," Barney Frank is one of Capitol Hill's best and most oft-quoted pundits. Once, during a rancorous floor debate with members of the Republican right, Frank became dismayed by his colleagues' opposition to both abortion and child nutrition programs. "Sure, they're pro-life," he quipped. "They believe that life begins at conception and ends at birth." According to the *Almanac of American Politics* (1986), "A lot of self-styled pro-lifers were stung by that comment, and started to back nutrition and child-care programs which they had reflexively opposed in the past." In 1985, responding to the Reagan administration's contention that a rising economic tide would "lift all boats," thus benefiting all Americans, Frank offered up the following riposte: "If you don't have a boat and you are standing on tiptoes in the water, a rising tide is not a cause for jubilation."

With the Republican takeover of the House in January 1995, Barney Frank became the Democrats' secret weapon. His job, as a member of the minority party, as he saw it, was "to shine the light where the Republicans don't want it to be shone." As a result of their new minority status, many Democrats voluntarily retired from Congress, claiming that the fun had been taken out of their lives. Not so Frank. He relished being a member of the minority: "I'm a counter-puncher, happiest fighting on the defensive. . . . Also, I'm used to being in a minority. Hey, I'm a left-handed gay Jew. I've never felt, automatically, a member of any majority."

Barney Frank's family came from Minsk around the turn of the century, settling in Bayonne, New Jersey. There he was born on March 31, 1940, one of Samuel and Elsie (Golush) Frank's four children. Sam Frank owned and managed a gas and truck stop, where Barney sometimes worked, pumping gas.

Barney's siblings are brother David, and sisters Doris Breay and Anne F. Lewis. Anne, a well-known Democratic Party strategist and consultant, served as Communications Director to President Clinton. Leaving Radcliffe after two years, Anne F. Frank married Gerald Lewis at age eighteen and moved to Florida, where her husband ran for public office. A lawyer, one of Gerald Lewis' law partners was Janet Reno, a future United States Attorney General. The Lewises were divorced in 1968.

The Frank children were raised in a family where public affairs and politics were widely discussed. As a boy, Barney Frank thought it was normal to bring a newspaper to the dinner table.

In Barney Frank's youth, Bayonne had two synagogues, one Conservative and one Orthodox. Because his parents considered the former to be a bit snobbish, they sent their children to the Orthodox Ohev Shalom at the corner of 49th and Avenue C. Barney was bar mitzvah there in 1953. Growing up in the 1950s Barney was deeply affected by both the televised 1951 Kefauver anticrime hearings and the 1955 murder of Emmett Till, a fourteen-year-old black youth who had allegedly whistled at a white woman. These two events helped shape Barney Frank's desire to enter politics, to fight the good fight against bigotry and poverty. Said Frank more than forty years later: "It's probably bigotry that bothers me the most—bigotry and undeserved poverty."

Following his high school graduation in 1958, Frank moved on to Harvard College, where he would spend the better part of the next twenty years—as both an undergraduate and graduate student, and as a member of the faculty. In 1959, Barney Frank came under the spell of *Allard Lowenstein*, one of the great political organizers and mentors of the period. Frank later said that Lowenstein taught him "how to try and be very serious about issues—to stand up for what you believe in." Like other bright, politically inclined students from across the country, Barney Frank found both a friend and a mentor in the peripatetic political organizer. Lowenstein eventually recruited Barney Frank to act as coordinator at Harvard College for the Mississippi Freedom Summer of 1964.

In 1965, Lowenstein became director of the Encampment for Citizenship, a progressive summer camp for future American leaders. Barney Frank was one of Lowenstein's campers. The EFC sought to bring together students of diverse backgrounds and interests to discuss all the pressing issues confronting America. While there as a camper, Barney Frank debated another future political leader, Tom Hayden of the Students for a Democratic Society (SDS), on the issue of "whether to work inside the established political system, or attack it." According to Lowenstein's biographer, William H. Chafe, "Frank functioned as Lowenstein's surrogate, Hayden represented all those who were angry at the system." The debate was supposed to be held in front of the rest of the campers. A minor flap ensued when Hayden refused to stand in front of the campers and debate Frank face to face, insisting, rather, on sitting among the campers on the ground. Remembering the debate some twenty years later, Frank said: "I told him [Hayden] that he was such a 'grass root,' I didn't know whether to debate him or water him." Barney Frank continued working with Al Lowenstein throughout the years, joining him for both the Dump Johnson movement in 1967 and Lowenstein's own congressional race in 1968.

Following his graduation in 1962, Frank stayed on in Cambridge, entering the Harvard Graduate School, intent upon receiving a Ph.D. in political science. For the next four years, Frank worked as a teaching fellow in government. In 1966–67, he served as assistant to the director of the Institute for Politics at the John F. Kennedy School of Government.

Barney Frank left the graduate program in 1967 in order to work on Kevin White's campaign for mayor of Boston. Victorious, White hired the twenty-seven-year-old Harvard graduate to be his executive assistant. Frank remained with White, "one of the canniest politicians of our time," until 1971, when he went to Washington to serve as administrative assistant to liberal Boston-area congressman Michael Harrington (1936–). His years in the rough-and-tumble of Boston politics proved to be invalu-

able; not only did he gain an "intimate familiarity with Boston politics," he "made the acquaintance of many of its players."

Leaving Harrington's employ in 1972, Barney Frank waged a successful race for the Massachusetts House of Representatives from Boston's Back Bay. He benefited greatly from all the Boston University students who came out to vote for Democratic presidential candidate George McGovern. Although McGovern lost in a landslide to Richard M. Nixon, carrying only Massachusetts, Frank could truthfully claim that "I'm one of the few people in the country who can say he benefited from George McGovern's coattails."

Frank compiled a boldly liberal record in his four terms in the Massachusetts House, concentrating on such areas as women's and homosexual rights, and social services. During his tenure in the State House he was recognized as legislator of the year by several state and national organizations. Ever brimming with energy, Frank even found time to earn a Harvard law degree and teach public policy at the Kennedy School while still an active state legislator. In 1977, the Frank children chipped in to send Barney and their mother on a tour of Israel, a gift for Elsie's sixty-fifth birthday. Frank returned to Israel a year later, this time as a member of a National Association of Jewish State Legislators delegation.

In 1980, Barney Frank moved from Back Bay to Newton, in order to run for the congressional seat of the retiring Representative Robert F. Drinan. A Jesuit priest who had served in Congress for a decade, Drinan had been forced into retirement when Pope John Paul II reaffirmed a ruling that prohibited members of the Roman Catholic clergy from seeking or holding public office. As constituted at the time, the Fourth Congressional District was a "politically complex geographic oddity, with residents of great social, cultural, and economic diversity." It encompassed everything from affluent suburbs to depressed factory towns and small family farms. Running on a pro-choice platform, Frank received the condemnation of the archbishop of Boston, Humberto Cardinal Medeiros. In theory, this meant that members of the four hundred–odd Roman Catholic churches in the diocese would be compelled to vote against him in the primary. Against all odds, Frank received

Drinan's endorsement, and, after an exhausting primary battle, defeated his conservative opponent, Mayor Arthur Clark of nearby Waltham, with 52 percent of the vote. In November 1980, Frank defeated Republican Richard Jones, again receiving 52 percent of the vote, thereby becoming only the second Jew elected to Congress from the Commonwealth of Massachusetts.

By the time Barney Frank was ready for his first reelection campaign in 1982, the Fourth Congressional District had been greatly altered in appearance. Within its new boundaries, Barney Frank was basically a political unknown; less than 30 percent of its residents were his former constituents. Said Frank upon learning of his new district: "If you asked legislators to draw a map in which Barney Frank would never be a congressman again, this would be it."

To make matters worse, Frank was forced to run against eight-term incumbent Republican Margaret M. Heckler. Despite being the odds-on favorite, Heckler adopted a defensive posture from day one. She attacked her Democratic opponent for "supporting prostitution." In fact, Barney Frank had favored the establishment of a "vice zone" in Boston. Heckler further attempted to cast Frank as an "unbeliever in family values" by continually pointing out that he was an unmarried forty-two-year-old who had supported gay rights. True to puckish form, Frank retaliated in a humorous vein. Taking a cue from his brother David, Barney made a funny commercial in which the seventy-year-old Elsie Frank said: "I'm for Barney Frank and he's going to help the elderly. And how do I know? Well, I'm his mother!" Ironically, this commercial served as the beginning of Elsie Frank's political "career." As Frank told a *New York Times Magazine* interviewer: "My mother started getting invited to speak; an elderly activist named Frank Manning asked her to join his organization. Today [1996], she is president of the Massachusetts Association of Older Americans."

Heckler's strident attacks wound up alienating enough voters among the Fourth District's liberal element to give Barney Frank a 60 percent to 40 percent victory. But it was an expensive race; Frank wound up raising and spending nearly $1.5 million to Heckler's million. It also caused Barney Frank's weight—always a concern—to balloon. "I'm a Jew. When I'm under stress, I don't get drunk, I get fat. You want to sum up my life in two words? Stress, *fress* [Yiddish for 'gorge']." Since his victory over Margaret Heckler, Frank has won eight straight elections, his lowest margin of victory being 66 percent in 1990. Over the years, his popularity had risen to such heights that, by 1994, not a single Republican chose to challenge him in the general election.

During his many years in the House of Representatives, Barney Frank has gained the respect and plaudits of colleagues on both sides of the aisle. The *Almanac of American Politics* has consistently referred to him as "one of the most gifted legislators of our time." Frank has been both a legislator and an intellectual leader in the House, involving himself in a wide array of issues. As chair of the subcommittee sitting on legislation that would grant compensation to Japanese-Americans interned in World War II, Frank steered the bill through the House and on to eventual passage. He is now a hero among the Asian ethnic community on the West Coast. Frank also spearheaded a bill that would provide adequate new housing for poor people displaced by urban renewal, and fought against the provision that would keep HIV-positive people from entering the country.

Although viewed by his political detractors as a down-the-line, unreconstructed liberal, Barney Frank has often taken stands at odds with his reputation. He has occasionally scolded members of his own party for such things as refusing to support the 65-mile-an-hour speed limit and "for pursuing an impossible goal like federal gun control." When asked what he thought about the pending retirement of fellow Democratic Senators Sam Nunn of Georgia and Bill Bradley of New Jersey, Frank was his typically candid self: "I was delighted when Sam Nunn said he wasn't going to run again. Nunn's been an outstanding bigot. This man has shown very little zeal in his career, but he was astonishingly active when he was leading the charge against gays and lesbians in the military. . . . I don't know how [Senator Bill] Bradley can claim to believe in what he does and then find everybody morally wanting. I mean, Bradley's been a Democrat all these years. What was he, like, on Mars or on Venus? What was he doing to change this?"

Of medium height with an unruly shock of thick gray hair and a thick New Jersey patter,

Barney Frank was, for many years, quite over-weight and given to wearing ill-fitting suits, tie always askew. In the mid-1980s, he began making changes. He took off nearly 75 pounds, got his hair styled, and started wearing custom-made suits. In May 1987, he made the biggest change of all: he confirmed to a reporter from the *Boston Globe* that he was a homosexual. Speaking of that decision nearly a decade later, he said: "When I first ran for office, I made a decision that I would sacrifice a private life for politics. After a while, I became increasingly jealous of the people who were 'out.' I thought, 'Why am I leading this unhealthy life where I have to be dishonest? People said to me: 'Well you don't have to be dishonest. Just don't mention it.'"

Frank decided to go public with his homosexuality after it was revealed that Congressman Stewart McKinney, a Connecticut Republican, was a bisexual who had died after contracting the AIDS virus. The press had a field day speculating on precisely how McKinney had contracted the deadly disease. Frank remembers attending McKinney's funeral: "I was saddened by his death. And there was this unfortunate fight in the press: was he gay, was he not? I thought: 'Boy, this is crazy. I've got to make sure this never happens to me.'"

In his interview with the *Boston Globe*, Frank stated: "I don't think my sex life is relevant to my job. But on the other hand, I don't want to leave the impression that I'm embarrassed by my life." In the early 1970s, Frank had occasionally escorted women to political fundraising events. By the mid-1970s, he was going alone. By 1984, he had begun taking men to these events. As Frank recounted: "By then, I was living kind of half in and half out. People knew. They didn't want to say anything." Frank was uncertain how this revelation would affect his political fortunes. He didn't have long to wait. In November 1988, he won reelection over Republican Debra Tucker with 70 percent of the vote—despite the fact that Tucker tried to create an issue out of Frank's personal life.

In June 1989, a memo was circulated among more than two hundred GOP leaders purporting to show that the new Speaker of the House, Thomas Foley of Washington, was likely a closet homosexual. Greatly angered by what he characterized as an "obviously scurrilous and vicious" attack, Frank told reporters that if the Republicans didn't "cut the crap," he would "reveal the names of Republican congressmen and other well-known Republicans" who he knew were homosexual. The storm blew over when Mark Goodin, the communications director of the Republican National Committee (and the drafter of the memo) resigned in disgrace.

On the subject of outing closeted members of Congress, Frank had this to say: "If someone is a closeted gay member of Congress, and is generally supportive of anti-discrimination measures, I regret the closeting, though I understand it. On the other hand, if someone is privately gay and publicly a gay-basher, that's hypocrisy and should be exposed." During the debate over homosexuality in the military services, conservatives raised the issue that gays represented a security risk. Frank angrily retorted: "I do not believe that gay people, in or out of the closet, are a security risk. But if the Republican Party gets through Congress a law that says that closeted gay people are a security risk, I will send a list to the Ethics Committee of all the closeted gay Republicans." Although Frank was accused of bullying tactics, the Republicans backed off.

In the Fall of 1989, Barney Frank's personal life again took center stage. A *Washington Times* article revealed that Stephen L. Gobie, a former male prostitute who had been Frank's housekeeper and driver from 1985 to 1987, had been running a prostitution business out of the Congressman's house, and moreover, that Frank had fixed innumerable parking tickets for him. Responding to the charges, Frank admitted that he had known of Gobie's former profession and had attempted to reform him. "Thinking I was going to be Henry Higgins and trying to turn him into Pygmalion was the biggest mistake I've made. It turns out I was being suckered." The *Boston Globe* called upon Frank to resign his seat in Congress. The Roman Catholic diocesan newspaper in his district likewise called for his resignation. Speaker Foley came to his defense, as did columnist Morton Kondracke in the *New Republic*. Answering those who charged that Frank's legislative effectiveness had been permanently damaged, Kondracke wrote: "I personally believe that a lot of Frank's ideas—especially on defense, foreign policy, and economics would be disastrous if they were implemented. But Barney Frank is a national treasure, and he ought to be preserved. His personal judgment was bad, but his political judgment on hundreds of issues . . . has never been more needed."

Barney Frank himself urged the House to launch an investigation into the charges against him. After exhaustive review, the House Ethics Committee issued a report stating that Frank's actions in fixing Gobie's parking tickets had "reflected discredit upon the House." On July 26, 1989, the House held a tense, raucous four-hour floor debate, during which Barney Frank apologized for his behavior. Republicans William Dannemeyer of California and Newt Gingrich of Georgia moved that Frank either be expelled or censured. Opting for an even lighter form of punishment, the House voted 408 to 18 to reprimand the gentleman from Boston. The Gobie flap held Frank's margin of victory in his next election to just 66 percent—the lowest of his political career.

In the early days of the Clinton administration, the President tackled the thorny issue of gays in the U.S. military. After hearing all sides, Frank concluded that Congress was not ready to lift the ban completely and offered a compromise: gay or lesbian service people would be permitted to maintain an openly homosexual lifestyle off-base, when not on duty, but would be forbidden to reveal this sexual orientation while on duty or in uniform. Frank called this proposal a "don't ask, don't tell, and don't listen and don't investigate" policy. Although Frank's proposal became official policy, he incurred the wrath both of conservatives, who wanted to maintain an absolute ban, and of homosexual groups, who accused him of betrayal. When asked about this two-sided attack, Frank responded: "That's the tension of my job, to try to interpret the groups to each other . . . telling each side things they don't want to hear."

Heading into the twenty-first century, Barney Frank continues to be the Democratic point-man on floor debate against the Republican majority. For the eleven years from 1987 to 1998, Frank lived with Herb Moses, an economist with the Federal National Mortgage Association and a gay rights activist. When Frank and Moses put their Washington townhouse up for sale in early September 1998, thus concretizing their breakup, advocates for gay and lesbian rights "rued the demise of their relationship and praised their contributions." Kerry Lobel, executive director of the National Gay and Lesbian Task Force said: "They provided the definition for how elected couples can serve a public life with dignity and authenticity. They did it in ways nobody had done before, and they accepted nothing less than other elected couples should accept." When asked by a reporter why he and Moses were breaking up after so many years, Frank commented tersely, "It isn't anybody's business." Frank termed the split "amicable," saying they called each other's families "to make sure we all understand we will still be friendly and stay in touch." At the time of their breakup, Herb Moses left his government job and opened a pottery studio.

During their decade together, Herb Moses became involved in political issues. Most notably, he did fundraising for Representative Loretta Sanchez, a California Democrat, when she was campaigning to unseat then-Representative Robert "B-1 Bob" Dornan, described as "a virulent foe of homosexual rights." Moses' participation in the Sanchez campaign brought about a verbal blast from Representative Dornan: "I know I speak for most members," he said on the House floor, "when I state that the only Moses we like to hear about . . . is our Moses of the Exodus, Moses the lawgiver, Moses of the Ten Commandments. I am beyond annoyance hearing on this floor about Herb Moses."

At home in Newton, Massachusetts, Barney Frank attends Conservative Temple Emanuel.

References

Interview with Barney Frank, Washington, D.C., February 1992.

Almanac of American Politics (1984–98 editions).

Boston Globe, March 29, 1998, A14; September 9, 1998, A7.

William H. Chafe, *Never Stop Running: Allard Lowenstein and the Struggle to Save American Liberalism* (New York: Basic Books, 1993).

Current Biography, April 1995, pp. 18–22.

New Republic, October 9, 1989.

New York Times Magazine, February 4, 1996, pp. 23–25.

FRANK, NATHAN (1852–1931): *Republican from Missouri; served one term in the House (Fifty-first Congress; March 4, 1889–March 3, 1891).*

In an out-of-the-way corner of the Baseball Hall of Fame in Cooperstown, New York, there is a faded picture of President William Howard Taft making a bit of American history. Taft, an inveterate baseball fan, initiated the custom of Presidents throwing out the first ball on Opening Day. The photo shows the 300-pound Taft throwing out the first pitch from his seat in the presidential box at Sportsman's Park in St. Louis. Among the small group surrounding Taft in the President's box was another inveterate baseball fan: Taft's good friend Nathan Frank, one-term Congressman and owner/publisher of the *St. Louis Star.*

The Frank family immigrated to the United States from Bavaria in 1849. Settling originally in Hopkinsville, Kentucky, Abraham and Branette (Weil) Frank quickly moved on to Peoria, Illinois, where their son Nathan was born on February 2, 1852. Branette's brothers, Joseph and Max Weil, had arrived in America in 1836, and within nine years were operating a dry goods store in Hopkinsville. After getting his feet wet working for his brothers-in-law, Abraham moved on to Peoria, where he opened his own store, specializing in "Yankee notions," hats, caps, and furs. Abe Frank was a leader of the Peoria Jewish community, serving as president of the Hebrew Society, forerunner of the Reform synagogue Anshei Emeth.

Shortly after Nathan's bar mitzvah in 1865, the Frank family moved to St. Louis, where the Weil brothers had become prosperous merchants. Abraham and Branette's family now consisted of sons Nathan, August, Louis, and Joseph and daughter Amelia. Within a few years, Abraham was running the clothing business, now renamed A. Frank & Sons. The senior Frank became a prominent leader of Congregation Shaare Emeth, the largest Reform temple in St. Louis.

Nathan Frank graduated at the head of his high school class in 1869. Within two years, he had earned a law degree at Harvard Law School and was back in St. Louis, a member of the Missouri Bar. He quickly began specializing in bankruptcy law, and by 1874, had published a work entitled *Frank on Bankruptcy Law,* which went through four editions. Nathan Frank had a knack for associating himself with the politically savvy and well-connected. Upon first entering the law, he was associated with John M. Krum, a former St. Louis mayor and judge of the Circuit Court. After his first three years as a lawyer, Frank became partners with William Patrick, a former district attorney for the Eastern District of Missouri and a prominent Republican. Frank's third and final legal partner was Seymour Thompson, an ex-judge of the St. Louis Court of Appeals.

As a young attorney in the west, Frank traveled great distances to service his clients. Traveling by rail and stagecoach, the young Harvard lawyer often found that "frontier justice" required more than a first-rate education. Once, "it was necessary for Frank to go to Little Rock, Arkansas, to represent a client . . . one of the leaders in the cotton trade. Threatened by [his client's] enemies, Frank boarded the train at Union Station and as the train pulled out, he started to walk through the cars. After a while he recognized the two men who had attempted to prevent his trip. Surprising them, he 'got the drop on them' and at revolver point, made them jump from the train."

In 1886, the thirty-four-year-old Nathan Frank became the Republican nominee for Congress from Missouri's Ninth District, running as the friend of the working man and in favor of a uniform national bankruptcy law. Word went out that the political neophyte was merely the hand-picked candidate of the Republican boss of St. Louis, Chauncey I. Filley. This raised political hackles throughout St. Louis. Editorial after editorial blasted Frank's nomination. The issue of the young man's religion was inevitably raised. The editorial writer of the *St. Louis Chronicle,* blasting a rival paper, the *Globe-Democrat,* for failing to endorse Frank, noted: "The real opposition of the *Globe* to Nathan Frank is because he is a Hebrew. [The editor] is said to hate Hebrews. . . . [He] should get over his prejudice. The Jewish people are very heavy taxpayers in this country. As a class they are remarkably thrifty and peaceable. . . . At any rate, if [the *Globe* editor] bolts the nomination of Mr. Frank he should give the real reason—race prejudice." Frank was defeated in the general election by a vote of 7,208 to 7,094. He contested the final tally before Congress, asking it to award him the seat. His plea fell on deaf ears.

In 1888, Frank ran for Congress again, this time as the nominee of both the Republican and the Union Labor Parties. He ran as a strong defender of protectionism, an important issue in a manufacturing town like St. Louis. Frank defeated his Democratic opponent, receiving nearly 56 percent of the vote. He was sworn in as a member of the Fifty-first Congress on March 4, 1889, and appointed to the Select Committee on Presidential Elections and the Select Committee on the Eleventh Census.

During his single term in the House, Frank was able to see his pet piece of legislation successfully enacted: a law creating a uniform system of bankruptcy through the nation. Frank was also a supporting player in a little bit of history known as the "No Quorum" episode. Frank introduced a bill to raise the salaries of members of the federal judiciary. Democrat members of the House, who were solidly against the measure, staged a mass exodus from chambers. Nonetheless, when Speaker Thomas Reed ordered the clerk to call the roll, he declared that a quorum was present. As a result of Reed's heavy-handed (and quasi-legal) tactic, he was forever more labeled "Czar Reed."

Frank was a loyal Republican, giving the programs and policies of President Benjamin Harrison his full support. Harrison and Frank did not see eye to eye on one parochial political issue: the appointment of one Louis Wittenberg as appraiser of the Port of St. Louis. Wittenberg, a fellow Jew, had been strongly recommended for the post by Congressman Frank, who was led to believe that President Harrison would agree to the appointment. When Frank learned that Harrison had reneged, he wrote the President a strongly worded protest, stating: "The main objection, if indeed not the only one is that Mr. Wittenberg is an Israelite; that is true and makes him none the less eligible." Frank waited quite awhile for Harrison's response. Finally, after much political jockeying, the President informed his fellow Republican: "I regret your disappointment about the matter, and especially that it should have been accompanied by any forgetfulness on my part of a promise to you."

Although seriously annoyed by Harrison's apparent betrayal, Frank continued to be a loyal Republican. His one long-lasting achievement came from his authorship of the Apportionment Bill, which, under terms of the eleventh decennial census, reapportioned the congressional districts for the decade of the 1890s.

Nathan Frank decided to leave Congress after his single term in order to devote more time to his burgeoning law practice. As a private citizen, Frank pushed hard for the creation of a cabinet-level Department of Trade and Commerce. Many years later, the federal government did indeed create secretariats of Commerce and Labor, with Frank receiving a fair portion of the credit.

Frank ran for the United States Senate in 1910, 1916, and 1928, but failed to win in the Republican primaries. In the latter campaign, Frank ran as a "wet," in opposition to Prohibition. After losing the primary, he campaigned vigorously for Republican presidential candidate Herbert Hoover. Following Hoover's victory over New York Governor Al Smith, rumors circulated that the new President would appoint Frank to either a cabinet position or an ambassadorship. Supposedly, Hoover even went so far as to confer with Frank about a possible appointment. When Hoover announced his cabinet lineup, Nathan Frank's name was not included. Frank claimed that he had been "knifed" by his political enemies, who had repeatedly stressed his advanced age (seventy-six) to the President-elect.

Along with his dual careers in law and politics, Nathan Frank was a prominent newspaper publisher. He founded the *St. Louis Star* in 1884, and greatly expanded it twenty years later with the purchase and absorption of the *St. Louis Chronicle*. He sold his paper to a University City, Missouri publisher, bought it back, and then resold it. As late as 1930, a year before his death, Frank gave serious consideration to purchasing the *New York World* from *Joseph Pulitzer*. Frank went so far as to make a $6 million bid for the former Missourian's paper, but Pulitzer turned him down.

Nathan Frank never married. His family consisted of his brothers August, Louis, and Joseph, and their children, and his sister Amelia. The three brothers were all associated with the family's business, which after their father's death in 1895 was renamed Frank Brothers. Brother August Frank served as managing editor of the *St. Louis Star* for a number of years, and then became vice president of the National Publishing Company, which was owned by brother Nathan. He was also an elected member of the St. Louis City Council for four years and the first president of the St. Louis Jewish Hospital.

Nathan Frank was a life member of his father's Reform synagogue, Temple Shaare Emeth, and a major supporter of both local and national Jewish charities. In 1920, he served as general chairman of the Jewish War Relief Committee, and was able to raise better than $300,000 in St. Louis alone.

Nathan Frank's last public appearance came just a few months before his death, when he, along with some five thousand Jews from the St. Louis area, met to protest British policies forbidding further immigration or land purchases in Palestine. Although not a Zionist ("I am as much opposed as you are to a political Jewish state in Palestine or in any other place on the habitable globe," Frank once wrote a friend), he was tireless in his efforts to aid and support the homeless and displaced of Europe. As chairman of the Midwestern Zone, Frank raised over $14 million for food and clothing for poverty-stricken Jews in Russia and Central Europe.

Nathan Frank died on April 5, 1931, just four weeks after celebrating his seventy-ninth birthday. In his will, he bequeathed $50,000 to Temple Shaare Emeth, which was used to construct the Nathan Frank Chapel. Nathan Frank—lawyer, publisher, politician, philanthropist, and avid sportsman—was buried in Mount Sinai Cemetery in St. Louis.

References

American Jewish Year Book, vol. 2 (1900–01), pp. 517–518; vol. 6 (1904–5), p. 94; vol. 11 (1909–10), p. 144; vol. 24, p. 141; vol. 33, p. 126.
Jewish Encyclopedia.
Publications of the American Jewish Historical Society, vol. 61, pp. 33–51.
Universal Jewish Encyclopedia.
Who's Who in America, vol. 1.
Who's Who in American Jewry, 1926.

FRIEDEL, SAMUEL NATHANIEL (1898–1979): *Democrat from Maryland; served nine terms in the House (Eighty-third through Ninety-first Congress; January 3, 1953–January 3, 1971).*

For years, Baltimore was known for H. L. Mencken, crab cakes, its distinctive accent ("Bawlmer" in local parlance), and for having block upon block of dilapidated old row houses with marble steps. Known as a city "with a savor all its own," Baltimore spent most of the twentieth century looking inward. In the 1930s, the *WPA Guide* noted that "there are no songs entitled 'Way Down Upon the Patapsco,'" nor 'The Baltimore Blues"; the city has inspired no outstanding novels . . . it does not boast of the biggest, the newest or the fastest anything." The writers of the guide concluded that "this does not indicate lack of city pride; it merely means that Baltimoreans are too sure of themselves and their city to feel the need of advertising their virtues." A Southern city with easy Northern accessibility, Baltimore has long been an ethnically diverse town with a strong, moderate-sized, Jewish community.

Starting in the 1970s, Baltimore began to change. Spurred on by its beloved, rumpled, unphotogenic mayor, William Donald Schaefer, Baltimore was transformed from a "dowdy, inbred industrial city" into a vibrant, forward-looking metropolis "where people vacation, where movies are made, where people are happy that the local economy . . . is providing enough good jobs to enable them to stay." Baltimore harbor, with a magnificent new aquarium as its centerpiece, became the talk of urban planners everywhere. Schaefer (who would be elected governor in 1986) was proclaimed by *Esquire* and other publications as "the best big-city mayor in America."

By 1980, the city had a black majority and a black Representative in Congress, Parren J. Mitchell (1922–). A member of a distinguished political family (his brother Clarence served many years as the Washington lobbyist for the NAACP), Parren Mitchel won his congressional seat in 1970 by the razor-thin margin of thirty-eight votes. The man he beat, Samuel Nathaniel Friedel, had been a fixture in the politics of Baltimore for more than thirty years.

Samuel Friedel, the son of Phillip and Rose (Franklin) Friedel, was born in Washington, D.C., on April 18, 1898. Before Sam was six months old, his family moved to Baltimore, which at the turn of the century was home to some thirty thousand Jews. Young Sam was educated in the Baltimore public schools and briefly attended the Strayer College of Business. In 1926, following a few years as a mail clerk in a local department store, Sam Friedel founded the Industrial Loan Company. He would serve as president of the company for the next thirty years.

In 1935, the thirty-seven-year-old Democrat was elected to the first of two terms in the Maryland State House of Delegates. Four years later, in 1939, he was elected to the Baltimore City Council as a representative from the First (and later the Fifth) District. Shortly before his election to the council, Friedel married Regina Bradley-Johnson. While on the City Council, Friedel was an ardent backer of measures meant to improve public housing, civil rights, and education. He continued serving on the City Council until 1952, at which time he was elected to the United States Congress as Representative from the Seventh District. The seat had previously been held for five terms by Republican J. Glenn Beall [pronounced "Ball"] (1894–1971), who was elected to the United States Senate in 1952. Beall's son, J. Glenn Beall, Jr., would later follow in his father's footsteps, serving as both representative and United States Senator. Friedel's victory was somewhat of a minor upset: not only had the Seventh been a safe Republican seat for most of a generation, but the Democrat Friedel managed to pull off his victory even as General Dwight D. Eisenhower was trouncing Adlai E. Stevenson in the presidential race.

Sam Friedel was a Democratic Party loyalist who paid a great deal of attention to the needs of his district. During his eighteen years in Congress, he was a strong supporter of civil rights legislation and an early advocate of federal aid to education. Countering arguments from Republican colleagues, Friedel contended that grants to local school systems were in no way a harbinger of ultimate federal control of education. As Friedel climbed the seniority ladder, he eventually became chairman of three rather bland committees: House Administration, Joint Committee on the Library, and Joint Committee on Printing.

Months before Friedel was elected to the House, the Eighty-second Congress passed the notorious McCarran-Walter Act. Named after Senator Pat McCarran, a Nevada Democrat, and Representative Theodore Walter, a Pennsylvania Democrat, the measure, in effect, exposed naturalized American citizens to "the sword of Damocles of deportation." The act did this by making deportation the penalty for naturalized citizens who failed to accurately report their past political (read: "Communist") associations on their naturalization applications. Moreover, McCarren-Walter lifted the statute of limitations on past political associations and made judicial review of questionable cases extremely difficult. President Harry Truman, who angrily branded the bill "anti-Semitic," vetoed the measure, but Congress easily overrode the veto.

Friedel came to Washington with the freshman class of 1953—the Eighty-third Congress. Outraged by the narrow, bigoted intent of McCarran-Walter, Friedel, along with other freshman colleagues, offered amendments that sought to water down its more onerous language and consequences. Try as they might, their efforts failed. The hysteria generated by the Red-baiting Senator Joseph McCarthy and his minions made the young Representative's moderate language seem dangerously near-sighted. The early and mid-1950s were simply filled with too much anger, fear, and tension.

Sam Friedel was easily reelected eight more times to Congress. Finally, in 1970, at the age of seventy-two, he was defeated by the forty-eight-year-old Parren Mitchell. By that time, Friedel's district had become nearly 70 percent black. Despite the overwhelming odds, as noted above, Mitchell's margin of victory was only 38 votes. Following his defeat, Sam Friedel continued living in Towson, Maryland. During his last years, he saw the career of his close friend, Maryland Governor Marvin Mandel, come to a crashing halt; Mandel was convicted of accepting bribes. Ever loyal to his friends and allies, Friedel stood by Mandel until the governor was forced to leave Annapolis in disgrace.

An active participant in the Baltimore Jewish community, Samuel Friedel belonged to three synagogues: Brith Shalom, Har Sinai, and Petach Tikvah. Sam Friedel died in Towson, Maryland, on March 21, 1978, a few days before his eightieth birthday. He was buried in Baltimore's Hebrew Friendship Cemetery.

References

Baltimore Sun, March 22, 1978.

Biographical Directory of the United States Congress, 1774–1989, p. 1029.

Howard M. Sachar, *A History of the Jews in America* (New York: Alfred A. Knopf, 1992), pp. 620–623.

FROST, JONAS MARTIN (1942–): *Democrat from Texas; has served eleven terms in the House (Ninety-sixth through One Hundred and Sixth Congress; January 3, 1979–present).*

It is an old and abiding custom among most European Jews to name children after deceased relatives. Generally speaking, it is the Sephardim (Jews of Mediterranean or Middle Eastern ancestry) who name their offspring after the living. "Better to honor someone while they are still alive than after their demise," goes the Sephardi rationale. For whatever reason, the Frost family of Texas adopted the Sephardi tradition. Jonas Martin Frost, Democratic Representative from Texas' Twenty-fourth District, carries the same name as both his father and his grandfather. Therefore, Martin Frost is really Jonas Martin Frost III.

The Frost family came to the United States from Berlin shortly after the Revolution of 1848. Representative Frost's great-grandfather settled in Memphis, where the first Jonas Martin was born and reared. As a young man, he became enamored of his first cousin, Pearl Cohen of Cairo, Illinois—their mothers were sisters. Because neither Tennessee nor Illinois would permit a union between first cousins, Jonas and Pearl traveled to Paduca, Kentucky, where they married. Shortly after the ceremony, the young couple returned to Memphis, where Jonas entered the liquor business. It was in Memphis, as mentioned above, that the first Jonas Martin Frost was born. The Frosts lived in Memphis until the onset of Prohibition when, after many generations, the family pulled up stakes and moved to San Antonio, where Pearl had family. There, Jonas Frost I opened a women's clothing store that eventually grew, prospered, and became Frost Brothers Department Store. While living in San Antonio, Pearl gave birth to the second Jonas Martin Frost—known as "Joe."

While Joe Frost was an engineering student at the University of Texas, he met and married Doris Marwil. The Marwil (Marwilsky) family was originally from Lithuania. Doris's grandfa-

ther came to America in the early 1870s, settling first in Detroit. By 1874, he had moved to the East Texas town of Henderson. Shortly after arriving in Henderson, Marwil married a German-Jewish immigrant named Brachfield, and moved to Vicksburg, Mississippi. After a short stay there, the couple moved back to Henderson, where their son Moses (M. H.) Marwil was born. Because there were few, if any, Jewish girls in East Texas, the Marwils sent their son to St. Louis to find a wife. There he met and married Stella Jackson, the daughter of a men's clothing salesman. The Marwils moved back to Henderson, where the family became politically active: "Mose" would eventually serve as mayor; his brother-in-law, Charlie Brachfield, served as county judge for Rusk County, and as state senator from 1903 to 1911. In 1909, Charlie Brachfield became the Texas Senate's first Jewish president *pro tem.*

Following their marriage, Joe and Doris Frost moved to California, where Joe, an aeronautical engineer, got a job working for Lockheed Aviation in Burbank. On January 1, 1942, their first child, Jonas Martin Frost III, was born. Joe Frost went into the United States Navy in 1944. Following his discharge, the family moved to Texas, where Martin's sister Carol and brother Richard were born. Martin Frost was educated in the Fort Worth public schools, and attended Sunday school at a Reform synagogue. Because the temple did not have a Hebrew school, he was privately trained for his bar mitzvah. As a teenager, Martin Frost was heavily involved in the Reform movement's National Federation of Temple Youth (NFTY), serving as both a regional and a national officer. Following his graduation from Fort Worth's Paschal High School in 1958, Martin matriculated at the University of Missouri, where, in 1964, he received both a Bachelor of Journalism and a Bachelor of Arts degree. While at Missouri, Frost was an active member of the Jewish fraternity Zeta Beta Tau.

Following his graduation, Frost moved to Bloomington, Delaware, where he spent a year working as a reporter for the *News Journal*. From there he went on to Washington, D.C., and spent the next two years working as a staff writer for the *Congressional Quarterly*. In 1967, Frost entered Georgetown University Law Center, where he spent the next three years. Frost received his law degree from Georgetown in 1970, graduating in the top 15 percent of his class, a member of the law review staff.

Upon completing his legal education, Martin Frost returned to Texas, where he clerked for Judge Sarah T. Hughes, the federal jurist who swore in Lyndon Johnson aboard Air Force One following the assassination of President John F. Kennedy. Martin Frost remained in Hughes's employ until 1972, at which time he went into private practice. Never far from the world of journalism, Frost also moonlighted as a legal commentator for Dallas television station KERA.

Upon his return to Texas, Martin Frost married Valerie Hall. She had been born in Panama, where her parents worked as civilian employees in the Canal Zone. Valerie's father, a convert to Judaism, came from a family that had been in America since pre-Revolutionary days. Valerie's mother was from Altoona, Pennsylvania. Although raised in Fort Worth, Valerie Hall had dual citizenship (Panamanian and U.S.) until her eighth birthday. The Hall family was active in the Fort Worth Jewish community. Valerie's first cousin, Harriet Sloan of New York City, served as national chair of the Women's Division of the United Jewish Appeal.

The Frosts have three daughters: Alana (born 1972), Mariel (born 1978), and Camile (born 1980). They are members of Reform congregation Rodef Shalom in Falls Church, Virginia, where the Frost girls, like their father, were active in NFTY. Reform Judaism runs in the family; Representative Frost's cousin, Rabbi Eugene H. Levy, serves congregation B'nai Israel in Little Rock, Arkansas. Rabbi Levy earned a moment of fame when, in 1990, he offered the invocation at Bill Clinton's last inauguration as Governor of Arkansas.

In 1972, Dale Milford, a former television weatherman, was elected to the House of Representatives as a Democrat from Texas' Twenty-fourth Congressional District. Following redistricting, which "pared away conservative suburban areas while adding black sections of Dallas," Martin Frost was encour-

aged to take on Milford in the Democrat primary. In that 1974 campaign, Frost complained that Milford was overly supportive of the Nixon administration and too conservative for the voters of the district. Running as an outsider, Frost ran a door-to-door campaign, hammering away at Milford's conservatism. When the final votes were tallied, incumbent Milford defeated challenger Frost with 58 percent of the vote. In 1976, rather than facing Milford in a rematch, Martin Frost ran Jimmy Carter's campaign in north Texas.

Two years later, Frost decided that the time was right to take on Milford once again. Reviving his charge that Milford was too conservative, Frost, aided by an effective precinct organization, the support of the state AFL-CIO, and endorsements from two of the largest newspapers in the Dallas–Fort Worth area, defeated Milford with 55 percent of the vote. In the November general election, despite being portrayed as a "tool of organized labor" and an ultra-liberal, Frost defeated his Republican challenger 54 percent to 46 percent.

The district from which Martin Frost was elected was decidedly non-Jewish and contained "the largest concentration of black and Hispanic voters anywhere in the Dallas area." Blacks composed nearly one-third of the district's voters, with Hispanics accounting for nearly 15 percent. The Twenty-fourth's economic base centers around two plants which manufacture aircraft products, missiles, and electronics. Needless to say, with the call for downsizing the military budget, the district's economy became shaky and uncertain.

As a young member of Congress, Martin Frost benefited greatly from his close personal relationship with the House Majority Leader (and future Speaker), fellow Texan James Wright. Because of his loyalty to Wright, Frost was appointed to the House Rules Committee, where he quickly became a protégé of committee chair Richard Bolling, a Missouri Democrat. Quickly earning a reputation for being good at the book work that other Rules Committee members often disdain, Frost was assigned increasingly important tasks by Chairman Bolling.

Martin Frost was easily reelected in 1980. In 1982, following the 1980 census, the Texas legislature redrew district lines, making the Twenty-fourth nearly 65 percent black and Hispanic. Professor Lucy Patterson, the first black woman elected to the Dallas City Council, decided to challenge Frost in the Democratic primary, believing that the district's minority voters would provide her a safe margin of victory. Reacting quickly, Martin Frost garnered early endorsements from a host of leaders in the district's black and Hispanic communities. Before the election was held, however, a three-judge panel "undid the Legislature's work," making the Twenty-fourth "a white-majority district with a combined black and Hispanic population just under 50 percent." Following the court's redistricting, Patterson switched parties and ran as a Republican; Frost coasted to victory, capturing more than 70 percent of the vote. This was to be his last difficult election for more than a decade.

Martin Frost climbed the House leadership ladder slowly but surely. He spent most of the 1980s and early 1990s working on the Democratic Party's national redistricting strategy. He was appointed chair of IMPAC 2000, the Democrats' redistricting organization, which "waged legal and political battles in the states to see that new maps drawn after [the] 1990 reapportionment protected Democratic incumbents and promoted prospects for minorities to win new House seats." Frost's efforts, mostly successful despite Republican challenges in the courts, earned him the post of floor whip in the One Hundred and Third Congress—one of the top jobs in the Democratic hierarchy. Frost also lost two leadership bids in the 1980s. In 1984 he lost his race for Budget Committee Chair to Representative William H. Gray III of Pennsylvania; in 1989, he came in a distant second to California Representative Vic Fazio in the race for Democratic Caucus Vice Chair.

Known as a "shrewd institutional player" and a technocrat, Martin Frost continued to rise as long as Jim Wright was a power in Congress. Frost worked in tandem with his Fort Worth neighbor to kill measures that would have "tightened lending and investment requirements for S&Ls and would have increased capital requirements." By January 1989, Frost was named by the *National Journal* one of twenty-three members "who have acquired legislative influence despite the fact that they are neither elected party leaders nor committee chairmen."

In June 1989 though, Wright was forced to resign from Congress following an Ethics Committee announcement that it had "found reason to believe that [the Speaker had] violated the rules of the House." At issue was Wright's "unusual royalty and marketing arrangements for his book *The Reflections of a Public Man*," which the committee charged was "an attempt to evade the House limits on outside earned income." With Wright's ouster, Frost was on his own. Despite the fact that the new House leadership "wanted to be rid of the influence of the deposed and disgraced former Speaker," Frost, through hard work and an innate talent for fundraising, continued to be a power in the lower chamber.

In 1990, the new Speaker, Thomas Foley, named Martin Frost chair of a newly created Special House Task Force on the Development of Parliamentary Institutions in Eastern Europe. Along with other task force members, Frost visited Czechoslovakia, Hungary, and Poland, establishing programs of technical assistance for the parliaments of those countries. While in Eastern Europe, Frost, along with fellow task force member *Nita Lowey*, managed to visit leaders of the dwindling Jewish communities in Bulgaria and Hungary.

In the 1990s, Martin Frost faced significant electoral challenges on the home front. Despite his best efforts to secure funding for the Superconducting Super Collider (SSC) for his district and his work on behalf of local defense contractors, Frost found himself in trouble. Long a champion of minority districts, he now had to run in an increasingly conservative, increasingly Republican section of Dallas–Fort Worth. Despite a moderate voting record (his 1994 Americans for Democratic Action rating was 55), Frost was continually depicted as a "dangerous tax-and-spend liberal." With superior fundraising power, a finely tuned campaign organization, and the advantages of seniority, he managed to turn back Republican challengers in both 1992 and 1994. In this last election, however, he was held to just 53 percent of the vote by wealthy Fort Worth home-builder Ed Harrison.

Frost's soft-spoken demeanor and shy smile suggest a "self-effacing personality." But according to *Politics in America*, "he is a man of calculating ambition and no small amount of self-esteem." His ambition, coupled with an intense single-mindedness, led Frost's Democratic colleagues to name him chair of the Democratic Congressional Campaign Committee. From that post, Frost became the House Democratic Caucus's *de facto* fundraiser and chief strategist. In 1995 and 1996, Frost's main goal was to recapture the House for the Democrats away from the Gingrich-led Republicans. And despite the fact that he stood a very real chance of losing his own seat due to court-ordered redistricting, Frost remained a stalwart champion of minority districts. As the *Almanac of American Politics* (1996) noted: "always the dedicated partisan, he seems willing to risk going down with his ship, but looks forward to serving as first or second mate when it returns to port in the lead."

Martin Frost was forced to run in a special court-ordered primary in 1996. He defeated Republican Ed Harrison, the man he had bested two years earlier. This time his margin was somewhat greater: 56 percent to 39 percent. In the campaign, Frost, who spent an unprecedented $1,963.529 to Harrison's $868,345, was criticized by *Roll Call*, which said that Frost sent fully 30 percent of the Democratic Congressional Campaign Committee's "soft money" to Texas, "much of it to Tarrant and Dallas County, where it could help his campaign." Frost was quick to respond that "Texas had many open seats, and that [my] own race was a legitimate target for Democratic spending." In the One Hundred and Sixth Congress, he won reelection to his eleventh term by a margin of 58 percent to 42 percent. On November 16, 1998, House Democrats bestowed a singular honor upon their Texas colleague: electing him to chair the House Democratic Caucus. In replacing longtime caucus chair Vic Fazio of California, Martin Frost became the first Jew ever elected to a House leadership position.

References

Interview with Martin Frost, Washington, D.C., July 1992.
Almanac of American Politics (1980–98 editions).
Congressional Quarterly.
Politics in America (1980–98 editions).

GEJDENSON, SAMUEL (1948–): *Democrat from Connecticut; has served ten terms in the House (Ninety-seventh through One Hundred and Sixth Congress; January, 3, 1981–present).*

When Connecticut Representative Sam Gejdenson (Gay-den-son) refers to himself as "just a farm boy who spends his week in Washington," he is speaking the truth. For nearly all his life, Gejdenson, along with his brother Ike, has lived and worked on his family's dairy farm in Bozrah, in the eastern end of the Nutmeg State. That certainly makes him unique among the current crop of Congressional Minyanaires. Additionally, Gejdenson is the first child of Holocaust survivors to be elected to Congress. From the forests of Russia to the grassy pastures of Connecticut is a long, long journey. That journey has made all the difference in the man who, as of January 1999, has served ten consecutive terms in the House of Representatives.

Sam Gejdenson frequently speaks to gatherings of Holocaust survivors. He usually begins his speech (in Yiddish) saying: "I was born in Eschwege, Germany, in an American refugee camp." He then "launch[es] into a rundown of his parents' full names, his mother's maiden name, the names and precise locations of their native towns in Lithuania and Poland." When asked once why he goes into such detail on his family history, Gejdenson  responded: "Oh I always do that. One never knows when one might run into a *landsman* [Yiddish for 'countryman'], or discover the final fate of a lost second cousin, or be able to render such service to a fellow survivor."

The Gejdenson family owned and operated a lumber business in Parafianovo, a village in a part of Belarus, midway between Vilna and Smolensk, that before World War II belonged to Poland. With the coming of the war, Sam's father, Szloma, served in the Polish army against the Russians, who occupied eastern Poland while the Germans were invading the country's western portion. The town came under German control after Germany attacked Russia in June 1941, and its five hundred Jews were ghettoized.

Szloma was permitted to leave the ghetto during the days in order to work on a farm. On May 30, 1942, around 5:00 A.M., the Nazis came to round up the Jews of Parafianovo. At that precise time, Szloma Gejdenson was outside the ghetto and thus able to escape; his future wife Julia hid in the woods. According to Congressman Gejdenson, his father ran until he heard the sound of an approaching squad of soldiers, then burrowed himself into a woodpile. Before the soldiers' arrival, "a non-Jew came along, threw some scraps on the woodpile, and he was further covered up."

Once the soldiers passed, Gejdenson unearthed himself and escaped into the woods. Eventually, he was taken in by a non-Jewish woman named Serafina, who had eight children. Serafina was close to the Jews of Parafiamovo; she was the woman who cleaned the local synagogue. "To do that sort of thing . . . I can't even imagine the kind of courage it took," the Congressman says. "I mean, if I were alone, without children, perhaps I might be able to do what this woman did . . . facing certain death if she were caught. But having all those children, I guess I would have probably answered the door and said, 'please, leave us alone.'" The Germans wound up marching the five hundred Jews of Parafiamovo (Szloma and Julia being among the very few to escape) to a ravine on the outskirts of town, and shot them.

The senior Gejdenson eventually joined the Russian Army in order to fight the Nazis. Toward the end of the war, he met Julia, a young Jewish girl from Vilna, whom he married. After war's end, Gejdenson, deciding that "Stalin was not his cup of tea," started heading west. He got as far as Germany, where he and his now-pregnant wife were interned in an American displaced persons' camp at Eschwege. Sam Gejdenson was born in the camp on May 20, 1948.

In October 1949, the Gejdensons entered the United States, moving first to Boston. Being country-bred and -raised, Gejdenson never felt comfortable in such a large city. Aided with a

$500 loan from the *G'milut Chesed* ("Free Loan") Society, the elder Gejdenson purchased a small dairy farm in Bozrah, Connecticut, which has been the family home ever since. Connecticut's eastern region, an admixture of Yankee villages, small industrial cities, and dairy farms, has few Jewish families. While a child at the Fields Memorial School, young Sam Gejdenson traveled 10 to 12 miles a day in order to attend Hebrew school. Nonetheless, he recalls that as a child, "the house was always filled with Holocaust survivors . . . men and women with gold teeth and numbered tattoos who chattered away in Yiddish while drinking endless cups of tea." Although Gejdenson's father came from a religious home, his wife did not. As a result, they reached a bit of a compromise: no pork or shellfish ever entered the home, "but if somebody accidentally had a bit of dairy while eating meat, the roof didn't cave in."

Sam Gejdenson graduated from the Norwich Free Academy in 1966. Following two years at Mitchell Junior College in nearby New London, Gejdenson transferred to the University of Connecticut at Storrs. He received a B.A. in political science in 1970. As a Vietnam-era college student, Gejdenson started out "on the radical side, but began to feel very lonely." "It's not that I'm against violence in cases where you are deprived of a constitutional, legal method [for] chang[ing] policy," he said. "But here, I came around to believing that we did have a legal method, and that method was politics." Putting his newfound belief into action, Gejdenson became active in the unsuccessful Senate campaign of antiwar candidate Joseph Duffy. Shortly after Richard Nixon was reelected to the White House (1972), Gejdenson left the country, bound for Israel. He remained there for three months.

Upon his return, Gejdenson became active in local politics, getting himself elected chairman of the Bozrah Town Committee. The following year, 1974, he won a seat in the Connecticut General Assembly. While out campaigning, he met Karen Fleming, the administrator of the Maria Montessori School of Norwich. Fleming, who was "not raised as much of anything," had a Jewish father. She became Jewish before her marriage to Sam Gejdenson. The Gejdensons, who were divorced in the mid-1990s, have two children, Mia and Ari. Before the beginning of the One Hundred and Fifth Congress, Sam Gejdenson married Betsy Henley-Cohn. As a result of this second marriage, Gejdenson became the stepfather of Jesse Henley-Cohen.

Sam Gejdenson served two terms in the Connecticut house, chairing the Labor and Industrial Relations Committee. In early 1980, Second District Representative Christopher Dodd announced his candidacy for the Senate seat being vacated by the retiring *Abraham Ribicoff*. The Second District, comprising all of eastern Connecticut, has an interesting political history. Over a two-decade period, it was represented by a series of highly successful people who eventually left office not through defeat, but in order to try for greener pastures. Included in this roster are Chester Bliss Bowles (1901–1986), who before serving his single term (1959–61) in Congress had already had a distinguished career as the cofounder of the advertising giant Benton & Bowles, and as governor of Connecticut, ambassador to India, and trustee of the Rockefeller, Woodrow Wilson, and Franklin D. Roosevelt Foundations. In 1961, Bowles left Congress in order to become Under Secretary of State in the Kennedy administration. Bowles was replaced in Congress by Horace Seeley-Brown, Jr., who gave up his seat in order to run for the United States Senate seat vacated by Prescott Bush, father of future President George Herbert Walker Bush. (Seeley-Brown narrowly lost to Abe Ribicoff.) Seeley-Brown was replaced by William St. Onge, who died in office. Next came Bob Steele, who left Congress in order to run for governor against Ella Grasso in 1974. Then came Dodd (himself the son of a former Senator), and finally, in 1980, Sam Gejdenson.

When Gejdenson first announced his candidacy for Chris Dodd's seat, he was given little chance of winning. Although his two terms in the General Assembly had given him a modicum of name recognition, he had little money and few connections. What he did possess were "an ability to organize a campaign, an instinctive feel for communicating issues to voters, a wry sense of humor, and the willingness to campaign hard personally." Gejdenson faced John Dempsey, the son of a former Connecticut governor, in the Democratic primary. Gejdenson emerged with a 62 percent to 38 percent victory. In the general election, his opponent was Republican Tony Guglielmo, who was not the party's first choice. A. Searle Field, the putative front-runner, had decided to drop out of the race shortly before the district convention, leaving the spot to Guglielmo. Gejdenson's ethnic background was neither a help nor a hindrance. The Second Congressional District has fewer Jewish voters than any district in the state. Most of its residents are "the offspring of migrants of the 1840–1924 wave, not of the Yankees who lived here during the revolution." Running on a small budget but with vast energy and good humor, Gejdenson bested Guglielmo 53 percent to 47 percent, even while Reagan was taking the district by a 46 percent–38 percent margin over Jimmy Carter.

Sam Gejdenson was assigned seats on Foreign Affairs and Interior and Insular Affairs. He quickly developed a reputation as a serious player with a down-the-line liberal voting record. For the most part, he voted against military appropriations. Back home in Connecticut, Gejdenson's rivals would claim that "Sam has voted against every weapons system except the bow and arrow." That wasn't necessarily the case. While voting against the MX missile, the B-1 bomber, and the Trident II submarine, he did support the Trident I, the Stealth bomber, and the Minuteman missile. Not too surprisingly, he became one of the most vocal congressional supporters of vast increases in the budget of the Coast Guard—the U.S. Coast Guard Academy, located in New London, is in the center of the Second District. As with any successful member of Congress, Gejdenson paid close attention to local issues as well.

In 1984, Sam Gejdenson tried to rotate to a seat on the Appropriations Committee, a plumb assignment. The seat went to a more moderate Democrat from Texas. With seniority, Sam Gejdenson became chair of the Foreign Affairs Subcommittee on International Economic Policy and Trade. As formidable as the name sounds, the post was without a great deal of clout: "Ways and Means has jurisdiction over trade agreements, the Senate guards its sole power to ratify treaties, and the U.S. trade representative is not eager to let congressmen into the loop."

Although Gejdenson has been reelected nine times, it has rarely been easy. His victory numbers have ranged from a high of 67 percent in 1986 to a low of precisely twenty-one votes in 1994. In 1986, Gejdenson faced former FBI agent Francis ("Bud") Mullin, who conservative Republicans believed would make an excellent candidate. Mullin suffered from two problems: he was greatly underfinanced and lacked credibility. He had originally come to the attention of the Republican Party during the Senate confirmation hearings for Labor Secretary Raymond Donovan. During the hearings, Mullin told Utah Senator Orrin Hatch that "the FBI had no evidence linking Donovan to organized crime." Later on, Mullin admitted that the FBI did indeed possess such evidence. When this information came to light, Mullin's candidacy fell apart. Gejdenson wound up carrying every city and town in the Second District except for the "affluent Republican stronghold" of Lyme.

In 1992, 1994, and 1996, Gejdenson faced State Senator Ed Munster. Though he outspent Munster by better than seven-to-one in their first confrontation, Gejdenson was only able to eke out a 3,875-vote victory. Sensing that 1994 would be his year, Munster immediately went back on the campaign trail. In their first rematch, Munster accused Gejdenson of "greas[ing] the wheel for Saddam [Hussein of Iraq] from his work on International Relations." In fact, Gejdenson had repeatedly excoriated the Bush administration for "misdeeds," arguing that it had "tilted toward Saddam Hussein." Specifically, Gejdenson accused Bush administration officials of letting the Iraqi leader use agricultural credits to purchase weapons prior to the August 1990 invasion of Kuwait. Although the argument carried some weight, Munster was able to attack Gejdenson for casting a vote against the Gulf War resolution.

Gejdenson's chances of victory were dealt a stunning blow when the *New London Day* came out against him, writing that he was "a career politician eager to protect his status quo." In a highly unusual move, the *Day* then endorsed not Munster, but third-party candidate David Bingham, a Norwich-area obstetrician and ice cream store owner. Bingham, the grandson of former Connecticut Governor and Senator Hiram Bingham, ran as the candidate of maverick Governor Lowell Weicker's Connecticut Party.

Despite the paper's endorsement, Bingham captured just 15 percent of the vote, enough to make the contest between Gejdenson and Munster a toss-up. Initial returns had Gejdenson ahead by two votes out of more than 186,000 cast. Recounts kept his margin to precisely two votes. Finally, the Supreme Court stepped in and declared Gejdenson the victor by twenty-one votes. The Republicans, who now controlled Congress, inexplicably refused to challenge the outcome of the race, despite the fact that ten years earlier, Gejdenson, then a member of the House Administration Committee, had helped to overturn a contested Indiana race in favor of a Democrat.

Perhaps the Republicans were too busy enacting their "Contract With America" to get involved in the political tussle. Speaking for the Republican majority, Washington Representative Jennifer Dunn said: "We're not the Democrats. We will not duplicate the Democrats' way of stealing seats." In their second rematch in 1996, Gejdenson defeated Munster by the slightly more comfortable margin of 52 percent to 45 percent.

In 1989, Sam Gejdenson entered the ranks of Democratic Party leadership with his appointment to the Steering and Policy Committee. Two years later, Speaker Thomas Foley tapped him to head a House Administration Committee task force on congressional campaign finance reform. Gejdenson produced a bill that "would have limited expenditures and provided some public financing." Both House and Senate voted for the bill, but it was vetoed by President Bush in 1992. Congress was unable to override the veto. As a reward for his loyalty, Foley appointed Gejdenson to run his 1993 reelection campaign for the speakership. Despite some "intraparty criticism" over his handling of the House bank scandal, Foley was easily reelected.

In 1998, Sam Gejdenson defeated Republican Gary Koval of Mansfield with nearly 62 percent of the vote—his highest percentage in years.

While in Washington, Sam Gejdenson, the "Connecticut dairy farmer," shares an apartment with former New York Representative (as of the beginning of the One Hundred and Sixth Congress, Senator) *Charles Schumer* and California Representative George Miller. On weekends, he returns to the family farm in Bozrah, the place where the "men and women with gold teeth and tattoos" used to sit around drinking tea and conversing in Yiddish.

References

Interview with Sam Gejdenson, Washington, D.C., February 1992.

Almanac of American Politics (1980–98 editions).

Politics in America (1986–98 editions).

Peter H. Wyden, *Stella* (New York: Simon & Schuster, 1992), pp. 336–337.

GILBERT, JACOB H. (1920–1981): *Democrat from New York; served six terms in the House (Eighty-sixth through Ninety-first Congress; March 8, 1960–January 3, 1971).*

A lifelong resident of the Bronx, Jacob H. Gilbert represented his neighbors, first in the New York State Assembly, then in the State Senate, and finally, for a decade on Capitol Hill. Gilbert, the son of Isidore and Rose (Miller) Gilbert, was born on June 17, 1920, in the Bronx, where his father owned a liquor store and his mother was active in the Muskoota Democratic Club. While still a youngster attending public school, Jacob Gilbert was already out ringing doorbells and making speeches on behalf of Democratic candidates.

Gilbert received both his B.A. and his LL.B. from St. John's University, and was admitted to the bar in 1944. While setting up a private practice, he continued up the ladder of the Democratic Party. In 1949, after becoming an election district captain in the Pontiac Democratic Club, he received his first public appointment: assistant corporation counsel of the city of New York. Shortly after receiving the appointment, he married Irma Steuler. They had three children: Miriam, Sandra, and Samuel.

In 1951, after working as assistant corporation counsel for nearly two years, Jacob Gilbert was elected to the New York State Assembly. He served three years in that body, and in 1954, was elected to the State Senate. His term of service in the upper chamber lasted until March 1960, when the people of New York's Twenty-second District elected him to the United States House of Representatives. Gilbert's victory came in a special election to replace Representative *Isidore Dollinger*, who resigned his seat after winning election as district attorney for Bronx County.

Jacob Gilbert made an immediate impact in the House; on his very first day in office, he introduced no fewer than twenty-one bills, something of a record for a freshman. During his six terms in the House, Gilbert became an influential member of the Ways and Means Committee. As a watchdog over the Social Security System, he worked hard to see that senior citizens received increases in their monthly pensions.

Gilbert devoted his life to Congress, finding little time to develop outside interests or activities. "I glance at detective stories in the evening, watch a little TV and relax with the family," he told an interviewer shortly after going to Congress. "I play a little golf as an excuse for fresh air and friendly conversation. The rest of my time and effort goes into my job."

Jacob Gilbert was defeated in the 1970 Democratic primary by *James H. Scheuer*. Following his congressional career, he went back into law, becoming a partner in the New York and Washington firm of Foley, Hickey, Gilbert, Power & O'Reilly. Despite a debilitating illness in his last several years, he managed to keep practicing law until the week before his death. Jacob Gilbert died on February 27, 1981, and was buried at the Mount Hebron Cemetery in Flushing, New York.

References

Biographical Directory of the United States Congress, 1774–1989, p. 1058.
New York Times, March 1, 1981.

GILMAN, BENJAMIN ARTHUR (1922–):
Republican from New York; has served fourteen terms in the House (Ninety-third through One Hundred and Sixth Congress; January 3, 1973–present).

As early as the first decade of the twentieth century, there were upwards of seven hundred Jews living in the Catskill foothills of New York. Almost half were farmers. The majority were boarding-house keepers—progenitors of the hoteliers who would one day make places like Grossinger's and the Concord a mecca for generations of Jewish vacationers. Running through New York's Orange, Sullivan, and Ulster counties, the Catskill region today is "one of the few predominantly Jewish non-metropolitan areas in the United States." It has also been home to generations of blue-blood public servants all named Hamilton Fish. Up until relatively recently, no Jew had ever represented upstate New York in Congress. That changed in 1972, when voters in the Twenty-second District sent Benjamin Gilman to Washington. Now one of the most senior Republicans on the Hill, he has also represented the Catskill region longer than any representative in American history.

Benjamin Arthur Gilman, the son of Harry and Esther (Gold) Gilman, was born in Poughkeepsie, New York, on December 6, 1922. He was raised in Middletown, where his immigrant parents owned a dry-cleaning store; as of the 1990s, the store still exists. Middletown was—and still is—"a shabby railroad terminus that lost most of its small industry to non-union shops in the South." During Gilman's youth, it had somewhere between five hundred and nine hundred Jews. In 1933, Ben Gilman accompanied his father to Nazi Germany, where the ten-year-old saw Nazi storm troopers marching through the streets of Berlin. That haunting image has stayed with him ever since.

Gilman was educated in the Middletown public schools and the University of Pennsylvania's Wharton School of Finance and Commerce, from which he received a B.S. in

1946. From 1942 to 1945, Gilman served as a staff sergeant in the 19th Bomb Group of the 20th Army Air Force, flying thirty-five missions over Japan. At war's end, the navigator had earned the Distinguished Flying Cross and the Air Medal with Oak Leaf Clusters. Following his graduation from Wharton, Gilman attended New York Law School, from which he earned a LL.B. in 1950.

Ben Gilman married his first wife, Jane Prizant, in 1954. Like her husband, she was a practicing attorney. They had four children: Jonathan Harrison, Susan, David, and Ellen. A drunk driver killed Ellen at age fourteen; David died of AIDS. Ben and Jane Gilman underwent a particularly rancorous divorce in 1978. Gilman married his second wife, Rita Gail Keller Kelhoffer, in November 1984, in the process becoming the stepfather of Alan Craig and Eric Ray Kelhoffer. Divorced from his second wife in 1997, Gilman is now married for a third time, to Georgia Gilman.

After practicing law in Middletown for four years, Gilman was appointed assistant attorney general in the New York Department of Law. From 1956 to 1957, he was attached to the New York Commission on Courts, and from 1956 to 1964, worked as counsel to the New York Assembly's Committee on Local Finance. In 1966, the people of Middletown elected Ben Gilman to the first of three terms in the New York State Assembly. In 1972, he entered the race for the Twentieth Congressional District seat held by Democrat John Goodchild Dow. Originally elected to the Eighty-ninth Congress in 1965, Dow, a liberal, served two terms before losing his seat to Republican Martin B. McKneally in 1968. Sitting out one term, Dow regained his seat in 1970.

Armed with an $11,000 gift from wife Jane, Gilman beat Yale Rapkin in the Republican primary, and then set his sights on Representative Dow. Although a moderate Rockefeller Republican, Gilman nonetheless was able to position himself to the right of Dow, whom he continually referred to as an ultra-liberal. Aided by the Nixon landslide, Gilman captured the Twentieth District seat with 48 percent of the vote. Down but not out, John Dow ran against Gilman again in 1974; this time Gilman came in at 54 percent. Sixteen years later (1990), the then eighty-five-year-old Dow ran against Gilman in what was called "the most unusual comeback attempt of the year." Predictably, Gilman buried Dow—by nearly 60,000 votes.

For years, Gilman was viewed by his House colleagues as "a man of constant motion and little impact," a man who "rarely says anything public that is not written out on paper ahead of time, but once he starts reading . . . is rarely willing to stop until he gets to the end." One backbencher referred to him as "a stealth member of Congress, [who's] made a career out of being inconspicuous, unquoted, [thereby] giv[ing] him a freedom to basically do whatever he wants in obscurity."

During his first decade-and-a-half in Congress, Gilman was one of the last of a dying breed: a "Gypsy moth"—a Northeastern Republican moderate. As a moderate, Gilman opposed Ronald Reagan's 1982 budget and tax bills, and was one of only two House Republicans to vote against a constitutional amendment requiring a balanced budget. Throughout the Reagan and Bush years, Gilman's percentage of votes against the administration was among the highest of any Republican. In 1994, he voted with the Clinton administration 71 percent of the time, thereby becoming the "most senior Republican with such a high record of support" for the Democrat President.

Gilman has had a long career on the House Foreign Affairs Committee, where he "made a minor specialty of obtaining the release of international prisoners." In 1978, Gilman helped negotiate a tricky three-way exchange of prisoners among the United States, East Germany, and Mozambique. In 1980, he fought to have thirty Americans freed by Castro; upon their arrival in Miami, Gilman was on hand to greet them. In 1985, he was involved in American efforts to obtain the freedom of jailed Soviet dissident Anatoly (Natan) Sharansky. Gilman discussed the refusenik's plight with an East German lawyer named Wolfgang Vogel. According to *Politics in America*, "Vogel later took part in official negotiations that led to Shcharansky's [sic]

release, and the swap of eight convicted spies."

In 1984, Gilman teamed with fellow International Relations Committee member *Tom Lantos* in sponsoring legislation requiring that the American embassy in Israel be moved from Tel Aviv to Jerusalem. Gilman argued that it was a basic courtesy to establish the embassy in the capital city: "By our resistance to move our embassy from Tel Aviv to Jerusalem, we do a disservice to the government and people of Israel as well as ourselves." The proposal was dropped in favor of a nonbinding resolution, which languished for years. The resolution was eventually approved during the early days of the Clinton administration but never implemented by the President.

During debate on the 1985 foreign aid authorization bill, Gilman and Washington Republican *John Miller* appended an amendment that permitted the President to "ban all trade with a country that supports or advocates terrorism." The amendment was directed mainly at Libyan strongman Muamar el-Qaddafi; in 1986, President Ronald Reagan used it as legal justification for cutting off trade with Libya and urging all American citizens to leave that nation. Gilman also became active in international drug interdiction "long before it became a hot political issue." His interest in the issue was personal: one of his children had become involved in drugs and had to be hospitalized.

At the beginning of the One Hundred and Third Congress (January 1993), following the retirement of Michigan Republican William Broomfield, Ben Gilman became ranking member of the House International Relations Committee. In order to assume that position, he gave up the senior Republican spot on the Post Office and Civil Service Committee. Two years later, when the Republicans, after forty years in the political wilderness, took over the House, Gilman stood poised to take over the committee's chairmanship. At first, members of the House Republican leadership balked; Gilman's moderate voting record on social issues (pro-choice, against prayer in the public schools) made him suspect. In the end, Gilman's seniority carried the day and won him the coveted position. As International Relations Committee chair, Gilman, although not much of a global strategist, has emerged as a spokesman on a broad array of foreign policy issues, particularly regarding Israel, Somalia, Haiti, and Bosnia.

Over the past quarter-century, Gilman has "quietly built himself a finely tuned money machine, a slick fundraising apparatus based on PAC money and donations from ultra-Orthodox Jews." With vast financial resources at his disposal, he regularly wins reelection with 65 percent to 70 percent of the vote. His only difficult reelection campaign came in 1982, when redistricting forced him to run against House colleague Peter Peyser. Peyser, a Republican-turned-Democrat, had represented parts of the newly constituted Twentieth District from 1971 to 1977. After failing to win a Senate seat in the 1976 election, Peyser went back to serving in Congress from 1979 to 1982. In the 1982 campaign, "Peyser had the party-registration advantage and Gilman the edge in familiar territory." It turned out to be a nastier, angrier campaign than Gilman was used to: Peyser criticized him for opposing the nuclear-weapons freeze and for supporting military aid to El Salvador. Gilman, whose campaign style was generally less combative, fired back, labeling the former Republican Peyser an "ultra-liberal Democratic Congressman." Peyser won the Westchester County portion of the district (his home base), while Gilman scored heavily in Sullivan County. On election day, Gilman won by the not-overwhelming margin of 54 percent to 44 percent.

Gilman has been an outspoken critic of Palestinian violations of the Oslo Accords. In 1996, in an effort to pressure the Palestinians to comply with the peace agreements, Gilman, in his capacity as chairman of the House International Relations Committee, blocked $10 million out of the Clinton administration's $100 million annual aid package to Yasir Arafat. He also arranged for the General Accounting Office to undertake a detailed examination of corruption in the Palestinian Authority's handling of foreign aid and an assessment of the PLO's hidden financial assets.

Representative Gilman is known to many of his colleagues as "Gentle Ben." To others, he is an enigma. One example: following his son David's death from AIDS, Gilman began to support gays in the military. "I like what Senator [Barry] Goldwater said. . . . If he can shoot straight, that's the most important aspect of someone's military qualifications."

Benjamin Gilman was elected to a fourteenth term in November 1998. Running against Greenburgh Town Supervisor Paul Feiner, Gilman got an unexpected lift when Feiner's campaign computer suffered a "breakdown": voters throughout the Twentieth District received computerized telephone calls from the Feiner campaign at three and four o'clock in the morning. When asked what had happened, Feiner commented sheepishly that the automated telephone system "had gone crazy." Even without the gaff, Gilman's reelection was never in real jeopardy. He defeated Feiner 58 to 38 percent.

Gilman, white-haired and avuncular, will likely remain a power in the House as long as he wishes.

References

Interview with Benjamin Gilman, July 1994.
Almanac of American Politics (1974–98 editions).
New York, June 19, 1995, pp. 61–66.
People magazine, June 19, 1978.
Politics in America (1980–98 editions).
Progressive, June 19, 1996, p. 10.

GLICKMAN, DANIEL ROBERT (1944–):
Democrat from Kansas; served nine terms in the House (Ninety-fifth through One Hundred and Third Congress; January 3, 1977–January 3, 1995). U.S. Secretary of Agriculture, 1995–present.

Democrat Dan Glickman, the only minyanaire from the great state of Kansas, is one of the few people in political life who can honestly say, "in defeat, there is advancement." For when Glickman lost his Fourth District seat in one of 1994's major upsets, he looked like a man who had fallen off the top of the mountain. One might have expected him to go back into private practice or become one of Washington's omnipresent consultants. To the contrary, a mere seven weeks after defeat, Glickman, like the legendary phoenix, rose from the ashes of political oblivion. He was nominated by President Bill Clinton to be Secretary of Agriculture, the one position in government he truly coveted.

Glickman was not the original family name. The Secretary's paternal grandfather, Yankev Moshe Leikech, arrived in Wichita from Chudow Bolinsk, Russia, in 1910. He was the only member of his family of eight children to come to America. Upon arriving in Wichita, where he had a second cousin, Leikech began giving some thought to his American name. An acquaintance told him: "You know, I have a friend who is a good American, an honorable man who always pays his bills. Why don't you adopt his name?" "Sounds good to me," Yankev Moshe Leikech said. "So what's his name?" "Glickman," answered his friend. So Yankev Moshe Leikech became Jacob Morris Glickman. According to his son, Milton Glickman, there are virtually no Glickmans who are related to them. "We get calls from time to time from people named Glickman who want to know if we're related. I always have to tell them, 'Sorry, but no.'"

Jacob Glickman went to work in a scrap yard. After about a month, he decided to start his own business. By 1915, he had a going concern.

Glickman Scrap Metal is still in business after more than eighty years, with Milton, age eighty-one in 1999, still heading the company. Dan Glickman's paternal grandmother, Molly Goetzel, came to Wichita from Poland around the same time as her future husband. Jacob met Molly at her engagement party. For reasons that Milton can no longer remember, Molly broke off her engagement and started going with Jacob. They were married in 1916. Nine months and three days after their marriage, their first son, Milton, was born. "In those days, if a baby was born even one day shy of nine months after the marriage, people would talk," Milton recalls. "Well, my mother was ready to give birth a few days before nine months. Since she didn't want any tongues wagging, she took to bed for three days just to make sure." The Glickmans belonged to Wichita's more traditional synagogue, Ahavas Achim, where Jacob, Milton, and his brother Billy would all serve as president. Although observant of the Jewish holidays, the Glickmans did not keep kosher.

Dan Glickman's mother, Gladys Koppelman, came to Wichita at age eleven, shortly after her parents' divorce. Her mother then married Leo Gelman, who owned a delicatessen. Milton Glickman met Gladys Koppelman almost immediately upon her arrival in Wichita. "In those days, there were only about 75 Jewish families in town, so whenever someone new arrived, you got to know them pretty quickly," Milton said. The Glickmans had three children: Norman, born in 1940; Dan, born in 1944; and Sharon, born in 1948.

Daniel Robert Glickman, was born in Wichita, Kansas, on November 24, 1944. At the time of his birth, Wichita was about to become the Sunflower State's largest city. Founded in 1864 and named for a local Indian tribe, Wichita is situated on a broad plain in south-central Kansas at the junction of the Arkansas and Little Arkansas rivers. Originally the center of a booming wheat and cattle market, Wichita's postwar economy has come to be based largely on aviation—both Boeing and Cessna have major plants there. For the past generation, Wichita has been the nation's leading center for building small planes. In 1990, Wichita had a population of approximately 304,000, of whom no more than 1,000 were Jewish.

Dan Glickman was educated in the Wichita public schools and bar mitzvah at Ahavas Achim, where his father served as president. He received a B.A. in history from the University of Michigan in 1966. Two months after his graduation, he married Rhoda Joyce Yura, a native of Detroit. Their son, Jonathan, was born in 1969; daughter, Amy, in 1972. As of 1998, Jonathan Glickman was president of Caravan Studios, a division of the Disney Corporation.

In 1969, after receiving his law degree from George Washington University, Dan Glickman remained in Washington, working for a year as a trial attorney with the Securities and Exchange Commission. Returning to Wichita in 1970, he became an officer in Glickman Inc., "a family concern specializing in recycling metals." Passing the Kansas bar, Glickman spent the five years between 1971 and 1976 working first as an associate, then as a partner, with the firm of Sargent, Klenda, and Glickman.

In 1973, the twenty-eight-year-year-old Glickman won a seat on the Wichita Board of Education; within two years he was that body's president. In this capacity he "kept his name visible in the Wichita media by pushing for open board meetings and a school ombudsman." He also used the post to make known his positions on various local problems. In 1976, Glickman decided to make a run for the Fourth District congressional seat held by Republican Garner Shriver. Republicans had represented the Fourth District, which included "all of Wichita and most of its suburbs, plus some farming territory and the small city of Hutchinson to the north," for forty years. Edward Rees (1886–1969), a native of Emporia, Kansas, represented the district from 1936 to 1961. Shriver (1912–), a Wichita native succeeded Rees and was elected with relative ease until 1974. In that year, facing a "lackluster, low-spending" Democratic opponent named Bert Chaney, Shriver was only able to eke out a 49 percent to 42 percent victory—an ominous sign for a six-term incumbent.

While Shriver and Chaney were going head-to-head, Glickman was being baptized in statewide politics. During that election season, he served as regional coordinator for Democrat William Roy's Senate campaign (Roy lost to Republican Bob Dole). Two years later, the thirty-one-year-old Glickman decided to go for Garner Shriver's seat, though the odds were against him. Besides having all the benefits of incumbency, Shriver had the comfort of knowing that the Fourth District hadn't voted for a Democrat since 1936, the year FDR swamped Kansas Governor Alf Landon. (Ironically, William Randolph Carpenter, the last Democrat to represent the Fourth, also came to Congress from the Board of Education.)

Glickman passed the first hurdle with ease, winning a four-way Democratic primary with 62 percent of the vote.

Despite his seeming advantages, Shriver turned out to be "considerably less ambitious" than Glickman. At age sixty-four, he "didn't campaign as hard or as vigorously as one would expect of someone who really wanted to be Congressman." For his part, Dan Glickman ran as a strong supporter of the B-1 bomber, part of which would be built in Wichita. Glickman also benefited from his "identification with local problems in a year in which Washington was held in suspicion." One of Glickman's campaign themes ran: "You've had 16 years of a professional politician. Now is the time for a citizen congressman." Due to a Supreme Court ruling outlawing limits on candidates' expenditures on their own campaigns, Glickman was able to raise and spent nearly $105,000—an extraordinary amount for a nonincumbent in 1976. Fourth District voters handed him a 51 to 49 percent victory.

Dan Glickman received what for a Kansan were two choice committee assignments: Agriculture, and Science and Technology. In his early days in Congress, Glickman voted as a moderate and established a reputation for offering "symbolic amendments that struck at the heart of members' personal privileges." At one point, he proposed taking elevator operators, virtually all of whom were patronage employees, off most of the automatic elevators in the Capitol. He also proposed denying members a hardbound set of the *Congressional Record* for personal use, and sought to restrict insertions in the *Record* to items "relevant to government matters."

From almost his first day on the Hill, Glickman was "more skeptical about government programs than most Democrats," and somewhat more inclined to hold down spending. This stance, along with his penchant for issuing a vast array of press releases, did not endear him to his colleagues. In his early days as a representative, he was, in the words of the *Almanac of American Politics*, "no leadership favorite."

As a member of the House Agriculture Committee, Glickman was predictably "solicitous and attentive to wheat programs," and became an expert on the regulation of the futures markets. In 1982, he pushed through legislation tightening up their regulation. With maturation came a broadening of his legislative interests and a growing, if at first grudging, respect. By 1978, he was already being touted as a possible candidate for statewide office back home.

During his first term Dan Glickman received a 50 (out of 100) rating from the liberal Americans for Democratic Action, and a 48 rating (also out of 100) from the Conservative Americans for Constitutional Action. His middle-of-the-road voting record earned him an easy reelection victory in 1978; he defeated Republican Jim Litsey by a better than two-to-one margin.

With the build-up of seniority, Glickman starting receiving positive reviews from political journalists. By the early 1980s, the *Almanac of American Politics*, which had once called him "a media-seeking maverick," was reporting that "Glickman has managed to extend his legislative tentacles from farm policy to aeronautics research to product liability law without seeming to be a dilettante." In 1982, Glickman joined the Judiciary Committee. He quickly worked his way up to chairmanship of the Subcommittee on Administrative Law. In that post, he cranked out legislation to improve federal debt collection and to combat medical malpractice in the military.

At the beginning of the One Hundredth Congress, Glickman, now starting his fifth term, inherited the chairmanship of the Agriculture Subcommittee on Wheat, Soybeans, and Feed Grains. In order to gain this post, he had to give up his Judiciary Subcommittee chairmanship. At the time, there were deep divisions among his fellow Democrats as to the future of federal agri-

culture programs and the ailing farm economy. As one writer noted at the time, "assuming the helm of this subcommittee [can] be likened to walking through a mine field."

In 1987, Glickman got a seat on the Steering and Policy Committee, the panel that makes Democratic committee assignments.

From his position as a member of the Agriculture Committee's hierarchy, Glickman had a major impact on all farm legislation. None of his legislative activity, however, was as prescient or as historically important as an amendment he offered to the 1990 Farm Bill. That year, he inserted a clause that disqualified Iraq from receiving any important assistance, "including loan guarantees and export enhancement shipments, based on its human rights record and suspension from guaranteed loan programs." The amendment took a degree of courage; its passage would undoubtedly cost Kansas farmers a bundle in sales. Not surprisingly, the Bush administration vigorously opposed it, claiming that its passage would worsen relations between the United States and Iraq. Glickman persisted, however, and the amendment passed 234–175.

At the start of the One Hundred and Third Congress, Dan Glickman became chair of the House Intelligence Committee. He immediately launched a campaign to "demystify" the nation's intelligence operations, promising "to hold frequent open sessions of the panel in addition to the usual closed-door meetings." In reality, he would have greatly preferred being named Bill Clinton's Secretary of Agriculture. Instead, that post went to his Agriculture Committee colleague, Mike Espy of Mississippi. Nonetheless, Dan Glickman loved being a member of Congress. Staff members report that "sometimes he went to work on the weekends just to open the mail."

Glickman's congressional career came to a sudden and crashing end in November 1994, when he was defeated by Kansas State Senator Todd Tiahrt. Conservative and a devout Christian, Tiahrt's great cause in his State Senate race had been a concealed weapons law allowing citizens, on application, to carry firearms. In the Congressional election, Tiahrt ran ads showing Glickman's face morphing into Bill Clinton's. He further targeted Glickman's vote for the 1994 Crime Bill with its assorted gun-control provisions. Despite being outspent by a better than three-to-one margin, Tiahrt defeated Dan Glickman 54 percent to 46 percent. Upon losing, Glickman was quoted as saying: "Any candidate, no matter how perceptively strong, must stand for specific principles and articulate them to the public. I did not do that. I ran on my history, not on my future. Would that have made a difference in this race, I don't know. But ideas are what matter in politics." Then, a smile on his face, he added: "The public has spoken—the bastards!"

During his period as a lame-duck legislator, Glickman "did not go out of his way to endear himself to the White House." He voted against ratification of the global trade accord that President Clinton had made a priority. Nonetheless, in January 1995, the President nominated Dan Glickman to replace Mike Espy as Secretary of Agriculture. Glickman's nomination was approved with relative ease. Prior to making the nomination, President Clinton asked Dan Glickman to become his chief of staff. According to Milton Glickman, his son was advised by friends Albert Gore, Dick Gephardt, and Leon Panetta that the position would entail a virtual end to his personal life. "You can expect calls from the President at 2:00, 3:00, and 4:00 in the morning; you'll never see your family," they warned. Glickman respectfully declined the President's offer. Shortly thereafter, President Clinton nominated him for the Agriculture post.

As Secretary of Agriculture, Dan Glickman has proven to be amazingly popular among his new constituency. During the 1996 elections, he was the cabinet officer whom congressional candidates requested most often for campaign appearances. Upon assuming the reins of the Agriculture Department, he began a campaign to urge restaurants, hotels, and other institutions to "glean" unwanted food and give it to programs that feed the homeless. Glickman is the first Agriculture Secretary in more than a generation to appear before an Appropriations Subcommittee to declare himself "ultimately responsible for the decisions of the Forest Service." Glickman's predecessors had commonly distanced themselves from the forest agency. He has also become the first Agriculture Secretary to address the Council on Foreign Relations, cautioning its members (most of whom are free-traders) that "agriculture exports to China may not increase as quickly as traders hope because the Chinese still regard agricultural self-sufficiency as a worthy goal."

For more than twenty years, Dan Glickman has worn a sunflower in his lapel every day. "The sunflower," President Clinton remarked at the press conference nominating Glickman, "reminds him of where he's from, the values of the heartland that make him what he is." In late March 1998, Glickman went before the national media to announce that, within three months, a preparation for the eradication of salmonella in chickens would become available to farmers across the country. For a man who had suffered political defeat, Dan Glickman was certainly back on top.

References

Interview with Milton Glickman, March 1998.
Almanac of American Politics (1978–96 editions).
National Journal, vol. 29 (June 14, 1997), pp. 1192–95.
New York Times December 27, 1994, 12:1.
Politics in America (1980–96 editions).

GOLDER, BENJAMIN MARTIN (1891–1946):

Republican from Pennsylvania; served four terms in the House (Sixty-ninth through Seventy-second Congress; March 4, 1925–March 3, 1933).

In 1939, six years after he left Congress, Benjamin Golder's picture appeared on the front page of the *New York Times*. It was the only time that Golder was accorded such distinction, and had virtually nothing to do with politics. That year, Golder served as attorney in one of the Depression era's most sensational cases: the bribery and extortion trial of Martin T. Manton, a judge on the United State Circuit Court of Appeals. A millionaire appointed to the federal bench by President Woodrow Wilson in 1916, Manton had seen his fortune disappear with the coming of the Depression. Desperate to "bolster or protect his interests in the face of rapidly declining values," Manton began mulcting litigants before his court in exchange for favorable rulings. Brought to trial by New York County's crusading new district attorney, Thomas Dewey, he was convicted of "selling his integrity for cash," more than $185,000 in eight specific cases. Most of these were suits having to do with patent-infringement claims that involved heavy losses for the losing side. Despite Golder's best efforts, Manton was disbarred, fined $10,000, and sentenced to serve time in the federal penitentiary. Golder's photo appeared on page 1 of the *Times* the day of Manton's sentencing.

Benjamin Martin Golder, the son of Joseph and Minnie Golder, was born in Alliance, New Jersey, on December 23, 1891. When he was two, the Golders moved approximately 32 miles north of Alliance to Philadelphia, where Benjamin attended public school. In 1913, he graduated from the law department of the University of Pennsylvania and immediately went into private practice. Three years later, at age twenty-five, Golder was elected as a Republican to the state legislature for the first of four consecutive terms. In 1917, with the coming of World War I, he enlisted in the fledgling Naval Aviation Service. He was discharged at war's end, an ensign.

In 1924, Golder resigned his legislative seat in order to challenge six-term incumbent George Washington Edmonds in the Republican primary for Congress from Pennsylvania's Fourth District. The Fourth District had been solidly Republican for three-quarters of a century. The last Democrat elected from the district had been *Henry M. Phillips* in 1856. With his win in the Republican primary, Golder was assured a seat in the Sixty-ninth Congress. He went on to serve four terms in the House, where his main concerns were "the better treatment of disabled service men" and "changing America's new immigration law," which he termed "economically and morally unsound." The immigration law that Golder wished to revise was the National Origins Act of 1924, whose unabashed purpose was to limit the number of Southern and Eastern European immigrants entering America. By terms of the law, which went into effect in 1929, immigration was limited to 178,000 per year, based on the pernicious formula of 2 percent of the "nationals" in the 1890 census.

After serving four terms in the House, Benjamin Golder was defeated in the 1932 Republican primary by G. W. Edmonds, the man he had originally defeated eight years earlier. The Fourth District seat continued to be held by Republicans until 1948, when Democrat *Earl Chudoff* defeated Franklin J. Maloney. In the 1970s, a Democrat, *Joshua Eilberg*, would once again hold the seat.

On January 16, 1930, Golder married Margery Lee "Peggy" Mastbaum, the daughter of the late Jules E. Mastbaum, president and chief executive officer of the Stanley Company of America. Mastbaum, a Wharton graduate and perennial chairman of the Philadelphia Federation of Jewish Charities, had made a fortune in real estate and the motion picture industry. The Stanley Company, named after his late brother, owned motion picture palaces (as they were then known) all along the eastern seaboard and in the Midwest. Shortly before his death in 1926, Mastbaum donated $1 million for the creation of a Rodin Museum in Philadelphia. He counted among his closest friends New York Mayor Al Smith and the Gimbel brothers.

Following his defeat in 1932, Golder resumed his legal career as vice president of Albert M. Greenfield & Company, a real estate firm. Golder's participation in the Manton case apparently came about because of his work with Greenfield; Judge Manton's lost wealth had been based largely on Philadelphia real estate holdings.

Benjamin Golder was commissioned a captain in the United States Army on February 5,

1943, During the war, he served nearly two years on the staff of Major General Louis B. Hershey, the future head of the Selective Service System. Golder was honorably discharged as a lieutenant colonel on July 1, 1945. He returned to Philadelphia, engaged in a little law and a little banking; he died after a brief illness on December 30, 1946. Golder was interred in Philadelphia's Mount Sinai Cemetery. A member of the Conservative B'nai Jeshurun Congregation, Golder was survived by his wife and two daughters, Norma and Joan.

References

American Jewish Year Book, vol. 49, p. 611.
New York Times, May 23, 1939, 4:2; November 18, 1946, 31:3; December 31, 1946, 18:3.
Universal Jewish Encyclopedia.
Who Was Who in America, vol. 2.
Who Was Who in American Jewry, 1926, 1928, 1938.

GOLDFOGLE, HENRY MAYER (1856–1929):
Democrat from New York; served seven terms in the House (Fifty-seventh through Sixty-third Congress and Sixty-sixth Congress; March 4, 1901–March 3, 1915, March 4, 1919–March 3, 1921).

Until its dismantling at the hands of *Fiorello La Guardia* in the 1930s, Tammany Hall was the political power in New York City. Ruled by crafty, corrupt bosses like William Marcy "Boss" Tweed, "Honest John" Kelly, "Big Tim" Sullivan, and "King Richard" Crocker, Tammany ran New York City's Democratic Party with an iron fist and plenty of patronage. Originally Irish in makeup, the shrewd Tammany sachems quickly came to recognize that, in order to remain on top of the political heap, they would have to incorporate the burgeoning Jewish masses of New York's Lower East Side. Always on the lookout for nascent political talent, the boys from Tammany kept their eyes wide open and, by the last decade of the nineteenth century, started bringing the sons of Abraham, Isaac, and Jacob into their club.

For the Jewish immigrant, the world of politics and political intrigue was as foreign as subways and shrimp. Coming from politically oppressive Eastern Europe, most Jews had a native and thoroughly understandable aversion to the intrigues of city hall. To the struggling East Side Jew, the captains, lieutenants, and foot soldiers of Tammany were a bit unsavory. To enter the Tammany fold one had to go through a process of metamorphosis. According to Irving Howe, "a Jewish aspirant casting his fortune with Tammany had to take on or simulate a certain rough plebeian gloss. He learned to chew, smoke, and gamble. . . . He rooted himself in the neighborhood as the agent of the Irish leader though in so doing he sometimes harmed his own prospects, for by cutting himself off from Jewish communal life and devoting himself entirely to the machine, he might become excessively dependent on the leader."

Despite the obstacles, many Jewish boys fought and scraped their way up the Tammany ladder, beginning mostly as "hangers-on, messengers, and flunkies." Again, it wasn't easy—for either side. To Jewish mothers and fathers, becoming a Tammany flunky wasn't exactly the kind of career they envisioned for their sons. To the Irish of Tammany Hall, the Jews were "different." The Irish might learn to keep their hats on when attending a bar mitzvah or *bris*, and might even pick up a few Yiddish words and expressions. But there remained a high degree of discomfort. Again quoting Irving Howe: "such men felt uncomfortable with most immigrant Jews, as, for that matter, most immigrant Jews with them."

But New York's Jews weren't all immigrants. Possessed of acute civic "radar," Tammany's leaders started out by inviting native-born New York City Jews onto their political tenure track. One of the first of these was the New York–born and –bred *Jacob Cantor*, who in 1901, became the Tammany-appointed borough president of Manhattan, the first of seven Jews to hold that post. Later that year, Tammany sent its first Jew to Congress in the person of Henry Mayer Goldfogle.

One of Mayer and Hannah (Herz) Goldfogle's three children, Henry Goldfogle was born in New York City on May 23, 1856. The Goldfogles were thoroughly Americanized. Along with his brother Alexander and sister Matilda, Henry attended New York City's public schools. After graduating from Townsend Harris Hall High School, the preparatory school associated with City College, he read law, and was admitted to the New York Bar shortly after his twenty-first birthday in 1877. "Drafted" by Tammany Hall, Goldfogle, now in private practice, became the protégé of Fourth Assembly District leader John F. Ahearn, one of the first Tammany bosses to successfully integrate Jews into the fold. By the early 1890s, Ahearn, working out of a clubhouse at 290 East Broadway, had appointed Tammany's first Jewish "lieutenant," Leon Stand, the father of future Tammany luminaries Bert and Murray Stand.

Under Ahearn's sponsorship and tutelage, Goldfogle built up an impressive legal practice. In 1887, just a scant decade after his admission to the New York bar, Henry Goldfogle was elected justice of the fifth district court. In his first term on the court, he drafted and secured enactment of a law by the New York State legislature "providing for an expeditious remedy to collect judgments obtained by laborers, mechanics and other wage earners for wages earned or for labor performed." With the backing of Tammany Hall, he was easily reelected in 1893. Simultaneously, he served as judge of the municipal court of New York from 1888 to 1890. Rising through the

Tammany ranks, Goldfogle was sent as a delegate to the Democratic National Convention in both 1892 and 1896. In 1901, Goldfogle, occasionally referred to as "Tammany's pet Jew," was elected to the Fifty-seventh Congress.

Most of Henry Goldfogle's congressional career was spent carrying Tammany's water bucket in Washington. This is not to say that he was totally ineffectual. In 1902, Goldfogle became embroiled in what was, for Jews of the day, a political "hot button" issue: the 1832 Treaty of Commerce and Navigation between the United States and Russia. According to the terms of the treaty, each country agreed to grant the citizens of the other the right "to sojourn and reside in all parts whatsoever" of its territory. The wording of the treaty continued, somewhat innocuously, "on condition of their submitting to the laws and ordinances there prevailing, and particularly to the regulations in force concerning commerce." As the Russians read and interpreted this clause, they had the right to impose upon American Jews the same restrictions they imposed on their own Jewish subjects. And therein lay a potentially serious problem.

The problem came to the surface in the last half of the nineteenth century, when the Russian government repeatedly refused to permit American Jews, carrying valid American passports, to purchase property in Russia. After much futile diplomatic posturing on the part of both sides, it came to light that Russian consulates in the United States were even denying visas to American citizens who were Jews. The American Jewish community was up in arms, and petitioned the President to abrogate the treaty. In 1894, Representative *Isidor Raynor* of Maryland sponsored a resolution calling for the treaty's revocation, but it died in committee. In 1902, responding to the pleas of New York's "uptown" (read: German) and "downtown" (read: East European) Jews, Henry Goldfogle sponsored a similar resolution. Although Goldfogle's bill passed the House, it died in the Senate. Over the next decade, Henry Goldfogle kept his Jewish constituents happy by resubmitting his resolution of revocation.

The campaign for the treaty's nullification was carried on outside the halls of Congress. It reached a crescendo in 1911, at a mass rally held in Carnegie Hall. The speakers included Woodrow Wilson, then Governor of New Jersey;

Champ Clark, the Speaker of the House; Jacob G. Schurman, the president of Cornell University; and publisher William Randolph Hearst. Notably absent from the list of dignitaries was Congressman Goldfogle. Later that year, New York Representative William Sulzer, a non-Jew, introduced Goldfogle's old resolution in the House. It passed by a vote of 300 to 1. Realizing that both public and political sentiment were forthrightly behind the treaty's abrogation, President Wilson ordered his Secretary of State, former Senator Philander Knox, to revoke American compliance. The fight was won; Henry Goldfogle's role was relegated to no more than a footnote.

Although Henry Goldfogle went on to serve six consecutive terms in the House (1902–1912), getting reelected was never easy. His Lower East Side Ninth Congressional District was fast becoming home to a majority of America's Jewish socialists. In virtually all of his reelection campaigns, he was opposed by at least one socialist candidate. In the 1904 election, Goldfogle drew Joseph Barondess, the popular leader of the cloakmakers, as his opponent. Barondess managed to capture about 20 percent of the vote. In both 1906 and 1908, his opponent was Morris Hillquit, a true hero to the Jews of the Ninth District. Hillquit (1869–1933), née Moshe Hilkowitz, was an East Side icon. A native of Riga, Latvia, who had been swept up in the Bundist movement, Hillquit arrived in the United States in 1887, where he quickly mastered English and became a union organizer. Along with Eugene Debs and *Meyer London*, Hillquit was one of the true intellectual and political forces in American socialist circles. Harry Roskolenko, Hillquit's contemporary and friend, remembered him as a *tzaddik* ("righteous" or "saintly" man) who "almost single-handedly made the [Socialist] party our messiah."

Hillquit first squared off against Goldfogle in the election of 1906. The Socialists ran on a platform that urged protection for pushcart peddlers, sanitary tenements, clean streets, and better factory conditions. Hillquit's candidacy was backed by well-known outsiders like William Dean Howells, the distinguished man of letters, and the Russian writer Maxim Gorky, whose arrival in New York caused quite a stir. Hillquit and Gorky marched arm in arm up East

Broadway, drawing cheers from the crowds that lined the street. But if Hillquit had the message and emotion on his side, Tammany-backed Goldfogle had the organization. Nonetheless, Hillquit and the Socialists put a bit of a scare into Goldfogle's Tammany handlers: "In the closing days of the campaign, the Democratic camp became thoroughly panicky. A deal was speedily made with the local Republican machine, which openly urged its supporters to vote for Henry M. Goldfogle. . . . Mr. Goldfogle received all the votes of the Democratic party . . . and most of the Republican votes." A poster from the campaign read: "Vote for a 100% American . . . candidate of both Democratic and Republican Parties." Although Hillquit bettered his vote tally of 1906 (he received 26 percent), Goldfogle was easily reelected.

After losing again to Goldfogle in 1908, the leaders of the Socialist Party on the East Side decided to jettison Hillquit in favor of a more "politically acceptable" candidate. Hillquit had come under attack by the Bundists, the Yiddish daily *Varheit*, and Daniel De Leon, the Socialist Labor Party polemicist, for belonging to "those who hide their Jewish identity . . . who crawl after the *goyim* [non-Jews]." And, in fact, Hillquit was far more cosmopolitan than his would-be constituents. As a thinker, he rarely addressed issues in a way that the pieceworkers of East Broadway could understand. The Socialists decided that for the next election, Goldfogle would have to be opposed by a "man of the people." That man turned out to be *Meyer London*.

London garnered 33 percent of the vote in 1910, and 31 percent in 1912. Goldfogle and the boys from Tammany were becoming worried. In 1914, London carried 47 percent and took over Goldfogle's seat. For the next three election cycles, Goldfogle and London ran heated campaigns against each other, with London defeating "Tammany's pet Jew" in 1916, losing his seat in 1918, and recapturing it again in 1920, only to be unseated by yet another Tammany Jew, *Samuel Dickstein*, in the election of 1922.

Following his final campaign in 1920, Henry Goldfogle went back into private practice with his firm, Goldfogle and Dorf. Within a year he was appointed president of the New York City Board of Taxes and Assessments, a position he would hold until his death some eight years later.

Henry Goldfogle was a Reform Jew. A member of Congregation Rodeph Shalom, Goldfogle served as synagogue president from 1921 to 1929. He was also active in B'nai B'rith, serving as District 1 president for nearly a decade. A lifelong bachelor, Goldfogle lived for many years at the Hotel Imperial with his colleagues Abraham Turchin and Isaac Sabath.

Henry Goldfogle died on June 1, 1929 at the Imperial. Some 1,200 people attended his funeral, which was held at Central Synagogue. Rabbi Stephen S. Wise conducted the service; the main eulogy was delivered by Maurice B. Blumenthal, a deputy attorney general who for many years was Goldfogle's secretary. When his will was probated, it was discovered that Henry Goldfogle had amassed an estate of some $250,000, which he divided principally between his brother Alexander and his sister Matilda (Wertzberger) Goldfogle. He also made small bequests to his colleagues, Turchin and Sabath. Henry Goldfogle, referred to by most of his former constituents as "The Judge," was buried in Union Hills Cemetery on Long Island.

References

American Jewish Year Book, vol. 4, p. 172; vol. 6, pp. 101–102; vol. 24, p. 147; vol. 31, p. 93.

Irving Howe, *World of Our Fathers* (New York: Simon & Schuster, 1976), chap. 11.

Irving Howe and Kenneth Libo, eds., *How We Lived: A Documentary History of the Immigrant Jews in America* (New York: Richard Marek Publishers, 1979), chap. 8.

Jewish Encyclopedia.

New York Times, June 2, 1929, 39:4.

Universal Jewish Encyclopedia.

Who Was Who in America, 1926.

Who Was Who in American Jewry, 1926, 1928, 1938.

GOLDWATER, BARRY MORRIS (1909–1998):
Republican from Arizona; served five terms in the Senate (1953–1965, 1969–1987).

In 1971, seven years after his staggering defeat for the presidency, Senator Barry Goldwater was addressing the Alfalfa Club at its annual "Potential Candidate for President" banquet. Speaking in a jocular vein, the Arizona senator quipped: "You are to be congratulated. You have made a perfect selection. I have had experience. I have had an audience with the Pope. I have talked with Golda Meir. I have visited the Wailing Wall. I have been to Vietnam. The *New York Times Encyclopedia* has me listed as a Democrat. The Senate clerk calls me a Republican. Bill Buckley's *National Review* calls me a Conservative. And the *Washington Post* calls me a Neanderthal."

Sensing that he had the audience in the palm of his hand, Goldwater continued: "I start off with twenty million votes. I want to prove I can lose some of them. You see, I am really just an Episcopalian who is restricted to playing nine holes on Gentile golf courses because I am half Jewish!"

The Alfalfa Club story is true. The barb about the Senator playing only nine holes on a Gentile golf course is apocryphal. Some say the story started with Barry's brother Bob; the Senator didn't believe it. "I know my brother, he's not that smart," the Senator said whenever asked about the tale.

Nonetheless the story persisted. Goldwater said, "I don't know where my brother heard it, because I get credit for it and he's the one who [originally] told it. I still hear it. People will kid me. Even today I'll go out to dinner with good friends of mine and they'll have ham and they'll say, 'Go ahead, Goldie, you can eat it; just eat half of it.'"

Despite the fact that Barry Morris Goldwater was an Episcopalian, he is included in this book. Why? First, because the Goldwater family's Jewish history is both extensive and well-documented. Second, that was his wish. As the Senator noted on more than one occasion, "I'm very proud of the part of me that's Jewish. I just wish I had inherited a bit more of it." That was Barry Goldwater: straightforward, honest, and plainspoken. That Goldwater's paternal relatives were Jewish is just a fact he took in stride—that was who he was. Just like his roots in Arizona, his well-conceived conservatism, and his love of flying.

The Goldvassers were originally from Konin, Poland. Michel "Big Mike" Goldvasser, the future Senator's grandfather, was one of Hersh and Elizabeth Goldvasser's twenty-two children. In nineteenth-century Poland, it was normal for Jewish boys and young men to be drafted into the tsar's army for no fewer than twenty-five years—generally a fate tantamount to death. Rather than allow themselves to be shanghaied, Michel and his brother Joe fled Poland in 1845, eventually winding up in France. Faced with the prospect of taking sides in the Revolution of 1848, the brothers moved on to England. There, around 1849, Big Mike married an English Jew named Sarah Nathan. By this point, he had anglicized his name to Goldwater. The wedding ceremony took place in the London Jewish ghetto of Whitechapel. Years later, during World War II, Barry Goldwater attempted to locate his grandparents' marriage records; both the synagogue and all its records had been destroyed in the German Blitz. The Senator also tried to track down the families of the other Goldvasser siblings. He wrote: "I found some members of my immediate family, one distant relative in Africa, and one in Australia, and that's where I end."

While residing in London, the Goldvassers had two children, Elizabeth and Morris. In 1852, Michael and his brother Joe set off for America after hearing countless tales of how people were striking it rich in the gold mines of California. Sarah, her sister, and the two children traveled by way of Panama, where they crossed the Isthmus on horseback and then boarded a ship bound for San Francisco. By the time of their arrival in early 1853, the Goldwater brothers were living in Sonora, California, where they had established a liquor store on the ground floor of the town's brothel. Because of this unique arrangement, the brothers decided that it would be best for the women and children to remain in San Francisco, where they had another liquor store and dabbled in "notions." Eventually Big Mike and Joe moved to Los Angeles, where they were joined by their brothers Henry, Sam, and Ben. Big Mike was a wanderer by nature, "forever chasing rainbows," in the words of his most famous grandchild. Although a hard worker, he never succeeded in making his fortune. He and his brother Joe went broke, first in Sonora, then in both San Francisco and Los Angeles. In 1860, the brothers struck out for Arizona, living briefly in La Paz, then settling in the nearby town of Ehrenberg on the Colorado River.

Although Big Mike and Sarah lived apart for the better part of the next thirty years, they still managed to have eight more children, the Senator's father, Baron (Barry), being the youngest. Although Baron was raised as a Jew, when it came time to marry, there simply were no Jewish women around. These were the days of Territorial Arizona, where the Gunfight at the OK Corral was still a vivid memory, and Barry's Uncle Joe was friends with both the Earp brothers and Doc Holliday. Baron Goldwater met his wife Josephine at the Goldwater department store. They were married at St. Paul's Episcopal Church in Prescott, Arizona, in 1907. Their three children, Barry, Bob, and Carolyn, were all raised in prosperity as Episcopalians. The Goldwaters were a study in opposites: "'Mun' [Josephine's nickname] was a tomboy who loved the outdoors. Father . . . impeccably dressed, conservative, never drove a nail or a car in his life . . . slept in fresh sheets, never a bedroll under the stars, a man of measured words, tone and bearing."

Besides his mother, Barry Goldwater credited his father's brother, Morris, with being the single most important influence in his life. A short, energetic man, Uncle Morris was fluent in both Hebrew and Spanish, helped found the Arizona Democratic Party, and served more than twenty years as the mayor of Prescott. From his mother, Barry Goldwater learned the values of frankness, honesty, and patriotism. From his uncle, he received a thirst for involvement in the affairs of the community.

Barry Goldwater was born on New Year's Day, 1909. A popular, rebellious child, his father had him sent off to the Staunton Military Academy in Virginia, where he came under the tutelage of Major Alexander M. "Sandy" Patch, the man who would one day replace General George Patton as commander of the Seventh Army. Patch taught Goldwater the importance of discipline. By fits and starts, the young cadet did learn discipline; in his senior year, he won the outstanding cadet award, and was offered an appointment to West Point. Elated at first, Goldwater had to turn down the appointment and return to Arizona, where his father was seriously ill. To the end of his life, the Senator regretted that decision. Instead of an education at the Point, Barry Goldwater entered the University of Arizona in 1929. Again, his plans went awry; he had to drop out within the year due to his father's death. "As the eldest son . . . I went to work in the family department store to learn the business. That [leaving the University of Arizona] was the biggest mistake of my life."

Over the next several years, Barry Goldwater turned his family's department store into a top-flight establishment. In 1930, he was commissioned a second lieutenant in the Army Reserve, serving part-time with the 25th Infantry Division, until the outbreak of World War II. He also received a pilot's license and was a founder of the Arizona Air National Guard.

In 1932, Barry Goldwater began seriously courting Margaret ("Peggy") Johnson, of Muncie, Indiana. Peggy refused to marry her young suitor unless he would "quit flying and take up bridge." Goldwater agreed and the two were married in 1934. Of his twin promises, Goldwater later wrote, "Those were the two biggest white lies of my life." The Goldwaters had four children: Joanne, Barry Jr., Michael, and Peggy.

During World War II, Barry Goldwater entered the Army Air Corps, serving as a pilot with the 27th Ferry Squadron of the Air Transport Command. Originally assigned to New Castle, Delaware, he wound up flying missions in the China-Burma-India Theater. By war's end, he had become a major general.

After the war, Goldwater returned to Phoenix to run his family's department store, and became involved in both civic affairs and city politics. In those days, Phoenix was a wide-open city replete with crooked politicians, innumerable brothels, and a city manager–commission form of government that had gone through thirty-one city managers in less than thirty-five years and eleven police chiefs in a single decade. In 1949, a hundred of the city's most prominent citizens created a charter government committee which pressed for an elected city council and a strong city manager. Prompted by his close friend Harry Rosenzweig, Goldwater declared his candidacy for the Phoenix City Council in 1949. In November of that year, he was elected to his first political office—vice chairman of the new seven-member city council.

During his first year in office, the new city council "drove crime underground, balanced the city budget," and received an All American City Award from the National Municipal League. Goldwater quickly gained a reputation for being both hotheaded and plainspoken: "I raised hell in those council meetings. It never occurred to me to do otherwise. They beat around the bush, and it took hours, days, and weeks to get to the bottom of a problem. . . . So to get people to the point I would say in exasperation, 'You're a liar' or 'You're using Gestapo tactics.'"

Up until the early 1950s, Arizona was a solidly Democratic state. At the beginning of the decade, Republicans began mounting a serious campaign for the Governor's office. Their candidate, Howard Pyle, a veteran Arizona newsman, chose Goldwater to be his campaign manager. Pyle won an upset victory; the Republican Party was on the ascent in Arizona. Somewhat against his wife's wishes, Barry Goldwater decided to run against incumbent Democratic Senator Ernest W. McFarland. As Goldwater wrote of that campaign: "I wanted to take on McFarland. I was fed up with President Franklin D. Roosevelt's New Deal, especially the ballooning federal government and its increasing invasion of our lives." True to his already well-thought-out conservative philosophy, Goldwater called for "a balanced national budget, greater self-reliance across the spectrum of American life, more power to local government, a mightier military, and stronger, better directed opposition to communism." Goldwater defeated McFarland by a razor thin margin of less than 7,000 votes.

From his first day on Capitol Hill, Senator Goldwater let his colleagues know where he stood: "I had little interest in streamlining government or in making it more efficient, for I meant to reduce its size. I did not undertake to promote welfare, for I proposed to extend freedom. My aim was not to pass laws but to repeal them. It was not to inaugurate new programs but to cancel old ones that do violence to the Constitution." Goldwater busied himself with military and intelligence issues, voted against the censure of Senator Joe McCarthy ("the most stubbornly cussed character I ever met in my life"), and built a solid reputation as a conservative's conservative.

From 1955 to 1957, and again from 1959 to 1960, Goldwater was chosen by his colleagues to head the Senate Republican Campaign Committee. From this position, he crisscrossed the country, giving literally thousands of speeches in a seemingly single-handed attempt to refashion the GOP along conservative lines. Goldwater saw his party being strangled by the Eastern GOP establishment (read: Rockefeller), which he regarded as "a pale imitation of the Democratic Party." Throughout his long public career, Barry Goldwater always managed to have a balanced, honest view of himself: "I was a salesman. That's all. That's what my people were. Goldwater wasn't the big enchilada. Just a guy with a smile and a speech about freedom, opportunity, hard work, and hope. Hell, I was out there to wipe away the conservative stereotype stuffed shirts in celluloid collars and cufflinks who combed their hair the wrong way."

Goldwater's prominence kept growing. In 1960, Republican Party leaders asked him to give a major speech at their national convention. Goldwater and his fellow conservatives arrived at the convention loaded for bear. They were incensed that the would-be nominee, Vice President Richard M. Nixon, had sold out their conservative principles in the infamous "Treaty of Fifth Avenue." The "treaty" was Nixon's pledge to Nelson A. Rockefeller that in exchange for the New York governor's support, he would push for a more liberal Republican platform. Goldwater saw red, and referred to Nixon's surrender as an "American Munich."

Angry South Carolinians sought to place Goldwater's name in nomination, but the Senator demurred, asking those who would back him to instead vote for Nixon. In his speech to the fractious convention delegates, Goldwater stated: "We had our chance, and I think the conservatives have made a splendid showing at this convention. We've fought our battle. Now let's put our shoulders to the wheels of Dick Nixon and push him across the line. Let's not stand back. This county is too important for anyone's feelings; this country in its majesty is too great for any man, be he conservative or liberal, to stay home and not work just because he doesn't wholly agree. Let's grow up, conservatives. Let's, if we want to, take this party back and I think we can someday. Let's get to work."

With that speech, Barry Goldwater became *de facto* leader of the emerging conservative movement in America. Following John F. Kennedy's narrow victory, he continued setting out the conservative agenda for America. Shortly after the 1960 convention, Brent Bozell, an editor of the conservative *National Review*, published a 123-page, red-white-and-blue book of Goldwater's speeches that was to become the "bible" of the right. The book was entitled *The Conscience of a Conservative*. In this work, which sold in the hundreds of thousands, Goldwater clearly and concisely set out the conservative agenda in both practical and philosophical terms: "The basic difference between conservatives and liberals is that conservatives account for the whole man while liberals tend to stress the material man. Liberals tend to regard economic satisfaction as the dominant mission of society. . . . The primary concern of conservative political philosophy is the enhancement of man's spiritual nature." By 1964, the book had become "a rallying cry of the right against three decades of Franklin D. Roosevelt and the liberal agenda."

In 1964, Barry Goldwater became the Republican nominee for President of the United States through what amounted to a political draft. A realist, Goldwater knew from first to last that he had virtually no chance of winning. While officially he was campaigning against President Lyndon Johnson, in his heart Goldwater understood that he was really taking on the ghost of President Kennedy—an impossible task. He saw what was before him not as a campaign for the Presidency, but as a crusade for both the soul of the Republican Party and the future of conservatism in America. Short on funds and strategy, but equipped with a vast cadre of young volunteers, Goldwater waged what he felt was a "wild, magnificent, screwy,

splendid undertaking. . . . We knew exactly where we were going—to defeat at the polls and victory with the party."

During the campaign, Johnson and the media portrayed the Arizona Senator as a right-wing lunatic, who drew support from the John Birch Society, a racist whose election would mean the end of Social Security and the introduction of nuclear weapons to the escalating conflict in Vietnam. Even Goldwater's famous campaign slogan—"Extremism in the defense of liberty is no vice, and moderation in the pursuit of justice is no virtue"—was used as "proof" that the Republican nominee was a dangerous, far-right maniac. In its most vicious attack, the Johnson campaign aired a television commercial showing a little girl sitting in a sunny field of daisies. She begins plucking petals from a daisy. As she plucks, a male voice in the background starts a countdown: "ten, nine, eight . . ." At "one," the screen explodes, the little girl disappears in a mushroom cloud, and the voice intones: "These are the stakes. Vote for President Johnson on November third. The stakes are too high for you to stay at home."

Not surprisingly, the Arizona Senator felt that the Johnson ad campaign had gone well beyond the bounds of good taste. Barry Goldwater never hid his personal contempt for Lyndon Johnson. In his self named autobiography, Goldwater wrote: "LBJ made me sick . . . [he] was the epitome of the unprincipled politician. . . . His only political dogma was expediency. . . . Government was his political action committee, his slush fund, his firepower, his troops."

Barry Goldwater went down to one of the most crushing defeats in American political history. The Johnson-Humphrey ticket tallied 43 million votes to Goldwater's 27 million. Goldwater and his running mate, Buffalo-area Congressman William Miller (who years later would do an American Express Card commercial asking that famous question "Do you know me?"), carried but six states: Arizona, Alabama, Georgia, Louisiana, Mississippi, and South Carolina. Uncowed by defeat, Goldwater proudly proclaimed that "the new GOP has been forged in the fires of the 1964 presidential campaign." Nationally syndicated columnist David Broder noted some years later that Goldwater's campaign "contributed to enormous political change in the country. [It] changed the way we look at the American political world . . . not only geographically but in terms of values and beliefs. [The campaign] introduced modern conservative political thought to the national debate."

Having given up his Senate seat in order to run for President, Goldwater returned to Arizona, where he was, in his own words, "shunned like a bird of ill omen." Staging his political comeback in 1968, Goldwater trounced Democrat Roy Elson by more than 70,000 votes. He was once again a United States Senator with a national audience. Goldwater's support for the war in Vietnam was, if anything, stronger than ever; his denunciations of its opponents even more scathing. During one floor debate, he denounced those who opposed the escalation of the war as "weak-kneed and jelly-backed." He defiantly proclaimed: "I would rather blow the living daylights out of Haiphong than lose one more American life."

Despite his unflinching support for President Nixon, Goldwater was becoming restive and harbored thoughts of retirement in 1974. Due to his two year absence from the Senate, he had lost his seniority. Even more troubling, he was almost a nonperson at the Nixon White House.

With the coming of the Watergate crisis, Barry Goldwater returned to the national spotlight. Shortly after Nixon's reelection in 1972, the Senator began urging the President to make a full disclosure, to "get rid of the smell." Goldwater spent the next year and a half relentlessly criticizing the Nixon White House for its handling of the affair. As a result, Barry Goldwater was once more a political hero, "one of the world's ten most admired men," according to the Gallup Poll.

In early August 1974, President Nixon publicly admitted withholding pertinent Watergate evidence. A delegation of Republican leaders, with Goldwater acting as spokesman, went to the White House and warned Nixon that he had reached the end of the line. A brutally honest man, Goldwater told his former Senate colleague that, at best, there were fifteen Senators who might vote in his favor during an impeachment trial. Moreover, he told Nixon, he himself would probably vote for conviction. The following night, Richard M. Nixon announced his resignation. Although he had known and worked with Richard Nixon for nearly a quarter-century,

Goldwater harbored no illusions about the man known as "Tricky Dick." "Nixon," Goldwater wrote, "was the most dishonest individual I ever met in my life."

Barry Goldwater was overwhelmingly reelected to the United States Senate in 1974 and by a smaller margin in 1980. During his last six-year term, with the Republicans finally controlling the upper chamber, he served as chairman of the both the Senate Select Committee on Intelligence and the Senate Armed Services Committee. From the latter post, Goldwater achieved what he once described as "the only goddamn thing I've done in the Senate that's worth a damn"—the Armed Services Reorganization Act of 1986. By means of this act, organizational, strategic, and fiscal responsibilities for the four armed service branches were clearly defined, combined, and streamlined. Following the Senate's historic 95–0 vote in favor of Goldwater's measure, the Senator wrote: "I can go home happy, sit on my hill and shoot jackrabbits."

Hobbled by painfully arthritic knees and devastated by the death of his wife in 1985, Goldwater retired from the Senate at the end of 1986. He was seventy-seven years old. During his last days in Washington, he was feted by a host of organizations and received West Point's prestigious Sylvanus Thayer Award, presented annually to a U.S. citizen "whose service and accomplishments in the national interest exemplify personal devotion to the ideals expressed in the West Point motto, 'Duty, Honor, Country.'"

Goldwater gave away "most of what [he] owned in the office to [his] staff, the U.S. Air Force Academy the Arizona Air National Guard, and friends." Before he left his private office (room 350, Russell Senate Office Building), he fired his pellet gun a number of times, "notching my remembrance into [the] door." On his final day, he left Capitol Hill carrying away one black felt-tip pen, boarded a military plane, and returned to his hillside above downtown Phoenix.

Barry Goldwater lived long enough to see many of his conservative principles achieve mainstream acceptance. The election of Ronald Reagan in 1980 and the Republican takeover of Congress in 1994 both owed a great deal to the "Oracle of Paradise Valley," as some dubbed the octogenarian. As the end of his life drew near, he was still as cantankerous, plainspoken, and controversial as ever. To many of his ardent admirers, he seemed to have "lost his marbles," for he became an outspoken advocate of gay rights: "You don't have to agree with it, but they have a constitutional right to be gay. And that's what brings me into it." Goldwater supported President Bill Clinton's initiative concerning gays in the military, and spoke out, whenever and wherever possible, against governmental policies that would discriminate against them. Having been the recipient of many awards from gay rights' groups, Goldwater humorously quipped: "I'm an honorary gay now."

Goldwater also urged his fellow Republicans to forsake their alliance with the religious right, which he saw as being both exclusionary and dangerously self-righteous. He went so far as to back a Democrat for Congress over a "Christian-Right conservative" Republican. In the early spring of 1994, he called a press conference to urge Republican critics of Whitewater to "get off his [Clinton's] back and let him be president."

In 1992, at age eighty-two, Barry Goldwater married Susan Schaffer Wechsler, a health care executive and Jewish convert. He spent the final years of his life swimming, riding his bicycle, and visiting with his children and grandchildren. In 1996, Goldwater suffered a debilitating stroke that affected his frontal lobes. By 1997, his family reported that he was suffering from Alzheimer's disease. Barry Goldwater died on May 29, 1998. His funeral, held at All Saints Episcopal Church in Phoenix, was co-officiated by the Reverend Carol Carlozzi and Rabbi Albert Plotkin. Speaking after the service, Rabbi Plotkin told the *Arizona Jewish Post*: "I gave him the full Jewish rites, read the Hebrew *El Mole* prayer and recited the blessing for him at the very end . . . Susan Goldwater wanted something Jewish at Barry's funeral. . . . I was very honored to be there, to represent the Jewish community."

One of Goldwater's children, Barry, Jr., now a financial advisor, served seven terms in the House of Representatives from a Los Angeles–area district. Like his father, Barry Jr., is a conservative Republican.

Washington is a funny place. It can turn country lawyers into statesmen and downtown shopkeepers into political strategists. In the case of Barry Goldwater, it reminded him of his ancestry: "Neither my father nor any of our family ever took part in the Jewish community. It was only on entering the power circles of Washington that I was reminded I was a Jew." Big Mike would have been proud.

References

Barry Goldwater, *The Conscience of a Conservative* (Shepherdsville, Ky.: Victor Publishing Co., 1960).

——— (with Jack Casserly), *Goldwater* (New York: Doubleday, 1968).

———, *With No Apologies* (New York: William Morrow, 1979).

Current Biography, 1978, pp. 165–168.

Jewish Post and Opinion, June 24, 1998, p. 3.

Michael Lind, "The Myth of Barry Goldwater," *New York Review of Books*, November 30, 1995, pp. 22–27.

Howard Simons, *Jewish Times: Voices of the American Jewish Experience* (Boston: Houghton Mifflin, 1988), pp. 185–190.

Private correspondence with author, 1990–1996.

GOLDZIER, JULIUS (1854–1925): *Democrat from Illinois; served one term in the House (Fifty-third Congress; March 4, 1893–March 5, 1895)*

Julius Goldzier was born in Vienna on January 20, 1854. Nothing is recorded about his family. He immigrated to the United States at age twelve, settling first in New York. Goldzier lived there for six years, during which time he read law. At age eighteen, armed with a legal education, he moved to Chicago, where he began to practice.

Active in local Chicago politics, he was elected to the Chicago City Council in 1890. Before his term was up, he was elected to the House of Representatives from the Fourth District. Goldzier served but a single term in the House, being defeated for reelection in 1894 by Republican Charles Woodman. Returning to his legal practice, Goldzier was elected to a second term on the Chicago City Council in 1899.

He died in the Windy City on his seventy-first birthday, January 20, 1925, and was buried in Graceland Cemetery. Virtually nothing is known of his family or descendants.

References

Biographical Directory of the United States Congress, 1774–1989.
New York Times, January 21, 1925; 21:4.

GRADISON, WILLIS DAVID, JR. (1928–):
Republican from Ohio; served nine terms in the House (Ninety-fourth through One Hundred and Second Congress; January 3, 1975–January 3, 1993).

Cincinnati has long been one of America's most Republican cities. According to the *Almanac of American Politics* (1986 edition): "Of the nation's twenty-five largest metropolitan areas, only Dallas–Forth Worth and San Diego turn in Republican margins with greater regularity." Settled largely by German immigrants in the antebellum era, the Queen City was "a German, pro-Union, and Republican island in a sea of southern Democratic sentiment." Cincinnati was the home of Harriet Beecher Stowe, the author of *Uncle Tom's Cabin*, and of the underground railroad, which helped thousands of slaves on the road to northern freedom. Its nineteenth-century German heritage is still omnipresent; to this day, Cincinnati boasts America's best strudel.

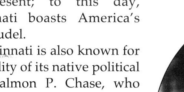

Cincinnati is also known for the quality of its native political sons. Salmon P. Chase, who served as Lincoln's Treasury Secretary, Chief Justice of the United States Supreme Court, and helped found the Chase Manhattan Bank, spent most of his life there. President (and later Chief Justice) William Howard Taft, House Speaker Nicholas Longworth (the son-in-law of Teddy Roosevelt), and Senator Robert A. Taft ("Mr. Republican") all hailed from the Queen City. Besides their Republican politics, all were "men of urbanity and learning," conservatives who sought to maintain the "values and the political system which had allowed the growth and prosperity of places like Cincinnati, the articulate advocates of a system that worked."

Cincinnati has long been home to a stable German Jewish community. The home of Hebrew Union College–Jewish Institute of Religion (the nation's oldest rabbinical school) and the Gothic-Byzantine-Moorish Plum Street Synagogue, Cincinnati's Jews have a long and proud tradition of community service. Somewhat predictably, the Jewish families of Cincinnati are traditionally more conservative,

more Republican, than their counterparts in New York, Chicago, or Los Angeles. For nearly twenty years (1975–1993), half of Cincinnati was represented in Congress by Willis D. "Bill" Gradison, one of the most thoughtful men of his era.

Unlike many of the Jewish families who settled in Cincinnati in the post–Civil War era, the Gradisons were from Russia. The Congressman's paternal grandfather, David Gradison, came to Cincinnati with his brother Joseph in the mid-1880s. The Gradisons may have come from Moscow; records indicate that David and Joseph's sister, Esther Gradison, was living in Moscow at the time of her death. David Gradison and his wife Anna, who was from the Austro-Hungarian Empire, had a son, Willis, who was born and raised in the Queen City. David Gradison died suddenly in 1915, and son Willis was forced to go to work.

Willis Gradison was a stockbroker by trade. Originally with the firm of Gibson and Gradison, he became politically active in the late 1920s. One of his close friends in Cincinnati political circles was an up-and-coming state senator by the name of Robert Alphonso Taft, the son of former President Taft. In the late 1920s, Senator Taft encouraged Willis Gradison to run for the Ohio House of Representatives. By the time of his son Willis David, Jr.'s birth on December 28, 1928, Willis Sr. was serving the first of two terms in that body.

Bill Gradison, called "Willie" by his classmates, was the first of the two Gradison children; his sister, Joan (Coe) was born two years later. Their mother, Dorothy Benas, was from a family with deep roots in the American Midwest. Her father was born in Lawrence, Kansas; her mother was a Kaufman from Chicago.

Following his two terms in the Ohio House, Willis Gradison, Sr. entered Cincinnati municipal politics. A Republican, he was elected to seven consecutive terms on the City Council, and long served as the chairman of its finance committee. Cincinnati is one of the few cities that still has a municipal political party, the

Charterites. A holdover from the early-twentieth-century "good government" movement, the Charterites have often held an absolute majority on the City Council. Even when the Charterites controlled city hall, Gradison, Sr. was retained as finance committee chairman. He rose to become vice mayor, but never managed to make the final hurdle into the mayor's office; to this day, his son Bill believes that anti-Semitism may have played a role.

Willie Gradison and his family attended the ultra-Reform Rockdale Temple in North Avondale—one of Cincinnati's premier Jewish neighborhoods in the 1920s through the 1940s. Bill Gradison never became bar mitzvah; among the German Reform Jews of Cincinnati, such rituals were extremely rare. Gradison attended Sunday school at Rockdale and was confirmed at age sixteen. Following his graduation from Walnut Hills High School, he entered Yale University, the Taft family's alma mater. One of his classmates at Yale was future President George Herbert Walker Bush, who in 1988, considered naming his fellow Yalie Secretary of Health and Human Services. Gradison received his B.A. in 1948, and then entered the Harvard Business School, from which he received an M.B.A. in 1951, and a doctorate in commercial science in 1954. While working on his doctorate, Gradison, through a letter of introduction from Senate Majority Leader Robert A. Taft, secured a job as assistant to the Under Secretary of the Treasury. In 1955, he moved over to the Department of Health, Education, and Welfare, where he worked as assistant to the Secretary.

Returning to Cincinnati, Bill Gradison joined his father's stock brokerage firm, now renamed Gradison & Company. He continued to work as a stockbroker until his election to Congress in 1975. Gradison first entered politics in 1961, when he won election to the Cincinnati City Council. He continued to serve on that body for the next dozen years. From 1970 to 1973, Gradison was chairman of the board of the Federal Home Loan Bank of Cincinnati. From 1970 to 1974, he achieved that which had eluded his father: he became Mayor Gradison.

In January 1974, Representative William J. Keating resigned his First District seat in order to become president and chief executive officer of the *Cincinnati Enquirer*. His seat was taken by Democrat Thomas Luken, who beat Bill Gradison in a special election. After serving less than a half year, Luken faced off against Gradison a second time, losing to the popular Cincinnati mayor by the slim margin of 51 percent to 49 percent. Gradison went on to enjoy a successful eighteen-year career in the House. Luken eventually made his way back to Congress in 1977 from Cincinnati's other House district, and remained on Capitol Hill until he retired in 1989. His seat was taken over by his son Charles, who, like Bill Gradison, was serving as mayor at the time of his election. Charles Luken remained in the House but a single term, preferring to return to Cincinnati, where the pace of life was more to his liking.

As a member of the House of Representatives, Bill Gradison received two choice committee assignments: Budget, and Ways and Means. More interested in government service than in politics *per se*, Gradison soon became known among both his colleagues and political journalists for being remarkably "free of political cant and catechism." An intelligent, principled conservative on economic issues, Gradison got into a heated public exchange of letters with supply-side hero (and future Republican vice-presidential candidate) Jack F. Kemp during the Reagan years. Gradison rejected Kemp's contention that lower tax rates would stimulate economic growth, thereby increasing tax revenues. His reservations had the effect of exposing deep divisions within the Republican Party.

Two years later, the Ohio Republican echoed Democratic thinking when he declared that the Gramm Rudman-Hollings deficit reduction target "could not be reached without deep defense cuts or a recessionary dose of taxes and program cuts." Already suspicious of his lack of dogmatism on economic issues, the party's emerging right wing also found him to be "insufficiently orthodox in his opposition to abortion." Nonetheless, with time and seniority on his side, Gradison rose to become ranking Republican on the House Budget Committee and on the Ways and Means Subcommittee on Health.

During his eighteen years in Congress, Bill Gradison built a reputation for being a moderate Republican. His ADA ratings ranged from a low of 11 in 1990 to a high of 35 in both 1981 and 1988. During the Reagan-Bush years (1980–1992), he voted with the administration anywhere between 61 percent and 76 percent of the time.

Gradison served as chairman of the House Wednesday Group—a by-invitation organization of thirty-nine House Republicans that was established in 1963. He also chaired the Economic Roundtable of the American Enterprise Institute (a Washington-based think tank) and was vice-chairman of the U.S. Bipartisan Commission on Comprehensive Health Care, also known as the Pepper Commission. The latter body was created by statute in the One Hundredth Congress; Gradison served as one of six members appointed to the Commission by the Speaker of the House.

Gradison's major areas of interest and expertise were in the fields of taxation and health care. In the first instance, he helped lead the fight for the indexing of personal income taxes. In the area of health care, the Ohio Republican led the campaign to extend Medicare coverage to include hospice care. His interest in hospice grew out of personal experience: when his father was dying of cancer, he saw firsthand what the program could do for those in extremis. He also realized that hospice care, in which the terminally ill are cared for at home, surrounded by family, costs far less than hospitalization.

Shortly after his reelection to a ninth consecutive term in November 1992, Gradison announced that he was resigning his seat in order to become president of the Health Insurance Association of America, an umbrella group that represents more than 270 small- and medium-sized health insurance companies across America. He took over the post in February 1993. When asked why, after rising to a position of respect and prominence in the House, he was moving to the private sector, Gradison replied that he felt that, at sixty-five, he was at an age where "if I was going to try something new, I'd better get started on it." Moreover, with his former Yale classmate George Bush turned out of office, he realized that he would no longer be a player in the emerging healthcare debate. Having been a member of the minority party throughout his congressional career, Gradison believed that Democratic majorities were inevitable. Had he decided to remain until the One Hundred and Fourth Congress, he would likely have become chair of the House Budget Committee and of the Ways and Means Subcommittee on Health.

When President Bill Clinton announced that he was launching an ambitious program to "guarantee every American full access to quality health care," the White House neglected to bring Gradison and HIAA into the process of dialogue. As a result, Gradison's association underwrote a $10 million television ad campaign against the program. The series of commercials, featuring a thirty-something yuppie couple named Harry and Louise, spurred a great deal of comment and controversy. By the end of the campaign, HIAA was being referred to in White House circles as "The Coalition to Scare Your Pants Off." When the Clinton health-care proposals went down to defeat, White House political advisor Paul Begala paid HIAA a backhanded compliment: "HIAA has clearly been the pit bull in the fight against health care reform. . . . I think the role they've played has been significant, and I think it's been destructive. He [Gradison] has done damage, and nobody's had the money to counter it."

Gradison's take on the health-care battle was, not surprisingly, a bit different from that of the White House. When interviewed by the *New York Times* in April 1994, he said that HIAA "totally supported the President's goal of 'guaranteeing private health insurance' for every American." Gradison further stated: "The notion that the Government is going to come along and require people to buy what we have to sell is rather appealing, as long as it is set up on a basis that permits us to stay in those markets and be able to raise the capital and go out there and compete."

Bill Gradison has been married three times. He married his first wife, Helen Anne Martin, in 1950. From their twenty-four year union, he has five daughters: Ellen, Anne, Robin, Beth, and Margaret. In 1980, Bill Gradison married Heather Jane Stirton, with whom he had four more children: Merle Jo, Benjamin David, Logan Jane, and Andrew Kirk. In December 1995, Gradison married his third wife, Cari Elliot, whom he met at a health-care conference in Pebble Beach, California. Along with his nine children, Bill Gradison has ten grandchildren.

During his formative years, Gradison's paternal grandmother, Anna, lived with the family. She would get together with her friends on a weekly basis to chat in Yiddish. This was to be Gradison's only exposure to the *mama loschen* (mother tongue). Gradison is a member of the historic Washington Hebrew Congregation and attends High Holiday services. In 1978, in honor of his fiftieth birthday, he took five of his daughters on a tour of Israel—his only journey to the Jewish state.

Although he lives in the Washington area, Bill Gradison continues to sit on the board of directors of the Cincinnati firm his father founded so many years ago. The former Gradison & Company is now McDonald & Company, but the name Gradison, along with Taft, Chase, and Longworth, still has a place of prominence in the Queen City of the West.

References
Interview with Bill Gradison, December 1996.
Almanac of American Politics (1974–96 editions).
New York Times, April 6, 1994.
Politics in America (1978–96 editions).

GREEN, SEDGWICK WILLIAM (1929–):
Republican from New York; served eight terms in House (Ninety-fifth through One Hundred and Second Congress; February 14, 1978–January 3, 1993).

New York City's Upper East Side Silk-Stocking District is, in the words of the *Almanac of American Politics*, "home to the people who make Manhattan the center of the nation's securities, publishing, advertising, entertainment, broadcasting and communications industries." Statistically, the Upper East Side is rich (per capita income of $41,151 according to the 1990 census), expensive (median house value $242,500), educated (nearly 70 percent are college graduates), and single (only 30 percent are married). Traditionally, it has been "more Republican, more liberal and more tolerant than the rest of the nation." Two of its congressional representatives, John V. Lindsay and *Edward Koch*, became mayors of New York City. During the 1970s, the Upper East Side began changing, becoming a politically trendy enclave, where people "showed greater concern . . . for the problems of lettuce workers in California or the Black Panthers . . . than . . . the problems faced by the cab drivers, doormen, waiters, sanitation workers . . . and others whose work makes life in the Upper East Side possible."

With a better than three-to-one Democratic-Liberal voter registration, the Upper East Side gave huge margins to McGovern, Carter, Mondale, Dukakis, and Clinton. And yet, for most of the period from 1978 to 1992, the Upper East Side was represented in Congress by a Republican—Sedgwick William Green. Diffident to the point of shyness, and lacking the "gregariousness that drives most winning candidates for public office in the era of personality-oriented politics," Bill Green succeeded by a combination of intelligence, hard work, money, and being that rarest of late twentieth-century political creatures: a liberal Republican.

Bill Green's paternal grandparents were German Jews named Gruen. No one remembers precisely when they first came to New York. The Schoenbergs, the maternal side of the family, arrived at Ellis Island in 1890. Bill's mother, Evelyn Schoenberg, came here as an infant "in her father's arms," her mother having died in childbirth. Louis A. Green, Bill's father, was already a prosperous broker when he married Evelyn. Their son, whom they named Sedgwick after Louis's business partner, was born on October 16, 1929, just two weeks before the boom years of the twenties came to a resounding crash. Louis was a shrewd investor, and, unlike most, was able to weather the financial storms of the Depression.

During his formative years, "Sedg," as he was then called, attended Hunter Model Elementary School and took religious instruction on Sundays at Rabbi Stephen S. Wise's Free Synagogue. Bill's Jewish education came to an abrupt and permanent end when Louis discovered that his son's American Jewish history text had words of praise for an attorney he regarded as a shyster. "That was that," the Congressman recalls, "I never went back."

Following his graduation from Horace Mann High School in 1946, Bill Green entered Harvard. During his four years in Cambridge, Green worked on the *Harvard Crimson*. By the time he graduated *magna cum laude* in 1950, he had become the paper's managing editor. From there, Green attended Harvard Law School, where he made Law Review. Following his admission to the District of Columbia bar in 1953, Green entered the Army, where he served two years in the Judge Advocate General's office at the Pentagon. Upon his discharge from the service in 1955, he spent two years as law secretary to U.S. Court of Appeals Judge George T. Washington. Green then went into private practice, "dealing mostly with securities and corporate law."

After a three-year post as chief counsel to the New York Joint Legislative Committee on Housing and Urban Development, Bill Green ran for the State Assembly as a Republican from the Sixty-sixth District, the "richest part of the Upper East Side." He won by a better than two-to-one margin over his Democratic-Liberal opponent, thereby becoming the last Republican to win an Assembly seat from Manhattan. Due to his prior experience with the Joint Legislative Committee, Green made a specialty of the housing field during his three years in the Assembly (1965–1968).

In 1968, Bill Green entered the Republican primary for the Eighteenth Congressional District seat, losing to United States Attorney Whitney North Seymour, Jr., who in turn lost in the general election to *Ed Koch*. Although Green did not need to work (he is heir to the Grand Union supermarket fortune), he secured a federal appointment as regional administrator in the Department of Housing and Urban Development (HUD) for New York, New Jersey, Puerto Rico, and the Virgin Islands. In that position, Green was responsible for more than 80,000 housing units in New York State alone. When Jimmy Carter became president in 1976, Green lost his job.

When Eighteenth District representative Edward Koch was elected mayor of New York in 1977, his seat came open. Green easily won the Republican nomination, and then faced former Congresswoman *Bella Abzug* in the special election. Abzug, fresh from narrow defeats in both the 1976 Senate and 1977 mayoral primaries (she lost respectively to Daniel Moynihan and Koch), won her nomination by court decree. The Democrats, who had chosen a different nominee via party convention, had a political donnybrook on their hands, with "charges and countercharges of chicanery filling the air and the columns of the *Village Voice*." Abzug's chief opponent was Carter Burden, the former owner of *New York* magazine and the *Village Voice*. Green barely defeated Abzug with 50 percent of the vote. Analysts decreed that his victory was as much a vote against Abzug, who had many enemies in city politics and was looked upon as having become a "perennial candidate looking for a place to run," as a vote for Green.

The newly elected Congressman had little time to settle into the Washington routine; he was faced almost immediately with a new election for a full two-year term. In the 1978 general election, Green faced Democrat Carter Burden, the man who had lost in court to Bella Abzug. Burden was almost as despised as Abzug by the voters of the Eighteenth District, in this case for having sold his publications to media mogul

Rupert Murdoch, "a controversial episode" which, whatever one's views of the merits of the sale, "reflected no credit on Burden." Though Burden spent more than $1.1 million on the race, Green triumphed, taking 53 percent of the vote. The Eighteenth District seat was now his.

Green was at first assigned to the Housing Banking Committee and its subcommittee on Housing and Community Development. It was a good marriage. Green quickly established himself as one of the two or three most liberal Republicans on the Hill. During the Reagan years, he was anything but a sure vote for the Republicans. Nonetheless, he moved up the ranks quickly, and in 1981, was handed a special plum—the ranking GOP position on the Appropriations HUD subcommittee.

Coming on the heels of his support for Independent John Anderson for president in 1980 and his one-man battle against Reagan's platform plank on women's rights, his elevation caused consternation in some GOP quarters. It shouldn't have. As the *Almanac of American Politics* (1982) astutely noted: "If Green came from anywhere else but Manhattan, he would probably have [had] to serve out his career as a liberal Republican renegade, risking ostracism with every new move he made against his party's national policy. But a Republican from Manhattan is so incongruous these days that GOP leaders seem happy to let him cast as many liberal votes as he pleases if it will help reelect him."

As if to prove the truth of this observation, Green was one of the few Republicans who, short of benefiting from the Reagan coattails, had to run far ahead of his party's standard bearer just to survive. And survive he did: while Carter was carrying the Eighteenth District 49 percent to 37 percent over Reagan in 1980, Green was winning the district 57 percent to 43 percent. In 1984, when Walter Mondale took the district (by now the Fifteenth) 60 percent to 39 percent over Reagan, Green triumphed 56 percent to 44 percent over Manhattan Borough President Andrew Stein in what was, up to that time, the single most expensive House race in history. Finally, in 1988, when Michael Dukakis was carrying the Fifteenth with 66 percent over George Bush, Green was defeating Peter Doukas 61 percent to 37 percent. In order to pull off this electoral sleight of hand, Green "took pains to brand himself an 'Independent Republican.'" His positions on social and cultural issues were among the most liberal in the House; his votes on economic issues decidedly free-market in their orientation. This sat well with his constituents.

An active legislator, Green sponsored a "Reproductive Health Equity Act" that would "legally guarantee the right to abortion." A long-time supporter of the rights of gay men and lesbians, Green voted against mass testing for AIDS. He also voted to override Bush's veto of the Family and Medical Leave Act, and voted for the civil rights bills which Bush had vetoed. In the 1980s, Green became a leader of the "Gypsy Moths" faction—moderate-to-liberal Republicans who would withhold votes on Republican-backed appropriations bills until moneys for mass transit, low-income energy assistance, education, and health care were preserved. Bill Green also served as a focal point for moderate GOP opposition to the Reagan-backed MX missile system. Working with the Democratic Defense Appropriations Subcommittee chair, he put together a bipartisan anti-MX coalition. When the MX came to the floor, Green was one of just three Republicans to vote against it.

Green served two terms as chairman of the House-Senate Environmental and Energy Study Conference, and chaired the Climate Study Group. A leader in the field of women's issues, he was one of the few male members of the congressional caucus on that subject.

Bill Green's first visit to Israel came only after his election to Congress. Coming from a wealthy German Jewish family, this is not surprising; Zionism did not have quite the allure for the families of Park Avenue as it did for the Jews of Flatbush. Nonetheless, Green became a strong and vocal supporter of the Jewish state. He voted in favor of using American forces to liberate Kuwait from Iraqi occupation, and then criticized the administration for its post-war resumption of military aid to Jordan despite Jordan's support for Saddam Hussein.

In 1992, toward the end of his congressional service, Green made headlines when he attacked wording in the State Department budget for fiscal year 1993 that "couldn't do more to sanction the Arab boycott of Israel if the Arab League had written it itself." Poring through the massive budget proposal, Green had discovered that the State Department had deleted the "prohibition on contracts with firms complying with the Arab League Boycott of Israel or discriminating on the basis of religion," and the "prohibition on issuance of passports for travel to Israel only." Addressing the press, Green argued that "in plain English, what this says is that the State Department thinks it's okay to do business with firms that comply with the Arab boycott of Israel. Also, that we should play along with the Arab countries' denial of entry to anyone with an Israel stamp on their passport." He concluded by declaring that "for someone to sneak these odious provisions in and hope that no one notices, makes one wonder if the old image of 'Arabists at the State Department' has more than a little basis in fact." Green successfully fought to have the language removed from the appropriations bill.

In 1992, Bill Green lost his seat to Carolyn B. Maloney. Green faced two problems in this election: redistricting and the "enthusiasm of feminism and women candidates among the liberal Democrats on the Upper East Side." After the 1990 census, Green's district was changed to add sections of Astoria and Greenpoint, where he was a virtual unknown. Despite outspending Maloney by nearly four-to-one, he lost 50 percent to 48 percent. After nearly fifteen years, the Silk Stocking District was once again in Democratic hands. In March 1994, two years after his defeat, Bill Green ran an abortive campaign for New York Governor. Offering himself as "a moderate who is conservative on fiscal issues and sensibly compassionate on social issues," he wound up garnering only a minuscule 2.7 percent of the votes cast at the Republican state convention. The nomination eventually went to New York State Senator George E. Pataki, who wound up defeating Governor Mario Cuomo in the general election.

A tall, gray-haired man with a soft voice and impeccable tailoring, Bill Green is married to the former Patricia Freiburg. Mrs. Green's father was an attorney who worked for his old law school classmate William O. Douglas at the Securities and Exchange Commission. She was formerly employed as a schoolteacher, and actively campaigned on her husband's behalf. The Greens have two children: Catherine, an attorney, and Louis, named after the Congressman's late father. Bill Green is active in the Jewish community as a member of the U.S.

Holocaust Memorial Council, and a director of both the Eastern European Jewish Heritage Foundation and the Raoul Wallenberg Committee of the United States. He continues to live on the Upper East Side.

References

Interview with S. William Green, Washington, D.C., July 25, 1992.

Almanac of American Politics (1980–92 editions).

New York Times, February 15, 1978; March 19, 1994 A, 29:3; June 1, 1994, B, 2:6.

GRUENING, ERNEST HENRY (1887–1974):
Democrat from Alaska; served ten years in the Senate (1959–1969).

When a reporter called Hubert H. Humphrey on June 26, 1974, to inform him that his friend and former Senate colleague Ernest Gruening had passed away at age eighty-seven, Humphrey was quoted as saying, "He might have been the 20th-century Benjamin Franklin." Upon reading Humphrey's estimation of Senator Gruening, columnist Jules Witcover noted that the former Vice President "might have compared him to the versatile Thomas Jefferson as well." To a great degree, both men were correct. Originally trained as a physician (Harvard '12), Gruening was at various times a newspaper reporter and editor, a magazine editor, foreign correspondent, author, historian, publicist, territorial governor, lobbyist, and finally, a United States Senator. To say that he was one of this century's most multifaceted individuals would not be an overstatement.

In his long lifetime, Ernest Gruening went from the civilized comforts of Harvard College, Harvard Medical School, Rockport, Massachusetts, and the Union Boat Club to the untamed wilds of Mexico, Puerto Rico, and Alaska. As a journalist, he was one of the first to interview Helen Keller and the imprisoned Leo Frank. As editor of the *Nation*, he recruited such writers as H. L. Mencken, Sinclair Lewis, Willa Cather, and Theodore Dreiser. As a reformer and innovator, he brought electricity, land reform, and birth control to Puerto Rico, and air travel to Alaska. As a Senator, he was, in the words of his colleague George McGovern, "an indefatigable champion of peace." Toward the end of his life, he was nominated by him for the Nobel Peace Prize. He is the only member of the Congressional Minyan whose remains repose on a mountain named in his honor—the 6,500-foot Mount Ernest Gruening, some 30 miles north of Juneau, Alaska.

In 1861, Ernest Gruening's father, Dr. Emil Gruening (1842–1914), immigrated to America from Hohensalza, East Prussia (now Irowroclaw, Poland). As Senator Gruening wrote in his autobiography, *Many Battles*, "He would shortly have been drafted into the King of Prussia's army, but fighting in wars against Prussia's neighbors for the greater glory of King and fatherland did not appeal to young Emil." Once arrived in America, then embroiled in the Civil War, Emil joined the Seventh New Jersey Volunteer Infantry and saw action at the Battle of Five Forks. He was "among the cheering boys in blue at the surrender of General Lee at Appomattox." Following the Civil War, Emil Gruening entered Columbia University Medical School, earning his way through by tutoring in German, Latin, Greek, and mathematics. Upon graduation (class of 1867), Dr. Gruening went to Europe, where he studied both otology and ophthalmology in Paris, London, and Berlin with the leading physicians of the day.

A professor of ophthalmology at the New York Polyclinic from 1882 to 1895, Dr. Emil Gruening was a pioneer in the diagnosis of mastoiditis (a severe, sometimes life-threatening, virus of the middle ear) and helped develop its cure through the mastoid operation. He was also the first to introduce platinum instruments in ophthalmic surgery. In 1903, he was elected president of the American Otological Society, and in 1910, president of the American Ophthalmological Society.

In 1874, Emil married Rose Fridenberg, the eldest of Henry and Bertha Fridenberg's ten children. Like Gruening, the Fridenbergs had emigrated from Hohensalza. Mrs. Gruening died at age twenty-one in 1876, giving birth to a daughter, whom the doctor named Rose in her memory. In 1880, the thirty-eight-year-old physician married Phebe Fridenberg, one of his late wife's younger sisters. They would eventually have four children together: Clara, Marie (May), Ernest, and Martha.

Ernest Henry Gruening was born on February 6, 1887 in New York City. During the first decade of his life, he and his German-speaking family lived at the corner of Fourth Avenue and 23rd Street, where his father owned three brownstones—two for the family and one for his burgeoning medical practice. In 1894, when Ernest was seven, the family went on the first of what were to be many trips to Europe, spending most of their time in Paris. While living in Paris, young Ernest attended the Petit Lycée Condorcet, where he learned to speak French fluently. Upon their return a year later, Ernest entered the Drisler School. From there he transferred to Sachs's Collegiate Institute and eventually wound up at Hotchkiss (a well-known prep school in Lakeville,

Connecticut, founded in 1891), from which he graduated in 1903.

Judaism does not seem to have played any role in the life of the Gruening family. The children's sole "religious" education consisted of several years of attendance at a Sunday school run by the Society for Ethical Culture, whose nontheistic, humanist "theology" was deeply influenced by the American transcendentalism of Ralph Waldo Emerson and the German transcendentalism of Immanuel Kant. As Ernest Gruening would write more than seventy years later: "That [Ethical Culture] was as near as we came to an organized religion in my family. Father was a freethinker and we children followed in that course until later in life when we came to our own conclusions in the realm of faith." What those "conclusions" were, Gruening never revealed. In matter of plain fact, nowhere in his massive autobiography, *Many Battles*, does one find a sentence, a suggestion, a single word that would indicate that Ernest Gruening or his family were Jewish.

Gruening entered Harvard College in the fall of 1903, where, he writes, "my scholastic achievements were mediocre." Following graduation in 1907, he entered Harvard Medical School, eventually graduating in 1912. During his nine years in Cambridge, Gruening became friendly with the likes of Heywood Broun, Walter Lippmann, T. S. Eliot, and Earl Derr Biggers. His association with Biggers (1884–1933), the creator of fictional detective Charlie Chan, was to play a pivotal role in Gruening's professional development. Biggers became the dramatic critic for the *Boston Traveler* after graduating from Harvard ('05). Whenever he found himself with more than one play or musical to review on a single evening, he would send his chum Gruening in his stead. Gruening's reviews were published (with Biggers's byline) in the *Traveler*; he became infatuated with journalism. At one point he even gave serious consideration to chucking medical school and becoming a full-time newspaperman. Heeding his father's advice, however, he completed his M.D.

Immediately afterward, young Dr. Gruening landed a job as a beat reporter on the *Traveler*, for which he was paid $15 a week. By age twenty-seven, he was the paper's managing editor. His first act in this post was decreeing that "identifi-

cation of individuals by race be dropped unless [it is] of particular and special interest and when the story is manifestly incomplete and inaccurate if the color of the person involved is concealed." While with the *Traveler*, Gruening, an early member of the NAACP, led an editorial assault against D. W. Griffith's celebrated film *Birth of a Nation*, attacking the picture for its overt racism. He even helped organize a censorship panel in Massachusetts to delete the offensive scenes from Griffith's masterwork.

When word got out that Gruening was leaving the *Traveler*, he was offered the job of executive secretary of the NAACP. He turned it down, however, and over the next several years worked as managing editor of the *New York Tribune*, the *New York Sun*, the Spanish language *La Prensa*, and the *Nation*, where, as noted above, he was responsible for recruiting some of the twentieth century's most notable writers.

In November 1914, Ernest Gruening married Dorothy Elizabeth Smith, the daughter of a prominent publisher. They had three sons: Ernest Jr., nicknamed "Sonny," Huntington "Hunny" Sanders, and Peter Brown. Sonny died, ironically, of mastoiditis at age sixteen, in 1931. Hunny, who graduated from Harvard in 1938, married Elizabeth Ingalls, whom he had met in Cambridge. Hunny became a banker and the father of three boys: Clark, and twins Winthrop and Bradford. Peter, the youngest of Ernest and Anne's three sons, was born in 1927. After World War II, he married and divorced Nadine Unger Roosevelt, the former wife of George Emlen Roosevelt, Jr. A correspondent for the United Press in Australia, Roosevelt committed suicide "down-under" in October 1955 at age twenty-eight.

Gruening's sisters all had interesting careers. Clara authored "a scholarly and readable" biography of writer Samuel Butler, subtitled *A Mid-Victorian Modern*. Martha, while a student at Smith College, was secretary of the National College Suffrage League. Sister Rose devoted her life to social work. In 1916, she founded a settlement which she named Arnold Toynbee House. Working without compensation throughout her life, she was known as "The Angel of Grand Street."

In 1924, Ernest Gruening served as director of national publicity in Senator Robert La Follette's presidential campaign. During the next two years, he was on assignment for *Collier's* in Mexico. While there, he learned about the people, politics, and issues of the "Sleeping Giant to the South." The article he was supposed to write for the magazine turned out to be a finely crafted book entitled *Mexico and Its Heritage* (1928). The reviewer for the *New York Herald Tribune* called it "the most vigorous, useful and comprehensive picture yet made of the complex present day conditions below the Rio Grande." Antonio Carillo Flores, the Mexican ambassador to the United States, described it as "the best book written by a non-Mexican about my country."

In the late 1920s and early 1930s, now based in Maine, Gruening founded and published the *Portland Evening News*, a paper noted for its battles against utilities magnate Samuel Insull. Gruening left his position in Maine in order to go back to his editorship at the *Nation*. Under his stewardship, the magazine played a pivotal, albeit unsung, role in the election of *Fiorello La Guardia* as mayor of New York.

Running in 1933 against incumbent John P. O'Brien and Democratic nominee Joseph V. McKee, La Guardia was lagging in the polls with only a few weeks to go. The smart money was on Democrat McKee. Then, with time running out, Gruening was made aware of "a skeleton in McKee's closet: he was alleged to have written a viciously anti-Semitic article in the *Catholic World* some years previously entitled 'A Serious Problem.'"

Unfortunately, no one could find a copy of the article. Gruening sent out reporters to all the major libraries in and around New York, desperately searching for a copy of the May 1913 edition of the *Catholic World*. As he wrote many years later: "In every library where the bound volumes of this monthly magazine . . . were kept, either the volume was missing or the article—listed in the table of contents—had been excised."

Finally, at the eleventh hour, a copy was located in the library of the Presbyterian Seminary in Princeton. Gruening had the pertinent passages reprinted in the *Nation* in a two-and-a-half-page article. The issue "sold like hot cakes." The publication of "A Serious Problem" turned out to be a tonic for La Guardia's sagging fortunes. On election day, the "Little Flower" outpolled Mayor O'Brien by nearly 275,000

votes, and the hapless McKee by more than 350,000.

In the summer of 1934, Gruening joined the Roosevelt administration as director of the Interior Department's Division of Territories and Island Possessions. In this newly created post, Gruening became the *de facto* administrator-cum-governor of Puerto Rico, Hawaii, Alaska, and the Virgin Islands. Turning his attention first to Puerto Rico, Gruening established the Puerto Rican Reconstruction Administration (PRRA), which, under his leadership, provided hydroelectric power, built schools, hospitals, and libraries, set up birth control clinics, and planted over 30 million trees.

From Puerto Rico, Gruening turned next to Alaska, of which FDR had told him "I would like to move a thousand or fifteen hundred people from the drought-stricken areas of the Middle West and give them a chance to start life anew." After an extensive tour, Gruening convinced both Roosevelt and his key adviser, Harry Hopkins, that rather than the Middle West, the pioneers should come from the Dakotas, Montana, Wyoming, Idaho, and eastern Washington, on the assumption that these states were climatically similar to Alaska. Greatly concerned about Alaska's inaccessibility, Gruening pushed for direct air service to the territory, and for the creation of a highway linking the United States to Alaska. This latter effort eventuated in the construction of the AlCan Highway during World War II.

FDR appointed Ernest Gruening Territorial Governor of Alaska in 1939, a position he would hold for the next thirteen years, the longest term of any Territorial Governor in American history. Immediately upon assuming office, Governor Gruening began pushing for Alaskan statehood. In 1945, he persuaded the Alaska legislature to pass an eighteen-year-old voting act; Congress vetoed it. In 1946, Alaska held its first referendum on the issue; it passed overwhelmingly. Over the next decade, Gruening made more than two hundred speeches throughout the continental United States on the subject of Alaskan statehood, and convinced his old friend Edna Ferber to write a novel (*Ice Palace*) about Alaska. In later years, critic Clifton Fadiman referred to Ferber's novel as "the *Uncle Tom's Cabin* for Alaska." When Alaska finally did become the forty-ninth

State, Gruening, by then a United States Senator, became known as "The Father of Alaska Statehood."

As Territorial Governor, Gruening was not without enemies. In the late 1940s, the *Alaska Daily Empire* launched a campaign against him, painting him as "pro-communist." The paper's editors purported to show that Gruening was involved with a left-wing group called the Fund for Public Service. Although the flap died down somewhat after Gruening gave incontrovertible proof that he was "neither an officer nor director of the fund," the charges would continue to reemerge for many years to come.

Gruening was elected Senator for the Alaska Territory on November 25, 1958. On his second day in the Senate, he cosponsored bills calling for the admission of both Alaska and Hawaii to statehood. The Senate, voted 64 to 20, to admit Alaska as the forty-ninth state, effective January 3, 1959. Formerly unable to vote in the Senate because he represented a territory, Ernest Gruening now had the same rights and privileges as all his other colleagues.

Today, Ernest Gruening is perhaps best remembered for his opposition to the war in Vietnam. Without question, he was one of the very first, if not *the* first, to voice strenuous opposition to the emerging conflict. His first pronouncement came in October 1963, when he said: "We have been and are heavily engaged in Vietnam to the extent of 12,000 'advisors.' They are supposedly 'technicians,' but of course they are troops, and it is sheer hypocrisy to pretend they are anything else." In March 1964, in a speech entitled "The United States Should Get Out of Vietnam," he boldly predicted that "if this sacrificing [of lives] is continued, it will be denounced as a crime." No report of that Senate speech appeared in the *New York Times*, or in any of the three Washington dailies.

On August 4, 1964, President Lyndon B. Johnson informed the nation that an American destroyer, the *C. Turner Joy*, had been fired upon in the Gulf of Tonkin. Furthermore, he told a nationwide television audience that when he had ordered a second destroyer, the *Maddox*, to accompany the first, both vessels had been attacked. The President saw these "incidents" as sufficient justification for a sweeping Senate resolution that would permit him "to take all nec-essary measures to repel armed attack and prevent further aggression," and would further authorize him "to use U.S. armed force anywhere he saw fit in Southeast Asia."

History knows this blank check as the Gulf of Tonkin Resolution. After much debate, during which Gruening repeatedly expressed his strenuous objections, the resolution was passed by a vote of eighty-eight yeas to two nays—those of Ernest Gruening and Oregon Senator Wayne Morse. Of that vote, Gruening noted: "I had no other alternative. I was convinced of the folly of our military involvement in Southeast Asia. Of course when I voted 'nay,' I did not suspect, any more than did any of my colleagues, that the Tonkin Gulf incident was largely spurious." Years later it would become known that the two "incidents" hadn't happened in the way the President claimed—that far from being on "routine patrol," the *Maddox* was, in reality, a spy ship.

In addition to his staunchly dovish position on the war, Gruening was instrumental in the passage of Public Law 89209, the National Endowment for the Arts and Humanities, and was a champion of birth control and zero population growth. Although, as mentioned above, Gruening always remained strangely mute on his Jewishness, he was a resolute defender of Israel. After visiting ten Middle Eastern countries on a 1962 Senate fact-finding junket, Gruening "came to the sorrowful conclusion that the Arab leaders did not desire a solution beneficial to the [Arab] refugees, but rather preferred to keep the fist of resentment burning and the refugees as pawns in their campaign against Israel." In his report to the Senate, Gruening recommended a cessation of all economic aid to Libya. Of Israel, Gruening said: "In my view, of all the recipients of our foreign aid, Israel was the best qualified to receive it and had made the best use of it."

In 1968, the eighty-one year-old Ernest Gruening lost his Senate seat, by 1,694 votes, to the speaker of the Alaska legislature, thirty-seven-year-old Mike Gravel. Relying heavily on the as yet-untried technique of saturation television advertising, Gravel scored a stunning upset over the "Father of Alaska Statehood."

In the remaining six years of his life, Ernest Gruening devoted himself to such causes as ending the war in Vietnam, population control, and women's rights. At age eighty-two, he joined the stop-the-draft movement, because, as he wrote, "I considered that—contrary to prevailing public opinion—those who, following their conscience, refused to fight in an utterly unjustified war and incurred imprisonment or exile in consequence, were the unsung heroes of the war. It took courage to do what they did." At age eighty-five, he was still giving upwards of five speeches a day. A page from his diary attests to his amazing schedule: "Moratorium Day . . . spoke at a high school in Bethesda at 9:00 AM; at Georgetown Law School at 11:00; in Farragut Square at 1:00; on the Johns Hopkins Campus at 3:00, and thereafter to a crowd ten thousand strong, massed around Baltimore's City Hall."

In the last two years of his life, Gruening wrote his autobiography (*Many Battles*, published in 1973), and worked for the "impeachment, conviction, and incarceration of President Richard M. Nixon." Gruening was unsparing in his condemnation of the man he always referred to as "Tricky Dick," writing, for instance:

> Nixon's undeniable guilt had been "his attempted and partly successful subversion of our free society into a police state, abrogating our basic concept of "a government of laws and not of men," even less, of one man—a course which encompassed Watergate's multiple crimes, his various unconstitutional actions, his perversions of the electoral and judicial process, his assaults on the First Amendment's guarantees—all

evidences, manifestations and consequences of his purpose.

Gruening did not live long enough to win his final battle. He died June 26, 1974, just five weeks before Richard Nixon resigned from office. At his funeral, which was held at the National Cathedral in Washington, D.C., he was eulogized by Supreme Court Justice William O. Douglas, Senator Wayne Morse, Representative (and former Senator) Claude Pepper, and Alaska Governor William Egan. During the service, these words from Dylan Thomas, one of Gruening's favorites, were read:

> Do not go gentle into that good night,
> Old age should burn and rave at close of day;
> Rage, rage against the dying of the light.

Ernest Gruening's remains were cremated and scattered over Mount Ernest Gruening, a long, long way from Harvard.

References

Ernest Gruening, *Many Battles* (New York: Liveright Publishers, 1973).

Sherwood Ross, *Gruening of Alaska* (New York: Best Books, 1968).

Current Biography, 1946.

Encyclopaedia Judaica (1972), vol. 7, col. 947.

New York Times, June 6, 1974, 48:1.

Universal Jewish Encyclopedia.

Who Was Who in America, vol. 6.

Who Was Who in American Jewry, 1938.

GUGGENHEIM, SIMON (1867–1941):
Republican from Colorado; served one term in the Senate (March 4, 1907–March 3, 1913).

On May 31, 1913, William Jennings Bryan, President Woodrow Wilson's Secretary of State, announced the ratification of Article XVII of the United States Constitution. Otherwise known as the Seventeenth Amendment, it declared that "The Senate of the United States shall be composed of two Senators from each State, elected by the people thereof, for six years." Prior to the adoption of Article XVII, Senators had been elected by the legislatures of the various states. Historians are in general agreement that the impetus for this change stemmed largely from the Colorado state legislature's 1906 vote that sent the fabulously wealthy and spectacularly unqualified Simon Guggenheim to the United States Senate. Guggenheim's campaign for the Senate was, in the words of biographer John Davis, "so barefacedly corrupt . . . that there is something almost refreshing about it."

In that campaign, Guggenheim reportedly spent more than $300,000—well over $6 million in today's money. While $6 million or even more may not seem like an outrageous sum for a Senate race, consider that Guggenheim was not seeking the votes of a mass electorate. Rather, he was merely campaigning among the ninety-five members of the Colorado legislature. That works out to something like $4,411 (easily more than $90,000 in current dollars) for each of the sixty-eight state legislators who would eventually cast votes in favor of the Jewish mining magnate.

Moreover, Guggenheim, who publicly proclaimed "I have preserved a list showing the names of every person to whom I have paid a dollar, and what it paid for," also promised that he would "personally finance any state legislator's campaign for reelection in return for his vote." The mining magnate further sweetened the deal by promising that once elected, he would "help his electors and their families in any way he could."

Is it any wonder that Article XVII became law? Ironically, Guggenheim voted for its passage, and thereby became the last United States Senator elected by a state legislature.

Although no incontrovertible proof exists, it is highly likely that the Guggenheim family originated in the northwestern Bavarian village of Guggenheim, now called Jugenheim. It is speculated that sometime during the Thirty Years' War (1618–48), the Guggenheim clan moved to the then-safe haven of Switzerland, where they settled in the Surb River Valley village of Lengnau. Switzerland did not prove to be all that Edenic for the Jews; by 1776, only one member of the Swiss Confederation, the earldom of Baden, remained open to them. Moreover, the rulers of Baden restricted Jews to just two small farming communities, Endigen and the aforementioned Lengnau. Forbidden by law to engage in farming, the Jews of the Surb Valley were variously labeled "alien protection fellows" or "tolerated homeless persons not to be expelled."

Simon Meyer Guggenheim (1792–1869), the future Senator's grandfather, was a tailor. Although *his* grandfather, Isaac Guggenheim (known as "Old Icicle"), had been the wealthiest Jew in Lengnau, Simon Meyer was only able to eke out a precarious existence. In 1828, his first wife, Sch'feli Levinger Guggenheim, bore him a son, named Meyer. By the time of Sch'feli's death in 1836, Simon Meyer had six children— Meyer and five girls. Like many Jews in Lengnau, Meyer Guggenheim became a peddler, "traveling through Switzerland and Germany." Because of the harsh restrictions and legal disabilities placed on the Jews of Baden, neither the widowed Simon Meyer nor his five daughters could reasonably expect to marry. According to local law, Jews had to pay a substantial dowry before the Christian authorities would approve a marriage.

As a single father, Simon Meyer needed to remarry. Around 1846 or 1847, he was attracted to a forty-one-year-old widow named Rachel Weil Meyer, who herself had three sons and four daughters. Realizing that marriage was out of the question so long as they remained in Lengnau, Simon and Rachel decided to pool their meager resources, pull up stakes, and move to America. In 1847, having sold his tailoring shop, Simon, Rachel, and twelve of their thirteen children set sail from Hamburg to Philadelphia. Somewhere in the middle of the Atlantic, twenty year-old Meyer Guggenheim fell head over heels in love with Rachel's fifteen year-old daughter Barbara. Shortly after their arrival, the fifty-six-year-old Simon Meyer married Rachel and became a door-to-door peddler. His son Meyer likewise began peddling.

Unlike his father, who went door-to-door in Philadelphia, Meyer headed for the "more arduous, but more lucrative, Pennsylvania anthracite country." The two Guggenheims peddled a "bit of everything: shoestrings, lace, stove and furniture polish, ribbons, pins, spices, needles." Because of the vast distances he had to travel, Meyer regularly left his father's home early Sunday morning, not returning until Friday afternoon, just before the onset of the Sabbath. Friday evenings were sacrosanct in the Guggenheims' traditional Jewish household. Because father and son both spoke German (although with a Swiss accent) in a region where there were many German immigrants, they quickly prospered as peddlers; especially Meyer, whose best-selling item was stove polish. As he began making money selling the polish, Meyer came to understand that he could realize a far greater profit if he became his own manufacturer. Working in tandem with a German chemist, he was soon producing a polish superior to anything on the market, because it did not stain the housewife's hands. Before too long, Simon was at home making the polish while Meyer was out on the road selling it. The Guggenheims had established their first profitable business in America.

From stove polish, Meyer moved into the manufacture and sale of "coffee essence." In mid-nineteenth-century America, coffee was a rich man's drink. By taking the cheapest coffee beans available and then "distilling an essence from them [and] mixing that essence with flavoring agents such as chicory," Meyer came up with a product remarkably similar to today's instant coffee. Because it was only the *essence* of coffee, it was well within the financial means of the average worker's tight budget. With a line that now included both stove polish and coffee essence, Meyer was financially able to marry his beloved Barbara. Less than four years after their arrival in America, Meyer Guggenheim and Barbara Meyer were married at downtown Philadelphia's Keneseth Israel Synagogue. Meyer was twenty-four, Barbara nineteen.

One should never underestimate the role that luck and beating the odds play in the creation of dynastic wealth. The vast Guggenheim fortune was built as much on luck as on pluck. Without question, the luck that Meyer and Barbara Guggenheim had in parenting no fewer than eight sons went a long way toward the creation of both their dynasty and their fortune. In the two decades between 1854 and 1873, Barbara gave birth to eleven children: Isaac (1854), Daniel (1856), Murray (1858), Solomon R. (1861), Jeanette (1863), Benjamin (1865), twins Simon and Robert (1867), William (1868), Rose (1871), and Cora (1873). Of these, only Simon's twin, Robert, would fail to live until maturity; he died from a fall from a horse at age eleven.

From the late 1850s to the late 1870s, Meyer Guggenheim continued to expand his business interests, first by importing lace and embroidery from Europe, and then in the wholesale spice trade. In 1873, he added yet another line to his business—lye. In those days, women made their own soap, the primary ingredient of which was lye. Generally, the lye came from "wood ashes and fat derived from home butchering." Meyer Guggenheim saw that in manufacturing lye, he could make a small fortune. He was right. Within a few years, his newest business, incorporated as the American Concentrated Lye Company, had become so successful that the Pennsylvania Salt Company sued for patent infringement. Meyer Guggenheim won the court case and then turned around and sold his company to Pennsylvania Salt for $150,000. His capital was growing.

Fresh from his triumph in the lye business, Guggenheim, acting on a tip, bought two thousand shares in the floundering Hannibal and St. Joseph Railway. According to the tip, financial titan Jay Gould would likely be in the market to purchase the St. Joseph, which he needed to complete his Missouri Pacific rail system. The tip proved to be right; Meyer Guggenheim sold his shares for an incredible profit of $300,000. He was now a wealthy man with a net worth of nearly half-a-million dollars. But the best was yet to come.

In 1881, Meyer Guggenheim bought a one-third interest for $5,000 in two lead and silver mines in California Gulch, near Leadville, Colorado. They turned out to be a bonanza. Within six years, the mines had produced 9 million ounces of silver and 86,000 tons of lead. The mining operations were so successful that "two miners in a single twelve-hour shift could pull down enough ore from the stopes to pay all the mine's expenses for one day." By 1888, the two mines, dubbed the A. Y. and the Minnie, were earning Meyer about $750,000 a year. The basis for the world's largest private mining fortune was secure.

From mining of silver and ore, the Guggenheims (now incorporated as M. Guggenheim's Sons) became smelters. With the passage of the Sherman Silver Purchase Act in 1890 (by which the Treasury agreed to buy 4 million ounces of silver each month), the price of silver rose by nearly 40 percent. Within a year, net profits at the Guggenheim smelters were in excess of $60,000 a month. With successful mining ventures in Mexico and Chile (site of the Chuquicamata copper mine, the world's most productive and profitable), M. Guggenheim's Sons was truly international in scope.

Meyer Guggenheim parceled responsibilities for his burgeoning empire amongst his sons, with Simon being shipped off to Spain to learn Spanish and acquire some European polish. Upon his return after two years, he was sent out to Colorado, where he was put to work "scouting for and buying ores, and overseeing the operations of the Western and Mexican mines and smelters."

Meyer moved his family and his business empire to New York in the early 1880s. There they became members of Temple Emanu-El on Fifth Avenue, home to the "Our Crowd" German Jews. This represented somewhat of a compromise, for Barbara Guggenheim was a "profoundly religious" woman. Meyer's sole interest was in seeing that his boys got the best secular education available. In Philadelphia, this had meant sending them to the "better" Catholic day schools, where "of course, they were indoctrinated in another religious viewpoint." As a result, none of the Guggenheim children ever had much of an attachment to the religion of their ancestors; today, four generations later, there are simply no Jewish Guggenheims.

The Guggenheims were never really accepted into the "Our Crowd" circle. To begin with, they were far richer than the Loebs and Schiffs, the Lehmans and Seligmans. Second, they were not truly German, but rather Swiss. Third, and perhaps most important, they were the only Jewish family whose fortune was based on heavy industry rather than finance or retailing. The polite German Jewish families referred to the mining magnates collectively as "The Googs."

Young Simon married Olga Hirsch, the daughter of a wealthy New York realtor. Stuck in Colorado and richer than Croesus, Simon needed something that would make him stand out from his older brothers. By the late 1890s, he came to the conclusion that getting himself elected to high office would provide the distinction he sought. In the 1890s, silver was the most important political issue of the day. The question boiled down to a matter of "inflation versus deflation, cheap currency versus hard money, easy credit versus tight credit." As a "Silver Republican" from a family that owned the nation's choicest silver mines, Simon Guggenheim should have had a fairly easy time winning election. In 1896, he declared his candidacy for Lieutenant Governor of Colorado, only to discover that, at twenty-nine, he was underage. Two years later, he made noises about running for Colorado Governor as a Silver Republican, but was forced to withdraw by his brothers; his "silverism" was causing the family firm too many problems in the "hard-money, gold-standard climate" of Wall Street.

In 1906, as noted earlier, Simon Guggenheim bought himself a seat in the United States Senate by convincing sixty-eight members of the Colorado state legislature to vote in his favor. During the campaign, Guggenheim was referred to in the local Denver press as "nothing but a walking bank account," and as "Napoleon Bonaparte without a brain." An anonymous letter printed in the *Denver Post* bitingly remarked, "Let us not forget that he is a Jew . . . a voluptuary and sensualist." Guggenheim chose to ignore the calumnies and instead financed lavish dinner parties for the employees of the *Post*. Most importantly, he also backed the eight-hour workday to the delight of every miner in the West. His strategy worked to perfection: Guggenheim took his seat in the United States Senate on March 4, 1907.

At that time, the Senate was truly a millionaires' club. No fewer than eighteen fortunes were represented in that chamber by the likes of Nelson W. Aldrich of Rhode Island (the father-in-law of John D. Rockefeller, Jr.), Henry Du Pont of Delaware, Henry Cabot Lodge of Massachusetts, and Elihu Root of New York. But Guggenheim, without question, was the richest of them all.

As a Senator, Simon Guggenheim contributed precious little to the nation. Shortly after his election, he went back to favoring the hated twelve-hour workday for miners. Known as "the most conservative man in the United States Senate," Guggenheim rarely made a speech, offered no legislation of consequence, and voted nearly one hundred times for the ultra-conservative schedules of the Payne Aldrich tariff. Outside of protecting his family's silver interests, about the only issue which engaged him was the creation of a Department of Labor; Guggenheim was at the forefront of those standing in vehement opposition.

During his one six-year term, Senator Guggenheim maintained a high level of popularity in Colorado's business community by "bringing home the bacon"—lucrative federal construction contracts. Perhaps the only truly notable act of his political career was his vote for the Seventeenth Amendment, which, as noted above, largely came about because of his notorious election campaign of 1906.

Throughout Simon Guggenheim's years in the Senate, his family was regularly excoriated in the press as a pack of greedy, rapacious capitalists. A poem published in the *Washington Times* in March 1910, paints a fairly dire portrait:

The Goggling Guggenheims

The Guggenheims will get you if you don't watch out;
They're gobbling all the coal lands of the West and North and South.
It is simply appalling when you think what they're about.
They'll surely gobble everything inside the earth and out.
They've gone to Alaska and optioned all the coal;
They've searched the mountains over and gobbled all the gold.
The water rights they do not own are very few, I'm told;
In fact this clan of Guggenheims is growing all too bold.
In Denver, Colorado, they own the whole blamed town.
The copper mines they cabbaged [stole] and nailed securely down.

The state was bought by Simon and he did the job up brown.
For he wears the senate toga now and owns our Washington.
It really looks a good deal like they'd gobble all in sight.
On top of the earth or under it, so fearful is their might.
They'll gobble all there is to get and turn you inside out.
The Guggenheims will get you if you don't watch out.

After one term in the Senate, Simon Guggenheim decided to call it quits. Had his public career ended at this point, he would be no more than a footnote in American history—a wealthy man who at one time was a dilettantish United States Senator from Colorado. But his public life did not end here. Following his six years in Washington, Senator and Mrs. Guggenheim moved back to New York. Once back in private life, he became chairman and president of the family-controlled American Smelting and Refining Company. By this time, the Guggenheims had two sons: John Simon, born in 1905, and George Denver, born two years later. Tragedy would befall both boys. John Simon, a promising young scholar, died suddenly in the spring of 1922 from pneumonia and mastoiditis. He was barely seventeen and had already been admitted to Harvard College. Seventeen years later, Simon and Olga's other son, George Denver, a greatly troubled young man, would commit suicide in a rented room in New York's Paramount Hotel.

The death of their first son was, without question, a devastating blow to the Senator and his wife. It could well have ruined their lives. As biographer John Davis notes: "It is a tribute to both of them that they were able to transform the . . . tragedy into one of the most inspired benefactions in American history." That "inspired benefaction" was the John Simon Guggenheim Memorial Foundation, which the Senator endowed in 1925 with an initial gift of $3 million worth of securities. For nearly eighty years, the Guggenheim Foundation's stated aim has been "to promote the advancement and diffusion of knowledge and understanding, and the appreciation of beauty by aiding without distinction on account of race, color, or creed, scholars, scientists and artists of either sex in the prosecution of their labors."

The Guggenheim Fellowship soon became the academic prize of distinction on a par with the British Rhodes Scholarship. In the first half-century of its existence, thirty-nine Guggenheim Fellows went on to win the Nobel Prize, while nine won the coveted Pulitzer Prize. Forty-four of the eighty National Book Awards between 1926 and 1976 were awarded to former Guggenheim Fellows. Among the outstanding works written on Guggenheim Fellowships were Stephen Vincent Benét's *John Brown's Body*, W. H. Auden's *The Age of Anxiety*, John Kenneth Galbraith's *The Affluent Society*, James D. Watson's *The Double Helix*, and Robert Penn Warren's *All the King's Men*. A partial listing of Guggenheim Fellows reads like a "Who's Who" of American arts and sciences: Aaron Copland, Gian Carlo Menotti, Thomas Wolfe, Hart Crane, Linus Pauling, Norbert Weiner, Samuel Barber, John Berryman, Arthur M. Schlesinger, Jr., Henry Kissinger, Vladimir Nabokov, and Eudora Welty. In perhaps the most glowing tribute of all, Brand Blanshard, Sterling Professor of Philosophy at Yale University, called the John Simon Guggenheim Foundation "the Socratic midwife of American scholarship."

Guggenheim family bequests have been responsible for the creation of art museums, free dental clinics, and much of the American space program. None of the family's various foundations, however, has had as lasting and important an impact as that created by Senator Simon and Olga Guggenheim in memory of their son.

Simon Guggenheim, known for the rest of his life as Senator Guggenheim, died on November 2, 1941 in New York City from pneumonia. He was seventy-three years old. His estate was valued at approximately $50 million, the largest of the seven brothers. In his will, he left an additional $20 million to the John Simon Guggenheim Foundation.

Olga lived another twenty-nine years, succumbing shortly after her ninety-third birthday. A convert to Episcopalianism, Olga convinced her husband to join the fashionable St. Thomas Episcopal Church at Fifth Avenue and 53rd Street. It was from the WASP crowd, not "Our Crowd," that Senator and Mrs. Guggenheim drew most of their closest companions.

Having no immediate heirs, Olga Guggenheim left the bulk of her estate to the Foundation. Her personal art collection was deemed "one of the finest ever assembled by a single donor in New York." Among the twenty-four works in her estate were eight Picassos, five Matisses, four Legers, a Chagall, a Gauguin, and a Miro, two Modiglianis, Rousseau's *Sleeping Gypsy*, and sculptures by Brancusi, Maillol, and Rodin. Senator and Mrs. Guggenheim are buried in the family crypt in Woodlawn Cemetery.

References

American Jewish Year Book, vol. 6 (1904–5), p. 107; vol. 9 (1907–8), p. 436; vol. 24, p. 151; vol. 44, p. 338.

Biographical Directory of American Jews.

Stephen Birmingham, *Our Crowd* (New York: Harper & Row, 1967).

John H. Davis, *The Guggenheims: An American Epic* (New York: William Morrow, 1978).

Dictionary of American Biography, 3.

Encyclopaedia Judaica (1972), vol. 7. col. 965.

Edwin P. Hoyt, Jr., *The Guggenheims and the American Dream* (New York: Funk & Wagnalls, 1967).

New York Times, November 4, 1941, 23:1.

Universal Jewish Encyclopedia.

Who Was Who in America, vol. 1.

Who Was Who in American Jewry, 1926, 1928, 1938.

HAHN, MICHAEL (1830–1886): *Unionist Republican from Louisiana; served two terms in the House (Thirty-seventh Congress; December 2, 1862–March 3, 1863; Forty-ninth Congress; March 4, 1885–March 15, 1886).*

Although Michael Hahn was born to Jewish parents, he was a practicing Christian for most of his life. The timing and circumstances which led to his conversion to (or adoption of) Christian principles and practice are, regrettably, not known. From the record, it is clear that Hahn was a man of courage and strong convictions; he often stood alone in condemning slavery and attempting to keep his adopted state of Louisiana part of a disintegrating Union.

Michael Hahn was born in Bavaria on November 24, 1830. Of his parents and family in Germany, nothing is known. All sources agree that the Hahn family emigrated to New York City in either 1831 or 1832, and moved to New Orleans by 1836. There, Hahn went through high school, and decided to study law. While a student at the law school of the University of Louisiana, he read law in the offices of an attorney named Christian Rosaliers. Upon receiving his law degree in 1850, he was admitted to the bar. Two years later, at the age of twenty-two, he was elected to the New Orleans Board of Education, serving several years as that body's president.

In the 1850s, Louisiana politics was controlled largely by the Slidell brothers. As Michael Hahn's political visibility increased, he became a stridently outspoken opponent of the Slidells' pro-slavery, anti-Union stance. In 1856, a presidential year, Hahn threw his support behind Illinois Senator Steven A. Douglas, the candidate of the Northern Democrats, while the Slidells stumped for James Buchanan—former congressman, senator, and secretary of state, and, most recently, President Polk's ambassador to Great Britain.

Buchanan was unanimously nominated on the seventeenth ballot, and chose John C. Breckinridge of Kentucky as his running mate. Opposing Buchanan were the first candidate of the newly formed Republican party, John C. Frémont, and former president Millard Fillmore, the nominee of the American ("Know Nothing") and Whig parties. "Buck and Breck" were elected with less than half the popular vote, and the Union began a rapid slide toward civil war.

During Buchanan's four years in the White House, the split between slave and free states steadily widened. Some hoped that the problem might be settled by the Supreme Court; all such hopes were dashed when almost the entire North rejected the high court's 1857 verdict in the Dred Scott case. In that case, a majority of the Supreme Court ruled that the federal government had no power to make slaves free.

By the end of Buchanan's one term, the Democratic party was unalterably divided into two groups; neither faction would accept Buchanan as its nominee. The Northern Democrats backed Senator Douglas; the Southerners opted for Vice President Breckinridge. This split all but guaranteed the election of the Republican candidate, Abraham Lincoln. Between Lincoln's election and inauguration, South Carolina seceded from the Union. The push was on for the other Southern slaveholding states to follow suit.

In those dark days, as Mississippi, Florida, Alabama, and Georgia decided to secede, Michael Hahn joined a committee which canvassed the populace in favor of union. It was like trying to stem a flash flood with a trowel. When Louisiana joined the Confederacy, all public officials were called upon to swear allegiance. Hahn, in renewing his oath as a notary public, neglected (or refused) to do so.

When Union forces captured New Orleans, Hahn gladly swore allegiance to the U.S. government, and in November 1862, was elected to Congress as a Unionist. He presented his credentials to the House on December 2, 1862, the beginning of the third session of the Thirty-seventh Congress, and was declared entitled to his seat by resolution on February 17, 1863. When the third session ended just a little over two weeks later, Hahn, now a private citizen, returned to New Orleans, where he "advocated the reopening of the Federal courts." He further counseled that "no more congressional elections be held until the state was more thoroughly reconstructed."

Turning his attentions to a new pursuit, Hahn purchased and edited a newspaper called the *True Delta*. As publisher and editor, he advocated emancipation and supported the policies of President Lincoln. In February 1864, Hahn ran on the Free State ticket for governor of Louisiana. He was opposed by two candidates who supported the secessionist status quo. When the federal government disqualified nearly all of the state's 350,000 white voters, Hahn wound up being elected with only 10,270 votes.

His gubernatorial administration was the classic case of the king wearing a "hollow crown." Three-quarters of the state was still under Confederate control, and even as he began his term, Louisiana's Confederate state legislature, with Governor Henry W. Allen at its head, was convening in Shreveport. Lincoln attempted to shore up Hahn's authority by granting him the powers of a military governor.

The President advised Hahn to extend suffrage rights to all of the state's blacks. In April 1864, a convention was held to revise the Louisiana constitution. The proposed document abolished slavery and made general public education the law of the land, but did not give the legislature authority to extend suffrage to the state's black population. In the election to ratify the new constitution (it passed by only 6,836 votes), Michael Hahn was elected United States Senator. He never presented his credentials in Washington, however, because he disagreed with the Reconstruction policy of President Andrew Jackson, the assassinated Lincoln's successor.

After the war, Hahn started another newspaper, the *New Orleans Republican,* and repaired to his sugar plantation in St. Charles Parish, where he built the village of Hahnsville. Over the next several years, he represented his parish in the state legislature, served as superintendent of the U.S. Mint, and was elected to a term as judge of the twenty-sixth judicial district. In 1885, he resigned his judicial post in order to enter Congress, becoming the state's only Republican in Washington. Eleven days into his term, Michael Hahn died at age fifty-five. He was buried in Metrarie Cemetery in New Orleans.

Hahn is described by a writer of the time as "short and lame . . . [with] dark, curly hair and a brown complexion. He was of a vivacious temper . . . a most amiable and persuasive gentleman, and accomplished in the amenities of congressional life. He did not debate a great deal, but had a fervid love for his state."

References

Biographical Directory of the United States Congress, 1774–1989, p. 1109.

National Cyclopedia of American Biography, vol. 10, p. 79.

HALPERN, SEYMOUR (1913–1997): *Republican from New York; served seven terms in the House (Eighty-sixth through Seventy-third Congress; January 3, 1959–January 3, 1973).*

The Latin term *sui generis* means "of its own kind." It is a phrase that should be used with some care, lest it lose its value. According to Eugene Ehrlich's *Amo, Amas, Amat and More*, "properly used, *sui generis* requires that the person, place, or thing be of an entirely distinctive character." Ehrlich provides such fitting examples as Jimmy Durante, the Grand Canyon, and Bach's Mass in B Minor. One might add to the list New York Representative Seymour Halpern, for without doubt, he was "one of a kind." How so? In the latter years of his congressional career, he was the only Republican in New York City's House delegation.

Today, the words "Republican" and "conservative" seem to be tautological. It was not always that way. Less than a generation ago, there actually were card-carrying members of the GOP fully as liberal as their Democratic counterparts. Seymour Halpern was one such liberal Republican; he regularly garnered the endorsement of labor unions and New York's Liberal Party, something almost unthinkable in the late 1990s. In fact, Halpern was so consistently liberal that it was frequently suggested that "he might be more comfortable as a Democrat." Whenever the topic arose, Halpern would bristle. "Yes, I am a liberal," he would proclaim, "but I am first, last and always, a Republican." What those who made the party-switching suggestions never knew was that for Seymour Halpern, being a member of the GOP was "both a family tradition and a lifelong commitment." In other words, Republicanism was Halpern's political birthright.

Seymour Halpern was born in the Richmond Hill section of New York City on November 19, 1913. His father, Ralph Halpern, was a one-time member of the New York State Assembly. He was also "the perennial secretary of the Queens Republican Committee, holding the post throughout his son's political career." Following his graduation from Richmond Hill High School in 1931, Halpern spent two years (1932–34) as a student at the Seth Low College of Columbia University. But college wasn't for him. Following a brief stint as a reporter for the *Long Island Daily Press*, Halpern landed his first polit-

ical job: campaign aide to *Fiorello H. La Guardia* in his successful 1933 race for mayor of New York City. From there, he went to work for New York City Council President Newbold Morris. By age twenty-six, Seymour Halpern was ready to begin his own political career.

Halpern won a seat in the New York State Senate in 1940. He remained in that body until 1954, when he made an abortive race for Congress from New York's Sixth District (Queens), losing to Democrat *Lester Holtzman*. During his fourteen years in Albany, Halpern "served on scores of committees, and claimed sponsorship of 279 bills that became law." Among these were measures dealing with "schools, housing, civil rights, transportation, narcotics, nutrition and mental health." Known as a "generally natty dresser," Halpern once transformed himself into a derelict (rumpled clothes and unshaven) in order to make an anonymous visit to the Creedmore State Hospital. Posing as a patient's relative, he was able to "verify reports of appalling conditions at the hospital for the mentally ill."

Four years after his defeat to Lester Holtzman, Halpern ran for the open Fourth District seat that had been vacated by Republican Henry Jepson Latham, following Latham's election to the New York State Supreme Court. Halpern won, and was easily reelected to six additional terms. In the House, Halpern "was a man who took his legislative duties seriously." Not one to put all his legislative eggs in one basket, Halpern played an active role in a wide array of issues. Among the most noteworthy achievements of his fourteen-year House career were his cosponsorship of both the 1964 Civil Rights Act and the original Medicare legislation in 1965. That same year, Halpern garnered headlines by championing a measure designed to "protect American businesses against an Arab boycott." As a Republican serving an increasingly Democratic constituency in Queens, Halpern "kept a close eye on constituents' needs, no matter how small."

Throughout his public career, the dapper Halpern was known as a "charming ladies' man, who favored fine restaurants and rarely dined alone or let anyone else pick up the check." That all changed in 1956. While speaking at a fashion show at the Pennsylvania Hotel in New York, "Mr. Halpern took one look at the beautiful 22-

year old fashion coordinator, Barbara Olsen, and his days as a bachelor were numbered." The two married in 1959, when Halpern was forty-six, his bride a mere twenty-five. Halpern, first, last, and always a politician, made headlines on his honeymoon by becoming "the first Jew since 1948 to be allowed by Arab authorities to cross the border from Israel into Jordan." Representative and Mrs. Halpern, who remained childless, "settled into a penthouse apartment," where they "pursued the good life."

Halpern's "good life" earned him a bit of unwelcome publicity in the late 1960s, when a *Wall Street Journal* article disclosed the fact that the Queens legislator was more than $100,000 in debt. The debt included a $40,000 unsecured loan "at a highly favorable rate" from a bank that had "lobbied hard in opposition to a measure Mr. Halpern had also opposed on the House Banking Committee." Halpern's position with his Fourth District constituents was strong enough to withstand the assault on his integrity; he was returned to Congress with 77 percent of the vote in the next election.

Following the 1970 reapportionment, Seymour Halpern retired his congressional seat. He did not wish to run against veteran Democratic Representative *Lester L. Wolff*. "He wanted to go out a winner," his wife said. In the remaining years of his life, Seymour Halpern worked as a public relations man and pursued his private passions: painting and collecting autographs. Several of his portraits hang in the United States Capitol today. Seymour Halpern died in Southampton, Long Island, on January 17, 1997. He was eighty-three years old. Mrs. Halpern continues to live in Southampton.

References

Biographical Directory of the United States Congress, 1774–1989, p. 1117.
New York Times, January 18, 1997, 10:1.

HAMBURG, DAN (1948–): *Democrat from California; served one term in the House (One Hundred and Third Congress; January 3, 1992–January 2, 1994).*

During the 1992 presidential campaign, Arkansas Governor Bill Clinton was asked in a television interview if he had ever smoked marijuana when he was a student in the 1960s. Looking the interviewer in the eye, Clinton said: "Yes, I must admit that as a student I did try it once or twice, but I didn't inhale." That comment would take on a life of its own; political pundits and late-night talk show hosts had a field day making sport of a "baby boomer" who toked but didn't inhale. One conservative pundit quipped: "I'm almost positive that he inhaled. I'm not too certain that he ever exhaled!"

Clinton's answer was given new meaning two years later when Dan Hamburg was running for Congress from California's First Congressional District. Mitchell Landsberg, of the Associated Press, asked Hamburg about his memories of 1968, "a watershed for the Baby Boom Generation" marked by war in Vietnam, antiwar, antidraft demonstrations at home, the assassinations of Dr. Martin Luther King and Senator Robert F. Kennedy, the Beatles' "White Album," the Democratic National Convention in Chicago, and the election of Richard M. Nixon. In answer to Landsberg's question, Hamburg "responded with a laugh: 'I don't remember. I did inhale.'"

The second of Walter and Jean (Milton) Hamburg's three children, Dan Hamburg was born in St. Louis on October 6, 1948. The Hamburg and Milton families had come to the United States from Russia around the turn of the century, with the Hamburgs settling in St. Louis and the Miltons in Sedalia, about 200 miles to the west. The Hamburgs were Reform Jews, belonging to Temple Israel. Dan became bar mitzvah not at the synagogue, but in his family's home in October 1961. He continued his Jewish education at Temple Israel, becoming confirmed in 1964.

Following his graduation from high school in

1966, Hamburg went west, where he attended Stanford University. Originally majoring in religious studies, he changed his academic emphasis to American history by the beginning of his senior year. Hamburg's four years at Stanford coincided with the "summer of love" in San Francisco's Haight-Ashbury and the rise of the counterculture. As noted in the *Almanac of American Politics* (1994), Hamburg's graduation class of 1970 was "suffused with opposition to the Vietnam war and devotion to marijuana." One of Hamburg's friends at Stanford was student body president David Harris, who married singer Joan Baez and eventually went to jail rather than serve in Vietnam.

Following graduation, Hamburg went to Mendocino County to visit some friends; he wound up moving there permanently. Within a short time of his arrival, he became a cofounder

of the alternative Mariposa Elementary School. Hamburg soon met Carrie Blood, a San Francisco native with three children from a previous marriage. They were married on May 18, 1974. Along with Carrie's three children—Laura (born 1964), Kirt (born 1965), and Elizabeth (born 1967)—the Hamburgs have one child of their own, Matthew, born in 1976. Like his father, Matthew is a graduate of Stanford. In 1990, the Hamburgs became grandparents with the arrival of Melissa.

Dan and Carrie Hamburg stayed with the Mariposa school until 1975, when Dan became a member of the Ukiah City Planning Commission. He spent four years on the board, serving as its chairman in 1977. At the same time, he served as director of the Ukiah Valley Child Development Center. In 1980, Dan Hamburg was elected to the Mendocino County Board of Supervisors as a "managed growth" candidate. His staunch opposition to untrammeled growth in pristine Mendocino brought on the wrath of developers, who attempted to have him recalled. Hamburg survived the threat and wound up becoming chairman of the Board of Supervisors in 1983.

In 1984, Dan and Carrie went to China at the

behest of friends who were living in Taishan, near Canton. From 1985 to 1986, they taught college-age students from America, Europe, and New Zealand at a Cultural Studies Program sponsored by the local Chinese university. Hamburg managed to return to China every summer until 1990, a year after Tiananmen Square, at which time he set his sights on a congressional race in 1992.

In the 1990 congressional elections, four-term incumbent Democrat Douglas H. Bosco was narrowly defeated by conservative Republican Frank Riggs, a former policeman. Upon deciding to make the race for Congress, Hamburg set about raising money. He got an early infusion of funds when friends Bonnie Raitt, Jackson Browne, and Holly Near held benefit concerts on behalf of his campaign. Hamburg amassed a large enough war chest to scare off any other challengers for the Democratic primary. The election provided a classic race between opposites: Hamburg, a product of the countercultural sixties, and Riggs, a former cop.

California's First Congressional District is the home of some two hundred wineries, most of the world's redwood trees, and a vast collection of "veterans of the counterculture," many of whom grow marijuana as a cash crop. Hamburg emphasized the differences between himself and Riggs when he stated: "He was a narc. I favor growing your own." Indeed, one plank of Hamburg's platform was the legalization of marijuana for personal and medicinal use.

Riggs countered by calling Hamburg "Deadbeat Dan," a pointed reference to the fact that during the campaign, Hamburg, who had been laid off from his job as a computer typesetter, was collecting $87 a week in unemployment benefits. Riggs angered First District voters when he went back on his 1990 campaign pledge not to take the "obscene" congressional pay raise. He got himself into further hot water when, as a member of the so-called "Republican Gang of Seven," he "insisted on disclosure of the names of House bank check-bouncers, only to find that he had three overdrafts himself." Hamburg, who raised nearly $650,000 for the campaign, wound up defeating Riggs by a final tally of 119,676 to 113,266—48 percent of the vote. (Phil Baldwin, running on the Peace and Freedom ticket, captured nearly 5 percent of the vote). Upon his election, he was termed "proba-

bly the purest child of the sixties in Congress today."

Once in Congress, Hamburg received assignments on Merchant Marine and Fisheries and on Public Works and Transportation. When he arrived in Washington, *People* magazine named him "one of the fifty most beautiful people in the world." Possessed of "rugged good looks," Hamburg quickly became one of the most distinctive members of the One Hundred and Third Congress. Having long since rejected the conventional formality of neckties, he took to wearing bolo ties in order to conform to a congressional dress code that mandates the wearing of "neck apparel." Not surprisingly, the liberal Hamburg became a member of the Congressional Progressive Caucus. He quickly called for defense reconversion in Fairfield, the home of Travis Air Force Base.

During his single term, Hamburg was one of only six members of Congress to vote against giving the FBI authority to obtain unlisted phone numbers without a warrant in cases of terrorism or espionage. He was one of only four to vote against authorizing money to establish a national DNA base to track convicted criminals. In his single term, he had only one piece of legislation passed by the House—the Headwaters Forest Act, which would have protected the last ancient forest in California by having the government acquire some 44,000 acres of timberland near Eureka. Despite overwhelming opposition from loggers in his district, Hamburg's legislation passed in the House by a vote of 288–213, only to be defeated in the Senate on the last day of the session.

The 1994 election was a rematch between Hamburg and Riggs. Hamburg survived the Democratic primary, defeating former Representative Bosco, this time by a margin of 62 percent to 38 percent. In the general election, Riggs attacked Hamburg for the Headwaters bill, terming it a "job killer." Riggs hammered away on the issue, saying: "I say jobs first and not earth first like Dan Hamburg and other environmentalists do." Although outspent by more than $200,000 (Hamburg raised nearly $835,000), Riggs defeated Dan Hamburg 53 percent to 47 percent

In early 1995, shortly after leaving Congress, Dan Hamburg went to South Africa, where he spent ten months working as a consultant to the provincial legislatures in and around Johannesburg. Returning in early 1996, he acted as campaign manager for friend Mike Reilly, who was running for the Sonoma County Board of Supervisors. Hamburg endorsed attorney Monica Marvin in the congressional race to unseat Frank Riggs. Marvin lost the Democratic primary to Michela Alioto, the twenty-eight-year-old granddaughter of Joseph Alioto, former mayor of San Francisco (Alioto wound up losing to Riggs). Hamburg also spent the fall of 1996 working on Green Party candidate Ralph Nader's presidential campaign, "and trying to figure out how he was going to make his next mortgage payment." Hamburg gave one of the presidential nomination speeches at the Green Party presidential Nomination convention in Los Angeles.

In early 1997, Dan Hamburg became executive director of VOTE Action Committee, a foundation "dedicated to creating a progressive coalition that can challenge the current two-party 'duopoly.'" Hamburg, the highest-ranking former elected office-holder with either the Democrat or Republican parties to have jumped to the "Greens," became that party's candidate for governor of California in 1998. Hamburg's running mate, environmental scientist Sara Amir, was a native of Iran. Despite campaigning from one end of california to the other, the Hamburg-Amir ticket came in a distant third.

Hamburg, a gifted writer, has had articles in the *Nation, Tikkun,* and *Harper's.* While running for California governor, he also hosted a twice-monthly public affairs radio program dealing with the need to shift political and philosophical perspectives.

Although married for more than twenty-five years to a non-Jew, Hamburg still observes Passover and Chanukah with his family. He currently resides in Ukiah, California.

References

Interview with Dan Hamburg, March 1996.
Almanac of American Politics (1994–96 editions).
Fort Lauderdale News Sun Sentinel, January 10, 1993, G12.

HARMAN, JANE (1945–): *Democrat from California; served three terms in the House (One Hundred and Third Congress through One Hundred and Fifth Congress; January 3, 1993–January 4, 1999).*

Shortly after Jane Harman arrived on Capitol Hill as a member of the One Hundred and Third Congress, she invited a few friends over to celebrate her husband Sydney's seventy-fifth birthday. Among those who stopped by were then-Defense Secretary Les Aspin, Robert E. Ruben (soon to become President Clinton's Treasury Secretary), Mollie Raiser, the President's chief of protocol, and former Senator John Tunney. House Speaker Thomas S. Foley also showed up, which was only appropriate; the party was held in his office at the Capitol. As one reporter remarked, "not bad for a freshman member of Congress." Well-schooled in the ways of Washington, Harman had already spent nearly two decades working in Congress and the White House before winning her seat.

Jane Harman was born in New York City on June 28, 1945, the daughter of Adolph N. and Lucille (Geier) Lakes. When Jane was four, her father, a physician, moved his medical practice to Culver City, California. At the same time, he moved the family to West Los Angeles, a few miles away from his place of employment. While a student at Emerson Junior High School, Jane lost her first run for office—treasurer of her class. Always intrigued by politics, the fifteen-year old sat in the spectator's gallery of the 1960 Democratic National Convention held in Los Angeles. In 1962, following graduation from University High School, Jane Lakes went off to Smith College in Northampton, Massachusetts, from which she received her B.A., *magna cum laude*, in 1966.

At the end of her sophomore year, Lakes went to Washington as a college intern, and "something clicked." From that point on, politics was on her mind. She went on to Harvard Law School, from which she received her J.D. in 1969. The valedictorian of the class was future Los Angeles–area Representative *Mel Levine*; the careers of the two would dovetail for the next several years.

On July 4, 1969, Jane Lakes married Richard Asher Frank, and she became Jane Frank. They had two children: Brian Lakes and Hilary Lakes. Following a brief stint in Switzerland and two years as an associate with the firm of Surrey, Karasik and More, she joined the staff of California Senator John Tunney, and from 1972 to 1973, was his legislative director. (Mel Levine was a legislative assistant on Tunney's staff during those years). In 1973, Tunney, who chaired the Senate Judiciary Subcommittee on Citizens' Interest, named Frank its chief counsel and staff director. During her time with the committee, she also taught at Georgetown. When Tunney was defeated for reelection in 1976, Frank joined the Carter White House, serving one year as deputy cabinet secretary. In 1977, she made headlines when she quit her White House post in order to stay home with her young children.

Jane and Richard Frank were divorced in 1978. She initially wanted to return to her family in California but stayed in Washington, due to "her sense of responsibility." She and her former husband worked out a joint custody agreement. In August 1980, the future congresswoman married Sydney Harman, whom she had met in the Carter White House, where he was serving as Under Secretary of Commerce. Harman, an "audio equipment mogul," was the founder of Harman International Industries, a Washington-based Fortune 500 company. (Harman International Industries manufactures high-end stereo equipment.) Together, the Harmans have two children of their own, Daniel Geier and Justine Leigh.

In 1987, after practicing law with Jones, Day, Reavis & Pogue, a top Washington firm, Jane Harman became a partner with the high profile Washington-California firm of Manatt, Phelps, Rothenberg and Tunney. Her work required her to commute between Washington and Los Angeles. In 1984, she served as counsel to the

Democratic Convention's platform committee. Three years later, she chaired a $2.2 million Democratic Party fundraiser. From 1986 to 1990, she chaired the National Lawyers' Council, a legal network for the Democratic Party. Jane Harman also joined her husband's firm, serving on its board of directors as corporation secretary. In 1996, with a net worth estimated at $15 million, Jane Harman placed fourteenth on *Roll Call*'s list of the fifty wealthiest members of the One Hundred and Fourth Congress.

In 1991, Jane and Sydney Harman moved from Washington to Southern California, where Sidney had long-standing business ties. Knowing that Mel Levine was forsaking his congressional seat to run for the United States Senate, Jane Harman initially moved to Brentwood, within the boundaries of Levine's old district. A year later, the Harmans moved to Marina Del Rey, in Southern California's newly created Thirty-sixth Congressional District.

Known to locals as South Bay, the district ranges from Venice southward to San Pedro. Historically, most of the newly constituted Thirty-sixth District (and its earlier incarnations) had been represented by conservative Republicans. In recent years, Republican stalwarts Robert ("B-1 Bob") Dornan and Dana Rohrbacher, a former senior speechwriter in the Reagan White House, represented a vast percentage of Jane Harman's district. A smaller portion belonged to Levine. The Thirty-sixth District is the local home of the defense contractors Hughes, Lockheed, and TRW, all of which had been laying off employees as a response to defense cutbacks.

The Democratic primary field contained no fewer than seven candidates. Perhaps the best known of whom was Ada Unruh, a daughter-in-law of the late Jesse ("Big Daddy") Unruh, former California assembly speaker and state treasurer. The Republican primary's marquee name was Maureen Reagan, daughter of the former president. Spending lavishly of her own money, Harman bested the Democratic field with 45 percent to Unruh's 16. In the Republican primary, Joan Milke Flores, a well-known Los Angeles city councilwoman, won with 34 percent to Reagan's 31. In the general election, Flores accused Harman of being a carpetbagger, and stressed her own conservative pro-life credentials. Harman ran as a "pro-choice, pro-change"

moderate, supporting both national health insurance and a balanced budget. Choosing the slogan, "This woman will clean House," Harman argued that she could "do more to protect defense jobs in the area." She also supported a targeted capital gains tax cut and the line item veto. On election day, Harman pulled an upset, winning by more than 16,000 votes.

One of the keys to Harman's victory was voter registration. At the beginning of 1992, districtwide registration favored Republicans 46 percent to 41 percent. By September, Harman's vigorous voter registration drive had narrowed the margin to less than two percentage points. She also ran the third most-expensive congressional race in the country, spending nearly $2.3 million, reportedly including $823,000 of her own money.

As a freshman member of the House, Harman was shrewd enough to be assigned to the Committees on National Security (formerly Armed Services), and Science, and was appointed Democratic chair of a freshman task force on implementing the Clinton administration's "reinventing government" proposals. From her committee seats, she was in a strong position to keep two of her campaign promises: "to protect South Bay defense industries and promote reconversion of defense businesses and jobs." During her first term, Harman got the National Security Committee to approve the purchase of six C17 cargo jets, to be built in her district, and succeeded in keeping the Los Angeles Air Force Base in El Segundo off the list of military facilities to be closed. She returned home weekly, often bringing high-level Washington officials with her. One of her guests was Vice President Al Gore, who came along to hold a town meeting at a TRW plant in Redondo Beach. While Harman supported most of the Clinton administration's policies, she did vote against the North American Free Trade Agreement (NAFTA).

Harman became the California Republican Party's number-one target in 1994. State party chairman Tirso Del Junco declared: "She ran on a very conservative platform and then voted for every Clinton tax proposal. How is she going to be able to come back to the district and hide her voting record?" In her first reelection campaign, Harman drew as her opponent Susan M. Brooks, mayor of Rancho Palos Verdes. Brooks, who had won a "high tension" primary, ran into immediate trouble when the runner-up, Ron Florance, refused to endorse her. Brooks, who like Harman was pro-choice, attacked the incumbent for supporting the Clinton tax increase and for voting with Maxine Waters (perhaps the most left-wing member of the California congressional delegation) 95 percent of the time. While Brooks was campaigning door-to-door, Harman was spending more than $1 million on television ads that portrayed her unique ability to do "heavy lifting for the district economy."

The election went down to the wire, with Brooks coming out ahead by ninety-three votes on election night. Convinced she had won, Brooks went to Washington to join in postelection sessions with the freshman class of 1994. While Brooks was in Washington, however, the absentee ballots were counted, giving Jane Harman a razor thin 812-vote victory. When California state election officials declared Harman the winner, Brooks contested the outcome, claiming that votes had been cast illegally. The House Oversight Committee held hearings on the case in May 1996. Harman's victory was once again upheld.

Described as smart, intense, and highly skilled, Harman maintained a moderate voting record, receiving a 60 rating (out of 100) from the liberal ADA, and a 19 from the conservative ACA. In 1996, Harman once again faced Susan Brooks in a general election fight. This time she emerged with a 54 percent to 44 percent victory. On February 4, 1998, Jane Harman declared her candidacy for governor of California. At the press conference announcing her intention, Harman said: "Like many of my friends, I had planned to spend a portion of this year working to elect *Dianne Feinstein* governor. But when our distinguished senior Senator decided to forgo the race, I was approached by many of her supporters and urged to enter it."

Declining to run for reelection to her House seat, Harman devoted all her energies to the June gubernatorial primary. Funding her campaign with $15 million of her own money, Harman waged a tough battle against California Lieutenant Governor Gray Davis and businessman (and political novice) Al Checchi. Checchi, the former head of Northwest Airlines, pumped upwards of $40 million of his own fortune into a primary race that was long on television advertising and rather short on substantive issues. Sensing that Harman was his more important rival, Checchi aired a series of costly ads attacking her for illegally employing two nannies—a woman from Ghana in the 1970s and another from England in 1989. Although Harman acknowledged employing the women, she said that, at the time, she believed them to be in the country legally, and was, in any case, "uncertain about immigration law." Reporters looking into Checchi's allegation discovered that, at one time, Mrs. Harman was quite familiar with the intricacies of immigration law. Twenty years earlier, Mrs. Harman had written a memo to then-President Jimmy Carter outlining a plan for changing immigration law that included "penalties for employers who hired undocumented workers." Despite the massive spending on the part of both Harman and Checchi, Lieutenant Governor Davis won the primary with 35 percent. Jane Harman came in a distant third, capturing just 12 percent of the vote.

Now a private citizen, Jane Harman divides her time between California and Washington, D.C.

References

Almanac of American Politics (1994–98 editions).
Los Angeles Times, October 8, 1992, B 1:2; October 3, 1993, B 1:5; March 1, 1993, D 2:3.
New York Times, February 5, 1998, A14:4.
Politics in America (1994–98 editions).
"Roll Call Files," *Roll Call Online*, 1996.
Washington Post, June 4, 1998, p. A1.
Who's Who in America, 1996.

HART, EMANUEL BERNARD (1809–1897):
Democrat from New York; served one term in the
House (Thirty-second Congress; March 4,
1851–March 3, 1853).

Unlike the first Jew who preceded him in Congress (a foreign-born Sephardi, David Levy Yulee), Emanuel Hart was a native-born son of one of America's most distinguished Ashkenazi families. The Harts were originally from Fuerth, Bavaria, a city with a long and remarkable history of Jewish scholarship. Emanuel Hart's father, Bernard, who was born in London in 1763, was an established merchant in New York by 1800. Along with his cousin Ephraim, Bernard played a pivotal role in the creation of the New York Stock Exchange, and served as its secretary for over thirty years.

A devout Jew who was a pioneer member of the Spanish and Portuguese Synagogue (despite his Ashkenazi roots), Bernard Hart inexplicably married a gentile woman, Catherine Brett, in 1799. The marriage, which lasted less than a year, produced one son, Henry. In due course, Henry Hart (1800–1845) married Elizabeth Ostrander, with whom he had a son. They named him Francis Brett. This youngster would grow up to be the great American writer Bret Harte, the "Laureate of the Pacific Belt."

Bernard Hart married a second time in 1806. His new wife was Rebecca Seixas, a niece of Gershon Mendes Seixas, Shearith Israel's hazzan, strictly speaking its cantor, but in this era when there were as yet no rabbis in America, also its spiritual leader. With Rebecca, he fathered ten children, including another son named Henry. The second of these ten children was Emanuel Bernard, America's second Jewish Congressman.

Like his father, Emanuel B. Hart became a prosperous merchant who played an active and important role in the life of New York. A Jackson Democrat, Hart was elected alderman of the Fifth Ward in 1845, and by 1849, was chairman of the Tammany General Committee. His one congressional term (Thirty-second Congress; 1851–53) was remarkable only for its relative lack of distinction. One speculates that his friends at Tammany Hall honored him with the seat for services rendered above and beyond the call of duty.

In 1857, President James Buchanan appointed Hart surveyor of the Port of New York. While holding down a series of appointive political jobs (e.g., immigration commissioner, excise commissioner, city assessor), Emanuel Hart found time to study law. He was admitted to the New York Bar at the age of fifty-nine.

A leader of the Jewish community, Hart served many terms as president of Mount Sinai Hospital and was treasurer of the Society for the Relief of Poor Hebrews. He was married for many years to the non-Jewish Mary Louise Coombs. They had no children. Emanuel B. Hart died in New York City on August 29, 1897, two months shy of his eighty-eighth birthday. He is buried in Cypress Hills Cemetery, in Brooklyn, New York.

References
American Jewish Year Book, vol. 2 (1900–01), p. 518.
Helen I. Davis, "Bret Harte and His Jewish Ancestor, Bernard Hart," *Publications of the American Jewish Historical Society* 32 (1931): pp. 99–111.
Encyclopaedia Judaica (1972), vol. 7, col. 1354.
Jewish Encyclopedia.
Universal Jewish Encyclopedia.

HECHT, JACOB (1928–): *Republican from Nevada; served one term in the Senate (January 3, 1983–January 2, 1989).*

The first Jew elected to Congress from the state of Nevada, United States Senator Jacob "Chic" Hecht, was known as much for his arch-conservatism as for his colorful verbal gaffes. Called by one reporter the "Rodney Dangerfield of Capitol Hill," Senator Hecht once stressed his opposition to the locating of "nuclear suppositories" in his home state. Once, during an interview, he told an inquiring reporter about his having debated "diametric materialism" with several colleagues. Short, unprepossessing, with a slight lisp, Senator Hecht was, from time to time, an almost invisible presence in Washington. Once, he got up to address a group of Jewish lawmakers who were gathered for a meeting with Israeli Prime Minister Yitzhak Shamir at the Israeli embassy. The group's leader, Representative *Sidney Yates*, interrupted Senator Hecht with the admonition that only members of Congress were allowed to speak. Someone had to tell Yates who Hecht was.

The Hecht family was originally from Poland. Senator Hecht's grandfather came to the United States before the turn of the century, working at first as a peddler on the streets of New York City. Moving west, grandpa Hecht made his way to St. Louis and eventually settled down to raise a family in Poplar Bluff, Missouri. There he opened a retail store and sired ten children. All ten of them eventually went into the retail trade, many establishing their own men's and women's shops in and around Poplar Bluff. One son, Louis, moved to Cape Giradeau just before World War I and opened a store. After serving in World War I, Louis Hecht returned to Cape Giradeau, reopened his shop, and married a Russian immigrant from Kiev. Their son, Jacob, was born on November 30, 1928.

Cape Giradeau, perhaps best known as the hometown of radio talkshow personality Rush Limbaugh, was a small farming community whose main industry was a shoe factory. Among the approximately 18,000 residents was a tiny Jewish community numbering no more than ten or twelve families. Despite their small numbers, the Jews of Cape Giradeau managed to support a synagogue and hold lay-led services on Friday evening. The Hechts were a "semi-Orthodox" family—no ham or bacon ever entered their home. Louis Hecht imported a rabbi from St. Louis to train his sons for bar mitzvah. Years later, Senator Hecht remembered that "he would stay over, and all weekend I would study with him. I *davened* [prayed] for many years after that."

Following high school, Chic Hecht attended Washington University in St. Louis, where he graduated with a degree in retailing. Following World War II, Louis Hecht decided to retire to Las Vegas, Nevada. The retirement was short-lived; in 1948, he opened a new retail establishment. Chic went to work for his father in 1949. Two years later he was drafted into the United States Army. Following basic training, he was assigned to the intelligence school at Fort Holabird, Maryland. He went on to serve eighteen months as a special undercover agent in Berlin. At one point he was elected president of the National Counter Intelligence Corps. Hecht, who retained a lifelong membership in the National Military Intelligence Association, was installed in the Army Intelligence Hall of Fame in 1988.

Following military service, Chic Hecht returned to Las Vegas and opened his own men's clothing store. As he prospered, his interests eventually came to include holdings in a bank and hotels in both Nevada and Arizona. In 1964, Hecht ran for the Nevada State Senate. Winning the election, he became the first Republican to serve the predominantly Democratic Clark County in more than twenty-five years. Hecht would serve ten years in the Nevada State Senate, rising to the post of minority leader in 1969–70. An early and active supporter of Ronald Reagan, Hecht was a Reagan delegate at the 1968 Republican National Convention. In 1976 and again in 1980, he served as southern Nevada chairman and deputy director of the Nevada Reagan for President Committee.

In 1982, taking the advice of his friend and ally Paul Laxalt, a former Nevada governor and United States senator, Hecht himself ran for the United States Senate. Spending more than $300,000 of his own money, Hecht ran a "one note campaign": strong support for President Reagan. Beyond that, he took few substantive stands. Nonetheless, he defeated Democratic incumbent Howard W. Cannon 50 percent to 48 percent. Cannon, who had won an exhaustive, bitter primary race against Representative James Santini, was tainted by the bribery trial of Teamsters president Roy Lee Williams and mob figure Allen Dorfman. Both were charged with conspiring to offer Senator Cannon a favorable price on union-controlled land in Las Vegas in exchange for his blocking a truck deregulation bill. Cannon was subpoenaed, and gave extensive testimony at a trial held just a month before the election. Although the Senator was not charged with any wrongdoing, the aura of complicity hurt his ability to run an effective campaign. Moreover, Cannon never took Hecht's candidacy seriously. By the time he realized he had a fight on his hands, it was simply too late.

Once in the Senate, Hecht quickly became one of that body's two or three most conservative members. In 1985, he backed the majority of Republicans 98 percent of the time, tops in the Senate. The next year, his score was 95—tied for highest among Senate Republicans with North Carolina's Jessie Helms and Texas's Phil Gramm. Indeed, Hecht and Helms forged a close political and personal friendship based on a similarity of views. When the Hecht family, long active in Jewish affairs both at home and in Israel, decided to build and dedicate the Hecht Synagogue on the Mount Scopus campus of the Hebrew University, Senator and Mrs. Hecht took Senator and Mrs. Helms along as their guests. This was Jesse Helms's first visit to Israel.

Chic Hecht's conservatism troubled those in the Jewish community who were long accustomed to a more liberal or even centrist political philosophy. Hecht once stated that "probably my thinking, my philosophy, is that of Orthodoxy. . . . What does that mean? You talk about social issues. I feel strongly against abortion, which is certainly the Orthodox thinking.

School prayer—there's a picture over there of [the] Lubavitcher Rebbe, and he's talking to me in that picture. He's telling me that the moral caliber of America in the cities has deteriorated so badly that we must have a prayer in the morning so the students will know there is a Supreme Being, and we should have school prayer. This is strictly an Orthodox bill. I'm talking about Jewish Orthodox."

When Chic Hecht was running for the Senate, there were fears that Nevada, with its heavily Mormon population, would not vote for a Jew. During the campaign, the Mormon bishops invited him to a meeting to explain his views. As Hecht tells it: "So I went over one day to tell the Mormons that I was running. They didn't know me from Adam. I brought out the similarities in the Mormon religion and the Jewish religion—very, very strong family ties, living a good clean life, working hard, the work ethic, saving so much time for prayer. Then at the end . . . I said, 'I'm Jewish; I do not believe in assimilation; I have two daughters; I do not want my daughters marrying your sons.' And they liked that, and they supported me. I meant it. I was right up front with them."

During his six years in the United States Senate, Chic Hecht submitted few bills. During his first three years on Capitol Hill, he didn't offer a single amendment or bill on which there was a roll call vote. His one legislative triumph was in getting Congress to repeal the 55 mile-per-hour speed limit on rural interstate highways.

In 1985, when many Nevada politicians were criticizing federal plans to study the state for a nuclear waste site, Senator Hecht said it would be "Nevada's patriotic duty" to accept the facility if it did not endanger public safety. "I'm of the opinion," he said, "that we cannot do enough for this wonderful country of ours." Further, he noted, "Nevada has a lot of wide-open spaces and we're still part of the union." By the end of the year, however, Hecht began having second thoughts about Nevada's being used for nuclear storage.

Chic Hecht was narrowly defeated for reelection in 1988 by Nevada Governor Richard H. Bryan. Following his defeat, he was nominated by President George Bush to become American ambassador to the Bahamas. During his confirmation hearings, Hecht offered the following rationale as to why he should be confirmed: "I am sure I will feel at home in the Bahamas. I've been involved in gambling in Nevada, and I've been involved in banking for 25 years. . . . Also, I understand it is a nice life style. I love golf and they have a lot of nice golf courses and good fishing."

The committee's chair, Senator Paul Sarbanes of Maryland, referred to Hecht's nomination as an example of what he called "political throw-aways": people who were being rewarded by President George Bush because they "could do no harm." Senator Bob Graham of Florida said: "He does not deserve, nor does our nation deserve to be represented by him in the Bahamas."

In Hecht's defense, Senator Helms said that his friend was well-qualified and was being pil-loried because of his conservatism. Helms claimed that Hecht's record had been "twisted and misrepresented and hee-hawed by journalistic pygmies in the news media."

Hecht was approved by a final vote of 78 to 19. Following his stint in the Bahamas, Hecht returned to Nevada, where he lives in retirement with his wife Gail and their two daughters, Lori and Leslie.

References

Biographical Directory of the United States Congress, 1789–1988, p. 1165.

Politics in America (1986 edition).

Howard Simons, *Jewish Times: Voices of the American Jewish Experience* (Boston: Houghton Mifflin, 1988), pp. 371–375.

Private correspondence with author, 1995.

HELLER, LOUIS BENJAMIN (1905–1993):

Democrat from New York; served three terms in the House (Eighty-first through Eighty-third Congress; February 15, 1949–July 21, 1954).

When Louis Heller graduated from Boys High School in 1922, the commencement address was delivered by Brooklyn's newly elected congressman, *Emanuel Celler*. More than a quarter-century later (1949), Heller would become Celler's colleague in the House of Representatives. A generation later (1968), Celler, by then the "Dean of Congress" and its longtime Judiciary Committee chairman, had one of the few primary challenges of his illustrious career. The challenge came from Louis Heller's son Bob, a twenty-seven-year-old attorney with virtually no political experience. Although the younger Heller came in last in a three-way race, he succeeded in making the octogenarian chairman politically vulnerable. By the time the senior Heller retired from the New York Supreme Court, some fifty-five years after his high school graduation, his old commencement speaker was still practicing law in Brooklyn.

Born on New York's Lower East Side on February 10, 1905, Louis Benjamin Heller was the second of Max and Dora Heller's four children. The senior Hellers had emigrated from Romania just a few years before the birth of their first child, a daughter named Freida. Max Heller was a manufacturer of "skating sets"—matching wool hats, gloves, and scarves. His business prospered until the beginning of the First World War, when the government began expropriating wool in order to manufacture uniforms. Although not Orthodox, the Hellers kept a kosher home in the Williamsburg section of Brooklyn.

Following his graduation from Boys High, Louis Heller attended Fordham University School of Law, from which he received an LL.B. in 1926. He then went into private practice, becoming a litigator. Heller tried hundreds of cases in his career. One of his most famous clients was baseball great Leo "The Lip" Durocher, who had been charged with assault and battery against an unruly fan.

In 1936, Louis Heller ("Louie" to his friends) married Ruth Gulkis, the daughter of American-born parents. They had two children, Bobby and Marcia. Around the time of his marriage, Heller was appointed special deputy assistant attorney general in the election fraud division. He served in that capacity until just after the end of World War II. A devoted Democrat, Heller built a power base in the Sixth Assembly District, eventually becoming that area's longtime (1944–54) state committeeman and executive member (leader).

Heller was elected to the New York State Senate in 1943. During his single term in Albany (1943–44), he authored and successfully spearheaded passage of the state's first anti-bias legislation, under the terms of which "public defamation of ethnic or religious minorities" became a punishable offense. Heller was redistricted out of his state senate seat in 1944. His leadership in the anti-defamation fight led Governor Thomas E. Dewey to appoint him secretary of the New York State Temporary Commission Against Discrimination.

On Tuesday, November 2, 1948, eight-term Democrat John J. Delaney defeated Republican Francis E. Dorn by a 48.3 percent to 34.9 percent margin in New York's Seventh Congressional District race. Sixteen days later, the seventy-year-old Delaney died. Governor Dewey called for a special election, to be held on February 15, 1949. The Seventh District, which included the Williamsburg, Borough Hall, Brooklyn Heights, and Park Slope sections of Brooklyn, was overwhelmingly Democratic. Voters in the district had elected no one but Democrats since well before the turn of the century. To say the least, whoever the party selected as its standard bearer was guaranteed victory in the general election.

As district leader, Louis Heller was the Democrats' natural choice. The Republicans decided that Dorn, whose name recognition in the district was good, should run once again. The race held little suspense: noting the district's vast Democratic edge, the *New York Times* said that about the only interest "centered on whether the Democratic percentage of the total vote cast would increase, or fall off, from that cast last fall."

Louis Heller ran on a platform supporting President Truman's Fair Deal platform, despite the fact that the Missourian was wildly unpopular with the voters of the Seventh District. (When petitions calling for the President's impeachment were circulated in Brooklyn, sentiment ran twelve to one in favor of his removal.) Gratified by his support, Truman sent a contribution to the Heller campaign. According to Bob Heller, as far as he knew, his father never cashed Truman's check. Although Heller's percentage in victory was greater than the late Representative Delaney's (50.7 percent for the former versus 48.3 percent for the latter), so too was Dorn's. What made the difference was the fact that the third-party candidate, Minneola Ingersoll of the American Labor Party, had lost ground since the previous election.

Heller was duly sworn in as a member of the Eighty-first Congress on February 21, 1949. He was assigned to the Committee on Interstate and Foreign Commerce. During his second term, Heller chaired a subcommittee charged with investigating the Securities and Exchange Commission, and participated in the Kefauver hearings on racketeering. Recognized by both Senator Kefauver and his committee counsel Rudolph Halley for his superior skills as a litigator, Heller was induced to prepare the two for the upcoming hearings. According to Bob Heller, his father spent countless hours tutoring and grilling Halley.

In the 1950s, the number of Jews serving in Congress was less than a third of what it would become in the 1980s and 1990s. Anti-Jewish feeling was never far from the surface. Bob Heller remembers an occasion during his father's years in Congress when the entire family went on a fact-finding junket by ship to the Panama Canal. As the younger Heller recalls: "There were about 150 people on board ship—all members of Congress and their families. The only two Jewish members on board were my father and [Bronx area] Representative [*Isadore*] *Dollinger*. They were the only two who weren't invited to a gala cocktail party. I remember the day of the party, my mother and father and the Dollingers argued back and forth, back and forth about going to the party. My father's and Izzy [Dollinger]'s position was that they were damned if they were going to go to a party to which they hadn't been invited and at which their presence wasn't welcome. My mother argued just as forcefully that they had to go regardless of whether they had been invited or not. Finally, the two men relented. My mother said that she wanted to make a 'grand entrance' after the party had already begun. Well, they did

just that. In order to enter the ballroom, you had to take a grand staircase at the bottom of which was a baby grand piano. Well, as they made their entrance, the piano player [who apparently was a member of Congress] suddenly stopped playing. All the 'party sounds'—conversation, clinking glasses and the like came—to an abrupt end. All eyes were fixated on the staircase. From that point on, the Hellers and the Dollingers were included as equals."

In July 1954, the thrice-elected Heller announced his resignation from Congress in favor of an appointment as Judge of the Court of Special Sessions. Heller spent the next twenty-three years on the bench. In 1958, he was elected a justice of the city court; twelve years later he became a justice of the New York State Supreme Court. During his tenure on the bench, Heller became supervising justice of the Matrimonial Division. In that post, he issued two landmark legal opinions. In one, he ruled that "New York City must provide and pay for legal counsel for indigent defendants in matrimonial cases;" in the second, he ruled that the delivery of a Jewish religious divorce document (known in Hebrew as a *get*) could be part of civil proceedings without abridging the First Amendment's separation of church and state clause. This latter case was of particular interest to Orthodox Jewish women whose husbands could hold the *get* over their heads as a form of blackmail with impunity. By the terms of Heller's verdict, the adjudication of a religious divorce could properly be made a part of the court record. In 1968, Justice Heller wrote a book about lawyers' courtroom tactics called *Do You Solemnly Swear?*.

In 1968, as mentioned above, Bobby Heller decided to run against his father's old friend Manny Celler. The younger Heller, by then an attorney, ran on an antiwar platform, attacking the forty-five-year incumbent for his unrelenting hawkishness. Bobby Heller remembers the difficulty of running against a man who had been a fixture in his family's life as long as he could remember: "I even remember him coming over to my house at the time of my bar mitzvah. One day, up comes a black limousine and out steps Manny Celler. He came over to give me my bar mitzvah gift—a copy of Upton Sinclair's *The Return of Lanny Budd*." As mentioned above, Bob Heller was endorsed by the *New York Times*, which found Celler to be distant, aloof, and increasingly unresponsive to the needs of his constituents. Despite the *Times* sanction, Heller came in third. He never ran for office again.

Louis Heller retired from the bench in 1977. Ruth Heller passed away in 1981, after forty-five years of marriage. Following Ruth's death, Judge Heller moved to Lauderhill, Florida, to live with his sister, Freida Meyerowitz. Louis Heller died of colon cancer on October 30, 1993. He is buried in Brooklyn. Marcia Heller, Louis and Ruth's daughter, passed away the next year. Bobby and Susan Heller continue to reside in Brooklyn.

References
Interview with Bob Heller, January 1998.

Fort Lauderdale Sun Sentinel, October 30, 1993, B 7:1.

New York Times, February 16, 1949, 6:4. November 1, 1993, D 9:4.

HOLTZMAN, ELIZABETH (1941–): *Democrat from New York; served four terms in the House (Ninety-third through Ninety-sixth Congress; January 3, 1973–January 3, 1981).*

At a 1975 question-and-answer session with visiting rabbinical students, Massachusetts Representative Robert Drinan, a Catholic priest, was asked how he was addressed by his colleagues and members of the press: "Are you called 'Congressman Father,' 'Father Congressman,' 'Father,' or just plain 'Mister'?" the students wanted to know. Drinan, well known for his sense of humor, paused and said: "Well, you know, with the recent move to make our language more gender neutral, this has caused a lot of discussion. I thought about it recently, and told people that it would probably be best for them to address me as 'Parent Congressperson Drinan.'" Without missing a beat, Drinan continued: "I guess by extension that means that we will have to start addressing Elizabeth Holtzman as 'Congressperson Holtzperson,' but she probably won't find it too funny. One thing about dear Liz, she doesn't have much of a sense of humor."

Throughout her remarkable political career, Elizabeth Holtzman was known as a serious, grimly tenacious woman. "The Congresswoman is not a legislator who gets things done through camaraderie," the writer of Liz Holtzman's biography noted in the *Almanac of American Politics*; "she is deadly serious." Others have described her as "aloof", "abrupt", and "sanctimonious". Despite her lack of personal warmth or humor, Elizabeth Holtzman was a woman whose career was dotted with a series of notable historical firsts: first woman nominated by a major party for United States senator from New York; first woman elected district attorney of Kings County (Brooklyn); first woman elected comptroller of the city of New York. And to top it all off, Holtzman began her political career by being the youngest woman ever elected to the United States Congress.

Elizabeth Holtzman comes from a family of achievers. Her father, Sidney, a Russian immigrant, became a successful criminal attorney. Her mother, Filia, also a Russian immigrant, was chair of the Russian Department at Hunter College. Holtzman's twin brother, Robert (called "Red"), is a neurosurgeon. Sidney and Filia met when they were teenagers on the Lower East Side of New York City in the mid-1920s.

Sidney's family had emigrated from Pinsk when he was four years old; Filia and her family had come from Bielaya Tserkov in the Ukraine when she was twelve. Her father had owned "a successful dry goods store" there.

The Holtzman twins were born in Brooklyn, thirty minutes apart—Robert arriving first—on August 11, 1941. Among the earliest memories the Holtzman twins recall are stories of how their maternal grandfather sheltered fellow Jews during the Russian pogroms. Russian was spoken in the home; as a young parent, Red Holtzman would recite the same Russian poems to his children that Filia had shared with him and his sister when they were growing up. The twins were unusually close.

Elizabeth and Robert attended P.S. 152, the Brooklyn Ethical Culture School, and Abraham Lincoln High School. They studied piano at the Mannes School of Music. While students at Lincoln, the twins ran in tandem for president and vice president of the General Organization. Campaigning on the slogan "win with the twins," the two won handily. Robert, being "older," was elected president. They celebrated their victory with a boisterous party at their large Tudor home on Ditmas Avenue. As their mother recalled, "Half the school came to the house and danced all night. We almost had the police here."

Elizabeth Holtzman graduated third in her class with a 98.6 average; Red graduated "somewhere in the 40's" with a 92 average. "Those were the days of eggheads," he recalled in a 1980 *New York Times* profile, "and I didn't want to be considered an egghead." Following their graduation, the twins headed to Cambridge, where Elizabeth attended Radcliffe, and her brother Harvard. Elizabeth, who majored in American history and literature, was elected to Phi Beta Kappa, and graduated *magna cum laude* in 1962. She then entered Harvard Law School, where she was one of fifteen women in a class of nearly five hundred. While in law school, she spent several months working with a civil rights lawyer in Albany, Georgia. In later years, she would say that this harrowing experience had a major effect on her future—an extension of her grandfather's bravery during the pogroms.

Holtzman's work in the South "had a serious downside, too," as she explained in her memoir, *Who Said It Would Be Easy?*

The *Harvard Law Record* published an interview with me in which I criticized the FBI for failing to protect civil rights attorneys and workers. The *Record* went to a large number of law school alumni. Almost as soon as they got it in the mail, the Georgia Alumni Association of Harvard Law School asked the faculty to expel me. The faculty refused to do so. Then J. Edgar Hoover wrote a letter to the *Record* defending the FBI and attacking me. I was startled that Hoover would pay attention to me, a mere law student.

After receiving her J.D. from Harvard in 1965, Holtzman joined the staff of Wachtell, Lipton, Rosen & Katz, a small Manhattan law firm, where she worked as a litigator.

In 1969, New York City Mayor John V. Lindsay, "acting on the advice of some of her law school colleagues," asked Holtzman to join his staff as a mayoral assistant. For the next two years, she served as a liaison representative between the mayor's office and the Department of Parks, Recreation and Cultural Affairs. She resigned in 1970, frustrated and indignant over the inability of the agencies (which she termed "all screwed up") to respond to the public's needs. Her indignation led her to run for Democratic state committeewoman from the Flatbush section of Brooklyn. She won, after successfully filing suit against a New York State election law that gave incumbents the top line on the ballot. While serving as committeewoman, Holtzman worked for the law firm of Paul, Weiss, Rifkind, Wharton & Garrison, and founded the Brooklyn Women's Political Caucus.

As Democratic committeewoman, Liz Holtzman became increasingly aware that Congressman *Emanuel Celler* was not giving his Sixteenth District constituents the type of representation she thought they deserved. Upon investigating his record, she discovered that he had the second-highest absentee rating of all New York Representatives, and was "disregarding opportunities to funnel available federal money into Brooklyn public improvement projects." After nearly a half-century in Congress, Holtzman concluded, Celler was taking a cavalier attitude toward both his job and his constituents. For the most part, during his long career, Celler had been able to avoid primary challenges. In 1968, however, he had faced two

adversaries, one of them the son of former Congressman *Louis Heller*. Holtzman decided that Celler was vulnerable to another primary challenge. On March 28, 1972, she declared her candidacy, sounding the same "time for a change" theme that Celler had used in his first successful election in 1922. When asked what he thought about his chances of beating Holtzman (whom he called "a nonentity"), Celler was reported to have said: "They are about as good as they have been in any year ending in two, four, six, eight, or zero."

Unaccustomed to campaigning for reelection, the eighty-six-year-old Celler basically sat on his hands, relying on the Brooklyn Democratic machine to do its customary job of appealing to the voters. For her part, Holtzman, who resigned from Weiss, Rifkind, blanketed the Sixteenth District, charging Celler with being totally out of touch. Specifically, she attacked the octogenarian for his hawkish stance on Vietnam, his resistance to the Equal Rights Amendment (he had kept it bottled up in his Judiciary Committee for more than twenty years), his endorsement of costly space exploration programs, and his "consistent" opposition to consumer protection, environmental, and educational bills. Celler countered by laying out his fifty-year record of authoring more than four hundred bills, including legislation involving civil rights, gun control, immigration, and crime.

Toward the end of the campaign, Holtzman charged Celler with representing special-interest groups. Specifically, she brought up his consistent approval of the antiballistic missile defense system, which would benefit Fishbach & Moore, a New York–based engineering firm in which he owned stock. The charge stuck. On primary day, Holtzman defeated Celler 15,557 to 14,995 (50.9 to 49.1 percent). His name remained on the Liberal Party line for the general election, but when he decided to drop out of the race, Holtzman's victory in November was certain. In the general election, she defeated Nicholas Maccio, Jr., by a nearly three-to-one margin.

During her three campaigns for reelection, Holtzman, like Celler before her, would run unopposed in the Democratic primaries. Her election was historic in two ways. First, she had defeated the senior-most member of the House of Representatives; second, her victory gave the chairmanship of the House Judiciary Committee to sixty-five year-old Peter Rodino of New Jersey. If she had gotten just 611 fewer votes, Manny Celler would have chaired the Judiciary Committee's hearings on the impeachment of Richard Nixon.

As a freshman member of Congress, Elizabeth Holtzman received Celler's seat (though not, of course, his seniority) on the House Judiciary Committee. Within four months of her entry to the House, Holtzman made national headlines. After President Nixon ordered the bombing of Cambodia in early 1973, a number of bills were introduced to prohibit bombing after August 15, 1973. Holtzman refused to vote for any of them, arguing that they all gave the President congressional approval to continue the air war for another six months and, as such, conferred war-making power on him. Congress then began crafting legislation to define the President's power to wage war—the War Powers Act. It passed over Nixon's veto in November 1973.

Meanwhile, Holtzman filed suit in U.S. District Court to enjoin the Cambodian bombings on the grounds that they had not been authorized by Congress and were therefore unconstitutional. On July 25, 1973, she obtained a precedent-setting decision from a Republican-appointed federal judge, who agreed that American military activity in Cambodia was both unauthorized and unconstitutional. The judge ordered a halt to the bombings within 48 hours, and then allowed a stay of his order until the government could obtain a hearing on appeal. The decision was overturned on appeal. Holtzman then filed an appeal with the Supreme Court, which was granted by Justice Thurgood Marshall. Marshall was overruled by Chief Justice Warren E. Burger and a majority of the court. In November 1973, Holtzman voted to override Nixon's veto of the War Powers Act.

During her first term, Holtzman also introduced legislation requiring "immediate Congressional action" on the Supreme Court's proposed new rules of evidence for federal courts. The rules were scheduled to take effect on July 1, 1973. In her maiden speech before the House, Holtzman argued: "The proposed rules of evidence do not deal with abstruse legal technicalities. . . . They seek to resolve social issues over which there is now vast national debate: executive secrecy, the newsman's privilege, and

individual privacy." In committee, she argued that the new code, which, in effect, invalidated existing state laws of evidence, had been drafted "according to the Justice Department's specifications for the secrecy of official information." Her bill, making the code subject to congressional approval, passed the House on March 4, 1973, 399 to 1, and was later accepted by the Senate. President Nixon signed it on April 1, 1973. Holtzman thereby became the first member of her freshman class to successfully enact legislation.

Holtzman also played a prominent role in the House Judiciary Committee's impeachment hearings, earning a reputation for "her well-reasoned, competent argument in support of a broad definition of impeachment." Holtzman voted for all five articles of impeachment, and specifically supported an article that charged the President with "illegally and secretly invading Cambodia in 1970." The committee defeated the article.

Following his resignation in August 1974, Richard Nixon was pardoned by his handpicked successor, President Gerald R. Ford. In October 1974, Ford appeared before the Criminal Justice Subcommittee to respond to questions about the pardon. Holtzman, "incensed" at the subcommittee's intent to conduct a "mild, *pro forma* hearing," objected to the five-minute time limit on questions, and hurled a series of politically explosive questions at Ford: "Why was no crime cited, no guilt confessed? Why was the action done in haste and secrecy without consultation with the Attorney General or the special prosecutor?" Holtzman asked the President.

By the end of her first term, Elizabeth Holtzman had become a politician with a national reputation. In the House, she voted a consistently liberal line, and earned the plaudits of women, minorities, and gays. She "astounded even her own admirers" when she managed to win extension of the ratification of the Equal Rights Amendment. Always in the headlines, she also wrote legislation that barred Nazi war criminals from the United States and authorized their deportation.

In her second term (which she won 79 percent to 21 percent), Holtzman was assigned to the Budget Committee, where she fought unsuccessfully for passage of a budget that stated national priorities. Throughout her career, she consistently called for large cuts in defense appropriations and tended to the needs of her district. In 1978, she made a stir when she questioned the presence in this country of the Vietnamese official who had shot a Viet Cong prisoner on television during the Tet offensive.

In 1980, Elizabeth Holtzman decided to "go for broke," giving up her safe House seat in order to run in the Democratic primary for United States Senate. Her chief opponent was New York's former Commissioner of Consumer Affairs (and former Miss America), Bess Meyerson. Vastly outspent by the independently wealthy Meyerson, Holtzman was forced to borrow $200,000 in the campaign's final two weeks, putting up her entire life savings as collateral. Meyerson made a major issue of Holtzman's votes against defense spending. For her part, Holtzman, in a last-minute television blitz, charged Meyerson with profiting from her "image as a consumer advocate" by "working for various corporations." Holtzman, easily the more liberal of the two, "played down her liberal voting record and talked . . . about waste in defense spending rather than using more traditional liberal rhetoric about a 'bloated' defense establishment."

Holtzman won the primary, scoring big among Jewish and Catholic voters, and taking Manhattan, Brooklyn, and Queens, Westchester County, and Long Island, and running close to Meyerson in upstate New York. Meyerson's voting strength was mainly in the Bronx, Staten Island, and several populous upstate counties. In the Republican primary, Nassau County Supervisor Alfonse M. D'Amato unexpectedly defeated Senator *Jacob Javits*, who proved to be "too liberal for Republican primary voters." Although defeated as a Republican, the ailing Javits remained on the ballot as the candidate of the Liberal Party.

As the general election approached, Holtzman called the Javits campaign headquarters, seeking a meeting with the Senator. "Would he," she asked "be willing to drop out of the race" and endorse her campaign? The Javits people said they would get back to her. They never did. On election day, 1980, D'Amato narrowly defeated Holtzman 2,699,965 to 2,618,661, with Javits taking 664,544 (11 percent) of the vote. In her "nonconcession speech," Holtzman left out the customary congratulatory words for the

winner and attributed her defeat to three factors: "the Reagan landslide, the distraction of a third candidate [Javits] and Mr. D'Amato had an immense amount of money." The third point was not accurate; final campaign finance reports showed that Holtzman had outspent the victorious D'Amato (who she said had "slipped through") by nearly $475,000.

The next year, Elizabeth Holtzman ran successfully for district attorney of Kings County. During her six years as Brooklyn D.A. (1982–88), she had the highest conviction rate of any prosecutor in New York City. She was lauded for "revolutionizing" the D.A.'s office by "cutting the time lag between arrest and trial." Moreover, she introduced computerized technology to the courts, created "units sensitive to the needs of rape and child abuse victims," and "proved that a liberal who opposes capital punishment can be hard on criminals." While serving as D.A., she had bills drafted to spare youngsters from having to appear in court. The laws passed, making it possible for children to be videotaped for the grand jury and then appear on closed-circuit television at trials. Her proudest achievement was starting a program of community service sentencing for juvenile offenders, whereby, instead of getting probation, they were sent out to work. During her years as D.A., this program sentenced 3,324 youthful defendants to work; they cleaned the graffiti off more than 2,300 subway cars.

In 1988, Elizabeth Holtzman was elected comptroller of New York City. As comptroller, she was responsible for New York's enormous bond business. During her four-year term, New York City's pension funds grew by $14 billion. She also made it possible for blacks, Hispanics, and women to "do business with the city as pension fund managers and bond underwriters." In 1992, Holtzman once again entered the Democratic primary for the Senate. This time she ran in a four-candidate field that included New York Attorney General Robert Abrams, former Congresswoman Geraldine Ferraro, and the Reverend Al Sharpton. Running a distant fourth in the polls, Holtzman launched a last-minute television assault (for which she took out a $450,000 loan) against Ferraro. In her ads, she attacked Ferraro for "not throwing out a pornography distributor tenant from a building she and her husband owned in 1985, as they had promised." She further criticized her for having had a convicted labor racketeer as a fundraiser in her first congressional campaign in 1978. The low water mark came when Holtzman ran an ad showing a *Village Voice* headline reading: "What You Don't Know About Ferraro and the Mob." Ferraro decried this as an "ethnic slur." Even New York Governor Mario Cuomo said he was "disappointed" with Holtzman.

Abrams won the primary with 37 percent to Ferraro's 36 percent. Holtzman came in fourth, garnering just 12 percent of the vote. Holtzman's nasty campaign left a bitter taste in the mouths of New York voters and the press, and essentially ended her political career even though she was still comptroller. It was now just a matter of time before the voters had the last word.

Elizabeth Holtzman was never the darling of the press. She constantly railed against its tendency to comment on her clothing, hairstyles, and new contact lenses rather than deal with her accomplishments. As one former Holtzman aide said to the *New York Times*: "Everybody hates Liz. Everybody in the media hates Liz." Her 1992 campaign for Senator made the situation even worse. Forced into a runoff in the 1993 Democratic primary for comptroller, Holtzman was assailed by the New York press over the $450,000 loan she had obtained from Rhode Island's Fleet Bank during her second Senate campaign. Just a few days before the runoff, the New York media ran a story claiming that, at the time Holtzman received the "low interest loan," officials of a Fleet affiliate, Fleet Securities, were "aggressively seeking and were later given a larger piece of the city's lucrative bond business."

The attack on Holtzman by New York's political establishment and the media "struck out at her with a ferocity unusual even by the standards of a city whose cultural signature often appears to be the Bronx cheer," one columnist noted. Following an official report that accused her of being "grossly negligent in taking money from the same people her office regulates," Holtzman further angered the press by apologizing, "backtracking," and "pleading a hazy memory on what she termed a 'trivial detail.'" For Holtzman, who had "built a career on being more virtuous than other politicians," the charge proved to be fatal: She lost the runoff to a relatively unknown state legislator named Alan Hevesi.

On leaving office, Holtzman summed up her career by saying: "We took on the dragons. We had a great time." A former aide, asked to comment on Holtzman's precipitate fall from political favor, stated: "I think she has been one of the smartest, hardest working, and honest public officials that I have ever had a chance to work with. But for whatever reason, the media has decided that what Holtzman did is so bad that they will blur the line between news analysis and editorializing. In part it's because they don't like Liz Holtzman's personality and in part its because she has taken a lot of positions that have angered people. She just doesn't have any friends anymore."

In April 1996, Holtzman was fined $7,500 for the improper loan. An investigative panel found that "she not only had used her office to help the bank get part of the lucrative city bond business at a time when she was being pressed for repayment of the loan, but had also defeated the bank's 'legitimate efforts to obtain repayment.'" Not surprisingly, Holtzman appealed the fine. In June 1997, the appeal was rejected.

Since leaving the comptroller's office, Elizabeth Holtzman has dropped from the political stage, except for a recent appearance at a campaign rally on behalf of City Council President Carol Bellamy. The New York media made much of the fact that standing to Holtzman's "distant right" was her former foe Geraldine Ferraro. The two never looked at each other.

Elizabeth Holtzman has never married. She continues to live in New York, where she works as an attorney, takes occasional trips abroad, and sails her boat on Peconic Bay, at the eastern end of Long Island. In May 1997, Holtzman began a new career as a radio talk show host, broadcasting on New York's WBAI. Never far from public view, Liz Holtzman continues to be a vocal presence on the New York political scene.

References

Elizabeth Holtzman, Who Said It Would Be Easy? (New York: Arcade Publishing, 1996).
Almanac of American Politics (1974–94 editions).
Current Biography, 1973, pp. 101–103.
Harper's Bazaar, April 1973.
New York Times, June 22, 1972, 46:5; November 5, 1980, II, 3:1; February 11, 1986, C, 1:3; September 19, 1993, 3:1; April 4, 1996, B, 3:7.
Village Voice, July 22, 1997, pp. 26, 28.

HOLTZMAN, LESTER (1913–): *Democrat from New York; served five terms in the House (Eighty-third through Eighty-seventh Congress; January 3, 1953–December 31, 1961).*

During the early 1930s, when Lester Holtzman was a prelaw student in St. John's University's night program, he joined the James Phillips Association, a rebel Democratic club. Holtzman's reason for joining the reformist group had little to do with political idealism; he reasoned that membership in the club might improve his chances for finding a job. Holtzman toiled in the Phillips Club's vineyards for the next twenty years without reward. As a lifelong resident of Middle Village, Queens ("the only peninsula surrounded by cemeteries"), Holtzman built a reputation for honesty, integrity, and being a consummate raconteur. Finally, in 1952, a great year for Republicans, Holtzman decided to run for Congress. The odds promised to be long, for the universally beloved Dwight Eisenhower sat atop the Republican ticket. Holtzman's opponent, incumbent Robert Tripp Ross, hadn't been in Congress long enough to offend his constituency. Against all odds, Holtzman defeated Ross by less than 300 votes, thereby becoming the only Democrat to unseat a sitting Republican member of Congress in 1952. After nearly twenty years, Holtzman had his political job.

Isidore and Rebecca Holtzman, Lester's parents, came from Lomza Gubernia in Poland. Prior to emigrating to America, they had six children, all but one of whom died in infancy from "childhood diseases that would easily have been cured here." The Holtzmans settled on New York's Lower East Side, where their only American-born child, Lester, entered the world on June 1, 1913. The Holtzmans, like hundreds of thousands of other Jewish immigrants, worked in the garment industry. Isidore was a "sleeve thrower" in a sweatshop; Rebecca worked on bow ties ("bowl ties" as she called them).

In 1916, three-year-old Lester was stricken during a nationwide polio epidemic. Upon hearing that country air would offer their ailing son

a greater chance of recovery, the family moved to Henry Street in the then-rural enclave of Middle Village, Queens County. There Isidore joined the Orthodox B'nai Israel, where "papa's only dream in life was one day to become the *gabbai rishon* [the rabbi's primary assistant] in the old Orthodox synagogue," his son recalled nearly eighty years later. "He made it," Holtzman recounted with a chuckle, "he lived long enough."

Lester Holtzman attended P.S. 67 and B'nai Israel's Talmud Torah. As a youngster, he was "completely observant" and remembers studying "Torah, Rashi and a *shtickel* [Yiddish for "a bit of"] Gemara," meaning the Pentateuch with the medieval commentary of Rashi and a bit of Talmud. The future Congressman's rigorous Orthodoxy was not longlived: "I didn't need much of a reason. One day I saw the president of our shul look around furtively in a place called Myrtle Avenue in Ridgewood, Queens. And when he saw nobody around, he took out a cigarette on Shabbos and lit it. A terrible *averah* [transgression], *gottenu* [God help us!]."

The Talmud Torah's principal and *lehrer* (teacher), Israel Gress, was something of a local legend. In addition to his duties at the Talmud Torah, Gress was in the "installment peddler business." He sold "everything on time, collecting half a dollar, a dollar a month." Most of his "clients" were non-Jews. The swarthy Gress, fluent in Italian, got along well; non-Jews called him "Luigi." "He dealt with the worst gangsters in the world, but they protected him. He was fair with them, and they liked him." Israel Gress also had a daughter, Mae. Lester Holtzman first met Mae when he was seven. They were married in 1936. As of 2000, they were still together, living in a modest, impeccably decorated home at the Woodlands Country Club in Tamarac, Florida.

During his formative years, Les Holtzman sang in the synagogue choir and learned enough *nusach* (Jewish liturgical melodies) to do a little cantorial work. The Holtzman household was strictly kosher and strictly Orthodox. Yiddish was the family's primary language; even in his mid-eighties, Lester Holtzman, when remembering the past, sprinkles his conversation with Yiddish expressions.

Les Holtzman attended Newtown High School for two years, before a precipitous drop in family finances forced him to drop out. With the garment industry in bad shape, Isidore was forced to borrow $800 from a credit union in order to buy "a dump grocery really in the *tuches* [Yiddish for "rump" or "rear end"] of Williamsburg at that time." The entire Holtzman clan went to work in the grocery, with Lester continuing his prelaw education at night. After a few years, Isidore Holtzman sold his Williamsburg grocery and purchased a store in Middle Village.

Because of its geographic configuration and small population, Middle Village has always been a unique enclave. Its residents tend to know one another. In Lester Holtzman's formative years, the south end of Middle Village was totally Jewish; its northern area was made up of Irish, Italian, and German families. To this day, the "children of Middle Village," often in their seventies, eighties, and even nineties, maintain close relations.

Working at a series of odd jobs, Holtzman continued his education at St. John's University. An honors student, he graduated from the St. John's School of Law in 1936 as president of his class. The very day he passed the New York bar, Holtzman hung out his shingle on Metropolitan Avenue, the main thoroughfare of Middle Village. Specializing in matrimonial and criminal law, he supplemented his income by doing collection work for his father-in-law: "I got twenty bucks a week . . . made a hundred and ten stops on a Saturday to collect a half a dollar or a dollar."

With the coming of World War II, Mae's two brothers were the first boys from Middle Village to be drafted. Les "bought bonds and managed to get draft extensions" for many of his neighbors. For this, he "never took a dime." When Holtzman's notice arrived, he went down to his draft board, where everyone knew him. "Ah, we got you now!" they told him. "What do you want?" one of the draft board members asked. "Do for me what you did for my clients," Holtzman answered. "Give me an extension."

Holtzman got a sixty day extension. Before it ran out, the law was changed: men who were twenty-six years old with a child were exempted. "Boy, was I happy. Talk about a *g'dilah* (big deal), a *nes* (miracle)."

By the end of the war in 1945, Holtzman still had not received the political job he had hoped for. Finally, his political mentor, Jimmy Phillips, came to him with an offer: a position with the Federal Housing Administration for $1,200 a year. Holtzman had to turn the job down: "I'm making $60 to $100 a week now and can't afford the cut in income." He suggested that Phillips offer the job to another man. That man wound up staying with FHA for nearly a decade. Fifty years later, Les Holtzman is still in contact with the man who got that federal job; they, like so many former residents of Middle Village, are neighbors in South Florida.

Lester Holtzman's victory over Republican Robert Tripp Ross was one of the great upsets of 1952. As a political novice running against the Eisenhower juggernaut, no one gave Holtzman a chance. Out on the hustings, he promised voters that if elected he would "stop the low flying planes taking off from LaGuardia." Holtzman calls that promise "the only fib I ever told consciously." Despite the Eisenhower landslide, Holtzman defeated Ross by nearly 300 votes, thereby becoming the first Jew from Queens County to go to Washington.

Holtzman arrived on Capitol Hill "not knowing my ass from my elbow." "The quality of members of Congress intellectually today, is so much over and above what I had . . . what we had, many of us Jews . . . especially *Izzy Dollinger* and *Sidney Fine* and *Lenny Farbstein*. . . . We had no background. The *goyim* [non-Jews] would come in steeped in history, government and politics, and all we knew was pretzels and beer on a Saturday night at the club. I was totally unequal to the job at the time. It paid $12,000 a year at the time . . . a fortune."

Lester Holtzman was sworn in as a member of the Eighty-third Congress on January 3, 1953. During his nine years in the House of Representatives, he never moved his family to Washington. "I was scared it wouldn't last." Instead, he roomed with fellow Representatives Paul Fino (an eight-term Republican from New York and classmate from St. John's), *Jacob Gilbert*,

Hugh Addonizio (a seven-term Democrat from New Jersey and one-time mayor of Newark), and Peter Rodino, who twenty years later would gain national recognition as the Watergate-era chairman of the House Judiciary Committee.

Holtzman was originally assigned to "the garbage committee"—Government Operations. He was also assigned to the House Armed Services Committee, one of the few nonveterans seated on that panel. After his first year on the Hill, Holtzman, thanks to his close relationship with fellow New Yorker *Emanuel Celler*, received a seat on Judiciary. At that point, he gave up his other committee assignments. Holtzman was assigned to the Subcommittee on Antitrust, chaired by his roommate, Peter Rodino.

In 1954, sensing that Holtzman's '52 victory was a fluke, the Republicans drafted New York State Senator *Seymour Halpern* ("the most popular politician in Queens") to challenge him for the Sixth District seat. The district, which took in Jackson Heights, Rego Park, Flushing, and College Point, had been represented in the State Senate by Halpern for years. As such, he was the favorite. During his first term in the House, Holtzman had spent the lion's share of time learning the ropes and tending to his constituents' needs. By comparison, Halpern was a veteran legislator with many important legislative triumphs to his credit.

The early betting line gave Halpern a ten-to-one lead over Holtzman. During the campaign, Holtzman was offered the American Labor Party's endorsement. Despite his down-the-line liberal voting record, Holtzman realized that an ALP endorsement could spell nothing but trouble. McCarthyism was in full swing, and the ALP was made up of a bunch of "pinkos and commies." Despite his request that they remain out of his race, the party went ahead and endorsed Holtzman. A week before the election, the *Long Island Press* ran a banner headline: "Commies All Out for Holtzman." Nonetheless, Holtzman campaigned furiously and again pulled off an upset, defeating Halpern by more than 10,000 votes.

During his nine years in the House, Lester Holtzman saw none of his legislative measures passed into law. "I came within a whisker once," he remembers. "After having become so friendly with Manny [Emanuel Celler], I said to him:

'Let me have something, Manny.' He said: 'We're creating a new committee . . . COMSAT satellite type thing,' and I said: 'Manny, that's not for me. My inclinations don't go that way.' He said: 'How about handling a bill on ethics?' I said: 'Oh, that's terrific.' A month or two later he says to me: 'I'm sorry . . . I need John Lindsay to lead in a particular vote, so I'm going to offer this [the ethics bill] to him.' That's the closest I ever came."

Predictably, Holtzman was pro–civil rights, pro-Israel, and pro-labor. On the latter he said: "Papa working in a sweatshop until the union came in . . . and being cheated on the piecework. . . . I couldn't forsake the union no matter how arrogant they became." Lester Holtzman was very popular with the voters in his district. In his last reelection campaign (1960), he won by more than 90,000 votes. He could easily have kept the seat for life. Nonetheless, in 1961, he decided to give up his safe seat and make a run for a fourteen-year term on the New York State Supreme Court. Why? "It was the old story . . . security, an increase of $12,000 a year, which was enormous in those days."

Holtzman was one of six candidates running for three vacancies in the Tenth Supreme Court District (Queens, Nassau, and Suffolk Counties). "There were local intramural difficulties in the party . . . and both Jack and Bob [Kennedy] interceded to finalize my designation." As a member of the Supreme Court, Holtzman was the first justice to preside over a case involving the state's reformed divorce laws. In retrospect, he would rather have remained in Congress, despite the raise in salary: "The challenge was virtually nil. The pressure was on all the time to dispose . . . to keep the calendars moving. . . . The mood was to dispose, that's all they really cared about."

Holtzman retired from the bench in 1973 in order to become president of the Queens Savings and Loan Association, a bank of which he was a founding incorporator and director. "I'm a restless man," Holtzman explained to the *Long Island Press*. "I was prevailed upon by the board to fill [a] vacuum." In addition to his position with the bank, Holtzman returned to the practice of law, joining the firm of Shapiro, Schlissel, Shiff, Beilly and Fox. Always active in Jewish charitable organizations, Holtzman was a director of the Menorah Home and Hospital for the Aged in Brooklyn.

Les and Mae Holtzman are the parents of Joy, a teacher in Bethesda, Maryland, and Matthew, an executive with a carpet company in Potomac, Maryland. The Holtzmans have four grandchildren and one great-grandchild. More than sixty-five years after he began worrying about financial security, Lester Holtzman is able to live the good life. He has earned it.

References

Interview with Lester Holtzman, July 18, 1997.
Long Island Press, November 29, 1973.

HOUSEMAN, JULIUS (1832–1891): *Democrat from Michigan; served one term in the House (Forty-eighth Congress; March 4, 1883–March 3, 1885).*

When Julius Houseman arrived in Grand Rapids, Michigan, in August 1852, he became the first Jewish settler in that small city (population: approximately 3,000). More than a hundred years after his arrival, the name Houseman has not been forgotten. The Houseman Building in Grand Rapids is in the middle of one of the largest business areas in the state. Grand Rapids Lodge 238, B'nai B'rith, which he helped organize in 1875, and served as its first president, is still called the Julius Houseman Lodge.

Julius Houseman, Michigan's first Jewish member of Congress, was born in Zeckendorf, Bavaria, on December 8, 1832. His father, Solomon, was both a merchant and a manufacturer of silk and cotton goods. His mother, Henrietta Strauss, of Heiligenstadt, Bavaria, died at age thirty-five, when Julius, her eldest child, was but three years old, and his sister, Mary, was less than two. Young Julius was educated at the national schools in Zeckendorf and Bamberg, and completed a two-year commercial course. By age fifteen, he was a dry goods clerk in Zeckendorf.

In 1851, three years after the revolution in Germany, Houseman left Europe, bound for Cincinnati, Ohio, which already had a thriving German-Jewish community. There he became a clerk in a clothing store. From Cincinnati, Houseman moved to New Vienna, Ohio, where he found another job as a clerk. In March 1852, the nineteen-year-old Houseman moved north to Battle Creek, Michigan, where he went into the merchant tailoring business with Isaac Amberg. They named their firm Amberg & Houseman. The business quickly flourished—so much so that within five months, Houseman moved to Grand Rapids and established a branch of the firm. By 1854, he became its sole proprietor. Under his ownership, the firm continued to expand.

In 1864, Julius Houseman organized a new firm, Houseman & Alsberg, with his sister Mary's husband, Albert Alsberg, a prominent New York merchant. Soon they had branches of their clothing concern in New York, Baltimore, and Savannah. Houseman and Alsberg disbanded their corporation in 1870, with Houseman retaining rights to the original Grand Rapids establishment. He eventually sold the Grand Rapids store to his cousin Joseph and a friend named Moses May. The firm, which went through numerous name changes, today is known as Houseman and Jones. Located on Monroe Street, it is the second-oldest mercantile establishment in Grand Rapids.

After divesting himself of his mercantile interests, Houseman invested heavily in timberlands and the manufacture of pine lumber. From this he made yet another fortune. In 1870, as befitting a wealthy merchant, he took the grand tour of Europe, visiting Germany, Switzerland, France, and England.

As a prominent local merchant, Julius Houseman took a keen interest in local business and civic affairs. People wanted him associated with their businesses. In 1870, be became a stockholder in the City National Bank. This was followed in rapid succession by his involvement with the Grand Rapids Chair Company, a directorship in the Grand Rapids Brush Company, and the presidency of the Grand Rapids Fire Insurance Company. From 1863 to 1870, Houseman served as an elected member of the city council. He left that body upon being elected to Michigan's state legislature in 1870. Two years later, he was elected to the first of two consecutive terms as mayor of Grand Rapids. Julius Houseman suffered his first political defeat in 1876, when he ran as the Democratic Party's nominee for Lieutenant Governor. Urged to run for Governor four years later, Houseman refused, deciding instead to run for the Forty-eighth Congress from Michigan's Fifth District. He captured the seat in 1883, but declined renomination after serving only one term.

Julius Houseman returned to Grand Rapids in 1885 to live out what would be the final six years of his life. Besides his numerous business interests, he was devoted to the activities of the local Jewish community. As mentioned above, he was one of the founders of the local B'nai B'rith lodge and served as its first president.

Julius Houseman died shortly after his fifty-eighth birthday, on February 9, 1891. He was interred in Oak Hill Cemetery in Grand Rapids. Nothing is known of his descendants.

References
Publications of the Michigan Jewish Historical Society 1, no. 1 (1960): pp. 10–11.
Universal Jewish Encyclopedia.

IRVING, THEODORE LEONARD (1898–1962): *Democrat from Missouri; served two terms in the House (Eighty-first through Eighty-second Congress; January 3, 1949–January 3, 1953).*

It is a well-known fact that Harry S. Truman's best friend and personal confidant was a Jewish haberdasher named Eddie Jacobson. What is not commonly known is that for four of the seven years he occupied the White House, Truman's Independence, Missouri–based Congressman was also Jewish. Regrettably, Theodore Leonard Irving, the only Minyanaire to represent a sitting President, was far better known for defending himself in court than for declaiming on Capitol Hill.

Leonard Irving (he was never called by his first name) was born in St. Paul, Minnesota, on March 24, 1898, the son of Edgar Lorenzo and Florence May Chapel. Little is known about his family history. While he was still quite young, the Irvings moved from St. Paul to North Dakota, where his father had purchased a small farm. Leonard Irving attended public schools in North Dakota. As a teenager, filled with wanderlust, he went to work for a railroad; it provided him with a free pass to travel. By the end of World War I, Irving had married Effie Bjorjnstad and moved to Montana, where he spent a few years managing a theater. From Montana, he moved out to California, where he became the manager of a hotel. In 1934, the thirty-six-year-old Irving finally wound up in Missouri, where he found employment as a construction worker. When it was discovered that he had a penchant for organizing and speaking, Irving was made a field representative for the American Federation of Labor.

Leonard Irving first came to public attention in 1937, when he led a gravediggers' strike in Kansas City. Three years later, he was elected head of the gravediggers' local. During the 1940s, Irving moved up the trade union ladder, eventually becoming president and representative of Local 264 of the Construction and General Laborers Union. Finally, after years of wandering from place to place and from job to job, Irving had settled down. During these years, he made Independence, Missouri, his home. In 1948, when seven-term Democrat C. Jasper Bell announced that he was giving up his Fourth District seat, Irving decided to throw his hat into

the ring. Rated a dark horse in the Democratic primary, Irving finished first in a five-candidate race and won the general election in November.

Irving was sworn in as a member of the Eighty-first Congress on January 3, 1949. Six months later, the legal problems that would dog him for the next few years began.

On July 16, 1949, members of the Hod Carriers' Building and Common Laborers Union filed suit in circuit court, charging that Irving had "diverted funds . . . to his own use." Their petition alleged that since June 1948 (the month that he won the Democratic primary), Irving had "engaged in a combination and conspiracy" with other members of the union "to divert the funds of the local union to their own use." Specifically, they charged that Irving, Roy E. Livingston, financial secretary and treasurer of the local, and Alvin Butcher, secretary, had "authorized and permitted large sums of money to be paid out of the treasury of the local union for political purposes, for the work of procuring people to register as qualified voters in county, state and national elections, and to promote the campaigns of people seeking election to public office."

Speaking to a *New York Times* reporter, Irving explained: "There has been a small clique working against me as far back as 1940. We don't have anything to worry about. Our books are in good shape. We have 1,800 members and no one can satisfy all of them." On July 19, Irving went to a Hod Carriers meeting in order to give a financial report and tell his side of the story. A battle royal ensued in which five men were sent to the hospital with knife wounds. An article in the *New York Times* reported that "scores used their fists and wielded chairs as clubs . . . pieces of shattered chairs cluttered the floor of the meeting hall." Irving had to be escorted from the meeting hall by a forty-man police detail.

Less than a month later, on August 16, 1949, the laborers' suit against Irving was dismissed. In sustaining a defense motion for dismissal, Judge John Cook said that the matter could "best be handled by the union itself." By early fall of that year, Irving was back in the news, having inexplicably locked his congressional staff out of his office. When queried about his actions, all Irving would say was that attacks on him had been embarrassing not only to him but to the President. When a reporter asked Truman whether he was embarrassed, the President reportedly smiled and replied: "Long service in politics has made [me] embarrass proof."

Union members filed yet another suit in equity against Irving and his colleagues in June 1950. Once again, Judge Cook issued a dismissal. A year later, a federal grand jury in Kansas City handed down a two-count indictment against Irving and Livingston, alleging violation of the Corrupt Practices Act and the Taft-Hartley Law, "in that about $3,000 of union funds were used" in Irving's election campaign. Irving waived immunity, and his case came to trial on November 19, 1951. On December 28, 1951 he was acquitted on all counts. During these legal hassles, Irving managed to win reelection. Ironically, after finally being acquitted on all charges, he lost his congressional seat to Jeffrey Hillelson in the 1952 Democratic primary.

Following his exit from Washington, Irving returned to Independence, where he once again became president of a labor union. He died while on a business trip to Washington on March 8, 1962, and was buried in Mount Moriah Cemetery, Kansas City, Missouri. Of his family and descendants nothing is known.

References

Biographical Directory of the United States Congress, 1774–1989, p. 1246.

New York Times, July 17, 1949, 5:1; August 16, 1949, 2:5; October 28, 1949, 2:3; May 27, 1950, 7:3; June 9, 1951, 36:3; June 10, 1951, 62:4; December 29, 1951, 6:8.

ISACSON, LEO (1910–1997): *American Laborite from New York; served eleven months in the House (Eighty-first Congress; February 17, 1948–January 3, 1949).*

In a 1968 Bronx County Historical Society pamphlet entitled *Leo Isacson and the Election of 1948*, author George Tabor wrote: "Probably the most important single election ever held in Bronx County took place in 1948 when Leo Isacson won an upset special election for Congress and thereby changed both the foreign policy and the political history of the United States." Hyperbole? Perhaps: Leo Isacson's tenure in the United States Congress amounted to just 320 days (February 17, 1948–January 3, 1949). Nonetheless, during those nearly eleven months, he did make a significant mark on the future of American foreign policy vis-à-vis the nascent State of Israel. As Tabor noted: "His victory helped persuade President Truman to grant immediate recognition to Israel." Furthermore, Tabor claimed that Isacson's victory "enormously encouraged" the independent candidacy of Henry Wallace, and caused the Republicans to become "overconfident of victory in November."

One of the two or three most outspoken leftists in the Eighty-first Congress, Isacson made his presence known his very first day in office. The first words he said (shouted actually) on the House floor were: "I AM A JEW!" When Isacson spoke, his colleagues listened. A lifelong agitator who roomed in Washington with Mark (Vito) Marcantonio, I. F. Stone, and Paul Robeson, Isacson firmly believed that "it would be a good idea if a law were passed that all Congressmen taking office should spend a certain number of hours on the picket line."

Leo Isacson was born in New York City on April 20, 1910. His parents, Laura Nager and Hyman Isacson, were Romanian immigrants from Bakow. Although the two had known and liked each other in their hometown, they had never been permitted to "keep company;" she came from a wealthy, aristocratic family, while he was the son of a poor widowed mother who

ran a bakery. Once in New York, the two renewed their acquaintance at a Hebrew Immigrant Aid Society (HIAS) function and were soon married. The Isacsons would eventually have three children: Leo, Ruth, and Regina. Leo attended P.S. 52 and Morris High School, and was graduated from NYU in 1931. Laura was "the Jew in the family." According to Leo Isacson: "My father was very secular, even at that time; my mother observed the religious customs—lighting Friday night candles and so forth. I was sent to *cheder*; I learned Hebrew and I was bar mitzvah, but didn't really continue with much religious education or involvement after that."

Up until the time Leo was midway through his undergraduate years, his father, Hyman, manufactured phonographs. With the rising popularity of radio and the stock market crash in 1929, the business collapsed. After the crash, Hyman Isacson began manufacturing radios. Leo worked for his father after school, putting up antennas on rooftops. In 1931, Isacson entered NYU Law School. As he noted, "Those were difficult times. My lunches were always at the automat. . . . "By putting a nickel in a slot you got a very nice vegetable, and then by going to the water fountain and then to the sugar tray and to the lemon which they furnished for tea, you were able to get a free lemonade. And so I worked my way through law school."

Raised in a classically left-leaning, largely secular Jewish home, the Isacson children received a strong sense of social justice from their parents: "We lived it. . . . You see, those of us who were progressive were progressive in a holistic sense. We were almost Renaissance people, because it wasn't just the injustice to Jews that we felt immediately, but the injustice of the blacks, and the injustice to those who were not afforded an opportunity for the pursuit of happiness that we were promised."

Isacson graduated from law school in 1933, and shortly thereafter went into private practice. Sharing an office with six attorneys and one stenographer, Isacson took "whatever [cases] my relatives could bring me. I don't think I reached a thousand dollars the first year in my practice. It was very tough going."

Leo Isacson's first political hero was Mayor *Fiorello La Guardia*: "I admired La Guardia and his Fusion Party. I admired the honesty and the integrity of the man, and I came out [of law school] right after he left politics, and the American Labor Party was formed. And to me, that represented an opportunity to further some of the principles in which I believed."

The Fusion Party was a political amalgam of liberal, "good government" Democrats and Republicans that eventually became the American Labor Party. The ALP was created in 1936 as the local chapter of the Labor Non-Partisan League. It was intended to provide a means whereby anti-Tammany Democrats could vote for Franklin Roosevelt and independents could vote for Fiorello La Guardia. Leo Isacson joined the party in 1936.

In 1944, Isacson was elected to the New York State Assembly from a northern Bronx district as an American Laborite. In the election, Isacson received the Republican Party's endorsement. His election was viewed by the leftist paper *P.M.* as a revolution. "I was somewhat of a freak, an anomaly. I raised the first question. . . . When the Democrats . . . and the Republicans caucus, and they each go to the caucus room, am I to go to the nearest telephone booth to caucus?"

As a member of the State Assembly, Isacson supported proposals for a low-rent housing program, state rent controls, and anti-discrimination legislation. After serving but one term, he lost his seat when the Republican Party refused to endorse him again. In the election of 1946, he was defeated by a Republican: "I ran on the Labor Party [ticket], and I beat the Democrat. But by splitting up that vote, the Republican got in. It was just one of those things."

In 1947, Isacson's dander was raised by the Truman-inspired arms embargo against Palestine: "I was terribly excited about the prospects about a Jewish state, and a homeland for those remnants of the Holocaust who had made their way to the seaports of Europe . . . out of the lime pits and the crematoria . . . all waiting there to try to get to Israel. The British blockade not allowing them to get into Palestine. And then the American embargo against arms. This was the final straw."

Isacson desperately wanted to do something to help the Jews of Palestine. Fortuitously, Democratic Congressman *Benjamin Rabin* resigned from the House, effective December 31, 1947, in order to take a seat on the New York State Supreme Court. A special election was called for February 17, 1948. Isacson quickly announced his candidacy for Rabin's Twenty-fourth District seat, running on the American Labor Party ticket. The Democrats nominated Karl Propper, a past-president of the Bronx County Bar Association. The Liberal Party (a "right-wing" spin-off of the ALP) nominated Dean Alfange, a former ALP candidate for governor, while the Republicans, conceding defeat, "went through the motions" and nominated one Joseph A. DeNegris.

The Twenty-fourth District, located in the southeastern Bronx, was a predominately working-class community in 1948. Ethnically, it was largely populated by Puerto Ricans, Jews, and blacks. Propper and Isacson, the two front-runners, were in relative agreement on most major issues. They were both in favor of price and rent controls, and of lifting President Truman's arms embargo against Israel. They were both against the Taft-Hartley Law. Isacson diverged in his opposition to the "bankrupt Truman Doctrine," and was dubious about the proposed Marshall Plan. Said Isacson during the election: "If the emphasis is on food, I'm for it. If the emphasis is on politics, I'm against it."

What gave this election its importance and impact was not the issues. With a presidential election coming up in November 1948, Isacson's candidacy was looked upon as a test of strength for former Vice President Henry A. Wallace, who had already been endorsed by the American Labor Party. Upon his nomination, Isacson immediately identified himself with Wallace's candidacy, and announced that he would campaign on a "fighting Roosevelt–Wallace program." Henry Wallace appeared at a rally for Isacson, along with ALP Congressman Vito Marcantonio, singer Paul Robeson, and Michael J. Quill, head of the Transport Workers' Union. Wallace's support for Isacson was both professional and personal; he had an old score to settle with the Bronx County Democratic leader, Edward J. Flynn. In 1944, Flynn had been at the forefront of a move to persuade Roosevelt to drop Wallace as Vice

President. Roosevelt chose Truman over Wallace. But for that twist of fate, Henry Wallace, not Harry Truman, would have been President of the United States upon the death of FDR.

Leo Isacson was elected with nearly 56 percent of the vote (22,697) in the four-candidate race. Suddenly, it looked as if Henry Wallace might have a chance in the November 1948 election. Analyzing the results, *New York Times* political reporter Warren Moscow attributed Isacson's victory in "predominately Jewish voting territory" to his militant support for the Jews of Palestine. In addition, he said, "the Communists, out in full support of Mr. Wallace and Mr. Isacson, were able to mass their full worker strength for the entire city in one Congressional district. They portrayed Isacson as the true candidate of peace, prosperity and Palestine."

Leo Isacson became a member of the Eighty-first Congress on February 17, 1948. A momentary delay was caused in the swearing-in process when Representative Charles Kersten, a Wisconsin Republican, suggested that the House refuse to seat Isacson because his loyalty was in doubt. As noted above, Isacson spoke that first day. In his "I AM A JEW!" speech, he examined the ethical considerations and aspirations of the Jewish people, and excoriated the Truman administration's arms embargo against Palestine. The next day, he drafted his first piece of legislation, a bill that would "recognize the independent Jewish State in Palestine and guarantee its security against attack."

While a member of the House, Isacson voted against the Marshall Plan ("a plan of the imperialists to cut off democratic forces abroad") and the peacetime draft, and in favor of statehood for Puerto Rico. In the domestic realm, he argued for civil rights legislation, price controls, and federal housing, and was one of onlyfourteen representatives who supported Adam Clayton Powell's amendments to end segregation in the military services.

In June 1948 Isacson went to Israel. He flew from New York to Cyprus, where he met with Jewish detainees in the British internment camps. Upon arriving in Israel, he met with Prime Minister David Ben-Gurion—the first member of Congress to do so. Ben-Gurion told Isacson, "We have a clandestine radio station, *Kol Israel*. In four days, it will be the Fourth of July . . . would you like to address the people of our new state, and talk about the American Independence and now the Independence of the Jewish State?" Isacson readily agreed. As he recounted years later, "They blindfolded me, spun me around . . . and took me God knows where. I was put before the microphones and spoke about the American War for Independence and the Israeli War of Independence. It was one of the great moments of my life."

While in Israel, Isacson witnessed the ship *Altalena*, bringing in arms for Menachem Begin's Irgun, being shelled and sunk by units of the Labor Zionists' armed force, the Haganah. That night "I got drunk with the captain of the ship and one or two of the boys." While Isacson was staying at the King David Hotel in Jerusalem, it came under enemy shellfire. "I got into some room and crawled under a large bed. There were four other people there with me. So after we're there for a few minutes, I turned to the fellow on my right and I say, 'Incidentally, we're here together, who are you?' He says, 'My name is Herzog, I'm the Chief Rabbi of Israel.'"

When Isacson returned to New York, he learned that the Republicans and Democrats had joined forces to ensure his defeat in the November election. Although garnering nearly 45,000 votes (Henry Wallace received only 20,000), Isacson was defeated by *Isadore Dollinger*.

Following his defeat, Isacson resumed the practice of law in New York City as a partner in the firm of Isacson and Weinberger. He remained active in the American Labor Party, running (unsuccessfully) for Bronx borough president in 1949. In 1951, he resigned from the ALP in disagreement with the party's refusal to condemn Communist aggression during the Korean War. In 1968, he was a delegate to the Democratic National Convention in Chicago, pledged to the candidacy of Eugene McCarthy.

Isacson had two daughters, Dale and Jill. As a young parent, Jill was murdered; as of 1999, the investigation was still ongoing. In 1969, Leo Isacson moved to Tamarac, Florida, where he remained active in local Democrat Party politics and became an adjunct professor of political science at Nova University. Leo Isacson died on Erev Yom Kippur, 5757, September 21, 1996. He is buried in New York. In February 1997, the South Florida chapter of Americans for Peace Now honored his memory by renaming their group the Leo Isacson Lodge.

References

Interview with Leo Isacson, December 1991.

New York Times, February 22, 1948, p. 1.

George Tabor, "Leo Isacson and the Election of 1948," *Bronx County Historical Society Journal* 5, no. 2 (July 1968).

Private video made by Leo Isacson prior to his death, 1996.

JACOBSTEIN, MEYER (1880–1963): *Democrat from New York; served three terms in the House (Sixty-eighth through Seventieth Congress; March 4, 1923–March 3, 1929).*

Of all the programs created by the Roosevelt administration during its fabled "Hundred Days," perhaps none was as controversial or drew as much fire as NRA—the National Recovery Administration. Directed by the mercurial General Hugh Johnson, the director of the draft during World War I, the NRA was the bureaucratic vehicle that drove the entire New Deal. Through its numerous codes, the NRA established maximum hours and minimum wages for virtually every major industry, abolished the sweatshop and child labor in many industries, gave workers the right to bargain through their own union representatives, and specified that businesses must open their books to government inspection.

The NRA, symbolized by the Blue Eagle, only lasted for two years; it was found unconstitutional by the Supreme Court in the 1935 Schechter case. In its decision, the court ruled that the government lacked the power to set working conditions for Schechter's business (raising and selling chickens) because it was were not involved in interstate commerce. The Schechter decision not only ended the NRA; it led directly to Roosevelt's ill-conceived court-packing plan.

In the context of American politics, the NRA was, in the words of historian Page Smith, "as radical as one could have wished. . . . The surprising thing is not that the NRA failed, but that, Alice in Wonderland prospect that it was, it was even tried." When historians write about the NRA, they almost universally mention the names of Roosevelt, General Johnson, and Rexford Tugwell, who certainly was one of its strongest advocates in White House inner circles. Sadly lacking from most historical accounts of the rise and fall of the National Recovery Administration are the names of the two individuals who first gave the idea life: Harold G. Moulton and Meyer Jacobstein.

Moulton, the president of the Brookings Institute in Washington, and Jacobstein, an economist, publisher, businessman, and former member of Congress, drafted a "comprehensive plan for business recovery" in early 1933. To a great degree, it was their plan that was trans-

muted into the NRA. History has an unforgiving tendency to favor implementers and popularizers over thinkers and innovators. Such has been the fate of Moulton and Jacobstein, whose names are now largely forgotten.

Meyer Jacobstein, the son of Joseph and Bertha (Nelson) Jacobstein, was born in New York City on January 25, 1880. He was educated at the University of Rochester and Columbia University, from which he received a Ph.D. in economics in 1907. Shortly after his graduation, he married Lena Lipsky, with whom he had two daughters, Mary Elizabeth and Ruth. The Jacobsteins spent their first year of married life living in Washington, D.C., where Meyer was employed as a special agent in the Commerce Department's Bureau of Corporations. In 1908, they moved to Grand Forks, North Dakota, where Meyer spent the next five years as professor of economics at the University of North Dakota. One can only imagine the sense of dislocation that two New York-born-and-bred Jews must have felt in Grand Forks; in 1908, the entire state had less than 1,000 Jewish residents out of a population of nearly half a million.

At the end of his tour in the Peace Garden State, Jacobstein was hired to teach in the economics department of his *alma mater*, the University of Rochester. He was a member of the faculty at Rochester from 1913 to 1918, the last two years of which he acted as a director of emergency employment management under the auspices of the War Industry Board. In 1922, when Rochester Congressman Thomas B. Dunn decided to retire after five terms (he was nearly seventy), Jacobstein resolved to run for the open seat. The Thirty-eighth Congressional District, which took in all of Rochester, had been a safe Republican seat ever since the Civil War—and would continue to be so after Jacobstein's tenure until the present.

With a Jewish population of slightly less than 15,000 (about 5.5 percent of the population), Jacobstein did not have any special advantages going into the race. Nonetheless, against all odds, the professor won, taking his seat in the Sixty-eighth Congress. During his first term, Jacobstein acquired control of the Rochester Business Institute, a private school of business and commerce, serving as its president for several years. At the conclusion of his first term, the local Democratic establishment urged Jacobstein to run for Rochester mayor. Jacobstein refused, preferring to remain in Congress. He won reelection by a better than two-to-one margin.

Not surprisingly, Jacobstein specialized in economic and labor issues during his six-year congressional career. One of the first members of Congress to issue an annual report to his constituents, Jacobstein reported to the folks back home that the most pressing issues facing Congress were "flood relief, tax relief, farm relief and labor relief." The *New York Times* applauded his efforts to remain in contact with his constituents, and urged other members of Congress to follow suit. "Although," they noted, "we doubt that others will be able to be as succinct and clear-minded as the gentleman from Rochester."

When President Calvin Coolidge made an offhand remark that there would be a better than $390 million surplus at the end of fiscal year 1926, Jacobstein quickly moved for a 25 percent rebate on all personal taxes. The measure, which was cosponsored in the Senate by New York's Royal Copeland, also called for repeal of the 3 percent tax on automobiles and the elimination of the so-called "amusement tax." The Coolidge administration designated Treasury Secretary Andrew Mellon as their point man on this issue. Mellon criticized the Jacobstein-Copeland plan, claiming that any surplus the plan's authors believed existed had in fact already been spent.

At one point in 1926, the boys in Tammany Hall seriously considered giving Jacobstein the Democratic senatorial nomination. This was the Prohibition era, however, and Jacobstein was considered "not wet enough to suit most of the Democratic leaders," so the nomination (and eventual victory) went to New York Supreme Court Justice Robert F. Wagner, Sr.

An ardent supporter of Al Smith's presidential aspirations, Jacobstein spent a great deal of time out on the campaign trail speaking on behalf of the New York Governor. While giving an outdoor speech in Rochester in August 1928, Jacobstein was interrupted by members of the Ku Klux Klan (an emerging political power in the Rochester area), who raised a fiery cross on a nearby hill. When the assembled crowd noticed the cross, Jacobstein quickly remarked: "That does not represent the spirit of America. It looks to me so far away that I believe it must be in a foreign country." The Klansmen, planning to give their support to whoever ran against the "Jew Congressman" in the next election, were dismayed to learn that the Republican candidate was a Catholic. Being just as bigoted against Catholics as Jews, the Klan ran its own candidate, who came in a dismal third. Jacobstein was reelected to his third term, his margin again being about two-to-one.

While campaigning for Al Smith in the summer of 1928, Jacobstein announced that he would not run for reelection in the fall. It may have been that Jacobstein was tiring of the commute between Washington and Rochester. More likely, he retired from the House because he had become Al Smith's personal choice to run with Franklin Roosevelt for Lieutenant Governor of New York. Smith felt that having a Jew on the ticket would ensure victory in 1928. As things turned out, Smith was right, although it was *Herbert H Lehman* who filled the spot, not Jacobstein.

Eight months after Jacobstein left Congress, the stock market crashed and the Depression was on. Ironically, Jacobstein's first enterprise after leaving Washington was to become president of the First National Bank and Trust Company of Rochester. Shortly after he took it over, Brooklyn Congressman *William Sirovich* issued a press release stating that Jacobstein would soon become a candidate for state superintendent of banks. Sirovich either had bad information or was merely floating a trial balloon, for nothing came of Jacobstein's putative candidacy. Jacobstein resigned his bank presidency in 1933 in order to become publisher of the *Rochester Evening Journal* and the *Rochester Sunday American*, continuing in that capacity until the papers suspended operations four years later.

Even with his banking, teaching, and publishing interests, Jacobstein still found the time to again begin commuting from Rochester to Washington, where he worked closely with the aforementioned Harold Moulton in drafting a proposal for economic recovery. One suspects that it was Moulton, rather than Jacobstein, who transmitted the plan to the Roosevelt administration; relations between the liberal Brookings Institute and the White House were quite close.

In 1939, Jacobstein left Rochester to join the research staff of the Brookings Institute. After seven years with Brookings, he moved over to the Library of Congress, where he spent the years 1946 to 1952 as economic counsel to the library's legislative reference service. In that position, Jacobstein was responsible for providing members of Congress and their staffs with answers to questions on economic theory, policy, and legislation. Long convinced of the institution's centrality in the intellectual and cultural life of America, Jacobstein, along with Representative *Emanuel Celler*, had spearheaded a 1926 drive to raise $150,000 for the library's Hebrew and Oriental division.

Jacobstein retired in 1952, shortly after his seventy-second birthday. He returned to Rochester, where he died on April 18, 1963. Jacobstein was buried in Rochester's Mount Hope Cemetery.

References

American Jewish Year Book, vol. 24, p. 158; vol. 44, p. 412; vol. 47, p. 629; vol. 65, p. 434.

Biographical Directory of American Jews.

Jewish Telegraphic Agency Daily News Bulletin, April 22, 1963.

New York Times, June 10, 1926, 11:1; June 24, 1926, 6:8; July 27, 1928, II 6:7; August 5, 1928, 17:2; March 3, 1929 6:8; April 19, 1963, 43:2.

Page Smith, *Redeeming the Time: A People's History of the 1920s and the New Deal* (New York: Penguin Books, 1987).

Universal Jewish Encyclopedia.

Who's Who in America, vol. 4.

JAVITS, JACOB KOPPEL (1904–1986):
Republican from New York; served four terms in the House (Eightieth Congress through Eighty-third Congress; January 3, 1947–December 31, 1954); four terms in the Senate (January 9, 1957–January 3, 1981).

In an April 1966 *Esquire Magazine* article, writer Milton Viorst compared Senator Jacob Javits to other well-known members of the American-Jewish political establishment: "What's so amazing about Javits," Viorst wrote, "is that he's such a Jewish Jew. Javits is not a white-collar New England Jew like *Ribicoff*, a pioneer Jew like *Gruening*, a Western, conservationist Jew like the late *Dick Neuberger*, or even a multi-generation German Jew like the late *Herbert Lehman*. Jack Javits," Viorst concluded, "is a genuine, one-hundred-percent, all-wool-gabardine, Yiddish-speaking Old Country Jew, the kind who knows how to cut a matzo ball with the side of the spoon without splashing the soup. Javits is a regular Huckleberry Finn Jew." What Viorst did not have to mention was that this "regular Huckleberry Finn Jew" was also one of the most accomplished politicians of the twentieth century; a man whom the *New York Times* eulogized as "a towering colossus of American politics."

Morris Jewetz, the future Senator's father, was born in Mielnieza, Galicia, in 1862. As a child, Morris was entrusted by his parents to a rabbi "in whose steps it was hoped he would follow." Following more than a decade of rigorous talmudic study, Morris Jewetz immigrated to America. At age twenty-two, he found himself, like so many other newcomers from Eastern Europe, living and working on New York's Lower East Side. Morris made pants. In 1891, at age twenty-nine, Morris met Ida Littman Koppel, a recent teenage immigrant from Russia.

According to family tradition, Ida's family had walked all the way from Russia to Palestine in the early nineteenth century. Born and raised in the holy city of Safed in Galilee, Ida was the child of a farmer's daughter who had married a traveling salesman from Vienna. Shortly after her birth, the traveling salesman abandoned his wife and child. Ida's mother subsequently married a Russian and went off with him to Odessa, leaving the little girl behind with her grandparents. Ida was forced to go to work in her grandmother's grocery store at age six. She was given virtually no schooling, and did not learn to read or write until age fifty-five.

When Ida was sixteen, her mother finally sent for her. Again according to family legend, Ida walked the 65 miles between Safed and Beirut, where she took a sailing ship to Odessa. There, her life of toil continued. Two years after Ida arrived in Odessa, she and her mother pulled up stakes and immigrated to New York, where, like Morris, she found work in the garment industry. They were married in 1893. Their first child, whom they named Benjamin, was born the following year. Over the next ten years, Ida suffered six miscarriages. On May 18, 1904, the Javits's second and only other surviving child, Jacob Koppel, was born on New York's Lower East Side. In later years, Senator Javits would claim that "in New York State that is like being born in a log cabin."

Morris Javits was a "dreamy type, ill at ease in a materialistic world." Ida, on the other hand, was "a practical woman who considered pants-making a precariously seasonal trade." Somehow, she convinced Morris that he could provide the family with far greater security by becoming a building superintendent. Following her advice, he "devoted himself" to superintending "three dingy tenements" near the corner of Orchard and Stanton Streets. Morris remained a janitor/super until his death in 1918. At no time in his life did Morris make more than $40 or $45 a month. Ida supplemented the family's income by selling toys and notions from a pushcart.

In *Javits: The Autobiography of a Public Man*, the Senator wrote that his father "prayed with his phylacteries every morning of his life." Ida, on the other hand, "was not as attached to Orthodox rituals" as her husband. Javits's maternal grandmother, who lived with the family during his earliest years, "believed in a simple remedy for every illness, whether it be chilblains, arthritis, a sore throat, or weak eyes. . . . Colgate toothpaste. She did not know what it was," the Senator said, "but she was convinced it could cure everything." The Javits family needed more than Colgate; both boys suffered from serious illness. Ben almost died from empyema, the suppuration of pus in the chest cavity. As a result, he had to have several of his ribs removed. Always a fighter, he determined "that he was going to live no matter what anybody said."

In addition to his work as a super, Morris represented Tammany Hall on the premises of "his" three tenements. "Before every election, he would go to a nearby saloon and from its proprietor, who controlled political disbursements in that neighborhood, receive a two-dollar honorarium for each tenant eligible to vote and ostensibly to vote Democratic." In return for his undertaking these tasks on behalf of Tammany, Morris was permitted to "perform minor philanthropic functions in its behalf, such as fixing any parking tickets acquired by pushcart peddlers on his corner."

As a youth, brother Ben was a fiery Socialist, "mesmerized by Hilquit, Debs and Eastman and the beautiful goals of the Young People's Socialist League." As an adult, Ben would become an even more ardent apostle of capitalism, believing that "the salvation of the world lay in high finance." Once he had established himself as an attorney, Ben helped to draw up the National Industrial Recovery Act and created a "pressure group of stock and bondholders called the Investors League." He also authored a number of books on high finance, among them a "sensationally untimely one," published on the eve of the stock market crash, entitled *Make Everybody Rich: Industry's New Goal.*

By the time "Jakela" was fourteen, his father was dead. A year or two before his death, Ben, who was earning a living "selling petticoats and hounding people for money" (he was a bill collector), decided to move the family out of the Lower East Side to Brooklyn. Morris, "too proud to accept Ben's ultimatum," refused to go; he spent the last two years of his life apart from his family.

The year after Morris's death (1919), Ben was admitted to the bar, and promptly moved his mother and brother from Brooklyn to New York's Upper West Side. Ben's influence over younger brother Jack was seminal: "Ben was utterly relentless in his determination that both of them were going to make it big. Ben gave Jack the drive. Ben gave him the objectives, the ambition, the conviction that he could really be somebody. If Jack is Cinderella, then Ben is the fairy godmother."

Jack Javits was president of the 1920 graduation class at George Washington High School. Under his picture in the school yearbook was written: "You can't tell from first appearances." Immediately following graduation, Jack went to work as a traveling salesman of printing inks and lithographic stones. Traveling a route that took him from New York all the way to Delaware, Jack quickly found himself earning $75 a week—a very respectable amount in the early 1920s.

Once Ben's legal practice began taking off, he was able to turn his bill collection business over to his younger brother, who had visions of a college career. While collecting debts during the day, Jack took evening classes at Columbia University. Ben urged Jack to follow in his footsteps and become an attorney. Heeding his older brother's advice, Jack entered the New York University School of Law. He received his LL.B. in 1926 without benefit of having received an undergraduate degree. After interning with his brother's firm for a year, Jack made application to join the Bar Association of New York; he was blackballed on the grounds that "no partner of Ben Javits deserved to be a member of the association." Jack withdrew his application and did not apply again for almost twenty years.

By 1930, Ben changed the name of his firm to Javits & Javits. The brothers specialized in corporate bankruptcy and reorganization work. The two complemented each other quite well: while Ben was "particularly adept at the research," Jack took the lead "at the advocacy." Together, they made a very handsome living. One of their most famous, and most lucrative, cases involved the bankruptcy of Ivar Kreuger, the "match king." As Javits tells the story in his autobiography:

> Hundreds of lawyers and accountants on both sides of the Atlantic spent years trying to unravel the tangled affairs of Ivar Kreuger. ...Ben was retained to represent a committee

of U.S. investors who held more than $80 million worth of stocks and debentures in Kreuger and Toll, the financier's Sweden-based parent firm. We filed a petition in federal court to have Kreuger and Toll declared bankrupt in the U.S. and set about searching for assets that could be used to reimburse our clients.

After more than a year's work and research, Ben determined that they needed "an experienced and well-known lawyer to represent us in court." Ben chose Samuel Untermeyer (1858–1940), "one of the most brilliant and famed courtroom lawyers of his day." (Untermeyer, it should be noted, was one of that era's leading advocates of government ownership of public utilities.)

The main opposition came from a group of Kreuger and Toll stockholders represented by attorney (and future Secretary of State) John Foster Dulles. For two months, Dulles and his group "stubbornly opposed our attempt to have Kreuger and Toll declared bankrupt in the United States." After nearly a year of legal maneuvering, the two sides agreed to enter into a settlement. By the time the settlement was concluded (in 1939), Javits & Javits was no longer involved with the case, although the brothers did collect a substantial fee.

Toward the end of the firm's connection with the Kreuger case, Jack Javits married Marjorie Ringling, the adopted daughter of circus magnate Alfred Ringling. Theirs was a "recreation marriage, a good-time marriage," that ended in divorce after only two and one-half years. Javits wrote of it: "I doubt that Marjorie ever became fully adjusted to the fact that we were of different faiths. Before we married, I had suggested that any children we had be brought up with the knowledge of both the Jewish and the Catholic religions so that they could eventually choose for themselves. But later, although we had not been married in church, Marjorie could not face the idea that her offspring would not be baptized."

Like many young, politically-minded New Yorkers in the 1930s, Jack Javits was enamored of both President Franklin Roosevelt and Mayor *Fiorello La Guardia*. Unlike most Jews, however, Javits became a Republican. To a great extent, he based this decision on the revulsion he felt for Tammany Hall. As a child, he had been witness to his father's dealings with the Tammany bosses, and found them to be corrupt and immoral.

Jack's feelings about the Democrats were cemented in 1932. During the summer of that year, Judge Samuel Seabury's investigation of corruption in New York City unearthed "an appalling saga of kickbacks, bribery, the buying of judgeships and outright fraud—all for the pecuniary benefit of the political bosses of Tammany Hall." To the twenty-eight-year-old Javits, the Republicans "seemed . . . to hold the only hope for an end to Tammany corruption." Javits found a political soulmate in La Guardia, the "little flower." "La Guardia inspired me as no other contemporary politician has done. . . . He was more than a reformer . . . he was a pro-labor man, with a passion for social justice that I shared."

Ben, on the other hand, was in a political world of his own. He had developed a theory of the corporation that he believed made socialism invalid. He named his theory "ownerism," something akin to corporate statism, the original foundation of Italian Fascism. According to Ben's theory, society was divided into workers, employers, and technicians. He had an almost blind faith that business managers, left to their own devices, could be entrusted to operate business in the public interest.

This was one of two major issues upon which the brothers violently disagreed; the other was President Roosevelt. According to Ben's daughter, Joan Javits Zeeman: "The only time I ever heard any dissension was when Jack would come back and he would say: 'I don't understand it. How can you hate Franklin Roosevelt?' My father would say: 'How can you like Franklin Roosevelt?' My father called himself a Republican because he HATED Franklin Roosevelt."

Jacob Javits worked for his idol, FDR, in his quest for a third term in 1940. That "defection from the Republican ranks" would come back to haunt him in his later political career; many old-line members of the GOP would continue to take a jaundiced, if not downright suspicious, view of him. The following year, the thirty-seven-year-old Javits became director of the Citizens Committee for Mayor La Guardia.

Shortly after La Guardia's reelection as mayor, America entered the war. In late 1941, while attending a party in Washington, Javits met Major General Walter C. Baker, the chief of the army's Chemical Warfare Service. Baker mentioned in passing that his service was having "a great deal of difficulty in procuring filter paper for gas masks and magnesium for incendiary bombs." Javits, sensing an opportunity to help the war effort, volunteered to see what he could do. "It required just a couple of phone calls to obtain from the Zellerbachs [a Jewish San Francisco-based family of highly successful paper merchants] a promise to make the filter paper Baker needed," Javits writes, "and thanks to [Charles] Wilson, it took only a little longer to find the magnesium." Baker was so bowled over by what Javits had accomplished that on December 2, 1941, he appointed the young lawyer his special assistant.

Four months later, Jacob Javits became a major in the United States Army. Before accepting his commission, he went through the same basic training grind as all enlisted personnel, just to prove to himself that at age thirty-seven he was still physically fit. As assistant to the director of the Chemical Warfare Service, Major (soon to be Lieutenant Colonel) Javits was sent to the European and Pacific Theaters. His rise to the rank of lieutenant colonel happened in record time. In a series of January 1950 *New Yorker* articles, E. J. Kahn, Jr., tried to put Javits's rapid promotions into perspective: "[He] is possibly the only soldier in American history to make an academic jump roughly the equivalent, in civilian circles, of skipping from kindergarten to the Institute of Advanced Study."

Jacob Javits was discharged from military service in June 1945. He was forever a changed man. Speaking of his time in the army, Joan Javits Zeeman remembered: "Something happened to him that was very dramatic. He knew it. He told everybody. I knew it. I remember being on a train with him when . . . I said to him: 'What's the matter with you? You're so crabby.' And he said: 'I'm not crabby.' He said 'I've just woken up to the world. I just realized that I'm very important and that I'm going to do some very important things. And you'll have to become used to the fact that I'm becoming a very serious person.'"

Shortly after coming to this realization, Javits went to work for Judge Jonah Goldstein, the Republican/Fusion nominee for mayor of New York City. Javits wrote endless speeches for Goldstein, "all dealing soberly with significant issues and brimming with research." As it turned out, Goldstein never used any of them, and went down to defeat.

In 1946, after going through an abortive engagement to singer Hollis Shaw, Javits was encouraged to run for Congress from New York's Twenty-first District. Hugging the banks of the Hudson River from 114th Street north through Inwood, the district took in the areas of Washington Heights, Marble Hill, Manhattanville, Morningside Heights, and Hamilton Grange. It was so overwhelmingly Democratic that the Republican nomination could be had for the asking. Who but a person with a taste for defeat would have wasted his time? At first, Javits's entry into the race seemed quixotic; two years earlier, the Tammany-backed James H. Torrens had captured the seat with nearly 70 percent of the vote. The last Republican to represent the Twenty-first had been *Martin Ansorge*, who was elected in 1920, and only after three successive defeats.

Even with its strongly Democratic track record, Javits felt he had a chance. While the district was Jewish and liberal, he reasoned, Torrens was Irish and conservative. In 1946, the Twenty-first District had so many recently arrived World War II German Jews that it was often referred to as "The Fourth Reich." Javits jumped into the campaign with both feet, employing pollster Elmo Roper at a cost of $2,000 to sound out residents of the district on how they felt about things. Roper came back with encouraging news: only 8.8 percent of the thousand constituents polled could correctly name their congressman; 6.9 percent thought they could but came up with the wrong name; 84.3 percent found the question utterly beyond them. (By comparison, when Javits ran for reelection in 1948, a similar Roper-conducted poll found that 33.1 percent of the voters in the Twenty-first District knew their Republican Congressman.)

Javits spent $7,500 on his first campaign, including $2,500 from his own pocket. He spent more than $300 on pencils with his name inscribed on them. He passed them out by the thousands. Running as an "unorthodox Republican," Javits came out in favor of the Office of Price Administration and against the

National Association of Manufacturers. He got a great deal of mileage out of his unwavering support for the unlimited admission of displaced persons into Palestine.

During the campaign, a complication surrounding this issue arose. While Javits was out on the hustings, Congress was debating a loan to Britain for "rehabilitation and development." Someone in the State Department had come up with the idea of making the loan conditional on the admission of the refugees to Palestine. Javits came out against this idea: "As I saw it, the loan was not a favor to Britain but was essential to help a destroyed Europe recover from World War II."

In the campaign's final weeks, Javits took the refugee issue "a step further" by demanding that America "open the doors of our country to not less than a hundred thousand refugees." He also bitterly attacked the 1924 Immigration Act, and urged its revision, thus "beginning a struggle that would later occupy much of [his] time and effort."

Endorsed by the Liberal Party, Javits declined to give more than "lukewarm assistance" to the concurrent campaign for reelection being waged by Governor Thomas Dewey. On election day, 1946, Javits carried the Twenty-first District by more than 6,000 votes. His winning was likened by one rhapsodic admirer to "a flower suddenly blooming in a cesspool."

Before moving down to Washington, Representative-elect Javits visited Palestine at his own expense in order to "study conditions there." As one of the first members of Congress to visit the Jewish homeland, he was the logical choice to christen the S.S. *Haifa*, the first vessel to fly the colors of the American-Israeli Shipping Company. Jacob Javits's interest in foreign affairs was just beginning.

From his first day in the House of Representatives, Jacob Javits showed contempt for the rule that freshmen should keep their mouths shut. Contrary to tradition, this freshman spoke on "anything and everything that struck his fancy." In his maiden speech before the House, Javits proposed the dispatch of a special U.S. mission to Palestine "to supervise increased immigration and land settlement." He further warned that "the situation of the Jews in Europe and in Palestine will grow worse on all counts the longer a solution is deferred and tension remains at a peak."

Before the end of his first term, Javits had "managed to alienate himself from most of his colleagues by his presumptuousness and from his party leadership by voting consistently against them." During the Eightieth Congress, Javits wound up voting with the majority of his fellow Republicans only about 60 percent of the time. In the Eighty-first Congress, his support dropped to less than 25 percent. Javits was one of eleven Republicans who voted against the Taft-Hartley Act, and one of just eight to vote against the Nixon-Mundt Communist Registration Act. Javits further infuriated his Republican colleagues by voting consistently in favor of bills providing for public housing, and against both the House Un-American Activities Committee and a bill that would have made Communist Party membership a crime. To complete his "apostasy," Javits voted in favor of the Truman Doctrine and the Marshall Plan, and against the McCarran Immigration Act.

Representative Javits was appointed to the Committee on Foreign Affairs. In this post he traveled to Europe in 1947, '49, and '51. It was his good fortune to be appointed to the committee in the immediate postwar era. With the rise of the European Recovery Plan (i.e., the Marshall Plan), Javits discovered that he was one of "a handful of global-minded Republican members who, at a time when there was considerable sentiment within the committee for returning to isolationism and the Congress as a whole was dominated by the Republicans, tipped the balance in favor of distributing American largess abroad."

During his first three years in Congress, Jacob Javits set some sort of a record for speechifying. According to the 1950 *New Yorker* article, he "held forth on something like a hundred and fifty themes," including:

James G. Blaine
Health conditions in Brazil
CARE packages
Indonesia
The death of Jan Masaryk
Pan-American Day
Herbert Hoover
Overtime pay
Immigration quotas for the British
    West Indies
Rent control for hotels
Segregation in Washington schools

The profits of the General Foods Corporation
Wendell Willkie
The United States Employment Service
Air-mail rates
Retirement pay for Army officers
The preservation of the dairy industry
American policy toward Spain
The Russian threat to the Dardanelles
Elihu Root
The character of the German people
Wheat
Children
Wool
The Jackson Hole National Monument
New York City

During his 1948 campaign, Javits had a comic book written and distributed in which the hero was none other than Jack Javits. In the comic, Congressman Javits "bravely disarms and soothes an enraged veteran who, on the brink of being tossed out of his home, had threatened to shoot a marshal trying to enforce the eviction order and was holding the entire neighborhood at bay." The Democrats tried to portray him as a crony of Governor Dewey, with whom, in fact, he had never truly gotten along. They took to calling him a "Big Business Representative, a demagogue who poses as a liberal to deceive an independent progressive community." Democratic claims to the contrary, Javits over-whelmed his Democratic rival.

In 1949, Javits wanted to run for mayor of New York City on the Fusion Party ticket; when the nomination went to Newbold Morris, he "sportingly" agreed to chair his campaign. After winning reelection in both 1950 and '52, and receiving the Republican nomination for 1954, Javits resigned his House seat in order to run for Attorney General of New York. Running against Democrat Franklin Roosevelt, Jr., Jacob Javits won, thereby becoming the only Republican on the state ticket to break the Democratic tide in the November election. Javits's four-year term as attorney general commenced on January 3, 1954.

Javits thoroughly enjoyed his term as attorney general. The position permitted him to have a regular home life for the first time in more than eight years, and by now he had a family. In 1947, he married Marian Ann Borris, whom he had met at Fusion Party headquarters in the fall of 1945. An aspiring actress and singer originally from Detroit, she was more than twenty years Javits's junior. Their wedding ceremony was performed by Rabbi Joshua Loth Liebman, after whom Jack and Marian would name their first-born son. Joshua was preceded by sister Joy. Joshua's birth came just a few years before the Javitses' third child, daughter Carla.

In 1956, Jacob Javits decided to make a run for the United States Senate seat being vacated by *Herbert Henry Lehman*. As the Republican nominee, Attorney General Javits squared off against New York's mayor, Robert F. Wagner, Jr. During the campaign, Javits had to fend off charges that he had solicited support from the Communists in his 1946 race for the House—charges that he vehemently denied. He even went so far as to make a voluntary appearance before the Senate Internal Security Subcommittee to answer the charges. Following his testimony, the swirl of rumors and allegations dissipated. On election day, 1956, Jacob Javits was elected to the United States Senate—a post which he would hold until January 1981.

During his nearly quarter century in the United States Senate, Jacob Javits helped compose and pass legislation on "foreign affairs, urban redevelopment, civil rights, organized labor and big business." According to many political experts, he sponsored "more significant and successful legislation than almost any other Republican of his time—and more than most of the Democrats who served around him." Never a single-issue specialist, Senator Javits played a major role in "reasserting Congressional control over the Federal budget, in omnibus private-pension legislation and in the War Powers Act."

As a member of the Government Operations Committee, Javits was instrumental in Senate passage of legislation on lobbying, gun control, and open government, plus the bill that established government title to the Nixon White House tapes. A truly bipartisan Senator, Javits backed Hubert Humphrey's "step-by-step" suspension of nuclear tests in order "to end the nuclear threat to mankind." Although supportive of Israel, Javits criticized the Israeli government for permitting Jews to establish communities in the administered territories. He also aroused concern among some Jewish voters by supporting U.S. arms sales to Arab regimes.

Javits kept an extremely high profile in New York City. Because he often found himself scheduled to give three or more speeches in a single evening, he often had to send a telegram of regret. The joke developed that "the definition of a *minyan* is nine Jews and a telegram from Jack Javits sending his regrets."

Throughout his long Senate career, Javits managed to walk a tightrope between his liberal, welfare-state instincts and the Wall Street interests that kept him in office. Despite his affinity for the social welfare legislation of the Democrats, he managed to maintain the strong backing of such financial powers as the Whitneys, the Loebs, the Rockefellers, and the Morgan heirs.

In 1970, Jacob Javits began noticing a strange tingling sensation in his feet and legs. Upon consulting with his physician and undergoing tests, it was determined that he was experiencing the early stages of amyotrophic lateral sclerosis, also known as Lou Gehrig's disease. Over the next sixteen years, his health deteriorated to the point where he became wheelchair-bound, unable to breathe without assistance. In 1980, faced with obvious health problems and a new conservative tide, Jacob Javits lost the Republican primary (his only political defeat) to Nassau County Supervisor Alfonse M. D'Amato. Javits kept his name on the ballot as the nominee of the Liberal Party in the November general election. Despite the fact that he did no campaigning, Javits still received 11 percent of the vote, thereby denying Democrat *Elizabeth Holtzman* a victory.

Following his defeat, Javits returned to private life, becoming an adjunct professor of public affairs at Columbia University's School of International Affairs. In April 1981, the federal government's largest office building in New York State—the 41-story tower at 26 Federal Plaza in lower Manhattan—was formally renamed for Senator Javits. In 1983, President Ronald Reagan presented him with the Medal of Freedom, the nation's highest civilian honor. In December 1984, New York City's new convention center was named the Jacob K. Javits Convention Center of New York.

As his life wound down, Jacob Javits had an opportunity to look back upon more than forty years of public service. When asked how he wished to be remembered, he said: "I would like to be remembered for the concept that changed the outlook of the country." The three major acts or measures to which he might have been referring were the War Powers Act, which limited the ability of a President to make war without Congressional approval; the ERISA Act, which guaranteed private pensions; and the National Endowment for the Arts and Humanities, which provides regular government subsidies for cultural projects.

In one of his last interviews, Javits discussed his difficult physical situation. "Life," he said, "does not stop with terminal illness. Only the patient stops, if he doesn't have the will to go forward with life until death overtakes him."

Jacob Javits succumbed to a heart attack in West Palm Beach, Florida, on March 7, 1986. He was nearly eighty-two years old. At his funeral, Senator Ted Kennedy observed that Javits had persisted in pushing his principle of "life not stopping with terminal illness" to the very end. "With each labored breath, he urged us to do better," Kennedy said. "Few of us have done as much to make America equal to its dream." Jacob Javits is buried in Linden Hill Cemetery, in Queens, New York.

References

Jacob K. Javits, *Javits: The Autobiography of a Public Man* (Boston: Houghton Mifflin, 1981).

Interview with Joan Javits Zeeman, Palm Beach, Fla., January 1992.

Esquire, April 1966.

New Yorker, January 21, 1950, pp. 31–43; January 28, 1950, pp. 30–41.

New York Times, March 8, 1986, 1:1.

JOELSON, CHARLES SAMUEL (1916–1999):
Democrat from New Jersey; served five terms in the House (Eighty-seventh through Ninety-first Congress; January 3, 1961–September 4, 1969).

Although Charles Samuel "Chuck" Joelson was the first Jew (and the first Democrat) to represent New Jersey's Eighth District in Congress, he was not the first Jew to run for the seat; that distinction was held by his father, Harry Joelson. The elder Joelson, a "left-leaning" Paterson municipal court judge, had twice run unsuccessfully for the seat—in 1938 and 1940. In the first race, he lost to Republican incumbent George Nicholas Seger (born 1866), who held the seat from 1923 until his death in August 1940. Harry Joelson's second defeat came at the hands of Seger's longtime secretary, Gordon Canfield (1898–1972), who went on to represent the Eighth District for another twenty years, finally retiring in December 1960. In the race to replace Canfield, history came full cycle when Harry's son Chuck won the election. After more than twenty-two years, the Eighth District was finally in the hands of a Joelson.

Charles Samuel Joelson was born in Paterson, New Jersey, on January 27, 1916. As much as he might have wished it were so, the Joelsons of Paterson were not related to the most famous Joelson of them all, Broadway and Hollywood star Al Jolson, born Asa Yoelson in Baltimore in 1886. "According to one of my father's uncles," Chuck Joelson recalled, "the original family name was something like Telelovsky. Can you imagine that on a campaign sign?"

Harry Joelson emigrated to Paterson, New Jersey, from Russia around the turn of the century. Establishing himself as an attorney, he married Jennie Ellenstein, who was a member of a politically prominent family. Her brother, Meier Ellenstein (1886–1967), was a man of great accomplishments. A 1912 graduate of the Columbia University College of Dentistry and Oral Surgery, he spent twelve years as a practicing dentist before enrolling in law school. Admitted to the New Jersey Bar in 1925, Meier

Ellenstein rose through the ranks of Newark Democratic politics, eventually winning a seat on the city commission. He went on to serve two four-year terms as Newark mayor. His administration was "marked by charges of corruption within the city government." In 1939, following a three-year investigation, Ellenstein and six other defendants were tried for "conspiracy to defraud the city in a series of meadowland purchases." All seven were eventually acquitted.

Chuck Joelson described his father, Harry, as "a free thinker . . . I guess today you'd call him a leftist." Not surprisingly, Chuck received no Jewish education and never became bar mitzvah. Instead, he received an excellent secular education, graduating from the Montclair Academy, Cornell (Phi Beta Kappa, B.A., 1937), and Cornell Law School, from which he received an LL.B. in 1939. The younger Joelson practiced  law in Paterson from 1940 to 1942, at which time he enlisted in the United States Navy, which sent him to the University of Colorado to learn Japanese. Upon completion of his coursework, Joelson was detailed to Pearl Harbor, where he served in the Far Eastern Branch of Naval Intelligence.

Following his discharge from the Navy, Joelson returned to Paterson where, in 1949, he became city counsel. Three years later, in 1952, he was appointed deputy attorney general in the state's criminal investigation division. From 1958 to 1960, he served as Director of Criminal Investigations for the State of New Jersey. In November 1960, Chuck Joelson was elected to the House of Representatives.

In his first term in Congress, Joelson was assigned to the Education and Labor Committee, chaired by the flamboyant Adam Clayton Powell of Harlem. Joelson and Powell (1908–1972) developed a fast friendship. Years later, Joelson recalled: "Adam used to invite me to come up to Harlem with him all the time—something that probably wouldn't be done in this day and age." In 1963, when Representative Joelson took the bus to attend Dr. Martin Luther King's "I Have a Dream" speech, his traveling companion was none other than Powell, America's best-known and most powerful black legislator.

Reelected in 1962, Joelson rotated off Education and Labor, having been assigned to the all-powerful Committee on Appropriations. As a member of this committee, he introduced the initial legislation that led to the creation of OSHA, the Occupational Safety and Health Administration.

A legislator with a moderate record, Joelson was known for his wry sense of humor. Once, in 1968, the House was engaged in the "dilatory tactic" of having the daily *Congressional Record* read word for word when it was supposed to be voting on an equal-time measure that would give all presidential candidates the chance to debate one another on national television. Republican candidate Richard Nixon had "ordered" House Republicans to use every parliamentary weapon in their arsenal to keep the measure from coming to a vote. (Nixon was "afraid of debates and with good reason." He once told a college audience, "milking a laugh out of his well-remembered disastrous encounter with Jack Kennedy in 1960, 'I am a dropout—from the electoral college. I flunked debating.'"). Hour after hour, Democrats tried in vain to have the reading of the *Record* ended. With tempers becoming short and civility on the wane, Representative Joelson called for a parliamentary inquiry.

"Mr. Speaker, would it be possible to terminate these quorum calls by agreeing to substitute Mr. Agnew for Mr. Nixon in the TV debates?" The house broke out into laughter.

Speaker McCormick, "in a no-fun mood," shot back, "The Chair doubts if that qualifies as a parliamentary inquiry."

Mr. Joelson: "Well, then, Mr. Speaker, how about an old Ronald Reagan movie?" Again, the House chamber was rocked by laughter.

As a member of the House Appropriations Committee, Joelson led the floor fight for a measure that added $1 billion to President Richard M. Nixon's 1969 education budget. By one estimate the added money "kept an estimated 40,000 public elementary and secondary school libraries, most of them serving poor and minority pupils, from shutting down." The money also "saved their (i.e. the schools') guidance counseling, vocational and remedial programs. For years thereafter, his name was associated with this measure, which came to be known as the "Joelson Package."

Chuck Joelson was reelected to Congress three times. In January 1969, he resigned his House seat in order to take an appointment as judge of the Superior Court. After eight years in Congress, the bench looked pretty inviting: "In Congress, every time you make a decision, you have to worry about what your constituents are going to think. As a judge, you only have to do what is right." Joelson became a judge of Superior Court, where he heard criminal cases. He went on to serve in the Chancery Division as an assignment judge in Passaic County, and wound up in the Appellate Division in Hackensack, from which he retired in 1984.

Shortly after World War II, Chuck Joelson married Ora Abulafia, a sabra from what was then Palestine. As the husband of a native Hebrew speaker, Joelson learned a bit of the holy tongue "out of self-defense." "You know," he recalled in a 1997 interview, "my wife used to call me *chamor* all the time, which for some reason I thought was the word for 'sweetheart.' It turns out that all along she was calling me a 'jackass.'"

The Joelsons eventually separated, but remained good friends. They had one daughter, Susan (Kelley), with whom Judge Joelson went to live following his retirement from the bench. In late 1997, the nearly eighty-two-year-old Joelson suffered several strokes. Although able to see only with difficulty, he retained his sense of humor: "I must have every ailment known to man except, perhaps, ovarian cancer." Chuck Joelson died on August 17, 1999 at the ContraState Medical center in Freehold Township, New Jersey.

References

Interview with Charles Joelson, December 1997.

Biographical Directory of the United States Congress, 1774–1989.

William "Fishbait" Miller, *Fishbait: The Memoirs of the Congressional Doorkeeper* (Englewood Cliffs, N.J.: Prentice-Hall, 1977), pp. 131–132.

New York Times, February 12, 1967, 92:5; August 21, 1969, A12:1.

JONAS, BENJAMIN FRANKLIN *(1834–1911): Democrat from Louisiana; served one term in the Senate (March 4, 1879–March 3, 1885).*

"Jewish geography" is a term known to most children of Abraham. Put two Jews together in a social setting, and within a short while they will likely figure out: who they know in common, where and with whom they went to school, and how, if possible, they might be related.

In nineteenth-century America, the kings of Jewish geography would no doubt have been the Jonas family. Their intertwining family roots, associations, and intimate friendships read like a Who's Who of Jewish and secular America.

The marvelously named Benjamin Franklin Jonas, a one-term Senator from Louisiana (1879–85), was related by marriage and by blood to the Seixas family, by business association to the family of *Judah P. Benjamin*, and by parental connection to no less a personage than President Abraham Lincoln. The future Senator's uncle, Joseph Jonas (1792–1869), a native of Exeter, England, was one of Annie Ezekiel and Benjamin Jonas's twenty-two children. Immigrating to America in 1817, he became the first Jewish settler in Cincinnati. Two years later, he was joined there by his brother Abraham (1801–1864), who came with a sizable contingent of Jews from Plymouth and Portsmouth.

Joseph and Abraham Jonas went into the auction business together along with their brother-in-law, Morris Moses. Both of them married daughters of the Revolutionary War patriot-rabbi, Gershom Mendes Seixas of New York. Abraham's wife, Lucia Orah Seixas Jonas, died in 1825. Shortly after her death, Abraham picked up and moved to the frontier town of Williamstown, Kentucky, some 35 miles south of Cincinnati, where he opened a store. In 1829, Abraham married Louisa Block of Virginia, destined to be the future Senator's mother.

Meanwhile, brother Joseph remained in Cincinnati, where, in 1824, he became the president of Ohio's first synagogue, Bene Israel. Three years earlier, in 1821, Joseph Jonas was one of the purchasers of a small plot of ground for the state's first Jewish cemetery. The land was purchased from Nicholas Longworth, the great-grandfather of the famous Ohio Congressman of the same name. Moreover, the younger Longworth would become the son-in-law of President Theodore Roosevelt.

Abraham Jonas flourished in Kentucky. Within one year of his arrival there (1828), he was an elected member of the Kentucky legislature. By 1833, he was elected Grand Master of the Masons of Kentucky. Upon acceding to the Masonic post, Abraham resigned from the Kentucky legislature. On July 19, 1834, Louisa gave birth to their second son, Benjamin Franklin. All in all, the Jonases would have five sons: Charles, Benjamin, Julian, Edward, and Samuel.

Plagued by wanderlust, Abraham Jonas picked up his family and moved to Quincy, Adams County, Illinois, in 1838, where Benjamin received his education. Nominally a merchant, Abraham turned the day-to-day running of his mercantile establishment over to two of his brothers and one Henry Asbury, who would remain his partner for the next twenty-two years. Freed from the daily toil of running a store, Abraham studied law and was admitted to the Illinois bar in 1843. A year earlier, the relative newcomer had been elected to the state legislature on the Whig ticket. While serving in the legislature, Abraham Jonas renewed acquaintances with an old friend from Kentucky, the fledgling Whig attorney Abraham Lincoln.

Jonas and Lincoln grew close both politically and personally. Some historians have suggested that it was Jonas who first publicly urged Lincoln to run for President. We will never know for sure because the record is rather murky. Without question, however, Jonas did follow Lincoln when the lanky "rail-splitter" broke away from the Whigs in order to form the Republican party. At one of the party's first conventions, Jonas suggested that Lincoln might make an ideal candidate for President. His efforts being unsuccessful, Jonas followed Lincoln in supporting John C. Frémont. Four years later, when Lincoln engaged in the historic series of debates with Stephen A. Douglas, Jonas served as chairman of the Republican committee of arrangements.

From 1849 to 1852, the well-connected Jonas served as postmaster of Quincy by appointment of Presidents Zachary Taylor and Millard Fillmore. When Lincoln became President in 1861, Jonas was reappointed to the post.

Meanwhile, young Benjamin Franklin Jonas, having received his primary and secondary education in Quincy, set out on his own. In 1853, he moved to New Orleans, where he entered the law department of the University of Louisiana. Jonas graduated two years later as valedictorian of his class. Following his admission to the bar, Jonas went into partnership with Henry Hyams, a cousin of the newly elected junior Senator from Louisiana, Judah Phillip Benjamin (Hyams's mother and Benjamin's grandmother were sisters).

In 1859, the young lawyer married Josephine Block, who, like Benjamin Jonas's mother, was a Block of Virginia. Although one can surmise that Ben and Josephine were distant cousins, no incontrovertible evidence survives. The Jonases had two sons, one of whom became an officer in the United States Marine Corps and saw service in Cuba during the Spanish-American War.

In 1862, Benjamin Jonas enlisted in the Confederate Army, spending the next three years as adjutant to General John Bell Hood (1831–1879) in the Army of Tennessee. Four of Abraham Jonas's five sons fought for the Confederacy. The one exception was the eldest Jonas brother, Edward, who attained the rank of major in the Union Army. Brother Samuel gained fleeting fame as author of the poem "Written on the Back of a Confederate Note." The fact that four of Abraham Jonas's five sons fought with "the enemy" did nothing to dampen Lincoln's ardor for his old friend or his family. He permitted Abe Jonas to keep his position as Quincy postmaster throughout the war; whenever Lincoln met someone from New Orleans, he would inquire about the well-being of young Ben.

Lincoln's personal affection for Abraham Jonas was put to the test in June 1864, when Louisa Jonas sent the President an urgent telegram. Informing the President that his old friend lay dying, Mrs. Jonas pleaded with Lincoln to extend a pardon for their son Charles (at that point, a prisoner-of-war on Johnson's Island in Lake Erie) so that he could return home to see his father one last time. Lincoln immediately issued a three-week parole to Charles, who arrived in Quincy on the day of his father's death. Following Abraham Jonas's death, Lincoln appointed Louisa postmistress of Quincy.

After the war, Benjamin Franklin Jonas returned to New Orleans, where he resumed the practice of law and was elected to the state legislature in 1865. In 1868, he was chosen delegate-at-large to the Democratic national convention held in New York City and chairman of the Louisiana delegation. As chairman, he cast his delegation's vote for Winfield Scott Hancock. Jonas was elected a state senator in 1872. From 1875 to 1879, he served simultaneously as a state legislator and as city attorney of New Orleans.

In 1879, Benjamin Jonas was elected as a Democrat to the United States Senate—the first Jew to serve in that body since the resignation of Judah P. Benjamin some eighteen years earlier. During his six years in the Senate, Jonas was the chamber's only Jew. From 1881 to 1883, he served as chairman of the Senate Committee on Interior and Insular Affairs. Following his defeat in 1884, Jonas returned to New Orleans, where he resumed the practice of law and was named Collector of the Port of New Orleans.

Benjamin Franklin Jonas died in New Orleans on December 21, 1911, and was buried at the Dispersed of Judah cemetery.

References

American Jewish Year Book, vol. 6 (1904–05), p. 126.

David Max Einhorn, *Joys of Jewish Folklore* (New York: Jonathan David, 1981), pp. 318–319.

Bertram Korn, *American Jewry and the Civil War* (Philadelphia: Jewish Publication Society, 1961), pp. 189–194.

Encyclopaedia Judaica (1972), vol. 10, col. 181.

Jewish Encyclopedia.

National Cyclopedia of American Biography, vol. 4, p. 544.

New York Times, December 22, 1911, 13:5.

Publications of the American Jewish Historical Society 17 (1909): 123 ff.

Universal Jewish Encyclopedia.

Who's Who in America, vol. 1.

KAHN, FLORENCE PRAG (1866–1948):
Republican from California; served five terms in the House (Sixty-ninth through Seventy-third Congress; March 4, 1925–January 3, 1937).

One day during a heated debate in the House, an exasperated Representative *Fiorello La Guardia* accused California Congresswoman Florence Prag Kahn of being "nothing but a standpatter, following that reactionary, Senator George H. Moses of New Hampshire." Mrs. Kahn is reported to have wriggled loose from her chair, jammed her nondescript hat down over her nose, and bellowed: "Why shouldn't I choose Moses as my leader? Haven't my people been following him for ages?" The House erupted into gales of laughter, La Guardia included.

On another occasion, a reporter asked the rather old-maidish Kahn how she managed to get more votes for her pet projects than anyone else in the House of Representatives. Without missing a beat, Kahn replied "Why it's my sex appeal, don't you know?" It was quips like these that made Representative Kahn one of the most beloved figures on Capitol Hill.

Florence Prag Kahn was born in Salt Lake City on November 9, 1866. Her parents, Conrad and Mary (Goldsmith) Prag, Polish immigrants, had been early settlers in California, but moved to Utah several years before their daughter's birth. Suffering severe financial reverses, the family returned to California in 1866, establishing a home in San Francisco. Somewhat uniquely for that time, Mary Prag became the principal breadwinner in the family as head of the history department at San Francisco's Girls' High School. An early advocate of pensions for schoolteachers, she eventually wound up serving several terms on the San Francisco Board of Education.

Florence Prag was educated in the public schools of San Francisco, and upon graduation from high school (at age fourteen), made application to the University of California, an institution that in 1883 admitted few girls. While taking the entrance exam, she was baffled by a question that referred to Sir Francis Bacon; his name was totally unknown to her. "Rather than leave the query unanswered, she wrote, 'The tenets of my faith prohibit me from knowing anything about bacon.' The faculty board agreed that a youngster with that much aplomb could do college work." Florence was admitted, and wound up graduating from Berkeley at age nineteen in 1888.

Florence Prag set her sights on attending law school, but the family's straitened financial circumstances (her father had died) made this dream impossible. Instead, following in her mother's footsteps, she became a teacher, specializing in history and English.

On March 19, 1899, Florence Prag married newly elected Congressman *Julius Kahn* at San Francisco's Temple Emanuel, and moved with him to Washington, where she would live for the next forty years. The Kahns had two sons: Julius, Jr., and Conrad Prag. Florence Kahn took an active interest in her husband's congressional career, eventually becoming his unpaid secretary and campaign manager.

Upon Julius Kahn's death in December, 1924, his widow decided to run for his now-vacant seat. She was elected to the Sixty-ninth Congress on February 17, 1925 and seated on March 4. She would be reelected to five consecutive Congresses, until she lost her seat in the Roosevelt landslide of 1936.

Upon entering the House, Florence Prag Kahn was appointed to the Committee on Indian Affairs. Breaking with congressional tradition, she refused the assignment, loudly proclaiming: "The only Indians in my district are in front of cigar stores, and I can't do anything for them!" She also served three years on other relatively minor committees: Census; Education; Coinage, Weights and Measures. Like her late husband, she was both a conservative Republican and an ardent supporter of military preparedness. ("Preparedness never caused a war, unpreparedness never prevented one.") At the beginning of the Seventy-first Congress (1929), she was finally appointed to Military Affairs, the committee her husband had chaired. She also became the first woman on the House Appropriations Committee.

A fiscal conservative, Florence Kahn nonetheless supported federal funding for highway construction, flood control, and the development of radio and aviation. She staunchly supported a whole host of anticrime measures, including the Lindbergh Law (which made kidnapping a federal crime punishable by death) and increased funding for the FBI. For this latter effort, FBI Director J. Edgar Hoover honored her with the nickname "mother of the FBI." Hoover must have meant it; in posthumous respect, he served as an honorary pallbearer at her funeral in 1948. Pilloried in the press for "laying the foundation for a national police force and taking the first step toward dictatorship," the acid-tongued Prag responded: "Ridiculous, I'm speaking for the nation's mothers who demand protection for their children."

An ardent "wet," Kahn railed against the Volstead Act, proclaiming it to be "unenforce-able" and "a complete failure." She was also dead-set against all efforts to impose censorship on the movie industry. Accused by a group of women of having been influenced on a movie-censorship bill by a young, handsome motion picture executive, she declared: "Of course I have been. Look at him and tell me if I'm to blame!" One of Florence Prag Kahn's proudest achievements was passing the legislation which secured funding for the San Francisco Bay Bridge connecting San Francisco and Alameda County.

The people of San Francisco adored Florence Kahn. In 1932, the year Roosevelt was swept into the White House, she rolled up a plurality of some 55,000 votes. There was speculation in the press that she might run for the United States Senate. "No use kidding myself," Kahn was quoted as saying, "I couldn't make it." In the 1934 off-year elections, Kahn was held to a mere 3,620-vote plurality against Chauncey Tramutolo, a perennial Democratic candidate. The writing was on the wall; her days in Congress were numbered. Running for a seventh term in the election of 1936, she was defeated by newspaperman Frank R. Havenner, who ran on both the Democrat and Progressive tickets. Upon losing her seat, Kahn returned to San Francisco, where she moved into her final home, the Huntington Hotel.

Like her husband an active member of Temple Emanuel, Florence Prag Kahn supported the programs of Judaism's Reform movement. A wit until the very end, Kahn told the reporter who came for what would be her last interview, "I know why you're here. You want to do my obituary." She died at the Huntington Hotel on November 16, 1948, and was buried next to her husband at the Home of Peace Cemetery in Colma, California.

References

American Jewish Year Book, vol. 44, p. 413; vol. 47, p. 629; vol. 51, p. 522.

Biographical Directory of American Jews.

Hope Chamberlin, *A Minority of Members: Women in the U.S. Congress* (New York: Praeger, 1973), pp. 48–52.

Dictionary of American Biography, vol. 4.

Encyclopaedia Judaica (1972), vol. 5, col. 57; vol. 10, col. 689.

Duff Gilfond, "Gentlewoman in the House," *American Mercury*, October 1929.

New York Times, November 17, 1948, 27:5.

Who's Who in America, vol. 2.

Who's Who in American Jewry, 1926, 1928, 1938.

KAHN, JULIUS (1861–1924): *Republican from California; served twelve terms in the House (Fifty-sixth and Fifty-seventh Congress; March 4, 1899–March 3, 1903; Fifty-ninth through Sixty-eighth Congress; March 4, 1905–December 18, 1924).*

California has long been noted for electing and sending celebrities—actors, singers, and entertainers—to Washington: Will Rogers, Jr., Helen Gahagan Douglas, George Murphy, Ronald Reagan, Sonny Bono. The list would be incomplete without Julius Kahn, the very first actor ever elected to Congress. San Francisco Representative Kahn, who spent nearly twenty-five of his sixty-three years in Congress, had a successful career on stage in which he toured and performed with the likes of Edwin Booth, Joseph Jefferson, and the great Italian tragedian, Tomasso Salvini.

Julius Kahn was born in Kuppenheim, Grand Duchy of Baden, on February 28, 1861, the son of Herman and Jeannette (Weil) Kahn. His parents emigrated to America when he was five, settling first in Calaveras County, California, and shortly thereafter in San Francisco, where Herman became a baker. Shortly after his bar mitzvah, Julius left public school to drive his father's delivery wagon. This marked the end of his formal education. By age sixteen, he was actively engaged in theater—a career that would last for more than a decade. By all indications, Kahn was a more than competent actor and must have had a broad range, considering that among the luminaries with whom he performed, Joseph Jefferson was best-known for comedy, while Booth and Salvini were world-class tragedians. His last role was that of Baron Stein in *Diplomacy*, an English adaptation of Victorien Sardou's *Dora*.

While still on the stage, Kahn started looking about for a more "suitable" profession. He decided to become an attorney; in the mid-1880s, he began reading law in the San Francisco offices of Foote & Coogan. In 1892, while still reading with Coogan, Kahn was elected to a single term in the California State Assembly. Declining nomination to the State Senate in 1894, he studied for, and passed, the California Bar, and went to work for his mentors. Kahn practiced law until 1898, at which time he was elected as a Republican to serve in the Fifty-sixth Congress. Shortly before taking his seat, he married

Florence Prag, a San Francisco schoolteacher. The Kahns had two sons, Julius Jr., and Conrad.

Julius Kahn was one of the lower chamber's "flashiest" speakers, described by one contemporary writer as "a picturesque figure, being a forceful speaker, employing many mannerisms which he had acquired in his theatrical career." Kahn was reelected to the Fifty-seventh Congress in 1900, but lost his seat in the election of 1902. Returned to his seat by the voters of San Francisco in 1904, he would go on to be reelected eleven more times. At the time of his death in December 1924, Julius Kahn had reached a unique plateau in the history of Congress: of the 4,080 Congressman who served in the House between 1788 and 1924, only four big-city Representatives had won more than ten terms—Theodore Burton of Cleveland, Nicholas Longworth of Cincinnati, Martin E. Madden of Chicago, and Julius Kahn. In fact, in the lower chamber's first 136 years, only seven members had longer tenures than Kahn.

Kahn's forte was military and defense issues. He was appointed a member of the Committee on Military Affairs in 1905, and remained with it for the next twenty years. Twice serving as chairman (Sixty-sixth and Sixty-seventh Congresses, 1919–23), he was the ranking minority member in the years immediately preceding and during the First World War. It was from this position that he played a pivotal role in America's defense posture.

Long an advocate of military preparedness, he helped organize the National Defense League in 1913, and later became its chairman. The NDL was, in the words of historian Page Smith, "a highly conservative organization of businessmen and old guard politicians; [it] was the principal propagandist for preparedness."

Long convinced of the unpreparedness of the country, Kahn labored long and hard to impress the Committee on Military Affairs of the need to plan for any defense emergency that might arise. In 1916, Congress passed Kahn's National Defense Act, by which a skeletal defense organization was outlined.

When America entered the Great War (as World War I was known until the advent of World War II), President Wilson's defense proposals fell on deaf ears among his Democrat colleagues. When Military Affairs chairman Stanley H. Dent, Jr., of Alabama, a pacifist, declined (along with other Democrat panel members) to support the President's military policy, most notably the Selective Draft Act, it fell to the Republican Kahn to pick up the cudgels. Kahn was given the lion's share of the credit for getting the House to pass the Selective Draft Act of 1917 and the Army Emergency Increase Act of August 1918. He was also the father of the National Defense Act of 1920, which reorganized the American military establishment. As Congress's strongest proponent of universal military training, he proposed that every young man serve six months in military training, whether in time of war or peace.

Interestingly, Julius Kahn was perhaps the first proponent of campaign finance reform. He was the first member of Congress to call for a law compelling publication of campaign contributions and expenditures in both primary and general elections. The law was enacted shortly after the end of World War I.

Julius Kahn was reelected to Congress in November 1924, but died before the new session began. He was replaced by his widow Florence, who would continue to hold the seat for another dozen years. At his death, the *Washington Post*, in an article entitled "A Useful Immigrant," stated: "When the history of American participation in the World War comes to be fully written, the name of Rep. Julius Kahn . . . will have a conspicuous place." Wilson's Secretary of War, Newton D. Baker, in a letter to historian Harry Schneiderman, wrote: "There was no member of either House of Congress upon whom, as Secretary of War, I relied with more confidence than Mr. Kahn. His services to the country, as Chairman of the Military Affairs Committee of the House of Representatives, were conspicuous even at a time when everybody was giving all he had, and many were in a position which attracted attention to their work."

Kahn, an out-spoken anti-Zionist, was long a member of San Francisco's oldest and largest Reform synagogue, Temple Emanuel. Along with the congregation's rabbi, Jacob Voorsanger, Kahn helped establish the Jewish Educational Society of San Francisco, the first of its kind on the Pacific coast. In 1919, he was appointed a member of a commission of the Union of American Hebrew Congregations charged with lobbying the new League of Nations to include a "clause of universal religious liberty" in its charter.

Julius Kahn died on December 18, 1924, just two months before his sixty-third birthday. He was buried in the Home of Peace Cemetery in Colma, California.

References

American Jewish Year Book, vol. 2 (1900–01), p. 519; vol. 6 (1904–5), p. 127, vol. 11 (1909–10), p. 144, vol. 24 (1922–23), p. 160; vol. 27 (1925), p. 151; vol. 28 (1926), pp. 238–245.

Dictionary of American Biography.

Encyclopaedia Judaica (1972), vol. 10, col. 689.

New York Times, December 22, 1924, 17:3.

Universal Jewish Encyclopedia.

Washington Post, December 19, 1924, p. 14.

Who's Who in America.

KAUFMAN, DAVID SPANGLER (1813–1851):
Democrat from Texas; served three terms in the House (Twenty-ninth through Thirty-first Congress; March 30, 1846–January 31, 1851).

David S. Kaufman's Jewish lineage is somewhat suspicious. Nonetheless, he is included as a member of the Congressional Minyan; at least three early sources, including the *American Jewish Yearbook* of 1901–1902, refer to him as being "of Hebrew extraction." Additionally, he is prominently mentioned in Natalie Ornish's fine work *Pioneer Jewish Texans*. This certainly suggests that Kaufman deserves a spot on the Minyanaire roster.

David Kaufman was born in Boiling Springs, Pennsylvania, on December 13, 1813. Nothing is known about his family. Kaufman received a classical education at Princeton College, from which he graduated at age sixteen, in 1829. In 1978, an archivist looking through Kaufman's old college file found a pencil notation reading "of Hebrew extraction."

Following his graduation, Kaufman moved to Natchez, Mississippi, where he read law in the offices of General John A. Quitman. His mentor, a man of great accomplishments, had variously been a state legislator, a "heavy contributor" to Texas' independence, a Mexican War general, and governor of Mississippi. David Kaufman was admitted to the bar in 1835. Moving on, he practiced law in Natchitoches, Louisiana, for two years, then resettled in Nacogdoches, Texas. Within a year of his arrival in the Texas Republic, he was elected to its Congress.

It is likely that Kaufman was one of the most highly educated members of the Texas legislature—let alone in the entire Republic. As such, he quickly became Speaker, a position he held for the next five years. Kaufman owed his initial prominence to his oratorical skill. One writer of the time described him as being "a pleasing and forcible speaker" who "was much in demand." His heavy speaking schedule "included addresses at colleges, at Masonic lodges . . . and a graduation address at Princeton University." As Natalie Ornish observed: "Kaufman directed his oratory chiefly to three targets: speeches for the annexation of Texas to the United States, speeches explaining the causes of the Mexican War, and speeches in defense of Texas retaining all of its claimed territory."

In 1839, David Kaufman, holding the rank of major, fought in the Battle of the Neches as an aide to General Kelsey H. Douglass. During a skirmish against a Cherokee band, he was wounded in the face. Returning from the war, Kaufman resumed both his legal practice and his political career. He became a close personal friend of Sam Houston, with whom he vied for the hand of one Anna Raguet, "the belle of Nacogdoches." "The Major" eventually married Jane B. Richardson of Sabinetown, where he had moved to establish the law firm of Kaufman and Gould. The Kaufmans had four children: David Spangler, Jr., Sam Houston, Daniel, and Anna.

In 1843, the citizens of Sabine County elected David Spangler Kaufman to the Texas Senate, where he was assigned to the Committee on Foreign Relations and soon became its chairman, "a position in the Republic second only to the president." Kaufman presented a report to the Senate in favor of annexation to the United States and actively lobbied for the resolution's adoption. On March 1, 1845, Congress passed a joint resolution calling for Texas to be annexed as the twenty-eighth state. The annexation would take effect only after "certain conditions stipulated in the joint resolution" were met. The last President of Texas, Anson Jones, sent Kaufman to Washington as chargé d'affaires of Texas to the United States, but his credentials were not officially received because the federal government had already adopted the bill for annexation.

Upon Texas's formal admission to the union, David Kaufman became the Lone Star State's first-ever member of the United States House of Representatives. His district—actually more like a territory—encompassed "all of Texas east of the Trinity River," where the vast majority of the population then resided. The main issue facing Texas in the House of Representatives dealt with a territorial dispute with the United States. As the former chairman of the Foreign Relations Committee of the Texas Senate, Kaufman had an immediate and forceful impact on the delicate negotiations. Through careful, painstaking research, Kaufman helped define which of the lands in question legally belonged to the newly formed state. The present-day map of Texas owes its shape and dimensions to David Spangler Kaufman.

Kaufman was reelected twice, in 1848 and 1850. He must have impressed his congressional colleagues, for they appointed him chairman of the House Rules Committee at the beginning of the Thirty-first Congress. Kaufman looked like he was set for a brilliant career in Washington. Unfortunately, he died unexpectedly on January 31, 1851, at the tender age of thirty-eight. His death came on the heels of his greatest political victory: the compromise that ceded tens of thousands of square miles to the Lone Star State. Kaufman's funeral service took place in the House chamber on February 3, 1851. In attendance were President Millard Fillmore, both Houses of Congress, members of the Supreme Court, and General Winfield Scott. Kaufman's burial took place in the Congressional Cemetery in Washington, D.C. In 1932, Kaufman was reinterred in the State Cemetery in Austin, Texas.

The year after David Kaufman's death, his widow, Jane, died quite suddenly, leaving four orphaned children. Shortly after her death, little Sam Houston Kaufman perished. Daughter Anna, the eldest of the four Kaufman children, was raised, along with her brothers Daniel and David, Jr., by their aunt and uncle, Eliza (Richardson) and Franklin Sexton. Daniel Kaufman eventually changed his name to Richardson "so he could inherit from his grandfather, Daniel Long Richardson." After his grandfather Richardson's demise, Daniel changed his name back to Kaufman. David Spangler Kaufman, Jr., died while still in his teens.

Today, nearly a century-and-a-half after his death, the name and memory of David Kaufman, Sr., survive by means of a county and town near Dallas named in his honor when he was but thirty-four. The main thoroughfare in Rockwall, Texas, is Kaufman Street. One can also find his portrait at the Sam Houston Museum in Huntsville, Texas.

References
American Jewish Year Book, vol. 2 (1900–01), p. 519.

Biographical Directory of the United States Congress, 1774–1989, p. 1288.

National Cyclopedia of American Biography, vol. 37, p. 389.

Natalie Ornish, *Pioneer Jewish Texans: Their Impact on Texas and American History* (Dallas: Texas Heritage Press, 1990), pp. 67–71.

KLEIN, ARTHUR GEORGE (1904–1968):
Democrat from New York; served six terms in the House (Seventy-seventh and Seventy-eighth Congress; July 29, 1941–January 3, 1945; Seventy-ninth through Eighty-third Congress; February 19, 1946–December 31, 1956).

In 1925, Arthur G. Klein, the Orthodox son of Orthodox Jewish parents, spent a brief stint as a Roman Catholic priest. A struggling student at New York University School of Law, Klein landed a bit part playing the priest in famed director Max Reinhardt's production of *The Miracle*. Years later, Klein would recall that he was paid the princely sum of $2 a performance—"pretty good [money] in those days." In 1926, forsaking his clerical collar, Klein graduated, was awarded his LL.B, and never looked back. Although his days as a thespian were over, his connection to show business was not. In later years, he would deal with both director Otto Preminger and the notorious novel *Fanny Hill*.

Arthur George Klein was born on New York's Lower East Side on August 8, 1904, one of Louis and Gussie (Greenfield) Klein's eight children. His parents, Hungarian immigrants, were, as mentioned above, strictly Orthodox. Their son Arthur remained an observant Jew throughout his life. Joseph Friedman, who served as Klein's law clerk in the 1950s, recalled a weekly ritual: As dusk approached each Friday evening, Judge Klein would look at his watch. "I'm Orthodox too," Friedman would say. "A few minutes later, with the time for Sabbath even closer, the judge would say to his young clerk: 'What are you doing here so late? Go to shul. I've got enough sins of my own to account for.'"

In 1927, following an education at both the Washington Square College of New York University and NYU Law School, Klein was admitted to the bar. Following a path blazed by numerous young lawyers before him, Arthur Klein quickly became involved with Tammany Hall as a member of the St. Mark's clubhouse. While practicing law throughout the late 1920s and early 1930s, Klein rose to the rank of district captain. His involvement with St. Mark's not only gave a boost to his political ambitions; it provided him with a wife. In February 1934, Arthur Klein married Mary Goldenkranz, who was also a member of the local Tammany clubhouse. Together they had two daughters: Susan (Mrs. Harold) Wilson and Nanci (Mrs. Elliot) Staple.

As Klein practiced law and rose through the ranks of Tammany, he maintained an involvement in the Jewish community as a member of the West End Temple and serving for many years on the board of the Orthodox Yeshivat Ohel Torah. Shortly after his marriage, Klein went to work for the newly created Securities and Exchange Commission, dividing his time between New York City and Washington. After a six-year stint with the SEC (1935–41), Klein returned full-time to New York, where he announced his candidacy for the Nineteenth District congressional seat vacated by the sudden death of *M. Michael Edelstein*. In turn, Edelstein had won the seat following the untimely death of Representative *William I. Sirovich*, who, ironically, like Klein, had also been involved in theater in the mid-1920s. With heavy backing from Tammany Hall, Klein won the special election, taking his seat in the Seventy-seventh Congress on July 29, 1941.

Klein was easily reelected in 1943 to the Seventy-eighth Congress, and looked like he was on the road to a long congressional career. Suddenly and unexpectedly, he announced in the summer of 1944 that he would be leaving Congress in order to return to the private practice of law. Before he could return to New York City and hang up his shingle, Representative *Samuel Dickstein* was appointed to the New York Supreme Court, thereby leaving an open seat. For reasons not known, Klein permitted himself to be talked into running for Dickstein's seat. He was elected, and returned to Capitol Hill at the beginning of the Seventy-ninth Congress. All told, Klein's "retirement" from the House lasted less than a single year.

Arthur Klein was reelected from the Nineteenth Congressional District five more times, and served until December 31, 1956. During his nearly fourteen years in Congress, he was known as a machine politician—one who carefully saw to the needs of his constituents. Tiring of life in Washington and desirous of returning to the New York scene, Arthur G. Klein resigned his congressional seat effective December 31, 1956, so that he could run for the New York State Supreme Court. Again backed by the Tammany machine, Klein won his judicial post, being sworn in on January 1, 1957.

In his nine years on the Supreme Court, Klein threw out the New York State ban on the sale of the bawdy novel *Fanny Hill*. In his decision, he ruled that *Fanny Hill* was not obscene, and thus any ban on it was unconstitutional. Klein's ruling began with the words: "While the saga of Fanny Hill will never replace Little Red Riding Hood as a bedtime story . . ." New York State appealed Klein's decision, and the case went all the way up to the United States Supreme Court, which refused to reverse Klein's judgment. The sale of *Fanny Hill* was once again declared legal.

In another well-publicized case, Judge Klein ruled against movie director Otto Preminger. Associated with some of Hollywood's best-known pictures in the 1950s and 1960s, Preminger sued a television network, claiming that it had ruined a nationwide showing of his *Anatomy of a Murder* by inserting far too many commercial breaks. Klein found little merit in Preminger's charge, and ruled against the temperamental director.

Arthur Klein, who for years lived at 47 East 88th Street, remained on the New York Supreme Court until his death on February 20, 1968. He was survived by his wife Mary, his two daughters, his brother Harold, and four sisters: Stella Lipowitz, Lee Jackson, Rae Kohn, and Charlotte Hayman. He left an estate of about $10,000 to his wife. Arthur G. Klein was buried in Mount Moriah Cemetery in Fairview, New Jersey.

References

American Jewish Year Book, vol. 37, p. 629; vol. 50, p. 643; vol. 70, p. 522.

Jewish Telegraphic Agency, "Daily News Bulletin," February 23, 1968.

New York Times, February 22, 1968, 31:1.

KLEIN, HERB (1930–): *Democrat from New Jersey; served one term in the House (One Hundred and Third Congress; January 3, 1993–January 3, 1995).*

A highly successful Harvard-trained trial lawyer, Herb Klein served but a single term in Congress. And yet, in that brief time, he played a crucial role in one of the One Hundred and Third Congress's most critical, complex, and contentious pieces of legislation: the bill that provided funding for the Resolution Trust Corporation (RTC). Created as a result of the savings and loan debacle of the late 1980s, the RTC was given a broad mandate to both oversee and liquidate the various properties left in financial limbo. The RTC was not without its detractors; its most severe critics saw it as a sinecure at best, a boondoggle at worst. Herb Klein was both author and point man on a tricky amendment that eventually cut RTC funding by nearly $7 billion. In order to get his amendment from the House hopper to the Oval Office, Klein had to jump through innumerable political hoops. That House Banking chair Henry Gonzales (Democrat from Texas) and Financial Institutions Subcommittee chair Steve Neal (Democrat from North Carolina) entrusted the legislation to a freshman says a great deal about Herb Klein's intelligence, pertinacity, and political acumen.

Herb Klein was born on June 24, 1930 in Newark, New Jersey, where his father, Alfred, was an accountant. Alfred Klein's father was an immigrant from Hungary. Herb's mother, Fae (Sackin) Klein, merely said that she was "from Russia." In the summer of 1997, Herb and his wife, Jackie, traveled to Hungary in order to search out the Klein family's roots. "My parents were really rather closemouthed about family history and background," Klein related in a January 1998 interview. "My father's family was almost divorced from religion." Through a cousin, the Kleins wound up in a Hungarian village called Oijuhuta, which they believe is the place from which grandfather Klein emigrated. In 1996, Herb and Jackie's son Roger, a law school professor, was a visiting scholar at a university in Minsk, Russia. While there, he learned that his grandmother (Herb's mother) Fae had likely come from somewhere within 60 miles of Minsk, in present-day Belarus.

Herb and his younger sister Ann (Richmond) were raised near Paterson, in northeastern New Jersey. Paterson, as one writer noted years ago, "is one of the few American cities that have turned out exactly as they were planned." In this case, the planner was Alexander Hamilton, who, about the time George Washington became President, journeyed some 20 miles from Manhattan into the New Jersey interior, to the Great Falls of the Passaic River. "Watching the water surge down 72 feet—the highest falls along the East Coast—he predicted that an industrial city would rise at this place." In short order: Hamilton formed the Society for Establishing Useful Manufactures; opened a calico factory in 1794; convinced Pierre L'Enfant, the architect who planned Washington, D.C., to plan Paterson, which he named after then-Governor Paterson.

By the mid-1830s Paterson was the home of Colt Firearms; in 1837, the first locomotive, the "Sandusky," was built there. Paterson ultimately became known as America's Silk City, employing upwards of 25,000 silk mill workers prior to the great strike of 1913. Paterson was a magnet for attracting immigrants from England, Ireland, Italy, Hungary, and Eastern Europe. By the time of Herb Klein's birth in 1930, the Paterson area was home to more than 25,000 Jews.

Herb attended public schools, and received a basic Jewish education at an Orthodox Hebrew school in nearby Hillside. "I guess you would say we were Conservative, although the school was housed in an Orthodox synagogue," he remarked in 1998. "Actually, I didn't really become interested in religion until I was an adult. By that time, I became far more involved than my parents or my upbringing would ever have suggested." As a high school student, Klein joined the debate team and became active in student politics. Herb Klein attended Rutgers University in New Brunswick, receiving a B.A. in 1950. From there, he went to Harvard Law School, where he helped pay his tuition by spending summers selling Fuller Brushes. Klein received his J.D. from Harvard in 1953, and promptly entered the United States Air Force. Originally assigned to Wright Air Force Base in Dayton, Ohio, Klein wound up spending nearly three years working out of an Air Force office in downtown Los Angeles.

Upon his discharge from service in 1956, he went back to New Jersey and began practicing as a trial lawyer. While building his practice (he was originally a sole practitioner), he also earned a master of laws degree from New York University. Herb Klein practiced law for more than thirty years. By the time he was elected to Congress in 1992, the former sole practitioner had headed a firm with more than twenty attorneys.

By this point, Klein had married Jacqueline Krieger, a New Jersey girl educated at the exclusive Wellsley Women's College in Massachusetts. Jackie Klein is an accountant and has an M.B.A. from Fairleigh Dickinson University. The Kleins had two children: Cynthia, who died of a sudden heart attack at age twenty-six in 1991, and son Ronald, who teaches securities and environmental law at the Hastings School of Law in San Francisco. The Kleins, who live in Clifton, New Jersey, belong to two Conservative synagogues: Temple Emanu-el in Passaic, and the Clifton Jewish Center.

Herb Klein was initially drawn to politics "after studying about the career of Harry S. Truman at Rutgers University." Imbued with the Democratic ideals of Roosevelt and Truman, Klein was a volunteer in Adlai E. Stevenson's 1952 presidential campaign. In 1969, by now a wealthy attorney with an array of communal experiences, Klein ran a losing campaign for county freeholder. Two years later, he defeated an incumbent Republican for a seat in the New Jersey Assembly. An enthusiastic (and generous) supporter of New Jersey Governor Brendan Byrne, Klein was rewarded for his loyalty by being named assistant majority leader in his second (and last) term in the Assembly. While in the Assembly, Herb Klein authored legislation that created the New Jersey Economic Development Authority, and pushed hard for Governor Byrne's state income tax. The latter effort proved to be his undoing; he was defeated for reelection in 1975.

Klein remained active in civic and political affairs, serving as president of the Jewish Federation of Clifton, Passaic and Vicinity, and raising prodigious sums for the Democratic Party. Jackie Klein became a political power in her own right, serving many years as a member of both the Passaic County Democratic Committee and the Democratic National Committee.

On September 4, 1969, Eighth District Representative *Charles S. Joelson* resigned his seat, upon being elected judge of the Superior Court of New Jersey. The special election called to fill the unexpired portion of Joelson's term was won by Democrat Robert A. Roe, the longtime commissioner of the New Jersey Department of Conservation and Economic Development. Roe, whom the *Almanac of American Politics* described as "a classic congressional type, the professional politician who is a lifelong bachelor and lives in a Washington hotel, staying up late at night studying bills and precedents," was reelected without difficulty eleven times. By the time of his retirement at the end of the One Hundred and Second Congress, he had chaired both the House Committee on Science, Space and Technology (1987–1990) and the Committee on Public Works and Transportation (1990–1992).

Roe's retirement, which came as a surprise, set off a maelstrom of political activity. Several well-known local politicos sought, unsuccessfully as it turned out, to get the nod as Roe's anointed successor. Despite the fact that he had been relegated to the political hinterlands for nearly fifteen years, and was by no means the party's first choice, Herb Klein managed to get Roe's endorsement. According to *Politics in America*: "The notion of Roe passing the congressional mantle to Klein was a powerful symbol, particularly with elderly residents in the district."

Klein, who lent nearly half of the $1,250,000 the campaign eventually cost, won a five-way Democratic primary with 39 percent of the vote. In the general election he faced Republican state senator Joseph L. Bubba. While Klein was out "campaign[ing] hard in Jewish communities such as Passaic, Montclair and his hometown of Clifton," Bubba was working the Italian voters of Totowa, Nutley, Belleville and Wayne. Hearkening back to Klein's days in the Assembly when he had been an enthusiastic supporter of a state tax, Bubba campaigned on a no-tax pledge. It was a sensible strategy; in 1992, New Jersey voters were "still seething" over Governor Jim Florio's massive 1990 tax increase.

For his part, Klein "retaliated with promises that he would work to create jobs in the desperately depressed region . . . [and] blamed GOP presidents for the nation's financial woes, mocking 'trickle down' theories and the savings and loan crises." He ran as an unabashed liberal, calling for "universal health care, abortion rights and stringent gun control." In the campaign's final days, Klein hit Bubba hard with a series of "tart-tongued" radio spots. In these political ads, Klein accused the Republican Bubba of having accepted $46,000 from a contractor convicted of bribing the Paterson mayor, although, as the editors of *Politics in America* note, "the contractor was convicted *after* Bubba received the money" (emphasis added). Klein also scored Bubba for "not paying overdue property taxes until he ran for Congress . . . and for taking $1,500 from a video gambling promoter charged with illegal kickbacks."

In turn, Bubba kept referring to Klein as "an out-of-touch millionaire." On election day, Herb Klein, running ahead of Bill Clinton, captured the Eighth District seat with 47 percent of the vote. Despite the fact that voters in the district had sent no one but Democrats (Joelson, Roe) to Congress for more than a generation, the Eighth was hardly a Democrat stronghold. From the day of his victory, Herb Klein was a marked man.

As a freshman member of the One Hundred and Third Congress, Herb Klein, like many others, lobbied for a seat on the House Appropriations Committee. Few if any freshmen are ever placed on that prestigious committee. Instead, Klein was seated, as mentioned above, on the House Banking, Finance and Urban Affairs Committee, and the Committee on Science, Space and Technology—the panel that his predecessor had chaired. From this latter position, Klein worked hard to keep one of his campaign promises: to "try to convert military and foreign aid dollars into domestic job programs."

As noted at the outset, Herb Klein's congressional career lasted but one session. Despite his success with the Resolution Trust Corporation legislation, he was beset by forces that were simply beyond his control. In the 1994 election, he faced Passaic County freeholder Bill Martini, nephew of longtime Passaic mayor Nicholas Martini. Once again, Klein was attacked for his support of former Governor Byrne's state income tax back in the seventies. Martini also hit Klein hard over his support for Clinton's budget and tax proposals—despite the fact that Klein had voted against them. Martini reasoned that Klein was "allowed" to vote against the measures by Democratic Party leaders "only after it was clear that it had enough votes to pass." Klein ran against the "Contract With America," also noting that while serving as a freeholder, Martini had voted to raise local taxes.

Despite outspending his opponent by a better than three-to-two margin ($1,116,614 to $851,781), Klein went down to defeat by less than 1,850 votes. In recapping the campaign, Klein said: "It was an anomaly. I don't think you can say that Martini has made it a Republican seat." Klein's words proved to be prophetic: in 1996, Bill Martini was defeated 51 percent to 48 percent by Paterson mayor Bill Pascrell, Jr., a moderate Democrat.

Since leaving Capitol Hill, Herb Klein has been practicing law back in New Jersey with Hannoch-Weissman, where he specializes in banking, government relations, and real estate litigation. Herb and Jackie Klein are inveterate travelers, who love both England and Israel. Never far from Jewish communal activities, Herb Klein was recently reappointed chair of the Initial Gifts Division of the Clifton-Passaic Jewish Federation.

References

Interview with Herb Klein, January 1998.
Almanac of American Politics (1992-98 editions).
Politics in America (1994 edition).

KOCH, EDWARD IRVING (1924–): *Democrat from New York; served five terms in the House (Ninety-first through Ninety-fifth Congress; January 3, 1969–December 31, 1977).*

Of the 179 members of the Congressional Minyan, there are 124 attorneys, three physicians, two Rhodes Scholars, a handful of journalists, professors, industrialists, and stockbrokers, and even a former tragedian. Only one minyanaire, however, can lay claim to having:

- Hosted *Saturday Night Live.*
- Acted in a daytime soap opera.
- Played himself in both a *Muppet* movie and a Woody Allen film.
- Served as commercial pitchman for Ultra Slim Fast, the *New York Post*, and Coca-Cola.
- Written movie reviews for a local magazine.
- Hosted a popular talk-radio program.
- Served as "judge" on the nationally syndicated television program *The People's Court.*
- Co-authored murder mystery novels using himself as the crime-solving sleuth.

That minyanaire is New York's self-proclaimed "most popular, most controversial and oft-quoted" former mayor, Edward I. Koch. Ironically, there is little in Koch's background to suggest that one day he would grow up to be one of twentieth-century America's most flamboyant and ego-driven politicians.

Edward Irving Koch's parents, Louis Koch and Yetta (Joyce) Silpe, arrived in New York as teenaged Polish immigrants around the year 1910. Louis, who traveled alone from the village of Uscieszko in the Polish Ukraine, had, according to his own account, suffered greatly as a child. In his earliest years, he worked alongside his father as a peddler, moving from village to village. As such, he received little, if any, schooling. Upon arriving in America, he became a pants presser.

Like Louis Koch, Yetta Silpe came to America and entered the garment industry; she put herself through design school, becoming a blouse designer. Unlike Louis, however, she made a conscious effort to eradicate as much of her Polish roots as possible. Upon marrying in 1920, Yetta changed her name to Joyce, feeling that it was much more American-sounding. At one point, she even hired a tutor at 25 cents an hour to help her eliminate her Polish accent. Unlike Louis, she eventually lost her accent and learned to read English—after a fashion. The one problem was that she hired a man who could only write English phonetically. Until the end of her life, Joyce wrote English phonetically. Louis never learned to write at all.

From the beginning, it was apparent that Louis and Joyce were mismatched. About the only thing they had in common was their Polish background. "My mother was the smarter of the two by far; my father was the nicer of the two by far," Koch would note in one of his many autobiographies. Soon after their marriage, Louis and Joyce moved to the Bronx, where their first child, Harold, was born. Their second son, named Edward Irving, was born in the Bronx on December 12, 1924. A third child, Paula (Pat), was born several years later.

Joyce's embrace of all things American did not extend to religion. "My parents would never be like the assimilated German Jews who looked down on us," Koch writes. "Neither of my parents was very religious . . . but being Jewish was something that was important to them. On balance, our household was run in the Conservative Jewish tradition." Until the beginning of World War II, Joyce kept a kosher home. "Outside the home," Koch remembers, "my father was semi-kosher." *Kashrut* was more than a basic tenet of Judaism in the Koch household; it was also a weapon. Whenever Joyce was "very upset at her husband," she would cook bacon and "wave the pan under his nose." Of this particular form of torture, Koch humorously writes: "I don't know if she even liked bacon that much. I think she brought home the bacon simply for the chance to torture Papa, although she did keep a separate frying pan for it."

During Ed Koch's earliest years, his father experienced a modicum of prosperity as a furrier. With the onset of the Depression, his business failed. The family moved to Newark, New Jersey, where they rented two rooms from Bernard Koch, Louis's brother. For one year, nine people shared two bedrooms. The Kochs went to work for Joyce's brother Louis—the oldest and most successful of the Silpes. Louis Silpe leased and operated a prosperous catering hall in Krueger's Auditorium on Belmont Avenue in Newark's South Ward. There, Louis Silpe's wife Mary oversaw the preparation of kosher food for bar mitzvahs and weddings. The hall also had a hat-check concession, which Louis Silpe sold to the Koch family. On weekends, when big bands and such notables as Molly Picon would perform, Louis, Joyce, and the children were hard at work, begging nickel and dime tips from their customers. Edward Koch remembers how demeaned his parents felt.

Within a year of their arrival in Newark, Louis moved his family out of his brother's crowded flat into an apartment of his own about a half-mile away. In December 1937, Ed Koch became bar mitzvah at "synagogue B'nai Jeshrum" [sic] in Newark. The only thing Koch remembered about that day was his father hitting him that morning: "he was afraid that we'd be late."

In 1938, Ed Koch entered South Side High School, where most of his classmates remembered him only as "a face in the class, not as a person." A handful remembered Koch for being one of the few boys to register for a cooking class. Koch describes himself in these years as being "an egghead, a square, a loner and very bright." Beside his picture in the high school yearbook was the notation "Strong in will to find, to strive, to seek, and not to yield." Following his graduation in 1941, Joyce Koch moved her family to Ocean Parkway in Brooklyn, where their residence qualified her second son for a free education at City College. Even at age sixteen, Ed Koch knew he wanted to become a lawyer—"the Jewish ethic," he called it.

Ed Koch's undergraduate education came to an abrupt end when he was drafted in March 1943. Following basic training in Spartanburg, South Carolina (where he earned the respect of the other trainees by losing a fist fight to a large anti-Semitic bully), Koch became a member of Company F, 2nd Battalion, of the 415th Infantry Regiment—the night-fighting Timberwolf Division. Shipped to Europe, Koch saw action in both Belgium and along the Siegfried Line. The company "scrounger," Koch was injured in a fall, and at war's end became a de-Nazification specialist assigned to the Army's European Civilian Affairs Division in Bavaria. Although his German was poor, Koch was given the job of "removing German public officials from their jobs and finding others to take their places." Sergeant Edward Koch was honorably dis-

charged with a combat infantry badge and two battle stars in April 1946.

Returning to his parents' home in Brooklyn, Koch entered an accelerated program at the New York University Law School without benefit of an undergraduate degree. An average student, he graduated from NYU Law School in two years, and passed the New York Bar on his second try, in 1949. Entering private practice, Koch eked out a living doing "small, run-of-the-mill matters—wills, minor negligence cases and the like." He continued living with his parents on Ocean Avenue until 1956, when he took a small flat in Greenwich Village.

Upon his arrival in the Village, Koch joined the Tamawa Club, the local clubhouse for Tammany Hall. Working days at his floundering legal practice, Koch would spend his lunch breaks and evenings standing on street corners, giving speeches on behalf of Democrat presidential candidate Adlai E. Stevenson. Koch joined a liberal reformist bloc within the Tamawa Club. The faction, which eventually broke away, named itself the Village Independent Democrats—VID.

In 1960, Joyce Koch died from cancer at age sixty-one. Throughout her final illness, her son ferried her from doctor to doctor, from treatment to treatment, never revealing to her the severity of her condition. After Joyce's death, Louis married Rose Klein and retired to Sunrise Florida, where he lived until his death in 1986. Following his mother's death, Ed Koch took off a year from politics in order to fulfill a fantasy. On March 13, 1961, he applied for a patent for something called the "Simulated Vehicle Toy," more familiarly known as the "Boxmobile." What he had "invented" was "nothing more than adhesive decals that could be placed on the front, sides, and rear of a cardboard box so that it would look like either a car or a locomotive." Patent no. 3,099,433 in hand, Koch put the Boxmobile into production. He then distributed some to friends and family, and placed them on sale in at least one Manhattan store. The idea bombed, and Koch returned to politics.

In 1962, Koch mounted a race for the State Assembly as the candidate of the VID. Koch's three main planks called for repealing state criminal laws against sodomy, relaxing prohibitions on abortions, and making it easier to get divorced. Behind his back, his campaign became known as the "SAD" campaign. Many members of the VID refused to work for Koch's candidacy. Of the major reform figures in New York City politics, only Eleanor Roosevelt backed him, most likely because she wanted to see Democrat boss Carmine DeSapio's candidate defeated. Despite Mrs. Roosevelt's endorsement, Koch lost. The following year, Koch, now the VID president (he won by forty-one votes), defeated the powerful DeSapio by thirty-nine votes to become the neighborhood's Democratic leader. DeSapio challenged the final tally, but Koch's victory stood.

In 1964, Ed Koch and a delegation from the VID went south to Alabama, where they joined a civil rights protest in Selma. Koch and several others spent eight days there, working with the Lawyers' Constitutional Committee, which was organizing attorneys to represent blacks who had been arrested. The atmosphere, Koch writes, was threatening: "I remember thinking to myself, 'here is a big [Koch stands 6'1"], obviously Jewish person, and they don't like Jews very much down here, arguing for these people.'"

Upon his return from Alabama, Koch was forced to run against DeSapio again for leader of the local Democratic establishment. Aided by a last-minute endorsement from Mayor Robert F. Wagner, Jr., Koch once again defeated DeSapio, this time by 164 votes.

In 1966, New York City experienced a political upheaval. With the election of Republican John Lindsay as mayor, a congressional seat opened up. When City Council member Theodore Roosevelt Kupferman decided to run for Lindsay's House seat, a position on the City Council became available. Koch, who had crossed party lines to endorse Lindsay for mayor two days before the election, announced his candidacy for Kupferman's seat. Despite the fact that Lindsay did not return the favor by endorsing Koch, the Village Democrat managed to win a seat on the council. Never one to forget a slight, Koch has maintained an animus for Lindsay for more than thirty years. In his autobiography, *Koch*, he wrote: "Years later, after I became Mayor, I tortured him at every opportunity. He deserved it."

During his two years on the City Council (1966–68), Koch became a press hound. He began distributing reams of press releases, thereby keeping his name before the public. He also decided that instead of pocketing the $5,000 bonus given each member of the council for "expenses," he would pay $500 stipends to "bright professional people" who would "provide him with ideas for being an effective councilman and pitch in to help him draft legislation." Many of these "bright professional people" would become the backbone of the Koch political team for the next twenty years. During his two years on the City Council, Koch's major legislative success was the enactment of a bill that renamed a street in Greenwich Village after his political idol, *Fiorello La Guardia*.

In 1968, when Representative Kupferman left the Seventeenth Congressional District seat for a position on the New York State Supreme Court, Koch ran for Congress. The Seventeenth, known as the Silk Stocking District, ran north from the Village and took in the largely Hispanic Lower East Side and the middle-class communities of Turtle Bay and Stuyvesant Town. Its political and economic heart, however, was the wealthy and prestigious Upper East Side of Manhattan. Campaigning tirelessly, Koch managed to capture the Democratic nomination for the House. His Republican opponent, the urbane WASP Whitney North Seymour, Jr., looked like a shoo-in. But he hadn't counted on the indefatigable Koch, who doggedly campaigned at subway stops and on street corners, tirelessly shaking hands and handing out literature from sunup to sundown. Koch won by a little more than 2,500 votes. Mayor Lindsay termed Koch's victory "a disaster for the city."

In Congress, Koch quickly became known as one of that body's most liberal members. Staunchly antiwar and pro–civil rights, he consistently won 100 percent approval ratings from the liberal Americans for Democratic Action and near-perfect scores from the Leadership Council on Civil Rights. As the acknowledged leader of the New York City congressional delegation, Koch supported mass transportation, public housing, tax reform, home care for the aged, and federal payments for abortion. He opposed the federal loan bailout of Lockheed Aircraft, and was one of the first members of Congress to back amnesty for Vietnam draft resisters.

Legislatively, Koch was not a great success in the House. "Although he did win passage of bills creating federal commissions to study privacy laws and the decriminalization of marijuana, his causes for the most part were too liberal to win general acceptance." Throughout his congressional career, Koch was also one of Israel's staunchest supporters on Capitol Hill.

Koch easily won reelection in 1970, beating businessman Peter Sprague. Originally assigned a seat on the Science and Astronautics Committee, Koch now moved over to Banking and Currency. Named secretary of the New York delegation by senior colleague *Emanuel Celler*, Koch got the group to meet on a biweekly basis (heretofore untenable) by offering "a great, not a good" lunch and a make-your-own-sundae ice cream bar.

A master at self-promotion, Koch made sure that he was among the first to speak each morning when the House was called into session. In that way, his one-minute remarks (200 words or less) would appear on the front page of the *Congressional Record*. Over the years, Koch delivered these one-minute addresses on literally hundreds of topics. Transferring this ability to television, Koch later became known as the "king of the one-minute sound byte." Ed Koch wound up spending a decade as a representative.

Never in love with life in Washington, Koch had his sights set on a triumphant return to the city of his birth. He spent a few weeks in 1974 as a candidate for mayor of New York, but soon dropped out. The race was eventually won by New York's first Jewish mayor, Abraham Beame.

The Koch candidacy benefited from the serendipity of the blackout of July 1977, and the horrifying "Son of Sam" killings. Koch took a tough-on-crime approach to both incidents, thereby garnering both a newfound reputation and increased support. The turning point in the campaign, though, came when press baron Rupert Murdoch's *New York Post* endorsed Koch. This was followed by an endorsement from both Mayor Abraham Beame and the *Daily News*. Mario Cuomo was endorsed by the *New York Times* and by Representative *Bella Abzug*, an early aspirant to the office of mayor.

Koch received 22 percent to Cuomo's 21 percent in the primary. Facing Cuomo in a runoff race just three weeks later, Koch defeated him by more than 80,000 votes. Koch and Cuomo squared off for a third time in the four-way November general election. Koch won that race as well, receiving nearly 50 percent of the vote to Cuomo's 41 percent. Ed Koch was now New York's 105th (and second Jewish) mayor.

Once in office, Koch became, in the words of writers Browne et al., "the most popular and recognizable character ever to inhabit City Hall. Everything about him was New York. He was the most arrogant, wise-ass, know-it-all odd duck to come down the pike in a long time. He had a mouth like ten opinionated cabbies rolled into one. But his mouth had a bunch of microphones to talk into."

Edward Koch wound up serving three four-year terms as mayor of New York City. During those dozen years he confounded his former political allies by moving perceptibly to the political right—going so far as to seek and then accept both the Democratic and the Republican nomination for mayor in 1981. He became the first Democrat ever to address the Republican Party's National Platform Committee, where, in 1980, he attacked the urban policies of his fellow Democrat, President Jimmy Carter.

Koch inherited a city that stood on the brink of financial disaster. By the end of his first term, he had restored New York's economic well-being and was easily reelected with more than 75 percent of the vote. Koch lost the reputation for being a wide-eyed ultraliberal through his tough stands on crime (favoring the death penalty) and rent control, and his refusal to heal the growing alienation between him and the black community. This latter issue was caused mainly by some of his public statements. Once, when asked by an interviewer whether Jews, because of their history of oppression, should feel a special obligation to help blacks, Koch, the man who had traveled to Selma, Alabama, answered: "I have no guilt complex. My father didn't own slaves."

As mayor of New York City, Edward Koch belonged to the Orthodox Park East Synagogue. Though raised Jewish, he admitted that once he had made a conscious decision to "celebrate his roots," he had to do research so he could deliver a speech on Judaism without embarrassing himself.

Koch's third term was marred by a political scandal involving kickbacks and corruption in the Parking Violations Bureau. The scandal reached its nadir with the suicide of Koch's former ally and friend, bureau chief Daniel Manes. Although never directly implicated in the imbroglio, Koch's reputation (and his health) suffered greatly. As a result, he was defeated for reelection to a fourth term by David Dinkins, New York's first black mayor, in 1985.

Since his defeat, Edward Koch has, in his own words, worked at nine jobs simultaneously: "Here I am . . . in my new life as an attorney, radio talk-show host, newspaper columnist, television news commentator, syndicated movie reviewer, public speaker, university lecturer, commercial spokesperson, and author." In this latter capacity, Koch has penned no fewer than five books: *Mayor, Politics, His Eminence and Hizzoner, All the Best,* and *Citizen Koch,* as well as serveral murder mysteries. Today, Ed Koch resides in Manhattan, where he is senior partner with the firm of Robinson, Pearce, Aronsohn and Berman. He can also be seen on the daily syndicated television program *The People's Court,* where he was selected to replace the fantastically popular Judge Wapner. "Judge" Koch's program goes head-to-head with another court-centered show, *Judge Judy.* Ironically, Judy Sheinlin was appointed to the New York City Family Court by Mayor Ed Koch.

References

Edward Koch, *Citizen Koch: An Autobiography* (New York: St. Martin's Press, 1992).

———, *Mayor: An Autobiography* (New York: Simon & Schuster, 1984).

Arthur Browne, Dan Collins, and Michael Goodwin, *I, Koch* (New York: Dodd, Mead, 1985).

Jack Newfield and Wayne Barret, *City for Sale: Ed Koch and the Betrayal of New York* (New York: Harper & Row, 1988).

KOHL, HERBERT (1935–): *Democrat from Wisconsin; has served two terms in the Senate (January 3, 1988–present).*

Upon meeting United States Senator Herb Kohl for the first time, one is struck by his friendliness, his unassuming nature, and his ability to make one feel completely at ease. One would never guess that he is also a man of immense personal wealth—his net worth is estimated at $250 million. He is perhaps the epitome of what the Founding Fathers had in mind when they thought of Senators more than two hundred years ago: an individual of great accomplishment and financial independence, imbued with a sense of *noblesse oblige.*

The third of Max and Mary (Hiken) Kohl's four children, Herb Kohl was born in Milwaukee on February 7, 1935. His parents had migrated separately to Milwaukee in the early 1920s—Max from Poland, and Mary from Russia. Both had family already living there. When the two wed, Max was working in a factory, saving his money so that he could open a store. By 1927, Max Kohl was the proprietor of a small grocery on Milwaukee's South Side. Max's English was so poor that his customers had to point to the things they wanted from the shelves. Like many immigrants, Max kept a backbreaking schedule: he got up at 3:00 A.M. and worked fourteen hours a day. This was during the dark days of the Depression. Max had to drive himself just to keep up with the needs of his growing family.

By 1938, Max and Mary, now the owners of two stores (one with the area's first electronic door), had four mouths to feed: Sidney (born in 1932), Delores (1934), Herb (1935), and Alan (1938). Today, Sidney is a businessman and real estate developer in Palm Beach, Florida. Alan is a Milwaukee businessman and investor. Sister Delores lives in Chicago and operates the Delores Kohl Educational Foundation, which includes a children's museum in Wilmette, Illinois, and three centers (two in Wilmette, one in Israel) for grade school and high school teachers seeking to improve their skills.

As a child, Herb Kohl excelled at both athletics and academics. "I was a really good athlete. Until I was about thirteen, I was about the best . . . quick and good coordination. . . . I was good at baseball, good at basketball, good at football, good at golf, and loved to swim. I had a wonderful childhood."

The Kohls hired an Orthodox rabbi to come to their home each morning at 6:00 to give religious instruction to the children. The rabbi remained with the family for nearly ten years. Years later, in describing this learning experience, Herb Kohl said: "He was an outstanding person. He did a good job. I learned Hebrew, learned the Torah, and how to put on tefillin. I remember when I was bar mitzvah, I gave my speech in Hebrew; I knew Hebrew very well. I still know it somewhat. . . . If I went to Israel, I'm sure after a few months I would become conversant in it."

When Herb Kohl was growing up on North 51st Street between Auer and Concordia on Milwaukee's Northwest side, his best friend, Alan, lived a block away on North 52nd. The two boys were inseparable. They grew up together, went to school together, competed at sports together (often on opposing teams) roomed together in college at the University of Wisconsin, and served, one after the other, as president of their Jewish fraternity, Phi Lambda Phi. Today, after more than fifty years of friendship, Herb is not only a United States Senator; he is also the owner of the Milwaukee Bucks professional basketball team. His best friend Alan not only owns the Milwaukee Brewers baseball team; he is the commissioner of major league baseball. Alan is better known as "Bud" Selig.

Max Kohl's business kept expanding. After World War II, he opened Wisconsin's first modern supermarket. By the 1950s, he owned seven stores. He was well on his way to becoming the dominant purveyor of food in the Milwaukee area. As the fifties gave way to the sixties, the Kohl family enterprises expanded to include department stores, real estate, and the development of shopping centers. In 1972, the Kohl family sold 80 percent of the stock in Kohl

Corporation to a British retail group for a reported $80 million. By that time their "empire" included more than sixty-five stores. Herb Kohl ran the Kohl Corporation until 1979, when Brown and Williamson (the British group) purchased the remaining stock. By then, there were a hundred Kohl stores and more than 7,500 employees. The stores were responsible for nearly 50 percent of all sales in the Milwaukee area.

Max Kohl placed great emphasis on education. His sons heeded his advice: Sidney went to Harvard Law School; Herb, after graduating from the University of Wisconsin in 1956, earned an M.B.A. at the Harvard Business School; Alan graduated from the Wharton School of Finance.

Following the final sale of Kohl Corporation, Herb Kohl "collected and [gave] away art; spent more time with the real estate and investment business; [did] more philanthropic work and bought the Milwaukee Bucks." By some estimates, Kohl gives away in excess of a million dollars each year, with little fanfare or recognition. One exception is a high school in Beersheva, Israel, named after his parents. As Kohl said in an interview in the *Milwaukee Journal*: "We grew up observing charity in our parents. My grandmother, if she had 5 cents, would give it away. The way I see it, I am a single person with tremendous resources. If money can be used wisely to help someone, it should. And that, for me, doesn't require publicity. Something is lost when it is publicized." He personally funds the Herb Kohl Foundation, which has given away more than $1.5 million in scholarships and grants to students, teachers, and schools. In April 1995, he gave $25 million to the University of Wisconsin.

In 1985, Herb Kohl purchased the Milwaukee Bucks professional basketball team for a reported $18.5 million. When questioned by friends and members of the press as to why he, such a shrewd businessman, would knowingly enter into an investment that was bound to lose money, Kohl simply explained: "I didn't want to see the Bucks leave Milwaukee. . . . It was an opportunity to do something for my hometown." In keeping with his modest, unassuming style, Kohl would park in a municipal lot a block-and-a-half away from the stadium, rather than park in the space reserved for members of the Bucks organization. As his cousin, David Hansher, recalled: "The day of the first game

after he was owner and he was given owner seats, well, Herb walked down to those seats, sat and a lady came in and kicked him out. She said they were her seats. He left. He didn't want to make a fuss. He got the seats back later after the lady discovered she was sitting in the wrong place."

When William Proxmire announced his retirement from the Senate in early 1988, Herb Kohl quickly declared his candidacy for the vacant seat. Refusing to take money from political action committees (PACs), Kohl spent nearly $7 million of his own money, finishing first in a four-candidate Democrat primary. He then captured the seat by a narrow margin (52 percent to 48 percent) over his Republican opponent, moderate State Senator Susan Engeleiter. Kohl ran on the theme "Nobody's Senator but yours," stressing his support for defense cuts and for requiring businesses to provide medical insurance for their employees.

Although attacked for his unique ability to spend freely of his own money, Kohl saw it as a distinct advantage—and not necessarily for the obvious reasons: "I'm here [in the Senate] totally independent of the need for money, special-interest groups, pressure, lobby—all that stuff that makes guys . . . go crazy here. Run around collecting money, spend an inordinate amount of time doing it. They get pressure from special-interest groups then because the money comes with a purpose. They spend 20, 40, 50 percent of their time raising money for the next election. . . . I don't have those problems. That gives me a tremendous advantage. I can be independent of that stuff, and that is very important. . . . I don't spend any time raising money. I spend all my time just doing this job the best I can."

Kohl was appointed to four committees: Governmental Affairs, Special Committee on Aging, Select Committee on POW/MIA Affairs, and Judiciary. As a Senator, Kohl, a longtime Zionist, has been a staunch supporter of Israel. Although he was chairman of the Democratic Party of Wisconsin, he claimed he was "not a conservative or liberal, and not really a Democrat or Republican but just a businessman with a sense of social justice," concerned with educational issues, the budget deficit, and campaign finance reform.

As a member of the Judiciary Committee, Senator Kohl took an active role in the 1991 confirmation hearings of Supreme Court nominees David Souter and Clarence Thomas. Perhaps because he was one of the two members of the Committee who was not a lawyer (Illinois Senator Paul Simon being the other), he saw the hearings as pertaining more to matters of character than to nitty-gritty legal issues: "Most of the issues that you face are not lawyer questions. Supreme Court nominations . . . don't really rest on law; [they] rest on character and on what kind of person you're really talking to. Whether their values are the values that this country needs or represents or not. They're not really so much legal questions." Kohl voted for Judge Souter and against Clarence Thomas. He made his feelings about the latter quite clear in an article he wrote for the *Milwaukee Journal*:

The Senate Judiciary Committee asked the nominee [Thomas] the right questions, but we did not get many specific answers. Instead of illuminating the thought process he would use and the values he would bring to the bench, Justice Thomas essentially refused to answer questions about his views and distanced himself from previous statements. He was not forthcoming. Yet that was a function of the decisions Justice Thomas made and not a failure of the process. . . . From the beginning, when President Bush claimed Justice Thomas was "the best man" for the job, decisions were made for political reasons—not for the right reasons. . . . In the end, our faith in the court as an independent branch of the government was weakened, and the faith of the American people in the ability of the system to look after the national interest was shaken.

In the Senate, like William Proxmire, his predecessor, Kohl has been something of a fiscal conservative. He has relentlessly attempted to hold down federal spending, unsuccessfully urging the Clinton administration to pay for its stimulus package by cutting spending. Not surprisingly, he was one of just fourteen Democrats who voted in March 1995, for the Balanced Budget Amendment.

Kohl has also been at the forefront on crime and gun-related issues. He was the primary Senate sponsor of the Brady Bill, which mandated a waiting period for the purchase of handguns. He has also introduced legislation that would outlaw the possession of any handgun by people under the age of eighteen. As a member of the Judiciary Committee, he has decried violence on television and in video games.

On Capitol Hill, Herb Kohl has the reputation of being an ideal boss, so much so that in an article about working on "The Hill" in *Washingtonian Magazine*, Senate staffers gave him the title "Office Angel." He was easily reelected to a second six-year term in 1994. Once again dipping into his deep pockets, he spent nearly $7 million of his own money to defeat conservative State Representative Robert Welch by a 58 percent to 41 percent margin.

On the first day of the One Hundred and Fifth Congress, Senator Kohl introduced the "Child Care Infrastructure Act," a bill to encourage on- or near-site day care centers to meet the rapidly growing demand for child care. The bill was commended in the January 1997 issue of *Working Mother* magazine. Already working on his reelection to his third six-year term in 2000, Kohl will probably get a "free ride" in the Democrat primary. State Senator Robert Welch (the man he defeated in 1994) and Waukesha County executive Dan Finley have already entered the Republican primary.

Reflecting on his Jewish background and upbringing, Kohl said: "I have a deep respect and regard for my background, my Jewish culture, my feelings as a Jew, what I think Judaism represents to the world in terms of its values. Judaism teaches values of honesty, integrity, hard work and character, doing good for other people . . . to a degree that I think is marvelous. I am very happy that I grew up in the Jewish culture, because I think that it left me with values that I think have served me very well in my life."

References

Interview with Herbert Kohl, August 1992.
"A Businessman First," *Midwest Express* magazine, December 1990.
Almanac of American Politics (1990–98 editions).
Richard L. Kenyon, "The Challenge of Being Herb Kohl," *Milwaukee Journal Magazine*, February 14, 1988.

KOPPLEMANN, HERMAN PAUL (1880–1957):
Democrat from Connecticut; served five terms in the House (Seventy-third through Seventy-fifth Congress; 1933–1939; Seventy-seventh Congress, 1941–1943; Seventy-ninth Congress, 1945–1947).

In the 1930s, American anti-Semites were becoming increasingly emboldened. They benefited from a potentially explosive mixture of economic and political trends: staggering economic dislocation caused by the Great Depression; conservative distaste for the New Deal policies of the Roosevelt administration in Washington; the success of Hitler's Nazi Party in Germany. These situations led to a cadre of notorious anti-Semites who gained prominence. Among them, the most notorious were Father Francis Coughlin, Fritz Kuhn, the "American Führer," William Dudley Pelly and his Silver Shirt movement, and George Deatherage, leader of the Knights of the White Camellia, George Sylvester Viereck, who made no bones of his admiration for Hitler.

Not even the halls of Congress were immune from the mephitic diatribes of nativists, conspiratorialists, and Jew-haters. Prior to the 1930s, the savvy politician would cloak his anti-Semitism with terms like "Bolshevist," "un-American," "alien," or "international bankers." By the early 1930s, such niceties had disappeared. During that time, America had Brown Shirts, Silver Shirts, Khaki Shirts, Blue Shirts, White Shirts, Minutemen, and dozens of other anti-Semitic organizations.

Chief among the Capitol Hill anti-Semites were:

- Representative John Rankin (Democrat from Mississippi)
- Senator Robert Reynolds (Democrat from North Carolina)
- Representative Jacob Thorkelson (Republican from Montana)
- Representative John Schafer (Republican from Wisconsin)
- Senator Rufus C. Holman (Republican from Oregon)
- Representative Louis T. McFadden (Republican from Pennsylvania)

Reynolds (1883–1963), who served in the Senate from 1932 to 1945, published a weekly newsletter, *American Vindicator*, which borrowed heavily from Father Coughlin's notorious *Social Justice*. In a 1939 Senate speech, Reynolds wondered aloud whether Jews would have been driven out of Europe if "they were good citizens . . . or if they had not impoverished those lands, or if they had not conspired against their governments." McFadden (1876–1936), an admirer of William Dudley Pelly, actually quoted from the *Protocols of the Elders of Zion* and Henry Ford's *International Jew* on the floor of the House.

A hard-bitten enemy of what he termed Roosevelt's "Jew-controlled New Deal," McFadden applauded Hitler's "heroic" efforts to eliminate "Jewish domination" in Germany. For quite some time, McFadden and his ilk spoke their words of hatred without much in the way of challenge. Then, in 1933, a balding fifty-three-year-old Democrat from Connecticut was elected to the House who refused to sit idly by while hearing his people vilified. Herman Paul Kopplemann took upon himself the task of challenging, answering, and reproving McFadden each step along the way. Even after McFadden was defeated for reelection in 1934, Kopplemann kept to his self-appointed task. His efforts met with success: when McFadden attempted to regain his House seat in 1936, he was defeated in the Republican primary. Ironically, McFadden died at age sixty, just a few months after his final defeat.

Herman Paul Kopplemann, the son of Henry and Jessie (Gitlin), was born in Odessa, Russia, on May 1, 1880. His parents and siblings—brothers Marcus and Abraham, and sister Sara—emigrated to America in 1882, settling in Hartford, Connecticut. Receiving only a high school education, Herman Kopplemann went to work at age fourteen as a paperboy. Over the next ten years, he expanded upon his paper route until by age twenty-five, he was the head of the H. P. Kopplemann Agency, a publisher's agent for the distribution of newspapers and magazines. It eventually became the largest in the state of Connecticut and made Kopplemann a wealthy man.

In 1904, Kopplemann was elected to the Hartford City Council. He would remain a member of that body for the next eight years, the last of which (1911) he served as its president. Progressing up the political ladder, Kopplemann served one term in the Connecticut House of Representatives (1913–14) and one term in the State Senate (1917–20). While in the

Senate, Kopplemann sponsored legislation much akin to the present-day Aid to Families With Dependent Children Act.

Herman Kopplemann was married to Adelene Greenstein on March 23, 1902. They never had children. They were active members of Hartford's conservative Emanuel Synagogue, and Kopplemann served several terms as its president. An ardent member of the Conservative movement, he was involved for many years with the United Synagogue of America, eventually becoming one of its vice presidents. He also served as secretary of the board of overseers of the Jewish Theological Seminary of America.

In 1932, when First District Representative Augustine Lonergan resigned from the House in order to run for the United States Senate, Herman Kopplemann entered the race for Lonergan's open seat. Although the First District was historically Republican, Kopplemann won the election, becoming the first Jewish member of Congress from Connecticut, and only the second in the history of New England—the first having been *Leopold Morse* of Massachusetts, some fifty years earlier.

In Congress, Kopplemann became a member of the House Banking and Currency Committee, which, ironically, had been chaired for ten years by the aforementioned Louis T. McFadden. An ardent New Dealer, Kopplemann voted for the entire gamut of FDR-sponsored legislation, and devoted much of his energy to getting federal loans for private industry. He was cosponsor, along with Massachusetts Senator David Ignatius Walsh, of the Walsh-Kopplemann Flood Rehabilitation Act.

Herman Kopplemann was reelected to Congress in both 1934 and 1936. From 1938 to 1946, the First District seat seesawed back and forth between Kopplemann and William J. Miller. Kopplemann lost to Miller in the elections of 1938, 1942, and 1946, and defeated him in 1940 and 1944. Following his final victory over Kopplemann in 1946, Miller held on to the First District seat for only one more term. In 1948, he was defeated by *Abraham Ribicoff*.

Returning to Connecticut, Kopplemann was named chairman of the State Water Commission and the Metropolitan District Commission. Herman Kopplemann died in Hartford on August 11, 1957, and was buried in the Emanuel Cemetery in Wethersfield, Connecticut.

References

American Jewish Year Book, vol. 44, p. 413; vol. 47, p. 629; vol. 60, p. 356.
Biographical Directory of American Jews.
Encyclopaedia Judaica (1972). vol. 10, col. 1189.
New York Times, August 13, 1957, 27:2.
Universal Jewish Encyclopedia.
Who's Who in American Jewry, 1926, 1928, 1938.
Who Was Who in America, vol. 3.

KRAMER, KENNETH BENTLEY (1942–): *Republican from Colorado; served four terms in the House (Ninety-sixth through Ninety-ninth Congress; January 3, 1979–January 3, 1987).*

To the American mind, the vast majority of Jews are liberal Democrats. Don't tell that to the people of Colorado; the two Jews who have represented the Rocky Mountain State in Congress have both been ultraconservative Republicans. The first, Senator *Simon Guggenheim,* was known in his day as "the most conservative man in Washington." The second, Representative Ken Kramer, was variously referred to as "Mr. Star Wars" or simply "one of the crazies."

According to a family legend "that must be taken with a grain of salt," Kramer's maternal ancestors originated in Spain, where the family name was Pokrasso. Somehow, the family wound up in the Ukraine, where Ken Kramer's maternal grandmother—the name had been changed to Pokras—supposedly was born in a wheat field during a pogrom. The Kramer side of the family, about which little is known, originated in Eastern Europe, and immigrated to the United States in the late nineteenth century. As far as anyone can tell, the family name has always been Kramer.

Ken Kramer's father, Albert Aaron Kramer, moved to Chicago in the 1930s in order to attend the Northern Illinois College of Optometry. While living in Chicago, he met and married Ruth Pokras. Their son, Kenneth Bentley Kramer, was born in Chicago on February 11, 1942. The Kramers also had a daughter, Barbara, who at the time of her marriage converted to Catholicism.

Ken Kramer was raised on Chicago's South Side, where he spent "two or three years" attending Sunday school at Temple Sinai. The Kramer parents were both "totally apolitical and not at all religious," according to their son. Temple Sinai was "so Reform that their main Sabbath service was on Sunday, not Saturday," Kramer recalled. "They didn't believe in bar mitzvah." At age sixteen, Ken Kramer became confirmed at Temple Sinai.

By the time Ken Kramer reached high school, his family had moved to Chicago's Near North suburbs. In 1959, he entered Grinnell College in Grinnell, Iowa. At the end of Ken's first year at Grinnell, Albert Kramer died, thus necessitating his transfer to the University of Illinois. While at Illinois, Kramer was urged by his Jewish friends to rush their fraternity. Being "more ecumenical than my friends," Kramer instead decided to rush several distinctly non-Jewish fraternities. At one frat house he was taken aside and "gently told" that he "would probably be happier in a Jewish fraternity." Despite the student's advice, Kramer wound up joining a non-Jewish fraternity. During the years 1960–63, Kramer was a member of ROTC.

Ken Kramer graduated from the University of Illinois in 1963 with a B.A. in political science. He then entered Harvard Law School, from which he received his J.D. in 1966. Upon receiving his law degree, Kramer had to fulfill his military obligation. Since he was billeted to the Judge Advocate General's Office, he first had to pass the Illinois Bar. Six months after graduation, he became an officer in the United States Army, assigned to Fort Lewis in Tacoma, Washington. Kramer had always harbored a dream of moving to the West. Although he was impressed by the natural beauty of Washington state, he found it "too wet" for his taste. Sensing that Colorado might be a nice place to settle, he asked for, and received, a transfer to the Rocky Mountain State. Following his three-year hitch in the Army (1967–70), Kramer passed the Colorado bar, briefly practiced law in Chicago, then made a permanent move to Colorado Springs.

While growing up in Chicago, Kramer considered himself a Democrat. By the time he moved to Colorado, he was a Republican. One of the factors that made him a Republican was his experience with the Chicago Democratic machine. As a young man in Chicago, he had attempted to get involved in politics "several times," and "got the feeling that it was a pretty closed deal. . . . Without contacts, you were noth-

Upon his arrival in Colorado Springs, Kramer was hired by the Republican district attorney as a deputy for the Fourth Judicial District. At that time, Colorado Springs had virtually no Democrat organization. Its Jewish community numbered less than 1,000 out of a total population of nearly 300,000. (Colorado as a whole is one of America's least Jewish states; as of the 1990 census, Jews represented less than 0.15 percent of its population). Within a year of his arrival in Colorado's second-largest city, he was elected to the Colorado General Assembly. During his two terms in the General Assembly, Kramer was a part of a group known as "the crazies." He quickly developed a reputation for being extremely conservative, "stubborn and sometimes belligerent." As a state legislator, he was active in promoting anti-pornography and state right-to-work laws.

In 1978, Fifth District Representative William L. Armstrong left his safe House seat in order to run for the United States Senate. The Fifth District encompasses all of Colorado Springs and some suburban Denver communities. It comprises one of the most reliably Republican enclaves in the nation; in 1988, when Michael Dukakis was running even with George Bush in the Denver metropolitan area, the voters of the Fifth Congressional District were voting for Bush by a better than two-to-one margin. The district's economic raison d'être is the military—specifically the Army's Fort Carson, the Air Force Academy, and Cheyenne Mountain, where the North American Air Defense Command (NORAD) maintains its underground headquarters. The district also includes the Colorado School of Mines, the Adolph Coors brewery, Buffalo Bill's grave, and the Continental Divide. The district was created after the 1970 census specifically for William Armstrong, a principled and highly popular conservative, and he had been its Representative ever since.

In the Republican primary to replace Armstrong, Ken Kramer took on the "equally determined conservative Republican," state legislator Bob Eckelberry. It was a bitter campaign, with each candidate claiming that the other had distorted his record; Eckelberry portrayed Kramer as "a wild man." The race was so bitter

that the national Republican Party sent a representative to Colorado Springs in order "to cool things down." Kramer emerged victorious with 56 percent of the vote, and then beat Democrat Gerry Frank in the November general election.

As a member of the Ninety-sixth Congress, Kramer "came to Washington acting and sounding as if he hoped to dismantle most of the edifice of liberal government by the end of his first term." Within a matter of weeks, he started making speeches and offering amendments "by the basket-full." Kramer fought against President Carter's proposed new Department of Education, railed against improved relations with mainland China, and fought legislation implementing the U.S. transfer of the Panama Canal. Few of his amendments passed. Before too long, Kramer was known as "E. F. Hutton in reverse. . . . When he talks, nobody listens."

Ironically, the archconservative was seated on one of the House's most liberal committees, Education and Labor. As the committee's most strident conservative, Kramer became "an advocate of right-to-work laws . . . a sort of gadfly against the panel's solid pro-union majority." Always at odds with the liberal direction of the committee, Kramer favored "cutting back the role of the Environmental Protection Agency, Occupational Safety and Health Administration and Federal Trade Commission." Additionally, he sought to restrict federal court jurisdiction over both busing and abortion. Even in his first term, though, it was apparent that Ken Kramer's major legislative interest was going to be military issues.

After winning reelection by a wide margin in 1980, Kramer was given a seat on the House Armed Services Committee. From that post, he emerged as one of the military's staunchest defenders in Congress. Kramer felt that his appointment was absolutely necessary, because his district was, in his words, "the No. 1 Soviet targeting priority in all the world." With the advent of the Reagan administration in early 1981, Kramer began making speeches on "the uses of space for nuclear defense." Within two years, Reagan himself joined Kramer's cause, which was now named the Strategic Defense Initiative—SDI. Ken Kramer introduced what he called the People Protection Act as a means of both funding and implementing the idea. He praised the plan as "perhaps the greatest hope for mankind." Because he was so tireless in his promotion of both the SDI concept and attempts to create a congressional space caucus, skeptics gave him the nickname "Mr. Star Wars."

Kramer was so convinced that the future defense of mankind would come from space that he even proposed changing the name of the Air Force Academy to the "U.S. Aerospace Force," with the mission of "centralizing military space activity." In 1982, the Air Force did create a new Space Command, which was located—not surprisingly—in Colorado Springs. He also fought hard to expand his district's Fort Carson by some 245,000 acres, warning that if the House rejected the expansion, members might "find the blood of American soldiers on our hands in a few years." Something of an alarmist, Kramer also warned his colleagues that unless the United States created a massive civil defense evacuation plan equal to that of the Soviets, "an American president would have no choice but to virtually surrender" in case of any Russian-launched attack. By the beginning of his third term, Kramer left Labor and Education to devote himself full-time to the affairs of Armed Services.

In 1986, after serving four terms in the House, Ken Kramer decided to run for Gary Hart's vacant Senate seat. He won his party's nomination at the June 1986 convention by holding two candidates to less than 20 percent of the delegate votes. He then faced popular Denver-area Representative Timothy E. Wirth. The two presented a studied example of political and physical opposites: Wirth, the tall, classically handsome WASP, versus Kramer, the "frizzy-haired, disorganized" Jew; Wirth, "one of the busiest and most powerful members of the House," versus Kramer, the man "no one listened to."

As chairman of the House Energy and Commerce Committee's Subcommittee on Telecommunications, Consumer Protection, and Finance, Wirth had exercised considerable jurisdiction over "TV networks, the telephone industry, and Wall Street." Needless to say, this gave him tremendous clout. Kramer, on the other hand, was a mid-level member of the minority party given to making speeches about outer space. And yet, despite Wirth's seemingly insur-

mountable advantages, Kramer kept the race competitive. Most of the "Jewish money" backed Wirth; Kramer, who was "sympathetic, but not in lock-step with the government of Israel," was deemed "unreliable." Kramer felt that he was being held to a different standard by the leaders of the Colorado Jewish community, claiming that "they are much less tolerant of me than, say, a non-Jewish member of the same delegation. . . . [I] have always had more problems with the Jewish community than with the non-Jewish community."

Running on the slogan "Not Slick, Just Good," Kramer got a campaign boost when President Reagan's "performance at Reykjavik [Iceland]in October 1986 made his Strategic Defense Initiative" a reality. As the political tide began turning in Kramer's direction, the dollars started flowing. By election day, he and Wirth raised and spent virtually the same amount—$3,785,000. On election day, Kramer carried the Colorado Springs area by a better than two-to-one margin. Wirth, however, carried Denver and wound up winning the race by fewer than 20,000 votes. Shortly after his defeat, Kramer had what is known in the world of politics as "a soft landing." He was appointed to a fourteen-year term, ending in 2000, on the newly created U.S. Court of Veteran's Appeals. Kramer currently resides in Washington, D.C.

Ken Kramer married, and eventually divorced, Nancy Pearson, a Catholic. Neither of their two children, Kenny and Kelli, was raised as Jews. Today, Kramer's children are in their mid-thirties, and daughter Kelli is "beginning to show a little interest in Judaism." Although Ken Kramer does not belong to a synagogue, he attends from time to time on the High Holidays. Of average height with thinning, reddish-brown, frizzy hair, Ken Kramer considers himself to be "probably the most assimilated Jew who ever served in Congress." The most assimilated? Perhaps. The most conservative? More likely.

References
Interview with Kenneth B. Kramer, July 1992.
Almanac of American Politics (1978–86 editions).
Politics in America (1980–86 editions).

KRAUS, MILTON (1866–1942): *Republican from Indiana; served three terms in the House (Sixty-fifth through Sixty-seventh Congress; March 4, 1917–March 3, 1923).*

Probably less is known about Milton Kraus than any member of the Congressional Minyan. Although he is the only Jew elected to Congress from Indiana, that state's major Jewish newspaper, the *Post and Opinion* of Indianapolis, ran no obituary. Even his entries in the *American Jewish Year Book* and *Who Was Who in America* offer nothing more than a bare-bones sketch.

Milton Kraus was born in Kokomo, Indiana, on June 26, 1866, the son of Charles and Hannah (Rosenthal) Kraus. How his family wound up in Indiana in the Civil War years is unknown. Milton attended the "common schools" and public high school in nearby Peru, Indiana, graduating in 1883. From Peru, Kraus went to the University of Michigan, where he was a student in the department of law. He received his law degree in 1886, and was admitted to the Indiana bar the following year. Along with practicing law, Kraus became involved in what *Who Was Who in America* (vol. 4) termed "industrial interests and manufacturing activities."

During the Spanish-American War, Kraus organized a company of volunteers to serve in the army. Returning home from the war as a hero, he became involved in local politics. In 1908, he was named a Republican member of the Electoral College and cast his vote for William Howard Taft. Kraus was elected to the Sixty-fifth Congress in 1916 from Indiana's Eleventh Congressional District, defeating four-term incumbent George Washington Rauch, a Democrat from Marion. Kraus served three terms in Congress. During his brief career, he appears to have been mainly concerned with military issues.

His sole reference in the *New York Times* appeared on page 17 of the February 25, 1920 edition. Coming in the early days of his second term, the tiny article (two column inches) reported that Kraus had put in a bill to repeal the so-called Overman Act. Authored by the veteran North Carolina Senator Lee Slater Overman (1854–1930), this wartime act granted the President of the United States the "power to transfer duties of one Government bureau to

another." Overland had specifically been chosen to author the bill by President Wilson because he was well-known as one of the Senate's most ardent defenders of states' rights. Wilson's political instincts told him that a having a states' rights man authoring a hyper-federalist bill made good sense. Wilson's hunch was right; Congress passed the Overland Act in February 1918.

According to historian Frederic Paxson: "Few statutes have in so few words surrendered so much; and none has vested so much discretion in the President." The Overman Act granted the President the statutory right to "redistribute the functions of executive agencies as he saw fit." It permitted him "to utilize, co-ordinate, or consolidate any executive or administrative commissions, bureaus, agencies, offices or officers now existing by law," and to "create new agencies; to transfer redistribute, or abolish the functions of others; and to utilize funds voted for any purpose for the accomplishment of that purpose by whatever means might to him seem good."

The Overland Act was supposed to remain on the books only so long as the nation was engaged in war. Two years after the Armistice, it was still the law of the land. Enter Milton Kraus. In filing his bill for abolition, Kraus stated: "The United States may tolerate a dictator in time of war, but never in time of peace." Not wishing to seem overly partisan, Kraus added: "My bill is not aimed directly at the present occupant of the White House [the ailing Wilson], but is founded on principle and designed as a step toward a return to representative government." Kraus's bill passed, and the Overland Act was stricken from the United States Code.

Milton Kraus was defeated by journalist and former circuit court judge Samuel Ellis Cook of Huntington. Cook served but one term, being defeated by Republican Albert R. Hall in the election of 1924.

Following his three terms in Congress, Kraus returned to Peru, Indiana, where he resumed his legal practice and business activities. He remained in Peru until his death, on November 18, 1942. He is buried in Mount Hope Cemetery in Peru. Nothing is known about his family or descendants.

References

American Jewish Year Book, vol. 24, p. 165.

Biographical Directory of the United States Congress, 1774–1989.

Universal Jewish Encyclopedia.

Arthur Walworth, *Woodrow Wilson* (Baltimore: Penguin Books, 1969).

Who Was Who in America, vol. 4.

Who Was Who in American Jewry, 1926, 1928.

KREBS, JOHN HANS (1926–): *Democrat from California; served two terms in the House (Ninety-fourth and Ninety-fifth Congress; January 3, 1975–January 3, 1979).*

Although not a sabra, John H. Krebs is the only member of the Congressional Minyan to have fought in the Haganah. The product of an assimilated upper-middle-class German family, Krebs arrived in Palestine in 1933, remaining there until shortly after his high school graduation in 1945. From 1943 to 1946, while a student at the Ben-Yehuda College (a pre-statehood high school) Krebs was a member of the famed underground fighting force.

John Krebs's grandfather was a prosperous doctor in Berlin. His father was a dentist and ardent Zionist. John Hans Krebs was born in Berlin on December 17, 1926. In 1933, his father, sensing that there was no future for Jews in Hitler's Germany, packed up his young family and moved to Palestine. Dr. Krebs the dentist could not convince his father, Dr. Krebs the physician, to leave. Dr. Krebs the elder died "accidentally" in Berlin in 1941. Shortly after his death, the Palestine Krebses received a postcard from the doctor's widow, telling them she was going to a "health spa." The family never heard from her again; the "spa" turned out to be Theresienstadt.

As a youngster growing up in the *Yishuv* (the Jewish settlement in Palestine), John Krebs was educated at the Balfour Elementary School and at the aforementioned Ben-Yehuda College. The year after his graduation from Ben-Yehuda, he left Palestine for America, where he entered the University of California at Berkeley. In 1950, Krebs received a bachelor's degree in zoology. Shortly after his graduation, he entered the United States Army, where he served as a translator. Following his discharge in 1954, John Krebs became a citizen of the United States. Upon his return from service, Krebs attended the Hastings College of Law (University of California) in San Francisco, from which he earned his degree in 1957. Along the way, he had a wide assortment of employment experiences, working variously as a "diamond cutter, whiskey taster, bellboy and ditch digger." Upon being admitted to the bar in 1957, Krebs moved to Fresno, in the heart of California's Central Valley, where he went into private practice.

With a Jewish population of no more than 1,200 in the 1950s and 1960s, Fresno was an unusual place for a German-born, Israeli immigrant to set up shop and raise a family. The Central Valley, known as America's Breadbasket, is dotted with small cities and even smaller towns, variously proclaiming world-class status as Artichoke Capital of the World (Castroville), Lettuce Capital of the Earth (Salinas), or America's Garlic Capital (Gilroy). For countless decades, the politics and economics of the Central Valley had been run by the big corporate growers. Starting in the 1930s, the Central Valley became the destination of both necessity and choice for hundreds of thousands of victims of the Depression-era Dustbowl. Along with the downtrodden Okies and Arkies of Steinbeck's *The Grapes of Wrath* came a huge population of *campesinos*—migrant farm workers—from south of the border.

During the postwar era, the often-conflicting interests of farm owners and farm workers formed the parameters of political warfare. On one side sat the mostly Eastern-owned agribusiness farms; on the other, the largely Chicano farmer workers, led by Cesar Chavez of the United Farm Workers Organizing Committee (UFWOC). Throughout the 1960s and early 1970s, Chavez's nascent union fought for the right of collective bargaining and improved living conditions for migrant farm workers. A leader of heroic stature, Chavez organized and led national boycotts of grapes and lettuce in order to give his movement publicity and credibility. The boycotts became a cause célèbre for liberals throughout the nation. The war between the growers and farmworkers, which included picketing and often violent clashes between *campesinos* and the International Brotherhood of Teamsters, had its culmination in California's historic Proposition 14, an initiative to grant UFWOC official status as a union.

With his thick "Kissingerian accent," John Krebs stood out among the other local attorneys. Armed with a wide array of human skills picked up in his many occupations, Krebs prospered as an attorney in Fresno. In 1965, now married to Hannah, and the father of Daniel Steven and Karen Barbara, Krebs won a seat on the Fresno County Planning Commission. After a four-year stint, Krebs, "known throughout the county as a backer of planned growth," was easily elected to the Fresno County Board of Supervisors. Not surprisingly, as a proponent of planned growth he did not lend support to the farmworkers' cause. In the Central Valley, open support for Chavez and his United Farm Workers was tantamount to political suicide.

In 1966, while Democrat Krebs was winning election to the Planning Commission, the residents of the Central Valley's Eighteenth District were electing Republican Bob Mathias to the Ninety-second Congress. A native of nearby Tulare, Mathias (1930–) was both a hometown and an American hero. As a double Olympic gold medalist in the decathlon (1948 Olympic games in London, 1952 games in Helsinki), Mathias was the all-American boy. He had been recruited to run for Congress the same year (1966) that Ronald Reagan was sweeping to a million-vote victory as California Governor. Riding Reagan's expansive coattails, Mathias easily defeated incumbent Harlan Hagen, "a 12-year veteran Democrat whose conservatism was closely tailored to the interest of the big growers in the region." As a member of Congress, the conservative Mathias was assigned a seat on the House Agriculture Committee, where he "worked for the interests of the large agribusiness interests in the Valley." Mathias was easily reelected in 1968, 1970, and 1972. His seat appeared to be as safe as safe could be.

In 1973, the California Supreme Court was given the task of creating the state's new congressional districts. The largely Democratic court altered Mathias's district by removing both his hometown and a high percentage of the Republican precincts. In his 1974 bid for reelection to a fifth term, Mathias was saddled with two insurmountable problems: Watergate and the new district. More than half of the new Seventeenth District was made up of largely Democratic Kern County, an area Mathias had never represented. The court also added another 64,000 people from Kings County, where Mathias had not campaigned since 1966.

In June 1974, John Krebs easily won the three-person Democratic primary with 65 percent of the vote. Well-financed (he raised and spent more than $130,000, a large sum at the time), Krebs campaigned from one end of the district to the other as a proponent of planned growth and economic opportunity. The battle seesawed back and forth, with Mathias bringing in President Gerald Ford to speak in the cam-

paign's last week. In the end, voter disgust with Watergate proved to be too much: Krebs eked out a 4,800-vote majority over Mathias.

John Krebs's first day in Washington was truly memorable: he wound up in jail. Upon his arrival in the District of Columbia, Krebs drove his new Mercedes-Benz to the home of Representative Phillip Burton. While trying to park in front of Burton's house, he attracted the attention of a passing policeman. When Krebs showed the officer his driver's license, confusion arose over its legality. An argument ensued, tempers flared, and Krebs was taken downtown and held until the matter could be resolved. "It was a hell of an introduction to Washington," Krebs said with notable restraint.

In the House, Krebs received Mathias's seat on Agriculture as well as a post on the Interior and Insular Affairs Committee. During his first term, Krebs was one of but a handful of representatives in the Ninety-fifth Congress to be present and cast every vote. Krebs voted a mostly liberal line, earning ratings of 80 and 89 from the Americans for Democratic Action, and 81 and 87 from the League of Conservation Voters. What success Krebs experienced in his brief congressional tenure stemmed "not from his willingness to fight on issues—as his background might suggest—but from his ability to compromise." With the issue of farm workers versus farm owners continuing to play a large role in his district, Krebs repeatedly stressed that "the welfare of farm workers . . . depend[ed] on that of the growers."

In 1976, John Krebs was reelected with 66 percent of the vote over Republican Henry J. Adreas. Like Bob Mathias, John Krebs appeared to have a safe seat. In 1978, spurred by an economic downturn in the Central Valley, largely the result of a horrendous drought, Krebs was upset by local attorney Charles ("Chip") Pashayan, Jr. Following his defeat, John Krebs returned to Fresno, where he resumed the practice of law.

Krebs has kept his hand in public affairs, having "walked precincts and contributed thousands of dollars to candidates." Recently, he has thrown himself into an issue that has long consumed his energies: the future of Mineral King Valley in Sequoia National Park. Testifying before Congress in mid-1995, Krebs told his former colleagues: "It (the proposed purchase of

Mineral King) is such a long grab. It really can't be justified, and it's all at the expense of the general public." In 1997, he chaired the Fresno County Grand Jury.

Beginning in January 1998, Krebs began working as a volunteer Hebrew tutor for the Fresno Board of Education. Working a few hours a week with Israeli children, Krebs teaches them English and chats in Hebrew on topics that they cannot as yet discuss in their new language. "I'm not a teacher," Krebs maintains, "I'm just giving them the opportunity to speak their language."

References

Almanac of American Politics (1976–78 editions).

Fresno Bee, November 19, 1995, B1; June 13, 1998, B1.

Los Angeles Times, April 20, 1978, I, 3:4.

LA GUARDIA, FIORELLO HENRY (1882--1947): *Republican from New York; served six terms in the House (Sixty-fifth and Sixty-sixth Congress; March 4, 1917–December 31, 1919; Sixty-eighth through Seventy-second Congress; March 4, 1923–March 3, 1933).*

Every schoolchild knows that it was Benjamin Franklin who said: "In this world nothing is certain but death and taxes." Those coming of age in the New York City of the 1920s through the 1940s were aware of three other eternal verities: that Franklin D. Roosevelt was always President; that Joe McCarthy's Yankees were always in the World Series; and that Fiorello H. La Guardia was always mayor. Today, the name La Guardia summons up vague recollections of a fellow who read the Sunday funnies on the radio during a newspaper strike. Or perhaps a mental image of a swarthy little man in a terminally rumpled suit conducting an orchestra in Central Park. Fiorello H. La Guardia was both of these—and far, far more. As good a mayor as he was ("he ran the best reform government in American municipal history"), La Guardia was an even better member of Congress. Indeed, during his dozen years in the House of Representatives, La Guardia was lionized by no less an observer than Heywood Broun as "the most powerful and persuasive member of the lower house." To biographer Lawrence Elliott, "he knew more about pending legislation than most House members, and affected more bills than any of them."

Through the haze of memory, La Guardia seems to be the consummate New Yorker, the cosmopolite of that most cosmopolitan city. In point of fact, the Little Flower (the literal meaning of his given name, Fiorello) was far more than a mere New Yorker. Although born in New York, La Guardia was a "Western-bred, Balkan-plated Episcopalian of Italian-Jewish descent with the advantage of being a balanced ticket unto himself." And despite the fact that he spoke a more than passable Yiddish (in addition to Italian, French, Croatian, German, and Spanish), La Guardia rarely mentioned his Jewish background. He simply did not want to be accused of using his Jewish lineage as a political prop. Despite all this, he was roundly jeered and pilloried by Nazi Germany; they labeled him "a dirty Talmud Jew . . . a shameless Jewish lout" with a "thieves-den mentality . . . a whoremonger." In response, La Guardia launched his own verbal assault: "The only authority in New York competent to deal with German press accusations [is] the deputy sanitation commissioner in charge of sewage disposal."

La Guardia's father, Achille Luigi Carlo La Guardia, was born in the southern Italian city of Foggia in 1851. The La Guardias were civil servants—solid middle-class *cittadinos*. Achille, a lapsed Catholic, was far more interested in music than municipality; by the time he came to America in 1880 (to be accompanist to the legendary singer Adelina Patti), he was an accomplished musician and linguist—and a married man. In June 1880, shortly before his departure from Italy, Achille married Irene Luzzato Coen, the scion of a Jewish family from Trieste, then a part of Austria. Irene was twenty-three, and though raised in a religious home was "thoroughly Italian in speech and culture"—the prevailing tendency among Jews in cosmopolitan Trieste. On their marriage certificate, Irene recorded her religion as *Israelita*; Achille, "carrying the memory of indignities heaped on him by his teachers, all priests," wrote down *nessuna*—"nothing."

Shortly after their marriage, the La Guardias immigrated to America, settling in the then Italian enclave of Greenwich Village in New York City. Within a year of their arrival, their first child—a daughter they named Gemma—was born. Not quite two years later, on December 11, 1882, their first son entered the world. They named him Fiorello Enrico. A third child, Richard Dodge La Guardia, was born in 1887.

Unable to find steady employment as a musician, Achille enlisted in the United States Army, which made him a bandmaster. Beginning in 1885, the army sent Achille and his family to a series of frontier posts: first to Fort Sully, South Dakota, then to Whipple Barracks near Prescott, Arizona. It was in Prescott that Fiorello La Guardia "attended school, learned to make spaghetti sauce in his mother's kitchen, to play the cornet, [and] to love Italian opera." With the coming of the Spanish-American War in 1898, Achille received orders for Cuba, and the La Guardias left Prescott. Traveling across country, the family stopped in St. Louis, where Fiorello, imbued with patriotic fervor, talked his way into an unpaid position on *Joseph Pulitzer's Post-Dispatch*. The cub reporter's first piece ran under the "slightly mangled" byline "T. La Guardi."

Before Achille could ship out for Cuba, he became gravely ill—a casualty of "embalmed beef" that corrupt contractors had sold to the army. Discharged from the service, Achille moved his family back to Europe, where for a while they lived with Irene's widowed mother Fiorina (for whom Fiorello had been named) in Trieste. His energy sapped, Achille eventually leased "a neglected seaside hotel at nearby Capodistria." Before too long, the hotel began to prosper. In 1900, Fiorello, not quite eighteen years old, accepted a post as clerk at the American consulate in Budapest. He spent the next six years of his life working at diplomatic posts in Budapest, Trieste, and finally Fiume (modern-day Rijeka in northwestern Croatia), where he served as United States consular agent.

During his years in the consular corps, La Guardia's official duties consisted mainly of "processing visa and passport applications and gathering information for the consul's periodic reports." La Guardia, who stood five feet two inches and barely looked his age, "reveled in the most tangled consular cases and wound up with the practical equivalent of advanced degrees in sociology, politics, and applied economics, and at least conversational command of seven languages." During his three years in Fiume (1903–06), he caused quite a stir when he demanded that emigrants be checked by physicians *before* they sailed, rather than upon arrival at Ellis Island. In that way, the young consular agent reasoned, fewer of the dispossessed would face the trauma of being forced to return to Europe. On more than one occasion, La Guardia used the implied power of his post to hold ships in port until medical checks had been completed. His strategy worked: "During his three years as consular agent, Fiume had far fewer health rejections at Ellis Island than any other port embarking emigrants for the United States, a total of only forty-five for trachoma, for example, against an average of twenty-five on every ship docking in New York."

In 1904, Achille La Guardia died, never having gotten over the effects of the tainted beef. Despite a lengthy battle with the American gov-

ernment, Fiorello La Guardia could never get the War Department to admit that his father's death had been service-related. His mother was denied a military widow's pension. As a result, La Guardia began harboring an intense aversion to bureaucrats and corruption that would carry over to his political career; years later, when he was elected to Congress during World War I, his first legislation was a bill providing the death penalty for "the scavengers of history who [supply] tainted food or defective supplies and equipment in wartime." It died in committee.

La Guardia's superior in Fiume was a Boston Brahmin named Frank Dyer Chester. Although Chester "admired Fiorello's fire and ambition," he nonetheless felt constrained to tell the young agent that he would never advance too far in the consular corps. To Chester's way of thinking, La Guardia's ethnicity—and lack of a Harvard degree—stood in the way of future success. Fed up, La Guardia left the consular corps and made his way back to the United States. He arrived in New York in 1906. It had been twenty-one years since the family had started their trek, and he was far more a Westerner or a European than a New Yorker.

Back in New York, La Guardia found temporary employment with the Society for the Prevention of Cruelty to Children. His job was to "translate the juvenile sections of the French penal code into English." In 1907, convinced that his future lay in politics, La Guardia was admitted to the law school of New York University. While taking classes at night, he worked days as an interpreter for the Immigration Service. His salary was $1,200. La Guardia worked in the white slave division of the Immigration Service during his three years in law school. Receiving his LL.B. in 1910, he joined the firm of Weil, La Guardia & Espen. As an attorney, La Guardia worked almost exclusively in the garment industry, protecting the rights of the immigrant masses. For La Guardia, "the practice of law was never meant to be an end in itself. . . . It was a tool, like his knowledge of languages, a stepping-stone toward what he really wanted; a career in public service."

La Guardia soon became politically active in the Twenty-fifth Assembly District, "a mile-square tangle of neighborhoods in the center of Manhattan." It was also the home base of

Tammany leader Charlie Murphy. Within a short while, La Guardia, who against all reason had become a Republican, was making a name for himself as a rebel with a following. Through his impoverished law practice, La Guardia made friends "among the housewives, workingmen, poor immigrants"—people who would become his constituents within a matter of a few years. With the election of Charles S. Whitman to the Governor's mansion in Albany in 1914, local Republican leaders, wishing "to do something for their young rebel," managed to secure him a position as a New York State deputy attorney general.

La Guardia took his work in the A.G.'s office seriously, but kept his eye on a congressional race in New York's Fourteenth District. His chance came in 1916. Declaring his candidacy for the seat held by Tammany stalwart (and local bartender) Mike Farley, La Guardia was the clear underdog. Having "neither jobs nor buckets of free coal" at his disposal, La Guardia decided to dispense free legal advice. Soon it became known throughout the district that "any poor man or woman who needed advice or a lawyer to take his case to court could come to La Guardia." As one admirer said at the time: "the greatest favor you can do this man is to come to him with a tale of injustice and ask him to fight your battle for nothing."

La Guardia campaigned on two fronts. First, he went to the East Side, campaigning in Italian, Yiddish, and Serbo-Croatian, "dismember[ing] the Hapsburg Empire and liberat[ing] all the subjugated countries almost every night." Second, he took every chance at his disposal to ridicule and belittle Farley. On one occasion, La Guardia parked his Model T in front of Farley's saloon and loudly dared the congressman to come out and debate. When nothing happened La Guardia angrily told the gathering crowd it was because Farley didn't know anything about the issues. Finally goaded into doing something, the hapless Farley issued a ten-point platform. La Guardia "fell on it with glee." "Eight of the ten proposals," he told a street corner crowd, "have already been dealt with in one legislature or another. When the other two were brought up in Congress, Farley was back home tending bar." On election day, La Guardia won by a mere 357 votes, thereby becoming the first Italian ever elected to Congress. Moreover, he was the first Republican since the Civil War to be elected from the Lower East Side.

As a member of the Sixty-fifth Congress, Fiorello La Guardia was in a unique position. He found himself assiduously courted by both the Republicans and the Democrats; both parties had precisely 215 members. The matter of who would organize the House appeared to rest with five independents, of whom La Guardia was one. La Guardia, "in one of his infrequent spasms of party loyalty," voted with the Republicans. The Democrats won, thereby placing him in the minority—a position he would occupy all his political life.

As war clouds began darkening the horizon, La Guardia introduced an amendment to the draft law that would nullify all exemptions; "conscientious objectors were to be given non-combat duties, and the physically unfit less strenuous work." It was easily defeated. When it came time to vote on the Selective Service Act, La Guardia was one of but five voting in opposition. Fearing that the impending war would make the rich richer, La Guardia "urged government controls on the price and distribution of food, clothing and shelter." His plan was buried in committee. When war came, along with soaring prices and alarming shortages, La Guardia began looking like a prophet—and not for the last time.

The day after war was declared, La Guardia enlisted. Already skilled as a pilot, he was assigned to the Italian Royal Flying School near Foggia. In January 1918, he became a member of the Joint Army-Navy Aircraft Committee; within a few months, he was chief in all but name of American aviation in Italy. In addition to his almost daily bombing missions, "the flying Congressman" was sent the length and breadth of Italy as a spokesman for America. Addressing crowds of up to 300,000, La Guardia, speaking in "colloquial Italian," told the throngs that "the Americans were here, and he was one of them!" By all accounts, wherever La Guardia spoke, the results were spectacular.

While he was off fighting the war, an alliance of pacifists and suffragettes in his New York district petitioned Congress to vacate his seat, so that they could be represented. Suddenly, the Little Flower was a national hero, receiving support from all over the country. The editorial writers of the *Philadelphia Record* noted that "Congressman La Guardia, absent to fight for his country, is absent little more than some congressmen during the baseball season. Why raise a fuss over him?" When informed by a reporter of what was going on at home, La Guardia told him: "You might say that if any signers of the petition will take my seat in a Caproni bi-plane, I shall be glad to resume my upholstered seat in the House." La Guardia need not have worried. The petition for removal had been "filed away" by House Speaker Champ Clark.

Following his much-heralded return from the war, La Guardia introduced an amendment to an appropriations bill providing that "federal civil-service employees who had been drafted or enlisted be reinstated in their former jobs." The measure was sidetracked by a parliamentary tactic and died. On the surface, it would seem that La Guardia lost all his legislative battles. This was not the case—if only because of the law of averages. One of La Guardia's first legislative victories came when Congress approved his measure to feed postwar Europe.

In 1920, Fiorello La Guardia voluntarily gave up his seat in Congress in order to run for president of the New York City Board of Aldermen. The board's previous president, Alfred E. Smith, had just been elected governor. La Guardia won the election by appealing to the city's Democratic minority voters—many of whom were outraged by President Wilson's Versailles Treaty. After serving less than a year as president, La Guardia ran for mayor in the Republican primary against Manhattan Borough President Henry Curran. La Guardia, vilified as a "red," a "dago," and a "radical," got only 37,000 votes to Curran's 103,000. He failed to carry a single borough. When La Guardia was attacked for being outside the "Republican mainstream," he caustically replied: "Some men who claim to be exponents of Republican principles know as much about the teachings of Abraham Lincoln as Henry Ford knows about the Talmud."

Life had hit rock bottom for Fiorello La Guardia. In addition to losing the primary, both his wife (the former Thea Almerigotti, whom he had married in 1917) and his baby daughter (also named Thea) had died one right after the other. He was now without family, job, or

prospects. In June 1922, a new law firm—La Guardia, Sapinsky & Amster—was formed so that the Little Flower might have an income. Throughout his life, La Guardia was always on the verge of bankruptcy. When he became mayor in 1933, he owned "neither an automobile nor an overcoat." When he died, all he had to his name was a small house in the Riverdale section of the Bronx and $8,000 in U.S. War Bonds.

La Guardia wasn't down for long. Suddenly, in the spring of 1922, William Randolph Hearst was booming "the Major" (as he was called by everyone but relatives and strangers) for New York Governor. On June 29 of that year, La Guardia issued a forty-two-point platform calling for such basic social reforms as "equal rights for women, old-age pensions, workmen's compensation, a minimum wage, an eight-hour day, and the abolition of child labor." The Republicans were aghast. In exchange for his dropping out of the gubernatorial race, the party offered him the nomination for Congress from the Twentieth District—East Harlem. Next to Manhattan's Lower East Side, the Twentieth was "the most congested slum in the United States"—a perfect constituency for the Major.

La Guardia's race for this seat is the basis for one of the truly unforgettable stories in all American political history. Having secured the Republican nomination, he faced two strong opponents: William Karlin, "a Socialist endorsed by important trade unions and running on a something-for-everybody platform"; and Democrat Henry Frank, "a pedestrian and politically untested lawyer [who] had the advantage of Tammany Hall's very considerable support." La Guardia campaigned from early morning till late at night, running on his typically progressive platform.

Shortly before the election, the Democrats were getting scared. Party strategists concluded that the only way for Frank (who was Jewish) to win the race was to go all out for the Jewish vote. A few days before the election, Tammany distributed tens of thousands of leaflets with the following message:

> The most important office in this country for Judaism is the Congressman. Our flesh and blood are . . . on the other side of the ocean. Only through your Congressman can we go to their rescue.

There are three candidates who are seeking your vote: One is Karlin, the atheist. The second is the Italian La Guardia, who is a pronounced anti-Semite and a Jew-hater.

Be careful how you vote.

Our candidate is Henry Frank, who is a Jew with a Jewish heart, and who does good for us. Therefore it is up to you and your friends to vote for our friend and beloved one, Henry Frank, for Congressman.

La Guardia was livid. One of his aides advised him to make a speech about his Jewish mother. La Guardia refused. He had always considered himself Italian, "and to imply otherwise now would be too transparently self-serving." Instead, La Guardia delivered a brilliant *coup de grâce*. He issued "an open letter to Henry Frank" that read:

At the beginning of the campaign, I announced that I would not indulge in personalities nor in abuse of my opponents. I have kept this pledge. [. . .]

You have seen fit, however, to resort to the kind of campaigning which was discredited in American politics over 25 years ago. You . . . are making a radical-religious appeal for sympathy votes [and] I regret exceedingly that this has happened. However, I always met a fight on any issue openly. [. . .]

Very well, then . . . I hereby challenge you to publicly and openly debate the issues of the campaign, the debate to be conducted by you and me entirely in the Yiddish language. We will suit your convenience in every respect.

La Guardia himself translated his "open letter" into Yiddish and released it to all the Jewish dailies. Frank (who didn't speak a word of Yiddish) was made to look ridiculous. The next day, La Guardia was endorsed by the *Forward*, which touted him as "one who speaks Yiddish like a true Jew and who over the years has been a good friend to the Jewish people."

La Guardia pulled off a razor-thin victory, coming out a mere 168 votes ahead of Frank. The Major was back as a member of the Sixty-eighth Congress.

La Guardia's second congressional "tour of duty" continued until the Roosevelt landslide of 1932.

Although reelected several times, his margins of victory were never outstanding. In 1924, his best year, he had 3,500 votes more than his opponent. By comparison, in 1926, he won by just 55 votes. But during the years between 1923 and 1933, La Guardia became a focal point in the House—a lightning rod for a host of disparate issues. Although he would never become chairman of a congressional committee, he was perhaps the nearest thing to a "Congressman-at-large" the United States has ever had.

La Guardia relished his role as a gadfly. "The function of a progressive," he once said, "is to keep on protesting until things get so bad that a reactionary demands reform." And protest he did: against Prohibition, the "money class," the "interests," and the inequities of the tax code, and on behalf of the poor, the disenfranchised—even the Eskimos of the frozen north. During the 1920s, La Guardia pushed such "radical" ideas as minimum wages, old-age pensions, a child-labor law, social security, government regulation of utilities and the stock market—every one of which eventually became the law of the land.

One of La Guardia's closest friends in Congress was Minnesota Representative Ole J. Kvale—the man who had billed himself as "Drier than Volstead" in his victorious race against Congressman Andrew Volstead, the originator of legislation that empowered the government to crack down on the sale and importation of liquor. Despite this anomalous friendship, the Little Flower was a forceful and bitter opponent of Prohibition. To La Guardia, the Volstead Act was a case of "them against us," the "them" being the "money-class." The rich, La Guardia reasoned, could still buy the best liquor and drink it undisturbed. He set himself to do something for "the little guy."

In June 1926, he did just that. He announced "in the very precincts of the torpid House Committee on Alcoholic Liquor Traffic," of which he was the only "wet" member, that he was going to brew beer right before their eyes! The next day, he entered the committee chamber accompanied by a former brewer. Most of the committee members ran off in alarm. La Guardia was left with an audience of fifty reporters. Before their very eyes, he showed them how to brew lager, ale, and pilsner. Then he dared anyone to arrest him. His little demonstration brought national headlines.

On February 28, 1929, La Guardia married a second time. His bride, Marie Fischer, had been his secretary for fifteen years. "I lost a great secretary," La Guardia quipped, "and gained a lousy cook." The marriage ceremony was performed by Congressman Kvale, who was also a Lutheran minister.

In 1929, La Guardia challenged Democrat Jimmy Walker for mayor of New York City. La Guardia tried to get the people of the city to understand that Walker was running a totally corrupt administration—that the bosses of Tammany Hall were deeply involved with elements of organized crime. Again, La Guardia was a man before his time. The mayoral race of 1929 took place during an "endless summer of paper prosperity." People were simply having too good a time to listen to the voice of doom. Even the collapse of the stock market one week before the election didn't help. Dapper Jimmy Walker crushed the Little Flower by nearly a half-million votes, even carrying East Harlem. La Guardia's defeat was the worst any major-party candidate had suffered in the history of Greater New York.

With the onset of the Depression, La Guardia was back in Congress, playing his accustomed role of moral absolutist. Early in 1932, faced with the prospect of an unbalanced budget, President Hoover proposed a national sales tax of 2.25 percent on manufactured goods. It was meant to raise $600 million. Hoover's ill-conceived proposal "set the stage for the most spectacular victory of La Guardia's legislative career." In response to Hoover's tax increase, the Major proposed taxes on safe-deposit boxes and stock transfers, and a surtax on incomes over $100,000. The battle lines had been drawn.

In the beginning, La Guardia was almost alone in his opposition to the tax hike. Hoover's bill made it out of the House Ways and Means Committee on a twenty-four-to-one vote. An irate La Guardia asked his House colleagues: "What is this—a kissing bee?" The Major wound up turning what was supposed to be a two-day debate into a two-week "carnival." Moments before one colloquy, a La Guardia aide asked: "What are you going to do, Major?" to which he uttered the immortal words "Soak the rich!"

La Guardia's "soak the rich" speech caused a sensation: "As the second week [of the debate] opened, the leaders could no longer hold their people in line. There was turbulence on the floor . . . members shouting, jeering, coming close to fist fights. Then the lines broke all together." In the end, almost single-handedly, La Guardia turned the tide. When the House finally got around to voting on the Hoover surtax on March 24, 1932, it was turned down by a final vote of 211 to 178.

That same week, President Hoover signed the Norris-La Guardia Anti-Injunction Act into law. This landmark legislation outlawed the yellow-dog contract, under which workers, as a condition of employment, had to agree not to join a union. It also forbade the federal courts from issuing an injunction against legal strikes unless they turned violent or caused "irreparable harm."

In 1932, Fiorello La Guardia was voted out of office by the people of the Twentieth District. He had originally wanted to run on both the Republican and the Democratic ticket. The effort "foundered on the refusal of a West Side Tammany boss named James J. Hines." It proved to be a costly error on Hines's part: had La Guardia been given the Democratic nomination, he likely would have remained in Congress. As things turned out, once the Major was out of Washington, he ran for mayor, thus setting in motion the process that eventually put men like Hines out of business and behind bars. Had Hines not been so obtuse, the history of the era might have turned out differently.

La Guardia lost his seat by some 1,200 votes to James J. Lanzetta, a young Tammany alderman. There was plenty of evidence of voter fraud: "In some precincts there were more votes than residents. Men claiming to be election inspectors later disappeared and were found to have given fake addresses—but the votes they had certified were already counted."

Down again, but not out, La Guardia came back with a vengeance. Newly elected President Franklin Roosevelt offered La Guardia the post of Assistant Secretary of Labor. La Guardia regretfully turned him down, saying he was "too old to start taking orders from anyone." Between the time of his defeat and the end of his term, La Guardia played a pivotal role in formulating what was to become FDR's "Hundred Days." During that lame-duck session, La Guardia drafted two critical pieces of legislation. One, aimed at "stanching the flood of foreclosures," would have provided some $200 million in government capital for a federal credit bank. Bottled up in committee, it eventually passed during the Hundred Days. The second bill, an amendment to the National Bankruptcy Act of 1898, empowered courts to give "credit extensions to farmers and individuals, staving off forced liquidations by their creditors." This bill became law on the last day of the Hoover administration.

Upon La Guardia's return to New York City, the Seabury Commission hearings were in full swing. Under the leadership of Judge Samuel Seabury, a descendant of John and Priscilla Alden, the commission investigated all of Tammany Hall's nefarious dealings. La Guardia's charges from 1929 proved to be true. The commission "sifted a mountain of evidence and eventually questioned four thousand witnesses, producing enough transcribed testimony to fill ninety-five thousand pages." The final report showed what one writer termed "the insolence of office." It thoroughly exposed a spoils system that reached all the way to Mayor Walker himself. Shortly after Seabury's findings were made public, Walker resigned and took the first boat to Europe.

In the next election for mayor, Fiorello La Guardia ran as the candidate of the newly created Fusion Party. At first, the Fusionists didn't want the Major; they were looking for a "respectable" candidate. When virtually everyone else turned them down, La Guardia became their man. He swept to victory, running with a slate of minority candidates. His swearing-in took place in the library of Judge Seabury's home. His task complete, the old aristocrat spoke precisely seven words: "At last, New York has a mayor."

The next morning, January 1, 1934, Fiorello La Guardia went down to his new office. Upon entering for the first time, he was met by a group of reporters. As he was going through the door, he "threw a one-sentence, all-purpose answer at them over his shoulder: *finita la cuccagna*—"the party's over."

As history records, La Guardia served three terms as Mayor of New York. During his twelve-year tenure, he became perhaps the second-best-known American in the world. La Guardia was by no means perfect. He had a wide puritanical streak and could be cynical, churlish, hot-headed, petty, and just plain wrong. To his enemies, he was "egotistical, strutting and power hungry, a demagogue and a rascal." To his many admirers, the Little Flower was "colorful, dynamic, contagiously self-confident, progressive and the deadliest Tammany-killer of his day."

La Guardia involved himself in virtually every facet of the city. When the Democrat-controlled Board of Aldermen complained about his harsh tactics, he replied: "I am the majority in this city, and don't you forget it." From the creation of parks and bridges to meat rationing and American foreign policy, La Guardia was a whirlwind of activity. And the people loved him.

La Guardia was one of the first major American politicians to openly speak out against the Nazi menace. According to David M. and Jackie R. Esposito, "his implacable hostility toward the Nazis was based on his belief that they were the international equivalent of his domestic enemies." As early as June 1933, La Guardia was making statements like "Hitler is a perverted maniac." While giving the keynote address before the National Conference Against Racial Persecution in Germany, he made the "terrifyingly prophetic" statement that "Part of his [Hitler's] program is the complete annihilation of the Jews in Germany. When the internal affairs of one country affect the peace of the world, then it is time to protest."

In March 1937, speaking to the Women's Division of the American Jewish Congress, La Guardia suggested that the upcoming New York World's Fair should include a "chamber of horrors" just for "that brown-shirted fanatic." This comment brought an official protest on the part of the German government. Secretary of State Cordell Hull made a formal apology to the Nazis: "I very earnestly deprecate the utterances which have thus given offense to the German government." La Guardia's statements were page-one news.

Time magazine cynically speculated that La Guardia's attack on Hitler was his "opening gun" in the 1937 mayoral race. "In New York City, as any political nose-counter knows, the hooked far outnumber the Aryan noses."

Many believed that La Guardia would be called on the carpet by President Roosevelt, whose Secretary of State, Hull, had gone "beyond the bounds of diplomatic courtesy by giving the Nazis expert advice on how to handle their American critics." When La Guardia finally went to Washington and entered the Oval Office, he was greeted by a smiling FDR, arm outstretched in a mock Nazi salute. "Heil, Fiorello!" he said with a grin. La Guardia immediately snapped to attention and thrust out his own arm. "Heil Franklin!" he responded. The two men are reported to have burst out laughing. Later, when La Guardia left, Roosevelt reportedly told Secretary Hull "he wished he could pin a gold medal on La Guardia for saying what everyone in the administration was thinking."

With the coming of World War II, La Guardia thought he might be named Secretary of War. Instead, the post went to another Republican, Henry Stimson. FDR did appoint the Major to head up the nation's civilian defense. La Guardia was not happy in the post, and applied for an army general's commission. His application was rejected.

In his 1999 book, *The American Mayor*, author Melvin G. Holli, with the assistance of dozens of political historians, rated the one hundred best big-city mayors in American history. La Guardia came in first, with Cleveland's reform mayor Tom L. Johnson (in office 1901—09) "considerably below La Guardia in second." Holli writes, La Guardia was " a stout-hearted fireplug of a man who built modern New York . . . fought 'Murder Incorporated,' read the comics to children over the air during a newspaper strike, and was a symbol of ethnic probity and honesty—an antidote to the widespread public view that ethnic politicians and crooks were one and the same, and part of the problem of big cities."

La Guardia decided against running for a fourth term in 1944. By that point he and Marie had adopted Thea's sister's two children. Life at home was good, and La Guardia was just plain worn out. At the conclusion of his dozen years as mayor, La Guardia briefly hosted a radio program, and then fell victim to pancreatic cancer. He died on September 20, 1947, and was buried at Woodlawn Cemetery in the Bronx. It was the end of an era. Roosevelt was no longer President. La Guardia was no longer mayor. Thank God for the Yankees.

References

American Jewish History, vol. 78, no. 1 pp. 38–53.

Current Biography, 1940, pp. 473–476.

Dictionary of American Biography.

Lawrence Elliot, *Little Flower: The Life and Times of Fiorello La Guardia* (New York: William Morrow, 1983).

August Heckscher, *When La Guardia Was Mayor* (New York: Norton, 1978).

Melvin G. Holli, *The American Mayor: The Best and Worst Big City Leaders* (University Park: Pennsylvania State University Press, 1999).

Arthur Mann, *La Guardia: A Fighter Against His Times, 1882–1933* (Chicago: University of Chicago Press, 1969).

Universal Jewish Encyclopedia.

LANTOS, THOMAS PETER (1928–): *Democrat from California; has served ten terms in the House (Ninety-seventh through One Hundred and Fifth Congress; January 3, 1981–present).*

Only two individuals have ever been made honorary citizens of the United States of America: Sir Winston Churchill and Raoul Wallenberg. Churchill, a major player in world events for more than fifty years, was one of the best-known men of his time. Wallenberg, on the other hand, languished in relative obscurity for more than forty years. Then, in the late 1970s, his name and heroic deeds resurfaced. Within a brief time, he became the subject of numerous biographies and a made-for-television miniseries, became an honorary citizen, and had a plaza named for him in the nation's capital. Wallenberg's emergence from obscurity was primarily the work of one man: San Francisco-area Representative Tom Lantos. Without Lantos's tireless efforts, the name and deeds of the Swedish diplomat would likely have been lost to history.

Tom Lantos is the only member of the Congressional Minyan to have personally experienced the Holocaust. Born in Budapest on February 1, 1928, Lantos was a child when the Nazis entered Hungary. Rounded up with his family (all of whom were eventually exterminated), Lantos was sent to a Nazi forced-labor camp. He escaped and made his way back to Budapest, where he spent the rest of the war living with an aunt in a "house of refuge" provided by the heroic Wallenberg. Not one to lie low, the blond-haired, blue-eyed Lantos became a runner for Wallenberg, continually putting his own life in peril.

Raoul Wallenberg (1912–?) was, by profession, a University of Michigan-trained architect. Descended from a long line of Swedish bankers and diplomats, he spent six months in Haifa, Palestine, in 1936, where he studied management at the Holland Bank. It was in Haifa that he first came in contact with Jewish refugees from Germany. Upon his return to Sweden, he became the foreign representative of a Central

European trading company whose president was a Hungarian Jew. In July 1944, the Swedish Foreign Ministry, "at the request of Jewish organizations," sent him on a rescue mission to Budapest, as an attaché at the Swedish embassy.

By the time of Wallenberg's arrival there, more than 475,000 Hungarian Jews had already been deported to Nazi extermination camps. Determined to save as many as possible, Wallenberg came up with a plan: he began issuing *Schutz-Paesse*—Swedish identification passes that soon came to be known as "Wallenberg passports." Jews holding these passes were legally under the protection of the Swedish government. Wallenberg housed them in the more than thirty apartment houses he had purchased in Budapest. He claimed that each of the apartment buildings, with a giant Swedish flag flying on its roof, was legally Swedish territory, thereby legally barring Nazi entry. There were nearly 10,000 Jews living in these "houses of refuge" at any one time. All told, Wallenberg saved as many as 33,000 Jews from extinction.

In January 1945, the Russians entered Budapest. On January 17, Wallenberg went to meet with some Soviet officers to urge them to provide aid for the Jews; that was the last anyone ever saw of Raoul Wallenberg. For nearly a dozen years, the Soviet Union denied he was a prisoner. In 1957, Russian officials finally admitted that Wallenberg had been their prisoner, and claimed that, according to their records, he had succumbed to a heart attack a decade earlier. Unconfirmed reports had Wallenberg still alive as recently as the late 1980s. As of 2000, no one knows for sure what happened to him.

Following the war's end, Tom Lantos came to the United States to attend the University of Washington on a Hillel Foundation scholarship. He received his B.A. in 1949, an M.A. in 1950, and a Ph.D. in economics from the University of California in 1953. During those years, Lantos had an exacting schedule: he arose at "6:00 A.M. and taught courses at San Francisco State, attended classes at Berkeley, and instructed students at two evening schools, then snatched a few hours sleep before the next 19-hour day."

Shortly after receiving his master's degree from the University of Washington, Tom Lantos married his childhood sweetheart, Annette Tilleman. Born in Budapest and educated in Lausanne, Annette had met Tom when she was seven, he eleven. During the war, Annette and her family were sheltered in the Portuguese embassy in Budapest, "an opportunity that resulted from a family connection with a Portuguese diplomat." In 1945, Annette left Budapest for the United States, traveling on a Portuguese passport. Annette became a United States citizen in 1948, and earned a B.A. at San Francisco State University in social sciences and French. She was reunited with her childhood friend Tom, and the two were married on July 13, 1950. Annette went on to do graduate work in psychology, and taught French and social studies in high school for many years. The Lantoses have two daughters, Annette and Katrina, and thirteen grandchildren. Daughter Katrina is married to former New Hampshire Representative Dick Swett, who lost a 1996 Senate race to incumbent Republican Bob Smith. Annette is married to Timber Dick, a businessman in Colorado. The Dicks have eight children; the Swetts five. Neither Lantos daughter is a practicing Jew; the Swetts are Mormons.

Tom Lantos became an economics professor at San Francisco State University in 1950. He remained on the faculty until his election to Congress in 1980. During those three decades, in addition to his faculty position, he worked as a television commentator (1955–63) and served as an economic advisor to United States Senators Mike Gravel of Alaska, Frank Church of Iowa, and Joseph Biden of Delaware, all Democrats. In 1970, Lantos was elected to the Milbrae Board of Education—his first electoral victory.

In November 1978, fanatics in Jonestown, Guyana, gunned down Eleventh District Representative Leo Ryan. In the special election to fill the unexpired portion of his two-year term, voters elected Republican Bill Royer, a member of the San Mateo County Board of Supervisors. In 1980, Tom Lantos challenged Royer. He "spent liberally, ran an astute campaign, and at the same time managed to argue

for a larger defense budget and to attack Royer's allegedly conservative voting record." The Eleventh District (eventually to be renamed the Twelfth) was an "ethnically diverse and economically prosperous constituency." Ranging from the northern San Francisco Peninsula suburbs to San Mateo, Burlingame, and Hillsborough, the Twelfth District had a 1998 median house value of $320,400—easily one of the highest in the nation. It contained the second-highest percentage (26 percent) of Asians of any mainland district in the nation, and was nearly 15 percent Hispanic.

As an astute political animal with liberal instincts and an enviable track record in international economics, Lantos was a perfect fit for the voters of his district. On election day, 1980, he defeated Royer 46 percent to 43 percent. Lantos drew Royer as his opponent once again in 1982. Raising an astounding $1,192,400 to Royer's $509,000, Lantos won by the even more impressive margin of 57 percent to 40 percent. In his last eight reelection campaigns, Lantos's measure of victory ranged from a low of 67 percent in 1994 to 74 percent in 1986. In three of those races (1986, 1988, and 1990) Lantos faced Republican G. M. "Bill" Quraishi, a nuclear and electrical engineer. Quraishi garnered 26 percent of the vote in 1986, 24 percent in 1988, and 29 percent in 1990. "At this rate," quipped the esteemed *California Journal*, "he'll have Lantos out of office in 2002."

In Congress, Lantos was assigned to the House Foreign Affairs Committee. His first bill (cosponsored with then-Rhode Island Senator Claiborne Pell) called for making Raoul Wallenberg a citizen of the United States. Lantos's measure, which eventually gained two Republican cosponsors, Representatives Jack Kemp of New York and Millicent Fenwick of New Jersey, passed the House by a vote of 396–2. Granting Wallenberg American citizenship was more than a way to honor the heroic diplomat; it gave the American government official standing in requesting documentation from the Soviets. In the mid-1980s, Lantos tried to get the Swedish government to use the leverage they had gained by trapping a Soviet submarine in their territorial waters to get more information about Wallenberg; nothing of substance was forthcoming. In 1995, Lantos sponsored the bust of Raoul

Wallenberg which now resides in the Capitol.

Annette has also been intimately involved in getting Raoul Wallenberg's name before the public as a way of honoring her father, who was drowned in the Danube River by the Nazis in 1944. In the late 1970s, when she was still a homemaker and Tom a professor, she entered a National Public Radio sweepstakes-type event in which the prize was the opportunity to ask one question of President Jimmy Carter during a nationally televised press conference. According to the *San Mateo Weekly*, "she entered the contest with some hope [sending in no fewer than ten postcards], but forgot about it entirely." Annette Lantos was one of those selected, and "in the two minutes she was given to speak with President Carter, she told him her story." Carter promised that he would ask Soviet Premier Leonid Brezhnev about Wallenberg at their next summit. Even more importantly, the world press began to learn about Raoul Wallenberg. The "second she hung up with President Carter," she received calls from the *New York Times*, the *Boston Globe*, and the *Chicago Tribune*. The *Times* wound up doing a cover story on Wallenberg; Dan Rather interviewed her on *60 Minutes*.

Annette Lantos has long claimed that in telling the story of Raoul Wallenberg, "I am also telling the story of my father."

Tom Lantos has spent the lion's share of his two decades in Congress as a guardian, spokesman, and watchdog for the oppressed of the earth. He is an urbane, well-spoken intellectual with the social formality of his native Hungary. (The *San Jose Mercury*'s description of Lantos is a bit less flattering: "His white hair combed straight back and his smooth, rosy complexion, added to his Old World manner and decorum, give him a strait-laced appearance that borders on pomposity.")

Lantos has never been afraid to speak his mind when it comes to foreign policy issues, especially regarding the Middle East. Speaking of Sadaam Hussein, Lantos told his House colleagues:

> We are witnessing the emergence of a new Hitler in the Middle East. Mr. Speaker, the time has come for the Congress to take a firm stand against this vicious, irresponsible and dangerous leader.

We cannot sit by idly while he continues to intimidate and dominate his neighbors in the Middle East. Mr. Speaker, will we be remembered as the Neville Chamberlains of this era or will we stand up against this brutal totalitarian dictatorship in the tradition of Sir Winston Churchill?

Lantos was a "vocal and vehement" supporter of the Gulf War Resolution. In casting his vote in favor of the resolution, Lantos told a hushed House chamber: "We were not intimidated by Hitler. We were not intimidated by Mussolini. We were not intimidated by the Japanese militarists, by Stalin, or Mao Tse-Tung. And we shall not be intimidated by Sadaam Hussein."

Lantos is also known for his biting sarcasm. Witness his address to John Kelly, Assistant Secretary of State for Near Eastern Affairs, upon listening to Kelly's optimistic testimony on Iraqi strongman Hussein: "With all due respect, Mr. Secretary, I detect an Alice in Wonderland quality about your testimony . . . you express the hope that we can deal with him [Hussein], which boggles my mind . . . I find this, to put it mildly, a non-sequitur."

Not surprisingly, Lantos has, from time to time, been likened "more as a crusader than a legislator." In 1989, he brought the Dalai Lama to the Capitol in order to dramatize Chinese oppression in Tibet. While on a visit to China a few years later, he raised the issue of the Dalai Lama and Tibetan human rights with Communist leader Deng Xiaoping. Deng labeled Lantos "ignorant" and "arrogant." In 1990, Lantos became the first American official to visit Albania in nearly a half-century.

From his position as chair of the Employment and Housing Subcommittee, Lantos held a televised investigation of waste, fraud, abuse, mismanagement, and neglect under Reagan Housing and Urban Development Secretary Samuel Pierce. In convening the hearings, Lantos claimed that as much as $2 billion had been lost to mismanagement and fraud during Pierce's eight-year tenure. C-SPAN viewers tuning in to the hearings saw Lantos excoriating Pierce, labeling the mismanagement "a staggering fiasco of the greedy, unethical and sleazy people who went to HUD and found it a honey pot." When Pierce denied that any mismanagement had occurred, Lantos snapped back: "If

HUD were a bank, it would be closed by the FDIC."

Upon hearing a Republican fundraiser protest his innocence on grounds that he lacked positive political influence, Lantos responded: "That is about as believable as Elvis's being seen in a K-Mart store."

One former HUD official, who had received $1.7 million in consulting fees for obtaining federal rent-subsidy grants for developers, tried to justify his hiring of former Interior Secretary James G. Watt to help win the federal plums. When he began reading a letter extolling Watt for his "well-known flair for innovation," Lantos cut him short and said: "This is a very flowery letter. You hired him to peddle his influence to get your projects through." Lantos told the witness that Watt's only experience in housing was "making Bambi homeless. . . . What I find the most obnoxious so far is the unmitigated hypocrisy of people like James Watt who exude unction, piety and noble motives, who carry on a crusade to destroy these programs and at the same time shamelessly milk them." Stunned by the chairman's directness, the witness wilted. "Influence peddling is a pejorative," he stammered, "but in a sense the description is correct."

Summarizing his subcommittee's findings, Lantos opined that "For some individuals, obtaining . . . HUD funds was as easy as phoning Domino's for a pizza. The bidding process [has] all the competitiveness and suspense of professional wrestling."

Throughout his career in Congress, Tom Lantos has managed to work well with Republicans as well as Democrats. A bit more conservative on economic and foreign-policy issues than his fellow Democrats, Lantos does not have that "instinctive mistrust of American foreign policy or doubt of American good intentions" that haunts many post-Vietnam-era legislators.

In 1990, Lantos's son-in-law, former Yale football hero Dick Swett, was elected to Congress from New Hampshire's Second District. Swett defeated incumbent Republican Chuck Douglas, a former associate justice of the New Hampshire Supreme Court. Shortly after his victory, Republicans charged that some of Swett's campaign funds ($465,160, a huge amount for a nonincumbent) may have been steered his way by his father-in-law-a clear violation of federal campaign finance laws. Nothing came of the charges; Swett served two terms and was then defeated in 1994 by Charles F. Bass. In 1996, Swett nearly beat incumbent Republican Bob Smith for one of New Hampshire's two Senate seats.

In December 1997, Lantos drew the ire of both Republicans and Democrats after comparing a witness to Nazi war criminal Kurt Waldheim. While listening to testimony before the Government Reform and Oversight Committee (of which he was the ranking member during the One Hundred and Fifth Congress), Lantos suggested that Donald Smaltz, special prosecutor of former Agriculture Secretary Mike Espy, was "hiding his GOP past much as former United Nations Secretary General Kurt Waldheim hid his Nazism." Lantos defended his comments to the press, proclaiming that his comments were nothing more than a "very clear suggestion that just as Waldheim covered up his political affiliation, Mr. Smaltz attempted to do the same thing."

Now past seventy, Lantos shows no signs of slowing down. Ably assisted by his wife Annette (who has been part of his office staff since day one), Tom Lantos is wildly popular with the voters of his San Francisco district. Lantos easily defeated Republican Robert Evans (74 to 21 percent) in 1998, thereby earning a tenth term in the House. He continues to play a major role, speaking out on foreign policy issues, defending the rights of the oppressed, and constantly prodding the United Nations to take a more activist posture. On this last point he has a keen edge. His good friend, United Nations General Secretary Kofi Annan, is married to Nane, the niece of Raoul Wallenberg.

References
Biographical material provided by Tom Lantos.
Almanac of American Politics (1978–98 editions).
Congressional Record, vol. 127, no. 86 (June 9, 1981); vol. 137, no. 7 (January 11, 1991).
Los Angeles Times, August 5, 1989, 1:21.
Moment Magazine, October 1987, pp. 58–59.
San Mateo Weekly, September 19, 1990, pp. 24, 38.

LAUTENBERG, FRANK RALEIGH (1924–):
Democrat from New Jersey; has served three terms in the Senate (January 3, 1982–present).

Horatio Alger could have written Senator Frank Lautenberg's life story, except that in most cases, Alger's tatterdemalions usually rose from rags to mere respectability. In Lautenberg's case, the rise was all the way to great wealth. From all appearances, the Senator has never forgotten his humble roots. Once, while campaigning for the Senate, he pointed to the gap between his front teeth and said: "If my parents had money, I wouldn't have this. I keep it as a badge of my roots."

The Senator's parents, Samuel and Mollie (Bergen) Lautenberg, were immigrants from Russia. The Lautenbergs lived in Paterson, New Jersey, where Sam worked in a silk mill. For a brief spell, he ran a tavern in nearby Paramus, until the Depression put him out of business. At various times, he also sold coal and farmed. In order to make ends meet, Mollie opened a lunch counter in Belleville, worked in a women's clothing store, and sold insurance. Despite all their efforts, the Lautenbergs remained poor. Their son, Frank Raleigh, was born in Paterson on January 23, 1924. During his childhood, the family moved more than a dozen times. At one point they lived in a "cramped apartment above a tavern in a racially mixed neighborhood" in Paterson.

When Frank was ten, his father took him to a silk mill in order "to teach him a lesson he never forgot." Walking through the mill, holding his son by the hand, Sam said: "Do you see how dark and awful it is in here? Never let yourself be put in a position where you have to do work like this!" Frank Lautenberg attended Elementary School 21 in Paterson and Nutley High School, from which he graduated in 1941. Six years earlier, Sam Lautenberg had died from intestinal cancer. He was only forty-three years old. The loss haunted Frank for years. In the early 1970s, when he had become a multimillionaire, he established the Lautenberg Center for General and Tumor Immunology at the

Medical School of the Hebrew University.

At age eighteen, Frank Lautenberg entered the army, was assigned to the Army Signal Corps, and sent to Europe. At war's end, he entered Columbia University on the G.I. Bill, graduating with a degree in economics in 1949. Lautenberg has long said that "getting an education he could not otherwise afford, thanks to the G.I. Bill, was a seminal influence on the formation of his liberal political philosophy." Following graduation, Frank Lautenberg worked as a salesman for the Prudential Insurance Company in Paterson. In 1952, he literally stumbled upon the opportunity that was to make his great fortune.

That year, the twenty-eight-year-old Lautenberg approached an accountant named Henry Taub, whose "fledgling . . . firm was preparing the payrolls of a handful of companies in the Paterson area." Lautenberg persuaded Taub that in order to expand, he would have to "aggressively go after business." Lautenberg sold himself to Taub as an individual who had the requisite marketing skills for the job. Taub hired Lautenberg as the fifth employee—and only salesman—at the firm that would eventually become Automatic Data Processing. ADP grew to become the largest data-processing firm in the world. By 1961, Lautenberg was the firm's vice president in charge of administration. Eight years later, he became ADP's president. In this capacity, Lautenberg "embarked on an ambitious acquisition program, buying up many smaller firms, including the Electronic Data Service in Chicago, Payroll Specialists in Cleveland . . . and the First National City Bank of New York." He also rewarded ADP's workers by creating an employee stock-ownership plan. The employees (numbering more than 20,000 by 1990) in turn rewarded their leader by "consistently refusing to unionize." By 1975, Lautenberg had risen to become chairman of the board and chief executive officer. When the Clothing and Textile Workers Union tried to unionize the Clifton office of ADP, "not a single worker responded positively."

At the time of Frank Lautenberg's election to the United States Senate in 1982, ADP was preparing payrolls for "more than 100,000 companies involving more than five million workers—one out of every fourteen nongovernment workers in the United States. In 1996, *Roll Call* rated Lautenberg the sixth-wealthiest member of Congress, with a net worth of approximately $40 million. No wonder Lautenberg has said that "ADP really means American Dream Personified."

While he amassed his fortune, Frank Lautenberg also became active in community organizations and politics. Always a "giver" to good causes—he served as president of the American Friends of Hebrew University and as national chair of the United Jewish Appeal from 1975 to 1977—Lautenberg started his political career by making a $90,000 contribution to Senator George McGovern's 1972 presidential campaign. That contribution earned him a spot on Richard Nixon's infamous "Enemies List." Four years later, he helped finance Jimmy Carter's successful presidential race, and was often sought out by the Georgian for his views on Israel and the Middle East.

As he became more and more involved in Democratic politics—lending support to the likes of Senators Birch Bayh, Ted Kennedy, Gary Hart, and John Glenn—Lautenberg began thinking: "if I'm willing to support them, why shouldn't I support myself?" As the 1970s turned into the 1980s, Lautenberg began giving serious consideration to launching his own political career.

In 1978, "in recognition of his contributions to the Democratic party of New Jersey," Governor Brendan T. Byrne named Lautenberg a commissioner of the Port Authority of New York and New Jersey. In 1980, Lautenberg once again lent strong financial assistance to Jimmy Carter, hoping that he might receive a cabinet position in a second Carter administration. Those hopes were, of course, dashed when Ronald Reagan buried the man from Plains. Lautenberg remained on the Port Authority, awaiting his chance. He did not have long to wait.

In March 1982, four-term Senator Harrison Williams, Jr. (1919–) resigned from the upper chamber following his conviction on corruption charges involving the Abscam sting operation.

Republican Governor Thomas H. Kean then appointed banker Nicholas F. Brady (1930–) as a "caretaker" senator. Brady, who would later become Secretary of the Treasury, served in the Senate for precisely eight months and one week. He did not seek election to a full six-year term. Frank Lautenberg, sensing that the time was right, quickly announced his candidacy for the Democratic nomination. Putting more than $1 million of his own money into the Democratic primary race, Lautenberg "managed to come from behind in the polls to top a crowded field of ten Democrats." The final tally gave the ADP chairman 26 percent to 23 percent for former Congressman Andy Maguire and 20 percent for Joseph A. LeFante. Coming in a distant fourth with 11 percent of the vote was Princeton Mayor Barbara Boggs Sigmund, the daughter of the late House Majority Leader Hale Boggs and his wife, Representative Lindy Boggs, and the sister of Washington power broker Tommy Boggs and ABC reporter Cokie Roberts.

In the general election, Lautenberg squared off against Republican Representative Millicent Fenwick (1910–1992), who became the early favorite. A member of the GOP's moderate wing, the "eccentric" pipe-smoking Fenwick was "nationally recognized as the model for the Lacey Davenport character in Garry Trudeau's topical cartoon strip *Doonesbury*." With less than three weeks left to go in the campaign, Lautenberg was lagging far behind, showing poll ratings of no more than 18 percent. He then added more than $3 million of his own money, blanketing New Jersey with commercials "that portrayed the seventy-two-year-old congresswoman as being out of touch with the concerns of a state that was suffering from the worst recession since the Depression.

Lautenberg's numbers began to rise. Aided by a last-minute endorsement from the National Organization for Women (and a better than two-to-one edge in spending), Lautenberg wound up winning 51 percent to 48 percent. All told, Lautenberg spent $6,596,088, of which $5,142,812 (78 percent) came from his own deep pockets.

Assigned to the Committees on Banking and Commerce, Frank Lautenberg spent his first eighteen months in the Senate in "quiet obscurity." He did not even make his maiden speech until June 7, 1983, a full six months after his swearing-in. In his first speech, the junior Senator from New Jersey, warning of "a growing gap in computer literacy," called for more computers in inner-city classrooms.

Lautenberg's first significant legislative achievement did not come until the next year; the enactment of an anti-drunk driving bill that "forced states to raise the legal drinking age to twenty-one or face a cut in federal highway funds." Faced with the daunting prospect of getting his bill past the powerful liquor lobby, Lautenberg began buttonholing his colleagues, refusing to take no for an answer. In the end, Lautenberg pulled off a legislative upset; his bill passed 81–16. After his first two years in the Senate, Lautenberg transferred to the Committees on Appropriations, Budget, and Environment and Public Works.

Throughout most of his Senate career, Lautenberg was easily overshadowed by his senior colleague from New Jersey, Bill Bradley. The six-foot, five-inch Bradley, the Senate's only former professional basketball player and Olympic Gold Medal winner (and one of its few Rhodes Scholars), always seemed to be at the epicenter of major national and international issues. A slow, deliberate thinker, Bradley came to be known as one of the Senate's intellectual giants. Lautenberg, by comparison, spent most of his career looking to the needs of his home state. The 1991 edition of *Current Biography* noted that "his workmanlike performance on behalf of the citizens of New Jersey has been pretty dull stuff" when compared to the issues on Bradley's political pallet. A man with a well-developed sense of self, Lautenberg "bristled" at invidious comparisons between him and Bradley: "The things I work on are the things that affect everyday life. Things for New Jersey. Would I like to craft legislation that gets featured in every newspaper and on every television station? Of course I would. But I'm not a grandstander; I never have been."

In 1985, while Bradley was dealing with revisions to the Federal Tax Code, Lautenberg was sponsoring revisions to the Superfund Law. This law provided for the "continuing . . . cleanup of toxic waste sites around the United States, including about 100 in New Jersey." At the same time, Lautenberg authored the provision "requiring chemical companies to notify area residents of the specific contents of local dumps." A former two-pack-a-day smoker, Lautenberg also led the fight to ban smoking on all commercial flights in the United States. When he suggested that tobacco farmers "grow soybeans or something," he incurred the wrath of Senator Jesse Helms of North Carolina and other tobacco Senators, who complained that he had "bypassed their committees by attaching the ban to an appropriations bill." (The Senate, unlike the House, does not require that amendments be germane.) Lautenberg responded to Helms's angry charge by snapping: "The committee system is safe. The flying public is not."

In 1988, Senator Lautenberg was challenged for reelection by former Heisman Trophy winner–Rhodes Scholar–turned banker Pete Dawkins. When asked his thoughts about running against an American icon, Lautenberg replied: "What the Republicans did was to go to central casting and pick out a candidate to run against me. He thinks he can just wash up on the Jersey shore, announce, and walk away with his next trophy." Dawkins began the campaign by excoriating Lautenberg for his liberal record, especially his opposition to the death penalty for drug-related murders. Despite a huge campaign war chest, Dawkins quickly got into the political mire by attempting to "dress up his already impressive resume."

Sensing Dawkins's political weakness, Lautenberg accused him of being a carpetbagger who had only chosen to settle in New Jersey "after considering other states in which to launch a political career." Dawkins further imperiled his chances for victory when he was quoted as saying he would "blow his brains out" if he had to live in a small town. Running a series of commercials with the words "Be real, Pete" over Dawkins's pronouncements, Lautenberg coasted to a 54 percent to 46 percent victory. It turned out to be the most expensive Senate race in New Jersey history, with the two candidates spending nearly $15 million between them. In his first race for reelection, Lautenberg provided a "mere" $300,000 from his own pocket.

Ever in Bradley's shadow, Frank Lautenberg continued working on issues like Amtrak and mass transit, both important in New Jersey. Noting local voter hostility to New Jersey Governor Jim Florio's 1990 tax increase, he "obdurately refused" to vote for the 1993

Clinton budget and tax package. Lautenberg's "defection" made good political sense. Looking ahead to his 1994 reelection campaign, he realized that he would likely be facing the Speaker of New Jersey's House of Representatives, Garabed "Chuck" Haytaian, the man who had first sponsored the rollback of Florio's sales tax and then helped push Governor Christie Todd Whitman's tax cuts.

Upon entering the race, Haytaian came out for a flat tax, and raised millions of dollars from his fellow Armenian-Americans. Lautenberg, campaigning on his record, noted that while he had supported the Brady handgun-control bill, Haytaian had opposed Florio's ban on assault weapons. Throughout the campaign, Lautenberg hammered away at Haytaian's more conservative record. Haytaian's campaign fell apart after he made an appearance on the Bob Grant radio talk show on the heels of Grant's being accused of making racist remarks on the air. Frank Lautenberg was reelected for a third six-year term by a 50 percent to 47 percent margin.

Senator Lautenberg voted against the use of military force in the Persian Gulf. At war's end, he garnered considerable press for lambasting the governments of Kuwait and Saudi Arabia for "their failure to honor their financial commitments to the United States." Lecturing Secretary of State James A. Baker III, Lautenberg said: "It is a significant frustration of mine that we seem to have gotten nothing from Saudi Arabia or Kuwait or the other countries whose sovereignty we saved, whose assets we saved. They sent out a 911. We responded as no emergency team has ever responded in history. And what do we get? We don't even get payment on the pledges that they made to help us through the financial crisis."

On February 17, 1999, Frank Lautenberg announced, much to the dismay of his supporters, that he would not be running for reelection in 2000. At the press conference announcing this decision, Lautenberg said: "I believe I would have won a campaign . . . if I had run, and it's difficult to walk away from continued service." Keeping his promise not to let his political guard down and to continue to fight for what he believed, Lautenberg acted vigorously to get a Republican-controlled Senate to pass gun control legislation in the spring of 1999. Coming on the heels of the Columbine High School massacre in suburban Colorado, in which a dozen students were killed, Lautenberg induced his Republican colleagues to pass a measure that would institute background checks on potential buyers at gun shows.

In 1957, Frank Lautenberg married the former Lois Levenson. The Lautenbergs separated in 1988, after thirty-one years of marriage. They have since divorced, and the senator has remarried. Senator Lautenberg and his first wife have four children: Ellen Lautenberg, Nan Lautenberg Morgart, Lisa Lautenberg Birer, and Joshua. The senator also has six grandchildren. Lautenberg, who admits to having "found [his] Jewish identity late in life," believes "Jews are bound together by memory, tradition, faith and the refusal to succumb to indifference." When not in Washington, Frank Lautenberg resides in Montclair, New Jersey.

References

Almanac of American Politics (1984–98 editions).
American Jewish Biographies, pp. 241–242.
Current Biography, 1991, pp. 353–357.
New York Times, June 10, 1992, B8; July 19, 1984, p. 31; October 29, 1988.
Politics in America (1984–94 editions).

LEHMAN, HERBERT HENRY (1878–1963):
Democrat from New York; served part of one term and then one full term in Senate (November 9, 1949–January 3, 1957).

In his short story "The Worm in the Apple," author John Cheever tells the tale of the Crutchmans, a family "so very, very happy and so temperate in all their habits and so pleased with everything that came their way that one was bound to suspect a worm in their rosy apple and that the extraordinary rosiness of the fruit was only meant to conceal the gravity and the depth of the infection." Throughout the tale, Cheever as narrator/observer seeks to find their fatal flaw, the "worm in the apple" that will bring them down to the level of everyone else. No one, he suggests, can be that good or that happy.

Try though he may, the narrator is left wondering whether "the worm was not in the eye of the observer who, through timidity or moral cowardice, could not embrace the broad range of their natural enthusiasms." In the end, much to his amazement, the Crutchmans turn out to be precisely what they seem.

To a great extent, Senator Herbert Henry Lehman is like the Crutchmans. The product of immense wealth and privilege, Lehman spent more than sixty years in public life as a much-beloved public servant. Known for his humility, charity, and love of the common man, Lehman did seem a bit too good to be true. But cynicism makes fools of even the most discerning. When one of Lehman's most rancorous political enemies was asked to say something defamatory about him for a 1936 *New Yorker* profile, he thought, and then ruefully commented: "The worst thing I can say about Governor Lehman is that he is a good man." Once again, the "worm" was in the mind of the cynic, not in the "apple" of the subject.

The three Lehman brothers—Mayer, Emanuel, and Henry—came to America with the exodus of liberal Jews from the troubled Germany of 1848. Settling in Montgomery, Alabama, they went into partnership in a general store. They supplied cotton farmers in the area with clothes, utensils, and other merchandise. In return, they often received raw cotton in lieu of cash. In order to get their cash, the Lehmans resold the cotton in bulk quantities, often making a profit on both ends. By the mid-1850s, the brothers had moved into cotton brokerage and out of retailing.

In 1858, Emanuel opened an office in New York City, but the Civil War sent him hurrying back to Montgomery, where both he and Mayer served the South. Emanuel, at the behest of President Jefferson Davis, went to England, where, in addition to selling Southern cotton, he managed to sell Confederate bonds. In December 1864, Davis appointed Mayer Lehman to a special committee to raise funds to aid Confederate prisoners in the North. The plan was to send $500,000 worth of cotton through the battle lines for sale in New York. Mayer was supposed to travel under a prearranged safe-conduct pass. Unfortunately, General Ulysses Grant ignored Mayer's plea for safe conduct, and the scheme fell apart. The Lehmans' growing fortunes were so inextricably bound up with the Confederacy that when the war ended, they were fairly bankrupt. Following the war, they moved to New York, where they founded the Cotton Exchange, built a new fortune, and became prominent members of "Our Crowd."

Herbert Henry Lehman, the youngest of Mayer and Babette (Newgass) Lehman's eight children, was born in New York City on March 28, 1878. Young Herbert enjoyed the amenities of a wealthy boyhood—attending the exclusive Sachs Collegiate Institute, Sunday school at Temple Emanu-el (where his uncle Emanuel was the president), and summers either in the Adirondacks or Europe, where he went with his parents in both 1884 and 1887. Beginning when Herbert was six, his father would take him on regular Sunday visits to the charity wards at Mount Sinai Hospital (one of his main charitable interests) and to the poor neighborhoods of the Lower East Side. There, Lehman would recall many years later, "I saw the squalor, the congestion, the disease, the misery of people forced to live under conditions which seemed to me at the time subhuman, in quarters that seemed utterly unthinkable." These Sunday jaunts left a lasting impression on Herbert, who spent most of his life feeding, caring for, and seeking to bring hope to the impoverished of the earth.

Mayer Lehman wanted his youngest son to become a mining engineer, and considered sending him to a technical school. One of Herbert's teachers, aware that the younger Lehman was poor in mathematics and had no interest in science, persuaded the elder Lehman to send his son to Williams College, the teacher's alma mater. Herbert entered Williams in 1895. Although not a world-class student, he led an active college life, becoming manager of the track team, acting manager of the football team, an editor of the *Literary Monthly*, and a member of the debating society. At the end of Herbert's second year at Williams, Mayer Lehman died, leaving an estate of more than $5 million. Herbert's share of the inheritance amounted to slightly more than $400,000.

By the time Herbert Lehman graduated Williams College in 1899, Lehman Brothers was a highly successful banking house. Rather than going to work for the family firm, Herbert struck out on his own, joining the firm of J. Spencer Turner, a textile manufacturer, where he became a salesman of duck cloth. On the day he collected his first week's pay, he framed and hung on the wall a two-dollar bill. Years later, when he was already Governor of New York, he revealed that it was not really his first week's pay, but only two-fifths of it. His pay had been five dollars that first week. He had wished to make the "conventional gesture," but "wanted to have some extra spending money, too." Herbert remained with J. Spencer Turner for nearly ten years. By the time of his departure, he had become the company's treasurer and vice president.

In 1908, following his brother Sigmund's retirement, Herbert officially became a partner in Lehman Brothers with his brother Arthur and several Lehman cousins. The other Lehman brother, Irving, had taken a liking to constitutional law while studying at Columbia and became an attorney. Herbert Lehman wound up spending the next quarter-century with Lehman Brothers. During his career as an investment banker, the firm floated more than $5 billion worth of securities, and underwrote such firms as Sears Roebuck, F. W. Woolworth, Continental Can, Studebaker, and Goodrich. Additionally, it acted as financial agent and banker for R. H. Macy & Company, Gimbel Brothers, S. H. Kress, W. T. Grant, and other chain stores. As historian Alan Nevins noted in *Herbert H. Lehman and His Era*: "Of today's twenty largest retailing enterprises, Lehman Brothers has been or is presently regarded as investment broker for more than half." Before leaving the firm in 1932 to enter politics, Herbert Lehman arranged for the sale of Bamberger's department store in Newark, New Jersey, to R. H. Macy. With the money he received from the sale, Louis Bamberger established the Institute for Advanced Studies at Princeton. It is said that Bamburger created it just in time to provide a "haven for Albert Einstein and other scientists escaping from Hitler." Herbert Lehman was a member of the Institute's first board of directors.

As a banker, Herbert Lehman is remembered for his sagacity, his conservatism, and, above all, his personal ethics. Once, for instance, when his name was used in the prospectus of a venture that went bankrupt, Lehman insisted paying off all the stockholders because he thought his name might have persuaded them to invest. Lehman was a financial sponsor of the American Bemberg Company, a "German-controlled concern" which "set up rayon works at Elizabethtown, Tennessee." When Lehman learned that the company had refused to meet with a committee of its employees' union for collective bargaining, he resigned from the board of directors.

As charter members of America's German-Jewish elite ("Our Crowd"), the Lehmans married "their own kind": Arthur, one of Herbert's brothers, married a daughter of Adolph Lewisohn. Brother Irving (soon to become a federal judge) married a daughter of Nathan Straus. Mrs. Henry Morgenthau, Jr., wife of FDR's Secretary of the Treasury, was a daughter of Herbert's sister, Mrs. Morris Fatman. In April 1910, Herbert married Edith Altschul of San Francisco. Her father, Charles Altschul, was president of a bank controlled by the great Paris house of Lazard Fréres. Shortly after their marriage, Herbert acquired a seventy-acre estate at Purchase, in Westchester County, New York. Lehman took ten acres of the estate and set it aside as a public playground for the children of the town of Harrison. Mr. and Mrs. Herbert Lehman, who were married fifty-three years, adopted three children: Peter Gerald, John Robert, and Hilda Jane. Peter was killed while on active service in Britain in 1945, after having flown fifty-seven missions.

When America entered the "Great War" in 1917, Lehman, nearly forty and well past the age of conscription, immediately volunteered for service. His first assignment had him working with the Assistant Secretary of the Navy, Franklin D. Roosevelt—an association that would radically alter the lives of both men. Within a short time he became a captain in the United States Army, assigned to the General Staff, where he assisted General George W. Goethals, the engineer who had built the Panama Canal. His work revolved primarily around the purchase and procurement of supplies. At war's end, he was responsible for "dismantling the huge machine that had been built up to provision the military." By the time Lehman was discharged in 1919, he had risen to the rank of colonel. In addition to his other wartime duties, he served as treasurer and vice chairman of the Jewish Joint Distribution Committee. During the three years from 1916 to 1918, he "directed the collection and distribution of $75 million for relief of war sufferers."

The original Lehman brothers were rebel Democrats. In the next generation, Herbert and Irving were the only Lehmans who did not become Republicans. Prior to the time he ran for Lieutenant Governor of New York in 1928, Herbert Lehman's involvement in Democratic politics had been limited almost exclusively to finance. In 1912, along with many other "reforming and progressive Democrats," Lehman supported William Sulzer, a Lower East Side Congressman, for governor. Sulzer, who like Lehman was anti-Tammany, immediately got into a violent fight with the organization over a direct-primary bill, and was "rousing the state to support him" when a legislative committee revealed that "he had not reported a number of substantial campaign contributions, one of $5,000 from Lehman." When Lehman testified at Sulzer's impeachment trial, "he had no trouble in convincing his hearers that he had given the money to support what he thought was an honest reformer and expected nothing but progress in return." When he finished his testimony and was leaving the chamber, a Republican senator "plucked his sleeve" and asked: "You really gave Bill Sulzer $5,000 with no strings whatever?" When Lehman answered in the affirmative, the incredulous Republican said: "Well, you're just the kind of man the Republican Party needs!" Following Sulzer's conviction in 1913, Lehman was appointed to a committee charged with revising the New York State banking laws.

Some say that Woodrow Wilson owed his reelection in 1916 to Herbert Lehman's financial support. As the votes were being counted, it appeared that the outcome would depend on California. There was "apprehension that the bal-

lot boxes might be tampered with by Republican officials." Learning of this, Lehman wired his uncle, the Republican banker I. W. Helena in San Francisco, to "give the California Democrats, who were without funds, $5,000." The money safely in hand, Democratic officials hired guards for the ballot boxes "in order to insure an honest count."

In 1926, Al Smith asked Lehman to become manager of his campaign for Governor of New York. Lehman surprised everyone when he said yes, "put aside his business, moved into an office, and actually ran the whole show." Two years later, Smith ran for President of the United States, having been nominated by Franklin Roosevelt in the famous "Happy Warrior" convention speech. (Lehman served as director of the finance committee of the Democratic National Committee during the campaign.) Smith "returned the compliment by so arranging the state ticket as to make Roosevelt the candidate for Governor." Roosevelt agreed, but only if Lehman would run with him for lieutenant governor. The Republican gubernatorial candidate was to be Albert Ottinger, a Jew (and the uncle of future Congressman *Richard Ottinger*); and Roosevelt, as a savvy politician, knew the value of having a well-known, highly respected Jew on his ticket. Then again, Roosevelt knew and trusted Lehman from their days at the Department of the Navy. Roosevelt needed "a dependable workman to look after things in Albany during his long absences at Warm Springs."

The year 1928 was not a lucky one for the "Happy Warrior": Smith was defeated by Herbert Hoover, not even able to carry his home state. Lehman, on the other hand, eked out a 14,000-vote plurality. Following the election, the *Review of Reviews* noted that "it was Lehman's popularity (in a city that has many more than a half million Jewish voters) that carried the State tickets for the Democrats while they lost the Presidential ticket." Before moving up to Albany, Herbert Lehman divested himself of his business interests, so as not to give even a hint of impropriety in any future activities.

Lehman spent a great portion of the next four years as acting governor during Roosevelt's many absences. In 1929, just two months after he took the oath of office, he was called upon to deal with the failure of the City Trust Company, a bank with four branches and 20,000 depositors.

Lehman ordered an investigation, which resulted in Frank Warder, the state superintendent of banks, going to Sing Sing, a state prison. As acting governor, that was all he really had to do. But not Lehman: "he brooded over the bank failure," and was heard to remark on several occasions that "all those poor people shouldn't have to lose all that money." Lehman persuaded a number of other bankers to join him in making up a $6 million fund to pay off the depositors; the acting governor put in a million dollars of his own. A trust company was organized, which bought out the City Trust Company, and paid off the depositors. When the market crashed in October of that year, Lehman and his fellow guarantors lost every cent of the $6 million they had put up. In his second race for lieutenant governor in 1930, Lehman's plurality exploded to 565,000 votes.

In 1932, Franklin Roosevelt was nominated for President of the United States. Tammany did not want Lehman to become governor; he was too much of a reformer for their taste. But Roosevelt, with an assist from Al Smith, persuaded Tammany to back Lehman. As the *New Yorker*'s Hickman Powell noted: "He [Lehman] was the only thing that Roosevelt and Smith agreed on in 1932, and he is the only thing they have agreed on since." Running against Republican "Wild Bill" Donovan, Lehman was elected the forty-ninth Governor of New York with a plurality of 849,000 votes. Two years later, running against the charismatic Robert Moses, he was reelected by 808,089 votes. As governor, Lehman was able to "reorganize state finances, urge programs for public development of natural resources, improve the prison [system], expand the mental hospitals, develop welfare and housing programs, and improve the administration of relief."

Lehman made it known that he did not want to run for a third term in 1936. Roosevelt, insisting that he needed a strong pro-New Dealer in Albany, convinced him to run. This time, Lehman won by more than a half-million votes. From the distance of nearly sixty years, it is difficult to realize just how popular, how universally loved and respected, Lehman was. To New Yorkers of the 1930s there were three constants in the world of politics: Roosevelt was always President, Lehman always governor, and *La Guardia* always mayor. Lehman combined "a liberal social-conscious philosophy that appealed to ten million workingmen

voters" with "a solid conservative banker background reassuring to the nation's financial capital." Lehman presided over a truly dynamic, accomplished state government. As one writer of the period noted: "Under the pressure of Mr. Lehman's conscience, the Democrats [have] kept so many promises . . . that they have almost exhausted[ed] their issues."

Lehman truly wanted to leave Albany after finishing his third two-year term in 1938. Once again, he was convinced that he had to run. Facing Thomas Dewey (whom he had brought into government service) for the right to serve as New York's first four-year governor, Lehman won by one of the closest elections in the history of the state—63,394 votes. This was to be his final term as governor. After six elections, and a full decade as governor, the sixty-four-year-old Lehman was ready to move on to the next phase of his life.

During his decade as governor, Lehman accomplished some truly remarkable things, not the least of which was being able to convert a $100 million deficit into a surplus estimated at over $75 million, while simultaneously cutting taxes $90 million a year. As much satisfaction as he took in this achievement, Lehman derived even greater pride from his accomplishments in the area of social progress. In his valedictory address to the state legislature in Albany, he said: "my greatest satisfaction has come through the part which I have been privileged to play in enacting enlightened and beneficial social and labor legislation." Then, encapsulating his political philosophy, he stated: "I believe with all my heart that government is for the people. It must be clean, honest, and efficient, but it must be more than merely an administrative machine. It must concern itself with the solution of human as well as material problems. It must satisfy the needs and aspirations of its people and, in order to satisfy those needs and aspirations, it must be flexible enough to meet the changing conditions of the world today."

Lehman resigned a few days before his term expired in order to become the head of the newly created Office of Foreign Relief and Rehabilitation Operations (OFRRO). Lehman defined the agency's purpose in military terms: "Our enemy is fighting to enslave mankind; we are fighting to make men free. We must feed and clothe and find shelter for the millions whose lives have been disrupted by the war." As the director of OFRRO (soon to become the United Nations Relief and Rehabilitation Administration), he saw himself being called upon to act as "diplomat, dietitian, expressman, banker, farmer, distributor, and builder as well as social worker." In a sense, what Herbert Hoover was to the relief efforts of World War I, Lehman was to World War II. He spent the war years traveling the world, speaking, writing articles, and "convincing the American people that they should be willing to sacrifice extra steaks and butter, even after the War has ended, in order to insure world-wide economic stability and thus prevent a third world war." Through his agency's work, tens of millions of people in a war-ravaged world were fed, given shelter, and, more importantly, given hope. For his efforts, he was decorated by the United States, Italy, Czechoslovakia, and China.

Citing poor health, Lehman resigned as director general of UNRRA in March 1946. Eight months later, he suffered his only political defeat; losing his campaign for United States Senator to Republican Irving M. Ives. One year later, in November 1949, he won a special election over John Foster Dulles to complete the term of Senator Robert F. Wagner, who had resigned. He arrived in Washington, in the words of *U.S. News & World Report*, "bring[ing] into Congress a ready vote and voice for nearly, but not quite all, of President Truman's 'Fair Deal' policies." True to this prediction, Lehman supported Truman in most measures, the one notable exception being his vote against the President's compulsory health insurance program.

In 1950, the seventy-two-year-old Lehman ran for a full six-year term in the Senate. During the campaign, he enunciated the principles that would guide him in voting: "To increase in every way our preparedness, strength and security at home; to do the same for our allies abroad; to cooperate with the United Nations to discourage communistic or other totalitarian aggression; to maintain a sound domestic economy and control inflation; to insure an equitable sharing of the profits of national enterprise and the burdens of national sacrifice; to maintain at home an orderly government dedicated to the welfare of the people and the protection of their liberties; and to keep before [himself] and the people as 'a guiding light to the ultimate goal of a world at peace.'" On November 8, 1950, he defeated Republican Joseph R. Hanley.

Senator Lehman was a potent liberal with a conscience to match. He was one of the few senators to stand up to Joseph McCarthy. Along with Vermont Senator Ralph Flanders, Lehman proposed stripping McCarthy of his chairmanship and called for the Senator's censure. In his speech calling for censure, Lehman said: "I have been shocked . . . by attacks on individuals constituting character assassination, by charges unfounded, ungrounded, unproved. In the past two years a policy of indicting by smear has been indulged in, and the victim has no opportunity whatever to defend himself. There has been a policy of trying to prove guilt by association, not only of persons, but of ideas."

Lehman also opposed the Immigration and Naturalization Act of 1952, better known as the McCarran-Walter Act. Named after its sponsors, Nevada Senator Pat McCarran and Pennsylvania Representative Francis Walter (Democrats both), the bill retained the national-origins quota bias of the 1924 Johnson Act, and limited annual immigration to 150,000. Additionally, prospective immigrants would be "elaborately investigated for past radical associations." Far worse, even after being admitted, even after becoming naturalized citizens, their status would continue to hang by "the thread of their sworn commitments of past nonradicalism," thus exposing them to "the sword of Damocles of deportation." Lehman called McCarran-Walter an "indefensible and evil act" that reflected "a racist philosophy of fear, suspicion and distrust of foreigners." He called for its defeat, acknowledging that "my conscience will be easier, though I realize my political prospects may be more difficult." The bill passed, Truman vetoed it, and Congress easily overrode his veto. It should be noted that in addition to his war against McCarthy and McCarran-Walter, Lehman was one of the Senate's most persistent civil rights advocates.

Lehman's liberalism during an era of conservatism, combined with his refusal to compromise, alienated many senators and made him a "lonely and embattled figure among them." Known as "The Conscience of the Senate," he retired in January 1957. He was seventy-nine, and felt it was time to move on.

During the final six years of his life, he returned to the world of philanthropy, though maintaining an active interest in politics. In his eighties, he won one of his greatest political triumphs: the defeat of the old hierarchy that had long dominated the Democratic Party in New York. In a sense, he became the "spiritual godfather" of the Reform movement that saw so many Tammany-bred politicians go down to defeat at the hands of a new generation of leaders like *Bella Abzug, Ed Koch, James Scheuer, Benjamin Rosenthal,* and *Ted Weiss.*

Like most members of "Our Crowd," Lehman spent most of his life as a non-Zionist. Along with others of his ilk, he had put his faith and his money into the rehabilitation of the Jews of Europe, and had seen Palestine "only as a supplementary means of relief." In consonance with this philosophy, he had organized the Palestine Loan Bank and the Palestine Economic Corporation in the late 1930s. By the time he came to the United States Senate, however, Herbert Lehman was an ardent supporter of the new Jewish state.

In his person, Herbert Lehman looked, acted, and sounded like anything but a politician. His flat, monotonous speaking style was likened to one who "lifts up before him a gray facade of uneventful prose." At the opening of his 1934 campaign for governor, he began a long dissertation on governmental affairs by saying that he probably was going to be dull. A reporter noted, "he thereby added to his unblemished record of absolute accuracy." According to Louis Finkelstein, chancellor emeritus of the Jewish Theological Seminary, Lehman became a statesman "without ever passing through the intermediary stage of being a politician."

Like his father and uncles before him, Herbert Lehman was a member of Temple Emanuel on New York's Fifth Avenue. Despite his affiliation with a specific denomination, he always minimized the divisions of Judaism, maintaining that "the forces unifying Jewry were far stronger than the differences that hold us apart." As Lehman said on more than one occasion: "All I require of a Jew is that he follow the basic laws, precepts and traditions of our faith. It makes no difference to me whether a man goes to a Reform, Orthodox or Conservative synagogue."

To provide a list of Lehman's communal organizations and charities would be an exercise in futility. He chaired, belonged, or contributed heavily to virtually every organization in the Jewish pantheon. One of his proudest achievements in the field of Jewish communal life was being named Brandeis University's first "trustee emeritus" in 1963. In 1960, in honor of their fiftieth wedding anniversary, Herbert and Edith Lehman (whom he always called "E-e-e-e"), donated the children's zoo in Central Park.

Two weeks after the assassination of President John F. Kennedy, as Lehman was preparing to go to Washington to receive the Medal of Freedom, he died of a heart attack. He was eighty-five years old. His funeral, held at Temple Emanuel, was attended by President Lyndon Johnson, New York Senators *Jacob Javits* and Kenneth Keating, Governor Nelson Rockefeller, Mayor Robert F. Wagner, Robert F. Kennedy, Adlai Stevenson, Chief Justice Earl Warren, Justices Arthur Goldberg and Thurgood Marshall, and Bernard Baruch. In his will, he left bequests of $850,000 to various charities—this on top of a lifetime of giving. Lehman was buried in the family plot in Kenisco Cemetery, Valhalla, New York.

Not a terribly reflective man, Lehman was nonetheless able to put his life and his Jewishness in perspective: "My Jewish heritage has unquestionably affected my political and social thinking. All through my years of public life I have felt strongly the importance of keeping faith with the ethics of Judaism and its basic concept that 'creed without deed' is meaningless. As a Jew and as a human being, I have accepted no boundaries except those of justice, righteousness, humility and charity."

References
American Jewish Year Book, vol. 66, 1965, pp. 3–20.
Current Biography, 1943, 1955.
Nathan Glazer, "Herbert H. Lehman: Public Servant, Statesman and Jew," *Commentary,* May 1963.
Robert Ingalls, *Herbert H. Lehman and New York's Little Deal* (New York: New York University Press, 1975).
Jewish Digest, July 1958, pp. 37–40.
Charles A. Madison, *Eminent American Jews, 1776 to the Present* (New York: Frederick Ungar, 1971), pp. 259–280.
Alan Nevins, *Herbert H. Lehman and His Era* (New York: Scribner's, 1963).
New Yorker, May 2, 1936, pp. 21–26; and May 9, 1936, pp. 23–30.
New York Times, December 6, 1963 1:1.

LEHMAN, WILLIAM (1913–): *Democrat from Florida; served ten terms in the House (Ninety-third through One Hundred and Second Congress; January 3, 1971–January 1992).*

In Congress, the "College of Cardinals" has everything to do with consecration and virtually nothing to do with religion. According to "Washington-speak," the College of Cardinals is not some ecclesiastic body, but, rather, the elite group of representatives who chair the Appropriations Committee's thirteen subcommittees. As leaders of their various subcommittees, the "cardinals" have enormous clout and autonomy. They often have the final word on how moneys in the federal coffers shall be spent. In recent years, only two members of the Congressional Minyan have been elevated to this dizzying height: Representative *Sidney Yates* of Illinois, and Bill Lehman of Florida's Seventeenth District. For the ten years from 1982 until his retirement in 1992, Lehman chaired the Appropriations Subcommittee on Transportation. At his disposal were literally tens of billions of dollars for everything from highway construction and rapid transit systems to bicycle paths and high-tech traffic monitoring devices. All in all, it was quite an assignment for a man who started out life as a used-car salesman from Alabama.

William Lehman was born on October 4, 1913 in Selma, Alabama, where his parents owned a candy-making company. Selma has had a remarkably stable Jewish population over the past hundred-plus years: between 200 and 225. In 1995, it contained but a single synagogue (Mishkan Israel) with no more than thirty-six members. Lehman credits "growing up in a little town and, in a way, having more than other people during a bad time for our country" with giving him the desire to help others.

Lehman was educated at the Dallas Academy and Selma High School before going off to the University of Alabama, from which he received a B.S. in business in 1934. Following graduation, he took a job with a finance company in New York that quickly sent him to Miami. As a young man in Miami, Lehman "used to hang around the used-car lots his company provided financing for. Then he got the idea that he could sell cars and finance them under the same roof." In 1936, Lehman went into business for himself, opening a 24 x 50 foot lot at Northeast Second Avenue and Eighth Street. He prospered, largely because he was the only used-car dealer who would make financing deals with blacks.

In 1939, Bill Lehman married Joan Fiebelman, an Alabama-born sculptor. They had three children: Bill, Jr., Kathryn, and Tom. Bill, Jr., grew up to take over the family business; Tom became an attorney. Daughter Kathryn died of a brain tumor in 1979 at age twenty-two, leaving two sons. During World War II, Lehman served in the Army Air Corps.

With the coming of television, Bill Lehman became a familiar face in Miami. He advertised himself as "Alabama Bill" on a hillbilly TV show, sitting on a stack of cotton, cheerfully proclaiming that he would make "deals as solid as a bale of Alabama cotton" and giving away stacks of Confederate money. In later years, Lehman would say that the secret to his political success (he wasn't elected to Congress until past age sixty) came from "automobile psychology." As he explained: "When I was selling used cars, I always tried to be on the same level as the person I was trying to sell the car to without being a phony."

As a used-car dealer, Lehman did things "nobody else would do in business." According to a rival dealer, "If somebody didn't like a car, he'd either give back their money or give them a new car. People called him a bad businessman, but he was a good businessman because he was so straight with people." When prospective buyers came down to his ever-expanding lot, they would find Lehman "pad[ding] around . . . in sandals, khaki pants, an open-necked shirt and a baseball cap." Lehman was also the first automobile dealer to employ black salespeople.

Bill Lehman got out of the used-car business in the 1960s and started selling new Buicks. He later claimed that the move was necessitated because he "couldn't take the competition from

Cuban used-car dealers in CIA-front companies." A November 1989 article in the *Miami Herald* reported that years after he had left the used-car business, Lehman was questioning then-CIA Director William Colby, who was testifying before the House Intelligence Committee:

Lehman: "Mr. Colby, you put me out of the used-car business."

Colby: "How'd I do that?"

Lehman: "You funded the Cuban used-car dealers. They came in and bought up all the used cars."

Colby: "Well, they paid top dollar, didn't they?"

Lehman: "That was what the problem was."

Always restless, Lehman decided he wanted to teach school. In 1963, at age fifty, he began teaching at a local public high school. He recalls, "I was just troublesome enough to teach books nobody else was teaching, such as *Huckleberry Finn*, *The Merchant of Venice* and *The Quiet American*." From 1964 to 1966, he taught at Miami Dade Junior College. His interest in education and civic affairs, coupled with the backing of his loyal black and Jewish customers, got him elected to the Dade County School Board in 1964. Lehman's "reputation for fairness helped him bridge racial gaps and put into practice a court-ordered school busing plan to desegregate the schools." Lehman's role in the busing plan put him in physical jeopardy: "There was a time when I would go out to school-board meetings and I would have to have a person from security escort me in and out. A lot of people when I was on the school board said: 'I'll never buy a car from anybody else, but I won't vote for you on account of that busing.'"

In 1972, Lehman launched a long-shot candidacy for Congress from the newly created Thirteenth District. He was one of seven Democrats seeking the nomination. Going into the race, state Senator Lee Weissenborn, "a liberal legislator, who had sponsored legislation on handgun control and a state kindergarten system," was the favorite. Lehman's advisors insisted that he go on television, saying, "No more forced cross-town busing." Lehman refused: "I said, no way, that is not me." When asked, "Don't you want to get elected?" Lehman told his advisors, "That bad I don't want to get elected, because I've been trying to work with desegregation on the school board for six years, and

I'd be going against what I've been doing, what I am." His principled stand led to an endorsement from the *Miami Herald*.

Weissenborn finished first in the primary with 27 percent of the vote. Lehman, who received 20 percent, forced a runoff. Perceived as "more of a centrist than Weissenborn," Lehman pledged that he "would work in Congress for higher Social Security benefits and better rapid transit." Lehman took the runoff with 57 percent of the vote. He then went on to a 62 percent to 38 percent victory in the November general election.

The Thirteenth Congressional District (the Seventeenth after the 1980 census) "stretche[d] from the predominantly Jewish neighborhoods along the coastline north of Miami to black communities like Liberty City, Carol City and Opa-Locka." The district also included the Hispanic neighborhoods in Hialeah. It was a perfect fit for Lehman; his constituents loved him. With the exception of 1976 and 1980, when he won by margins of 78 percent and 75 percent respectively, Lehman was reelected without opposition eight times.

Lehman quickly became known as an "unbending liberal on most policy questions . . . the rainmaker of the Florida delegation." Lehman was anything but a typical politician. According to a *Miami Herald* writer, "he's not much of a speaker and hardly what one would call an out-front leader. . . . In an age of the blow-dried politician, there's not a whole lot left on Lehman's head to blow-dry. He is not one of the more recognizable members of Congress." Not one to go out of his way to make headlines, Lehman once told his press secretary: "The biggest story you'll ever get is when I die."

In point of fact, Lehman did garner some pretty good press during his years in the House. Ironically, though, it rarely had anything to do with his work in Congress. Lehman was a natural do-gooder. During the course of his twenty years in Congress, he "got the hard-line government of East Germany to allow a rabbi to live in East Berlin for the first time in 40 years. He sneaked a heart valve into the Soviet Union for a sick woman [and] pried dissidents loose from the claws of right- and left-wing dictatorships from Cuba to Argentina." One of Lehman's legislative triumphs had a do-good quality about it. In 1986, he inserted a brief amendment in a

Reagan budget proposal that gave federal employees the right to donate vacation time to a sick colleague. The case involved an IRS employee suffering from cancer. Under terms of Lehman's bill (P.L. 99-500), the terminally ill woman, Shannon Chiles, received more than 150 hours of leave-time from her fellow workers.

When Indiana Democrat Adam Benjamin died suddenly in 1982, Lehman became chair of the Appropriations Subcommittee on Transportation. As an "insider's insider," Lehman doled out billions of dollars for road, airport, and mass transit projects. Not surprisingly, he saw to it that Miami received a goodly portion of the available funds. Lehman became the father of Miami's Metro-Rail system, and saw to it that South Florida highways had the most up-to-date traffic control technology. As subcommittee chair, Lehman "moved his annual spending bills with a calm efficiency that belied the fierce backroom negotiating that often accompanies spending bills." According to one colleague: "If kindness won't resolve a problem [Bill Lehman] is ready to exhibit a bit of toughness. He knows when to fight and when to turn on the charm."

Bill Lehman suffered a stroke in March 1991. Eleven months later, he announced his retirement from Congress. In his statement to the press, Lehman said he had made his decision "without pressure, without concern about reapportionment, without concern about opposition." As things turned out, had he sought reelection, Lehman would have had to compete in a newly drawn district, "likely facing strong challenges in both the Democratic primary and, if successful, possibly in the general election as well." The Seventeenth was cut up into two new minority-based districts, now represented by an African-American and a Hispanic.

As of 2000, Bill and Joan Lehman were still living in Biscayne Park, Florida. On most mornings, one will find Lehman at Jimmy's, the "down-home everybody-knows-everybody restaurant in North Miami." Since leaving Congress, Lehman, who admits that retiring depressed him, has become involved with "a few organizations that gave me something to hang on to." Those "few" include the Daily Food Bank, Camillus House, the Ryder Trauma Center and ICARE. The Lehman name is still well known in South Florida: each day, hundreds of thousands of commuters travel to work on the William Lehman Causeway; millions of Floridians still watch, hear, and read advertisements for Lehman Buick, Lehman Hyundai, Lehman Mitsubishi, and Lehman Saab.

On his eighty-fifth birthday, a *Miami Herald Reporter* asked him what was the nicest thing anyone had ever said to him in Washington. Reflecting for a moment, Bill Lehman said: "Nice job Mr. Chairman." Pausing for a moment, Lehman added: "I'd like that on my tombstone."

References

Congressional Quarterly, February 29, 1992, p. 462.

Ft. Lauderdale News Sun Sentinel, May 17, 1989 D:1.

Miami Herald, November 20, 1989, 1:2., October 5, 1998, 2:1.

Washington Post, January 6, 1985.

LESSLER, MONTAGUE (1869–1938):
Republican from New York; served one term in the House (Fifty-seventh Congress; January 7, 1902–March 3, 1903).

Although Montague Lessler only served thirteen months in the House, his election caused quite a furor. Elected to the unexpired term of Democrat Nicholas Muller, who had resigned in order to run (unsuccessfully) for president of the borough of Staten Island, Lessler became the first Republican to represent New York's Seventh Congressional District in more than a generation; he was also the last Republican to hold that seat until 1944. Although Lessler claimed his victory was "a splendid victory for principle," it owed more to a rift within Democrat circles. The contemporary record clearly indicates that the sachems of Tammany Hall commanded their rank-in-file to remain at home rather than vote for the Democratic nominee, Perry Belmont.

Montague Lessler, the son of Sigmund and Annie (Schrier) Lessler, was born in New York City on New Year's Day, 1869. The product of an assimilated German-Jewish family, Lessler received a bachelor's degree from the City College of New York and studied law at Columbia University. Admitted to the New York bar in 1891, Lessler rented office space at 31 Nassau Street and went into private practice. A man of constant habits, he practiced out of the same office until his death forty-eight years later. He later went into partnership with Parris Russell; the two specialized in "corporation and surrogates work." In 1898, Lessler married Tillie Sondhemier of Chicago. They had two children: Florence Marie (Nessler) and Montague, Jr.

On November 22, 1901, Democrat Nicholas Muller resigned his seat in Congress. Montague, who by that time had moved to St. George, out on Staten Island, announced his candidacy as a progressive Republican. Lessler's politics were akin to those of Theodore Roosevelt, who had been sworn in as President on September 14, following the assassination of President William McKinley. Taking a page from Roosevelt's Square Deal philosophy, Lessler called for an "attack on serious social problems facing the nation; legislation allowing the regulation of big business; broader control of the railroads; and conservation of natural resources."

The Seventh Congressional District (soon to become the Eleventh) covered Richmond County, a decidedly non-Jewish part of New York City, as well as a sliver of Manhattan. In 1901, fewer than 700 Jews lived on Staten Island. Lessler had little trouble getting the nomination of the Republican regulars for the special election. The only other potential candidate, financier Cornelius Vanderbilt III, "refused to permit the use of his name." The Democrats, on the other hand, were in total disarray. No fewer than three candidates vied for the nomination. After an angry fight between various factions—Greater New York Democracy, Tammany Hall, Social Democrats—Perry Belmont II grudgingly got the nod as the candidate of Greater New York Democracy.

Belmont, the grandson of August Belmont and son of former Congressman Perry Belmont I, had the disadvantage of not living in the district. Moreover, he took his victory as a given. Although there were a few election-day arrests for attempted bribery and "other alleged violations of the election law," most Tammany workers stayed at home. Election Day found Belmont holed up at his Astor House headquarters, expressing "rosy-hued opinions as to the result," and making plans for a "blow-out" that evening.

Lessler, on the other hand, rose early that morning; by 5:30 A.M., he had left his home by automobile (rather unique for 1901), planning to visit various polling places in Manhattan. Ten minutes after his departure, the car broke down, necessitating that Lessler go the rest of the way on foot. According to the account given in the *New York Times*, the Republican candidate happened upon Alderman Thomas Foley, a Tammany regular, who assured him: "We [Tammany] are making a bluff for Belmont, but we are not doing you much harm. We are not trying to get out the vote."

Lessler wound up winning the election by a mere 394 votes, nearly all of his plurality coming from Staten Island. Upon learning of his defeat, Belmont, accompanied by his campaign manager, "Battery Dan" Flynn, slipped out of the Astor House, refusing to speak to the assembled press. William Walker, New York's superintendent of buildings and leader of Greater New York Democracy in the Third Assembly District, remained behind to speak on behalf of Belmont: "Richard Croker [the Tammany boss] and the Tammany leaders of the lower New York districts stabbed Belmont in the back. . . . Tammany has betrayed a regular Democratic candidate, and Tammany will be punished for its treachery in the near future."

Walker's threat turned out to be hollow. In the next election, Tammany put all its energies behind the candidacy of "Big Tim" Sullivan, who trounced Lessler. Sullivan (1862–1913) went on to serve two terms in Congress. Elected to a third term in 1912, he was committed to a mental institution before he could take his seat, escaped from the care of three nurses, and was struck and killed by a locomotive near Pelham Parkway in New York City.

During his thirteen months in Congress, Lessler served on the Naval Affairs Committee.

Needless to say, he was not in Washington long enough to do much more than take up space. Following his defeat, Lessler returned to the practice of law. Following his wife's death in 1916, he moved from Staten Island to the Towers Hotel in Manhattan, where he resided until his death on February 17, 1939. His remains were cremated.

References

Biographical Directory of the United States Congress, 1774–1989, pp. 1365, 1895.

New York Times, January 8, 1901, 1:4. February 18, 1939, 15:6.

LEVIN, CARL MILTON (1934–): *Democrat from Michigan; has been elected to four terms in the Senate (January 3, 1978–present).*

LEVIN, SANDER MARTIN (1931–): *Democrat from Michigan; has served nine consecutive terms in the House (Ninety-seventh through One Hundred and Sixth Congress; January 3, 1983–present).*

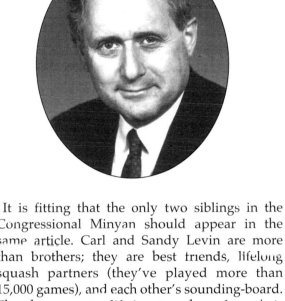

It is fitting that the only two siblings in the Congressional Minyan should appear in the same article. Carl and Sandy Levin are more than brothers; they are best friends, lifelong squash partners (they've played more than 15,000 games), and each other's sounding-board. They have spent a lifetime together—from their childhood, in which they shared a bedroom and went to summer camp together, to their mutual year at Harvard Law School, to their more than fifteen years on Capitol Hill.

The paternal grandparents of the Levin brothers came from Russia-Poland in the late nineteenth century. They originally settled in Ontario, where grandfather Levin was a cigar maker. He moved to Detroit, where he became foreman in a cigar factory. The Levins had eight children. The oldest eventually became a federal judge. The second-oldest, Saul, married Bess Levenson, the daughter of an immigrant dry-goods peddler who, through scrimping and saving, worked his way up to owning four stores along the main street of Birmingham, Michigan. The Levensons were the only Jewish family in Birmingham. Moreover, Bess was the first and only Jewish child ever born in what now is a prosperous Jewish suburb of Detroit; she was born in her parents' home, her siblings in a Detroit hospital. Although not strictly Orthodox, the Levensons kept a kosher home, and traveled each week into Detroit in order to buy meat.

Saul and Bess Levin had three children: daughter Hannah (Gladstone) and sons Sander Martin (born September 6, 1931) and Carl Milton (born June 28, 1934). Saul Levin was a businessman and attorney who specialized in prison reform. His son Carl described him as "a great big-hearted, social-minded, progressive Roosevelt lover" who was "into public affairs." For many years, he served on the state's corrections commission, which supervised all the prisons. Carl remembers that, each year at Passover, his father would absent himself from the family's second *seder* in order to spend the evening with Jewish inmates at Jackson Prison. Bess Levin, as the boys recall, was rarely home when they returned from school. "We were 'Hadassah orphans,'" the Senator fondly recalls. Dinners around the Levin family table were replete with discussions on issues of the day. Among the brothers' fondest memories are the Sunday evenings the family "spent together around the radio to hear commentary by Walter Winchell and Drew Pearson and discuss it." In the Levin household, "our parents thought the opinions of their children were important."

Throughout their childhood, the brothers shared a bedroom, attended the same summer camp, and went to Sunday school together. To this day, Senator Levin keeps the toy box and beds from that room. As the older brother, Sandy spent endless hours throwing ground balls to Carl "with the idea that I could make [him] the world's best shortstop." The brothers were so close that upon his graduation from Central High School, Sandy argued long and loud to be permitted to take his younger brother with him on a trip out West.

The Levin family home was near, but not in, a Jewish neighborhood. Although ardently Zionist, the family was not terribly religious. "My father had a set of tefillin," Senator Levin recalls, "but I don't remember ever seeing him put them on." Both boys studied for bar mitzvah "with a great Jew." Bess Levin made sure that neither pork nor shellfish ever entered her kitchen. The Levin siblings were imbued with strong family bonds: "We never, ever sat down to dinner until my father got home from work," Senator Levin reports. "We were a very, very close family.. He describes his parents as having been "decidedly anti-materialistic, although my mother was somewhat aristocratic . . . she had very high standards. They gave us great values."

Where Saul Levin was an emotional, outgoing man, Bess was more private and guarded. After her sons had been elected to their current posts in Congress, a journalist asked her what she thought about their achievements. Instead of bragging, Bess Levin calmly remarked: "If that's what they want, that's O.K. by me." Bess Levin believed in the inherent goodness of people: "She truly believed that people were just as good and as worthy—but not any better—as her."

The brothers both graduated from Central High School—Sandy in 1949, and Carl three years later. Sandy then went off to the University of Chicago, and Carl to Swarthmore. Receiving a B.A. in 1952, Sandy then got an M.A. from Columbia (1954) and an LL.B. from Harvard in 1957. Carl followed up Swarthmore (B.A. with honors) with a Harvard law degree in 1959. During their one mutual year in Cambridge the brothers—not surprisingly—roomed together.

The brothers returned to Michigan, where they passed the bar and went into private practice.

Carl Levin practiced for five years (1959–64) with the firm of Grossman, Human, and Grossman. In 1961, he married Barbara Halpern, a native Detroiter whom he had met in New York. Barbara's father was originally from Bialystok. While traveling from Bialystok to Odessa in order to buy *matzah* for his town, he

was drafted for five years into the tsarist army. Sentenced to a prison camp, the resourceful Halpern (who spoke six languages) managed to escape and find employment in Lithuania as a clerk. For the next several years, he saved his money, intent upon emigrating to America. Of all his many accomplishments, father Halpern was proudest of the fact that he had sailed for the New World not in steerage, but as a first-class passenger with his own cabin. Barbara Halpern was raised in a Yiddish-speaking, glatt kosher home.

Carl and Barbara Levin have three daughters: Kate (born 1964), Laura (1965), and Erica (1968). Sandy Levin, who married Victoria Schlafer, has two daughters and two sons: Jennifer (born 1964), Madeleine (1965), Andy (1963), and Matthew (1969).

While Carl and Sandy were growing up, all the Levin first cousins and their parents spent Sundays having potluck dinners at their grandparents' home. After Saul Levin's death, the tradition continued—sixteen Levins gathered around the Sunday table. "The cousins are incredibly close," according to the Senator. "Although they are scattered across the country, you never have to tell them 'why don't you call your cousin.' They talk to each other all the time, and whenever they travel, make sure to see each other."

Following in the family tradition of public service, the brothers entered politics. Sandy was elected to the Michigan Senate in 1964 from the "heavily Jewish Oakland County suburbs north of Detroit." In the Senate, Sandy Levin became known for his skill as a negotiator. He was seen as "one who could exert a calming influence when tempers flared." A rising star in Democratic Party circles, he was a delegate to the national convention in both 1964 and 1968. By the end of the 1960s, he had become chair of the state party.

In 1970, he challenged incumbent Republican William G. Milliken for the governorship. Milliken, a highly popular, well-liked department store heir from Traverse City, was a tough target. Sandy Levin, imbued with a "low-key, even-tempered manner that had made him a successful legislator . . . was unable to develop a knack for fighting Milliken's 'nice-guy' image." Levin took the high road, presenting voters with "detailed factual information about state government programs." It almost worked; Milliken won with just over 50 percent of the vote. Sandy Levin challenged Milliken again in 1974 in a race that one reporter dubbed "the bland leading the blind." Levin lost this race as well, slipping to under 47 percent of the vote. Following this second defeat, Sandy Levin went off to Washington to run the technical assistance program of the Agency for International Development under President Carter. His name "left the front pages."

In a sense, Sandy's political missteps paved the way for brother Carl's successful entry into the public fray; it gave his younger sibling name recognition. Following his five years in private practice, Carl Levin, feeling "the pull of public service," secured an appointment as assistant attorney general and general counsel for the Michigan Civil Rights Commission. From 1968 to 1969, he served as chief appellate defender for the city of Detroit. As a public defender, he helped free a man who had served thirty years in prison for a crime he had not committed. This incident forever shaped Carl Levin's thinking on capital punishment, which to this day he calls "a mistake you can't correct."

In 1970, Carl successfully ran for a seat on the Detroit City Council. His first term on the council came during the immediate post-riot period in Detroit. He proved to be an ardent friend of the black community, teaming with Mayor Coleman A. Young on many issues. While on the council, Carl Levin "became so furious watching HUD [the federal Department of Housing and Urban Development] let thousands of Detroit houses fall into default, government repossession and decay" that he actually went out with a bulldozer "to help raze some of them." In 1974, Carl Levin became president of the City Council.

Four years later, Carl Levin decided to take on incumbent Republican Senator Robert P. Griffin (1923–). Originally elected to Congress in 1957 from Traverse City, Griffin had been appointed to the Senate, in May 1966, to fill the vacancy caused by the death of Patrick V. McNamara (1894–1966). Elected in his own right in November 1966, Griffin won reelection in 1972. In 1977, he narrowly lost a race for Senate Republican leader to Howard Baker of Tennessee and then announced that he would retire at the end of his present term.

This turned out to be "a major misstep."

Griffin began skipping votes and absenting himself from the daily activities of the Senate. Shortly after Carl Levin announced his candidacy for the Democratic nomination, Griffin changed his mind about retirement. Having already missed more than a third of the Senate votes's during the year, Griffin gave Carl Levin an ideal opening. Levin campaigned throughout Michigan saying that Griffin was "obviously tired of the job" and should be "permitted" to retire. The voters agreed: Levin defeated Griffin 52 percent to 48 percent.

As Senator, Carl Levin secured seats on Governmental Affairs, Small Business, and Armed Services. The latter appointment was most significant; Levin became one of the first Vietnam-era doves to be named to Armed Services. For years, he was the third-ranking Democrat on the committee, just behind Senators Sam Nunn of Georgia and James Exon of Nebraska. At the beginning of the One Hundred and Fifth Congress in January 1997, Levin became the committee's ranking minority member. Should the Democrats ever regain control of the Senate, he will likely become chairman of Armed Services. As of the beginning of the One Hundred and Sixth Congress in January 1999, Senator Levin was still the committee's ranking member.

As a member of the Armed Services Committee, Senator Levin has often sided with the reform-minded group, which, for many years, was led by Republican Senator *William S. Cohen* of Maine, who in December 1996 became President Bill Clinton's third Secretary of Defense. This group emphasized "the need for creative strategy and simple, reliable weapons." Levin has been one of the Senate's most constant advocates of arms control, and led the opposition on the committee to the Reagan-era Strategic Defense Initiative ("Star Wars"). He also opposed both the MX missile and the Reagan administration's interpretation of the ABM treaty.

Throughout his two decades in the Senate, Levin has remained one of that body's most liberal members. The *Almanac of American Politics* (1988 edition) described him as "an example of a politician who has taken a set of principles seemingly in political eclipse and has managed to apply them with some success." Levin voted against tax cuts in 1981 and tax reform in 1986. He termed the latter measure "a lousy bill—the wealthiest people got tremendous tax cuts and lots of middle income people got increases." The bill passed 97 to 3, but Levin was unrepentant: "I was one of the three, and that makes me look outside the mainstream. But it was the right vote."

Levin is perhaps the Senate's leading opponent of capital punishment. This is easily within the bounds of Michigan tradition; the state constitution outlawed the practice as early as 1855. Although the Senator has always opposed the death penalty for drug-related murders, he has supported numerous anti-drug measures and authored a law that mandates jail time for anyone selling drugs near a school. He firmly believes that he is "as tough on crime as folks who voted for that [death penalty] bill, which permits parole." Despite his liberal credentials, Levin is not doctrinaire; he does not believe that every problem can be solved merely by the allocation of funds. He played a pivotal role in securing hundreds of millions of dollars in federal funding to help bail out Chrysler in the 1980s, thereby saving tens of thousands of jobs in Michigan. Known variously as "Mr. Ethics" (he takes no honoraria) and "America's most underrated Senator," Levin is anything but a campaign handler's dream: "rumpled, unfashionable, speaks articulately but without apparent political artifice and takes unpopular stands on issues he cares about, without much regard for the political consequences." Levin sees his job in simple, straightforward terms: "I'm here to listen, think, be accessible—but when it comes down to it, to do what I believe is best for my state, whether or not it's popular at the moment." Once, when a reporter suggested that his "disheveled" look was a conscious political ploy, Levin responded: "I've never dressed for effect. I'm not more or less rumpled now than I was five years ago or twenty years ago. I wish I looked like Tom Selleck. The top half. The bottom half. The left or right half. I don't care."

Carl Levin is also known for being "a man of passionate convictions who is also capable of understanding the passions of others—the key to a naturally effective legislator." The Senator, according to one reporter, is "not often given to grandstanding; he is more self-effacing than ambitious." According to one aide, "the worst reason you can give him for anything is that it would be politically helpful."

Widely respected by colleagues on both sides of the aisle, Carl Levin has been at the forefront of sponsoring tough ethics legislation. In 1993, he successfully coauthored a bill stipulating that lobbyists "disclose the identities of their clients and their income from them and requiring stringent detailing of government officials that are contacted and issues discussed." Along with Senator Cohen of Maine, Levin wrote legislation "to revise lobbying laws and to prohibit members of Congress from accepting meals, gifts, and entertainment from lobbyists." The legislation died in the last week of Congress when its supporters were unable to gather the sixty votes needed to stop a Republican-led filibuster in the Senate. When Senate Majority Leader George Mitchell appointed a Democratic task force to address "the thorny question of revising Senate ethics laws," he named Carl Levin to chair it.

Because of his liberal voting record (0 from the Christian Coalition and generally 100 from the Americans for Democratic Action), Carl Levin has always been a prime target for Republicans. As such, his three races for reelection have drawn considerable interest and a lot of Republican cash.

In 1984, his opponent was former astronaut Jack Lousma. Levin was greatly aided by the fact that Lousma, a Michigan native, had not lived in the state for most of his adult life, thereby opening him to charges of carpetbagging. Even Lousma's status as a space hero did him little good; although a heavily industrialized state, Michigan plays almost no role in the space program. Lousma's fate was sealed when the Levin campaign released a campaign tape showing him singing the praises of his Toyota—a foolhardy thing to do in automobile-conscious Michigan. Before the tape was released, Levin had it sent back to the studio to have technicians mask out a Japanese flag behind Lousma's head. He did not want the image to be construed as Japan-bashing. Despite the former astronaut's assertion that the car belonged to his son, the damage was done. Lousma was defeated 52 percent to 47 percent, a margin that told Republican leaders Levin would likely be even more vulnerable in 1990.

Six years later, Carl Levin faced three-term Representative Bill Schuette of Midland on Michigan's Lower Peninsula. Schuette, thirty-seven, single, and boyishly handsome, was the stepson of the chairman of Dow Chemical, and able to raise vast sums of money. Levin, who went into the race as a decided underdog, had to scramble for every dollar. During the campaign, Schuette ran an ad with himself in a plaid shirt, "looking younger than his 37 years," trying to tie Levin to Michigan Senator Donald Riegle's involvement in the savings and loan scandal. The tactic backfired; while Michigan voters might have disagreed with Levin's liberal voting record, they know him to be a man of impeccable character. Later, Schuette ran another ad showing Levin in the Persian Gulf on board the battleship *Wisconsin* in 1985. The ad proclaimed that Levin had voted against the Gulf Resolution, against the commissioning of the *Wisconsin*, and against the Maverick anti-tank missile currently being used in the Gulf. Schuette vainly tried to equate Levin with former Massachusetts Governor (and 1988 Democratic presidential candidate) Michael Dukakis, calling the Senator "Dukakis without a helmet." Levin responded by pointing out that he'd supported many technologically simple weapons, like the M-1 tank produced in Chrysler's plant in Warren, Michigan. Moreover, he ran an ad showing a retired Reagan administration Pentagon official saluting him for "critically assaying defense spending requests." Levin rolled to a 57 percent to 41 percent victory over the hapless Schuette.

In 1996, Senator Levin was challenged by Ronna Romney, a Detroit-area radio talk-show host and the former daughter-in-law of the late Michigan Governor George Romney. She had narrowly lost (52 percent to 48 percent) the 1994 Republican Senate primary to Spencer Abraham, the former deputy chief of staff of Vice President Dan Quayle. Romney attacked Levin for his support of President Clinton's health care "scheme." In fact, sensing that the Clinton proposal was about to "crash and burn," Levin had hastened to put together his own health care plan with "universal coverage for children." Romney also scored Levin for being one of the first members of the Senate to endorse Clinton's proposal to end the ban on homosexuals serving in the military. Levin was easily reelected to his fourth six-year term in November 1996, by his best margin yet: 58 percent to 40 percent.

Carl and Barbara Levin keep an apartment in Detroit's Lafayette Park and a two-bedroom Capitol Hill townhouse. Although not a regular shul-goer, Senator Levin is proud of the role he played in founding the only synagogue in downtown Detroit, the Reconstructionist T'cheyia, located near the Renaissance Center. During the High Holidays, Levin generally attends services at a local Orthodox synagogue in Georgetown—"not that I understand everything going on, but I just love the ritual. It means a great deal to me." Barbara Levin is a unique woman in her own right. She has worked for a Washington defense information agency, built her own harpsichord, and earned a law degree at age forty.

Senator Levin has long been a champion of human rights. He was recipient of the first Alexander Solzhenitsyn Award presented by the Christian Solidarity International in 1980. He also received the very first Herbert H. Lehman Ethics Medal from the Jewish Theological Seminary of America. His support for Israel, which he first visited in 1962, is both constant and visceral. In 1979, former Texas Governor John Connally, then a candidate for the 1980 Republican presidential nomination, delivered a speech condemning the so-called Jewish lobby. Soon afterward, speaking at the annual dinner of the Jewish Reconstructionist Foundation, Senator Levin asserted sardonically: "Oil and idealism do not mix. If idealism stands between Governor Connally's America and a secure oil supply—then IDEALISM must go. And if Israel—the one democratic state in the Middle East, the one stable friendly government that exists in the Middle East—if Israel stands between Governor Connally's America and a secure oil supply—then Israel must go."

Shortly after his election to the United States Senate, Levin was invited to deliver the Raoul Wallenberg Lecture at the University of Michigan's College of Architecture, from which Wallenberg had graduated in the 1930s. Speaking of the Swedish diplomat who had risked his life to save thousands of Jews during the Holocaust, Levin said: "We can learn from him that the moral dimensions of action demand our attention and that the ethical issues of conduct require our continued concern. That is, after all, the task we ultimately must accept when we realize that while a truly human life may be neither simple nor easy, it is both possible and desirable."

Where most Senate offices display pictures of the famous and immortal, Carl Levin's is filled with pictures of his family. In his office lobby, one finds a computer-controlled sculpture wired in such a way that when the Senate calls for a quorum of members, a balloon-like part of the sculpture fills with hot air and lifts a genuine cow chip aloft. Sitting close to his desk is a black-and-white sketch of himself and brother Sandy. Underlining the sketch is a biblical quotation: "How good and how pleasant are brothers dwelling together in unison" (Ps. 131:1). The same sketch and quotation can be found in brother Sandy's House office.

Following his stint with the Carter administration, Sandy Levin returned to Michigan. In 1982, a "scant 12 weeks before the primary," veteran Democratic Representative William Broadhead decided not to seek reelection. Sandy Levin jumped into the race. According to *Politics in America* (1984 edition) "critics accused him of trying to regain public office on the popularity of his younger brother." Of course, it was the other way around; Carl had initially succeeded because Sandy had given the name Levin currency in Michigan politics.

Sandy Levin found himself in a six-way race for the nomination. His chief competition came from state Senator Doug Ross, "who held the legislative district Levin had once represented." Ross, a former director of Michigan Common Cause, mounted a door-to-door campaign. Levin drew support from the Democratic Party establishment. Levin, who still had high name recognition in the district, won the primary with 44 percent, and then coasted to an easy 67 percent to 32 percent victory over an underfunded opponent in the general election.

Sandy Levin's House district (originally the Seventeenth, today the Twelfth) comprises the suburban communities of Oak Park ("perhaps the only small city in America with sizable numbers of Jews, Arabs and blacks"), Hazel Park, Madison Heights, and parts of Macomb County. The district has large concentrations of Polish-Americans, "descendants of Appalachian migrants," a large Chrysler plant, and the M-1 tank plant where Michael Dukakis took his infamous ride in the 1988 campaign. Following the

1992 reapportionment, in which Michigan lost two congressional seats, Sandy Levin's district was combined with that of Democratic Representative Dennis Hertel. First elected to the House in 1980 at age thirty-two, Hertel decided to retire, leaving the new Twelfth District seat to Levin.

As a member of the Ninety-seventh Congress, Sandy Levin received a seat on the House Banking Committee, the only Michigan representative on that prestigious panel. As a member of Banking, he focused the lion's share of his energies on the problems of the disadvantaged and unemployed. Working in tandem with New York Senator Daniel Patrick Moynihan, he sponsored legislation that would "link welfare payments to job training." He also created the Work Opportunities and Retraining Compact, which required states "to establish comprehensive work, training and education programs for recipients of Aid to Families with Dependent Children (AFDC), and to provide child care, transportation and other support services."

Sandy Levin quickly gained a reputation for his capacity for hard work and his deft understanding of issues before the House. The *Almanac of American Politics* (1984 edition) described him as "less interested in trumpeting his own opinions than . . . in working out compromise and agreement among everyone involved in an issue." Toward the end of the Ninety-ninth Congress (1987), Levin began lobbying for a seat on the House Ways and Means Committee, chaired by the legendary Dan Rostenkowski of Illinois. "Rosty," a Chicago-area machine Democrat who ran his committee like a private fiefdom, was loath to give seats to representatives like Levin—whom he viewed as being too independent, too liberal, and potentially too obtrusive. Sandy Levin pursued the coveted slot for almost a year, lobbying his colleagues and supporting Rostenkowski's pet legislation, the 1986 tax-overhaul bill. In the end, Levin got the seat. It is likely that the politics of geography had as much to do with his victory as his dogged pursuit; Michigan had gone four years without having a seat on Ways and Means—the largest state not to have one.

Assigned to the Human Resources and Oversight subcommittees, Levin shepherded into law a "carefully crafted provision" requiring Medicare and Medicaid providers to inform patients of their right under state law to either execute living wills or give advance directives about their care "should they later be unable to communicate." He also fought for revisions in the Medicare program that would permit the use of "cutting-edge drugs" in the treatment of cancer, for which reimbursement had been prohibited. Levin quickly carved out a position as one of the leading trade hawks on Ways and Means. He strongly opposed the North America Free Trade Agreement (NAFTA), arguing that "Mexican environmental and labor standards [are] so far below ours that the agreement [does] not make sense." After its passage, he was one of the few House Democrats to back the original Mexican "peso bailout."

Working in tandem with another trade protectionist, Missouri Democrat Richard Gephardt, Levin pushed for the renewal of the Super 301 retaliation provisions of the 1987 trade act, which had expired in 1990. Super 301 language requires "negotiations with and possible sanctions against" countries that discriminate against U.S.-made goods. During floor debate, Levin included an amendment that specifically required negotiations with Japan over both "the number of cars that country exports to the United States and the quantity of U.S.-made car parts included in cars produced in the United States by Japanese-owned companies." As a champion of Michigan's auto interests, Levin also founded the Congressional Auto Parts Task Force and cochaired the Competitiveness Caucus's Task Force on Japan. Despite all this, Sandy Levin sees himself as an internationalist rather than a protectionist.

Like his brother, Sandy Levin regularly receives a 0 rating from the Christian Coalition and near-perfect scores from the Americans for Democratic Action. As one of the oldest members of the class of 1982, he has often acted as a mentor to his younger colleagues. As one of the more liberal members of the Michigan delegation, Sandy Levin has traditionally drawn strong opposition in his campaigns for reelection. Thanks to the advantages of incumbency and his tireless efforts on behalf of his constituents, Levin's margins of victory have generally been in excess of 60 percent.

Vicky Levin is a research administrator with the National Institute of Mental Health and a licensed psychiatric social worker. The Levins live in Southfield, and along with Carl and Barbara own a 100-acre retreat called "Lion Den" in Livingston County, just over the Oakland County line. The two families have been spending their free time there for nearly thirty years. In the past several years, the brothers have taken to "farming" their land, growing both fruits and vegetables.

The Levin brothers see each other nearly every day—both in Washington and back home in the Detroit area. They are remarkably similar in their politics, their demeanor, and their senses of humor. They are even somewhat like-minded when it comes to their legacy. When asked how he would like to be remembered, Senator Carl Levin responded: "The world's best shortstop. Politically, I think it's too early." Not to be outdone, Representative Sandy Levin quipped: "As a good father and a good human being. He cared and he tried. If only he had been eight inches taller—I love to play basketball."

References

Interview with Carl Levin, Washington D.C., August 1992.
Almanac of American Politics (1978–98 editions).
American Jewish Biographies, pp. 249–250.
Detroit Free Press Magazine, October 22, 1989, pp. 10–21.
Politics in America (1980–98 editions).
Southfield Eccentric, May 30, 1979.

LEVIN, LEWIS CHARLES (1809–1860):
American Party ("Know-Nothings") from Pennsylvania; served three terms in the House (Twenty-ninth through Thirty-first Congress; March 4, 1845–March 3, 1851).

In the biblical book of Ecclesiastes, Koheleth, the self-named author, states a profound truth: "What has been will be, and what has been done will be done again; there is nothing new under the sun" (Eccles. 1:9). Koheleth's verity, which extends to both the political and the religious realm, might well serve as the epitaph for the second Jew to serve in the House of Representatives, Lewis Charles Levin of Pennsylvania. For the major issue that obsessed Levin and made his brief moment in the political spotlight possible has resurfaced time and again. In Levin's day, it was called nativism. Toward the end of the nineteenth century, it was termed populism. Today it goes under the name white supremacy, or as one historian termed it, "the cult of national patriotism." The issues Levin raised in the Twenty-ninth, Thirtieth, and Thirty-first Congresses—prayer and Bible in public schools, keeping America free of foreign influence, strengthening moral values—are still being raised and debated on the House floor at the end of the twentieth century.

Equal parts crusading moral zealot, paranoid conspiratorialist, and agitating dogmatist, Levin fashioned a somewhat coherent political philosophy that sought nothing less than "the attainment and preservation of America's 'national character.'" As he declared early in his first congressional term, "I go for everything American in contradistinction to everything foreign." In the end, he proved himself to be remarkably unsuccessful in achieving his aim.

From the way Lewis Levin railed against paupers, drunks, Catholics, and those who "had not been sufficiently long in the country to have lost the odor of . . . steerage," one might have taken him for some priggish Back Bay snob. Far from it. Although little is known about his antecedents or early life, it is clear that Lewis Charles Levin was the son of Jewish parents. Born in Charleston, South Carolina, on November 10, 1808, Levin spent the first sixteen years of his life growing up in a city that was home to early-nineteenth-century America's largest Jewish population—somewhere between 600 and 700. From his later actions, it is clear that

Levin felt like an outsider and tried desperately to escape from his Jewish past. Although there is no concrete evidence that he ever formally converted to another religion, he did become an advocate of Protestantism and married two non-Jewish women, Anna Hays and Julia Gist.

Levin graduated from South Carolina College (University of South Carolina) in 1824. Infected with wanderlust, he spent the next fifteen years earning a precarious living as an itinerant Christian preacher and teacher, settling variously in Maryland, Kentucky, Louisiana, and Mississippi. Somewhere along the line he read law and was admitted to the bar in several states. In 1839 or 1840, Levin—by now married to Anna Hays of Kentucky—moved to Philadelphia, then home to some 1,600 Jews.

In 1842, Lewis Levin purchased a newspaper which he called the *Temperance Advocate*. For the budding journalist, the subject of temperance was an early passion. His speeches and articles against the evils of drink brought him to the attention of like-minded souls; in 1843, he was elected president of the Pennsylvania Temperance Society. In this capacity, Levin continued speaking out against drink, the stage, and anything that, in his estimation, led to the creation of a less puritanical society. Like a Sunday-school teacher, he distrusted man's natural impulses. Without discipline and self-control, he feared, American society would collapse beneath the weight of its immorality.

Levin sold the *Temperance Advocate* in 1843 and purchased a larger paper, the *Daily Sun*. Now he added the evil of foreign influences to his arsenal. Levin was not alone in disparaging foreigners. In the 1840s, America began playing host to wave after wave of European immigrants. Their arrival served to fan the flames of dislocation, uncertainty, and intolerance. As a result, many Americans, looking for scapegoats, became attracted to the burgeoning nativist movement. This movement, which would eventually coalesce into a national political party, sought to identify and promote a purely American ethos. Foreigners, particularly Irish Catholics, became easy scapegoats in a highly confusing time. Levin took this antipathy and molded a paranoiac fantasy whereby the monarchs of Europe were plotting to take over America by means of the spiritual influence of the Catholic Church. In an article he wrote in his

Daily Sun, Levin claimed that the monarchs of Europe were planning

> to people the country with Catholic immigrants, in order to provide for the contingency so patriotically prayed for . . . of our government changing to a monarchy—whereby His Holiness (the Pope) will have a King ready, sprinkled with holy water, to mount the throne in the name of Catholic liberty!

In 1844, Levin published a broadside entitled *A Lecture on Irish Repeal, in Elucidation of the Fallacy of Its Principles and in Proof of Its Pernicious Tendency in the Moral, Religious, and Political Aspects.* In it, he attacked both the Irish "Repeal" movement (the fight for the repeal of Ireland's union with England and Scotland) and its leader, Daniel O'Connell. Levin claimed that in establishing Repeal Clubs throughout America, O'Connell and his minions were actually establishing beachheads for an eventual takeover of America by the papacy. Levin uncovered "a nefarious plot to debauch and contaminate the institutions of the United States and to set up a monarchy." His pen dripping with vitriol, Levin concluded that "The Irish Catholic vote is to be organized to overthrow American liberty. The extensive ramifications of Repeal Clubs have suddenly become affiliated societies, to carry out the intentions of His Holiness, the Pope!"

Fueled mainly by the diatribes of journalists, propagandists, and pamphleteers like Levin, the nativist movement continued to grow. In the mid-1840s, a new political faction, variously called the Native American Party, American Republicans, or the Know-Nothings, came into existence. Wherever and whenever they held their conventions, violence against Catholics and Catholic churches was sure to follow. The party attracted followers by raising the fear that immigrants posed a concrete threat to the American way of life. When Levin and his cohorts added the issue of Bible in the public schools, their ranks swelled dramatically.

One plank of the Native American Party's platform boldly proclaimed:

> We maintain that the Bible, without note or comment, is not sectarian—that it is the fountain head of morality and all good government and should be used in our public schools as a reading book.

The Bible to which the nativists referred was, of course, the King James Version (Protestant), which, they claimed, the Catholics wanted excluded from the schools. Levin's diatribes to the contrary, this was simply not the case. As one Catholic bishop of the time stated, "I do not object to the use of the Bible provided Catholic children be allowed to use their own version." Levin retorted that the King James Bible was actually a nonsectarian book! He and his nativist allies pushed for what they called "Bible Education"—a program of learning that would inculcate proper moral values and promote Americanism. Underlying all of this was, of course, an implied attack on the Catholic Bible, the Catholic Church, and Catholics in general. Although the nativists attracted numerous followers, their appeal remained largely among a narrow segment of society. With regard to the Catholic versus Protestant Bible issue, one observer of the time wryly noted: "A large majority of the Protestants who fought out the question of reading the Bible in the public schools . . . would not have known the difference between the Protestant and the Catholic Bible if it had been placed in their hands."

In July 1844, Levin was indicted by a grand jury for inciting to riot. He made political capital by claiming that he had actually tried to stem the violence which had taken place in Philadelphia's Southwark district; moreover, he claimed, the indictment was part of a "Popish plot." His name prominently before the public, Lewis Charles Levin declared his candidacy on the American Party ticket for Congress from Pennsylvania's First District. During the three-man campaign, Levin kept hammering away on the "pernicious foreigner" issue. Levin's standard stump-speech message from 1844 sounds hauntingly familiar even after more than a century and a half: "Unless a remedy be found to impede the influx of foreigners in the United States, the day [will] not be distant when American-born voters find themselves a minority in their own land." Largely on the strength of this message, and his public notoriety, Levin captured the First District seat. Shortly after his election, he stood trial on the charge of "riot, treason and murder." He was found not guilty.

Levin served three terms in Congress, during which he became one of the least popular men on Capitol Hill. In speech after speech, Levin subjected his colleagues to rancorous attacks on the Catholic Church. When members of the House challenged him or took him to task, Levin would simply accuse his antagonists of being "paid agents of the Jesuits who hang around this Hall." At one point, Levin attempted to win Southern support for the American Party by claiming that the abolitionist movement was inspired by the Pope and his agents. Most Southerners, offended by Levin's bravado and naked political opportunism, turned away in disgust.

It has long been a truism in Congress that the best way to succeed on Capitol Hill is to make oneself an expert on a single issue or area of interest—farm price supports, foreign policy, defense, etc. For Levin, given his unique political pathology, his area of expertise, not surprisingly, was immigration and naturalization. Levin proposed changing the naturalization law to require a residence period of twenty-one years in order to qualify for American citizenship. Moreover, he pushed a concept he called "federal citizenship," whereby the federal government would be granted the exclusive right to determine qualifications for voting. After a prolonged and rancorous debate, the House concluded that Levin's proposal was unconstitutional; it usurped the clearly enumerated right of the individual states to set voting qualifications.

Levin's hatred of immigrants was so great that he opposed a bill setting minimum passenger-space requirements for transatlantic ships bearing newcomers to America. The bill's sponsor, Representative George Rathbun of New York, argued that current overcrowded conditions on the ships were "a revolting spectacle, a disgrace not only to our laws and our country, but to humanity itself." In speaking out against Rathbun's proposal, Levin sarcastically suggested that the legislation be amended to read "A bill to afford additional facilities to the paupers and criminals of Europe to emigrate to the United States." Levin's diatribe notwithstanding, Rathbun's bill passed overwhelmingly.

Levin and his cohorts attempted to turn their nativist faction into a national political party but met with little success. Levin easily dominated the Native American Party's three national conventions, held in 1845, 1846, and 1847. The party's demise can largely be blamed on Levin himself. By resolutely demanding that "birth upon the soil be the only requisite for citizenship," Levin caused an irrevocable split among his nativist colleagues. By 1848, the Native American Party was finished as a political force. Levin should have seen the handwriting on the wall. He was easily defeated for reelection to a fourth term in 1850, and returned to Philadelphia, where he took up the practice of law.

In the last years of his life, Levin's tenuous mental makeup got the best of him. He spent at least the last three to four years of his life as a patient in hospitals for the insane in Baltimore and Philadelphia. Lewis Charles Levin died in Philadelphia on March 14, 1860 at age fifty-one, thus ending both a tortured life and a sorry chapter in American political history. Levin was buried in the nondenominational Laurel Hill Cemetery in Philadelphia. His wife, Julia, tried to raise funds for a monument to his memory, but someone connected with the campaign absconded with the funds. To this day, no tombstone graces Levin's final resting place. Ironically, Julia Gist Levin and Louis Levin (his son) converted to Catholicism in 1880.

References
American Jewish Year Book, vol. 2 (1900–01), pp. 519–520.
Dictionary of American Biography.
John A. Forman, "Lewis Charles Levin: Portrait of an American Demagogue," *American Jewish Archives*, October 1960, pp. 150–194.
Jewish Encyclopedia.
Universal Jewish Encyclopedia.

LEVINE, MELDON EDISES (1943–): *Democrat from California; served five terms in the House (Ninety-eighth through One Hundred and Second Congress; January 3, 1983–January 3, 1993).*

On June 2, 1956, Shabbat *Shelach Lecha*—the Sabbath on which Numbers 13:1–15:41 is read at services—thirteen-year-old Mel Levine became bar mitzvah at Temple Beth El in Hollywood. The synagogue had been built years earlier by his father and grandfather. Thirty-six years later, on June 2, 1992, the forty-nine-year-old Levine lost the California Democratic primary for the U.S. Senate to *Barbara Levy Boxer*. In a lifetime filled with great accomplishments, this was his first and only real defeat.

Meldon Edises ("Mel") Levine was born in Los Angeles on June 7, 1943, delivered by Dr. Morrie Silden, the same obstetrician who four years earlier had delivered *Howard Eliot Wolpe III*, another future member of the Congressional Minyan. Ironically, both men were defeated in June 1992, thus ending their congressional careers together. Mel Levine is the son of Sid and Shirley (Blum) Levine, both California natives. Sid Levine's parents, originally from Russia-Poland, came to New York in 1903 and moved to Los Angeles three years later. The Blums, who trace their ancestry back to Edises, Spain, in pre-expulsion times, arrived in San Francisco shortly before the earthquake of 1906. Grandfather Levine started a cooperage business in Los Angeles. "They would buy wooden wine barrels, rub them out, clean them up and sell them as reconditioned, restored wine barrels." When the barrel business shifted from wood to steel, the family found itself manufacturing steel oil drums.

Sid Levine joined his father's business while going to law school in Los Angeles. He eventually expanded the family's interests to include the manufacture of tanks and cooling towers, toys and lumber. Sid Levine wound up owning a lumber mill in Santa Rosa, California, where the family spent half the year.

When Mel was two, his family, which now included his sister Dana (Schecter), moved to Hancock Park, where the family would maintain their Southern California residence for the next dozen years. Because the family kept moving between L.A. and Santa Rosa, Mel's Jewish education was a bit spotty: "I had various false starts in Hebrew School. It's sort of a sad story. . . . I had a great teacher in Santa Rosa . . . who really got me interested in studying Hebrew. But then we would go to L.A. and whatever Hebrew School I went to . . . I had one crummy teacher after another, and after a few years they totally drove out any interest I had in learning Hebrew."

In a very real sense, the Levines were founders of the los Angeles Jewish community. The (Reseda) Jewish Home for the Aged was created in their living room in 1910. Grandpa Levine served as its first president. The Levines also donated the land upon which would be built L.A.'s first Jewish hospital: Cedar-Sinai. "People operated under the assumption that I came from a very wealthy family, largely because my family gave that land. What people didn't realize . . . [is that] my grandfather and my dad and my uncle borrowed the money to give that land on which Cedar-Sinai sits. My grandfather believed that he owed so much to America that he gave away one out of every three dollars he made. He just made it a point of giving *tzedakah* and beyond."

The Levine family's involvement went well beyond *tzedakah*. Sid Levine was the Western states' representative for the Haganah in 1948. "One of my earliest memories as a 5-year old was hearing the doorbell ring in my house and opening the door and being knocked over by a gunny sack filled with God knows what. And my dad grabbing me and basically throwing me away from the door. I learned many years later that that was some type of materiel that was on its way to Israel during the War [of Independence]."

In 1958, the Levines moved from Hancock Park to Beverly Hills, so that Mel and his sister could attend Beverly Hills High School, from which he graduated in 1960. In 1964, Levine was valedictorian of his graduating class at the University of California-Berkeley, as well as student body president. From Berkeley, Levine spent two years at the Woodrow Wilson School at Princeton University, where, in 1966, he earned a master's degree in public administration. While at Princeton, Levine spent as much time as he could in New York City: "My parents were very friendly with this really nice guy at the [Jewish] Theological Seminary . . . Dr. [Louis] Finkelstein, and he used to invite me to New York for a *seder* once in a while."

From Princeton, Levine entered Harvard Law School; he was valedictorian and commencement class speaker in 1969. His address was "sort of a defense of the anti-war student movement types." While at Harvard, Levine met Jan Greenberg, a freshman at Radcliffe. Returning to Los Angeles after graduating Harvard, Levine was invited to speak before a local Anti-Defamation League chapter. The president of the group dragged his daughter to the lecture. She turned out to be the same Jan Greenberg. They were married shortly after Greenberg graduated from Radcliffe. The Levines have three children: Adam Paul, and twins Jacob Caplan and Cara Ingrid. Jan Greenberg Levine is an environmental rights attorney in Los Angeles.

Following law school, Levine returned to Los Angeles, where he became involved in numerous Jewish organizations: the Community Relations Committee, Anti-Defamation League, American Jewish Committee, and American Jewish Congress. In the mid-1970s, he served as an unpaid lobbyist in the state capital for legislation dealing with the Arab boycott of Israel and its impact on California's commerce. While lobbying in Sacramento, Levine became friends with the legislator responsible for the anti-boycott legislation: Los Angeles-area Assemblyman *Howard Berman*. The two would become fast friends, political allies, and along with *Henry Waxman*, leaders of the most powerful and successful political clique in California politics, the "Waxman-Berman Machine." Over the years, this "machine" would grow to control most Westside (Los Angles) politics. "Its power came not from patronage but from fundraising and savvy. Their specialty was targeted direct mail, with hundreds of customized letters and endorsement slates sent out to different lists of people."

After a short stint in a Los Angeles law firm, Levine became legislative assistant to Senator John Tunney of California. He remained with Tunney for two years, from 1971 to 1973. Levine loved the job because "it was doing the legislative work without having to do the politics." In 1977, Levine was elected to the California Assembly from a Westside Los Angeles district. During his five-year tenure in that body, Levine authored sixty-one pieces of legislation that were signed into law. During his first term in Sacramento, Levine's good friend Howard Berman was the Majority Leader and thus able to be of great assistance.

In 1982, Mel Levine was elected to the United States Congress as representative from California's Twenty-seventh District. This district included such diverse communities as Santa Monica, Venice, and Manhattan Beach, Brentwood, Torrance, and Inglewood. Levine's main committee assignments were Foreign Affairs, Judiciary, and Interior and Insular Affairs. Levine was assigned to the Foreign Affairs Subcommittee on Europe and the Middle East. Teaming up with fellow committee members *Tom Lantos, Gary Ackerman, Eliot Engel, Sam Gejdenson,* Howard Berman, *Ted Weiss,* and *Steven Solarz* to provide solid backing for Israel, he quickly became a recognized expert on Middle East policy. A lifelong Zionist, Levine had made his first visit to Israel at age twelve, in 1955.

Mel Levine was one of the first members of Congress to warn about the danger Iraq posed to peace and stability in the Middle East. Months before the invasion of Kuwait, he supported sanctions against Iraq. He was one of but a handful of Congressional Minyanaires in the One Hundred and Second Congress to vote in favor of HJR 77, which authorized President Bush to use force in the Persian Gulf. Levine's early warnings about Iraq had gone unheeded; in the aftermath of the Persian Gulf War, his position proved to have been prescient.

Levine was reelected in 1984, 1986, 1988, and 1990—generally by large margins. In his first reelection campaign, 1984, Levine was held to a surprising 55 percent of the vote by his Republican opponent, evangelist (and former Los Angeles Ram) Rob Scribner. During the campaign, Scribner repeatedly hit on Levine for being "diametrically opposed to nearly everything the Lord's Church stands for in this nation." Scribner urged the voters of the Twenty-seventh District to "take territory for our Lord Jesus Christ." In a 1986 rematch, Westside voters, not much inclined to accept Scribner's message, reelected Levine with 64 percent of the vote.

In 1992, Mel Levine gave up his safe House seat in order to run for the United States Senate. After a hard-fought campaign, he wound up running third in a four-candidate primary. He received 22 percent of the vote versus 44 percent for Representative (and future Senator) *Barbara Boxer*, and 31 percent for former Assembly Speaker Leo McCarthy. Since leaving politics, Levine has once again become involved in lobbying for pro-Israel causes and in the practice of law. In 2000, Mel Levine is a partner of the prestigious Los Angeles-based firm of Gibson, Dunn and Crutcher, where he specializes in international transactions, administrative law, and government contracts.

A devoted, passionate baseball fan, Mel Levine was, at one time, a batting-practice pitcher for his hometown team, the Los Angeles Dodgers. As a pitcher, so Levine says, "I was a great confidence builder . . . all I could ever do was get the ball over the plate and it would be hit a mile." When he threw his arm out, then-Dodger manager Tommy Lasorda gave Levine the job of playing first base during batting and fielding practice "whenever I was in town." Says Levine: "He [Lasorda] didn't realize when he made that offer that he would never get rid of me. I still have a locker and uniform at Dodger Stadium. . . . And for 17 straight years I have gotten throws from every Dodger infielder from 1976 to 1992. And have gone with them and have worked out in Atlanta, San Francisco, and New York. It's hard to describe, but I totally love it. It's like being a kid."

References

Interview with Mel Levine, Washington, D.C., July 1992.

Almanac of American Politics (1984–94 editions).

LEVITAS, ELLIOTT HARRIS (1930–): *Democrat from Georgia; served five terms in the House (Ninety-fourth through Ninety-eighth Congress; January 3, 1975–January 3, 1985).*

Elliott H. Levitas was the first Minyanaire to attend Oxford University as a Rhodes Scholar. An admirer of political philosophers John Stuart Mill and Edmund Burke, Levitas began evincing a thoughtfulness as a youngster that marked him as being just a bit different from his compatriots; when boys in his urban Atlanta neighborhood put together an "army," Levitas chose to serve as "strategist" rather than "captain." More than thirty years later, as a member of the United States Congress, he likewise gravitated toward the abstract and esoteric: the legislative veto, his one-man effort (some called it an obsession) to give Congress the power to reject rules and regulations of the federal government. This is not meant, however, to give the impression that Levitas has always been all work and no play. To the contrary, as a youngster, he disappeared from Hebrew school for weeks at a time because it interfered with his playing football and sandlot baseball.

Elliott's father, Louis J. Levitas, emigrated to Atlanta from Ireland as a teenager and quickly married. For more than sixty years, he earned a living selling life insurance. A thoroughgoing family man, he once turned down a major promotion to avoid uprooting the household. In modern terminology, the Levitases would be considered lower-middle income, although Mrs. Levitas did have household help. The future Congressman was born in Atlanta Baptist Hospital on December 26, 1930, the second of two children. His older brother, Ted, became a well-known Atlanta periodontist. Speaking of his older sibling, the Congressman said, "He has had a considerable influence on my life and development. . . . He was the 'good boy.'"

Young Elliott, as gregarious as he was rambunctious, was a bit of a disciplinary problem at the Samuel Inman Elementary School. Perhaps it was because he knew how to read long before he entered school; he had taught himself so that he could read the comics. On more than one occasion, the teacher punished him for talking by moving him from the "all-boy side of the classroom to the all-girl side." This rarely did the trick: "Still he chattered—and was isolated at his own table away from both groups."

As a child, Elliott loved sports, going to the Saturday Westerns at the local cinema ("equipped with a quarter or thirty cents, which would get your admission and lots of candy and popcorn"), and radio. He was such an avid fan of *The Lone Ranger* that he had his brother Ted drink "inordinate quantities of Ovaltine" in order to supply him with the labels required for "radio giveaways of secret rings, code badges, etc." Elliott's love of sports led him to his aforementioned truancy from Hebrew school. When his absence was at last discovered, he was, not too surprisingly, punished. But punishment in the Levitas household rarely involved spankings. The usual punishment was "verbal disapproval, sometimes accompanied by deprivations of what you wanted to do."

Levitas attended O'Keefe Junior High, where he was a "B-plus to A-minus student." In 1945, he entered Boys' (later renamed Grady) High School, where he became sports editor of the school paper, and a member of both the chess club and the debating society. During those years, he was both a cub scout and a boy scout. Following high school graduation, Levitas attended Atlanta's Emory University. During his undergraduate years, he was active in the Tau Epsilon Phi fraternity, and participated in intramural sports and the debating society. During his four years at Emory, he also wrote for the student newspaper, the *Emory Wheel*, and served as editor of the literary-humor magazine, the *Phoenix*.

Even with all his extracurricular activities, Levitas posted an academic record worthy of a Rhodes Scholarship. His secret? "Every afternoon, I'd always take a nap for two hours before dinner. I'm not one of those people who can get up early in the morning and work before class. I liked to sleep as late as I could, but I wouldn't mind working till two in the morning. I have always done my best work, in whatever I did, sometime between eleven and two in the morning."

Graduating from Emory in 1952, Levitas attended Oxford on his Rhodes Scholarship, earning a master's degree in jurisprudence in two years. Upon his return to the States in 1954, Levitas enrolled at the University of Michigan Law School, where he made law review. While at Michigan, he married Barbara Hillman, who had been "a childhood acquaintance, though not a sweetheart." Originally a student at Agnes Scott College in Atlanta, Barbara transferred to Michigan. After their marriage, while Elliott was still in law school, Barbara became a teacher. Realizing that between her teaching and his financial aid they couldn't make ends meet, they returned to Atlanta, where Elliott finished up his legal studies at Emory. While doing so, he became a law clerk at the firm of Arial, Golden, and Gregory—the Arial being former Georgia Governor Ellis Arial. During his last week in law school, Levitas, who was a member of ROTC, received notice that he was being called up. He served two years in the Eighth Air Force, Strategic Air Command, mustering out as a captain.

Levitas practiced law with Arial, Golden and Gregory for nearly twenty years, specializing in public and administrative law, copyright, and food law. In 1965, he was elected to the Georgia House of Representatives. During his ten years in the Georgia House, he was considered somewhat of a liberal on social issues. His main thrust during that decade was urban planning: "When I started, there wasn't even a committee that dealt with urban problems: transit, housing, zoning, planning." As a state legislator, Levitas created a state planning commission, helped authorize a funding agency for middle-income housing, and enacted a law that sharply restricted "electronic eavesdropping and other invasions of privacy." During each of his five terms in the state House, he was named "One of the Ten Most Effective Members" by his colleagues.

In 1974, having concluded that he had "just about done what I could successfully do in the legislature," Levitas decided to run for the United States Congress from Georgia's Fourth District. The Fourth, which consisted of the middle- and upper-middle-class suburbs of DeKalb County, was the leading bastion of Republicanism in Georgia. Indeed, in 1974, the Fourth was the only one of Georgia's ten congressional districts to be represented by a Republican—Ben Blackburn.

First elected in 1966, Blackburn, a "quiet but staunch conservative," had been regularly reelected with little difficulty. In 1972, his margin of victory had approached 76 percent. No one gave Levitas's candidacy a chance. But the tide of history was on the state legislator's side. Prompted by a slumping economy and the sense of disillusion brought about by Watergate and the resignation of Richard M. Nixon (and President Gerald Ford's subsequent pardon), voters were looking to express their outrage. Levitas was able to use Blackburn's diehard support for the disgraced President to his advantage. On election day, he pulled off a stunning upset, winning with 55 percent of the vote.

Sworn in as a member of the Ninety-fourth Congress, Levitas was assigned to Public Works and Transportation and the Committee on Government Operations. During his ten years in Congress, Levitas was known as a conservative-to-moderate Democrat; his rating by the Americans for Democratic Action averaged just a little over 28 on a scale in which 100 was the most liberal. Although his move to the right earned him some criticism from his old liberal allies, it turned out to be a smart move politically for a representative from the Republican-leaning Fourth.

Levitas spent most of his first term learning the ropes of Congress, moving to the right, and anticipating a return match against Ben Blackburn. Again, luck was on his side. Nominated for a position on the Federal Home Loan Bank Board, Blackburn "scuttled his chance for a rematch in 1976 by performing ineptly during Senate hearings on his proposed nomination." Blackburn was criticized by members of the committee for insensitivity to the rights of minorities. His answers "failed to satisfy a committee majority, which killed the nomination." With Blackburn's chances for a comeback sunk, Levitas had no difficulty dispatching Republican state Senator George T. Warren II, 68 percent to 32 percent.

During his decade in Congress, as mentioned above, Levitas became virtually obsessed with the legislative veto. By means of this proposal, Levitas meant to "rein in the faceless bureaucrats by giving Congress control over the rules and regulations of the federal government." For nearly a decade, Levitas relentlessly attached legislative-veto amendments to bills on virtually every subject. When, as often occurred, the House Rules Committee refused to permit his amendment to be attached to a bill, he turned around and worked to block the bill's passage. To say the least, this did not make Levitas one of the more popular members of the House, but as the writers of *Politics in America* noted, "There is no sign that popularity is one of his major goals."

Wearying of this approach, Levitas tried to wrap his entire legislative-veto movement into one "comprehensive law that would make all federal regulations subject to the veto." His bill, quixotically labeled House Resolution 1776, remained bottled up in the Rules Committee for years. Although Rules held hearings on H.R. 1776, it never made it to the floor of Congress for a vote: "the leadership . . . argued that a legislative veto might shift the blame for regulations from bureaucrats to Congress, and some committee chairman [thought] reviewing regulations would increase their workload enormously."

Finally, in 1982, Congress used Levitas's legislative veto for the first time, overturning a Federal Trade Commission rule that required used-car dealers to list known defects in the cars they sold. Not surprisingly, Levitas voted against the rule. The federal government challenged Congress's action in court. In 1983, the Supreme Court ruled that in this case, the legislative veto was unconstitutional because "it did not provide for presidential review."

With seniority, Levitas became chairman of the House Public Works subcommittee on Investigations and Review. In that position, he had oversight responsibilities over virtually every facet of the main committee's jurisdiction. In the early days of the Reagan administration, Levitas launched an investigation into the problems of waste, fraud, and abuse in the Environmental Protection Agency. Specifically, his subcommittee investigated the agency's multibillion-dollar municipal waste water-treatment facility Construction Grants Program. When Levitas subpoenaed documents from the EPA administrator, Anne Gorsuch Burford, she refused. Outraged, Levitas called upon the House to cite her for contempt; it voted to do so. Burford and many of her associates wound up resigning.

Levitas was one of the prime movers in killing Congressman *Benjamin Rosenthal*'s proposed Consumer Protection Agency. The bill calling for creation of the agency was assigned to the Committee on Government Operations. Despite Levitas's best efforts, the bill made it out of committee by one vote. He then rounded up more than a hundred fellow Democrats to help kill it on the House floor, leading consumer advocate Ralph Nader to label him "a total big business lackey." When informed of Nader's comment, the "prickly" Levitas fired back that Nader was just "frustrated because I did not bow down and kiss his ring and worship him and his monument, the Consumer Protection Agency."

In 1984, Levitas met his electoral Waterloo in the person of thirty-four-year-old Patrick Swindall, who campaigned as a Christian fundamentalist with a "biblical scorecard." Swindall charged Levitas with having a voting record similar to that of Geraldine Ferraro, the liberal New York-area Congresswoman running as the Vice Presidential candidate on the Democratic ticket. At first, Levitas refused to take Swindall seriously; his record was far more market-oriented and decidedly more conservative than Ferraro's.

But Swindall know how to play hardball: "When a Treasury undersecretary canceled plans to attend a Swindall fund raiser because Levitas threatened to withdraw his support for an Administration bill to refinance Washington Kennedy Center, Swindall called the Treasury to protest, and taped the conversation . . . charging that Levitas's threats constituted a felony." Those in the political know pooh-poohed Swindall's charge; Levitas was acting "as any sensible politician would." Nonetheless, the charges stung, and Levitas found himself "reduced to attacking his challenger rather than publicizing his own ten-year record." On election day, Swindall, with tremendous help from the Christian right, swept to a 53 percent to 47 percent victory.

In an interesting sidebar, Swindall lost his seat after two terms, during which his sole legislative "achievement" was getting a roll call vote on whether or not to fire fourteen House elevator operators. In 1986, Swindall turned back a challenge from former *Dukes of Hazzard* actor Ben Jones (he played "Cooter" the mechanic). By 1988, Swindall was in hot water. In the process of building a $1 million house near Stone Mountain, he fell into money problems. Strapped for cash, he met with an Atlanta businessman and an undercover agent who offered him an $850,000 loan. Although they told the Congressman (on videotape) that the $850,000 was "probably drug money," he nonetheless accepted. When this was reported in the June 1985 edition of the *Atlanta Constitution*, Swindall tearfully apologized and returned the money. It was too little, too late. Jones once again challenged Swindall, who lost not only his seat by a final margin of 60 percent to 40 percent, but was indicted and later convicted of soliciting a bribe.

Following his defeat, Elliott Levitas returned to Atlanta, where, for the past fifteen years, he has practiced law with the firm of Kilpatrick and Cody. In 1991, Levitas was appointed to serve as one of eight commissioners of the National Commission on Financial Institution Reform, Recovery and Enforcement, which was created by an act of Congress to investigate the savings and loan debacle. He has also been active as a member of the board of directors of the Chatham House Foundation, a group which works to increase American participation in the Royal Institute of International Affairs. A devotee of the conservation of historic buildings, he also serves on the executive committee of the Georgia Conservancy and the National Building Museum. Because of this passion, Levitas was made an honorary Fellow of the American Institute of Architects.

The Levitases have three children: Karen (born in 1959), Susan (1961), and Kevin (1965).

References
Personal information provided by Elliott Levitas.

Almanac of American Politics (1972–86 editions).

Bruce Galpin, "Elliott Levitas: A Biographical Mosaic of the Trivial and Profound," *Atlanta Magazine*, January 1975.

Politics in America (1972–86 editions).

LEVY, DAVID A. (1953–): *Republican from New York; served one term in the House (One Hundred and Third Congress; January 3, 1993–January 3, 1995).*

New York's Fourth (originally Fifth) Congressional District is "one of America's first suburbs." Located on Long Island, it includes Garden City—created in the 1890s by retailer A. T. Stewart, the Five Towns (Lawrence, Inwood, Cedarhurst, Hewlett, and Woodmere), and everything along the Queens line from New Hyde Park to Valley Stream. While the Five Towns are predominantly Jewish and tend to vote Democratic, there are also strong Republican enclaves in "heavily Irish and Italian communities like Elmont and East Meadow." From 1990 to 1996, the Fourth Congressional District seat changed hands four times.

In 1992, five-term Republican incumbent Raymond J. McGrath, a mid-level member of the House Ways and Means Committee, decided to trade in his congressional seniority for a career as chief lobbyist for the beer industry. The open Republican primary pitted former New York Assemblyman and direct-mail consultant Dan Frisa against Hempstead Town Councilman David A. Levy, who won both the Republican primary and the November general election. Frisa, feeling he had been betrayed by the local Republican hierarchy, immediately began preparations for the 1994 race. After two years of almost constant campaigning, Frisa defeated Levy, thereby gaining the distinction of being the "only member elected in 1994 who ousted a Republican incumbent." Two years later, Frisa was easily defeated by former Republican Carolyn McCarthy, a nurse who had gained national press recognition after Long Island Rail Road gunman Colin Ferguson killed her husband and wounded her son.

David A. Levy was born in Johnson County, Indiana, on December 18, 1953. When he was still a youngster, his family moved to Long Island's Nassau County, where he received a public education. Levy graduated from Hofstra University in 1974 and immediately found employment as a radio news reporter. During his stint as a radio journalist (1974–81), he also found time to attended law school at Hofstra, from which he received his J.D. in 1979.

David Levy first visited Washington, D.C., when he was eight years old. He recalls being "impressed with the city's aura of power and resolved to return one day as one of the decision-makers." Armed with a political dream, Levy became involved in the local Nassau County Republican Party machine. For years, the local party apparatus was under the aegis of party chairman Joseph Margiotta. In 1982, shortly after Nassau County Supervisor Alfonse M. D'Amato was elected to the United States Senate, Margiotta was convicted and imprisoned on extortion charges arising from "a municipal insurance scheme." Margiotta was replaced by Joseph Mondello, with whom Levy struck up a strong and useful relationship.

Shortly after receiving his law degree, Levy was appointed press secretary for the town of Hempstead—a patronage job. From there, he went through a series of patronage positions—counsel to the Nassau County Republican Committee, minority special counsel, and executive assistant to the New York State Assembly—until his election as a Hempstead town supervisor in 1987, and member of the town council in 1989.

When Raymond J. McGrath declared his retirement from Congress, both David Levy and New York Assemblyman Dan Frisa declared their candidacies. Frisa, like Levy, a product of the local Republican machine, claimed that he had been promised the party's backing. When party chair Mondello endorsed Levy, Frisa labeled his opponent "a hack . . . Mondello puppet." Levy "shot back that [convicted former chair] Margiotta was running Frisa's campaign." Frisa roundly and loudly denied the charge. Levy then distributed a *Newsday* editorial accusing Frisa of "falsely reporting that Levy stole $56,000 from H.U.D." Levy wound up winning the Republican primary with 57 percent of the vote.

In the general election, Levy faced Democrat Phillip Schiliro, "a Long Island native who had spend 10 years as a top aide to California Congressman *Henry Waxman*." Because of his connection to the House Energy and Commerce Committee (of which Waxman was an influential member), Schiliro was able to raise more than twice as much money as Levy. Armed with a half-million-dollar war chest, Schiliro began attacking Levy as a party hack and "claiming credit for his work on the Clean Air Act and other legislation for Waxman."

For his part, running as a conservative who opposed taxes, Levy "bragged that the Town of

Hempstead had held down taxes." During the campaign, Levy opposed the Bush administration's ban on abortion counseling at federally funded clinics and promised to hold the line on cuts in the defense budget. Levy, like Schiliro, also opposed the Bush administration's policy of "placing restrictions on loan guarantees for Israel."

Despite his financial edge, Schiliro was vulnerable to charges of being a carpetbagger; although a Long Island native, he had not lived there for nearly a dozen years. In November 1992, Levy defeated Schiliro 50 percent to 46 percent, an uncomfortable margin for an incoming freshman. While Republican Levy was besting his Democratic opponent, Bill Clinton was defeating George Bush in the district 47 percent to 41 percent.

David Levy entered the House at the dawn of a Democratic administration. He now found himself required to vote with his Republican colleagues even when it meant going against some of his previously articulated positions. Despite his stated opposition to the so-called gag rule (banning abortion counseling at federally funded clinics), Levy voted no on a Clinton-backed proposal that "included language lifting the counseling ban." He also opposed Medicaid funding of abortions and the Freedom of Choice Act, "believing that regulation of abortions should be left to the states."

As mentioned above, after his November 1992 defeat, Dan Frisa never stopped running for the Fourth District seat. Eschewing media attention in favor of direct mail and a cadre of "foot soldiers from his old Assembly district," Frisa "flew under the radar screen of the Republican machine." This made good political sense; in 1993, Frisa had "bolted the party and supported the Democratic candidate for Nassau County executive." Frisa defeated Levy by 276 votes in a low turnout. After a recount, his margin of victory dropped to a mere 54. Charging irregularities, Levy sued in state court but lost. Levy remained on the ballot in November as the candidate of the state's Conservative Party and received only 9 percent of the vote. Dan Frisa defeated Phil Schiliro, again armed with a formidable bank account, with 50 percent of the vote. Two years later, in 1996, Frisa faced Republican-turned-Democrat Carolyn McCarthy. Buoyed by a "prime-time, center-stage spot" at the Democratic National Convention, McCarthy made her passionate support of handgun control the centerpiece of the campaign. She overwhelmed Frisa 57 percent to 41 percent.

David Levy has been married twice. His first marriage produced two children: Samantha Lynn, born in 1980, and Jessica Sue, born in 1984. In 1989, he married the former Tracey Burgess. Since his defeat, David Levy has been living in Baldwin, Long Island.

References

Almanac of American Politics (1992–96 editions).
New Members of Congress Almanac, Hundred and Fifth Congress.
Politics in America (1992–94 editions).

LEVY, JEFFERSON MONROE (1852–1924):
Democrat from New York; served three terms in the House (Fifty-sixth Congress; March 4, 1899–March 3, 1901; Sixty-second and Sixty-third Congress; March 4, 1911–March 3, 1915).

No member of the Congressional Minyan has a longer American pedigree than the marvelously named Jefferson Monroe Levy. The first Levys landed on American shores in 1662. As with many early American families, both Jewish and non-Jewish, the Levy family tree has branches and offshoots in a wide array of other prominent clans. To wit: J. M. Levy's father, Jonas, was the son of Michael and Rachel Phillips Levy. Rachel was the daughter of Jonas Phillips (1736–1803), the progenitor of a prominent Philadelphia family. One of Jonas's sons, Zalegman, was the first Jew admitted to the Pennsylvania bar. His son, *Henry M. Phillips,* a prominent lawyer in his own right, served one term in Congress in the late 1850s. Henry was J. M. Levy's second cousin.

Among Jonas Phillips's many grandchildren were Mordecai Manuel Noah, the most prominent Jew in early-nineteenth-century America; the aforementioned Henry M. Phillips and Jonas Levy; and Jonas's infinitely more famous (or infamous) brother, Commodore Uriah P(hillips) Levy. The Levy brothers were both prominent naval officers. Jonas was the commander of the steamer *America,* which ferried troops to, and participated in, the battle for Veracruz during the Mexican War. When Veracruz was captured, General Winfield Scott appointed Levy an army captain. In 1850, the Mexican Congress granted him the exclusive privilege of building a road from New York to San Francisco that would pass through Mexico. For reasons unknown, nothing ever came of the plan. After the war, Jonas made a fortune in New York real estate and eventually moved to Washington, D.C., where he became a founding member of the Washington Hebrew Congregation. He was also one of the more vocal leaders in the fight to alter the U.S.-Swiss Treaty of 1850.

Jonas's brother (and J. M.'s uncle), the Philadelphia-bred Uriah P. Levy, ran away to sea at age ten, subsequently joined the U.S. Navy, and eventually rose to the rank of commodore, the Navy's highest rank in that era, commanding the Mediterranean squadron for six months in the late 1850s. Brash, pugnacious, and a bit of a martinet, the Commodore felt the sting of anti-Semitism throughout his naval career and was court-martialed no fewer than six times. Indeed, any aspiring biographer seeking to acquire an accurate portrait of Commodore Levy must of necessity read through the transcripts of those half-dozen trials. His troubles with the Navy kept him on shore from 1827 to 1857. He is best known for his successful one-man campaign to abolish flogging and other forms of corporal punishment in the U.S. Navy. Like his brother, he was a founding member of the Washington Hebrew Congregation.

Jefferson Monroe Levy was born to Jonas and Fanny Mitchell Levy in New York City on April 16, 1852, precisely the time his father was moving his base of operations to the nation's capital. Little is known of J. M.'s early family life. He had a younger sister, Amelia Levy Mayhoff, who would be the prime beneficiary of his will. Levy was educated in the public and private schools of New York City, graduated from the New York University School of Law in 1873, and practiced law for more than twenty-five years.

Levy was elected as a Gold Democrat to the Fifty-sixth Congress in 1898, representing the Thirteenth Congressional District. His forceful advocacy of hard money was anathema to most Democrats and nearly all Jews, but Levy, as the scion of one of America's oldest and most prosperous Jewish families, was largely out of step with the positions and dreams of his coreligionists. One of the few Jews holding membership in both the Sons of the Revolution and the Society of the War of 1812, Levy was, to say the least, something of a patrician. Fed up with the hurly-burly of congressional life, he quit Congress after his one term and returned to New York, where he resumed the practice of law.

J. M. Levy was reelected to the House of Representatives in 1910 and served in both the Sixty-second and Sixty-third Congress. While the general thrust of Levy's political energies and expertise continued to be in the economic realm, this time around he found a new cause to champion: the creation of a Federal Reserve Bank. Energized by the banking theories of his coreligionist, the German Paul M. Warburg, Representative Levy became a tireless worker on behalf of the Federal Reserve System. Created in the years immediately preceding World War I, the Federal Reserve would eventually come under attack as being the pernicious creation of a cadre of conspiring Jews. Indeed, Paul Warburg, generally credited with being the Father of the Federal Reserve, would be asked to leave its board of governors by President Wilson; the political pressure had become too much for the former Princeton professor to bear.

Neither politics nor the law, however, was Levy's prime passion. Throughout most of his life, the love, the obsession, the "mistress of his soul" was Monticello, the estate of America's third President, Thomas Jefferson.

The history of the Levy family's ownership of Monticello is shrouded in mystery and misconception. Two facts, however, are certain: first, the Levy family owned Monticello for more than ninety years (1836–1929); second, without the tireless stewardship of J. M. Levy, Monticello would likely be nothing more than a memory today.

J. M.'s uncle, Uriah P. Levy, purchased the mountaintop estate in May 1836, ten years after Jefferson's death. Hard as it is to imagine from the perspective of the late twentieth century, in 1836, Thomas Jefferson was not a particularly popular figure. His star had been totally eclipsed by George Washington. Like his reputation, Jefferson's estate lay in ruins, the surrounding lands overgrown with weeds and the detritus of neglect. That the Levy family revered the Jefferson legacy and name is obvious; while in Paris in the early 1830s, Uriah P. Levy privately commissioned a French sculptor to create a statue of his hero in bronze. Upon his return to the United States, he asked Congress to accept the statue as a gift to the people of the United States. The statue still has a place of honor in Statuary Hall in the rotunda of the Capitol. Standing to the right of the statue of George Washington, it is the only icon in that distinguished collection that was not paid for with federal or state government funds.

By one account, Commodore Levy purchased the rundown property at the behest of his good friend President Andrew Jackson, and wound up acquiring the estate for $2,600 or $2,700. Levy proceeded to restore and refurbish the estate at his own expense, and made it his summer home—his permanent residence being on St. Mark's Place in New York City.

When the Commodore died in March 1862, his will transferred title of Monticello to the "People of the United States," to be used "as an

Agricultural School for the purpose of educating as practical farmers" the children of deceased naval officers. The will was contested by Levy's relatives. After years of wrangling in the federal courts, and internecine squabbling among Uriah's seven brothers, sisters, and their children, the estate wound up in the hands of the young, appropriately named Jefferson Levy. It would appear that the federal court divided up shares of the estate among the many Levy family members. Quietly and without notice, J. M., like a modern-day arbitrageur, began buying shares from his many cousins, aunts, and uncles. By 1879, he had acquired enough "stock" to be able to purchase Monticello outright. This he did for the sum of $10,500, to be paid in three annual installments. In March 1881, nearly twenty years after Uncle Uriah's death, J. M. Levy finally became the sole owner of Monticello. Those twenty years took a toll on both the feelings of the members of the Levy family for one another and on the estate for which they were vying. By 1881, Monticello was once again in ruins.

Over the next decade-and-a-half, J. M. Levy committed nearly a half-million dollars of his own money for the restoration of Monticello. By the end of the nineteenth century, Jefferson's reputation, like his home, had been rehabilitated. At that time, William Jennings Bryan began making inquiries about purchasing Monticello and turning it into a national monument. When asked what price might suit him, J. M. Levy is reported to have replied that "all the money in the Treasury could not pay for the mansion." This was just the beginning of a brouhaha that would last for another quarter century.

J. M. Levy's desire to maintain Monticello as a private residence was viewed with disdain by many. Although largely unstated, one gets the impression that many Sons and Daughters of the American Revolution were repulsed by the idea of a New York Jew owning the Jefferson property. Chief among these bluebloods was Mrs. Martin Wiley Littleton, wife of one of Levy's congressional colleagues from New York. Mrs. Littleton spared no time, effort, expense, or invective in her attempt to make Monticello the property of the American people. She took her case to Congress, where the issue was turned over to the House Rules Committee. Chary of manhandling a colleague, the Rules Committee issued a nebulous finding that "perhaps" the

House might consider authorizing the purchase of Monticello on behalf of the American people. The House voted 141 to 101 against the committee's resolution.

Levy was then offered $100,000 (four times Monticello's assessed valuation) by Virginia's governor, Thomas Fortune Ryan. Again Levy demurred. He was quoted by the *New York Times* as saying: "I will sell Monticello under no circumstances. I have repeatedly refused $1,500,000 for the property. My answer to any proposition seeking the property of Monticello is: When the White House is for sale, then will I consider an offer for the sale of Monticello, and not before." Truth to tell, Levy rarely ever lived at Monticello. He did journey there each Fourth of July, when he would take Jefferson's old music stand outside the mansion and, using it as a lectern, read the Declaration of Independence to his neighbors.

Shortly after World War I, Levy let it be known that he might be interested in selling the property to a private foundation—if the price was right. Why the change after so many years of steadfastly refusing to sell? Simple. J. M. Levy had exhausted most of his funds in restoring and maintaining Monticello. Once word got out that Levy would sell, groups in Washington, Richmond, and Charlottesville, Virginia, attempted to establish foundations with the aim of acquiring sufficient capital for the purchase of Monticello. They all failed. It was left to a New York City-based group, the Thomas Jefferson Memorial Foundation, to succeed.

Funded largely by Felix M. Warburg, Oscar Straus, and *Herbert Henry Lehman*, the Memorial Foundation pledged $1,000,000—half for the outright purchase of Monticello, and half in the form of an endowment for its upkeep.

By the time the Thomas Jefferson Memorial Foundation completed its fundraising, J. M. Levy had died. Title to the estate passed to his heir, his sister Amelia Mayhoff. Following her late brother's wishes, she accepted $500,000 for Monticello, which was then turned into the national monument that millions have visited over the past seventy years.

When one visits Monticello today, tour guides rarely, if ever, mention the name Jefferson Monroe Levy. They seem almost willfully ignorant of the seminal role this patriotic Jewish man played in salvaging, restoring, and preserving Thomas Jefferson's magnificent home. They seem unaware that a Jewish family owned the estate for nearly a century, and that without its loving efforts, Monticello would no longer exist.

The keen-eyed tourist can, however, find a tiny reminder of the Levy family's legacy. Just up the road from the gift shop, you will come across the vine-covered enclosure that is the Jefferson family graveyard. Buried here are the Jefferson family's cousins, servants, and retainers. If you crane your neck just a bit, you will spot a tiny, moss-encrusted headstone marking the final resting place of Jefferson Monroe Levy's beloved great-aunt (and Uncle Uriah's mother), Rachel Phillips Levy. Small though it be, the Levy family's legacy remains.

References

American Jewish Year Book, vol. 2, p. 520; vol. 6, pp. 138–139; vol. 24, p. 171; vol. 26, p. 156.

David Max Eichorn, *Joys of Jewish Folklore: A Journey from New Amsterdam to Beverly Hills and Beyond* (New York: Jonathan David, 1981), pp. 75–84.

Encyclopaedia Judaica (1972), vol. 11, col. 158.

Jewish Historical Quarterly, vol. 53, pp. 219–252.

New York Times, March 7, 1924, 15:3.

Publications of the American Jewish Historical Society 39 (1949–50): 1–66.

Universal Jewish Encyclopedia.

Who Was Who in America, vol. 1.

LEVY, WILLIAM MALLORY (1827–1882):
Democrat from Louisiana; served one term in the House (Forty-Fourth Congress; March 4, 1875–March 3, 1877).

Only two sources recognize the Jewish background of William Mallory Levy: the *Universal Jewish Encyclopedia* and Dr. Jacob Rader Marcus, the late dean of American Jewish historians. Despite a varied career as soldier, attorney, legislator, and jurist, Levy remains a rather obscure character.

William Mallory Levy was born in Isle of Wight, Virginia, on October 31, 1827. Of his family, virtually nothing is known. Following "preparatory studies," Levy attended the College of William and Mary in Williamsburg. Graduating at age seventeen (1844), he began reading law in anticipation of becoming an attorney. His studies were interrupted by the Mexican war in 1846, during which he served as a second lieutenant in Company F, First Regiment, Virginia Volunteers. At war's end in September 1847, Levy returned to Virginia, where he completed his legal education. Admitted to the Virginia bar in 1851, he began practicing in Norfolk. Within a year, he left Virginia, settling in Natchitoches, Louisiana, where he hung out his shingle.

Levy was elected to a two-year term in the Louisiana House of Representatives in 1859. Before his term concluded, the Civil War had begun and he was back in the army, this time serving as captain of Company A, Second Louisiana Infantry. By the end of the war, he had been promoted to major in the Adjutant General's Department.

In November 1874, William M. Levy defeated one-term Republican George Luke Smith, publisher of the *Shreveport Southwestern Telegram* and president of the Shreveport Savings Bank & Trust, for Louisiana's Fourth District seat in Congress. (Smith had won a special election in 1873 to fill the vacancy caused by the death of Representative-elect Samuel Peters.) Levy's election ended an eight-year period during which no Jew served in Congress.

The election of 1874 ushered in the first Democrat-controlled House since well before the Civil War. Emboldened by the election results, Democrats across the South sought, in the words of Page Smith, "not only to gain political power but to drive blacks out of the political arena entirely." This meant, among other things, keeping black voters from the polls. Histories from the period abound with reports of whites patrolling polling places "with rifles and shotguns, turn[ing] blacks away while they themselves voted repeatedly." Reconstructionist governments in Texas, Arkansas, Mississippi, and Alabama all fell to the Democrats by 1874. In William Mallory Levy's Louisiana, a so-called White League organized a paramilitary force and took to killing blacks in "an orgy of brutality." In New Orleans, the White League got into a pitched battle with the black state militia. When the militiamen were routed, the league controlled the city for five days—until federal troops arrived to restore order.

As a member of the Forty-fourth Congress, Levy became involved in a controversy surrounding the credentials of certain House members. By law, former rebels were barred from holding office. This effectively kept the vast majority of Southern whites out of Congress. As a former Civil War officer, Levy was viewed as a seditionist as well. The Forty-fourth Congress was bedeviled by an endless stream of successful challenges to the credentials of its members. Serious legislative activity ground to a halt.

With tensions running high, and a presidential election looming, the Democrat House decided to flex its political muscles. Partisan lines were drawn; Democrats and Republicans squared off with bipolar proposals. Levy stepped into the middle of the widening gap, issuing a call for a workable compromise that would recognize the various Southern state governments and their popularly elected representatives. According to the *New York Times*, Levy, who "by reason of his ability has no small influence," opined that "this House, fresh from the people, cannot be bound by the action of the last House."

Running for reelection toward the end of 1876, Levy was defeated in the Democrat primary by Joseph Elam, the former Speaker of the Louisiana House of Representatives. Elam went on to face George Smith, who was attempting to regain his seat, and defeated him by the slimmest of margins. Although Smith contested the election, Elam was duly seated in Levy's stead.

Following his single term in Congress, William Mallory Levy returned to Natchitoches, where he resumed the practice of law. In 1879, after serving as a member of the state's constitutional convention, Levy was appointed associate justice of the Louisiana Supreme Court. He served on the court until his death in Saratoga, New York, on August 14, 1882. William Mallory Levy was buried in the American Cemetery, in Natchitoches.

References

Jacob Rader Marcus, *American Jewish Biography* (New York: Carlson Publishing, 1994), vol. 1, p. 384.

New York Times, January 6, 1876, 1:3.

Universal Jewish Encyclopedia.

Who Was Who in America.

LIEBERMAN, JOSEPH I. (1942–): *Democrat from Connecticut; has served two terms in the Senate (January 3, 1988–present).*

Upon entering the offices of Senator Joseph Lieberman, one is immediately struck by two things: the *mezuzah* on the door and the *pushkes* (Jewish charity boxes) on the desks and tables. There is no getting around it; Joe Lieberman is a Jewish United States Senator—the first (and so far, only) practicing Orthodox Jew to ever serve in that body.

The story is told that on his first Friday night in Washington, the Senate worked late—so late that Lieberman, not wishing to violate the Sabbath injunction against travel, was planning to sleep on the cot in his office. When Tennessee Senator Al Gore heard what his junior colleague was about to do, he prevailed upon Lieberman to stay at his parents' nearby apartment. A veteran campaigner who had spent much time amongst the Orthodox Jews of New York, "Gore was familiar enough with [Jewish] traditions to turn the apartment lights on and off for Lieberman." Recalling that event, Lieberman muses, "I may have had one of the most distinguished *Shabbos goys* (a non-Jew who performs tasks a Jew cannot on the Sabbath) in history."

The Liebermans were among the vast wave of Eastern European Jews who came to America in the first decade of the twentieth century. Henry Lieberman, the Senator's father, was born in New York. Henry's mother, Rebecca Segalovich, came to America alone from Russia; the rest of her family settled in Palestine. One of her brothers fought, died, and was buried alongside Yosef Trumpeldor, the legendary Zionist pioneer killed by Arab terrorists in 1920 while defending a Jewish community under siege.

When his mother died in the influenza epidemic of 1918, the three-year-old Henry was placed in an orphanage, where he remained until the age of ten. He was not reunited with his family until his father, Jacob (known as Jake), remarried and moved to New Haven, Connecticut, where he opened a grocery store. By the time Henry graduated from New Haven's Hillhouse High School, the Depression was in full swing; instead of attending college, as was his dream, he had to find a job.

As a young man, Henry attended a Purim dance at the Jewish Center in Stamford. It was a fateful event, because there he met his future wife, Marcia Manger. Like Henry, Marcia was from an Eastern European family that had immigrated to America around 1910. The Manger family was far more Jewishly knowledgeable and observant than the Liebermans. Due to the exigencies of Henry's early life, he had all but been denied a proper Jewish education. In fact, he did not become bar mitzvah until shortly before their wedding.

The newlyweds settled in Stamford, where their first child, the future Senator, was born on February 24, 1942. Soon, two daughters, Ellen (Ellie) and Rietta (Riri), were added to the family. Henry ran a small liquor store on Hamilton Avenue in Stamford, where, in the early days, despite his growing commitment to raising his family in a religiously observant manner, he had to keep his store open on Friday nights, the Jewish Sabbath. With the passing of time, he was able to hire a man to take over for the Sabbath.

Henry was not a typical shopkeeper. Customers coming into his shop would often find him "read[ing] and listen[ing] to classical music on WQXR," the radio station of the *New York Times*. In speaking of his father, who died in 1986, Senator Lieberman recalls that "[he] became a great student of Judaism . . . a great student of history and texts. . . . My dad was very learned." Of his mother, the Senator said, "[she] really created an aura in the house, she was very ritualistically involved. [She] created a warmth that we associated with religion. [My father] gave a kind of intellectual content—depth—to this love of basic religion that my mother gave."

Joe Lieberman was, by all indications, an ideal child—a "boy scout" in every sense of the term. The three Lieberman children got along well: "We never fought. Never." As the firstborn, Joe was apparently the family's favorite.

One family tradition has it that whenever Joe came down to breakfast, his parents would rise from their places and applaud his entry. From an early age, he was made to feel special—and he was. At Stamford High School, Joe was "'Mr. Personality,' who always had a kind word for everyone and who tirelessly strove for the commonweal." Active in everything from the math and jazz clubs to the school newspaper and synagogue youth group, Joe was remembered by his classmates as "a person who by week's end would have accomplished, with apparent ease, twice as much as anyone else. And no one knew exactly how he did it, much less why." Joe Lieberman graduated from Stamford High School in 1960. Next to his picture in the school yearbook was the simple comment: "A successful future assured."

While growing up in Stamford, Lieberman attended an Orthodox Hebrew school where he was taught by Rabbi Aron Kranz. Lieberman credits the rabbi with having helped shape his life: "He was very much involved in the community . . . a lot of teaching about *tikkun olam* [the concept of "bettering the world"] and your responsibility to be involved in the life of the community. . . . I know that there are real religious roots to my political involvement."

In September 1960, Joe Lieberman entered Yale. Although he was offered a scholarship, his father, a man of great pride, insisted on paying for the son's education himself. As an undergraduate, he *davened* (prayed) every morning and was one of but four Jews in his class who kept kosher—at a time when Yale did not have a kosher kitchen. The four were provided with frozen kosher meals by the director of Yale's Hillel, Rabbi Richard Israel. Like many people attempting to keep kosher in a largely non-kosher world, Lieberman ate a lot of eggs, vegetables, and fish. Reminiscing about those days, he told two writers for *Urim v'Tumim* (the student quarterly of Yale's present-day Jewish community): "One of my funnier stories from that time was about a lady who worked in the Morse College dining hall, where I ate my meals. She would see me eat fish every day, and after three or four months of this, she said to me, 'I've never met a Catholic as religious as you are. I thought most Catholics only eat fish on Friday, but you eat fish every day!'"

While an undergraduate, Lieberman served as editorial board chair of the *Yale Daily News* and was active in the Society of Orpheus and Bacchus, one of Yale's *a capella* singing groups. He was also "somewhat involved" in the Yale Jewish Appeal. Lieberman received his B.A. from Yale in June 1964. That summer, he went to Washington, where he interned for John Bailey, the head of the Democratic National Committee. Bailey has often been referred to as "the last great political boss." Lieberman got to know him well during his time in Washington and eventually published an admiring biography entitled *The Power Broker* (1966). In its review, *Library Journal* recommended Lieberman's book to both the "general reader" and "all students of political science." To date, Lieberman has published three other books: *The Scorpion and the Tarantula* (1970), a study of early efforts to control nuclear proliferation; *The Legacy* (1981), a history of Connecticut politics from 1930 to 1980; and *Child Support in America* (1986), a "guidebook on methods to increase the collection of child support from delinquent parents."

In 1964, Lieberman entered Yale Law School, from which he graduated in 1967. During one of his law school summers, he returned to Washington to intern for Connecticut Senator *Abraham A. Ribicoff*. In 1970, Joseph Lieberman ran for the Connecticut State Senate against its Majority Leader, Edward Marcus. Lieberman won by 242 votes. Running a tough, aggressive campaign, he was greatly aided by the fact that 1970 was the first year in which students at Yale could vote in a local election. Lieberman mobilized a large contingent of volunteers from Yale, including a twenty-four-year-old law student named Bill Clinton. Political memory can be a good thing; twenty-two years later, U.S. Senator Joseph Lieberman became the first Senator outside the South to endorse Clinton's candidacy for President of the United States.

Lieberman served ten years in the Connecticut Senate, the final six as majority leader. During this time, he supported a state income tax and opposed the death penalty, positions he would change in the coming years. In 1980, Joe Lieberman gave up his seat to run for the U.S. House of Representatives from Connecticut's Third District. His opponent was State Senator Lawrence J. DeNardis, an associate professor at Albertus Magnus College in New Haven. The Third District is very ethnic, most notably Italian-American. For years, it had been represented by men with names like Giaimo and Cretella. Lieberman ran as a mainline Democrat, tying his political fortunes to those of President Jimmy Carter. Well ahead in the polls until the campaign's final weeks, he suffered his first—and only—defeat.

The election also proved to be the end of Lieberman's sixteen-year marriage to Betty Haas, the daughter of a prominent Connecticut tobacco-growing family. The two had met in the summer of 1964 when they were both working in Senator Ribicoff's Washington office. They were married within the year and had two children, Matthew and Rebecca.

Stunned by his first defeat, Joe Lieberman spent the next two years licking his wounds, working as a commentator for Connecticut Public Television and doing some lobbying on behalf of the beer industry. He also pondered his political future. In July 1981, he made the curious announcement that "he would be running for office but hadn't yet decided which one it would be." In the fall of 1981, he announced for state attorney general, and wound up winning an impressive victory. He was easily reelected in 1986 with a record 65 percent of the vote.

During his six years as A.G., Joe Lieberman paid particular attention to consumer and environmental issues. In the realm of consumer affairs, he went after fake charities and unscrupulous merchants who took advantage of their customers. As a proactive environmentalist, he worked to strengthen laws concerning nuclear disposal sites and toxic waste dumps. Lieberman credits his environmental concerns to his understanding of Jewish law and the Jewish *Weltanschauung*: "If you believe in God and you believe that God created the earth, then you believe that one of your religious responsibilities is to work to continue to protect the creation. . . . Throughout the Torah and Jewish liturgy there are continued environmental calls. . . . There is a *midrash* [commentary] that says that if you enter the Holy Land and begin to plant a tree, you must finish planting even if someone comes and tells you that the *Moshiach* [Messiah] is coming."

Midway through his second term as A.G., Lieberman's political life took a radical change. Lieberman's friend and former Yale classmate,

Massachusetts Senator John F. Kerry, began urging him to run for the Senate against maverick Republican Lowell Weicker. On February 22, 1988, after much contemplation, Lieberman announced his intention to challenge Weicker. Lieberman won the Democratic nomination for Senator later that year at a convention he did not attend because it was held on the Sabbath. The *frum* (religious) Lieberman has always refused to campaign on Shabbat or other Jewish holidays, and in this instance, he missed seventeen of the final sixty-five days of the Senate race.

Lieberman and Weicker disagreed on few substantive issues. Both supported abortion rights. Both called for increased federal funding in the areas of environmental protection, AIDS research, and education. Both were staunchly pro-Israel. On the issues where they did differ—prayer in the public schools, the United States invasion of Grenada, and the bombing of Libya, a national tax on gasoline—Lieberman came off as the more conservative of the two. Indeed, as the 1994 *Current Biography Yearbook* noted: "If more evidence were needed that the Democratic challenger was more conservative than the Republican incumbent, that proof was provided when the right-wing columnist William F. Buckley . . . endorsed Lieberman's candidacy."

Lieberman turned Weicker's maverick reputation into a liability. Where the incumbent's campaign slogan proudly proclaimed: "He's nobody's man but yours," the challenger retorted: "He's nobody man, period." All told, 1,366,953 voters cast ballots in the election, with Lieberman winning by a mere 10,045.

Almost from his first day in the United States Senate, Joseph Lieberman was recognized as a political comer. Within a month of his arrival in the Senate, he was chosen to give the Democrat response to President Ronald Reagan's final radio address. As the upper chamber's only Orthodox Jew, he was and is one of that body's most distinctive members. He continues to eat only kosher food, and when necessity requires his presence in the Senate on a Sabbath, he walks the nearly five miles from his Georgetown home to Capitol Hill. Once there, in strict adherence to Jewish law, he takes the stairs rather than ride in an elevator. His Sabbath votes are recorded by hand or voice rather than by electronic means.

Although generally receiving high marks from the liberal Americans for Democratic

Action, Senator Lieberman has sided with the Republicans on many occasions. He was one of but six Senate Democrats to vote for cuts in the capitals gains tax in 1989. One year later, he was one of the few Senate Democrats to support President George Bush's use of force in Panama. Notably, he was sponsored legislation that authorized President Bush to use military force against Iraq and that opposed cuts in funding for the Strategic Defense Initiative—"Star Wars." Notably, he was also one of the few Senate Democrats to come out against shifting money from the defense budget to cover the costs of domestic programs.

Asked to explain his various departures from the Democrat Party's "line," Lieberman responded: "What has always distinguished the Democrats, and I hope will continue to distinguish them, is that they care about people's problems and believe that government has an obligation to solve those problems. But what we have to do is redefine how that happens."

When President Bush nominated Clarence Thomas for a seat on the Supreme Court, Lieberman initially gave him his qualified support. This pleased the White House and angered his fellow Democrats. After reading virtually all of Judge Thomas's legal decisions and interviewing scores of people who had known and worked with him, Lieberman was still inclined to vote for confirmation. It was only when allegations of sexual misconduct came to light that Lieberman cast a negative vote. Political observers note that the junior Senator from Connecticut did not cast his vote until Thomas's confirmation was assured. More than one writer termed this a "stealth vote."

Joseph Lieberman is one of the few Northeastern Democrats who does not oppose voluntary prayer in the public schools. "I always go back to my grandmother on that issue. My grandmother used to say, 'What do I care if they want to have a nativity scene at the town green. I mean, this is a great country. I can walk to *shul* [synagogue] on Saturday, and nobody bothers me like they used to do when I was in the old country.' It's a funny attitude, but to a certain extent she was saying . . . let's go beyond these sets of theoretical fears about 'Church/State' because it is not really real. It doesn't affect us. Let us be grateful for what is here."

In 1991, Lieberman became one of the very first American Jews who had an Israeli stamp on their passport to be granted permission to visit Saudi Arabia. Originally, his request had been denied. Approaching the Saudi ambassador, with whom he had developed a working relationship, he queried: "How can you possibly tell a U.S. Senator, let alone any American, that they can't come into your country because they've been to Israel?" The ambassador responded: "Let me know when you want to go." Lieberman quickly answered: "I want to go this summer." And so he went.

On March 20, 1983, Joseph Lieberman remarried. His new wife, Hadassah Freilich, was born in Prague, the child of Holocaust survivors. The tale of how the two met has an almost storybook quality: "Shortly after his divorce from his first wife, Lieberman was approached in the synagogue by a woman who said, 'I have someone I want you to meet—but not yet.' Six months later, as a candidate for attorney general of Connecticut, Liberman found himself in the unusual position of being alone with no political event scheduled. It was Easter Sunday, April 11, 1982. . . . Liberman delved into the drawer where he kept all the names of prospective dates given to him and picked out the most unusual. Wouldn't it be fascinating to go out with someone named Hadassah? So he phoned with a strange request: meet him that day or not until December because he had virtually no free time until after the November election. Not missing a beat, Hadassah told him she had just bought a dining room table and could use some help moving it in. The couple met and romance blossomed."

Hadassah Lieberman works as a consultant for the National Research Council in Washington. Together they have one daughter, Hana, born in 1988. In addition to Hana, the family consists of the Senator's two children, Matthew and Rebecca, and Ethan, the son of Hadassah Lieberman's first marriage. All three of Senator Lieberman's children attended Hebrew day schools. As of late 1998, twenty-two-year-old Ethan, a Harvard graduate, was making plans to study for the rabbinate; Rebecca, twenty-nine, a University of Pennsylvania Law School graduate, was working for the Children's Aid Society in New York; Matt, thirty, a Yale-educated attorney, was working with the "I Have a Dream" Foundation in New Haven. Matt is the father of the

Lieberman's only grandchild, named Tennessee. (Her Hebrew name, *Nesya*, means "a miracle of God.") Hana, ten, was a student at the Jewish Primary Day School of Adas Israel in Washington, D.C.

Long known as one of President Bill Clinton's most avid supporters, Joe Lieberman took the floor of the Senate shortly before Rosh Hashana 5759 (September 1998) to denounce his old friend as "immoral." At issue were the President's repeated denials that he had had an extramarital affair with former White House intern Monica Lewinksy. Speaking to a hushed Senate chamber, Lieberman said the President's behavior had "reinforc[ed] one of the worst messages being delivered by our popular culture, which is that values are fungible." Lieberman thereby became the first member of the President's own party to upbraid him for his actions. Shortly after Lieberman's speech, fellow Democrats Daniel Patrick Moynihan of New York and Bob Kerrey of Nebraska rose to second him. According to one reporter sitting in the gallery, "most Democrats winced."

When asked why he decided to publicly excoriate the President when he knew full well that the Republicans would exploit his words, Lieberman responded: "The President wasn't dealing with this openly. Among Democrats nobody was talking about it, worst of all, nobody was saying anything directly to him. My feeling was that, unless the President and the Democrats spoke of these things openly, the situation could only get worse. If the President would speak of this openly, he might be able to rebuild enough trust to finish his term." Lieberman's comments turned out to have a prescience that perhaps even he could not have predicted; shortly after delivering his remarks, President Bill Clinton went on national television to confess his errors and express penitence. Most news accounts noted that Lieberman was the Senate's only Orthodox Jew. When reporters covering his historic speech asked about whether he were merely a Jewish version of a born-again Christian, Lieberman remarked:

There is a general rightward movement in Orthodox Judaism today, but I am not part of that. The word I use to describe myself is observant. To me, being observant means following the rituals by which I was raised, such as Sabbath rules and dietary laws and drawing on the historical body of ethical precepts and experiences of Judaism. But I see no reason why a person can't be Orthodox and also an independent thinker. The whole history of the Talmud is one of questioning and discussion. My religious experience encourages independence of judgment.

In an article entitled "Not Your Average Joe," *New Republic* senior editor Gregg Easterbrook wrote:

We're so accustomed to images of the televangelist Christian hypocrite, the threatening Islamic extremist, or the intolerant Orthodox Jew that we think they symbolize the main current of the three great monotheistic faiths. Contemporary culture seems to ignore the possibility that a person might embrace the customs and forms of a traditionalist faith, as Lieberman does, yet remain open-minded, or the possibility that faith can constructively shape political and personal philosophy. Thus, a better symbol is Lieberman, whose religious background may indeed make him too quick to hurl words like "immoral" but otherwise has instilled in him responsibility and introspection. Observance of tradition with independence of mind is a worthy combination and one reason Lieberman ranks among the Senate's best.

Joseph Lieberman has received honorary degrees from Yeshiva University and the University of Hartford. In 1991, *Connecticut Magazine* named him "best politician of the previous two decades."

References
Interview with Joseph Lieberman, Washington, D.C., March 1992.
Interview with Ellen Lieberman, February 1996.
Connecticut, December 1991.
Current Biography, 1994, pp. 331–334.
Hartford Courant, February 5, 1989.
Jewish News of Greater Phoenix, July 24, 1998.
New Republic, November 2, 1998.
New York Times, April 29, 1990, October 13, 1991.
Policy Review, Summer 1990, pp. 26–33.

LITTAUER, LUCIUS NATHAN (1859–1944):
Republican from New York; served five terms in the House (Fifty-fifth through Fifty-ninth Congress; March 4, 1897–March 3, 1907).

When Lucius Littauer graduated from high school (the Charlier Institute in New York City) at age fifteen, he went off to Harvard College. Like many students before and since, he roomed with "a kid from the old neighborhood." In this case, the kid was Theodore Roosevelt, the future President of the United States. The two would remain fast friends—Roosevelt once stated publicly that Littauer was his closest political adviser—until 1916, when Littauer refused to leave the Republican fold in order to support T. R.'s insurgent candidacy for President on the Progressive—"Bullmoose"—Party ticket. Roosevelt's disappointment was matched by Littauer's sadness at having to put "political conviction and duty" ahead of friendship.

Lucius Nathan Littauer was born in Gloversville, New York, on January 20, 1859, the eldest son (and the second of five children) born to Nathan and Harriet (Sporborg) Littauer. His mother's family had been well established in Albany for at least two generations. His father had immigrated to New York from Prussia at age sixteen in 1845. The Littauers, originally from Littau, Lithuania, were at one time one of Europe's oldest and most respected Jewish families. They lost their money in the Napoleonic Wars and migrated to Breslau, Prussia, where Lucius's father Nathan was born. According to family legend, Nathan decided to leave Prussia after he had struck his teacher, mistaking the man for an assailant. Walking from Breslau to Hamburg, he boarded a ship and arrived thirty-six days later in New York.

Nathan Littauer followed the time-honored path of employment: he became a peddler, first on foot, then graduating to a horse and wagon. His merchandise consisted largely of calicos and "Yankee notions." Hearing that there was a growing community in Stump City (later renamed Gloversville), he settled there in 1852 and opened a dry goods store. In November 1856, he married Harriet Sporborg, whom he had met on a trip to Albany. They were the first Jews to settle in Fulton County.

The glove industry was pivotal in the Mohawk valley. Nathan added a line of imported glove material to his store and soon discovered a much better way to make a living. Observing that lambskin made much better glove linings than wool or old blankets, Nathan began importing it. This branch of his business expanded so rapidly and proved to be so profitable that he soon closed his shop and went solely into the manufacture of gloves. The glove industry came to be dominated by German Jews; men with names like Meyers and Deichsel, Levor, Adler, and Rubin. Of all these, none was bigger or more prominent than Littauer. The industry would eventually employ more than 12,000 men and women in the Gloversville area and produce more than $15 million worth of gloves a year. By the time Lucius was seven, his father, already a very wealthy man, had moved the family to New York City.

Lucius Littauer was educated at the Wells Seminary in Gloversville, the aforementioned Charlier Institute in New York City, and, of course, Harvard College. While at Harvard, he was a member of both the football team and the varsity crew. During his second year in Cambridge, Lucius's sister Louise died at age nineteen. In later years, he would establish a hospital wing in her name. Upon graduating in 1878, Lucius moved back to Gloversville, where, along with his younger brother Eugene, he entered his father's firm. Within four years, the two boys owned and controlled the business, now renamed Littauer Brothers. In time, Littauer Brothers grew to be the largest glove-manufacturing concern in the United States, employing upwards of 1,000 people. Lucius diversified his business interests, becoming associated with public utilities and banks. At the peak of his financial career, he served as president or managing director of more than a dozen corporations. Not surprisingly, he also served as president of the Glove Manufacturers Association.

After Nathan turned the business over to his sons in 1882, he devoted the remaining nine years of his life to making bequests and endowments to various Jewish organizations in Gloversville. He thereby set an example for his son Lucius, who in his later years would become one of the American Jewish community's greatest philanthropists. Littauer was of the generation and ilk that subscribed to Andrew Carnegie's Gospel of Wealth theory: Society benefits most when men of talent, ability, and vision are able to amass great fortunes; these fortunes are then to be used for the betterment of the society that underwrote their vast success. Toward the end of his life, when he was continuously lauded for his extraordinary beneficence, Lucius Littauer tried to deflect the praise by claiming, in all humility: "I am simply an ordinary fellow who has followed the accidents of life as he met them." From all indications, Littauer's comment was without guile; that's truly the way he saw himself.

In 1896, Lucius Littauer was elected as a Republican to the Fifty-fifth Congress. His nomination came by way of a compromise; local Republican leaders were at sixes and sevens over whom to nominate, and finally settled on Littauer. Following a rather silent first term, Littauer was reelected to the Fifty-sixth Congress in 1898. He was quickly appointed to the House Appropriations Committee, on which he would serve with distinction for the remainder of his congressional career. Littauer's reelection in 1898 coincided with his friend Theodore Roosevelt's election as governor of New York. Almost immediately, rumors began spreading that the Republicans would nominate T. R. for Vice President on the McKinley ticket in 1900.

The Hero of San Juan Hill wanted no part of it. He wrote his old friend Littauer that he was seriously considering staying away from the Republican National Convention, to be held in Philadelphia. Littauer urged his former college roommate to change his mind. Not only did Roosevelt go to Philadelphia; he seconded McKinley's nomination and was in turn overwhelmingly nominated (save his own vote) for the second spot.

Littauer's joy was tempered with a few second thoughts. "My only regret," he wrote T. R., "is that you must waste four years in a position unsuited to your abilities." Not having a crystal ball, Littauer had no way of knowing that within six months of beginning his second term, McKinley would be assassinated and Theodore Roosevelt would be sitting in the Oval Office. With Roosevelt in the White House, Littauer's political career began to soar.

Not surprisingly, the main thrust of Lucius Littauer's congressional career came in his role as watchdog par excellence over protective tariffs, especially as they affected the American glove-manufacturing industry. From his seat on the Appropriations Committee, he supported virtually every proposed tariff. He was an ardent lobbyist for the Dingley Tariff of 1897, which increased import duties on men's gloves by 20 percent and, for the first time, levied a tax on ladies' gloves. For Lucius Littauer, protective tariffs were as much a matter of patriotic pride as personal gain or partisan politics. In a speech backing Roosevelt for a full four-year term, Littauer stated: "The Republican Party, first, last and all the time stands for protection, for a protective tariff which guards American interests of labor and capital. . . . We stand for that policy of protection which guards and develops our industries."

On several occasions, the Jewish community turned to Representative Littauer for assistance on matters of international concern. After the bloody Kishinev pogrom in 1905, Littauer, at the behest of Louis Marshall of the American Jewish Committee, used his influence with President Roosevelt to lend assistance to downtrodden, imperiled Russian Jewry. After leaving Congress, he was instrumental in getting the State Department to abrogate an 1832 commercial treaty with Russia after it violated the agreement's terms by denying entry visas to American Jews.

Toward the end of his congressional career, Littauer was rumored to be in line for an appointment to the cabinet as Secretary of Commerce and Labor. The post eventually went to another Jew, Oscar Straus, brother of former Congressman *Isidor Straus*. It is highly likely that Littauer was not appointed, at least in part, because of his involvement in the so-called gauntlet scandal of 1903. Members of Congress were legally prohibited from entering into contracts with the federal government. During the Spanish-American War, Littauer Brothers had manufactured and sold 3,000 gloves to a Mr. Lyon, a contractor for the War Department. Lyon, in turn, sold the 3,000 muskrat gauntlets to the U.S. Army.

When charges related to this transaction surfaced, Littauer turned over all relevant books, ledgers, and documents to the War Department, contending that the whole thing had been dreamed up by his political enemies. Secretary of War Elihu Root investigated and found one violation of the law. The case dragged on so long that the statute of limitations expired. Littauer, not satisfied by this outcome, demanded that it be reopened. When Attorney General Philander C. Knox reinvestigated, he determined that indeed, no violation had occurred. Thus vindicated, Littauer ran for reelection in 1904 and won. This proved to be his last term in Congress; the scandal had soured him on elective politics.

Littauer remained active in Republican politics for another eight years. His political career came to a crashing halt in 1914, when he and his brother William were indicted for smuggling a diamond and pearl tiara into the country. The jewelry, supposedly once owned by the Empress Josephine, the wife of Napoleon, was intended as a gift for William's wife. The brothers pleaded no contest to the charges and were each fined $1,000. In order to prove to a jaundiced public that the wealthy and well-connected were not given preferential treatment, the court also handed down unprecedented six-month suspended sentences.

In July 1913, Lucius Littauer married Flora Mathilda Crawford. It was the fifty-four-year-old Littauer's first and only marriage. Because Crawford was not Jewish, Littauer decided it best to hold off on marrying her until both his parents were deceased. They had no children, and Flora Littauer died of pneumonia in 1924. Following her death, Lucius Littauer entered into the final phase of his life—philanthropy. In the next twenty years, he would give away more than $6 million, mostly for the aid and benefit of the Jewish community, education, and medical research.

Among Littauer's major bequests were the Nathan Littauer Chair in Jewish Literature and Philosophy at Harvard (the first of its kind in America) and nearly 15,000 volumes of Hebrew texts to the Harvard library. In 1935 and 1937, he gave $2.25 million to establish Harvard's Graduate School of Public Administration. He also gave generous grants to hospitals in Breslau, Paris, and New York, and to medical schools for research on pneumonia, cancer, diabetes, psychiatry, and speech disorders. In 1929, he established the Lucius N. Littauer Foundation "for the welfare of mankind," giving it over $1 million in securities and instructing its directors to use the income for "altruistic activities of every nature, charitable, humanitarian, educational, religious and communal." He adopted a strictly hands-off policy; decisions by the foundation's directors would be final. Littauer also endowed the Jewish Theological Seminary and built the Jewish Community Center in Gloversville.

In the late 1920s, while living at his estate on Premier Point, near New Rochelle, New York, Littauer hired a young rabbinical student, Emanuel Schenk, to tutor him in Hebrew and Bible. Schenk made a twice-a-week pilgrimage to the Littauer estate, for which he was paid the princely sum of $25 per session. Littauer explained to his young teacher that as a lad he hadn't paid much attention to his Jewish studies, and now, in later life, he wished to right that wrong.

A stout, dapper, balding man with a white walrus mustache and an ever-present carnation in his lapel, Lucius Littauer succumbed to a heart attack at age eighty-five on March 2, 1944. In his will, he left the bulk of his estate to the Lucius N. Littauer Foundation, which exists to this very day. He was buried in Salem Field Cemetery, Cypress Hill, Long Island.

References

Interview with Rabbi Emanuel Schenk, November 1991.

American Jewish Historical Quarterly, vol. 66, pp. 498–512.

American Jewish Year Book, vol. 2, p. 520; vol. 6, p. 143; vol. 24, p. 174; vol. 46, p. 341.

Biographical Directory of American Jews.

Dictionary of American Biography, vol. 3.

Encyclopaedia Judaica (1972), vol. 11, col. 391.

Jewish Encyclopedia.

New York Times, March 3, 1944, 15:1.

Universal Jewish Encyclopedia.

Who Was Who in America, vol. 2.

Who Was Who in American Jewry, 1926, 1928, 1938.

LONDON, MEYER (1871-1926): *Socialist from New York; served three terms in the House (Sixty-fourth and Sixty-fifth Congress; March 4, 1915–March 3, 1919; Sixty-seventh Congress; March 4, 1921–March 3, 1923).*

Unlike *Victor L. Berger*, the first Socialist elected to Congress, Meyer London devoted his entire life to being an advocate, lightning rod, spokesman, and leader of the Jewish community. His tireless efforts on behalf of his people did not go unnoticed by the Jewish masses of the East Side; the *New York Times* estimated the number of mourners at his funeral to be in excess of half a million. Not since the funeral of the great Yiddish writer Sholom Aleichem in 1916 had there been such an outpouring of love, grief, and respect. The *Times* reporter who accompanied the funeral cortege to the Writer's Lane section of Mount Carmel cemetery wrote: "For six hours, the East Side put aside its duties, pressing or trivial, to do honor to its dead prophet." All that love, all that grief, for a simple, humble, and brilliant man from Poltava—the same province that, ironically, had given the world Sholom Aleichem.

Meyer, the eldest of Ephraim and Rebecca (Berson) London's five sons, was born in Kalvaric, in the province of Suwalkie (Russia), on December 29, 1871. Shortly after his birth, the family moved to Zenkov in Poltava. Rebecca was descended from a long line of distinguished rabbis. Ephraim, originally trained as a talmudic scholar, was "tainted with new ideas . . . revolutionary in politics and agnostic in religion." He was, by most accounts, a *luftmentsch*—a man without definite occupation who, as the Yiddish term implies, seemed to live "on air and air alone." Ephraim eked out an uncertain existence writing for Hebrew journals. At one point, after immigrating to New York, he published a radical weekly called *Morgenstern*. Anarchistic in tone, it soon failed.

While growing up in Poltava, Meyer London attended a local *cheder*, and afterward, Russian school and the local Gymnasium. His early education was somewhat unique in that few Jewish boys were permitted to attend the Russian Gymnasium, roughly equivalent to an American secondary school. London was an outstanding student. During his lifetime, he became proficient in six languages (Russian, Yiddish, English, German, French, and Italian); during his years

on Capitol Hill, he was generally recognized as Congress's most erudite member.

Ephraim London emigrated to America in 1888, along with his second son, Louis. The rest of the family arrived in 1891, establishing their residence on New York's Lower East Side. While the father was making a precarious living as a printer, Meyer was working in a library, giving private instructions in language, and attending night law school at NYU. In 1896, the twenty-five-year-old Meyer London became an American citizen, was admitted to the New York Bar, and had his first taste of electoral politics as the Socialist Labor Party's nominee for the New York Assembly in the Fourth District. London lost the election (and again in 1898) because, as his biographer noted, "The marvel of Socialist strength would grow until the day of the election. Then during the 12 hours between the opening of the polls and their closing, the strength would melt away. On election day, the Tammany leaders and their heelers would slink from the corner saloons . . . and get the job done."

From the very beginning of his legal career, Meyer London represented the overworked, the underpaid, and the forgotten. His client list read like a "who's who" of East Side trade unionism: the International Ladies' Garment Workers' Union, the International Fur Workers, the Cloak Makers, and the United Hebrew Trades. It was said that Meyer London accepted only such clients and cases as would not interfere with his socialist principles, and that he would never take on a case involving an arrest.

Because he paid little attention to the more pecuniary aspects of the law, London was often in debt. Once, having neglected his private practice for months on end in order to offer his services *pro bono* to striking needle trade workers, London was ordered by the union strike committee to accept a $2,000 "gift." London demurred, and was told in no uncertain terms that should he refuse the largesse, the committee would have no choice but to drop him as their attorney of record. London quickly accepted the fee.

Although he spent a great deal of time in court, fighting for the rights of striking workers, the greatest part of London's legal work consisted in "keeping up the morale of the men. . . . He made it possible for the strike to go on." London also served as attorney of record for the Workman's Circle from 1905 until his death.

In 1897, a schism broke out in the Socialist Labor Party; the rank and file opposed the dictatorial tactics of party leader Daniel De Leon. London, like Victor Berger, moved over to Eugene V. Debs's newly organized Social Democracy Party of America, which in 1901, changed its name to Socialist Party of America—an association he maintained for the rest of his life.

Meyer London endowed socialist doctrine with high moral purpose and ethical dignity. He truly believed that the "system" dehumanized the worker, and that without socialism, the "little guy" could not possibly stand a chance. Unlike most of his Socialist Party colleagues on the East Side, London made his political appeal as an American to an American audience. A forceful street orator, he drew his public "chiefly among the young, the more Americanized and the more thoughtful elements." He was one of the few Socialist speakers who was accepted and listened to by the Irish, the Italians, and the Germans. He was one of the very few who could address them in their own languages; he regularly delivered his campaign speeches in Italian to the Italians, Yiddish to the Jews, German to the Germans, and English to the Irish.

Meyer London ran for Congress on the Socialist Party ticket in 1908, 1910, and 1912, losing all three races to incumbent Democrat *Henry M. Goldfogle*. He was finally elected to the Sixty-fourth Congress in 1914. The Republicans essentially sat out that race, leaving Tammany Hall to battle the Socialists. London did most of the campaigning. The Tammany candidate, the seven-term incumbent Goldfogle, sat on the sidelines, waiting for those final "12 hours" when his backers, the "boys from Tammany," would undoubtedly work their election day magic.

This time Goldfogle was wrong. Tammany's organizational genius was finally outmatched by London's Socialist minions. Not surprisingly, most of the morning papers, with the exception of the Yiddish ones, declared Goldfogle the victor. Their error was "characteristic of the ignorance of the papers of what was going on in the immigrant quarters." It seems that in calculating the election returns, they compared the Republican vote (totally insignificant) to the Democratic tally, and concluded that Goldfogle must have won in a landslide.

The *New York Times* addressed a long sermon of advice to the newly elected Socialist, warning him "not to lose his head, not to be blinded by popularity and victory . . . [and] not to attempt to force his ideas and his party principles on the attention of his colleagues." The Sunday after the election, the Socialists of New York packed Madison Square Garden to celebrate London's victory. In his short address to the gathered masses, London answered the *Times* editorial and at the same time took a swipe at the defeated Henry Goldfogle: "I don't expect to work wonders in Congress. I shall, however, say a new word and I shall accomplish one thing that is not in the platform of the Socialist party. I hope that my person will represent an entirely different type of Jew from the kind that Congress has been accustomed to seeing."

In 1915, the most burning issues facing Congress were peace and preparedness. In May 1915, the Germans sunk the passenger liner *Lusitania* without warning, and more than a hundred American citizens went to their death. The *Lusitania* tragedy precipitated an intense campaign of war propaganda against Germany.

In response to the rising hysteria, the executive committee of the Socialist Party of the United States issued a manifesto which declared, in part: "Any member of the Socialist Party, elected to an office, who shall in any way vote to appropriate money for military or naval purposes of war shall be expelled from the Party." The directive was passed by the rank-and-file by a vote of over 11,000 to 800. Meyer London had been put on notice. As Congress's only sitting Socialist, the eyes of both his party brethren and his Washington colleagues were fixed firmly his way. How would London respond to the emerging cries for war?

On December 6, 1915, in his maiden speech in the House of Representatives, Meyer London drew a political line in the sand with regard to war and peace, preparedness and politics. As the House listened, London accused President Woodrow Wilson of being "frightened by a mere shadow flung across the ocean by the nightmare of war that is being enacted by the other side." He termed the various preparedness proposals "largely foolish, artificial and to a great extent political and entirely unjustifiable."

He ended his speech by submitting a resolution for peace. In it, he asked Congress to call upon the President to summon a conference of neutral nations "for the purpose of offering mediation to the belligerents of Europe."

London's resolution outlined in minute detail the terms of peace for the proposed conference to consider. Congress assigned it to the Committee on Foreign Affairs, which held hearings on February 24 and 25, 1916. A large number of progressive organizations and labor unions sent representatives to testify in its support. Nothing, however, was done; neither the Committee on Foreign Affairs nor the Congress took action. In 1919, however, major portions of the London Peace Resolution found their way into President Wilson's Fourteen Points. Thus London's proposal "became the basis of discussion among all the nations at the close of the war."

In March 1916, Congress debated a bill that would increase the peacetime strength of the regular army from 100,000 to 140,000. True to his Socialist roots, London argued forcefully against it. In the end, only two members wound up voting against the Army Bill, Meyer London and Fred A. Britten, a Republican from Illinois. The two "no" votes were cast for totally different reasons. London stood four-squarely against war; Britten was of the opinion that "the increase of a mere 40,000 [is just] too trifling to bother with."

London also cast the sole vote against a presidential request for permission to send an expeditionary force to Mexico. Thanks to his efforts on behalf of peace, London, originally accepted and even admired by his congressional colleagues, found himself an outcast, denounced as un-American, a traitor. During one of his speeches, London was unceremoniously interrupted, while members of the House debated just how to deal with their radical colleague.

"I wish I could make a motion to expel him from the House," one member stated for the record. London responded angrily, saying: "I hate professions of loyalty, but I believe I am as deeply in love with the United States as any man who can trace his ancestry to the *Mayflower*."

Interestingly, London voted "present" (rather than yea or nay) on two war-related measures: the War Appropriations Bill of 1917 and a bill authorizing the sale of War Bonds. London offered an emotional explanation: "If I am expected to appeal for fair play for the Socialists in Congress, I want to appeal to the Socialists for common sense in their attitude in this great crisis of the world. I am not interested in why Morgan is for the war. I know. It is for the same reason as the Krupps are for the war. But after the United States declares for war there can be no choice. I owe a duty to every man who has been called to the service of his country, and that is not only that nothing shall be left undone to provide him with everything he needs, but to get this fight over as soon as possible." The Socialists, refusing to accept his explanation, denounced London for violating the peace manifesto. Meyer London was becoming a man without a political friend to call his own.

As a mainstream member of the Socialist Party, Meyer London's attitudes toward Zionism and Jewish nationalism were rather undeveloped. The Zionist question was hardly ever raised during the election of 1914. He did, nonetheless, insert a clause in his peace proposal that called for the "removal of the political and civic disabilities of the Jewish people wherever such disabilities exist." In the election of 1916, London was opposed by a new Tammany candidate, Judge Sanders, who tried to make his chief issue London's lack of Jewishness. It failed to impress the immigrant masses. London shunted aside Sanders's claim with the declaration: "I deem it a duty of the Jews everywhere to remain a Jew as long as in any corner of the world the Jew is being discriminated against." London was reelected to a second term.

As tirelessly as Meyer London worked on behalf of peace, he gave most of his energy to issues of social reform. He introduced bills calling for a minimum wage and unemployment insurance, and opposed high tariffs, the reduction of the income tax for the wealthy, and draconian cuts in immigration quotas. London fought for liberal maternity aid, the enforcement of anti-lynching laws, and measures that would aid coal miners. With regard to his call for national unemployment insurance, London explained to his colleagues that he was demanding this reform "not as an act of mercy or charity, but as an act of justice." Had they understood Yiddish or Hebrew, London would no doubt have employed the proper term for this "act of justice": *tzedakah*.

By the time Meyer London's second term was winding up, factions within the Socialist Party were casting about for a candidate who could defeat him. His refusal to vote against the War Appropriations Bill caused him to be labeled an "enemy of the revolution" by one side, while a second faction accused him of exposing immigrant Jews to the taint of disloyalty. Meyer London was being squeezed from both sides; attacked as both a dangerous radical and as a traitor to radicalism; denounced as un-American and pro-German; accused of sacrificing socialism in the interest of the Jews in his district, and of neglecting Jewish problems in the name of socialist ideals.

The New York papers had a field day reporting the political evisceration of Meyer London. One daily "discovered" that Representative London had attended a session of Congress on Yom Kippur, the holiest day of the Jewish year. The leaders of Tammany, suddenly overcome with Jewish piety and fervor, accused him of "disgrac[ing] the Jewish religion and insult[ing] the religious feelings of every Orthodox Jew in America." The die was cast. Meyer London lost the election of 1918 to his old nemesis, Henry Goldfogle, by a vote of 7,269 to 6,519. The *Brooklyn Standard* ran an editorial headed "Socialism Menace Checked."

Meyer London returned to the East Side, down but not defeated. He ran for Congress again in 1920, once more defeating Henry Goldfogle. During what was to be his last term in Congress, London waged a vigorous but lonely campaign on behalf of those imprisoned for violating the Espionage Law. He also worked for the normalization of relations with Russia. Here, his chief aim was to ensure that Russia, just emerging from the Bolshevik revolution, would not slip back into the clutches of the tsars.

Amazingly, Meyer London recaptured a fine measure of the collegial respect that had evaporated during the war. In a folksy speech to the House, one of his colleagues, Thomas Lindsay Blanton of Texas, spoke for many when he said: "Mr. Chairman, I have no use for Socialists. For ten years I have not permitted a Socialist to speak in my district without answering him before my people. But we men who know Meyer London, know that he is a sincere, honest man, a man of strict integrity and high ideals according to his beliefs, and a student. And while I hate Socialism . . . common justice to man prompts me to say that if all Socialists were like Meyer London, they would not be so bad after all."

Meyer London was defeated for the last time in the election of 1922, by *Samuel Dickstein*. Shortly before he left the House of Representatives, Warren G. Harding became the first President of the United States to sign a bill introduced in Congress by a Socialist—London's bill to afford a small measure of protection for workers whose employers went into bankruptcy. It wasn't a bill of earth-shattering proportions; it did, however, prove that a Socialist could work within the system to enact meaningful change on behalf of the people.

Slight of build and small of stature, Meyer London created an enduring legacy for the people of the East Side. He was one of them. Like the beloved Sholom Aleichem, London spoke their language, understood their joys, and felt their pain. Like the writer, he was from Poltava and married to a dentist—Anna Rosenson. And like Sholom Aleichem, he died too early—Sholom Aleichem at fifty-six, and London at fifty-five.

Meyer London died after being hit by a cab at Second Avenue and 15th Street, driven by a fellow Jew, Louis Greenspan, of Newark, New Jersey. The date was June 6, 1926. His hospital bed was surrounded by his small family: his wife Anna, daughter Isabella, and brothers Louis and Harris. His body lay in state at the Forward Building on East Broadway for twenty-four hours, while countless tens of thousands passed by the bier, paying final respects to their fallen hero.

The *Baltimore Sun*, in an article on London's death, noted that "the first request made by Meyer London on his way to the hospital was that no charge be made against the driver of the car that struck him." It concluded: "The thought was characteristic of the man. No personal suffering, no pressure of work, no private duties were ever sufficient to stifle the kindly sentiments towards his fellows which always animated this Socialist leader. The brilliancy of Mr. London's mind was as pronounced as the humanitarianism which had its well-springs in his heart."

Ever the servant of his people, Meyer London left an estate of less than $4,000, and a political legacy that would reemerge during the heady days of Roosevelt's New Deal.

References

American Jewish Historical Quarterly 65, no. 1 (September 1975): pp. 59–73.

American Jewish Year Book, vol. 24, p. 176; vol. 29, p. 117.

Biographical Dictionary of American Labor Leaders, p. 208.

Dictionary of American Biography.

Encyclopaedia Judaica (1972), vol. 11, col. 483.

New York Times, June 7, 1926, 1:8.

Harry Rogoff, *An East Side Epic: The Life and World of Meyer London* (New York: Vanguard Press, 1930).

Universal Jewish Encyclopedia.

Who Was Who in America, vol. 1.

LOWENSTEIN, ALLARD KENNETH (1929–1980): *Democrat from New York; served one term in the House (Ninety-first Congress; January 3, 1969–January 3, 1971).*

When one ventures to Arlington National Cemetery to visit the graves of John and Robert Kennedy, one cannot help but notice another grave just a few feet away. It is the final resting place of a one-term member of the House of Representatives, Allard Kenneth Lowenstein. His tomb is about as close to the Kennedys' graves as one can get without being an actual member of the family. In a sense, Lowenstein *was* a member of the Kennedy clan. His ties to Robert F. Kennedy were both deep and abiding: the night Robert F. Kennedy decided to run for President of the United States, Al Lowenstein was among a small, select gathering of close friends and advisors who had gathered at RFK's home, Hickory Hill. Lowenstein also helped to draft Kennedy's announcement. On June 5, 1968, the night Robert Kennedy won the California primary, Al Lowenstein was the first person the Senator called. It was Lowenstein, in fact, who was holding the line, waiting for him to come to the phone, when Kennedy was shot.

In one of history's cruel, cruel ironies, Lowenstein, a man of whom Senator Ted Kennedy said, "All by himself he was more effective than an organization of thousands . . . even when he walked alone, he was a multitude," was himself the victim of political assassination.

Though he served but a single term in the House of Representatives at the end of the 1960s and was assassinated twenty years ago, Al Lowenstein's legacy continues to permeate the American political scene. An enumeration of his disciples reads like a "Who's Who in American Politics": Senators *Joseph Lieberman, Paul Wellstone,* Bob Kerrey and Tom Harkin; former Senators Gary Hart, Harris Wofford, and Bill Bradley; Representatives *Howard Berman, Barney Frank,* and Andy Jacobs; Marian Wright Edelman and former California Governor Jerry Brown. His circle also included the Kennedys, Coretta Scott King, Andrew Young, Warren Beatty, Peter Yarrow, Mary Travers, and William F. Buckley(!), who, "despite their philosophical and political differences . . . endorsed Lowenstein for Congress on multiple occasions and had [him] as a guest on his show [*Firing Line*] more often than any other politician." As Ted Kennedy said in eulogizing Al Lowenstein, "He was a one-man demonstration for civil rights . . . he had a gentle passion for the truth."

Allard Kenneth (originally "Augustus") Lowenstein was born in Newark, New Jersey, on January 16, 1929, the eve of the Great Depression. He was Gabriel and Augusta (Goldberg) Lowenstein's third son. Al's father, a native of Lithuania, had come to the United States in 1906, one year after he was arrested and imprisoned for "helping to organize his community's participation in the general strike." Quickly learning English, Gabriel entered college at age nineteen (1908), received a B.S. degree from Columbia in 1913, and went on to earn a Ph.D. in biochemistry. Shortly after receiving his doctorate, "Doc" Lowenstein secured a position as instructor of biochemistry at the College of Physicians and Surgeons at Columbia. By this point, married, with one child and another on the way, Doc decided to forsake his beloved academia and turn to the world of business. Years later, explaining this radical departure, Doc wrote his son Al: "When I was young, I didn't have all the milk and honey that God has provided. . . . I had to struggle, fight, think hard, try to earn a living . . . to borrow, to work, and to repay." His brothers invited him to join their thriving restaurant business. He prospered, and became a man of means. By the time the Depression hit, the Lowensteins were living quite comfortably on Central Park West in Manhattan. A few years later, the family moved to a spacious home in Harrison, in New York's upscale Westchester County.

Doc's wife, Augusta Goldberg, was the daughter of immigrants who worked in the garment industry. Augusta died of breast cancer the year after Allard was born. Though torn with grief, Gabriel made the decision to quickly remarry and move the family from Newark to New York. Gabriel's new wife was named Florence; she became the only mother Allard would ever know. In fact, Allard Lowenstein did not learn that Florence was actually his stepmother until he was thirteen. Even then, he felt that he could not tell his father and "mother" of his discovery, for fear that he might hurt their feelings. When he finally broke down and admitted to Florence that he knew about his birth-mother's death, he told her that she should never worry; as far as he was concerned, she was—and would always be—his mother.

Florence Lowenstein was far more religious than her husband; "she tried to keep a kosher household, notwithstanding Gabriel's contempt for religious ritual." When young Allard insisted on drinking milk with his meat, Florence compromised; the house would not be kosher except during the Passover holiday. Al identified more with his father's agnosticism than with his mother's devotion. As one of the only Jewish families in Harrison, Al felt the sting of anti-Semitism. On more than one occasion, he was beaten by bigger, stronger boys.

Florence and Doc's married life was anything but ideal. Because of their differences in background, academic ability, and religious *Weltanschauung*, the couple often got into prolonged verbal battles. Allard and his younger sister Doris (born two years after) were often witness to their scraps. Doc was a demanding father. The Lowenstein dining table was replete with political discussions, reports, and pointed questions. When company came over, the children were expected to "perform" by showing their superior abilities. Doc was forever admonishing his children to "systematize your hours of work, systematize your hours of study . . . get out of the habit of procrastinating . . . keep your teeth clean, scrub, soap and wash [your hands], keep your nails short, tie your laces."

Politics was important to Al Lowenstein even as a young child. He handed out leaflets for FDR at the corner of Central Park West and Eighty-first Street during the 1936 presidential campaign. The next year he was "doing the same for the Republican side in the Spanish civil war." As a student at the Ethical Culture School, Al edited the school newspaper. He initiated a fundraising drive for Spanish Republicans that netted more than $18; his goal had been merely $5. In an editorial, the sixth-grader urged his fellow students to write or wire their Congressmen "demanding the immediate lifting of the arms embargo on Republican Spain." When the Republicans were eventually defeated by the Nationalists, Al wept bitterly; he considered it one of the worst moments in his life. Even at the tender age of eleven, Allard Lowenstein was a caring, committed liberal. Lowenstein's lifelong identification with the poor, the oppressed, and the downtrodden came mainly from his father, who had

been an ardent socialist. As a "greenhorn" working and living on New York's Lower East Side, Gabriel had supported Socialist candidates Morris Hilquit and Eugene Debs, and "helped organize workers in the garment industry."

For the first several years of his life, Al's oldest brother Bert was the apple of his father's eye. While Bert was a student at the Fieldston School, one of his teachers, who had also taught physicist-to-be Robert Oppenheimer, referred to him as "his most brilliant student." Bert went off to Harvard when Al was seven, graduating Phi Beta Kappa in three years. From there, he enrolled in Harvard Medical School. The Lowenstein children all began their education at the Ethical Culture School and then went on either to the Fieldston School or Horace Mann. Al resented private school, "sensing the elitism and privilege of such a setting." Al's teachers identified him as a brilliant student, but noted "a certain disorder and fussiness in his personal matters as well as careless habits of speaking."

Allard Lowenstein attended high school at Horace Mann, a "staid, socially conservative, and politically complacent school." Among his fellow students in those days were several who became movers and shakers: attorney Roy Cohen, *New York Times* columnist Anthony Lewis, Congressman *William Greene*, and publisher Si Newhouse. Lowenstein was considered somewhat of a bohemian and an oddball. A fine student (he regularly ranked in the top ten of his class) and editor of the school's paper, he was nonetheless considered "less than respectable" because of his political views and unusual interests.

Upon graduating from Horace Mann, Al defied his father's wishes by enrolling at the University of North Carolina rather than Harvard, Yale, Princeton, or, most preferably, Columbia, Doc's alma mater. Al's choice of Chapel Hill was deliberate. He wanted to get away from the Northeast and his Jewishness, and move to a place where he could, in his own mind, remake himself. That is precisely what he did. Calling himself Lowen or Lowenstine, Al found his social and religious base at Charley Jones's Presbyterian church. During his college years, he was a member of the wrestling team, frequented the Catholic student center, "consciously selected Christian, not Jewish peers," and "loved nothing better than to belt out old-fashioned hymns with his pals on campus." He even made application to a fraternity that excluded Jews. Predictably, he also became involved in campus politics. Two issues to which he gave his time, thought, and energy were North Carolina's Jim Crow laws and Zionism. Lowenstein found a political mentor in UNC President Frank Porter Graham. An attorney with an advanced degree from Columbia, Graham (1886–1972) was a political liberal, always seeking to break through the social, economic, and political barriers that beset the state's African-American population. Lowenstein, as vice president of the student legislature, assisted President Graham in his attempts to integrate the UNC campus. In March 1949, Graham was appointed to the United States Senate seat held by the recently deceased J. Melville Broughton. Lowenstein went to Washington to serve as Graham's special assistant. Graham wound up serving in the Senate for less than two years; he was defeated for a full six-year term in November 1950.

As mentioned above, one issue that deeply concerned Lowenstein during his tenure at Chapel Hill was Zionism: he was against it. Lowenstein equated Zionism with Jim Crow. To his way of thinking, the movement for a Jewish homeland in Palestine reflected "an unhealthy expression of race nationalism." In Lowenstein's words from that period: "Zionism is unwise, undesirable, and evil . . . and keeping silent on Zionism . . . is equally unwise, undesirable, and evil, as well as cowardly." Without question, Lowenstein exhibited an ambivalence about his Jewishness. He was first and foremost a disciple of individualism and personal freedom. To him, Jews were "individuals with a particular religious faith . . . not a race or nation." In name, heritage, and even physiognomy, he was unquestionably Jewish; in attitude, philosophy, and self-conception, he was an American liberal.

Following his brief tenure with Senator Graham, Allard Lowenstein served one year (1950–51) as president of the National Student Association and chaired a national student organization of young volunteers for presidential candidate Adlai E. Stevenson. In 1951, acceding to his parents' wishes, Lowenstein entered Yale Law School. Never really wanting to be an attorney, Lowenstein spent the next three years "appearing to study law," all the while keeping up an active schedule of "politicking and speechmaking." He quickly became a campus legend: the peripatetic politico who somehow "graduated from Yale having attended the fewest classes." Upon his graduation in 1954, Florence wrote "congratulations for having accomplished almost the impossible; that is, passing subjects that you know nothing about." Following Yale, Lowenstein entered the United States Army, serving two years (1954–56) in Germany. Wishing to get out of the army in time for the 1956 presidential election, Lowenstein pulled enough strings to be discharged two months early. He immediately went to the Democratic National Convention.

Following his admission to the New York Bar in 1958, Lowenstein went to work as a foreign policy assistant to Senator Hubert H. Humphrey. The next year, he toured South-West Africa, an international territory under the legal jurisdiction of the Republic of South Africa, in order to investigate racial conditions there. It was his stated intent to "arouse the conscience of the world." Shocked by the poverty, neglect, and oppression he witnessed, Lowenstein turned his observations into a book, *Brutal Mandate*, which was published by Macmillan in 1962. In his review, *New York Times* writer Orville Prescott called Lowenstein "a capable writer . . . a fiery idealist, a zealous crusader for social and political righteousness."

After attending the 1960 Democratic National Convention in Los Angeles, Lowenstein returned to New York, where he managed the successful congressional campaign of "pioneer Reform Democrat" William Fitts Ryan in Manhattan's Twentieth District. Following the election, he began nearly a decade of wandering, teaching, lecturing, organizing, and helping to shape the minds of a new generation of young political animals. During these years, he taught political science at Stanford and at North Carolina State University. He was a controversial figure on both campuses, taking the side of the students in a power struggle at Stanford (where he was also assistant dean of men), and encouraging local civil rights demonstrators at North Carolina. Along with his teaching, Lowenstein "donated his services to jailed civil rights workers in the deep South . . . recruited student volunteers for voter registration drives in Mississippi; helped organize the Mississippi

Freedom Vote . . . and served as an adviser to Martin Luther King and the Southern Christian Leadership Conference."

All these activities brought Lowenstein into contact with a generation of emerging political talent. To them, he was a pied piper who taught the ABCs of political philosophy, organizational technique, and liberal commitment. In his travels, he often bedded down on the floor of a dormitory room, sharing the students' meager existence, becoming essentially one of them. These are the years when he began shaping the political aspirations of literally dozens of future senators, representatives, governors, and writers.

In 1967–68, Lowenstein taught political science at the City University of New York. During this time, he also served as a civilian observer of the elections in the Dominican Republic and South Vietnam. An early and articulate opponent of the war in Southeast Asia, Lowenstein hit upon the idea in late 1966 and early 1967 of finding a candidate to oppose President Lyndon B. Johnson in the upcoming Democratic primaries. One of the first people Lowenstein shared his "dump Johnson" idea with was a young friend and disciple, *Barney Frank*. Totally energized, Lowenstein traveled the length and breadth of the United States, rallying an army of students "ready to serve as volunteers for a Democratic peace candidate." Lowenstein's first choice was Senator Robert F. Kennedy. When Kennedy turned him down, Lowenstein next approached South Dakota Senator George McGovern. Again a polite refusal. Finally, Lowenstein got Minnesota Senator Eugene McCarthy to agree. Armed with McCarthy's pledge to run, Lowenstein mobilized a huge student contingent for the upcoming Democratic primary in New Hampshire. The students, many of whom arrived shorn and clean-shaven under the banner of "Clean for Gene," blanketed the state. On election day, McCarthy made such an impressive showing (twenty of the state's twenty-four delegates) that on March 31, 1968, Johnson announced that he would not seek reelection. Suddenly, Lowenstein was a force in American liberal politics.

Following the assassination of Senator Robert F. Kennedy, who had eventually changed his mind and entered the race, Lowenstein attended the stormy 1968 Democratic National Convention in Chicago. Pushing for a strong peace plank, Lowenstein opposed the Democratic front-runner, Senator Hubert Humphrey. At the same time, he was also running for a seat in Congress from New York's Fifth Congressional District, centered in Long Island. The Fifth District was "a complex of thirty middle-class suburbs, twenty-five miles long, running from Queens out to Oyster Bay." Catholics and Protestants, 70 percent of whom were registered Republicans, made up nearly 65 percent of the district, with the remaining 35 percent being Jewish Democrats. The Democrats had first won the district in the Johnson landslide of 1964, electing attorney *Herbert Tenzer*. When Tenzer decided not to seek a third term, Lowenstein got into the race.

Allard Lowenstein defeated Union of American Hebrew Congregations vice president Albert Vorspan in the Democratic primary by a vote of 14,881 to 10,908. The late Senator Kennedy played "a critical role" in Lowenstein's victory. Following the Senator's death, "a rich folklore developed about the relationship between Kennedy and Lowenstein," which added to Lowenstein's stature, visibility, and *gravitas*. In the general election, running on both the Democratic and Liberal tickets, Lowenstein squared off against Republican Mason L. Hampton. During the campaign, Lowenstein's army of young volunteers "canvassed almost every home in the district, persuading voters that their candidate was far from being the radical depicted by his opponent." Restating his credo time and time again, Lowenstein stressed that the war in Indochina was "morally, politically, and economically indefensible," and argued forcefully that "national priorities must be reordered to allow us to take care of our urgent needs——housing, education, job training, transportation, pollution and conservation." On election day, 1968, Lowenstein scored an upset, polling 99,193 votes to Hampton's 96,247. What made this victory all the more remarkable was the fact that Humphrey lost the districtwide vote in the presidential race.

During his single term in the House of Representatives, Lowenstein had, predictably, that body's most liberal voting record. During his two years on Capitol Hill, Lowenstein cast votes "against the District of Columbia anti-crime bill, a proposal to cut off aid to students involved in campus disorders, an anti-pornography measure," and virtually every military appropriation bill. He voted in favor of reforming the Selective Service System and abolishing the House Un-American Activities Committee. Viewed at first with disdain and uncertainty, Lowenstein was seated on the House Agriculture Committee, an unusual assignment for a man representing suburban Long Island and Queens.

As a bachelor who worked twenty-four hours a day and lived a spartan life, Lowenstein found a comfortable home right on Capitol Hill. When House Doorkeeper "Fishbait" Miller discovered that Lowenstein was living in his office, the freshman explained: "I work out in the House gym and get up a good sweat before I take a nice shower down there. And the old couch in the office is good enough for me." When the "big three" on the House Office Building Commission—Speaker John McCormack, and Representatives *Emanuel Celler* and Gerald Ford—heard what Lowenstein was doing, they were "shocked," and quickly "sent word of their disapproval."

According to Doorkeeper Miller, "they would have disapproved more had they heard his secretary telling me how during her lunch hour she had to take his shirts to the Chinese laundry three blocks away." Although the big three had no authority to kick him out of his living quarters, Lowenstein came up with a compromise: some nights, just to throw them off, he slept in Fishbait Miller's office instead of his own.

Al Lowenstein spent a lifetime caught between the Scylla of his outer self and the Charybdis of his inner passions. This tension manifested itself in ambivalence about his Jewishness, his career, and even his sexuality. For many years, Lowenstein suspected that he was a homosexual. As biographer William H. Chafe notes in his stellar *Never Stop Running: Allard Lowenstein and the Struggle to Save American Liberalism*: "Going back to his high school diary entry, Lowenstein had always evinced a powerful interest in close same-sex relationships. The intensity of his relationships with men—and the difficulty of his relationships with women—became a prominent feature of his life." During his wandering years at Stanford, North Carolina State University, and points in-between, Lowenstein developed a "rit-

ual" with his young disciples: "The scenario was almost always the same. . . . Frequently a long automobile trip was involved, with an overnight stay at a motel. Lowenstein would go to the desk clerk and return saying that the only available room had just one bed." In the words of one longtime friend, Al Lowenstein lived "on the borderline" of homosexuality, "seemingly unsure just where his own boundaries should be."

Likewise, Lowenstein's ambivalence about his Jewishness caused him great pain. When he finally married, he chose for his mate a quintessential WASP: Jennifer Lyman, a Boston Brahmin from a "rigid upper-class family from Beacon Hill." The product of divorced parents, Jenny Lyman attended Barnard and went to work as Lowenstein's volunteer secretary. Soon he was smitten. Their wedding, on November 25, 1966, symbolized the conflict deep within Lowenstein's soul; the ceremony, which took place at the Vale, a two-hundred-year-old estate in Waltham, Massachusetts, that the Lyman family had given to the National Historic Trust, was co-officiated by a Reform rabbi and the Reverend William Sloane Coffin, a fixture in liberal Democratic politics. Before their divorce in 1972, the Lowensteins had three children: Frank Graham, Thomas Kennedy, and Katherine Eleanor (named after Al's dear friend and mentor, Eleanor Roosevelt).

In 1970, Al Lowenstein lost a bid for reelection to Republican Norman Lent. His defeat came largely as a result of the Republican-controlled New York legislature's gerrymandering of the Fifth District. Lent's victory was orchestrated by Murray Chotiner, a long-time ally of Richard Nixon. During the campaign, Lent accused Lowenstein of "inciting students to riot," and called him "an inflamer of youth, an encourager of draft-card burners," and an extremist guilty of "coddling the leaders of violent confrontation on campus." For added measure, Chotiner had Lent accuse Lowenstein of being "a supporter of smut peddlers and dope pushers." Despite the volcanic accusations hurled at Lowenstein, Lent's victory was not terribly lopsided; his final margin of victory was about 8,000 out of more than 180,000 votes cast.

Out of office, Lowenstein spent the last decade of his life playing the role he had mastered: political activist. Despite four more unsuccessful races for a House seat (in 1972, 1974, 1976, and 1978), Lowenstein remained a vital part of the political scene—both in New York and Washington. In May 1971, shortly after leaving the House, Lowenstein was elected chairman of the liberal Americans for Democratic Action. In that post, he launched a nationwide drive to register eighteen- to twenty-one-year-olds (who had recently been granted the vote) and "to mobilize them in support of peace candidates in 1972." Al Lowenstein was a dogged critic of the Nixon administration—over its conduct of the war in Indochina, its handling of dissent, and its disdain for the basics of constitutional law. In speech after speech, Lowenstein assailed Nixon and his associates for their political cynicism. As a result, Lowenstein was included on Nixon's infamous enemies list in 1971; Lowenstein often boasted that he was "number seven."

In his person, Al Lowenstein was of medium height and quite muscular, with "Coke bottle" glasses and a disheveled appearance. Always on the go, he often conducted business out of phone booths and guest rooms, traveling by night and generally working in rumpled clothes and unshod feet. His briefcase was always crammed full of articles, newspapers, notes, and slips of paper.

During the Carter years, Lowenstein was appointed to head the United States delegation to the Thirty-eighth regular annual session of the United Nations Commission on Human Rights in Geneva. From August 1977 to June 1978, he served as the alternate United States Representative for Special Political Affairs in the United Nations, a post that carried the rank of ambassador.

Throughout virtually his entire public career, Al Lowenstein was viewed with alarm by both ends of the political spectrum. To those on the Right, he was a dangerous, subversive radical—a Communist at best. To members of the New Left, he was also suspect, due mainly to his insistence on working within the system, and his former ties with the National Student Association. (Long after Lowenstein ceased being a member, it was revealed that the NSA had been bankrolled by the CIA.)

Lowenstein's last hurrah was his effort to reopen the investigation into the assassination of Senator Robert F. Kennedy. For years, he was of the opinion that Sirhan Sirhan, the man convicted and imprisoned for the slaying, was not the sole gunman. Despite repeated press conferences, legal briefs, and political agitation, Lowenstein never got his chance. On March 14, 1980, he was gunned down by Dennis Sweeney, a mentally unbalanced young man who had originally been attracted to politics by Lowenstein himself during his years at Stanford. Mortally wounded, Lowenstein was rushed to a hospital, where doctors tried to stem the bleeding caused by two gunshot wounds to the heart. Sitting outside in the waiting room were Al's former wife, Jenny, and their three children, Kennedy family member Steve Smith and his son, Steve, Jr., friend Sherman Bull, and folk singer Peter Yarrow of Peter, Paul and Mary. As they sat there in the waiting room, Yarrow led the group in songs. At the moment the doctors came in to announce that Al Lowenstein had passed away, the group was singing—somewhat appropriately—Bob Dylan's "Blowing in the Wind." Al Lowenstein was only fifty-one years old.

Lowenstein's funeral was held at the Central Synagogue on Manhattan's East Side. Among the two thousand in attendance were Coretta Scott King, Jacqueline Kennedy Onasis, Senator Ted Kennedy, William F. Buckley (who sat next to Senator Kennedy), Kathleen Brown, sister of California Governor Jerry Brown, Transportation Secretary Neil Goldschmidt, Andrew Young, Congressmen Peter McCloskey and Andy Jacobs, and actor Robert Vaughn, one of the most politically active members of the Hollywood community. Peter Yarrow and Mary Travers, along with folksinger Harry Chapin, sang "Stewball Was a Race Horse," one of Lowenstein's favorites, and then led the congregation in the singing of "Amazing Grace"—a peculiar hymn for a Jewish synagogue. Then again, perhaps it was not strange at all. Perhaps that one hymn best symbolized the conflict within Al Lowenstein. As was mentioned above, Allard Kenneth Lowenstein was buried in Arlington National Cemetery, just a heartbeat away from John and Robert Kennedy.

References

William H. Chafe, *Never Stop Running: Allard Lowenstein and the Struggle to Save American Liberalism* (New York: Basic Books, 1993).

Richard Cummings, *The Pied Piper: Allard K. Lowenstein and the Liberal Dream* (New York: Grove Press, 1985).

Harper's, December 1968.

New Yorker, January 10, 1970.

New York Times Magazine, August 17, 1980.

William "Fishbait" Miller, *Fishbait: The Memoirs of the Congressional Doorkeeper* (Englewood Cliffs, N.J., 1977).

Who Was Who in America, vol. 7.

LOWEY, NITA M. (1937–): *Democrat from New York; has served six terms in the House (One Hundredth through One Hundred and Sixth Congress; January 3, 1989–present).*

Reading through the biographical profiles of latter-day Senators and Representatives, one is struck by how young most of them were when they first started out in politics. In many cases, their first run for public office came within a year or two of graduation from college or law school. Nita Lowey's story is somewhat different; after her graduation, she spent the next fifteen years raising a family. Her first foray into the world of campaign politics did not come about until she was thirty-seven. At that point, Lowey, then living in Queens, opened her home to a local attorney who was running for New York lieutenant governor. Although the attorney was defeated in the primary, his political career was far from over. His name was Mario Cuomo, and he possessed a good eye for political talent. In 1975, when Governor Hugh Carey appointed him New York's secretary of state, Cuomo asked Lowey to come to work in his department's antipoverty division. She agreed, and a political career was born. Thirteen years later, at the age of fifty-one, Lowey was elected to the One Hundredth Congress.

Nita M. Lowey, the daughter of Jack and Beatrice (Fleisher) Melnikoff, was born in New York City on July 5, 1937. Both the Fleishers and the Melnikoffs had come from Russia in the early years of the twentieth century, but by decidedly different routes: the Melnikoff family came by way of England, the Fleishers directly from Kiev. Nita and her brother Richard grew up in a "warm supportive home" in the Bronx at the corner of 164th Street and Walton Avenue, about five blocks from Yankee Stadium. Although the Melnikoffs were not Orthodox, their house was kosher, and they belonged to the nearest synagogue, Young Israel of the Concourse. They sent both their children to Hebrew school. Nita studied alongside boys for eight years. Young Nita Melnikoff never became bat mitzvah, since that was not a common practice in her family's synagogue. She proudly remembers, however, that she was "the only girl in [her] class who went

on to Hebrew High School." Nita's mother was much involved in Jewish communal activities. Her father, an accountant, worked long hours.

Nita Melnikoff attended the prestigious Bronx High School of Science, where she was elected president of the senior class. In the Melnikoff household, going to college was a given; going to "a good school like Vassar, Wellesley or Mt. Holyoke" was also assumed. In 1954, Nita entered Mount Holyoke, which, despite its name, is not a Catholic college—it is named after a local mountain in Massachusetts. At Mount Holyoke, Melnikoff discovered that "less than 10% of the student body was Jewish," and that "there were mandatory church services." From almost the day she matriculated at Mount Holyoke, Nita Melnikoff knew that she had "to associate myself with Jewish issues and traditions." Along with a group of Jewish friends, she helped organize Friday night Shabbat services. Throughout her four years in college, Melnikoff remained devoted to the group. She became, in her words, "a quiet campus activist," taking on such positions as "social chair of her class, president of the Jewish organization, and head of the Red Cross and Community Chest campaigns in her dormitory." During her senior year (1958), she interned with the Democratic Senatorial Campaign Committee in Washington, D.C., working alongside Minnesota Senator Hubert H. Humphrey. "The experience gave me a sense of 'someday . . .'" she recalls.

In 1959, Nita Melnikoff graduated with a degree in political science and went back to New York to find employment with Young and Rubicam, a major advertising agency. In 1961, she married Stephen Lowey, a young attorney. The couple moved to Queens, where Stephen began his law practice. Today, he is a partner in the firm of Lowey, Dannenberg, Bemporad & Selinger, P.C. The Loweys have three children: Dana, born in 1966, Jackie, born in 1968, and Douglas, born in 1970. Stephen Lowey prospered at the practice of law; according to *Roll Call*'s "Wealth Watch," Nita Lowey, with a net worth of approximately $7 million, was the twenty-first richest member of the One Hundred and Fifth Congress.

In 1977, while a staff member in the secretary of state's office, Nita Lowey worked on her boss Mario Cuomo's unsuccessful campaign for New York City mayor. Following his defeat, she was promoted within the secretary of state's office, becoming a specialist in "economic development and neighborhood preservation." After seven years in that position, during which time she learned how to lobby Congress, Lowey was appointed assistant to Secretary of State Gail S. Shaffer. At the same time, she was also named to the state's Child Care Commission. During those years, the Loweys moved to the upscale Westchester County suburb of Harrison, where Nita worked with such organizations as the YWCA, Westchester Jewish Community Services, and the League of Women Voters. Through all these activities, she began building up a formidable coterie of friends and political contacts.

When the Loweys first moved to Harrison, their congressional representative was Democrat *Richard Ottinger*. When Ottinger decided to retire before the 1984 election, his seat was taken by Republican Joseph J. DioGuardi, an accountant with the firm of Arthur Anderson and Company. DioGuardi's narrow victory (50 percent to 48 percent) over Ottinger's former aide, Oren J. Teicher, owed much to the Reagan landslide. Indeed, in a slightly less Republican year, Teicher would likely have won. DioGuardi was prone to verbal gaffes ("Minorities enjoy having children. It gets them another check."), and tended to have a less-than-stellar grasp of the issues. During his first term in the House, he became a staunch supporter of Reaganomics. As one of the few CPAs in Congress, he was "constantly making statements about how government should be run like a business." Most political observers assumed that Oren Teicher would once again win the Democratic nomination and once again face DioGuardi in the general election. At the last moment, however, *Bella Abzug* announced that she had moved to White Plains and was throwing one of her many hats into the ring. Abzug won the primary and began campaigning on the issues of nuclear disarmament and increased aid for public housing. DioGuardi, for his part, portrayed Abzug as a carpet-bagging radical feminist and "emphasized his support of budget-cutting." On election day, DioGuardi won a surprisingly narrow victory (54 percent to 45 percent) over Abzug. If nothing else, Bella had proven

that DioGuardi was politically vulnerable.

Enter Nita Lowey. The 1988 Democratic primary featured Lowey, businessman Dennis Mehiel, and Hamilton Fish III, publisher of *The Nation* and the son, grandson, and great-grandson of House members. Although candidate Lowey labeled herself a moderate, Mehiel accused her of being a liberal. In her response, Lowey was quoted as saying: "If being a liberal means caring about our senior citizens, honoring our commitment to Social Security, and working to clean up the environment, I am proud to be a liberal. If being a conservative means balancing the budget, raising a family with strong values, putting drug pushers behind bars, then I am proud to be a conservative."

Thanks in large part to her network of contacts in Westchester, Lowey captured the primary with 44 percent of the vote. In the general election, she accused DioGuardi of "overspending on defense," and was given a tremendous boost when a car dealer was charged with funneling illegal money to DioGuardi's campaign. Any other candidate might have been able to make a plausible argument for ignorance. Not DioGuardi. As a CPA—a man with a "self-advertised fetish for figures"—such "protestations of ignorance" would have seemed highly unlikely. Aided by a $1.3 million war chest (of which nearly $660,000 was her own money), Lowey defeated the vulnerable DioGuardi by nearly 6,000 votes. Between them, Lowey and DioGuardi spent nearly $3 million, making their contest the second-most-expensive House race in the country. Despite outspending his opponent by nearly $250,000, DioGuardi was one of the very few incumbent Republicans to be ousted in 1988.

Nita Lowey was assigned to the Committees on Education and Labor, Merchant Marine and Fisheries, and the Select Committee on Narcotics Abuse and Control. During her first term, she established a liberal voting record (receiving a perfect 100 rating from the liberal Americans for Democratic Action) casting votes "for tough oil spill legislation . . . supporting more money to create drug-free school zones, as well as funding to fight Lyme Disease."

In her first reelection bid, Nita Lowey faced only token opposition, and won with 63 percent of the vote. The highlight of Nita Lowey's second term was her participation in a task force whose purpose was "supporting the emerging parliaments in Eastern Europe." Joined by colleagues *Martin Frost* and *Henry Waxman*, among others, Lowey went to Eastern Europe and met with Jewish leaders in every city they visited. The trip renewed her desire to learn Yiddish because, as she discovered, it was "the one unifying language we had."

Before the end of her second term, redistricting gave Nita Lowey a district with new boundaries and a new number. The Eighteenth District, formerly the Twentieth, still included most of Westchester County, but also took in "a ribbon of the East Bronx bordering Long Island Sound, across the mouth of the East River and down a narrow corridor into central Queens." For Lowey, this represented no problem; she had been raised in the Bronx and had resided in the Hillcrest section of Queens. In the 1992 election, she was again challenged by DioGuardi, who, after four years out of office, wanted back in. Once again, Lowey emerged victorious, capturing 56 percent of the vote.

Returning for the One Hundred and Second Congress, Lowey found that there were a few openings on the House Appropriations Committee. She lobbied intensely for a spot, and got it, becoming one of just two Jewish members (*Sidney Yates* being the other) on the committee. One of the leading abortion rights advocates in Congress, Lowey sponsored legislation that would "bar the government from awarding Community Development Block Grant funding to communities that do not enforce laws to protect those involved in the abortion process, from doctors to patients." The bill failed to pass in the One Hundred and Second Congress; she reintroduced it in the next session. Vocally critical of the so-called gag rule that "barred abortion counseling and referral in federally funded family planning clinics," Lowey had it eliminated in 1993. A staunch Zionist, Lowey also introduced a resolution that urged "Arab states to recognize and make peace with Israel." Nonetheless, she voted against the Gulf Resolution committing U.S. troops to battle against Iraq.

Nita Lowey was easily reelected in 1994, 1996, and 1998, when she captured 83 percent of the vote. Following the Republican takeover of the House in 1994, it looked as if she would lose her seat on Appropriations. "Rather than trust her own leaders to negotiate on her behalf, Lowey went directly to incoming House Speaker Newt Gingrich . . . and Appropriations Chairman Robert Livingston." Lowey not only saved her own seat, but that of California's Esteban Torres as well.

Nita Lowey is recognized on Capitol Hill for having "a flair for public relations and sound bites," a key survival skill for a Representative from New York. One example would be her marshaling of forces against the National Rifle Association, which was recruiting women members through ads in mass-market magazines such as *Ladies' Home Journal* and *Redbook*. With television cameras rolling, Lowey led a protest march in front of the NRA's downtown Washington headquarters; it made the national nightly news. As chair of the bipartisan Congressional Women's Caucus, she organized seventy-two members, mostly Democrats, who pledged "not to vote for a health care plan that did not cover abortions." Known as a prodigious fundraiser (she has never spent less than $911,000 on a campaign), Lowey is also one of the few members of Congress who makes personal contributions to the campaigns of other House members.

Starting in late 1998, political insiders began speculating on whether Lowey would run in 2000 for the seat of retiring Senator Daniel Patrick Moynihan. Because of First Lady Hillary Clinton's anticipated entry into the Democratic field, Lowey's candidacy carried a big question mark. In mid-1999, she declared that, should Mrs. Clinton enter the New York primary, she would drop out of the race. A few months later, with Clinton soon to be a declared candidate, Lowey announced that she would run for reelection to her House seat.

Nita and Stephen Lowey's daughter Dana was an associate producer for the *Geraldo Rivera Show*; daughter Jackie worked as a special assistant in the U.S. Department of Transportation. Son Doug is a bond trader. Representative and Mr. Lowey continue to live in Harrison, New York.

References

Interview with Nita M. Lowey, Washington, D.C., July 1992.
Almanac of American Politics (1990-1998 editions).
Current Biography, 1977, pp. 28–30.
Mount Holyoke Alumnae Quarterly, Summer 1988, p. 16.
Politics in America (1990-1998 editions).

MARGOLIES-MEZVINSKY, MARJORIE (1942–): *Democrat from Pennsylvania; served one term in the House (One Hundred and Third Congress; January 3, 1992–January 3, 1994).*

Marjorie Margolies-Mezvinsky (known as "MMM" or "3-M") holds several distinctions among the members of the Congressional Minyan:

She is the only Minyanaire to have won no fewer than five Emmy Awards for excellence in television reportage.

She is the only member of the group to have adopted Amerasian children. (Indeed, she was the first unmarried American citizen to adopt a foreign child.)

She (along with her husband, former two-term Iowa Representative *Ed Mezvinsky*) has more children (eleven) than any other Minyanaire. They are, in her words, "adopted, step, sponsored and home-made."

She is the sole member whose published oeuvre includes a "summer-weight" romance novel, a best-selling memoir on adoption, and a how-to book on "finding someone to love."

In the realm of Pennsylvania politics, MMM also holds several distinctions:

She was the first (and so far, only) woman elected to Congress from Pennsylvania in her own right. Her three female predecessors, Veronica Grace Boland (1899–1982), Vera Daerr Buchanan (1902–1955), and Katherine Elizabeth Granahan (1894–1979), all moved into seats previously occupied by their husbands.

MMM was the only Democrat elected to represent her state's Thirteenth Congressional District in eighty years. Not surprisingly, she was once described as "the sort of hyper-achiever who makes other career women feel like sloths."

MMM also cast the deciding vote on the 1993 Clinton economic plan—thereby handing the administration a seminal victory. That vote, which she knew was "tantamount to political suicide," cost her her seat in Congress.

Marjorie Margolies, the younger of Herbert

and Mildred (Harrison) Margolies's two daughters, was born in Philadelphia on June 21, 1942. She was, in her words, "the product of a mixed marriage"—one parent being a German Jew, the other a Litvak of Russian-Jewish lineage. Speaking of her parents' fifty-one-year marriage, MMM said: "[My mother's] family thought it was awful that she married a Russian Jew." Her father's family, who originally spelled their name "Margulies," emigrated from Russia at the turn of the century, while the Harrisons came from England at least a generation earlier. Mildred Harrison Margolies's father was born in Minneapolis. As a young man he moved to Philadelphia, where he became a member of Mikveh Israel, one of America's oldest Orthodox synagogues. Mildred's maternal relatives, the Sostmans and Herzsteins, hailed from Pottstown, Pennsylvania. Many members of her family remained behind in Germany, where, in the early 1930s, they were saved by a wealthy uncle who brought about thirty-five of them to America. Herb Margolies's family belonged to the Reform Kenesset Israel. Herb and Mildred, who were both born in Philadelphia, married in 1936. Their first daughter, Phyllis, was born three years later.

Herbert Margolies, "one of the driest, funniest individuals ever," was an engineer with a degree from Drexel Institute in Philadelphia. During the course of his career, he worked for Bendix and RCA. Mildred Margolies has long been a commercial artist specializing in fashion advertising. MMM remembers her father (who died in 1987) as "always speaking in the Talmudic idiom . . . especially about 'saving a life is like saving the whole of humanity.'" In 1947, the Margolies family moved to Baltimore, where Herb served in the management division of RCA.

The family did not move back to Philadelphia until the early 1960s. Marjorie Margolies went through the Baltimore public schools, graduating from Forest Park High School. She spent the eleventh grade in Spain, studying under the aegis of "Experiment in International Living."

While there, she picked up a fluency in Spanish that she has maintained into her adult years. MMM was confirmed at the Baltimore Hebrew Congregation, a Reform synagogue.

Following her 1963 graduation from the University of Pennsylvania, Marjorie Margolies became a teacher. For a brief time, she entertained thoughts of becoming an attorney. Her plans changed when, during an interview with a law school dean of admissions, she was encouraged to "go and take a good paralegal course . . . get yourself into a law firm as a secretary, [and] marry a lawyer . . . you'll be just as happy."

"I'm astonished that you would say that to me," she replied, "absolutely astonished."

"I tell most women this," the dean of admissions said. "The law isn't quite ready for women the way women think that the law is ready for them."

In 1967, Margolies got her first job in broadcast journalism at WCAU-TV in Bala-Cynwyd, Pennsylvania. She also started volunteering at a local radio station—"an early version of National Public Radio." From 1969 to 1970 she was a CBS News Foundation fellow at Columbia University. The following year, she began what was to become a twenty-year career with NBC, working for its affiliates in New York City and Washington, D.C. Between 1971 and 1991, Margolies worked as a contributing correspondent on the *Today* show, *Sunday Today*, and *A Closer Look*. She also worked for CNBC and *Real Life with Jane Pauley*.

In 1970, while putting together an award-winning series on the plight of Southeast Asian war orphans, Marjorie Margolies decided that she wanted to adopt one of these children. At age twenty-eight, she adopted a little Korean girl, Lee Heh, thus becoming "the first single woman in the United States to adopt a foreign child." Four years later, she adopted Holly, a six-year-old from Vietnam. Margolies, "want[ing] to make sure that there was some sort of written record of their first six years, before we came into one another's lives," wrote the 1976 best-selling *They Came to Stay*. In writing the book, Margolies also hoped to "document the process of single-parent adoption for others who might choose to do the same thing." Over the past two decades, Marjorie and her husband Ed Mezvinsky have added Drang, Hai, and Vu to their family.

In 1975, while covering Capitol Hill for the CBS affiliate in Washington, Marjorie Margolies met Iowa Representative *Edward Mezvinsky*. As Margolies related in her 1994 book *A Woman's Place*, "I interviewed him for a story and came home and called my mother. I knew he was the one, from the first time we met. 'Mom,' I said, 'if he calls me, he's a goner.'" Marjorie Margolies and Ed Mezvinsky were married within the year. Ed entered the marriage with four daughters—Margot, Vera, Elsa, and Eve—from his first marriage. The Mezvinskys had two boys, Marc and Andrew, together. Marjorie and Ed raised their eleven children (plus the nearly dozen foreign foster children) in a sprawling home in Narbeth, Pennsylvania. The younger children all received a Jewish education at Har Zion in Philadelphia. Lee Heh (who turned thirty-five in 1999), a graduate of Brown, married in 1992. Son Marc entered Stanford University in 1996, planing to major in Jewish Studies. Son Andrew, born in 1982, began observing the laws of *kashrut* in 1997.

The more MMM covered the politics and personalities of Capitol Hill, the more dissatisfied she became: "After spending half my life asking questions, sitting on the other side of the desk armed with notepad and tape recorder," she wrote, "I decided I was dissatisfied with the answers I was getting, singularly unimpressed with the progress our lawmakers were making in so many areas vitally important to our nation—particularly concerning women, children, and the disenfranchised." MMM's growing sense of discontent reached crisis proportions during the Clarence Thomas hearings—"the image of that all-white, all-male panel of the Senate Judiciary Committee" grilling Professor Anita Hill. Prodded by friends and local women's groups, Marjorie Margolies Mezvinsky decided to run for Congress from Pennsylvania's Thirteenth District.

The Thirteenth District, which takes in Montgomery County, "the hinterlands of Philadelphia," is one of America's wealthiest enclaves. It includes the Main Line towns and has long been quintessentially Republican. Indeed, until MMM's election in 1992, the Thirteenth had not sent a Democrat to Washington since 1916. From 1968 to 1992, the people of the Thirteenth District were represented by Lawrence Coughlin (1929–), a Yale contemporary of George Bush with a Harvard M.B.A. During his twelve terms in the House, Coughlin was able to hold Democratic challengers to less than 40 percent of the vote. In 1992, Coughlin announced his retirement from Congress. MMM quickly declared her candidacy, scoring an easy 79 percent to 21 percent victory over Bernard Tomkin in the Democratic primary.

Facing Montgomery County Commissioner *Jon Fox* in the general election, MMM focused on education, health care, and joblessness, "the issues that made me get out of the bleachers and onto the playing field." She spent the campaign "repeatedly charg[ing] that Fox had spent most of his political career running for whatever office was higher than the one he held." Fox, in turn, argued that Margolies-Mezvinsky (who regularly commuted to New York and Washington) had "too few roots in Montgomery County and too many out-of-state supporters to properly represent the district." Outspent by more than $150,000, MMM eked out a 1,373-vote victory. Noting that former Arkansas Governor Bill Clinton had carried the district by more than 11,000 votes, political pundits declared that MMM had "clearly slipped in on candidate Clinton's coattails."

Once in the House, MMM quickly proved that she was no political outsider by capturing a seat on the prestigious Energy and Commerce Committee. Within weeks of arriving in Congress, MMM had organized and led several bipartisan meetings of the lower chamber's twenty-four new women. Out of these meetings came a "manifesto" calling for full funding of Head Start for preschoolers, family and medical leave, initiatives that would codify *Roe* v. *Wade*, and measures that would address sexual harassment in Congress.

MMM distinguished herself in the One Hundred and Third Congress by becoming the only Democratic freshmen to vote against both President Clinton's budget and his $16.3 billion economic stimulus package. Explaining her vote in a taped interview, she said that the plan cut too little and that the tax-to-spending ratios were off. She was greatly concerned, she told her constituents, that were the President's budget and tax package to be enacted, federal entitlement programs would suffer greatly.

With MMM on the record as being a nay vote,

everyone from the House Democratic leadership to Vice President Gore and the President himself began lobbying her. The night before the vote, she received a call from Clinton.

"Marjorie," the President asked, "what will it take?"

"We must face up to entitlements," she responded. "An entitlements conference. Not in my district necessarily, but it has to be in a community like my district, where people have the same concerns as my constituents and most Americans."

When word of their conversation leaked out, the media focused on MMM's request for the entitlements conference and claimed that she had made a political deal. To MMM, the deal was "from the very beginning, more of a sacrifice: the political future of one freshman member of Congress versus the future of the presidency." Nonetheless, MMM had her staff draft a press release explaining her no vote on the plan, to be released immediately after the vote. The release stated that she had voted no "because the budget didn't go far enough and almost completely ignored entitlements."

As the vote drew even closer, the White House stepped up its pressure on MMM and Montana Democrat Pat Williams—the two decisive votes. Mezvinsky began to waver. She was politically astute enough to realize that "changing my vote at the eleventh hour [was] political suicide." In her mind, the issue was boiling down to one simple equation: "was [her] political future more important than the agenda that the President had laid out for the American public during his campaign and that he was seeking to implement over the next four years?" When Margolies-Mezvinsky entered the House chamber, she carried both the green (yea) and red (nay) cards with which to cast her electronic vote. As her turn to vote approached, "it hit me that if I turned him down, if I let him down, I would personally be cutting a President off at the knees in his first seven months." MMM spotted Pat Williams, a former schoolteacher from Helena. "Let's give the President his victory," MMM said. Walking down the aisle, green voting card clearly in view, MMM began hearing catcalls from her Republican colleagues: "Bye-bye Margie. That's the end; she's gone. Bye-bye Marjorie." Both MMM and Williams voted in favor of the President's economic plan; it passed by a margin of 218 to 216. Margolies-Mezvinsky, it turned out, had cast the decisive vote.

The next morning, with less than three hours sleep, MMM appeared on the *Today* show, CNN's *Morning Break*, and the Fox Network's *Morning News*. The *Washington Post* ran a front-page story about the budget and the role she had played in its passage. *USA Today* ran an editorial suggesting that she be added to Mount Rushmore; the *Wall Street Journal* offered her an "Oscar for angst." Colorado Democrat Pat Schroeder, on her way back home for an audience with the Pope, who was visiting the United States, declared: "I'm going to ask the Pope to pray for Marjorie Margolies-Mezvinsky."

As it turned out, not even the Holy Father's most ardent prayers could salvage her political career; the vote had sealed her fate. In the next election, MMM once again faced Jon Fox. During the campaign, Fox hammered away at MMM's vote for "higher taxes and more spending," while noting that as a county commissioner, he had voted to cut county taxes by 3 percent. Despite outspending Fox by more than $600,000, MMM was defeated by a margin of 96,254 to 88,073. "The vote" had done her in.

Following her defeat, MMM became head of the Washington-based Woman's Campaign Fund. Unlike EMILY's List, which funds only liberal Democratic women candidates, WCF is bipartisan. MMM describes the twenty-three-year-old Fund's goal as "putting women on the farm team in order to climb up into the major leagues." In 1995, MMM served as director of the delegation that went to the Beijing Conference on the Status of Women.

MMM ran for Pennsylvania Lieutenant Governor in 1998. At the press conference announcing her candidacy, she said her decision to seek statewide office was "influenced by her work with other female candidates" during her tenure as president of WCF. Teamed with guber-natorial candidate Ivan Itkin, a twenty-five-year veteran of the Pennsylvania House with a Ph.D. in mathematics, Mezvinsky campaigned from one end of the state to the other. The Itkin-Mezvinsky ticket was soundly defeated by Governor Thomas Ridge and his running mate Mark Schwieker, the son of former United States Senator Richard Schwieker.

In 1999, MMM, undaunted by her losing campaign, announced her candidacy for the United States Senate seat held by Republican Rick Santorum. As of late 1999, the Democrat field had grown to five creditable candidates: MMM; Representative Ron Klink; former Representative (and Zero Population Growth Chief Executive Officer) Peter Kostmayer; State Senator Allyson Schwartz; and former Pennsylvania Lieutenant Governor (and failed 1994 gubernatorial candidate) Mark Singel. In early 2000 MMM dropped out of the Senate race, daunted by personal financial reverses suffered by her and her husband.

Majorie and Ed Mezvinsky live in Narbeth, Pennsylvania, where they belong to Har Zion synagogue. As has been the case for the past quarter-century, MMM still commutes between home and Washington. She is the author of four books: *They Came to Stay* (1976), *The Girls in the Newsroom* (1978), *Finding Someone to Love* (1980), and *A Woman's Place: The Freshmen Women Who Changed the Face of Congress* (1994).

References

Interview with Marjorie Margolies-Mezvinsky, August, 1997.

Interview with Mildred Margolies, August, 1997.

Almanac of American Politics (1994-1996 editions).

Marjorie Margolies-Mezvinsky, *A Woman's Place: The Freshman Women Who Changed the Face of Congress* (New York: Crown, 1994).

MARKS, MARC LINCOLN (1927–): *Republican from Pennsylvania; served three terms in the House (Ninety-fifth through Ninety-seventh Congress; January 3, 1977–January 3, 1983).*

In January 1976, Marc Lincoln Marks was a successful attorney in Sharon, Pennsylvania. In January 1979, he was a two-term member of the United States Congress, and giving serious consideration to running for the United States Senate seat held by Richard Schweiker. By mid-1979, Republican presidential candidate (and former Secretary of the Treasury) John Connally was suggesting that Marks was "the kind of man who might make a good vice president." In January 1983, Marc Marks was back in Sharon, practicing law. Like a shooting star, Marks's national political career was gone almost before it became visible on the horizon.

Marc Lincoln Marks was born in Farrell, Pennsylvania, on February 12, 1927. Located in Mercer County in the northwestern corner of Pennsylvania, Farrell is close to the Ohio line. It is part of the industrial Great Lakes region, its economy historically fueled by the steel industry. According to the edition of the *American Jewish Year Book* published the year of Marc Marks's birth, Farrell had, at most, five hundred Jews. Within a generation, the number would shrink to fewer than two hundred. Marc Marks began his education in the Farrell public schools. He attended high school in nearby Sharon, graduating in 1945. From 1945 to 1946, he served in the United States Army Air Corps. Following his stint in the service, Marks entered the University of Alabama, from which he received a B.A. in 1951. Three years later, he earned his law degree from the University of Virginia. Moving back to Pennsylvania, Marks began practicing law in Farrell. From 1960 to 1966, he served as Mercer County solicitor.

For more than a generation, Mercer County was part of the Twenty-Fourth Congressional District. Consisting of Mercer, Erie, and Crawford Counties, the Twenty-Fourth, despite a nearly two-to-one Democratic registration, tended to vote with the rest of the nation; in 1976, the district gave Jimmy Carter a 51 percent to 47 percent victory; in 1980, Ronald Reagan defeated Carter 49 percent to 43 percent with 7 percent for Independent John Anderson. In 1964, Democrat Joseph Vigorito, an assistant professor at Pennsylvania State University, defeated one-term Republican Representative James D. Weaver. Vigorito went on to represent the Twenty-Fourth District for the next twelve years, generally winning reelection by safe margins and without much effort. Beginning in 1973, Vigorito's political profile began taking a nosedive. That year, journalist Nina Totenberg, writing in *New York Times Magazine*, referred to him as "one of the ten dumbest congressmen," and gave him the nickname "Jumping Joe." From that point on, Vigorito was in danger. In 1974, he won reelection by 22,000 votes—not too healthy for a ten-year incumbent.

Noting Vigorito's vulnerability, Marc Marks decided to challenge him in 1976. "Jumping Joe" Vigorito won the Democratic primary with an anemic 52 percent of the vote. Waging an energetic and well-financed campaign, Marks scored an upset 56 percent to 44 percent victory. His victory was unique for two reasons: first, he had defeated a well-entrenched Democrat; second, he had done it at the same time that the district was voting Democratic in the presidential election.

Marc Marks entered the House as a "thoughtful and independent newcomer." Assigned to the powerful Energy and Commerce Committee, he let it be known that he was going to be a swing vote on the committee, "open to rational persuasion from all sides." A reasonable political posture in theory, it wound up causing Marks a lot of trouble. His strategy brought him "incessant pressure from nearly every interest lobbying the committee on major issues." The deregulation of natural gas is one example. When the committee held hearings on deregulation legislation, Marks was literally besieged by energy companies and consumer advocates seeking to get him to vote their way. Meeting and listening to one and all, Marks held off announcing his vote for weeks. When he finally decided to vote with committee Democrats to preserve controls, he incurred the wrath of his fellow Republicans.

According to *Politics in America*, Marks "struggled through three difficult terms without finding a comfortable niche in the institution." One reason for this was the political tightrope he was forced to walk. Marks represented a district with a strong Democratic majority and a highly conservative Republican minority. As a moderate, pro-choice Republican, he was often at odds with the more conservative elements in the district. And yet, he was adroit enough to earn ratings above 60 percent from both organized labor and organized business groups.

In 1978, Joe Vigorito tried to get his seat back; Marks, outspending his Democratic opponent by a better than five-to-one margin, won a decisive 64 percent to 36 percent victory. He returned to Capitol Hill for his second term "a new Marks, a candidate for the Senate and an outspoken liberal on a variety of issues." During the Ninety-sixth Congress's first session, Marks's Americans for Democratic Action rating shot up to 60, while his grade with the conservatives dropped down to 38. He began speaking far more frequently on the House floor, making himself "a target of ridicule from the Republican right, which felt he was moving left simply for political reasons." Cranky and abrasive, Marks gave as good as he got. *Politics in America* noted that "for a man of moderate views and a professional desire to be reasonable, he ha[d] a remarkable tendency to anger people." Two examples will suffice. While debating the merits of an anti-busing amendment to the Constitution, Marks used the word "hypocrisy," thereby bringing on a stinging rebuke from Maryland Republican Robert Bauman. At another point, California Republican John Rousselot, an ultra-conservative, demanded a roll-call vote on a Marks amendment "purely to embarrass him by demonstrating its lack of support."

In 1980, a popular young Democratic state legislator named David DiCarlo challenged Marc Marks. Although Marks won a third term, it was a hollow victory; his margin was only 120 votes out of 173,254. In a less Republican year (Reagan beat Carter 49 percent to 43 percent in

the district), DiCarlo would have undoubtedly won. Marks returned for his third term a more conservative legislator. He began speaking less on the House floor; his support for the conservative coalition began to rise. He also returned as ranking Republican on the Oversight and Investigations Subcommittee of Energy and Commerce. In this position, Marks had the dubious pleasure of going head-to-head with the equally abrasive and temperamental John Dingell. It could not have been a fulfilling two years for Marks.

Before the end of his third term, Marc Marks announced that he would not run for reelection. He left the House "offering vehement blasts" against a Reagan administration whose economic programs he had supported. David DiCarlo ran once again for Marks's seat, losing the Democratic primary to state Senator Anthony "Buzz" Andrezeski. The Republicans nominated a thirty-seven-year-old Erie attorney named Thomas J. Ridge. Andrezeski "campaigned abrasively and raised relatively little money, as if he assumed he were a shoo-in." Ridge defeated Andrezeski by a mere 729 votes out of 159,631. Ridge held the seat until 1993, when he was elected Governor of Pennsylvania. Marc Marks returned to Sharon to practice law.

Marc Lincoln Marks is now a resident of Chevy Chase, Maryland, and practices law in Washington. He and his wife, the former Jane London, have three children.

References

Almanac of American Politics (1974–82, 1994 editions).
Politics in America (1980 edition).

MARX, SAMUEL (1867-1922): *Democrat from New York; elected to the Sixty-eighth Congress, but died before he could take the oath of office (1922).*

Despite the fact that Samuel Marx never made it to Capitol Hill, he nonetheless deserves a spot in the Congressional Minyan. He was duly elected to Congress and was active in New York politics for many years.

Sam Marx was born in New York City in 1867 and received a public school education. As an adult, Marx had two passions: Democratic politics and auctioneering. In the latter capacity, he acted as the appraiser of a number of fabulous estates, including those of *Joseph Pulitzer*, J. P. Morgan, and John Huyler. Working out of offices at 15 West 23rd Street in the old Woolworth Building, Marx prospered greatly. For one appraisal alone—that of the estate of one Benno Loewy—he received the sum of $12,500. Marx was also one of the founders of the Association of Auctioneers of Greater New York.

As a politico, Sam Marx was first, last, and always, a creature of Tammany Hall. His base of operations was the Cayuga Club on Seventh Avenue. For many years, he served on the Board of Aldermen as representative of the Thirty-first Aldermanic District. In August 1919, he was appointed Internal Revenue Collector for the Third New York District. As the Tammany leader for the Thirty-first Assembly District he controlled a great many patronage positions. In 1889, Sam Marx married Irene Smith. Her brother, Phillip, became one of Sam's most loyal lieutenants. In October 1916, the two were arrested and held on $500 bail on charges of "electioneering too close to a polling place." The charges were later dropped. The complaint had been made by one Jacob Levin, a leftist who despised both Marx and Tammany Hall. Marx's opinions about the political left were well-known to voters in his district: "I don't care whether a man is a Republican or a Democrat. If he is for our present form of government, I'll work for him. But I will fight a Socialist every time I see one, for I believe their principles are entirely subversive of what a real American ought to stand for."

In 1916, twenty of Sam Marx's political friends formed a delegation to go to Washington on his behalf. Their mission was to convince New York Senator James Aloysius O'Gorman and Postmaster General Burleson that Marx was deserving of an appointment as Postmaster of New York. The delegation, headed up by a jeweler named Charles Wilder, argued somewhat disingenuously that "the movement to get the place for Mr. Marx was entirely outside of politics," and that "the request for his appointment [is] made on the ground of his business qualifications." O'Gorman and Burleson appointed another man to the post.

In November 1922, Sam Marx defeated Republican Representative Walter Marion Chandler (1867–1935), who had represented the Nineteenth Congressional District from 1913 to 1919, and again from 1921 to 1923. Three weeks after winning his congressional seat, Sam Marx died of a massive heart attack at his home on Seventh Avenue, just a few blocks away from the Cayuga Club. Marx's funeral was held at the Institutional Synagogue, on whose board of directors he had served for many years. More than sixteen hundred people attended the funeral, presided over by Rabbi Herbert Goldstein. Sam Marx was buried at the Mount Carmel Cemetery. He was survived by his wife and "several brothers and sisters." The Marxes had no children.

References

New York Times, October 6, 1915, 5:2; January 17, 1916, 20:2; December 1, 1922, 17:4; December 4, 1922, 17:1.

MAY, MITCHELL (1870–1961): *Democrat from New York; served one term in the House (Fifty-sixth Congress; March 4, 1899–March 3, 1901).*

In his time a much-revered figure from the Williamsburg section of Brooklyn, Mitchell May is best remembered today, if at all, as a judge rather than as a member of Congress. He was born in Brooklyn on July 10, 1870, the son of Nathan and Matilda Mulhauser. His father had come to Brooklyn from Strasbourg in Alsace, around 1850. May was educated at Brooklyn Polytechnic Institute and graduated from the Columbia University School of Law in 1892. After clerking with an attorney named Ira Leo Bamberger, he went into private practice, setting up shop at 189 Montague Street. He continued to practice law in Brooklyn until 1898, when he was offered the Democratic nomination for Congress. That was the year in which Brooklyn was consolidated with New York City. May won his election, and at the age of twenty-eight years, eight months, became one of the two or three youngest members of the Fifty-sixth Congress.

May quickly lost the support of his Democratic backers when he refused to go along with the silver policy of William Jennings Bryan, the party's acknowledged leader. Because of his break with party orthodoxy, he was denied renomination. Shortly before leaving Congress in March 1901, May married a widow, Pauline Joli Thompson. During their forty-five years of marriage, they had two children, Mitchell, Jr., and Ruth (Moore) May. May also had a stepson from Pauline's first marriage, John J. Thompson.

Returning to Brooklyn and the practice of law, May was out of the political arena for the next five years. After putting out feelers to his former political allies, he was eventually appointed to the King's County Board of Education in 1906, where he served his political "penance" for the next four years. He was finally "rehabilitated" and invited back into the Democratic Party in 1911. Working his way into the mainstream of party activity, May served as both counsel to the county clerk and as an assistant district attorney for Kings County from 1911 to 1913. During his term in the district attorney's office, he investigated the failure of the Union Bank and successfully prosecuted its president

for malfeasance. In 1913, he was elected New York Secretary of State. During his single term, he helped enact some of the nation's first laws against reckless automobile driving and moved to eliminate a new menace to motoring—the speed trap. He was perhaps the first state official to recommend and enact a law to mandate that all moneys paid for speeding and other vehicular violations must go to the maintenance and improvement of the state highway system.

In 1915, May was elected to a five-year term as judge of the Kings County Court. At the end of the term (1921), he was elected to the first of two fourteen-year terms on the New York State Supreme Court. Fully back in the Democratic fold, May became the founder and first president of the Unity Club of Brooklyn and was twice drafted as a prospective candidate for Governor of New York State. In both instances, he asked that his name be withdrawn so that the party could offer unified support to his good friend *Herbert H. Lehman*.

May served on the Supreme Court until 1940, when he reached the mandatory retirement age of seventy. After his retirement from the bench, he entered private practice with the firm of Weisman, (*Emanuel*) *Celler*, Quinn, Allan, and Spett, with which he remained for the next twenty-one years. During this latter stage of his life, he served eight terms as president of the Brooklyn Federation of Jewish Charities and was eventually appointed its director. May was also involved with the Jewish Hospital of Brooklyn and the Hebrew Educational Society. A Reform Jew, he was a member of the Union Temple and the Eighth Avenue Temple, both in Park Slope, Brooklyn. Mitchell May, widowed in 1945, died in Brooklyn on March 24, 1961. He was buried in Valhalla Cemetery on Staten Island.

References

American Jewish Year Book, vol. 2 (1900–1901), p. 521; vol. 6 (1904–1905), pp. 152–153; vol. 24 (1922–23), p. 180; vol. 63 (1962–63), p. 561.
Biographical Directory of American Jews.
Jewish Encyclopedia.
New York Times, March 27, 1961, 31:1.
Universal Jewish Encyclopedia.
Who Was Who in American Jewry, 1926, 1928.

METZENBAUM, HOWARD MORTON

(1917–): *Democrat from Ohio; served one unexpired and three full terms in the Senate (January 4, 1974–December 23, 1974; January 3, 1977–January 3, 1995).*

In 1974, when Ohio Governor John J. Gilligan appointed Howard Metzenbaum to fill the unexpired term of Senator William Saxbe, Metzenbaum told a reporter from the *Washington Post*: "I won't come in riding a white horse and being gung-ho. I hope to be effective but in a quiet voice." Those who knew Metzenbaum well understood that he was only telling a partial truth; it just wasn't in Metzenbaum's nature to be anything but gung-ho. Apparently even the *Post* reporter realized that the Cleveland-born lawyer-businessman wasn't telling the whole truth, for he noted: "After nearly three decades of political earthmoving, Metzenbaum has earned the reputation . . . of an activist who never leaves a job half done."

Howard Metzenbaum was born in Cleveland, on June 4, 1917, where his father and grandfather, who had emigrated from Hungary, ran a dry-goods store. His parents, Charles I. and Anna (Klefter) Metzenbaum, raised their son in "financially precarious conditions in a middle-class neighborhood on Cleveland's east side." At one point, things got so bad that Charles Metzenbaum had to sell his 1926 Essex automobile in order to keep the bank from foreclosing on their small house. Howard Metzenbaum worked his way through Ohio State University by selling chrysanthemums at OSU football games, hawking magazines and Fuller brushes, renting bicycles, and playing trombone for 50 cents an hour in a National Youth Administration orchestra. Ever resourceful, upon graduating from the OSU School of Law in 1941, Metzenbaum placed an ad in a Cleveland newspaper offering to exchange "legal services for law office space." The ad was answered by attorney Sidney Moss, who gave the young lawyer a corner in which to ply his trade. Within a matter of months, Moss and Metzenbaum had

gone into business together, opening income-tax consulting offices in several Ohio cities. Charging one dollar for each form he prepared, Metzenbaum earned in excess of $10,000 the first year.

In 1942, Metzenbaum ran for the Ohio State Legislature, winning without the endorsement of the local Democratic Party organization. His election caused something of a stir, for at twenty-five, he was the youngest person ever elected to the legislature. During his first term, he introduced a measure to ban discrimination by employers and unions on the basis of race, religion, or national origin. The bill, which Metzenbaum proudly says "was far ahead of its time," failed. Reelected in 1944, Metzenbaum authored the successful Ohio Retail Installment Sales Act, which made residents of the Buckeye State among the first Americans to have consumer protection in matters of credit. Known informally as the Metzenbaum Act, it was a prototype for the Federal Truth in Lending Act.

In 1946, Howard Metzenbaum became one of four Democrats elected to the Ohio Senate. There, he successfully pushed for the expansion of the state's workmen's and employment compensation plans. Following the end of his second term, Metzenbaum decided to leave politics in order to devote his energies "to his family, his work with the law firm of Metzenbaum, Gaines, Finley & Stern, and, above all, his business interests." It was not that Metzenbaum wanted to see if he could make money; he was supremely confident that given the time, the money would come. And it did, in a big way. Of his famed business acumen Metzenbaum says, matter-of-factly: "Some people have it on a golf course. I can barely break 100. Others have talent in tennis or some other sport. I play them, but I'm not very good at any of them. What I can do is make money."

In 1947, Metzenbaum rented a plot of land at the Cleveland Airport for $400 a month, turning it into a parking lot. People thought he was taking an unreasonable gamble; it would simply be too expensive to maintain an airport parking lot twenty-four hours a day. Moreover, the naysayers argued, there wouldn't be much need for it. Metzenbaum knew better: "I knew there would be more people flying airplanes every day, and more cars on the street, and that eventually it would pay off." Two years later, in partnership with old college roommate Alva T. "Ted" Bonda, Metzenbaum established APOCA—the Airport Parking Company of America. Over the next sixteen years, Metzenbaum and Bonda expanded their operations across the country, adding concessions and airports throughout the United States. Among their holdings were seventeen Avis Rent-A-Car franchises, "the largest number held under a single ownership." (It was Bonda, by the way, who originated Avis's "We Try Harder" slogan.) In 1966, Metzenbaum and Bonda, who continued to maintain a controlling interest in APCOA after it went public, merged their company with the International Telephone and Telegraph Corporation. Metzenbaum reportedly received $6 million in stock as his share of the approximately $30 million sale price. Metzenbaum also became Chairman of ITT's Consumer Services Corporation, from which he retired in 1968. A year later, Metzenbaum and Bonda became the largest single shareholders in the Society Corporation, which owns banks throughout Ohio. That same year, 1969, Metzenbaum paid $14 million for a controlling share in Com-Corps Inc., a concern which owns twenty weekly newspapers in the Greater Cleveland area.

During his money-making years, Metzenbaum did not turn his back on politics; he served as campaign manager for Senator Stephen M. Young's surprise victories against John Bricker in 1958 and Robert Taft, Jr., in 1964. When Young (1888–1984), one of the Senate's truly crusty characters, announced that he would not seek reelection in 1970, Metzenbaum decided to run for his seat. The odds against him were formidable, for his opponent in the Democratic primary was none other than former astronaut John Glenn, one of the best-known men in America. Worse, early polling indicated that Metzenbaum's name was known to less than 10 percent of the Ohio electorate, while Glenn had near-universal name recognition. Adding to his uphill struggle, Metzenbaum was warned that his being Jewish would likely work against him. To this, the candidate was philosophical: "Those people who won't vote for me because I'm Jewish would have found ten other reasons for not voting for me," he said.

Armed with formidable financial resources, Metzenbaum hired political consultant Joseph Napolitan to advise him. Napolitan's research uncovered that Glenn had his weaknesses, especially among "blacks, union members and urbanites in the thirty-to-forty-year-old bracket." Metzenbaum saturated the state with television commercials portraying him as a candidate who was "more thoughtful than Glenn and more in touch with ordinary people." Glenn accused him of trying to "buy the election." Metzenbaum did not deign to respond to the charge until after the campaign. Instead, he called for a specific timetable for withdrawing American troops from Vietnam and criticized his opponent for supporting continued funding for the space program "while the funding for urgent domestic programs" was declining.

Metzenbaum's battle against John Glenn was, in the words of one political observer, "the slickest piece of campaigning to which the Ohio electorate has been exposed." He wound up winning the primary in an upset, 427,294 to 414,848. Only then did he respond to the charge of buying the election: "Certainly I admit that it would have been impossible for me to have won without television. But it would have been impossible for my opponent to have become a candidate without it. Look at the billions of dollars of free publicity he got as an astronaut. I spent the money to let people know who I am and what I stand for."

In the general election, Metzenbaum ran against Republican Congressman Robert A. Taft, Jr., son of the late Senator, grandson of the former President. It was a classic battle of opposites: "Moderate vs. Liberal, or Ivy League vs. Big Ten, or Episcopalian vs. Jew, or Money vs. Money," as the title of a *New York Times Magazine* article proclaimed. Uniquely, the two agreed to limit their spending for broadcast time to seven cents for each vote cast in the last statewide general election—approximately $260,000. Metzenbaum fought hard, but was hurt by a smear, raised late in the campaign by a reporter, that he had "known Communist connections" in his past. What the reporter was alluding to was Metzenbaum's membership in the leftist National Lawyers' Guild in the 1940s; the NLG had, at one time, appeared on the Attorney General's List of Subversive Organizations. This charge, coupled with Metzenbaum's liberalism and Judaism, caused him to lose votes in Cleveland's ethnic areas. Despite an heroic effort, Metzenbaum wound up losing to Taft 1,565,682 to 1,495,262—a respectable 49 percent showing.

In late 1973, President Richard Nixon named Senator William Saxbe his new Attorney General. John Gilligan then tapped Metzenbaum to fill out the final year of Saxbe's term. Although Metzenbaum did not personally lobby the Ohio Governor for the position, his friends in the labor movement did. On January 4, 1974, Metzenbaum took his seat in the United States Senate. Before taking the job, the new Senator divested himself of "those business interests that might possibly seem to be in conflict . . . and putting his investments . . . into a blind trust." During the remainder of the term—less than a year—he cast votes to roll back oil prices, raise the minimum wage, end the extension of daylight saving time into winter, and register privately owned guns. While serving out the remainder of Saxbe's term, Metzenbaum was again facing Glenn in the Democratic primary. This time Glenn had a much stronger campaign organization and relentlessly attacked Metzenbaum for a "lack of financial ethics"— Metzenbaum had managed to avoid paying federal income taxes in 1969. Glenn defeated Metzenbaum by more than 90,000 votes and went on to win the general election.

In 1976, Metzenbaum squared off against Taft once more. After easily winning the Democratic primary, Metzenbaum began a hard-hitting campaign based on economic issues and his "accomplishments on behalf of the wage-earner, the consumer, the average citizen in eleven months in the Senate as compared to those of Taft in a full six-year term." Specifically, Metzenbaum called for the introduction of national health insurance, the creation of a consumer protection agency, and the adoption of the Humphrey-Hawkins full employment bill. On election day, Metzenbaum defeated Taft by a margin of 1,925163, to 1,809,283—slightly more than 51 percent of the vote. Finally, after three attempts, Howard Metzenbaum was a United States Senator.

Metzenbaum hit the Senate floor running, receiving assignments on four major committees: Energy and Natural Resources, Judiciary, Budget, and Labor. One of the first things the new Senator learned was how to bottle up legislation that did not meet with his approval. Acting as a kind of "Horatius at the bridge," he began putting holds on dozens of pieces of special-interest legislation at the end of a session, and then would filibuster them if they came up. "In effect, Metzenbaum forced senators backing these [special-interest] bills to negotiate with him, even if they had a large majority and he represented only himself." In one such effort, Metzenbaum, along with South Dakota Senator James Abourzek, staged the Senate's first filibuster on behalf of the consumer—against deregulation of oil and gas prices. Although their effort failed (he termed deregulation "a cruel policy"), Metzenbaum "saw that the possibilities for delay were tremendous." Metzenbaum perplexed his colleagues by putting in as many as one hundred amendments on a single bill and then turning around and fighting to change the rule that had permitted him to do so.

During his first term, Metzenbaum voted to ratify the Panama Canal treaties and endorsed federal efforts to control hospital costs. He supported efforts to prevent states from rescinding their ratification of the Equal Rights Amendment and opposed the planned sale of advanced U.S. military equipment to Saudi Arabia. Arguing against the sale, Metzenbaum claimed that "providing AWACS to Saudi Arabia would be a true catastrophe for Israel [and] would amount to a reversal by the United States of our commitments to the security of a loyal and courageous Democratic ally." He also cosponsored the bill that made World War II-era Swedish diplomat Raoul Wallenberg an honorary American citizen, a move that permitted the United States to make official inquiries as to his fate. During the 1981 floor debate on voluntary prayer in public schools, Ernest F. Hollings, a South Carolina Democrat, referred to Metzenbaum as "the Senator from B'nai B'rith." A hush descended on the floor. Although Hollings later claimed "I said it only in fun," Pennsylvania Senator *Arlen Specter* came to Metzenbaum's defense, excoriating the South Carolinian for the use of "inappropriate and offensive" remarks.

Predictably, Metzenbaum received high ratings from such liberal groups as the Americans for Democratic Action, the Committee on Political Education, and the American Civil Liberties Union. Also predictably, he drew the ire of the conservative Americans for Constitutional Action. As a result of his perceived ultra-liberal record, he was marked for political extinction in 1982. Facing Ohio state Senator Paul Pfeifer, Metzenbaum tied his opponent's tail to the Reagan administration, denouncing the Republicans' economic policy and budget cuts. Pfeifer, who was one of the few Republican Senate candidates who "could not persuade the national Republican Party to give him the maximum legal funding," went down to defeat by a 57 percent to 41 percent margin.

In 1984, Metzenbaum almost single-handedly forced Judiciary Committee chair Strom Thurmond, a South Carolina Republican, to put an indefinite hold on Edwin Meese's nomination to become Attorney General. At the time, Meese was under investigation by a special prosecutor on charges that he had used his White House post as presidential counselor for personal financial gain. Metzenbaum was not the best man to take on Meese; he had recently made headlines for accepting a $250,000 "finder's fee" for what was, arguably, a negligible role in the sale of Washington's Hay-Adams Hotel and had lobbied the Senate Finance chairman on a tax break for companies that paid for employees' legal services. This latter issue raised eyebrows; Metzenbaum's son-in-law, Joel Hyatt, headed the nation's largest legal services firm. When word of this windfall hit the press, Metzenbaum returned the fee. Reagan withdrew the Meese nomination until the special prosecutor could finish his investigation. When no improprieties turned up, Reagan resubmitted the nomination. Again, Metzenbaum led the campaign against him. Meese was nonetheless confirmed.

In Metzenbaum's next reelection campaign, he faced Cleveland mayor George Voinovich. (In 1998, by-then Ohio Governor Voinovich would be elected to the U. S. Senate seat being vacated by John Glenn.) The Senate Republican Campaign Committee decided to again bring up the canard that Metzenbaum had been a Communist sympathizer in the 1940s. When word of the strategy was leaked to the press, Senators Bob Dole and *Rudy Boschwitz* publicly

apologized. Toward the end of the campaign, Voinovich accused Metzenbaum of opposing "laws that will put child pornographers out of business." This charge sealed the Cleveland mayor's fate.

Metzenbaum's colleague and old nemesis John Glenn came to Metzenbaum's defense, taping a television commercial in which he attacked Voinovich for "gutter politics." Metzenbaum cruised to a 57 percent to 43 percent victory. Remarkably, Metzenbaum won his election by more than 600,000 votes even while George Bush carried Ohio by over 400,000 votes. At his victory celebration, he announced that he would retire when his new term ended.

During his last term in the Senate, Metzenbaum acted as lead sponsor of various gun control measures, including the Brady Bill and bans on automatic rifles and plastic weapons. His "most spectacular moment" came during the Clarence Thomas confirmation hearings, when he "doggedly pursued Thomas to articulate his personal views on abortion." Moreover, it was Metzenbaum's staff that originally learned about and contacted Oklahoma law professor Anita Hill. The Senate special counsel's report on the hearings said that "Metzenbaum's staff may have had a hand in leaking the story to the press."

Toward the end of 1990, Metzenbaum, saying he was "tired of seeing too many of his Democratic colleagues becoming shadow Republicans," formed the Coalition for Democratic Values. In its charter, the CDV proclaimed that it was "committed to revitalizing the Democratic Party by emphasizing the progressive values that make it the Party of the People." Founded with more than seventy Democratic members of Congress and "more than 200 members of the business, academic, entertainment and political community," the CDV was seen as a counterweight to the Democratic Leadership Council, once headed by Arkansas Governor Bill Clinton. Its conferences have drawn upwards of five hundred participants.

Metzenbaum began planting the seeds for his successor during his last years in the Senate. He expected his son-in-law, Joel Hyatt, to succeed him. As things turned out, Hyatt, who won the Democratic primary with an anemic 47 percent to 43 percent, lost to Ohio Lieutenant Governor

Michael DeWine. Political observers noted that Hyatt's family ties actually worked against him, for Metzenbaum's job approval rating in the exit poll was 40 percent positive and 51 percent negative. Metzenbaum retired from the Senate on January 3, 1995, having spent nearly nineteen years in that institution. Throughout his career, he maintained a staunchly liberal posture, becoming known as the Reagan-era Senate's "leading obstructionist."

Shortly after announcing his retirement from the Senate, Metzenbaum's colleagues gathered to pay homage to the man they called "Headline Howard." The gathering was held in the ornate caucus room where John F. Kennedy announced his candidacy for president and Senator Sam Ervin once grilled Watergate witnesses. When it came Metzenbaum's turn to speak, he sought to teach his fellows a political lesson: "Today, politics is about fear, fear of the 30-second attack ad, fear of special interest groups. If you are afraid, you can't lead. Too many in this town are so fearful for their political lives that they forget about helping the people who sent 'em."

Following his retirement, Metzenbaum became the first-ever chairman of the Consumer Federation of America, "a non-profit coalition of 240 pro-consumer groups with 50 million members." Not surprisingly, Metzenbaum agreed to take the position without pay. Speaking of his new position, the then-seventy-seven-year-old Metzenbaum announced that he would wage a campaign against the import and sale of products made with child labor in "Bangladesh, Pakistan, China and various other places." "I think it's an abomination," he said, "for these fancy sweater houses, dress houses, Persian rug manufacturers to have their products made by kids from anywhere from 5 to 14 years of age at absolutely sub, sub, substandard wages."

In 1946, Howard Metzenbaum married Shirley Turloff. They have four grown daughters—Barbara, Susan, Shelly, and Amy—and seven grandchildren. (Susan is the daughter who married Joel Hyatt.) A Reform Jew, Metzenbaum spent many years as a board member of the Union of American Hebrew Congregations and was a generous contributor to the Hebrew Union College-Jewish Institute of Religion. In 1994, Metzenbaum abruptly quit the UAHC board in disagreement over its policy of accepting children who have only one Jewish parent as being fully Jewish. Metzenbaum has also served as vice chairman of fellows at Brandeis University.

Through the years, Metzenbaum has fought discrimination in the greater Cleveland community. For years he "steadfastly and loudly" refused to set foot in Cleveland's Union Club, the city's "leading bastion of the Establishment," because it would not accept black or Jewish members. He was so outspoken in his condemnation of the city's most exclusive tennis club for its discriminatory membership policies that when it finally began accepting Jewish members, he was refused admission. Undaunted, and in typical Metzenbaum fashion, he simply built his own tennis court next to the swimming pool of his Shaker Height's estate. The Metzenbaums now divide their time between Lyndhurst, a suburb of Cleveland, and their winter home in Pompano Beach, Florida.

Summing up his career as a populist, Metzenbaum said: "To be a populist is to be a guy who speaks for all people. A liberal might not be speaking for all the people but might be standing up for the right to burn the flag. It just hurts me to see people who aren't being fed or clothed or educated, who can't have decent health care. It actually hurts me. I guess sometimes I wish I could wave a wand and make things better for so many of the have-nots."

To his enemies, Howard Metzenbaum was "ruthless," "opportunistic," "a manipulator." To his supporters, he was "shrewd," "extremely sharp," "compassionate," "a political genius." Upon one thing, however, they all agreed: everything about Howard Metzenbaum had the "patina of success."

References

Almanac of American Politics (1976–94 editions).
American Jewish Biography (New York: Facts on File, 1983), pp. 285–286.
Current Biography, 1980, pp. 255–259.
New York Times Magazine, October 4, 1970, p. 32.
Politics in America.
Washington Post, December 24, 1973, A 2:1. November 15, 1994 B:1.

MEYER, ADOLPH (1842–1908): *Democrat from Louisiana; served nine terms in the House (Fifty-second through Sixtieth Congress; March 4, 1891–March 8, 1908).*

In the Algiers section of New Orleans, there is a street called General Meyer Avenue. It is highly unlikely that any of the people traveling the thoroughfare have the slightest idea who General Meyer was. Such are the ravages of history. In his day, Adolph Meyer was one of the most respected citizens of his adopted city—a war hero, banker, owner of a highly successful cotton firm, and nine-term member of the United States House of Representatives.

Adolph Meyer was born in Natchez, Mississippi, on October 19, 1842. Although little is known about his antecedents or his earliest years, it would seem that he came from a well-to-do family, for in 1860, he matriculated at the University of Virginia. In 1862, his fledgling college career cut short by the Civil War, Meyer returned home and joined the Confederate army. Assigned to the staff of Brigadier General John S. Williams of Kentucky, Meyer attained the rank of adjutant general. Years later, in a letter to President Ulysses S. Grant, Williams praised his former adjutant: "He was pre-eminent for soldierly qualities—the loftiest courage, fidelity and endurance. In fact, he seemed a natural born soldier." At war's end, Meyer moved to New Orleans, where, in 1868, he married Rosalie Jonas, the daughter of Abraham Lincoln's good friend Abraham Jonas, and the sister of Louisiana's future United States Senator, *Benjamin Franklin Jonas.* The newly married Meyer became a planter of cotton, sugarcane, and rice in Concordia Parish, and subsequently entered the cotton factorage and commission business with the firm of Meyer, Weis & Company, established by his brother Victor. The brothers expanded their enterprise, forming the spectacularly successful cotton firm of A. & V. Meyer.

Well-known in New Orleans for his military record and his increasing wealth, Adolph Meyer was appointed brigadier general of the 1st Louisiana Brigade in 1881, which included "all the uniformed militia of the state." At age forty-eight, Meyer was elected as a Democrat to represent New Orleans in the United States Congress. Wildly popular, he was reelected eight times. With seniority, he became a power on the House Committee on Naval Affairs. Surprisingly for a former army general, Meyer spent the better part of his career as an advocate for the United States Navy. During his seventeen years in the House, Meyer could be counted on as a solid vote for any and all appropriations measures that would increase the size, strength, and prestige of the navy. As with all successful members of Congress, Meyer knew how to "bring home the bacon" to his district. He was largely responsible for the construction of the naval station and dry dock in New Orleans—one of the world's largest in its day.

The Meyers had one daughter, Louise, who married a naval captain named Franklin Swift. Adolph Meyer died in New Orleans on March 8, 1908, and was buried in the Metrarie (Louisiana) Cemetery.

References

Biographical Directory of the United States Congress, 1774–1989, p. 1495.

National Cyclopedia of American Biography, vol. 16, p. 64.

MEZVINSKY, EDWARD MAURICE (1937–):
Democrat from Iowa; served two terms in the House (Ninety-third through Ninety-fourth Congress; January 3, 1973–January 3, 1977).

Imagine the following scene: It is the late 1940s or early 1950s. A bearded itinerant fundraiser from an Orthodox yeshiva makes the rounds of prominent Jewish householders. He arrives at the home of a well-known Jew, who invites him in for a meal, a chat, and a glass of tea. They go into the kitchen, where the kettle is boiling, sit down, and immediately begin conversing in Yiddish. They drink, they eat, they talk long into the night. Finally, the emissary leaves with dollars for his yeshiva and the names of other prospective contributors in the area. It is not a particularly unusual scenario, if one imagines the scene taking place in Brooklyn, Rogers Park, or Fairfax. In this case, however, the kitchen is located in Ames, the hometown of Iowa's sole minyanaire, Edward Mezvinsky.

The future Congressman's father, Abraham Mezvinsky, came to America from Kiev as a young man. Wandering out to the American heartland, he became a peddler, hawking fruits and vegetables from a horsedrawn wagon in St. Joseph, Missouri. There he met Fannie Grundman, an immigrant from Warsaw. Following their marriage, they moved to Iowa, where Abe continued to peddle. Times were rough; the Depression had come to the farm belt a full decade before the stock market crash of '29. To make matters worse, Abe Mezvinsky encountered religious bigotry. He was charged an excessively high fee for the right to peddle. Eventually, a court would find that the fees were discriminatory.

Abe and Fannie Mezvinsky had four children. Their youngest, Edward, was born in Ames, Iowa, on January 17, 1937. Ed was raised in a Yiddish-speaking, kosher home; the Mezvinskys had to travel all the way to Des Moines or Omaha for their food. During Ed's youth, Ames had a Jewish population of less than one-tenth of one percent. In truth, the Mezvinsky family formed the sum and substance of the Ames Jewish community. Because the town had no synagogue, no rabbi, and no *melamed* (teacher), young Ed Mezvinsky made the 60-mile round trip to Des Moines three times a week to receive bar mitzvah instruction at a *cheder*.

Following his graduation from high school, Ed Mezvinsky entered the University of Iowa in Iowa City. Graduating in 1960, he headed out to Berkeley, where he spent the next five years. During his time on the west coast, Mezvinsky studied Russian at both the University of California and the Monterey Defense Language Institute, and earned an M.A. in political science (1963) and a J.D. from Boalt Hall. Following his graduation from law school, Mezvinsky went to work for Fourth District Representative Neal Smith. Mezvinsky worked for Smith for two years (1965–67) and then joined the firm of Shulman, Phelan, Tucker, Boyle and Mullen in Iowa City. Two years later, he was elected to the Iowa State House of Representatives. He quickly set his sights on Washington, D.C.

Iowa's First District, which comprises the cities of Davenport, Iowa City, Burlington, and a lot of farmland, had been represented in Congress for nearly twenty years by moderate Republican Fred Schwengel. A man "with a wide range of interests," Schwengel (1906–1993) was founder and president of both the National Capitol Historical Society and the Republican Heritage Foundation, and a noted Lincoln buff. Considered something of a loner by his congressional colleagues, Schwengel lost his seat in 1964 to John R. Schmidhauser, a Bronx native who taught constitutional law at the State University of Iowa and served as Democratic Party chair in Johnson County. Two years later, Schwengel recaptured the seat. From that point on, Schwengel, who had rarely had serious opposition in the Republican primary, found himself being regularly challenged. In 1970, he barely escaped a primary challenge from David Stanley, the man who had nearly won an upset victory over Iowa Senator Harold Hughes two years earlier. Emerging from the primary with a mere 56 percent of the vote, Schwengel faced the thirty-three-year-old Mezvinsky. Running as an antiwar candidate, Edward Mezvinsky came within 765 votes of defeating Schwengel. No sooner had he lost than he began running again.

Mezvinsky faced Schmidhauser again in the 1972 primary, defeating the former Representative by a better than two-to-one margin. His general election campaign against Schwengel was "not so much a matter of attack and counterattack as a contrast in attitudes and styles." Running once again as an opponent of the war in

Vietnam, against a man who, more often than not, was "uncommittal on issues," Mezvinsky won a decisive 15,000-vote victory. Ed Mezvinsky, the first (and so far only) Jew elected to Congress from Iowa, took his seat on January 3, 1973.

As a new member of the Ninety-third Congress, Mezvinsky was elected chair of the Freshman Democratic Caucus. His vice chair was future Louisiana Senator John Breaux. Mezvinsky was assigned to the House Judiciary Committee, where he quickly became embroiled in the debate over the confidentiality of journalists' sources. According to the *Almanac of American Politics* (1974 edition), Mezvinsky was "a firm believer in the right of a reporter to keep his sources secret." Where some members of the committee sought a reporter's "shield law," Mezvinsky took a different tack. He argued that no law should be enacted in this area, for "protection by statute, unlike a constitutional amendment, can be revoked at some later time."

The highlight of Ed Mezvinsky's congressional career came when the House Judiciary Committee voted to impeach Richard Nixon. Though the most junior member of the committee, Mezvinsky participated fully in the historic hearings, even offering an article relating to the President's "misuse of government funds on his person." The article failed to carry. In his 1977 book, *A Session to Remember*, Mezvinsky noted a peculiar change that occurred at the beginning of the impeachment hearings:

> Our seating had always seemed to me and several of my colleagues to be backwards. The traditional arrangement in the Judiciary Committee was to have the chairman in the middle, with the Republicans to his left and the Democrats to his right. . . . Yet in 1973, when I joined the committee, it was the other way around. . . . Today however, [Judiciary Committee Chair Peter] Rodino had ordered a switchover and we were now seated according to the House tradition and common sense. I asked someone why we had previously been "out of order," and I received an answer that was perfectly acceptable: *Manny Celler*, for thirty years the previous chairman, had a bad ear. The afflicted ear was on his

right side, so that's where he put the Republicans. The chairman, a Democrat, wanted to be sure that during debate he did not fail to hear and recognize a member of his own party. Peter Rodino's hearing was unimpaired.

Mezvinsky compiled a solidly liberal record during his first term. In his first campaign for reelection (1974), he faced James A. S. Leach, the scion of a well-known Davenport family. Leach, a graduate of Princeton, had served as a Foreign Service officer assigned to the United Nations in 1972 at the time George Bush was U.S. ambassador there. They became fast friends. In 1973, Leach resigned his post "out of dismay" after President Nixon fired Watergate special prosecutor Archibald Cox. Following his resignation, Leach went back to Davenport to run the family propane business. Mezvinsky defeated Leach by some 8,000 votes. Leach immediately began making plans for a rematch in 1976. After two years of almost nonstop campaigning, Jim Leach defeated Ed Mezvinsky by 8,500 votes. Some speculated that Ed Mezvinsky did not truly have his heart in the campaign. As of 2000, James Leach was still in the House of Representatives. In his twelfth term, and the de facto leader of the Republican's moderate wing, Leach is a major power in the House, where he serves as Budget Committee chair.

In 1975, Mezvinsky, who was divorced with four children, married *Marjorie Margolies*, a news correspondent for the local Washington-based NBC affiliate. As a result of his remarriage, Mezvinsky suddenly found himself the father of Margolies's two adopted youngsters in addition to his four children. Over the past twenty-four years, the Mezvinskys have housed more than twenty-five children.

Following his defeat, Ed Mezvinsky moved to Montgomery County, the hinterland of Philadelphia, from whence his wife came. He went back into private practice, specializing in international business law. From 1981 to 1986, Mezvinsky served as chair of the Pennsylvania Democratic State Committee. Today, the Mezvinskys reside in Narberth, Pennsylvania, where they are the parents of eleven children.

References

Interview with Edward Mezvinsky, May 1994.
Almanac of American Politics (1974–78 editions).

Edward Mezvinsky (with Kevin McCormally and John Greenya), *A Session to Remember* (New York: Coward, McCann & Geoghegan, 1977).

MIKVA, ABNER JOSEPH (1926–): *Democrat from Illinois; served five terms in the House (Ninety-first and Ninety-second Congress; January 3, 1969–January 3, 1973; Ninety-forth through Ninety-seventh Congress; January 3, 1975–September 26, 1979).*

Although he can trace his ancestry back through five generations, Judge Abner Mikva has never been able to determine precisely when or how his family acquired their rather distinctive name. *Mikvah* is the Hebrew term for the ritual bath that Orthodox Jewish women are required to visit after each menstrual cycle before resuming sexual relations, and that Jewish men visit in order to purify themselves on various occasions. One might posit that just as Bakers, Coopermans, and Schneiders, are descended from ancestors who baked, made barrels, and were tailors, the Mikvas are descended from people who were in charge of the community bath. It's plausible, but not certain. The judge's youngest daughter, Rabbi Rachel Mikva, has another theory: "Mikva comes from a similar Hebrew word; the one meaning hope [*tikva*]." Either theory works well for a politician, especially one from Chicago. Ironically, one of Chicago's best-known political characters of the late nineteenth and early twentieth centuries had a similar name: "Bathhouse" John Coughlin.

Abner Joseph Mikva was born not in Democrat Bathhouse John's Chicago, but in Socialist *Victor Berger*'s Milwaukee, on January 21, 1926. His parents, Henry Abraham and Ida (Fishman) Mikva, were both immigrants from Russia. Abner's paternal grandparents, the product of an arranged marriage in the old country, never lived together in America. Grandpa Mikva lived in Monroe, Wisconsin, while his wife resided in Milwaukee. Mikva recalls that his grandfather would come back to Milwaukee for Passover and other major Jewish holidays, and that his grandmother "would throw food at him while she was serving and mutter under her breath." Apparently, grandpa, throwing off the shackles of the Old World,

wanted to sow his wild oats. Grandma Mikva, an old-fashioned woman, couldn't abide his roguishness and threw him out.

Abner Mikva grew up in a Yiddish-speaking, left-wing socialist home. His father, who worked during the Depression as a clerk for the Works Progress Administration (WPA), was a member of the International Workers Order. Though raised in a strictly Orthodox home, Henry Mikva became an atheist. He sent his son "Ab" to *kindershul* in order to learn to read and write Yiddish, but ordered the boy to "get up and leave the classroom" whenever the instruction turned to Hebrew or Torah. Mindful of his father's admonition, Ab did pick himself up and leave the room whenever the subject matter turned religious. On more than one occasion, the teacher admonished him by saying: "Boychik, come sit down! Don't listen to that *meshuggener* [crazy] father of yours!" But Ab, who even at a young age "knew where the power was," kept on walking. Toward the end of his life, as a tuberculosis patient at Denver's Jewish Consumptive Relief Society, Henry had a change of heart. In his last years, he became the facility's High Holiday *chazan* (cantor). Speaking of his "daughter the rabbi," the cantor quipped: "She is a Jewish miracle—that she should grow up in our household."

Following his graduation from high school in 1944, Abner Mikva joined the Army Air Corps and spent the war as a navigator with the Air Force Training Command. Enlisting as a private, he was mustered out in 1946 a second lieutenant. Following his discharge, Mikva spent two years (1946–47) as a student at the University of Wisconsin and two years (1947–48) at Washington University in St. Louis. Despite not having received his undergraduate degree, Mikva was admitted to the law school of the University of Chicago in 1949. Before entering law school, he married Zorita "Zoe" Wise, who became a schoolteacher. While studying law, Mikva found time to volunteer for the campaigns of Governor Adlai Stevenson and United

States Senator Paul Douglas. In 1951, he graduated with his J.D. From all indications, he was the shining star of his class: *cum laude*, Phi Beta Kappa, editor-in-chief of the law review, and Order of the Coif. Following his graduation, Mikva went to Washington, where he spent a year clerking for United States Supreme Court Justice Sherman Minton (1890–1965), a former Senator from Indiana. Upon his return to Chicago in 1952, Abner Mikva entered private law practice, becoming an associate of the late Justice Arthur Goldberg. He eventually joined the firm of Devoe, Shadur, Mikva, and Plotkin. The firm's practice dealt largely with labor issues. During his sixteen years with the firm (1952–68), Mikva worked extensively with the West Side Organization (WSO), "an early community-civil rights organization engaged in seeking to break down prejudice in employment, housing and schools." In the mid-sixties, acting as WSO chief counsel, Mikva became involved in a case that went all the way to the Illinois State Supreme Court, *West Side Organization* v. *Centennial Laundry Company* (215 N.E. 2d 443 1966). In this case, the members of WSO organized a protest against Centennial Laundry's discriminatory hiring practices. Centennial obtained an injunction prohibiting WSO from publicizing the laundry's hiring practices. Mikva successfully prosecuted the appeal, which resulted in the "vacating of the injunction, allowing damages to the West Side Organization for the wrongful issuance of the injunction." This was a landmark case not only in the area of labor law, but with regard to rights of free speech.

In 1956, Mikva decided to run for the Illinois State Legislature from the Twenty-third district, a traditionally liberal enclave centered in Hyde Park. The Twenty-third also included Woodlawn, the site of the University of Chicago and home of one of Mikva's political mentors, Saul Alinsky (1911–1972). A political organizer of legendary proportions, Alinsky authored two manuals in his chosen field: *Reveille for Radicals* and *Rules for Radicals: A Pragmatic Primer for Realistic Radicals*. Known nationally as the father of pragmatic radicalism, Alinsky taught Mikva his organizing techniques. When the young attorney decided to run for the legislature, Alinsky gave him a bit of advice: "You're going to have to develop two separate strategies, because what you've got to sell in Woodlawn won't sell in South Shore and Hyde Park, and what you've got to sell in South Shore and Hyde Park won't sell in Woodlawn." Running without the endorsement of the all-powerful Daley machine, Mikva nonetheless rode to victory.

As a member of the state legislature, Mikva was one of the "kosher-nostra," a group of like-minded liberals whose ranks included future United States Senators Adlai E. Stevenson III, and Paul Simon. Mikva, who was seated on the Judiciary Committee, was voted Outstanding Freshman Legislator by the Springfield press corps. During his decade in the Illinois House, Mikva sponsored measures dealing with crime control, mental health, civil rights, credit reform, and educational opportunities. At the end of each of his five terms in the State House, he was voted Best Legislator by the Independent Voters of Illinois.

In 1966, Mikva gave up his safe seat in order to challenge incumbent Democrat Barratt O'Hara for the Second Congressional District seat. O'Hara (1882–1969), had been a figure in Illinois politics for more than half a century. A veteran of the Spanish-American War (at fifteen, he enlisted and served as a corporal in Company I, Thirty-Third Michigan Volunteer Infantry, at the Siege of Santiago), O'Hara had been elected Lieutenant Governor of Illinois some thirteen years before Abner Mikva was born. Mikva, again without the endorsement of the Daley machine, nonetheless made a creditable showing, losing by less than 4 percentage points. Following his defeat, Mikva continued practicing law and began working on Mayor Richard Daley in order to get his political blessing for the 1968 race. In 1968, O'Hara was eighty-six years old and beginning to fail. Daley suggested that he should retire. When O'Hara refused "hizzoner's" recommendation, the Chicago mayor gave Mikva his "reluctant backing." This time, running on a platform calling for increased foreign aid, a guaranteed annual wage, fair-housing laws, abolition of the House Un-American Activities Committee, and recognition of the People's Republic of China, Mikva won the Democratic primary in a landslide. In the November election, he defeated the Republican challenger with 65 percent of the vote.

Although Mikva was the new kid on the block in Congress, he was not without old friends. Ironically, three men representing California districts had all been raised within a half-mile of Mikva's home back in Milwaukee: two liberals, Phillip Burton and Fortney "Pete" Stark, and the ultra-conservative John Schmitz. The late San Francisco-area Representative Phil Burton (1926–1983), the husband of the late Representative *Sala Burton*, was, during his congressional career, one of the true powers in the House. Pete Stark, who made a fortune in banking before entering Congress, remained a stalwart liberal after more than twenty years in Congress. Schmitz, who represented an Orange County district and replaced Alabama Governor George Wallace as the American Party's presidential candidate in 1972, was an acknowledged member of the ultra-right John Birch Society. When the four got together to share old memories and the impact that growing up in Depression-era, socialist Milwaukee had on them, Schmitz remarked: "Well, it had an effect on me, but apparently not the same as on you guys."

Abner Mikva made an immediate impact in the House of Representatives. As one of the Congress's "most determined . . . opponents of the Vietnam war," he often found himself denounced on the floor by hawks like Representative Wayne L. Hays. Never at a loss for acidic commentary, Hays called Mikva both "an emissary from Hanoi" and "a dupe of the Viet Cong." Because of his consistent opposition to increased war appropriations and his efforts to prohibit the bombing of dams and dikes in North Vietnam, Mikva was put under surveillance by army intelligence officers. Needless to say, when he learned of the army's interest in his person, he was outraged; he called for a thorough public investigation. Taking the House floor, he spoke with anger and emotion: "There must be a complete purging of every command official who was responsible for establishing and operating this spy network. I, for one, would urge the resignation of every such command officer, in the interests of restoring America's credibility in its own military." The surveillance effort came to a quick denouement. In his first term, Mikva was also appointed to the Brown Commission, which provided the main impetus for efforts to recodify the criminal laws of the United States.

Growing up in Milwaukee, Abner Mikva had experienced little anti-Semitism. That was to come later: "The first time I really experienced it [anti-Semitism] was in Congress. It came in the person of Speaker John McCormack, who, every time I would seek recognition would say: 'THE GENTLEMAN FROM NEW YAWK!' The parliamentarian would have to lean over and remind him that I came from Illinois. It was either my politics or my religion that made him assume that I came from New York. It was probably a little of each, but mostly the latter."

Although Mikva was an active legislator during his first term, he had serious reservations about Congress. "What have we done for the people?" he asked one reporter after completing his first term. "What has Congress really done about the real, real problems? . . . The quality of life—is it any better for Congress having met two years? Nothing came out of the Congress for the people—nothing like Social Security, nothing like Medicare. . . . Here I am in Congress, and now I find that Congress ain't where it's at."

After the 1970 census, Mayor Richard Daley directed that Mikva's white, largely Jewish district be reapportioned out of existence. Heeding Daley's directive, the state commission merged Mikva's Hyde Park power base into the predominantly black First Congressional District, represented by the former Olympic gold medal winner (1932 and 1936 games) Ralph Metcalf. Deciding that he did not want to deprive Chicago of a "much-needed Black Congressman," Mikva moved his family north to Evanston in order to run in the newly created Tenth District. Upon announcing his candidacy for the Tenth District seat, Mikva told the press: "Any decision to end the career of an elected official ought to be made by the people, not by judicial fiat." Surviving charges of being a "carpetbagger," Mikva won the Democratic primary, but lost the general election to Samuel Young, who rode to victory on Richard Nixon's coattails.

During the next two years, Mikva practiced law with the Chicago firm of D'Ancona, Pflaum, Whatt & Riskind, accepted an appointment as adjunct professor of law at Northwestern University, and served as vice president of the liberal Americans for Democratic Action. In 1973, he began gearing up for a rematch with Samuel Young. The Tenth, a largely Republican district, was not Mikva's for the taking. It took a lot of money and a lot of organization. In 1974, he succeeded in defeating Young by a narrow margin. Two years later, "in one of the most expensive and hard-fought Congressional races in the country," Mikva effectively turned back a gerrymandering attempt by Mayor Daley and defeated Young by 201 votes. Remarkably, while the Democrat Mikva was squeaking to victory, presidential candidate Gerald Ford was carrying the district by more than 60,000 votes. In his last election, Mikva defeated newcomer John Porter by a slightly larger margin of 1,200 votes. When Mikva left Congress to accept a seat on the United States Court of Appeals, he was replaced by the Republican Porter, who was still in Congress as of 1999. A pro-choice, pro-gun control moderate who supports the National Endowment for the Arts, Porter entered the 106th Congress as Chairman of the Appropriations Subcommittee on Health and Human Services and Education.

Abner Mikva was considered the darling of the liberals. As head of the Democratic Study Group, he was the acknowledged leader of the liberal faction in the House. This group was responsible for "keeping Democrats and other coalitions abreast of weekly legislative action." They published a weekly study guide concerning the current week's legislation on the floor. Among Ab Mivka's most important accomplishments was acting as floor-manager in the debate about giving eighteen-year-olds the right to vote—an effort which resulted in the passage and ratification of the Twenty-sixth Amendment to the Constitution in June 1971.

Mikva led the fight for a stronger code of ethics for members of Congress. By means of the law he enacted (since revised and strengthened), the outside income for members of Congress was limited to 15 percent of their congressional salaries. The bill also eliminated office slush-fund accounts and, for the first time, required members to disclose their financial holdings. Mikva also proposed a measure for partial public financing of congressional elections by which contributions of $100 or less would be matched with monies drawn from the voluntary tax check-off fund. Defeated in 1978, this proposal is still brought up during every session of Congress.

Ever interested in reforming and streamlining government, Mikva was responsible for introducing the first "sunset" bill. Although never acted on, this imaginative proposal would have caused federal regulatory agencies to self-destruct—go completely out of existence—unless they could justify their continued existence. The bill gave regulatory agencies seven years to prove their intrinsic worth; if they did not, they were automatically out of business.

Although a political realist, Mikva often acted like a starry-eyed idealist. Case in point: his efforts to eliminate handguns. Throughout his congressional career, Mikva regularly submitted legislation prohibiting "the manufacture, sale and distribution of handguns in the United States except for use by the police, military and licensed pistol clubs." Each time Mikva's proposal went to committee for hearings, the National Rifle Association would lobby Congress furiously to make sure the measure never saw the light of day. "No other piece of legislation, no change in our law, no amount of resources for law enforcement could have a greater impact on crime," Mikva told his colleagues. So thoroughly did Mikva outrage the NRA that when President Carter nominated him for a seat on the United States Court of Appeals for the District of Columbia, the well-heeled gun lobby spent more than six months and $1 million in an effort to block his nomination. During the Senate confirmation hearings, the NRA spokesman claimed that Mikva's well-known antipathy for weapons would make it virtually impossible for him to be objective in hearing cases dealing with guns. The Senate wound up confirming Mikva by a vote of 58 to 31.

Abner Mikva resigned from the House of Representatives on September 26, 1979, in order to take his seat on what is commonly referred to as the second most powerful court in the land. President Carter selected him from among a list of more than two hundred prospective candidates. In nominating Abner Mikva, Carter was returning to the old tradition of elevating members of Congress to the federal bench. After eleven years on the court, Mikva became the court's chief judge.

During his first congressional stint in Washington, Mikva brought his family with him to Washington. During his second tour of duty, Zoe and the three girls remained in Evanston, where Mrs. Mikva continued teaching school. With Mikva's elevation to the federal judiciary (and with their daughters now grown, Mary and Laurie both having become attorneys, and Rachel, a Reform rabbi), Zoe Mikva moved once again moved to Washington, taking a job with the Advocacy Institute, a Washington-based group that helps community groups organize.

The United States Court of Appeals is quite often a stepping-stone for appointment to the Supreme Court. In the past decade, Antonin Scalia, Clarence Thomas, and Ruth Bader Ginsburg have made that transition. Not Mikva. Realizing that he was "too old, too white, too male, and too liberal" to ever be named to the highest court in the land, Mikva shocked his colleagues by announcing his retirement in August 1994, in order to become President Clinton's new White House Counsel. In its assessment of this development, the *New York Times* noted that Clinton had chosen a man who would likely be "the most scholarly White House Counsel of the modern era." Mikva remained at the White House for a little more than a year, being replaced in September 1995 by Vice President Al Gore's chief of staff, Jack Quinn. During that year as White House Counsel, Mikva was faced with the Whitewater hearings and Travelgate. News of his retirement led conservative columnists to claim that he had seen how much trouble the President was in and decided to bail out. "Not so," said Mikva. "It's just time to retire and spend some time with my family, write a few books, and teach a course or two."

In summing up the career of Judge Mikva, Morton Kondracke of the *New Republic* wrote: "Abner Mikva is different from many other liberals because he doesn't only love mankind; he loves individual people, too."

References

Interview with Abner Mikva, July 1992.
Almanac of American Politics (1978–82 editions).
Chicago Daily News, May 28, 1977.
Chicago Sun Times, March 13, 1977.
Current Biography, 1980, pp. 259–262.
District Lawyer, May–June, 1980.
New York Times, August 17, 1994.

MILLER, JOHN RIPIN (1938–): *Republican from Washington; served four terms in the House (Ninety-ninth through One Hundred and Second Congress; January 3, 1985-January 3, 1993).*

When John Miller was a boy growing up in Manhattan, he attended the Society for Ethical Culture School and P.S. 6. One day, the fourth-grader was reading a geography book. The only thing he remembers about the book was a page about the Pacific Northwest—specifically the Puget Sound area. Captivated by a picture of "rain forests and misty rain," Miller read the caption. It stated that the climate in the area was temperate. Not knowing what the word "temperate" meant, he tried "rolling it around on my tongue" and then went to a dictionary. There he discovered that "temperate" meant "neither too hot nor too cool." The ten-year-old liked the sound of that. At dinner that night, he proudly announced to his parents, Henry (Hyman) and Paula Miller, that when he grew up, he was going to live in Seattle.

"Had they merely said 'that's nice,'" Miller recalls, "that probably would have been the end of it all." Instead, the Millers "patronized" their son and told him "Well, you'll get over it." Their attitude got on his nerves. The very next day, at breakfast, he once again proclaimed, "You know, I'm still going to do that—that Seattle thing." An idea was thereby planted that would eventually take root and flourish nearly two decades later. For indeed, John Miller did move to Seattle. What he did not know at the time was that he was merely following in the footsteps of his first American relative, who had settled in the Pacific Northwest nearly a half-century earlier.

Solomon Ripinski (1850–ca. 1938), John Miller's maternal great-grandfather, was a native of Rypin, Poland. He arrived in the United States in the late 1870s and headed west to Cincinnati. From Cincinnati he traveled south to New Orleans, before eventually winding up in Alaska by the late 1880s. There he settled in the town of Haines, where he became an artist, judge, and the local postmaster. A staunch Republican, he served as a delegate to the national convention in 1896. He died in the late 1930s and was buried on Mount Ripinski, which the territorial government had named after him during the last years of his life.

From Rypin to Alaska, the family saga continued. John Miller's maternal grandmother came from Berlin just before the First World War and married a son of Solomon Ripinski, who by that time had shortened the family name to Ripin. The Ripins' daughter, Paula, married Henry (Hyman) Miller, an immigrant from Latvia. Miller had come to America in 1903 at the age of eleven. The Millers established residence in Manhattan, where Henry was an attorney. Their son, John Ripin Miller, was born in New York City on May 23, 1938.

Although Henry Miller was Jewish, virtually no vestige of the religion was practiced, observed, or discussed in the home. The Millers belonged to the Society for Ethical Culture, where young John received his "moral education." The only Jewish recollections John Miller has from his childhood are two or three Passover seders, at which his father led the service. Miller remembers being "amazed that he [his father] could read the Hebrew—or at least fake it so well."

Following a New York City public school education, John Miller headed to Lewisberg, Pennsylvania, where he entered Bucknell University. Following his graduation in 1959 (*cum laude*, Phi Beta Kappa) Miller spent a year in the United States Army, serving as an infantry captain. In 1961, Miller entered the Yale University School of Law, from which he received an LL.B. in 1964. During Miller's three years in New Haven, he became interested in Judaism. Although Jewish by birth, he did not consider himself a full-fledged member of the House of Israel. One of Miller's friends at Yale was an Orthodox Jew from the Bronx, New York, who helped him "discover" his religion. He began going to the friend's home in New York and occasionally accompanying him to synagogue.

Toward the end of his second year of law school, Miller began thinking about taking a summerz internship at a law firm. "But where," he asked himself, "should I apply?" Suddenly, the old dream about Seattle came to mind; Miller wound up sending out more than a hundred letters to law firms in the Seattle area. From the hundred-odd letters, he wound up getting precisely seven responses. He hopped into his car, drove out to Seattle, and interviewed with the seven firms. When he was finally offered an internship at the princely sum of $75 a week, Miller took the job. Following his graduation from Yale in 1964, he moved permanently to the Pacific Northwest.

Miller spent his first three years working as an assistant state attorney general in Olympia, Washington. From 1968 to 1969, he practiced law with the firm of Johnson, Johnson, and Inslee. The following year he became a partner in the newly created firm of Miller, Howell and Watson. In 1972, John Miller was elected as a nonpartisan to the Seattle City Council. Upon his election, he terminated his relationship with Miller, Howell, and Watson. Miller served on the City Council from 1972 to 1980, during which time he developed a reputation for being an environmentally conscious legislator. During his last two years on the council (1978–80), his colleagues elected him City Council president. Rotating off the council in 1981, John Miller entered the next phase of his professional life, becoming both an adjunct professor of state and local government law at the University of Puget Sound Law School and a political commentator for KIRO Television, the CBS affiliate in Seattle.

While living and working in Seattle, John Miller kept his promise to himself and became much more involved with the Jewish religion. He joined the Reform Temple Beth Am and became sufficiently versed in Jewish history and tradition to serve as a Sunday school teacher for children in the sixth, eighth, and twelfth grades. While teaching at the University of Puget Sound School of Law, John Miller met June Marion Makar, a native of Pittsburgh. The two were married in June 1984, while John Miller was beginning to campaign for Congress. They have one son, Brett, born on April 26, 1988, just a month before John Miller's fiftieth birthday.

In early 1984, Joel Pritchard, the Republican incumbent from Washington's First Congressional District, announced his impending retirement after twelve years in office.

(Pritchard eventually became Washington State Lieutenant Governor.) That set up a rip-roaring Republican primary that attracted no less than half-a-dozen candidates. The First Congressional District, like many districts in the Pacific Northwest, has "strong environmental tendencies" and a rather large and devoted corps of peace activists. "Shaped like a butterfly hovering over Seattle, the 1st encompasses most of the city's northern suburbs, a collection of largely middle-class communities from northern King County up into Snohomish County, almost to Everett." The district's political mix includes both liberals and an active Christian Fundamentalist community. Although nominally Republican, the average district voter is both middle-of-the-road and not terribly partisan-minded.

Because of the great name recognition he had garnered from his three years on television— and a failed 1980 race for state Attorney General—John Miller managed to come in first in the Republican primary. Second place (25 percent) went to "liberal" Republican Sue Gould. Miller's opponent in the November general election was Democrat Brock Evans, the longtime Washington lobbyist for the Sierra Club. Evans had the advantage of carrying not one but two well-known names in the Seattle area: Dan Evans was a popular Governor and Senator; Brock Adams, later Secretary of Transportation, was then a popular local Congressman. On election day, Miller emerged victorious, capturing 56 percent of the vote. Because he was never widely popular with the voters of his district, Miller's 1984 percentage proved to be the highest of his eight-year career. In his next three reelection bids, he would win by the rather narrow margins of 51, 55, and 52 percent.

John Miller was a decidedly moderate Republican, voting with the Reagan and Bush administrations anywhere from 44 percent to 64 percent of the time. During his eight years in the House, Miller garnered liberal Americans for Democratic Action ratings of between 25 percent and 60 percent—quite high for a Republican. He was originally assigned to the committees on Foreign Affairs, and Merchant Marine and Fisheries. In his last term, Miller was offered a seat on the prestigious House Budget Committee. Where one might assume that a Seattle-area representative would remain on

Merchant Marine and Fisheries and give up Foreign Affairs (the former has a more direct bearing on key constituencies in the maritime First District), Miller decided just the opposite. His decision to remain on Foreign Affairs while jettisoning Merchant Marine showed both his "pattern of bucking political convention" and his growing affinity for international relations.

During the 1980s, Miller made a name for himself in the House as both a staunch anti-Communist and an outspoken supporter of the contras—the forces fighting against the Marxist government of Nicaragua. His involvement with "issues concerning freedom and democracy" led him from Lithuania, where he stood on street-corners passing out copies of the United States Constitution, to Moscow, where he met with Soviet dissidents and refuseniks. He was also a cofounder of the Ad Hoc Group in Support of Democracy in Chile during the darkest days of the Pinochet regime.

As mentioned above, Miller could not always be counted to go along with the policies and proposals of the Republican administration. He voted against the MX missile in 1985, in spite of a "direct appeal from Reagan." He also supported South African sanctions, opposed loosening gun control laws, and voted to override President Bush's veto of the Family Leave Act in the One Hundred and First Congress. In the Ninety-ninth Congress, Miller and fellow Republican *Benjamin Gilman* successfully offered an amendment to a 1985 foreign aid bill barring U.S. aid to any country that supported terrorism.

After serving four terms in the House, John Miller decided not to seek renomination. Although he considered being a member of Congress "an absolutely fabulous job," he also sensed that he was shortchanging his son. On the day he was interviewed in his Capitol Hill office, he had just learned that his then–four-year-old son had taken his first successful stroke in a swimming pool. He felt badly about missing it. "Congress is not a family-friendly place," he

noted. "Look at most of the House leadership. They are either older men with grown children or single guys without families to worry about. It's not a question of how you prioritize your time. If you just do your job, you won't have the opportunity to have a normal family life." Before leaving the House of Representatives in 1993, Miller joined Ohio Democrat Dennis Eckart in creating a bipartisan task force on family issues vis-à-vis the Congress. At the beginning of the One Hundred and Fourth Congress in January 1995, newly elected Speaker Newt Gingrich announced that he would do everything in his power to make Congress a "family-friendly institution." As of late 1999, Congress had yet to reform itself along these lines.

Miller's stated reason for leaving Congress was met with skepticism in some quarters. Speaking on a radio talk show in Seattle, congressional term limit advocate Sherry Bockwinkel claimed that Miller was retiring "so he [can] pocket the $700,000 sitting in his reelection campaign treasury." Miller strenuously denied Bockwinkel's charge. An editorial in the *Seattle Times* supported Miller's decision, stating that "Bockwinkel's comments reflect a serious lack of understanding of the law and what Miller has had to do over the years to get reelected in a heavily Democratic district. . . . One possible reason for Bockwinkel's attack may be that Miller refused to support her most recent effort . . . to limit terms to six years."

John, June, and Brett Miller currently reside in the Seattle area, where the former Congressman is involved in a wide assortment of professional and community activities. He is once again making an effort to learn to read Hebrew.

References

Interview with John Miller, Washington, D.C., July 1992.
Almanac of American Politics (1988–94 editions).
Politics in America (1988–94 editions).

MORSE, LEOPOLD (1831–1892): *Democrat from Massachusetts; served five terms in the House (Forty-fifth through Forty-eighth Congress; March 4, 1877–March 3, 1885; Fiftieth Congress; March 4, 1887–March 3, 1889).*

America was precisely one hundred years old before New England got around to electing its first Jew to Congress. Historically speaking, New England trailed behind the nation's other regions in electing Jews to any office at all. The five New England states combined have been responsible for sending only ten Jews to Congress in the past 120 years, and of these, Senator *William S. Cohen* of Maine had a non-Jewish mother.

Boston's role in electing Jews to any public office has been particularly spotty. In 1720, Isaac Lopez was elected city constable; in 1805, Judah Hays was elected to the office of fire-warden. The first practicing Jew elected to public office in post-1776 Boston appears to have been attorney Godfrey Morse (1846–1911), who was elected to the Boston School Committee in 1875. Morse, an 1867 graduate of Harvard Law School, went on to serve three years (1882–85) as assistant counsel of the United States in the Court of Commissioners of *Alabama* Claims, while contemporaneously serving as president of the Boston Common Council. A year after Godfrey's election to the school committee, his older brother, Leopold Morse, became the first Jewish member of Congress from any of the New England states.

The Morse (originally Maas) *mishpachah* (family)—seven brothers and two sisters—hailed from Wachenheim in Rhenish Bavaria. There, on August 15, 1831, Leopold Maas was born. In 1848, Leopold's eldest brother, Moses, emigrated to the United States, blazing a trail for the rest of his siblings, all of whom would eventually settle in Boston. Settling originally in Sandwich, New Hampshire, Moses, like thousands of other Central European immigrants, became a peddler. Befriended by two local families, he was encouraged to anglicize his family name. Thus "Maas" became "Morse." A year later, with the help of these local families, he was able to send for his younger brother Leopold.

Arriving in Sandwich, Leopold lived with his brother's friends while he went to a local school and learned English. When he arrived in Boston in 1851, he immediately found employment in

the clothing store of one Henry Haverman. In 1854, with the help of a loan provided by their New Hampshire friends, Moses and Leopold opened up their own small clothing concern on North Street. Before the year was out, Moses died, leaving the twenty-three-year-old Leopold to carry on alone. Over the next decade, Leopold greatly expanded his enterprise. In 1864, along with partner Ferdinand Strauss, he organized the Leopold Morse Company, which both manufactured and sold men's clothing.

Morse got a big break right after the end of the Civil War. Learning that the army was going to be auctioning off a vast array of surplus coats in Philadelphia, Morse borrowed money, traveled to Philadelphia, and wound up purchasing some five thousand coats. He apparently sold enough of them in Philadelphia to repay the loan, and then sold the remainder upon his return to Boston, thus realizing a significant profit. Before the end of the decade, the Leopold Morse Company had become the "most prosperous concern of its kind in New England."

Although a lifelong member of Temple Israel and a generous subscriber to innumerable Jewish charities, Leopold Morse married Georgianna Hay, the Episcopalian daughter of a prominent Boston attorney. Together they had two sons, who were apparently raised in the religion of their mother.

Leopold Morse's initial entry into the world of elective politics met with disaster; he was defeated for Congress in both 1870 and 1872. Both times he ran as a Democrat in a highly Republican district. To make matters worse, he wasn't even a resident of the district in which he ran. Morse received a "consolation prize" by being named as a delegate to the 1876 Democratic National Convention in St. Louis. Upon his return from St. Louis, he ran once again for Congress from the same Republican-dominated district; this time, against all odds, he won. Morse was reelected three more times (1878, 1880, and 1882). In the last of his four consecutive terms (Forty-eighth Congress), he served as chairman of the House Committee on Expenditures in the Department of the Navy, a particularly important post for a Boston-area representative. Morse declined renomination in 1884, and spent the next two years back in Boston, tending to his business affairs and founding the Boston Home for Infirm Hebrews and Orphanage, the first institution of its kind in New England.

Leopold Morse was returned to Congress for one last term in 1886 (Fiftieth Congress). By this point, he had become something of a national figure. This should not be surprising, for during the entire time Morse served in Congress, he was either the only Jew serving in that body (Forty-fifth Congress) or one of a very select few—together with *Edwin Einstein* (Forty-sixth Congress), *Julius Houseman* (Forty eighth Congress), and *Isidore Raynor* (Fiftieth Congress), and Senator *Benjamin Franklin Jonas* (served Forty-sixth to Forty-eighth Congress).

Leopold Morse died in Boston on December 15, 1892. He was sixty-one years old. At the time of his death, it was rumored that President Grover Cleveland had been considering him for the position of Secretary of War in his newly formed cabinet but had changed his mind when the issue of Morse's religion was repeatedly raised. According to what passed for "common knowledge" among political insiders, Morse had died of a broken heart.

Upon his death, the Massachusetts State Legislature officially changed the name of the Boston Home for Infirm Hebrews and Orphans to the Leopold Morse Home for Infirm Hebrews and Orphanage. He was buried in the Mount Auburn Cemetery in Cambridge, Massachusetts.

Leopold Morse's younger brother, Godfrey, was quite possibly the first Jewish Bostonian to graduate from both Harvard and Harvard Law School. As an undergraduate, he served as both editor of the *Harvard Advocate* and manager of the school's first crew to be sent abroad to row against Oxford. He went on to become president of the Leopold Morse Home, as well as chairman of the Massachusetts Democratic State Committee. He also served as the first president of the Federated Jewish Charities and received an honorary Master of Arts degree from Tufts College in 1900. Married in 1907 to Janet Rosenfield, he died childless in Dresden, Germany, in 1911, at age sixty-five.

References

Albert Ehrenfried, *A Chronicle of Boston Jewry from Colonial Settlement to 1900* (Boston: Ehrenfried, 1963).

Biographical Directory of the United States Congress, 1774–1989, pp. 1540–41.

Universal Jewish Encyclopedia.

MULTER, ABRAHAM JACOB (1900–1986):

Democrat from New York; served ten terms in the House (Eightieth through Eighty-ninth Congress; November 4, 1947–December 31, 1967).

Of the 534 Senators and Representatives listed in the 88th edition of the *Congressional Directory*, none has a longer biographical entry than Abraham Jacob Multer. While the typical entry, composed by the members themselves, runs about a dozen lines, Multer's is easily four times as long. Encapsulated within this rather prolix document are the achievements and associations of a public life; a life that would shortly thereafter bring the veteran Brooklyn politician under fire from New York's Liberal Party and his colleagues in the House of Representatives.

Abraham Multer was the third of Max and Emma (Rock) Multer's eight children. He was born in New York City on December 24, 1900. Raised in Coney Island in a poor family, Multer worked even while attending grade school. He graduated from Boys' High School in Brooklyn, took evening classes at the City College of New York, and graduated from Brooklyn Law School in 1921. Multer served as managing clerk for the law firm of Judge Abram C. Ellenbogen. Following his admission to the New York bar in 1923, he went into private practice. Over the next quarter century, Multer was associated with two firms: Multer, Nova & Seymour, and Rayfiel and Multer. The Rayfiel of the latter firm was *Leo F. Rayfiel*, a member of the Congressional Minyan. Ironically, Abraham Multer would eventually replace him in the House of Representatives in November 1947. Multer was primarily a litigation attorney who specialized in corporate and commercial law. According to a lifelong friend, he was "an old-fashioned kind of lawyer who could handle any kind of case that came along." Through his legal practice in Brooklyn, and his many community activities, he came to the attention of the Kings County Democratic Party.

In June 1925, Abraham Multer married Bertha Leff. They had two sons, Robert K. and Howard C., both of whom would graduate from Cornell University. As his law practice grew, Multer, like many ambitious young men, became involved in local Democratic Party politics. He joined the Kings Highway Democratic Club, rising through its ranks: from chairman of the club's civil service committee to secretary to twenty years as its president. Multer eventually became Democratic leader of Brooklyn's Second Assembly District.

Coming to the attention of Governor *Herbert Henry Lehman*, Multer was named a special attorney general of New York State. He began attending state Democratic conventions in 1936. With the entry of the United States into World War II at the end of 1941, Multer, who was exempt from service by reason of age, joined the United States Coast Guard, serving for the duration of the war.

After the war, Multer became special counsel to New York Mayor William O'Dwyer. At one time, O'Dwyer had been the Brooklyn district attorney, best known for his 1930s roundup of members of Louis "Lepke" Buchalter's notorious Murder, Inc. By the time Multer was named special counsel, O'Dwyer was suspected of having organized-crime connections himself, most notably with Frank Costello. O'Dwyer was said to have done favors for Costello—alias Francisco Castaglia, alias Frank Severio—after the career criminal had taken over the rackets from his former boss, Charles "Lucky" Luciano. In a sense, O'Dwyer set the tone for Multer. Not that Multer had any criminal connections; rather, as his later political colleagues would claim, Multer had the unfortunate habit of "supporting in vigorous House debate the interests of his close friends in private business."

On September 13, 1947, Fourteenth District Representative *Leo Rayfiel* resigned his seat, having been appointed a judge of the United States District Court for the Eastern District of New York. Multer, Rayfiel's former law partner, entered the special election, winning an easy victory. He was sworn in as a member of the Eightieth Congress on November 17, 1947. Almost immediately, he had to start campaigning for a full two-year term. In the 1948 election, Multer ran with the endorsement of the Democrat, Republican, and Liberal parties. His chief opponent was the American Labor Party's candidate, Lee Pressman, former counsel to the leftist Congress of Industrial Organizations. Multer swamped Pressman, and went on to represent his Brooklyn district for the next twenty years. Through seniority, Multer eventually rose to become ranking Democrat on the House Banking and Currency Committee, chaired by the legendary Wright Patman.

Multer was sometimes criticized for supporting causes that appeared to benefit his friends and benefactors. In one such case, he led the successful opposition to a bill authorizing a $400 million public subway system for the District of Columbia, while enjoying a close personal relationship with O. Roy Chalk, the president of D.C. Transit System, Inc., a private bus line. Multer also came under fire for "sponsoring a major revision of liquor laws in the District of Columbia . . . while maintaining a close personal friendship with Milton S. Kronheim, a major Washington liquor distributor."

Throughout his twenty-year tenure in the House of Representatives, Multer regularly won reelection as the candidate of both the Democrats and the Liberals. In 1966, in his last race, the Liberal Party withheld its endorsement, charging that Multer was "dirty." They came out with a laundry list of offenses that made the front page of the *New York Times*. They accused Multer of everything from engaging in a questionable Florida land deal to organizing a bank in the Bahamas "as a tax haven for American accounts." In January 1964, Abe Multer's name came up during congressional hearings into the sordid dealings of President Lyndon Johnson's former aide, Bobby Baker. During the hearings, it was alleged that Multer, a partner in a highly lucrative Milwaukee-based group called MAGIC (Mortgage Guarantee Insurance Company), had used his influence to get a "hos-pitable hearing" in Washington. Multer, known for his "volatile bursts of temper," angrily denied all charges, and threatened to slap the Liberal Party with a defamation of character suit. Nothing ever came of his threat, and Multer was reelected one last time.

In November 1967, Abraham Multer was elected to the New York Supreme Court. He served on the court until January 1, 1977. Two years later, he was named a special referee of the Brooklyn Appellate Division. He served in that capacity until 1984, at which time he retired from public life. Following his retirement, the Multers moved from Brooklyn to West Hartford, Connecticut, where their son Howard lived and worked as an electrical engineer.

Abraham Multer was active in Jewish communal organizations, serving as president of B'nai Zion. In 1962, he received an honorary Doctor of Laws degree from Yeshiva University. Multer died at the Hebrew Home and Hospital in Hartford on November 4, 1986. He was survived by his wife and two sons, two sisters, a brother, and seven grandchildren.

References

Biographical Directory of the United States Congress, 1774–1989, p. 1549.

New York Times, November 3, 1948; April 1, 1964; November 11, 1986.

NADLER, JERROLD LEWIS (1947–): *Democrat from New York; has served four terms in the House (One Hundred and Third Congress through One Hundred and Sixth Congress; November 4, 1992–present).*

When Jerrold Nadler was growing up on his father's chicken farm in New Jersey, there were two names "never pronounced except with disdain;" one was Dwight D. Eisenhower, and the other was Ezra Taft Benson, Eisenhower's Secretary of Agriculture. Jerrold's father, Emanuel Nadler, was a "dyed-in-the-wool Democrat," who told his son that these two were making it "impossible for chicken farmers to produce eggs without losing money." Emanuel Nadler's chicken farm went under, and the family was forced to move to Brooklyn. Out of that experience came yet another "dyed-in-the-wool Democrat."

Jerrold Lewis Nadler, the son of Emanuel and Miriam (Schreiber) Nadler, was born in Bensonhurst, Brooklyn, on June 13, 1947. He was raised as an Orthodox Jew and attended the Crown Heights Yeshiva. While attending Stuyvesant High School, Jerry ran for president of the student government. His campaign literature was written by lifelong friend Richard Gottfried, who would, years later, vie with Nadler for an open seat in Congress. From Stuyvesant, Nadler went off to Columbia University, where he was a Pulitzer scholar. During his second year, Columbia became the scene of the student riots "immortalized" in the book (and later, movie) *The Strawberry Statement.* In 1968, Nadler organized antiwar students for Eugene McCarthy in the New Hampshire presidential primary. A born activist, he quickly moved into other areas of community concern, "warning tenants about lead paint and campaigning for *Ted Weiss* in one of his early unsuccessful bids for Congress." Nadler was exempted from the military draft due to severe asthma.

Following his graduation from Columbia in 1970, Nadler went to work as an assistant branch manager of an Off-Track Betting office. Nights, he attended law school at Fordham University in

the Bronx. While at Fordham, he found time to work as both legislative assistant to Richard Gottfried, who had been elected to the New York State Assembly, and as a law clerk. In 1976, a year before he received his law degree, Nadler narrowly won a race for an open seat in the State Assembly.

During his sixteen years in Albany, Jerry Nadler was its "leading expert in mass transit and its most vocal proponent for the protection of blue collar jobs in manufacturing through the development of port and rail freight infrastructure." Nadler became convinced that the increased use of rail freight was essential "both as a means to reduce truck traffic and pollution and to preserve manufacturing jobs." He founded and served as the first chair of the Assembly's Subcommittee on Mass Transit and Rail Freight. He also served at various times as chair of the Ethics Committee, the Consumer Affairs and Protection Committee, and the Committee on Corporations, Authorities and Commissions.

From his first day in Albany, Nadler was known as a liberal's liberal. He authored laws in the areas of child support, domestic violence, and day care. Devoted to women's issues, he was the only man ever named Assembly member of the Year by the National Organization for Women. Nadler also became well known among his colleagues for his tenacity and single-mindedness; on one occasion he debated whether Jewish tradition condoned the death penalty, "rattling off memorized passages from the Talmud in [Aramaic] in a duel with Assemblyman Dov Hikind . . . much to the chagrin of the Assembly stenographer." He also developed a reputation for being "a terrible nudnik," according to former Assembly Speaker Saul Weprin, who qualified his statement by adding "but in a good sense; when [Jerry] has something on his mind that he wants to get done, he'll never leave you alone." "Jerry may be a little long-winded," one colleague noted; "every one of his questions has 16 parts."

As Assemblyman, Nadler ran two unsuccessful races for other offices: a 1985 campaign for

Manhattan Borough President, and a 1989 race for New York Comptroller. On September 14, 1992, two days before the Democratic primary, Representative *Ted Weiss* died from heart disease. Weiss (1927–1992) had represented the Seventeenth Congressional District for eight terms. After the 1990 reapportionment, Weiss's district was altered and renumbered. The new district, the Eighth, comprises the most heavily Jewish section in America. Three-fifths of its population resides on Manhattan's West Side, the rest in Brooklyn. The Eighth contains much of what makes New York a world-class city: Wall Street, both the Twin Towers and the Empire State Building, the Broadway Theater district, and Greenwich Village, as well as Madison Square Garden, New York University, and Clinton—better known as Hell's Kitchen. In its Brooklyn precincts, the Eighth consists of Brighton Beach, Coney Island, and the Hasidic enclaves of Crown Heights and Williamsburg. Much of the new Eighth District had belonged to Representative *Stephen Solarz*. It was widely assumed that he would challenge Weiss in the Democratic primary. But Solarz realized that his "strong positions for the Gulf War and U.S. engagement in Asia" probably would have hurt him in Manhattan. Instead, he opted to run in the "minority-Hispanic" Twelfth District, and lost. Two days after his death, Ted Weiss won the Democratic primary with nearly 90 percent of the vote, thereby permitting party leaders to choose his successor for the fall election. As soon as word of Weiss's death hit the papers, Jerry Nadler was on the phone with the party leadership, lobbying for the seat.

Nadler competed in a six-way race for the Democratic nomination, which in the Eighth District was tantamount to victory. Included in the pack were Ted Weiss's widow Sonya, State Senator Franz Leichter, Councilwoman Ronnie Eldridge (the wife of columnist Jimmy Breslin), and Nadler's old friend Assemblyman Richard Gottfried. The best-known candidate, former Representative *Bella Abzug*, threw her support to Eldridge. It quickly became a heated race between Gottfried, Eldridge, and Nadler. When James R. McManus, "a fourth-generation scion of Tammany Hall," switched his political club's votes to Nadler, Gottfried was finished. The final tally gave Nadler 62 percent to Eldridge's 21 percent.

Within days, Nadler was in Washington, filling out the unexpired days of Weiss's term. From November to the end of December, he represented both the Eighth District and the old Seventeenth. Because of his early entry in the House, Nadler had a bit more seniority than the other members of his freshman class.

On January 3, Nadler took the oath of office with the other members of the class of 1992. He was assigned to Public Works and Transportation, and Judiciary. His freshman colleagues also elected him second vice president of their class. In his eight years in the House, Nadler has consistently been one of that body's two or three most liberal (and corpulent) members, easily following in the political footsteps of the late Representative Weiss. One of his first acts in the One Hundred and Third Congress was to sponsor Stephen Solarz's Religious Freedom Restoration Act, meant "to reverse a Supreme Court decision allowing the Army to bar the wearing of yarmulkes." The measure passed.

Nadler has been a strong supporter of both gay and women's rights, and favors less spending on defense and more on the poor. From his seat on Judiciary, he has opposed the death penalty, and "tried unsuccessfully to replace the federal death penalty provisions in the 1994 crime bill with a requirement for life imprisonment without parole."

When Congress debated the controversial "three strikes and you're out" provision in the crime bill, Nadler inserted language that would allow inmates older than seventy who had served thirty years to be released if they posed no threat to society. Jerry Nadler represents the largest gay constituency in America. As such, he has been a watchdog. He took umbrage when the Clinton administration failed to lift the ban on homosexuals in the military: "The new 'don't ask, don't tell, don't be caught' policy represents a reaffirmation of the official bigotry by the United States, with changes only in the methods by which that bigotry will be enforced." When the 1994 education bill contained an amendment that would have "mandated a cutoff of federal funds to any school district that used instructional materials depicting homosexuals," he angrily commented: "Do we not believe in local control of education? Or are we in favor of local control only when local school officials agree with us and with our prejudices?"

In the 1994 Democratic primary, Nadler was challenged by Thomas K. Duane, "an openly gay, openly HIV-positive" member of the New York City Council. Nadler won with 62 percent of the vote.

Nadler's greatest triumph to date has been passage of the so-called Nadler rule. This rule restricts ranking members of full committees from taking "any ranking subcommittee posts on their panels as well." What made his victory even more unique was that Nadler had to take on Representative John Dingell of Michigan, one of the most powerful members of Congress.

During the early days of the Republican-controlled One Hundred and Fourth Congress, Nadler introduced a bill that would "index federal tax brackets to reflect regional differences in the cost of living." In introducing the bill, Nadler noted that "the cost of living in New York City is more than 2 times as great as in other areas of the country. So pretending that a New York City family earning $50,000 a year is high-income is a joke—a bad joke if you happen to be a New Yorker." The Republicans, understanding that they had little to fear from voter retaliation in New York City (with its lopsided Democratic registration) overwhelmingly defeated the bill.

Jerry Nadler is regularly reelected by comfortable margins. In 1998, he received 86 percent of the vote over Republican Theodore Howard.

Jerry Nadler is married to the former Joyce L. Miller, who is a real estate investment officer. They have one son, Michael, born in 1985. The Nadlers reside in Manhattan, on West End Avenue at 94th Street, just a few blocks away from the home of the late Ted Weiss.

References

Almanac of American Politics (1994–98 editions).
New York Times, September 25, 1992, B 3:1.
Politics in America (1994–98 editions).

NEUBERGER, RICHARD LEWIS (1912–1960): *Democrat from Oregon; served five years in the Senate (January 5, 1955–March 9, 1960).*

The Congressional Minyan contains more than a half-dozen members who earned their primary living through the written word, either as publishers, editors, or journalists. Of these, none was more prolific than Oregon's Senator Richard Neuberger. From his first newspaper article, published in 1928, until his death nearly thirty-two years later, Neuberger authored or coauthored half-a-dozen books and more than three hundred articles. During the course of his career, his byline could be found in such respected national publications as the *New Republic*, *Harper's*, *Collier's*, *Current History*, the *Saturday Evening Post*, and *Reader's Digest*.

Richard Neuberger's parents, Isaac and Ruth (Lewis) Neuberger, were both the children of German immigrants. His father had immigrated with his parents to the Pacific Northwest from Hainstadt, Germany, at age seventeen. Settling near Portland, he met and married his wife, and opened a restaurant. The Neubergers had two children: Richard Lewis, born on December 26, 1912, and Jane. Richard Neuberger attended public school in Portland. During his early years, he earned money by washing dishes in his parents' restaurant and caddying at a local golf course. His most frequent client on the course was his German-speaking grandfather. While a student at Lincoln High School, he was drawn to journalism, serving two years as a sports reporter for the school newspaper. During his high school years, he met and was befriended by Lair H. Gregory, sports editor of the *Portland Oregonian*, who taught him the fundamentals of newspaper work. By the time Richard Neuberger graduated from Lincoln High School in 1930, he was already a seasoned reporter. Following his graduation, he worked for a year as Gregory's assistant. He then entered the University of Oregon in 1931.

Although naturally bright, Neuberger wasn't terribly successful as a college student. His passion for journalism captured most of his waking hours. By the beginning of his sophomore year, he already had been named editor-in-chief of the university's paper, the *Oregon Daily Emerald*. From this position, Neuberger, in the words of one obituarist, "stood the campus on its ear." Never one to shy away from controversy, he

became a crusading journalist, campaigning for the abolition of the university's mandatory military-training program and compulsory student fees, and going to battle against the fraternities, which he saw as bastions of elitism.

In 1933, after the end of his sophomore year, Neuberger took a leave of absence in order to travel to Europe. While there he witnessed the growing Nazi persecution of the Jews and Germany's unsettling preparation for war. He turned his observations into an article entitled "The New Germany," which was published in the *Nation*. Neuberger's piece was one of the first to realistically describe the growing horror of Nazi Germany.

Upon his return to the University of Oregon in 1934, Neuberger became involved in the gubernatorial campaign of Peter Zimmerman, whom Neuberger described as a "liberal independent." Neuberger spent so much time working on the campaign that his grades took a dramatic downturn; he left the university without receiving his journalism degree.

On September 23, 1934, Neuberger's byline appeared for the first time in the *New York Times*. Less than two years later, the twenty-four-year-old (by this time a reporter and feature writer for the *Oregonian*) was named the *Times*'s regular correspondent for the Pacific Northwest, a post he held until his election to the United States Senate nearly twenty years later.

As a journalist, Neuberger established a reputation for being "one of the Northwest's most prolific writers." He wrote stories on Pacific coast politics, Northwest scenic beauties, power development, conservation of salmon and other natural resources, the problems of the aged and the poor. As a fervid New Dealer, Neuberger decided to run for the Oregon Senate in 1936. He lost by a surprisingly narrow margin. That same year, in collaboration with Kelley Loe, Neuberger published a book entitled *An Army of the Aged*. In it, he and Loe, exposed what they termed the "cruelest runaround": politicians who kept the Townsend Plan alive for their own political purposes. The Townsend Plan was named after Dr. Francis Everett Townsend of Long Beach, California, whose remedy for the Depression was "to give every person over the age of sixty a pension of $200 a month, with the proviso that it must all be spent within the month." This, Townsend and his minions argued, "would provide such a stimulus to the economy [not to mention to those over sixty] that the Depression would be immediately ended." Townsend, with his slogans "Thirty Dollars every Thursday" and "Ham and Eggs for California," quickly became the darling of West Coast politics. He and his program took on an almost cultlike status among the elderly. The $2 billion required to launch his program could, he averred, be raised by a 2 percent tax on all incomes. Unbelievably, Townsend's plan was passed by the legislatures of no fewer than seven Western states in 1934. By 1936, however, Townsend began showing his true colors when he, along with anti-Semites Gerald L. K. Smith and Father Frances Coughlin, formed the Union Party. Their first and only presidential candidate, William Lemke, a reformed North Dakota radical, went down to crushing defeat.

The following year (1937), Neuberger authored his first solo effort, *Integrity: The Life of George W. Norris*. In 1938, Neuberger, this time collaborating with Stephen B. Kahn, coauthored *Our Promised Land*, described as "an interpretive study of the Pacific Northwest." After his entry into politics in the 1940s, Neuberger would author three more books: *The Lewis and Clark Expedition* (1951), *The Royal Canadian Mounted Police* (1953), and *Adventures in Politics: We Go to the Legislature* (1954). In this latter book, Neuberger, about to take his seat in the United States Senate, offered advice to those who might one day seek political office: "If you enter public life, you will have to decide when a compromise threatens your ideals and when it simply blends your own views with those of some other honest person."

Neuberger's reputation as a writer of colorful and vivid prose grew. In early 1940, he was offered a job offer in New York "which would practically have doubled my income," as he wrote in the *Saturday Evening Post*. Tempted though he was, and desirous of making more money, Neuberger nonetheless decided to remain in Portland, where, as he explained, he had "a genuine sense of belonging" which he could feel "in no other place."

Neuberger's decision to remain in Portland was immediately rewarded: he was asked to run for the Oregon Legislative Assembly. The Democrat Neuberger, running in an arch-Republican district as "the only Jew on the bal-

lot," managed to eke out a victory. Before he could even get his feet wet as a legislator, however (he did manage to sponsor one bill seeking to regulate logging in the forests of Oregon), Neuberger enlisted in the United States Army as a second lieutenant. For the next three years, Lieutenant (eventually Captain) Neuberger served as aide to General James A. O'Connor, who was in charge of the construction of the Alaska Military Highway (later known as the AlCan Highway). Neuberger served a year-and-a-half at O'Connor's headquarters at Whitehorse in the Yukon Territory before being transferred to Washington, D.C.

Following his discharge in 1945, he returned to Portland, where, on December 20, 1945, he married the nearly thirty-nine-year-old Maurine Brown, a non-Jewish teacher of physical education and English.

Shortly after his marriage, Richard Neuberger turned down an offer to run for governor of Oregon. Instead, he opted to run again for the State Senate from the Thirteenth District. Once again he lost—this time by a mere 3,000 votes. In 1948, Neuberger was urged to take on incumbent Republican Senator Guy Cordon. Again he demurred, having been informed that "an adequate senatorial campaign would require a minimum of $40,000." The next year, Neuberger finally got elected to the Oregon Senate, drawing "the biggest vote ever polled by any legislative candidate in Oregon." Two years later, Maurine Neuberger was elected to the Oregon Legislative Assembly. They thereby became the first husband-wife team in American history ever elected simultaneously to both houses of a state legislature.

As a state senator, Richard Neuberger earned the princely sum of $600 per year plus a modest travel allowance. Even with his earnings from writing and his wife's salary as a teacher/legislator, the Neubergers had a hard time making ends meet. Soon after his wife entered the legislature, Senator Neuberger sponsored a bill to increase legislators' compensation to $1,200. The measure passed after he had already left the State Senate. During his nearly five years in that body (1949–54), Neuberger gained a reputation for being both a liberal and an ardent independent. His call for a constitutional convention "to revise Oregon's outdated and cluttered basic charter" fell on deaf ears until a Republican governor co-opted the idea two years later. Because of Neuberger's penchant for "calling a spade a spade"—he could just as easily denounce his fellow Democrats as praise a Republican governor—his bills rarely even got out of committee. Nonetheless, when he and his wife ran for reelection in the presidential year of 1952, they were the only candidates on the Portland ballot who received more votes than General Dwight D. Eisenhower.

In 1954, feeling that time and tide were in his favor, Richard Neuberger announced his candidacy for the United States Senate, and named Maurine his campaign manager. Neuberger's opponent, incumbent Guy Cordon, had led the Senate fight for the transfer of offshore oil resources to the states. Buoyed by campaign appearances by Interior Secretary Douglas McKay (a fellow Oregonian) and President Eisenhower, Cordon looked like a easy victor. The Neuberger campaign countered with appearances by senior Senator Wayne Morse and Illinois Governor Adlai E. Stevenson. The campaign offered voters a study in contrasting political styles and content: Cordon, the staid conservative, and Neuberger, the brash, combative liberal. The fight went down to the wire, with Neuberger winning by a mere 2,400 votes. Cordon attempted to contest the election, but Republican Governor Paul Patterson turned down his request. Neuberger thereby became the first Democrat to be elected to the United States Senate from Oregon since Harry Lane exactly forty years earlier.

In the Senate, Neuberger earned the nickname "Mr. Conservation." Toning down his brash "in your face" demeanor a bit, Neuberger nonetheless continued championing the causes for which he most deeply cared: clean air, clean water, preservation of natural resources, civil rights, the removal of billboards from highways, increased funding for cancer research, the recall of Senators, bringing the members of Congress under conflict-of-interest laws, and, perhaps most important, Alaska statehood. So pivotal was his support in this latter cause that today a mountain range bears his name in the nation's forty-ninth state.

As a writer, Neuberger was outraged by the old Senate custom of editing remarks before they were printed in the *Congressional Record*. He fought valiantly against this practice, arguing that what Senators actually said should be reported for all to read. Neuberger's reputation for clear thinking and passionate adherence to a stated set of principles won him both admirers and detractors. His Democratic colleagues thought highly enough of him that, less than two years after he entered the United States Senate, he was chosen to second Tennessee Senator Estes Kefauver's nomination for Vice President at the 1956 Democratic National Convention. Interestingly, the other major candidate for Vice President that year, Massachusetts Senator John F. Kennedy, had his name placed in nomination by a future member of the Congressional Minyan, Connecticut Governor *Abraham Ribicoff*. Although Kennedy was easily the popular choice among delegates on the convention floor, Kefauver, buoyed by the support of the powerful Speaker of the House, Sam Rayburn, became his party's nominee. (Upon Kennedy's election to the White House four years later, Ribicoff was appointed Secretary of Health, Education, and Welfare.)

In 1958, a routine physical examination revealed a malignant tumor. Neuberger underwent surgery and extensive radiation treatment, but succumbed to a cerebral hemorrhage on March 9, 1960. At his funeral, held at Portland's Temple Beth Israel (where he had been confirmed in 1926), Neuberger was eulogized by Senators Paul Douglas, Ernest Gruening, and Wayne Morse, and United States Supreme Court Justice William O. Douglas. In remarks made on the Senate floor a few days later, Vermont Senator George Aiken said: "He will be missed by all others who love the natural resources of this country, the wild life, the pure water, the good, deep soil, the trees growing tall."

In its front-page story on his passing, the *New York Times* noted: "Perhaps the one thing on which political friends and foes of Senator Neuberger were able to agree was that he could not be ignored. One was either on his side or as vehemently against him. There was a sound reason for this. Mr. Neuberger was always in the middle of a controversial subject, but never on the fence."

Neuberger, who was raised as a Reform Jew, died childless. He was survived by his parents and sister, Jane (Goodsell) Neuberger. His wife

Maurine succeeded him in the Senate, serving from November 8, 1960 to January 3, 1967. Richard Neuberger was buried in the Beth Israel Cemetery, Portland, Oregon.

References

American Jewish Year Book, vol. 62, p. 451.
Current Biography, 1955, pp. 442–44.
Dictionary of American Biography 6.
Encyclopaedia Judaica, vol. 12, col. 1006.
New York Times, March 10, 1960, 1:3.
Washington Post, March 10, 1960.
Who Was Who in America, vol. 4.

OTTINGER, RICHARD LAWRENCE (1929–):
Democrat from New York; served eight terms in the House (Eighty-ninth through Ninety-first Congress; January 3, 1965–January 3, 1971; Ninety-fourth through Ninety-eighth Congress; January 3, 1975–January 3, 1985).

Westchester County, New York, has long been thought of as a suburb for the wealthy. There is in fact some truth to this stereotype. Westchester was where the robber baron Jay Gould built Lyndhurst, his Gothic revival mansion, and John D. Rockefeller erected the spectacular Kykuit. The locus of much classical fiction, Westchester also contains Washington Irving's Tarrytown, and John Cheever's Ossining. Westchester County is also the home of the "ordinary" rich—people who live in the big comfortable homes in places like Pelham, Eastchester, and Bronxville, and the liberal Jewish enclaves of Chappaqua, Larchmont, Mamaroneck, and Scarsdale. It was in this latter community that Richard Lawrence Ottinger was born.

Lawrence (1884–1954) and Simon (1884–1974) Ottinger were the founders of the United States Plywood Corporation, a business that made a fortune for them and their family. The Ottingers were an active clan, lending their talent, money, and energies to a host of public and communal causes. One Ottinger, Albert (1878–1938), a Republican, was twice elected New York State attorney general, and nearly defeated Franklin Delano Roosevelt for governor in 1928.

With wealth, Lawrence Ottinger, married to the former Louise Loewenstein, moved to Scarsdale, where their son, Richard Lawrence, was born on January 27, 1929. After attending public school in Scarsdale, young Dick moved on to the Loomis Preparatory School in Windsor, Connecticut; from there to Cornell, where he received a B.A. in 1950; and then to Harvard Law School, from which he graduated with an LL.B. in 1953. Following his graduation from law school, Richard Ottinger enlisted in the United States Air Force. He served for two years, reaching the rank of captain. After his return from the service, Ottinger married Betty Anne Schneider, with whom he has four children.

After practicing international and corporate law from 1955 to 1960, Ottinger moved his family to Washington, D.C., where he did graduate work in international law at Georgetown University. In 1961, he came to the attention of recently elected President John F. Kennedy, who asked him to join the newly created Peace Corps. Ottinger agreed, becoming a founder and the second staff member of that noteworthy organization. For the next three years (1961–1964), he served as director of Peace Corps programs in South America.

In 1964, Richard Ottinger left the Peace Corps and returned to Westchester County, where he settled in Pleasantville and announced his candidacy for the United States Congress from New York's Twenty-fifth district. In 1964, the Twenty-fifth comprised western Westchester and Putnam Counties. It had been represented by Republicans since 1907. But 1964 was a good year for Democrats, for it was the year that President Lyndon B. Johnson beat Arizona Senator Barry Goldwater in a landslide, carrying a record number of Democrats on his coattails.

In the Republican primary, incumbent Representative Robert R. Berry was defeated by James R. Frankenberry, who then took on the Democrat Ottinger in the November general election. Ottinger, benefiting greatly from the coattail effect, easily won. Frankenberry contested the election. Speaking on behalf of Frankenberry, New Hampshire Republican Representative James Cleveland sought to have Ottinger's victory set aside on the grounds that he had spent more than the legal limit on his campaign. Speaker John W. McCormack allowed Cleveland's challenge to die a quiet death. Ottinger was officially sworn in as a member of the Eighty-ninth Congress on January 3, 1965 and given a seat on the House Commerce Committee. As a member of that committee, Ottinger "took a prominent role in challenging legislation designed to aid the major oil companies at the expense of the consumer."

When Ottinger campaigned for reelection two years later, his opponent, ever mindful of how helpful the President had been in 1964, employed the campaign slogan: "In 1966 skirts are higher, pants are tighter and L. B. J.'s coattails are shorter." Ottinger handed his Republican opponent a hard-fought defeat. After being reelected again in 1968, Ottinger relinquished his House seat, announcing his candidacy for United States Senator from New York. Financing his campaign with a $1.7 million loan from his mother, Ottinger won the Democratic primary but then lost the general election to James L. Buckley, brother of conservative columnist William F. Buckley. Running on the Conservative Party ticket, Buckley won the three-way race with just 39 percent of the vote, displacing Senator Charles E. Goodell, who had been appointed to the Senate after the assassination of Senator Robert F. Kennedy in 1968. Much of Ottinger's potential support was drained away by Goodell, who got the backing of the Liberal Party.

Remaining in Washington, Ottinger returned to the practice of law. Deeply involved with environmental and consumer issues—during his first stint in Congress, he had founded the House Environmental Study Conference—Ottinger now organized and directed Grassroots Action, Inc., "a non-profit corporation established to assist citizen action groups to organize and act effectively, primarily in consumer and environmental matters." Ottinger tried to reclaim his old House seat (now the Twenty-fourth district) in 1972, but lost to incumbent Ogden Reid, heir to the *New York Tribune*. Reid, it should be noted, had switched party affiliation from Republican to Democrat just before the election. When Reid decided to retire at the conclusion of the Ninety-third Congress, Ottinger ran hard, winning the election with 58 percent of the vote. He was reelected four more times before deciding to retire at the conclusion of the Ninety-eighth Congress in January 1985.

During his years in Congress, Ottinger was known as "a man who work[ed] better with issues than with people . . . a creative legislator with a first-class mind . . . not always good at selling himself or his ideas to the rest of the House." Ottinger was one of the first members of Congress to express grave concern about the depletion of the earth's ozone layer. By 1980, he had become convinced that the energy resources of the planet and its ability to absorb pollution were running out, and that only radical conservation measures and renewable energy could solve the problem. As chairman of the subcommittee on Energy Development, Ottinger pro-

moted federal subsidies for solar development and research on an electric car. Not surprisingly, he was a militant opponent of nuclear power.

In addition to his work on environmental and consumer issues, Richard Ottinger was a champion of human rights. He sponsored legislation urging Romania to restore religious freedom, and fought hard for the right of Soviet Jews to emigrate to Israel. He personally went to bat with Soviet President Leonid Brezhnev on behalf of dissidents Andrei Sakharov, Anatoly (Natan) Sharansky, and Ida Nudel.

As a friend of Israel, Representative Ottinger was one of the first members of Congress to publicly condemn Ambassador Andrew Young's assertion in 1979 that the United States needed to develop a "positive relationship" with the Palestine Liberation Organization. Ottinger also sponsored an amendment in 1980 which urged that the PLO should not be given membership in the International Monetary Fund.

When Richard Ottinger announced his retirement from Congress, he threw his support behind his former aide, Oren Teicher. In the election, Teicher was edged out by Republican Joseph J. DioGuardi, an accountant with no previous political experience, by the slim margin of 50 to 48 percent. DioGuardi went on to be reelected in 1986, handily defeating former Representative *Bella Abzug*. Ottinger's former seat, now the Twentieth District, returned to the Democratic column in 1986, when DioGuardi was defeated by the former New York Assistant Secretary of State, *Nita M. Lowey*.

Following the end of his congressional career, Ottinger settled in Mamaroneck, Westchester County, and became a professor at the Pace University Law School.

References

Almanac of American Politics.

Biographical Directory of the United States Congress, 1774–1989, p. 1598.

Murray Polner, *American Jewish Biographies* (New York: Facts On File, 1983), pp. 308–309.

PERLMAN, NATHAN DAVID (1887–1952):
Republican from New York; served four terms in the House (Sixty-sixth through Sixty-ninth Congress; December 6, 1920-March 3, 1927).

In 1927, the sports pages of the nation's newspapers were filled with the exploits of Babe Ruth and his Yankee teammates, known variously as the Bronx Bombers and Murderers' Row. The entertainment pages were pondering the latest revolution in the motion picture industry—the introduction of sound in the Warner Brothers' production of *The Jazz Singer*. For much of 1927, the front pages of American dailies reported on the sordid libel cases of Herman Bernstein and Aaron Sapiro against auto magnate Henry Ford. Bernstein, the author of an exposé on the *Protocols of the Elders of Zion* entitled *The History of a Lie*, had sued for libel in 1923, when Ford published an article in his paper, the *Dearborn Independent*, identifying Bernstein as a "spy for International Jewry." This came at the tail end of the *Independent*'s serialized version of the *Protocols*, entitled "The International Jew." Ford managed to evade being served in the Bernstein matter by remaining outside the jurisdiction of the New York court system.

The next year (1924), Aaron Sapiro, a San Francisco attorney active in the formation of farmer cooperatives, was accused by Ford's *Independent* of plotting, along with such eminent Jewish leaders as Bernard Baruch, Otto Kahn, and Albert Lasker, to seize "control of the agricultural . . . resources and production of America." In a series of bold, histrionic articles, the writers of the *Independent* went so far as to claim that "Every stalk of celery . . . pays direct tribute to Jewish domination of the cooperative marketing system in . . . the United States." Sapiro, seeking, he said, to vindicate "myself and my race," sued Ford and the Dearborn Publishing Company for $1 million.

A firestorm of controversy and invective ensued. At least three members of the Congressional Minyan took active roles in the ongoing debate over Ford's anti-Semitism: New York-area Representative *Sol Bloom*, who threatened Ford with a congressional subpoena; former Representative *Martin Ansorge*, who joined the Ford legal team; and former Republican Congressman *Nathan David Perlman*, who, in his position as vice president of the American Jewish Congress, challenged Ford to prove he

wasn't an anti-Semite. Perlman demanded that Ford issue an apology for all the libels he had caused to be printed, and to publicly fire E. D. Leopold, the vice president of the Dearborn Publishing Company. In the end, Ford issued a public apology that stated, in part: "I deem it to be my duty as an honorable man to make amends for the wrong done to the Jews as fellow-men and brothers, by asking their forgiveness for the harm that I have unintentionally committed."

Many people can be said to have shared in the credit for Ford's recantation: Congressman Bloom, superlawyer Louis Marshall (representing the American Jewish Committee), and the aforementioned Nathan Perlman. It is difficult, if not impossible, to say who was ultimately most responsible for Ford's retraction, although Perlman's role was certainly pivotal; he "performed" in front of the curtain, while Marshall maneuvered behind the scenes.

Nathan David Perlman, the son of Victor and Rachel Perlman, was born in Poland on August 2, 1887. As with many families in that era, Victor Perlman left his wife and son behind while he set out for the United States. Like millions of his landsmen, Victor settled on the Lower East Side. He was able to send for Rachel and Nathan in 1891. The youth was educated in the public schools of New York City and graduated from the New York University School of Law shortly before his twentieth birthday.

In 1911, after four years in private practice, Nathan Perlman was appointed special deputy attorney general of New York State. He spent the next four years (1911–14) prosecuting violations of the Pure Food and Drug Act. This act, along with its companion, the Meat Inspection Act, became law during the presidency of Theodore Roosevelt. In part, it owed its existence to the young writer Upton Sinclair's hair-raising description of the meat-packing industry, *The Jungle*. Sinclair, a socialist, had intended his novel to garner sympathy for the plight of the immigrant worker. Instead, it sounded the tocsin over the conditions under which America's meat was prepared for consumption. Sinclair later complained that he had "aimed at America's heart and hit its stomach."

Through his work in the attorney general's office, Perlman came to the notice of the elders of the Republican Party, always on the lookout for emerging young talent. Nathan Perlman was elected to the New York State Assembly in 1915. During his one term (1915–17), he spent the lion's share of his time working to increase the rate of workman's compensation in New York State.

In December 1919, Representative *Fiorello H. La Guardia* became president of the New York City Board of Aldermen, thus prompting his resignation from the Sixty-sixth Congress. La Guardia's Fourteenth District seat remained vacant until November 1920, when an election was held to replace him. Perlman was easily elected, and was sworn in on December 6, 1920, the beginning of the Sixty-sixth Congress's third session. Perlman was given a seat on the House Judiciary Committee, where he coauthored the Child Labor Amendment and the Wadsworth-Perlman Act. The latter was designed "to facilitate the entrance into this country, outside the regularly prescribed quotas, of qualified relatives of former members of the United States armed services . . . and to certain other qualified persons having relatives [in the United States]."

Senator James Wolcott Wadsworth, Jr., Perlman's cosponsor, was the scion of an old and prominent New York family. His father, James Wolcott Wadsworth, Sr., had served in Congress from 1891 to 1907. While serving in the Senate, James Jr., was chairman of the Senate Military Affairs Committee, to which the legislation in question was sent. Without question, the two made a most unusual political pairing: Perlman, a Jewish immigrant from Poland, and Wadsworth, a WASP patrician schooled at St. Mark's and Yale. The two remained lifelong friends. Ironically, Senator Wadsworth died just one week before Representative Perlman.

Nathan Perlman was reelected to Congress three times. In 1924, he narrowly defeated Democrat *William Sirovich*, who contested the election by charging voter fraud. Perlman's election stood. Running against Perlman again in 1926, Sirovich emerged victorious. Following his

defeat, Nathan Perlman returned to New York City, where he resumed the practice of law. Shortly after his return to New York, Perlman, now a vice president of the American Jewish Congress, became involved in the Ford-Sapiro imbroglio. In 1935, Mayor La Guardia appointed Perlman a city magistrate. While a magistrate, Perlman established and was the first presiding judge of New York's Felony Court. In 1936, Perlman was the Republican nominee for New York State attorney general. Although Perlman lost that race, La Guardia named him justice of the Court of Special Sessions, a position in which he served until his death on June 29, 1952. While on the court, he wrote important decisions upholding the right to peaceably picket during industrial disputes.

Perlman married Florence Sylvia Bierman in 1917. They had one son, Jack Marvin, who, at the time of his father's death, was the legislative assistant to Rudolph Halley, president of the New York City Council. In addition to his involvement with the American Jewish Congress, Nathan Perlman served as vice president of Beth Israel Hospital and was a trustee of the Federation for Jewish Philanthropies. Attracted more to Judaism's Orthodox wing, Perlman was a congregant and friend of Rabbi Joseph Hyman Lookstein, a future president of Israel's Bar-Ilan University. Rabbi Lookstein presided at Nathan Perlman's funeral, which was attended by more than eight hundred people. Perlman was buried at Mount Hebron Cemetery, in Queens County.

References
American Hebrew, October 9, 1936, pp. 408, 417.
American Jewish Year Book, vol. 24, p. 189; vol. 54, p. 540.
New York Times, June 30, 1952, 19:1; February 22, 1968, 31:1.
Universal Jewish Encyclopedia.
Who Was Who in America, vol. 3.
Who's Who in American Jewry, 1926, 1928, 1938.

PEYSER, THEODORE ALBERT (1873–1937):
Democrat from New York; served three terms in the House (Seventy-third through Seventy-fifth Congress; March 3, 1933–August 8, 1937).

Theodore A. Peyser could easily have been a poster child for the American Dream of Success. In his sixty-four years, he went from a childhood of poverty in West Virginia to the halls of Congress as representative from Manhattan's fabled Silk Stocking District, and from being a traveling liquor wholesaler in the midwest to becoming one of the insurance industry's legendary superstars.

Theodore A. Peyser was born in Charleston, West Virginia, on February 18, 1873. That year, the Jews of Charleston, estimated to number no more than ninety, erected the city's first synagogue, the Reform B'nai Israel. The Peysers were a staunchly Reform family. Indeed, one of Theodore Peyser's nephews, Rabbi Edward L. Israel, was ordained at the Hebrew Union College in Cincinnati, class of 1919.

Not much is known about the Peyser family beyond the fact that it consisted of two boys and three girls. From the evidence at hand, the Peysers appear to have been somewhat impecunious, but not without influential friends. Theodore had to quit school at age eleven. Before the end of the year (1884) he had landed a job as a page in the West Virginia state legislature. Peyser worked at a series of jobs for the next nine years until, in 1893, he moved to Cincinnati, Ohio, where a married sister, Emily Bernard, was residing. For the next seven years, Peyser traveled the midwest, wholesaling liquor to an ever-expanding network of restaurants, stores, and hotels.

In 1900, Peyser pulled up stakes and moved to New York City, where he entered the insurance industry. It was a match made in heaven. Peyser found he had a knack for attracting well-heeled clients. As a special agent for the Northwestern Mutual Life Insurance Company, he was credited with having sold million-dollar policies (the equivalent of $10 to $15 million in today's money) to thirty-three clients. Peyser made enough money in the next three decades to be able to retire comfortably by the beginning of his sixtieth year.

In the fall of 1932, with the Depression attacking the economic and spiritual resources of a desperate nation, Franklin Roosevelt offered his plan for a New Deal for the American people. Roosevelt's dynamism and sense of vision influenced many people to enter the political arena. One of these was Theodore A. Peyser, who declared his candidacy for Congress. In 1932, Peyser was living in the section of Manhattan known in political circles as the Silk Stocking District. The then-Seventeenth Congressional District was home to some of America's wealthiest families. Most of the voters in the district lived on the few blocks east of Fifth Avenue along Central Park. Although historically Republican, the Seventeenth District was more tolerant than the rest of New York City and the rest of the nation. "While it did not trust union leaders and Democratic Party politicians, it accepted much of the New Deal." According to the *Almanac of American Politics* (1996): "The district believed that the nation should be led by the well-educated Protestant gentlemen one saw strolling down Madison Avenue to their clubs, who continued to hold high government posts."

From 1929 to 1932, the Seventeenth District was represented in Congress by an almost prototypical member of WASP society, Ruth Sears Baker Pratt. Schooled at Wellesley, the daughter of a prominent Massachusetts cotton manufacturer, Ruth Sears Baker had married well; her husband, John T. Pratt, was the son of an oil company executive. Moving from a wealthy enclave in Greenwich, Connecticut, to New York City in 1904, Ruth Pratt quickly gained recognition as a "comer" in Republican circles. During World War I, she chaired the Second Federal Reserve District's Woman's Liberty Loan Committee, and was appointed vice chair of the Republican National Ways and Means Committee. In 1925, she became the first woman elected to the New York City Board of Aldermen. As a member of this board, she often found herself at odds with New York's flamboyant mayor, James J. Walker.

Pratt was elected to Congress in 1928, defeating Democrat Phillip Berolzheimer. Shortly after her arrival in Washington, the Pratts leased Evermay, an eighteenth-century Georgian manor in Georgetown. Pratt went on to serve two terms in the House, where she introduced funding for "books for the blind," favored the repeal of the Eighteenth Amendment (Prohibition), and gladly supported President Herbert Hoover's reliance on private funding to alleviate unemployment. In 1930, Pratt won reelection by a scant 695 votes over the Tammany Hall candidate, Louis B. Brodsky, and the Socialist candidate, journalist Heywood Broun. At the 1932 Republican National Convention, Pratt was given the honor of seconding Hoover's renomination for President.

In his campaign against Ruth Pratt, Theodore Peyser charged her with abusing the franking privilege. She had mailed out more than seventy thousand pamphlets to her constituents describing her achievements. Moreover, she sent a reprint of a Walter Lippmann column praising the Republican Party's position on Prohibition. Peyser also attacked Pratt for having been absent from her seat in Congress "whenever a roll-call vote was taken on an important measure." On election day, aided by the Roosevelt coattails, Peyser defeated Pratt by a vote of 36,397 to 29,776. He was sworn in as a member of the Seventy-third Congress on March 4, 1933.

During his nearly four years in the House of Representatives, Peyser was known as an active legislator and a member of a bloc that generally supported FDR's New Deal legislation but was basically independent in thought and action. In his first reelection campaign in 1934, Peyser was endorsed by a nonpartisan women's committee chaired by Mrs. Leo Sulzberger. She took pains to point out that Representative Peyser, although he had "supported the best of the New Deal," had "never voted blindly." As an independent thinker, Peyser had opposed Roosevelt's court-packing scheme.

Two weeks after entering Congress, Peyser submitted his first bill: legislation calling for the establishment of an airfield for passenger and mail planes on Governor's Island in New York Harbor. The bill called for an appropriation of $300,000 for clearing the island and filling in new ground through dredging. This proposal hung around Congress for the next four years, and finally was given a green light by the House Military Affairs Committee in 1937. Peyser vigorously opposed Prohibition, and offered a plan "to tax the thirsty and feed the hungry" as a solution to the liquor question. His greatest legislative accomplishment was his cosponsorship, along with New York Senator Robert Wagner, of the Wagner-Peyser Unemployment Act, which put tens of thousands of idle workers back on the payroll.

In 1937, the year he died, Peyser garnered national attention through his actions on behalf of Helmuth Hirsch, a twenty-one-year-old American citizen who was executed for treason in Germany. In March 1937, Hirsch, described as a "stateless Jew," was sentenced to death by the German People's Tribunal on charges of high treason and possessing explosives. It was charged at his trial that he had conspired to blow up the offices and printing plant of Julius Streicher's anti-Semitic newspaper, the *Stuermer*, in Nuremberg. The trial was cloaked in secrecy. According to the *New York Times* (June 5, 1937): "To this day, virtually nothing is known of the evidence against Hirsch presented to the People's Tribunal."

Once news of Hirsch's death sentence came to light, Peyser leaped to his defense. Peyser argued that Hirsch, although born in Germany, was the son and grandson of Austrian nationals who had become naturalized American citizens. As such, Peyser contended, Hirsch was *de facto* (if not *de jure*) an American citizen himself, and under the protection of American law.

During his trial, Hirsch had stated that he was an American citizen, claiming that after his birth he had been duly registered at the American embassy in Kiel. A petition seeking to recognize his legal claim to American citizenship was submitted to Secretary of State Cordell Hull. At first, the State Department turned the petition down, saying that he could not claim American citizenship; his father's naturalization, they argued, had been canceled by a Pennsylvania court in 1926 because he had remained abroad more than two years. Finally, in May 1937, one month before his scheduled execution, Hirsch was granted citizenship. Representative Peyser and the State Department made repeated appeals to the Hitler government for clemency. Peyser's pleading fell on deaf ears. Helmut Hirsch was executed on June 4, 1937.

Emotionally and physically exhausted from this trying ordeal, Peyser's health quickly began to decline. Two months and four days after Hirsch's execution, Theodore Peyser died in New York City. He was sixty-four years old. His seat was taken by Republican Bruce Barton, a best-selling author (*The Man No One Knows*, *The Book No One Knows*) and pioneering advertising man.

Peyser never married. Widely traveled, an avid sportsman, he was known for his tremendous collection of etchings. On the Jewish communal front, Peyser was a member of New York's Temple Emanu-el and affiliated with the Federation for the Support of Jewish Philanthropies. His funeral, held at Temple Emanu-el, was presided over by Rabbi B. Benedict Glazer, assisted by Peyser's nephew, Rabbi Edward L. Israel of Baltimore. Included among the five hundred-plus mourners were his sisters, Theresa Newman, Emily Bernard, and Josephine Dreyer, his sister-in-law Rose Peyser of Birmingham, Alabama, Mayor *Fiorello La Guardia*, and Senator Wagner.

Peyser left an estate "in excess of $10,000," divided equally between his three sisters and his sister-in-law. His will named Florence Guggenheim, wife of Daniel Guggenheim, as coexecutrix. Theodore Peyser's body was returned to Cincinnati, where he was buried at the United Cemetery.

References

American Jewish Year Book, vol. 40, p. 390.

New York Times, June 5, 1937, 1:2; August 9, 1937, 19:1.

Universal Jewish Encyclopedia.

Who Was Who in America, vol. 1.

Who's Who in American Jewry, 1938.

Women in Congress, 1917–1990 (Washington, D.C.: Office of the Historian, U.S. House of Representatives, 1991).

PHILLIPS, HENRY MEYER (1811–1884):
Democrat from Pennsylvania; served one term in the House (Thirty-fifth Congress; March 4, 1857–March 3, 1859).

A native of Philadelphia, Henry Phillips was the grandson of Congregation Mikveh Israel's first president, Jonas Phillips. Henry's father, Zalegman, was a noted criminal lawyer who also served as *parnas*, or president, of that noted Portuguese synagogue. One of ten children, Henry Phillips was the only one of Zalegman's six sons to follow in his father's footsteps and become an attorney-at-law. Henry was admitted to the Philadelphia bar some seven months before his twenty-first birthday. One of the preeminent criminal attorneys in nineteenth-century America, Henry practiced for more than thirty years and was acclaimed by his colleagues as "the associate of the great lawyers of this Bar . . . rightfully recognized as one of the foremost citizens of Philadelphia."

Phillips was elected as a Democrat to the Thirty-fifth Congress for the term beginning March 4, 1857. As was the case in those days, Congress did not convene for nine months; Congressional sessions lasted anywhere from three to six months. Consequently, Representatives like Henry Phillips, who served only one term, were actually "on the job" for anywhere between six and perhaps ten months.

Henry Phillips' congressional career contains few transcendent moments. He was appointed to the standing Committee on Elections and the special Committee on the Pacific Railroad. An intellectually talented man—he was elected to membership in the prestigious American Philosophical Society—Phillips spoke little on the burning political issues of the day. In fact, he made precisely two speeches on the House floor. One dealt with "the admission of Kansas as a State under the Lecompton Constitution;" the other on "the expenditures and resources of the country." Despite delivering just these two speeches, Phillips seems to have nonetheless earned the respect of his colleagues. They found in him a man of uncommon intellectual prowess who seemingly mastered complex issues with only minimal effort.

Following his single term in Congress, Phillips returned to the practice of law in Philadelphia. A lifelong bachelor, he lent his talents and prestige to many notable community institutions. In 1862 he was appointed trustee of the Jefferson Medical College, taking over the seat of his brother, J. Altamont Phillips, who had died. He also served as president of the Academy of Music, director of the Pennsylvania Railroad Company, and, as previously noted, was accepted for membership in the American Philosophical Society, founded by Benjamin Franklin in 1743. At the personal request of Cornelius Vanderbilt, Henry M. Phillips was also seated on the board of Western Union.

When Phillips died in August 1884, his American Philosophical Society colleagues published a lengthy tribute to their late comrade. Nowhere in necrologist Richard Vaux's wordy encomium is there the slightest hint that Henry Meyer Phillips was the scion of a prominent Jewish family. Neither the American Philosophical Society nor the *New York Times* found any importance in the fact that Phillips's remains were buried in the family plot at Mount Sinai Cemetery, Frankford (now Philadelphia), Pennsylvania. That fact went unreported.

References

American Jewish Year Book, vol. 2 (1900–01), p. 521.
Jewish Encyclopedia.
New York Times, August 29, 1884, 5:3.
Publications of the American Jewish Historical Society, vol. 22, pp. 139–46.
Richard Vaux, "Biographical Notice of Henry M. Phillips," *Proceedings of the American Philosophical Society*, vol. 22 (January–October 1885), pp. 72–78.
Universal Jewish Encyclopedia.

PHILLIPS, PHILLIP (1807–1884): *Democrat from Alabama; served one term in the House (Thirty-third Congress; March 4, 1853–March 3, 1855).*

One of only two Jews ever elected from the state of Alabama, Phillip Phillips was also the firstborn of all the Congressional Minyanaires. Born to German immigrants in Charleston, South Carolina, that early cradle of American Jewish political leaders, Phillips received a Northern education. He attended both the Norwich Military Academy in Vermont and the Middletown School in Connecticut. This early Northern exposure probably played an important part in making him one of the few Southern Unionists in Congress. Returning to Charleston, Phillips read law under one John Gadsen and was admitted to the South Carolina bar in 1828 at the age of twenty-one.

Phillips was a Unionist delegate to South Carolina's 1832 Nullification Convention, convened by John Calhoun, where he vehemently opposed secession. He was elected to the South Carolina legislature in 1834, but inexplicably moved to Alabama the following year. He then went on to serve in that state's legislature from 1844 to 1853, at which time he defeated incumbent Representative Elihu Lockwood for a seat in the Thirty-third Congress. Phillips served but a single term. It would appear that his Jewishness played virtually no role in his election to Congress; in 1853, the Jewish population of Alabama was less than 325.

Even in the politically fluid antebellum period, two years was not enough time to make a mark in Congress. Phillip Phillips's brief tenure did not result in any significant legislation. After serving his one term, he declined renomination and returned to private life. It was as a private citizen that Phillip Phillips played a leading role in the contentious American-Swiss Treaty debate. Under the terms of this treaty, the governments of Switzerland's autonomous cantons retained the right to prohibit foreign Jews from entering and doing business in their territory. In 1857, when an American Jewish businessman was "invited" to leave one of the Swiss cantons, the issue took on a life of its own. Voices were raised in protest across America, one of the loudest belonging to former Representative Phillips. Interestingly, despite the hue and cry emanating from the Jewish community, most people in Washington saw this as a singularly "American" issue. By 1866, the Swiss Constitution was amended, ever after ensuring equality for citizens, residents, and travelers of all religious persuasions.

Phillip Phillips continued being a faithful Unionist, though both his wife, Eugenia, and their daughters were outspoken Secessionists. Some writers have claimed that the pro-slavery Mrs. Phillips was not in fact a Jew, and that, because of this, her husband's contacts with the Jewish community were negligible. To the contrary, Eugenia Phillips hailed from a prominent Charleston family named Levy. And far from being estranged from Jewish activities, Phillip Phillips served as secretary of the Charleston Reformed Society of Israelites, the earliest group to advocate a thoroughly liberalized Judaism in America. While living in the nation's capital, Phillips was a financial supporter, if not in fact a member, of the fledgling Washington Hebrew Congregation.

Following his single term in Congress, the Phillips family remained in Washington, where Phillip argued cases before the U.S. Supreme Court, and Eugenia and the girls continued speaking out in favor of secession. With the outbreak of the Civil War in 1861, Phillips and his family were placed under house arrest, labeled as seditionists because of the outspoken Eugenia.

Before the war's first year, the Phillips family left Washington and moved to New Orleans, where they would wait out the war. New Orleans, however, was no kinder to Mrs. Phillips; she was imprisoned there for three months by General Benjamin Butler for an insulting remark she made as the funeral cortege of a fallen Union officer passed by. Following her release from jail, Eugenia was hailed as a heroine. After Lee's surrender, they returned to Washington, where Phillips resumed his highly lucrative practice before the Supreme Court and authored weighty legal tomes with ponderous titles like *Statutory Jurisdiction and Practice of the Supreme Court of the United States*. Phillips died in Washington on January 14, 1884, and was buried in Laurel Hill Cemetery, Savannah, Georgia.

References

American Jewish Year Book, vol. 2 (1900–01) p. 518.

Encyclopaedia Judaica, vol. 13, col. 407.

David T. Morgan, "Phillip Phillips and Internal Improvements in Mid-Nineteenth Century Alabama," *Alabama Review*, vol. 34 (April 1981), pp. 83–93.

PODELL, BERTRAM L. (1925–): *Democrat from New York; served four terms in the House (Ninetieth Congress through Ninety-fourth Congress; February 20, 1968–January 3, 1975).*

On January 10, 1975, President Gerald Ford signed the Trade Reform Act. Included in the legislation, passed unanimously by the House and by a 77-4 vote in the Senate, was an amendment denying most-favored-nation status (and its concomitant privileges) to any "nonmarket" government "denying its citizens of the opportunity to emigrate to the country of their choice." Known as the Jackson-Vanik Amendment (after its primary sponsors, Washington Senator Henry "Scoop" Jackson and Ohio Representative Charles Vanik), the measure, more than two and one-half years in the making, was specifically crafted to help the Jews of the Soviet Union.

In the 1960s and '70s, the plight of Soviet Jewish refuseniks was widely publicized throughout the world. Anatoly Sharansky, Ida Nudel, and Alexander Lerner— refuseniks all—became international symbols of a pariah nation. In Washington, D.C., the Soviet embassy was watched and picketed by the refuseniks' friends and sympathizers for several hours every day, 365 days a year, year in, year out. Rabbis and politicians, students and business types began taking trips to the Soviet Union and meeting clandestinely with the forgotten Jews. Throughout the period, allies and sympathizers searched for a possible legislative weapon with which to club the Soviet Union into letting the Jewish people emigrate. In the Torah, Moses and Aaron had Ten Plagues with which to convince a heart-hardened Pharaoh; as of 1975, Jewish agitators had Jackson-Vanik.

The progress of Jackson-Vanik from conception to delivery involved tense negotiations between Congress and leaders of the American Jewish community, the Nixon White House, and the Kremlin. Its passage represented a tremendous victory for American Jewry, which had, in the words of historian Howard M. Sachar, "brought the mighty Soviet Union to terms."

Sachar devotes nearly three thousand words to the account of Jackson-Vanik in his *History of the Jews in America.* As Sachar tells it, the amendment was a collaborative effort of several Senate staffers, notably Morris Amitay and Richard Perle, top aides, respectively, to Senators *Abraham Ribicoff* and Henry Jackson. Nowhere in Sachar's excursus does one find the name of the man in whose office the amendment likely originated in the spring of 1972: New York Representative Bert Podell. According to Podell, the genesis for what eventually became the Jackson-Vanik Amendment was originally intended to be a bill, not an amendment, and was drafted by a "twenty-something" intern from Stern College. The coed, who was working in Podell's office, brought the idea of most favored nation status in exchange for emigration rights to him for his input. He liked the concept, and sent it along to the office that translates ideas into legislative language.

In Podell's account: "I was the original author of Jackson-Vanik. It was only after I started going around getting cosponsors that I was urged to get a more prominent member of Congress as author." According to Podell, the request came from Malcolm Hoenlein, legislative affairs director of B'nai B'rith, who in the late 1990s would serve as executive vice-chairman of the Conference of Presidents of Major American Jewish Organizations. Hoenlein convinced Podell that his bill would be better served by having a "non-Jewish friend with clout" as its named author. Senator Jackson's aide, Richard Perle, further suggested that the bill would work best as an amendment. Although Podell's claim cannot be proved, it does have the ring of truth about it.

According to Sachar, Jackson may have had a political motive in sponsoring the amendment, for "as he charted his [presidential] campaign plans for 1976, Jackson was keenly aware of the value of Jewish financial support." Podell, on the other hand, had, by 1972, a long and distinguished track record with regard to Jewish issues and Jewish causes. In remembering the fate of his proposal nearly a quarter-century later, Podell said: "It wasn't that hard giving up personal aggrandizement for the common good. Then again, it's like Shakespeare said: 'The good men do is often interred with their bones [sic].'"

Bertram L. Podell, the eldest of Hyman and Henriette (Menaker) Podell's three children, was born in Brooklyn on December 27, 1925. Both Hyman and Henriette were first-generation Americans, their parents having emigrated from Russia-Poland around the turn of the century. Hy Podell (the family name was originally Podolsky) was an attorney. Running a traditional (though non-Orthodox) home, he sent his eldest son to the Yeshiva of Flatbush, where Bert received an Orthodox education. "He just wanted to make sure I had a proper Jewish education," Podell recalls. Podell attended Abraham Lincoln High School and St. John's University, from which he received his undergraduate degree at age nineteen. After serving in the United States Navy from 1944 to 1946, Bert Podell entered Brooklyn Law School, receiving his LL.B. in 1950. According to the *New York Times*: "His entry into politics coincided with his graduation."

From his earliest years, Bert Podell was an inveterate joiner. As a youth growing up in Brooklyn, he was president of the Flatbush Young Zionists and chair of the Junior Division of the United Jewish Appeal. As a young attorney, he became part of Stanley Steingut's "regular clubhouse Democratic organization" in Brooklyn. Podell was the machine's candidate for the New York State Assembly in 1954. Nearly a year earlier, on February 15, 1953, he had married Bernice "Bunny" Posen. They have three children—Stephen Daniel, Ellen Crown, and Gary Adam—and, as of early 1999, four grandchildren.

Bert Podell went on to serve fourteen years in the state legislature. He was known as an "energetic, tough campaigner," one who "seem[ed] to revel in the rigors of speech-making and hand-shaking." During Podell's fourteen years in Albany, Republicans controlled the state legislature. Nonetheless, Assemblyman Podell chaired both the Assembly Committee on Finance and the Joint Legislative Committee on Penal Institutions. From this latter post, Podell launched a widely reported investigation into the operations of several penal institutions,

including the Brooklyn Adolescent Remand Shelter, which he indignantly termed "a monstrosity—a modern-day Devil's Island." Though a Democrat in a Republican-controlled Assembly, Podell had a knack for getting his legislation enacted. One of his legislative initiatives abolished capital punishment in New York. As with many who enthusiastically supported an end to the death penalty in the 1960s and '70s, Podell no longer holds that position.

On November 7, 1967, Thirteenth District Representative *Abraham J. Multer* was elected to the New York State Supreme Court. A year earlier, he had eked out a 1,050-vote victory over industrialist Mel Dubin in the Democratic primary. With Multer's elevation to the bench (amid charges that he had used his position on the Banking and Currency Committee to his own financial advantage), the seat opened up for any Democrat strong enough to win a special election. The Thirteenth District, as noted in the *Almanac of American Politics* (1970 edition) was an area of "big apartments and small homes." Its communities, "each with a clear-cut identity," included Coney Island, Sheepshead Bay, Flatbush, Bensonhurst, Borough Park, and Midwood. After his near upset in the 1966 primary, Dubin decided to run again—this time as an independent. The Democratic machine anointed Bert Podell as its candidate.

Dubin, running on a peace platform, invited Minnesota Senator Eugene McCarthy to campaign on his behalf. Although Bert Podell ran as a "100 percent supporter" of President Lyndon Johnson, he called for a cessation of the bombing of North Vietnam for at least thirty days "in order to get all parties into negotiations." When challenged on the consistency of this position, Podell had a stock response: "I don't divorce my wife every time we have a disagreement."

In the campaign, Podell hammered away at issues important to families in the district, notably the spreading use of illegal drugs. Podell repeatedly charged: "It is ridiculous that a Federal Government that spends $180 billion a year and can sample the moon's crust [this was a year-and-a-half before the first manned flight to the lunar surface] cannot inaugurate and contribute to an international commission to buy the world poppy crop, select what is needed medically, burn the rest, and dry up the illicit drug traffic." Podell also supported passage of a constitutional amendment granting eighteen-year-olds the right to vote.

Roughly one-third of the district's voters showed up at the polls—a remarkable turnout for a special election. Podell wound up winning an 8,429 plurality over Dubin. The *New York Times* saw his victory as a major triumph for Brooklyn Democratic boss Stanley Steingut, who, the paper noted, had "staked his political reputation on [Podell's] candidacy." Mel Dubin, who waited until all 358 election districts had reported before conceding defeat, blamed his loss on the "Democratic organization vote." Standing before his disappointed supporters, Dubin told them: "We depended on the votes of those who opposed the war in Vietnam and there were 27,664 of them." Podell, on the other hand, likened his victory to "a Christmas party, Fourth of July and bar mitzvah all rolled into one." On February 20, 1968, Bert Podell was seated as a member of the Ninetieth Congress.

The day after the election, the *Times* ran an editorial that damned Podell's victory with faint praise: "The Steingut organization, which has kept in office some of the dingier members of this state's Congressional delegation, chose on this occasion to run one of its brighter members." The *Times* saw Podell's victory as "a limited one" for President Johnson's Vietnam policy, noting that "Mr. Podell campaigned vigorously for the peace vote . . . call[ing] for a halt in the bombing of North Vietnam." Seeking to send a pointed message to the newly seated representative, the editorial concluded by saying: "If he doesn't already know it, the new Congressman will soon learn in Washington that this is not Administration policy." Once in Congress, Podell became a solid, vocal opponent of the war.

The House Democratic leadership assigned Bert Podell to the House Administration Committee and the Interstate and Foreign Commerce Committee. He was appointed to the latter panel's Subcommittee on Transportation and Aeronautics. During his nearly seven years in the House of Representatives, Bert Podell voted a generally liberal line, opposing most of President Richard Nixon's policies—prayer in the public schools, the anti-ballistic missile, and selling jet aircraft to Nationalist China—and supporting political disclosure laws, consumer protection, and abolishment of the House Un-American Activities Committee.

Podell was a strong, vocal supporter of Israel and Soviet Jewry, and an equally vocal detractor of the Nixon administration. Shortly after his arrival in Congress, he led a massive petition drive in favor of the sale of Phantom Jets to Israel. Backed by articles and editorials run in the Orthodox *Jewish Press*, Podell was able to collect more than two million signatures. For his efforts, he received the personal thanks of Israeli Prime Minister Golda Meir.

In 1971, a friend from the Israeli embassy approached Podell with the information that transcripts of the Stalin-era Doctors' Plot trial had been discovered. Would he be interested in going to Russia and retrieving them? Podell agreed. "This was on a Wednesday, and he told me that I would be going over there with *Jack Javits* on Friday. Well, I went home and told Bunny to pack. We got to the airport—no Javits. We went alone." Once in Moscow, Podell was given a State Department escort and a Russian driver. "Throughout our stay, we were followed by the KGB. I was such a cocky kid in those days, that once I had the State Department guy get the Russian driver to pull over in front of a telephone booth. I jumped out, and made a big deal of putting a large folded piece of paper under the telephone. Then I got back in the car, and we returned to the hotel. Before going into the hotel, Bunny and I walked the two or three blocks back to the telephone booth to see if the KGB had taken the bait. Sure enough, when we got there, the paper was gone. What they got for their efforts was a paper with the message 'F—You!'"

Before Podell could obtain the Doctors' Trial transcripts, the State Department told him that he would have to leave Russia—things were getting too hot. According to Podell, on the way to the airport, he turned to the driver and said: "Look, I know you understand English perfectly well. You've been listening in on everything we've been saying for days. Please, if you ever wanted to do something for humanity, do this one favor: lose those guys behind us." The driver managed to elude the KGB at a railroad crossing and delivered Podell to a place where he was given a small packet of documents. Back in the car, Bunny Podell put the documents into a sanitary napkin, which she wore on her person all the way out of Russia. Flying on to Paris, the Podells were met at Orly airport by two cars: one from the U.S. State Department and one from the Israeli embassy. Before getting into the State Department vehicle, he walked over to the Israelis and delivered the papers. To this day, Podell has no idea what the papers really were.

Podell also claims to have been instrumental in Israel's 1973 air strike on Egyptian SAM missile emplacements. According to Podell, a NASA lobbyist gave him a gift—a series of high-resolution photos taken from space. The photos showed various places on earth, notably the Middle East. Podell asked the NASA lobbyist if the photos were classified. The lobbyist insisted that they were not. Representative Podell then took the photos to Amos Eron, legislative representative at the Israeli embassy. According to Podell, Eron passed the photos on to Israeli intelligence, who blew them up, discovering the SAM missile site. "I got real personal satisfaction out of that one," Podell said.

Bert Podell was easily reelected in 1968, 1970, and 1972, capturing 77 percent, 65 percent, and 74 percent of the vote, respectively. In 1973, he was indicted on charges that he had received more than $40,000 "for an attempt to get the Civil Aeronautics Board to award a Bahamas route to a Florida airline." Facing the local and national press, Podell charged that the indictment was "trumped up by the Nixon Administration" in order to discredit him and to "divert attention away from the Watergate scandal." In the 1974 primary, Podell, with the indictment and a pending trial hanging over his head, came in second in a three-way race; the victor was thirty-six-year-old New York State Assemblyman *Stephen Solarz*. His victory was as much a rebuke of the Brooklyn Democratic machine as a repudiation of an indicted incumbent.

Shortly after losing the Democratic primary, Bert Podell went on trial. His attorney paraded a host of character witnesses, including House Speaker Thomas "Tip" O'Neil and Harlem Congresswoman Shirley Chisholm, in an attempt to portray his client as a decent, honorable gentleman. On the trial's ninth day, exhausted by the grueling cross-examination of

Assistant U.S. Attorney Rudolph Giuliani ("Giuliani virtually destroyed Podell's credibility," wrote a *New York Post* reporter), Podell entered into a plea agreement. In exchange for a guilty plea to one charge of conspiracy and one count of conflict of interest, the government agreed to drop the far more serious charges of bribery and of lying to both the FBI and a federal grand jury. Podell was sentenced to six months in prison and a $5,000 fine. He was also disbarred. Had he not entered into the plea agreement, he could have gotten as much as fifteen years in prison.

Podell tried repeatedly to have his legal license reinstated. Finally, in 1979, the state legislature passed a law "reversing the automatic disbarment of lawyers convicted of Federal crimes that are not state felonies." Podell was reinstated on July 26, 1980.

Today, Bert Podell is a partner in the firm of Podell, Schwartz, Banfield, Schecter and Banfield. The practice represents more than ten thousand properties worth more than $40 billion. Podell is still active in Jewish communal activities. He sits on the board of his *alma mater*, the Yeshiva of Flatbush, and recently finished a five-year stint as president of the Greater New York Region of the Jewish National Fund. A former trustee of the East Midwood Jewish Center in Brooklyn, Podell is currently a member of the Reform Central Synagogue in Manhattan. Some years ago, he built and dedicated a park in Jerusalem in memory of his parents. Now in his mid-seventies, he toys with the idea of writing his memoirs, tentatively entitled "All That Glitters . . ."

References

Interview with Bertram Podell, January 1998.
Almanac of American Politics (1970–76 editions).
New York Post, October 2, 1974, 1:4.
New York Times, February 21, 1968, 1:4; February 22, 1968, 30:2;October 26, 1968, 22:3; August 8, 1997, B7:6.
Howard M. Sachar, *A History of the Jews of America* (New York: Knopf, 1992), pp. 912 ff.

PULITZER, JOSEPH (1847–1911): *Democrat from New York; served part of one term in the House (Forty-ninth Congress; March 4, 1885–April 10, 1886).*

Most movie critics agree that Orson Welles's *Citizen Kane* is one of the two or three greatest films of all time. A thinly veiled avatar of journalist William Randolph Hearst, Welles's Charles Foster Kane is a tragic figure who metamorphoses from a rich crusading reformer into a crude acquisitive monster. Welles's career suffered greatly as a result of this, his first movie. Hearst became enraged, and put the full power and prestige of his newspaper empire behind the blacklisting of the cinema's twenty-five-year-old enfant terrible. One wonders how things might have turned out for Welles if, instead of Hearst, he had chosen to make his film about the other great newspaper baron, Joseph Pulitzer. The cinematic possibilities fairly boggle the mind.

Of the 179 members of the Congressional Minyan, Joseph Pulitzer stands alone in terms of accomplishment, brilliance, and sheer eccentricity. Variously described as the best-informed man in America and the loneliest man in the world, Pulitzer ran a hugely successful newspaper empire. Moreover, during his lifetime, he elected American presidents, governors, and mayors, and helped shape the thinking of a nation. He was painted by Sargent and modeled by Rodin, was sued by President Theodore Roosevelt for libel, and almost single-handedly raised the funds for the Statue of Liberty. He was, in short, endowed with a rare aspect of genius. And yet, despite this stunning record of achievement, Pulitzer was a victim of his own poor health, suffering from "insomnia . . . fierce headaches, asthma, rheumatism, dyspepsia, diabetes, catarrh and other ills as well as fulminating nerves." As a result, he spent the better part of his life shuttling from spa to spa and from clinic to clinic the world over, in search of a magic cure that might restore his sight, health, and mental equilibrium.

One of history's true eccentrics, Pulitzer had such a penchant for secrecy that he developed a private code of more than twenty thousand words. Painfully sensitive to noise, he spent literally millions of dollars on deep-pile carpeting, triple-thick glass, and other noiseless materials. He kept an ongoing retinue of private secretaries (whom he referred to as his "white mice") who served as his eyes and legs, his mentors and students. To be employed as one of J. P.'s white mice, a man had to be schooled in the arts and classics, literature, music, current events, and architecture, speak several European languages, possess a well-modulated voice, be able to withstand almost constant criticism and challenge, and have the ability to eat without making undue noise. A towering figure in American journalism, Pulitzer only stepped foot into his newspaper office three times in a thirty-year period. Like the fictionalized Hearst, Pulitzer lived a largely hermetic existence. Unlike Charles Foster Kane, he never truly left the reformist fold. From first to last, Pulitzer saw both himself and his newspapers as forces for enlightenment, education, and progress.

Joseph Pulitzer was born in Mako, Hungary, on April 10, 1847. Mako was a thriving market town near the Romanian border, some 125 miles southeast of Budapest. His father, Phillip Pulitzer, is said to have been a "cultivated Magyar-Jew grain dealer;" his mother, Louise Berger, "an Austro-German beauty and a Catholic." Joseph was one of four Pulitzer children. The eldest, Louis, died as a child, leaving Joseph and his brother Albert, four years younger, and a still younger sister, Irma. In 1853, Phillip Pulitzer went into semi-retirement and moved his family to Budapest, "where the children were educated by private tutors and were expected to learn French and German." It would appear that Louise's Catholicity was stronger than Phillip's Jewishness, for at one time Albert seemed destined for the priesthood.

Joseph was still in school when his father died and his mother remarried a Budapest merchant named Max Blau. Headstrong and impulsive, young Joseph grew to hate his stepfather. By age seventeen, standing nearly six feet three and weighing a cadaverous 140 pounds, Joseph decided to strike out on his own. Energized by the exploits of Otto Von Bismarck, he sought a commission in the Austrian army; he was rejected on the grounds of age, poor eyesight, and fragile physique. Pulitzer went on to Paris, where he tried to enlist in the French Foreign Legion; again he was rejected. From Paris he moved on to London, where he attempted to join the British army. He was turned away yet a third time. Undeterred, Pulitzer went to Hamburg, where "agents, seeking recruits for the Union army in America's Civil War, were so anxious for federal bounties that they would accept anything that could walk." Pulitzer had finally found an army that would take him.

Placed on a "grubby" ship, Pulitzer sailed from Germany to America, arriving in Boston in the late summer of 1864. According to legend, he decided it made good sense for him to "collect his own bounty rather than have it benefit the recruiting agent." Consequently, he jumped overboard in Boston Harbor, swam to shore, and made his way to New York, where he enrolled in the First New York Lincoln Cavalry. Since he spoke Hungarian, German, French, and a smattering of English, he was placed in a largely German-speaking unit. Described in those days as "a scrawny beanpole with a hooked blade of a nose, an up-jutting chin that seemed to meet the nose, an enormous Adam's apple and weak eyes peering through cheap spectacles," Pulitzer became the "Goat of Company L." Taunted by his comrades as "Joey the Jew" and "Pull-it-sir," the lanky Hungarian got into fist fights galore. Brawling aside, it was a rather uneventful war; Pulitzer spent most of his eight months in the Union Army as an orderly for Major Richard Hinton.

Upon his discharge from the army, Pulitzer spent time trying to keep body and soul together in New York City. Failing at this, he moved west to St. Louis, where there was a large German community. During his early days in the west, Pulitzer worked as "a gate-operator at a ferry-slip, deckhand on a packet to Memphis, construction laborer, stevedore on the river docks, and hack driver." He even served a short stint as a waiter at Tony Faust's, a famous St. Louis restaurant.

Imbued with enormous self-confidence, Pulitzer talked his way into a job with a German-language newspaper run by Carl Schurz, who was to exert a "lasting influence over his career." Schurz (1829–1906), a Bonn-educated expatriate, had one of the most interesting, and variegated careers of any nineteenth-century American. He "fought in the German revolution of 1848, was captured and imprisoned, staged a hair-raising escape, fled to England and then America," where he became involved in politics. Lincoln named him minister to Spain. Never one to shy away from a battle based on principle, Schurz

left his comfortable post, returned to America, and joined the Union Army. By war's end, he was a major general. Following the war, he went out to St. Louis, where he became coeditor of the Republican *Westliche Post*—and Pulitzer's employer. Schurz later served one term as United States Senator from Missouri (1869–75), and was President Rutherford Hayes's Secretary of Interior. At one time, Schurz also served as editor of the *New York Evening Post*.

Pulitzer's first years in St. Louis were a blur of activity. Besides working for the *Westliche Post*, he became an American citizen (1867), read law and passed the Missouri Bar (1868), entered politics, and got himself elected as a Republican to the Missouri Legislature (1870). No one seemed to notice that the lanky Hungarian was underage at the time. As a state legislator, Pulitzer was not one to "merely support or oppose legislation." Always intense to a fault, Pulitzer weighed each measure "in all its ramifications and then either assailed as one attacks a thug or upheld as if for salvation." Following his one term in the Missouri legislature (1870–72), Pulitzer secured a gubernatorial appointment as a member of the board of three police commissioners in St. Louis. It was a two-year appointment that carried an annual salary of $1,000.

Pulitzer continued making a name for himself as a journalist and orator. In 1872, he became a delegate to the state constitutional convention. Two years later, he attended the Reform Republican convention in Cincinnati. Originally a liberal Republican, Pulitzer broke with his mentor Schurz and became a Democrat. By the late 1870s, he was given an ownership stake in the *Westliche Post* and made managing editor. Selling his stake in the *Post* for nearly $40,000, Pulitzer purchased his own newspaper, the *St. Louis Post Dispatch*. Now a man of means, Pulitzer began living in the city's best hotel, wearing nattily tailored suits, and dining at the best restaurants.

As a journalist, Joseph Pulitzer was a both a rabble-rousing crusader and a born reformer. The journalistic crusade was the foundation of his editorial policy for more than thirty years. His tirades always had two aims: to build circulation and to promote reforms. Naturally hotheaded and argumentative, Pulitzer had "a luckless affinity for violence and tragedy" that would pursue him throughout his St. Louis years. He accumulated a series of enemies throughout St. Louis because of his journalistic crusades against the gas company, a lottery racket, a horse-car monopoly, and an insurance fraud. Having exposed the powerful and corrupt with equal relish, he found it necessary to carry a pistol wherever he went. People who knew him in these years found him to be insightful and driven—like a man who thought that each day might be his last. He remained a man possessed for the rest of his life. No one could quite figure him out: for although he loved to draw others out in conversation, he rarely spoke about himself.

In 1877, Missouri Congressman John E. Clarke introduced Pulitzer to the "positively beautiful" Kate Davis. The twenty-three-year-old daughter of Judge William Worthington Davis of Georgetown, Kate Davis possessed "intelligence, spirit, warmth, common sense [and] humor." Her father, "in comfortable circumstances and socially impeccable," was a distant cousin of Jefferson Davis, President of the Confederate States of America. Having experienced anti-Semitic barbs both in Hungary and America ("Joey the Jew," "Jewseph" and "Pull-it-sir" being among the more onerous), Pulitzer made the conscious decision not to tell Miss Davis of his Jewish ancestry. Perhaps he thought that she would reject him out of hand. They were married on June 19, 1878 at Washington's Episcopal Church of the Epiphany, where her parents had been married thirty years earlier. Pulitzer, who as an adult had virtually no religious affiliation, "knelt at the altar with the devout daughter of Anglo-Saxon Protestants who thought she was marrying an unalloyed Hungarian." Kate Davis Pulitzer did eventually learn of her husband's Jewish antecedents. Though it was said that she was "greatly upset," she managed to "survive the shock." Nevertheless, Pulitzer's Jewishness was "a factor that both of them would have to cope with for the rest of their lives."

Kate Pulitzer gave birth to six children: Ralph (1879), Lucille Irma (1880), Katherine Ethel (1882), Joseph Jr. (1885), Edith (1886), and Constance (1888). Katherine died of pneumonia in 1886, just six weeks short of her sixth birthday. Lucille died suddenly in 1897, at age seventeen. Joseph was a demanding, autocratic father. He desperately wanted his sons to be strong-

willed and independent, but made them completely dependent on his largesse. He wanted his daughters to be paragons of culture. Because he spent most of his time away from home, Joseph Pulitzer can truly be said to have raised his children via telegram and letter. He encouraged them to keep journals in which they would record such daily minutiae as what books they read, what sights they saw, even what ideas they contemplated. He further demanded that they correspond with him on a constant basis. Nonetheless, the tyrant could be very generous.

Throughout most of their married life, Kate Pulitzer saw her husband for only a few weeks a year, and only for brief periods on those rare occasions when they were in the same place at the same time. Nonetheless, they remained devoted to one another, and once he became wealthy, Joseph permitted Kate a monthly allowance in excess of $7,000—this at a time when the average *annual* income was less than $850.

Kate raised the Pulitzer children as Episcopalians. Whether any of their father's Jewish heritage permeated their lives is doubtful. According to one of Pulitzer's biographers, W. A. Swanberg, "Pulitzer . . . seemed unable to adjust himself comfortably to his fractional Jewish ancestry. He was so abnormally sensitive that any slur struck him like a whiplash." In his later years, although he contributed money for the relief of Jewish victims of pogroms, Pulitzer strictly forbade his white mice to enter into any discussion that involved Jews, Judaism, or Jewishness. Though he himself was certainly not an anti-Semite, and numbered Jews among his friends and employees, he "tended to recoil from racial or religious discussions . . . to escape them, to push them away." From a theological point of view, Pulitzer was a thoroughgoing skeptic. He had no overt hostility toward Judaism or any other religion. His "religion" was a powerful identification with "the people," in whom he saw his special "mission" or "calling." Because he had married a staunch Episcopalian, many Jews misinterpreted Pulitzer's religious skepticism as a denial of his ethnicity.

Pulitzer was afflicted by what biographer Swanberg called "electionitis Pulitzerium"—a pathological addiction to electoral politics. It plagued him every four years. During his earliest days in St. Louis, he told a friend: "I can never be president because I am a foreigner, but some day I am going to elect a president." This "election malady" led Pulitzer into an ill-advised primary race for Missouri's Second District congressional seat in 1880. He was humiliated at the polls, receiving only 709 votes to 4,254 for Thomas Allen, the wealthy president of the Iron Mountain Railroad. Meeting members of the St. Louis press after his defeat, Pulitzer told them: "I am out of public life. The only suffrage I solicit you can extend to me by purchasing my newspaper daily."

Joseph Pulitzer, "the loudest voice on the Mississippi," soon wore out his welcome in St. Louis and set his sights on New York. His brother Albert was already in New York, having founded the one-cent Morning Journal in 1882. Albert had already made a considerable reputation for himself as Washington correspondent for the Herald, which later sent him to Europe to report on the Russo-Turkish war. Albert's Morning Journal (which he would sell in 1894 for more than $1 million) shunned politics, devoting much of its space instead to "entertainment and gossip, to the theater and sporting events." It was an immediate success.

Brother Joe desperately wanted a New York newspaper of his own. After several abortive efforts, he succeeded in purchasing the New York World from robber-baron Jay Gould in 1883. The price was a staggering $346,000, to be paid in installments ending in 1886. The World had been founded as a religious daily in 1860, sunk into receivership, and then strongly revived as a Democratic paper following the disastrous Samuel Tilden campaign in 1876. By the time Pulitzer purchased the World in 1883, it did possess one valuable asset: an Associated Press franchise.

Joseph Pulitzer's ideal was to create a newspaper "so astonishingly liberal, reformist and newsy" that it would captivate working-class readers and "still appeal to a segment of the white-collar class." In this he succeeded. Looking ahead to the presidential race of 1884, less than a year away, Pulitzer realized that if he was to have a voice in the election, he would need to build up circulation at a fantastically rapid pace. This he did. One remembers the pastiche of short takes in Citizen Kane where Kane and his senior staff are looking out the window of the newspaper office. Emblazoned on the

glass is the fictional paper's daily circulation. Within a matter of three shots, the paper's circulation more than quadruples. Such was Pulitzer's success. By November 1884, he was close to his goal of having the most powerful Democratic newspaper in America.

From the first day Joseph Pulitzer took over the World, it was a voice for reform. World articles exposed "tenement horrors and . . . gave statistics on infant mortality. . . . It pictured the poor at Christmas without bread much less turkey and plum pudding. . . . It assailed the laggard sanitary inspectors for letting conditions sink to savagery." Unlike the other great New York papers of the day, Pulitzer's World "insisted on treating the poor as human beings rather than ciphers." Pulitzer won over the masses in record time by imbuing his paper with three qualities: readability, excitement, and education.

Pulitzer's campaign on behalf of presidential candidate Grover Cleveland was decisive. It also got Pulitzer himself elected as a Democrat to the Forty-ninth Congress from New York's Ninth Congressional District. Pulitzer, barely one year in the city, won a decisive victory over Republican Herman Thum by the final count of 15,510 to 8,510. During his race for Congress, the rival New York Journal belittled Pulitzer by declaring: "As a business manager of a clothing establishment . . . Jewseph Pulitzer [sic] would be an honor to his race and a glory to his surroundings."

Big things were expected of the gaunt, bearded, myopic publisher-cum-Congressman. He also expected big things from himself. Perhaps with his powerful sense of self, he truly believed that a freshman Congressman in his first session could get both the Senate and the President to dance to his tune. He was wrong. Arriving on Capitol Hill, Pulitzer declared that his first goal would be to "wipe out the high Republican tariff" and replace it with a low "tariff for revenue only." Toward that end, he was given a seat on the important Interstate and Foreign Commerce Committee.

As things turned out, Congress was not for Joseph Pulitzer. First, there was the matter of running both his New York and St. Louis newspapers from a great distance. He wound up spending most of his time consulting with his own correspondents. Secondly, "he could take little interest in such congressional debates as that over a bill to regulate the manufacture and sale of oleomargarine when he felt that the most important issue facing the country (the tariff) was leaking away in committee." Pulitzer resigned his seat on his thirty-ninth birthday, April 10, 1886, barely four months into his first term. He was replaced by the ebullient Samuel Sullivan "Sunset" Cox (1824–1889), who had in turn already resigned from the Forty-ninth Congress in order to accept a diplomatic post in Turkey.

Joseph Pulitzer returned to New York and his fast-growing newspaper empire. By 1887, he had paid off his debt to Gould and was now a very rich man. With the *World*'s circulation in excess of 250,000, his net worth was hovering around $2.5 million. As a result of his rapid rise in both the newspaper world and "polite" society, Pulitzer came under attack from his rivals, most notably Charles A. Dana of the *New York Sun*. Dana (1819–1897), a onetime member of the Brook Farm community and Civil War-era Assistant Secretary of War, assailed Pulitzer at every turn. He referred to the increasingly eccentric Hungarian as "a renegade Jew who has denied his breed . . . a poltroon in an hour of danger."

Dana reprinted ad nauseam an editorial from the *Hebrew Standard* that read in part: "[Pulitzer] is a Jew who does not want to be a Jew." Dana often went over the top in his condemnation of his rival:

> The Jews of New York have no reason to be ashamed of Judas Pulitzer if he has denied his race and religion. . . . The shame rests exclusively on himself. His face is repulsive, not because the physiognomy is Hebraic, but because it is Pulitzeresque . . . cunning, malice, falsehood, treachery, dishonesty, greed, and venal self-abasement have stamped their unmistakable traits. . . . No art can eradicate them.

Dana would reprint the *Hebrew Standard* editorial as often as three times a week, always on Saturdays and Mondays. Most frequently, the editorial would be double-leaded for greater prominence, always with the title "Move On, Pulitzer—Repudiated by His Race." Beginning in the late 1880s, Joseph Pulitzer did just that, becoming a wanderer and seeming recluse for the rest of his life.

As Pulitzer's sight began to fail, he increasingly withdrew from the hurly-burly of the New York publishing scene. By 1890, he was almost totally blind. Moreover, he developed an extreme sensitivity to unexpected sound that would eventually "make him wince at the scratching of a match." As he moved into his sixth decade, the impossibly wealthy Pulitzer (now worth in excess of $20 million) began showing signs of melancholy and mental instability. It is fair to say that clinically he was a manic depressive. Times of suspiciousness, unreasonableness, deviousness, and cruelty were interspersed with periods of gaiety, affection, and generosity. There developed a legend of "Pulitzer the monster who drank editors' blood," and another legend of "Pulitzer the most generous, if the most demanding of employers." Both had their roots in truth. Try as he might, he could not find a cure for what ailed him. In a sense, by moving from spa to spa, from clinic to clinic, from rented estate to rented estate, he was seeking to cure his surroundings.

Joseph's brother Albert was also suffering from mental instability. He too suffered from terrible bouts of melancholy and insomnia. Unlike his more famous elder brother, Albert drowned his sorrows in compulsive eating binges that made him "fat as a Buddha." Moving to Europe, Albert lived as a virtual recluse at the Hotel Bristol in Vienna along with a secretary and a woman aide who read newspapers and books to him daily. One day, in 1909, the woman read him an item about a man troubled by insomnia who had killed himself. To this Albert reportedly said: "*Wenn ich nur Mut dazu hatte*"—"if only I had the courage." A few days later he went to a pharmacy to buy prussic acid. The pharmacist, sensing that the customer was deranged, sold him a harmless almond extract. Returning to his hotel, Albert drank the concoction, realized that he had been deceived, and shot himself in the head. He was buried in a Jewish service, paid for by brother Joseph. The only mourner at the service was one of Joseph Pulitzer's retainers. The *World* ran a brief obituary on Albert Pulitzer a few days later, failing to mention his relation to the paper's publisher.

Joseph Pulitzer's journalistic war with William Randolph Hearst is the stuff of which legends are made. As in *Citizen Kane*, Hearst repeatedly raided the *World*'s staff, hiring away

Pulitzer's "best and brightest." Like Charles Foster Kane, Hearst struck Pulitzer as "a crude boy having fun with millions, a mere stunt specialist masquerading as a reformer." Both newspapermen delighted in pulling off "stunts" in search of greater circulation. Where Hearst caused a stir by making a martyred heroine of "Miss Cisneros," purportedly the victim of Spanish atrocities in Cuba, Pulitzer scored a direct hit with his sponsorship of Nellie Bly's seventy-two-day circumnavigation of the globe. Both men pushed for war with Spain. Both papers seized on the tragedy of the sinking of the *Maine* as a pretext for immediate war. Both papers supported their own presidential candidates as if the fate of the entire world depended on their respective endorsements.

As mentioned above, Pulitzer developed his own secret code for communicating with his editors, his attorneys, even his family. Among the more fascinating code names he developed were "Andes" (himself), "Gadroon" (J. Pierpont Morgan), "Glutinous" (Theodore Roosevelt), "Gush" (Hearst), "Malaria" (the Republican Party), and "Melon" (Woodrow Wilson). Each of New York's leading papers had its own code name as well: "Geography" (The *New York Times*), "Geologist" (the *New York Herald*), and "Geranium" (the *New York Journal*). A typical coded telegram from Pulitzer might read: "Yesterday and today's senior hopping, yesterday's junior hydropsy, last seniority gross hypocrite hands crew hydrant." Decoded, the message reads: "The *World* has sold 295,000 copies, the *Evening World* 430,000, and the *Sunday World* 400,000."

During the Theodore Roosevelt years, Pulitzer launched an editorial assault on the President and his administration, charging them with conspiracy to defraud the American people in the matter of the Panama Canal. Roosevelt in turn sued Pulitzer and his minions for libel. The case strung along till after Roosevelt was out of office. During research leading up to the trial, Pulitzer actually bore the expense of sending United States Attorney General Henry Wise to Paris, as well as another federal attorney to Panama. Responding to the federal indictment with defiance, Pulitzer had his *World* editorialist write:

Mr. Roosevelt is an episode. The *World* is

an institution. Long after Mr. Roosevelt is dead, long after Mr. Pulitzer is dead, long after the present editors of this paper are dead, the *World* will still go on as a great independent newspaper, unmuzzled, undaunted, and unterrorized.

Joseph Pulitzer was only half right; his *New York World* would only outlive him by nineteen years and four months. In 1931, it was sold to the Scripps-Howard chain.

Joseph Pulitzer died on board his 269-foot long, $1.5 million yacht, Liberty, in the harbor of Charleston, South Carolina. He was sixty-four years old. In his will, he divided his $18 million fortune unequally among his wife, sons, and daughters, and provided $2 million for the creation of a school of journalism at Columbia University. He also endowed the program which to this day awards "Pulitzer Prizes" for outstanding achievements in journalism, history, biography, music, and drama. In his will, he admonished his sons to keep the *World* going:

I particularly enjoin upon my sons and my descendants the duty of preserving, perfecting and perpetuating the *World* newspaper, to the maintenance and publishing of which I have sacrificed my health and strength. In the same spirit in which I have striven to create and conduct it as a public institution, from motives higher than mere gain . . .

Joseph Pulitzer's funeral service was held on November 1, 1911, at St. Thomas Episcopal Church at Fifth Avenue and Fifty-third Street, which it is likely Pulitzer had never entered once in his life. He was interred in Woodlawn Cemetery in New York City.

Six weeks after Pulitzer's death, daughter Edith married William Scoville Moore, grandson of Clement Moore, the scholar and poet who wrote "A Visit From St. Nicholas." Kate moved to France, where she spent the remaining sixteen years of her life living variously at Deauville, Cap martin, and the Château de la Garoupe at Nice. Joseph Jr. continued in his father's footsteps, achieving great success running the *St. Louis Post Dispatch*. Pulitzers continue to appear in the news from time to time, but not for the reasons that J. P. would have appreciated. Or would he? At least their stories sell papers.

Perhaps the most telling tribute to this blind, ailing man who "educated the people, dropping boulders rather than pebbles into the pool of public opinion" came from one of his oldest and best friends, the publisher Henry Watterson: "His life reads like a story out of the books of giants, goblins and fairies."

References

American Jewish Year Book, vol. 14 (1912–13), p. 125.

Dictionary of American Biography.

Encyclopaedia Judaica (1972), vol. 13, col. 1382.

Jewish Encyclopedia.

New York Times, November 2, 1911, 11:5.

Don C. Seitz, *Joseph Pulitzer: His Life and Letters* (New York: Simon & Schuster, 1924).

W. A. Swanberg, *Pulitzer* (New York: Charles Scribner's Sons, 1967).

Universal Jewish Encyclopedia.

Who Was Who in America, vol. 1.

RABIN, BENJAMIN J. (1896–1969): *Democrat-Liberal from New York; served two terms in the House (Seventy-ninth and Eightieth Congress; January 3, 1945–December 31, 1947).*

In 1937, Governor *Herbert H. Lehman* appointed attorney Benjamin J. Rabin to chair the New York State Mortgage Commission. The body had been created by the New York State Legislature and mandated to "supervise the financial reorganization of 15,000 real estate financial structures and the actual management of 4,000 buildings." Originally appointed commission counsel in 1935, Rabin did such a good job as chairman that by 1939, he recommended its abolition; all its work had been completed. When viewed from the perspective of the late twentieth century, Rabin's action seems incredible. Certainly by today's standards, "once a bureaucracy, always a bureaucracy."

Benjamin J. Rabin was born in Rochester, New York, on June 3, 1896, one of Meyer and Sarah Rabin's four children. He was educated in the public schools of Rochester before moving down to New York City in 1915 in order to attend New York University. In May 1917, Rabin's studies were interrupted by World War I. He enlisted in the United States Navy, serving until January 1919, at which time he mustered out as an ensign. In June of that year, he received his law degree from NYU. Following his admission to the New York State bar later that year, he joined the law firm of Greenbaum, Wolff, and Ernst. Starting as a law clerk, he rose to become managing partner. In 1926, he struck out on his own, and was in private practice until 1935.

For the two years from 1934 to 1935, Rabin served as counsel to a New York State joint legislative committee investigating guaranteed mortgages. With expertise came recognition, for in 1935, as noted above, Governor Lehman appointed him Mortgage Commission counsel. Following the demise of the commission (Lehman took his advice), Rabin went back into private practice with the firm of Diamond, Rabin, Freidin, and Mackay, which was later to be renamed Poletti, Diamond, Rabin, Freidin, and Mackay. During World War II, Rabin headed the appeals board of the Selective Service System in the Bronx, disposing of some 15,000 draft case appeals in less than three years.

In 1944, Twenty-fourth District (southwestern Bronx) Representative James M. Fitzpatrick announced that he would be retiring from Congress after serving nine terms. Rabin entered into the race for the vacant seat, winning the election without difficulty. As a member of the Seventy-ninth Congress, Rabin was appointed to the Committee on Interstate and Foreign Commerce. He was easily reelected in 1946.

Shortly after his reelection, Rabin's name began to be bandied about in political circles as "the eventual final choice" of Democratic Party leaders for appointment to the federal bench to fill the vacancy caused by the death of Judge Samuel Mandelbaum. At the last minute, however, President Truman accepted the recommendation of the bar association and appointed another man to the position. His appetite whetted, Rabin decided to run for the New York State Supreme Court from the First Judicial District. Nominated by both the Democrats and the Liberal Party, Rabin declined to accept the American Labor Party's endorsement, fearing that its left-leaning reputation might hurt his chances at the polls. The American Labor Party wound up giving its endorsement/nomination to Rabin's chief opponent in the race, Edward Lumbard, Jr. Rabin won election to a fourteen-year term on the Supreme Court and resigned from Congress, effective December 31, 1947.

Midway through his first fourteen-year term, Governor Averell Harriman appointed Rabin a justice of the Appellate Division for the First Department, New York and Bronx Counties. Reappointed by Governor Nelson A. Rockefeller, Rabin won reelection to a second fourteen-year term in 1961. He served until his death in Palm Beach, Florida, on February 22, 1969.

Benjamin Rabin was married to the former Syd Sobel. They had no children. A member of Kehilas ha-Kodesh B'nai Elohim, Rabin was active in Big Brothers and the United Jewish Appeal. He was survived by his wife, his sisters Ethel B. and Nettie B. Rabin, and his brother, Dr. Coleman B. Rabin. Benjamin Rabin is buried in Riverside Cemetery in New Rochelle, New York.

References
American Jewish Year Book, vol. 47, p. 630.
New York Times, November 5, 1947, 2:4; February 24, 1969, 37:1.
Who Was Who in American Jewry, 1938.

RAYFIEL, LEO FREDERICK (1888–1978):
Democrat from New York; served two terms in the House (Seventy-ninth and Eightieth Congress; January 3, 1945–September 13, 1947).

Leo Rayfiel's career as a public servant began with his election to the New York State Assembly in 1938; it ended forty years later with his death. Remarkably, Rayfiel did not run for public office until past age fifty. In this, however, he was merely following family tradition: his father didn't begin attending law school until he was past forty.

Hyman Rayfiel, Leo's father, was born in Riga, Latvia. At age eight, he became a lumberjack, riding lumber-filled boxcars to the port, where they were off-loaded onto waiting barges. As a teenager, Hyman left Latvia for England, where he lived briefly near Hyde Park. From there, it was on to Halifax, Nova Scotia, and eventually New York, where he found work as a trolley car conductor. In the late nineteenth century, being a conductor was not only a steady living, it had political ramifications. One lucky enough to land a job on a trolley generally had friends with good connections.

Hyman was married to Anna Rich, whom he met either in Latvia or in England. Their son, Leo Frederick, was born in New York City on March 22, 1888. By all accounts, Hyman was an autodidact and something of a Renaissance man and free spirit. According to his grandson, Howard Rayfiel, Hyman was "a totally self-taught man who spoke many languages . . . was a magical horticulturist, a poet, a painter . . . and a great lover of animals." As an amateur horticulturist, the senior Rayfiel somehow managed to grow an orange tree in the middle of Brooklyn—one that actually bore fruit. Once, while vacationing in Florida, Hyman Rayfiel became so intrigued with alligators that he brought one back to his home. "For weeks, we couldn't take a bath," his grandson recalls. "He also kept a lot of birds which he would allow to fly free through the house."

A self-taught talmudist, Hyman Rayfiel was also a devotee of Emerson. Given his views, it is not surprising that Leo received little (if any) Jewish education and never became bar mitzvah. Devoted to local Democrat politics, Hyman was "a power for many years . . . in the Brownsville and Flatbush sections." At age forty, he decided to go to law school. After developing a successful private practice, Hyman Rayfiel eventually became a magistrate and Special Sessions judge. At Leo's judicial robing ceremony in 1947, he began his remarks with the quip: "It was easy for me—my father was a judge."

Leo Rayfiel went through the New York public school system, graduated high school, and then enrolled in the New York University School of Law. He received his LL.B. in 1908 at age twenty but did not take the bar examination until 1918. During the ten years between his graduation and his first days as an attorney, Rayfiel worked at a series of jobs. An excellent musician, he toured the country with a group of young friends that included Eddie Cantor, George Jessel, and Gus Edwards. The latter was an actor/singer who became both a vaudeville producer and an impresario. Edwards was largely responsible for making stars of both Cantor and Jessel.

From show business, Leo Rayfiel became a salesman. While living and working in Atlanta, he did business with Harris Marks, a garment manufacturer. Marks's daughter Flora, who worked as his bookkeeper, caught Leo's eye. They were married in June 1916. The Rayfiels had three sons: Robert D., David, and Howard. Robert (deceased) became a chemical engineer. David, one of Hollywood's most respected script doctors (his film credits include *Yentl, The Morning After, Three Days of the Condor, Absence of Malice,* and the Academy Award–winning *Out of Africa*), was at one time married to actress Maureen Stapleton. Howard, like his father and grandfather before him, became an attorney, and was, for many years, counsel to the Desilu Studios in Hollywood.

Like his own father, Leo Rayfiel was a freethinker who permitted his sons to make decisions for themselves. Son Bob, who was such an outstanding Hebrew student that "he could have become bar mitzvah at age ten," decided shortly before his thirteenth birthday that he simply "didn't believe in it." As a result, he never became bar mitzvah. Leo never said a word.

In 1918, the thirty-year-old Leo Rayfiel set up a law practice in Brooklyn. He specialized in real estate law and from all indications did quite well. Active in Brooklyn Democratic Party circles, Rayfiel was offered the local State Assembly seat in 1928. He turned the party bosses down; the practice of law brought him too much enjoyment. Ten years later, he did run—and won a seat in the New York State Assembly. During his four-plus years in Albany (1939–44), Rayfiel set a record by never missing a legislative session. After his election to Congress in November 1944, he consciously decided to miss his last session, thereby spoiling an otherwise unblemished record. When asked why, he responded: "It will give someone the chance to do better."

In 1944, Rayfiel ran for Congress from the newly created Thirteenth District in Brooklyn. From 1944 until its dismemberment fifty years later, the Thirteenth was represented by four Jewish men: Leo Rayfiel (1945–47), Rayfiel's law partner *Abraham Multer* (1947–68), *Bertram Podell* (1968–75), and *Stephen Solarz* (1976–92). Both Rayfiel and Multer left Congress to become judges; Podell ended up before the bench rather than on it; Solarz was redistricted into oblivion.

During its half-century of existence, the Thirteenth District in south-central Brooklyn might have been called the Ocean Parkway district. It took in neighborhoods on both sides of that well-known thoroughfare as it made its way from Prospect Park to Coney Island. It had the largest Jewish constituency of any congressional district in America. It also had one of the nation's most heavily Italian-American constituencies. (Leo Rayfiel actually took Italian lessons at Berlitz in order to be able to campaign among this group). The Thirteenth was one of the "bastions of support for the Democratic machine." In its heyday, with its "patronage tentacles covering the Brooklyn Courts and Borough Hall," the machine could get its man (never a woman) elected at will. As a loyal party brave, Rayfiel was assured victory in 1944.

Despite lacking any military background, Leo Rayfiel was seated on the Veterans' Affairs Committee, chaired by Mississippi's John E. Rankin. A noted bigot, Rankin (1882–1960) got perverse pleasure from "baiting and making life unbearable" for black and Jewish members of Congress. As Rankin became more senile, his bigotry became more vile and pronounced. Adam Clayton Powell, a black representative from Harlem, took his seat in Congress the same day as Leo Rayfiel. Upon seeing Powell, Rankin said he would not sit next to him—though nobody had asked him to. Powell replied that he refused to sit next to Rankin, because "only Hitler and Mussolini [are] qualified to sit next to him, and we [have] already taken care of them."

Like his good friend Representative Powell, Leo Rayfiel was oftentimes the target of Rankin's obloquy. For the most part, Leo Rayfiel held his tongue—and waited. His time came toward the end of the Seventy-ninth Congress.

In 1946, a reporter by the name of Albert Deutch wrote a lengthy article in the leftist paper *PM* detailing horror stories about conditions in various Veterans Administration hospitals. Rankin decided to hold hearings, not so much to see whether Deutch's allegations were true, but to pillory the hapless reporter for being a "fellow traveler." Rankin demanded that Deutch reveal his sources. Deutch refused. Rankin threatened to hold Deutch in contempt of Congress. At this point, Leo Rayfiel took the unprecedented step of moving that Rankin be stripped of his chairmanship. Against all odds, Rayfiel's motion passed; Rankin relinquished his gavel.

During his thirty-two months in Congress, Leo Rayfiel worked in Washington but lived in Brooklyn. His wife Flora, plagued by a bad heart and diabetes, never became a "politician's wife." Between his legislative duties on Capitol Hill, his law practice in Brooklyn, and local politics, Rayfiel had little time for relaxation. Son Howard remembers that in all the years his father was a legislator, "we went to precisely two baseball games. Dad was always bone-tired." Once, upon returning from Washington during his second term, Rayfiel came home to find a telegram on his bed. Opening it, he read that the Republicans, knowing that all the liberal Northeastern Democrats had gone home for the weekend, had decided put a "penny milk repeal bill" on the agenda for the next day—Friday.

In the 1930s and 1940s, Democrat-controlled Congresses regularly passed legislation making milk available to the nation's children—often for free. Because the Republican Party controlled the Eightieth Congress (1948–48), they also controlled the legislative agenda. When he finished reading the telegram, Rayfiel, dog-tired, picked up the phone and made reservations to take the redeye back to Washington. When he came onto the House floor the next morning, he was the only member of the New York City delegation in attendance. As it turned out, the Republican attempt at repeal failed—by one vote.

Rayfiel maintained a mostly liberal voting record, in which he regularly supported President Harry S. Truman. On July 1, 1947, Truman nominated Rayfiel to replace the late Grover M. Moskowitz on the United States District Court for the Eastern District of New York. Not surprisingly, his nomination had been made on the recommendation of the Brooklyn Democratic organization headed by Borough President John J. Cashmore. According to the *New York Times* announcement of Rayfiel's nomination, "it represented a victory for the [Brooklyn Democratic] organization in that similar political recommendations made in the Southern District of New York were ignored by the President." Concomitant with Rayfiel's nomination, another of Truman's nominees, Harold R. Medina, was confirmed for a position on the Southern District bench.

On July 2, the *Times* lauded Judge Medina ("an excellent choice of a man") while editorializing against the Rayfiel nomination, which it termed "sponsored by local political leaders." Furthermore, it said, the nomination "elevate[d] to the bench a man who ha[d] devoted many years mainly to service in the State Assembly and in Congress." While acknowledging that "Mr. Rayfiel undoubtedly is a man of high principles," the editorial writer saw fit to add that "political and legislative experience constitutes neither preparation nor qualification for judicial service." In short, the *Times* said, it is "discouraging to find the excellent example of the Medina appointment so quickly followed by one which does not seem to measure up to the standards desired for the federal bench." In reality, the problem was not so much Leo Rayfiel's lack of judicial qualifications as the pique of the *New York Times* counsel, Henry Ward Beer, at not having been offered the nomination.

Despite the opposition of both the American and New York Bar associations "on the grounds [we can] find no evidence whatever that he is qualified for the position," Rayfiel was confirmed by the Republican Senate in early September 1947. Rayfiel promptly resigned his congressional seat. He remained on the District Court until his death in Wayne, New Jersey, on November 18, 1978. Leo Rayfiel is interred in Wellward Cemetery, Farmingdale, New York. Amazingly, for a New York City native who devoted four decades to public service, the *Times* ran no obituary.

References

Interview with Howard Rayfiel, December 1997.

American Jewish Year Book, vol. 47, p. 630.

William "Fishbait" Miller, *Fishbait: The Memoirs of the Congressional Doorkeeper* (Englewood Cliffs, N.J.: Prentice-Hall, 1977), pp. 162–164.

New York Times, July 1, 1947, 47:3; July 2, 1947; 22:2; July 16, 1947; 16:5.

New York Times Magazine, April 6, 1986, pp. 24–30.

Who Was Who in America, vol. 8.

RAYNER, ISIDOR (1850–1912): *Democrat from Maryland; served three terms in the House (Fiftieth, Fifty-second, and Fifty-third Congress; March 4, 1887–March 3, 1889, March 4, 1891–March 3, 1895); elected to two terms in the Senate but died early in the second (March 4, 1905–November 25, 1912).*

Time and history have not been kind to Senator Isidor Rayner. Virtually unknown today, he was, in his heyday, both a spellbinding orator and a politician of national stature. He was twice asked to run for Vice President of the United States but opted to remain in the Senate, "preferring the floor to the chair." Moreover, at the 1912 Democratic National Convention, held in his hometown of Baltimore, Senator Rayner was one of several men whose names William Jennings Bryan offered as suitable candidates for President. The nomination wound up going to New Jersey Governor Woodrow Wilson, who, when elected, named Bryan his Secretary of State. Rayner had a nervous breakdown and died less than three weeks after Wilson's election, thus beginning a rapid descent into historical anonymity.

Isidor Rayner, the fourth Jew elected to the United States Senate, was born in Baltimore on April 11, 1850. His father, William Solomon Roehner, who had emigrated from Obrelsbach, Bavaria, about ten years earlier, was originally a schoolteacher. Upon arriving in the United States, he was offered a job teaching Hebrew at the Henry Street Synagogue in New York. Declining the offer, he moved south, to Fell's Point, Maryland, where he established himself as a dry goods merchant. Within two or three years he had accumulated enough capital to send for his childhood sweetheart (and first cousin), Amalie Jacobson, whom he married in 1844. A liberal Jew and freethinker, William Rayner was one of the founder's of Baltimore's Har Sinai Congregation. He was also instrumental in the hiring of Rabbi David Einhorn (1809–79), one of nineteenth-century America's preeminent rabbis. Einhorn was forced to flee Baltimore during the riots of April 1861, because of his vehement opposition to slavery. He eventually made his way to New York City, where he served many years as the rabbi of Congregation Beth El.

By the eve of the Civil War, William Rayner had become a very wealthy man. He was able to send his son Isidor first to Frederick Knapp's private school in Baltimore, then to the University of Maryland, and, finally, in 1865, to the University of Virginia. Following his graduation from Virginia, the young Rayner read law in the Baltimore offices of Brown and Brune. He was admitted to the Maryland bar in 1871, just a few weeks before his twenty-first birthday. On December 5 of that year, he married a non-Jew, Frances Jane Bevan, the scion of a prominent Baltimore family. Their one son, William, was raised as a Christian.

In the 1870s, Rayner built up a lucrative legal practice, specializing in litigation. Since he came from a family long known for its involvement in civic affairs, it came as no surprise when Rayner announced his candidacy for the Maryland General Assembly in 1878. He was easily elected as a Democrat and served in that body for seven years. During his tenure in the General Assembly, he served as chairman of its Judiciary Committee. Rayner was elected to the State Senate in 1885 but resigned midway through his term in order to run for Congress from Maryland's Fourth District. He won the election and was officially sworn in as a member of the Fiftieth Congress on March 4, 1887.

In 1888, President Grover Cleveland was defeated by Republican Benjamin Harrison. Rayner, a staunch ally of the Democrat President, also lost his bid for reelection. After just one term in the House of Representatives, he returned to the practice of law. Rayner remained a private citizen for only two years; in 1890, he was once again elected as Representative from the Fourth District. This time he would remain in the House until early 1895. During his second stint on Capitol Hill, Rayner served on the House Committee on Foreign Affairs and chaired the Committee on Organization. He was one of the first members of Congress to push for a constitutional amendment mandating the popular election of United States Senators, a position that stood him in good stead with the people of Maryland.

Rayner took a lead role in the repeal of the Sherman Silver Purchase Act during the first session of the Fifty-third Congress. This act, named after Ohio Senator (and future Secretary of State) John Sherman, required the Treasury Department to purchase 4.5 million ounces of silver a month at prevailing prices and issue legal-tender Treasury notes redeemable in gold or silver. When a worldwide depression began during the Harrison administration in 1890, the fight for repeal of the Sherman Silver Act began in earnest. With Rayner at the helm, the act was finally repealed on October 30, 1893, thus earning the Maryland Representative the undying gratitude of the newly elected President, Grover Cleveland. (By being returned to the White House in 1892, Cleveland thereby became the only President in American history to serve two nonconsecutive terms.)

Rayner declined renomination in 1894 and returned to Maryland, where he was immediately touted as a major candidate for governor. Inexplicably, he withdrew his name from the race shortly before the election, and was pilloried in the Democratic press for a lack of political courage—a stigma that adhered to him for the rest of his life. After practicing law for several years, Rayner was elected Maryland's attorney general in 1899, a post he retained until 1903.

Isidor Rayner first came to national prominence in 1902, when he offered his *pro bono* legal services to Rear Admiral Winfield Scott Schley. During the Spanish-American War, Schley had been in immediate command of the U.S. forces that defeated the Spanish fleet at the Battle of Santiago. Many people credited him with the victory, but others said it belonged to Admiral Sampson, Schley's superior. A naval court of inquiry, headed by Admiral George Dewey, the victor of the Battle of Manila Bay, was convened to resolve the controversy. The inquiry, a long, drawn-out affair, garnered a great deal of public attention, especially for the senior counsel, Isidor Rayner. His summation before the court of inquiry reportedly lasted more than five hours, and was called a "classic" by legal cognoscenti. In the end, the court ruled in favor of Admiral Schley.

Fresh from this legal triumph, and armed with a great deal of public goodwill, Rayner announced that he would be "a candidate before the people" for United States Senator in the upcoming 1904 election. At that time, Maryland Democratic politics were held in a viselike grip by the so-called Gorman ring, headed by United States Senator Arthur Pue Gorman (1839–1906). Rayner's decision to go to the people with his candidacy caused the Gorman faction to laugh—

and the national press to take notice. Against all odds, the Maryland General Assembly went against the Gorman ring and elected Isidor Rayner to the United States Senate. He was sworn in on March 5, 1905.

Rayner was soon recognized as one of the Senate's most powerful orators. He could also, on occasion, show devastating wit. Once, when arguing an amendment to the McKinley Tariff bill, he casually made the remark: "Everything is either a luxury or a necessity." Just then a Southern Senator, known for his scrofulous appearance, stepped onto the floor and said: "May I interrupt the gentleman?" "Certainly," said Senator Rayner. "Did I understand you to say that everything is either a luxury or a necessity?" "Yes sir," responded Senator Rayner. "Well, I have just taken a bath; what would you call that?" the Southern gentleman asked. "In your case," Rayner replied, "it is both a necessity and a luxury; a necessity because you need it so badly, and a luxury because you take it so rarely!"

In the Senate, Isidor Rayner saw himself as a defender of the Constitution against President Theodore Roosevelt, whom he accused of "arrogating the right to make treaties under the guise of executive agreements without the consent of the Senate; of centralizing power in the federal government in derogation of state[s'] rights; and of interfering with the functioning of the judiciary at the expense of constitutional government."

Rayner rarely mentioned his Jewishness in public—nor did anyone else, for that matter. One exception was when he was arguing against a bill that would have disenfranchised the black voters of his home state, Maryland. This measure, known as the Poe Amendment, would have required prospective voters to pass an examination on the Constitution. In a statement run on page 1 of the *Baltimore Sun*, Rayner said that if his own father, an immigrant Jew from Bavaria, had arrived in Maryland after 1869, he could have been disenfranchised under the Poe Amendment. Moreover, he added, he himself would be disenfranchised unless he passed "a satisfactory constitutional examination, conducted, perhaps by some unconvicted felon in a register's box."

Rayner also fought long and hard for the abrogation of an 1832 commercial treaty with

Russia because of the tsarist government's discrimination against passports held by American Jews. After the Kishinev pogrom in 1905, Rayner launched into a plea for granting aid to the persecuted Jews of Russia. He said on the floor of the Senate that "Jews [will] submit to every indignity and wrong rather than abandon their creed—a creed which [has] maintained its simplicity inviolable in the face of all opposition." He urged the Roosevelt administration to take the lead in making "a demand upon this barbarous Prince [the tsar] to grant to these people their rights or no longer be allowed to maintain contact or intercourse with civilized governments."

Isidor Rayner was reelected for a second six-year term in 1911, but died less than a year later. A nervous, excitable man, he passed away at age sixty-two on November 25, 1912. His health had been in decline for some time. Although he had been a lifelong member of Congregation Har Sinai, Rayner's funeral service was conducted by two Christian ministers, one of whom, the Reverend Ulysses G. B. Pierce, minister of All Souls' Unitarian Church, was both Senate chaplain and President William Howard Taft's own pastor. Isidor Rayner was buried in Rock Creek Cemetery in Baltimore, a non-Jewish cemetery.

References

American Jewish Year Book, vol. 2, p. 522; vol. 6, p. 167; vol. 15, p. 273

Dictionary of American Biography.

Encyclopaedia Judaica (1972), vol. 13, col. 1590.

Jewish Encyclopedia.

Publications of the American Jewish Historical Society, vol. 40, pp. 288–295.

Universal Jewish Encyclopedia.

Who Was Who in America, vol. 1.

RESNICK, JOSEPH YALE (1924-1969): *Democrat from New York; served two terms in the House (Eighty-ninth and Ninetieth Congress; January 3, 1965–January 3, 1969).*

A self-made millionaire who served two terms in the House, Joseph Resnick is one of the few Minyanaires who never graduated from high school. Born to immigrants Morris and Anna (Zaida) Resnick, in Ellenville, Ulster County, New York, on July 13, 1924, Joseph Resnick was raised on his family's farm. He dropped out of high school in order to join the Merchant Marine, and spent World War II studying electronics, eventually becoming a radio officer.

Following his discharge from the service, Resnick, along with his brothers Harry and Louis, entered the fledgling television industry. Working in his parents' barn, Resnick devised a preassembled television antenna that virtually anyone with a ladder could install. His antenna had the added advantage of offering clearer reception than any such device on the market. In 1947, the brothers incorporated themselves as the Channel Master Corporation. Within a scant six years, they had become the country's leading manufacturer of TV antennas. Expanding their interests into plastics as well, all three brothers eventually became multimillionaires.

Joseph Resnick remained in Ellenville, marrying Ruth Lehrer in 1947, and raising three sons and a daughter. Freed from the necessity of having to make a living, he entered local politics, winning a seat on the Ellenville school board. In 1964, the forty-year old Resnick announced his candidacy for Congress from the Twenty-eighth District. At that time, the Twenty-eighth took in the overwhelmingly Republican (and overwhelmingly WASP) Columbia, Duchess, Green, Schoharie, and Ulster Counties. Easily winning the Democratic primary, Resnick then faced incumbent Republican J. Ernest Wharton, who had represented the Twenty-eighth Congressional District for seven consecutive terms. Wharton looked like a sure bet for reelection, but 1964 was the year that President Lyndon B. Johnson beat Republican challenger Barry M. Goldwater in a landslide. Johnson's coattail effect gave Resnick all the edge he needed to defeat Wharton. Joseph Yale Resnick was duly sworn in as a member of the Eighty-ninth Congress on January 3, 1965.

Resnick was appointed to the House Agriculture Committee—a good assignment for someone representing a fairly rural district. Before too long, Resnick gained a reputation for being a political maverick. As a freshman, he took on the powerful American Farm Bureau Federation, denouncing it as a "gigantic, interlocking nationwide combine of insurance companies and other companies." Resnick argued that the AFBF should be deprived of its tax-exempt status. He then garnered national headlines by taking on the United States Navy in the matter of Lieutenant Commander Marcus Aurelius Arnheiter, who had been removed from the command of a destroyer escort operating off the coast of Vietnam. Arnheiter, a 1952 graduate of the U.S. Naval Academy, was summarily relieved of his command of the U.S.S. *Vance* after a 99-day stint that writer Neil Sheehan claimed could easily have been taken from *The Caine Mutiny*, *Mr. Roberts*, and *The Bedford Incident*. Writing in the *New York Times Magazine*, Sheehan described Arnheiter as "a paranoid captain, a real-life Queeg, who exhibited strange quirks and ran his ship with tyrannical whimsy." According to his junior officers, Arnheiter enforced discipline "with a martinet's fetish for shined belt buckles and shoes, but violated Navy regulations and the orders of his superiors whenever it suited him." He was also charged with trying to wage a "private war" while on duty off the coast of Vietnam.

Resnick charged the Navy with treating Arnheiter unfairly and demanded his reinstatement. Arnheiter was given his "day in court," charging his crew with mutiny and defamation of character. Despite Resnick's assistance (he convinced nearly ninety of his colleagues to sign a petition on the beleaguered lieutenant commander's behalf), Arnheiter was reassigned to a "graveyard" position at Treasure Island, California. His board of inquiry declared that he would never be returned to active sea duty.

Resnick also caused a bit of a stir when he came to the aid of a "dark-skinned" couple who wanted to adopt a blond, blue-eyed baby girl. Resnick saw no reason why an "insignificant" issue like color should have anything to do with a legitimate adoption.

Joseph Resnick defeated Republican Hamilton Fish, Jr., for reelection in 1966. Fish, who came from the most politically prominent family in the district—there had been men named Hamilton Fish serving in the federal government for more than 125 years—would take over Resnick's seat in 1968, when Resnick resigned in order to seek the Democratic senatorial nomination. Despite his national reputation and sound financial backing, Resnick came in third in the primary, losing to Paul O'Dwyer, who in turn was defeated by incumbent Senator *Jacob Javits*.

Following his defeat, Joseph Resnick returned to Channel Master, which by now was an enormous corporate entity. On October 6, 1969, while en route to Las Vegas on a business trip, Resnick suffered a fatal heart attack. He was just forty-five years old. Joseph Resnick, who was survived by his wife, children, two brothers, and two sisters, was buried in the Hebrew Aid Cemetery in Wawarsing, New York.

References
Biographical Directory of the United States Congress, 1774–1989, pp. 1706–1707.
New York Times, August 11, 1968, VI:7 ff.; October 7, 1969.

RIBICOFF, ABRAHAM ALEXANDER (1910–1998): *Democrat from Connecticut; served two terms in the House (Eighty-first and Eighty-second Congress; January 3, 1949–January 3, 1953) and three terms in the Senate (January 3, 1963–January 3, 1981).*

At the 1968 Democratic National Convention in Chicago, Connecticut Senator Abraham Ribicoff gained a measure of lasting fame after having already spent more than a quarter-century in public life. The pitched battle taking place on the convention floor was relatively tame in comparison to the battle going on outside the hall. Young antiwar demonstrators, who had descended upon Chicago by the tens of thousands, were met with the fury of Mayor Richard Daley's police force and the Illinois National Guard. For three days, a rapt American television audience was witness to acts of police brutality and simmering political tensions.

On the convention's final night, Ribicoff took center stage. In the middle of his speech nominating South Dakota Senator George McGovern for the presidency, Ribicoff, throwing away his prepared notes, leaned over the rostrum and stared directly at Mayor Daley. Barely able to contain the anger welling up within him, Ribicoff said: "With George McGovern as president of the United States, we wouldn't need police using Gestapo tactics in the streets of Chicago. With George McGovern, we wouldn't need the National Guard."

Daley and his supporters "cupped their mouths and shouted an obscenity at Senator Ribicoff that few television viewers had trouble lip-reading." Glaring at Daley and his minions, Ribicoff scolded: "How hard it is to accept the truth when we know the problems facing our nation." The Illinois delegation demanded that Ribicoff "Get down! Get down!" A cacophony of mixed boos and cheers ascended in the hall.

For the vast majority of the television audience, it was the first time they had ever seen or heard of Abraham Ribicoff. That fact is rather surprising, considering that at the time he so bluntly assailed Mayor Daley, Ribicoff already held a unique distinction: he was (and still is) the only Senator in American history to have previously served as state legislator, municipal judge, United States Representative, governor, and cabinet officer.

According to his parents, Samuel and Rose (Sable) Ribicoff, Abe was destined to greatness from the moment of his birth. For Abraham Ribicoff was born on April 9, 1910 with a caul covering his head. To his parents, this membrane was a sign of great fortune. To the last day of his life, nearly eighty-eight years later, Abe Ribicoff kept the membrane preserved in tissue paper—as a reminder of his humble beginnings and of a prediction that came true.

Samuel Ribicoff, a Polish immigrant, worked in a Hartford factory. In order to help eke out the tenement house existence for his family, which included Abe, another son, Irving, and a daughter, Hilda, Samuel also *untergepedlered*—Yiddish for one who peddles part-time. According to the Senator, "we were really poor, but everything I earned peddling papers and working in stores, he [Samuel] made me put aside for education." While attending Smalley Elementary School and New Britain High School Ribicoff worked part-time as a paper boy, caddy, milkman's helper, gasoline pumper, and construction worker. An avid athlete, he also played sandlot baseball and was starting tackle on his high school's football team.

The Ribicoffs belonged to a small Orthodox congregation; until the end of his life, Samuel attended services three times each day. Young Abe studied Hebrew at the New Britain Talmud Torah, and was bar mitzvah in 1923. According to his Talmud Torah teacher, Jacob Stein (who went on to head the Hebrew school at Temple Emanuel in Hartford), Ribicoff was a very good student who, as an adult, could "still hold his own" in reading from a *siddur* (Hebrew prayer book).

Following his graduation from New Britain High in 1927, Ribicoff went to work in the G. E. Prentice Company's zipper factory in New Britain, "in order to meet future expenses at New York University," where he enrolled as a freshman in 1928. Before the beginning of his sophomore year, Ribicoff accepted an offer from Prentice to become its Midwest sales representative at a salary of $70 a week. Moving to Chicago, he petitioned the University of Chicago to be admitted to its evening law school despite lacking a bachelor's degree. Accepted in 1930, Ribicoff soon became its star and editor of the *University of Chicago Law Review*. Three years later, he received his law degree *cum laude* and was elected to the Order of the Coif.

During his first year in law school, Ribicoff married his childhood sweetheart, Ruth Siegel of Hartford. Rabbi Morris Silverman, who had confirmed Ruth, conducted the ceremony at Temple Emanuel. In later years, the Ribicoffs would belong to two Hartford synagogues: the Reform Temple Beth Israel and the Conservative Emanuel. Ruth Ribicoff spent many years actively involved in the latter synagogue, working for the women's branch of the United Synagogue. At one point, she served as honorary chair of a United Synagogue drive to raise funds for a women's residence at the Jewish Theological Seminary in New York. The Ribicoffs had two children: Peter and Jane (Bishop).

In his final year in law school, Ribicoff published a paper entitled "The Jurisdiction of the Supreme Court in Hearing Appeals from State Courts in Certain Categories," which came to the attention of several officials in the Treasury Department. Shortly after graduating, Ribicoff was offered a $3,800-a-year position with Treasury but decided to return to Connecticut, where he passed the bar and went to work in the office of a Hartford attorney. Sometime later, the Roosevelt administration offered him a $4,800-a-year position with the Tennessee Valley Authority. Again he declined the offer, telling himself he was "a small-town lawyer" at heart.

After practicing law for several years, Ribicoff was urged by Connecticut Democratic Party leader John Bailey to run for the state legislature. Bailey saw in the young (twenty-eight) attorney "a potentially successful challenger to Republicans." Ribicoff was elected to the first of two terms in the lower house of the Connecticut General Assembly in 1938. In a poll of political reporters he was voted the legislature's "most promising freshman." During his second term, he was named "most able representative." Leaving the legislature, he became a member of the American Arbitration Association's Motion Picture Panel and was appointed a judge of the Hartford Police Court.

After serving on the bench for a number of years, Ribicoff was urged to take on First District Republican William J. Miller for a seat in Congress. Ribicoff defeated the incumbent Miller by more than 25,000 votes and was largely credited for providing the margin that made newly elected Governor Chester Bowles's upset victory possible. The First District, taking in all of Hartford, contained about 26,000 Jews in 1948. As a prominent member of the Jewish community, Ribicoff received the lion's share of their votes. During his two terms in the House, Ribicoff supported most of the Truman administration's domestic measures. In foreign affairs, he had a tendency to part ways; he voted for the passage of the Communist-control bill over the President's veto.

Assigned to the House Foreign Affairs Committee, Ribicoff was sent to Europe in 1949 with North Carolina Representative Thurmond Chatham to report on the progress of the Marshall Plan. At the time, many members of Congress felt that the Marshall Plan had accomplished its task and that its discontinuance could lead to a much-needed reduction in taxes. Upon his return, Ribicoff reported that such thinking was "dangerous." "It looks to me more like a task of ten more years calling for an additional outlay of $25 billion," he said. "We must look upon the cost of keeping Europe free as a cost of keeping ourselves in business."

Ribicoff was reelected by more than 38,000 votes in 1950. During his second term in the House, he authored and cosponsored (along with Connecticut Senator Brien McMahon) a resolution affirming that "the American people deeply regret the artificial barriers which separate them from the peoples of the Union of Soviet Socialist Republics" and calling on the Soviet people "to cooperate in a spirit of friendship." Coming in the nascent stages of McCarthyism, it was a gutsy resolution. Amazingly, the bill passed both the House and Senate, and was transmitted to Soviet President N. M. Shvernik by Harry S. Truman in July 1951.

In 1952, forsaking his safe House seat, Ribicoff suffered his only political defeat: a loss in the Senate election to Prescott S. Bush, father of future President George Herbert Walker Bush. Stressing issues of "national survival," Ribicoff lost by less than 30,000 votes out of more than 1 million cast. Following the defeat, Ribicoff resumed his partnership with his brother Irving in the Hartford firm of Ribicoff & Ribicoff. Handling largely real estate and probate cases, Ribicoff made a small fortune.

Two years later, on June 25, 1954, he was nominated "by acclamation" to run against Governor John Davis Lodge, who was seeking a second term. Ribicoff pledged to run a campaign that would be "positive, constructive and free from personalities." As he told assembled reporters: "If we cannot win decently, I do not want to win at all." Although hard fought, the campaign was declared "among the cleanest in the nation" by the *New York Herald Tribune*. During the race, Ribicoff was made aware of an anti-Semitic whispering campaign. Rather than ignore it, Ribicoff decided to take the issue head-on. Going on statewide television, Ribicoff dramatically declared: "Any boy, regardless of race, creed or color, has the right to aspire to public office. It is not important whether I win or lose. The important thing is that Abe Ribicoff is not here to repudiate the American dream, and I know that the American dream will come true. I believe it from the bottom of my heart, and your sons and daughters, too, can have the American dream come true."

That did it; the whispering campaign stopped. Ribicoff defeated Lodge by the narrow margin of 3,115 votes, thereby becoming the first Jewish governor of a New England state. Ribicoff was the only Democrat to win statewide office that year. As a newly elected Governor, he was faced with a split legislature; the Lower House had a two-to-one Republican majority; the Senate a slight Democratic edge.

While serving as governor, Ribicoff conducted affairs of state with great simplicity. "He had no press secretary and issued no press releases. . . . He preferred a state policeman's small sedan to the big, official Governor's limousine [and] he rode in the front seat with the driver. . . . And he disliked the term 'executive mansion' for the nineteen-room Georgian house assigned to the Governor on Prospect Hill in Hartford. He referred to it as his 'residence.'"

In his campaign for reelection in 1958, Ribicoff won with what, at the time, was the greatest majority in state history—nearly 250,000 votes. Ribicoff's coattails were responsible for the election of a totally Democratic slate from his state in the U.S. House, and a Democratic majority in both houses of the State Assembly. It was the first time that this had occurred since 1874.

As early as 1950, Abraham Ribicoff predicted that his House colleague John F. Kennedy would one day become America's first Catholic President. Ribicoff was given the honor of putting Kennedy's name into nomination for Vice President at the 1956 Democratic National Convention. This came only after a heated back-room debate. Although many party stalwarts thought Kennedy would make an attractive national candidate, many felt that he should not even try. Sitting in a hotel room in Chicago, Ribicoff "listened to the leading Irish Catholic politicians object to Kennedy," the Senator remembered. "They did not think the nation was ready for a Catholic, they said. Speaking last, I said, 'I never thought I'd see the day when a man of the Jewish faith had to plead before a group of Irish Catholics about allowing another Irish Catholic to be nominated for the position.'"

When Kennedy announced his candidacy in 1960, Ribicoff acted as his floor manager at the Democratic National Convention. Even before his inauguration, "the nation's first Catholic President had announced as his first Cabinet appointment the designation of a Jew." According to Abe Ribicoff, Kennedy originally wanted to name him Attorney General. Ribicoff declined, and suggested that Kennedy name his brother Bobby to the post. Recalling the scene more than thirty years later, Ribicoff said: "Kennedy was taken aback: 'I can't name my own brother.'" Ribicoff reportedly told the President-elect: "The person closest to you is Bobby; you're from the same womb. In every crisis, you automatically turn to Bobby."

As Secretary of Health, Education and Welfare, Ribicoff became only the third Jewish member of an executive cabinet. The two previous were Oscar S. Straus, Theodore Roosevelt's Secretary of Commerce, and Henry Morgenthau, Jr., Secretary of the Treasury under Presidents Franklin Roosevelt and Harry Truman.

Ribicoff resigned his governorship in January 1961. Within sixteen months, he would leave the Kennedy cabinet. He deeply regretted leaving Connecticut and taking the HEW post, describing it as a position that required making "politically unpopular" decisions. While in Kennedy's cabinet, Ribicoff drafted the original Medicare plan, which was defeated after intense lobbying by the American Medical Association. Returning to Connecticut, Ribicoff announced his candidacy for the Senate seat being vacated by Prescott Bush. Ribicoff won, thereby beginning an eighteen-year tenure in "the world's greatest deliberative body."

As a Senator, Ribicoff had "an almost uncanny ability to anticipate issues." As an example, Ribicoff wrote the nation's first Clean Air Act (1963) and conducted the Senate's earliest hearings on automobile safety—a full year before publication of Ralph Nader's *Unsafe at Any Speed* (1965). He was also largely responsible for the creation of four new cabinet posts: Housing and Urban Development, Transportation, Energy, and Education.

Throughout his Senate career, the issue closest to Ribicoff's heart was national health care. Having failed in his earlier attempt at passage of Kennedy's Medicare plan, Ribicoff went on the offensive, fighting for a health-care system that would benefit the greatest number of people without bankrupting the treasury. He opposed Senator Edward Kennedy's health program, which promised total coverage for all Americans, because "it was too expensive and would become a bureaucratic nightmare." Rather, he joined with Louisiana Senator Russell Long in offering an alternative bill providing insurance only for catastrophic illnesses.

Under the Long-Ribicoff plan, "Medicaid would handle services for the poor and Medicare for the elderly. The remainder of the nation would continue to participate in government-subsidized, private or union plans." Ribicoff argued that the federal government did not have "the administrative capacity to manage a national health care program," and suggested that private insurance companies were better prepared to handle the program.

Supporters of Senator Kennedy's proposal accused Ribicoff of "opposing the more ambitious program because his state contained more national insurance companies than any other state in the union." In the end, Congress failed to pass either the Ribicoff or the Kennedy bill.

From his earliest days in the House, through his time as Governor and his stint as Secretary of HEW, Ribicoff was known as one of the true champions of civil rights in the nation. In 1970, he found himself in the strange and uncomfortable position of being allied with Southern conservatives. Ribicoff supported an amendment by Mississippi's Senator John Stennis that called for "a uniform policy on enforcement of school desegregation guidelines regardless of the cause of discrimination." In effect, the amendment sought to eliminate the distinction between *de jure* and *de facto* segregation.

Ribicoff got into a dramatic debate with New York Senator *Jacob Javits* (in 1970, the only other Jewish Senator), whom he dared to drop his "monumental hypocrisy" and admit that Northern school systems were just as racially segregated as those in the South. Speaking directly to his old friend and colleague, Ribicoff told Javits: "I don't think you have the guts to face your liberal constituents who have moved to the suburbs to avoid sending their children to school with blacks." Despite his support of Stennis's desegregation amendment, Ribicoff emphasized that he would not support an anti busing amendment that would "halt federal efforts to enforce school desegregation." The Senate adopted the Stennis amendment, but a House-Senate conference committee reinstated the *de facto-de jure* distinction.

A staunch Zionist, Ribicoff backed arms sales for Israel and opposed efforts to force it to surrender the administered territories. Ribicoff was also a cosponsor of the historic Jackson-Vanik Amendment, which refused most-favored-nation status to the Soviet Union unless (or until) it permitted Jews to emigrate to Israel. Toward the end of his Senate career (1978), Ribicoff shocked members of the Jewish community when he voted in favor of arms sales to Egypt and Syria and supported President Jimmy Carter's policies in the Middle East policies.

The next year, Ribicoff announced that after nearly forty years in public life, he would retire from the Senate. In announcing his retirement, Ribicoff said: "There is a time to stay and a time to go."

Ribicoff was both a practicing Jew and an active *shul* member all his life. On way to his formal inauguration as Governor of Connecticut in 1955 and 1959, he stopped at Temple Beth Israel in order to confer with his rabbi, Abraham Feldman. While living in the Governor's residence, he suffered two deaths: his father-in-law and his mother. On both occasions Governor Ribicoff sat *shiva* (the seven-day period of mourning), bringing in a *minyan* each morning and evening in order to say *Kaddish* (the mourner's prayer).

In April 1972, Ruth Ribicoff died after having been ill for nearly fifteen years. Later that year, the Senator married the former Lois ("Casey")

Mathes. Following his retirement from the Senate, Abraham Ribicoff joined the New York law firm of Kaye, Scholer, Fierman, Hays & Handler, where he became the firm's "resident elder statesman and wise man." Until his death, Ribicoff remained out of the political limelight, explaining that he had "no use for politicians who didn't know when their day was up." "Nothing is as sad as seeing a person who used to have power have none," he told a reporter.

As Abe Ribicoff reached his eighties, people asked why he hadn't written his autobiography. Ribicoff's response was unique for a politician of his stature: "You should not do an autobiography if you want to tell the truth. There are a lot of things I know about people. If I can't say something good about a person, I don't want to say anything. And since I don't want to say anything bad, I won't write a book."

In an August 1997 *Los Angeles Times* interview, Casey Ribicoff disclosed that her husband was suffering from Alzheimer's disease. During the Senator's final illness, Mrs. Ribicoff became very close to former First Lady Nancy Reagan, whose husband had been diagnosed with the same disease three years earlier. "You can't begin to understand what living with this is like unless you do live with it, day in and day out," Mrs. Ribicoff told the *Times* reporter. "I don't know what I would do without Nancy."

Abe Ribicoff died at the Hebrew Home for the Aged in Riverdale, the Bronx, on February 22, 1998. His funeral service was conducted two days later at Temple Emanu-el on Manhattan's Fifth Avenue.

Abraham Ribicoff was described as "a man of handsome elegance, always meticulously dressed, given to smoothing his wavy graying hair, his lips downturned in an expression of perpetual, vague distaste . . . [an] intensely private man, a humorless, distant man who carrie[d] himself with the patrician bearing of one who never seriously doubted his success."

References

American Jewish Biographies (New York: Facts on File, 1983), pp. 349–350.

Current Biography, 1955, pp. 503–505.

Jewish Digest, March 1961, pp. 1–5.

New York Times, July 7, 1974; June 6, 1979; February 23, 1998.

Abraham Ribicoff, *Politics: The American Way* (Boston: Allyn & Bacon, 1973).

RICHMOND, FREDERICK WILLIAM (1923–):

Democrat from New York; served four terms in the House (Ninety-fourth through Ninety-seventh Congress; January 3, 1975–August 25, 1982).

Fred Richmond is unquestionably one of the saddest, most perplexing members of the Congressional Minyan. He is also a study in opposites: a self-made multimillionaire who lived in an elegant apartment on Manhattan's posh Sutton Place while representing a polyglot, largely blue-collar Brooklyn district; an urbanite who became a power on the House Agriculture Committee; a man of charm, generosity, and consideration who was also insulting and tyrannical; a collector of fine art and antiques who had an appetite for the sordid and the depraved. And yet, despite it all, he was an extremely effective legislator—before he was forced to resign from Congress and begin a prison term for income-tax evasion, possession of marijuana, and making an improper payment to a federal employee.

Fred Richmond used to tell people that his father, George Richmond, had gone to Harvard and coached teams there; had been a judge and played for the Boston Braves. None of it was true. Fred Richmond was baldly attempting to reinvent his father's past, in order to make him the kind of man Richmond wished his father had been. In truth, George Richmond had attended Boston's School of Commerce and Finance and the Northeastern College of Law, from which he graduated *magna cum laude*. Although he was an attorney, he was never a judge, and though he may have loved "America's pastime," he certainly never played it professionally.

Frederick William Richmond was born in Mattapan, Massachusetts (now part of Boston), on November 15, 1923, the second of George and Frances (Rosen) Richmond's two children. Fred's sister Blanche (Endler) was born five years earlier. The Richmonds, who, according to Fred, had been farmers in the English county of the same name (there is no Richmond County in England), first came to the United States in about 1875; the Rosens arrived from Odessa around 1880. Fred's mother, the former Frances Rosen, was described as "small, tough, and kind of Waspy." During his earliest years, Fred's parents kept a kosher home and belonged to the Conservative Mishkan T'filla synagogue in

Roxbury, where he was bar mitzvah in 1936.

Fred Richmond attended Roxbury Memorial High School before transferring to Boston Latin, the "gateway to Harvard." Instead of going directly to Harvard after Boston Latin, Fred spent one year at Boston University. In 1942, he transferred to Harvard, majoring in history. While in Cambridge, Richmond served as advertising manager of the *Harvard Lampoon*, helping to pay off its mortgage. In 1943, he enlisted in the United States Navy, and spent the next two years as a radioman third-class in Hawaii and Guam. At war's end, he returned to Boston University, earning a bachelor's degree in 1946.

Shortly before graduating, Fred Richmond hit upon a scheme for making money—a lot of money. Learning that exporters were having a difficult time finding war-surplus material, he wrote dozens of them, explaining that he could solve their problem. Borrowing $1,200 and an office from his father, he went to work as a "matchmaker" between suppliers and buyers, making money "on both ends." Within a year he moved his operation from Boston to an office on New York's Fifth Avenue, and was soon grossing more than $10 million a year in the import-export business. Realizing that there was a limit on the amount of money to be made in this endeavor, Richmond began buying and selling companies. His technique was simple: buy a company, close it down, and then sell all its machinery and equipment at a profit.

It never seemed to bother Richmond that his *modus operandi* generally resulted in people losing their jobs. In one case, he bought a steel plant in West Virginia for slightly over $9 million, dismantled it, and made plans to sell the physical assets to Republic Steel for an enormous profit. Before the deal could be consummated, Richmond began taking tremendous heat from the press, which labeled him a "fast-buck boy, a raider, a liquidator." Before long, Richmond found a way out of his dilemma: Cyrus Eaton, soon to become "Nikita Khrushchev's favorite capitalist," came to the rescue and bought him out. Richmond made his profit, and the steelworkers kept their jobs—for a while. Within a year, the plant closed for good.

With his newfound wealth, Richmond moved into a luxurious apartment at 25 Sutton Place and began buying paintings by Chagall, Picasso, and Childe. Possessing an "appetite for respectability," he hired a press agent and entered the world of philanthropy and civic activity. Notably, none of his efforts extended to the Jewish community. Rather, he became active in the Urban League, serving as its president from 1958 to 1964. As a former friend commented to writer Pete Hamill, "In Boston, he was kind of a closet Jew; in New York, none of that crap mattered."

In February 1955, Richmond married Monique Alice Pfleiger, the daughter of Mrs. Pierrepont Isham Prentice and John James Pfleiger, in the chapel of St. Bartholmew's Church. His wife, described as a "New York socialite," came from a family that had homes on Park Avenue, Westhampton Beach, and Port Washington. Later that same year, Richmond's only son, William McNeir Richmond, was born. The Richmonds were divorced in Mexico in February 1957.

In 1962, Richmond organized the Frederick W. Richmond Foundation, which was his vehicle for making a name in the world of philanthropy. Begun with a $500 loan from Richmond, the foundation grew by leaps and bounds, largely through further loans and grants from him. Sensing that the foundation was Richmond's personal operation, a committee of the House of Representatives launched an investigation in 1968. Its final report noted that "despite the fact that Treasury regulations require that the names and address of officers and directors, their compensation, etc., must be listed in the foundation's tax returns, the information does not appear in the Frederick W. Richmond Foundation's returns." Pressed for information, Richmond complied.

Richmond used his foundation to gain further entree in the world of good works. Becoming actively involved in Democratic politics, he served as deputy finance chairman of the Democratic National Committee (1958–60) and as a commissioner on the New York City Human Rights Commission (1964–70), budget director of the New Your State Council on the Arts (1964–70), and member of the New York City Taxi and Limousine Commission (1970–72). He also began to actively search for a congressional district of his own. He narrowed his focus on Brooklyn, where, through his foundation, he "started a program of storefront schools, helping kids to learn . . . set up an apartment in Flatbush

. . . [and] began to hire people for the storefronts, who would later be pressed into service in a congressional campaign."

In 1968, feeling that the time was right, Richmond decided to take on Fourteenth District Congressman John J. Rooney. A twenty-four-year veteran of the House, the sixty-five-year-old Rooney, described as a "crusty, old regular Democrat," was the third-ranking member of the House Appropriations Committee. To Richmond's way of thinking, Rooney had two strikes against him: he supported the war in Vietnam, and he voted a generally conservative line. Richmond, armed with an unlimited checkbook, entered the primary as a supporter of insurgent antiwar Democrat Eugene McCarthy.

The Fourteenth Congressional District, extending along the Brooklyn waterfront from the Italian neighborhood of Red Hook to the Queens border, took in Bedford-Stuyvesant, Greenpoint, and Williamsburg. Ethnically mixed, the Fourteenth was 48 percent black, 18 percent Puerto Rican, and nearly 35 percent blue-collar white. Richmond "laid out money everywhere: to the Hasidim in Williamsburg, to black churches, to other community groups." Brooklyn Democratic boss Meade Esposito, sensing that his man Rooney was, after many years, being seriously challenged called out the troops. On election day, Rooney won by a whisker. In victory, Rooney was bitter, accusing Richmond of using his foundation to buy his way into Congress. (Richmond had laid out more than $200,000 of his own money.) In turn, Richmond called Rooney "a sick and vindictive old man."

Always full of surprises, Fred Richmond turned around and acted as campaign manager for the "sick and vindictive old man" two years later in Rooney's tough battle against former Congressman *Allard Lowenstein*. Lowenstein, who wound up losing by 890 votes, challenged the results before the New York State Supreme Court, which ordered a new election. In the rematch, Rooney defeated Lowenstein by more than 2,000 votes. In 1972, Esposito, who "obviously wanted Richmond's money on their side," gave him a political plum: a seat on the New York City Council. The seat came with Esposito's assurance that Rooney would retire after 1974.

Esposito was telling the truth; after serving

two years on the City Council, Fred Richmond, spending nearly a quarter of a million dollars of his own money, became Congressman from the Fourteenth Congressional District. In the House, he became the only urban member of the Agriculture Committee. While at first blush this might not seem to be a great political marriage, it actually turned out rather well. From his first day on the committee, Richmond realized that the body had jurisdiction over a whole host of policies which affect food prices "and thus are of great interest to every city dweller"

Over the next seven years, he "made a career of defending the food stamp program against its critics and helping to sell farm subsidies to big-city colleagues." Relishing his position as a "Brooklynite among farmers," Richmond began traveling the country, "bailing hay in Kansas, and arranging seminars between militant ranchers and Congressmen from San Francisco, Detroit and Buffalo." Richmond fought tooth-and-nail against proposed cuts in the food stamp program, going so far as to call Ronald Reagan's budget director, David Stockman, "totally inexperienced," and "talking through his hat."

A spokesman for consumer interests, Richmond proposed that half the members of a new beef promotion board be consumer representatives. "Consumers," he said, "must have a voice equal to agribusiness . . . anything less is an affront." Richmond, along with Chicago area Representative *Sidney Yates*, also became a forceful spokesman for the arts. During his early years in the House, he proposed an income-tax checkoff for support of the arts (rejected), and started the Congressional Arts Caucus. This panel's stated purpose was to save the National Endowment for the Arts budget from proposed cuts. "Americans are 100% behind the arts," he insisted. "Every dollar you spend on arts generates $5 more."

Frederick Richmond was easily reelected in 1976, but in 1977, his world started to unravel. In November of that year, Washington police were alerted to the fact that a member of Congress had solicited sex from a sixteen-year-old boy. After a brief investigation, it turned out that Fred Richmond was that member. In January 1978, he was arrested, admitted to a minor morals charge in District of Columbia Superior Court, and applied for the First Offenders Program. He was ordered to undergo thirty days of psychological counseling. At the same time, Richmond issued an open letter of apology to his constituents, the people who worked for him, and his family. Interestingly, he did not offer an apology to the family of the sixteen-year-old boy.

Back in Brooklyn, Esposito said that despite the charges against Richmond, he would support him for reelection. Pushed to explain his position, Esposito said the Congressman "was sick." Despite these problems, Richmond easily won the Democratic primary (tantamount to winning the general election) over a black foundation worker, Bernard Gifford. Richmond wound up spending nearly a half-million dollars in the campaign.

Continuing to vote a liberal line, Fred Richmond was widely popular with his constituents. Through his foundation, he kept pumping money into the Fourteenth Congressional district, all the while continuing to live in his Sutton Place apartment when in the city and a luxurious home in Washington, where he was known for throwing lavish parties. But Fred Richmond was living a double life. He started having staff members purchase marijuana and cocaine for him, continued having clandestine trysts with young men, and finagled his way into a $100,000-a-year "pension" from his foundation. It was later proven that he had used the ruse of retirement from the foundation in order to skirt the congressional restriction on earned income placed on members by the Ethics Code rules of the House of Representatives.

Fred Richmond was, and still is, an enormously wealthy man. His wealth has been estimated to be in excess of $30 million. In 1960, he founded a company called the Walco National Corporation, described as a holding company, that at one time included "seventeen manufacturing plants, 3,500 employees and assets of $128 million." Richmond controlled most of the stock in a corporation whose individual companies made a variety of products "from timber-cutting tools to coffins."

Starting in 1981, Richmond again began running afoul of the law. It was determined that he had used Walco employees during working hours to do political work without compensation to Walco. Moreover, he regularly used a Walco car and chauffeur, and Walco paid 90 percent of the upkeep on his Sutton Place apartment, but he had reported none of this as income. Additionally, Richmond had "caused Walco to make charitable contributions in [his] name rather than Walco's, so that [he] could get the political benefits."

Compounding these legal problems (of which Richmond commented "I don't feel one ounce embarrassed . . . I've done nothing wrong") was the discovery, in March 1981, that Richmond had, for some years, been having a "relationship" with one Earl Randolph, who had escaped from a Massachusetts prison where he was serving an eighteen-year sentence for assault with intent to murder. Following Randolph's escape from the halfway house to which Richmond had helped him be transferred, Richmond secured him a job under the name of "John McLaughlin" working for the doorkeeper of the House of Representatives. It turned out that Richmond had also personally rented Randolph-McLaughlin an apartment in Washington, D.C.

All this was discovered after Randolph was arrested for male prostitution by an undercover police officer. A federal grand jury was soon impaneled to look into "the tangled web of Richmond's affairs." Indicted on charges of income-tax evasion, possession of marijuana, and violations of Securities and Exchange Commission regulations, Richmond was told by Meade Esposito that he had reached the end of the road; he would have to resign his seat. On August 25, 1982, Fred Richmond resigned from the House of Representatives. Even if he had not resigned, he probably would have lost his seat, for the New York State Reapportionment Commission eliminated Richmond's district.

In October of that year, Gregory Bergeron, a twenty-two-year-old body-builder with whom Richmond had been involved for nearly a year, was found dead in the bathroom of Richmond's Sutton Place apartment, a suicide. Written on the boy's chest in blue felt-tipped pen was the message "I always love U, XOXOX, sin angel." Reeling from the latest revelation of his sordid double-life, Richmond retreated to California, waiting for the court's judgment on his plea-bargain deal. In November 1982, Fred Richmond

reached a settlement with the Securities and Exchange Commission over the issue of the pension payments, agreeing to repay $425,000 in connection with his illegal "pension." He was further sentenced to a year and a day in a federal penitentiary for income-tax evasion, possessing marijuana, and making an illegal payment of $7,420 to a Navy employee who had been helpful in winning government contracts for a Brooklyn ship-repair firm.

Before issuing the sentence, U.S. District Court Judge Jack B. Weinstein said: "You have done commendable things for many people; for this you received personal gratification, affection, respect and high office. You have committed criminal acts; for this you must be punished." Sent to the minimum-security prison in Allenwood, Pennsylvania, Richmond served nine months and was released to a halfway house `in September 1983. Today, Fred Richmond divides his time between New York City and North Ergremont, Massachusetts, where he operates a waste-management business called U.S. Systems Inc.

It is difficult to make sense of the ups and downs of Richmond's career, of his tormented, essentially bifurcated life. Perhaps a former friend put it best when he said: "The question to ask about him is very simple. Was Fred Richmond a good man who did a few bad things? Or was he a bad man who did a few good things?"

References

Interview with Fred Richmond, Great Barrington, Mass., July 1996.

Almanac of American Politics.

Peter Hamill and Denis Hamill, "The Rise and Fall of Fred Richmond," *New York*, November 11, 1982, pp. 36–44.

Newsweek, April 19, 1982, p. 34.

New York Times, September 7, 1983, II, 6:4; October 23, 1987, II, 1:2; April 25, 1991, B, 22:1.

Politics in America.

Time, November 6, 1982, p. 7.

Who's Who in American Jewry, 1980, pp. 393–394.

ROSENBLOOM, BENJAMIN LOUIS

(1880–1965): *Republican from West Virginia; served two terms in the House (Sixty-seventh through Sixty-eighth Congress; March 4, 1921–March 3, 1925).*

Not surprisingly, West Virginia has sent only a single Jew to Washington—Benjamin Louis Rosenbloom. What is surprising is that the state which the *Almanac of American Politics* calls "the most unhorizontal in the union" has sent even that one. For West Virginia, an historically poor state born out of the tragedy of the Civil War, has never been home to more than 7,000 Jews at any one time. As of the last census, the Mountain State had 4,265 Jews—less than 0.2 percent out of a population of 1,965,000.

Little is known of the life and family background of Benjamin Rosenbloom. He was born on June 3, 1880, in Braddock, Pennsylvania, located in Allegheny County, the heart of Pennsylvania's steel country, about 75 miles southeast of Wheeling, West Virginia. Ben Rosenbloom was educated in the local public schools, graduating from North Braddock High School in 1897. Following high school, he moved on to Morgantown, West Virginia, where he attended the University of West Virginia. It is unknown whether he ever graduated from UWV, but he studied law, was admitted to the West Virginia bar in 1904, and commenced practice in Wheeling, the state's third-largest city.

A Republican, Ben Rosenbloom was elected to a four-year term in the State Senate in 1914. At the time, West Virginia's First Congressional District was represented by Democrat Matthew Mansfield Neely (1874–1958). Neely had won his seat in a 1913 special election to replace Congressman John William Davis, whom President Woodrow Wilson had appointed Solicitor General of the United States. (Davis held that post from 1913 to 1918, at which time, Wilson named him to be his postwar ambassador to the Court of Saint James. Davis is best known for having lost the 1924 presidential race to Calvin Coolidge.)

Rosenbloom defeated Neely in 1920—a great year for Republicans, but this was by no means the end of Matt Neely's political career; in truth it was only the beginning. Neely turned around and was elected to the United States Senate in 1922. Losing his seat to Republican Henry

Hatfield, a surgeon and former West Virginia Governor, Neely returned to the Senate two years later. He was reelected in 1936, and served until 1941, when he himself became governor. After serving his four years in Charleston, Neely was once again elected to the House of Representatives. Two years later (1948), he returned to the United States Senate. Reelected in 1954, he served until his death in 1958. All told, Neely served four years in the Governor's mansion, eight years in the House, and twenty-seven years in the Senate.

Ben Rosenbloom was reelected to the House in 1922. In 1924, he gave up what had apparently become a safe seat in order to challenge incumbent Democratic Senator Davis Elkins. The scion of a politically prominent family, Elkins (1876–1959) had taken over the seat held by his late father, Stephen Benton Elkins. Both his grandfather, Henry Gassaway Davis, and his uncle, Thomas Beall Davis, had served on Capitol Hill: Henry G. as Senator, and Thomas B. as Representative.

In order to get to Senator Elkins, Rosenbloom first had to capture the Republican primary. There he miscalculated. Like many small states, West Virginia has spawned a handful of political dynasties—witness the Elkins/Davis family saga. Rosenbloom's primary opponent, Guy Despard Goff, was, like Senator Davis, the scion of a Mountain State dynasty. Goff (1866–1933) was the son of Nathan Goff, who had served as Secretary of the Navy during the Hayes administration, and as United States Senator from 1913 to 1919. Guy Goff's daughter, Louis Goff Reece, would one day replace her husband, Brazilla Carroll Reece, as a member of the House from Tennessee. Goff got by Rosenbloom in the primary, and went on to defeat Senator Elkins. Following a single term in the House, Guy Goff took over his father's old Senate seat. In West Virginia, family name is everything.

Following his defeat, Rosenbloom returned to practicing law in Wheeling. He served a two-year stint (1933–35) as publisher of a Wheeling weekly newspaper, and ended his public life with a four-year term (1935–39) as the city's vice mayor. Ben Rosenbloom retired in 1951, moving to Cleveland. He died there on March 22, 1965. Rosenbloom never married. In 1998, there were no Rosenblooms listed in any West Virginia telephone directory.

References

Biographical Directory of the United States Congress, 1774–1989, p. 1743.

Abraham I. Shinedling, *West Virginia Jewry: Origins and History, 1850–1958* (Philadelphia: Jewish Publication Society, 1963).

ROSENTHAL, BENJAMIN STANLEY
(1923–1983): *Democrat from New York; served eleven terms in the House (Eighty-seventh through Ninety-eighth Congress; February 28, 1962–January 4, 1983).*

In his day, Representative Wayne Levere Hays, an Ohio Democrat, was probably the most ill-tempered, confrontational member of Congress. Variously nicknamed the "Hairshirt of the House" and the "Bully of the House," he delighted in name-calling and getting the goat of his colleagues whenever and however he could. As longtime House Doorkeeper William "Fishbait" Miller noted in his autobiography, "He had fiendish names for everyone. . . . Almost everyone suffered the name of 'potato head' at one time or another, including me." Neither was Hays one to shy away from racial or ethnic slurs. He referred to Ralph Nader and his followers as "a bunch of Jew-boys led by an A-rab." Most of his colleagues took Hays's nasty tongue in stride; during his more than quarter-century in the House of Representatives (1949–76), he was one of its most powerful members. Calling him down or getting in his way always had severe political consequences.

Wayne Hays finally met his match in Ben Rosenthal, Democrat of New York. Rosenthal was known among his House colleagues for having a sharp tongue himself. The story goes that one day, during a meeting of the International Relations Committee, on which both men served, Hays directed an anti-Semitic remark at Rosenthal. A former World War II M.P., Rosenthal was fed up with the Ohio Democrat's truculent, abusive manner. Incensed, he picked up the closest thing at hand, a metal water pitcher, and took dead aim at Hays's head. Before he could launch his missile, however, Rosenthal was gang-tackled by several of his colleagues and convinced to take a deep breath. Somewhat shaken, Wayne Hays got the message; he was never heard to utter an anti-Semitic remark again.

The first Benjamin Stanley Rosenthal (the Congressman's grandfather) immigrated from Germany to Canada shortly after the American Civil War. A devoutly Orthodox Jew, he was one of the founders of Toronto's Holy Blossom Synagogue, serving as its third president. When the members of Holy Blossom (then an Orthodox shul) decided to bring in an organ to "beautify" its services, Rosenthal reportedly had the noxious instrument thrown out the window. Married twice, he sired twenty-one children; the youngest of these was the future Congressman's father, Joseph.

Benjamin Rosenthal was born in the Bronx, New York, on June 8, 1923, the older of Ceil (Fisher) and Joseph Rosenthal's two children. Joseph Rosenthal was not only a manufacturer of optical goods; he was an inventor as well. He invented clip-on sunglasses. Ben and his sister Lola (Ostreicher) were both educated in the public schools of New York. Their mother, who came from a family of Orthodox immigrants, instilled a love of Jewish culture in her children. Because Joseph was totally nonobservant, his son never went to Hebrew school and never became bar mitzvah. Although he would become a member of several Reform congregations as an adult, "Benjie" Rosenthal always felt cheated by not having gone through this traditional rite of passage.

Rosenthal entered Long Island University in 1941, but his college education was cut short by World War II. From 1943 to 1946, he served in the United States Army, spending more than a year-and-a-half as a military policeman in Iceland. Returning stateside after the war, Rosenthal entered Brooklyn Law School, from which he received his LL.B. in 1949. Later that year, while visiting the cousin of a friend, he met Lila Moskowitz. They were married in 1950 and had two children: Debra (Mandel), born in 1953, and Edward, born in 1961. After being admitted to the bar in 1949, Rosenthal continued his legal education, receiving a master of law from New York University in 1952.

Like many young lawyers in the New York City area, Ben Rosenthal developed a taste for local politics. From his home base in Queens, he became well known among the so-called regular Democrats. In November 1961, when Eighth District Representative *Lester Holtzman* was elected to the New York State Supreme Court, Rosenthal jumped into the race to succeed him. The district, comprising the heavily Jewish areas of Forest Hills, Rego Park, Flushing, and Bayside, attracted a large field of candidates. A bitter fight ensued. After a series of complex maneuvers involving the various candidates, Rosenthal emerged as the choice of Mayor Robert F. Wagner. This endorsement tipped the scales in Rosenthal's favor. Although Rosenthal won the special election, his victory was not front-page news; on that same day in February 1962, John Glenn became the first American to orbit the earth.

Rosenthal was named to the House Agriculture Committee, prompting jokes about "flower pots in the Bronx." He was able to turn the jeers into applause as he used this position to investigate a host of consumer issues. One of his earliest assignments was as a member of a task force that revised the food stamp program. Heretofore, the program had served mostly as a means of distributing surplus foodstuffs to the poor. What Rosenthal's task force recommended was that the stamps be employed to supplement the food needs of the poor. This radical change was quickly enacted into law.

During the 1960s, Representative Rosenthal became an active and vocal supporter of President Lyndon B. Johnson's Great Society social programs. Throughout his career, Rosenthal was known as one of Congress's strongest consumer protection advocates. His forte was investigation rather than legislation. As chairman of the Government Operations Subcommittee, he chaired hearings on such varied issues as food-price discrimination against the poor, condominium conversions, and foreign investments. For years, he fought a fruitless battle to create a federal consumer protection agency. Deemed "an expert analyst of motivation and of what could be accomplished," he worked tirelessly to get his congressional colleagues behind him on this proposal.

All hope for the agency's creation came to an abrupt end with the advent of the Reagan administration. "We ran out of time," Rosenthal told a reporter. "We were swimming upstream when everyone else was swimming downstream." Although Rosenthal never got the agency of his dreams, he did manage to put in place numerous consumer protection measures. Chief among them was the appointment of inspector generals whose job it was to monitor federal agencies—especially those dealing with social programs.

Benjamin Rosenthal was one of Congress's earliest and most vocal critics of the war in Vietnam. His forthright antagonism to the war alienated him from the Johnson administration. When he first declared his opposition in 1965,

fewer than 10 percent of his constituency agreed with his stand. "It was a very lonely road," said Rosenthal, remembering the days when he was one of the few congressional doves.

In 1969, when hundreds of thousands of American college students convened outside the Capitol for a mass antiwar rally, Rosenthal spearheaded a move to keep the House open all night in sympathy with the demonstrators. In the spring of 1970, when the Capitol was once again "stormed" by masses of antiwar college students protesting the American incursion into Laos and Cambodia, Congressman Rosenthal made his offices available as a message center. (This author was among the students who partook of his hospitality.)

For his efforts, Rosenthal became a hero to the student demonstrators. The *New York Times*, in an article entitled "A Leader of the War Foes," stated: "One Congressman with a fair amount of *chutzpa* can awaken the public conscience."

Despite the early unpopularity of his antiwar stand, Rosenthal was regularly reelected as a Democrat-Liberal. The key to his success was his understanding that, at root, all politics is local; Rosenthal spent the lion's share of his time seeing to the needs of his district and of New York City. He played a key role in the drive to win federal support for the city during its financial crisis in the mid-1970s. When the Ford administration opposed a plan to grant federal financial assistance to the beleaguered city, Rosenthal spoke angrily of its "preoccupation with fiscal brinkmanship." Rosenthal worked closely with the New York delegation, becoming particularly close to Representative *Ed Koch*. When Koch became New York's mayor and moved into Gracie Mansion, Rosenthal and his wife were among his first invited guests.

As chair of the House Government Operations Subcommittee on Commerce, Consumer and Monetary Affairs, Rosenthal launched investigations into manipulations of the silver market by the Hunt brothers of Texas, the involvement of the Kuwaiti government in American defense investments, and abuses of securities and banking laws by corporations and prominent civic officials. Rosenthal's investigations were not limited to Republican abuses of the system. He also launched inquiries into the banking fraud perpetuated by Carter administration official Bert Lance, and the conduct of the

American Invesco Corporation, whose principals included the wife of then New York Governor Hugh Carey.

From his position on the Subcommittee on Europe and the Middle East, Rosenthal was, predictably, a staunch defender of Israel. He fought against the American sale of AWACS planes to Saudi Arabia, and took umbrage when high-ranking government officials suggested that American Jews as a group should not take positions on foreign policy issues. Rosenthal contended that "if Jews and other groups were not to speak out, foreign policy would be left in the hands of banks, the oil industry and the defense industry," which "would be a disaster for this country and the democratic institutions we all believe in." During hearings on the AWACS sale, Rosenthal shed public light on the corporate maneuvering that had gone into the deal, such as Mobil Oil acting as the purchasing agent for the Saudis—a fact heretofore withheld from the American public.

Benjamin Rosenthal was a key player in the House Democratic leadership. During the latter stages of his career, he served as one of three deputy whips in the House and as a member of the Democratic Steering and Policy Committee. Although he and his family made their permanent home in Bethesda, Maryland (he kept a voting address in Elmhurst, Queens), Rosenthal never truly "went Washington." According to friends, "he was totally oriented to New York." According to his sister, the reason he lived in Bethesda was so that he could be with his family: "Benji was very family oriented. When he had to come back to New York, he would stay with me in New Hyde Park and call Lila and the kids four, five times a day. He was really devoted to them."

In 1981, Benjamin Rosenthal was diagnosed with cancer. Despite failing health, he was reelected to an eleventh term in November 1982. He was sworn in as a member of the Ninety-eighth Congress from his bed at Georgetown University Hospital on Monday, January 3, 1983. He died less than twenty-four hours later. He was survived by his mother Ceil and sister Lola, his wife and their two children. Benjamin Rosenthal was buried at Beth David Cemetery in Elmont, New York.

References

Interview with Lola Ostreicher, July 1996.

Biographical Directory of the United States Congress, 1774–1989, p. 1743.

New York Times, December 10, 1969; January 5, 1983.

ROSSDALE, ALBERT BERGER (1878–1968):
Republican from New York; served one term in the House (Sixty-seventh Congress; March 4, 1921–March 3, 1923).

A former postal worker and wholesale jeweler, Albert B. Rossdale served but one term in Congress. The son of Herman and Betty (Berger) Rossdale, Albert was born in New York City on October 23, 1878. Upon graduation from high school, Rossdale became a clerk in the Post Office. Active in postal union activities, he was the president of the New York Federation of Post Office Clerks from 1906 to 1907, and vice president of the national organization from 1908 to 1909.

Somewhere around 1910, Rossdale left the Post Office and entered the wholesale jewelry business. For the next fifty-plus years, he headed his own concern, the Rossdale Company. In November 1920, Rossdale defeated one-term Democratic Representative Richard F. McKiniry, the former secretary of the New York State Supreme Court, in New York's Twenty-third Congressional District. During his single term in the House, Rossdale appears to have been most concerned with the plight of veterans from the recently concluded Great War.

Rossdale's one legislative initiative was a proposal to give a bonus of a dollar for every day of service over ninety days to all enlisted men from the American Expeditionary Force (A.E.F.). This was but one of many early legislative efforts to get a jump-start on the promised bonus for soldiers from World War I. Rossdale's proposal was defeated in committee. The subject of a soldiers' bonus continued in fits and starts over the next decade. The issue came to a disastrous conclusion in the latter days of the Hoover administration with the massing of tens of thousands of war veterans, the so-called Bonus Army, in Washington.

Rossdale also joined forces with other members of Congress to fight against legislation restricting immigration. A committed Zionist, he was one of the leading voices in the move to have the House adopt a Zionist resolution (in support of Britain's Balfour Declaration).

Albert Rossdale lost his seat to Democrat Frank Oliver in the election of 1922. Determined to regain it, Rossdale tried to remain in the public eye. Shortly after his defeat, Rossdale got his "fifteen minutes of fame" in the *New York Times*. In late March 1923, Rossdale and Republican former-Congressman Andrew N. Petersen of Brooklyn (who, like Rossdale, had been elected in 1920 and defeated in 1922) were sent to the Canal Zone by President Harding's Secretary of the Navy, Edwin Denby, "seeking first-hand information about sailors' life."

According to the article in the *Times*, Rossdale and Petersen, "assigned to the battleship *New York* for manoeuvres . . . drew sailors' uniforms, had dinner with the crew, washed up their mess kits, obtained regulation passes and started out on shore leave." Once ashore in Panama, the two "sailors" repaired to a cabaret for an evening of pleasure. Within five minutes of their arrival, they were arrested by the shore patrol for "being ashore after 11 o'clock in violation of regulations." Protesting that far from being tars, they were, in fact, members of a congressional fact-finding delegation (not precisely the truth), Rossdale and Petersen were remanded to the brig until the captain of the *New York* wired instructions for their release. What had started out as an undercover investigation turned out to be a farce. The headline in the *Times* read: "Congressmen Seized, Dressed as Sailors."

Albert Rossdale never returned to Congress. Following his loss in 1922 (and the debacle in Panama), he ran in 1924, but was defeated once again by Congressman Oliver, who would hold onto the seat until 1934. Following his exit from politics, Rossdale returned to his jewelry business. In 1939, he moved up to Sandy Hook, Connecticut, not returning to New York until after the end of World War II. In 1946, Rossdale moved to Bronxville, New York, where he resided until his death on April 17, 1968.

Little is known about Rossdale's private life; *Who's Who in America* never carried any details about his family, marital status, or affiliations. Albert Rossdale was interred in Maimonides Cemetery, Elmont, New York.

References
American Jewish Year Book, vol. 24., p. 196.
New York Times, December 10, 1921; March 21, 1923, 4:3.
Universal Jewish Encyclopedia.
Who Was Who in America, vol. 6.
Who Was Who in American Jewry, 1926, 1928, 1938.

ROTHMAN, STEVE (1952–): *Democrat from New Jersey; has served two terms in the House (One Hundred and Fifth and One Hundred and Sixth Congress; January 3, 1997–present).*

Steve Rothman of New Jersey is one of the newest members of the Congressional Minyan. To date, precious little has been written about him. To compound the problem, he has a strict rule about keeping his private life private. The facts available in the public record portray a hard-working, ambitious young centrist Democrat: liberal-to-moderate on social issues, and distinctly conservative on fiscal matters.

Steve Rothman was born in Englewood, New Jersey, on October 14, 1952. At age twenty-two, he received his undergraduate degree from Syracuse University. Three years later, he earned a law degree at Washington University in St. Louis. From 1978 to 1980, he worked as an attorney with the firm of Hochman, Meyerson & Schaeffer, then moved into private practice. He remained in private practice until 1993, at which time he was elected to the Bergen County bench as county surrogate.

Rothman first entered politics in 1983, at age thirty, when he became the youngest mayor of Englewood. At the time of his election, Englewood had the highest crime and tax rates in all of Bergen County. During his six years as mayor, Rothman was able to cut crime by 22 percent, and posted a $5 million surplus while reducing the city's tax rate by nearly 42 percent. He also managed to push through a bond referendum to repair school buildings, and reduced the municipal work force by 14 percent, mostly through attrition. In 1993, he was elected county surrogate, "a local judicial oversight office." During his next three years in this office, Rothman "revamped the county's computer and filing system and boasted a healthy rate of return on foundation investments." Uniquely, Rothman was the only Democrat in the 1990s to win a countywide election in "conservative-leaning" Bergen County.

In early 1996, when seven-term incumbent Representative Robert G. Torricelli announced

his intention to run for the seat being vacated by retiring United States Senator Bill Bradley, Rothman quickly jumped into the race. Rothman easily won his party's endorsement. In the primary, he was challenged by Fair Lawn Mayor Bob Gordon, who labeled him "a tool of the party bosses." Despite being outspent by a better than two-to-one margin (Gordon put some $350,000 of his own money into the race), Rothman swept to victory with 79 percent of the vote.

In the general election, Steve Rothman faced Bergen County Clerk Kathleen A. Donovan, a moderate Republican in the political mold of New Jersey Governor Christine Todd Whitman. A single mother who had previously served in the New Jersey State Assembly and as a member of the Port Authority of New York and New Jersey, Donovan described herself as "a social progressive who supports abortion rights, environmental protection and gun control." During the campaign Donovan made frequent mention of her adopted son, elderly father, and the fact that she was likely "the only New Jersey Congressional candidate who sewed a Halloween costume for her son" and "who got her picture in *Glamour* Magazine." Donovan also took pains to distance herself from House Speaker Newt Gingrich, a man who had decidedly low approval ratings in New Jersey's Ninth Congressional District.

For his part, Rothman mounted a door-to-door campaign; serious use of the media was beyond his financial means. Rothman tarred Donovan with the brush of far-right Republicanism, repeatedly reminding voters that as a member of the State Assembly, she had "voted with her party 95% of the time." "This is not the record of an independent or maverick Republican," Rothman would tell voters. "She has a lifelong record of being a highly partisan Republican insider." Rothman also scored Donovan for presiding over a "lavish culture of waste" while a member of the Port Authority. He charged her with taking frequent "non-emergency" helicopter flights at a cost of $822 an hour. When queried, Donovan admitted to no fewer than seventeen flights, all of which she said were appropriate—only when her schedule was "especially tight or when she needed an aerial view of the bridges, waterways, and airports overseen by the Port Authority."

Rothman reminded voters that Donovan's first vote in Congress would be to reelect Gingrich as Speaker. Despite her support for the embattled Gingrich and what Rothman termed "the radical right wing of the Republican Party," Donovan nonetheless opposed Senator Robert Dole's 15 percent tax cut and criticized the Republican Congress's positions on Medicare, education, and the environment.

Along the way, Donovan won some powerful endorsements normally reserved for Democratic candidates. She was one of three New Jersey Republicans endorsed by the Sierra Club, and was the only Republican candidate in the country endorsed by the 2.2 million-strong National Educational Association.

Still, Rothman wound up winning the election by a 55 percent to 43 percent margin. As a freshman legislator, Rothman was assigned to the International Relations Committee, where his predecessor, Robert Torricelli (who defeated Representative *Dick Zimmer* for the Senate), "had played a major role in foreign affairs." Rothman also received a spot on the House Judiciary Committee. Rothman promised to be in the more moderate wing of the Democratic Party. He supports abortion rights, gun control, and Pentagon spending cuts. He also opposes term limits and the welfare "overhaul" bill that President Clinton vetoed in the closing days of the One Hundred and Fourth Congress.

Steve Rothman greatly improved his margin of victory in 1998, winning a second term with 64 percent of the vote over Republican Steve Lonegan.

Steve Rothman lives in Fair Lawn, New Jersey, where he is active in the Jewish community and helps sponsor a local food bank. Divorced, he has two children, John and Karen.

References

Information provided by office of Steve Rothman.

Hans Johnson and Peggie Rayhawk, *The New Members of Congress Almanac: 105th U.S. Congress* (Washington: Almanac Publishing Co., 1996).

New York Times, October 27, 1996, 38:1.

RUDMAN, WARREN BRUCE (1930–):
Republican Senator from New Hampshire; served two terms in the Senate (December 29, 1980–January 2, 1993).

Warren Rudman entered the United States Senate in late December 1980, a few weeks before fellow Republican Ronald Reagan was to be sworn in as America's fortieth President. He served two six-year terms and could easily have won reelection in 1992, but decided to call it quits, departing the Senate just as George Bush was about to leave the White House. During those twelve years of Republican rule, Rudman could be found at the epicenter of most of the era's most dramatic, divisive, and contentious issues—and was often at odds with the administration.

During his first term in the Senate, the New Hampshire Republican successfully took on the powerful American Medical Association, "co-fathered" the much-maligned Gramm-Rudman-Hollings deficit reduction act (which he himself called "a bad idea whose time has come"), and cochaired the Senate's investigation of the messy Iran-Contra scandal. During his second term, Rudman played a pivotal role in the Ethics Committee investigation of the so-called Keating Five, in which the Senate had to go through the delicate procedure of policing its own. Throughout all these highly charged, widely publicized episodes, Rudman retained the respect of both his Senate peers and the voters of New Hampshire. During his twelve-year Senate career, he maintained a reputation for being blunt, egotistical, independent, and pugnacious.

And despite being one of his party's acknowledged stars (columnist Marianne Means called him the "unexpected star of that huge GOP freshman class swept into office with President Reagan"), Warren Rudman never truly became a creature of Washington society. As he once explained: "To go to a White House dinner and to sit next to someone who I don't know and who is there because they are a friend of Mrs. Bush, or a famous movie star or someone who gave eight trillion dollars to the Republican Party is not my idea of fun."

Warren Rudman was always a difficult politician to pigeonhole. A fiscal conservative and defense hawk like most of his Republican colleagues, Rudman was nonetheless far more progressive than his fellows on social issues. He was both pro-choice and pro-environment, one of Capitol Hill's staunchest defenders of the embattled Legal Services Administration, and a caustic critic of the emerging Christian Right. Once, when a reporter asked his views on the Christian Right's social agenda, he responded: "Do you have fifteen seconds? That's all it will take. I'm deeply committed to the right to choose, to the separation of church and state and to personal liberty. The conservative social agenda threatens them all."

Not surprisingly, Rudman saw great consistency in this seeming political melange: "The liberals consider me a conservative, and the conservatives consider me a liberal. I consider myself a moderate." Summing up his notion of conservatism, Rudman wrote: "Providing legal services to the poor [is] profoundly conservative. . . . Government should not intrude in anything as personal as the decision to have a child, it should not be championing prayer or religion, and family values should come from families and religious institutions, not from politically inspired, Washington-based moralists."

Rudman was not the Senator's original family name. Like countless immigrants who came to America in the late nineteenth century, Abraham Rudman, the future Senator's grandfather, received his surname when he came through Ellis Island. As his grandson explained, "We never knew what it had been before that. He [Abraham Rudman] was not a man to look back." Like millions of other Jewish immigrants, Abraham Rudman, a native of Odessa, settled on New York's Lower East Side. Unimpressed with New York's endless "sidewalks and tenements," Abe asked a friend where he could find mountains, lakes, and trees. The friend suggested that he should get on the Boston train and take it all the way to the end of the line—Maine. Taking the long-forgotten friend's advice, Rudman went up to Maine, eventually winding up living with a Jewish family named Wolman on a farm just north of Bangor. Shortly after his arrival at the Wolman's farm, Abe sent to Odessa for his distant cousin Dora, who soon became his wife. Before too long, Mrs. Rudman was speaking English and reading classical literature. Eventually both Abe and Dora "spoke English like true Down-Easters."

After a time, the Rudmans purchased a hand-operated bottling machine and started bottling ginger ale in their home. Eventually they secured the franchise to bottle Moxie, a popular soft drink, and moved their expanding enterprise (now called the Rudman Bottling Company) first to Portland, and then to Boston.

The Rudmans had five remarkable children. In his autobiography, *Combat*, Senator Rudman discusses his aunts and uncles: "Of Abe and Dora's five children, the oldest, my uncle Ben, went to the University of Maine and Tufts Medical School. The second, Morris, graduated from Harvard and Harvard Law. My uncle Sid went to Harvard. My aunt Rita went to Wellesley. My father [Edward, born in 1897] went to work." By the time Edward Rudman joined his father's business, Abe's interests had expanded into "restaurants and similar ventures."

Striking out on his own, Edward Rudman ventured back up to Portland, where he began building houses and developing a passion for antiques. In the mid-1920s, Edward Rudman started a small company that made reproductions of antique furniture; he called it Old Colony Furniture. When his younger brother Sid graduated from Harvard in 1928, Ed made him his partner. Together, they ran Old Colony for the next forty years. In 1929, Edward Rudman married Theresa (Tess) Levenson from the Bronx. On May 18, 1930, their first child, Warren Bruce Rudman, was born in Boston. He was quickly followed by daughters Carol and Jean.

It is quite likely that Warren Rudman's sense of honesty and integrity came from his father. In the mid-1930s, the elder Rudman decided to move Old Colony from Boston up to Nashua, New Hampshire. Borrowing $100,000 from a "Yankee banker" named George Thurber, Rudman purchased an old sawmill near the Nashua River and started converting it into a factory. Two weeks before the factory was scheduled to open operations, New Hampshire was hit with the worst flood in its history; Edward Rudman went bankrupt. He went back to George Thurber. As Warren Rudman writes: "[He] said he was wiped out but if the banker would lend him more money, he'd rebuild and pay back every dime. Thurber approved the loan, and when that wasn't enough, added his own personal loan. In my time father paid him off, and Old Colony went on to achieve an international reputation for quality."

Warren Rudman and his sisters grew up in Nashua, where he still resides. Growing up in relative affluence, Warren became "a bit of a hell-raiser, at least by [his] father's standards." His interests tended more toward fishing and baseball than toward school. He was also "handy with [his] fists . . . thanks to schoolyard encounters with anti-Semitism." (In the 1930s, Nashua had no more than 500 Jewish residents.) Sensing that his son needed to learn discipline, Edward sent him off to Valley Forge Military School in Wayne, Pennsylvania. The younger Rudman excelled at Valley Forge, becoming both a champion debater and a fine boxer.

In 1948, Warren Rudman entered Syracuse University "where I continued to box, race stock cars on weekends, served in the ROTC, and became engaged to a tall, brilliant young woman named Shirley Wahl, whom I met on the debate team." Rudman married Shirley Wahl shortly after his graduation in 1952, and then shipped out for Korea as a second lieutenant in the United States Army.

Rudman graduated "with a wad of transcripts and a blank piece of paper." Syracuse refused to issue his diploma until he paid $18 for a school yearbook. Rudman refused to pay, claiming that the school catalogue had listed no such requirement. Shortly before leaving for Korea, Rudman wrote his alma mater requesting his diploma. Syracuse refused until he paid the $18. Rudman spent the next two years in the infantry, serving in Korea as a member of the third platoon of K Company, Third Battalion, 38th Regiment of the Second Division. While there he saw action in some of the war's bloodiest battles: the Kumsong Salient, Heartbreak Ridge, and Bloody Ridge.

Mustered out a captain with the Bronze Star,

three Battle Stars, and a Presidential Citation, Rudman once again petitioned Syracuse for his diploma. Once again they demanded he pay the $18. That was in 1954. Twenty-six years later, upon his election to the United States Senate, Warren Rudman received a letter from Syracuse explaining that "there had obviously been a mix-up," and that the diploma was in the mail. Senator Rudman not only refused to accept it; he repeatedly turned down their later offer of an honorary degree. As Rudman explained: "[Syracuse] wouldn't give me the one I earned. I certainly don't want the one I didn't earn."

Following his return from the war, Rudman went back to work for Old Colony. In 1956, he entered the night law school at Boston College, making the 90-mile round trip three or four days a week after a full day's work. Graduating in 1960, Rudman continued working for his father, while building up a legal practice with an old family friend, Morris Stein. It was only when his father and uncle sold Old Colony in 1964 that Warren Rudman (by then thirty-four and the father of three children—Laura, Alan, and Deborah) began practicing law full-time. Over the next several years, he built up a lucrative practice, working with the Nashua firm of Stein, Rudman and Gormley. During these years, Warren and Shirley Rudman also learned to fly—a passion that has remained a constant in the Senator's life.

In 1967, Walter Peterson, the Republican Speaker of the New Hampshire House of Representatives, asked Rudman, whom he had known since childhood, to be his finance chairman for the upcoming gubernatorial campaign. Once elected, Governor Peterson appointed Rudman his chief of staff. In 1970, Peterson named Rudman state attorney general. Rudman quickly went about the task of assembling "a first-rate staff." The new attorney general hand-picked a young Harvard Law graduate to be his assistant. His name was David Souter, who, through Rudman's tireless efforts, would one day sit on the United States Supreme Court.

In his six years as attorney general (1970–76), Warren Rudman "created a consumer protection division, fought successfully against the legalization of gambling . . . [and] joined Francis X. Bellotti, the attorney general of Massachusetts, in filing suit in federal district court seeking to postpone construction of the Seabrook nuclear power plant." In 1975, Rudman was elected president of the National Association of Attorneys General.

As an ex-officio member of the New Hampshire Ballot Law Commission, Rudman became embroiled in a controversy involving the 1974 reelection of United States Senator John A. Durkin. Rudman and his commission colleagues declared Republican Congressman Louis C. Wyman the winner by just two votes. Durkin secured the right to a new election, which he won. When President Gerald Ford nominated Rudman to chair the Interstate Commerce Commission in 1976, Durkin used his influence to delay confirmation of the appointment. Rudman eventually withdrew his name for consideration. It looked as if Durkin was exacting his revenge, but, ironically, if he had permitted Rudman's confirmation, it is unlikely that Rudman would ever have become a Senator.

In 1980, after practicing law for four years with the Manchester firm of Phinney, Bass and Green, Warren B. Rudman entered an eleven-candidate Republican primary race for the United States Senate. Topping the field with 20 percent of the vote, Rudman named the second-place finisher, (future Governor and White House chief of staff) John Sununu, his campaign manager. Greatly aided by Ronald Reagan's sweeping victory over President Jimmy Carter, Rudman defeated his old nemesis Durkin 52 percent to 48 percent, thereby becoming the first (and so far only) Jew ever elected to Congress from New Hampshire.

Entering the Senate as a member of the majority party, Senator Rudman quickly went to work learning the ropes. His first successful piece of legislation, coauthored with Connecticut Senator Lowell Weicker, Jr., was passed less than six months from the day he entered the upper chamber. Called the Small Business Innovation Research Act of 1981 (which the editorial writers on the *Washington Star* termed "one of the most ingenious acts of the 97th Congress"), this "invention" granted research and development firms as much as $400 million a year without adding a cent to the federal budget. The bill simply required that federal agencies with an R&D budget in excess of $100 million set aside 1 percent for small business. In arguing for the bill's enactment, Rudman noted that small businesses produced up to twenty-four times more innovation per R&D dollar than larger ones. Armed with a welter of facts and data, Rudman was able to attract no fewer than seventy-nine cosponsors for his bill, running the political gamut from Senator Edward Kennedy on the left to Senator Jesse Helms on the right.

In 1982, Senator Rudman went to war against the powerful American Medical Association. The issue raising Rudman's dander was a measure that would effectively wipe out the Federal Trade Commission's power to pursue violations of antitrust and consumer protection laws by health professionals. As one of the few members of Congress (and the only Senator) who refused financial support from political action committees (PACs), Rudman was in a unique position. He successfully inserted less sweeping language into the proposed bill, thereby preserving the FTC's ability to go after doctors when they were in violation of antitrust standards.

Speaking on the Senate floor, Rudman sarcastically noted: "For the first time in 20 years, doctors are making house calls. They made house calls in the Dirksen Building, [and] in the Russell Building. . . . I do not get excited by my own rhetoric. I get excited when I see someone attempting to perform a frontal lobotomy on the free-enterprise system, which is precisely what is going on here."

Rudman's ameliorative language was passed by a vote of 59-37. Suddenly, the junior Senator from New Hampshire was big news.

A vocal hawk on defense matters, Rudman nonetheless stunned the Pentagon by convincing the Senate to kill off the $1.5 billion VIPER—a shoulder-fired antitank weapon—which he proved was both ineffective and cost-prohibitive. Moreover, Rudman got Congress to agree to a highly unusual step: forcing the military to competitively test various weapons systems, including those made by foreign manufacturers. This took a fair degree of courage; the technical components for the VIPER were manufactured in Nashua, New Hampshire—Rudman's hometown. Rudman also got the Senate to scrap the ill-fated Sergeant York gun, which he said should have been called the Sergeant Bilko. For his efforts, Rudman won the respect of his Senate colleagues—and the enmity of the military brass.

In 1980, Ronald Reagan was elected on a platform that promised to balance the budget, dramatically increase military spending, and lower taxes. The theory behind the platform was given the name "supply-side economics." The Fourth Estate called it "Reaganomics." George Bush called it "voodoo economics." Rudman, charmed by Reagan's ability to state his case, voted in favor of the president's 1981 budget proposal. Although he prayed that all the figures were correct and that Reaganomics would work, Rudman feared that it was an illusion.

To his regret, Rudman's fears were not a chimera; far from reducing the deficit, it doubled within five years. Rudman was outraged. As the Senator told his colleagues: "After five years under a Republican president and a Republican Senate, we managed to double the national debt. I mean, who's kidding who?" In his memoirs, Rudman blamed Budget Director David Stockman for "budgetary deception and political cynicism that numbs the mind," and President Reagan for "inhabit[ing] his own reality." Something radical had to be done. America was fast becoming the world's leading debtor nation.

In 1985, Rudman came to national prominence when he, Texas Senator Phil Gramm, and South Carolina's Ernest "Fritz" Hollings introduced the Gramm-Rudman-Hollings Balanced Budget and Emergency Deficit Control Act. Called everything from "the political version of hemlock" to "just about the dumbest piece of legislation I have seen," the measure mandated a balanced budget by 1991. It included a "doomsday device" mandating automatic across-the-board spending cuts if needed to meet deficit-reduction goals. Gramm and Rudman made an effective team: "While Gramm provided much of the oratorical firepower behind the proposal, the more established Rudman gave it an aura of respectability."

Rudman truly believed that the bill's doomsday machinery would never have to be used. As he wrote in *Combat*: "We saw the legislation as a forcing mechanism. We thought the threat of automatic cuts would force Congress and the White House to compromise on a responsible budget. Automatic cuts would be, among other things, a shameful admission of political incompetence. The bill mandated that the Government

Accounting Office, a creature of the executive branch of government, would act as referee."

Debate over the proposal was intense. At one point, a Pentagon official went so far as to charge that Gramm-Rudman delivered "a message of comfort to the Soviet Union." Rudman was apoplectic. "The Russians ought to be dancing in the street when they see this country spending itself into bankruptcy," he responded. "They can defeat us without firing a shot."

Gramm-Rudman passed both houses of Congress, and was signed into law by President Reagan on December 18, 1985. Rudman came away from the signing ceremony with the sinking feeling that Reagan was far more enamored of tax cuts than balanced budgets.

On February 7, 1986, a federal court ruled that Gramm-Rudman was unconstitutional. The court held that it violated the separation of powers doctrine by "investing the power to determine how the automatic spending cuts were to be carried out with the comptroller general, who is appointed by the president but who can be fired by Congress." Later that year, the Supreme Court, in a seven-to-two vote, upheld the lower court's decision.

Senators Gramm and Rudman then drafted what was termed Gramm-Rudman II. In this version, the GAO would still decide whether automatic cuts were called for, but its recommendations would go to the House and Senate Budget Committees. They in turn would initiate legislation ordering the President to begin the process of sequestration. The problem with Gramm-Rudman II was obvious: the automatic cuts were no longer automatic. "Our backup plan returned the hard budget decisions to the same Congress that had failed to make them before."

In summing up the battle over the deficit, Rudman wrote: "Gramm-Rudman was defeated by politics as usual. The way it was undermined stands today as a textbook example of how politicians trick the American people into thinking they're acting on a problem when in fact they're ducking it."

Prior to becoming involved with the deficit fight, Warren Rudman gave serious consideration to ending his Senate career after one six-year term. With the passage of Gramm-Rudman, he decided to run again, easily defeating former Massachusetts Governor Endicott Peabody,

whom the Democrats had enlisted at the last minute as a sacrificial candidate.

In his second term, Rudman became a member of the minority. As ranking Republican on the Select Committee on Secret Military Assistance to Iran and the Nicaraguan Opposition, Rudman cochaired (along with Hawaii's Senator Daniel Inouye) the Iran-Contra hearings. These hearings, nationally televised, investigated the Reagan administration's sale of arms to Iran in exchange for the release of American hostages and its diversion of some of the profits from the sale to the Nicaraguan Contras.

The question on everyone's mind was whether or not President Reagan had had full knowledge—or worse, given consent—to the highly complex plan. Although Rudman had himself been a supporter of the Contras, he nonetheless was the most outspoken Republican critic of the administration's handling of the affair. When Lieutenant Colonel Oliver North (resplendent in Marine uniform and full complement of medals) testified before the committee, Rudman sternly criticized him. "The American people," he said, "have the constitutional right to be wrong."

What bothered Rudman the most about Iran-Contra was "the implications this had to our presidency and our Constitution: that someone can cook up an intelligence scheme, feed it to the president, brief him incorrectly, then lie to the secretary of state and the attorney general, and then try to cover up what they did." Rudman's posture lent a much-needed bipartisan tone to the hearings. Although he believed in his heart of hearts that Reagan was not, in a legal sense, culpable, he wrote that "clearly it was the president who had created the climate in which Iran-Contra could happen."

Rudman was roundly criticized by his state's largest newspaper, the *Manchester Union Leader*, for his role in the hearings. Rudman fired back: "I want someone from the Right politically to stand up and say, 'I think it was good to sell arms to the Iranians.' Let them stand up and say that. If they don't believe it, they should keep their mouths shut." The *Union Leader*'s condemnation notwithstanding, Rudman's mail proved that the overwhelming majority supported his tough stance.

Toward the end of his second term, Rudman,

as ranking Republican on the Select Committee on Ethics, cochaired the hearings on the so-called Keating Five. The hearings dealt with five Senators (Republican McCain of Arizona and Democrats Cranston of California, Glenn of Ohio, DeConcini of Arizona, and Riegel of Michigan) charged with conflict of interest stemming from their dealings with failed savings-and-loan executive Charles Keating.

Standing in judgment over one's colleagues is one of the least desirable jobs in the Senate—one which Rudman looked upon with great reservations. Nonetheless, he urged that the panel not "rush to judgment." Senators McCain and Glenn were quickly cleared of all charges. DeConcini and Riegel received slaps on the wrist and then retired from the Senate. Cranston, who already had announced his retirement and was suffering from prostate cancer, was given the heaviest reprimand.

Warren Rudman was also instrumental in helping to facilitate the confirmation of his old friend David Souter for a seat on the United States Supreme Court. Souter, "that quintessential, taciturn New Hampshire Yankee," was characterized by the press as an "oddball," a "hermit," and "dangerously out of touch with the lives of ordinary people." Rudman personally escorted Souter from Senate office to Senate office, and then helped prepare his friend for the confirmation hearings. What at first looked like a feeding frenzy turned out to be a rather facile procedure; Souter was confirmed by a vote of 90 to 9.

Warren Rudman left the Senate after two terms. Desirous of returning to the practice of law where he could once again make a good living, Rudman had become disenchanted with the direction of the "new" Republican Party. "I could see the Republican Party gradually being taken over by 'movement' conservatives and self-commissioned Christian soldiers whose social agenda I found repugnant. . . . The spirit of civility and compromise was drying up."

As a lame duck Senator, Rudman was supposed to be a delegate to the 1992 Republican National Convention in Houston, Texas. Reviewing the convention's agenda—"Pat Robertson, Pat Buchanan and all the rest"—Rudman decided instead to go on a fact-finding mission to Croatia. "I thought that with my views I might be safer in Zagreb than in Houston."

Upon leaving the Senate, Warren Rudman returned to the practice of law, this time with the Washington office of Paul, Weiss, Rifkind, Wharton & Garrison. Additionally, he teamed up with former Massachusetts Senator Paul Tsongas (1941–1997) and former Commerce Secretary Pete Peterson to found the Concord Coalition. It "works for a balanced budget by organizing informed citizens to bring grassroots pressure on political leaders." Rudman divides his time between Washington and Nashua. Summing up his political career, Rudman wrote, "I was a senator first, serving the country's interests as I saw it, and Jewish second. The irony was that most people outside Washington didn't know I was Jewish."

References

Warren B. Rudman, *Combat: Twelve Years in the U.S. Senate* (New York: Random House, 1996).

American Politics, December 1987, pp. 37–39.

Current Biography, 1989, pp. 484–487.

SABATH, ADOLPH JOACHIM (1866–1952):
Democrat from Illinois; served twenty-three terms in the House and elected to a twenty-fourth (Sixtieth through Eighty-third Congress; March 4, 1907–November 6, 1952).

Of the more than 11,100 men and women who have served in the United States Congress from 1789 to the present, only three had longer careers than Adolph Joachim Sabath, Democrat of Illinois—Mississippi's Jamie Whiten, Georgia's Carl Vinson, and New York's *Emanuel Celler*. Of the four, Sabath undoubtedly started out with the greatest handicaps; he was foreign-born, physically unprepossessing, and never quite mastered the English language. Throughout his congressional career, he frequently had difficulty in expressing himself, and never could pronounce the letter *v*—"let's wote to uphold the weto." In the heat of debate he would often have to resort to his native Czech. When asked how he felt after giving his maiden speech in the House, he replied: "I never in a Turkish bath perspired more."

Adolph Sabath, the second of Joachim and Barbara ("Babette") Eissenschimmel Sabath's twelve children, was born in Zabori, Bohemia (Czechoslovakia) on April 4, 1866—not quite a year after the assassination of President Abraham Lincoln. The Sabaths were the only Jewish family in the small town (population about 400), which in those days was the seat of the Catholic diocese. Joachim, the town butcher, sent all his children both to Catholic school and to church. In that way "there was nothing to set them apart from other citizens of Zabori."

At age thirteen, young Adolph headed off for Horazdovic, a neighboring town, where he worked as an apprentice clerk in a dry-goods store. After hours, he helped care for the shop-keeper's blind brother-in-law, whose name was Wigl. It so happened that Wigl had recently returned from the United States. After hearing the blind man's tales of America, Adolph resolved to save his money and make his way to the golden land. At age fifteen, armed with less than $45, Adolph set out for Bremen, where he embarked as a steerage passenger on a ship bound for Baltimore. In keeping with America's immigrant tradition, Sabath arrived in Baltimore harbor with precisely $2.15—enough to get him to Chicago, where he had a cousin. After a few false starts in Chicago, Sabath landed a job at $4 a week clerking in a Halsted Street store which sold shoes and house furnishings. By the time he became an American citizen at age twenty-one (1887), he was the store's manager. Restless and ambitious, he decided it was time to strike out on his own.

In the late 1880s and early 1890s, a vast number of Bohemian immigrants gravitated to Chicago's newly developing Southwest side. The locals nicknamed the area "Pilsen" after the Bohemian town made famous for its beer—Plzen, about 85 kilometers southwest of Prague. This was to be Adolph Sabath's power base for the next sixty-five years. Sabath went into the real estate business. He would buy tracts of land from insurance companies and subdivide them into parcels, which he would then sell to his Bohemian landsmen. By the early 1890s, already quite prosperous he was able to send for the rest of his family. Nearly wiped out by the Depression of 1893, he held on, and, with the help of the companies with which he dealt, managed to keep his head above water.

All the while, Sabath was going to school to improve himself. He attended both the Bryant and Stratton Business School and the Chicago School of Law, graduating from the latter in 1891. Sabath's motive for becoming an attorney was eminently reasonable: he wanted to save on lawyer's abstract fees. Admitted to the bar in 1892, he went into practice with several partners. Eventually the firm would be known as Sabath, Perlman, Goodman & Rein.

Adolph Sabath's interest in Bohemian affairs and the growing influence he attained as a result of his real estate business and his law practice led him into politics. He served as a ward committeeman for the Democratic Party, and in 1894 was secretary of the Committee to Elect Anton Dvorak, the first Czech-American to become an alderman in Chicago. Brought to the attention of Illinois Governor John Peter Altgeld, Sabath was appointed justice of the peace for Cook County (Chicago) the next year. For the remainder of his life, Sabath was always referred to as "Judge Sabath." In 1896, he was appointed police magistrate and attended his first Democratic National Convention. This was the convention that nominated William Jennings Bryan after his stem-winding "Cross of Gold" speech. Sabath would attend every national convention until 1944.

Sabath continued as police magistrate until 1906, when he was urged to run for Congress from the Fifth District against the Republican incumbent, Anthony Michalek, a one-term Republican originally from Radvanov, also in Bohemia. Campaigning in four languages, Sabath won by a final tally of 9,545 to 8,634. In 1906, approximately one-third of America's Czech population resided in Chicago, the majority of them in the Fifth Congressional District. Sabath represented that district until the day he died. One reason for Sabath's great electoral success was that Illinois had virtually no congressional redistricting until 1946. The Fifth Congressional District always remained a small district; in the 1940 census its population stood at only 112,116 against a national average of about 304,000 per district. Because he represented so few constituents, the *Chicago Tribune*, his longtime critic, frequently referred to him as "Half a Congressman" Sabath.

Adolph Joachim Sabath (he had added his father's name in order to distinguish himself from a cousin by the same name) was sworn in as a member of the Sixtieth Congress on March 4, 1907. In December 1907, the House took up a bill to enlarge the immigration station in Philadelphia. House Majority Leader, James R. Mann, an Illinois Republican, suggested to the freshman Democrat that since he was personally familiar with immigration, here was a chance to make his maiden speech. Sabath demurred, explaining to Mann: "I'm here only a few days; I'd better wait until I'm here awhile." But after listening to two "oratorical fire-eaters attack the bill—one went so far as to suggest that it would be more appropriate to burn the building down"—Sabath was moved to speak: "Let us build this building in Philadelphia . . . to give these worthy foreigners a welcome when they come, and to show them that our country ever extends the warm hand of sympathy and fellowship to the oppressed of the earth." The House wound up passing the bill, and, as Sabath later noted, "I was a big guy."

In 1908, Sabath introduced the first bill in Congress to provide for railroad workers' compensation in case of injury or accidental death. Although President Theodore Roosevelt personally supported Sabath's measure, it never came to a vote. The House, however, created a special commission "for the purpose of studying medical compensation for railroad laborers," and the commission introduced a bill that was eventually passed. Ironically, Sabath wound up voting against the bill; he felt that it dealt too much with railroad compensation rates and too little with worker's compensation.

Sabath went to the 1912 Democratic National Convention pledged to the candidacy of James Beauchamp "Champ" Clark, the House Minority Leader from Missouri. When asked why he was not supporting Woodrow Wilson, he said that so far as he knew, Wilson was in favor of restricting immigration. Invited to meet the New Jersey Governor, Sabath spent two hours sipping sherry and expressing his misgivings. By the conclusion of the meeting, Sabath had had a change of heart; he became an avid Wilson supporter.

As with many members of the Congressional Minyan, Adolph Sabath was acutely sensitive when it came to the issue of immigration. Wilson's pledge to Sabath that he opposed any and all legislation that would tend to restrict immigration was soon put to the test. In December 1913, Vermont Senator William Paul Dillingham and Alabama Representative John Lawson introduced a bill instituting a literacy test for all immigrants. Sabath was incensed to the point of eloquence:

> It is not the so-called "undesirables" in any country that migrate. They stay at home. It is the hardy, fearless, striving ones that give up their old homes and bring their indomitable spirits into new lands. It is that spirit which has been brought to this land by the immigrants of the last one-hundred years which has gone to make this country what it is today. . . . If I thought that immigration was detrimental to our country or to the interests of the laboring people of our country, I would rather resign my seat . . . than to advocate the defeat of this measure; but I am fully convinced that immigration has been and is of inestimable benefit.

Despite Sabath's valiant fight, the Dillingham-Burnett bill passed both houses of Congress in January 1915. Wilson, true to his word, vetoed the measure as soon as it reached his desk. The following month, the House attempted to override Wilson's veto. With Sabath as the point man, it failed to muster the required two-thirds vote. Once again, the five-foot-six gentleman from Illinois was "a big man."

The anti-immigration forces may have been down, but they weren't out. The next year, 1916, with nativist sentiment on the rise, Congressman Burnett introduced virtually the same measure. This time it passed 308 to 87. Sabath attempted to have the bill returned to committee so that the literacy clause could be struck, but his motion was voted down. Once again, Wilson exercised the veto. When the measure returned to the House with the President's veto message, Sabath took the floor to plead with his colleagues not to override. This time he spoke not just as an immigrant, but as a Jew.

> Ever since my election to Congress I have strenuously opposed this most obnoxious legislation and twice have I succeeded in preventing this bill from being passed over presidential vetoes. . . . Oftentimes upon the floor of the House I have shown by figures and facts the wonderful and progressive strides that have been accomplished by the foreign-born and their children. I particularly pointed out the achievements of our Jewish people, showing that they have gained the leadership in commerce, art, science and literature, and the expansion of commerce and industry is largely due to the push and the progressiveness of our people. I feel that I have successfully proven that the immigrant is beneficial to our country, especially the Jewish immigrant.

Despite his emotional appeal, Congress succeeded in overriding Wilson's veto.

Adolph Sabath maintained a close relationship with Woodrow Wilson throughout his two terms. Sabath felt close enough to disagree with him and to offer candid advice. One such situation arose during the First World War, when the President was considering negotiating a separate peace treaty with Austria-Hungary. Deeply concerned, Sabath went to Wilson's secretary, Joseph Tumulty, requesting a private meeting. Granted his private audience with the President, Sabath explained that discontinuing negotia-

tions would likely lead to revolts in Austria-Hungary. Furthermore, the diminutive congressman argued, such revolts would severely hamper America's ability to aid the German war effort. A few days after the meeting, Wilson announced to Congress that negotiations for a separate peace had been called off. History proved Adolph Sabath to be a prophet: not long after, revolts broke out in Czechoslovakia and Poland that led to their independence.

The year 1920 was one of those political moments in which the American voting public "threw the rascals out." What with the widespread dissatisfaction with Wilson's League of Nations and the wave of moralistic fervor sweeping the country, the years of Democrat rule were about to end in a big way. Warren G. Harding and Calvin Coolidge, the Republican apostles of "normalcy," trounced the Cox-(Franklin) Roosevelt ticket by more than 7 million votes. Prohibition was the law of the land. Adolph Sabath, running for reelection as a "wet," faced his toughest challenge, yet managed to squeak to victory over Jacob Gartenstein by the slimmest of margins—14,374 to 14,076. For the next twelve years, Sabath would languish as a member of the minority party.

In the spring of 1921, Congress went back to the issue of immigration, considering a bill that would establish a quota system. Under the terms of this system, the number of immigrants in one year from any given country could not exceed 3 percent of the number of persons of that nationality residing in the United States in the base year of 1910. What infuriated Adolph Sabath was that the bill's supporters kept referring to it publicly as temporary emergency legislation, but privately agreed that it would be permanent. Sabath introduced an amendment that would exempt political refugees, but it was rejected.

Less than three years later, Congress enacted the National Origins Act, which not only entirely banned immigrants from East Asia, but lowered the quota to 2 percent based on the 1890 census. The act was, without question, slanted in favor of immigrants from Northwestern Europe. In their minority report, Adolph Sabath and his colleague *Samuel Dickstein* condemned the obvious bias behind this disparity:

> It is curious to note that, taking the census of 1890 as a basis, Germany would be com-

paratively in the most favorable position, and Belgium, Czechoslovakia, Italy, Yugoslavia, Poland and Russia, with whom we were allied during the late conflict, are the most unfavorable. The obvious purpose of this discrimination is the adoption of an unfounded anthropological theory that the nations which are favored are the progeny of hitherto unsuspected Nordic ancestors, while those discriminated against are not classified as belonging to that mythical ancestral stock. No scientific evidence worthy of consideration was introduced to substitute this pseudo-scientific proposition.

In addition to his activities in Washington, Sabath was still a favorite with the political bosses of Chicago. He was definitely *persona grata* with the then-powerful Kelly-Nash political machine. "He was satisfactory to Mayor Edward J. Kelly and Patrick Nash not only because he attracted Bohemian-American votes by his presence on the ticket, but also he proved willing to do what he was told." For more than a decade, coinciding with the mayoralty of Carter H. Harrison Jr. (the son and namesake of a former mayor who was assassinated in 1893), Sabath served as chairman of the Cook County Democratic Central Committee. Surprisingly, though, despite his more than half-century of involvement in Windy City politics, many political histories of the period omit any reference to him. At least one essayist has concluded that Sabath, at best, played "a minor part in the lusty partisan fights of Chicago."

Sabath did not get along with Presidents Harding, Coolidge, or Hoover. He found their attachment to big business distasteful. Moreover, he was deeply troubled by the direction of the economy. In September 1929, Sabath advocated restrictions on short-selling practices and called for the closing of the New York Stock Exchange until legislation for the protection of investors "and the country as a whole" could be passed. A month later, when the stock market crashed, Sabath once again looked like a prophet. In early 1930, he introduced the first bill to establish the Reconstruction Finance Corporation. It was tabled until the early days of the Roosevelt administration.

With the election of Franklin Delano Roosevelt in 1932, Sabath once again found himself serving a President he truly admired. He had been friendly with FDR for nearly twenty years—back to the days when the young aristocrat had served as Wilson's Assistant Secretary of the Navy. Sabath had campaigned for Roosevelt when he ran for Vice President in 1920, and had wanted him to run for President in 1928 instead of Al Smith. Roosevelt rewarded the little judge for his long support by naming him chairman of the Midwestern region of the FDR for President Committee—a position he held in all of Roosevelt's presidential campaigns.

Adolph Sabath was a "New Dealer's New Dealer." His support for FDR's program knew no bounds. In Roosevelt, he found his idol. During the depths of the Depression, Sabath's greatest legislative opportunity to date arose: he was appointed chairman of a special investigative committee. Given broad powers, the committee had a mandate to look into an alleged racket that had grown up in the organization of so-called protective committees in connection with defaults on an estimated $20 billion in real estate bonds throughout the country. The impression was given that the committee—which was Sabath's idea—could do something about recovering funds for those who had invested in the defaulted bonds.

Unfortunately, Sabath's opportunity blew up in his face. "The entire investigation was enveloped in confusion and futility. . . . There were even ugly rumors that the firm of Sabath, Perlman, Goodman & Rein were profiting from fees obtained from companies under investigation." Sabath vehemently denied the charge, literally breaking out into tears when confronted with the accusation.

By the middle of FDR's second term, New Deal programs were coming under increasing attack from conservative Democrats. Infuriated, the President attempted to "purge" recalcitrant Democrats in the 1938 primary. With the exception of one election, FDR's purge was a complete failure. But that one exception, the defeat of New York Democrat John J. O'Connor, was a boon to Adolph Sabath. For the defeated O'Connor was, at the time of his defeat, chairman of the House Rules Committee. With O'Connor's defeat, Sabath, who was second in seniority, became chairman—but not without a fight. "For a time it appeared that certain conservatives on the committee might challenge Sabath, but the seniority system prevailed with the help of Majority Leader [and future Speaker] Sam Rayburn of Texas."

Sabath's years as chairman of this all-powerful committee were not smooth ones for the New Deal or for Sabath. He could only count on four consistent votes: his own, plus John J. Delaney of New York, Joe B. Bates of Kentucky, and Roger Slaughter of Missouri. The five Southern Democrats on the committee—Eugene Cox of Georgia, Howard W. ("The Judge") Smith of Virginia, J. Bayard Clark of North Carolina, Martin Dies of Texas, and William Colmer of Mississippi—were "irreconcilable in their opposition to the President's programs." (The Democratic Colmer, who served in Congress from 1933 to 1973, eventually chairing the Rules Committee himself, was replaced in Congress by his young assistant Trent Lott, who in June 1996 became the Republican Majority Leader of the United States Senate.) Sabath was also saddled with five Republicans—Hamilton Fish of New York, Leo E. Allen of Illinois, Earl C. Michener of Michigan, Charles A. Halleck of Indiana, and Clarence Brown of Ohio—who were just as steadfast in their opposition to anything FDR proposed.

History has not judged Adolph Sabath to be a particularly effective Rules Committee chairman. "With such an array of votes against him . . . he often found it necessary to resort to ruse." There is a story still circulating around Capitol Hill about how, on more than one occasion, Chairman Sabath, having failed in all conventional and parliamentary ways to delay a vote or adjourn his committee, would pretend to faint, almost falling out of his chair. Once the committee members left the chamber, he would lift his face from off the desk and whisper: "Have they gone yet?" Some say that Adolph Sabath didn't have a firm enough grasp of parliamentary procedure to be an effective chairman. Perhaps. Then again, it might be that he was simply too fair and gentle to wield all the power his gavel symbolized. Even his worst detractors praised him for his even-handedness.

As chairman, Sabath frequently had to report to the House on measures that he personally opposed. One such recurring situation involved the Committee on Un-American Activities. Sabath was convinced that the committee, under

its chairman, Martin Dies, was abusing its mandate and employing "the prestige and immunity of Congress to make partisan attacks on the administration, members of the Cabinet, organized labor, and many private citizens as well." He sought in committee to have the its funding cut or eliminated, but to no avail.

Adolph Sabath became dean of the House of Representatives in 1934 upon the death of Speaker Henry Rainey. He became dean of Congress upon the retirement of Senator George Norris of Nebraska in 1943. Less than two years later, his good friend President Roosevelt died. Without so much as missing a stride, Sabath became President Harry Truman's staunch supporter. He championed Truman's Fair Deal policies with the same fervor he had shown FDR's New Deal. The only recorded time he went against a Truman position involved a proposed $3.75 billion loan to Great Britain. Sabath was against it, stating that "we have saved Britain twice . . . what has Britain done for us in the last 160 years?" In the end, he did vote for the loan, rationalizing that its defeat would probably lead to a victory for the British Conservative Party.

Although Sabath and his Jewish colleagues were mostly hamstrung in their attempts to aid the Jews of Hitlerian Europe, he was, nonetheless, a staunch Zionist. As early as 1938, along with fifty other members of Congress, he urged President Roosevelt to "repudiate the Balfour Declaration and Mandate and to protest British restrictions of Jewish immigration into Palestine." On more than one occasion he warned Roosevelt of the announced plans of Joseph Goebbels that the Jews of Czechoslovakia would be executed if the Allies continued bombing German cities.

In his person, Adolph Sabath was a short, stocky man (five feet, six inches; 180 pounds) with a clipped mustache and an ever-present cigar. A *New York Post* writer described him as a "chubby, fussy little man." In 1917, at age fifty-one, he married May Ruth Fuerst, the "daughter of a newspaperman who was impressed with his reform platform." They had no children. Sabath's sole involvement in the Jewish community seems to have been his membership in B'nai B'rith. A man of means (he left an estate of some $150,000), Sabath owned a 1,200-acre farm in the delta lowland of California's San Joaquin Valley.

One of his brothers, Joseph, was Chicago's foremost divorce judge, having tried more than 45,000 cases from his post on the Cook County Superior Court.

In the fall of 1952, Adolph Sabath fell ill and was taken to Bethesda Naval Hospital. During his hospitalization, though weak, he kept at work, drafting foreign-language newspaper ads on behalf of presidential candidate Adlai E. Stevenson. Unable to campaign, Sabath was nonetheless reelected to his twenty-third and last term on November 4, 1952. He died two days later, just a few months shy of what would have been his eighty-seventh birthday. In his memorial address, Harry Truman said of Adolph Sabath: "He exemplified in his life the virtues that make America strong, and in him the forgotten man always found a champion."

Adolph Sabath is buried in the Forest Home Cemetery, Forest Park, Illinois.

References

American Jewish Year Book, vol. 24, p. 197; vol. 55, p. 459.

John R. Beal, "Adolph J. Sabath: 'Dean of the House,'" in *Public Men In and Out of Office*, ed. J. T. Salter (Chapel Hill: University of North Carolina Press, 1946).

Biographical Directory of American Jews.

Burton Boxerman, "Adolph Joachim Sabath in Congress: The Early Years, 1907–1932" and "The Roosevelt and Truman Years," *Illinois State Historical Society Journal*, Autumn and Winter 1973.

Dictionary of American Biography.

Encyclopaedia Judaica (1972), vol. 14, col. 557.

New York Times, November 6, 1952, 1:6.

Universal Jewish Encyclopedia.

Who Was Who in America, vol. 3.

Who Was Who in American Jewry, 1926, 1928, 1938.

SACKS, LEON (1902–1972): *Democrat from Pennsylvania; served three terms in the House (Seventy-fifth through Seventy-seventh Congress; January 3, 1937–January 3, 1943).*

Out of the 179 members of the Congressional Minyan, only a handful graduated from the Wharton School of the University of Pennsylvania. Two of these, *Joshua Eilberg* and Leon Sacks, were natives of Philadelphia, and both represented their home city in the Congress.

Leon Sacks, the son of Morris and Dora (Clayman) Sacks, was born in the City of Brotherly Love on October 2, 1902. He was educated in the local public schools and received his undergraduate degree from Wharton in 1923. Three years later, in 1926, he received an LL.B. from the University of Pennsylvania. Sacks practiced law in Philadelphia for nearly a decade before he was appointed deputy attorney general of Pennsylvania in February 1935. He served in this post for two years, until his election to the Seventy-fifth Congress in November 1936, the year that Franklin Roosevelt literally ran away from his Republican rival, Kansas Governor "Alf" Landon. Riding FDR's coattails, Sacks defeated Republican Harry Clay Ransley (1863–1941), who had held his First District seat for the preceding eight terms. It was one of the great political upsets of the year.

Near the end of his first term in Congress Leon Sacks married Shirley Kimelman. They had two daughters: Estelle Myra (Mrs. Sidney A. Chivian) and Fredlyn Jeri (Mrs. Martin D. Brown). During his three terms in Congress, Leon Sacks was assigned to the House Banking and Currency Committee. In April 1942, a few months after the United States became embroiled in World War II, the committee was conducting hearings on the war's effect on the American automobile industry. Sacks, voicing his displeasure with the "general confusion over rationing," urged that a committee be named "to investigate the entire rationing situation."

Prior to this, the Senate had passed legislation "to provide government financial relief for automobile dealers unable to sell their cars because of rationing restrictions." The Senate measure provided that the Reconstruction Finance Corporation would be "authorized to make loans on cars for those dealers who wished to retain their stocks or to purchase the cars after eighteen months at a retail price."

During the House Banking Committee hearings, Sacks brought the entire issue of rationing into question. "I'm wondering if we're trying to win this war by scaring people. This gasoline rationing is a good example. One official says we'll have only two and one-half to five gallons a week, and others say the estimate is entirely too low. Nobody seems to be in agreement." Continuing on to sugar rationing, Sacks added: "There's considerable talk that rationing actually isn't necessary. It's about time that this confusion in official circles, these conflicting statements, were cleared up. I urge that a committee be named to investigate the whole matter."

In the end, Sacks did not get his investigation underway. Representative Thomas Ford, Democrat of California, urged his colleagues: "Let's not make the confusion worse by creating another investigating committee." It turned out to be Leon Sacks's single moment in the sun.

Sacks lost his seat in the 1942 election to Republican James A. Gallagher, who in turn lost the seat in 1944 to William A. Barret, and then turned around and ousted Barret in 1946. The competition between the two came full cycle when Barret once again defeated Gallagher in 1948, and then managed to hold on to the seat for the next quarter-century. Barret died in office in 1976.

Following his six years in the House, Leon Sacks entered military service, attached to the Army Air Forces Eastern Flying Training Command. Rising to the rank of lieutenant colonel, Sacks served until January 1946. Upon his return to Philadelphia, Sacks resumed the practice of law, and was appointed to various civic and municipal boards. He died in Philadelphia on March 11, 1972, and was buried in Shalom Memorial Park.

References
New York Times, April 25, 1942, 15:5.
Universal Jewish Encyclopedia.
Who Was Who in American Jewry, 1938.

SANDERS, BERNARD (1941–): *Independent (Socialist) from Vermont; has served five terms in the House (One Hundred and Second through One Hundred and Sixth Congress; January 3, 1991–present).*

In the 135 years from 1865 to 1990, Vermont, arguably the most Republican state in the Union, sent twenty-nine men to the House of Representatives. Of these, twenty-seven were, unsurprisingly, members of the GOP. The other two, Bradley Barlow and William H. Meyer, were, respectively, a Greenbacker and a Democrat. In November 1990, Vermonters wrote a dramatic new page in their political history by electing as their congressional Representative-at-Large an independent, self-styled Democratic Socialist, forty-nine-year-old Bernie Sanders. *Roll Call*, the "newspaper of Capitol Hill," rated Sanders's upset victory (56-40 percent) over incumbent Representative Peter Smith "one of the twenty-five most significant elections in American history."

Sanders's election was more than a mere departure from Republican representation. Almost since its entry into the Union, Vermont had been represented by dyed-in-the-wool Yankees with almost stereotypic New England-sounding names like Worthington Smith, Dudley Denison, and Kittridge Haskins. Bernie Sanders doesn't look, sound, or act—at least politically—like anyone's image of a typical New Englander—and for good reason. He is a rumpled, tousle-headed New Yorker, who still speaks like the native Brooklynite he is, even after more than thirty years in Vermont.

The second of Eli and Dorothy (Glassburg) Sanders' two sons, the future Congressional Minyanaire was born in Flatbush on September 8, 1941. His father, a paint salesman, had emigrated from Poland at age seventeen. Economically, the Sanders were lower-middle-class, a fact that seemingly helped shape Bernie's future political ideology: "It's not that we were poor, but [there was always] the constant pressure of never having enough money. . . . The money question to me has always been very deep and emotional."

Bernie Sanders attended P.S. 197, where he played basketball on the team that won the borough championship. While a student at P.S. 197, Sanders attended afternoon Hebrew school. He was bar mitzvah in 1954 at the King's Highway Jewish Center. Speaking of his Hebrew skills, Sanders said: "I was able to read Hebrew in a true academic fashion: [I] could read it but not necessarily understand everything [I] was reading. I suppose I could brush up if pressed into duty."

Moving on to James Madison High School, he got his first taste of political campaigning—and political loss. In his senior year, Bernie Sanders ran for student body president. His platform included a proposal that the school adopt a Korean orphan. Although he came in last in a three-way race (shades of things to come), he did have the satisfaction of seeing the winner embrace his proposal; James Madison High School did adopt a Korean orphan.

Bernie followed in his older brother Larry's footsteps and entered Brooklyn College. By the beginning of his sophomore year, he was a student at the University of Chicago, where he was "radicalized by the grinding poverty he saw for the first time in places such as the city's South Side." His college years coincided with the civil rights movement and the early days of the war in Vietnam. Sanders helped lead sit-in protests against segregated housing on campus and applied for conscientious-objector status with the Selective Service. By the time his case came up for review, he was twenty-six—too old to be drafted.

Bernard Sanders graduated from the University of Chicago in 1964 with a degree in political science. Following graduation, he traveled to Israel, where he worked on several *kibbutzim*. By 1968, he was a resident of Vermont—a place that attracted a good number of hippies and members of what was in those days referred to as the counter-culture. Legend has it that Sanders decided to move to the Green Mountain State after seeing a brochure in a tourist office in Manhattan. According to Sanders, "When I was a kid, I always had a strong feeling for country life. I was not a great fan of big cities. After I was married . . . we bought some land in Vermont. We went up there for basically the same reason, I think, that many others have gone up there: its a very beautiful state."

Sanders and his son Levi, lived without electricity or running water in a converted sugar house. He earned a precarious living as a freelance writer, researcher for the Vermont Tax Department, and director of the American People's History Society. In this latter position, Sanders produced and directed college-level filmstrips and documentaries, including a praiseworthy video on the life of Eugene V. Debs.

In the early 1970s, Sanders helped found the Liberty Union Party. Between 1972 and 1977, when he left the party, he ran for office four times—always unsuccessfully. Examining Sanders's record during these years, one marvels at his tenacity.

January 1972: Special election for the U.S. Senate to fill the seat vacated when Senator Winston Prouty died. Sanders runs as the Liberty Union candidate, coming in third in a three-way race won by Republican Robert J. Stafford. Sanders wins 2.1 percent of the vote (1,571 out of 71,301 cast).

November 1972: Sanders runs for governor on the Liberty Union ticket. Again comes in third in a three-way race won by Democrat Thomas Salmon. Sanders garners 1.15 percent of the vote (2,175 out of 189,237 cast).

November 1974: Sanders runs again for the U.S. Senate as a member of the Liberty Union Party. Again, he comes in last in a three-way race won by Democrat Patrick J. Leahy. This time, Sanders's percentage inches up to 4.1 percent (5,901 out of 142,762 cast).

November 1976: A second run for governor as a member of the Liberty Union. Sanders wins 6.1 percent in a three-way race won by Republican Richard A. Snelling (11,317 out of 185,929 cast).

In March 1981, Bernie Sanders's record of electoral defeats came to an end—just barely—when he was elected mayor of Burlington by ten votes. Running as an independent in a four-way race, Sanders received 43 percent of the vote, ousting five-term incumbent Gordon Paquette.

Mayor Paquette, a conservative Democrat,

was known for running an office "marked by cronyism and neglect of city services." When urged by his friends and supporters to run for mayor, Sanders at first demurred, stating that although certainly knowledgeable about state and national affairs, he "felt out of touch with local concerns." About those days, Sanders was quoted as saying: "The God's honest truth is I knew very little about Burlington politics. I had attended two alderman meetings and fell asleep at one of them."

Somehow, for undisclosed reasons, Sanders made up his mind to enter the race. Once out on the campaign trail, he busied himself denouncing Mayor Paquette's proposed property tax increase, which he termed an undue burden on the middle class. Sanders's energetic style of campaigning and disarming honesty struck a resilient chord with the local voters. Aided by a surprise endorsement from the police union, which had been stymied in its attempt to negotiate a raise with the current city administration, Sanders was elected, as mentioned above, by an eyelash. As the only self-proclaimed socialist mayor in America, Bernie Sanders received instant attention in the national media. Vermont's largest city was suddenly dubbed "The People's Republic of Burlington."

Confounding his many critics, Sanders turned out to be a successful and remarkably durable mayor. Reelected three times—with majorities of 52.1, 55.8, and 55.2 percent—he got the voters of Burlington to accept a modest increase in property taxes and reached an amicable settlement with the police and firefighters' unions.

A "people's mayor," he successfully established "free health clinics for the poor and elderly, a community boat house and bike path at Lake Champlain . . . erected low-cost housing and shelters for the homeless, expanded the city's youth program, and established a municipal day-care center." And, in consonance with the spirit of a former *kibbutznik*, he planted thousands of trees. In order to finance all these public works projects, Sanders imposed special fees on utilities "and others whose excavation projects had hastened the deterioration of the roads."

According to Sanders, his proudest achievement during his eight years in office was "arousing public interest in government." During his tenure, voter participation grew by nearly 50 percent. Not all of Mayor Sanders's initiatives met with success, and his fiery anti-capitalist rhetoric, not surprisingly, alienated most of the business community.

During his years as mayor, Sanders found time to make a second gubernatorial run (1986), once again coming in third in a three-way race won by Governor Madeleine M. Kunin. In 1989, Sanders decided to call it quits as mayor, feeling that he had accomplished most of what he had originally set out to do. Speaking of his decision to retire from office, Sanders explained, "Being mayor, at least the way I do it, is a very hard job, because I feel a responsibility to make certain that the streets get paved, that we stop the war against Nicaragua, and that we have a national health-care system." During the Sanders administration, Burlington's municipal budget remained balanced even while businesses thrived. For one month in 1989, Burlington had the lowest unemployment rate (1.8 percent) in the nation.

In 1988, former Mayor Sanders made an unsuccessful bid for the U.S. House of Representatives. Running as an Independent in a six-way race, he came in second with 37 percent of the vote. Most remarkably, the candidate finishing behind him, Democrat Paul Poirier, was held to a paltry 18.9 percent. Emboldened by his strong showing, Sanders decided to bide his time and challenge the winner in the race, two-term Republican Lieutenant Governor Peter Smith. From 1989 to 1990, Sanders taught political science at Hamilton College, lectured at Harvard, and planned his strategy for the next campaign.

In his 1990 race against Smith, Sanders pilloried the incumbent for his support of the savings-and-loan bailout ("probably the greatest single rip-off in the history of this country"), and for his vote against the proposed ban on semiautomatic weapons. Of the former issue, Sanders opined: "How ironic that the Congress was able to find $500 billion in order to bail out the real-estate speculators and junk-bond dealers, but the same Congress can find no money for our children, for the environment, for health care, or for the needs of our senior citizens." Smith countered with ads suggesting that his opponent was pro-Communist. Sanders vociferously denied that he harbored so much as a even a scintilla of

sympathy for Communists or Communism: "When I talk about democratic socialism, what I am not talking about is authoritarian communism—a system which, thank God, is now falling apart; a system which has been responsible for the deaths of millions of people; a system which has been a vicious dictatorship; a system which has run an extraordinary dictatorship in the Soviet Union." It was this point that all but sunk Smith's campaign.

Bernie Sanders defeated Smith in the November 1990 election, carrying 227 out of 251 towns and capturing a solid 56 percent of the vote. He thus became the third socialist elected to Congress—and the first Independent to serve in that body in nearly forty years. Sanders's first task upon taking his oath of office in the House was to join the Democratic caucus without joining the party itself. House Speaker Thomas Foley averted a possible crisis among that party's conservative faction by reaching a compromise: Sanders would withdraw his application for membership in the party caucus in exchange for the right to committee assignments. Sanders was appointed to the House Committees on Banking and Government Operations.

Bernie Sanders has been reelected to Congress four times. In 1992, he captured 58 percent of the vote; in 1994, he was held to a slim 7,989-vote margin (50 percent). In 1996, he won by a solid 57,000 votes; in his last reelection campaign, 1998, he defeated Republican Mark Candon with a resounding 63.4 percent of the vote. As Congress's lone Independent, Sanders has become a true party of one—voting by the light of his own political philosophy. Sanders has called for progressive tax reform, a national health-care system like those found in England, Canada, and Australia, a national energy policy that is strong on conservation, affordable housing, and greatly increased support for family-owned farms. He has also repeatedly called for a 50 percent reduction in the defense budget, to be phased in over a five-year period. Arguing for the creation of a nonpartisan commission to "oversee a process by which the television industry . . . provides serious and uncensored discussion and portrayal of American reality," Sanders said: "We as a nation can no longer afford to amuse ourselves to death."

When asked what his proudest achievement

to date has been in Congress, Sanders replies: "I'm primarily proud of my own state. [They] made history by sending me down here as the first non-Democrat, non-Republican Independent in forty years. I'm more proud of my own state for having the courage to do that than I am for myself. I think that Vermont in many ways is leading this country into a new type of politics. . . . The idea of a 'third party' is now seen as not only feasible but something that the majority of people would like to see."

Rumpled, informal, with a shock of unruly gray hair, Bernie Sanders is both feisty and articulate, witty and charming, and according to at least one writer, "bears a slight resemblance to the filmmaker Woody Allen." Divorced from his first wife years ago, Sanders married Jane O'Meara Driscoll, a Burlington community organizer, on May 28, 1988. Along with his son Levi, who studied broadcast journalism at the University of Kentucky, Bernie Sanders has three stepchildren: Heather, Coreen, and David. Bernie Sanders does not belong to a synagogue, but does feel a special kinship with, and motivation from, the ethics of the Jewish people.

References

Interview with Bernie Sanders, Washington, D.C., July 1992.

Barre-Montpelier Times Argus, November 7, 1990.

Boston Sunday Globe, May 12, 1991, pp. 69-71.

Current Biography Year Book, 1991, pp. 494–498.

SCHAKOWSKY, JANICE D. (1944–): *Democrat from Illinois; has served one term in the House (One Hundred and Sixth Congress; January 5, 1999–present).*

One day while shopping at an Evanston, Illinois, grocery store, Jan Schakowsky became upset that the cottage cheese containers did not carry a freshness date—a way of knowing the relative age of the highly perishable foodstuff. Deciding that she could do something to rectify the situation, Schakowsky worked with her friends to organize a nationwide campaign. The results were spectacular; expiration dating on food became the norm. Energized by her group's success, Schakowsky became first a noted citizen activist, then a state legislator, and finally, on November 3, 1998, a member of the United States Congress. Speaking of her responsibility for changing a policy that affects so many people's daily lives, Schakowsky commented: "Changing that date on cottage cheese may not have changed the world, but it did change my life. It convinced me that a few committed individuals could make the world better."

Janice D. "Jan" Danoff, the second of Erwin and Tillie (Cosnow) Danoff's two daughters, was born in Evanston on May 26, 1944. The Danoffs were originally from Russia, the Cosnows from Russia via Montreal. Erwin Danoff, who died the summer before his daughter was elected to Congress, worked as a furniture salesman; her mother was an elementary school teacher. "My mother," Jan recalled in a 1998 interview, "was a consummate teacher."

Grandfather Cosnow was a peddler who lived near Humbolt Park. Jan's early memories include helping her grandfather "*schlep* bags of potatoes up flights of stairs," and going to the barn behind his home to visit with his horse Teddy. Grandpa Cosnow *schlepped* enough bags to put his three children through college.

As a child attending public school in the West Rogers Park area of Chicago's North Side, Jan and her family were members of the Reform Temple Menorah, where she was bat mitzvah in

1957. Upon graduating from Sullivan High School, Jan went off to the University of Illinois, from which she received a B.S. in education in 1965. At age twenty, Jan married Harry Schakowsky and began teaching elementary school. Their marriage produced two children: Ian, born in 1968, and Mary (Hart), born one year later. The Schakowskys were divorced in 1978 after thirteen years of marriage.

Following her successful campaign to put freshness dates on food, Schakowsky became a full-time citizen-activist. In 1972, she worked as a volunteer in Representative *Abner Mikva*'s unsuccessful campaign for Congress. Schakowsky's participation in that campaign would eventually bear fruit when, more than a quarter-center later, Mikva endorsed her candidacy for Congress. In 1976, Jan Schakowsky was hired to become program director of Illinois Public Action, the state's largest public interest organization. Schakowsky was hired for the position by Robert Creamer, the organization's executive director. The two were married in 1980. The non-Jewish Creamer has a daughter, Lauren, who was born in 1975.

As program director for Illiois Public Action, she led a "grassroots campaign to stop utility shutoffs during cold winter months," and passed the Community Right to Know law for toxic chemicals. In 1985, Schakowsky became executive director of the Illinois State Council of Senior Citizens, and campaigned/organized across the state for lower-priced prescription drugs, tax relief for seniors, and financial protection for the spouses of nursing home residents.

In 1990, Jan Schakowsky ran successfully for the Eighteenth District seat in the Illinois General Assembly, winning her race with 83 percent of the vote. During her four terms (1991–98) in the state Assembly, Schakowsky served on the Human Services, Appropriations, Healthcare, and Electric Deregulation Committees, and chaired Labor and Commerce. Schakowsky was an active legislator, sponsoring nearly five dozen bills. Among her legislative successes was a bill (the nation's first) that guaranteed homeless people the right to vote. "Because these homeless people had no address," Schakowsky said, "they were generally denied the right to vote. Our bill rectified that situation." A strong advocate of women-oriented issues, Schakowsky also amended the Illinois Hate Crimes Act to add the words "gender" and "actual or perceived." The latter words gave even more legal muscle to the bill's provisions, for henceforth, one did not have to prove actual discrimination based on race, creed, or gender, but rather merely the perception of such.

Schakowsky's interest in the national scene dates back to 1995. That year, she formed an exploratory committee to look into the possibility of opposing longtime Ninth District Representative *Sidney Yates*. Schakowsky and her advisors concluded that Yates was virtually unbeatable; with the exception of one two-year period he had represented the district since 1948. Biding her time, Schakowsky decided to wait until Yates announced his retirement. That time came in the summer of 1997. Shortly after Yates made his decision to retire, Jan Schakowsky announced her intention to run in the Democrat primary.

The Ninth District includes both city and suburbs encompassing the North Lakeshore of Chicago, Evanston, Skokie, parts of Niles and Morton Grove, and several Northwest Side neighborhoods. It has been described by the influential *Rothenberg Political Report* as "one of the crown jewels of safe Democratic House seats." Not surprisingly, the Democratic primary attracted three engaging candidates: State Senator Howard Carrol, Chicago-area developer (and Hyatt Hotel scion) J. B. Pritzker, and Schakowsky. From day one, Carrol, who had served more than twenty-five years in the Illinois State Senate, was viewed as the frontrunner. Pritzker, who announced that he was planning to fund his campaign with a minimum of $1 million of his own money, was seen as an intriguing long shot, with Schakowsky a possible spoiler.

Recognizing that she would never be able to match either Carrol's or Pritzker's campaign war chests, Schakowsky fell back on a strategy she had learned a quarter-century earlier while working in Abner Mikva's campaign: grassroots political activism. Schakowsky decided to "build an organization, in part using young and ambitious volunteers, to penetrate the neighborhoods" of the district. Toward that end, she ran ads in college and university newspapers across the country announcing a "Chicago campaign training school, a program to teach ambitious young adults about politics in exchange for countless hours of free labor." Unbelievably, Schakowsky received more than two hundred replies. Winnowing the group down to nineteen, Schakowsky brought the young volunteer "field marshals" to Chicago, found them free lodging, gave them small food allowances, and "took them to school."

"In return for dedicating eighty or more hours a week to [the] campaign, the recruits received an intensive course in streetwise politics." The tutoring included two weeks of nonstop lectures, role-playing, and meetings with seasoned politicians and consultants. Having identified slightly more than 31,000-plus voters—those who would vote for Schakowsky—the volunteers proceeded to go out and build a grassroots organization made up of district residents.

In the meantime, running on the slogan "A Champion for Progressive Values," Schakowsky received an "unusually early" endorsement from "EMILY's List," a political network for pro-choice Democratic women. Schakowsky also received the endorsement of former representative (and former White House Counsel) Abner Mikva, Representative Jesse Jackson, Jr., and Senator *Barbara Boxer*. Schakowsky campaigned on a pro-choice, pro–gun control, anti-tobacco platform, drawing support from women, gays, and the Jewish community. During the primary, she stressed what the local press called "women's issues"—health care, freshness dating on food labels, and education.

Running an unusually smear-free campaign, both Schakowsky and her husband, Robert Creamer, were put under the "ethics microscope." Both Carrol and Pritzker criticized Schakowsky for her affiliation with Citizen Action, a consumer activist group under federal investigation for "alleged financial wrongdoing." The group was criticized for "charging senior citizens $229.00 for a credit card they could have received for free." As of mid-1999, Creamer, the organization's former executive director, was still under investigation. For her part, Jan Schakowsky explained that while she was a member of the Citizen Action advisory board, she had no knowledge of the group's day-to-day activities.

Despite being vastly outspent by her two rivals, Schakowsky won a "surprisingly easy" victory in the three-way race. The final tally showed Schakowsky receiving 45 percent of the vote with Senator Carrol at 35 percent and billionaire Pritzker at a scant 21 percent. With her primary victory, Schakowsky's election to the United States House of Representatives was a mere formality. In November 1998, she easily defeated Republican Herb Sohn, a perennial candidate in the Chicago area.

Upon arriving in Washington for freshman orientation, Schakowsky discovered that her "campaign school" idea was the talk of the town. "[Minority Leader] Dick Gephardt said it was the wave of the future," Schakowsky beamed in an interview. "There are now more than one hundred young people who, through immersion, training and hard work, are dedicated to progressive politics." Schakowsky expects the campaign-school concept to be successfully replicated across the country. Her husband will run them.

In March 1998, Jan Schakowsky abruptly left the campaign in order to be on hand for the birth of her first grandchild, Isabel Ann Hart. Within hours of the 8-pound, 15-ounce baby's arrival, grandma was back out on the hustings, campaigning and shaking hands—"but not handing out cigars."

References

Interview with Jan Schakowsky, November 1998.

Chicago Jewish Times, November 6, 1998.

Chicago Sun Times, March 2, 1998; September 23, 1997; November 7, 1998.

Chicago Tribune, May 15, 1998

SCHENK, LYNN (1945–): *Democrat from California; served one term in the House (One Hundred and Third Congress; January 3, 1993–January 3, 1995).*

The daughter of impoverished Holocaust survivors, Lynn Schenk was born in New York on January 5, 1945. Her parents, Sidney and Elsa (Roth) Schenk, were both immigrants. Her father, a native of Hungary, had been imprisoned in a Nazi labor camp before emigrating to America. Her mother was born and grew up in Czechoslovakia. The Schenks raised Lynn and her younger brother Frank in an East Bronx tenement where "Hungarian, Yiddish and eventually English" were spoken. Although Schenk has forgotten her Yiddish, she still speaks Hungarian. As a child, she spent countless hours "cleaning other people's clothes" in her father's tailor shop and "cleaning other people's nails" in her mother's manicure shop.

Elsa Schenk was active in the Ladies Garment Workers' Union, and talk around the family's dining table usually revolved around union politics. From an early age, Lynn evinced a drive and intensity that were to become her hallmarks. Her brother Frank, who, like Lynn, became a lawyer, remembered: "My sister was that way from the first day I can remember her. She was always the leader. She always set the values for her friends and was always the one everybody came to for help. She was the motivator."

The Schenks have belonged to Orthodox synagogues throughout their lives. Lynn received her early Jewish education at the Beth Jacob school in the Bronx. When she was eleven, her family moved to Pennsylvania, and then, three years later, to the West Pico area of Los Angeles. The moves were necessitated by her father's health. In Los Angeles, the Schenk family belonged to two Orthodox synagogues: Beth Jacob and Beth David.

Following graduation from Hamilton High School, Schenk worked her way through UCLA as a part-time telephone operator, graduating in 1967 with a B.A. in political science. Degree in hand, she entered the law school at the University of San Diego, where she received her J.D. in 1970. A long-time advocate of women's rights, Schenk helped force the law school's administration to build a women's restroom. Following a stint at the London School of Economics (where she studied international

law), she spent three years as a California deputy attorney general (1971–74) and another five as counsel for the San Diego Gas and Electric Company. During those years, she cofounded the San Diego Lawyer's Club, a means of helping women lawyers in the city, and the Women's Bank.

Having built up an admirable *curriculum vitae*, Lynn Schenk was awarded a prestigious White House Fellowship in 1976. There, she worked as a special assistant to Vice Presidents Nelson Rockefeller and Walter Mondale. Upon her return to San Diego in 1977, Schenk became allied with Governor Jerry Brown's director of finance, Richard Silberman. He brought her into the Brown administration as a deputy secretary in the department of Business, Transportation and Housing. In 1980, Governor Brown brought her into his cabinet as Departmental Secretary—the first woman ever to hold the portfolio. Schenk served in that capacity until the end of the Brown administration in late 1983. Returning from Sacramento to her home base in San Diego, she went into private practice, occupying an office in the firm of Lorenz, Alhadeff and Oggel.

In 1984, Lynn Schenk was narrowly defeated by Sue Golding in a race for San Diego's Third Supervisorial District seat. Schenk and Golding (the wife of Schenk's mentor Richard Silberman) waged a campaign battle referred to by the local press as both "raucous" and "one of the dirtiest in recent San Diego history." Following her defeat, Schenk brought a libel suit against Golding. Schenk won a $150,000 judgment; it brought about an understandable split with Silberman.

Lynn Schenk "languished in a sort of political limbo" for the next six years, practicing law, spending two months of 1989 in Japan, where she studied trade, investment, and finance under the auspices of the Mitsubishi Research Institute, and founding the San Diego Urban Corps. She finally emerged from the political wilderness in 1990, when she was named a commissioner of the San Diego Unified Port District.

Along with her intelligence, drive, and network of contacts, Schenk was also a first-class fundraiser. In 1992, she put all her skills to work in a race for Congress from California's newly created Forty-ninth District. Prior to its creation, the Forty-ninth District, comprising about half the population of San Diego plus Coronado and

Imperial Beach, had been known as the Forty-First. For twelve years, it had been represented by Republican Bill Lowery. In 1992, smarting from the revelation that he had more than 300 overdrafts on the House bank and "some campaign contributions from unsavory S&L figures," Lowery decided to call it quits. His seat, now in the Forty-ninth District, was up for grabs.

Amassing a campaign war chest in excess of $1.1 million, Schenk easily outspent and outdistanced her opponents in the Democrat primary. Running on the slogan "Schenk means business," she went on to handily defeat critical-care nurse Judy Jarvis by more than eight points. Jarvis, who had been a surprise winner in the Republican primary, was outspent by a nearly three-to-one margin. Schenk actually wound up raising more money than any House member who won an open seat that year.

As a member of the One Hundred and Third Congress, Lynn Schenk was one of but five Democrat freshmen seated on the prestigious Energy and Commerce Committee. More importantly, she was one of just two Democrat newcomers assigned to perhaps its most influential subcommittee, Telecommunications and Finance. As a former port commissioner, she was also assigned to the committee on Merchant Marine and Fisheries.

As a member of Energy and Commerce, Schenk began developing a specialty in bioscience, a subject of great import in San Diego. She also worked on the politically volatile base closings issue, helping to determine which military bases would be scrapped and which permitted to remain in business. Representing a city that derived much of its financial health from the United States Navy, Schenk obviously had definite ideas about which bases should remain in operation. She worked closely on this issue with the mayor of San Diego, none other than Sue Golding.

Schenk gave one of her earliest—and most passionate—speeches on the House floor in favor of a private bill granting reparations pay-

ments to a Holocaust survivor. Schenk's passion stemmed as much from her support of the bill as her pique at her Jewish colleagues who did not line up behind her. "One thing I never understood," Schenk commented in a private interview, "is why there isn't a Jewish Caucus in the House. I mean, there is a Black Caucus, a Hispanic Caucus, and so many others. So why not one for the Jewish members?"

Described as "telegenic, articulate and determined to wield power," Lynn Schenk received more publicity than perhaps any other member of her freshman class. As one writer noted: "Schenk has begun popping up on Washington news shows and her first six months in office are being filmed by ABC-TV." A vocal supporter of the Clinton administration's agenda, Schenk was prominently featured on-camera during the President's major economic address to Congress. "Cameras were drawn to her like a magnet . . . when her blond hair and brightly colored suit were an oasis in a desert of dark blues and receding hairlines."

Lynn Schenk's vote in favor of the 1993 Clinton budget and tax package proved to be her congressional Waterloo. In the 1994 general election, she was challenged by tax consultant and former Imperial Beach mayor Brian Bilbray. The Republican Bilbray contrasted his endorsement of Newt Gingrich's Contract With America with Schenk's "Clinton connection." Although she outspent Bilbray by nearly two-to-one, Schenk's loyalty to the administration in an anti-incumbent year proved too costly. She wound up losing her seat by a final margin of 49 percent to 46 percent.

Married to Hugh Friedman in 1972, Lynn Schenk currently practices law in San Diego with the firm of Baker and McKenzie.

References

Interview with Lynn Schenk, May 1996.
Almanac of American Politics (1994, 1996 editions).
Politics in America, 103rd Congress.
San Diego Business Journal, April 5, 1992, p. 10.
San Diego Magazine, January 1993.

SCHEUER, JAMES HAAS (1920–): *Democrat from New York; served thirteen terms in the House (Eighty-ninth through Ninety-second Congress; January 3, 1965–January 3, 1973; Ninety-fourth through One Hundred and Second Congress; January 3, 1975–January 3, 1993).*

Trying to keep track of James Scheuer's political peregrinations is somewhat akin to plotting the course the children of Israel took in the wilderness—full of twists and turns, fits and starts. For during his twenty-six years in Congress, Scheuer ran in no fewer than five different districts (and won in four), variously representing constituencies in the Bronx, Brooklyn, Queens, and a little bit of Nassau County to boot. He also suffered three defeats, including an ill-fated race for New York City mayor in 1969, in which he came in dead last, polling fewer votes than writer Norman Mailer. And had he not decided to retire at the end of the One Hundred and Second Congress, he would have had to introduce himself to the voters of yet another new congressional district. For all his travels, he was labeled "the flying Dutchman of New York congressmen."

The Scheuers belonged to that social class of New York Jews known as the "Other Crowd." Unlike the great German-Jewish banking families ("Our Crowd") who lived on Manhattan's Upper East Side, sent their children to New England prep schools, and worshiped at Temple Emanuel, the "Other Crowd" families lived on Central Park West and West End Avenue, sent their children to the Ethical Culture school, and generally belonged to Temple Rodeph Shalom, the West Side liberal congregation founded in 1842. Jonas Scheuer, the Congressman's grandfather, came to New York from Germany shortly after the Revolution of 1848. A "fancy feathers merchant," Jonas served several terms as president of Rodeph Sholom. By the turn of the century, the Scheuers had prospered mightily—from textiles, retailing, real estate, and the law. By the 1980s, the Scheuer family had a foundation with holdings in excess of $40 million.

James Haas Scheuer, one of Jonas's many grandchildren, was born in New York City on February 6, 1920, the second of Simon and Helen (Rose) Scheuer's four sons and one daughter. Simon H. Scheuer was a "strong-minded investor and philanthropist whose golden eggs were hatched in real estate." The Scheuers were an accomplished family; all four of Simon and Rose's sons went on to achieve prominence in their chosen fields. In addition to Jim, the Congressman, Richard became manager of the family holdings, including the four corner buildings of London Terrace; Walter became a Wall Street investor; and Steven became a television columnist, producer, and campaign advisor. Their daughter, Amy, married Saul Cohen, a highly successful labor lawyer who would become one of his brother-in-law Jim's political advisors.

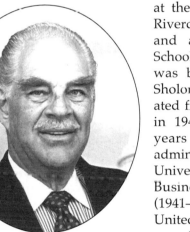

James Scheuer was educated at the Fieldston School in the Riverdale section of the Bronx and at the Ethical Culture School in New York City. He was bar mitzvah at Rodeph Sholom in 1933. Scheuer graduated from Swarthmore College in 1941 and then spent two years studying industrial administration at the Harvard University Graduate School of Business. While at Harvard (1941–43), Scheuer served in the United States Army Air Corps as a flight instructor. He was discharged in 1945 with the rank of sergeant. He then attended the Columbia University School of Law (from which he graduated in 1948) and worked as an economist for the Federal Foreign Economic Administration in Washington.

While James Scheuer was doing his graduate work at Harvard, he went to his brother Steve's high school graduation. There he met Emily Malino, one of his brother's classmates, and a cousin of Danbury rabbi Jerome Malino. After what the Congressman refers to as "a whirlwind courtship of six years," the couple was married on March 21, 1948, just a few months before he received his law degree from Columbia. While on their honeymoon, Jim Scheuer contracted polio; the couple spent the next year in Warm Springs, Georgia, while he recuperated.

As a result of that attack, Scheuer has used a cane ever since. Following his recuperation, the Scheuers went abroad, where Jim spent a year working as a political and economic correspondent for the Overseas News Agency in France, Italy, and South America. During their stay in South America, he learned to speak an "enthusiastic but inaccurate Spanish." Following their return to America in 1951, Scheuer spent a year working on the legal staff of the Office of Price Stabilization in Washington. His and Emily's first child, Laurie, was born in 1952, followed by Betsey (1955), James, Jr. (1958), and John (1960). Emily went on to become a successful interior decorator in New York and Washington under her maiden name.

In 1952, James Scheuer became president of the Renewal and Development Corporation, which had its headquarters in New York. During his years at RDC, Scheuer developed, in cooperation with federal renewal programs, residential community projects in eight cities, ranging from San Francisco to San Juan, Puerto Rico. The best-known of the RDC projects was Capital Park, a "fifty-acre, 1,739-unit middle-income apartment and townhouse complex built . . . on the site of a former slum in Southwest Washington, D.C." Capital Park was Washington's first urban renewal project, and the "first large-scale private housing development of any kind in the capital city to be racially non-discriminatory in its renting policy."

Scheuer's leadership in the urban renewal field came to the attention of New York Governor W. Averell Harriman, who named him chairman of the Housing Advisory Council of the New York State Commission Against Discrimination. When Nelson A. Rockefeller became governor, he appointed Scheuer to the State Special Task Force on Middle Income Housing, a group that sought ways to "increase the supply of middle income housing in the state." Scheuer's expertise was also noticed on the federal level; President Kennedy appointed him a White House consultant on housing and human rights problems and a delegate to United Nations conferences on housing, human rights, city planning, and urban renewal. As the old slogan goes: "The best way to do well is to do good." Not only did Scheuer's development

concerns provide countless thousands of housing units for the poor; he personally made a fortune in the process.

Scheuer's involvement in the politics of New York City led him to become a charter member and executive committeeman of the New York Committee for Democratic Voters, an insurgent group dedicated to "toppling Tammany Hall . . . and reforming the state Democratic party in New York." Known locally as the Reform Democrats, the group won the unqualified support of Eleanor Roosevelt, Senator *Herbert Lehman*, and New York Mayor Robert F. Wagner. The Reform Democrats began their successful assault on the "regular" Democrats in 1960, when Assistant District Attorney William Fitts Ryan (1922–72) defeated Tammany-backed Congressman *Ludwig Teller* in Manhattan's solidly Democratic Twentieth District. Scheuer was an also-ran in that Democratic primary.

Buoyed by Ryan's success, Scheuer challenged Twenty-first District (Bronx) Congressman James A. Healy in the 1962 Democratic primary. Healy's district, covering all of Bronx county, contained some of the worst slums in the United States, along with the then-middle-class Jewish enclave along the Grand Concourse. Scheuer campaigned against Healy's "bossism, payroll padding and absenteeism," telling audiences: "If the people of this city and state are not to live in bondage of perpetual shakedown, the Democratic party must summon up the strength and inspiration of fresh leadership from within its own ranks." Healy countered by charging Scheuer with "carpetbaggerism." There was indeed some truth in Healy's indictment: Scheuer lived in Manhattan, not the Bronx. On election day, Healy defeated Scheuer by 2,270 votes.

Realizing that his margin of loss was less than the amount of votes polled by the other anti-Tammany candidates, Scheuer immediately began preparations for the 1964 primary. Establishing a residence in the Bronx, Scheuer took to campaigning twelve to fifteen hours a day, seven days a week. After a full two years of nonstop campaigning, Scheuer defeated Healy, and then triumphed in the November general election.

Scheuer entered the Eighty-eighth Congress as a man with a mission. "I hope that ten or fifteen years hence," he told the *New York Times*, "I will be regarded as one of the serious people doing the work of Congress. I believe in hard work and imagination. I'm against killer phrases like 'Let's be practical.'"

As a freshman, Scheuer was an active legislator, enacting an amendment to the Economic Opportunity Act that provided work for the hardcore unemployed in public service jobs. He sponsored legislation to create a national institute of crime detection and prevention, to institute a national summer lunch program for children, and to create a national museum of black history and culture. For his efforts, Scheuer was given a perfect 100 rating by Americans for Democratic Action and was reelected with 84 percent of the vote.

An early opponent of the war in Vietnam, Scheuer was one of the few Congressmen to vote in favor of "forbidding the use of defense budget funds for military operations in or over North Vietnam." Scheuer was also one of a handful of Representatives to support Adam Clayton Powell when the House voted to deny the Harlem Congressman his seat.

In 1969, Scheuer declared his candidacy for mayor of New York. Running in a five-man field that included Robert F. Wagner, Herman Badillo, and writer Norman Mailer, Scheuer came in last, despite spending a reported $550,000—$14.25 for each vote he received. (By comparison, Mayor John Lindsay, who was reelected, spent a mere 38 cents per vote.)

In 1970, a new Hispanic district was created in the South Bronx—much of it Scheuer's old territory. Not wishing to challenge Bronx Borough President Herman Badillo for the seat, Scheuer moved into the neighboring Twenty-second Congressional District, where he defeated incumbent Democrat *Jacob H. Gilbert*. After the 1972 redistricting, the Bronx lost one of its two districts, thereby necessitating Scheuer to run against yet another incumbent in yet another district. This time he took on the aristocratic Jonathan Brewster Bingham in the newly drawn Twenty-second District and lost. (Although possessing the same number—22—this district was ostensibly new for Scheuer.)

Leaving Congress (though looking around for a new district from which to run), Scheuer spent two years (1972–74) as president of the New York Citizens Housing and Planning Council and the National Housing Conference.

In 1974, political developments in Brooklyn's Eleventh Congressional District presented him with the opportunity he was looking for. The Eleventh District, including the southeastern corner of Brooklyn, the extreme southern and southeastern edges of Queens, and the Rockaway Peninsula, had been represented for thirty years (1936–66) by Democrat Eugene Keogh, the father of the Keogh Plan. He was replaced in Congress by Frank Brasco, who had to resign his seat in 1974 after being convicted of taking bribes.

As soon as it appeared that Brasco would have to leave Congress, Scheuer acquired a residence (really no more than a mailing address) in the district, and announced his candidacy. Winning his primary over the candidate backed by the local Democratic organization, Scheuer easily bested his Republican opponent in the general election. After a two-year hiatus, James Scheuer was back in Congress.

From 1974 until his retirement in 1992, James Scheuer never had any difficulty being reelected by the people of the Eleventh District. In his last four elections, he won by margins of 63, 90, 100, and 73 percent. Assigned to the powerful Commerce Committee, Scheuer became chairman of the Subcommittee on Consumer Protection and Finance in 1979. Two years later, Commerce Committee chair John Dingell, a Michigan Democrat, and one of the House's most powerful and dictatorial members, infuriated Scheuer by strong-arming the Commerce Committee into abolishing Scheuer's subcommittee.

Dingell's public rationale was a claim that Scheuer's subcommittee had little to do, coupled with a desire to "equalize the work of the subcommittees." The personalities of the two principals may have had a lot to do with it. The "abrasive and abrupt" Scheuer was often in conflict with Dingell, "no sweeter . . . but possess[ing] considerably more skill at political infighting." More likely, however, Dingell was upset with Scheuer's ideas about consumer protection. Scheuer had long been a fervent crusader on behalf of requiring air bags in automobiles, a cause against which Dingell, whose district contained many of the nation's major automobile plants, had been equally militant.

Scheuer's righteous indignation earned him a kind of consolation prize: the chair of a Science and Technology Subcommittee, overseeing research and development at the Department of Energy, the Environmental Protection Agency, the Oceans Agency (NOAA), and the Department of Agriculture. From that supposedly minor chairmanship, Scheuer launched an investigation into misconduct at the EPA. During subcommittee hearings, Scheuer charged EPA official Rita Lavelle with perjuring herself in the matter of an EPA official who had been dismissed for criticizing the management of the hazardous waste programs. Lavelle was eventually dismissed from her post.

A dedicated environmentalist, Scheuer fought for increased funding for EPA research. He also put an amendment into the research funding bill that would require the EPA's Science Advisory Board to include "representatives from industry, consumers, academics institutions, the states and the general public." President Reagan, citing the amendment, vetoed the bill.

Deeply concerned about narcotics addiction, Scheuer traveled to France and Turkey, where he talked with dozens of experts in order to get a handle on the subject. Returning to Washington, he arranged dinners for specialists at his house in Georgetown, once the R Street home of General Ulysses S. Grant.

Scheuer is largely responsible for the smoking ban on American air carriers and in federal office buildings. As he said: "There is no silver lining to the dark cloud of tobacco smoke."

Not surprisingly, James Scheuer has been no stranger to controversy in his long career. During his 1964 race for Congress, he was arrested along with about a dozen officers of the American Jewish Committee (he was president of the New York chapter) for picketing the Jordanian Pavilion at the New York World's Fair. In 1970, while aboard an Eastern Airlines shuttle from Washington, a cabin attendant overheard him say: "Kill the co-pilot." Upon landing, Scheuer was immediately taken from the plane, searched, and detained. It turned out that what the flight attendant had heard was part of Scheuer's discourse to a friend about measures that could be taken to prevent hijackings.

Also in 1970, Scheuer became the first elected U.S. official ever expelled from the Soviet Union. Soviet officials charged him with "improper activities." The United States termed his expulsion "a grave step not helpful in relations." Shortly after his expulsion, Scheuer, in a telephone interview from Leningrad, told a *New York Times* reporter: "I understand I am being expelled for encouraging Soviet citizens to emigrate. I did have social contacts with some who want to leave, but they had made up their minds long before I arrived." According to the American embassy in Moscow, "Mr. Scheuer did nothing more than visit certain Jews here whose addresses had been given him in the United States. To the American Embassy's knowledge, there was no Soviet law prohibiting such visits." Local Soviet officials claimed to have in their possession "a sheaf of documents" that "represented material harmful to the Soviet Union," and accused Scheuer of distributing them to "enemies of the state."

Scheuer made his first trip to Israel in 1953. While there, he met with Prime Minister David Ben-Gurion, to whom he expressed his concern that the new Jewish state was run by a "bunch of old men." "Why do you have all these *alter kockers* [old geezers]? Why don't you get some young people to be the future leaders?" Scheuer asked the Israeli prime minister. "All right," Ben-Gurion responded, "you take care of it." As Scheuer recalls, "Ben-Gurion turned to Abba Eban and said: 'Get in touch with Scheuer when you get to New York, and he'll arrange to get us some young people.'" True to his word, Scheuer, along with his brothers and sister, arranged to send dozens of promising young American Jews to Israel to interest them in making *aliyah* (immigrating) and becoming future leaders of the Jewish state. The Scheuers have returned to Israel at least once each year ever since 1953.

After the 1980 census, Scheuer was once again a man without a district. Fortunately, through the intercession of Queen's Borough President Donald Manes, Scheuer secured the nomination in the incumbentless Eighth District, centered in Flushing, and including small parts of the Bronx and suburban Nassau County. While representing his newest (and last) district, Scheuer tried to keep the Concorde from landing at Kennedy Airport, arguing that its noise would disrupt the lives of his constituents.

In 1992, faced with 133 overdrafts on the House Bank, the prospect of having to move to yet another district, and advancing age, James Scheuer decided to retire. "The new district . . .

would have required spending every weekend for the next two years getting to know my 300,000 constituents and earning their confidence. . . . Emily and I then decided that the pace and pressures of congressional life were more than we were willing to accept—and that this would be a good time to regain control of our private lives."

Today, the Scheuers divide their time between their homes in Chelsea, New York (Duchess County) and Washington. A Reform Jew like his father and grandfather before him, Jim Scheuer still belongs to Rodeph Sholom, along with other members of the "Other Crowd."

References

Interview with James H. Scheuer, Washington, D.C., July 1992.

Almanac of American Politics (1974–94 editions).

Current Biography, 1968, pp. 343–345.

New York Times, January 24, 1969; January 15–16, 1972; February 15, 1972.

Politics in America.

SCHIFF, STEVEN H. (1947–1998): *Republican from New Mexico; served five terms in the House (One Hundredth through One Hundred and Fifth Congress, January 3, 1989–March 26, 1998).*

Few members of Congress would consider a seat on the Standards of Official Conduct Committee a plum assignment. Unlike most other committees of Congress, the House Ethics Committee, as it is more commonly known, neither passes laws nor dispenses pork for the people back home. Its specific mandate is to sit in judgment on the alleged ethical lapses and peccadilloes of the men and women of the House. Some members consider it a political lose-lose situation. And yet, to be appointed to this post says something quite positive about the individual member: that he or she is considered a straight arrow and, like Caesar's wife, "above suspicion."

Nonetheless, what Representative truly desires to sit in judgment over his or her colleagues? Quite often, it takes a fair amount of arm-twisting on the part of the Speaker and the Minority Leader to get members to agree to sit on the panel. In many cases, the potential ethicist demands a political *quid pro quo*: assignment to a major committee in exchange for consent. Consider the additional committee assignments for members of the Ethics Committee in the One Hundred and Fourth Congress:

Nancy Johnston (Republican from Connecticut)—Ways and Means

Jim Bunning (Republican from Kentucky)—Ways and Means, and Budget

Porter Goss (Republican from Florida)—Rules

David L. Hobson (Republican from Ohio)—Budget, and Appropriations

Jim McDermott (Democrat from Washington)—Ways and Means

Benjamin Cardin (Democrat from Maryland)—Ways and Means

Nancy Pelosi (Democrat from California)—Appropriations, and Intelligence

Then there was Representative Steve H. Schiff of New Mexico. Schiff's other committee posts were rather pedestrian by comparison: Government Reform and Oversight, and Judiciary. When asked why he too did not have a seat on one of the more prestigious committees like most of his Ethics colleagues, Schiff simply remarked: "I never asked for one. I consider it enough of an honor that both sides think I have the integrity to serve on that panel." Little did Schiff know when he agreed to the assignment that he would become embroiled in one of the most difficult issues to face Congress in the 1990s—the case against House Speaker Newt Gingrich.

Despite the Germanic sound of the name, the original Schiff clan came from Lodz, Poland. The Congressman believes that his forebears moved from Germany to Poland in the eighteenth century. Great-grandfather Schiff came to America sometime after the Civil War and settled in New York. There, in 1889, the Congressman's grandfather, Herman Schiff, was born. Herman was one of nine Schiff children. Eventually, Herman's father moved the family to the decidedly non-Jewish city of Sault Ste. Marie, Michigan.

Young Herman made his way to Chicago's North Side, where he became a wholesale food representative. It was in Chicago that Herman Schiff met and married a young Milwaukee native, Goldie Pompian. The Pompians were originally from the Baltic area, "probably near St. Petersburg." (Interestingly, one of Goldie's younger brothers went to elementary school with another Goldie—Goldie Meyerson, who one day would become known as Golda Meir.) Herman and Goldie Schiff had three sons. Son Alan would eventually marry Helen Marcus Ripper.

Helen's progenitors were members of the great wave of middle-class, urbanized German Jews who came to America in the 1840s. The most noted member of the clan was a man named Wurzel, who appears to have been the first rabbi ordained in America. He served many years as the rabbi of a congregation in Erie, Pennsylvania. One of his daughters, Bertha, married an entrepreneur named Victor Ripper. According to family legend, Ripper was a Viennese Jew who had deserted from the Austrian Navy. Victor and Bertha moved up to Buffalo, New York, where, in 1903, he designed an automobile he named the Rippermobile. Eventually his business went bust. Ripper "disappeared" from Buffalo, resurfacing in St. Louis around the year 1910. Their son Richard, moved from St. Louis to Chicago, where he married a girl named Marcus. Richard's daughter, Helen Ripper, was born on that city's North Side.

Alan Schiff worked as a shoe salesman in Chicago. The Schiffs' first child, Maury, was born in 1942. (Maury Schiff currently lives in the Los Angeles area, where he is a physicist.) Their second child, Steven H. was born on March 18, 1947. From the time of his birth until age eleven, Steve Schiff and his family lived in a part of Chicago where they were "the only Jews in the neighborhood." In 1958, the Schiffs moved to the more heavily Jewish East Rogers Park on Chicago's North Side. Although the Schiff family "identified as Jews," neither boy received any formal religious education, and neither became bar mitzvah. As an adult, Steve Schiff made sure that his children—daughter Jaimi and son Daniel—did receive a good Jewish education. Both became bar/bat mitzvah at Albuquerque's Reform Temple Albert.

While growing up in Chicago, Steve Schiff was a liberal Democrat, serving a term as president of the Young Democrats of the Forty-ninth Ward. Following his high school graduation in 1964, Schiff entered the University of Illinois. Four years later, he received a B.A. in political science. His graduation came at the height of the Vietnam War. As Schiff recalled in a 1997 interview: "At my graduation, there in the front row were my parents and my draft board." Rather than take a chance on being drafted (this was before the Selective Service lottery), Schiff decided to join the Air National Guard out in New Mexico, where he had been accepted to law school. (After Schiff joined the National Guard, the first draft lottery was held. Schiff received a high number, meaning that he never would have been drafted.)

Moving out west, Schiff put in four months of active duty in an outfit that had only two Jews—himself and the unit's commander, Fred Fink. While training with the Air National Guard, Schiff assumed that he would go to Vietnam along with the other New Mexico units already there. As luck would have it, within that four-month period, the Air National Guard completed its tour in Southeast Asia and returned home. As a result, his entire hitch in the service was spent on American soil. Schiff continued on in the Air Force Reserve for nearly thirty years. At the time of his death in March 1998, he was a lieutenant colonel.

Steve Schiff married Marcia Lewis in November 1968. A second-generation American (her grandparents were from Pinsk), Marcia majored in mathematics at the University of Chicago. Their daughter Jaimi was born in 1977; son Daniel four years later. Following his graduation from the University of New Mexico Law School, Steve Schiff served five years (1972–77) as an assistant district attorney for Bernalillo County. While he was working as an assistant D.A., Marcia Schiff decided to join the United States Army. Twenty-three years later, she is still a member of the Army Reserve. From 1977 to 1979, Steve Schiff set up a private legal practice. During that time, he waged an unsuccessful race for judge. Following his loss, he spent two years as assistant city attorney for Albuquerque and then entered the race for district attorney of Bernalillo County. By that point, Schiff had become a moderate-to-conservative Republican. He owes his political about-face to "a growing realization that the Democrats were both fiscally irresponsible and becoming isolationists." Facing stiff competition in the race for district attorney, Schiff "invested his $20,000 life savings in a last minute television ad blitz." He won, and went on to serve two four-year terms in the post, becoming "a familiar face in the media."

Albuquerque is the place writer Tom Wolfe called "a dirty, red, sod-hut, tortilla, desert highway city." More than one-third of its approximately 500,000 residents are of Mexican origin. For many years, its politics were Republican, but Democrats began making some local inroads in the late 1960s. By the 1988 election, it was one of the least Republican cities in the Sun Belt. That year, ten-term Republican Representative Manuel Lujan, Jr., a member of a politically prominent family, retired his First District seat, having suffered a heart attack two years earlier. (Lujan was eventually named Secretary of the Interior in the Bush Administration.) Schiff, who had originally been contemplating a race against Democratic Senator Jeff Bingaman, "quickly shifted his sights to the open House seat." It became one of 1988's hottest and most closely watched House races.

The Democratic primary featured no fewer than ten candidates. Included in the cast were Tom Udall, son of Kennedy-era Interior Secretary Stewart Udall (and nephew of long-time House Interior Committee chair Morris Udall), Judge Patricia Madrid, and former state Land Commissioner Jim Baca. Udall wound up taking the Democratic primary with a mere 25 percent of the vote. On the Republican side, Schiff faced off against Manuel Lujan's brother Edward, who ran the family insurance business. Running hard on his record as district attorney, Schiff overcame the formidable Lujan 41 percent to 37 percent.

During the general election, Udall "campaigned against transporting nuclear waste through Albuquerque and stressed his own experience as a federal prosecutor in drug cases and his pro-environment stance." Schiff, coming off eight years as D.A., proudly trumpeted "the death penalty convictions he [had] obtained, and his service as a lieutenant colonel in the New Mexico Air National Guard." Though he had always considered himself a "lousy politician," Schiff nonetheless bragged that he had "made the news 2,000 times during his tenure as D.A."

Schiff came under attack from Udall "for his willingness to plea-bargain." The charge did not stick because his "image as a law-and-order figure was well known to voters." Schiff countered by accusing Udall of failing to repay a student loan until he became a House candidate. (In fact, Udall had repaid the loan six years earlier, well ahead of schedule, but he was a candidate at the time—in New Mexico's Third District.) Managing to raise nearly $560,000 to Udall's $576,000, Schiff emerged victorious by a margin of 51 percent to 47 percent. With his victory, Steve Schiff became the first—and so far only—Jew sent to Washington by the voters of New Mexico.

"Being Jewish has rarely ever been an issue," Schiff said in speaking about New Mexico politics. "New Mexico is the most tolerant state that I can think of in terms of the electorate accepting a candidate. I'm living proof of that. Being Jewish and from Chicago is a bit different from many other New Mexicans, but nobody has ever raised it as a problem." While Schiff's being Jewish rarely was a political liability among the non-Jewish voters in his district, his conservatism oftentimes put him at odds with his coreligionists. "Many Jews believe that we're all liberal Democrats; that's obviously not always the case," Schiff commented in his 1997 interview. Moreover, non-Jews tend to believe that Jews will always vote for a Jewish candidate regardless of his or her politics. Sometimes this mistaken notion can backfire: In 1992, the Democrat-controlled New Mexico legislature set about the task of reapportioning the state's congressional districts. The legislators were loath to add the bedroom community of Rio Rancho ("the nearest thing to a Jewish enclave in Albuquerque") to Schiff's district, fearing that it would make him all but unbeatable. Ironically, had they added Rio Rancho, it might well have made him more vulnerable—due precisely to his problem with the largely liberal Jewish voters of Albuquerque.

During his nearly ten years in the House, Schiff was generally the most conservative member of the Capitol Hill Minyanaires. His Americans for Democratic Action ratings averaged between 15 and 20, while the American Conservative Union gave him a constant 75 to 80. Among all Minyanaires, he scored highest with the Christian Coalition, receiving 77 out of a possible 100 in its "Congressional Scorecard." According to the *Almanac of American Politics*, "Schiff is the sort of man who goes where his sense of right and wrong take him, regardless of politics." A stickler for ethics, he accepted no honoraria, and often quibbled over legislative language.

When the House considered a constitutional amendment to make flag desecration a federal offense, Schiff opposed it—not on principle, but rather because of "technicalities in drafting it." Although he was pro-choice on abortion, Schiff believed that the Freedom of Choice Act went too far. Then again, in 1994, he was one of only three Republicans on the House Judiciary Committee to vote for the law establishing "federal criminal and civil penalties for those who attempt to block access to clinics where abortions are performed." He also opposed a bill "allowing military personnel to sue military physicians for malpractice, because they may already qualify for disability."

As a former prosecutor, Schiff was, not surprisingly, extremely tough on crime. He opposed the Brady Bill, which mandated a five-day waiting period before the purchase of a handgun, and supported the three-strikes proposal—mandatory life imprisonment for those convicted of a third violent felony. Actually, Schiff sought to amend the proposal to impose the mandatory life term for a second violent felony, but his amendment failed.

During the One Hundred and Fourth Congress, Schiff sponsored the Sexual Crimes Against Children Prevention Act, which "increased sentences for child pornography and prostitution." It passed 417-0. He also called for the regulation of private jails housing federal prisoners and "encouraged state legislatures to adopt uniform treatment of juveniles, including the right to prosecute as adults, individuals 15 years or older who commit certain violent crimes." Never totally predictable, Schiff came out strongly against a proposal that members of Congress and their staffs be subjected to random drug tests. Said Schiff: "We are of course desirous of eliminating drugs in the workplace. Trampling on civil liberties is just not the correct place to start."

In the One Hundred and Third Congress, Schiff's career "took one turn for the weird . . . when he found himself battling the Pentagon for information about the so-called Roswell Incident." The Incident involved the 1947 crash of a "mysterious object" on a remote ranch in what became Schiff's First Congressional District. At the time, the crash made headlines; the public information officer for the Roswell Army Base issued a press release saying, "The wreckage of a flying saucer had been discovered." Schiff began pressuring the Pentagon to declassify documents relating to the incident in 1993. For his efforts, he got the run-around: the Pentagon sent him to the National Archives; the National Archives sent him back to the Pentagon. Schiff never got the documents declassified.

Schiff voted consistently in favor of NASA funding for the space station and for the now-defunct Superconducting Super Collider project—not surprising, considering that his district was home to Sandia National Laboratories, "a nuclear and solar research and testing center."

Schiff voted in favor of the Persian Gulf resolution (passed 240-183 on January 12, 1991), and then headed off to the Middle East as a member of the Air Force Reserve. (The only other member of Congress to serve in the Gulf War was former Oklahoma Representative David McCurdy.) As a member of the Judge Advocate General's Office, Colonel Schiff was not involved in the fighting. At the conclusion of the war, he managed to fly over the truce lines. Before he boarded his helicopter, his commanding officer reminded him that he should carry nothing on his person that might identify him as a member of Congress—just in case the plane went down. "I assure you that Iraqis will never know I'm a Congressman," Schiff told his superior officer. "However, my dog tags do show that I am Jewish!"

In early 1996, Representative Schiff was one of 141 House members who voted against sending U.S. troops to the Balkans. In February of that year, Lieutenant Colonel Schiff volunteered to go to Aviano Air Force Base in northern Italy, where he spent ten days working in the Judge Advocate General's Office. *Roll Call* quoted him as saying: "I have two separate responsibilities. My responsibility as a Member is to exercise my judgment on policy, which I opposed. . . . But as an Air Force officer, once a commitment is made, I have a separate obligation to make sure it's a success."

Steve Schiff was regularly reelected by margins of between 63 percent and 74 percent. This was due mostly to his growing popularity with the voters of the First District, and partly to his having faced weak or flawed opponents. In his first campaign for reelection in 1990, Schiff faced New Mexico Secretary of State Rebecca Vigil-Giron, "one of the weakest candidates anywhere." Vigil-Giron suffered from having "lied about having a 4-year college degree, bill[ing] the state for private trips when in office, and default[ing] on a student loan." She raised little money and ran no television ads. Schiff defeated her 70 percent to 30 percent. In his 1994 race for reelection, Schiff's opponent, Peter Zollinger, told the press: "I'm a long enough shot that instead of conducting a campaign I can go out on a lecture tour." Schiff overwhelmed Zollinger 74 percent to 26 percent.

When the Republicans gained control of the House at the beginning of the One Hundred and Fourth Congress, Steve Schiff became chair of the Science Committee's Subcommittee on Basic Research, an important post for one coming from a district in which Sandia Labs and Kirkland Air Force Base were the two largest employers. Schiff's most prominent assignment, however, as noted above, was as a member of the Committee on Standards of Official Conduct.

Schiff's appointment was in recognition of "his prosecutorial background and low-key personality," which are valuable attributes for a committee whose members are expected to draw minimum attention to themselves. According to *Roll Call*,

> The members of the ethics panel have . . . special obligations. It should go without saying that they have to put aside as much as they can of their partisan instincts. But it is more than that. Ethics panel members have to stiffen their backbones to resist direct and subtle pressures from their own party leaders. . . . They have to suffer indignities from grenade throwers on the other side, avoiding the temptation to respond in kind. They must bend over backwards to achieve unanimity or near-unanimity among themselves.

By *Roll Call*'s estimate, Schiff passed this test in the case of Speaker Newt Gingrich. Throughout the One Hundred and Fourth Congress and the early days of the One Hundred and Fifth, the ethics panel conducted hearings on the fate of Speaker Gingrich. At issue was whether the Georgia Republican had committed ethical lapses by using PAC money for partisan political purposes. Through endless months of testimony, gathering of evidence, and the writing of a voluminous final report, the members of the committee attempted to steer a course between the Scylla of statutory mandates and the Charybdis of partisan politics.

In the end, the committee determined that Gingrich had misled Congress and misused political money. They issued a reprimand and ordered him to repay the more than $300,000 that he had used for a cable-generated college course. Responding to the panel's findings, Gingrich said: "With great sadness, I have filed an answer which admits to that violation. . . . In my name and over my signature, inaccurate, incomplete and unreliable statements were given to the committee, but I did not intend to mislead the committee. . . . I was . . . in some ways naive. . . . I was dedicated to big ideas."

In late 1996, Steve Schiff was diagnosed with aggressive squamous-cell cancer. Returning to Albuquerque, Schiff began undergoing chemotherapy. On March 23, 1997, Schiff left Washington for Albuquerque; he would never return to Capitol Hill. In late January 1998, Schiff announced that due to his weakened condition, he would not seek reelection in November. Steve Schiff died on March 24, 1998. He was just fifty-one years old. His seat remained vacant until the November election, when Republican Heather Wilson defeated wealthy Democrat Phillip Maloof.

Steve and Marcia Schiff were members of Albuquerque's Temple Albert. While Schiff admitted to "not being the most devout practitioner of Jewish rituals," he nonetheless concluded that "public service gives one the opportunity to perform *mitzvot*."

References

Interview with Steven Schiff, January 1997.
Almanac of American Politics (1990–98 editions).
New York Times, March 25, 1998, C:19.
Roll Call, February 1, 1996.

SCHUMER, CHARLES ELLIS (1950–):
Democrat from New York: served nine terms in the House (Ninety-seventh through One Hundred and Fifth Congress; January 3, 1981–January 4, 1999). Elected to the United States Senate for a six-year term commencing January 4, 1999.

On the first day of Chuck Schumer's initial campaign for Congress in 1980, he made a visit to his barber, intent upon placing a poster in the man's window. The haircutter reportedly told the young state legislator: "Kid, I've never told you this, but I'm the local bookie. You're a fifty-to-one underdog. Don't bet on yourself!" In retrospect, one wonders how long that bookie remained in business. For not only did Schumer win his race for Congress in 1980; he won his next eight campaigns with little, if any, significant opposition. By the spring of 1997, when Schumer announced his intention to seek the Democratic nomination for the Senate seat held by Republican Alfonse D'Amato, he had become a New York City institution—one of its most ambitious, successful, and visible politicians. In the House, Schumer was viewed as a political anomaly: a legislative firebrand who combined flash and substance. Despite never having held a committee chairmanship, Schumer was considered one of the most significant and effective legislators of his generation.

When Schumer was first elected to the New York State Assembly (one short year after graduating from law school), he was told that "the Legislature is like a box full of crabs . . . if one should get a claw over the wall, the others will try and pull him back down." That which has kept him from being "pulled back into the box," he says, is substance. During his nearly twenty years in the House of Representatives, Schumer crafted legislation in areas ranging from credit-card reform and immigration to farm law and gun control. In the opinion of the editors of *Politics in America*, "if any member of the House—an immense and impossibly broad institution—can be called ubiquitous, it is Schumer." Former Wyoming Senator Alan Simpson, a conservative Republican, said of

Schumer: "I have never seen anyone like that guy. I don't know whether he ever slows down; there is an audible hum about him."

Charles Ellis Schumer, the son of Abraham and Selma (Rosen) Schumer, was born in Brooklyn on November 23, 1950. Chuck's grandparents came from Austria-Hungary around the turn of the century. Grandpa Schumer had a small exterminating business. "He was a scholarly man, not much of a business-type," his daughter-in-law Selma recalls. After Abe Schumer came back from service in World War II, he decided to help his father out "for a few months." Those few months led to more than thirty years as an exterminator. At age fifty-five, Abe Schumer sold his business to Orkin. Selma Rosen's parents were both born in New York.

Chuck, the eldest of Abe and Selma's three children, grew up in Flatbush. As a child, he was an inveterate reader. He was educated in the Brooklyn public schools and graduated from Madison High School, where he excelled at chemistry. The Schumers belonged to the Reform Ahavas Shalom synagogue on Avenue R in Flatbush, and it was there that Chuck was bar mitzvah in 1963.

In 1967, Schumer went off to Harvard. Originally intending to study chemistry, he wound up receiving a B.A. *magna cum laude* in political science in 1971 and an LL.B. with honors three years later. While still a student at Harvard Law School, he served on the staff of Rhode Island Senator Claiborne Pell and worked as a volunteer on Assemblyman *Stephen Solarz*'s unsuccessful bid for the Brooklyn borough presidency.

Following his graduation from Harvard Law, Schumer returned to Brooklyn. Within weeks of his arrival back home, Stephen Solarz announced that he would leave the State Assembly in order to run for the United States Congress. Hearing this, Chuck Schumer told his parents: "I hope you won't get angry, but I'm going to run for the state Legislature." His parents' response was: "Let him run and get it out of his system before he becomes a lawyer." Abe and Selma Schumer weren't able to help their son's campaign financially, because "we were still paying off his college education." A compulsive saver, Chuck Schumer had somewhere between $8,000 and $9,000 in the bank—savings from his bar mitzvah and various summer jobs. As Selma Schumer recalls: "He took the money and opened up a small campaign office. Before you knew it, a whole batch of these nice blond kids from Harvard came down to Brooklyn to campaign for Chuck. They were sleeping on our living room floor and going around the neighborhoods saying '*A gut shabbos*, vote for Chuck Schumer for Assembly.'"

Schumer won the seat vacated by Solarz and arrived in Albany at the tender age of twenty-three, the youngest man elected to the State Assembly since Theodore Roosevelt. Schumer went on to serve six years in the Assembly (1975–81), rising to the chairmanship of both the Committee on Oversight and Investigation and the Subcommittee on City Management and Governance.

Upon his arrival in Albany, Schumer sought out Assembly Speaker Stanley Fink, one of that body's most imposing members. The freshman Schumer, understanding that his future success would rely upon a solid relationship with Fink, made the elder legislator his mentor. According to a 1987 *National Journal* article, Schumer "broke the ice" with Fink by returning his imposing stare and suggesting that the speaker was undoubtedly "a marshmallow underneath."

Years later, Schumer would use the same technique to break the ice with an even crustier politician, Illinois Representative Dan Rostenkowski. During his six years in Albany, Schumer developed a formidable organization, and won a reputation for "keeping in close touch with the needs of his constituents."

In 1976, during his first term in the state legislature, Schumer met Iris Weinshall, a twenty-seven-year-old graduate of Brooklyn College who was working as a lobbyist for the Citizen's Union. Iris's great-great-grandfather, who had come to New York in the first decade of the twentieth century, divorced his wife and moved on to Chicago. There, many years later, one of his descendants married a young attorney named *Abner Mikva*, who would go on to Congress, the federal judiciary, and the White House as chief counsel to President Bill Clinton.

Chuck Schumer and Iris Weinshall were married in the fall of 1980, just days after he had won the Democratic nomination for Congress. The Schumers have two daughters, Allison and Jennifer. In 1998, Iris Weinshall was working for New York Mayor Rudolph Giuliani as First Deputy Commissioner in the Department of General Services. The Schumers belong to the Reform Beth Elohim in Brooklyn, where their daughter Jennifer became bat mitzvah in September 1997.

By the time of their wedding, Chuck Schumer was about to embark upon the next phase of his political career. In 1980, Representative *Elizabeth Holtzman* resigned her Sixteenth District seat in order to run for the United States Senate. Schumer quickly jumped into the four-way Democratic primary to replace Holtzman. In the Sixteenth District, one of only two Jewish-majority districts in America, winning the Democratic primary was the only challenge; Democrats had represented the Sixteenth (and its numeric antecedents) for more than fifty years. Its Jewish bloc was "not tremendously affluent" and "seemed more interested in celebrating their traditions than in trying to emulate the dazzling success of Jews who have long since moved on to Great Neck or Beverly Hills."

Schumer's main primary opponent was Theodore Silverman, whose support of the death penalty found favor with many of the district's Orthodox Jews. But Schumer, with "the best political organization of the pack" and a crucial endorsement from New York City Mayor *Edward Koch*, won the primary with nearly 60 percent of the vote. He easily won the general election, and Charles Schumer, not yet thirty, was headed for Capitol Hill.

Chuck Schumer's arrival in Washington coincided with the beginning of Ronald Reagan's first term. He was assigned to the Post Office, Judiciary, and Banking Committees. Shortly after he was sworn in as a member of the Ninety-seventh Congress, the *New York Times* interviewed Chuck Schumer. Asked how he felt about serving in a divided Congress (the Senate had been taken over by the Republicans), Schumer responded: "If I was a freshman Democrat during the [Democratic President Lyndon Johnson's] Great Society, there would have been very little need for Chuck Schumer. But with a Republican president and a

Republican Senate, there's a real need for my contribution."

Schumer saw his contribution as being a steady vote against a clear majority of administration-backed measures. Indeed, in his first term in the House, Schumer voted against the Reagan administration more than 60 percent of the time. In that first term, he opposed the President's budget proposal, the balanced-budget amendment, and funding for the MX missile.

Leaving his bride back in Brooklyn, Schumer moved into a Capitol Hill apartment with three other representatives: Marty Russo of Illinois and Californians George Miller and Leon Panetta, a future House Budget Committee chair and White House chief of staff. Through his friendship with these three senior, more experienced, House members, Schumer was able to "gain the ear" of the Democratic Party's leadership.

Russo, a member of the so-called College of Cardinals (made up of Ways and Means subcommittee chairs), provided Schumer with entree to, arguably, the most powerful member of the House: Ways and Means chair Dan Rostenkowski. Miller, an up-and-coming power on House Agriculture, provided Schumer with entree to committee chair "Kika" de la Garza. Schumer was appointed to the House Banking Committee, a prestigious spot for a freshman. From his post on the Housing Subcommittee, he quickly established himself as a leading spokesman for rent control—a vital issue in his Brooklyn district.

During the Reagan years (1980–88), Chuck Schumer was literally all over the legislative map. He fought for—and won—passage of an amendment to an International Monetary Fund appropriation that "relieved developing nations of some of their debt by forcing banks to accept lower interest rates and longer payment schedules." His measure also prevented the IMF from "forcing countries, in return for funds, to adopt such potentially harmful and unpopular measures as cutting social services." Schumer's logic was impeccable: "Unemployment in Pittsburgh and Detroit is related to debt in Nigeria and Brazil."

Concerned with skyrocketing credit-card interest rates, Schumer advanced legislation that would place a cap on these charges. Although the measure initially failed in committee, Schumer became so publicly identified with the issue that he began receiving mail addressed simply to "Credit Cards, Washington, D.C." A master of compromise ("I've always had the feeling that if you want to stand on your high horse and just make speeches and not compromise, then don't be in Congress"), Schumer was eventually able to get a credit-card bill passed in the One Hundredth Congress that "forced banks to disclose more fully the terms and provisions of credit-card networks."

As early as 1985, Chuck Schumer was predicting big troubles ahead for the savings and loan industry. In that year, he argued on the House floor that a future crisis could be averted "only by forcing thrifts to raise a substantial amount of new funds." Like a biblical prophet of old, his words went unheeded. Years later, after Schumer's prognostication had come hauntingly true, he spearheaded passage of a House thrift bill. According to the *Almanac of American Politics*, Schumer's fingerprints were on "virtually every one of the 732 pages of the . . . bill."

Working tirelessly both in committee and on the House floor, Schumer "championed the tough capital standards sought by the administration and ultimately adopted by Congress. He succeeded in his own efforts to increase civil and criminal penalties for banking law violations." Most importantly, he made the rhetorical case for "adding the cost of the bailout directly to the budget," in direct opposition to the wishes of 1600 Pennsylvania Avenue.

Despite his credentials as a "city slicker," Schumer earned a reputation as an expert and knowledgeable critic of American farm policy. During consideration of the 1990 farm bill, Schumer and Texas Republican (and future House Majority Leader) Dick Armey put together a unique coalition of "urban liberals and free-market conservatives" who "waged war on waste and inequity" in federal farm programs. Nonetheless, he was frustrated in his attempts to "reduce the cost of farm programs and their benefits for the rich." One of the issues that over the years has brought Chuck Schumer the most national press (both positive and negative) is gun control. Almost from the moment in 1991 when he became head of the Crime and Criminal Justice Subcommittee, Schumer was attempting to change the public's perception of the Democrats as soft on crime. From his Judiciary Committee post, he "spearheaded efforts to pass the Brady Bill." (The bill was named for former White House press secretary James Brady, who had been severely wounded in the 1981 assassination attempt on President Ronald Reagan.) Schumer's bill, which provided for a waiting period before a handgun could be purchased, so that authorities could check the purchaser's background, was finally enacted in 1994.

In the heady days immediately prior to the bill's passage, the National Rifle Association took out a full-page ad in *USA Today* that featured a picture of Schumer and the headline "The Criminal's Best Friend in Congress." The ad accused Schumer of trying to "rob" the crime bill of $8 billion earmarked for prison construction and putting it toward "treatment and recreation programs that would coddle criminals." In addition to the print ad, the NRA also purchased airtime on CNN for a commercial with a similar message.

When asked how he felt about being called "the criminal's best friend," Schumer responded "I wear this like a badge of honor." Attorney General Janet Reno eventually came to Schumer's defense, stating: "I have never met a public official more dedicated to fighting crime than Mr. Schumer."

When the Republicans announced their "Contract With America," Schumer went on the warpath, becoming a self-described Paul Revere on the subject. Indeed, he took the floor on twenty-two of the first fifty-nine days of the One Hundred and Fourth Congress to criticize it, and began issuing almost daily news releases and reports. Schumer was one of the first Democrats to put a chink in Speaker Newt Gingrich's armor when he criticized the woman Gingrich had designated to serve as House historian. The Brooklyn Democrat "felt outraged" when it was disclosed that the professor had "expressed controversial views about teaching the Nazi point of view as part of a junior high school curriculum." Schumer labeled her appointment "an affront to my constituents who survived the Holocaust."

Chuck Schumer is one of the best-known and most frequently interviewed politicians in New York City. Over the years he has appeared on so many television talk shows that, as one writer noted, "it is sometimes hard to tell whether he is a guest or a host." In the mid-1990s, Schumer teamed up with Staten Island Republican Congresswoman Susan Molinari on local Channel 2's *Chuck and Sue* show. Called "the Regis and Kathie Lee of Capitol Hill," the two young, articulate, and charismatic politicos would spar on a wide array of political issues.

Over the many years he has been in the public eye, Schumer has gained a reputation for being "a purebred press hound." Schumer responds to the charge by saying: "One of the best arrows in my quiver is the ability to communicate. Some people have great ideas but they don't get them out. I am not the most glamorous person in the world, but I know how to legislate. I work hard and I have a record of getting things passed that have an effect. My challenge is to get that record out."

Chuck Schumer learned early on that the best way to keep a firm grip on his congressional seat was to maintain an overpowering cash balance in his campaign account. A tireless and formidable fundraiser, Schumer has, over the past fifteen years, always ranked in the top five or six "cash-on-hand" members of Congress. As a result of keeping well in excess of $1 million in his campaign coffers at any given time, Charles Schumer never faced serious opposition. He regularly won reelection by margins of 70 percent and better, and had no primary opposition.

As early as 1988, the editors of *Manhattan, Inc.* were urging Schumer to consider running for mayor of New York. Predictions about his political future abounded. In the early 1990s, political writers speculated that he would probably run for New York Governor. Schumer firmly squelched these rumors. On April 17, 1997, he ended speculation over precisely what office he would seek by announcing his candidacy for the U.S. Senate seat held by Alfonse D'Amato. When asked to respond to Schumer's declaration, D'Amato fired his first campaign volley: "Everyone has a right to run, even Chuck Schumer."

At the beginning of 1998, Democrats Mark Green and Geraldine Ferraro were also in the race for D'Amato's Senate seat. By November 1997, Schumer had raised approximately $8 million of the $15 million he predicted would be needed in order to be "competitive in the race." As part of his fundraising effort, Schumer made a concentrated pitch for Jewish dollars.

In a four-page appeal that he started mailing to potential Jewish donors a mere two weeks after he announced for the seat, Schumer was described as "the target of anti-Semitic forces engulfing the country." The appeal opened with a vile letter from an unidentified Schumer-hater in Biloxi, Mississippi, who said he was beginning to believe that "Adolph [sic] Hitler was right. Just think of all the problems his solution would have solved."

Asked what anti-Semitism had to do with a race for the United States Senate, Schumer replied somewhat vaguely: "I think one of the issues is [whether you are] willing to stand up when there's bigotry and hatred around. I think that's very much part of my record. Fortunately the U.S. is not Weimar Germany. But the lesson is: when bigotry raises its head, it must be stamped out."

Another fundraising letter, designed by direct-mail consultant Hank Morris (whose mother Rita had run against *Gary Ackerman* in 1992) described Schumer as the National Rifle Association's "number one target" in the country.

Schumer started running television commercials as early as June 1997, in an attempt to become as well known in Buffalo, Syracuse, and Plattsburgh as he was in Flatbush, Coney Island, and Sheepshead Bay.

As expected, Schumer did not have a free ride in the Democrat primary. New York City Pubic Advocate Mark Green (who lost to D'Amato in 1986) was first to enter the race. Then, when former Representative (and failed 1984 Vice Presidential candidate) Geraldine Ferraro, who lost the Democratic primary for U.S. Senate in 1992, entered the race, political insiders declared her the "candidate to beat." Somewhat surprisingly, Mrs. Ferraro ran a rather lackluster campaign that never developed a cogent message or set of compelling issues. Voters saw her running more on the basis of past glories than any commitment to future actions. Proving his critics wrong once again, Chuck Schumer won the June primary in convincing style, capturing a majority in the three-candidate race.

The campaign between Schumer and D'Amato was not only the most expensive in American history—it was also among the nastiest and most vituperative. Both candidates looked to cash in their respective political chits with the Jewish community. D'Amato, long looked upon as being one Republican who was both responsive and simpatico to the community, campaigned on his defense of Jewish settlements in the administered territories, his sponsoring of the 1996 Iran-Libya Sanctions Act and his dramatic banking committee hearings on Holocaust restitution. Moving from event to event, accompanied by a bevy of notable Jewish supporters, D'Amato derided Schumer for being absent when the House voted on a resolution concerning a Holocaust memorial service, brought up an almost twenty-year-old charge that Schumer had illegally used paid government employees on his first Congressional campaign—a charge that was dropped for lack of evidence, inexplicably referred to Schumer as a "putzhead" and Representative *Jerrold Nadler* as "Congressman Waddler," and even imitated the corpulent Nadler's walk in front of a Jewish audience.

Fighting back, Schumer attacked D'Amato for ethnic insensitivity and mendacity; despite being captured on video, D'Amato denied ever having used the Yiddish vulgarism. Schumer hammered hard at his positions on a host of domestic issues, seeking to delineate where he and D'Amato differed. Schumer worked hard to paint D'Amato as an extremist conservative. When D'Amato implied that Schumer's missing the House vote on a Holocaust memorial service was tantamount to insensitivity to the memory of the six million, Schumer emotionally and angrily responded that he was the one who had lost family during the war, not D'Amato. Going into the campaign's final days, public opinion polls were inconclusive; most journalists rated the race a toss-up.

Chuck Schumer won election to the United States Senate by nearly 450,000 votes—54 to 45 percent. Exit polls showed that Jewish voters, who had given D'Amato nearly 40 percent of the vote in 1992 (when he also drew a Jewish opponent) abandoned him in droves, voting for Schumer by a better than three-to-one margin. Polls also showed that in the end, what mattered most to Jewish voters was not the religious affiliation of the two candidates, but their positions on domestic issues. Schumer, with his support for expanded healthcare, abortion rights, and gun control had struck the more resonant chord. In attempting to make sense out of D'Amato's loss, Republican strategists grumbled that it was "futile to befriend Jews, since Jews just don't vote Republican. Given a choice, Jews vote for other Jews." Somehow it eluded them that just six years earlier, Al D'Amato had defeated Robert Abrams—a Jew.

During the more than quarter-century that Charles Schumer has spent in public life, he has been called "a non-stop schmoozer," a man "bubbling over with ideas," and "a legislator with an outsized ego." Perhaps the best description was given by New York Times reporter Joyce Purnick, who referred to him as "an affable cross between the hard-working grind who makes the honor roll and the popular guy who becomes senior class president." Given his record, his fundraising prowess, and his legendary energy, one should never bet against Charles Schumer—local barber/bookies notwithstanding.

References

Interview with Charles Schumer, March 1998.
Interview with Selma Schumer, March 1998.
Interview with Iris Weinshall, March 1998.
Almanac of American Politics (1980–98 editions).
Current Biography, 1995, pp. 520–524.
National Journal, January 24, 1987 pp. 186–187.
New Republic, November 2, 1998, pp. 15-17.
New York Times, March 10, 1995 B1:3; January 8, 1998 A21:1.
Politics in America (1984–98 editions).
Roll Call, November 20, 1997 1:1.

SHAMANSKY, ROBERT NORTON (1927–):

Democrat from Ohio; served one term in the House (Ninety-seventh Congress, January 3, 1981–January 3, 1983).

Although they lived several generations and an ocean apart in time and space, Benjamin Disraeli might easily have had former Ohio Representative Bob Shamansky in mind when he wrote: "There is no gambling like politics." For in the Ohio Democrat's brief (one-term) congressional career, he won when the odds makers said he would lose, and lost when betting men knew he would win. As a matter of fact, Shamansky holds a doubly unique distinction: being one of just three Democrats to unseat an incumbent Republican during a GOP landslide, and then turning around just two years later to become the only Democrat to lose despite his party's overwhelming victory.

Bob Shamansky's paternal grandparents, Michael and Rachel (Clayman) Shamansky, emigrated from Riga, Latvia, to Manchester, England, in 1890. Like immigrants the world over, they found housing within a few blocks of the port of debarkation; in this case, the Chatham Hill section behind the local prison. There, in 1892, Harry Solomon, the second of the Shamanskys' three sons, was born. Before the turn of the century, the Shamanskys moved to Nelsonville, Ohio, just southeast of Athens.

To this day, no one is certain what brought the Shamanskys to Ohio. In the late 1890s, the economy of Nelsonville was based on mining and several brick-manufacturing plants. Michael Shamansky ran a store that had a junk yard behind it. In later years, his grandson Bob would humorously proclaim: "Our family coat of arms is three balls above a pile of junk rampant." The Shamansky clan must have been rather unique in the area; the most reliable census figures from the time reveal that between them, Nelsonville and Athens had fewer than thirty Jewish residents.

Harry Shamansky graduated from Ohio State University's School of Medicine in 1917, and settled down in Columbus to practice his new profession. By then, he was married to Sarah Greenberg, who had immigrated with her family to Columbus from Kovno in the 1890s. Their first son, Samuel C. Shamansky, was born in 1922. Five years later, on April 18, 1927, their second son, Robert Norton Shamansky, was born.

The Shamanskys originally lived at 245 East Gay Street in Columbus' old Jewish section. By the time Bob was in grade school, the family had moved out to a house on South Drexel Avenue in the more-fashionable Bexley section. As Shamansky recalls, "we lived on the poor end of South Drexel, not too far from the fancy *goyim* (non-Jews). . . . It was a rather short street."

As a youngster, Bob attended Hebrew school at the Orthodox Agudas Achim synagogue (where his maternal grandparents belonged), and Sunday school at the Reform Temple Israel. A good student, Bob skipped the fifth grade in public school. He was a short, terribly skinny child, who continually asked Grandmother Shamansky "when will I ever start growing?" She would respond by telling him that his father hadn't had his real growth spurt until age fifteen. That is precisely what happened to Bob. At age fifteen, Bob Shamansky spent his junior year attending high school in Tucson, Arizona. He grew tremendously that year: "It seems that every two weeks I had to go back to the tailor to have my pants lengthened," he recalls. "When I returned home at the end of the year, I was simply amazed at how low the bathroom sink had become. It didn't dawn on me that it was because I had become so much taller."

Shamansky graduated from Bexley High School in June 1944. Because he weighed only 115 pounds, he was rejected for military service; in World War II, "ground pound" was 120. In September of that year, he entered Ohio State University, majoring in political science. While attending OSU, Shamansky was a member of Phi Eta Sigma and Zeta Beta Tau. Following his second year at OSU, Bob, whose parents always encouraged him to travel, took a cattle boat to Europe. Reaching the Continent, he worked his way to Poland. On the trip back, his ship rammed another vessel in the North Sea—his first encounter with near-death. Happy to return in one piece, Shamansky resumed his undergraduate studies. He earned his B.A. (Phi Beta Kappa) in three years, graduating in June 1947.

Following a three-month trip to Europe in 1947, Bob Shamansky returned home to discover that he had been admitted to both the Harvard and Yale schools of law. He chose the former, receiving his LL.B. in June 1950. In November of that year, Shamansky, now weighing the required 120 pounds, was drafted into the United States Army. He was assigned to the counter-intelligence school just outside of Baltimore. "I was such a slow learner," Shamansky says in his self-deprecating manner, "that I had to start basic training three times before I could get through it."

Shamansky never got an opportunity to be a full-time soldier. Instead, he had his second narrow escape. In December 1951, he and a boyhood friend, Ted Huntington, were driving back to Columbus on furlough. With Bob at the wheel of Ted's car, the boys got into a head-on accident. Ted Huntington went through the car's windshield and died almost instantly. Bob Shamansky suffered numerous broken bones, and took more than a year to rehabilitate. The trauma of losing a close friend was lessened when he was visited at Walter Reed Army Hospital by Ted's mother. "No one can hurt Teddy anymore," Mrs. Huntington told Shamansky. "I've got to raise my other children and see that you get well." Her words made all the difference in Bob Shamansky's emotional recovery.

PFC. Shamansky was discharged from military service in December, 1952 with a 50 percent disability. He was unable to return to any form of gainful employment until 1954, when he took up the practice of law with Troy Feibel. Along with his brother Sam, he made some wise investments in real estate and prospered. As a single man ("You don't have to be married to know aggravation," Shamansky quips), Bob Shamansky had the opportunity to travel the world. His wanderlust has taken him to Antarctica, Africa, and Australia, South America, Asia, and the Middle East.

In 1966, Shamansky ran against Republican Samuel L. Devine for Congress in Ohio's Twelfth District. The two presented a study in opposites: Shamansky the liberal Democrat with virtually no political experience, and the Republican Devine, a former FBI special agent and chairman of the Ohio Un-American Activities Commission. Benefiting from the advantages of incumbency, Devine (who had served in Congress since the beginning of 1959), easily won reelection.

Bob Shamansky has a unique sense of humor. In June 1976, he published a witty op-ed piece in the *New York Times* entitled, "What to Call a Lawyer." In it he posed the tongue-in-cheek question: if a *lawyer* goes to *law* school to study *law*, in order to then practice *law*, why do so many of them prefer to be called attorney? After all, Shamansky argued, members of the American Bar Association don't go to "an attorney school to study attorneying to practice attorneying." Adding to this conundrum, Shamansky wrote, was the problem attached to the honorific "Esq." used "since time immemorial as a title of courtesy in writing to male lawyers." Shamansky poked fun at the plethora of titles in the field of law. Noting that many law schools were now granting their graduates the degree of Doctor of Laws (J.D.) instead of Bachelor of Laws (LL.B.), he came up with a unique solution:

All of the problems—lawyer, attorney, counselor, Esq., Esquire, male, female, can be solved by making the approximately 350,000 persons licensed to practice law in this country into "Doctors" based on the Juris Doctor. Thus, by one simple act of the imagination, this country will have solved forever its "doctor" shortage, while at the same time the legal profession will be unfailingly courteous to itself.

Matching barb for barb, attorney Jerome C. Eisenberg responded to Shamansky's article with a letter to the editor. "Does anyone want to rewrite Shakespeare? Would 'let's kill all the attorneys' sound better? Or should Hamlet's question, 'Why may not that be the skull of an attorney?'" Shamansky admits to having had a ball with this issue.

From 1977 to 1980, Shamansky developed a following in Columbus as a once-a-week, 90-second commentator on television station WBNS. He formed the liberal side of a point-counterpoint segment on the news. In 1980, armed with newfound name recognition, Shamansky decided to once again take on Representative Samuel Devine. Although by now he had represented the constituents of Ohio's Twelfth District for more than twenty years, Devine "was not necessarily well respected." Despite a reputation as strongly conservative and eight years tenure as rankling minority member of the House Commerce Committee, Devine was perceived as being a do-nothing member of Congress. Nonetheless, "the thinking in Columbus in 1980 was that Devine would survive, if only because it was a heavily Republican year." Local Democrats were in obvious agreement with this assessment; Shamansky ran in the primary unopposed.

Squaring off against Devine in the fall, Shamansky attacked him "for doing nothing" and identified himself "with the jobs issue long pushed by Columbus's own leading Republican, Governor James Rhodes." On election day, Shamansky pulled off an upset, defeating Devine 53 percent to 47 percent. The only other Republican incumbents to lose in the Reagan landslide of 1980 were Robert E. Bauman of Maryland and William Royer of California. Royer, who lost to *Thomas Lantos*, had originally won a highly charged special election to replace Representative Leo J. Ryan, whose assassination had precipitated the Jonestown Massacre. Bauman lost his election to Roy Dyson).

As a member of the Ninety-eighth Congress, Bob Shamansky was assigned to Foreign Affairs, Science and Technology, and the Select Committee on Aging. During his two years in the House, Shamansky "thoroughly enjoyed myself," in his words. "I mean, where else can you actually get paid to read the *New York Times* every day?" Shamansky had his fifteen minutes of fame when he introduced legislation to repeal tobacco subsidies. His proposal was voted down 184–231, due in part to a political *faux pas*: Shamansky "refused to yield the floor—an ordinary courtesy—to Carl Perkins, chairman of the Education and Labor Committee and a member of the House since 1948."

Serving as a member of the Foreign Affairs subcommittee on Europe and the Middle East, Shamansky was a ready vote in favor of Israel, a place he had visited on many occasions. Because he had traveled far more extensively than most members of the committee, his input and views often carried more weight than his freshman status would indicate.

Shamansky's race for reelection in 1982 hinged on one crucial point: redistricting. He failed to get the district boundaries he needed because of yet another political misstep. In this case, "he alienated [Ohio] Democratic Speaker Vern Riffe by endorsing gubernatorial candidate William Brown in the primary." Even though Brown decided against running, Riffe's pique was long-lasting. Shamansky was faced with a far less friendly district, and wound up losing to Republican state senator John R. Kasich, who today chairs the House Budget Committee. Shamansky's narrow defeat (53 percent to 47 percent) was singular; he was the only Democratic incumbent to lose that year.

Since losing the election, Bob Shamansky has been "of counsel to the Columbus firm of Benesch, Friedlander, Coplan & Aronoff." He is a regular guest at Bill and Hillary Clinton's Renaissance weekends held at Hilton Head, South Carolina, each new year, and has kept a hand in political issues.

His most recent political battle involves the issue of lost or "mismailed" stock dividends. In 1992, while attending the Democratic National Convention as a (nondelegate) guest, Shamansky had a long chat with then Representative *Ron Wyden* of Oregon. Wyden told him how publicly traded companies were bilking investors out of literally billions of dollars in dividends. As Wyden explained it, if a company's dividend check was returned because of an address error, they did not take the obvious step of attempting to locate the shareholder. "In effect," Shamansky said, "that meant that the companies in question were benefiting from their own negligence, and getting an interest-free loan from the investor."

Intrigued, Shamansky began calling around to various mutual fund companies. "Why don't you at least look in the telephone book or some data base?" he would ask. "Because that's beyond the scope of our time or ability," they would respond. "Well what if I owed you $500? How long would it take you to find me?" he would ask. "That's another matter," came the response.

Determining that more than $10 billion was being lost annually by investors, Shamansky mounted a lobbying campaign aimed at the Securities and Exchange Commission to right the wrong. As a result of his efforts, the SEC has changed its rules. Wyden, now a Senator, has also introduced legislation requiring publicly traded companies to place unclaimed dividends in interest-bearing accounts. Moreover, the legislation mandates that companies must make every effort to locate "lost" investors, and when they are found, to return not only the principal but the interest as well. As of the beginning of the One Hundred and Sixth Congress (January 1999), Wyden's measure had yet to be enacted into law.

"I think my involvement in all this has something to do with my being Jewish," Shamansky says. "I mean, aren't we commanded not to just stand idly by while someone is bleeding. I've got to guess that somehow, my motivation goes back to being Jewish."

Bob Shamansky continues to live in Columbus, Ohio. Although weakened by painful arthritis, he continues to practice law, attend conferences, and look forward to the Clintons' next Renaissance Weekend. Shamansky is a member of all three of Columbus's synagogues: Agudas Achim, Beth Shalom, and Temple Israel. Since neither of his brother's children have married Jews, it is highly likely that the Shamansky line will come to an end in the next generation. But being a man who has made a career of beating the odds, Bob Shamansky is betting it won't.

References

Interview with Robert N. Shamansky, January 1997.

Almanac of American Politics, 1982, 1984.

New York Times, June 21, 1976, 29:2; July 6, 1976, 24:5.

SHERMAN, BRAD (1954–): *Democrat from California; has served two terms in the House (One Hundred and Fifth and One Hundred and Sixth Congress, January 7, 1997–present).*

In November 1995, when Representative *Anthony Beilenson* made the surprising announcement that he intended to retire from Congress, most political observers assumed that his Twenty-fourth District seat would be taken by businessman Richard Sybert, the Republican Beilenson had narrowly defeated in 1994. The race had been extremely bitter, and the "thin-skinned" Sybert had filed a libel suit against the "venerable" Beilenson "over a last-minute campaign mailer." Although the suit was settled in early 1996, three appellate justices "felt so strongly about the case that they issued an opinion anyway, saying that such a suit 'has no place in our courts.'"

The 1996 race to succeed Beilenson pitted Sybert against attorney-CPA Brad Sherman, a member of the State Board of Equalization, California's elected tax board. The campaign had its normal share of charges and countercharges, unsubstantiated half-truths, and bitterness. Democrat Sherman attacked Sybert for his enthusiastic endorsement of the Republicans' "Contract With America." Sybert countered by portraying himself as "a moderate pro-choice Republican, a card-carrying Sierra Club member since high school and someone with compassion for the poor."

Sherman next laced into his Republican opponent for sending out a mass mailing that gave the erroneous impression that retired General Colin Powell endorsed Sybert's candidacy. Sybert responded by saying that Sherman was an "unreconstructed tax-and-spend liberal." In other words, it was campaign politics as usual. Both candidates spent heavily of their own money: Sybert at least $625,000, and Sherman more than $400,000.

What set this congressional race apart from perhaps any other in the history of the United States was that one candidate, Brad Sherman, was also the object (or target, if you will) of a

mass skewering by the nation's cartoonists. And in perhaps a portent of things to come, their medium was not the editorial page or the comic strip, but cyberspace.

Brad Sherman was born in Los Angeles on October 24, 1954. He grew up in Newport Beach in nearby Orange County, where his father served as president of the local Reform synagogue, Temple Bat Yam. Sherman was educated in the local public schools and at UCLA, where he received his B.A., *summa cum laude*, in 1974. Two years earlier, he had already entered the world of politics, when he headed the Orange County speakers' bureau for the George McGovern presidential campaign. Following his graduation from UCLA, Sherman was accepted at the Harvard University School of Law, from which he received his J.D., *magna cum laude*, in 1979. Along the way, he also picked up a degree in accounting. He was licensed as a certified public accountant in California in 1980.

As an attorney, working with a big-six CPA firm, Sherman specialized in audits of large businesses and governmental entities. Along the way, he became widely acknowledged as an expert in the arcane world of tax law. When Corazon Aquino was elected President of the Philippines, Sherman traveled to Manila, where he represented the government in its efforts to seize assets of the former President, Ferdinand Marcos. Upon his return to the United States, Sherman began a five-year term on the board of California Common Cause (1984–89). During his tenure with the good-government group, Common Cause convinced the California legislature to triple the child-care credit. Sherman took credit for helping to "draft tough conflict-of-interest laws for state officeholders."

In 1990, Brad Sherman was elected to the State Board of Equalization. During his first four-year term on the board, Sherman pushed for the elimination of the hated tax on snack food, and helped create "municipal finance reform to reward communities for accommodating movie studios, manufacturing and research centers." Sherman was reelected to a second four-year term in 1994.

In January 1996, the State Board of Equalization voted to retain a tax on "commercial illustrations that appear in publications and are not accompanied by text." Although Sherman actually voted against its retention (a fact quickly forgotten or overlooked), the board's action outraged cartoonists throughout the state. It was Brad Sherman's misfortune to then run for Congress in a district that is likely home to more cartoonists than anywhere in the world.

To express their anger at Sherman as a symbol of the Board of Equalization, artists in his district "established their own Web page," and soon "enlisted their colleagues across the country to contribute some not-so-flattering portrayals" of the candidate. During the campaign, more than three dozen nationally syndicated cartoonists, including those who draw the comic strips "Hagar the Horrible," "Cathy," and "Beetle Bailey," lampooned the balding, bespectacled Sherman in cyberspace.

Over the many months that the Website (*http://www.unitedmedia.com/ncs/tax.html*) was in business, Sherman was portrayed as "SherMan," a Pac-Man-like figure gobbling up tax money, and a "pointy-headed, pencil-necked bureaucrat." When questioned by the *New York Times*, Mort Walker, creator of "Beetle Bailey," said: "The nature of cartoonists is to be a little irreverent, to attack any kind of stupidity." For his part, Sherman took the lampooning in stride as "the price of a public life."

During the cartoonists' computer-generated ambush, Sherman began developing a self-deprecating sense of humor; he took to handing out combs (he is balding) with his name on them at all campaign appearances, and began referring to himself as "a recovering nerd."

Sherman ran as a pro-choice, pro-environment Democrat. Portraying himself as a moderate and Sybert as an ultra-conservative ally of Newt Gingrich, he also supported the death penalty, the three strikes law, term limits, and the balanced budget amendment. Running in a district with a large Jewish constituency, Sherman stressed his involvement in AIPAC, the Jewish Home for the Aged, and Democrats for Israel, as well as the fact that he was "the only Jewish California State Constitutional Officer."

On November 5, 1996, Sherman beat Rich Sybert with 50 percent; three marginal candidates who received a collective 7 percent of the vote, gave Sherman his margin of victory.

Almost from the moment of his victory, the National Republican Congressional Committee (NRCC) made Sherman a marked man. They saw him as one of the Democratic Party's most vulnerable incumbents, and launched an all-out effort to defeat him in the 1998 election. Randy Hoffman, Sherman's Republican opponent, a wealthy businessman was the founder of Magellan Systems, a company that "developed innovative products that allow users to pinpoint their geographic position on the earth by using satellite technology." Under Hoffman's guidance, Magellan grew to be a corporation with annual sales of $125 millions and over 500 employees. Running on a standard pro-business Republican platform calling for lower taxes and less government, Hoffman derided Sherman as a "tax and spend liberal," and attempted to tie him to the Moncia Lewinsky scandal plaguing the White House. Sensing that Hoffman had a realistic chance of defeating Sherman, Republican National Congressional Committee Chair John Linder and House Majority Leader Dick Armey visited the Twenty-fourth District to stump for their candidate. Calling the Twenty-fourth District race "one of our top-tier campaigns in the country," the RNCC pumped hundreds of thousands of dollars of "soft money" into Hoffman's campaign.

Sherman ran on his moderate record, and challenged Hoffman to state where the two differed. Hoffman refused to debate Sherman, telling a *Roll Call* reporter that he was "too busy raising money." Sherman stumped the district, pointing out that far from being an ultra-liberal, he had voted *with* the Republican majority anywhere between 52 percent and 55 percent of the time. Sherman was reelected to a second term by a 58 percent–38 percent margin. Despite a deep campaign treasury, Hoffman never created clear issue-oriented distinctions between himself and Sherman.

Brad Sherman was given a seat on the House Budget Committee and the Committee on Foreign Affairs. Unmarried, he lives in Sherman Oaks and is a member of Valley Beth Shalom Temple.

References

Hans Johnson and Peggie Rayhawk. *The New Members of Congress Almanac: 105th Congress* (Washington, D.C., Almanac Publishing Co., 1996), p. 29.

Los Angeles Times, August 19, 1996, 2:1; October 15, 1996, A 3:3; October 29, 1996, 2:1.

New York Times, October 1, 1996, A 21:1.

SIEGEL, ISAAC (1880–1947): *Republican from New York; served four terms in the House (Sixty-fourth through Sixty-seventh Congress, March 4, 1915–March 3, 1923).*

Isaac Siegel was a political enigma. A conservative Republican who sponsored the legislation that defined anarchy as a federal crime, he went out of his way to free a group of leftists hours before they were to be deported back to Russia on the "Soviet Ark." A staunch supporter of Warren G. Harding and his archconservative platform of normalcy, Siegel took the lead in the effort to reduce Southern representation in Congress to the proportion in which the black population was excluded from the polls. A political partisan, he was regularly endorsed for reelection by both the Democrats and the Republicans. But for all his successes, he was denied the one office to which he truly aspired—the U.S. Court of Appeals.

Isaac Siegel, the son of Kive and Leah Siegel, was born in New York City on April 12, 1880. A 1901 graduate of the New York University School of Law, he spent his entire legal career as senior partner of Siegel, Corn & Siegel. In 1907, Siegel married Annie Natelson. They had three children. Their oldest, Seymour, became program director for WNYC, New York City's municipal broadcasting station. The Siegels were founders of the Orthodox Institutional Synagogue (located at 11 West 116th Street), where Isaac served many terms as president.

A resident of Harlem in the days when it was a Jewish neighborhood, Siegel became active in the Eighteenth Assembly District Republican Club. In 1909, after New York went through a rash of contested elections, the politically ambitious Siegel was appointed deputy attorney general for prosecution of election fraud. Siegel did a good job; in the next election cycle (1911–12), cases of electoral fraud were all but eliminated.

Shortly after Woodrow Wilson became President, he appointed Twentieth District Congressman Francis B. Harrison Governor General of the Philippines. His vacated seat was taken over by Democrat *Jacob A. Cantor*, who won in the November 1913 special election. Isaac Siegel, with the endorsement of the local Republican organization, challenged Cantor in 1914 and won. Cantor contested the election, but to no avail.

Isaac Siegel spent most of his first term tending to the needs of his district and becoming accustomed to the intricacies of Congressional politics. With the coming of World War I, he began to spread his wings. After he cast a vote in favor of declaring war in April 1917, the *New York Times* took notice of the Republican from Harlem. In an editorial, the *Times* congratulated Siegel on his vote, especially in light of the fact that there was "no district in which the pacifists, pro-Germans and Socialists are more active and influential than in his."

Siegel's Republican colleagues, many of whom were planning to vote against "Wilson's War," had tried to get him to change his vote, telling him that it would likely end his career. Siegel, unimpressed by their argument, had taken the floor to explain his vote.

I should be unworthy of American citizenship were I to be deterred from acting by such warnings. I say to my colleagues who are now hesitating, that the people will know whether they are for this great land of freedom and religious liberty or whether they are going to be guided simply by the selfish question [of] whether they will obtain more votes in 1918 by standing on the side of our foes.

With the country arming for war, Siegel authored legislation to provide for up to twenty Jewish chaplains in the American Expeditionary Forces. Heretofore, the American military had few rabbis in uniform. In order to get the Army and Navy behind his proposal, Siegel got the board of Beth Israel Hospital to come to his aid. By early 1918, it had raised $1.25 million dollars for a new 15-story, 500-bed hospital facility to be erected on the square block bounded by Second Avenue and Livingston Place, 17th and 18th Streets. With the coming of war, the board decided to put the project on hold, feeling that the material required for the project would undoubtedly be needed for the European conflict. After consulting with the Beth Israel board, Siegel approached the War Department with his proposition: the hospital board would go ahead with construction and then turn the new facility over to the Army for the duration of the conflict, to use as it saw fit. After some deliberation, the Army took Siegel up on his offer. His legislation passed.

During the summer of 1918, Isaac Siegel spent seven weeks visiting American soldiers at the front as part of an overseas commission. He returned with personal messages from more than five hundred soldiers and their collective request for "more cigarettes and chocolate." While in France, Siegel was endorsed by both the Republicans and the Democrats for reelection. This was undoubtedly intended to keep the seat out of the hands of Socialist Morris Hillquit, who had already entered the race. With the dual endorsement, Siegel's reelection was all but certain. In November, he was easily reelected to his third term.

Appointed to the Committee on Immigration, Isaac Siegel immediately joined the minority in protesting the harsh Burnett Immigration Bill. By its terms, all immigration "from non-adjoining" countries would cease for four years. The committee gave the bill its imprimatur by a vote of 14 to 2. Siegel, joined by committee colleague *Adolph Sabath*, objected that their minority report had never been heard, and accused the majority of rushing to pass a "hodgepodge" and "laxly-drawn" bill.

Taking the floor, Siegel called the bill "un-American and against the spirit of American institutions." The bill's sponsors argued that its passage was crucial in order to stem the threatened "onrush of Bolshevik and radicals from Europe." Siegel called these charges "ridiculous and hysterical," noting that with virtually all ships being used to bring American soldiers back home from the recently concluded war, there simply weren't any available berths for the supposed revolutionaries. His voice rising in anger, Siegel charged that the bill was "a ploy by labor which seeks to maintain wartime wages." Congress failed to pass the Burnett bill.

The next year, the Burnett Bill, now renamed the Johnson Bill, once again passed the Committee on Immigration. Once again, Siegel and Sabath were in the minority. Once again, the full committee refused to let them read their minority report into the final record. When the committee chairman presented the legislation on the House floor, Siegel, recognized by the Speaker, said: "This bill is a direct result of Henry Ford's propaganda against the Jews. The point of the whole proposition is the fear of a large number of Jews coming in. Otherwise we would have had a full bill reported." Here Siegel was on firm ground; the bill's wording ("all non-adjoining countries") was obviously directed at

the people of Europe. Before the Johnson Bill came to a vote, Siegel managed to slip in an amendment that would permit brothers and sisters of resident aliens to immigrate. Siegel's amendment passed 203 to 76; the Johnson Bill passed 293 to 41.

During the days of Attorney General A. Mitchell Palmer's infamous Red Scare, Isaac Siegel sponsored legislation that would make plotting the overthrow of the government a federal crime punishable by deportation—assuming that the guilty were foreign-born. A devout patriot, Siegel was known to travel the lecture circuit and speak immediately after "Red Emma" Goldman, who was counseling anarchy, birth control, and draft evasion. And yet, when Palmer had rounded up enough "Bolsheviki" to fill the S.S. *Buford* (nicknamed the "Soviet Ark"), Siegel went aboard and questioned many of the putative radicals and revolutionaries. He had twelve of them removed from the ship, convinced that they had been wrongly accused and convicted.

During his final term in the House of Representatives, word got out that President Harding planned to name Isaac Siegel to fill the next vacancy on the federal Court of Appeals. Siegel was so certain of the appointment that he did not run for reelection. When a vacancy finally occurred, New York's two Senators, James Wadsworth and William Calder, sat down with Attorney General Harry M. Daugherty to speak on Siegel's behalf. Despite their best efforts, Siegel did not get the appointment. His congressional seat was taken over by *Fiorello LaGuardia*.

Isaac Siegel returned to his law practice in 1923. He continued as an active Republican, serving as president of the Eighteenth Assembly District Republican Club until 1939, and as a Republican presidential elector in 1932. Finally, on July 4, 1939, Siegel became a judge. Fiorello LaGuardia, now the mayor of New York City, appointed him to the domestic relations court. Siegel continued to serve on the court until June 29, 1947, when he died from a fall from a window of his ninth-floor apartment. A full-scale investigation was launched to determine whether Siegel's death was an accident or suicide. Siegel's obituary in the *New York Times* noted that "the window, one of three facing Eighty second Street, had a very low sill, bolster[ing] the family's belief that the Justice's death had been accidental." Isaac Siegel was buried at Union Fields Cemetery in Brooklyn.

Isaac Siegel was truly proud of having served his community as an elected official. As he told a group of high school students a few years after leaving Congress: "We do not believe in urging the nomination of those of our faith for public office solely because they are of that faith. We cannot, however, too strongly state that because one is of that faith is no reason why his capacity, ability and accomplishments for the public good should not be fully recognized."

References

American Jewish Year Book, vol. 24, p. 203; vol. 50, p. 523.

Biographical Directory of American Jews.

New York Times, April 17, 1916, 12:4; August 17, 1917, 4:1; January 31, 1919, 4:3; May 8, 1928, 24:2 June 30, 1947, 38:4.

Universal Jewish Encyclopedia.

Who Was Who in America, vol. 2.

Who's Who in American Jewry, 1926, 1928, 1938.

SIMON, JOSEPH (1851–1935): *Republican from Oregon; served five years of a six-year term in the Senate (December 5, 1898–March 3, 1903).*

Joseph Simon was the fourth Jew to serve in the United States Senate, and the first Minyanaire from the West. The son of David and Elise (Leopold) Simon, the future Senator was born in Bechtheim, Hesse-Darmstadt, Germany, on February 7, 1851. In 1857, the Simon family immigrated to Portland, Oregon, which at that time had a Jewish population of no more than 1,500. The vast majority of this small Jewish enclave was, like the Simon family, of German origin. David Simon was one of the residents who built Oregon's first synagogue, Beth Israel, in 1859.

Following a public school education, Joseph Simon began reading law in the offices of Mitchell and Dolph. In 1872, he was admitted to the Oregon Bar, and went into private practice with a group of attorneys who, within a year, formed the politically powerful firm of Dolph, Mallory, Simon, and Gearin. The "Dolph" of the firm was Cyrus Abda Dolph (1840–1914), the great-grandson of Jacob Vanderbilt, brother of the first Cornelius Vanderbilt. Cyrus Dolph's older brother, Joseph Norton Dolph (1835–1897), served as United States Senator from Oregon from 1883 to 1895. Simon's partners combined to form what was, without question, the most distinguished firm on the Pacific coast, it sent four members to the United States Senate, one to Congress, and one to the federal judiciary. Cyrus Dolph was also responsible for drafting the will of Mrs. Simeon Gannett Reed, who left the bulk of her estate to the newly created Reed College.

Joseph Simon was a Reform Jew. A member of the board of Beth Israel, Simon amended the temple's constitution to prohibit future rabbis from sitting in on board meetings "after the present incumbency." The incumbent rabbi against whom Simon's amendment was directed was the young Stephen S. Wise, who had gotten himself into trouble with the board for being too controversial. Cut to the quick, Wise left Beth Israel and, moving to New York, resolved to start a "free synagogue," where such political machinations would not be permitted.

Within three years of being admitted to the bar, Joseph Simon was appointed secretary of the Republican State Central Committee of Oregon. In 1877, he was elected to the Portland City Council. Three years later, in 1880, he became chairman of the Republican Central Committee, a post he would hold for the next decade. From 1880 to 1896, he represented Multnomah County (which included the city of Portland) in the Oregon State Senate. During those sixteen years, he frequently served as Senate president. Rising rapidly through the Republican ranks, Simon was a delegate to his party's national convention in both 1892 and 1900. After the 1892 convention, which was held in Minneapolis, he was made a member of the Republican National Committee.

In the fall of 1896, when the Oregon state legislature failed to cast a majority vote for any of the candidates contending for United States Senator, the seat was declared vacant. Faced with the prospect of being underrepresented in the upper chamber, the Oregon legislature asked former United States Senator Henry Winslow Corbett to act as interim Senator until such time as they could send a duly elected man to Washington. Corbett (1827–1903), a Republican who had served as Senator from Oregon from 1867 to 1873, presented his credentials as Senator-designate at the beginning of the Fifty-fifth Congress's first session on March 6, 1897. The Senate refused to seat him. After a series of hearings, it was determined on February 28, 1898 that Corbett was "not entitled to the seat." It was declared vacant until the state of Oregon could elect someone by majority vote. Seven months later, on October 7, 1898, the Oregon legislature officially filled the seat by electing Joseph Simon as the state's junior senator. Simon was duly sworn in on December 5, 1898 at the beginning of the second session of the Fifty-fifth Congress.

Joseph Simon served out the rest of his term, becoming chairman of the Committee on Irrigation and Reclamation of Arid Lands for the Fifty-sixth and Fifty-seventh Congresses. At the end of his five-plus years on Capitol Hill, he decided not to run for reelection. Upon his return to Portland, Simon resumed the practice of law. In 1909, the people of Portland elected him to a two-year term as mayor. It was to be Simon's "last hurrah" in elective politics. The story is told that in 1910, while he was mayor, the women of the city called a mass meeting to protest the high streetcar steps. Simon, "ever the gentleman," convinced the local transit company to lower them, "thus spar[ing] the virtuous women of Portland the shame of exposing their ankles." Following his single term as mayor, Simon returned to his law firm, practicing until shortly before his death on February 14, 1935. Simon was buried in Beth Israel Cemetery, Portland.

References

American Jewish Year Book, vol. 2, p. 523; vol. 6, p. 188, vol. 24, p. 204; vol. 37, p. 262.

Biographical Directory of American Jews.

Jewish Encyclopedia.

Jacob Rader Marcus. *United States Jewry* (Detroit: Wayne State University Press, 1993), vol. 3, p. 196.

National Cyclopedia of American Biography, vol. 6, pp. 56–57.

Universal Jewish Encyclopedia.

Who Was Who in America, vol. 1.

SIROVICH, WILLIAM IRVING (1882–1939):
Democrat from New York; served seven terms in the House (Seventieth through Seventy-sixth Congress, March 4, 1927–December 17, 1939).

Known as the most versatile man in Congress, William Sirovich was variously a surgeon, hospital superintendent, bank president, playwright, and self-appointed censor of theater critics. It was in the latter two roles that his name became a household word in the 1930s.

William Irving Sirovich was born in York, Pennsylvania, on March 18, 1882, one of three children born to Rabbi Jacob and Rose (Weinstein) Sirovich. Rabbi Sirovich accepted a pulpit in New York City in 1888, and moved his family to the Lower East Side, where he "lived in modest circumstances, most of his income [being] derived from real estate in York." Young William, along with his sisters Sadie (Rosenfeld) and Ada (Breuer) attended the public schools of the Lower East Side. He went on to the City College of New York and the College of Physicians and Surgeons of Columbia University, from which he received his medical degree in 1906. As a physician, Sirovich was known as the poor man's surgeon. In 1910, he was appointed superintendent of the People's Hospital, and served in that capacity until 1929, two years after he was elected to Congress.

Sirovich began his political career in 1919 when New York City Mayor John F. Hylan appointed him Commissioner of Child Welfare, a position which he held until 1931. During his tenure as Commissioner, he fought for, and obtained, compensation for the care of orphans in private homes. Sirovich often referred to himself as the stepfather of forty thousand orphans. He also served as president of New York City's Industrial Bank from 1929 to 1931—not particularly great years to be in that industry.

In 1924, Sirovich wrote and produced *Schemers*, a play satirizing critics, which lasted on Broadway for precisely sixteen performances. For the rest of his days, Sirovich would refer to it as "My Calvary." It was panned unmercifully. One critic, Stark Young of the *New York Times*, wrote: "A reviewer is thwarted from taking it seriously, perhaps by the fact that we are to believe from the critics in the play that the piece is rotten, as every one but the producer knows. It has neither wit, point, entertainment, [nor] humor, as the critics agree. . . . My critical expe-

rience was one of embarrassment." Stark's stinging comments were not unique; in comparison to the assessments of his fellow critics, Stark's review was actually rather muted. Percy Hammond called *Schemers* "more an aberration than a drama"; Heywood Broun described it as "one of the crudest plays that has come to Broadway in many days." William Sirovich was a man with a long, long memory. The reviewers' words would one day come back to haunt them.

Less than two months after *Schemers* closed on Broadway, Sirovich ran for Congress from New York's Fourteenth District, losing to incumbent *Nathan D. Perlman*. In a rematch two years later, Sirovich easily defeated Perlman. He would be reelected six times, serving in the House until his death in 1939 (Seventieth through Seventy-sixth Congresses).

In the House, Sirovich was known for his theatrics. An ardent "wet", he on several occasions startled his colleagues by conducting "experiments" on the House floor. Sirovich contended that the "drys" used poison in alcohol as part of Prohibition enforcement. He was also one of the wordier, more emotive members of Congress. Few of his speeches lasted less than an hour:

> Whenever the gentleman from New York rises to say, with that solemn courtliness of the born orator, "Mr. Speak-ah, lay-dees and gen-tul-men of the House," there is a rush from, not to, the cloakrooms. . . . Dr. Sirovich always pauses after these opening words and looks slowly right and left, his features noble and composed. His shorter speeches last an hour.

In a *New Yorker* profile of the good doctor published near the end of his life, columnist Richard Boyer described a typical Sirovich oration.

> Dr. Sirovich began with a Biblical instance of exploitation by the employers. Majestically he proceeded to the time of Columbus; touched on the Incas, the Aztecs, and the Mayans; continued to Richelieu and Louis XIII; progressed to the ideals of Montesquieu, Voltaire, and Rousseau; mentioned Henry the Eighth; rolled on to Bentham. . .; sketched the philosophies of Kant, Goethe, John Stuart Mill, Adam Smith, Franklin, Paine, Jefferson,

Madison, Monroe, Mirabeau, Lafayette, Claude Henri de Saint-Simon, Louis Blanc . . . Karl Marx, Friedrich Engels, Bismarck, Asquith, Lloyd George, and Al Smith; and finally arrived at the New Deal and "Franklin Del-ano Roos-e-velt."

Not surprisingly, Sirovich was giving a speech on the historical importance of the New Deal. Sirovich was once called "the most widely read author in the Fourteenth Congressional District." And with good reason: during his congressional career, it is estimated that he inundated his constituents with more than 7.2 million copies of his speeches.

In the House, Sirovich was one of the Roosevelt New Deal's most ardent supporters. Even before the advent of the New Deal and its wide array of alphabetic agencies and programs, Sirovich was sponsoring social welfare legislation. In 1927 alone, Sirovich introduced bills providing for unemployment insurance, old-age pensions, child welfare, and the creation of a Cabinet-level Department of Science, Art, and Literature. Never at a loss for a piquant expression when describing himself, Sirovich was quoted as saying: "I regard Congress as the uterus and myself as the fertilizer preparing it for pioneer measures yet to be born."

When Sirovich was elevated to chair the Committee on Patents in 1931 (Seventy-second Congress), he found a bully pulpit from which he could take revenge on all the critics who had panned *Schemers* years before. Sirovich's opening gambit was to introduce legislation that would force exhibitors to pay royalties on certain literary properties. The year was 1936. He then invited New York's leading critics to come and testify. Sensing that their presence might give Sirovich a platform from which to vent his pent-up anger, the critics demurred. Percy Hammond, on declining to go before Sirovich's committee, was heard to say: "It's about time we revived the old Spanish proverb, 'It's a waste of lather to shave an ass.'"

Apparently, Sirovich was counting on the critics' absence. He began a one-sided war of words, labeling the New York critics "smart alecs," "destructive," and "silly." At first this was done with a bit of good humor, but soon Sirovich took off the gloves. He charged that most New York theater critics were more experienced in prize fight and baseball reporting than in criticizing dramatic stage productions. Sirovich then challenged two of New York's leading critics, George Jean Nathan and Walter Winchell, to "listen to a speech" he expected to deliver in the House, and to "write it for their respective papers." In his challenge, he refereed to Nathan as an "intellectual anarchist," and Winchell as a "self-appointed super-critic." Both critics were "unavailable."

Upon receiving word that they would not be coming to "listen to a speech," Sirovich delivered what he thought would be his verbal *coup de grace*: "I will go back to my dissecting room and get the proper instruments to care for them." He then said that the Patents Committee should have a spelling bee for the critics! All this was played out in the New York press, often on the front pages of the *New York Times*, and the *Evening Graphic*.

When no critics showed up for his committee hearings on the copyright bill, Sirovich vented his frustration to a room packed with visitors: "Literally tens of thousands of men and women directly or indirectly employed by the theatre, are idle or in want and penury, and these conditions are chiefly attributable to the malicious, wanton, unfair and abusive criticism of these dramatic critics." His voice rising with emotion, Sirovich reached his peroration: "It is only fair to ascertain whether this enormous weapon has been utilize [*sic*] by dramatic critics in an honest, fair and impartial manner, and in accordance with the highest ideals that have motivated all artistic criticism from the beginning of time. . . . They know that a play is bad even before they have seen it and they come merely for the formality of confirming their pre-conceived notions."

In due course, Sirovich's war against the critics ran out of steam, and the newspapers began to relegate it to their inside pages. Dr. Sirovich had one last shot at his critics, however. This came at an annual luncheon of the Drama Study Club, held at the Waldorf-Astoria. There, he locked horns and tongues with Heywood Broun and Ed Sullivan before a lunch crowd that included Constance Collier, Leslie Howard, and Basil Rathbone.

Sirovich accused the critics of insincerity. Broun countered by charging that the attempt to curb dramatic criticism by legislation was silly.

Sirovich charged some of Broun's brethren with murder, citing the case of Tyrone Power (Sr.), who, he said, died because he was called a ham. Sirovich suggested that he would be suing a certain critic (presumably Walter Winchell) for libel.

The lawsuit never materialized. From that point on, Sirovich dropped the issue. He later attempted to produce another of his plays, *Suspended Sentence*, on Broadway. Perhaps remembering his own words ("They know that a play is bad even before they have seen it"), he pulled the plug shortly before opening night.

William Sirovich continued serving in Congress, albeit a bit more quietly, until his death in New York City on December 17, 1939. His funeral, held at the Gramercy Park Chapel on Second Avenue, was attended by more than 25,000 mourners. Pallbearers included Mayor *Fiorello LaGuardia*, Postmaster General James Farley, Senator Robert F. Wagner, Sr., Governor *Herbert H. Lehman*, David Sarnoff, and the great Yiddish actor Maurice Schwartz. Sirovich, who had never married, was buried in Mount Hebron Cemetery, Flushing, New York.

References

American Jewish Year Book, vol. 42, p. 84.

Biographical Directory of American Jews.

Irving Howe and Kenneth Libo, *How We Lived: A Documentary History of Immigrant Jews in America, 1880–1930* (New York: Richard Marek, 1979), pp. 235–236.

New Yorker, November 5, 1938, pp. 24–30.

New York Times, December 18, 1939, 23:1.

Universal Jewish Encyclopedia.

Who Was Who in America, vol. 1.

Who Was Who in American Jewry, 1926, 1928, 1938.

SISISKY, NORMAN (1927–): *Democrat from Virginia; has served nine terms in the House (Ninety-eighth through One Hundred and sixth Congress, January 3, 1983–present).*

The Virginia Tidewater is one of America's most historic areas. It was the scene of some of America's earliest settlements as well as its first popular uprising, Bacon's Rebellion, in 1676. It also provided the ground for some of the Civil War's bloodiest and most bitter fighting. Today, the Tidewater is home to tobacco and peanut farms, the naval town of Portsmouth, a sizable percentage of Virginia's black population, and the political headquarters of Pat Robertson's Christian Broadcasting Network. It is also the home of the only Minyanaire to come from Virginia, Norman Sisisky. A bluff, affable man with the drawl of a Southern gentleman and the skills of a seasoned political veteran, Sisisky began representing the Tidewater region in Congress in 1982, and has run virtually unopposed in many of his reelection campaigns.

Norman Sisisky's father, Samuel, came from Lithuania to Springfield, Massachusetts, in 1907. After a short time, he moved south to Baltimore, where he met and married Tina Ackerman, a Baltimore native. Their second son, Norman, was born in Baltimore on June 9, 1927. In the first three decades of the twentieth century, residents of Baltimore commonly moved freely between Baltimore and Richmond, Virginia, the city that had been the capital of the Confederacy. For many, especially Jews, it was a seasonal affair—finding employment part of the year in one city, and part of the year in the other. Shortly after Norman's birth, the Sisiskys made their way to Richmond, where Sam ran a kosher delicatessen. Although his business establishment was kosher, Sam kept only a "fairly kosher" home. They belonged to the Orthodox K'nesset Israel synagogue, where Norman became bar mitzvah in 1940. Norman attended Belview Elementary, graduated from John Marshall High School at age sixteen, and then enrolled at the University of Richmond. After he had completed his first year, he enlisted in the Navy, one day shy of his

eighteenth birthday. Sisisky's choice of the Navy was a logical one; Virginia, long the site of several major naval installations, has always been the most Navy-oriented of all American states. Its current Senior Senator, John W. Warner, served as Secretary of the Navy during the Nixon administration.

In 1946, Sisisky was honorably discharged from the service and entered Virginia Commonwealth University as a sophomore. Graduating in 1949 with a degree in business, he set about making his way in the world. Moving to Petersburg, about 25 miles south of Richmond, Sisisky found employment at a bottling plant owned by a Jewish family named Brown. In 1951, he married Rhoda Brown, the boss's daughter. Once he entered the Brown family, Sisisky took over the company. Over the next thirty-three years, he worked to make his bottling operation

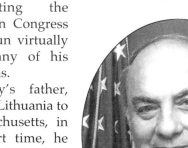

the largest Pepsi distributor in Virginia, becoming a multimillionaire in the process. *Roll Call* ranked him as the eighth richest member of the Hundred and Fourth Congress, with an estimated net worth of more than $30 million.

Sisisky's involvement in politics began as a result of his business. As president of the Virginia Bottlers' Association, and later as chairman of the board of the National Softdrink Association, Sisisky found himself lobbying the Virginia legislature on behalf of a bottle bill. At the conclusion of his lobbying efforts, he decided to run for the legislature in order "to solve my own problems." Running as an independent from a largely black district, Sisisky was elected to the Virginia House of Delegates in 1972. He was reelected without difficulty five times.

The same year that Sisisky was elected to the House of Delegates, Republican Robert W. Daniel, Jr., was elected to Congress from Virginia's Fourth District. A substantial landowner and former CIA agent, Daniel was "a serious man with little charm" who "compiled a solidly conservative voting record which made not a concession to the presumed views of the large black population in the district." Reelected four times against weak or divided opposition, he became Sisisky's target in 1982. Pumping nearly $350,000 of his own money into the campaign, Sisisky defeated Daniel by a solid 54 percent to 46 percent.

Sisisky won a seat on the House Armed Services Committee, and was the only freshman assigned to its four major subcommittees: Procurement and Military Nuclear Systems, Military Installations and Facilities, Seapower and Strategic and Critical Materials, and Investigations. Over the years, he has become a recognized expert on military-purchasing issues. As a freshman he made an early mark. Upon learning of a Pentagon request to build schools for military dependents in Western Europe at a cost of $8,500 per pupil, Sisisky "headed for a hall phone and called a contact in Virginia's Department of Education to find out how much schools cost." He came back with a figure roughly half what the Pentagon was requesting, thereby saving nearly $150 million.

As the representative of a district with a large military constituency, Sisisky has worked hard to keep defense dollars flowing. Sisisky was instrumental in securing funding for the construction of a new nuclear-powered aircraft carrier at the Newport News Shipbuilding and Drydock Company, located next-door to his district. He was one of just eleven House Democrats to vote against President Clinton's first budget proposal, which was billed as a serious deficit reduction measure. Speaking of that critical vote, Sisisky says: "I strongly believe that drastic action is needed to reduce our spiraling deficit, but the House budget resolution simply goes too far in cutting defense."

This is not to say that Sisisky has blinders on when it comes to military spending. Over the years he has initiated a number of high-profile investigations, which have uncovered hundreds of millions of dollars in overestimated and overfunded projects. His efforts to eliminate waste in the Pentagon budget have earned him the Golden Bulldog Award from the Watchdogs of the Treasury organization. Sisisky voted in favor of the Gulf War resolution, and then went to visit American troops deployed in Saudi Arabia. At the conclusion of the war, he held hearings on the opportunities for small businesses to participate in the rebuilding of Kuwait.

Sisisky's Fourth District has the largest percentage of blacks (nearly 40 percent) of any district in Virginia. Not surprisingly, he has been a strong supporter of low-cost housing, the Head Start Program, and the Womens' Infants' and Children's Program. A fiscal conservative, social moderate (he's pro-choice), and ardent Zionist, Sisisky has confounded establishment politicians, who variously dub him a liberal, a moderate, and a conservative. "I guess I'm really all three," Sisisky says. Although he voted for the constitutional amendment to require a balanced budget, he says: "I don't think it was necessarily the right thing to do—but at the time, it was the only thing on the table." Sisisky also opposed the Clinton administration on the Family and Medical Leave Act and on two gun-control measures. His ratings by the liberal ADA and conservative ACU are almost equal—a rarity in an age of partisanship.

Norman and Rhoda Sisisky are the parents of four sons—Mark, Terry, Richard, and Stewart—and seven grandchildren. While raising his family, Sisisky served as president of his Conservative synagogue in Petersburg. Norman Sisisky was also the president of the Virginia UJA—a position taken over by one of his sons. Another son has been UJA president in Jacksonville, Florida. In 1991, Sisisky missed a crucial civil rights vote because he was in Israel, attending the bar mitzvah of his grandson at the Western Wall. "It was the first important vote I ever missed," Sisisky says. "But I wouldn't have missed that bar mitzvah for the world."

Norman Sisisky represents a district in which there are at most 300 Jewish families. It is probably the least-Jewish district in Virginia. Despite that, he has never had a problem being reelected, and says he has never been aware of any overt anti-Semitism. In 1993, Sisisky flirted with the idea of running in the Democratic primary against incumbent senator Charles Robb, who was "beset with embarrassing publicity about his personal and political ethics." Sisisky changed his mind, and has remained in the House. He looks like a sure bet to remain as representative of the Fourth District until he decides to retire. In November 1998, Sisisky was reelected to a ninth term without opposition.

References

Interview with Norman Sisisky, July 1992.
Almanac of American Politics, 1982–1998.
Politics in America, 1982–1998.

SMITH, LAWRENCE JACK (1941–): *Democrat from Florida; served five terms in the House (Ninety-eighth through One Hundred and Second Congress, January 3, 1982–January 3, 1992).*

In the mid-1920s, the Stuyvesant Casino, located at the corner of 8th Street and Second Avenue, flourished as New York City's most famous kosher catering palace. Owned and operated by Gerson Schmidt, an immigrant from Galicia, the Stuyvesant offered sumptuous food, dazzling decor, and a first-class house band. The band consisted of the three Perelmuth brothers—Pinchas, Michoyl, and Sender—who played, respectively, violin, piano, and bass. The boys' father, the Stuyvesant's head waiter, had encouraged his good friend Schmidt to employ the lads. From their first performance, the three Perelmuths were a hit, especially Pinchas, the violinist, who could also sing. Moreover, Pinchas was enamored of Gershon's daughter, whom he "chased around the restaurant between sets." Young Miss Schmidt would have nothing to do with him. "He's short and can't see," she told her father, who thought that maybe the two might make a fine couple.

One night there was a huge gathering at the Stuyvesant Casino. One of the partygoers, Samuel L. "Roxie" Rothafel (of movie theater fame) fell in love with the voice of Gershon Schmidt's young singer. During the break, he approached Pinchas Perelmuth and asked him why, with such a wonderful voice, he was singing in a mere catering hall. "I would love to be an opera singer," the young man told the impresario, "but don't have the money for a vocal coach." Then and there, Roxie decided to take Pinchas under his wing and see that he got a break. Over the next several years, with Roxie's financial backing, Pinchas Perelmuth studied voice and started making his name known among the opera cognoscenti of New York. When he made his debut at the Metropolitan Opera in 1933, he stepped on stage with a new name; Pinchas Perelmuth had become Jan Peerce. By that time, young Miss Schmidt had married her father's "chauffeur"

(actually his cab driver), Sydney. In later years, whenever anyone in the Schmidt family was short of funds, they would remark, "If not for a quirk of fate, we would all have a rich relative from whom we could borrow."

In addition to the Miss Schmidt mentioned above, Gerson had a son named Mordechai ("Moti"), who married Myra Bank, the daughter of Galician immigrants. They were the parents of Lawrence "Larry" Smith, five-term Congressman from Florida's Sixteenth Congressional District. Thanks to their business involvements, he grew up as a product of the New York kosher catering scene. "From the time I was old enough to even be able to recollect anything, I was working in that business," he recalls. His parents ran catering establishments up until they retired to Florida in the late 1960s.

Larry Smith was born in the Brighton Beach section of Brooklyn on April 25, 1941. In 1942, Mordechai Schmidt was drafted. Before he shipped out, he changed his name to Martin Smith because "he didn't want to go fight the Germans with the name 'Schmidt.'" When Larry was eight, the family (now including his younger sister Helen) moved out to the "wilds of Long Island," where Moti had purchased a tract home in East Meadow. Larry remembers that when friends asked his father why he had moved so far away from the Stuyvesant, Moti would respond: "It's faster for me to drive from New York to East Meadow and pull up in my driveway than to drive home to Brighton and to drive around for two hours looking for a parking space."

As a child, Larry worked weekends at the Stuyvesant Casino. One of the establishment's endearing characters was Gershon's second wife (his first had died in giving birth to Moti), Tillie. Smith remembers her as being "full of spit and fire. She smoked like a chimney. She used to sit in the kitchen between parties and play cards with the waiters, taking back the money they had earned." Eventually, Moti and Myra opened up a new kosher catering hall on Long Island, the Tivoli Terrace.

Despite the fact that the family had long earned its living serving the kosher community, the Smiths were Reform Jews. Moti and Myra were founders of East Meadow's first synagogue, the Reform Temple Emanuel, at which Larry was bar mitzvah in 1954. As a teenager, Larry became involved in United Synagogue Youth, the youth division of the Conservative movement. During his college years, both as an undergraduate at New York University and then as a law student at the Brooklyn School of Law, Larry Smith worked for the United Synagogue—first as a field worker for Nassau and Suffolk County, and then as the youth director at the Westbury Jewish Center.

In 1962, while still a student, Larry married Sheila Cohen. Upon returning from their honeymoon, they learned that Larry's sister, Helen, had eloped with the bartender from the Tivoli Terrace, Chip Russo. After living many years in Las Vegas, the Russos moved to Sunrise, Florida, where they currently reside, close to Larry and Sheila Smith.

Following his graduation from law school, Smith went into private practice and became involved in local Democratic Party activities. Moving out to Great Neck, Long Island, he joined the Nassau County Democratic Executive Committee, became a zone leader, and eventually managed a friend's campaign for the New York State Assembly. All the while, he continued working weekends at the Tivoli Terrace. By the late 1960s, tiring of the law ("The courts were archaic, the buildings were archaic, and all the lawyers hated each other"), Larry and Sheila Smith and their children, Grant and Lauren, moved to Hallendale, Florida, where Moti and Myra were already living. While studying for the Florida bar, Smith, never far from the catering scene, made a deal to take over the food and snack concessions at the Sheraton Hotel on 194th and Collins—in those days the last hotel on "the strip." In 1972, Smith passed the Florida Bar, and became an associate with a firm in Hollywood.

Smith soon became involved in communal affairs. He and his wife helped found Temple Solel, a Reform synagogue, on whose board he has served for many years. He also became president of the South Broward County Bar Association and chairman of the Planning and Zoning Commission. In 1978, when a local state assembly seat opened up, Smith was urged to run. Strongly backed by both the legal and business community, he was easily elected. In those days, the Florida legislature was run and controlled by a group of conservative rednecks known as the "Pork Chop Hill Gang." There were fewer than a dozen Jews in Tallahassee, and certainly none as brash, aggressive, or "New York" as Larry Smith. Many predicted that he would soon run into trouble with the good old boys from the Florida Panhandle. Such was not the case. Smith made it a point to have breakfast with members of the gang at least once a week. Soon, their fears, suspicions, and reticence abated, and he found himself generally well accepted.

During his four years in the Florida House, Smith chaired the Committee on Criminal Justice, delivered that body's first-ever invocation in Hebrew, and hosted the legislature's first Passover seder. According to Smith, his proudest achievement was in getting the legislature to unanimously agree to the creation of a Holocaust Memorial Remembrance Day. Smith recalls that the first-such Remembrance Day was scheduled in the midst of a highly acrimonious floor debate. Many doubted that the House members were in any mood to listen to the invited speakers—Holocaust survivors. As Smith recalls: "When the first speaker began telling his tale, you could have heard a pin drop. It really opened their eyes and hearts to a horrifying reality. From that point on, the rest of the day's debate was much more subdued and civil."

The 1980 census added a new Congressional District to South Florida. Divided between southern Broward and northern Dade Counties, the Sixteenth Congressional District had vast numbers of transplanted New York retirees, many of whom were Jewish. Larry Smith, campaigning in the condo-communities of Broward County on the issues of crime, increased support for Israel, and continuing pressure on Castro's Cuba, swamped his Republican opponent, attorney Maurice Berkowitz by more than two-to-one. Smith took 72 percent of the Broward vote, but a mere 1,000-vote majority in Dade.

Larry Smith, who went on to serve five terms in the House of Representatives, was a classic liberal. Imbued with the spirit of such Democratic stalwarts as Wilson, FDR, and Kennedy, Smith's political philosophy was both simple and straightforward: "I always believed that it was government that could perform the things that needed to be performed. I never really had a great belief that private industry was the engine for social welfare or social change, or social equality in this country. I always believed it was the government that could do it."

In the House, Smith was originally assigned to the Select Committee on Narcotics Abuse and Control, Foreign Affairs, and Judiciary. From this latter post, Smith achieved his greatest success. Long concerned with the startling number of deaths and injuries caused by the drug Quaalude, Smith wrote and passed legislation which first made it a schedule I drug, and then took it completely off the market. As a result of Smith's measure, Quaalude deaths in the United States have gone down to virtually zero. Speaking of that accomplishment, Smith said: "Legislatively, that's something you dream about—that you do something that actually translates into a reality that you wanted to happen."

On Foreign Affairs, Smith lobbied for and received a seat on the subcommittee on Europe and the Middle East, where he could "continue the fight for a strong ongoing relationship between America and the State of Israel." During his tenure, Smith was well-known for his forthright and unyielding support of Israel. Smith led the opposition to the sale of advanced weapons to Jordan and Saudi Arabia "so aggressively that the proposals were dropped." The vehemence with which he supported Israel's security and economic well-being found strong support among his constituents, a sizable proportion of whom were strongly Zionist.

In his last term (1990–92), Smith left Foreign Affairs when a seat on the Appropriations Committee came open. He was assigned to the subcommittee on Foreign Operations, Export Financing, and Related Programs. He garnered national coverage in 1992 when, on February 24, he angrily took on Secretary of State James Baker over the issue of American loan guarantees to Israel. Testifying before the Foreign Operations subcommittee, chaired by Wisconsin's David Obey, Secretary Baker issued a "blunt warning" that unless Israel stopped building Jewish settlements in the administered territories, it would not get $10 billion in U.S.-backed loan guarantees. (The proposed loan was meant to help resettle hundreds of thousands of Jewish immigrants from the former Soviet Union).

"The choice is Israel's," Baker declared. "This administration is ready to support loan guarantees for absorption assistance to Israel . . . provided though there is a halt or end to settlements activity. From our standpoint, it's up to Israel." At this point, Smith angrily broke in.

Smith: "I don't hear anybody saying to the Arab states 'Well we're not going to broker any peace negotiations unless you stop the boycott.' . . . You talk now about loan guarantees and about having a decision made . . . that unless Israel freezes the settlements, they will not get the 2 billion dollars [per year for five years] . . . but I hear nothing about the Arab states."

Baker: ". . . Nobody else is asking us for 10 billion dollars in additional assistance over and above the 3 to 4 billion dollars that we give every year with no strings attached."

Smith: [simultaneously: "Mr. Secretary, they're not asking for a dime in additional assistance.] You know they are not asking for any assistance."

Chairman Obey: "Please finish your answer very shortly . . ."

Baker: "Well, I think I've probably finished the answer anyway."

Smith: "Mr. Secretary, Mr. Chairman, point of personal privilege. You know, you've done that before Mr. Secretary, and I find it extremely offensive. I didn't ask you anything confrontational personally, this is all on policy, and for you not to finish the answer is another attempt to try to reject any kind of significant intrusion."

Baker: [interrupting] "No Larry, I think I finished the answer."

Smith: [interrupting] "Well, sir, you did not finish the answer. Basically the same way you want to deal with this subject . . ."

Baker: [interrupting] "I finished it as far as I was concerned and I will determine when I've finished my answers and not you."

Smith: [slamming down his glasses on the table] "I hope someday the American public is going to determine whether you've finished the answer or not. Disgraceful."

Speaking with the press after this heated exchange, Smith said: "Baker threw down an ultimatum to the Israelis: either you stop building the settlements or you don't get the $2 billion first installment. The Israelis are damned if they do and damned if they don't, because President

Bush knows that [Prime Minister Yitzhak] Shamir is in a bind. I believe they [Bush and Baker] are angling to put Shamir in a bad light . . . . Baker never likes to be cross-examined. He is flip and disingenuous."

Larry Smith was regularly reelected by large margins. In his last campaign, he was unopposed. In the fall of 1992, faced with 161 overdrafts on the House bank and questions about a possible diversion of campaign funds for personal use (for which he was eventually convicted, disbarred, and served a brief prison sentence), Larry Smith decided to retire. In any event, had he chosen to run, it would have been in a new district, where he would likely have had to run against the longtime House Foreign Affairs chairman, Dante Fascell.

Smith continues to reside in Hollywood, Florida, where he has had his right to practice law restored. He is an active lobbyist on behalf of many municipal groups, including the powerful Broward County Board of Supervisors. Despite his former legal problems, he is still well thought of by his former constituents, who remember his passion, his forthrightness, and his family's famous meals.

References
Interview with Larry Smith, April 1992.
Almanac of American Politics, 1986–1994.
Congressional Quarterly, February 29, 1992.
Washington Post, February 25, 1992.

SOLARZ, STEPHEN JOSHUA (1940–): *Democrat from New York; served nine terms in the House (Ninety-fourth through One Hundred and Second Congress, January 3, 1975–January 2, 1993).*

At the time of their marriage in February, 1967, Stephen and Nina Solarz had an understanding: he would "take care of the little problems like what to do about the future of the country," and she would "take care of the big problems like paying the mortgage and where the kids went to school." For the next thirty years, they stuck by their agreement. Solarz went on to become one of Congress's leading movers and shakers in foreign affairs; Nina saw to the family checkbook. Many political observers feel that if only Representative Solarz had paid a bit more attention to the "big problems like paying the mortgage" he might have one day become Secretary of State in a Democratic administration. The sad truth is, that while Stephen Solarz, Representative from New York's Thirteenth Congressional District could name "seven political parties in Turkey," Stephen Solarz the husband and family man had no idea that his wife was bouncing checks at the rate of more than $15,000 a month.

Stephen Joshua Solarz, the son of Sanford and Ruth (Fertig) Solarz, was born in New York City on September 12, 1940. Sanford Solarz was an attorney and Tammany Hall captain. Steve Solarz's parents divorced soon after his birth, and he was raised first by his father, who remarried and divorced again, and then by a widowed aunt who had two sons of her own. Solarz was educated in the New York public school system. By the time he entered junior high school, he was already involved in student government. Upon graduating from Midwood High School in 1958, he entered Brandeis University in Waltham, Massachusetts. While there, he edited the school paper and became interested in foreign affairs. Solarz received a B.A. from Brandeis in 1962 and promptly enrolled in the Columbia University School of Law.

Finding legal studies uninteresting, he entered the Columbia University Graduate School, where he became a student of public law and government under the tutelage of future Secretary of State Zbigniew Brzezinski. Over the next five years (1962–67), Solarz's career path was, for all intents and purposes, set: he would earn a Ph.D. and then become a professor of government and political science. During his graduate school years he worked as a journalist, serving first as Max Lerner's assistant at the *New York Post,* and then as national news editor of a now-defunct monthly called *Newsfront.* He also served a short stint as associate editor of *Greater Philadelphia.*

In 1967, while still ostensibly working toward his doctorate at Columbia, Solarz managed the congressional campaign of anti-Vietnam activist Mel Dubin in a special election to replace Democrat *Abraham Multer,* who had received a judgeship. Dubin lost the primary to long-time New York Assemblyman *Bertram Podell,* who ran as a "100 percent supporter" of Lyndon Johnson's Vietnam policy. Shortly after Dubin's defeat, Solarz received an M.A. from Columbia and started teaching political science at Brooklyn College. One plus came out of his work in the Dubin campaign: he met his future wife, Nina Koldin, a divorced mother of two, whom he married on February 5, 1967.

In 1968, Solarz defeated Max M. Turchin, a fifteen-term incumbent in the New York State Assembly. The senior member of the state Assembly (he was first elected in 1937), Turchin chaired the powerful Judiciary Committee. Solarz defeated Turchin in the Democratic primary by a vote of 7,224 to 5,410, and then went on to capture sixty-six percent of the vote in the November general election. The Forty-fifth Assembly seat was his. His candidacy was given a tremendous boost when he was endorsed by the *New York Times.* During his first term in the Assembly, Solarz "attacked the New York City subway system, urging the dismissal of

Metropolitan Transit Authority Chairman William J. Ronan." Solarz, who from his earliest days in politics had a flair for quotes and sound bites, referred to the MTA as the "Black Hole of Calcutta." Not content to ride this one issue, Solarz also fought job discrimination against former heroin addicts in the city's methadone program, and championed both homosexual rights and prison reform. His emerging interest in foreign affairs led him to call on Governor Nelson A. Rockefeller to convene a special legislative session "to consider a statewide referendum on United States military involvement in Vietnam." Solarz was easily reelected in both 1970 and 1972.

By 1973, Stephen Solarz was frustrated being a junior member of the minority party. "All you can do," he remarked, "is make speeches and not have any impact on anything." Always adept at garnering publicity, Solarz hosted a television program called *Spotlight on Albany*, which was designed to "inform viewers of legislative accomplishments." As Solarz's frustration grew, he sought new challenges. In 1973, he unsuccessfully sought the Democratic nomination for Brooklyn borough president. One of the volunteers in that abortive campaign was a twenty-three-year-old, third-year law student at Harvard named *Charles Schumer*. Over the next two decades, the two Brooklyn-bred politicos would become both colleagues and rivals. In a 1991 *New York Times* article, Nina Solarz compared the rivalry between them to the scene in Chaplin's *Great Dictator* in which two dictators (played by Charles Chaplin and Jack Oakie) "find themselves next to each other in a barbershop, and each tries to crank his chair higher than the other guy's." When Steve Solarz was elected to the House of Representatives in 1974, Chuck Schumer took over his seat in the New York State Assembly.

Until 1993, when it was redistricted out of existence, New York's Thirteenth Congressional District was "the most heavily Jewish in the nation." As originally laid out, the Thirteenth District took in terrain on both sides of Ocean Parkway along its route from Prospect Park to Coney Island. It included the Jewish enclave of Brighton Beach as well as Sheepshead Bay. At one point, the Thirteenth was one of the country's few Jewish majority districts and contained "the highest proportion of immigrants from Communist Russia." It was also long the province of Jewish machine Democrats.

From 1945 to 1947, the district was represented by *Leo Rayfiel*, who resigned his seat upon being appointed a judge of the United States District Court. His spot was then held for the next twenty years by *Abraham Multer*, who, like his predecessor, left Congress for the bench. Multer's successor, *Bertram Podell*, saw his congressional career end in 1974, not as a jurist, but as a defendant. Podell had been indicted for "taking $41,000 to get the Civil Aeronautics Board to award a Bahamas route to a Florida airline." Podell claimed that the charge was bogus—a bald-faced "plot by the Nixon administration to discredit his attacks on Watergate." Sensing that the pending charges against Podell made him vulnerable, Solarz entered the Democratic primary as an insurgent. He beat the Democratic machine, capturing 44 percent of the vote to Podell's 34 percent and Robert Chira's 22 percent. In the Thirteenth, whoever won the Democratic primary was assured victory in the general election. At age thirty-four, Stephen Solarz was a member of the Watergate class in Congress.

As a member of the Ninety-fourth Congress, Stephen Solarz fought for, and received, a seat on the House Committee on Foreign Affairs. He was also assigned to Merchant Marine and Fisheries, and the Joint Economic Committee. In later years, he would serve, as well, on the House Budget Committee, and the Permanent Select Committee on Intelligence. From his first weeks in Congress however, it was readily apparent that Stephen Solarz intended to make a name for himself in foreign affairs. In his first six months, Solarz made twelve speeches, co-sponsored 370 bills, and made an eighteen-day tour of the Middle East. By the end of his first term, he had conferred with—

Secretary of State Henry Kissinger,
Israeli Prime Minister Yitzhak Rabin,
President Helmut Schmidt of West Germany,
Egyptian President Anwar el-Sadat,
King Hussein of Jordan,
President Hafez el-Assad of Libya, and
Zimbabwe African National Union officials Robert Mugabe and Edgar Tekeri.

Steve Solarz was regularly reelected by the voters of the Thirteenth District by margins of 80 percent and more. With a secure seat, he could easily focus on those "little problems" like how to run the world. A Solarz staff member once remarked: "Steve is only interested in two things: Brooklyn and the rest of the world." By 1979, he was chairman of the Foreign Affairs Subcommittee on Africa. From that post, he became a leading critic of the Muzorewa regime in Zimbabwe-Rhodesia, and a supporter of the process that brought Robert Mugabe to power. Solarz became the chief architect of the legislation which led to the settlement of the Zimbabwean civil war and the transition to black rule.

In 1981, Solarz, coming off yet another lopsided victory, had his pick of Foreign Affairs subcommittees. Forsaking his chairmanship of the Africa subcommittee, Solarz lobbied for, and received, the top post on the Subcommittee on Asian and Pacific Affairs. From that post, Solarz became intimately involved in the dismantling of the Marcos regime in the Philippines. He made innumerable trips to Manila as chairman of the Asia and Pacific Affairs subcommittee. On August 21, 1983, he spent more than two hours with Philippine President Ferdinand Marcos, "suggesting that relations between the U.S. and the Philippines would improve if Marcos' political opponents were given a chance to take part in the 'free' elections scheduled for 1984." The next day, as Solarz was leaving Manila, exiled opposition leader Benigno S. Aquino was making what was supposed to be a triumphant return. Aquino was assassinated as he debarked from his plane. Solarz immediately flew back to Manila for his funeral.

Aquino's widow, Corazon, was elected President of the Philippines in 1986, but Marcos refused to accept defeat. Solarz then took pen in hand and wrote a scorching op-ed piece for the *New York Times*, urging the Reagan administration to "distance itself from the Marcos regime." A rebellion ensued, and President and Mrs. Marcos fled to Hawaii. At that point, Representative Solarz returned to Manila to confer with President Aquino. While at Malacaöang Palace in Manila, he witnessed the discovery of Imelda Marcos's enormous collection of shoes, "symbolic of the fallen regime's excesses." From that point on, Solarz, a hero to the people of the Philippines, doggedly investigated what he termed the Marcos' kleptocracy. In 1988, the *Almanac of American Politics* said: "He deserves much of the credit for the revolution that put Aquino in office."

As Steve Solarz's involvement in foreign affairs increased, so too did his reputation. The editors of the *Almanac of American Politics* called him "one of the most important members of the House on major foreign policy issues. Not often in American politics," they wrote, "do you get a combination of precinct politician and foreign policy scholar." Solarz's involvement in foreign policy issues caused many to conclude that one-day he would become Secretary of State. Among his accomplishments in the field, he—

- was one of the earliest backers of the Afghan rebels, which helped them stymie the Soviets and perhaps made the difference in forcing them out;
- created the plan later adopted by the United Nations Security Council to resolve the civil war in Cambodia;
- co-authored the legislation barring compliance by U.S. firms with the boycott of Israel;
- wrote the law requiring certification of progress on human rights in El Salvador as a condition for further U.S. military aid;
- secured the release of several young Jewish women from Syria to come to live in the United States with other Syrian-Jewish expatriates;
- was the first American government figure to visit North Korea in thirty years, returning with a report that Kim Il Sung, the North Korean dictator, was interested in improving relations with the United States;
- sponsored, along with House Republican Leader Robert Michel, the resolution authorizing President Bush to use force in the Persian Gulf; and
- helped to plan the strategy of the nuclear freeze resolution brought to the House floor in 1983.

Steve Solarz was also an ardent defender of Israel, making sure that the Jewish state received as much foreign aid as possible, and always on the lookout for imbalances or tilts in American foreign policy. "For my constituents," he once told a Congressman from a western state, "getting money for Israel is the equivalent of getting a dam built for yours."

During his long tenure in the House, Stephen Solarz had a continual battle with Republican Congressman Paul Findley of Illinois, "the PLO's chief spokesman on Capitol Hill." In one fairly typical colloquy, Findley stated: "What troubles me are the many signs, not just comments and questions here in this room today, but many signs throughout the country, that the PLO is viewed as nothing but a band of demons bent on killing women and children." While acknowledging that the PLO might have engaged "in some very dreadful acts" in the past, Findley insisted that there was also a "humanitarian side to [its] character. . . . Some of them are to provide health services and educational services for Palestinians."

At that point, Solarz requested the floor. Pointing out that the PLO was "responsible for the murder of women and children as well as athletes and diplomats," he fixed a withering stare at Findley and said: "I think to suggest that the PLO may engage in humanitarian enterprises from time to time is no more relevant than it would be if somebody pointed out that Hitler was kind to dogs and little children."

On the domestic front, Solarz's greatest cause in his latter years was the Religious Freedom Restoration Act. This act sought to overturn a 1990 Supreme Court decision that prohibited exceptions to laws for reasons related to religious practice. As an example, according to the high court's ruling, if a law stated that no one may testify in court or serve on a jury while wearing a hat, no exception could be granted to an Orthodox Jew, for whom keeping the head covered is a religious obligation. Solarz fought hard to see this law enacted. It was finally passed after he had left the House.

For all his growing acclaim, Solarz was beginning to find himself under increasing attack. First came the report that he was the "junket king," having made more trips at taxpayer expense than any other member of Congress. While acknowledging that he made frequent trips abroad, Solarz claimed he had helped to save millions of dollars that would have been "otherwise squandered on boondoggles abroad." Next came a damning article in the

Washington Post detailing how the "foreign policy specialist" had made innumerable trips at the taxpayer's expense for the sole purpose of soliciting campaign funds. Somewhat brazenly, Solarz had solicited funds from Filipino-Americans, Indian-Americans, and Taiwanese-Americans, claiming before each group that he was their champion. In the latter case, accompanied by a camera crew from public television, Solarz had "attended a fund-raiser on the *Queen Mary*, docked at Long Beach, California." With the cameras rolling, the Taiwanese contributed some $15,000 to his campaign war chest.

Stephen Solarz became the fundraising king of the House, often carrying over a post election treasury in excess of $2 million. Some believed this was his way of staving off any and all putative rivals for his seat. Others assumed that he was amassing the funds in case he had to square off against Representative Charles Schumer in a future contested House race. During his last two terms in Congress, Solarz was indeed concerned that he might have to face the widely popular Schumer—himself a force in the House. As early as 1990, it became apparent that with redistricting the two rivals might have to get into a head-to-head competition.

Solarz's ace-in-the-hole was New York State Assembly Speaker Mel Miller, "a Brooklynite determined to preserve Brooklyn districts for both Solarz and Schumer." When Miller was convicted of a crime in late 1991, he was replaced by Saul Weprin of Queens, who simply "didn't care." Solarz found his old district dismantled; his Brighton Beach home base, with its many Russian Jewish immigrants, and the Orthodox community in Borough Park were now tied to Greenwich Village and the West Side of Manhattan. This new district, the Eighth, gave a clear advantage to *Ted Weiss*. Not wishing to run against the equally formidable Weiss, Solarz decided to take his chances in the newly refashioned, largely Hispanic, Twelfth District.

Faced with the already daunting task of running in a district in which he was a largely unknown quantity (the district's boundaries were a "cartographic absurdity" according to the *New Republic*), Solarz was hit with yet another serious challenge: his 743 overdrafts on the House bank. An investigation by the *Village Voice* gleefully calculated that Representative and Mrs. Solarz had "overdrawn an average of

$15,247.33 per month—or $508.24 per day—for more than three years." One of those checks, written in 1990 for $5,000 when the account was overdrawn by about $10,000, became the basis for federal charges. Further investigation showed that at one point Congressman Solarz's wages were actually garnished in order to pay off a $2,285.04 Master Card bill.

In the Twelfth District's Democratic primary, Solarz faced off against no fewer than five Hispanic candidates. The campaign got ugly when he was attacked on all fronts for "being white and running in a Hispanic district." The Reverend Al Sharpton called Solarz "a racist for running at all." Jack Newfield of *Newsday* labeled him an "ethnic arsonist." Perhaps the most incendiary of all was Armando Montano, a Latino voting rights activist, who said: "It is now time for the Jewish community to share with the Latino community, because they can't have everything." On election day, Nydia Velazquez, a former short-term member of the New York City Council and head of Puerto Rico's community affairs office in New York, defeated Solarz 34 percent to 28 percent.

(On February 26, 1997, a panel of three federal judges in Brooklyn overturned the Twelfth District's boundaries and ordered the New York state legislature to redraw its lines by June 30, 1997. In their ruling, the judges found that "the district was drawn primarily to concentrate Hispanic voter clout to elect a Hispanic to Congress." The judges determined that the district's creators had used "a race-based computer program, voter registration lists and surname dictionaries to identify Hispanic voters.").

With his congressional career over, it looked as if Solarz might become Secretary of State in the Clinton administration. When the post failed to materialize, word got out that Solarz was in line to become ambassador to India. Then the roof caved in for the last time: Nina Solarz pleaded guilty to bouncing a check drawn on her husband's House bank account. In reality, she had bounced hundreds of them. To make matters worse, she was also caught stealing money from the American Friends of Turkish Women, a charity that "bought medical equip-

ment to assist women in rural Turkey." Solarz claimed to be totally unaware of his money problems (which seemed unlikely, given that he had been named in lawsuits, warned by the State Department, and had had his wages garnished), and made the statement quoted above about the couple's early understanding concerning little problems and big problems. In June 1995 Nina Solarz received one year's probation (instead of the three sought by the prosecution) and fifty hours of community service (the government had requested 200). The court also imposed a fine of $5,350 plus probation costs.

In a telephone interview with the *Washington Post*, Nina Solarz wept and said: "I had a problem—I'm not saying the House Bank was the cause of my problem. I'm saying the House Bank sort of enabled me to continue with my problem." Court documents showed that at the time of her arrest, she and her husband had a combined income of somewhere between $215,000 and $260,000 a year. In her defense, Nina Solarz noted the high cost of living "the political life—all the gifts, dinners and trips."

Steve and Nina Solarz are the parents of two grown children: Randy and Lisa. They have homes in suburban Virginia and on Fire Island in New York. He is a trustee of Brandeis University and a member of the governing council of the American Jewish Congress. He is also a prolific writer whose articles have appeared in the *New York Times*, the *New Republic*, *Foreign Affairs*, and *Foreign Policy*. As of the beginning of 1997, Stephen Solarz was vice-chairman of the International Crisis Group, a "nongovernmental organization dedicated to helping prevent large-scale, man-made disasters."

References

Almanac of American Politics, 1974–1992.
Current Biography, 1986, pp. 536–539.
Long Island Jewish World, vol. 10, no. 21.
New York Magazine, April 4, 1986, p. 44+.
New York Times, June 19, 1968, 30:5; November 8, 1968, 28:7.
Politics in America, 1980–1992.
Washington Post, June 5, 1995. C. 1:2, 4:1.

SPECTER, ARLEN (1930–): *Republican from Pennsylvania; has served four terms in the Senate (January 3, 1980–present).*

One of the very few Jews to ever seriously contemplate a run for the White House (1995), Arlen Specter has spent a lifetime playing the role of the enigmatic outsider—in his hometown, his adopted state, and his own political party. A forty-year resident of Philadelphia, he still speaks in the peculiar Midwestern drawl of his native Kansas. A Republican in an era when the GOP has become increasingly more conservative in outlook, he has remained unabashedly liberal in matters of social policy. Praised by his admirers as an utterly brilliant and courageous political leader, he is vilified by his detractors as an abrasive grandstander. Although decidedly pro-choice, he is anathema to most politically active women.

Arlen Specter was born on February 12, 1930 in Wichita, Kansas. His parents, Harry and Lillie (Shanin) Specter, were Russian immigrants. Shortly after his birth, the family moved to Russell, Kansas, the same tiny farming community that claims Senator Robert Dole as a native son. At age three, Specter made Ripley's "Believe it or Not" when he was "deputized" by the sheriff of Sedwick County. A studious, disciplined child, young Arlen was a fanatic about baseball statistics.

Following his high school graduation in 1947, Arlen Specter entered the University of Oklahoma but soon transferred to the University of Pennsylvania. After graduating Phi Beta Kappa in 1951, Specter married Joan Lois Levy, with whom he has two sons, Stephen and Shanin. Specter spent the years 1951–53 in the United States Air Force. Returning from military service, he attended Yale Law School, where he edited the law journal. Graduating with his LL.B. in 1956, he moved to Philadelphia, where he spent three years in private practice. In 1959, he was appointed an assistant district attorney. During his four years in that post, he made a name for himself as a tough prosecutor, winning numerous convictions against corrupt Teamsters Union officials.

Following the assassination of President Kennedy on November 22, 1963, Specter resigned from the district attorney's office in order to take a position as an assistant counsel to the Warren Commission, the fact-finding body charged with investigating the assassination. When the commission concluded that a single bullet had killed President Kennedy and wounded Texas Governor John Connally, Specter suddenly found himself the subject of both celebrity and notoriety. He had been the "chief architect and staunch defender of the commission's . . . so-called single bullet theory." Interviewed by *U.S. News & World Report*, Specter said "the evidence is overwhelming that Lee Harvey Oswald was the assassin of President Kennedy." Specter's role in the Warren Commission investigation was later immortalized in filmmaker Oliver Stone's blockbuster movie *Kennedy*.

Following his stint with the Warren Commission, Specter returned to Philadelphia, where he sought the Democratic nomination for district attorney. Rebuffed by the Democratic machine that had controlled Philadelphia politics for more than a generation, Specter accepted the Republicans' offer to become their candidate for the office. Running as a reform candidate with the backing of both the liberal Americans for Democratic Action and moderate Republicans like Governor William W. Scranton and Senator Hugh Scott, Specter pulled off an upset victory over his former boss, Philadelphia District Attorney James C. Crumlish. With his better-than-36,000-vote victory, Specter became the first Republican to capture a citywide Philadelphia election in more than a dozen years.

Arlen Specter spent eight years as district attorney, overseeing more than 250,000 cases. He was a different sort of D.A. than the people of Philadelphia were accustomed to—truculent, pugnacious, and unafraid to take on anyone and everyone—from the mayor to the police commissioner. Following his first year in office, he ran for mayor, losing by a hair to the incumbent, James H. Tate. It was the city's closest mayoral contest in more than thirty years.

Returning to his duties as D.A., Specter gained added notoriety by adopting "an unorthodox method of defusing explosive tensions among rival teenage street gangs by hiring two warring gang leaders to work in a 'consulting capacity' in his office." He also helped restore death-penalty statutes in Pennsylvania and prosecuted innumerable cases involving consumer fraud. He was easily reelected for a second four-year term in 1969. Specter was fast becoming the darling of the Republican Party.

In the early 1970s, smarting from the tangled web of Watergate, Republicans began losing elections in droves. Despite his personal popularity with the people of Philadelphia, Specter fell prey to the anti-Republican trend; he was defeated for reelection in 1973. Following his defeat, he returned to private practice, quickly becoming one of Philadelphia's highest-paid attorneys. Over the next several years he ran unsuccessfully for the Republican nomination for the United States Senate (1976) and Pennsylvania Governor (1978).

In 1980, when Senator Richard S. Schweiker announced his retirement, Specter quickly jumped into the race. This time he emerged victorious, easily defeating former Pittsburgh Mayor Peter F. Flaherty. Specter ran on a mainline Republican platform—lower taxes and reduced federal regulation. Some found it remarkable that a man would leave a $250,000-a-year law practice to take a seat in the United States Senate. Specter's explanation was characteristically straightforward: "You can do a lot more in the U.S. Senate than you can in a Philadelphia skyscraper charging $300 an hour."

Once in the Senate, Specter devoted a tremendous amount of time seeing to the needs of his constituents. As a Jewish Republican elected from a largely non-Jewish, industrial state, he had little choice. Ever the unorthodox, battling district attorney, Specter soon gained a reputation for being one of the Senate's most combative members. As chairman of the Judiciary Committee's subcommittee on Juvenile Justice, Specter held hearings on his "big four" subjects—kids, drugs, sex, and violence. During the hearings, Specter paraded before the cameras such unusual witnesses as "former porno star Linda Lovelace, the children's television host Captain Kangaroo and some of the jurors who had sat in judgment on John Hinckley, the man

convicted of attempting to assassinate President Ronald Reagan." Noted one Specter biographer: "The media loved it, but some of Specter's colleagues in the Senate clearly did not." Many observers wondered just what Linda Lovelace, Captain Kangaroo and a bunch of former jurors had to do with juvenile justice.

When Specter sought to hold hearings on the whereabouts of Dr. Josef Mengele, the Nazi "Angel of Death," Judiciary Committee chair Strom Thurmond refused to offer official committee sanction. Specter persisted, hounding Thurmond until the aged North Carolinian finally relented. Specter held two hearings before Thurmond pulled the plug. When the Pennsylvania Senator couldn't get his chairman's permission for a third set of hearings, he defied Senate custom and held them anyway. Through actions such as these, Specter became one of the least-liked members of the Senate. Undaunted, he continued to hew to an independent line.

During the Reagan years (1980–88), Specter achieved the dubious distinction of voting against the administration more often (upwards of 40 percent) than any other Senate Republican. As a true fiscal conservative, Specter called for cuts in the defense budget and a radical overhaul of such politically sensitive subsidies as farm price supports for tobacco, sugar, and peanuts. As a social and foreign policy liberal, Specter voted against prayer in the public schools, aid to the Nicaraguan Contras, and cuts in funding for abortion. Although his voting record didn't sit well with either the White House or his Republican colleagues in the Senate, the people of Pennsylvania found much to like; Specter was easily reelected for a second term in 1986.

During his second six-year term, Specter remained in the public spotlight through his positions on both the Judiciary Committee and Senate Select Committee on Intelligence. An intrepid interrogator, Specter's pointed questions during the Iran-Contra hearings led him to conclude that the American intelligence establishment was in need of a major overhaul. The one piece of legislation to result from these hearings was a Specter proposal that created an independent CIA inspector general. The bill also provided for "presidential disclosure of covert activities, jail sentences for officials who lie to congressional committees, and a division of the powers of the director of the CIA into two positions: one heading the CIA, the other acting as a presidential adviser."

It was from his position on the Judiciary Committee that Specter first came to the attention of a national audience. In 1987, he was one of the key players in the committee's hearings on President Reagan's nomination of conservative judge Robert H. Bork to sit on the United States Supreme Court. Following several rounds of pointed, incisive questions, Specter, resisting tremendous pressure from both the White House and his Republican colleagues, came out against the Bork nomination. In a statement to the press, Senator Specter explained: "I reluctantly decided to vote against him because I had substantial doubts about what he would do with fundamental minority rights, about equal protection of the law, and freedom of speech."

If the Bork hearings brought the Senator's name before the public, the confirmation hearings for Clarence Thomas made it a household word. During the hearings Specter challenged Anita Hill, a University of Oklahoma Law School professor, about her alleged affair with the Supreme Court nominee. His hard-bitten questioning of the demure Professor Hill caused a cloudburst of invective from some of the most prominent women in America. Notwithstanding his rather liberal positions on most women's issues, Specter became a pariah to many American women.

With the extreme rightward turn of the Republican Party in the post-Reagan/Bush years, Arlen Specter once again went on the offensive. In 1994, he created the Big Tent Political Action Committee, based on his view that "the 'Far Right' represents a danger to the [Republican] party and to America." Outlining the Big Tent's philosophy, Specter wrote: "We believe that the conscience of the individual, not the power of the state, should be paramount on questions such as a woman's right to choose, pray in schools, the teaching of creationism, and other issues recently imposed into the governmental arena. We reject litmus tests, intolerance, bigotry, anti-Semitism and extremism and reaffirm our Party's deep commitment to tolerance, civil rights and the equal protection of the law. . . . We are also working to eliminate the anti-choice plank from the 1996 Republican platform

because this issue of conscience has done more to divide our party than to unite it."

This became, in essence, part of Specter's platform in his run for the White House in 1995. Unable to find a sympathetic audience in the ranks of Republican regulars, and frustrated by an inability to raise significant funding, Specter dropped out of the race late that autumn. Asked whether his being Jewish had anything to do with the negligible, even hostile, reception his candidacy had received, Specter said simply: "No, not at all."

Specter's 1998 race for reelection was as easy and lopsided as 1992 had been difficult and nerve-racking. Drawing William R. Lloyd, a long-time member of the state House of Representatives as his opponent, Specter won by nearly 800,000 votes. Within days of his reelection, Specter published an op-ed piece in the *New York Times* exhorting his Republican colleagues to reconsider their campaign to impeach President Clinton. Rather than pursuing impeachment, Specter reasoned, the Senate should work out a deal with the President: resign from office in exchange for keeping his pension, his freedom and his license to practice law. Specter further argued that if the President refused to resign, he would thereby be liable to criminal prosecution once he left office. Although Specter's article was widely discussed in the media, the White House chose not to issue a response.

A trim man with curly brown hair and what one writer described as "basset hound eyes," Arlen Specter has few hobbies outside of reading (mostly biographies of his fellow Senators) and the game of squash. His wife Joan, who owns a highly successful pie-baking company, was, for many years, a member of the Philadelphia City Council. She was defeated for reelection in November 1995. The Specters are a two-city family; the Senator lives in Georgetown while the Senate is in session, and commutes home to Philadelphia on weekends.

References
Almanac of American Politics, 1982–1998.
Biographical Directory of the United States Congress, 1774–1989, p. 1851.
Current Biography, 1988, pp. 538–542.
New Republic, November 10, 1985.
New York Times, April 8, 1984
Washington Post, May 19, 1985.

SPELLMAN, GLADYS NOON (1918–1988):
Democrat from Maryland; served four terms in the House (Ninety-fourth through Ninety-seventh Congress, January 3, 1975–February 24, 1981).

Even before taking her seat in the Ninety-fourth Congress, Gladys Noon Spellman was hard at work making herself known to the members of the freshman caucus. At their first official meeting, Iowa Democrat Berkley Bedell nominated Spellman for caucus secretary, the traditional woman's post. Spellman had other ideas; when the votes were tallied, the effervescent Maryland freshman had been elected caucus vice chair. To anyone who knew her, it did not come as much of a surprise; such were the political skills of the gentlelady from Maryland. Throughout her nearly eighteen-year career in elective politics, Gladys Spellman had an almost "magical ability to float into a crowded room bubbling with happiness and cheer." For this, she was given the unique sobriquet "Madame Tinkerbell."

Gladys Blossom Noon, the daughter of Henry and Bessie G. Noon, was born in New York City on March 1, 1918. She was educated in the public schools of New York until she reached high school, at which time the family moved to Washington, D.C. There, her father spent the last twenty years of his life running a cooperative grocery store chain. Following her graduation from Roosevelt High School in 1937, Glady entered George Washington University. Prior to completing her undergraduate degree, she married Reuben Spellman, a government employee. Although she never received her bachelor's degree, she continued her education at the graduate school of the United States Department of Agriculture.

In the 1940s, while raising her children Stephen, Richard, and Dana, Spellman became a teacher in the Prince Georges County public school system. Until the early 1960s, Prince Georges County, lying north and east of Washington, was ruled by the sort of Democratic machine found in many small southern communities: "a few old men, one of them perhaps chewing tobacco, who liked to hang out in the dusty courthouse in tiny Upper Marlboro and talk about the old days."

To maintain their hold on county politics, the entrenched leaders needed only for things to remain the same. All that began changing when Washington's population began bursting outside the District of Columbia line in the late 1950s and early 1960s. With the rapid growth of the federal bureaucracy, Prince Georges soon became one of the fastest-growing counties in the nation. During the 1960s alone, its population shot up nearly 70 percent. Prince Georges's old politicos didn't much care for the new suburbanites "who quickly outnumbered their old friends, and the feeling was mutual."

It did not take the newly arrived government workers long to begin exercising their electoral numbers and throw the old-timers out of office. One of the leaders in the insurgent movement to bring about a home-rule charter form of government in the county was Gladys Spellman, who over the years had been active in the PTA and various civic associations. She was elected to the Prince Georges County Board of Commissioners in 1962. Though the reform group was outnumbered three to two during Spellman's first term, she proved to be "a shrewd and pragmatic member of the board."

As an elected official, Gladys Spellman carefully cultivated an "aura of maternal femininity" that "belied her political savvy and shrewd personality." She had a mother-hen quality; that of "a matriarchal crusader who has sacrificed and sweated for her sometimes innocent and often selfish brood, and expects their recognition and devotion in return." Her admirers applauded her as crafty, wise, and indefatigable even though they knew she suffered from "an enormous ego and a grating penchant for grandstanding." One writer noted that her more generous friends and co-workers ranked her "very close to the near perfection with which she credits herself."

With her compulsion for mingling and a strong sense of self, Gladys Spellman was easily reelected to three four-year terms on the County Board of Commissioners. Following her reelection in 1966, she served two years as board chairperson, in effect the head of the county's government. In 1972–73, she served as president of the National Association of Counties.

In 1974, Fifth District Republican Representative Larry Hogan decided to run for Governor of Maryland. (Hogan, first elected in 1968, was the first congressional Republican to publicly announce his support for impeachment proceedings against President Richard M.

Nixon.) While Hogan was chasing his dream of moving to Annapolis, Spellman was running hard in the Democratic primary. Easily nominated with 67 percent of the vote, she went on to defeat conservative Republican John B. Burcham, Jr., in the general election. Burcham, who ran as the candidate of the "Christian community," lost to Spellman 53 percent to 47 percent. Spellman defeated him in a 1978 rematch by an even larger margin—58 percent to 42 percent.

No less than 40 percent of Spellman's congressional district was made up of federal employees—mainly secretaries, clerks, elevator operators, and mid-level professionals. Catering to their needs, she regularly honored one with a "Beautiful Bureaucrat" award in her monthly newsletter. As the voice of so many federal workers, she insisted that, "far from slowing down the wheels of government, [they] are really the people who keep them churning." Spellman received seats on the Banking, Post Office, and Civil Service Committees. During her second term she was named chair of the subcommittee on Compensation and Employee benefits, an important position for one representing so many government workers.

Spellman proved to be an expert at working with "idealistic liberals and more practical minded politicians who did not want to do away utterly with the patronage that is so much a part of Maryland politics." Seeing to the needs of her constituents turned out to be a full-time job. The people of the Fifth District responded well to Spellman's motherly ministrations; not only was she reelected three times by increasingly larger margins, but by the time of her heart attack in 1980, she was widely regarded as the "most popular local politician in Washington's Maryland suburbs."

In late October, 1980, Gladys Spellman attended a children's Halloween party at a mall in Laurel, Maryland. While judging the children's costumes, she collapsed, having suffered a severe heart attack. Although she never regained consciousness, she improved to the point where she could be taken off life support. Although she was totally incapacitated, the people of the Fifth District overwhelmingly reelected her just a few days later. On February 24, 1981, Congress passed House Resolution 80, which removed Gladys Spellman from Congress by reason of physical incapacity. This was the first and only time that Congress had to remove a member for such cause. Spellman's husband Reuben ran for her seat, but he was not nearly the politician his wife had been. He came in second to Maryland Senate president Steny H. Hoyer, now a member of the House Democratic leadership.

Moved to the Hebrew Home in Rockville, Maryland, Spellman remained in a coma until her death nearly eight years later, on June 19, 1988. She was survived by her husband and three children: Richard, Stephen, and Dana (O'Neill) Spellman. Even before her death, Congress honored her by naming a 29-mile stretch of the Baltimore-Washington Parkway in her honor. Gladys Noon Spellman was buried in Arlington National Cemetery.

References

Almanac of American Politics, 1974–1980.

Washington Post, October 27, 1976, B:12; June 20, 1988, A:1.

Women in Congress: 1917–1990 (Washington, D.C.: Office of the Historian, U.S. House of Representatives, 1991), pp. 245–246.

STEIGER, SAM (1929–): *Republican from Arizona; served five terms in the House (Ninetieth through Ninety-fourth Congress, January 3, 1967–January 3, 1977).*

A self-confessed SOB and fiscal fascist who took a "perverse delight in making people mad," Sam Steiger once angered his congressional colleagues by telling radio talk-show Joe Pine that many of them were "usually too drunk to be trusted pushing a wheelbarrow." Rodeo roustabout and rancher, biplane wing-walker, and winner of the Purple Heart, Steiger has long been known as the bad boy and "brashest and fastest lip" in Arizona politics. With his lizard-skin cowboy boots, silver belt buckles, and pearl-buttoned shirts, Steiger was unlike any New York Jew Congress had ever seen. He was also unlike any Jew his coreligionists had ever met: conservative to the core. Says Steiger: "The worst intolerance I ever met as a Jew was from other Jews."

Sam Steiger was born in New York City on March 10, 1929, the only child of Lewis and Rebecca (Klein) Steiger. The American-born Lewis Steiger was a prosperous salesman for clothing manufacturers with a national clientele. Sam was educated in the public schools of New York City and became bar mitzvah in 1942. Of that event he remembers next to nothing: "We never belonged to a synagogue, but somehow I became bar mitzvah. I think I might have studied with four or five other boys, but can't remember where or with whom."

From the time he was a pre-teen, Steiger spent summers at a dude ranch in Arizona. Never terribly comfortable with New York or the East Coast, Steiger decided during these summer treks that someday, somehow, he would become a rancher out west. Steiger received his undergraduate education at Cornell University and Colorado A & M. During his years in Fort Collins (the home of Colorado A & M), Steiger competed in the nation's intercollegiate rodeo program. He spent nearly three years earning a "sporadic living" as a rodeo rider following college. Drafted into the United States Army as a commissioned officer, Steiger was sent to Korea, where he became a tank platoon leader. While on routine patrol, he rescued a group of stranded soldiers. For his efforts, he received both the Silver Star and the Purple Heart. Of the latter citation he says: "It was no big deal; I was just wounded in the arm."

Upon his return from Korea, Steiger settled in an area just north of the then-sparsely populated Prescott, Arizona. "There were so few people there in those days [the mid-1950s] that this one friend's father's phone number was just plain 7." Steiger became a rancher and a horse trader, selling livestock throughout the Southwest. As he recalls, "some of the horses wound up at Corriganville, the movie ranch where all the Westerns were shot."

In the late 1950s, the local Republican Party used Steiger's ranch for a picnic. On the day of the gathering, Steiger, who had heretofore been "totally disinterested in politics," put on a mini-rodeo for the party-goers. Included among them was United States Senator *Barry Goldwater*, who lived in nearby Prescott. After meeting Steiger, Goldwater kept in contact with the young rancher, calling upon him from time to time to discuss public land problems. In 1960, Goldwater convinced the thirty-one-year-old Steiger to run for the Arizona Senate. Steiger won, and was easily reelected in 1962.

In 1965, Sam Steiger went to Vietnam as a correspondent for two Prescott-area newspapers. The following year, he ran for the United States Congress from Arizona's Third District. The heavily Republican district, which spanned the desert expanse from Yuma, just north of the Mexican border, up to the Navajo and Hopi Reservations near the Utah state line, included Prescott, Flagstaff, Phoenix's west side, and "just the wings of the city's small black and Mexican-American ghettoes." In 1960, the Third Congressional District had less than 1,000 Jewish voters out of a combined population in excess of 350,000.

Once in Congress, Steiger settled on a farm in distant Fauquier County, Virginia, thereby giving himself "the longest commute of anyone on the Hill." Assigned to the committees on Government Operations, and Interior and Insular Affairs, Steiger quickly earned a reputation for being one of the most conservative and outspoken members of Congress. He was regularly given a perfect 100 rating by the Americans for Conservative Action, and was among the "Dirty Dozen"—the twelve members of Congress with the worst voting records on environmental issues. For his part, Steiger referred to environmentalists as "green bigots."

Following his much-publicized jibes about his colleagues' alleged drinking habits ("I have never seen them drunk on the floor . . . but I have seen them drunk during the day . . . . Some members [have to] be assisted to their offices during the morning"), Steiger got his comeuppance. Shortly after his appearance on Joe Pine's radio talk show, Steiger put in a bill that would have transferred some 20 acres of federal land in Glendale, Arizona, to the city for recreation purposes. By terms of Steiger's bill, the city would pay the government $35,000. It was a simple measure, something the House routinely passes five days a week as a courtesy to its members.

The bill easily passed the Senate. But when the House Agriculture Committee reported out the bill, it claimed that the parcel was worth anywhere between $140,000 and $200,000 on the open market. In a parliamentary maneuver meant to teach Steiger a lesson, Democratic House Whip Hale Boggs of Louisiana (the late father of ABC reporter Cokie Roberts) called up the bill under "suspension of the rules," meaning that the measure would require a two-thirds vote rather than a simple majority in order to pass. Boggs called for a vote. There immediately arouse in the House chamber a thunderous shout of "NO!" from the Democratic side of the aisle. Steiger called for a roll-call vote. His measure lost 202 to 138.

Wherever Steiger went, controversy seemed to follow. In 1972, he became embroiled in congressional hearings on the involvement of organized crime in professional sports. Going head-to-head with the powerful Jacobs brothers, who headed the Buffalo-based sports conglomerate Emprise, Inc., and owned the NBA Cincinnati Royals, Steiger charged them with racketeering, extortion, bribery, and threats of bodily harm. During the hearings, it was brought out that the Jacobs brothers had hired thugs to wiretap Steiger and get hold of his bank records. They then spread a story that Steiger's divorce records had been sealed because of his suspected involvement with a minor child. Steiger admitted having an operative bug the Jacobses' hotel room in San Diego.

The story played out on the sports pages of the nation's papers for weeks on end. By the time the hearings concluded, Steiger's friend and ally, Pulitzer Prize-winning journalist Don Boles had been assassinated by a bomb placed under his car; both the Chicago White Sox and the Detroit Tigers baseball teams were implicated in receiving large cash payments from the Jacobses; and a host of witnesses, including NBA commissioner Walter Kennedy, baseball commissioner Bowie Kuhn, and entertainer Sammy Davis, Jr., gave testimony.

Shortly after Boles's murder, Steiger went to police headquarters in downtown Phoenix to see if he could be of assistance in the investigation. Headlines in the *Arizona Republican* "gave the false impression that he was a suspect." Four years later, when Steiger ran for United States Senate, his Republican opponent used the old headlines against him. Left out of the charge was the fact that shortly after the headline ran, the newspaper, seeking to offset the damage it had done, endorsed Steiger.

Sam Steiger's 1976 Senate race against fellow Republican John Conlan turned out to be a vicious political brouhaha of epic proportions. Conlan, a two-term Representative from the adjacent Fourth District, was Steiger's antithesis in style. A former Fulbright Scholar and Harvard-educated lawyer who often wore white patent-leather shoes and white socks, Conlan described the difference between them in stark terms: "We are both conservatives, but . . . he uses a meat ax and I use a scalpel." Steiger riposted: "John thinks of himself as a scalpel. I prefer to think of him as a Roto-Rooter."

Conlan's antipathy for his fellow Republican stemmed from Steiger's refusal to endorse his candidacy for the House in 1972. As the Senate primary heated up, Conlan, an evangelical Protestant who headed a "controversial movement called Christian Freedom Foundation," sent out a letter to more than 800 clergymen. In the letter, Conlan asked the preachers, pastors, and reverends to do everything in their power to persuade their parishioners to vote for him because "it sure would be nice to have a man with a clear testimony for Jesus Christ representing Arizona and America." Steiger cried foul, decrying Conlan as "a dangerous man . . . a plastic politician" who was "fanning the fires of anti-Semitism."

Conlan's tactic backfired. A leading Baptist minister denounced Conlan for acting un-Christian, and Senator Goldwater, breaking his long-standing custom of remaining neutral during primaries, endorsed Steiger. Told of

Goldwater's endorsement of Steiger, Conlan quipped: "I don't know what it is with Barry. Maybe it's the pain [from a hip operation]. Maybe it's the drinking he's been doing." Hearing this, Goldwater became livid: "I've had all I can take from this guy. I'd hate to serve in the U.S. Senate with him. He's never been honest in politics." Steiger went on to capture the Republican nomination with a margin of about 10,000 votes out of a record 195,000 cast. It turned out to be a Pyrrhic victory.

In the general election, Sam Steiger faced former Pima County (Tucson) district attorney Dennis DeConcini, the scion of a wealthy, politically connected family. During the campaign, DeConcini, a Catholic, chided the Jewishly non-practicing Steiger for opposing appropriations bills and resolutions in support of Israel. "I may be a fiscal fascist," Steiger retorted, "but I refuse to bear the label of anti-Israel." During the campaign, the B'nai B'rith came out against Steiger, castigating him for not being Jewish enough. Steiger counts the B'nai B'rith's charge as the "most offensive thing I ever encountered in politics. Just because I didn't support every single thing with regard to Israel does not mean that I was anti-Israel. I tell you, I never faced more intolerance for being Jewish than from other Jews. I guess they couldn't get used to the fact that not every Jew is a liberal."

Steiger's chances of victory were severely hampered by all the ill-feelings coming out of the Republican primary. Conlan refused to endorse him. Steiger referred to Conlan's intransigence as a "non-attack position." On election day, DeConcini defeated Steiger by nearly 80,000 votes—a 54 percent to 43 percent margin.

Following his defeat, Steiger went back to cattle ranching—for a while. Following a downturn in the livestock industry, he returned to politics, running for Governor as a Libertarian in 1982. He received a surprising 5 percent of the vote. From 1987 to 1988, Steiger served as an aide on the staff of Arizona Governor Evan Mecham, whose maladroitness and propensity for controversy (he refused to sign the bill making Dr. Martin Luther King's birthday a state holiday) got him impeached and removed from office by the Arizona legislature.

During that time, Sam Steiger had his own legal problems. He was convicted of extortion for "threatening a parole official's job."

Appealing the case, Steiger convinced the appellate court to reverse the lower court's decision on the grounds that "his characteristic bluster [had been] distorted by an anti-Mecham prosecutor."

In 1990, Sam Steiger made a try for the Republican nomination for Governor. His campaign was run on a shoestring; his radio spots were "cut from a Steiger monologue his sons taped in their father's kitchen in Prescott." With no pollster to point him to winning issues, and a dearth of ads, Steiger stumped the state with his own particular brand of political honesty. During the campaign, he made a big issue out of the rapid growth of the state university system; he suggested that many enrollees at the University of Arizona (40,000 students) and Arizona State University (65,000 students) belonged instead in a "beefed up community-college system." A long-time foe of attorneys, Steiger "bashed the bar" at every opportunity. One of his pat phrases during the campaign was about "lawyers leaving Arizona for lack of business, and business coming for lack of lawyers." Steiger wound up coming in fourth in the Republican primary—won by Phoenix developer Fife Symington—some 41,000 votes behind the second-place finisher, former Governor Evan Mecham.

Since his defeat in 1990, Sam Steiger has continued on in Prescott, where he now keeps a few head of cattle and a few horses "just for the fun of it." He hosts a radio talk-show in Phoenix, appears on television, writes a weekly column for the state's second-largest newspaper, and publishes his own monthly newspaper, the *Burro Chronicle*. The paper gets its unusual name from a famous bit of Steiger lore: the time he shot two of his neighbor's "wild burros in the ass" for causing a disturbance on his property.

Sam Steiger is the father of twin boys, Lewis and Gail, born in 1956, and a daughter, Delia Rebecca, born in 1959. He is also the grandfather of Joel, born in 1991. His sons are partners in a documentary film concern called Steiger Brothers. In the early 1990s, they received an award from the Public Broadcasting System for a documentary entitled *Ranch Album*, which ran nationally.

As colorful a character as can be found among the Congressional Minyan, Sam Steiger is the only one who can claim to have been a wing-walker. Years ago, when he was asked to do some promotion for an air show, he found himself strapped to a harness on the wing of a Steerman biplane. "Although it looked pretty foolproof, it was one heck of a wild ride. There's just no way you can practice that sort of thing," he recalled. "I guess it's like practicing bleeding. It can't be done. Believe me, I've never even thought about doing it again."

References

Interview with Sam Steiger, September 1996.

Newsweek, September 16, 1972, pp. 16–17; February 19, 1968, p. 26.

Time, September 20, 1972, pp. 20–21.

Wall Street Journal, June 18, 1990, A:10.

Washington Post, October 13, 1976, A:13.

STONE, RICHARD BERNARD (1928–):
Democrat from Florida; served one term in the Senate
(January 3, 1975–December 31, 1980).

Many American Jews think of Florida as New York's sixth borough—a place filled to overflowing with synagogues, delicatessens, and liberal-minded Democrats. Nothing could be further from the truth. True, South Florida's Dade, Broward, and Palm Beach Counties do contain the nation's third-largest Jewish community. Moreover, these three counties have elected four of Florida's five members of the Congressional Minyan. Nonetheless, when viewed in its totality, Florida is, politically speaking, still far, far south of the Mason-Dixon Line. Viewed in this light, it should come as little surprise that only one practicing Jew has ever been elected to statewide office in the Sunshine State: Senator Richard Bernard "Dick" Stone.

The Schvartzstein (Yiddish for "Blackstone") family, the Senator's paternal ancestors, hailed from Antwerp, Belgium. Like many Belgian Jews, the Schvartzsteins were diamond merchants. Why diamonds? As historian Howard M. Sachar notes in his *History of the Jews in America*: "Safe, portable investments for a perennially insecure people, gems had been a historic Jewish vocation for centuries. Indeed, it was the mass influx of Sephardic Jews to the Low Countries in the sixteenth century that transformed Amsterdam and Antwerp into Europe's pre-eminent diamond centers."

Alfred Schvartzstein, the Senator's father, was born in Antwerp around the turn of the century. When World War I began in 1914, Nathan Schvartzstein, the Senator's grandfather, moved his family to Manhattan. The next year Nathan went to court and had the family name legally changed to "Stone."

Although he still "dabbled" in diamonds, Nathan Stone's true American avocation was construction. Starting out in Manhattan Beach, Nathan worked hard and prospered greatly. His son Alfred, who married New York native Libby Abby in the mid-1920s, likewise, worked in the

family's construction business. Alfred and Libby had four sons: Nathaniel (called "Buddy"), Robert, Ben, and Richard, who was born in New York City on September 22, 1928. Before Dick was six months old, the family had relocated to Miami, where Nathan and his son were building the Blackstone Hotel, one day to become a South Florida landmark.

Dick Stone attended the public schools of Miami up until the time he was ready to enter high school. In 1942, his parents acceded to his wishes and sent him to the Georgia Military College in Milledgeville, Georgia. The genesis of Dick's request was simple: his best friend was going to attend there.

In Miami, the Stone family originally belonged to Beth Jacob, an Orthodox synagogue in Miami Beach. Today, the tiny former shul houses the South Florida Jewish Museum. In the late 1930s, Alfred Stone provided construction expertise for the building of Temple Emanuel, arguably Miami Beach's most prominent and architecturally significant synagogue. Dick Stone became bar mitzvah at Temple Emanuel in 1941. Officiating was the synagogue's newly appointed rabbi, thirty-year-old Irving Lehrman, who would go on to serve the congregation for more than fifty-five years.

Following his graduation from Georgia Military, Dick Stone entered Harvard, from which he earned a B.A. (cum laude) in economics in 1949. Five years later, armed with a law degree from Columbia University, Stone headed back to Miami. There he married Marlene Lois Singer, the daughter of William D. Singer, founder of the Royal Castle restaurant chain. Marlene was born in West Virginia, while her family was in transit from Ohio to Florida. William Singer went on to become a pillar of Florida society. Serving variously as chairman of the Jackson Memorial Hospital Trust and as a founding member of the United Jewish Appeal of South Florida, Singer is today remembered chiefly for a stretch of highway I-95 which bears his name—the William D. Singer Causeway. Dick and Marlene Stone have three children. Nancy, Amy, and Elliott. All three children were bar or bat mitzvah, and attended Hebrew high school.

Once back in Miami, Dick Stone began practicing law, specializing in corporate matters. Within a few years he had worked himself up into a partnership with the firm of Stone, Bittell, Langer, Blass, and Corrigan. Stone prospered and became a millionaire. In 1966, he became city attorney for Miami. The next year he was elected to serve a one-year term in the Florida Senate from Dade County's Forty-eighth District. Running for a full four-year term in 1968, Stone was easily reelected. He barely had time to become accustomed to his new surroundings in Tallahassee, the state capital, before he resigned his seat in order to run for Florida Secretary of State. On November 3, 1970, Stone became the first self-acknowledged Jew to win statewide office in Florida.

As Secretary of State, Stone was vice-chair of the Florida cabinet, presiding over its meetings in the absence of the Governor. A stalwart champion of the Florida Sunhine Law, which mandated that no government business could be transacted away from the public view, Stone's first act upon taking office was to remove the doors to his office and conference room. Admired by the capital press corps for "his policy of seeking solutions, particularly in difficult situations," Stone was dubbed "a bridge over troubled waters"—after a popular Simon and Garfunkle song of the period. One of his best-publicized efforts as Secretary of State involved his vigorous enforcement of the Charitable Solicitations Act. The act "required charities (except bona fide religious groups) to register with the state and, upon demand, submit financial statements." As a result of Stone's enforcement of the Charitable Solicitations Act, the number of charities registered with the state rose from less than 300 in 1971 to over 5,000 in 1974.

On July 8, 1974, Dick Stone resigned in order to devote full time to his race for the United States Senate seat held by Republican Edward J. Gurney. Senator Gurney (1914–1996) had one of Florida's most meteoric political careers. A native of Maine, the Harvard-educated lawyer moved to Winter Park, Florida, in 1948 and was quickly elected to the city commission. In 1962, he was elected to the first of three terms in the House of Representatives. He was elevated to the United States Senate in 1968, taking over the seat of the retiring Senator George ("Gorgeous George") Smathers, a cohort of the late John F. Kennedy.

Gurney's political rise and fall coincided, in great part, with that of the Nixon administration. A staunch conservative, Gurney was Nixon's most vocal ally on the Senate Watergate Committee. Day in, day out, television viewers across the country could see Gurney defending the embattled President, proclaiming both his innocence and the purity of his motives. Shortly after Nixon's resignation in August 1974, Gurney himself took a political fall; he was indicted on bribery charges and declined to run for reelection. (In 1976, Gurney was acquitted on all counts, but was ruined both financially and politically. It is likely, however, that even without his legal problems, he would have been defeated for reelection.).

As noted in the *Almanac of American Politics* (1978 edition), "Gurney's fall happened so quickly that the Republicans hardly had time for a fight for the nomination." After a spirited political encounter, drugstore magnate Jack Eckerd edged out Paula Hawkins, Florida's public service commissioner. (Hawkins would eventually win election to the Senate in 1980.) The Democratic primary featured no fewer than eleven candidates, though only two were truly competitive: Orlando-area Congressman Bill Gunter and Dick Stone.

In the primary's early days, the moderate Gunter was viewed as more "in tune temperamentally with the state's less cosmopolitan areas." By comparison, Dick Stone, Jewish with a Harvard education and a Miami address, was presumed to be a wild-eyed liberal. Stone went out on the campaign trail, "playing the harmonica and spoons . . . on trips in north Florida," trying to come off as just "one of the folks."

His strategy worked. Putting together an "unlikely alliance between condominium dwellers on the Gold Coast and rural Protestants in the northern panhandle," Stone eked out a plurality of 30 percent in the primary, and then defeated Gunter 51 percent to 49 percent in the runoff. Stone's big issue in the runoff was, unbelievably, dead chickens: Representative Gunter had voted for a law, sponsored by Mississippi Senator James Eastland, to "compensate owners of chickens that had died from a rare disease." Stone promulgated the idea that "the government ought not to pay for dead chickens."

The general election was, for 1974, a comparatively costly affair, with Eckerd spending $421,000 to Stone's $920,000. Somewhat unusually for the time, Dick Stone made his personal financial holdings a matter of public record. In doing so he said: "The public has a right to know and we need to do all we can to restore public confidence in government and government officials." He also refused contributions from any business regulated by the Office of the Secretary of State, and did not accept more than $3,000 from any one person; in 1974, Florida State law permitted a maximum personal contribution of $9,000.

Shortly before the November election, Eckerd ran a series of newspaper ads comparing himself to Stone, and noting that Stone was Jewish, whereas he was not. Eckerd's strategy backfired; Stone defeated him 43 percent to 41 percent, with American Independent Party candidate John Grady coming in a distant third at 16 percent. Dick Stone was assigned to the Senate Agriculture, Veterans' Affairs, and Foreign Relations Committees. After he had accumulated a bit of seniority, he was offered the opportunity to chair whichever Foreign Relations subcommittee he wished. His natural inclination was to take the Middle East subcommittee. Before deciding to take the chairmanship, however, he did something unique: he gave the Arabs a chance to veto his appointment.

Stone related the process to a writer from *Jewish Living* magazine in 1979:

> I discussed it [the chairmanship] with Marlene as I do all important career decisions. She felt that in order to be effective in this role, I needed to have some expression of support from the Arab ambassadors in Washington with whom I would have to relate. So I telephoned [Egyptian Ambassador] Ashraf Ghorbal and asked him to survey his colleagues, the Arab ambassadors in Washington, and if they felt I would not be fair, to let me know and I'd think twice about accepting this chairmanship. He did survey his colleagues and did advise me that he and they felt I would be fair. And based on that, I decided to take the chairmanship.

Stone later admitted that he had not anticipated Ambassador Ghorbal's response: "I did not know what he would say when I made the call." Asked what would have happened if the Arab ambassadors had sent back a negative response, Stone answered: "Then I would have had to think twice about it. I wanted to be effective in this role. I wanted to advance the cause of peace and not simply make noise."

While speaking at a $1,000-a-plate fundraiser in Washington in September, 1979, Vice President Walter Mondale called Richard Stone "one of the heroes of the success of Camp David." He offered no explanation for this encomium. According to an article in the April 2, 1979 *New York Magazine*, Stone, working with one of his aides,

> revived a 30 year-old plan to give Palestinian refugees a homeland on the Gaza Strip, rather than on the West Bank. Stone made his proposal in a ten-page letter to [President] Carter before the Camp David summit meeting. . . . Apparently word got back [for] when Senator Henry Jackson visited President Sadat . . . the Egyptian leader . . . mentioned that Gaza was the only solution to the stalemate. This response reached Washington and the Gaza proposal was raised during the president's shuttle diplomacy. And so, on the basis of a staff memo and a 30-year old plan, a compromise was achieved.

When asked if he had truly played such a pivotal role in the breakthrough that led to the peace treaty, Stone merely responded: "I participated."

Richard Stone carved out a mostly moderate and independent voting record. More conservative than the majority of his fellow Democrats, Stone voted against President Carter's nomination of Paul Warnke as U.S.-U.S.S.R. arms negotiator and for development of the neutron bomb. He voted against pardons for Vietnam draft resisters and the funding of abortions, and in favor of the Panama Canal treaties, a move "later felt by many to have been harmful in his reelection bid."

In 1980, Dick Stone lost the Democratic primary to Bill Gunter, who at the time was Florida's commissioner of insurance. Paula Hawkins wound up defeating Gunter (who outspent her $2,165,000 to $696,000). Following his six years in the Senate, Dick Stone remained in Washington, joining the New York law firm of Proskauer, Rose, Goetz, and Mendelsohn. From March 1981 to March 1982, he worked as a registered foreign agent for the governments of Guatemala and Taiwan. In the fall of 1982, he resigned from Proskauer-Rose to become vice-chairman of Capital Bank of Washington and a consultant to the U.S. State Department in the area of public diplomacy.

President Reagan appointed Stone a special envoy to Central America in June 1983. During his seven months in the post, Ambassador Stone sought "a political settlement to the instability in Central America." Moving back and forth between private practice and government service over the next decade, he was appointed ambassador to Denmark by President George Bush in 1990. He left that post after the first year of the Clinton administration.

Since 1996, Dick Stone has been president of the Dart Group Corporation, which owns Crown Books, Trak Auto, Total Beverage, and a 50 percent stake in Shoppers' Food Warehouse. Dick and Marlene Stone live in the Washington area. One of Dick Stone's favorite bits of advice goes: "If you want a long life, take care of your grandmother." By way of explanation he says: "That's in our tradition—take care of your grandmother. What you do for them governs how long and well you will live. I took care of my grandparents. I've had more than my share of luck."

References

Interview with Richard B. Stone, February 1998.
Almanac of American Politics, 1974–1982.
George Douth. *Leaders in Profile: The United States Senate* (New York: Speir & Douth, 1975).
Jewish Living, Summer 1979, pp. 24–27, 56.
New York, April 2, 1979.
Washington Post, December 12, 1995, C1:6.

STRAUS, ISIDOR (1845–1912): *Democrat from New York; served one term in the House (Fifty-third Congress, January 30, 1894–March 3, 1895).*

In Edith Wharton's *The Age of Innocence*, Mrs. Welland and her aunt, the imperious Mrs. Manson Mingott, are discussing the recently announced engagement of Mrs. Welland's daughter May to Newland Archer:

"And when's the wedding to be?" [Mrs. Manson Mingott] broke off, fixing her eyes on Archer's face.

"Oh . . . as soon as ever it can," Mrs. Welland murmured, while the young man, smiling at his betrothed, replied: "As soon as ever it can, if only you'll back me up, Mrs. Mingott."

"We must give them time to get to know each other a little better, aunt Catherine," Mrs. Welland interposed, with the proper affectation of reluctance; to which the ancestress rejoined: "Know each other? Fiddlesticks! Everybody in New York has always known everybody!"

From her point of view, Mrs. Manson Mingott was certainly speaking the truth. The "everybody" to whom she referred was the Four Hundred—that elite group of bluebloods who made up America's "royalty." The same could easily and truthfully be said for the Jewish version of the Four Hundred, America's fabled New York-based German-Jewish elite.

Over the generations, this group has been known by many names: the One Hundred, the Jewish Grand Dukes, and most simply, "Our Crowd." Like European royalty (and their Christian counterparts in America), these Jewish merchant and banking families formed partnerships, alliances, and interlocking directorates through both marriages and mergers. In plain fact, the marriages between the various "Our Crowd" families—Kuhns and Loebs, Guggenheims and Strauses, Goldmans and Sachses, Lehmans and Rothschilds, Warburgs and Schiffs—were as much financial mergers as matters of the heart.

The "Our Crowd" families were leaders in banking and finance, commodities and the arts, department stores, publishing, and philanthropy. Mainline Reform Jews for the most part (belonging almost exclusively to Temple Emanu-el), they were imbued with a natural sense of *noblesse oblige*. Thus they were instrumental in the founding and funding of museums and national organizations (such as the American Jewish Historical Society and the National Council of Christians and Jews), and the underwriting of hospitals, relief agencies, America's nascent space industry, and institutions of higher learning. Some members of "Our Crowd" even found time for occasional forays into the world of government and politics.

Consider but one family, the Strauses. Isidor Straus (1845–1912), the eldest of Lazarus and Sarah (Straus) Straus's three sons, became, upon his election in 1893, the first of three "Our Crowd" members-in-good-standing to serve in the United States Congress. The middle son, Isidor's brother Nathan (1848–1931), was intimately involved in the plight of New York City's poor; he all but single-handedly established an emergency relief system for the distribution of food and coal, and underwrote numerous "bed and breakfast" establishments where the downtrodden could find room and board for as little as a nickel a day. Lazarus and Sarah's youngest son, Oscar Solomon Straus (1850–1926), was the first Jew appointed to a presidential cabinet, serving as Theodore Roosevelt's Secretary of Commerce and Labor. Prior to that, he had been a justice of the International Court of Arbitration at the Hague and President Grover Cleveland's ambassador to Turkey

The Straus family was originally from Otterberg, Bavaria, where the future Congressman, was born on February 6, 1845. As previously mentioned, Isidor and his two brothers, Nathan and Oscar (along with their sister Hermina), were the children of Lazarus and Sarah Straus. Lazarus, the son of Jacob Straus, married his first cousin Sarah, the daughter of Jacob's brother Solomon.

Isidor's great-grandfather, Jacob Lazare, was one of the members of the Great Sanhedrin convened by Napoleon in Paris in 1806. Moreover, great-grandpa Lazare was a member of the nine-man commission that met with the emperor's agents to lay the groundwork for this historic fraud.

The Otterberg Strauses were landowners and members of the middle class. Despite this, Lazarus Straus was devoted to the principles of the German revolution of 1848. Whereas many

Jewish families left Germany immediately upon the collapse of the revolutionary movement, Lazarus remained in the Old World for another four years. In 1852, leaving his wife and children behind, he departed Germany and made the long voyage to America. Settling originally in Philadelphia, he met up with a few of his landsmen, who advised him that his future lay in the South. Taking their advice, he moved to Oglethorpe, Georgia, where he began traveling about the countryside, selling dry-goods and "Yankee notions" to the local planters and plantation owners. Happening upon Talbotton, Georgia, Lazarus was sufficiently impressed with the town to settle there permanently. Opening a store with a line of general merchandise, it wasn't too long before Lazarus was able to send for Sarah and the children. They arrived in New York aboard the steamer *St. Louis* on September 12, 1854.

Upon arriving in Talbotton, the twelve-year-old Isidor was immediately sent to a preparatory school in order to learn enough English to permit admission to a proper school. Isidor attended Collinsworth Institute from 1856 to 1861, at which time he left school in order to assist his father in the family business. After working for his father for a year and a half, Isidor enrolled in the Georgia Military Academy in Marietta, with thoughts of eventually transferring to the U.S. Military Academy at West Point. This plan was quickly dashed when Isidor, subjected to a particularly nasty bout of hazing, withdrew from GMA. Joining the local Talbotton militia, he was elected first lieutenant. The company never saw action in the Civil War, however, for there were simply not enough arms or materiel to equip the young men.

In 1863, an agent for a commercial company that was seeking to purchase a vessel capable of running the Union blockade of Southern ports selected Isidor Straus to be his secretary. The two successfully ran the blockade in June 1863, and eventually wound up in London. Realizing that the plan could not possibly succeed, Straus left the company's employ and traveled to Otterberg for a reunion with his German relatives. Returning to England, he spent the next two years selling Confederate bonds in London and Amsterdam. Having the Amsterdam market to himself, Straus was able to realize a profit of more than 3,000 pounds sterling (about $12,000).

Armed with this small fortune, he returned to America in 1866, meeting up with his father and brothers, who by then had moved to New York City. On June 1, 1866, the firm of L. Straus & Son was established. The company specialized in the merchandising of crockery, china, and glassware. In 1874, the firm (by now renamed L. Straus and Sons) took over the glassware department of R. H. Macy and Company. By 1888, Isidor and his brother Nathan were full partners in Macy's, and soon built it up into the largest department store in the world. The brothers also built up the Brooklyn department store of Abraham and Straus.

In July 1871, Isidor Straus married Ida Blun, who was four years his junior. Once their financial affairs were in order, Straus began evincing an interest in communal and political affairs. His extreme interest in such issues as currency reform and the tariff led him to Washington, where he was a frequent witness before the House Finance Committee. Straus's expertise in banking matters led to his election as a director of the Hanover National Bank.

Isidor Straus was a close friend and supporter of President Cleveland—so much so that he was at one time rumored to be in line for the position of Postmaster General. Cleveland often sought Straus's input on financial and monetary issues. It is likely that Cleveland's continued support of the gold standard was due to Straus's influence. Cleveland called a special session of Congress in August 1893 for the express purpose of repealing the clause in the Sherman Act of 1890 which ordered the Treasury Department to make monthly purchases of silver bullion. Straus's infatuation with the Democrats lasted until the party adopted William Jennings Bryan's Free Silver platform in 1896.

In November 1893, Representative Ashbel P. Fitch left his House seat after being elected comptroller of the city of New York. Isidor Strauss ran for Fitch's vacant seat, easily winning the election. He entered Congress on January 30, 1894, arriving just in time to engage in the heated debate over the Wilson Tariff Reduction Bill. Named after its chief sponsor, West Virginia Representative William Lyne Wilson, an ex-professor of ancient languages and former president of West Virginia University, the measure would have drastically reduced U.S. tariffs. A highly contentious debate insued, during which Maryland Senator Arthur Pue Gorman sought to have many of the proposed cuts—most notably in the case of sugar—restored. The debate reached a head when it was revealed that many Senators were actually speculating in sugar stocks at the very time they were considering a bill to protect sugar refining interests. When queried about the obvious conflict-of-interest involved in such a scheme, one senator—Republican Matthew S. Quay of Pennsylvania—confessed in a defiant statement: "I do not feel that there is anything in my connection with the Senate to interfere with my buying or selling the stock when I please; and I propose to do so." The Wilson Bill eventually passed, albeit with more than 630 Senate-mandated changes. "L'affaire Wilson" led one member of Congress—Alabama Populist Milford Howard—to write a satiric novel, *If Christ Came to Congress*. In the novel, Howard used the image of the Christ to excoriate his congressional colleagues for their excessive venality.

During his single term in Congress, Isidor Straus was an ardent supporter of Senator Nelson Aldrich's currency reform measure, which sought to make commercial paper the basis for the issuance of banknotes. This proposal would eventually be embodied in the Federal Reserve Act through the tireless efforts of another member the German-Jewish elite, Paul M. Warburg.

Straus left Congress after his single term. Although he was urged to run for mayor of New York on two separate occasions (1901 and 1909), he never ran for public office again. For the rest of his life, he devoted his time to communal good works. With the arrival of hundreds of thousands of Eastern European Jews in New York, Strauss became vitally concerned with their welfare. Along with other members of "Our Crowd," he began working for the revamped Educational Alliance. By the time he entered Congress, he was that organization's

president, a post he would hold until the end of his life. Isidor Straus also devoted his time and money to the J. Hood Wright Memorial Hospital, the Montefiore Home, and the American Jewish Committee, of which he was a founding member.

On April 14, 1912, Isidor and Ida Straus were passengers on the *Titanic*'s ill-fated maiden voyage. According to eyewitness accounts, Mrs. Straus refused to get into any of the lifeboats provided for the women and children. As one report stated, "[she] declined to be separated from her companion of forty years, so the aged couple went down with the ship."

The Straus family's involvement in politics and governance did not end with the sinking of the *Titanic*, but continued on into future generations. Isidor's son, Jesse Isidor Straus (1872–1936), raised untold millions of dollars for the Democratic National Committee and served as FDR's first ambassador to France. Nathan's son, Nathan, Jr. (1889–1961), was twice elected to the New York State Senate and for six years headed up the Depression-era U.S. Housing Authority. Oscar's son, Robert Williams (1893–1957), served as vice-chairman of the Republican National Committee. Oscar's grandson, Oscar II (1914–), was for many years a high-ranking member of the U.S. State Department. Oscar II's brother, Robert Williams, Jr. (1917–), went into publishing and in 1945 founded Farrar, Straus, and Company, known today as Farrar, Straus and Giroux.

References

American Hebrew and Jewish Messenger, April 26, 1914.
Dictionary of American Biography.
Jewish-American Hall of Fame: News (Internet).
New York Times, April 15–21, 1914.
Publications of the American Jewish Historical Society 22 (1914): 235–239.
Universal Jewish Encyclopedia.

STROUSE, MYER (MEYER STRAUSS) (1825–1877): *Democrat from Pennsylvania; served two terms in the House (Thirty-eighth and Thirty-ninth Congress, March 4, 1863–March 3, 1867).*

Only one member of the Congressional Minyan served on Capitol Hill during the Civil War. That man was Representative Myer Strouse, from Pennsylvania. Precious little is known about Strouse's private life. Originally named Meyer Strauss, he was born in Oberstrau, Bavaria, on December 16, 1825. He immigrated to the United States at age seven in 1832 with his father (who may or may not have left his wife behind). They settled in Pottsville, Schuylkill County, Pennsylvania, where he was most likely educated in the local Pottsville schools. As a young man, he moved to Philadelphia, where he spent four years (1848–1852) as editor-in chief of a paper called the *North American Farmer*. At his death, a childhood friend, a colleague, and political opponent named Howell Fisher, Esq., intimated that Strouse had a financial stake in the paper. If so, he did not come out on top. Said Fisher: "Had he launched his enterprise in more modern times, [he] would not only have been successful financially, but would have made his mark in the world as an able writer."

Returning to Pottsville in 1852 or '53, Strouse read law in the offices of Benjamin Cummings, and was duly admitted to the Pennsylvania bar in 1855. Within five years, he had become a leading member of the local bar and the possessor of a highly lucrative practice. As the aforementioned Fisher stated in a eulogy to the Pottsville Bar Association, "There are few among us who attain such rapid success in the profession as he did."

Strouse's reputation as "a representative German American and a general favorite" led to his receiving the Democratic nomination for Congress in 1862. Howell Fisher ran on the Republican ticket. Said Fisher of the campaign, "Though political feeling ran high and was very bitter . . . I can say that he conducted himself throughout as a gentleman and acted fairly." Strouse carried the Tenth Congressional District, capturing a comfortable 56.2 percent of the vote. He was reelected in 1862, winning by nearly the same margin as in his initial victory.

While in Congress, Strouse was seated on fairly pedestrian committees: Roads and Canals, Territories, Expenses, and Mines and Mining. The latter was quite important to the Tenth

District, where coal mining provided most of the employment and nearly all the native wealth. While in Congress, Strouse devoted his energies almost exclusively to the needs of his constituents—most notably those waging war on behalf of the United States against the Confederacy. Popular both at home and on Capitol Hill, Strouse surprised everyone when he announced that he would not run for reelection in 1866.

Why Meyer Strouse made this decision is uncertain, although one can make an educated guess. Up until the early 1860s, the ethnic make-up of Schuylkill and Lebanon Counties was largely German. Strouse, perceived by his constituents as a German-American rather than as a German Jew, was a favorite at the ballot box. By the mid 1860s, however, there were the beginnings of a vast infusion of Welsh and Irish immigrants, brought over to work in the area's numerous coal mines. It is reasonable to assume that this dramatic shift in his district's ethnicity is what caused Strouse to leave the Congress.

Strouse resumed the practice of law in the Pottsville area, garnering even greater fame and fortune. His was a general practice that ran the gamut from criminal to real estate law. In 1868, Meyer Strouse participated in a criminal case that would almost undo all the public goodwill he had cultivated over the past decade: the murder of one Alexander Rea. Both the *Biographical Directory of the United States Congress* and the *Encyclopaedia Judaica* make reference to his having "in 1876–1877 defended the notorious miners' organization, the Molly Maguires." This is not precisely the case.

The group known as the Molly Maguires was a violent, terrorist-oriented labor organization that operated in the coal-mining region of Pennsylvania and West Virginia during the late 1850s and early 1860s. Originally a secret society formed in Ireland in 1843, during the time of the potato famine, its initial purpose was to frighten rent collectors, landlords, and others who oppressed the impoverished of the Emerald Isle. The society was purportedly named for a widow who had been killed because she was unable to pay her rent.

The Molly Maguire organization was brought to the United States along with the wave of Irish immigrants who made their way to coal country in the 1850s and '60s. Its members soon began waging a war of terror and sabotage against the mine owners, who were subjecting their workers to terribly dangerous working conditions. Mines were notoriously unsafe, and the owners cared little about the fate of individual miners or their families. Additionally, the owners ran company towns and company stores that turned miner families into nothing more than indentured servants. A poem of the time expresses the miners' plight:

> Only a man in overalls, lay him anywhere—
> Send for the company doctor—we have no time to spare.
> Only a little misfire, only a miner crushed,
> Put another one on, for from dawn till dark
> The smelter must be rushed.

Starting in 1865, the Molly Maguires moved from the suborning of labor unrest against ruthless mine owners to outright criminal violence. Included in their arsenal were acts of robbery, arson, and even murder. In an attempt to stop the Molly Maguires, the mine owners brought in a Pinkerton agent, James McParlan, who successfully infiltrated the group and gathered sufficient evidence to have its ringleaders arrested on a charge of murder in the first degree. McParlan's charges led to a series of sensational trials in 1875–1877. Found guilty, the leaders of the Molly Maguires were hanged. English author Sir Arthur Conan Doyle used the Molly Maguires as the basis for *The Valley of Fear*, one of the early Sherlock Holmes mysteries. Contrary to popular belief, these were not the trials in which Myer Strouse participated.

In 1868, Myer Strouse was one of five attorneys representing a defendant named Thomas Donohue in *Commonwealth* vs. *Donohue, Hester, Prior and Duffy*. This was one of the earliest trials involving members of the Molly Maguires. Strouse's role in the trial was minimal; he made a one-hour opening statement on behalf of Donohue, who was eventually found guilty and hanged. Strouse did not participate in the more infamous Molly Maguire trials, which would not take place for another seven years. Nonetheless,

his local reputation suffered as a result of his participation in the defense of Donohue, and over the years his name became linked with the more notorious trials of the mid-1870s. This was simply not the case, for by 1875, Myer Strouse was dangerously ill.

Myer Strouse had a long, lingering illness (presumably cancer) to which he succumbed on February 11, 1878. The local bar association convened to remember their former colleague. Although their sentiments were both warm and effusive, one senses an underlying tone of regret or melancholy—and not just because a colleague had died.

Strouse's remains were laid out in the living room of his home on Second Street. He wasn't buried until three days after his death—the fourteenth of February. The funeral ceremony, which took place at the Odd Fellows cemetery, was performed by two non-Jewish clergymen: Rev. Hinterleiter of the German Reform Church, and the Rev. Dr. Cron of the English Lutheran Church. Nowhere in his obituary did it mention that Myer Strouse, né Strauss, was a Jew.

In his will, Myer Strouse requested his wife Catherine to "bring up our children, by us begotten, in the fear and love of God, and take the same care of them after my death as if I were living." Nowhere does the will mention "the fear and love of God" as understood by people of the Jewish faith. One may speculate that Strouse had converted to Christianity; no proof exists to sustain this claim.

References

American Jewish Year Book, vol. 2, pp. 523–524.
Daily Miner's Journal (Pottsville, Pa.), February 12, 13, 15, 1875.
Jewish Encyclopedia.
New York Times, February 12, 1878, 5:3.
Universal Jewish Encyclopedia.

The author wishes to thank Professors George A. Turner and Gerald H. Strauss of Bloomsburg University for their assistance in tracking down biographical data on Myer Strouse.

TELLER, LUDWIG (1911–1965): *Democrat from New York; served two terms in the House (Eighty-fifth and Eighty-sixth Congress; January 3, 1957–January 3, 1961).*

The son of Morris and Rose (Smolov) Teller, Ludwig Teller was born in New York City on June 22, 1911. Educated in the city's public school system, Ludwig entered New York University shortly after the stock market crash of 1929. During his years at NYU, Teller earned an A.B. (1936), LL.B. (1935), LL.M. (1937), and J.S.D. (1939). In December 1938, he married Clarice Hilda Schlesinger. The couple, who resided at 320 Central Park West, were childless.

Admitted to the New York bar in 1936, Teller, a "small, imperturbable, bookish" legal scholar, gravitated toward a specialty in labor relations law. By the early 1940s, he was serving as an expert consultant to the Labor Relations Board at the United States War Department. Enlisting in the United States Navy, Teller rose to become a lieutenant (senior grade) assigned as labor relations officer for the Ninth Naval District, headquartered in Chicago. At war's end, Teller joined his alma mater's law faculty, where he taught from 1947 to 1963. During his last five years at NYU, he chaired the graduate faculties for advanced degrees in law.

As Tammany Hall leader of the Fifth Assembly District South, Teller was elected to the New York State Assembly in 1950. He was easily reelected in 1952 and 1954. Not surprisingly, Assemblyman Teller specialized in legislation affecting labor relations.

Effective December 31, 1956, Twentieth District Representative *Irwin D. Davidson* resigned his seat, having been elected to a fourteen-year term as judge of the Court of General Sessions. His seat remained vacant for the duration of the Eighty-fourth Congress. Running on both the Democrat and Liberal Party lines against Milton H. Adler, a "tall and elegant lawyer," Ludwig Teller was elected to the Eighty-fifth Congress with nearly 65 percent of the vote.

In the mid-1950s, the Twentieth Congressional District comprised a multi-ethnic chunk of Manhattan. It ranged from 21st to 110th Street, and from the Hudson River to "a wavering line (that touched) Seventh, Eighth and Ninth Avenues, Central Park West, Columbus Avenue and Amsterdam Avenue." According to the *New York Times*: "Its people are of every race, color and creed."

Teller defeated Milton Adler again in 1958, and wound up serving in Congress a total of four years. During that brief period, he served on the House Committee on Labor. As a member of Congress, Teller supported the Eisenhower Doctrine on the Middle East, and voted for the 1957 Civil Rights Act and statehood for Alaska. His major success came with the passage of the Douglas-Teller Bill, which "provided for the disclosure of pension plan finances to beneficiaries." In the 1960 election, Teller lost his seat to a New York County assistant district attorney named William Fitts Ryan (1922–72), who would go on to become one of Congress's earliest and most vocal doves against the war in Vietnam.

Following his one and only political defeat, Ludwig Teller resumed the practice of law. Throughout his career, Teller wrote a series of well-received legal tomes with titles like *The Law Governing Labor Disputes and Collective Bargaining* (1940, 3 vols.), *A Labor Policy for America* (1945), *Law of Contracts* (1947), *Law of Torts* (1947), *Law of Bills and Notes* (1948), *Law of Corporations* (1949), and *Worker Participation in Business Management* (1961).

For the five years from 1958 to 1963, Ludwig Teller served as president of the Central Library for the Blind in Israel. He died in New York City on October 4, 1965, and was interred in Union Fields Cemetery, Jamaica, Queens.

References

American Jewish Year Book, vol. 67, p. 544.
Biographical Directory of the United States Congress: 1774–1989, p. 1920.
New York Times, October 31, 1958, 18:1.
Who Was Who in America, vol. 4

TENZER, HERBERT (1905–1993): *Democrat from New York; served two terms in the House (Eighty-ninth and Ninetieth Congress, January 3, 1965–January 3, 1969).*

At twelve noon, Monday, September 27, 1965, the first day of Rosh Hashanah, the Jewish New Year, a *shofar* was blown on the steps of the U.S. Capitol for the first time in American history. This followed and preceded two other historic firsts that day: the first Jewish worship service ever held in the Capitol, and the first kosher meal ever served on the premises. All three were arranged by the Irish-Catholic Speaker, John McCormack of Massachusetts, for the benefit of the one Orthodox Jew serving in Congress: Herbert Tenzer of New York. There was an ulterior motive behind Speaker McCormack's beneficence. He desperately needed Tenzer's vote on a critical issue: granting the citizens of Washington, D.C., the right to vote.

Informed by Democratic House Whip *Abraham Multer* that Tenzer could not possibly be in Washington for the vote, Speaker McCormack took the matter into his own hands. Calling Tenzer into his office, "He [the Speaker] asked if there was any possible way I could attend the session. I said I needed ecclesiastic permission." After consulting with Rabbis Klaperman, Belkin, and Soloveitchik, Tenzer received permission, "just as long as I didn't have to write or ride—if I could attend a Rosh Hashanah service, recite the prayers, and hear the *shofar* blown."

Such was McCormack's respect for Tenzer, that he helped him make all the arrangements: flying in a rabbi from New York, providing a Torah scroll, Torah reader, prayer books (twelve Conservative and twelve Reform), skullcaps, and prayer shawls. McCormack "even provided a row of plants to section off an area for women." Unbeknownst to Tenzer, Speaker McCormack had also consulted a kosher caterer and arranged for his private dining room to be prepared for a special Rosh Hashanah meal. It was indeed a momentous way in which to usher in the new year 5726.

One of the outstanding Jewish lay leaders of the twentieth century, Herbert Tenzer lived his long life in accordance with two ethical maxims. The first was a motto he found on an index card which he purchased in a Broadway novelty shop in 1942 for ten cents: "There is no limit to what a man can do or where he can go if he doesn't mind who gets the credit." Tenzer took that index card and made it into a bronze plaque for his desk. Over the years, he gave copies of the plaque to friends and colleagues. In time, they would be found on the desks of Senators, titans of industry, President Chaim Herzog of Israel, Dr. Norman Lamm, the president of Yeshiva University—even President Ronald Reagan.

The second maxim was a lesson taught him by his father, Michael Tenzer. "My father, of blessed memory, taught me as a child that I must count every day. After my bar mitzvah he added: 'It is not only important that you count every day—but you must make every day count.'"

Herbert Tenzer was born on New York's Lower East Side on November 1, 1905. He was the sixth of seven children—four boys, three girls—born to Polish immigrants Michael and Rose Tenzer.

My father came to the U.S. in 1883 alone, without his family. My mother had come over in 1871. Father started peddling house to house with a basket of notions, as this was the period when most immigrant families did their own sewing and made all their own clothes. When he had accumulated enough money, he bought an outdoor candy stand, which he ran until he caught a cold. Then he decided to open a retail candy store.

Before too long, he married Rose, who ran the store, while he went into the wholesale end of the business. Within a short period of time, Michael Tenzer had established the first wholesale confectionery business in New York. Michael Tenzer set a good example for his children. He was a Jewish communal leader who helped found the synagogue at Clinton and Houston Streets in the 1890s. It was at this synagogue that the Tenzer boys were bar mitzvah. All seven of the Tenzer children would go on to serve as presidents or chairpersons of major Jewish organizations.

Herb Tenzer received his formal education in the New York City public schools—P.S. 92, 75, 34—and graduated Stuyvesant High School in 1923. He received his law degree from NYU in 1927, and was admitted to the New York State bar two years later. The turning point in his life occurred in 1924, when he applied for a job in a law office. Tenzer landed the job, but was told that he would have to work on Saturdays. When he informed them that he could not work Saturdays because it was the Jewish Sabbath, he was told they could not use him. "The managing clerk told me that I didn't look Jewish, and from then on I was determined to conduct my life in such a way, by my actions and conduct, that everyone would always know that I am Jewish."

In December 1929, Tenzer met Florence Novor, a distant relative by marriage on his mother's side of the family. "Florrie" and Herb "met and were practically engaged in three days." They were married on June 20, 1930 in Philadelphia. The couple moved to the Crown Heights section of Brooklyn, where their son Barry and daughter Diane were born. In 1932, Tenzer was elected president of the Yeshiva of Crown Heights, which his father had founded in 1923 as the first Orthodox Talmud Torah and synagogue in that part of Brooklyn. He served in the post until 1949.

In 1937, Tenzer founded the law firm of Tenzer, Greenblatt, Fallon & Kaplan. Over the years, it would grow to a seventy-lawyer firm. Tenzer's firm specialized in labor-management disputes, especially in the candy industry. Tenzer was responsible for writing the first collective-bargaining agreement in the candy manufacturing industry, a peace treaty that lasted more than thirty-two years. Between 1940 and 1960, he served as chairman of the board of Barton's Candy Corporation. In 1947, the Tenzers moved to Lawrence, on Long Island, where he became president of Congregation Beth Shalom.

Herbert Tenzer's long involvement with the Yeshiva of Crown Heights paved the way for his involvement with Yeshiva University. The second meeting to establish the university's Albert Einstein College of Medicine was held in Tenzer's home, and he was elected to the university's board of trustees in 1965. In 1977, he was named chairman of the board, and in 1989, chairman emeritus. In addition to his role in founding the Albert Einstein College of Medicine in 1955, Tenzer was instrumental in founding the Benjamin N. Cardozo School of Law in 1976 (for which he endowed a chair in Jewish law and ethics), and the Sy Syms School of Business in 1987. Moreover, he played a pivotal role in bailing the university out of a serious

financial crisis in the late 1970s by arranging for loans, debt forgiveness, and cash settlements.

In a life filled with achievement, Tenzer was proudest of his founding and running of Rescue Children, Inc., from 1945 to 1948. The organization raised funds to relieve the severe shortage faced by the *Vaad Hatzala* Rescue Committee, a major Jewish relief organization during and after the Second World War.

Our objective was to raise a dollar a day, $365 per year, for the support of each of the more than 2,000 orphans in Vaad Hatzala homes. We had photos and a biography of each child, gathered by organization members who went to Europe, at their own expense, for one or two months.... At the end of three years, one-third of these children found their parents, another third were adopted by relatives in America and elsewhere, and the remaining "full orphans" emigrated to Israel.

Herb Tenzer was also the father of the Israeli poultry industry. "Israel's first secretary of agriculture, Benyamin Mintz . . . was distressed that the U.S. was burying surplus cattle, hogs, and chickens because there was not enough food to sustain them and not enough of a market to sell them," Tenzer recalled.

"I said I'd see what I could do to obtain a release of some of the baby chicks to ship to Israel, where there was a severe shortage." Representative *Emanuel Celler* approached the Department of Agriculture, "which agreed to make the chicks available but warned that any attempt to take a planeload of chicks to Israel would result in a 90 percent death rate."

Tenzer and Mintz decided to take a chance. "The baby chicks were fed and watered throughout the trip and when they arrived in Israel, more than 90 percent had survived." That was 1948. By the beginning of 1949, Tenzer had "airlifted" more than 800,000 chicks to Israel. Within four years, Israel was one of the largest egg exporters to Europe.

In 1963, Tenzer decided to run for Congress from New York's Fifth Congressional District, which had never previously elected a Jew. In those days, the Fifth Congressional District contained 485,000 people living east of the New York City line to Massapequa, south of the

Southern State Parkway. The Jewish population of the district was just 30 percent; the percentage of registered Democrats less than one-third. Tenzer refused to campaign on the Jewish Sabbath, thus missing out on many Friday-evening speaking engagements.

At one point in the campaign, President Lyndon Johnson came to Long Island for a major speech. It was to take place on a Saturday. Undeterred, Tenzer spent Friday night at a near-by motel, less than a mile's walk from the spot where Johnson would be speaking and greeting Democrat candidates. When Tenzer arrived, hot and disheveled from his walk, he was introduced to President Johnson as "candidate for Congress who had walked there because he is an Orthodox Jew." Tenzer recalled that the President took his hand and said, "I want to commend you for adhering to your faith. It's really a great thing." Tenzer went on to an easy victory over Republican Ralph Edsel, capturing 65 percent of the vote.

During his two terms in the House of Representatives (Eighty-ninth and Ninetieth Congress, 1965–1969), Tenzer served on the House Judiciary Committee. His primary areas of concern were health care for the elderly, aid to education, and civil rights. He was the first member of Congress to introduce the concept of the minimum tax. He was also one of five co-sponsors of landmark legislation that launched an all-out national attack on cancer, heart disease, and stroke.

After two terms, Tenzer declined renomination. Upon announcing his retirement from elec-tive politics, Judiciary Committee chair Emanuel Celler stated: "Much of the legislation which has come forth from the [Judiciary] Committee bears the impact of Mr. Tenzer's formidable knowledge of the law. The contributions he made to the sub-committee on which he served not only revealed his breadth of knowledge, but emphasized his keen compassion and sense of equity."

After leaving Congress, Tenzer was appointed vice chairman of the New York State Special Advisory Committee on Medical Malpractice (1975) and served as chairman of the New York State Board of Social Welfare (1977–83). He also served as both a founder and national president of the United Jewish Appeal. Tenzer received the first-ever U.J.A.-Federation lifetime-achievement award.

Mrs. Tenzer, who was married to her husband for more than sixty years, passed away in 1991. Herbert Tenzer died on March 28, 1993. He was survived by his son Barry of Manhattan and Quogue, Long Island; his daughter, Diane Schachter of Hewlett Bay Park, Long Island; his two sisters, Eva Pion and Estelle Schiff, both of Rockaway Beach; and nine grandchildren.

References
Interview with Herbert Tenzer, January 1991.
Biographical Directory of American Jews.
Jewish World, October 11, 1985, pp. 4, 36.
New York Times, March 29, 1993.
Yeshiva University Tribute Dinner Booklet in Commemoration of Herbert and Florence Tenzer Yeshiva University Fellows Program, September 20, 1989.

TOLL, HERMAN (1907–1967): *Democrat from Pennsylvania; served four terms in the House (Eighty-sixth through Eighty-ninth Congress, January 3, 1959–January 3, 1967).*

Jess Unruh, the "Big Daddy" of California Democratic politics in the 1950s and '60s, used to say that there are three basic reasons why people get involved in electoral politics: ego, a desire to get ahead in some other endeavor, such as law or business, and the need to right a wrong or make a difference. Herman Toll, a four-term representative from Pennsylvania's Sixth Congressional District, definitely fell into the last category. An attorney with a general practice, Toll came to the attention of local political boss Charles O. Finley after getting involved in a dispute over the placement of a neighborhood supermarket. Sensing that Toll had political potential, Finley made him district committeeman. From that point on, politics became Herman Toll's consuming passion.

Herman Toll, the son of Mechel (Max) and Rifkah (Rebecca) Tolchinsky, was born in Buflov, about 60 miles from Kiev, on March 15, 1907. The family immigrated to Philadelphia around 1910, where Mechel, who had been a builder in the Ukraine, became a plasterer. Although the Tolls were Orthodox, young Herman gravitated toward Judaism's Reform movement. For virtually his entire adult life, he belonged to Temple Judea.

In the 1920s, it was still possible to enter a school of law without benefit of a college education. One merely had to pass the law school's entrance examination. In this way, Herman Toll was admitted to the law school at Temple University in the late 1920s. Graduating in 1930, he went into private practice in Philadelphia. While working as a young lawyer, Toll married Philadelphia-born Rose Ornstein. They had two sons, Sheldon and Gilbert, both of whom would become attorneys.

As mentioned above, Herman Toll's first foray into politics came when he involved himself in a neighborhood dispute over a supermarket. In Toll, the local party boss saw a young

man who was a natural; a bright, motivated man who spoke easily without benefit of notes. Long a student of "the social condition," Toll soon found himself running for Pennsylvania's state legislature from Philadelphia's Sixteenth District. Although long a Republican stronghold, Toll beat the odds and got himself elected. The year was 1950.

Toll threw himself heart and soul into his work in Harrisburg, easily being reelected in 1952, 1954, and 1956. "He was rarely home," his son Gilbert recalls. "He had meetings virtually every night. Even when he was home, he sometimes would have meetings there. I think he took my brother and I fishing once and to one ballgame. Politics was his life."

Toll's entry into electoral politics coincided with the national hysteria over the Communist menace. Spurred by the rantings of Wisconsin Senator Joseph McCarthy, many people believed there were Communists in the State Department, Communists in Hollywood, Communists under every bed. Had it been widely known that Herman Toll was a native of the Russian Ukraine, he too might have become suspect. No matter that he was born a full decade before the Communist revolution or that he had come to America at age three. The national hysteria had become so great that liberals were transmuted into radicals, and the foreign-born into enemy agents. As a result, Toll rarely, if ever, mentioned his foreign birth.

In 1958, Republican Congressman Hugh Scott, Jr., announced his candidacy for the United States Senate seat held by Edward Martin (1879–1967), a former Pennsylvania Governor and president of the Council of State Governments. Martin was nearing eighty and looking forward to retirement after nearly sixty years of public service. Toll quickly announced his candidacy for Scott's seat. Although the seat had been held by Republicans more than two decades, Toll managed an upset victory.

As a member of the Eighty-sixth Congress, Toll was befriended by Judiciary Committee chair *Emanuel Celler*, who appointed the freshman to his committee. Throughout his eight years in the House of Representatives, this would be Herman Toll's only committee assignment. According to Gilbert Toll, "Manny [Celler] wanted to make sure that the members of his committee devoted full time to Judiciary. He didn't want them spreading themselves too thin."

In Herman Toll's era, House members representing East Coast districts were said to be members of the T & T Club—"in on Tuesday and out on Thursday." Toll was different; he commuted between Philadelphia and the capital virtually every day. "He was so busy," his son recalled in a July 1997 interview, "that often people would make an appointment to see him on the train. Sometimes he would have to tell them that he could only see them for the first hour of the train trip, because he had another appointment before the train arrived in D.C."

Herman Toll was widely popular in his district, easily winning reelection in 1960, 1962, and 1964, Toward the end of his third term, Toll began noticing a weakening in his legs; he started walking with a limp. He was diagnosed with amyotrophic lateral sclerosis—Lou Gehrig's Disease. Toll took to spending increasing amounts of time at home in bed. Occasionally, when his vote was absolutely essential, House Speaker John McCormack would send a military ambulance to Philadelphia to deliver the ailing Representative back to Washington. Although Toll was all but bedridden in the fall of 1964, he announced his candidacy for a fourth term. Without making so much as a single campaign appearance, he defeated his Republican opponent by more than 70,000 votes. During his final

term (1965–66), Toll was a Representative-in-absentia; he never set foot on the House floor.

During his congressional career, Herman Toll sponsored legislation to establish a Federal Recreation Services Administration, a Youth Conservation Corps, a Department of Urban Affairs and Housing (eventually known as HUD), and a United States Disarmament Agency for World Peace. For the most part, Toll spent his time and energies attending to the needs of his district and the various issues coming before the Judiciary Committee.

Herman Toll announced his retirement from Congress in 1966. He died at age sixty on July 26, 1967, and was buried in Roosevelt Memorial Park. Rose Toll, who was a political activist in her own right, survived her husband by almost thirty years to the day, passing away in the early summer of 1997.

Herman's son Sheldon ran an unsuccessful race for sheriff of Oakland County in Michigan and then got out of politics. Son Gilbert, who still resides in Philadelphia, says that his only involvement in politics is "supporting the candidate of my choice. After seeing how much time he spent away from the family, my brother and I decided that we were going to be different. We were going to devote our energies to the family." Today, there are four Toll grandchildren, two of whom are attorneys..

References

Interview with Gilbert Toll, July 1997.

Biographical Directory of the United States Congress: 1774–1989, p. 1945.

New York Times, July 28, 1967.

VOLK, LESTER DAVID (1884–1962):

Republican from New York; served two terms in the House (Sixty-sixth and Sixty-seventh Congress, December 6, 1920–March 3, 1923).

A Renaissance man in every sense of the term, Lester David Volk enjoyed four successful careers, the first of which began shortly after his fifth birthday. The son of Aaron Barney and Esther (Topsky) Volk, Lester David was born in Brooklyn on September 17, 1884. As a youngster, Lester studied violin with the equally young Joseph Pasternak (1881–1940). His teacher, newly arrived from Czestochowa, Poland, and a graduate of the famed Warsaw Conservatory, earned his first American dollars giving young Jewish boys and girls violin lessons. Pasternak would eventually gain great renown as a composer for the Metropolitan Opera. From age five through thirteen, young Lester Volk performed as a concert violinist with symphony orchestras up and down the eastern seaboard. Violin and piano would remain a passion rather than a profession throughout the rest of his life.

Following a public school education, Lester Volk enrolled at Long Island Medical School, from which he received his M.D. in 1906 at age twenty-two. A specialist in otolaryngology (ear, nose, and throat), Volk spent many years in private practice and as coroner's physician for Kings County (Brooklyn, N.Y.). Somehow, he also found time to go the Brooklyn Law School of St. Lawrence University, from which he received his LL.B. in 1911.

In 1913, Lester Volk turned twenty-nine. It was a year of exhaustive activity. In that one twelve-month period he—

- was admitted to the New York bar;
- founded and organized the Federation of Medical Economists;
- began serving as the organization's counsel and editor of its journal, the *Medical Economist*; and
- began a term in the New York state legislature.

Although he considered himself a staunch Republican, Volk was, in reality, a maverick. His 1912 race for the state legislature was carried out under the aegis of Theodore Roosevelt's Progressive ("Bull Moose") Party. Volk was the first and only member of that faction to sit in the New York State Assembly. During his two-year term, he was appointed to a special commission that investigated vice and corruption in the New York City police department. When his term in Albany drew to a close, he declined renomination, opting to return to his legal, medical, and journalistic endeavors in Brooklyn.

During World War I, Volk served as a first lieutenant with the U.S. Army Medical Corps, Twelfth Remount and 88th Air Squadron of the AEF. An active member of both the Veterans of Foreign Wars (New York State Judge Advocate) and the American Jewish War Veterans, Volk was largely responsible for securing the soldiers' bonus from the state of New York. He organized and led the approximately 82,000 veterans who marched in the New York Bonus Parade in 1920. His name appeared on the front page of the *New York Times* for several days in succession. The public renown helped elect him as a Republican to Congress in 1921 when he ran for the vacated Nineteenth District seat of Republican Representative Reuben Haskell, who had resigned from Congress in order to take a position as judge of the Kings County Court.

As a member of the Sixty-sixth and Sixty-seventh Congress, Volk became an outspoken critic of Prohibition. He also led the fight against proposed legislation that would remove control and treatment of narcotics addicts from the medical profession. As a physician, Volk had become an early expert in the field of narcotics abuse and would author numerous papers in the field. His research convinced him that substance abuse should be considered a medical, and not a legal or criminal problem. Through Volk's efforts, Congress created the Whitney Commission in 1922, which eventually resulted in the abolition of the State Narcotic Bureau. In 1921, Speaker Frederick Gillette appointed Volk to head a congressional delegation to Canada that studied that country's sales tax.

Reelected to a full two-year term in November, 1921, Lester Volk was defeated in 1923 by the thirty-six-year-old *Emanuel Celler*. He returned to the practice of law and medicine. As mentioned above, Volk was anything but a doctrinaire Republican. In 1928, he broke party ranks to throw his support behind Democrats Alfred E. Smith for President and Franklin D. Roosevelt for New York State Governor. When asked to explain this move, Volk attributed it to a desire to fight "bigotry and fanaticism." In 1932, Volk spent a year in Vienna, practicing otolaryngology at the Allegemeine Krankenhaus, for which he was made an honorary member of the Medical Association of Vienna. He published numerous books and articles on allergies and narcotics abuse, and, as chief deputy grand chancellor of the New York State Knights of Pythias, wrote a 1938 book entitled *Abie's Travels Through the Knights of Pythias.*

Lester Volk married Florence Solomon in December, 1924. They had two children, Alayne Harriet (Newman) and Alan Maurice. Florence, sixteen years her husband's junior, died following a lengthy illness in 1945 at age forty-five. Alan was killed in 1952 while with the United States Air Force on Okinawa. Alayne and her husband settled in San Juan, Puerto Rico. Following his first wife's death, Lester Volk married Anne Safran. In 1942, Lester D. Volk was appointed Assistant Attorney General of the State of New York, a position he would hold for the next sixteen years.

Reform Jews, the Volks were members of Brooklyn's Temple Beth Emeth. Lester David Volk died on April 30, 1962, and was interred at Bayside Cemetery, Ozone Park, New York.

References

American Jewish Year Book, vol. 24, p. 210.
New York Times, May 1, 1962, 37:2.
Universal Jewish Encyclopedia.
Who Was Who in America, vol. 7.
Who Was Who in American Jewry, 1926, 1928, 1938.

WANGER, IRVING PRICE (1852–1940):
Republican from Pennsylvania; served nine terms in the House (Fifty-third through Sixty-first Congress, March 4, 1893–March 3, 1911).

Although he served eighteen years in Congress, very little is known about Irving P. Wanger. The son of George and Rebecca (Price) Wanger, he was born in North Coventry, Chester County, Pennsylvania, on March 5, 1852. Chester County is Pennsylvania-Dutch country, an area settled in the eighteenth century by Germans, who were predominantly members of the Amish and Mennonite sects seeking religious freedom. As a student, Wanger apparently shuttled back and forth between North Coventry and Pottstown, where he attended the Hill School. At age nineteen, he became the deputy prothonotary (recorder) of Chester County, while beginning the study of law in Norristown, in nearby Montgomery County. During his legal studies, which lasted from 1872 to 1875, Wanger appears to have made a permanent move to Norristown, for by 1873, he had been named Montgomery County's deputy prothonotary (chief clerk).

Admitted to the Pennsylvania bar in December of 1875, Wanger established both his legal practice and residence in Norristown. Wanger's being Jewish was obviously not a barrier to upward mobility, for within three years, he was elected burgess (councilman) of Norristown. In 1880, Wanger was a delegate to the raucous Republican National Convention in Chicago. The Republicans, faced with a contest between "two charming and corrupt rivals," James G. Blaine (a perennial candidate), and Roscoe Conkling, boss of the New York State political machine, wound up selecting dark horse candidate "General" James A. Garfield of Ohio on the thirty-sixth ballot. In the November election, Garfield defeated Democrat Winfield Scott Hancock and James B. Weaver of Iowa, the Greenback-Labor nominee. Upon his return from Chicago, Wanger was elected district attorney of Montgomery County.

On June 6, 1884, the thirty-two-year-old Irving Wanger married Emma C. Titlow of North Coventry. The Wangers had five children— Lincoln, Rebecca, George, Ruth, and Marion. Lincoln and Rebecca apparently died in infancy. In the 1880s, Norristown and the surrounding towns of Montgomery County had a negligible Jewish population; the first recorded Jewish "census" of the area took place in 1927, at which time the county housed no more than 600 Jews. Nothing is known about the Wanger family's Jewish practices, or if there even was a synagogue in the area. Nearby Pottstown did have a small Jewish community—approximately twenty-six in 1880—and the area's only Jewish cemetery.

Returned to office as district attorney in 1886, Wanger became chairman of the Montgomery County Republican Committee. In 1890, he ran for Republican Robert M. Yardley's vacated Seventh Congressional District seat. Wanger chose the wrong year to run; 1890, a year of financial panic brought about a voter revolt. Nebraska went Democratic for the first time in its history; in Wisconsin, Democrats swept the state. And in Nebraska's First Congressional District, voters rejected incumbent Republican William J. Connell in favor of a forty-two-year-old Lincoln lawyer named William Jennings Bryan, soon to become a figure of national importance. In consonance with this trend, Wanger lost his election to Democrat Edwin Hallowell. Undaunted, he challenged Hallowell again in 1892, this time emerging victorious even though the Republicans were turned out of the White House.

Irving Wanger was reelected eight times to Congress from the Seventh District. For six of those terms (Fifty-fifth through Sixty-first Congress), he served as chairman of the Committee on Expenditures in the Post Office Department, a position with little prestige and even less political clout. During his eighteen years in the House, Wanger's name appeared but once in the *New York Times*, a fair indication of a lackluster career. (The one time his name does appear, he is cited for chiding William Howard Taft over his extreme girth.).

Wanger was defeated for reelection to a tenth term in 1910 by Democrat Robert Difenderfer, a prosperous lumber contractor from nearby Jenkinstown. Following a brief sojourn in Wilmington, Delaware, he returned to Norristown, where he resumed the practice of law. Wanger died shortly before his eighty-eighth birthday, on January 14, 1940, and was buried in Mount Zion Cemetery, Pottstown, Pennsylvania.

References
Biographical Directory of the United States Congress: 1774–1989, p. 2005.
Who's Who, 1908.

WAXMAN, HENRY ARNOLD (1939–):
Democrat from California; has served thirteen terms in the House (Ninety-fourth Congress through One Hundred and Sixth Congress, January 3, 1975–present).

When people in Los Angeles talk about the Westside, they are referring to the place that people from Peoria to Plattsburgh think of as Hollywood or Tinseltown. To be perfectly honest, Hollywood, the entertainment capital of the world, doesn't really exist. While there is an incorporated part of Los Angeles by that name, it has long been in a state of decline; Hollywood and Vine, the center of that mythic world, stands at the eastern end of a rather seedy, rundown, shopping area. When people the world over conjure up images of stars, mansions, recording studios, and glitter, they are unknowingly referring to the Westside.

The Westside is, in the words of the *Almanac of American Politics* (1996 edition), "shorthand for what might be the biggest and flashiest concentration of affluence in the world." Made up of the upper-income enclaves of Beverly Hills, Los Feliz, Brentwood, Pacific Palisades, and Hancock Park, the largely Jewish Fairfax section, and the singles and gays of Santa Monica and West Hollywood, the Westside has gone through explosive change. In the decade from 1986 to 1996, the median price of a home sky-

rocketed from about $117,000 to just a little over half a million. It is the most solidly Democratic and liberal part of Southern California, and "probably contributes more money to Democratic candidates and liberal causes than any other district" in the country. It is also the home of one of the ablest, most successful legislators in postwar America: Henry Arnold Waxman.

Not quite five-and-a-half-feet tall, balding, with a toothy grin and a quiet, almost shy demeanor, Henry Waxman is the antithesis of Southern California glamour and glitter. Yet, ever since 1974, he has been regularly reelected by such large majorities that he has a hard time remembering who his opponents are. Waxman's formula for the extraordinary success he has

experienced, both at home and in Congress, is simple: hard work, knowing the issues and parliamentary procedure better than anyone else; a genius for fundraising, and a great deal of patience, persistence, and perspicacity.

Henry Waxman, the son of Louis and Esther (Silverman) Waxman, was born in the Boyle Heights section of Los Angeles on September 12, 1939. From the end of World War I through the end of World War II, Boyle Heights was the Jewish working-class neighborhood of Los Angeles. The Waxmans and the Silvermans originally came to America from Bessarabia, shortly after the Kishinev pogrom of 1905. The Waxmans came to Los Angeles in the early 1920s by way of Montreal; the Silvermans at about the same time via Pittsburgh. As a child, Henry Waxman heard his grandparents' horrifying tales about "how the anti-Semites would come into town and destroy property, beat people up, threaten their lives. . . . They were younger people, so they could just pick up and leave . . . but they suffered." Waxman credits these memories with spurring his lifelong concern for the poor and the powerless.

When Henry and his sister Miriam were still quite young, the Waxmans moved to Los Angeles' South-Central District, where the family lived above Lou's grocery store at 80th Street and Avalon Boulevard. (Today, South-Central is better known as Watts.) Since there were no synagogues in South Central, Henry Waxman attended afternoon Hebrew school at the Conservative Huntington Park Hebrew Congregation, where he was bar mitzvah in 1952. He went to Fremont High School "where I was in a minority—both as a Caucasian and as a Jew." Following his graduation in 1957, the family moved to the Jewish Beverly-Fairfax area, which has remained Waxman's political base ever since.

Lou and Esther were both staunch Democrats who took a keen interest in politics. Waxman remembers that as a child, his mother "encouraged him to wear an Adlai Stevenson button to school, even though the teachers made him remove it." While still in high school, Waxman worked as a volunteer in local political campaigns. The Waxman name was already known in Westside political circles; his uncle Al published a "string of neighborhood newspapers throughout Los Angeles . . . and the Waxman name commanded influence in local politics."

Henry Waxman attended UCLA, where he majored in political science. During his undergraduate years, he became involved with the California Federation of Young Democrats, a network of clubs that specialized in political debate and lobbying for influence in party circles. Upon receiving his bachelor's degree in 1961, he enrolled in the UCLA Law School, from which he received his J.D. in 1964. From 1964 to 1965, the young attorney served as president of the Young Democrats: "We were considered way-out radicals at the time . . . we came out with resolutions endorsing a test-ban treaty, recognition of Red China and disbanding the House Un-American Activities Committee."

More importantly, as president, Waxman made friends with a group of young politicos who together would change the face of California politics: *Howard Berman* and his brother Michael, John Burton, Willie Brown, and David Roberti. Howard Berman and John Burton went on to become members of Congress; Willie Brown became the California Assembly's powerful Speaker and mayor of San Francisco; Roberti, a savvy state senator.

After practicing law for three years, Waxman ran for the California State Assembly. Searching for a district from which to run, he decided to take on twenty-six-year veteran Lester McMillan, who was "losing touch with the voters." Waxman entered the race as a distinct outsider, challenging "not only an incumbent but his own family," for his uncle Al's local paper had long supported McMillan, and continued to do so in this race as well. Aided by his friend Howard Berman and hundreds of volunteers from the ranks of the Federation of Young Democrats, Waxman polled 64 percent of the Democratic primary vote, and then easily won the general election.

The key to victory lay in Waxman's and Berman's then-novel use of differentiated political mailings. The strategy called for "seniors to get one letter from Waxman addressing their concerns, while middle-class homeowners . . . got another." Today, this technique, called direct mail, is a well-accepted tool in all phases of polit-

ical campaigning; in 1968, it was brand-new. Not only was a political career born; it also marked the beginning of political alliance that continues to this day.

The California State Assembly is a rather fluid institution, where freshman and sophomore members often chair important committees. At the beginning of his second term in the Assembly, Waxman chose the right side in the Speakership fight, which went to Valley-area Assemblyman Bob Moretti. In thanks for his support, the new Speaker named Waxman chair of the Assembly's redistricting committee, which was charged with "redrawing California's congressional districts to reflect the demographics of the 1970 census." Waxman also chaired the Health Committee.

During his first term in Sacramento, Waxman married Janet Kessler, the cousin of old friends from UCLA. Kessler, originally from Brooklyn, had moved to Los Angeles as a small child, where she was raised in the predominantly Jewish Fairfax section. When the two married, on October 17, 1971, the neighborhood newspaper ran the headline "Local Assemblyman weds Fairfax Grad." To the native Angelino, this could only mean one thing: the Assemblyman had married a Jew. The new Mrs. Waxman had a daughter, Carol, from a previous marriage. The couple later had a second child, Michael.

In 1972, Henry Waxman helped his old friend Howard Berman win a seat in the Assembly. Thus was born the Waxman-Berman Machine, a "network of liberal politicians who pool their resources, including sophisticated computer technology and campaign coffers, overflowing with contributions from wealthy southern Californians, to help elect like-minded candidates to state and national office." Over the years, the machine came to include *Mel Levine*, black Congressman Julian Dixon, and Howard's brother Michael, who serves as their technical wizard.

In 1974, Henry Waxman ran for Congress from the newly created Twenty-fourth District. Accused of creating a district for himself as chair of the reapportionment committee, Waxman quickly pointed out that, in fact, the district had been created by the Supreme Court-ordered redistricting of 1973. Making judicious use of the Waxman-Berman computer lists and $95,000 in campaign contributions, Waxman was elected with 64 percent of the vote. In the intervening years, Waxman's margin of victory has never been less than 63 percent; in his latest campaign (1998), he was reelected with 74 percent of the vote.

After languishing in relative obscurity for two terms, Henry Waxman took the bold and unprecedented step of challenging a senior member for chairmanship of a subcommittee. Setting his sights on the House Energy and Commerce Committee's powerful Subcommittee on Health and the Environment, Waxman waged an all-out effort to defeat North Carolina Democrat Richardson Preyer. The latter, "a popular and highly respected former federal judge," not only outranked Waxman; he also had the backing of the Democratic leadership.

In his effort to become subcommittee chair, Waxman contributed some $24,000 to the campaign coffers of ten Democratic members of the Energy and Commerce Committee, a practice generally observed only by senior members of Congress. (During his years in Congress, Waxman has contributed more than $750,000 to his colleague's campaigns—money that comes mainly from his wealthy Westside constituents.) Waxman was also quick to point out that Preyer "represented a tobacco-growing state, favored tobacco subsidies and opposed anti-smoking measures, and that Preyer's family had substantial holdings in a large pharmaceutical company, setting up a potential conflict-of-interest problem." Waxman's bold scheme worked; he was elected subcommittee chair by a final vote of 15 to 12. Accused of buying a chairmanship, Waxman insisted otherwise: "California officer-holders have been doing it for years. That's how the Democrats won a majority in the state assembly."

From his position as subcommittee chair, Henry Waxman was at the center of some of Congress's most crucial legislation. An unabashed liberal, Waxman has become the House's acknowledged expert on health-care and environmental issues. He has fought for expanded health-care coverage, increased funding for AIDS research, and stringent measures for protecting the air we breathe and the water we drink. He has also been absolutely pivotal in improving the quality of nursing home care, bringing down prices for prescription drugs, and helping make available otherwise unprofitable "orphan" drugs for rare diseases.

A master of parliamentary procedure, Waxman learned early on how to stall bills that did not meet with his approval. Case in point, the 1981 battle over reauthorization of the Clean Air Act of 1970. Waxman, along with a host of environmental groups, favored keeping the act largely intact. The Reagan administration, backed by a coalition of the automobile, coal, and steel industries, public utilities companies, and House Energy and Commerce Committee chair "Big John" Dingell, a Michigan Democrat, sought to "significantly relax the act's provisions on automobile emission standards and its rules barring new industry in clean-air zones.

The bill's first stop was Waxman's Subcommittee on Health and the Environment. There, he initiated an ingenious set of stalling tactics that remained in place until public opinion began rallying around his point of view. In addition to holding hearings that promised to go on *ad infinitum*, Waxman one day entered the committee room wheeling a shopping cart containing some 600 amendments. He insisted that the committee clerk read the entire text of each amendment, and barred the committee (as was his right) from holding afternoon sessions. Waxman was able to stall successfully for more than fifteen months, until public sentiment shifted toward strengthening the Clean Air Act.

Eventually, even Chairman Dingell relented. Knowing that he had little chance of passing a weakened act, Dingell adjourned the committee. *Washington Post* writer Michael Barone noted that "Waxman maneuvered and delayed masterfully, preventing action until he had the votes to win. He proved himself to be one of the shrewdest legislators in Congress—and one of the most powerful."

Waxman, who represents a district with a large number of gays (West Hollywood and surrounding neighborhoods have a higher per-capita AIDS rate than New York or San Francisco) was instrumental in passing the first comprehensive federal legislation dealing with AIDS. The bill established "a $1 billion program [including] appropriations for anonymous testing, home health care, research, counseling, and education." During hearings on the bill, California Republican William Dannemeyer tried to scuttle Waxman's proposal extending anti-discrimination protection to people with the fatal disease. Dannemeyer, an ultra-conservative protector of family values, suggested that "many of these individuals brought the disease on themselves and [do] not deserve special treatment." Waxman, who is normally a soft-spoken individual, grabbed his microphone and made the caustic remark that "anyone making such an argument was speaking like a supreme being." As a hush fell over the committee room, Waxman, looking directly at his Republican colleague, said: "I don't see any supreme beings on this committee."

Waxman has also been instrumental in writing laws to provide health-care coverage for children, the poor, and the aged. "I believe that government has a responsibility to help those people who are otherwise going to be unprotected," he told writers from the *National Journal*. "Without basic health care, housing, education and the basic necessities of life, I think we're denying people an [equal] opportunity."

The second month that Waxman was in Congress (1974), he made his first trip to Israel with a delegation from the House Armed Services Committee. The junket's purpose was to "look at some of the military equipment that Israel had captured from the Arab countries in the '73 [Yom Kippur] war." Although Waxman was not a member of the committee, its chairman, Illinois Democrat Melvin Price, gave the freshman legislator permission to come along. When informed that the junket would also be making stops in Egypt and Saudi Arabia, Waxman "hurriedly [got] together a visa application." It "asked not only your religion but some documentation to prove you are what you are." Waxman sent an aide to Washington's Adas Israel synagogue (of which the Waxmans are active members) to get a letter on their stationery saying that he was Jewish and that his mother was Jewish.

The Saudis turned his visa application down on the grounds of his religion. Says Waxman : "I was astounded because prominent Jews by that point had been admitted to Saudi Arabia, including the Secretary of State, Henry Kissinger." Waxman took his outrage to Armed Services Committee Chair Price. He expected Price to take the attitude "that none of them [the committee members] would go to Saudi Arabia unless I would go." Instead, Price's response was, "Oh yeah, you may not be able to go . . . . They've had this law for a long time." Incensed,

Waxman exploded and told the chairman: "I'm not going as a member of the Jewish community; I'm going as a member of the United States Congress." Waxman put pressure on the State Department, which finally got the Saudis to agree to let him make his visit.

While in Saudi Arabia, Waxman and members of the committee met with the soon-to-be-assassinated King Faisal, who handed out copies of the *Protocols of the Elders of Zion*. Waxman recounts that the king "was a very sinister and mean-looking man . . . and he had these guards around him all the time with daggers or knives in holsters. It was sort of a menacing experience."

When it got to the question-and-answer session "nobody asked him any tough questions." Finally, Waxman, steeling up his courage, said: "Your Highness, we're pleased to be in your country. It's certainly the heart of the Islamic world because of Mecca and Medina. The Arab people have a number of countries. Do you foresee ever, under any circumstances, coexisting with one Jewish country in the Middle East?" Faisal got extremely agitated.

Continuing with his train of thought, Waxman said: "Since you made the distinction between Jews and Zionists, why do you prohibit Jews to come into your country?" Faisal angrily explained to Waxman: "Jews are our enemies. They're friends of our enemies, and friends of our enemies are our enemies . . . . Palestine is an Arab country. Jews can live there, but only with Palestine as an Arab country." Waxman's give-and-take with King Faisal had the effect of "shocking [his] colleagues, because that was not the view they were getting from a lot of people [who] were giving them a different analysis of the Middle East."

Henry and Janet Waxman are practicing Conservative Jews. They keep a kosher home, observe Shabbat, and meet twice a month with other Jewish members of Congress for a study session. Waxman is, except under the most pressing of circumstances, unavailable from sundown Friday until sunset Saturday. The Waxmans sent both their children to Hebrew day school in Washington. He is also the only member of Congress to have a grandchild who is a *sabra* (Hebrew for "native-born Israeli"). Their daughter Carol made *aliyah* after college (Brandeis), changed her name to Shai, and married Ricky Abramson, a Canadian *oleh* (immigrant) who changed his name to Raki. In early 1992, the Abramsons had the Waxman's first grandchild, Ari Barak ben Raki Abramson. Waxman muses that his daughter and son-in-law have gone through a "reverse Ellis Island transformation." "When I talk to [Raki's] father, he wants to know how Ricky and Shai are. And I say: 'Ricky and Shai? You mean Raki and Carol.'"

Janet Kessler was a founding member of Congressional Wives for Soviet Jewry, and has worked actively on behalf of Syrian Jewry. Waxman remembers that in the early days of the Soviet Jewry committee, his wife would host get-togethers at their home, where participants would place calls to Jewish refuseniks in Russia. In 1987, the Waxmans went on a political junket to Syria. Visiting the Jewish quarter of Damascus on Shabbat, they were met by the neighborhood's Jewish residents, who took Mrs. Waxman into their homes and voiced their grave concerns.

In 1991, in what he termed "the most difficult vote of his entire career," Henry Waxman voted against the Gulf resolution. Speaking of that vote, he said: "I'm anguished by it. War [with Iraq] may be inevitable, [but] I just can't vote for war. I'm just not convinced that war is our only option . . . . I don't think we should say diplomacy is at a dead end."

Waxman's most recent crusade began in early 1994, when he "lined up the chief executive officers of leading tobacco companies and accused them of adding nicotine and other substances to cigarettes and of lying in their testimony." After the Republican take-over of Congress in November 1994, Waxman held one last hearing as subcommittee chair on smokeless tobacco. In January 1995, Representative Thomas Bliley, Republican of Virginia, took over as Commerce Committee chair. Said Bliley after assuming the post: "I don't think we need any more legislation regulating tobacco." Waxman's response was typically cutting: "He's acting like he's taking over the Tobacco Committee, not the Health Committee."

Working in a minority for the first time in his congressional career, Waxman remained both philosophical and optimistic: "We have to recognize that we will be a permanent minority unless we put forward our agenda in a way the American people can understand it." During his many years in Congress, Henry Waxman has been a true leader of the House Democrats. Feared by some, respected by all, he has been, from day one, a champion of liberal causes. He has not always been immediately successful. As a colleague remarked: "At the beginning of every year, he'll ask for the sky. And when he gets only the moon instead of the whole sky, he still ends up getting more than most legislators get in ten years."

One of the most "Jewishly Jewish" members of the Congressional Minyan, Waxman understands that his training and upbringing have had a great impact on his career: "I find in our liturgy an ancient foreshadowing of President George Bush's famous call for a kinder and gentler society. In all our prayers we ask Him 'who makes peace Above to grant peace also unto us and to all our people.' The commentators point out that peace means not merely the absence of open conflict, but the presence of justice, compassion, harmony, and wholeness."

References

Interview with Henry Waxman, March 1992.
Almanac of American Politics, 1976–1998.
Current Biography Year Book, 1992, pp. 600–604.
Los Angeles Times, April 25, 1990, E 1:1; January 13, 1991, A 6:3.
National Journal, March 3, 1989 pp. 577–581.
New Republic, July 7, 1986, pp. 17–19.

WEINER, ANTHONY D. (1965–): *Democrat from New York; has served one term in the House (One Hundred and Sixth Congress, January 5, 1999–present).*

On November 2, 1998, Anthony D. Weiner was elected to fill the Congressional seat of *Charles Schumer*, the man who gave him his first political job. Born and raised in Brooklyn, Weiner graduated from the State University of New York at Plattsburgh. Upon graduation, he went to Washington, D.C., where he went to work for Representative Schumer. During his stint with the Congressman, he served variously as budget director, press assistant, and foreign affairs assistant. Returning to Brooklyn, he became Schumer's district office liaison and eventually became the Congressman's chief advisor.

In the summer of 1991, charter revision in New York City led to the creation of new City Council districts. Weiner ran in the newly created Forty-eighth District, comprising Sheepshead Bay, Manhattan Beach and Midwood. Running on the slogan, "No promises, just hard work," Weiner won a six-way primary and then a three-way general election. At twenty-seven, Anthony Weiner became the youngest person ever elected to the New York City Council. Two years later he was reelected, "garner[ing] more primary votes than any other Council Member." Despite the fact that voters in the Forty-eighth District voted four-to-one for Republican mayoral candidate Rudolph Giuliani, Democrat Weiner was reelected with better than 80 percent of the vote.

During his years on the City Council, Weiner became known as one of that body's leading consumer advocates, and was named chair of the Subcommittee on Crime in Public Housing after his first term. The *New York Times* called him "one of the Council's brightest members and a gifted speaker who is particularly knowledgeable on public safety issues." According to his critics, he was arrogant.

By the time Weiner started gearing up for his second reelection campaign in 1997, his eyes were already on Washington. Almost from the moment that Ninth District Representative Charles Schumer announced his intention to seek the Senate seat held by Republican Alfonse D'Amato, Weiner made no secret of the fact that he wanted to replace his political mentor. Running for reelection to his council seat against

Jeffrey A. Reznik, a former aide to State Comptroller H. Carl McCall, Weiner realized that in order to look competitive in the 1998 Congressional race, he would have to win big in 1997. Weiner did just that, carrying an eye-popping 92 percent of the vote. He managed to do this without the endorsement of some of the most prominent politicians in the district. The reason was simple: most of these "most prominent politicians" were considering getting into the congressional race themselves.

The race to succeed Schumer attracted four viable candidates:
- State Assemblywoman Melinda Katz
- City Councilman Noach Dear
- State Assemblyman Daniel L. Feldman
- City Councilman Anthony D. Weiner.

At first, the putative leader was Councilman Dear, due in large measure to his formidable fundraising prowess. A City Council member since 1982, Dear, an Orthodox Jew, was one of the top national fundraisers for President Clinton. By April 1998, Dear was easily leading the financial field, with nearly $1 million in the bank—more than his three rivals combined. Dear, who would eventually raise more than $1.5 million, "spent lavishly on television advertising and on a videotaped campaign commercial that he sent to more than 20,000 registered Democratic voters in the district."

Assemblywoman Melinda Katz, elected to the Twenty-eighth Assembly District (Queens) in 1994, was the second-leading fundraiser with Weiner in third, and Forty-fifth District (Kings County) Assemblyman Daniel L. Feldman in fourth. When questioned as to whether Dear's vast financial resources would prove the deciding factor, Weiner responded: "I feel I have to raise less money than my opponents to win this thing." He suggested that "Mr. Dear's political positions, especially his opposition to abortion," would make him "too conservative to many voters in the district." "He has a record that is certainly not going to attract many Democratic primary voters to his side," Weiner added.

During the campaign, the four had the daunting task of setting themselves apart from their rivals. At a September debate held at a Brooklyn elementary school:

Assemblyman Feldman boasted of authoring more than 125 bills during his eighteen years in the state legislature.

Councilman Dear spoke of his attentiveness to the nitty-gritty of constituents service, from repaving streets to installing traffic lights.

Asemblywoman Katz trumpeted her advocacy of health care legislation.

Councilman Weiner spoke of his close affiliation with Chuck Schumer.

Feldman, who received the endorsement of Representative *Jerrold Nadler* admitted, "I'm not good with sound bites, and I'm not cute. But if people want to pick a Congressman on the basis of qualifications, why is this race so close? My qualifications are a lot stronger than my opponents."

Katz, a protégée of New York City Comptroller Alan G. Hevesi stated: "I have focused on health care since I've been in the Assembly. The first law I passed was a direct access law that provided care for women from gynecologists and obstetricians without first seeking permission from their H.M.O.'s."

Councilman Dear, by far the most conservative of the four, said, "I try to work with people to help them solve their problems. That's why I have a 24-hour hot line. That's why people identify with me."

For his part, Anthony Weiner bluntly stated, "A lot of people will come out to the polls to get Chuck [Schumer] elected to the Senate. And they are likely to be persuaded by [his] endorsement. I think everyone would agree that Chuck Schumer's endorsement is by far the most important one in this race."

The initial vote tally showed Anthony Weiner winning the four-person race by a scant 285 over his closest rival, Ms. Katz. A recount was ordered. After two weeks, the final results were announced:

- Anthony D. Weiner: 13,049
- Melinda Katz: 12,560
- Noach Dear: 9,888
- Daniel L. Feldman: 9,616

In the end, Dear spent slightly more than $1,500.00 per vote. Weiner's primary victory was the only one that mattered; in November, the people of the Ninth District elected him in a landslide—66 percent to 24 percent over Republican Louis Telano.

Anthony Weiner, who describes himself as a secular Jew, is single. He lives in Sheepshead Bay, Brooklyn.

References

Interview with Anthony Weiner, December 1998.

New York Times, July 14, 1997, B3:9; April 17, 1998, B5:6; September 8, 1988, B6:4.; September 30, 1998 B5:2.

WEISS, SAMUEL ARTHUR (1902–1977):
Democrat from Pennsylvania; served three terms in the House (Seventy-seventh through Seventy-ninth Congress, January 3, 1941–January 7, 1946).

In his 1991 book *Chutzpah*, Harvard Law School professor Alan Dershowitz humorously noted that "bar mitzvah is the age when a Jewish boy realizes that his chances of playing on a major league sports team are considerably less than his chances of owning one." Dershowitz's point was that in America, Jews have succeeded in most areas of human endeavor—save athletics. It is likely that America's most quote-worthy civil libertarian never met the late Pennsylvania Representative Samuel A. Weiss. For Weiss, more than any other member of the Congressional Minyan, spent a lifetime actively involved in sports—as an athlete, official, and legislative ally.

Samuel Arthur Weiss, the son of Israel and Sadie (Golden) Weiss, was born in Krotowicz (Warsaw), Poland, on April 15, 1902. Within a year, the Weiss family immigrated to America, settling in Glassport, Pennsylvania. At the time of their arrival, Glassport had a tiny Jewish population—less than seventy-five Jewish families. Young Sam was educated in the Glassport public schools; in 1921, he matriculated to Duquesne University in Pittsburgh. During his four years there, he captained the football and baseball teams—a unique distinction for any college athlete. Following his graduation in 1925, Weiss entered the Duquesne University School of Law, from which he received an LL.B. in 1927 and a J.D. in 1929.

Entering private practice in Pittsburgh, Weiss soon married Jeanette E. Hoffman, with whom he had three children: Sandra Jacqueline, Joy (Mrs. S. R. Cohen), and James. Active in local Democratic politics, Weiss was elected to the State House of Representatives in 1935, and again in 1939.

In 1940, Weiss defeated Thirty-first District Republican John R. McDowell, taking his seat in the Seventy-seventh Congress on January 3, 1941. (McDowell lost a second race to Weiss in 1942. He sat out the 1944 election, and ran once again in 1946, after Weiss had announced his resignation from the House. This time he was successful. McDowell once again served but a single term, losing the 1948 election to Democrat Harry J. Davenport, who also served but a single term, losing the 1950 election to the improbably named Hamar Denny Denny, Jr., whose great-grandfather, Hamar Denny, had served as an anti-Masonic member of Congress in the 1820s.).

As a member of the House, Weiss spent his first year in the relative anonymity of the back bench. Shortly after the Japanese attack on Pearl Harbor, he volunteered for military service in the United States Navy; his application was turned down, probably because of his age (nearly thirty-eight) and his position in Congress. Denied the opportunity to serve his country in a military capacity, Weiss turned his attention to keeping up the morale of those stateside. Specifically, he directed his energies toward sports and the role athletic competition could play in keeping the home fires burning.

In the early decades of the twentieth century, the annual Army-Navy football game was considered one of the country's premiere sports spectacles. In 1942, the War Department quietly placed a ban on the game, citing as its rationale "the need to conserve rail and motor transport for essential uses." After a strong appeal by the Navy, President Roosevelt overrode the War Department's edict. The 1942 game took place, with Annapolis humiliating West Point by a score of 14–0.

In July 1943, when Acting Secretary of War Robert P. Patterson hinted that the game would in all likelihood be canceled, Representative Weiss entered the picture. In 1943, Sam Weiss was chairing an "informal Congressional committee on sports for Army trainees." In an interview with the *New York Times*, he said: "I believe this [the upcoming game] has a vital bearing on the future of college sports and on the morale of the country. I believe that the Commander in Chief [and not the War Department] should determine the uniform policy." Weiss went on to enlist the support of 256 of his congressional colleagues. In the end, he won the day—sort of.

The War Department relented, and said that the 1943 game could go on, as scheduled, at West Point. Secretary Harry Stimson added the caveat that "only persons living within a ten-mile radius" would be allowed to attend "because of transportation problems." Weiss then made public a letter he had written to Stimson, in which he stated: "I plead with you, Mr. Secretary, to revise your policy and permit this great game to be played in New York,

Baltimore or Philadelphia, where it will encounter little or no transportation obstacles."

Showing a bit of political acumen, Weiss reminded the War Secretary that moving the game to a major East Coast city would give the government the opportunity to "promote a real job of selling war bonds." Reminding Stimson that England and Scotland, "who are within a half hour of the real danger of the Luftwaffe," were about to play a match before more than 100,000 people, what, "for goodness sake," Weiss asked could possibly happen "to the good old U.S.A.?" Stimson held firm; the 1943 game was played at West Point. Aside from the Annapolis team, no Navy cadet was in attendance.

During the war years, major league baseball was stocked with men who in peacetime would never have made it past the minors. Roosevelt, who gave baseball a green light in 1942, was of the opinion that "perfectly healthy young men should [not] be playing ball at this time." As a result, wartime baseball was played largely by "4-F's, overage and underage players and those discharged from the armed forces." Weiss, "the sports world's vocal but unofficial spokesman on the floor of Congress," gave Roosevelt his unqualified support: "I feel that the President has been a great friend of sports, and I'm certain that Congress will support him solidly." Major league baseball (unlike horse-racing, which was banned for the duration) continued to be played throughout the war years. Of the 291 men playing on the sixteen major league teams in those years, 223 were classified 4-F, thirty-one were discharged veterans, thirty-two overage, and five underage.

Following his reelection to the Seventy-eighth Congress, Sam Weiss was appointed chair of a House Post Office and Post Roads Subcommittee. From that position, he was instrumental in passing legislation to ban "racially discriminatory literature or pictures from the mail." Weiss's other major legislative effort involved the establishment of a nationwide physical-training program. The bill called for a $25 million allocation for "extensive sports and exercises in schools to increase the strength, athletic skill, stamina, endurance and morale of the people of the United States."

In a speech on the House floor, Weiss noted that more than 51 percent of all draftees had been rejected for physical defects, and that more than 1 million men, once inducted "had to be released for bodily defects." Weiss said that his measure would "not only prepare youth for the time of war but train them to meet the challenges in the peaceful pursuits of life."

In November 1945, Representative Weiss was elected judge of the Common Pleas Court for Allegheny County, Pennsylvania. He resigned his seat in Congress on January 7, 1946. Twice reelected, he served on the bench until 1967, when, having reached age sixty-five, he retired. Uniquely, during his six years in Congress and sixteen of his twenty years on the bench, Weiss also served as a referee in the National Football League, traveling from city to city on a weekly basis.

Long active in the Jewish community, Weiss served a term as president of District Grand Lodge 3 of B'nai B'rith. District 3, comprising all B'nai B'rith units in New Jersey, Pennsylvania, Delaware, and West Virginia, with some 40,000 members. Weiss also served as B'nai B'rith's national vice president from 1949 to 1967, and as vice president of the Jewish Hospital in Denver.

Following his retirement from the bench, Samuel Weiss was elected president of the Pennsylvania State Judicial Administration. He died in Pittsburgh on February 1, 1977, and was buried in the B'nai Israel Cemetery.

References

Encyclopaedia Judaica (1972), vol. 16, col. 416.

New York Times, July 16, 1942, 15:3; July 30, 1942, 13:1; November 11, 1943 29:7; January 17, 1945, 24:1; February 8, 1946, 13:4.

Universal Jewish Encyclopedia.

Who Was Who in American Jewry, vol. 7.

WEISS, THEODORE S. (1927–1992): *Democrat from New York; served eight terms in the House (Ninety-fifth through One Hundred and Second Congress, January 3, 1977–September 14, 1992).*

For nearly sixteen years, Ted Weiss represented a New York City district that included the city's Upper West Side, Battery Park, Greenwich Village, and part of the Bronx. Without question, it was (and remains) one of the nation's most liberal and reform-minded districts. A thoroughgoing liberal, Ted Weiss was a perfect fit for his district. Even in an era when the term was "treated as an obscenity by many politicians," Ted Weiss continued to proudly proclaim his liberal pedigree. Because of his integrity and appetite for work, he was greatly admired by both his colleagues and his constituents. His congressional colleagues considered him the conscience of the House of Representatives. His constituents' loyalty was so great that they paid him the greatest of all political compliments: voting him back into office after he was already deceased.

Ted Weiss was born on September 17, 1927, in Gava, Hungary—a rural village about 50 miles southeast of Budapest—where his father was a butcher. Weiss, along with his older sister, attended the public schools of Gava as well as a local *cheder*. In 1930s, Hungary, Weiss recalled, his school was "remarkably free of overt anti-Semitism. About the only time you really saw it was on Hungarian Independence Day." In 1934, Ted's parents, Joseph and Pearl Weiss, divorced, and the mother began making plans to move to America. By prearrangement, Pearl Weiss married a man in New Jersey, which permitted her to leave Hungary and enter the United States. Pearl and her two children arrived in South Amboy, New Jersey, in 1938. Prior to leaving Gava, Ted had his "first bar mitzvah," so that his grandfather could be in attendance. His father remained in Hungary, was imprisoned in a concentration camp during World War II, and died three years after the end of the war.

Within four months of his arrival in America, Ted Weiss had learned to speak English and was attending public school. In 1940, he had his second bar mitzvah at a South Amboy synagogue. His participation in synagogue life would dwindle after this until many years later when, like many American Jews, he would join for the sake of his children. Following his graduation from Hoffman High School in 1946, Weiss enlisted in the United States Army; he served an eighteen-month tour of duty in Japan, working for the Armed Forces Radio Service. Following his detachment from service in 1947, Weiss, using his benefits under the G.I. Bill, entered Syracuse University. He earned a B.A. *cum laude* in political science in 1952. The next year, he earned his law degree from the same school. Upon passing the New York State bar examination, Weiss worked for a short while as a legal aid attorney and began a four-year stint (1955–59) stint as assistant district attorney in Manhattan. In 1960, he left the D.A.'s office and entered private practice with the firm of Gaffin and Weiss.

During his years in the D.A.'s office, Weiss teamed up with Eleanor Roosevelt and other "like-minded individuals" to organize a reform group called the Committee for Democratic Voters. Weiss was also a co-founder of the New Democratic Coalition, which, like the CDV, worked to further social reform. As the candidate of the new reform faction in city politics, Ted Weiss was elected to the New York City Council in 1961. During what eventually became a sixteen-year career on the City Council, Weiss came to be known as that body's conscience. As a councilman representing Manhattan, he championed tenants' rights, civil liberties, and environmental protection. He helped to write the city's strict gun-control law. As chair of the council's committee on environmental protection, he also wrote the city's stringent noise-control law.

Even as a member of the City Council, Ted Weiss spoke out on national and international issues. An early and vociferous opponent of the war in Vietnam, he denounced the conflict as "morally indefensible and militarily untenable." In 1966, his anger over the war reaching a plateau, Weiss challenged five-term incumbent

Leonard Farbstein in the Democratic primary for Farbstein's Twentieth District seat. Weiss, running on a "get out of Vietnam" platform, repeatedly scored the machine-backed Farbstein (whom he termed a "paper liberal") for his staunch support of the war in Southeast Asia. Weiss lost the June primary by a mere 151 votes.

Charging voter fraud, he got the state Supreme Court to hear his case. The court, finding that 1,153 invalid ballots had been cast, ordered a new election. Weiss lost the second primary race as well—this time by more than 1,000 votes.

Unbowed, Weiss turned around and challenged Farbstein again in the 1968 Democratic primary. This time "the organization brought Farbstein a 3,000 vote victory." In summing up his third defeat in less than two years, Weiss said that Farbstein's latest victory was due to a "dishonest, hand-tailored" job of redistricting that "deprived [me] of the votes of a large block of Reform Democrats."

Farbstein's days in Congress were numbered, however. In the 1970 Democratic primary, he was defeated by *Bella Abzug*. Ted Weiss continued on with the New York City Council.

By the mid-1970s, Weiss was "beginning to chafe under the limitations of the city council." Fortunately, the political game of musical chairs would help ease his chafing. In 1976, Bella Abzug decided to leave her safe Twentieth District seat in order to run for the United States Senate. Weiss quickly announced that he would run for her seat. In what one analyst called "an usual show of unity for West Side politics," Weiss won the nomination without opposition. When Abzug lost her Senate race, party leaders tried to persuade Ted Weiss to "step aside and let her resume her seat." Rumor had it they even offered him a judgeship if he would accede to their wishes. Weiss refused.

In the general election, Weiss ran against Republican Denise T. Weiseman. His slogan—"The city's future is in the hands of Washington"—reflected his belief that most social problems could best be handled on a federal level. During the campaign, he called for a federal takeover of all welfare expenditures in order "to encourage people to stay where they have roots." Weiss's rationale was that making welfare payments the purview of the various

states and municipalities tended to encourage people to move to places where welfare payments were the highest—thereby stimulating inequities in both population distribution and fiscal responsibility. His message struck a responsive chord with his West Side constituency; he was elected to Congress with 87 percent of the vote.

Weiss was assigned to the House Education and Labor Committee and Government Operations. During his first month in Congress, he petitioned the Senate Banking Committee for a "five-year extension of the federal emergency loan that had rescued New York City from the brink of bankruptcy." A few weeks later, he "secured a place on the special congressional subcommittee set up to scrutinize President Jimmy Carter's planned overhaul of the nation's welfare system." By the end of his first term in the House, Weiss had scored a perfect 100 rating from the liberal Americans for Democratic Action and 0 from the Conservative Americans for Constitutional Action. Weiss's unalloyed liberalism sat well with his constituents; he was reelected with more than 80 percent of the vote.

Ted Weiss was regularly reelected with larger percentages in the 80s. His only electoral scare came after the 1980 reapportionment, when it looked as if he would have to take on his liberal Democratic colleague Jonathan Bingham in the newly re-formed Seventh District. Outside of their commitment to liberal principles, Weiss and Bingham had next to nothing in common. Bingham (1914–1986), the son of the late Connecticut Senator Hiram Bingham, was a patrician—a graduate of Groton, Yale, and Yale Law. But Jonathan Bingham was also politically astute and a gentleman; he graciously retired after eighteen years in the House, leaving the district to Weiss.

Throughout his congressional career, Ted Weiss was known for his liberalism, his hard work, and for telling it like it is. When President Ronald Reagan proposed his New Federalism (by which the federal government would turn back moneys to the states), Weiss called it a "shift and shaft program . . . it shifts the burden and shafts the recipients." When Reagan ordered the invasion of the island of Grenada on October 25, 1983, Weiss quickly co-sponsored a resolution of impeachment on the grounds that Reagan had "usurped the power of Congress to declare war, violated treaty obligations and disregarded the First Amendment rights of the American people by blocking press coverage." At the time he introduced his impeachment resolution, Weiss told his colleagues: "In ordering the invasion of Grenada, Ronald Reagan has adopted the tactic of the Japanese attack on Pearl Harbor as the new American standard of behavior." Weiss's resolution never even made it to committee.

As chair of the House Subcommittee on Intergovernmental Relations and Human Resources, Ted Weiss displayed a passionate concern for national health care issues. He was "among the first to perceive the serious implications of the deadly acquired immune deficiency syndrome (AIDS) epidemic." As the representative of a district that included a large bloc of gays and minorities, both subject to the AIDS virus in alarming numbers, Weiss introduced the first bills to authorize emergency federal funding for AIDS research. He also sponsored the legislation that made AIDS victims eligible for coverage under Medicare.

Known for his gentlemanly demeanor, Weiss could easily fly off the handle when confronting adversarial witnesses. When an official of the Health Resources and Services Administration testified before Weiss's subcommittee that his agency had "not projected the number of health-care workers needed to deal with the growing number of children with AIDS," Weiss responded angrily. "The problem I have with all of you," he said, "is that all we get back when we ask for action are words. If the Public Health Service does nothing else, the least it can do is project what the needs will be. Is that too much to ask?"

Ted Weiss was also one of the leading supporters of women's issues in the House of Representatives. As one of the few male members of the Congressional Caucus for Women's Issues and the National Commission on Working Women, he co-sponsored the Economic Equity Act, which "guaranteed women economic equality in the workplace." Without question, Weiss was a staunch supporter of the Equal Rights Amendment, maintaining that "only a constitutional amendment can insure equality for women, not just in theory, but in the reality of our daily lives."

With the demise of the Soviet Union in the late 1980s, Weiss turned his attention to the conversion of the American defense establishment. One of his pet ideas was a cabinet-level Defense Economic Adjustment Council, empowered to "draw up plans for converting military facilities and defense plants to civilian uses." Weiss's conservative colleagues derided the measure as "a typical liberal effort to eliminate defense programs and convert military funding to domestic purposes." Countering their charges, Weiss insisted that "in a new era of superpower relations and zero or negative growth in defense budgets, economic conversion has become a virtual reality."

In the early 1980s, Ted Weiss underwent heart-bypass surgery and the installation of a pacemaker. Neither procedure slowed him down. He kept up his normal breakneck pace for nearly another decade. Ted Weiss succumbed to heart failure on September 14, 1992, the day before the New York Democratic primary. His death caused considerable turmoil in Democratic circles. At the time of his death, his only opponent was Arthur R. Block, a member of the New Alliance, a fringe party standing in opposition to most of Weiss's liberal principles. With Weiss out of the picture, Block was assured of victory in both the primary and the general election. Enter the Democratic Party, whose leaders amassed an overnight campaign urging, begging, and cajoling the public to vote for Ted Weiss even though he was dead. Voters responded to their call by giving Weiss an 88 percent margin of victory—the largest of his career. One might posit that voters merely cast their ballots for Weiss out of habit, not knowing of his death. This is highly unlikely, since the *New York Times* ran a front-page article on his passing. Weiss's victory permitted Democratic leaders to choose the successor who would run in the general election. Their candidate, *Jerrold Nadler*, went on to victory in November.

Ted Weiss was married twice. His first marriage, which ended in divorce, produced two sons: Thomas D. and Stephen R. In 1980, Weiss married Sonya M. Hoover ("a Yankee from Indiana"), a press officer for the deputy attorney general for Medicaid fraud control for the State of New York.

Throughout his career, Ted Weiss stood up for the poor, the homeless, and the sick. The causes closest to his heart included AIDS, Agent Orange, breast implants, food stamps, federal housing, and the elimination of nuclear weapons. Shortly after his death, President Bill Clinton signed the Family Leave Act into law—a bill originally sponsored by Ted Weiss, the immigrant from Gava, Hungary.

References
Interview with Ted Weiss, July 1992.
Almanac of American Politics, 1978–1992.
Current Biography, 1985, pp. 439–442.
Politics in America, 1982–1992.

WELLSTONE, PAUL DAVID (1944–): *Democrat from Minnesota; has served two terms in the Senate (January 3, 1991–present).*

Shortly after his election to the United States Senate in 1990, the *Minneapolis Star Tribune* ran an article entitled "Another tactless, brusque senator from Minnesota." Its lead paragraph described

an upstart Democrat politician with an advanced degree in political science and a reputation for being a good speaker, but also for talking too much, never elected to statewide office, [who] defeats a supposedly entrenched, personally popular Republican incumbent in a year that wasn't supposed to be good for Democrats. He goes to the Senate and immediately stakes a position to the left of almost everyone else. He offends a few senior senators by brashly wading into controversial issues right away, instead of listening and learning as freshmen are supposed to do.

Although the article was written about Paul Wellstone in 1991, the quotation was about Senator Hubert H. Humphrey in 1949.

The similarities between the two men are more than superficial. Like Humphrey, Wellstone was written off early by Washington insiders as a "tactless, brusque loser who would never amount to anything." And like Humphrey, Wellstone, much to the amazement (and regret) of his supporters, did learn, after several false starts, how to play the game of being an insider in the difficult maze of senatorial politics and protocol. One suspects, however, that no matter how good a Senator he becomes, Paul David Wellstone probably will never be voted second on a list of the ten best Senators in U.S. history—as Hubert Humphrey was in 1985, second only to Henry Clay.

Dubbed "the spirit of Woodstock 1969 come back to earth," Paul David Wellstone was, in the 1990s, *sui generis*: "Among the $700 suits on the Senate floor, he's the guy in the $99.99 special from K. G. Men's Store in Northfield. Among pols who stride the halls like deities, he insists

that janitors and elevator operators call him Paul." Most of what makes him uniquely liberal in a time of increasing political conservatism stems from his upbringing. For although Paul Wellstone was raised in 1950s suburban Virginia, his upbringing was more like that of a 1920s Lower East Side socialist.

The Senator's father, Leon Weschelstein, was born in Odessa in 1897 to a family of devoutly Orthodox Jews. Leon's family moved to Siberia when he was a youngster. In 1914, traveling alone, he crossed the Bering Sea, settling in Seattle, where he entered the University of Washington. Although he graduated with a degree in electrical engineering, Leon "wanted to be a Chekhov." Moving to New York in order to pursue his dream of being a playwright, Leon found work writing for the *American Mercury*. While in New York, he met Mincha, the daughter of a labor organizer named Menashe Daneschevsky. (In public school, "Mincha Daneschevsky" had somehow become, "Minnie Danish.") The two were married, and soon moved to Boston, where Leon got a job as an editorial writer on the *Boston Transcript*.

Following a laudatory article he wrote on Justice Louis D. Brandeis, Weschelstein received a letter from Justice Felix Frankfurter. "As one Jewish immigrant to another," Frankfurter wrote, "I applaud your article. If you ever have any difficulty, please let me know." Shortly afterwards, the *Boston Transcript* folded. Leon Weschelstein, sorely in need of employment, took Frankfurter up on his kind offer. Soon thereafter, Frankfurter secured Leon a position as an economist with the Department of Commerce in Washington. Within a short time, Leon moved over to the Voice of America, where he worked as a writer under Edward R. Murrow. Fluent in ten languages, and able to speak English without an accent, Weschelstein (who Americanized his name to Wellstone shortly after going to work for the government) worked for the VOA until he retired in 1962.

Leon and Minnie Wellstone's second son, Paul David, was born in Washington on July 21,

1944, and raised in East Falls Church (Arlington), Virginia. Although raised an Orthodox Jew, Leon had become, in his own term, "a reverent agnostic." As such, neither Paul nor his brother received a Hebrew school education: "By the time my father began to think about whether I should become bar mitzvah, I was already thirteen, and it was too late," the Senator relates. While Leon worked at the VOA, his mother labored as a cafeteria worker at a local junior high school.

The twin traditions of reading and discussion were of paramount importance in the Wellstone household; every evening at precisely 10:00, the family would gather around the kitchen table, "eating sponge cake and drinking hot tea," and discussing world affairs. In his earliest years, Paul learned about Eugene V. Debs, the International Workers of the World, and the labor organizers of the old Lower East Side. From these evening tea-sessions, Paul became imbued with a "strong moral conscience and an inclination to side with the underdog." As a teenager, he immersed himself in the works of Jewish theologians Martin Buber and Abraham Joshua Heschel.

Paul Wellstone entered the University of North Carolina in 1962, where he was an average student and a superior wrestler; he finished his first two seasons undefeated, and won the ACC championship. During his sophomore year, Paul married Sheila, his childhood sweetheart. Sheila came from an "Appalachian-Southern Baptist family." Within a year, their first child, David, was born, necessitating Paul to quit wrestling and start working at part-time jobs. With the birth of a child, Paul Wellstone decided that it would be smarter to double up on classes, in order to graduate as early as possible.

One evening in the spring of 1964, Paul and Sheila were taking a walk on Franklin Street in Chapel Hill. As they passed the post office, Paul saw members of the Klan menacing and verbally harassing a group of students who had gathered to stage a fast in opposition to racial discrimination in Chapel Hill. Wellstone, who had been politically uninvolved up to that point, remembers: "My first reaction was that I didn't have time to get involved. I remember thinking to myself, the demonstrators are right, but I'm married, working, trying to graduate in three years, expecting a child. I just can't do this. But the sight was so powerful that I felt I couldn't just stand on the sideline." Wellstone joined the activists, and then became increasingly involved in university and community issues.

Graduating in 1965, Wellstone entered the UNC graduate school, working toward a Ph.D. in political science. During his four years as a graduate student, Wellstone participated in anti-war teach-ins, and voter registration drives and came under the spell of future Congressman *Allard Lowenstein*. During his final year of graduate school, Wellstone played a prominent role in organizing support for striking cafeteria workers. Wellstone received a Ph.D. in 1969, having written his dissertation on "Operation Breakthrough," an organizing effort carried out by members of the black community of Durham, North Carolina, in the mid-1960s. Ph.D. in hand, Wellstone got a job as assistant professor of political science at Carleton College, where he would remain until his election to the United States Senate.

Within a year of his arrival at Carleton, he began organizing in nearby Rice County, "succeeding in building a coalition of senior citizens, welfare mothers, working poor, family farmers and others to challenge the county's existing power structure." Out of these experiences came Wellstone's first book, *How the Rural Poor Get Power*. (His second book, *Powerline*, chronicled his observations on the struggles of Minnesota farmers in the late 1970s.) Wellstone proved to be an extremely popular professor at the small, highly respected liberal arts college. So much so, that in 1974, when Wellstone went on the warpath against Carleton's investment policies in South Africa and the faculty voted unanimously to deny him tenure, more than half the student body signed protest petitions on his behalf. Responding to the students' petitions, the faculty agreed to bring in "outside evaluators," who recommended that Wellstone be granted tenure. It was granted. During his years at Carleton, Wellstone was arrested twice: once for leading a demonstration against American involvement in Cambodia; once for battling banks that were foreclosing on local farmers.

Wellstone's efforts on behalf of struggling Minnesota farmers led to his first unsuccessful political campaign. In 1982, Wellstone wrote a memo "suggesting that the farmers try to get someone from their organization elected to the state board . . . in order to push for a moratorium on the foreclosures." At a meeting held a few days later, the assembled protesters decided that the professor was their man. Wellstone ran for state auditor, losing the election to future Minnesota Governor Arne Carlson, but "whetting his appetite for politics."

In 1984, Wellstone, by now the father of three (in addition to David, Marsha, born in 1969, and Mark, born in 1971), became a Democratic National Committeeman. In 1988, he was asked to co-chair Jesse Jackson's presidential campaign in Minnesota. Unsure about what to do because of Jackson's earlier disparaging comments about Jews, Wellstone agreed to sit down and talk with the black activist. The two spoke for over an hour, and Wellstone told Jackson he would think about it. After a week, he agreed. When Massachusetts Governor Michael Dukakis won the Democratic nomination, Wellstone became the co-chairman of his campaign.

In 1990, Paul Wellstone was urged to run for United States Senate against incumbent *Rudy Boschwitz*. He agreed, and quickly announced his candidacy. Few people gave Wellstone a chance; Boschwitz was well known, running well ahead in the polls, and had amassed a formidable $7 million campaign treasury. What Wellstone lacked in name recognition and money he more than made up for in organizational skill and imagination. Traveling around the state in a battered old green school bus (which frequently broke down), Wellstone went from one end of the state to the other. Boschwitz, underestimating Wellstone's campaign prowess, ran few ads and rested on his laurels.

Wellstone captivated the voters of Minnesota with a series of television commercials dubbed "Looking for Rudy." The ads were modeled after the film *Roger and Me*, in which the main character tries to secure an interview with Roger B. Smith, the former chairman of General Motors. In Wellstone's version, he is desperately trying to track down Boschwitz for a debate—even leaving his home phone number—but never making it past two Boschwitz workers.

Wellstone was taking a calculated gamble here: Boschwitz had already agreed to a debate. The ads had cute touches, such as Wellstone speaking rapidly on camera "because I don't have enough money for longer commercials,"

and proclaiming "I may not have his money, but I'm better looking." These ads, masterminded by North Woods Advertising, a volunteer group led by Bill Hillsman, won the American Marketing Association's Grand Effie Award for the "most effective advertising of 1990."

With Wellstone gaining in the polls, Boschwitz made a fatal mistake: he sent a letter to members of the Minnesota Jewish community charging Wellstone with being a "non-Jew," and upbraiding him for having "no connection whatsoever with the Jewish community or our communal life." Boschwitz's tactic backfired; even his own rabbi condemned his "attempt to appeal to Jewish chauvinism." Wellstone's campaign volunteers put the final nail in Boschwitz's coffin by managing to contact more than 700,000 voters in the seventy-two hours preceding the election. On election day, Boschwitz lost to Wellstone 50 percent to 48 percent, becoming the only incumbent Senator to go down to defeat. A few days later, Yoav Karny, Washington correspondent for the Israeli paper *Ha'aretz* summed up the election by writing: "In Minnesota this week, the bad Jew defeated the good Jew. Thank God."

Paul Wellstone's first few days in Washington were unique. Accompanied by dozens of his campaign workers, he drove to Washington in his old green school bus. Pulling up alongside the limousines parked in front of the Capitol, he was told to move on—until he informed the incredulous cop that he was a newly elected United States Senator. Walking up the Capitol steps, Wellstone and his band marched to his new office, only to have their entry barred by yet another policeman, who could not believe that he was a Senator. The first article written about him in Washington described him as looking "like a 47-year old fireplug who was yanked from a demonstration and abruptly deposited in the Capitol, with barely time to think about his new role, let alone change clothes."

At his swearing-in, on January 3, 1991, Wellstone asked former Vice President and Minnesota Senator Walter Mondale to escort him down the aisle, thereby "bypassing the tradition of having the other home-state sitting Senator (in this case Republican Dave Durenburger) do the honors." As he was about to be sworn, Wellstone "thrust an audio tape of an antiwar meeting into the hands of . . . Vice President Quayle." Within a few days of his swearing-in, he participated in a candle-lit peace march that ended at the White House (the only Senator to do so), and breached Senate protocol by publicly attacking Senator Jesse Helms as someone "I have despised ever since I was 19." Later that same month, his "relentless, highly publicized attempts to lobby the Bush administration to change its policy in the Persian Gulf prompted Bush to ask members of the Minnesota delegation, "Who is this chicken-shit?'" It was a baptism that perhaps only Hubert Humphrey might have appreciated.

Wellstone's first vote came on the issue of sending American troops to the Persian Gulf. Taking the Senate floor, Wellstone said: "I [can] not accept the loss of life of any of our children in the Persian Gulf right now, and that tells me in my gut I do not believe it is time to go to war. I do not believe the administration has made the case to go to war. And if I apply this standard to my children, then I have to apply this standard to everyone's children. I have to apply this standard to all of God's children."

Senator Wellstone's main areas of concern have been health-care, campaign reform, education, and the environment. After several false starts (including wearing a bright red tie and brown suit to his first black-tie affair), Wellstone started to get the hang of Washington. Walter Mondale's advice, that "you have six years here, and don't have to get everything done the first day," was beginning to sink in. As he started "calming down," Wellstone also began learning to work with people. He became particularly close with Senate Majority Leader George Mitchell of Maine, who, sensing an emerging talent, appointed him a member of the Senate delegation to the Earth Summit in Rio de Janeiro.

One of Wellstone's first legislative successes came in the environmental field. Along with some of the Senate's "most ardent environmentalists," he successfully knocked language out of a sweeping energy bill "that would have permitted drilling in the Arctic National Wildlife Refuge."

In 1991, Wellstone made his first trip to Israel. Before his visit to the Jewish state, Wellstone had been considering voting to withhold $10 billion in U.S. loan guarantees to Israel for the resettlement of Soviet Jews, unless the Israeli government agreed to freeze settlements in the administered territories. Upon his return, he said that "as the son of a Russian Jew," he supported granting the loan guarantees, and "would prefer that the aid not be linked to the issue of settlements." Shortly thereafter, he began studying Judaism with Rabbi Bernard Raskas of Minnesota, in an attempt to learn more about his heritage. Asked to speak before a meeting of the Arab American Anti-Discrimination Committee, he was applauded for criticizing Israeli settlements. Looking out over his audience, he felt moved to "speak out and say that as Israel moves to make peace with the Palestinians . . . Arab countries must make peace with Israel and recognize Israel and welcome Israel." For this he was booed. Wellstone felt proud.

Paul Wellstone is considered the most liberal Senator of his era. As such, he was a particular target of the Republicans, marked for defeat in 1996. Once again, his opponent in his race for reelection was Rudy Boschwitz; but Boschwitz wasn't facing the same Wellstone. Gone were the pre-wrinkled suits and amateur haircuts. Gone was the man who had refused to accept any contributions greater than $100. Not that Wellstone had sold out. Rather, he had "learned to respect the office of Senator," and to understand "the importance of building coalitions in order to get things done."

In fact, Wellstone revived his infamous school bus for the 1996 election against former Senator Boschwitz. Barnstorming the state, Wellstone stood proudly on his record of liberalism. Boschwitz, aided by more than $2 million of Republican National Committee money, portrayed Wellstone as "dangerously out of touch with Minnesota." Running as a pro-life, pro-business conservative, Boschwitz hammered away at Wellstone for being the only Senator to vote against the 1996 Welfare Reform Act. He employed the services of controversial Republican political consultant Arthur Finkelstein, an advisor to National Republican Senatorial Committee chair Alfonse D'Amato of New York. Finkelstein was known for his "utilization of bare-knuckles politics" and for "hammering Democrats at every turn as 'liberals.'" In his campaign speeches, Boschwitz proclaimed that while Wellstone "counts compassion on the number of people you put into the welfare system, I'm for more freedom. I'm for less government." Wellstone's energetic liberalism carried the day; he defeated Boschwitz by nearly 200,000 votes. Far from being an outsider, Paul Wellstone was now heading into his second term in the United States Senate.

Although Paul and Sheila Wellstone did not raise their children as Jews, the three consider themselves Jewish. Much of this has to do with their grandparents, Leon and Minnie. After Leon's retirement, the couple moved to Paul and Sheila's neighborhood, where their children could take care of them; both were suffering from Parkinson's disease. Leon Wellstone died in 1983, haunted by the fact that he had not seen his parents, brothers, or sisters since his departure from Russia. Minnie Wellstone lived long enough to vote for her son for Senator, but died before he took office. On election day, Minnie's granddaughter Marcia picked her up at the nursing home where she was incapacitated with Parkinson's and Alzheimer's, and drove her to the polls. When questioned by the poll worker as to whether the woman was in any shape to cast a vote, Marcia responded: "No matter what, she's going to vote for her son, even if I have to do it for her." Minnie was wheeled into the booth and cast her last vote—for Paul Wellstone.

Senator Wellstone is a muscular five-foot five-inch man with curly hair and a ready smile. When speaking, he resembles a basketball player going for a rebound: "his arms flail, his hands chop the air, and his legs convulse into deep knee bends." Much more comfortable today with his Jewishness than at any time in the past, he feels his life "inextricably bound up with the values and beliefs [I] absorbed as part of my Jewish background." His basic philosophy of Judaism comes from Albert Einstein: "The pursuit of knowledge for its own sake, an almost fanatical love of justice, and the desire for independence. . . these are features of the Jewish tradition that make me thank my stars I belong to it."

References

Interview with Paul Wellstone, July 1992.
Almanac of American Politics, 1992–1998.
Carolina Alumni Review, Summer 1991.
Long Island Jewish World, August 9, 1991.
Mother Jones, January–February, 1992, pp. 32 ff.
New York Times Magazine, November 10, 1991, pp. 36 ff.
Roll Call, October 17, 1996
U.S. News and World Report, June 24, 1991.

WEXLER, ROBERT (1961–): *Democrat from Florida; has served two terms in the House (One Hundred and Fifth Congress, January 7, 1997–present).*

In early October 1995, Florida Congressman Harry Johnston (Nineteenth District) announced that after four terms he would not be seeking reelection. His statement set off a predictable chain reaction; members of the state legislature began dreaming about a move to Capitol Hill, while municipal leaders considered making a leap to the state capital in Tallahassee. This game of musical chairs resulted in a political dogfight of epic proportions: "three Jewish state lawmakers and a [party-switching] Greek millionaire against each other on the Democratic side; and a Jew-cum-Catholic-cum-Baptist-cum-Messianic Jew against a little-known Broward County chiropractor on the Republican ticket." Add to this mix a blatantly anti-Semitic slur and a multimillion-dollar defamation of character suit, and you have one of 1996's most convoluted races. Ironically, the winner, liberal state Senator Robert Wexler, had originally come to the public's attention when he advocated chemical castration for convicted rapists.

Robert Wexler was born in Queens, New York, on January 2, 1961, the only child of Ben and Sandra (Feldman) Wexler. His paternal grandfather, Russian-born Max Wexler, had settled on the Lower East Side of New York in 1905, where he operated a candy store and drove a soda truck. Ben Wexler originally worked for the *New York Times* and lived in Queens. When Robert was six, the family moved to Long Island. In 1971, after a family vacation to Florida, Ben and Sandra decided to pull up stakes and move to the Sunshine State. They settled in Hollywood, and Ben went to work for the Norton Tire Company. Today the elder Wexlers live in Pembroke Pines, Florida, where Ben is a sales representative for Scholastic Book Fair.

Robert Wexler received his early indoctrination into politics at home. "Politics is something I always wanted to do. I grew up in a home where being in government was an honorable

calling." One of his first political memories goes back to age seven, when he debated his father over whether Hubert Humphrey or Bobby Kennedy should get the Democratic presidential nomination.

As a newcomer to Florida, Robert Wexler attended Attucks Middle School in Davie and Hollywood Hills High School. While in high school, he met his future wife, Laurie Cohen. The Wexlers belonged to a Conservative synagogue in Hollywood, although Robert's bar mitzvah was held at the Reform Temple Solel. Following his high school graduation, Wexler spent one year at Emory University in Atlanta before transferring to the University of Florida in Gainesville. He received his B.A. in political science in 1982, and then moved to Washington, D.C., where he attended the George Washington University School of Law. While going to law school, Wexler spent his first summer working as a civilian employee at the Navy Department. His second summer he interned with the Miami firm of Faller, White; during his final year, he worked at the Department of Justice, assigned to the office of the federal attorney with jurisdiction over the District of Columbia.

After receiving his law degree in 1985, Wexler returned to Florida, where he became a successful litigation attorney with the firm of Shutts & Bowen. In 1986, Robert and Laurie married, taking a three-week honeymoon in Israel. It was Wexler's first visit to the Jewish state. For Laurie Wexler, it represented a return; following her graduation from college, she had spent nearly a year in Israel, and had given serious thought to making *aliyah* (immigration).

Shortly after joining Shutts & Bowen, Robert Wexler became a member of the Palm Beach County Planning and Zoning Committee and the Democratic Executive Committee.

In 1990, at age twenty-nine, Wexler entered the Democratic primary for state senator from Florida's Twenty-eighth District. Democrat Don Childers had represented the district for sixteen years. Wexler pulled off an upset, winning a plurality in the primary (41.2 percent) and then defeating Childers (who ran as an Independent) in the run-off with 73.5 percent of the vote. In November 1990, he was elected to the Florida State Senate with 99.5 percent over write-in candidate Tim Bearson.

At twenty-nine, Wexler was the youngest member of the Florida Senate. Labeled a "political *wunderkind*," Wexler rose quickly in the Senate leadership, becoming chairman of three different committees, including criminal justice.

During his first term in Tallahassee, Wexler wrote an ethics and campaign reform package that "reduc[ed] the influence of special-interest groups on the political process and empower[ed] the public." Included in this measure was a $500 limit on campaign contributions. An October 1991 article in *Boca Raton Magazine* described Wexler's measure as "the most comprehensive ethics-in-elections bill in the nation." Wexler was also responsible for the legislation that created Florida's Department of the Elderly.

Wexler got his first taste of national media exposure in 1993, when he proposed that second-time rapists be chemically castrated, and third-time offenders be executed. The bill died, but not before Wexler landed on both *NBC Dateline* and *CNN News*. Following the bill's defeat (and a flurry of negative editorials) Wexler offered a watered-down version of the measure, calling for the castration procedure "to be administered in cases involving children under 17." That idea died as well.

Referring to himself as "a vigilant crime fighter," Wexler tore into the criminal justice system, noting that "repeat violent offenders [are] spending less than one third of their terms in jail." As a political pragmatist, Wexler also advocated freeing up prison beds occupied by nonviolent drug offenders. As he told the *Palm Beach Jewish Times*: "In an ideal world, we might imprison a car thief after his first or second offense, but if it means less money for nursing home care—and in reality it does—then we can't afford it."

Wexler's politics struck a responsive chord with the voters in his Palm Beach County district. Even when its boundaries were changed in 1992 to include the northern portion of Broward County, he was reelected virtually without opposition. In 1994, he won a landslide reelection against Tim Bearson, who was running against Wexler for the third time.

Shortly after his marriage to Laurie Cohen in 1986, Robert Wexler became "reacquainted" with his Jewishness to a far greater degree than his upbringing might have suggested. Originally members of Boca Raton's largest Conservative synagogue, B'nai Torah, Senator and Mrs. Wexler began attending the Orthodox Boca Raton Synagogue. There, under the tutelage of Rabbi Kenneth Brander, the Wexlers slowly began adding to their Jewish lives and lifestyle. Today, the Wexlers—Rob, wife Laurie, daughter Rachel, and son Zachary—keep a kosher home and observe the Sabbath. In the Wexler home, "the children know that mom and dad will be home Friday night. And that things are different until *Havdalah* [the ceremony at the end of the Sabbath on Saturday night]. It is the one constant of our lives."

The Wexlers have also participated as students in the Leslie Wexner Lecture series, aimed at increasing the Jewish awareness, knowledge, and practice of young professionals. They spent their first summer break from Congress (August, 1997) attending a month-long Wexner seminar in Israel, "parking" their children at an Israeli children's camp.

Just days after Representative Johnston announced his retirement from Congress, Robert Wexler declared his candidacy for the open seat. Within a matter of weeks, the field had grown with the declared candidacies of State Senator Peter Weinstein, State Representative Ben Graber, and millionaire businessman Peter Tsakanikas. Weinstein, a seven-term senator representing Broward County, was the son of Moses Weinstein, former Speaker of the New York State Assembly. Graber, who was born in a displaced persons' camp in Germany shortly after World War II, was a Coral Springs (Broward County) gynecologist who had represented his city in the state house for the past eight years. Months later, businessman Peter Tsakanikas (who had lost as a Republican to Harry Johnston in 1994) also entered the Democratic primary. For all their years in Tallahassee, Weinstein, Wexler, and Graber had been political allies and friends. Graber and Weinstein actually lived across the street from one another in Coral Springs.

From the outset, the three lawmakers declared that their being Jewish would "neither help nor hurt their chances" of election. That all changed when Tsakanikas "played his religion card, likening two voter-heavy retirement communities, Kings Point and Century Village, to "Nazi concentration camps." Tsakanikas (who years earlier had lost a race for Maryland Governor) issued a statement pledging "to liberate prisoners in Century Village–Kings Point political concentration camps." The bizarre imagery outraged local Jewish leaders and drew heated retorts from the three Jewish candidates. Wexler issued a statement declaring: "Any reference to the Holocaust or concentration camps for the purpose of political gain is both inappropriate and offensive. These references are especially outrageous when they are made in a community with a high number of Jewish residents and Holocaust survivors." Tsakanikas's campaign was effectively derailed in July, when he suffered a debilitating stroke.

Wexler, Weinstein, and Graber presented voters in the Nineteenth District with few political differences. All three sported liberal voting records. All three were pro-choice, against prayer in the public schools, and champions of Medicare, Medicaid, and Social Security. With so little separating them politically, the three began scrapping personally. At the beginning of the race, Wexler urged his colleagues to join him in signing a voluntary pledge to keep the campaign above-board. Weinstein sneered at Wexler's suggestion, calling it "a political ploy." The campaign quickly descended into a quagmire of personal charges and counter-charges.

Graber fired the first volley when he scored Senators Weinstein and Wexler for continuing to accept campaign contributions during session. (At the time, the Florida House, unlike the Senate, barred its members from accepting contributions during sessions of the legislature.) Graber lambasted his fellow legislators, calling their actions "odious." Wexler and Weinstein initially balked, but then joined in a unanimous vote to ban the acceptance of contributions during session. In passing, Weinstein noted that Graber's challenge had come at a time when the doctor-legislator was lagging behind in fundraising.

Wexler fired the next shot, charging that Weinstein, whom he called "a career politician," had been embroiled in an S&L scandal, and that Graber was "a debtor who was sued six times."

Weinstein responded by slapping Wexler with a multimillion-dollar defamation of character suit. Weinstein issued a campaign circular calling Wexler "the Republicans' favorite candidate," and charged the Palm Beach lawmaker with accepting contributions from sugar industry executives. By the time of the primary vote in September, the public was getting fed up with the backbiting and name-calling. On election day, Wexler won a plurality with 47 percent to Weinstein's 29 percent and Graber's 22 percent. Wexler then handily defeated Weinstein in the runoff with 65 percent of the vote.

Wexler's Republican opponent in the November general election was business consultant Beverly Kennedy. Kennedy, who had previously lost two congressional races to Democrat *Peter Deutsch* (as well as a City Commission race), was well-known in the community as a member of Fort Lauderdale's First Baptist Church. During a speech before a Jewish group in August, she suddenly blurted out: "I am Jewish. I am Jewish. It's my heritage. You can't take it away from me." It was the first time that Kennedy had ever mentioned her Jewish roots. After making this announcement, Kennedy explained that she was a "Messianic Jew"—meaning that she considered herself a Jew but accepted Jesus as her redeemer.

Jewish voters in the district, the vast majority of them Democrats, viewed Kennedy's declaration with skepticism—just another politician doing whatever was necessary to capture the Jewish vote. In fact, though, Kennedy was speaking the truth. She was the daughter of Jewish immigrants named Kleban and had been raised in a kosher home. In 1966, with the annulment of her marriage to a Jew, Kennedy had converted to Catholicism in order to marry Ed Kennedy, a former Broward County Commissioner. Kennedy's belated "recollection" of her Jewish roots did little for her at the polls; on election day, Wexler won a decisive two-to-one victory.

As a member of the One Hundred and Fifth Congress, Robert Wexler was assigned seats on Foreign Affairs and Judiciary. He decided to keep his family in Boca Raton, where his daughter attended the Hillel Day School and his son went to the Jewish Community Center. Wexler, who neither campaigns nor conducts business from sundown Friday to sunset Saturday, intended to return to Florida each weekend in order to spend the Sabbath with his wife and children. On January 3, 1997, just three days before he was sworn in as a member of the Hundred and Fifth Congress, Rob Wexler became a father for a third time. Hannah Wexler entered the world weighing 6 pounds, 13 ounces and measuring a most Jewishly appropriate 18 inches long. (In Jewish alphanumeric lore, the number 18 represents the word *chai*, meaning "life.").

Upon hearing that Rob Wexler was going to be taking over his congressional seat, retiring Harry Johnston humorously offered the incoming freshman the following unsolicited advice:

- Don't eat lunch at the House Members' buffet: Beautiful room, bad food.
- Don't forget your Congressional pin: It gets you in the door.
- Forget about learning your way around the tunnels underneath the Capitol and office buildings, which takes about 18 months.
- Do get your shoes shined and always tip well.
- Do eat lunch at the Library of Congress.
- And, perhaps, most important, Democrats sit on the right, Republicans sit on the left.

When the House Judiciary Committee began discussions on the possible impeachment of President Clinton in the early fall of 1998, Wexler suddenly found himself catapulted into the national spotlight. His appearances on programs such as *Firing Line* and *the C.B.S. Evening News* found him urging his colleagues to be more measured and less partisan in their deliberations: "Many of our colleagues have referred to our role here today as the most important work a member of Congress can perform. I sincerely hope not. This may be the most attention that this committee will ever receive. This may be the biggest news story in which we will ever play a part. But God help the nation if this is the most important work we will ever do in Congress."

On the Judiciary Committee's first day of deliberations into the Clinton-Lewinsky scandal,

Wexler declared: "I am not proud of the personal conduct of the president that has cheapened our national discourse, confused our children, disillusioned our idealists and empowered our cynics. While I'm very proud of the president's accomplishments, I am not proud of his moral lapses in judgement." Continuing, the freshman—one of the last panelists to speak—excoriated investigator Kenneth Starr for his handling of the case: "I am not proud of this prosecutor, Ken Starr, who has turned government in upon itself, distorted our system of justice in a politically inspired witch hunt that rivals McCarthyism in its sinister purpose, that asks mothers to betray daughters, Secret Service officers to betray their highest charge, and lawyers to betray their clients, dead or alive, all in search of a crime to justify five years of work and more than $40 million of taxpayers' money."

Hugely popular in his South Florida district, Rob Wexler was reelected without opposition on November 3, 1998. Throughout the first half of 1999, Wexler was prominently mentioned as a possible candidate for the United States Senate seat being vacated by two-term incumbent Connie Mack. In late May 1999, Wexler announced his intention to run for reelection to the House.

On January 7, 1997, the day Rob was sworn in as a member of Congress, Laurie Wexler was back in Boca Raton, tending to their newborn. Rob was accompanied to Washington by his parents and two older children. Upon entering the House dining room for the first time (where they all ate grilled cheese sandwiches) Ben Wexler was asked if he was a new member of Congress. "No sir," he beamed, but my son is."

References
Interview with Robert Wexler, December 1996.
Boca Raton Magazine, October 1991.
Miami Herald, March 27, 1996.
Palm Beach Jewish Times, August 10, 1996, p. 9; September 27, 1996, pp. 16–21.
Roll Call, December 2, 1996, pp. 1, 16.
Washington Post, October 16, 1998, A:8.

WOLF, HARRY BENJAMIN (1880–1944):
Democrat from Maryland; served one term in the House (Sixtieth Congress, March 4, 1907–March 3, 1909).

According to Article I, section 1 of the Maryland State Constitution, "No Person shall be a Representative who shall not have attained to the Age of twenty-five Years." Harry B. Wolf was one of the very few members of a state legislature elected at the constitutionally mandated minimum age. In fact, when he declared his candidacy for the Democratic nomination from Maryland's Third Congressional District, he was merely two years over the required age. A young man of enormous gifts, Wolf had already tried more than 2,000 legal cases before his first political campaign, and was widely considered one of Maryland's most successful trial lawyers.

Harry Benjamin Wolf, the son of Jacob and Mollie (Furstenberg) Wolf, was born in Baltimore on June 16, 1880. Not much is known about his early life, except that he was one of three children, and educated in the Baltimore public school system. As a youngster, he was a newsboy who peddled fruit on the side. Deciding that peddling on foot was too difficult, he and his brother purchased a horse and wagon, bought bananas on the Baltimore waterfront, and proceeded to sell them to shopkeepers throughout the city. In this way, Wolf had already amassed quite a tidy sum even before he entered the University of Maryland School of Law. Graduated in 1901, Wolf quickly went into private practice as a litigator, specializing in criminal law. During his first five years as an attorney, he was involved in more than 5,000 cases, and developed a reputation for getting most of his clients off. Ever restless and ambitious, Wolf soon branched out. By the time he ran for Congress, he was involved in the real estate business and hotel property investments, had founded a successful Baltimore–Eastern Shore ferry service, and had already served one term in the Maryland House of Delegates.

In 1906, Republican Representative Frank C. Wachter, an eight-year veteran of the Congress, decided to retire from politics. Wolf quickly put his name into nomination and won. The Third District, covering Baltimore's Eastside, contained a majority of the city's Jewish population—estimated at 25,000 in 1907. Wolf served his only term as a member of the minority party; the Sixtieth Congress was under the thumb of the tyrannical "Uncle" Joe Cannon of Illinois. In his first bid for reelection, Wolf was defeated by Republican John Kronmiller, and returned to his lucrative law practice. Amazingly, his career in electoral politics ended three and a half months before his twenty-ninth birthday.

As noted above, Wolf had an uncanny ability to get charges against his clients reduced. Occasionally, he resorted to extralegal means. In 1922, Wolf was found guilty of conspiracy to obstruct justice in connection with a murder trial. His client, nineteen-year-old Walter Socolow, was one of five young men arrested in the daylight holdup and murder of William Norris, a Baltimore building contractor. Arrested in New York City, Socolow was transferred back to Baltimore to stand trial. Although Socolow was found guilty of murder, Wolf managed to keep him from hanging. It later turned out that Wolf had conspired with one of Socolow's accomplices to create a "frump" story. In Wolf's trial before the Maryland Supreme Court, it was alleged that Wolf had worked up the false story "in order to destroy the value of the confession" of yet another of Socolow's accomplices, who had turned state's evidence. Wolf, who could have been disbarred for his actions, was fined and placed on probation.

Married to Sara C. Cohen of New York, Wolf had four sons: Edwin J., Frederick S., Harry B., Jr., and Alan M. During World War II, Edwin served as a lieutenant colonel with the Engineer Corps in China. Frederick was a captain, serving as a flight surgeon with the Medical Corps in England. Harry Wolf's only known connection with the Jewish community came in the late 1920s when he served as grand master of the Independent Order of B'rith Shalom, a fraternal organization. Harry B. Wolf died in Baltimore on February 17, 1944, and was interred in Hebrew Friendship Cemetery.

References
Biographical Directory of the United States Congress: 1774–1989, p. 2079.
New York Times, November 7, 1922, 18:4; February 18, 1944, 37:2.

WOLFF, LESTER LIONEL (1919–): *Democrat from New York; served eight terms in the House (Eighty-ninth through Ninety-sixth Congress; January 3, 1965–January 3, 1981).*

Lester Wolff is one of the few members of the Congressional Minyan whose family was living in America at the time of the Revolution. The Smalls, the paternal great-grandparents of Wolff's mother Hannah Bartman, came to New York from England in the late eighteenth century. The Wolff side of the family arrived at the time of the Civil War from Alsace-Lorraine—Trier and Strasbourg. By the time Samuel and Hannah Wolff's "lone Wolff" Lester was born in New York on January 4, 1919, they were already well-established in the nation's largest city. Sam Wolff, who moved his family to Washington Heights, was in marketing sale promotions, a field that his son would one day expand upon to a great degree.

Lester Wolff attended the public schools of New York and became bar mitzvah at a Reform synagogue in Washington Heights. Following his graduation from high school, he studied marketing at New York University. From 1939 to 1941, he was a lecturer in marketing at NYU. Shortly after his twenty-first birthday, he married Blanche Silver. As of 2000, the Wolffs, longtime residents of Great Neck, Long Island, had two children, Bruce and Diane, four grandchildren, and two great-grandchildren. After World War II service in the Army Air Corps, Wolff joined the faculty of City College, where he headed the marketing department of its Collegiate Institute for five years.

Not content to merely teach marketing and advertising, Wolff worked as promotion manager for both the *Long Island Press* and the *Bronx Home News* before forming his own firm, the Coordinated Marketing Agency. Wolff served as chairman of the board of his agency from 1950 until his election to Congress in 1964. His agency specialized in advertising for the retail grocery industry. At one point he was executive director of the New York Conference of Retail Grocers.

In 1948, Wolff got a toehold in the fledgling television industry when he became both producer and moderator of a local New York program he called *Between the Lines*. Over the twelve years between 1948 and 1960, Wolff interviewed hundreds of local and national newsmakers, becoming well-known to the burgeoning New York media market. From 1955 to 1958, he produced an early celebrity variety show starring actress Wendy Barrie. As a recognized expert in both marketing and media, Wolff came to the attention of Washington as early as 1957. That year he was asked to chair the advisory committee of a study conducted by the Subcommittee on Consumers of the House of Representatives. Five years later, he was named a member of the United States Trade Mission to the Philippines. The following year (1963), he joined the trade mission to Malaysia and Hong Kong. It was the beginning of an intimate relationship with the Far East—a relationship that has continued for nearly forty years.

By the mid-1960s, Lester Wolff was actually thinking of retirement. He had done very well in his chosen field, easily earning in six figures. In addition to his involvement in international trade, he had donated large chunks of his time to Jewish communal activities. A recognized leader in the retail grocery field, he chaired that industry's division in the United Jewish Appeal. When it became apparent that son Bruce was not going to be taking over his father's advertising agency, Wolff's thoughts began turning toward politics. Widely traveled and having spent years interviewing national and local officials, he felt that he had the knowledge and the ability to be a successful public servant.

In 1964, Lester Wolff decided to run for the United States Congress from New York's Third District. Steven Boghos Derounian, a moderate-to-conservative Republican, had represented the district, made up of the various bedroom communities in Nassau County, for the preceding dozen years. Prior to Derounian, the seat was held by Leonard Wood Hall (1900–1979), who served as chairman of the Republican National Committee during the Eisenhower administration.

A year older than Wolff, Derounian, "big and gregarious," had a seat on the House Ways and Means Committee. Having won his sixth term in 1962 by more than 26,000 votes, he was predicting an even larger plurality against Lester Wolff, a first-time political candidate. A pre-convention Goldwater Republican, Derounian's voting record showed support for the Civil Rights Act, President Johnson's Tonkin Gulf Resolution, the Urban Mass Transit Act, and the 1963 tax cut. He had also voted against a raise in the minimum wage. In writing about the race, the *New York Times* described Lester Wolff as "a man of average size and mien [whose] dark-rimmed glasses and generous moustache suggest a scholarly, investigative approach to the political scene." Aided greatly by Lyndon Johnson's wide coattails, Wolff became the surprise winner by 2,200 votes.

In 1966, the two squared off again. Derounian, who during his two years out of office continued to have himself listed in the local phone director as "Congressman Steve Derounian," defeated William J. Casey in the Republican primary. Described as an insurgent Republican, Casey would go on to become President Ronald Reagan's Director of the CIA. Vietnam, inflation, and busing were the campaign's main issues. Wolff accused Derounian of "extremism and irresponsibility"; Derounian labeled Wolff "nothing but a rubber stamp for President Johnson." On Vietnam, Wolff said: "I have differed with President Johnson as to who should sit at the peace table and the Administration's lack of sufficiently aggressive moves towards peace." Derounian called upon the administration to "make maximum use of American conventional air and sea power . . . and impose a Kennedy-type quarantine of North Vietnam." This time around, Lester Wolff beat Derounian by an even larger margin.

Following the 1970 census, the Republican-controlled New York legislature created a new district, the Sixth, consisting of "almost equal parts of the North Shore of Long Island in Nassau County and the Borough of Queens in New York City." The legislature shaped the new district with "the intention of ousting a Democratic incumbent [Wolff] and preserving a Republican seat." The Republican in question was Representative *Seymour Halpern*, who had represented the old Sixth District (Queens County only) since 1959.

On paper, the odds favored Halpern, for the district had a decided edge in Republican registrations. Working against Halpern, however, was a 1969 *Wall Street Journal* article alleging that he had received unsecured loans in the amount of $100,000. The *Journal* speculated that the loans were "perhaps related to the high position Halpern enjoyed on the House Banking and Currency Committee." After the charge came to light, Halpern resigned his committee post and

repaid the $100,000 loan. Halpern was spared his seat in the 1970 election when a "borough-wide deal was struck, leaving him and the other incumbents with the Republican, Conservative, and Democratic nominations."

In 1972, Lester Wolff let it be known that he would revisit the loan issue in his campaign against Halpern. Wolff's bluff worked: the moderate Republican precipitously retired, bequeathing the Republican nomination to Queens Assemblyman John T. Gallagher. Wolff beat the conservative Gallagher in convincing fashion, and did not have any electoral problems until his last race, in 1980.

By 1968, Blanche Wolff was urging her husband to retire from Congress and come home to Great Neck. Wolff thought about it, then decided to remain. When asked why, he told a *New York Times* reporter: "I feel pretty strongly about the war and this is the one basic reason I stayed on. . . to see a resolution . . . to see peace in Vietnam." Wolff, who had called for a negotiated settlement of the war as early as 1964, wound up going to Vietnam five times at his own expense. As a member of the House Foreign Affairs Committee, he began traveling the globe, gaining a reputation for being an expert on Far Eastern affairs. By the mid-1970s, Lester Wolff was named chair of the Foreign Affairs Subcommittee on Asia and Pacific Affairs. It turned out to be an important post; these were the days when openings to Mainland China, sensitive trade negotiations with Japan, the war in Vietnam, and tensions in the Middle East were at the top of the nation's foreign affairs agenda. In addition to his work in foreign affairs, Wolff co-authored major bills on Medicare, federal aid to education, the second-generation G.I. Bill of Rights, and the 1968 Omnibus Housing Act.

In 1967, Wolff added an historic amendment to the Foreign Aid Bill, a provision to sell Phantom Jets to beleaguered Israel. In retrospect, Wolff considered the amendment, which passed, one of the highpoints of his congressional career. Wolff also played a supporting role in the Camp David Accords of 1977. At a time when negotiations between Israel and Egypt had broken down, Congressman Wolff hand-delivered a message from Egyptian President Anwar el-Sadat to President Jimmy Carter. Unbeknownst to Wolff, Sadat's note requested a resumption of shuttle diplomacy, and indicated his willingness to enter into serious negotiations with the Jewish state. Shortly after Wolff delivered the Egyptian President's message to Carter, invitations to Camp David were extended to both Sadat and Israeli Prime Minister Menachem Begin.

In the mid-1970s, Wolff got some unwanted publicity in the form of the Koreagate scandal. As head of the Asia Subcommittee, Wolff led a junket to Korea in which other members of Congress and their wives were later proven to have taken bribes. Two members of Wolff's junket were subpoenaed. Shortly thereafter, Wolff's Washington office was burglarized and his files stolen. To make matters worse, an article came out in the *Washington Post* revealing that Wolff's Korean-born secretary, Suzi Park, was actually a member of the Korean version of the CIA. As a result of Koreagate, two members of Congress went to jail. Representative Wolff, however, was never indicted.

Even with the attendant publicity of Koreagate, Lester Wolff won reelection in 1978 by a nearly two-to-one margin—despite being outspent by precisely two-to-one. In 1980, however, a brash twenty-seven-year-old descendant of the Vanderbilt and Whitney families, John LeBoutillier, inexplicably defeated him. LeBoutillier, a graduate of Harvard and the Harvard School of Business, was part of the North Shore crowd popularized in F. Scott Fitzgerald's *The Great Gatsby*. In 1980, LeBoutillier's resume showed little—if any—political experience. What it did reveal was that he had authored two books: a novel about a Saudi Arabian prince and a work of nonfiction entitled *Harvard Hates America*. According to the publisher's blurb, the word was "based on his observations of other students at the college and business school."

Unlike Lester Wolff's North Shore (Great Neck) filled with liberal Jewish Democrats, Le Boutillier's (Westbury) was the ancestral home of rock-ribbed WASP Republicans. At first, Lester Wolff did not take the impudent upstart's candidacy seriously. He was not supported by Joseph Margiotta's Nassau County Republican machine, and was certainly not well known in the district. He was a WASP preppy in a predominantly Jewish and Catholic district.

LeBoutillier was able to turn these characteristics into advantages: "He raised large sums from Harvard classmates and admirers of his books," and wound up outspending Wolff nearly five-to-one. LeBoutillier benefited from the national Republican trend on issues and became well known for attacking Wolff for "junketeering on his Asian and other trips." Rather than concentrate on the Jewish/Catholic/Democratic Nassau County portion of the district, LeBoutillier spent his time, efforts and money in Queens, which was larger and more likely to vote for him. LeBoutillier wound up carrying Nassau by just 131 votes, but had a solid 56 percent to 44 percent margin in Queens. His strategy had worked to perfection.

Eight years after the New York legislature had first tried to squeeze Lester Wolff out of his seat, he was finally defeated. LeBoutillier wound up serving only a single term in the House. According to the *Almanac of American Politics*, he "seemed less than shrewd." Speaking of Speaker Thomas P. "Tip" O'Neill, the freshman called him "fat, bloated and out of control—just like the federal budget." That and other verbal slights earned him not only the enmity of the Speaker, but a reputation for being a contemptible, derisive preppy, "one of the careless rich of the North Shore of whom Scott Fitzgerald wrote." After one term, John LeBoutillier was easily defeated by Democrat Robert J. Mrazek.

Lester Wolff has been retired from Congress for twenty years. Ever since his 1980 defeat, he has hosted the weekly PBS program *Ask Congress*. More importantly, he serves as chair of the Touro College Pacific Community Institute, "a program to improve business and trade relations with Asia." In addition to his duties overseeing Touro's PCI program, Lester Wolff has also acted as a registered lobbyist for the Burmese government. Eighty-years old in January 2000, Lester Wolff shows no signs of slowing down. He still commutes from Great Neck to Washington several times a week.

References

Interview with Lester L. Wolff, March 1998.
Almanac of American Politics, 1972–1982.
New York Times, October 9, 1964; October 19, 1966; October 21, 1968.

WOLPE, HOWARD ELIOT III (1939–):
Democrat from Michigan; served seven terms in the House (Ninety-sixth through One Hundred and Second Congress, January 3, 1979–January 3, 1993).

Howard Wolpe is the only member of the Congressional Minyan—and indeed, one of the only members of Congress, now or ever before—to hold a Ph.D. in African Studies. As an expert on African political systems, Wolpe found "racism to be my most compelling issue in both academics and politics." As chair of the Foreign Affairs Subcommittee on Africa from 1981 to 1992, Wolpe lent both an educated and a compassionate voice on behalf of emerging African nations. When Howard Wolpe spoke, his colleagues listened.

Howard Wolpe, the son of Drs. Zelda Harriet (Shapiro) and Leon Sikirias Wolpe, was born in Los Angeles on November 2, 1939. His mother was a clinical psychologist, his father a radiologist. Both the Wolpes and the Shapiros had come from Lithuania around the turn of the century, with the Wolpes settling in Washington, D.C., and the Shapiros in Chicago. Zelda's sister, Dinah, went directly from Lithuania to Palestine, where she married a man named Phil Joseph. His brother, Dov Joseph, is considered one of the Founding Fathers of Israel.

Dov Joseph (1899–1980) was originally from Montreal. In 1918, he moved to Palestine, where he joined the Jewish Legion. Settling in Jerusalem in 1921, he quickly became one of the city's leading lawyers. During World War II, he was given the task of raising volunteers for the Jewish units in the British Army. He also served as a member of the Jewish Agency Executive, acting as the head of its political department. In 1946, he was one of a handful of *Yishuv* (Jewish settlement) leaders detained by the British at Latrun. A longtime (1949–65), member of Israel's Parliament, the Knesset, Joseph was Minister of Supply and Rationing and Minister of Agriculture (1949–50), Transportation and Communications (1950–51), Trade and Industry (1951–53), Development (1953–55), and Health (1955). A prolific author as well, Joseph wrote

Nationality: Its Nature and Problems, The White Paper on Palestine: A Criticism, British Rule in Palestine, and *The Faithful City,* "a dramatic record of the siege of Jerusalem, including a detailed report of the fall of the Old City in 1948."

The Wolpes' other renowned Israeli cousin is Professor Yuval Ne'eman. Born in Tel Aviv in 1925, Ne'eman served as brigade operations officer on the Egyptian front during the War of Independence in 1948. Following duty as deputy director of the Intelligence Division of the Israel Defense Forces in the 1950s, he went to England, where he earned a Ph.D. in physics from the Imperial College. In his doctoral thesis, he proposed "a symmetry scheme known as SU(3), for the classification of the elementary particles of nature—a major breakthrough in elementary particle physics." Ne'eman, who served as president of Tel Aviv University, currently occupies the Distinguished Chair in Theoretical Physics at the Mortimer and Raymond Sackler Institute of Advanced Studies at the University. Still a vital figure in Israeli public affairs in the late 1990s, Ne'eman chairs the National Committee for the Absorption of Immigrant Scientists, and Israel's version of NASA.

Howard Wolpe grew up in Los Angeles, and received his bar mitzvah instruction at the Reform University Synagogue near UCLA. Following his graduation from University High School in 1956, he attended Reed College in Portland, Oregon. At the time he received his B.A. (1960), "many African countries were going independent." Wolpe found himself becoming "intrigued by the prospect of blacks in a self-governing capacity." Following a year of law school in Chicago, he headed to Massachusetts, where he enrolled in a doctoral program at MIT. While preparing for his dissertation, Wolpe spent two years doing field work in Nigeria.

Receiving his doctorate in 1967, Wolpe secured employment in the political science department at Western Michigan University in Kalamazoo. From 1967 to 1972, he taught

African political systems, developing "a natural empathy for the emerging nations of the continent and for their leaders." He concluded that the future of Africa lay in "more aid, rather than a turn to free enterprise," as the developing continent's "best chance for economic growth." Highly sensitive to the issue of racism in America, he noted that "to talk about the black family as the cultural problem is a marvelously unconscious way of shifting attention to the product of discrimination." During his years as a professor at Western Michigan, Wolpe gave a low grade to a student named Mark Siljander, an act that would keep reverberating over the next dozen or more years. While teaching, Wolpe also found time to act as a consultant for the Peace Corps and to work at the State Department Service Institute.

Howard Wolpe is the author of *Urban Politics in Nigeria: A Study of Port Harcourt* (1974, University of California Press), co-author of *Modernization and the Politics of Communism: A Theoretical Perspective* (1970, American Political Science Review) and co-editor of *Nigeria: Modernization and the Politics of Communism* (1971, Michigan State University Press).

Two years after arriving in Michigan, Wolpe was elected to the Kalamazoo City Council. After a single term, he was elected to the Michigan House of Representatives—the first Democrat ever to represent Kalamazoo in the state legislature. Wolpe's trademark both on the council and in the legislature was constituent service, which he "carried out with a personal touch and occasional flamboyance."

In 1976, Wolpe ran a losing race against six-term incumbent Republican Representative Garry E. Brown, whom the *Almanac of American Politics* (1980 edition) described as "an aggressive, hard-driving young man who believed in increasing business's productivity and fighting hard against the Democrats." Following his rather narrow (52 percent–48 percent) defeat, Wolpe was hired by Michigan Senator Donald Riegle to run his Lansing office. In reality, Wolpe never stopped running from the moment he lost. Moving from Kalamazoo to Eaton (where he had scored poorly with the voters), Wolpe campaigned almost nonstop. Challenging Brown again in 1978, Wolpe improved his share of the Eaton-based vote from 40 percent to 46 percent,

and went on to win a "bitter" race with 51 percent.

Michigan's Third Congressional District was "anchored by the medium-sized industrial cities of Kalamazoo and Battle Creek," and contained such concerns as the Upjohn Company, the Kellogg and Post cereal manufacturers, and Ralston-Purina. Nominally Republican, the district never provided Wolpe with an easy election.

As a member of the Ninety-sixth Congress, Wolpe was assigned to Foreign Affairs, and Science and Technology. In 1980, he faced millionaire Republican James Gilmore, a former Kalamazoo mayor and the financial sponsor of race car driver A. J. Foyt. Gilmore vainly tried to "exploit Wolpe's liberal voting record." Wolpe had "given the voters what they wanted on local issues," especially when he went to bat on their behalf against the Federal Trade Commission, which was attacking the cereal industry in Battle Creek. Although outspent by more than $250,000, Wolpe managed to eke out a 52 percent–47 percent victory. Upon his return to Congress in January 1981, Wolpe, then in only his second term, was elevated to the chairmanship of the Africa Subcommittee, a post he would hold for the rest of his House career.

As subcommittee chair, Howard Wolpe found himself butting heads with the Reagan administration over its Africa policy. In 1981, he led his subcommittee to a 7–0 vote against repealing the Clark Amendment, which would have banned aid to factions in Angola. The Reagan administration favored its repeal, but Wolpe argued that "such a move at [this] time [will] drive the leftist regime in power in Angola farther toward Cuba and the Soviet Union and endanger chances for a peaceful settlement in Namibia." Wolpe was one of the leading congressional critics of American military aid to Zaire, which he called the "most corrupt" country in all of Africa. Although he was able to get the Carter administration to reduce military aid to Zaire and its dictator, Mobutu Sese Seko, he failed in his attempts for a full suspension.

During the Reagan years, Wolpe succeeding in getting his subcommittee to block the administration's requests for increased military aid to the Sudan, Kenya, Morocco, and Tunisia. However, the full committee restored aid to the requested level. Without question, Representative Wolpe was also one of Congress's leading critics of South African apartheid. He forcefully defended restrictions on exports to that country, calling them the "pillars of America's policy against . . . Apartheid." Wolpe was also the leading opponent of American aid to Jonas Savimbi and his UNITA group, which was seeking to overthrow the Cuban-supported Angolan government.

Equal parts politician and professor, Wolpe tried to persuade his colleagues "to look at the effects of U.S. foreign policy from an African point of view." During one hearing early in his congressional career, he said that Africans viewed as absurd the competition between America and the Soviet Union to win their favor. "They know in advance," he said, "that if they are going to call themselves communists, they get assistance from one side; anti-Communist, they get assistance from another side."

In January 1982, Howard Wolpe's former student, Mark Siljander, was elected to Congress from Michigan's Fourth District. An ultra-conservative Republican, Siljander's were the politics of "expressing attitudes rather than achieving results or shaping ideas." Siljander was assigned to Wolpe's subcommittee, where from day one he tried to make life difficult for his former teacher and political nemesis. During Wolpe's 1984 reelection bid, Siljander threw his support behind Republican Jackie McGregor. In an attempt to see Wolpe defeated, Siljander made a tactical error: he sent a letter to the Christian clergymen of the Third District referring to Wolpe as a Communist and "the liberal, far left radical puppet of the anti-American Third World." To make matters worse, Siljander urged the clergymen to "break the back of Satan and the lies that are coming our way."

Not only did Siljander's letter strike many as nutty, but he made it clear that his definition of Christian excluded a majority of Christians. Wolpe cried foul, and beat McGregor 53 percent to 47 percent. Siljander was trounced in his primary race by Frederick Upton, a former aide to David Stockman at the Office of Management and Budget (Stockman had held the seat before Siljander) and the grandson of the founder of the Whirlpool Corporation. McGregor faced off against Wolpe again in 1986. This time

McGregor's campaign produced a brochure stating that Wolpe and actor Ed Asner had sent out a fundraising letter to some 500,000 people "of their religion outside the district." This time, Wolpe won by an even bigger margin—60 percent to 40 percent.

Wolpe's legislative achievements included a Hazardous Waste Reduction Act, "which provided state grants to help companies learn how to reduce waste and established an Environmental Protection Agency office of pollution prevention." His Taxpayer's Right to Know Act required federal income tax booklets to include "pie charts detailing both the sources of federal revenue and the breakdown of federal expenses." Wolpe also authored the bill that barred former federal employees from lobbying for foreigners for a minimum of a year after they left government employ.

Howard Wolpe never won reelection by more than 60 percent. A 100 percent ADA liberal representing an essentially Republican district, he was always a target for political extinction by the GOP. Wolpe managed to get by in six reelection campaigns by dint of his constituent services and the ability to raise vast sums of money. In its editorial of endorsement, one local (Republican) paper called Wolpe "an example of the kind of pragmatic, principled, informed and intelligent leadership so greatly needed in our halls of government."

After redistricting in 1992, Wolpe's luck ran out. Rather than run in a new, more Republican constituency, Wolpe retired from Congress. In 1994, he mounted a campaign against Governor John M. Engler, but lost 61 percent to 38 percent. His old congressional seat, renumbered the Seventh, was taken over by Republican Nick Smith in an all-but-uncontested race; no Democrat had seen fit to even enter the primary.

Perhaps Wolpe's greatest moment came in a speech he gave in opposition to Senator Jesse Helms's amendment to civil rights legislation. Helms inserted language that would "bar employers from granting any kind of preferential treatment whatever, in hiring, compensation or promotion, if based on race, color, religion, national origin or sex." In his speech of opposition, Wolpe said: "The real enemy of beleaguered workers today is not affirmative action programs designed to overcome a legacy of race prejudice and discrimination, but an economy that does not provide secure employment for all Americans. The solution is not to fight over who gets the limited number of jobs available, but to create more jobs and to train people to fill them."

Howard Wolpe was at one time married to the former Jeanene Taylor. They have one son, Michael Stevenson (after Adlai) Wolpe, who is a gifted musician. Howard Wolpe continues to live in Michigan.

References

Interview with Howard Wolpe, March 1992.
Almanac of American Politics, 1980–1994.
Kalamazoo Gazette, October 30, 1990.
New York Times, July 4, 1991.

WYDEN, RONALD LEE (1949–): *Democrat from Oregon; served eight terms in the House (Ninety-seventh though One Hundred and Fourth Congress, January 3, 1981—December 31, 1995); elected to the Senate to fulfill an unexpired term in January 1996; elected for a full six-year term in 1998.*

All three of Oregon's Jewish Senators (Joseph Simon, Richard Neuberger, and Ron Wyden) are the products of German-born families. Of the three, Ron Wyden's is the most illustrious and most fully documented, thanks in large part to his late father, the noted writer Peter Wyden. In his critically acclaimed book *Stella* (Simon & Schuster, 1992), the senior Wyden wrote that when he was a youngster growing up in prewar Berlin, his uncle, Franz Weidenrich, showed him "a pedigree going back, in tiny market towns of southwestern Germany, to the fifteenth century, when the family name was Weil."

In medieval Europe, a surname was often derived from one's occupation. Weidenreich, literally "willow rich" in German, the name under which Senator Wyden's father was born, likely stemmed from a medieval antecedent who was a weaver of baskets. According to Peter Wyden, that early ancestor "produced them [the baskets] from willows, and was presumably loaded with huge stocks of them; hence the name." The Weidenreichs originally hailed from Edenkoben, on the southern wine road in the Rhine-Palatinate. Peter Wyden described Edenkoben as "authentically *deutsche*—civilized, colorful." According to Peter Wyden, his uncle, the aforementioned Franz Weidenreich, was "by far the most renowned personage Edenkoben or my family ever produced." Franz Weidenreich (1873–1948) was a world-renowned anatomist, physical anthropologist, and paleontologist. A professor of anatomy at Strassburg from 1899 to 1918 and at Heidelberg from 1921 to 1924, he was appointed professor of anthropology at Frankfurt University in 1928. With the coming of the Nazis, Franz left Germany and took a position at Peking Union Medical College in China. He became internationally famous for his discovery of *Homo Sinanthropus*—"Peking man."

Senator Wyden's paternal great-grandfather, Max Weidenreich, served as superintendent of the Jewish cemetery in Weissensee (Europe's largest), "a sinecure handed out by the Berlin Jewish Community authorities after he went broke in his haberdashery shop in Cologne." Max's son, Erich (Peter's father and the Senator's grandfather), grew up in the superintendent's "little yellow brick cottage on the enormous cemetery, always dark under its immense trees." Max married into the Brahn family. Peter's great-uncle, Max Brahn, was a scholar who edited and annotated the works of Schopenhauer. During World War I, he trained fighter pilots, advancing to the rank of *Oberregierungsrat*. After the war, he became a noted labor mediator for the German government, "which found him indispensable [until] two years in[to] the Hitler regime."

Raised in the somber, religiously constraining confines of the cemetery, Erich "rebelled against paternal tradition by becoming a comic . . . the family's entertainment." In *Stella*, Peter Wyden described his father as a "cherubic, bald, smiling presence whose easy charm and wit enabled him to bring off the coup of his life: he married the boss's daughter." The boss, Carl Silberstein, had started out in partnership with his father-in-law, one Rafael Zernick, in a "little dry goods shop" on Kaiser Wilhelmstrasse. By the time Erich Weidenreich became his employee in the years after World War I, Carl was running a highly successful textile business. Called "Opi" by his grandchildren and "Carlchen" by adult family members, Carl Silberstein was "massively built, all dignity." "If he had had a middle name," Peter wrote, "it should have been 'Rectitude.'" As a Silberstein employee, Erich Weidenreich's "grace and cheer" made him "an immensely popular salesman," easily the best in the firm.

In the early 1920s, Erich married Carlchen's daughter, Leni, a woman blessed with "a slightly more than adequate mezzo-soprano voice, [who] toured provincial outposts, doing her *lieder* to friendly reviews." Erich described his mother (whom he called Mutti) as "a career woman when no woman in her set would dream of such ambition." Leni was easily a woman ahead of her time: she had plastic surgery in the 1920s to reduce both her nose and her breasts, because "she deemed these organs too large to be in good taste."

Peter Weidenreich grew up in a privileged upper-middle-class home on Kantstrasse: "I had a live-in nanny. My mother had a cook and a cleaning lady. My clothes were selected with elaborate care; in winter they included a broad-brimmed white hat and a fluffy white fur coat." Peter and his father were among Berlin's many so-called "three-day Jews" who attended Rabbi Joachim Prinz's *Freidenstempel* in Wilmersdorf on Rosh Hashanah and Yom Kippur. Leni was a "no-day Jew who passed up the temple." Not that she wanted to deny being Jewish. Rather, as Peter explained, because "all religion struck her as too removed from reality, it offended her pragmatic self, her sense of now-is-now." Nonetheless, Peter did become bar mitzvah in 1936, "mostly to please him"— Opi, "the bearer of our Jewishness."

Peter was one of only two Jewish boys in a school attended by about 800 students. As a youngster in the earliest days of the Nazi regime, Peter remembers joining in with the rest of the children "extending the right arm in the Hitler salute . . . yelling 'Heil Hitler!'" Wyden remembered it as being "mechanical, a commonplace like pledging alliance [sic] to the flag, except we had to hail Hitler all the livelong day. I had always joined in, feeling foolish to be hailing this crazy person. Foolish, not guilty." One day in class, "some unaccustomed bulb" lit up within Peter Weidenreich: "I wanted to resist. Without much thought, I leaned against my desk . . . I didn't salute Hitler, and felt triumphant." At the close of school that day, he found that his bicycle tires had been slashed. He went back to the salute, rationalizing that his resistance had been "childish and futile, not brave."

Within the Weidenreich family circle, Hitler was "tolerated with bemusement." They considered him "a nut who had, by some inadvertence, been temporarily permitted to ascend to a position of power." By 1935, Peter and his Jewish friends had been "purged" from attending public school. He was then sent to the Goldschmidt

School, housed in a cluster of "elegant, airy former mansions with wide halls and tall windows."

As things became progressively worse, Leni made the decision that the family must leave Germany. As Peter recalled: "There was no family discussion. She had no vision of mass slaughters to come, but her hold on reality brooked no wavering." Carlchen strongly advised against a move. Leaving Nazi Germany was no easy matter. Fortunately, Eric, while on a "reconnaissance trip" to America in the late 1920s, had located an "obscure umpteenth cousin" in the Bronx. Additionally, Eric had purchased a life insurance policy during the hyperinflationary days of the 1920s "when a loaf of bread cost millions of marks." The insurance policy and the cousins became their tickets to freedom.

The Weidenreichs left Germany in February, 1937, traveling second-class aboard the S.S. *Washington*. Accustomed to luxury, they found themselves living in a tiny furnished apartment on Manhattan's West Side that was "unfit even for the vermin that called it home." Peter attended DeWitt Clinton High School. He remembers arriving at the school "wearing green knickerbockers and carrying the *New York Staatszeitung und Herold*," his English vocabulary running to about a dozen words. Leni, who had learned English (as well as Italian) in high school, made an easy transition; before too long, she began picking up singing students. Erich went into collapse, never learning English, never holding a job. "He wasn't transplantable. Like delicate wines, he didn't 'travel.'"

By 1941, Peter was already publishing articles in newspapers and magazines. Following service in World War II (during which time he shortened the family name to Wyden), he married Edith Rosenow, likewise a native of Berlin. Edith's great-grandfather Leopold Rosenow had been a member of the Berlin City Council at the turn of the century. Interestingly, he was well-known for the wars he waged against the public utilities (notably the Berlin phone company), which he claimed was mistreating small business owners. Nearly three-quarters of a century later, his great-great-grandson would be waging the same battles on the floor of the United States Congress.

Peter and Edith's firstborn son, Ronald Lee, was born in Wichita, Kansas, on May 3, 1949. At the time of his son's birth, Peter was working for a newspaper in Wichita. In August, 1949, Edith placed the three-month-old Ron in a laundry basket and took an all-night Missouri-Pacific train to St. Louis, where Peter spent the next five years writing for the *St. Louis Post Dispatch*. In 1954, the family, now including Ron's younger brother Jeff, moved to Washington, D.C., where Peter became Washington correspondent for *Newsweek*. During their five years in D.C., Ron began attending public school. Peter remembered that the local PTA had a roster of political heavyweights, including Minnesota Senator Hubert H. Humphrey, whose son, Hubert III ("Skip"), would grow up to become the long-time Attorney General of Minnesota.

Almost from day one, Ron's interests tended more toward basketball than academics. Over the years, he became an outstanding player. From Washington, the family moved to Chicago, where Peter opened the Midwestern editorial offices of the *Saturday Evening Post*. In 1961, Peter and Edith Wyden divorced. Edith took her sons to Palo Alto, California; Peter, moving farther east, was remarried to Barbara Woodman, a writer and librarian.

Ron Wyden attended Palo Alto ("Pali") High School, literally across the street from Stanford University. A star player on the Pali basketball squad, Ron received a scholarship from the University of California, Santa Barbara. He soon developed serious calcium deposits on the heels of his feet that made walking, let alone jogging up and down a wooden court, a painful activity. The good news was that the problem would keep him out of Vietnam; the bad news, that his basketball career was, sadly, over even before it had begun.

When Peter Wyden heard that the team's doctors were recommending cortisone treatments, he whisked his son off to Lenox Hill Hospital in New York. There, a world-renowned orthopedist prescribed a series of exercises. After nearly a half-year of following through the doctor's regimen, Wyden's problem abated. Nonetheless, he never went back to basketball. Leaving Santa Barbara, Ron Wyden "got himself shoestringed in Stanford." Once back in Palo Alto, he started taking his studies seriously, and wound up being a good student at the elite California college.

Graduating in 1971, Wyden headed up north to Eugene, where he attended law school at the University of Oregon. For two of his years in law school, he worked as a campaign aide for Oregon Senator Wayne ("Half a loaf is better than no loaf at all") Morse. Wyden earned a J.D. in 1974, and decided to remain in Oregon. Upon graduating, he co-founded the Grey Panthers, a "militant organization to aid the elderly." During the five years he co-directed the Panthers (1974–79), Wyden achieved a measure of public notice for spearheading a successful referendum to reduce the price of dentures. Wyden's involvement with the elderly was all-encompassing; in addition to his work with the Panthers, he served as director of the Oregon Legal Services for the Elderly, professor of gerontology at the University of Oregon and Portland State University, and as a public member of the Oregon State Board of Examiners of Nursing Home Administrators.

In 1978, Ron Wyden married Laurie Oseran. They have one child, Adam, born in 1984. In his youth, not having a religious grandfather like Opi, Ron had received little or no Jewish instruction himself and did not become bar mitzvah. Under Laurie Wyden's influence, he became quite interested in his religion, and found himself becoming more and more involved in Jewish communal activities. In 1997, their son Adam became bar mitzvah at the Washington Hebrew Congregation in the nation's capital. According to Peter Wyden, grandson Adam "is really into religion." In honor of their son's bar mitzvah, the Wydens threw a lavish party to which the elite of Capitol Hill came out and danced till all hours.

In 1980, Ron Wyden decided to run for Congress against Third District Democrat Robert Blackford Duncan. After serving as Speaker of the State House of Representatives from 1959 to 1962, Duncan (1920–) had been elected to Congress in 1962. After two terms he vacated his seat, deciding instead to try for the United States Senate. Duncan lost in 1968 to Robert Packwood and in 1972 to Mark Hatfield; he won back his House seat in 1974. After six years in the House, Duncan, "a traditional labor Democrat," seemed to be popular with the voters. Moreover, he was chair of the Transportation Subcommittee on Appropriations, a critical post for Portland, a city with no direct flights to most of America's major cities, including Washington, D.C.

Wyden, nearly thirty years Duncan's junior, organized a formidable volunteer force made up of "senior citizens, environmentalists and other young urban liberals like him." He set about the task of "exposing" Duncan's record on such bread-and-butter issues as mass transit, housing, and heating costs. Campaigning full-time for several months, Wyden was able to convince voters of the Third District (East Portland and its suburbs) that Duncan was insufficiently sensitive to their needs. Duncan was also saddled with the problem of geography; Washington is so far from Portland as to make it for any one but the heartiest commuter seem distant or foreign. Having had no Republican opponent in his last two races, Duncan "had not needed to communicate his record to voters." This, combined with Wyden's superior precinct organization and his "activist reputation and . . . outspoken campaigning," led him to an upset 60 percent to 40 percent victory in the primary. He then coasted to victory in November against Republican Daniel R. Conger by a nearly three-to-one margin.

In its 1982 edition, the *Almanac of American Politics* noted that Wyden was entering a Congress "that is going very much in the opposite direction," because "he is a strong believer in federal programs to help people—programs that the Reagan Administration and much of the Congress seem bent on dismantling or cutting." The editors of the *Almanac* opined that "over the long run, young men who enter Congress at a time when their views are not in favor often have a great advantage in the future." Looking into their political crystal ball, the editors predicted that "he will be a formidable candidate in the future." Their prediction was right on the mark.

Wyden entered the House with a well-earned reputation as an environmentalist and champion of the elderly. An intense lobbying campaign got him a coveted seat on John Dingell's Energy and Commerce Committee, a plum assignment for a freshman. Quickly allying himself with *Henry Waxman*, Wyden spent the lion's share of his early Washington career working on what was to become the 1982 Clean Air Act. Waxman, Wyden, and the liberals pushed hard for a bill that would preserve strict pollution controls; Dingell preferred a bill more friendly to industry. In April 1982, freshman Wyden successfully offered an amendment "to keep tight controls on air pollution in areas currently cleaner than the national standards." Predictably, Chairman Dingell opposed Wyden's amendment. Nonetheless, the voluble Michigander failed to muster the votes to block its approval. Undaunted, Dingell "proposed further action to try to marshal support for his position, but failed," resulting in a victory for Wyden and the environmentalists—a stunning accomplishment for a freshman member of Congress.

As a champion of the elderly, Wyden "had a field day . . . criticizing the Social Security cuts proposed by President Reagan," and introduced a bill "to create a new national research institute on arthritis." Although this measure passed the Senate, it died in the House. Wyden's record struck a responsive chord with voters in the Third District; in 1982, he was reelected with 78 percent of the vote. Over the next dozen years, Ron Wyden was routinely reelected by margins of anywhere between 72 percent and 100 percent. During his decade and a half in the House, Wyden gained a reputation as possessing "a pleasant personality and a low-key style" which easily belied his aggressiveness. The *Almanac of American Politics* praised him for "his inclination . . . to delve into several highly technical, usually unrelated issues at a time, from health care cost containment and hazardous waste disposal to telephone access charges [much like his great-great-grandfather Rosenow] and the federal tax on 'imputed' interest."

Among his more noteworthy legislative accomplishments were: a medigap fraud bill (1990) that provided "basic benefit packages and counseling for seniors confused about the myriad supplemental insurance carriers;" a bill, co-sponsored with Arkansas Senator David Pryor, "to force drug companies to give their most favorable discounts to Medicare and Medicaid purchasers;" and a measure, co-authored with Missouri Representative Richard Gephardt, that "provided a carefully screened number of unemployed workers with an advance on benefits, as a form of seed capital to start their own businesses." Wyden was also the first member of Congress to hold hearings on the controversial French abortifacient drug RU-486. His position was that "the ban on its importation to the United States should be lifted despite opposition from pro-lifers, because similar multi-hormonal drugs have produced promising results in cancer treatment."

Starting in the 1990s, Ron Wyden joined fellow Minyanaire Henry Waxman in fighting the powerful American tobacco industry. Their inquiry, abruptly shut down after the 1994 election (which brought in a Republican Congress), got Wyden into a legal peccadillo: a lawsuit with tobacco companies over the "alleged theft of industry documents by a disgruntled employee who turned them over to the Democrats." When the Republicans took over Congress in January 1994, Wyden, predictably, opposed most aspects of their Contract With America, and voted against their proposal to reduce projected Medicare spending by $270 billion over five years. Until the Republicans took over Congress, Wyden launched most of his campaigns from his position as chair of the Small Business Subcommittee on Regulation, Business Opportunities, and Technology. An activist panel, the Republicans abolished it almost immediately upon taking over.

Frequently mentioned as a possible senatorial candidate, Wyden, a passionate backer of Oregon's unique and innovative health plan (which rations coverage by treatment), passed up chances to run against Bob Packwood in 1986 and Mark Hatfield in 1990. His patience paid off in September 1995, when the Senate Ethics Committee recommended the expulsion of Oregon's' Junior Senator, Robert Packwood, for sexual harassment. Shortly thereafter, Packwood announced that he would resign. Despite the scandal that brought his days in the Senate to an ignominious conclusion, Robert Packwood had had a distinguished career: as noted in the *Almanac of American Politics*, he "was [the Senate's] leading supporter of abortion rights in the 1970s and as Finance chairman put together the Tax Reform Act of 1986."

Almost immediately, Ron Wyden announced his candidacy for Packwood's seat. The special elections (primary and general) made history: the nation's first (and so far only) elections in which ballots were cast by mail over a period of weeks. Wyden drew Fourth District Representative Peter A. DeFazio as his primary opponent. During the campaign, Wyden stumbled when, on a televised quiz that drew much attention, "he could not quote the price of a loaf of bread or a gallon of milk in Portland, and could not name the Canadian Prime Minister or find Bosnia on a map." Aided by a formidable campaign war chest and the endorsement of the *Oregonian*, the state's largest newspaper, Wyden won the primary by a rather tepid 50 percent to 44 percent.

In the special general election, Wyden faced the president of the Oregon Senate, Gordon Smith. Born and raised in Pendleton, in eastern Oregon, Smith, an ultraconservative Mormon, had made a sizable fortune as the president of Smith Frozen Foods. The contest between Wyden and Smith, which on paper was a fight between a new-fashioned liberal and an old-fashioned conservative, featured far less debate on the issues than their bipolar positions suggested. Instead, the campaign devolved into a spate of nasty *ad hominem* commercials. Smith called Wyden "out of touch." Wyden in turn attacked Smith for pollution and unsafe conditions at his plants, for his anti-abortion stance, for his endorsement by the anti-gay-rights Oregon Citizens Alliance, and for having expensive tastes (including an antique set of four golf clubs that had cost him $1.25 million).

Toward the end of the race, Smith was, somewhat surprisingly, endorsed by the Portland-based *Oregonian*; in the special Republican primary, the paper, noting Smith's lack of political experience, had endorsed his rival, Norma Paulus, the state's Superintendent of Public Instruction. Wyden fought back, reminding the publisher of the *Oregonian* that they were the ones who just weeks earlier had written that "Smith is still learning the basics of Oregon government," and now they were lauding him as having "emerg[ed] during his relatively short career, as an effective, thoughtful leader." Ballots were mailed to all Oregon voters on January 10, and had to be mailed back (or dropped off) by 8:00 P.M., January 30. Although Wyden wound up carrying only one-quarter of Oregon's thirty-six counties, he nonetheless eked out a 48 percent to 47 percent victory.

Almost immediately upon taking his oath, Wyden called for disclosure of all Senators who placed holds on legislation—an age-old practice by which any Senator, under the cloak of anonymity, can place an indefinite hold on any bill he or she wishes. Along with California Republican Christopher Cox, Senator Wyden introduced legislation to ban state and local taxes on the Internet and content providers. In winning election to the Senate, he had only won the last three years of Packwood's term, meaning that he would have to run again in November 1998.

One candidate Wyden need not fear was Gordon Smith, for his former adversary took Oregon's other Senate seat in the November 1996 election.

During the early days of his son's political career, Peter Wyden wrote speeches and spoke on his behalf. "He would always tell me to proclaim that I was for a strong defense. He thought I was some sort of Communist or pacifist," Peter recalled. "Actually, I guess I'm quite a bit more liberal than Ron."

Peter Wyden, the family chronicler, married for a third time in 1986; his new wife, Elaine Seaton, was the mother of two children: James Seaton and Andrea Miller. Peter Wyden died of a stroke on June 27, 1998 at a hospital in Danbury, Connecticut. He was the author of dozens of books and hundreds of articles on topics as far-reaching as the Berlin Wall (*Wall*), the Spanish Civil War (*The Passionate War*), Hiroshima (*Day One*), Castro's Cuba (*Bay of Pigs: The Untold Story*, winner of the 1979 Overseas Press Club Award as the year's best book on foreign affairs), and psychology (*What Every Parent Should Know About Homosexuality* and *Conquering Schizophrenia: A Father, His Son and a Medical Breakthrough*).

Peter Wyden's interest in psychology went back nearly a half-century. After World War II, he began investigating mental illness with a series of investigative reports on Kansas state hospitals. According to one source, "his stories revealed abysmal conditions and over-burdened staff at the institutions, and helped prompt a statewide overhaul of the Kansas mental health system." His last book on schizophrenia dealt with the Senator's younger brother Jeff, who has suffered with the disease for more than half his life. When he was interviewed in February, 1998, Peter Wyden reported that "Jeff is on a wondrous medication, and is better than he has been in many, many years."

As one of many accomplished Wydens, Peter said, somewhat sheepishly, that writing was just perfect for him: "I am a constitutionally nosy person. . . . Writing books is the world's best way to snoop for news and get paid for it." It's a pity that he did not live long enough to write a book about his illustrious son, the Senator.

References

Interview with Peter Wyden, February 1998.
Interview with Edith Wyden, February 1998.
Information provided by Ron Wyden.
Almanac of American Politics, 1980–1998.
Politics in America, 1986–1998.
Peter Wyden. *Stella* (New York: Simon & Schuster, 1992).
Washington Post, June 29, 1998, D8.

YATES, SIDNEY RICHARD (1909–): *Democrat from Illinois; served twenty-four terms in the House (Eighty-first through Eighty-seventh Congress, January 3, 1949–January 3, 1963; Eighty-ninth through One Hundred and Fifth Congress, January 3, 1965 to January 4, 1999).*

On January 3, 1995, Republicans took control of the House of Representatives for the first time in forty years. Of the 204 Democrats and one Independent serving in the One Hundred and Fourth Congress, only one had ever served in a Republican-controlled House: Representative Sidney Yates of Illinois. Remembering those days, Yates said: "Republicans fought what they called the socialistic measures of Democrats, and we tried just to stay alive in that Congress and come back." As the dean of Congress, Yates provided an institutional memory for his Democratic colleagues and for the young Republicans who had taken over Capitol Hill.

Louis and Ida (Siegel) Yates, the future Congressman's parents, were both immigrants from Lithuania, where Louis had been a blacksmith. In the United States, he became a truck driver. The Yateses had six children, the youngest of whom, Sidney Richard, was born in Chicago on August 27, 1909. One of Sidney's brothers, Charles, worked in Chicago as a vaudeville talent agent. In his time, he booked such then-rising stars as Bob Hope and Bing Crosby. Because of his older brother's show business connections, Sid spent a great deal of his early childhood attending theater. While still a teenager in the Chicago public school system, he worked as an office boy for the Keith-Orpheum vaudeville circuit. Early on, Yates also developed a passion for opera. When he was an undergraduate at the University of Chicago in the late 1920s, his roommate introduced him to the "canon" of Gilbert and Sullivan, which they both proceeded to memorize.

Upon receiving a bachelor of philosophy degree from the University of Chicago in 1931, Yates entered U.C.'s School of Law. He breezed through in two years, receiving his LL.B in 1933. During his college years, Yates also played bas-

ketball for the Fast Freights, a semiprofessional team. Upon admission to the Illinois bar in 1933, he began practicing law as the senior partner in the firm of Yates and Holleb. On June 24, 1935, Yates solidified his ties with the firm by marrying Adeline J. Holleb, his partner's sister. As of 2000, the Yatses, who have one son—Judge Stephen R., an associate judge on the Cook County Circuit Court—have been married for sixty-five years.

At the time of his marriage, Sid Yates was just beginning a two-year stint as assistant attorney for the Illinois state bank receiver. From 1937 to 1940, he served as "assistant attorney [general] attached as a traction attorney (dealing with rail transportation) at the Illinois Commerce Commission." Yates then served in the United States Navy from 1944 to 1946, rising to the rank of lieutenant. Following the end of the war, he returned to his law firm in Chicago. In 1947, he served as editor of the bulletin of the Decalogue Society of Lawyers, a fraternity made up of Jewish attorneys.

In 1948, while getting back to the practice of law, Sid Yates was drafted "at the last moment" by the Democratic organization to run against Ninth District Representative Robert J. Twyman. At the time, Yates was considered nothing more than a sacrificial lamb. In this, his first Congressional campaign, Yates admits that if the voting public knew him at all, it was as a basketball forward. With GOP standard-bearer Thomas Dewey leading in all the national polls, 1948 looked like a Republican year, and Twyman was expected to easily win reelection. The "best political wisdom" held that Dewey's coattails would permit most, if not all, Republican incumbents to retain their seats. Sometimes, however, the "best political wisdom" is proven wrong. The year 1948 is one glaring, historic example. Against all odds, President Harry S. Truman, who went to bed a loser, woke up to find that he had been elected to a full four-year term. Benefiting from Truman's surprise upset, Yates won his Ninth District race over Twyman by nearly 18,000 votes. In reflecting on that campaign, Yates recalled: I couldn't think of what I could say in a speech at a bunco party in my predominantly German ward, so I took along my guitar. I only knew three chords, and sang a German song."

The Ninth Congressional District of Illinois was, and remains, a largely Jewish enclave of middle- and upper-middle-income voters on Chicago's North Side lakefront. Before Yates's election in 1948, the seat had seesawed back and forth between Republicans and Democrats for nearly the entire twentieth century. Sid Yates changed all that; with the exception of a single two-year period (1963–64), when he voluntarily gave up his seat in order to mount an unsuccessful race for the United States Senate, the "tall, lean . . . unfailingly polite" Yates held the seat until 1998. After squeaking to reelection victories in 1950 and 1952 (both Republican years), he settled into what was a more than four-decade pattern of overwhelming (and sometimes uncontested) victories.

Yates entered the House as "a proud liberal committed to President Truman's Fair Deal programs." He immediately won a seat on the House Appropriations Committee—a coup for any freshman. Somewhat of a political visionary, Yates became one of the first federal legislators to speak out against age discrimination. In 1951, he introduced legislation "aimed at gathering information on—and eventually banning—the mandatory retirement of older workers." This practice owed its historic roots to the Depression, when forcing older workers into retirement seemed the logical way to get the growing legions of the unemployed into the work force. "It is time to recognize," Yates declared, "that our older citizens are a tremendous potential asset to this nation, and that they have the right to lead a proud, productive, and independent life." Nearly a half-century ago, Yates was speaking out on the "implications of the 'oldster boom' that would follow on the heels of the baby boom."

During his third term, the normally soft-spoken Yates came to the defense of Captain Hyman G. Rickover, the father of the Nuclear Navy. Rickover (1900–1986), a Jewish naval officer, was not terribly well-liked by his superiors, likely because he had a reputation for churlishness and "had never kowtowed to his superiors nor indulged in bootlicking." As a result, he was passed over for promotion in both 1951 and

1952. Navy rules stipulated that any officer denied advancement in two consecutive years faced mandatory retirement from the service. That meant that the pugnacious Rickover would have to retire no later than June 1953.

Enter Representative Yates, who roundly and loudly "condemned the injustice, and decried the folly, of the decision." Thanks to Yates's continual harping and cajoling, congressional hearings were scheduled during which all sides got to express their point of view. In the end, newly elected President Dwight D. Eisenhower entered the fray on Rickover's side. His participation tilted the battle in the curmudgeonly Rickover's favor; he was promoted to rear admiral in the summer of 1953. The legendary admiral remained on active duty until February, 1982—some seventeen years past the mandatory retirement age.

As an urban liberal in a conservative, Republican-controlled House, Sidney Yates championed the cause of public housing. In 1953, when the Republicans sought to kill the public housing program altogether, Yates made his feelings known. "We need a program that will satisfy the housing needs of all Americans," he said during floor debate, "not just those who can afford to buy their own houses." With the Truman administration on one side seeking 75,000 new public housing units, and the Republicans on the other, demanding the program's emasculation, Yates worked out a compromise. In the end, 20,000 new units were authorized.

With the election of John F. Kennedy as President in 1960, Yates became an ardent champion of Kennedy's proposal to provide medical insurance for the elderly—Medicare. Time and again, opponents of the Kennedy proposal likened it to socialized medicine. In a 1962 speech on the House floor, Yates answered this charge head-on: "Opponents say if people sixty-five and over can't pay the costs of medical care, let them apply for relief and their medical bills will be paid. But relief medicine is socialized medicine. The state, not the patient, pays all the medical expenses, hospital bills, doctors' fees, everything for a relief patient. Under this arrangement, the doctor is working for the state, not for the patient." When the issue of national health care returned to center stage during the Clinton administration, Yates's thirty-year-old argument was still both relevant and to the point.

In 1962, Chicago Mayor Richard Daley tried to interest United Nations Ambassador Adlai E. Stevenson in running against Senator Everett McKinley Dirksen, the Senate Minority Leader. When Stevenson declined, Daley next turned to Yates, who gave up his safe House seat in order to enter the race. He thereby became the first (and so far only) Jew to run for the United States Senate from Illinois. Yates, with the backing of both the Daley machine and organized labor, waged a vigorous campaign. He reminded voters of his strong support for the Kennedy administration and of "Dirksen's votes against both a redevelopment act that had helped impoverished Illinois communities and a strict drug regulation bill." This latter issue had become of paramount importance, due to the recent discovery that the drug thalidomide was causing dreadful deformities in infants.

Rumor had it that Kennedy, public declarations to the contrary, was actually in favor of a Dirksen victory. Kennedy, so the rumor went, believed Dirksen to be a far easier man to deal with than the ultra-conservative Iowa Republican Senator Bourke B. Hickenlooper, Dirksen's likely successor as Senate Minority Leader. Kennedy traveled to Illinois to stump for Yates in October 1962, but was suddenly called back to the White House—the Cuban Missile Crisis had just begun. This hurt Yates's chances in two ways. First, it deprived him of Kennedy's presence. Second, the crisis served to underscore Dirksen's importance in Washington; Kennedy sent a government jet to take the Minority Leader back to the White House for consultations. On election day, Dirksen beat Yates 53 percent to 47 percent. It was the narrowest margin of victory Dirksen would ever experience. Yates's Ninth District seat was taken by Democrat Edward Finnegan, a member of Daley's Cook County machine.

Out of the House after seven terms, Yates received a consolation prize from Kennedy: appointment as United States representative (with the rank of ambassador) to the Trusteeship Council of the United Nations. In the fall of 1964, the Daley organization "suddenly found a judgeship" for Representative Finnegan. Since Finnegan had already been renominated for office, the local party bosses "had the right to designate a candidate for the vacancy." Not surprisingly, Sid Yates was their choice. After little more than a year at the United Nations, Sid Yates was back in the House—this time for good.

Because Sid Yates had been away from the House for a little over two years, he lost the seniority he had accrued from his first seven terms. In essence, he reentered the House at the very bottom of the "greasy pole." Yates was reappointed to the Appropriations Committee, where he remained until the end of his Congressional career. Without the two-year gap in his congressional service time, Yates would have become chairman of the committee in 1992—or even sooner. In 1975 he did become chair of the Interior Subcommittee. In the twenty years that he chaired this subcommittee (1975–94), Yates "channeled billions to Chicago and Illinois." On the national scene, Yates developed "a detailed knowledge of government land use policy," and used "his appropriating power to create new national parks, wildernesses, seashores, lakeshores, wild and scenic rivers." In a world where "political pork" is at best a necessity, at worst deeply suspect, Yates's largess was of the sort that "many members and voters regard as particularly kosher."

Despite all the dollars he brought into Chicago over the years, Sid Yates was generally far more concerned with national and international issues. Members of the House knew that when Sid Yates got behind an issue, he did not let up. In 1969, he staged a marathon crusade against passage of the anti–ballistic missile system (ABM), which failed by precisely one vote.

Throughout the 1960s, he was the *de facto* leader of the movement to stop funding the supersonic transport (SST). From 1963 to 1969, Yates regularly introduced legislation to eliminate SST funding. The House just as regularly defeated his amendments, always on non-recorded votes. Time and time again, the Illinois Democrat argued that the plane—which was estimated by the late 1960s to cost $1.5 billion—was an "incredible distortion of our national priorities." Yates hammered away at the unconscionable spending of "that much public money for a private purpose."

In 1971, the SST once again came up for a vote. This time, due to a newly adopted rule, members of the House were forced to vote on the record. Up until 1971 (and actually through 1997), Sid Yates—most unusually—had never called a press conference. Nonetheless, during the final debate on the SST, Yates was more than happy to make himself available to reporters. The pending confrontation between pro- and anti-SST forces received wide press coverage. When the final on the record vote was taken, Yates emerged victorious: SST went down to defeat 217–203.

In 1973, Yates was "one of the leaders in a move to stop appropriations for the bombing of Cambodia." A steadfast supporter of Israel, he was a leading opponent of weapons both large and small. In addition to introducing the amendment that would block funding for the B-1 bomber (which failed in committee in 1982 by a vote of 27–22), Yates was consistently one of the House's "most resolute supporters of gun control." During the Ninety-seventh Congress, Yates introduced the most sweeping anti-gun legislation in history, a bill banning the sale, manufacture, and distribution of all handguns—clearly "a step toward an eventual ban on possession." Needless to say, Yates's legislation remained nothing more than an idealistic vision.

Without question, Sid Yates was the number-one supporter of the arts in Congress. Former National Endowment for the Arts chief Frank Hodsoll described him as "one of the most fiercely committed arts champions in Congress, if not the most committed. He's an extremely civilized and cultured man, he cares deeply about the arts, and he knows the arts." Yates's desire and ability to offer both support and federal assistance to the arts made him, into what the *Almanac of American Politics* called "a kind of Maecenas, the House's chief defender of the National Endowment for the Arts and Humanities and the National Trust for Historic Preservation."

In addition to his lifelong appreciation for theater, opera, and abstract impressionist art (he has an exemplary personal collection including works of Alberto Giacometti and Roy Lichenstein), Yates was in the best of all possible political slots: chair of the Appropriations Subcommittee on the Interior and Related Agencies. For in addition to having jurisdiction over "national parks, mines, Indian affairs, the Smithsonian Institution, and certain functions of the Department of Energy," Yates's subcommittee, fortuitously, also included both the National Endowment for the Arts and the National Endowment for the Humanities.

Sid Yates's rationale for why the federal government should fund the arts was both simple and direct: "Every civilization throughout history . . . has been judged not by its military conquests, but by its civilized achievements: the visual arts, the music, the architecture. And ours will be remembered, too, for the arts. The arts enrich the life of every community in the country. That's why we've got to do everything we can to sustain them."

Yates' philosophy was "sorely tested" during the Reagan-Bush administrations. Throughout the 1980s, both Reagan and Bush sought to cut federal spending for the arts. Yates, as subcommittee chair, simply "ignored the budget guidelines," appropriating the same amount as in previous fiscal years. In each case, the President signed the measure.

In 1989, a firestorm of controversy erupted when it was revealed that "works of art regarded by some people as pornographic and blasphemous" had been indirectly subsidized by the NEA. The works in question included a photo by Andres Serrano "of a crucifix submerged in urine, and several by the late Robert Mapplethorpe depicting "homosexual lovemaking, sadomasochism, and children in erotic poses." Republicans, heeding the demands of their increasingly conservative constituency, called for the fiscal emasculation of the NEA.

Yates, "seeking to defuse the furor, tried to put the situation into perspective." Speaking with the editors of the *New York Times*, Yates said: "In 85,000 grants, less than twenty have been found to be objectionable. That's one-quarter of one-tenth of a percent. Actually, the endowment has done a kind of a remarkable job." Throughout his long Congressional career, Sid Yates kept the National Endowment for the Arts and Humanities in business. As former NEA chair Hodsoll said of him: "He's a tough fellow, the arts are his baby, and he doesn't like people fooling around with them."

In 1988, Yates saw his National Film Preservation Act passed into law. Under its provisions, up to twenty-five Americans films are officially labeled as national treasures each year, and protected by the Library of Congress. The measure also stipulated that copyright owners who "cut or colorize movies" be "required to conspicuously label the films as altered "without the participation of the principal director, screenwriter and other creators of the original film."

The Film Preservation Act drew fire from the Motion Picture Association of America, which claimed that producers' commercial rights were being tampered with. In response to this charge, made by MPA president Jack Valenti, Yates responded: "All we're attempting to prevent is the desecration of movies . . . . Just as we preserve our 'still' masterpieces in museums and collections, we ought to do that as well for the great motion pictures." For all his tireless efforts on behalf of the arts, President Bill Clinton awarded Yates a Presidential Citizens Medal in 1993.

Sid Yates had only one serious election challenge in his second stint in Congress. That came in 1982, when his opponent, the thirty-something Republican Catherine Bertini, argued that Yates "could not identify with his constituents because he first went to Washington before many of them were born." Despite Bertini's claim, voters in the Ninth District found much to recommend returning the seventy-three-year-old Yates to Congress; he defeated Bertini with a resounding 67 percent of the vote. Remarkable as it may seem in this day of campaigning via soundbytes and thirty-second television spots, Sid Yates did not use a single TV commercial until a campaign in the early 1990s. In many respects, he was a throwback to a much older time, when the business of Congress was conducted within the walls of the House.

Long known as one of the most civilized members of Congress, Yates was probably its most entertaining as well. "His wit has often enlivened committee hearings, and he has gained a reputation as a highly entertaining raconteur with a seemingly endless store of anecdotes about his long years in the House." *Roll Call* listed Yates as the twenty-first wealthiest member of the Hundred and Fifth Congress, with an estimated net worth of $7 million. According to his public disclosure form, Yates's wealth was derived from "real estate holdings, Treasury notes, and Public Housing Authority Bonds." Yates was also a partner in a syndicate that owned two shopping centers in Kentucky.

At the beginning of the One Hundred and Fifth Congress, Sid Yates was eighty-eight years old and still going strong. "So long as my health holds up," he said, "I will remain in Congress, he said at the time"

In early 1998, Sid Yates announced that he would retire from the House at the end of the Hundred and Fifth Congress. In going public with his decision Yates merely said, "It's time for me to go." His announcement sent Democrats in Chicago's Ninth District scurrying for any advantage they might find for what would undoubtedly prove to be a political dogfight. Ironically, few, if any of those who aspired to replace Yates had even been born when he first went to Washington. Sidney Yates was succeeded by state legislator *Jan Schakowsky*.

References

Almanac of American Politics, 1972–1996.
Chicago Tribune, July 23, 1989, XIII p. 10+.
Current Biography, 1993, pp. 609–613.
Politics in America, 1994.

YULEE, DAVID LEVY (1810–1886):

Whig/Democrat from the Territory of Florida; served two terms in the House (Twenty-seventh and Twenty-eighth Congress, March 4, 1841–March 3, 1845); two terms in the Senate (July 1, 1845–March 3, 1851, March 4, 1855–January 21, 1861).

The year 1840 is generally reckoned as being the beginning of the Victorian era. The United States of America was made up of twenty-six states, three territories, and a population of slightly more than 17 million. Less than one-tenth of one percent of the population was Jewish. In November of that year, the voting public elected General William Henry Harrison, the sixty-eight-year-old hero of the Battle of Tippecanoe, who defeated the incumbent Democrat Martin Van Buren, thus becoming America's ninth President. Harrison, so the story goes, caught a cold while delivering a rather lengthy inaugural address, and died one month later, thereby making John Tyler the nation's first "accidental President."

In 1840, the United States was in a sorry fiscal plight. The Panic of 1837 had set the nation's economy on its financial backside. According to one political diarist of the time: "All things are disjoined. Trade is at a stand; property diminished in value; confidence shaken to the center; and nothing thrives but party spirit and corporation taxes." The presidential campaign that year did not really focus on the issues. Rather, much like modern-day elections, it sought to entertain and vilify where it might have enlightened and uplifted.

The Whig campaign was replete with slogans ("Tippecanoe and Tyler too"), songs ("With Tip and Tyler / We'll burst Van's Biler / Farewell dear Van / You're not our man"), banners, placards, balls, cider barrels, and plenty of free food. The campaign's centerpiece was a gigantic 50 x 100 foot log cabin in which literally thousands of Whig partisans could gather. Here they would listen to long-winded speeches that extolled the virtues of Harrison and the Whig platform and damned the vices, ineptitude, and relentless partisanship of Jackson, Van Buren, and the Democrats. Political passions became so inflamed that many rallies ended with besotted Harrison supporters coming to physical blows with enraged Van Buren partisans.

Harrison's candidacy met with popular approval despite his relative lack of personality and his sometimes incoherent stand on the issues. The public's equation of Van Buren and the Democrats with the sorry shape of the nation's economy and the contentious indecisiveness in Congress ("gridlock" in modern political parlance) made Harrison and the Whigs all the more appealing. The politically dexterous Van Buren ran a surprisingly lackluster campaign. When the final vote was tallied, the Whigs found themselves in charge of the White House and both chambers of Congress.

The Twenty-seventh Congress was sworn in on March 4, 1841. By the time its first session began on May 31, Harrison was dead, and John Tyler had become America's President. As politically talented a group as ever assembled under the Capitol Dome made up the Twenty-seventh Congress: one former and three future Presidents (respectively, John Quincy Adams, Millard Fillmore, Franklin Pierce, and James Buchanan); the political lions John C. Calhoun, Henry Clay, and Caleb Cushing; Leverett Saltonstall, great-grandfather of the twentieth-century Massachusetts Senator and Governor; and James I. Roosevelt, the first of that illustrious family to serve in national public office. Also taking his seat on March 4, 1841 was David Levy Yulee, the very first member of the Congressional Minyan. (As noted below, although Levy Yulee was the product of Jewish parents, he spent the majority of his life disavowing his religious heritage) Because he came from Florida, then a territory and not a state, he was technically a Delegate rather than a Representative.

There is a great deal of uncertainty about the background and original family name of the first Jew to serve in Congress. Most sources agree that he was the grandson of one Jacoub ibn Youli, who served at the court of Sidi Muhammed ibn Abdallah, Sultan of Morocco from 1757 to 1790. Sidi Muhammed, whose sultanate specialized in piracy and kidnapping, was one of the first heads of state to recognize the infant United States of America. It is said that among his prized possessions was a letter of appreciation from President George Washington.

Depending on the source, David Levy's grandfather was either a prince, Grand Vizier, or major domo to the Sultan, and either a Moroccan Muslim or a Portuguese Jew. There is even dis agreement over the derivation of the name Yulee (or Youli). It is variously described as a Moorish title, "a well-known Jewish name among Portuguese Jews," and the result of the simple transposition of the Hebrew letters *yud*, *vav*, and *lamed*, which can spell either Yulee or Levy.

Jacoub ibn Youli's wife, Rachel Levy, was the daughter of an English physician. Evidence exists that she was captured by Moroccan pirates while en route to the British West Indies. From there she was taken to the slave market at Fez, where she was sold to Youli, who may or may not have kept a harem. A son was born in Mogador, Morocco, perhaps as early as 1782. This boy grew up to become the father of the future member of Congress.

Both Sultan Sidi Muhammed and Jacoub ibn Youli died in a bloody palace coup in 1790. Pregnant with a second child, the widowed Rachel managed to escape to Gibraltar, where she gave birth to a daughter. Returning to England, Rachel resumed her maiden name and renamed her firstborn Moses Elias Levy. Although in later years he would occasionally sign an article or letter with the pseudonym "Eubates" or "Youli," Moses went by the name Levy for the rest of his life.

Raised as a practicing Orthodox Jew, Moses Levy was educated in English schools and eventually earned a university degree. In 1800, Rachel and her two children emigrated to St. Thomas, Virgin Islands, where Moses quickly made a fortune in lumber. Around 1808, Moses married a Sephardi, Hannah Abendanone. Their second child, David Levy, was born in St. Thomas on June 7, 1810.

In 1815, the British gave the island of St. Thomas to Denmark. Shortly thereafter, Moses moved to Havana, where he became a government contractor supplying materiel to the Spanish garrison. Amassing yet another fortune, Moses turned his attention to land speculation in the Spanish-held territory of Florida. Between 1818 and 1820, he purchased nearly 90,000 acres in Alachua and Marion Counties, some 10 miles south of present-day Gainesville. Levy's partners in these transactions, Abraham M. Cohen and Antonio Meir (Meyer), were both Jewish.

On this land, Moses Levy established a plantation called Pilgrimage. A utopian dreamer, he hoped to transform Pilgrimage into a haven for Jews yearning to escape the shackles of European oppression. In furtherance of this dream, he wrote New York's Shearith Israel synagogue in 1820, proposing the development of a Jewish agricultural colony. In the letter, he declared his intention to pledge a sizable portion of his land for the colony. He further proposed the creation of a Jewish theological seminary in New York to which he would happily lend substantial financial support. There is reason to speculate that Moses was seeking to create a school where his sons David and Elias might receive a proper Jewish education. Both proposals fell on deaf ears.

Undeterred, Moses left for Europe in late 1820, to recruit settlers for his Florida colony. He returned from Europe the next year with fewer than fifty people, all of whom were brought over at his expense. Attempting to breathe life into his dream, Levy built twenty-five houses, 45 miles of road, and three plantations on 300 acres of cultivated land. He had a cargo of sugar roots and seeds brought over from Cuba, envisioning that one day the plantations would produce sugar cane and tropical fruits. The plan came to naught. Moses Levy returned to Europe in the hope of finding more settlers for his Jewish utopia. One more journey, one more failure.

Moses Levy gave up on his proto-Zionist dream and settled down to run his own 50,000-acre plantation in Volusia County. He named his domain Hope Hill. Realizing that Florida was not the place for the sons of a landed Jewish gentleman to receive a proper religious education, Moses sent his boys to Norfolk, Virginia, where they attended a private school. While in Norfolk, they resided with their father's good friend Moses Myers, who at one time had represented the French Republic in the United States.

From Norfolk, the boys were sent briefly to Harvard College. For reasons unknown, Moses decided to cut short his sons' education and abruptly brought them back to Florida. It is possible that he had gotten wind of the fact that they were associating exclusively with non-Jews. That should not have come as a great surprise; in the mid-1820s, Jews at Harvard College were few and far between. David and Elias returned to Pilgrimage, where they spent several years as the plantation's overseers. Moses continued to reside at Hope Hill.

By 1831, Moses and his sons had become estranged. Evidence educed from David Levy's grandson suggests that the boys were put off by Moses' increasing "religious socialism." Neither David nor Elias was willing to go through life being known first and foremost as a Jew. The more pious and pronounced the father became, the more disaffected the sons grew. Then again, the estrangement had secular political overtones as well; Moses Levy was devoutly anti-slavery. As early as 1827, he had come out with a widely publicized plan to abolish slavery in Florida. That his son David would be both pro-slavery and increasingly unwilling to identify himself as a Jew must have embittered the elder Levy. So great was his antipathy for his sons that when he died in 1854, all he left them from his vast holdings was $100 apiece. The bulk of his estate was left to his two daughters. Despite the fact that David Levy did not need the money or the property (by 1854, he had made a fortune as a lawyer and land speculator), he and his brother successfully contested their father's will. The court decided that each of the four children should receive an equal portion of the estate.

To those who knew him, David Levy's entry into politics came as no surprise. Politics was his birthright. His father had been intimately involved in the hurly-burly of Florida politics almost from the moment of his arrival in the Spanish territory. Shortly after his admission to the Florida Bar in 1832, David Levy became clerk to the Territorial Legislature. In that position he reported on the peace negotiations between the United States and the Seminole Indian Nation. His work met with popular approbation. One of the officers attending the negotiations described Levy as "not only one of the most enlightened, but also one of the most patriotic inhabitants of Florida." David Levy's political career was on the rise.

In 1837, he was elected to the Territorial Legislature and chosen to represent St. John's County (St. Augustine) at the Florida Constitutional Convention. While Levy was in Tallahassee, the question of his citizenship was raised. This would prove to be a nettlesome issue for years to come. It is difficult to know whether those raising the citizenship issue were motivated by anti-Jewish feelings or mere partisan politics. It is somewhat doubtful that Florida, which at the time had fewer than 250 scattered Jewish residents, would have been a hotbed of anti-Semitism. Nonetheless, Levy's

right to practice law or be seated as a duly authorized delegate to the Constitutional Convention (or later, the United States Congress) was challenged on at least three separate occasions.

At issue was the original ordinance which granted citizenship to everyone who had been an inhabitant of Florida on July 17, 1821, the date the United States began exercising sovereignty. Evidence was presented which purportedly showed that Moses Levy had not taken up residence in Florida until several days after July 17. The territorial court ruled the evidence to be specious. The court further ruled that Moses Levy's vast land holdings, purchased prior to 1821, were tantamount to a declaration of legal residence. It decreed that Moses Levy, his wife, and his children were all legal citizens of the United States.

The issue refused to die. When David Levy attempted to take his seat in the Twenty-seventh Congress as Delegate from the Territory of Florida, the question was raised once again. John Quincy Adams noted in his diary:

[Francis Wilkinson] Pickens [of South Carolina] introduced David Levy as Delegate from the Territory of Florida. [Christopher] Morgan objected to his being sworn and presented papers contesting his election, and denying that he is a citizen of the United States. . . . Levy is said to be a Jew, and what will be, if true, a far more formidable disqualification, that he has a dash of African blood in him, which, *sub rosa*, is the case with more than one member of the house.

The issue was referred to the Committee on Elections, chaired by William Halstead, a New Jersey Whig. Ironically, Halstead's own credentials had been rejected in the preceding Congress. A long and rancorous debate was held during which hundreds of pages of testimony were taken, and Levy enlisted numerous supporters, including Dr. Daniel Levi Maduro Peixotto (1800–1843), the *hazzan* (cantor) of New York's Shearith Israel congregation and a prominent leader of American Jewry.

In order to settle the question of the new Delegate's citizenship, Moses Levy's sworn statements were taken, although from the tenor of his comments ("The irritating subject of David

Levy is become troublesome to me beyond measure . . ."), it was painfully obvious that the father was not overly concerned with his son's situation. The committee's final report, dated March 15, 1842, found in favor of Levy. He was finally seated as an official member of the Twenty-seventh Congress. Halstead, perhaps nursing a grudge against the colleagues who had denied him his seat two years earlier, authored the minority report against David Levy.

Levy was one of 148 new members taking seats in the Twenty-seventh Congress, one of the largest freshman classes in American history. Then as now, one of the most difficult and immediate challenges facing a newly elected member of Congress was to make a name for oneself and break away from the anonymity of the pack. David Levy managed to do just that. Because of the notoriety he gained as Congress's first Jew, coupled with the recent hearings on the status of his citizenship, the thirty-one-year-old Whig-Democrat became a known political commodity. He was more than a nameless, faceless freshman.

At the time David Levy entered the House, Congress was considering legislation to remove all federal troops from Florida. Those supporting this position believed that the Seminole menace had been eradicated. Even during his campaign for Congress, Levy spoke passionately against the plan. Time and again he argued that the Seminole threat, far from being eliminated, was an ever-present danger. Removing federal troops would be both premature and foolhardy. His wariness was based on personal experience; in 1835, one of his father's plantations had been destroyed by marauding Indian bands. (Moses Levy had presented Congress with a claim for the destroyed property, but it was disallowed.) Then too, Levy's support of the "peculiar institution" undoubtedly entered into his argumentation.

Levy introduced a bill calling for an investigation into the "Indian troubles in Florida." This was the first piece of legislation submitted in the Twenty-seventh Congress. His audacity in proposing legislation so soon was regarded as quite singular in a legislative body that has historically expected newcomers to sit on the back bench, learn the ropes, and be "rarely seen and never heard."

The Seminole Indian question had been a vexing issue for some time. For nearly a generation, the Seminoles had been waging guerrilla war against Florida settlers and federal troops. Eventually a treaty that would remove the Indians from Florida was signed, but the Seminoles balked. Two issues were at stake. First, Florida was their historic and ancestral homeland. Second, and perhaps even more to the point, under the treaty, no slave or person of black descent could be part of the Indian removal. This presented tremendous hardships for the Seminoles, who not only had been providing safe haven for escaped bondsmen over the years, but had, in fact, entered into numerous marriages with them. Led by their chief, Osceola (who was the son of an English trader named William Powell), the Seminoles "baffled, harassed, and occasionally defeated the troops dispatched against [them]." A bloody war ensued.

Levy's vehement opposition to the bill caused John Quincy Adams to once again take note. An entry in Adams's diary for May 16, 1842 reads: "I found Levy, the Jew Delegate from Florida, making a red hot speech against the President's message declaring his intention to put an end to the Florida war." As debate proceeded, the former President's pen became even more acidic. From mere "Jew Delegate," Levy descended to "the alien Jew Delegate." Not to be outdone, Tennessee's Senator Andrew Johnson, one day to be the first American President impeached, referred to Levy as a "miserable little cuss!"

Ad hominem attacks notwithstanding, David Levy kept pounding away, using every forensic weapon at his disposal. At no time did he deign to respond to his colleagues' *ad hominems* about his heritage. Ultimately, the troops were removed, and Osceola was captured, sent to Fort Moultrie near Charleston, and died there within a few months.

Levy's fight for Florida statehood, waged over a three-year period, ended in triumph. On March 3, 1845, Florida entered the increasingly unstable Union as its twenty-seventh State and chose Levy as one of its two Senators. One week later, the new state honored its new Senator by naming Levy County in his honor. The Florida legislature acted just in the nick of time; by the end of the year, David Levy, by an act of that same legislature, had officially changed his name to Yulee. Some claim without hesitation that the name change was prompted by the anti-Jewish sentiment he had encountered in Washington. Perhaps. Then too, in early 1845, David Levy became engaged to Miss Nancy Wickliffe, the daughter of Postmaster-General Charles A. Wickliffe (1788–1869). His betrothed, like her distinguished family, was devoutly Christian, so much so that contemporaries referred to her as the Wickliffe Madonna.

The suggestion has been made that David Levy agreed to the name change as part of an antenuptial agreement. One can imagine that the daughter of an old, upstanding Christian family simply did not want to go through life being known as Mrs. David Levy. If such was the case, then the Senator forged a compromise; from 1846 on, David Levy was known as David Levy Yulee.

By the time he legally changed his name, the Senator had already ceased having any relationship with the Levys. Although there is no solid evidence that he ever became a convert, his children were raised as Christians. From the day he became a Yulee, the former David Levy began claiming that far from being Jewish, he was the offspring of Moroccan aristocracy.

In the Senate, Yulee was named chairman of the Naval Committee. From this position he became one of the earliest champions of iron vessels and cheap ocean passage. He also became the Senate's strongest opponent of the movement to abolish flogging. In one of those lovely ironies of history, it was another, nonrelated Levy, U.S. Navy Commodore Uriah P. (1792–1862), who most ably presented the case for abolishing corporal punishment.

Despite Senator Yulee's newfound claim that he was not a Jew, he continued to be the butt of vicious barbs and calumnies. The withering comments of John Quincy Adams, as noted above, were among the most opprobrious. Adams's invective was grounded in his personal, intellectual dislike of Jews—an animus he likely inherited from his father, America's second President. Additionally, Adams, among others, was greatly concerned lest the "alien Jew from Florida" add his voice to the heated and politically divisive slavery issue.

His concerns were well founded. David Levy Yulee's impassioned support of slavery was no different than that of thousands of other Southerners. What made the nation take note of his position and his fiery words, of course, was the fact that they were being said by a Jew on the floor of the United States Senate. Regardless of how he saw himself or what he proclaimed his antecedents to be, David Levy Yulee would always be considered a Jew by his colleagues, the nation's journalists, and political cognoscenti, both north and south.

Levy Yulee's term as United States Senator expired in 1851. He was subsequently defeated in his bid for reelection by Stephen R. Mallory of Jacksonville. The final tally was close enough that Yulee contested. He brought suit before the Florida State Senate, where the case dragged on for nearly a year and a half, and was eventually decided in Mallory's favor. Despite this, the Florida Senate, in a highly unusual move, voted to pay Yulee a sum equal to the *per diem* he would have received as Senator during the time the case was being heard.

Once again a private citizen of Florida, David Levy Yulee devoted his energies to the further development of his state. He began paying particular attention to a project which would occupy his time, talent, and imagination for many years to come: the creation of a railroad system running from the Gulf of Mexico to the Atlantic Ocean.

Because of his fiery political positions, the Jewish ancestry of Senator David Levy Yulee (nicknamed the "Florida Fire Eater") was commented upon by countless colleagues, editorial writers, and political enemies. Time and again his detractors turned political animus into personal and religious enmity by heaping obloquy on the altar of his Jewishness. The fact that the Florida Senator no longer practiced the religion of his ancestors and was married to a devout Christian made not one iota of difference. Then, as now, the bigot's creed proclaimed "once a Jew, always a Jew."

This confrontational tactic would become a constant in the antebellum period. A venomous editorial directed against Levy Yulee and other prominent Jews of the day in the *Boston Transcript* went beyond the bounds of mere disagreement by rhetorically asking:

Can it be possible, that this "accursed"—having no land of their own, desire that other nations shall be in the same unhappy condition as they are themselves?. . . This "stiff-necked generation," by its principal men, takes a lead in attempting to destroy a Constitution which has been to them an Ark of refuge and safety.

It was not enough to merely condemn the pro-slavery position taken by Levy Yulee and other Jewish Southerners; they had to be attacked as cursed members of an accursed race, whom God Almighty Himself had condemned to be perpetual outsiders.

The Florida legislature returned Yulee to the United States Senate in 1855. He was one of the earliest proponents of secession and, if necessary, of insurrection. Such talk was nothing new for him, as shown by his response, seven years earlier, to the Wilmot Proviso. Introduced by Pennsylvania Democrat David Wilmot in the aftermath of the Mexican War, this bill proposed that slavery be barred from any territory acquired from Mexico. The South saw red, and Yulee offered a counter-resolution that would permit settlers to bring slaves into New Mexico and Southern California. These new territories, he argued, belonged to all the citizens of all the states; therefore, the transport of property, including slaves, was completely lawful. In a letter to John C. Calhoun in 1849, Yulee had warned that unless the Constitution was amended to protect the South from what he termed "Northern aggression," "the best policy [would be] to take steps at once for a separation."

During the early days of the Lincoln administration, Yulee and a group of Senate colleagues plotted secession. When Union forces captured Fernandina, Florida, in 1862, they found among Senator Yulee's correspondence a cache of letters which outlined a secessionist conspiracy. For example:

The immediately important thing to be done is the occupation of forts and arsenals in Florida. The Naval Station and forts at Pensacola are first in consequence. For this a force is necessary. . . . The occupation of the Navy Yard will give us a good supply of ordnance and make the capture of the forts easier. . . . Lose no time, for my opinion is, troops will be very soon dispatched to reinforce and strengthen the forts in Florida.

The fact that this plot was hatched within the halls of the United States Senate made it all the more monstrous. Why didn't Yulee and his cohorts resign their Senate seats in protest before plotting secession? Yulee's obituary provides the answer. At his death in 1886, the *New York Times* noted that "he and some other Southern Senators, while still in Congress, had been secretly plotting the secession while deciding to remain in Congress until Mr. Lincoln took office, in order to prevent legislation which would put the Government into condition to meet a hostile attack from its enemies."

Not only did David Yulee send advance-dated copies of the Resolutions of Secession to various influential Southerners, he also spelled out in minute detail a well-conceived strategy of misdirection:

The idea . . . [is] that the States should go out at once and provide for the early organization of a Confederate Government, not later than the 15th day of February. This time is allowed to enable Louisiana and Texas to participate, and volunteer bills might be passed which would put Mr. Lincoln in immediate position for hostilities, whereas by remaining in our places until the 4th of March, it is thought we can keep the hands of Mr. Buchanan [who would remain in office until Lincoln was inaugurated on March 1] tied, and disable the Republicans from effecting any legislation which will strengthen the hands of the incoming administration.

On the basis of this cache of letters, the actions of Senator Yulee were found to be treasonous. This most ardent of Southern chauvinists, whose state was the first to secede from the Union, played virtually no role in the war he had plotted and predicted; he spent his days as a prisoner of war at Fort Pulaski.

David Levy Yulee languished in prison longer than any other prominent rebel leader. He returned to Florida in 1866, and joined his family at Fernandina, where he devoted his time to rebuilding the state's ruined economy. In 1880, having sold his rail line to English investors, Yulee went to live with a married daughter in Washington. He divided the final years of his life between the nation's capital and New York City, where he died on October 10,

1886 at the Clarendon Hotel. His funeral was held at the New York Avenue Presbyterian Church in Washington, of which he was a member. In his obituary, he was remembered for precisely two things: his complicity in attempting to mutineer federal establishments in Florida, and the odd family history which somehow turned the son of pious Jewish parents into the scion of a Moroccan Vizier.

References

Charles Francis Adams, ed., *Memoirs of John Quincy Adams*.

Dictionary of American Biography.

Encyclopaedia Judaica (1972), vol. 16, cols. 894–895.

New York Times, October 11, 1886, p. 5; October 17, 1886, p. 1.

Publications of the American Jewish Historical Society, vol. 25, pp. 1–30.

Universal Jewish Encyclopedia.

Who Was Who in America, historical volume.

ZELENKO, HERBERT (1906–1979): *Democrat from New York; served four terms in the House (Eighty-fourth through Eighty-seventh Congress, January 3, 1955–January 3, 1963).*

Unlike most successful politicians, Herbert Zelenko was not given to taking about himself or his career. A *New York Times* reporter, his request for a personal interview having been denied, wrote: "He [Zelenko] proffers a record of his activities in the House of Representatives and makes it clear that the record can do his talking." As a result of this penchant for privacy, Zelenko failed to give the editors of *Who's Who in America* the name of his parents, wife, or daughter.

Herbert Zelenko's father emigrated from Kiev to New York City around the turn of the century. The future Congressman was born in New York on March 14, 1906, and graduated from Stuyvesant High School in 1923. Four years later, at age twenty, he earned a B.A. from Columbia. In 1929, Zelenko earned a law degree from Columbia and was admitted to the bar. Entering the legal profession shortly after the Crash of '29, Zelenko found work as a lecturer at the Practicing Law and the Law Science Institutes. In February 1933, one month before the inauguration of Franklin D. Roosevelt, he was appointed assistant U.S. attorney for the southern district of New York. During his years at the bar, Zelenko developed a specialty in railroad negligence cases.

In 1954, Twenty-first District Representative *Jacob Javits* resigned his seat in order to run for New York Attorney General. Zelenko, running on both the Democrat and Liberal Party tickets, defeated Republican Floyd Cramer by a margin of nearly 33,000 votes. In winning, Zelenko became the only Democrat that year to pick up a Republican seat in the New York City delegation. His maiden House speech created a sensation; he charged that under the 1954 tax law, business was permitted "to take a double deduction for expenses at a cost to the Treasury of $5 billion." Zelenko's speech did more than ruffle Republican feathers; it caused Congress to pass a law that effectively plugged the offending loophole.

Herbert Zelenko served four terms in the House, regularly winning reelection by a better than two-to-one margins. About the worst any of his Republican opponents could say of him

was that he was a talkative lawyer or a down-the-line liberal. In point of fact, Zelenko was a party moderate, favoring an increase in the minimum wage from 75¢ to $1, rigid farm price supports at 90 percent of parity, and federal aid for housing, road construction, and education. Like most Northern urban Democrats, Zelenko voted to expand Social Security. He voted against limiting the President's tariff-cutting powers, against exempting natural gas producers from federal price controls, and against increasing postal rates.

Zelenko's reelection campaigns generally had "as great a dearth of . . . issues as any district" in New York City. In 1956, the main issue separating Zelenko from his moderate Republican opponent, Dalton Shapo, was Israel. The campaign was run at the time of the Sinai conflict. Zelenko pushed for the sale of American fighter aircraft to the Jewish state; Shapo "agree[d] wholeheartedly with President Eisenhower's avowal that the United States [should] not become involved in the hostilities in the Middle East." The voters of the Twenty-first Congressional District, overwhelmingly Jewish, reelected Zelenko by nearly 70,000 votes.

Although the child of immigrants, Herb Zelenko was "not proficient in the language of [his] parents." He was, however, able to give campaign speeches in Spanish—helpful in a district with a growing Puerto Rican constituency. In exchange for their votes, Zelenko introduced an annual resolution advocating Puerto Rican statehood.

Following the 1960 census, the Twenty-first District was emasculated. Zelenko found himself in a heated primary contest with Representative William Fitts Ryan. Since Ryan already represented the great majority of the voters in this new Congressional District, the Twentieth, his 26,295 to 18,459-vote victory came as no surprise.

During his last term in the House, Herbert Zelenko was appointed chair of a special subcommittee of the Education and Labor Committee charged with looking into "racial discrimination and other improper practices" in the New York garment industry. Zelenko held four days of hearings in New York City before the Democratic primary. Following his defeat at the hands of Ryan, he decided to postpone any more hearings. David Dubinsky, president of the Ladies' International Garments Workers Union, charged that Zelenko's stalling tactics were politically motivated. Sources close to the subcommittee told the *New York Times* that Zelenko, having lost his seat, simply "did not have much interest in continuing the inquiry."

Herbert Zelenko left Washington at the end of 1962. Returning to New York City, he resumed the practice of law. He died in New York on February 23, 1979, and was buried at Sharon Gardens, in Valhalla, New York. He was survived by his wife, daughter, and two grandsons. Herb Zelenko remained a private person both in life and in death; no obituary appeared in the *New York Times*.

References

Biographical Directory of the United States Congress: 1774–1989, p. 2103.

New York Times, November 2, 1954, 15:1; November 3, 1956, 26:3; October 31, 1958, 18:3. September 13, 1962, 38:2.

ZIMMER, RICHARD (1944–): *Republican from New Jersey; served three terms in the House (One Hundred and First through One Hundred and Fourth Congress; January 3, 1991–January 3, 1997).*

On November 20, 1789, the State of New Jersey officially endorsed the first ten amendments to the Constitution of the United States. One amendment which it, along with many other states, failed to ratify, was the brainchild of James Madison: "No law, varying the compensation for the services of Senators and Representatives, shall take effect until an election of Representatives have intervened." The proposed amendment remained on the backburners of legislatures throughout the country for the next two hundred years, failing to find either a spokesman or a constituency.

Finally, in October, 1991, Dick Zimmer, a freshman member of the House of Representatives from New Jersey, decided that he must become that spokesman. Elected the previous fall from New Jersey's Twelfth Congressional District as a fiscal conservative, the Republican Zimmer made the case for ratification in the simplest of terms. "Members of Congress," he said, "have the ultimate perk: They can give themselves a pay raise without first asking their employers— the taxpayers who elected them."

In an era of growing distrust and distaste for elected officials, Zimmer's argument had an appealing logic. Moreover, he was probably in the best position to push for the amendment's passage; while serving in the New Jersey State Senate in the late 1980s, he was the one who had sponsored the state resolution for ratification. Zimmer's initiative worked. Not only did New Jersey become the thirty-sixth state to vote for ratification; other states followed suit, until on May 7, 1992, the measure became the Twenty-seventh Amendment to the United States Constitution. Such is the power that one person can have to effect change.

Dick Zimmer, a soft-spoken, bespectacled man whose youthful appearance belies his age, was born in Newark, New Jersey, on August 16,

1944. His father died when Dick was three. His mother, Evelyn Rader Zimmer, was descended from the Spingarns, the founders of American Tobacco and the NAACP. As Zimmer says: "There was money in the family once, but it never got down to us." Evelyn Zimmer raised Dick on her own in a garden apartment ("the New Jersey equivalent of a log cabin," the Congressman says) until, in 1956, she married Howard Rubin. Until the time she married Rubin, Dick had had almost no Jewish education. Prompted by his new stepfather, to whom Jewish education was very important, Dick went to Hebrew school and was bar mitzvah at the Reform Temple Menorah (today called Ner Tamid) in Bloomfield.

Zimmer, an outstanding student at his high school in Glen Ridge, was admitted to Yale in 1962. At first he majored in chemistry. That proved to be a mistake. "I figured that since I was the smartest kid in Glen Ridge, I was the smartest kid in America. I learned otherwise at Yale." Transferring to political science, Zimmer gradually became affiliated with the Ripon Society, a group of moderate-to-liberal Republicans. Both his mother and stepfather had been Democrats, Howard's family having been wiped out in the Depression. Zimmer worked his way through Yale, spending his last summer as an intern in the office of New Jersey Senator Clifford Case, one of the last of the great Republican moderates, and one of only two GOP senators (Jacob Javits being the other) to vote in favor of Lyndon Johnson's Great Society proposal.

Graduating in 1966, Zimmer entered the Yale Law School, where he served on the board of editors of the *Yale Law Journal*. During his last year in law school, Zimmer married Marfy Goodspeed, a Catholic. They have two sons: Carl, born in 1966, and Benjamin, born in 1971. Following his graduation from law school, the Zimmers settled in Delaware Township (Hunterdon County), where today, they raise sheep and grow hay on a small working farm.

The Zimmers raised their sons with the idea that when they came of age, they would have the right to decide which religion (if any) they would affiliate with. When Carl expressed an interest in becoming bar mitzvah, the Zimmers joined the Flemington Jewish Community Center. Carl went through the conversion ceremony and became bar mitzvah in 1979.

From 1969 to 1975, Dick Zimmer practiced law with Cravath, Swaine & Moore in New York City. In 1975, he left Cravath and joined the legal staff of Johnson and Johnson at its corporate headquarters in New Brunswick, New Jersey. He remained with the company until his election to Congress sixteen years later. From 1974 to 1977, Zimmer served as state chairman of New Jersey Common Cause, leading that public interest group's fight for passage of the state's Sunshine Law, which opened meetings of governmental bodies to the public. When Zimmer finished his term as president of Common Cause, he became campaign counsel on the staff of former New Jersey Assembly Speaker Thomas H. Kean, who was running for the Republican nomination for Governor. Kean, a blueblood whose family had been prominent in New Jersey since before the Revolution, lost his primary race to Raymond Bateman, who wound up losing the general election to Brendan Byrne. Zimmer remained loyal to Kean, acting as campaign counsel in his two successful races for governor—1981 and 1985.

Zimmer narrowly lost a race for the State Assembly in 1979, but prevailed in 1981. He won reelection in both 1983 and 1985, and then won a 1987 special election to become just one of three Republicans in the State Senate. While in the legislature, Zimmer combined a good government agenda with "a resolutely conservative approach to fiscal matters." He worked hard to give New Jersey voters the right of initiative and referendum, and backed campaign finance reform. An "unswerving opponent of new taxes," Zimmer attracted attention during the 1989 New Jersey budget hearings when he opposed Governor Kean's budget as "relying on erroneous revenue projections and thus being out of balance." Zimmer turned out to be correct in his assessment of Kean's proposed budget: the state was soon saddled with a $600 million deficit. Zimmer also carved out a reputation as

an environmentally sensitive legislator; he successfully sponsored bills dealing with radon gas testing and farmland preservation.

In 1989, Dick Zimmer co-chaired Twelfth District Congressman Jim Courter's campaign for New Jersey Governor. After Courter polled a dismal 37 percent in the general election (losing to his congressional colleague Jim Florio), he decided not to run for reelection to the House. Zimmer quickly announced for the open seat. The Republican-friendly Twelfth District takes in all of Hunterdon County and parts of Mercer, Middlesex, Monmouth, Somerset, Sussex, and Warren Counties. It contains the affluent, white-collar Trenton suburbs, Princeton, East Brunswick, and Plainsboro.

In the Republican primary, Zimmer faced two formidable opponents: Assemblyman (now Eleventh District Congressman) Rodney Frelinghuysen and former New York Giants player Phil McConkey. The Frelinghuysen name is as well known in New Jersey as Fish in New York or Daley in Chicago. The family's tradition of public service dates back to the Revolutionary War; four Frelinghuysens have served in the United States Senate, and Rodney's father served in the House from 1953 to 1975. Correctly sensing that McConkey's anti-establishment campaign would hurt the blue-blooded Frelinghuysen, Zimmer attacked the New Jersey legislator for his support of Kean's deficit budget. Aided greatly by environmental activists, Zimmer won the primary with 38 percent of the vote to McConkey's 31 and Frelinghuysen's 29.

The general election was anticlimactic. Zimmer faced millionaire businesswoman Marguerite Chandler, who had hoped to run against Courter on the abortion issue—Courter was pro-life. Zimmer's well-known pro-choice stance took away Chandler's one issue. Chandler spent more than $1.7 million on the campaign (much of it her own), to Zimmer's $1.2 million, making it the nation's most expensive open House seat. Despite Chandler's deep pockets, Zimmer defeated her by a better than two-to-one margin, winning everywhere but in liberal Princeton.

Zimmer was assigned to the Government Operations Committee, the Committee on Science, Space, and Technology, and the Select Committee on Aging. He was also elected chairman of the Republican Caucus of the One Hundred and Second Congress freshman class. Zimmer's maiden speech explained why he was voting to authorize the use of force against Iraq in the Gulf. Speaking of that vote, Zimmer later said: "It was a very painful vote. . . . Both my draft-age sons urged me to vote the other way. I just had to assume a worst-case scenario."

As a member of the Space subcommittee, Zimmer cast the only vote against funding of the space station. That singular action got him an in-depth half hour interview on C-SPAN. "I had read an analysis of the space station that it wasn't worth the $30 billion they were going to spend on it," he said. Speaking before his sub-committee colleagues, he argued that "in its current scaled-down configuration, Space Station Freedom could better be called Space Station Lite—one-third of the mission for nearly four times the price." Zimmer succeeded in winning House passage of an amendment to the NASA authorization bill that required a study of alternatives to the proposed space station.

One of the House's most consistent fiscal conservatives, Zimmer introduced numerous bills aimed at curbing congressional pork-barrel projects. Said Zimmer: "Everybody is very reluctant to vote against somebody else's pork barrel project. Someday they'll have something in their district that in their eyes is not a pork barrel project. They've got to have it. . . . The many members of Congress, perhaps the majority, subscribe to the view that this is what's going to get them reelected."

Even while running for Congress, Zimmer adopted a somewhat different attitude: "My district will be best served by reducing the size of the pie." For his efforts, Zimmer was regularly named the "most fiscally responsible member of Congress" by the National Taxpayers Union, and received the Citizens Against Government Waste's Taxpayer Hero award for three years in a row.

Zimmer was somewhat of a maverick, attacking both Democrats and Republicans for profligacy and elitism. He put tremendous pressure on Speaker Thomas Foley to abolish the House Bank—"the bank that would not bounce checks." After the publicly embarrassing disclosure that members of the House had written 4,325 bad checks in the first six months of 1990, Zimmer proposed legislation requiring the bank to comply with standard banking practices. The next day, Foley closed down the bank. Zimmer also railed against the system whereby members of Congress could fix parking tickets, enjoy free close-in airport parking, free help from the IRS in preparing their taxes, and $4.50 haircuts. Many of Zimmer's ideas were incorporated in the Republican's 1994 Contract With America.

Zimmer was unique among Republicans in Congress; conservative on fiscal issues and largely moderate on cultural. Nonetheless, in 1995, he had the third-highest rating of any Jewish member of Congress according to the Christian Coalition's Congressional Scorecard. (Zimmer scored a 79 out of a possible 100. Pennsylvania's Jon Fox received a perfect 100 rating, and New Mexico's Steven Schiff an 86. By comparison, fifteen of the twenty-five Jewish members of the House in the One Hundred and Fourth Congress received 0 ratings.)

While a member of the New Jersey state legislature, Dick Zimmer voted in favor of a moment of silence in public schools. Although he says he was "troubled by the prospect of prayers being written or mandated by a government agency or by a teacher," he continued to vote in favor of some form of prayer. "I have participated in public menorah lightings in malls and at the New Jersey state house," he said. "But I just don't know where to come down on this."

On Israel, Zimmer was a lead co-sponsor of the bill introduced by Speaker Newt Gingrich to relocate the American embassy in Israel to Jerusalem. The bill passed, with the proviso that if security warranted, the move could be delayed indefinitely at the discretion of the President. Zimmer supported the housing-loan guarantees for Israel, and consistently supported legislation for dismantling the Arab boycott. On the other hand, as a fiscal conservative, Zimmer voted to cut aid to Israel by 25 percent, in the name of fiscal integrity.

Dick Zimmer was reelected twice with little trouble. The New Jersey State Legislature changed his district boundaries after the 1990 census, making the Twelfth even more Republican in its makeup. In 1995, Zimmer announced that he would run for the Republican nomination for the United States Senate seat being vacated by Bill Bradley. Almost assured of the Republican nomination, Zimmer spent the last half of 1995 and all of 1996 trading political barbs and accusations with Democrat Robert Torricelli, the Democratic candidate. Zimmer accused Torricelli of being a tax-and-spend liberal, while Torricelli hammered away at Zimmer for being in lockstep with Jesse Helms. Zimmer was given a tremendous boost by his New York colleague Alfonse D'Amato, who pumped nearly $3 milion into his campaign and installed his own pollster and consultants to run the campaign. Despite D'Amato's largesse, Zimmer wound up losing the Senate race to Torricelli 53 percent to 43 percent. Dick Zimmer has continued to be a visible presence in New Jersey public affairs. Soon after his defeat he formed a group called Citizens for a Better New Jersey, which takes positions on taxes, crime, and other key issues. He also frequently makes the "short list" of putative candidates for state-wide and local political races.

Of his being a Jew in politics, Zimmer says: "I think the Jewish tradition has given me a kind of inner gyroscope so when we have to look inside ourselves to decide what the right thing is to do, it's the tradition I draw on . . . principally the prophets, who were concerned with the here and now."

References

Interview with Dick Zimmer, February 1992.
Almanac of American Politics, 1992–1998.
Forward, September 1, 1995, p. 4.
Politics in America.
Trenton Courier News, February 18, 1991, A-6.
Trenton Times, September 23, 1991.
Washington Post, June 5, 1991.

ZORINSKY, EDWARD (1928–1987): *Democrat from Nebraska; served two terms in the Senate (December 28, 1976–March 6, 1987).*

On the night he suffered a fatal heart attack, Nebraska Senator Ed Zorinsky was performing a song-and-dance routine at the Omaha Press Club's annual Gridiron Show. True to form, Zorinsky, a Republican-turned-Democrat now threatening to return to the GOP fold, was singing a self-deprecating ditty—a rewrite of the Platters' 1955 hit "The Great Pretender":

> Oh, I am the great pretender,
> Pretending to be two in one.
> Thus the party I choose,
> Can never lose,
> And I'll be its favorite son.
> Can't you see I'm a great pretender,
> And hanging parties my key.
> I'm a G.O.P. cat dressed as a Democrat.
> My party's the majority.

Zorinsky's last hurrah made an ironic epitaph for a man who once claimed: "I'm not very good at blowing my own horn." Truth to tell, Ed Zorinsky was, from first to last, "a man of consummate skill both at asserting his modesty and at claiming credit for it." Ed Zorinsky was only fifty-eight when he died.

Edward Zorinsky, the son of a Russian immigrant, was born on November 11, 1928 in Omaha, Nebraska, where his parents ran a wholesale tobacco and candy business. Zorinsky attended the public schools of Omaha. In 1945, he went off to the University of Minnesota. Following his freshman year, he transferred to Creighton University in Lincoln, and wound up receiving a B.S. in chemistry and zoology from the University of Nebraska in 1949. Shortly after graduation, Ed Zorinsky married Cece Rottman, with whom he had three children: Barry, Jeffrey, and Susan. Zorinsky spent nearly a quarter century (1950–73) working in his family's candy and tobacco business. He got his first taste of politics in 1968, when he was appointed to the Omaha Public Power District.

Situated on the Missouri River, Omaha is a city with a nineteenth-century economic base: livestock. Omaha was the site Abraham Lincoln selected as the eastern end of the transcontinental railroad. By the 1880s, it had become "the home of the stockyards and livestock exchange that made it the nation's third largest livestock town." Its population swelled as cattle hands from the West joined Europeans, largely German and Czech, to create a major Midwestern city. Omaha, in the words of the *Almanac of American Politics*, is "a small enough city . . . to be readily comprehensible; you don't feel distant, physically or psychologically, from neighborhoods on the other side of town, and you usually know people from a broader range of backgrounds than you would in a large homogeneous neighborhood within a big metropolitan area . . . . It is the kind of America many Americans want." In 1973, Ed Zorinsky, a Republican at the time, was elected mayor—the first Jew to occupy the office.

Zorinsky spent four years as a very popular mayor. He earned high marks for bringing a businessman's sensibility to City Hall, and for his rapid response to a series of devastating tornadoes and blizzards that struck Omaha in 1975. Sensing that his political capital was at an all-time high, Zorinsky set his sights on the Senate seat held by Republican Roman Hruska. Despite the fact that Hruska was a major player in the Senate for more than twenty years (1954– 76), he will always be remembered for giving voice to one of American political history's most hilarious (some would say ingenuous) comments. During the summer of 1969, the Senate took up the nomination of Judge Harold Carswell to the Supreme Court. Carswell's nomination came on the heels of President Nixon's failed attempt to name Judge Clement Haynsworth to the same position. A review of Carswell's career showed that the man was not, by any stretch of the imagination, a judicial giant. As his nomination began heading into a tailspin, Senator Hruska rushed to his defense. At one press conference, a reporter asked the Nebraska Senator if he didn't find Carswell to be "just a bit mediocre." "Let me tell you something," Hruska responded. "America is filled with mediocre people. Don't they deserve representation on the Supreme Court as well?"

In addition to his notorious gaffe, Hruska had two additional factors weighing in against him in considering a 1975 race: his age (seventy), and his poor showing in 1970—he won by a slim 53 percent to 47 percent margin over a weak Democratic candidate. Seeing the handwriting on the wall, Hruska announced that he would not seek reelection. With his proven vote-getting ability and wide-based popularity in Nebraska's largest city, Ed Zorinsky assumed that he would be offered the Republican nomination. Zorinsky assumed wrong: the party offered the nomination to Omaha Congressman John McCollister.

Although it cannot be proven, it is likely that Zorinsky's religion worked against him; no Jew had ever won statewide election in Nebraska. Whatever the case, Zorinsky saw red, and immediately left the Republican fold. The move was not terribly problematic; "Zorinsky had never been strongly identified with either party." Running in the Democratic primary against state party chair Hess Dyas, Ed Zorinsky scored an upset victory. At first, Dyas and many of his liberal supporters were angry about the victory of "this outsider." By the time fall rolled around, political tempers had cooled, and Dyas was publicly proclaiming that "although Zorinsky [is] an S.O.B., he is our S.O.B." The Republicans were caught off guard; they had been gearing up for a race against a liberal, not a conservative. McCollister's attempts to paint Ed Zorinsky as a dangerous liberal fell on deaf ears. In November, Zorinsky defeated McCollister by more than 35,000 votes, despite being outspent by a nearly two-to-one margin.

As a member of the Senate from 1976 until his death in 1987, Ed Zorinsky proved to be an "incorrigible maverick . . . cranky, conservative to the point of parsimony and as adept at seeking compromise in the partisan desert as a water dowser." Filling for a Senator from Nebraska, Zorinsky was assigned to the Agriculture Committee, where he "repaid his constituents' faith by making farm belt issues his top priority." In 1979, Zorinsky was also seated on the Senate Foreign Relations Committee, "where his maverick tendencies made him a swing vote." His decision to join Foreign Relations struck many of his colleagues as odd: just a year earlier he had turned down a trip to Communist China with a wisecrack: "Offhand, I can't think of one person in Mainland China who voted for me in the last election."

Zorinsky's frustration threshold was so low that within six weeks of his arrival on Capitol Hill, he was giving serious consideration to quitting. He changed his mind and then announced more than a year in advance that he wanted a second term.

During his first four years in the Senate,

Zorinsky voted with the Republicans more often than any other Democrat with the exception of the venerable Harry F. Byrd, Jr., of Virginia.

With the election of Ronald Reagan in 1980, the Republicans took over the Senate. The new Majority Leader, Howard Baker of Tennessee, phoned Zorinsky the morning after the election, wanting to know if the Nebraskan might be interested in "reconverting" to the GOP. From all indications, Zorinsky gave serious consideration to Baker's offer. It came to naught when Nebraska Republicans informed Senator Baker that they didn't want Zorinsky back. "I'm not accustomed to going to parties I'm not invited to," Zorinsky quipped.

Prior to the Democrats' loss of the upper chamber, Zorinsky chaired the Foreign Relations Subcommittee on the Western Hemisphere. From that post, somewhat improbably for a conservative, Zorinsky argued strenuously against cutting off aid to Nicaragua's Sandinista government. In staking himself to his rather unpredictable position, Zorinsky argued that "U.S. financial aid would shore up Nicaragua's economy, encouraging the left-wing Sandinista government to hold free elections. An aid cut-off . . . would force the Sandinistas into the arms of the communists."

Zorinsky's fellow conservatives disputed his reasoning, claiming that the Sandinista rebels were already Communists. When Ronald Reagan moved into the White House and "concluded [that] the Sandinistas were allowing arms to reach leftist guerillas in neighboring El Salvador," Zorinsky flip-flopped and agreed that aid should be suspended.

Throughout his Senate career, Ed Zorinsky was well known for his parsimony: he mailed out no newsletters, refused to hire the maximum staff allowed (or pay them the maximum salary), and annually turned back thousands of dollars in expense money to the government. A firm believer in "government in the sunshine," he removed his office doors and refused to use an automatic signature machine.

In 1982, Ed Zorinsky easily defeated Republican Jim Keck, a public relations executive and retired U.S. Air Force general making his first bid for public office. Zorinsky's victory made him the first Nebraska Democrat to win a second Senate term since Gilbert M. Hitchcock in 1916. When Kentucky Senator Dee Huddleston was defeated for reelection in 1984, Ed Zorinsky became the ranking Democratic member of the Agriculture Committee. From that post, he argued for higher price supports for wheat, and helped pass legislation setting up a commission to study agricultural trade policies. At the time of his death, Senate Minority Leader Robert Dole said: "Rural America never had a better friend."

For years, Zorinsky campaigned against Radio Marti, the U.S.-sponsored station that beamed news into Cuba. Zorinsky had no problem with Radio Marti's mission; rather, he opposed the technological means by which the mission was accomplished. Zorinsky argued that the Castro government would undoubtedly use powerful transmitters to jam the broadcasts, thereby causing interference with domestic American stations—particularly those listened to by farmers in the Midwest. Every time the Radio Marti proposal came to the floor of the Senate, Zorinsky would lead a filibuster against it. In 1983, Zorinsky worked out a suitable compromise: Radio Marti would be placed under the aegis of the Voice of America, which was legally bound to "adhere to journalistic standards of objectivity." In this way, he reasoned, Castro would be far less likely to jam Marti broadcasts.

At his death, Ed Zorinsky was still widely popular with the people of Nebraska. His cranky, independent brand of politics earned him a hallowed place in the hearts of his colleagues. A man with a thick skin, he never seemed to suffer from all the criticism he took over his party switching. He once joked that "when Republicans called [me] turncoat and Democrats called [me] opportunist, I told them they both were right."

Edward Zorinsky is buried in Beth El Cemetery in Omaha. Nebraska Governor Kay Orr appointed Omaha businessman David Karnes to fill the remainder of his term. Former Nebraska Governor Robert Kerrey defeated Karnes in 1988. In his memory, the federal government renamed the Omaha governmental center the Edward Zorinsky Federal Building. One of the city's newest and most lavish construction projects, it includes a man made body of water called Zorinsky Lake.

References
Almanac of American Politics, 1974–88.
New York Times, March 8, 1987.
Politics in America, 1976–1988.

Appendix I

No. of Members	State
67	New York
17	California
15	Pennsylvania
6	Florida
6	Illinois
6	Maryland
6	New Jersey
5	Connecticut
5	Louisiana
4	Michigan
4	Ohio
3	Arizona
3	Oregon
3	Wisconsin
2	Alabama
2	Colorado
2	Georgia
2	Massachusetts
2	Minnesota
2	Missouri
2	Nevada
2	Texas
1	Alaska
1	Indiana
1	Iowa
1	Kansas
1	Maine
1	Nebraska
1	New Hampshire
1	New Mexico
1	Oklahoma
1	Vermont
1	Virginia
1	Washington
1	West Virginia

Total: 179 members of Congress elected from 35 states.

Appendix II

State Rosters: House and Senate

Alabama: (2)
1. Erdreich, Benjamin (Democrat—House)
2. Phillips, Phillip (Democrat—House)

Alaska: (1)
1. Gruening, Ernest (Democrat—Senate)

Arizona: (3)
1. Coppersmith, Sam (Democrat—House)
2. Goldwater, Barry (Republican—Senate)
3. Steiger, Sam (Republican—House)

California: (17)
1. Beilenson, Anthony (Democrat—House)
2. Berman, Howard (Democrat—House)
3. Boxer, Barbara (Democrat—-House and Senate)
4. Burton, Sala (Democrat—House)
5. Feinstein, Diane (Democrat—Senate)
6. Fiedler, Bobbi (Republican—House)
7. Filner, Bob (Democrat—House)
8. Hamburg, Dan (Democrat—House)
9. Harman, Jane (Democrat—House)
10. Kahn, Florence (Republican—House)
11. Kahn, Julius (Republican—House)
12. Krebs, John (Democrat—House)
13. Lantos, Tom (Democrat—House)
14. Levine, Mel (Democrat—House)
15. Schenk Lynn (Democrat—House)
16. Sherman, Brad (Democrat—House)
17. Waxman, Henry (Democrat—House)

Colorado: (2)
1. Guggenheim, Simon (Republican—Senate)
2. Kramer, Kenneth (Republican—House)

Connecticut: (5)
1. Citron, William (Democrat—House)
2. Gejdenson, Samuel (Democrat—House)
3. Koppelman, Herman (Democrat—House)
4. Lieberman, Joseph (Democrat—Senate)
5. Ribicoff, Abraham (Democrat—House and Senate)

Florida: (6)
1. Deutsch, Peter (Democrat—House)
2. Lehman, William (Democrat—House)
3. Smith, Lawrence (Democrat—House)
4. Stone, Richard (Democrat—Senate)
5. Wexler, Robert (Democrat—House)
6. Yulee, David Levy (Whig, Democrat—Senate)

Georgia: (2)
1. Cohen, John Sanford (Democrat—Senate)
2. Levitas, Elliott (Democrat—House)

Illinois: **(6)**
1. Emerich, Martin (Democrat—House)
2. Goldzier, Julius (Democrat—House)
3. Mikva, Abner (Democrat—House)
4. Sabath, Adolph (Democrat—House)
5. Schakowsky, Jan (Democrat—House)
6. Yates, Sidney (Democrat—House)

Indiana: (1)
1. Kraus, Milton (Republican—House)

Iowa: (1)
1. Mezvinsky, Edward (Democrat—House)

Kansas: (1)
1. Glickman, Daniel (Democrat—House)

Louisiana: (5)
1. Benjamin, Judah P. (Whig, Democrat—Senate)
2. Hahn, Michael (Republican—House)
3. Jonas, Benjamin (Democrat—Senate)
4. Levy, William Mallory (Democrat—House)
5. Meyer, Adolph (Democrat—House)

Maine: (1)
1. Cohen, William (Republican—House and Senate)

Maryland: (6)
1. Cardin, Benjamin (Democrat—House)
2. Ellison, Daniel (Republican—House)
3. Friedel, Samuel (Democrat—House)
4. Raynor, Isidore (Democrat—-House and Senate)
5. Spellman, Gladys (Democrat—House)
6. Wolf, Harry (Democrat—House)

Massachusetts: (2)
1. Frank, Barney (Democrat—House)
2. Morse, Leopold (Democrat—House)

Michigan: (4)
1. Houseman, Julius (Democrat—House)
2. Levin, Carl (Democrat—Senate)
3. Levin, Sander (Democrat—House)
4. Wolpe, Howard (Democrat—House)

Minnesota: (2)
1. Boschwitz, Rudy (Republican—Senate)
2. Wellstone, Paul (Democrat—Senate)

Missouri: (2)
1. Frank, Nathan (Republican—House)
2. Irving, Theodore (Democrat—House)

Nebraska: (1)
1. Zorinsky, Edward (Democrat—Senate)

Nevada: (2)
1. Berkley, Shelly (Democrat—House)
2. Hecht, Jacob "Chic" (Republican—Senate)

New Hampshire: (1)
1. Rudman, Warren (Republican—Senate)

New Jersey: (6)
1. Bacharach, Isaac (Republican—House)
2. Joelson, Charles (Democrat—House)
3. Lautenberg, Frank (Democrat—Senate)
4. Klein, Herb (Democrat—House)
5. Rothman, Steve (Democrat—House)
6. Zimmerman, Richard (Republican—House)

New Mexico: (1)
1. Schiff, Steven (Republican—House)

New York: (67)
1. Abzug, Bela (Democrat—House)
2. Ackerman, Gary (Democrat—House)
3. Ansorge, Martin (Republican—House)
4. Bloom, Sol (Democrat—House)
5. Cantor, Jacob (Democrat—House)
6. Celler, Emanuel (Democrat—House)
7. Cohen, William (Democrat—House)
8. Davidson, Irwin (Democrat—House)
9. Dickstein, Samuel (Democrat—House)
10. Dollinger, Isidore (Democrat—House)
11. Edelstein, Morris (Democrat—House)
12. Einstein, Edwin (Republican—House)
13. Engel, Eliot (Democrat—House)
14. Farbstein, Leonard (Democrat—House)
15. Fine, Sidney (Democrat—House)
16. Fischer, Israel (Republican—House)
17. Gilbert, Jacob (Democrat—House)
18. Gilman, Benjamin (Republican—House)
19. Goldfogle, Benjamin (Republican—House)
20. Green, Bill (Republican—House)
21. Halpern, Seymour (Republican—House)
22. Hart, Emanuel (Democrat—House)
23. Heller, Louis (Democrat—House)
24. Holtzman, Elizabeth (Democrat—House)
25. Holtzman, Lester (Democrat—House)
26. Isacson, Leo (American Labor—House)
27. Jacobstein, Meyer (Democrat—House)
28. Javits, Jacob (Republican—House and Senate)
29. Klein, Arthur (Democrat—House)
30. Koch, Edward (Democrat—House)
31. LaGuardia, Fiorello (Republican—House)
32. Lehman, Herbert (Democrat—Senate)
33. Lessler, Montague (Republican—House)
34. Levy, David (Republican—House)
35. Levy, Jefferson (Democrat—House)
36. Littauer, Lucius (Republican—House)
37. London, Meyer (Socialist—-House)
38. Lowenstein, Allard (Democrat—House)
39. Lowey, Nita (Democrat—House)
40. Marx, Sam (Democrat—House)

41. May, Mitchell (Democrat—House)
42. Multer, Abraham (Democrat—House)
43. Nadler, Jerrold (Democrat—House)
44. Ottinger, Richard (Democrat—House)
45. Perlman, Nathan (Democrat—House)
46. Peyser, Theodore (Democrat—House)
47. Podell, Bertram (Democrat—House)
48. Pulitzer, Joseph (Democrat—House)
49. Rabin, Benjamin (Democrat—House)
50. Rayfiel, Leo (Democrat—House)
51. Resnick, Joseph (Democrat—House)
52. Richmond, Frederick (Democrat—House)
53. Rosenthal, Benjamin (Democrat—House)
54. Rossdale, Albert (Republican—House)
55. Scheuer, James (Democrat—House)
56. Schumer, Charles (Democrat—House and Senate)
57. Siegal, Isaac (Republican—House)
58. Sirovich, William (Democrat—House)
59. Solarz, Stephen (Democrat—House)
60. Straus, Isidor (Democrat—House)
61. Teller, Ludwig (Democrat—House)
62. Tenzer, Herbert (Democrat—House)
63. Volk, Lester (Republican—House)
64. Weiner, Anthony (Democrat—House)
65. Weiss, Theodore (Democrat—House)
66. Wolff, Lester (Democrat—House)
67. Zelenko, Herbert (Democrat—House)
Ohio: (4)
1. Fingerhut, Eric (Democrat—House)
2. Gradison, Willis (Bill) (Republican—House)
2. Metzenbaum, Howard (Democrat—Senate)
4. Shamansky, Robert (Democrat—House)
Oklahoma: (1)
1. Edwards, Mickey (Republican—House)
Oregon: (3)
1. Neuberger, Richard (Democrat—Senate)
2. Simon, Joseph (Republican—Senate)
3. Weyden, Ron (Democrat—House and Senate)
Pennsylvania: (15)
1. Chudoff, Earl (Democrat—House)
2. Eilberg, Joshua (Democrat—House)
3. Ellenbogen, Harry (Democrat—House)
4. Golder, Benjamin (Republican—House)
5. Fox, Jon D. (Republican—House)
6. Levin, Lewis Charles (American Party—House)
7. Margolies-Mezvinsky, Marjory (Democrat—House)
8. Marks, Marc (Republican—House)
9. Phillips, Henry (Democrat—House)

10. Sacks, Leon (Democrat—House)
11. Spector, Arlen (Republican—Senate)
12. Strouse, Meyer
13. Toll, Herman (Democrat—House)
14. Wanger, Irving (Republican—House)
15. Weiss, Samuel (Democrat—House)
Texas: (2)
1. Frost, Martin (Democrat—House)
2. Kaufman, David (Democrat—House)
Vermont: (1)
1. Sanders, Bernard (Independant—House)
Virginia: (1)
1. Sisisky, Norman (Democrat—House)
Washington: (1)
1. Miller, John (Republican—House)
West Virginia: (1)
1. Rosenbloom, Benjamin (Republican—House)
Wisconsin: (3)
1. Berger, Victor (Socialist—House)
2. Feingold, Russell (Democrat—Senate)
3. Kohl Herbert (Democrat—Senate)

Totals :

House	Senate
111 Democrats (74%)	20 Democrats (67%)
34 Republicans (22%)	10 Republicans (33%)
3 Socialists (2%)	
1 Whig (0.6%)	
1 American Labor (0.6%)	
1 American Party (0.6%)	
151 Representatives;	30 Senators

Grand total
179 (165 men, 14 women) elected from 35 states.

Notes
1. Five Democrats (Boxer, Raynor, Ribicoff, Wyden, and Schumer) were members of both the House and Senate.
2. Yulee, a Whig while in the House, was elected to the Senate as a Democrat.
3. Two Republicans (Javits and Cohen) were elected to both the House and Senate.
4. Two Democrats (Yulee and Benjamin) were originally Whigs.
5. One Democrat (Marx) died before he could begin his term in office.

Appendix III

States Electing Senators

State	Number	Name	Party
Alaska	1	Gruening	Democrat
Arizona	1	Goldwater	Republican
California	2	Boxer,	Democrat
		Feinstein	Democrat
Connecticut	2	Liberman	Democrat
		Ribicoff	Democrat
Florida	2	Levy-Yulee	Whig/Democrat
		Stone	Democrat
Georgia	1	Cohen	Democrat
Louisiana	2	Benjamin	Whig/Democrat
		Jonas	Democrat
Maine	1	Cohen	Republican
Maryland	1	Raynor	Democrat
Michigan	1	Levin	Democrat
Minnesota	2	Boshewitz	Republican
		Wellstone	Democrat
Nebraska	1	Zorinsky	Democrat
Nevada	1	Hecht	Republican
New Hampshire	1	Rudman	Republican
New Jersey	1	Lautenberg	Democrat
New York	3	Javits	Republican
		Lehman	Democrat
		Schumer	Democrat
Ohio	1	Metzenbaum	Democrat
Oregon	3	Simon	Republican
		Neuberger	Democrat
		Wyden	Democrat
Pennsylvania	1	Spector	Republican
Wisconsin	2	Kohl	Democrat
		Feingold	Democrat
Totals: 20 states	30	20 Democrats	10 Republicans

Appendix IV

Jews Per Congressional Session

Session	Years	House	Senate	Total	Total States
27	1841–'43	1	0	1	1
28	'43–'45	1	0	1	1
29	'45–'47	1	1	2	2
30	'47–'49	1	1	2	2
31	'49–'51	1	1	2	2
32	'51–'53	1	0	1	1
33	'53–'55	1	1	2	2
34	'55–'57	0	2	2	2
35	'57–'59	1	2	3	3
36	'59–'61	0	2	2	2
37	'61–'63	1	1	2	1
38	'63–'65	0	0	0	0
39	'65–'67	1	0	1	1
40	'67–'69	0	0	0	0
41	'69–'71	0	0	0	0
42	'71–'73	0	0	0	0
43	'73–'75	0	0	0	0
44	'75–'77	1	0	1	1
45	'77–'79	1	0	1	1
46	'79–'81	2	1	3	3
47	'81–'83	1	1	2	2
48	'83–'85	2	1	3	3
49	'85–'87	2	0	2	2
50	'87–'89	2	0	2	2
51	'89–'91	0	0	0	0
52	'91–'93	2	0	2	2
53	'93–'95	4	0	4	4
54	'95–'97	3	0	3	3
55	'97–'99	4	1	5	4
56	1899–1901	6	1	7	5
57	1901–1903	5	1	6	4
58	'03–'05	5	0	5	4
59	'05–'07	5	1	6	5
60	'07–'09	5	2	7	6
61	'09–'11	4	2	6	6
62	'11–'13	5	2	7	6
63	'13–'15	5	0	5	3
64	'15–'17	5	0	5	4
65	'17–'19	6	0	6	5
66	'19–'21	9	0	9	5
67	'21–'23	11	0	11	6
68	'23–'25	10	0	10	5
69	'25–'27	10	0	10	5
70	'27–'29	12	0	12	6
71	'29–'31	8	0	8	5
72	'31–'33	8	1	9	5

Jews Per Congressional Session

Session	Years	House	Senate	Total	Total States
73	'33–'35	10	0	10	6
74	'35–'37	11	0	11	6
75	'37–'39	10	0	10	4
76	'39–'41	7	0	7	3
77	'41–'43	9	0	9	4
78	'43–'45	7	0	7	4
79	'45–'47	9	0	9	4
80	'47–'49	9	0	9	2
81	'49–'51	11	1	12	5
82	'51–'53	13	0	13	5
83	'53–'55	11	1	12	4
84	'55–'57	11	2	13	5
85	'57–'59	10	2	12	5
86	'59–'61	13	3	16	6
87	'61–'63	12	2	14	6
88	'63–'65	9	3	12	6
89	'65–'67	16	3	19	7
90	'67–'69	17	3	20	8
91	'69–'71	17	2	19	7
92	'71–'73	12	2	14	5
93	'73–'75	14	4	18	8
94	'75–'77	21	4	25	10
95	'77–'79	23	5	28	11
96	'79–'81	23	8	31	15
97	'81–'83	27	6	33	18
98	'83–'85	32	8	40	21
99	'85–'87	32	6	38	21
100	'87–'89	29	8	37	21
101	'89–'91	30	8	38	22
102	'91–'93	34	8	42	23
103	'93–'95	29	10	39	20
104	'95–'97	24	9	33	19
105	'97–'99	24	10	34	16
106	1999–2001	23	11	34	17

Appendix V
Research Collections of Former Members of the House of Representatives

Abzug, Bella Savitsky (1920–1998)
Democrat–New York
Columbia University
Rare Book and Manuscript Library
New York, N.Y.
    Papers: 1970–1976. ca. 500,000 items.
    Congressional and legislative files.
Unpublished. Finding aid in repository.

Ansorge, Martin Charles (1882–1967)
Republican–New York
Columbia University
Oral History Project
New York, N.Y.
    Oral History: 1949. 74 pages, transcribed

Berger, Victor Luitpold (1860–1929)
Socialist–Wisconsin
Milwaukee County Historical Society
Milwaukee, Wis.
    Papers: In Socialist Party Collection.
    A large part of the collection is Berger's correspondence and his expulsion from Congress. Includes speeches, clippings, campaign literature, and public documents.

Bloom, Sol (1870–1949)
Democrat–New York
National Archives and Records Administration
Washington, Democrat.
    Papers: Correspondence and memoranda in the records of the U.S. Constitutional Sesquicentennial Commission
    (Record Group 148)
New York Public Library
New York, N.Y.
    Papers: 1920s–1949. 58 feet.
    Constituent correspondence and miscellaneous papers.
Yeshiva University Archives
New York, N.Y. Papers: 1 folder (1943–1946) in the Vaad Hatzala
    Collection, 1939–1963. 27 feet.
    Official correspondence regarding immigration and relief for Jewish refugees. Finding aid in repository.
  Use of documents in poor condition is restricted.

Celler, Emanuel (1888–1981)
Democrat–New York
John F. Kennedy Library
Boston, Mass.
    Oral History: 4 pages.
Library of Congress
Manuscript Division
Washington, D.C.
    Papers: 1924–1972. 524 containers.
    Register. Restricted.
Lyndon B. Johnson Library
Austin, Tex.
    Oral History: March 19, 1969. 18 pages.
Yeshiva University Archives
New York, N.Y.
    Papers: 1 folder (1945) in the Vaad Hatzala Collection, 1939–1963. 27 feet.
    Official correspondence regarding immigration and relief for Jewish refugees. Finding aid in repository. Use of documents in poor condition is restricted.

Dickstein, Samuel (1885–1954)
Democrat–New York
American Jewish Archives
Cincinnati, Ohio
    Papers: In Dickstein Committee records, 1934–1939. 16 feet.
    Correspondence, reports, speeches, certificates, andprinted matter dealing with committees investigation of Nazi propaganda activities.
Columbia University
Oral History Project New York, N.Y.
    Oral History: 1950. 74 pages.
Columbia University
Rare Book and Manuscript Library
New York, N.Y.
    Papers: 9 letters (1928–1933) in Lillian D. Wald Collection.
    Official correspondence. Finding aid in repository.

Edwards, Marvin Henry (Mickey)
University of Oklahoma, Carl Albert Center of Congressional Archives, Norman.
http://www.ou.edu/special/albertctr/
    Papers: 1971–1992. 209 cubic feet.

Congressional papers and correspondence, including photographs and videotape. Includes press releases, printed material, clippings, speeches, and other documents. Finding aid in repository. Restricted.

Einstein, Edwin (1842–1905)
Republican–New York
New York Historical Society
New York, N.Y.
    Papers: 1 letter (July 28, 1899) and autograph album (1879–1881).
    Finding aid in repository.
    Papers: Unknown quantity of personal correspondence in Hendricks family collection.

Hahn, Michael (1830–1886)
Louisiana
Library of Congress
Manuscript Division
Washington, D.C.
Papers: 1864. 1 certificate.

Javits, Jacob Koppel (1904–1986)
Republican–New York
Columbia University
Oral History Project
New York, N.Y.
    Oral History: Ongoing project in progress.
    Oral History: Interview in Social Security Project 12 pages.
    Oral History: Discussed in interview with Frank Thompson, Jr.
Columbia University
Rare Book and Manuscript Library
New York, N.Y.
    Papers: 3 official letters (1971–1975) in Citizens Committee for Protection of Environment.
    Finding aid in repository.
Dwight E. Eisenhower Library
Abilene, Kan.
    Oral History: In Civil Rights Documentation Project.
    Transcribed.
John F. Kennedy Library
Boston, Mass.
    Oral History: 18 pages.
    Concerning John F. Kennedy. Restricted.
    Oral History: 26 pages.
    Concerning Robert F. Kennedy. Restricted.
Princeton University

Dulles Oral History Project
Princeton, N.J.
    Oral History: 1966. 17 pages.
    Restricted.
State University of New York at Stony Brook
Stony Brook, N.Y.
    Papers: 2,000 cubic feet.
    Closed pending processing.
Western Reserve Historical Society
Cleveland, Ohio Papers: In Cyrus Eaton Papers, 1901–1978. ca. 422 feet.
    Finding aid in repository.

Kahn, Florence Prag (1868–1948)
Republican–California
Western States History Center
Judah L. Magnes Memorial Museum
Berkeley, Calif.
    Papers: In Julius and Florence (Prag) Kahn papers, 1866–1948. ca. 2 feet.
Unpublished inventory in repository.

Kahn, Julius (1861–1924)
Republican–California
Western States History Center
Judah L. Magnes Memorial Museum
Berkeley, Calif.
Papers: In Julius and Florence (Prag) Kahn papers, 1866–1948. ca. 2 feet.
Unpublished inventory in repository.

Kaufman, David Spangler (1813–1851)
Texas
University of Texas at Austin
Eugene C. Barker Texas History Center
Austin, Tex.
Papers: 1848–1852. 3 inches.
Business and congressional papers and correspondence.
Finding aid in repository.

Koch, Edward Irving (1924–)
Democrat–New York
City of New York Department of Records and Information Services
Municipal Archives
New York, N.Y.
    Papers: 1969–1977. 157 cubic feet.
    Congressional papers and correspondence, including legislative, subject, and case work files; materials relating to New York City, campaigns, committee work, and 1974 Judiciary

Committee impeachment inquiry; press releases appointment books; and photographs.
Unprocessed.
Columbia University
Rare Book and Manuscript Library
New York, N.Y.
Papers: 2 letters (February 21 and March 24, 1969) in Howard J. Samuels Papers.
Political correspondence. Finding aid in repository.

Kramer, Kenneth Bentley (1942–)
Republican–Colorado
Colorado Historical Society
Denver, Col.
Papers: 1978–1986. 2 cubic feet.
Photographs and television news film.
Finding aid in repository.
Pioneers Museum
Colorado Springs, Col.
Papers: Quantity unknown. Collection being processed.

LaGuardia, Fiorello Henry (1882–1947)
Republican, Fusion–New York Brooklyn
Historical Society
Brooklyn, N.Y.
Papers: 4 letters (August 30, 1938; January 18, 1943; May 6, 1947; and June 30, 1947) and 1 political appointment. (September 15, 1942)
Finding aid in repository.
City of New York Department of Records and Information Services
Municipal Archives
New York, N.Y.
Papers: Mayoral papers and correspondence, including photographs and sound recording.
Columbia University
Oral History Project New York, N.Y.
Oral History: Mrs. Fiorello LaGuardia. 1950. 56 pages.
LaGuardia Community College
Fiorello H. LaGuardia Archives
Long Island City, N.Y.
Papers: 1882–1947. 35 feet.
Includes transcripts of speeches and radio broadcasts, files of his work as Director-General of UNRRA, over 4,000 photographs, personal papers, original sketches, artifacts, and scrapbooks. Unpublished finding aid in repository.
Oral History: Over 50 pages, some transcribed, from friends and associates.
Some Restricted.

New York Historical Society
New York, N.Y.
Papers: 8 letters (1933–1943) and miscellaneous campaign notes (1933).
Finding aid in repository.
New York Public Library
New York, N.Y.
Papers: 1918–1945. 2 volumes and 17 boxes.
Congressional correspondence, subject file, letters of appreciation received while mayor, scrapbooks, and printed matter. Listing of subject file in library.

Levin, Lewis Charles (1808–1860)
American Party–Pennsylvania
Huntington Library
San Marino, Calif.
Papers: 1849–1850. 89 items.
Relate chiefly to political patronage. Catalog cards in library.
New York Historical Society.
New York, N.Y.
Papers: March 31, 1849. 1 official letter.
Finding aid in repository.

Levitas, Elliott Harris (1930–)
Democrat–Georgia
Emory University
Special Collections Department
Robert A. Woodruff Library
Atlanta, Ga.
Papers: 1974–1988. ca. 325 feet.
Personal and congressional papers and correspondence, including district files, photographs, portraits, motion picture film, video tape, sound recordings, and memorabilia.
Restricted.

Levy, Jefferson Monroe (1852–1924)
Democrat–New York
American Jewish Historical Society
Waltham, Mass.
Papers: 1901–1939, 560 items.
Correspondence, certificates, clippings, and photographs relating to personal matters and his activities as a Congressman. Most papers relate to his purchase of Monticello.

Littauer, Lucius Nathan (1859–1944)
Republican–New York
Lucius N. Littauer Foundation
New York, N.Y.

Papers: 3 scrapbooks of newspaper clippings and some letters, photographs, and memorabilia.

London, Meyer (1871–1926)
Socialist–New York
New York University
Tammiment Library
New York, N.Y.
    Papers: 1910–1959. 4 boxes.
    Correspondence, speeches, handbills, press clippings, scrapbooks, and photographs, chiefly relating to his political career.
Lowenstein, Allard Kenneth (1929–1980)
Democrat–New York
University of North Carolina
Southern Historical Collection
Chapel Hill, N.C.
    Papers: 1924–1985. 206 feet.
    Correspondence, organizational records, political campaign records, congressional files, writings, speeches and speech notes, press clipping file, research materials, scheduling files, financial and administrative records, diaries (1940s–1967), scrapbooks, family papers, photographs, sound recordings, and videocassette tapes.
    Printed guide available. Partially restricted.
    Oral History: A series of interviews, 1952–1980.
    Transcribed and on tape.

Mikva, Abner Joseph (1926–)
Democrat–Illinois
Illinois State Historical Society
Springfield, Ill.
    Papers: 1959–1979. 660 cubic feet.
    Personal and congressional papers and correspondence, photographs, sound recordings, and memorabilia; also papers as state legislator.
    Finding aid in repository. Restricted.

Multer, Abraham Jacob (1900–1986)
Democrat–New York
American Jewish Historical Society
Waltham, Mass.
    Papers: 1954-1966. 58 feet.
    Personal papers, printed matter, and papers relating to his congressional career.
Brooklyn College
City University of New York
Brooklyn, N.Y.

Papers: 17 boxes and slip cases.
    Congressional papers and correspondence.
Unprocessed.
    Restricted.

Ottinger, Richard Lawrence (1929–)
Democrat–New York
Columbia University
Rare Book and Manuscript Library
New York, N.Y.
    Papers: 5 official letters (1966–1970) in Citizens Committee for Protection of Environment Collection.
    Finding aid in repository.
Perlman, Nathan David (1887–1952)
Republican-New York
American Jewish Historical Society
Waltham, Mass.
    Papers: 1915–1952. 3 feet.
    Correspondence, judicial opinions, speeches, newspaper clippings, and printed material relating to his legal and political careers and his activities in Jewish community.

Phillips, Phillip (1807–1884)
Democrat–Alabama
Library of Congress
Manuscript Division
Washington, D.C.
    Papers: In Phillip Phillips family papers, 1832–1914.
    22 containers. Correspondence, papers relating to his law practice, and family papers.
Register.
University of North Carolina
Southern Historical Collection
Chapel Hill, N.C.
    Papers: In Phillips and Myers family papers, 1804–1928.
    1,400 items including 13 volumes.
    Unpublished description in library.

Raynor, Isidore (1850–1912)
Democrat–Maryland
Maryland Historical Society
Baltimore, Md.
    Papers: 1890s–1905. In Gorman papers (MS 706).
Letters, speeches, and newspaper clippings concerning Poe Amendment to Maryland Constitution to limit franchise.

Ribicoff, Abraham Alexander (1914–1998)
Democrat–Connecticut
Columbia University
Oral History Project
New York, N.Y.
    Papers: 3 official letters (1974–1976) in Bella
S. Abzug Collection.
    Finding aid in repository.
    Papers: 3 letters on personal business
(1957–1961) in the Overbrook Press
Collection. 1 letter on personal business
(April 24, 1969) in Random House
Collection. Finding aid in repository.
    Papers: 1 letter on personal business
(January 16, 1962) in Women's National Book
Association. Finding aid in repository.
Connecticut State Library
Hartford, Conn.
    Papers: 1954–1970. 6 feet.
    Scrapbooks and newspaper clippings per-
taining mostly to his election and service in
Congress.
John F. Kennedy Library
Boston, Mass.
    Papers: 1949–1953. 3 feet.
    Personal and constituent correspondence,
news clippings and miscellaneous material
from his service in the U.S. House of
Representatives.
    Restricted.
Library of Congress
Manuscript Division
Washington, D.C.
    Papers: 1949–1980. 262 feet.
    Political and public papers. Guidelines for
use of collection are on file in the repository.

Rosenthal, Benjamin Stanley (1923–1983)
Democra—New York
Queens College Library
City University of New York
Flushing, N.Y.
    Papers: 1962–1983. ca. 100 cubic feet.
    Congressional papers and correspondence.
Unprocessed.

Sabath, Adolph Joachim (1866–1952)
Democrat–Illinois
American Jewish Archives
Cincinnati, Ohio
    Papers: 1906–1952. 3,170 items.
    Correspondence, legislative material, speech

es, and other papers relating to his congressional service.

Siegel, Isaac (1880–1947)
Republican–New York
American Jewish Historical Society
Waltham, Mass.
    Papers: 1897–1944. 320 items.
    Chiefly correspondence regarding Jewish
personnel in Armed Forces.

Straus, Isidore (1845–1912)
Democrat–New York
Columbia University
Rare Book and Manuscript Library
New York, N.Y.
    Papers: 1 letter (March 21, 1904) in W. R.
Grace Collection.
    Finding aid in repository.
    Papers: 1 letter (November 6, 1901) in
Samuel Greenbaum Collection.
    Finding aid in repository.
    Papers: 2 letters (October, 1896) in Allan
Nevins Collection.
    Finding aid in repository.
    Papers: 1 letter (December 10, 1900) in
Plimpton Collection.
    Finding aid in repository.
    Papers: 2 letters (1902, 1911) in Edward
Morse Shepard Collection.
    Finding aid in repository.
    Papers: 2 letters (1909) in H. P. Willis
Collection.
    Finding aid in repository.
New York Historical Society
New York, N.Y.
    Papers: 1894–1897. 3 letters finding aid in
repository.

Teller, Ludwig (1911–1965)
Democrat–New York
Columbia University Libraries
New York, N.Y.
    Oral History: In Bibliographical oral history
collection,1964 1968.
    Described in published guide.
Tenzer, Herbert (1905–1993) Democrat-New
York
Yeshiva University Archives
New York, N.Y.
    Papers: In Rescue Children, Inc., Collection
1946–1985. 2 feet.

Papers from his work as chairman of this organization, which cared for Jewish orphans in post–World War II Europe. Finding aid in repository.
Restricted.
Oral History: December 23, 1985.

Yulee, David Levy (1810–1886)
Whig–Florida
American Jewish Historical Society
Waltham, Mass.
    Papers: 1843–1865. 8 items.
Boston Public Library
Boston, Mass.
    Papers: 1 letter.

Pierpont Morgan Library
New York, N.Y.
    Papers: 1855–1858. 3 items.
St. Augustine Historical Society.
St. Augustine,
    Papers: 1858. 1 letter.
University of Florida
P. K. Yonge Library of Florida History
Gainesville,
    Papers: 1842–1920. 41 boxes.
    Includes correspondence, business and legal papers, letter books, maps, and surveys.
    Finding aid in repository.

Index